12

POST OFFICE WORKERS:

A Trade Union and Social History

Post Office Workers

A Trade Union and Social History

ALAN CLINTON

London
GEORGE ALLEN & UNWIN
Boston   Sydney

**George Allen & Unwin (Publishers) Ltd,
40 Museum Street, London WC1A 1LU, UK**

George Allen & Unwin (Publishers) Ltd,
Park Lane, Hemel Hempstead, Herts HP2 4TE, UK

Allen & Unwin, Inc.,
9 Winchester Terrace, Winchester, Mass. 01890, USA

George Allen & Unwin Australia Pty Ltd,
8 Napier Street, North Sydney, NSW 2060, Australia

First published in 1984

British Library Cataloguing in Publication Data

Clinton, Alan
   The Post Office workers
1. Post Office – History   2. Trade unions –
Great Britain – History
I. Title
331.88′11383′0941   HD6668.P/
ISBN 0-04-331086-9

Library of Congress Cataloging in Publication Data

Clinton, Alan.
   Post Office workers.
Bibliography: p.
1. Trade-unions – Postal service – Great Britain –
History.   2. Postal service – Great Britain – Employees –
History. I. Title.
HE6939.P4C54 1983   331.88′113834941   83-15070
ISBN 0-04-331086-9

Set in 10 on 11 point Plantin
by Typesetters (Birmingham) Ltd
and printed in Great Britain
by Mackays of Chatham

Contents

List of Plates

Preface

In 1909 the Annual Conference of the Postmen's Federation rejected for the second year running the proposal that they should publish a history. One delegate thought 'it would take about half-a-dozen volumes to ascertain the history of the Federation, and conditions of service, and by the time they were ready they would have to have another volume, as the conditions of service were altering from day to day'. If the description of the history of one of the four main organisations of Post Office workers more than seventy years ago seemed such an enormous undertaking, it became more daunting still as the years passed.

Some efforts have been made over the years to tell parts of the story. H. G. Swift produced his *History of Postal Agitation* in 1899 and a new edition came out in 1929, though not with the extra volume he wanted to write to bring it up to date. In 1902 G. E. Hall, General Secretary of the Postal Telegraph Clerks Association produced a brief account of the *Thirty Years of Agitation* of his Association. Two Oxford University dissertations were also written, one by L. Middleton Smith in 1931 on *The History and Working of Trade Unionism in The British Post Office* and the other in 1952 by L. Martinuzzi on *The History of Employment in the British Post Office*. However these unpublished accounts were not well known to Post Office workers, or indeed to anybody else. The UPW conference in 1938 again rejected the idea of further work on a large-scale history on the grounds, according to *Post* editor Francis Andrews, that it would 'involve a big job of research', not to mention 'first-class writing ability'. However some articles on the history of Post Office workers and their unions did appear in *The Post* from time to time. William Clery wrote his 'Memoirs' in 1930, and G. H. Stuart-Bunning described the period in a series called 'From Tweedmouth to Whitley' and in various articles in the 1930s and 1940s. James Chalmers, *Post* editor in the early 1950s, wrote a number of articles and they were collected in two pamphlets published at the time called *How we Began* and *Official Recognition. How it Was Gained*.

Nevertheless, the history of trade unionism in the Post Office still needed to be properly researched and written. In 1970 the UPW celebrated its fiftieth anniversary and took the opportunity to approach Dr J. E. Williams of Leeds University, distinguished historian of *The Derbyshire Miners*. Soon afterwards I began work as his research assistant. Some plans were made and a few fragments drafted which now appear in Chapter 4 of this book, when, most suddenly and lamentably, Jim Williams died on 3 April 1973. It was then decided that I would take over the entire project, both research and writing.

The work that followed proved a formidable undertaking. One decision that had to be made quite early was whether to cover again the period up to 1900 as Swift had done. It soon became clear that although vivid and interesting, Swift's account was incomplete and often inaccurate. Continuous trade union activity could be traced back, often independently of Swift, for almost a century and a half. Furthermore, any effort to describe the economic and political background of employment in the Post Office was hampered by the very limited amount of previous work on this enormous and important subject.

Having been presented with the opportunity, I have therefore tried to be as comprehensive as possible, and have devoted the labours of a decade to covering many subjects which have only been described fitfully or inadequately before. The book thus contains an account of the development of the Post Office and of the machinery of the State and its economic policy. This was seen as a necessary preliminary to considering the lives and activities of the millions who have worked for this massive public enterprise. The book that has emerged is not only very large, it is also unashamedly 'institutional' in its approach. The working environment and the organisations built over many generations by Post Office workers to defend their interests and to improve their conditions have been viewed generally speaking from the top down. This is not because this is the only possible way of approaching such matters, but because the institutions involved are interesting enough, complex enough, and little enough known, to merit detailed consideration in their own right.

Some other points should be made to explain the form and content of this book. It should be made clear that because of the character of its central concerns, it is based first and foremost on the archives of the predecessors of the Union of Communication Workers and of the Post Office. There are virtually continuous records of all the main trade union bodies in the Post Office at least as far back as 1881 and they have never previously been surveyed and summarised. The voluminous records of the Post Office have rarely been seriously studied, and even the published reports on conditions of those working there have only occasionally been referred to in the past. I have regarded it as my primary task to summarise the contents of many thousands of tons of paper, supplemented by some things that people have told me.

I should emphasise that what has emerged in the following pages should in no way be regarded as an 'official' statement of the policy either of the present-day UCW, or of any of its predecessors – if there ever could be such a thing. This is the work of someone who is neither a member of the Union nor employed by the Post Office. However, the work has received continuous and unstinting support from the Union, and full co-operation from many of those who are its members or its employees. I have looked at archives and files without restriction and approached many individuals. I should add that although I have tried to look at this history independently, I have not done so in an attitude of spurious objectivity. I cannot deny a real identification with the aims and aspirations of those men and women whose efforts over all the generations built a great trade union. Nor have I been without a certain sympathy, shared at times by the workers, with the enormous problems faced by those who had to run the Post Office itself.

In putting together the final version of this book I have been very conscious that postmen, telephonists and postal officers of today may find it difficult to follow in parts, and will be surprised at the remoteness from their own experience of much that it contains. I hope that they will bear with me by studying the details that show how past generations have moulded contemporary ideas and institutions. They will see many examples to confirm what they no doubt already know – that however stable and established the processes of collective bargaining may seem, there have been no gains in wages and working conditions without pain and travail. I hope they will also discover how much this generation owes to men in top hats and women in long flowing dresses whose work and attitudes will seem almost as remote from us as penny blacks and strict Sunday observance. This will surely serve to emphasise that no matter how firm and fixed our world appears, there can be no doubt that in a future that some alive now may even know, messages will be conveyed, trade unions will function and societies will be organised in ways that we can now only dimly comprehend.

On so large a canvas as this one, I have tried to fill in at least an outline of every corner of the picture. I have tried to cover every major aspect of the development of the Post Office until it was dismantled in 1981. I have also tried to cover all the main industrial bargaining concerning the UCW's predecessors until the 1970s. In general, however, I have not found it possible to give the same detail for the most recent period. Many aspects of more recent events are still moving so fast that no clear pattern can yet be discerned, at least by this writer. Thus, though the reader will find a full account of the industrial democracy experiment of the late 1970s which derived from the long-term aspirations of Post Office trade unionists, there has been less to say about the new forms and arguments of industrial bargaining in the years of the unified corporation from 1969 to 1981 where a clear direction has yet to be established.

Over the years I have received help from many people in putting the book together. The initial impetus from the late Jim Williams has been taken up in a method of approach which has affected much other writing of trade union history. Other colleagues at the School of Economic Studies at Leeds University, with whom I discussed aspects of this work, included professors Vic Allen and Rodney Crossley as well as John Hillard and Alan Gillie, who has since commented on other aspects of the work. I also discussed parts of the work at the Centre for Social History at Warwick University in 1977, particularly with Professor Royden Harrison and Dr Jay Winter. I am also grateful for the opportunity to discuss some of it at the Commonwealth Labour History Conference held at Lanchester Polytechnic, Coventry, in September 1981, and at the Third Anglo-Dutch Social History Conference in Maastricht in April 1982. Those who have read and commented on various chapters include Jon Amsden, Bernard Waites and Ann Evans. Charles Perry and Ratna Sandersham also kindly discussed their own related work with me. The UCW Research Officer, Ted Geaney, has read and commented on virtually every section, as has his assistant Peter Hain, who has also helped me in many other ways. I owe much to others in the Research Department of the Union, especially to Molly Turpin and Peter Hooper, and at different periods to Phillip Bowyer and Alison Simpson.

Amongst those who were of particular help in the research, I should mention successive UPW/UCW librarians Joan Price and Judith Powell; those responsible for the Post Office Records at St Martin's-le-Grand, especially Jean Ferrugia; Christine Coates, Librarian of the TUC; Stephen Bird, Archivist of the Labour Party; Mr H. J. W. Legerton, former Secretary of the Lord's Day Observance Society; Miss E. A. Flint, Librarian of the invaluable Morten Collection at the Bruce Castle Museum in Tottenham; and Richard Storey of the Modern Records Centre, University of Warwick. I should also mention those who gave me access to the Cole Collection at Nuffield College Oxford and the Fawcett Collection in the Manchester City Archives, as well as those in various departments of the British Library – the Official Publications Library for numerous documents especially in the Parliamentary Papers collection including annual reports of the Postmaster General and Post Office, and the reading rooms at both Bloomsbury and Colindale which have provided many of the hundreds of magazines and newspapers cited in succeeding pages.

Amongst those in the Union with whom I have discussed the work and its progress have been Tom Jackson, general secretary from 1966 to 1982, Fred Moss, general treasurer to 1981, Harry Burnett and Tony Clarke, successive editors, together with former research officer Edgar Hardcastle, who also kindly read some of the draft chapters. Senior clerks Len Patterson, Ron Hobin and Alf Taylor also helped me on a number of points. A particularly warm debt of gratitude is merited by those who suffered to transform my scrawl into beautifully typed pages, notably Renée Morgan, Maralyn Alexis, Joan Robson, Audrey Channon, Pauline Granstan and Barbara Middleton.

All the people named – and many others – have contributed in many ways to the work of producing this book. None of them, however, can be held responsible for the pages that have finally emerged, complete with all the opinions and errors.

Finally, I should express the conviction that this book would be nothing at all without all the men and women who built the UCW and its predecessors. They have included many who engaged in small and dull negotiations aimed to improve the lot of their fellows, and many thousands whose unrecorded heroisms could never be recalled. If this book provides a memorial, it must be to those who suffered to improve the lives of Post Office workers – beginning perhaps with Robert Grapes, sacked in 1847 for leading a 'confederacy', to James Johnson, who lost his job in 1869, to William Booth, who left the Post Office in 1873 in debt and in despair, after failing to persuade his fellow letter carriers to set up a permanent union. In 1891 William Clery and Wallace Cheesman were sacked by the Postmaster General for lobbying Parliamentary candidates on behalf of the London sorters. These were perhaps the most conspicuous martyrs for the cause of trade unionism in the history of the Post Office, but they were by no means the only ones. Punctuating the detailed discussions and quiet negotiations set out in the following pages have been many battles whose outcome made it possible for the negotiations to take place. In 1871 the leaders of telegraphists who walked out on strike were disciplined by being 'exiled' to other offices. Their successors were exiled in 1897 for protesting against the proposals of Lord Tweedmouth's inquiry. In 1890, hundreds of postmen were sacked, suspended and otherwise punished for trying to set up a union and for going on strike. When their successors marched along the same road in 1964, they did so with much greater success. Most conspicuously of all in this long history, nearly 200,000 Post Office workers struck for six weeks in 1971 to obtain decent wages and conditions. However much the sacrifice necessary in these actions, whatever the uncertainty in their immediate outcome, they have provided the basis for the improvements obtained in more tranquil, less exciting times. It is to all those who provided an earnest that slavery will not prevail, that this work is particularly dedicated.

ALAN CLINTON
London
December 1981

Abbreviations and Notes

Most of the abbreviations used have been confined to the notes at the end of chapters. However, it has been impossible to avoid the use of sets of initials for the various organisations covered, and they are set out here. Acts of Parliament are referred to by regnal years until the recent period. Other abbreviations and details of publications are given in the Bibliography.

ACAS	Advisory Conciliation and Arbitration Service (1975)
ACC	Association of Counter Clerks (1924–47) secessionist union
AD	Associated Documents (with UPW Executive Minutes from 1958)
AE&SA	Amalgamated Engineering and Stores Association (1917–19), immediate predecessor of the Post Office Engineering Union
APEX	Association of Professional Executive Clerical and Computer Staff (1972 on) – called Clerical and Administrative Workers Union 1940–72
ASLEF	Associated Society of Locomotive Engineers and Firemen (1880)
ASTE	Amalgamated Society of Telephone Employees (1909–15). Formed by the Amalgamated Society of Telephone Operators and the National Society of Telephone Employees. In 1915 most members joined the AE&SA, but 1,500 telephone operators went into the P&TCA
BAR	Manuscripts of H. A. Barber in the Archives of the Labour Party under 'Barber (Labour Union) MSS'
BC	Branch Circular
BL	British Library
CC&T	Counter clerk and telegraphist. London Post Office grade from 1881 to 1946
CLPA	Central London Postmen's Association (1907–19). A breakaway from the Postmen's Federation at the East Central District Office. Joined the UPW
CO	Clerical Officer
CP	Communist Party
COPOU	Council of Post Office Unions (1966–81)
CPSA	Civil and Public Services Association, before 1969 known as the CSCA
CS	Conference Supplement
CSCA	Civil Service Clerical Association (1922–69), formerly the Assistant Clerks Association (1903–22)
CSF	Civil Service Federation
CSPD	Calendar of State Papers Domestic, i.e. printed lists of government documents
CSSS	Civil Service Socialist Society (1908–15?)
DC	District Council
DPRS	Direct Parliamentary Representation Society (1930–46), set up by the UPW to organise support for Candidates and MPs when direct aid was illegal under the 1927 Trade Disputes Act
E&SA	Engineering and Stores Association (1901–17), predecessor of POEU
ECDO	East Central District Office (of the London Post Office)
EC	Executive Committee
ECM	Executive Committee Minutes of the UPW from 1919
EO(T)A	Engineering Officers (Telecommunications) Association – secessionists from the POEU in 1946–54
F	*See* (UCW)F
FA	Fawcett Association (1890–1919)
GPC	General Purposes Committee
HPA	Head Porters Association (1909–17)
IL	Inner London
JIC	Joint Industrial Council

LDC	London District Council (of the UPW)
LDS	Lord's Day Society, or Society for Due Observance of the Lord's Day, later known as the Lord's Day Observance Society (set up in 1831)
LRC	Labour Representation Committee (1900–6)
MBS	Mutual Benefit Society (of the Postmen's Federation)
MC	Morten Collection (see p.598)
MR	Manchester (in telegraph code)
NAFF	National Association for Freedom
NAP	National Association of Postmen (1933–44)
NAPTO	National Association of Postal and Telegraph Officers (1947–54), secessionist body attempting to organise the main rank-and-file white collar grade during its first years
NATPE	National Association of Temporary Postal Employees, established in 1917 by provincial SC&Ts
NCLC	National Council of Labour Colleges (1921–64)
NFSPM	National Federation of Sub-Postmasters (founded in 1897)
NGT	National Guild of Telephonists (1927–71), secessionist union. Became Telecommunications Staff Association but soon thereafter disappeared
NIPs	Northern Ireland Post Office Clerks Association (1922–54)
NJC	National Joint Committee of Postal and Telegraph Employees (1902–20), included all the main Post Office associations. When first set up in 1897 was called the Amalgamated Postal Federation
NUR	National Union of Railwaymen (1913)
NWC(SS)	National Whitley Council (Staff Side)
OL	Outer London
OS	Official Side (nowadays, 'Management')
OSF	Officers' Salary File (of the UPW)
OTO	Overseas Telegraph Officer
P&TCA	Postal and Telegraph Clerks Association (1914–19), formed by merging of PTCA and UKPCA
P&TO	Postal and Telegraph Officer, the basic indoor grade from 1946–72, became Postal Officer
PCA	*See* UKPCA
PF	Postmen's Federation (1892–1919)
PFCE	Manuscript summaries of proceedings at Hobhouse and Holt inquiries taken by PF General Secretary G. H. Stuart
PHG	Postmen Higher Grade (created in 1946)
PIB	Prices and Incomes Board (1965–70)
PMG	Postmaster General. Political head of the Post Office from 1657 to 1969. From 1691 to 1823 two people held the office, and before 1871 they were all members of the House of Lords
POC	Post Office Circular, normally identified by number and date
POEU	Post Office Engineering Union. Since 1919 has organised engineers, stores and certain other Post Office grades
POGP	Post Office Green Paper
POMSA	Post Office Management Staff Association. Before 1968 the Controlling Officers' Association and since 1981 the Communication Managers Association
POR	Post Office Records and archives at St Martin's-le-Grand, London EC1
POUNC	Post Office Users' National Council (established 1965)
PRU	Pay Research Unit
PTCA	Postal Telegraph Clerks Association (1881–1913). Organised telephonists including SC&Ts in provincial offices
PTTI	Postal Telegraph and Telephone International, set up as the International

	Federation of Postal and Telegraph Servants in 1911, and re-established in 1920 under the new title
PU	Postmen's Union (1889–90)
R	*See* (UCW)R
RPI	Retail Price Index
SBC	Special Branch Circular
SC&T	Sorting clerk and telegraphist. Provincial Post Office grade abolished in 1946. From the 1890s entrants were supposed to be qualified in postal and telegraph work, but in the larger ('divided') offices usually specialised in one or the other. In smaller 'undivided' offices could do both sets of tasks
SPOE	Society of Post Office Executives – a title used since 1969 with the merging of various predecessors
STA	Sorter Tracers Association (1904–26), organising a small London grade, which joined the UPW
STD	Subscriber Trunk Dialling
SWDO	South Western District Office (of London Post Office)
TDA	Telecommunication (formerly Telephone) Development Association – a pressure group of large manufacturers in the field
T&T	Telegraph and Telephone
TPWA	Temporary Postal Workers Association (1916–20). London based. Originally called Temporary Sorters Association
TSA	Temporary Sorters Association (1915–16). Also Telecommunications Staff Association (*see* NGT)
TUC	Trades Union Congress
UCW	Union of Communication Workers (1980). New name for Union of Post Office Workers
(UCW)F	Files at UCW House in Research Department arranged according to a special numerical code
(UCW)R	Records and Archives, mainly of pre-UPW organisations, kept at UCW House and generally arranged by individual association
UGWF	United Government Workers' Federation (1895)
UKPCA	United Kingdom Postal Clerks' Association (1887–1914). Represented those in the SC&T grade doing sorting and counter work in the provinces
UPW	Union of Post Office Workers (1919–80), became UCW
WEA	Workers' Educational Association
WETUC	Workers' Educational Trade Union Committee

1 Introduction: Post Office Workers and their Unions

Neither snow, nor rain, nor heat, nor gloom of night stays
these couriers from the swift completion of their appointed
rounds. (Herodotus, *History*, VII, 89)

This reference to the communications system of ancient times is inscribed to this day on the walls of the New York City Post Office. It conveys a picture that still means something even in an advanced industrial society adapting to rapidly developing forms of telecommunications. The same feeling is captured in the sonnet *On His Blindness* by John Milton, published in 1673, about those who serve God:

Thousands at his bidding speed
And post o'er Land and Ocean without rest . . .

In the modern world people who accept and convey messages, always busy and usually invisible, have become so much part of the fabric of living as to be often ignored or forgotten. Yet a comprehensive system of communications was one of the many heritages that Victorian Britain has passed down to the modern world. It is the aim of this book to portray the lives and aspirations of those whose work made this system function.

There has always been something special about the position of those who convey letters to homes. Even before the days of the penny post, they had a reputation for being 'active and merry . . . honest and trustworthy . . . civil and obliging'. This cheerful, extrovert image has persisted across many cultures and periods.[1] It was utilised to win sympathy ever since the days in the early nineteenth century when letter carriers in London organised petitions to secure pay for extra duties. It was still there in the great industrial battle of 1971 when 'letter carriers' had long since been known as postmen, and when their special reputation was perhaps a little tarnished. By then it had long since been forgotten how superior to the rest of the working population had been the letter carriers of the early days of the penny post in the mid-nineteenth century, with their bright red uniforms and military bearing. The postmen had been pushed down into the ranks of the fetchers and carriers of late nineteenth century urban life before the onward march of capital accumulation and technological change made them seem unusual sorts of workers, perhaps no longer necessary.

Despite the picture dimly perceived by outsiders, the Post Office workforce has always consisted of many more people than those who deliver letters to front doors. For one thing there have always been those who have sorted letters and prepared them for distribution. There have been those who served at counters, acting as agents not simply for the dispatch of letters, but also for an increasing range of other services. The nationalisation of the telegraphs in 1870 brought another group of specialist workers – the telegraphists – into the Post Office. In smaller offices they combined their duties with those of the postal side. Teenage boys who delivered telegrams were familiar figures and apprentices to the workforce until the 1940s. The telephones, finally taken over in 1912, then brought in a new group of specialist workers. The 'hello girls' of the days before automatic telephones and Subscriber Trunk Dialling were also familiar figures down to the present generation. There were also male telephonists, but the general image of telephone operators was symbolic of a sexual division of labour whose course and consequences are traced in many parts of what follows. The development of telecommunications has also brought into the Post Office a major group of technicians who still work to maintain and extend the frontiers of telecommunications technology, and have been written about elsewhere.[2]

At the centre of this book is the story of how the main groups who worked for the Post Office built organisations to improve their conditions, to increase their wages, to take up their grievances, and to improve the quality of their lives. It deals, in particular, with the Union of Post Office Workers which, between 1919 and 1980, brought together a large proportion of postmen, sorters, telephonists, counter clerks and telegraphists under various changes of title and work organisation. However, the history of these workers did not begin in 1919, and a large proportion of the book is devoted to the years from the introduction of the penny post in 1840 and the consequent expansion of the Post Office. Nor can this history be understood without a consideration of the developing communications system, and the special economic and political pressures which exist for those employed by the state. However much Post Office workers have felt that they had a life apart they have always been affected, more or less seriously, by the same fluctuations of economic and social circumstance as the rest of the working class. They have become, at times, despite themselves, part of a wider trade union and labour movement, with its own momentum and ideals. It is this that has made the modern Union of Communication Workers contribute in its own particular way to making British society what it has come to be.

Chapter 2 outlines the main development in the postal and telecommunications system until the time of the foundation of the UPW after the First World War. The origins of the development of state control of the postal system in political surveillance are outlined and some details are given of the fading away of various forms of private enterprise during the seventeenth century and of the 'farming' of the system to individual entrepreneurs during the eighteenth. It was the modern development of communications beginning in stage coaches and continuing in the railways that made possible the introduction of the penny post in 1840. This arrangement for payment on dispatch at a low uniform rate allowed the multiplication of a system which was convenient for the consumer and profitable for the national exchequer. A good share of this profit went to private railway companies and even more to international shipping operators. Despite such difficulties, it was possible by the end of the nineteenth century to send letters at low cost to every part of the world and at a penny to every address in Britain, where they could often be received many times a day. The network of post offices necessary for this began to be used for other purposes also – as a savings bank, for the issuing of licences and eventually also for the payment of welfare benefits. In particular, the Post Office was able to take over the new medium of telegraphy from private companies who had inefficiently competed over profitable parts of the system. It did so after paying high compensation and under pressure to keep charges so low that telegrams never made the profit that posts did. These losses induced caution, so it was not so easy to get the Post Office to run the next great electrical marvel, the telephone. The Post Office did eventually take over the telephones in 1912 after a number of alternative arrangements had been tried and found wanting. By the outbreak of world war in 1914, the Post Office in Britain had become not only the largest economic enterprise but also the largest single employer of labour on the entire planet. It was even more than before seen as a great force for enlightenment and economic development – as Rowland Hill had put it in 1839, a 'powerful engine of civilisation'.

The modern Post Office developed as part of the Victorian State bureaucracy, and Chapters 3 and 4 are devoted to a consideration of the economic and political consequences of this fact from the point of view of the ordinary Post Office worker. The conventional arguments put forward at the time and to some extent since, were that there were special advantages in state employment. It has been maintained that there is a special protection from the hard world of the labour market as a result of the unlimited capacity of the State to pay its employees. Chapter 3 is largely devoted to refuting this view. Some detail is given of the advantages derived from the provision of uniforms, from the medical facilities provided and from the pensions paid to a large proportion of the workforce. Yet all of these items were introduced as measures of discipline and were resented by those who received them. The same disciplinary influence was also exercised by that special advantage of state employment so often talked about by recent generations – permanency and regularity of employment. At the end of the nineteenth century it was those conditions alone, and not pay or 'privileges' that gave Post Office workers any real advantage over their fellows.[3]

Chapter 3 is also devoted to a consideration of the complex evolution of the hierarchy of work and pay in the nineteenth century Post Office. Although there was supposed to exist a rational system of promotion by merit in the entire Civil Service after the 1850s, this did not have great significance for those at or near the bottom rungs of the ladder. In any case, promotion by seniority rather than merit was always preferred by all those below the top of the pyramid. Within the Post Office the system of grades and the relations between them were dominated by one overwhelming fact. This was the continual efforts of the authorities to employ, on all the new tasks that had to be performed, people who had inferior conditions to those already working there. Thus the 'clerks' of the early days of Anthony Trollope's Post Office employment in the 1830s were transformed into sorters and counter clerks, of whom there were large numbers in London by the 1880s. Some of the work of sending telegrams was done by women, and most of the delivery was done by teenage 'messengers' whose services could at first be dispensed with as they became more expensive to employ. Lower-paid women were introduced in even larger numbers as telephone operators. The Post Office authorities constantly tried, though never with great success, to integrate the work of postal and telegraph offices. They also pushed down the status of 'letter carriers', who after 1883 were 'postmen', dealing also with parcels.

This system of hierarchy was supposed to work in such a way as to persuade all these at every point to be diligent and efficient in an effort to rise higher. However, it was never seen in this way by those on the lowest rungs of the ladder, who perceived only muddle and inequity. Elements of pre-industrial employment conditions, including patronage and perquisites, remained for many decades. The payment of Christmas boxes to postmen is perhaps a last survival of arrangements whose origins have long been forgotten. It took many generations of effort to achieve standardised wages and conditions. Thus not until 1908 was a basis worked out for variations in pay by size of town, and it was only in the 1950s that a system came into existence which was generally accepted by all those subject to it. Lengthy incremental scales took even longer to break down, and they remained a major grievance right into the 1970s. For all the grievances which grew out of the inequities of hierarchy it was nevertheless the case as letter carriers' leader William Booth expressed it in 1872 that 'dissatisfaction will always exist . . . in accordance with the amount of pay received'.[4] He said this at a time when Post Office pay generally may well have been lower than it was twenty years earlier. It would seem, from the analysis set out more fully in Chapter 3, that most conditions did improve when permanent trade union organisations were set up in the Post Office in the 1880s and 1890s, and that they did so most substantially in the period before 1914, when real wages were falling elsewhere. This trend does not seem to have continued in the 1920s and 1930s after the setting up of agreed methods of wage bargaining.

How then were wages actually determined in the years before mutually acceptable procedures came with Whitlyism in the 1920s and agreed forms of argument with the Tomlin Royal Commission in the 1930s? An important factor, as already mentioned, was that pre-industrial patterns of payment in many respects persisted over a number of generations. Generally, standard arrangements developed which related to what was received elsewhere, complete with local variations. The letter carriers, sorters and telegraphists who first argued for improved wages and conditions usually did so by reference to a departed golden age, which in some cases really had existed. By the 1880s and 1890s they tended to argue in terms of their interpretation of promises that had been made in the past, like the 'Fawcett Scheme' which was alleged, without much justification, to have promised substantial improvements for sorters. In the great inquiries during the years before 1914, Post Office workers argued with some justice for the unique character of their work and skills, and usually also for their elevation to the status and conditions of those above them in the service. In contrast to the comparisons with the general labour market that came from the Post Office authorities, the workers and their associations began to maintain that they had a right to particular standards of subsistence including a 'middle-class life style'. They also began to argue that the government should be a model employer, setting an example to all others, a role which governments have never been keen to accept.

The central problem in bargaining about wages and conditions with a sovereign government is that in the end it alone can take the decisions. The myth put about in the nineteenth century, and sometimes heard even today, was that state employees were in a particularly advantageous position because in the end governments can always pay, whereas private employers can only find resources to the limit of their income. This myth has been behind the 'deep seated conviction' which has developed not only in Britain that there is a 'peculiar attractiveness in government employment' which in the end presents one of the 'chief obstacles in arousing an effective public sentiment to back up their claims'.[5] It is, however, quite false. State enterprise has always been subject to pressure from those responsible for 'house-keeping' inside the system and operating such mechanisms as 'Treasury control', or from various forms of outside political pressure. These can take the form of calls for the reduction of taxation and for 'economy'. Another example of the form of this pressure is in the case of the telegraphs. Here private enterprise could not operate efficiently or profitably, and the state was pressurised into a pricing policy as a result of which telegraphs could never be made to pay. None of this was the responsibility of those who worked for the Post Office. In any case, like any other section of government employees, Post Office workers were particularly susceptible to government economy campaigns, and as the years went by also became the object of virtually every effort at government regulation of the economy as a whole.

Over and above such economic pressures, Post Office workers were also subject to particular legal, political and even moral constraints which it is the aim of Chapter 4 to describe. There have always been rules about the behaviour of public servants, even outside their work. The same ultimate sovereignty of the state which could give secure employment could also be used in the end to dismiss without appeal those who worked there. As part of the efforts to end private patronage in government, public servants were deprived of the franchise before the 1860s. The right to hold meetings and to exercise political pressure on behalf of state servants was not easily accepted in the following decades. In 1891 two London sorters, William Clery and W. B. Cheesman, were dismissed for organising the lobbying of parliamentary candidates. In 1906 the Postmaster General Lord Stanley achieved some notoriety and also lost his parliamentary seat after describing Post Office workers who tried to exercise such influence as 'blackmailers' and 'bloodsuckers'. Despite this the 'civil rights' of Post Office workers were conceded step by step. In 1906 their Associations were recognised for purposes of negotiation. Already special public committees under the chairmanship of Lord Tweedmouth and Edward Bradford had considered their grievances. In 1908 and 1912–13 House of Commons Select Committees under Hobhouse and Holt did the same and further consideration was given in 1914 by the Gibb Committee on which Post Office workers were themselves represented. As already indicated, this was perhaps the golden age from the point of view of improvements in Post Office wages and conditions. During the First World War an arbitration board was established, and afterwards the Whitley System of joint negotiation was adopted for the entire Civil Service. This opened a new period in almost every way.

Chapters 5 and 6 are devoted to describing in detail the process whereby organisations for the redress of grievances were built in the Post Office. It is important to make the point that although it has proved possible to trace back such activities to the advent of the penny post and before, it was not until the 1870s that Post Office workers aimed to set up permanent organisations. Although there were secret bodies in fairly continual existence in London at least in the 1860s, and nationally co-ordinated activity as far back as the 1850s, the form and flavour of the 'agitation' of those distant days was not as in later generations. Most notably, 'postal servants' in the mid-nineteenth century displayed an attitude of deference to the rich and powerful which would not perhaps have been considered normal in later periods. They often found it necessary to rely on the assistance of respectable and influential people varying from the Society for the Due Observance of the Lords Day, to clergymen and correspondents of *The Times* newspaper.

The earliest efforts to improve conditions that were in any way sustained can probably be dated to meetings held in and around St Martin's-le-Grand in the early 1840s, usually in secret. These meetings established a 'confederacy' protesting against low pay and extra duties. Those in authority were consistently hostile to such efforts and eventually in 1847 dismissed Robert Grapes, who appeared to be the leader. In 1849 the letter carriers and sorters fought behind the zealots of the

Lords Day Society against having to work on Sundays, and for a time attained this happy end. However, the Sabbatarians were less successful than their political opponents, and soon Sunday work was restored. Letters were never delivered on Sundays in London, however, and Sunday work was restricted elsewhere and severely limited from the First World War onwards.

Agitation continued in the early 1850s on a national scale against regulations forbidding the solicitation of Christmas gratuities – though attitudes on such matters were to change in later years. In the discontent that followed the reorganisation of the London postal system in 1855, new forms of organisation began to emerge. A delegation of letter carriers even met the Postmaster General on 28 July 1858. However, those in authority, especially Rowland Hill, did not approve of meetings where grievances were discussed, and some dismissals of those organising such meetings followed. After the failure of John Lilwall and his respectable Early Closing Association to achieve much on their behalf, the postal workers found an unexpected ally in the columns of *The Times* newspaper in 1860. This resulted in another meeting with the Postmaster General and an internal inquiry proposing substantial improvements which, especially under the influence of Rowland Hill, were again not granted. Some increases in 1861 were followed by further meetings and organised activities, and by further repression. During the 1860s there was isolated agitation outside the capital and the London 'Committee' remained in existence, though its achievements remained limited and its leaders including George Padfield and James Johnson were sacked for their activities on its behalf.

A new phase in Post Office agitation began in 1870 both because of the entry of the telegraphists into the service and because of efforts to set up more powerful and permanent organisations. This is set out in Chapter 6, which also describes a number of strikes. The first of these was of telegraphists in 1871 before they had even been given a grade structure within the Post Office. This strike resulted in a few victimisations and the 'exiling' of its leaders to London offices. The early 1870s also saw the first efforts to set up a trade union based on the London letter carriers, led by William Booth. This was a failure, as also were disastrous isolated strikes by others closer to major industrial struggles of the time in Warrington and Huddersfield. By the early 1880s, there were negotiations with Postmaster General Fawcett, various reorganisations of grades and payments were made, and the telegraphists finally set up the Postal Telegraph Clerks Association in 1881.

In the four years from 1887 the main organisations of Post Office workers were established. The provincial postal clerks began the United Kingdom Postal Clerks Association in 1887. Soon after this the London sorters transformed their 'Fawcett Scheme Committee' into the Fawcett Association. Their claim for equality with the telegraphists achieved very little, but they had secured the right to meet and after the dismissal of Clery and Cheesman in 1892 they got two full-time officials. The postmen after many failures and victimisations set up their own Postmen's Union in 1889 under the leadership of 'outsiders'. The strike of London postmen which followed in July 1890 was not the inglorious failure that has often been described. It was somewhat ineffectively led, and also suffered from divisions amongst postmen themselves and the attitude of sorters, but most especially from the careful dispositions of the authorities. Hundreds of jobs were lost, but the basis for the Postmen's Federation was established and all the main grades now had their own unions.

Chapter 7 is devoted to describing Post Office bargaining in the era of the grade associations from the 1890s to 1919. It sets out the detail of the great public inquiries into Post Office grievances under the respective chairmanship of Tweedmouth (1895–7), Bradford (1904), Hobhouse (1907–8) and Holt (1912–13). The improvements granted by Lord Tweedmouth's Committee were not considered adequate and the result was large-scale militancy, especially from telegraphists. The Bradford inquiry, in an unusual period of a very weak Conservative Government, proposed large increases which were considered insufficient by the Post Office workers but never granted by the authorities. The Hobhouse and Holt Select Committees gave increasingly comprehensive consideration to the issues involved, rationalised such matters as provincial differentiation, but did not satisfy the Post Office workers who were speaking openly in the great period of industrial discontent just before 1914 of strike action in the Post Office.

The transition in agitation during the two decades before 1914 was most remarkable. The timid delegates who spoke to Lord Tweedmouth in 1896 came from trade union bodies fully recognised by 1906, and strongly affected by the great upsurge of unrest after 1911. At first they argued their case with the most elevated and implausible arguments about the value of their work. They then went on to various forms of comparison with other Post Office grades which rarely achieved more than bitter feelings between different sections of workers. They then set out standards of subsistence and comfort which they thought they had a right to achieve. In the period before the war Post Office workers became more effectively organised but, despite the improvements that they achieved, they never considered them sufficient. Furthermore, by 1914 it had become clear that the settling of wages and conditions by the near-theatrical proceedings of a public inquiry was no longer satisfactory. The Gibb Committee, on which representatives of the workers helped to reconsider the conclusions of the Holt Select Committee, showed that a new form was necessary, even though the effect of those particular deliberations was minimised by the war. Historically unprecedented price rises then resulted in further discontent and a rapid series of negotiations resulting in the granting of 'bonus' arrangements which were to persist into the 1930s. The war also brought with it an arbitration court, and eventually also the Whitley system.

Chapter 8 describes in detail the organisations that existed in the period before the foundation of the UPW. They were remarkable in particular for the comparative amateurishness of their organisation and the scope and effectiveness of their operation. Their early experiences made the pre-UPW bodies hostile to the employment of 'outsiders', or even of full-timers of any sort. Yet they had a string of achievements in some ways greater than their successors.

After the main bodies of Post Office workers had finally established permanent organisations in the early 1890s, the most active and dynamic organisation was undoubtedly the Fawcett Association. Though Clery and Cheesman became full-time officials as a result of their dismissal from the Post Office in 1892, they were subject to the control of an articulate and integrated set of workers who met in general meetings and elected an effective Central Committee. The Fawcett Association pioneered many important steps in Post Office trade unionism, particularly in relations with the wider labour movement, in efforts to get unity of the associations and in support for Parliamentary representation. They seemed to lose their way somewhat after a sharp internal crisis of 1903 resulted in the departure of the errant Clery both as Parliamentary candidate and as Chairman. The members grew less interested after this in progressive ideas, and a section of the early leaders even broke away. They came late into the eventual amalgamation and some at least of their number formed a secessionist body which continued until the sorter grade disappeared in 1946.

The Postmen's Federation began under the shadow of the failure of the 1890 strike and was affected by this for some time. It refused until 1902 to take on full-time officials, even after they left the Post Office. Then, however, G. H. Stuart (who was called Stuart Bunning after 1915) became Parliamentary Secretary and eventually General Secretary, dominating most of the negotiations from Hobhouse in 1906 to Whitley in 1920. Organisation was very diffused in the PF, contributions were low and policy for a long time uncertain. In 1906 the Federation embarked on its disastrous 'unification' programme for their integration with the grades above. This produced bitter feelings in the other associations and gained nothing for the postmen. After this policy was reversed, the PF came to dominate the trade union scene in the Post Office, and not only from force of numbers. At least from the time of the 1911 transport strikes, postmen saw themselves as trade unionists and supported schemes for amalgamation and reorganisation that were eventually achieved.

The United Kingdom Postal Clerks Association was set up in 1887 and organised the provincial equivalents of the London sorters as well as some who did work in writing and at counters. They were the weakest of the main bodies, especially after the disciplining of their entire leadership in 1893. They took some years to produce a periodical, they did not even have a national Executive Committee until 1908, and they never had any full-time officials. However, they did have a Woman's Organiser from 1908, they took an interest in the expansion of the service with special reference to a postal cheque – or 'giro' – system, and they began in 1911 to show some rebelliousness and militancy which carried on into the UPW. Two years later the postal clerks united with the oldest of the associations, the Postal Telegraph Clerks Association. The PTCA also worked with a localised Executive together with 'district centres' until 1907–8. One part of its decentralised power structure was a parliamentary committee which organised most effective lobbying in London. The PTCA was also the first association to call for equal pay for women. The merged P&TCA found organisation and activity very difficult in the early part of the war period. After 1916, it took over some telephonists from the ex-employees of private companies in the former Amalgamated Society of Telephone Employees. It then began to organise its first national conferences. Its leaders took an interest in issues of 'industrial democracy' and became full-time officials in such numbers as to provide the largest group of those who set up the UPW in 1919.

The latter sections of Chapter 8 are devoted to saying something of the smaller' associations who set up the UPW, and a few of those who did not, including super-visors. Some attention is also devoted to various efforts to bring together trade union activity in the Post Office eventually resulting in a National Joint Committee in 1903: this assumed considerable importance by the time of the Holt inquiry in 1911 and laid the basis for the complex wartime negotiations that set up the amalgamated union. It is worth also bearing in mind the great plethora of clubs and societies in which Post Office workers were involved, starting with insurance societies of the 1870s and culminating before 1914 in such bodies as the Civil Service Socialist Society which helped to give colour to trade union activity and social life in the vast institution that had come into existence by that time.

Nor is it possible to understand the life of the UPW itself without considering the great changes which have taken place in the Post Office since 1918, and it is to this that Chapter 9 is devoted. The greatest change of all is indicated in the title of the chapter – the gradual diminution of the emphasis once given to the 'service' provided by an organisation which only incidentally made a profit for the national exchequer. The first step in this process was perhaps the ending of the penny post in 1918, not, it is of some interest to note, because of losses in the postal service, but as a form of subsidy to telecommunications. This, however, was by no means sufficient to solve the perennial problems of the under-priced telegraph system whose relentless decline can be traced over many decades. It is important to point out also that despite the expansion of automatic telephones in the interwar period, it was not until as late as 1955 that the postal system ceased to have the larger turnover and profit. During this period there was often pressure for change in the Post Office, even while it was at its most profitable. The most well known of these efforts were associated with the Lord Wolmer, who was for a time Conservative Assistant Postmaster General. It culminated in the 1932 Bridgeman Committee which proposed a regional structure which had effectively come into existence by 1939, and a system of limiting the amount of profits that needed to go to the Treasury which did not finally come until 1955.

The 1930s saw the first efforts to publicise and market the services of the Post Office and the period after 1955 saw this develop to a greater extent. The 'friendly telephone' came with Subscriber Trunk Dialling and a bewildering succession of further technological innovations. As telecommunications year by year outpaced the postal side and became more profitable, more financial independence came in 1961, and the Post Office Corporation was established in 1969. The efforts made during this period to improve the performance of the postal and telecommunications services are outlined in Chapter 9. There were many changes in the life and activities of the Post Office in the 1960s and 1970s, at least as important as the great reforms of the 1830s. There were many inquiries and discussions also, most notably the 1967 Select Committee on Nationalised Industries and the Carter Review Committee of 1977. There were many organisational innovations culminating in the creation of two separate corporations in 1981. Yet many of the old constraints on investment and profit remained, and the reality of continuing government pressure on the public sector will be felt by those working for the two corporations in the 1980s, as well as by those planning its activities and performance, just as surely as it was in the days of Kingsley Wood in the 1930s and of Rowland Hill in the 1840s.

It is against this background that the main aspects of the life and work of the Union of Post Office Workers are traced in succeeding chapters. Chapter 10 is devoted to the organisation of the Union, Chapter 11 to some aspects of its life and work, and Chapters 12 and 13 to the history of its bargaining activities from 1919 to 1971.

In its outward forms and organisation, the UPW did not alter in any significant way the structure taken over from the pre-amalgamation bodies in 1919. For the individual member or branch there was little change of any sort until the advent of the closed shop in the 1970s. The Union has always retained a district council structure, though this has been far less significant than in many other unions, except where there have been special arrangements for Scotland and London. The same basic group of full-time officers has existed throughout the UPW's history covering the main functions of the Union and the main grades. The comparative weakness of the officer corps in the early years can be seen in the discussions about their salaries, which were kept low until the 1960s. By then, however, the leaders, once distrusted as 'outsiders' in the service, had become professional negotiators with greater power, and with incomes a good deal more than those of the UPW members.

The Union was always run by a lay Executive which also became more powerful in the 1950s, and since then more 'professional'. A good deal of power still remains in the hands of annual and special conferences, and ultimate authority is derived from them. Their operation is described in Chapter 10, as also is the form and organisation of the Union's headquarters, and the services that it provides to members. Particular attention is devoted to the education provided by the UPW, because the Union was something of a pioneer in this field, and also because an outline of how it has developed helps to illustrate the same trend to a more professional technically-oriented union that can be seen elsewhere.

A large proportion of Chapter 10 is devoted to a description of one subject which dominated the amalgamated UPW in almost every way from 1921 to 1970, and this was the secession of sections of members to form organisations of their own. Beginning with the particularist traditions of certain London grades, and sustained by special problems in almost every other section of the Union's membership, secessionism affected all aspects of trade union life and development in the Post Office to an extraordinary degree. There can be no doubt that the logic of secessionism was to set up separate bodies for every grade and to destroy the effectiveness of trade union organisation. Yet it cannot be denied that secessionist bodies had widespread support. They set up viable associations of London sorters and counter clerks which continued until these grades were abolished in 1946. They had significant support in almost every grade at some time, and probably had the allegiance of the majority of night telephonists for most of the time that the grade existed. They were thus a clear reflection of many of the special grievances of Post Office workers, and it must also be said that while they existed, and for whatever reason, the conditions of night telephonists spectacularly improved. The National Guild of Telephonists was in fact the only secessionist body to survive the period when the scales began to be weighted against setting up new organisations by the formula of Lord Listowel in 1946 and the 1952 report of Lord Terrington. The NGT later resisted the most determined efforts to find a place for them in the UPW, but only collapsed after recognition was withdrawn from them in 1970.

It is perhaps surprising to record that the present generation of UCW activists seems largely to have forgotten the secessionists, however much they dominated their predecessors. Nevertheless the existence of these rival organisations went a long way in explaining the character of much of the Union's internal life. For example, in the past dissent tended to get squeezed out into secessionist bodies, whereas nowadays it might be expressed in various forms of opposition within the Union itself.

Chapter 10 ends with some reflections on the relations between the professional and active members of the Union and the rank and file. Chapter 11 is concerned with the place of the UPW in the wider trade union movement, and with some of its particular contributions to that movement and the attitudes it has taken.

Perhaps the most remarkable individual trait of the UPW was its 'guild socialist tradition'. This derived not simply from an obvious set of influences that affected individual union leaders in the second decade of the century. It also came from particular problems which did not arise in the same way for any other trade unionists. In the Post Office there were particular conflicts of authority and special difficulties in establishing bargaining forms for those who for many generations were employees of the State. Thus the early guild socialist ideas were in part a solution to the same problems that led to the setting up of the Whitley Council system in the 1920s. Their revival in the 1960s and 1970s was not simply a testimony to those who had tried to keep them alive, but also an indication that the cluster of problems of authority and the bargaining process in the public sector that emerge from time to time under such headings as 'industrial democracy' will never quite disappear.

The UPW also had certain special experiences in its relations to the wider labour movement. Thus the pre-amalgamation associations were early adherents to the Labour Party, and all were affiliated to the TUC. By the 1920s, the Union had MPs and members of the TUC General Council who were actively involved in the various efforts of the wider working-class movement. The UPW nevertheless retained enough of the colour of its Civil Service environment not to get too involved, except by sympathy and support, in the General Strike of 1926. Nevertheless they and other public service unions were punished for defeat in this battle by the 1927 Trade Disputes Act which attempted to wall them off from the wider movement of which they were a part. This had some effect in re-enforcing attitudes of timidity in the 1930s, but was a source of continual irritation to Union leaders and activists culminating in an open but unsuccessful effort to defy the law in 1943. Three years later, however, the law was repealed by the Labour Government and UPW leaders were again able to participate in the wider labour movement in ways which affected attitudes and experiences down to the present day. Two examples described in Chapter 11 are the general political attitudes developed in the early 1950s, and the efforts to achieve ordered bargaining and the State planning of wages discussed then and since.

Chapter 11 also contains a discussion of the position of women in the UPW. The subordination of women at work, and the set of social attitudes which derived from this existed long before the UPW. Nevertheless, it took a long time before the slogan of equal pay accepted by the Union's founders was transformed into practice. Neither can it be said that the legislative changes of the 1970s have even yet put an end to traditional attitudes and persistent inequities. Chapter 11 also gives some consideration to the long-frustrated aims of the UPW in trying to expand industry-wide trade unionism in the postal and telecommunications field. It ends with an attempt to summarise some of the special characteristics of the UPW.

Chapter 12 describes the main events in the first twenty-five years of the life of the Union, especially in the field of bargaining. The chapter begins by arguing that the establishment of the Whitley system was by no means a solution to all the problems of bargaining. Nor did it do much of what was expected of it before 1939, since the main wage agreements were arrived at through direct negotiations or arbitration. For one thing, the ultimate power of unilateral decision by the government was asserted from the start in 1921 in the 'supercut' introduced on higher wage levels without reference to anybody at all. This helped to explain the intensity of the efforts of civil service trade unionists to restore arbitration machinery in 1922–5. The 'official side' in 1928 even tried to maintain that they could decide who could represent the staff on the non-engineering Post Office Whitley Council by admitting the secessionists. This led to the temporary collapse of the Committee. By the outbreak of war, the role of Whitleyism in dealing with general issues like pensions and women's pay had been established, and a period of the extension of their activities on such matters began.

Interwar wage bargaining in the civil service was dominated by the existence of a fluctuating cost-of-living bonus added to pay and providing a continual source of discontent until it was finally abandoned in 1935. By then there had been important changes in arguments about wages. The UPW in the 1920s and 1930s generally argued for better wages on the basis of the improved value of their work and their subsistence needs, and on occasions they also mentioned the profits accruing from their labours. The Tomlin Royal Commission in 1931 altered the perspective of those arguments by maintaining that civil service wages should follow those in the economy as a whole, though it took some time for this to be accepted. This was the essential basis of the frequent negotiations for a cost-of-living bonus during the Second World War, discussed through the National Whitley Council but in reality agreed by the more powerful civil service union leaders with their employers, the Treasury.

The course of negotiations in the early years of the UPW reflects not just those general issues and arguments. In particular the first claim negotiated in 1919–21 was a product of the confidence of the newly-formed amalgamation and achieved more for Post Office workers than any other such efforts for many years. It is important to emphasise, however, that at the time the settlement was seen as a large retreat from the Union's original aims. Before the negotiations were quite over, a very different atmosphere in industrial bargaining dictated an event which had considerable long-term implications for the UPW, and this was the abandonment of the Union's strike policy in 1921. Although the members voted in 1920 for a strike levy and the May 1921 Annual Conference supported this, the Executive decided to abandon it. The Union was losing members, some of them to bitterly hostile secessionists. However, the abandonment of the strike policy did not put an end to secessionism and probably only had a limited effect on membership losses. However, the 1922 Conference accepted the inevitability of a step which certainly weakened the Union for two generations.

The first indication of this weakening was in the protracted discussions on the Union's second wage claim. Initiated in 1922, it took five years to get to the arbitration court where it achieved only the most marginal of improvements. The claim was first of all bogged down in a disastrous effort to work out a new scheme of grade organisation which was abandoned early in 1924. It was argued with Labour and Conservative postmasters general in 1924 and 1925 and eventually in 1927 ended in the arbitration court. Here there was a full discussion, with the authorities asking for wage reductions and eventually getting some. On the whole, however, the tribunal confined itself to a number of marginal improvements.

These were difficult years for Post Office workers as for all others, which reached their nadir during the years of sharp economic and political crisis up to 1932. The bonus arrangement became a matter of contention, not only against the civil service authorities, but also among the unions themselves. As prices and the cost of living fell, then so also did the bonus, and it was not easy to decide what to do for the best to serve the interests of the members. In the early period of the 1929 Labour Government, reductions were to some extent averted, but after a series of complicated negotiations set out in Chapter 12, and after continual falls in money wages, a system for consolidating the bonus was finally agreed in 1934. During this period the UPW tried to take up the grievances of its members in a series of generally abortive claims. One of these was for an increase of 10s (50p) for all and another for a forty-hour week. It was only after 1932 that it became possible to obtain some improvements for those on the lower rates of pay. Discontent did not generally express itself in greater militancy during this period. However, a go-slow in Manchester in November 1931 led to the first disciplinary moves for trade union activity for a generation in the Post Office, and the dismissal of Arthur O'Donnell gave the Union the only officially designated full-time local official in its history.

The worst of the economic depression had passed by the time the UPW submitted its third major general wage claim in September 1937. This was presented to the Civil Service Arbitration Court during 1938 with some of the care and drama left over from the great pre-First World War public inquiries. The arguments had by now somewhat shifted to include some at least of the elements of the Tomlin formula of 1931, comparing public sector wages to those earned elsewhere. The result was wage increases in the Post Office in 1938 which broadly reflected the increases that had been obtained elsewhere. The wartime negotiations, described in the latter part of Chapter 12, were a good deal more complex and continuous than those of the previous two decades. They also closely followed wages movements elsewhere and, for the first time, were affected by government efforts to plan wages and prices.

In the postwar negotiations set out in detail in Chapter 13 a number of new concepts arose, sometimes old arguments in a new form. Government wage policies were of considerable significance in the late 1940s, in the early 1960s, and almost all the time after that. In the negotiations during the 1940s, comparisons between public sector wages and movements in the economy as a whole became commonplace. The Priestley Report of 1956 allowed the acceptance by civil servants, after many generations of arguing against the idea, that their wages could be decided by direct comparison with workers in the private sector. For their part, the government and the 'official side' had to accept a version of an argument they had traditionally rejected – that they should be model employers.

This was the context of the series of negotiations described in the first sixteen years after the end of the war. The historic re-allocation agreement of 1946 laid to rest not simply most of the secessionist organisations, but also disputes about the allocation of work in sorting offices that went back to the late nineteenth century. The changes that came were along lines which had been argued by the Post Office authorities since that time, but had been rejected by Post Office trade unionists with much anguish and rancour when put in the postmen's 'Unification Scheme' of 1906 and the UPW's own abortive 'reorganisation' ideas of 1923–4. The new postmen higher grade were now to be promoted from the ranks of postmen to perform tasks which in London had been carried out by sorters and some postmen and in the provinces by some SC&Ts. The work of other SC&Ts, and of London CC&Ts, was taken over by the new basic white-collar grade of postal and telegraph officers, called postal officers after 1972 when their telegraphy functions had diminished to nothing. There were opponents to re-allocation in 1946 in the ranks of the UPW, especially amongst returning ex-servicemen, but they were largely reconciled to it by the large pay increases that accompanied its introduction. Further large increases were negotiated in 1947 which brought an overall increase of some 20 per cent for most Post Office workers, probably at least twice the rate of inflation. There was a mood of unity and self-confidence in the UPW in 1947 indicated by the poll of members which restored the principle of strike policy after a gap of twenty-six years.

Improvements in the conditions of Post Office workers were not so easily obtained in the latter period of the first majority Labour Government in 1948–51. There was continual pressure from the government to keep down wages, and this was at first accepted at conferences of the UPW. Thus a claim for shorter hours in this period sank without trace. A wage claim in 1948 did not get to the arbitration court until 1949, when it secured 4–6 per cent for members, around what was then the annual inflation rate. A long delay during 1950 in settling a further general wage claim brought about some dissention within the Union and unofficial action in some London offices in April 1951. In the following month the arbitration court granted around 7 per cent, not very far short of what had been originally claimed.

In the early 1950s there was a new atmosphere in civil service wages bargaining. The pressures of economic crises and official interference were eased under the Conservative Government. Union leaders like UPW General Secretary Charles Geddes and Douglas Houghton of the Inland Revenue Staff initiated discussions on more centralised and automatic forms of bargaining, but their ideas did not come to much. The first of a number of general civil service 'additions' was agreed in 1952. The UPW's discontent with the limited results of its efforts resulted in a series of value of work claims in the arbitration court in 1953–4 which secured very little. A complex series of negotiations into 1955 resulted in further increases which now established a new concept of annual claims. Later in 1955 the Priestley Royal Commission established, against all the reservations of the unions, the principle of pay comparability and an apparently scientific way of deciding on it through the Civil Service Pay Research Unit.

In the period before and after Priestley, many UPW members continued to obtain increases through 'additions' negotiated for the civil service as a whole through the National Whitley Council. Some grades, like cleaners who were also in other Departments, or P&TOs who were tied to grades there, continued to have changes determined in general negotiations. The Pay Research Unit proved cumbersome and secretive, but it did play an important part every four or five years in allowing individual UPW grades to 'catch up' with overall settlements that had been negotiated elsewhere. The first result of the new system was the 1957 'package' agreement which, as indicated in Chapter 13, involved a good deal of change in hours and working practices and provoked some unofficial industrial action in London in April 1958. Further negotiations on hours provoked a good deal of pressure on the leadership from Union militants in the latter part of 1959. It was nevertheless possible for General Secretary Ron Smith to argue with some justice at the beginning of 1961 that conditions had improved a good deal in the 1950s. It was possible also to point to changes at the same time of a sort that had been aimed at over many generations. This included equal pay for women, the ending of the old system of provincial 'classification' of wage differentials and the link between P&TOs and the clerical grades in the civil service. Yet matters had changed by the 1960s from the time almost a century earlier when 'clerical status' was sought as a distant goal by Post Office workers. Now the P&TOs fought and eventually succeeded in breaking the link with clerical grades in an effort to get wages and conditions superior to theirs.

All this and much besides was thrown into question in the early 1960s by the efforts of Conservative governments to keep down the level of wage increases. The

1961 UPW conference gave the Executive the power to call industrial action and to submit a new wage claim. The negotiations came up against a 'pay pause' that tried, amongst other things, to limit the traditional independence of civil service arbitration procedures. This resulted in an official 'work to rule' in the opening weeks of 1962. After a series of negotiations and a visit to the arbitration court in June, the UPW secured a 4 per cent increase which was perhaps twice the annual rate of inflation and a good deal above the Government's 2½ per cent 'guiding light' incomes policy. Over the next two years further increases were obtained in pay research but few in the Union were content with them, especially amongst postmen. It was the postmen who moved decisively into action in the high summer of July 1964. There were various forms of local industrial action, a national one-day strike on 16 July, further unofficial actions and finally the threat of a national all-out official strike. An increase of 6½ per cent was secured, generally seen as a significant improvement against an inflation rate of around 4½ per cent.

The mid-1960s saw a large number of significant changes in Post Office trade unionism which are set out at a number of points in later chapters. The era of industrial disputes which began with the 1962 work to rule and ended with the 1971 national strike was one when the UPW itself changed, sometimes painfully and often with anguish and argument. The efforts of the national leadership to impose discipline on leaders of London postmen in September 1964 was perhaps the most traumatic example. The expulsion of a number of London leaders was short-lived and it was part of a whole series of changes of which another example was the accession of Tom Jackson to the position of general secretary in 1965. During the period when the Post Office workers were emerging from the civil service in the late 1960s there was further industrial action initiated for the P&TOs in 1968 and for the overseas telegraphists a year later.

The series of difficult and messy negotiations under various stages of incomes policy in the period after 1966 is described in Chapter 13. A large accumulation of discontent came up against restrictions imposed by another Conservative administration on both capital and labour. This culminated in the six-and-a-half-week national strike of all UPW members in January and February 1971. Chapter 13 gives a full account of the course and outcome of this struggle, and there is some discussion of whether it could have been different. Whether it could have been and indeed whether or not it had the dispiriting outcome which was perceived at the time and since, there can be no doubt that the 1971 strike has had a decisive effect on Post Office trade unionism since that time. The following years have not been without conflict or controversy of course, and some highlights of these are outlined in Chapter 14. However after 1971 the Union largely became what it had been before 1961 – a careful, non-militant negotiating body. The UPW was also able to do something it had never done before – to bargain directly year by year about wages and conditions with those who run the Post Office. Despite the many attitudes brought from the past into these discussions, in the final years before the UPW became the UCW in 1980 it had become more than ever a bargaining union like the others.

One way in which this development was indicated was in changes in the use of words. UCW negotiators nowadays talk of the 'employers' in a way that their predecessors would not have done. Indeed it is not many generations ago when there were neither 'employers' nor 'unions' in the Post Office, but an 'official side' and a 'staff side' who worked not for a 'business', but were part of a 'service'. Behind these words lay attitudes which seem nearly to have been forgotten by the present generation. Even more remote now are the days before 1920 when the talk was of 'associations' and of the 'authorities' with whom they negotiated. In the long years covered in this book, an effort is made to keep to roughly contemporary usage with such words and concepts as these. It is impossible to be quite consistent about this, however. It is particularly difficult when going into the remote past in the mid-nineteenth century to look at such quasi-trade union bodies as 'The Phalanx' and the 'General Commission Agent' and to remember that they had their own ways of thought and action which in no way depended on the remote consequences known only to posterity.

There are other problems in attempting so large a coverage as there is in this book. There is not just the change in the meaning of words – like the use of the term 'established' for pensionable, of 'classification' for differences in pay in various parts of the country. There is the emergence of such terms as 'telecommunications' in the 1930s and of 'business' in the 1970s, referring to phenomena that had existed in earlier times but were described in different ways. There is an almost insurmountable problem in talking about money values over very long periods. It has not proved possible to discover any simple or general formula to answer this difficulty. Some efforts are made to make long-term comparisons in the years of comparatively stable prices before 1914, and to measure changes against price changes in the more inflationary days from the 1940s. Ultimately, however, it is necessary to think back to wages, prices and conditions in the terms that contemporaries knew them rather than to render them almost meaningless by measuring them against some remote cosmic standard of value.

It must be said that an effort is made throughout this book to see things from the point of view of many thousands of men and women who pass by in the pages that follow. It cannot be claimed that it is possible to do this as if devoid of passion or subjective feeling. It is to be hoped however that it will be found possible both for the writer and for readers to stand back from and to understand the ideas and personalities of distant times. It will be necessary to begin with the strongest exercise of imagination of all in looking at the very origins of the communications system and the Post Office, and the earliest forms of work and agitation. Yet, however remote they seem, these distant events live with us still.

NOTES

1 *The Mirror of Literature, Amusement and Instruction,* 12 March 1831, pp. 186–9, 12 May 1838, pp. 318–9. For a similar picture see Doherty (1960), pp. 4–5.
2 Bealey (1976).
3 Besides Chapter 3, see also Baxter (1903), p. 12.
4 *B-H* (10 August 1872). See also Chapter 3, n. 20.
5 Spero (1927), pp. 30–1.

2 'A Powerful Engine of Civilisation': The Post Office Before 1920

When it is considered how much the religious, moral and intellectual progress of the people would be accelerated by the unobstructed circulation of letters and of the many cheap and excellent publications of the present day, the Post Office assumes a new and important character of a powerful engine of civilisation; capable of performing a distinguished part in the great work of National education. (Rowland Hill, *Post Office Reform: Its Importance and Practicability*, 1837, p. 8)

. . . our Post Office is the most perfect, the most complete and, I think, the most effective system of postal arrangement in the world.   (J. McCallum, Liberal MP for Paisley, *Hansard* V, 71 760, 28 April 1915)

We have long been of the opinion that this department should be conducted without any primary regard to profits. If the conveyance and distribution of letters in the mode most convenient to the public still leaves a surplus so much the better; but the first object should be the administration of the business itself.   (*The Times*, 4 February 1853)

. . . every successive Government . . . has done its utmost to squeeze profit out of letter carrying, as if they had been the managers of a gigantic parcels delivery company, whose tenure of office depended on their manufacturing big dividends. (*London Journal*, 16 May 1874)

The Post Office was the first and largest of Britain's state economic enterprises. Since the growth of central government in late mediaeval times, the carriage and delivery of letters has been considered an important function of government. Since the nineteenth century the Post Office has acquired a new range of functions in communication, notably in the organisation of the telegraph and telephone system, and also agency services such as transactions connected with the National Savings Bank, the collection of revenue licences and the payment of old age pensions and other welfare grants. In the 1960s it additionally assumed functions in banking and in data processing. Before being split in 1981 the Post Office employed over 420,000 people, making it the largest single employer in the land.[1] Half of these workers were members of what is now called the Union of Communication Workers.

Inevitably in such a large organisation with such a long history, the Post Office has long since developed a special ethos of its own. Before Victorian standards of 'public service' were superimposed on postal organisation, the Post Office was an important part of the functioning of the state, including both its intelligence services and in the collection of its revenues. Its different activities have often been endowed with an aura of romance. This was so in the days when the post boys rode on ill-defined muddy tracks, and when the great coaches of the eighteenth century took advantage of the expanding road system. It is even so in the era of the complex web of communications between rail and road and air in our own day. The growth of these services and the workers involved in them have played a vital part in the development of modern industrial society.

In the 1980s new and revolutionary methods of organising the Post Office and the services it provides are coming into existence. Not only are the integrated functions of posts and telecommunications being torn asunder, there is even talk of some parts of them being handed over to private enterprise. It is important to emphasise that this represents a departure of some significance not simply in economic organisation, but also in the workings of the state. The Post Office became part of the state and its functioning not in order to accumulate profits, still less because of ideological support for state enterprise as such. The first reason why the communications system came under state control was precisely so that the government could open the letters if it pleased, and intercept the telegrams and telephone calls. These were the origins of the nationalised system, even though in the nineteenth century the Post Office became part of the government's finances, and in the twentieth century part of its public sector. These developments are important not only for everybody using the system, but also for those working within it.[2]

In 1969, the Post Office became a public corporation, and in 1981 two public corporations. Until then its constitution and status were those of an ordinary department of state. The department was under the charge of a minister, the postmaster general. He was a member of the government responsible to Parliament and subject to Parliamentary control in precisely the same way as ministers in charge of other departments. The Post Office was subject to normal Treasury control in matters affecting expenditure and staff. Thus, for nearly all the period covered by this book, Post Office workers were civil servants. This has important consequences for their attitudes, for their civil liberties and for their relations with their employers. Many of these points are discussed in the next chapter, and in the meantime the changes in the organisation and functions of the Post Office will be described as a necessary preliminary to an understanding of the lives and aspirations of its employees.

BEFORE THE NINETEENTH CENTURY

The communication systems of past times have reflected the level of production and the political, social and cultural needs of these periods. Except in times of war, feudal society had little need of a postal system to serve its isolated communities. It was the establishment of a centralised nation state and the growth of commerce in the sixteenth and seventeenth centuries that made necessary a continually functioning postal system. Industrialisation in the eighteenth century created the need for a more complete system of communications. The stage coach and later the railway allowed the state to provide this more adequately and eventually in 1840 to begin a national system of penny postage. After that the developing technology of communications expanded the range and functions of the Post Office.

At their beginnings the British postal services were established to deal with government business and were exclusively for the transport of royal messages, especially in time of war. In 1482, during the war with Scotland, Edward IV introduced the practice 'of appointing a single horseman every twenty miles, by means of whom travelling with the utmost speed and not passing their respective limits, news was always able to be carried by letter from hand to hand 200 miles within two days'. These horsemen used the royal right of purveyance to requisition horses and enforce aid, paying virtually whatever they chose. They were the original 'posts'.

In the 1530s there were posts on the Dover Road. A proclamation of 1555 created a complete system, which also had a monopoly for letting out horses to 'currors' who had a horn hanging on the door or a painted sign to indicate a post house.[3] A 'post' thus stopped being a person and became a place. The word later referred to the whole system. During this period only the posts could loan horses to travellers, a right which they retained until the eighteenth century. The City of London in the time of Queen Mary kept horses from Hackney in East London in readiness for the posts. These horses, when not required, were specially licensed to ply for hire on 'hackney carriages'. In 1583 a royal proclamation granted this privilege more widely to local postmasters.[4] After this the state postal system began to take over the carriage of private mail.

Public control of the postal service thus developed not for economic but for political reasons. So it was that 'the Post Office as a public service began . . . when the Government preferred to keep watch on the subjects of the Crown'.[5] As early as 1324 local constables were 'commanded to make diligent scrutiny of all letters concerning which suspicions might arise'. After the rebellion known as the Pilgrimage of Grace in 1536, a post was first laid to the Lincolnshire area from which it had originated. Queen Elizabeth I always feared plots against her and it was as a result of opening her letters that she decided to have Mary Queen of Scots executed in 1587. In 1591 the government issued a proclamation ordering that no letter should be sent to foreign countries except through the posts and in 1609 this monopoly was extended to include all roads on which the King's posts had been established.[6] During the reigns of James I and Charles I the postal system was one of the frequently attacked royal monopolies, but it nevertheless survived and grew during the period of revolution and civil war in the 1640s and 1650s.

In the 1650s the postal system became firmly established as part of the government's intelligence service. The Secretary of State of that period, John Thurloe, employed an expert letter-opener called Isaac Dorislaus who worked in a special room at the General Letter Office and 'every post night about 11 a'clock he went into that room privately and had all the letters brought and layd before him, to open any he should see good'. Dorislaus continued to be employed by the Post Office after the Restoration of Charles II. Thurloe also sent instructions to local postmasters to set aside the letters of 'ill-affected persons' and 'then privately transmit the same to myself'. In addition, he asked the local officials to report on 'combinations, designs and plots of discontented and suspicious persons'.[7] A proclamation of 1663 stopped the practice of opening letters except on the express permission of the secretary of state. However, in the period of the 'Glorious Revolution' of 1688–9 there was special equipment used for opening and resealing letters. Packet boats to Spain were started in an attempt to isolate the letters of 'Jacobites' – supporters of the deposed King James II. Such practices continued in the eighteenth century and the use of postal servants as part of the government's intelligence network remained important. In 1758 at the trial of a suspected Jacobite for high treason, intercepted letters and the evidence of postal employees was vital for conviction. As the court was told, 'We letter carriers, or postmen, have great opportunities to know the character and dispositions of gentlemen in the several neighbourhoods of this part of the town, from their servants, connexions and correspondents'.

Postmasters continued to spy on all radical and reforming activity. In the social and political conflicts of the 1840s letter opening was widely used against Chartists campaigning for democratic reforms, as well as against such comparatively respectable figures as Mazzini, the Italian nationalist. It was the latter case which provoked the appointment of secret committees of both Commons and Lords to consider the matter and to record most of the letter opening that had gone on until that time. Since then there has undoubtedly been a continuation of the practice of opening letters, but no details are published. Post Office Acts of 1909 and 1953, as well as the 1981 Telecommunications Act, made continued provision for the practice, although permission was a matter for the home secretary and not the post-master general. Similar powers now exist to allow the tapping of telephones and in other ways to take account of the technological development.[8]

At the same time as the security functions of the Post Office largely passed to other parts of the government machinery, the Post Office came to occupy an increasingly important role in the economic calculations of the state. Since the 1630s the postal system was regarded as a source of revenue. At various times in the seventeenth and eighteenth centuries the postal system was simply 'farmed out' to private individuals, who paid back a fixed amount and made as much money as they could themselves. From 1663 the profits were owned by James, Duke of York, but they reverted to the Crown when he became James II in 1685, coming under Treasury control. In this period the postal revenues were used to pay for the upkeep of the mistresses of Charles II, some of it being for the Crown's own use as well as for the secret service. In 1660 the profit was calculated as £21,500 by a House of Commons Committee. By 1685 the Post Office had an income of about £80,000 and expenditure of only about a quarter of that.[9] In the eighteenth century the revenue from the post was used for many purposes of which the most important can be gathered from the title of the 1711 Act which was 'for establishing a General Post Office for all Her Majesty's Dominions and for settling a weekly sum out of the Revenues thereof for the Service of the War and other Her Majesty's Occasions'. The Act specifically set aside £700 a week for the state and there was also provision for any surplus above a certain amount to be paid to the Treasury.

Before the 1840s the high charges caused the postal system to be used only in comparatively rare and urgent cases. The earliest postal rates of 1635 based on a single sheet of paper were of 2d up to 80 miles, 4d up to 140 miles, 6d for any longer distance in England and 8d for anywhere in Scotland. Double sheets, envelopes or enclosures cost more. The 1711 Act increased the basic 2d rate to 3d. In 1765 there was some slight reduction for short-distance letters, but in 1784 the rates were raised to 2d per stage when the mail coach system began. Further increases, making the rates 3d up to 15 miles and 8d above 150 miles came in 1797. In 1801 the London penny post became twopenny post and in 1805 this became the threepenny post except in the delivery area of the GPO. In 1801 and 1812 there were further general increases in postage, which then reached their highest points of 4d for 15 miles, and 1s 5d (7p) above 700 miles. The mileage scale was so steep that the charge for a single sheet from London to Liverpool, Plymouth or York was 11d, though a century earlier it would have been 3d. In addition to the postage there were varying charges for collection or delivery of letters.[10]

Before the 1830s, the postal system served both the political and economic ends of the state, but grew slowly and haphazardly. The first official of the royal household that we know of who ran the postal system was Sir Brian Tuke, Clerk of the Signet, the private secretarial establishment of King Henry VIII from at least 1512 and Governor of the King's Post from 1517.[11] In 1533 in response to complaints about the service, Tuke wrote to the powerful Thomas Cromwell about his difficulties. He explained 'that except for the hackney horses between Gravesend and Dover, there is no such usual conveyance for post in this realm as in the accustomed places of France and other parts'. Without any fixed posts on most roads, when attempts were made to arrange the carriage of mail 'the constables many times [were forced] to take the horses out of ploughs and carts'.[12]

Other problems for postmasters resulted from royal financial stringency under the early Stuarts. In July 1617 a petition from Thomas Hutchins, Postmaster of Litchfield to the Privy Council 'on behalf of the posts of England . . . [asked] that their arrears of pay of a year and a half may be discharged'. Similar complaints were heard in the following years, together with countercharges that the postmasters had become 'insolent and negligent'. Hutchins was for a time imprisoned for his activities on behalf of his fellows. In 1628 in what has been described as the earliest 'combined action by officers of the Post Office for the redress of grievances', 'all the Post of England' petitioned the Privy Council, claiming arrears that now amounted to £22,626 and saying that those not already in prison for debt were soon likely to be. It is not surprising that in August 1627 it was reported to the Lord Treasurer that there were 'many faults among the posts' attributed to the fact that 'they are not able to perform the service for want of pay'.[13]

It was partly in response to such problems as these that proposals were put forward in 1635 to make the postal system balance its accounts, and later in the same year Thomas Witherings was given power by proclamation to run both foreign and domestic mails. Witherings, who has been described as 'the first of the notable postal reformers of this country' tried to make the system self-supporting by abolishing the arrangement whereby all private postings were organised by the postmasters themselves. He established a central Post Office in London, with offices in the main cities and many new fixed posts elsewhere. He took control of all private postings, simply paying the expenses of the postmasters and their messengers. Through a system of regular timetables and day and night travelling it became possible to get letters from London to Edinburgh or Plymouth in three or four days. He also established the first permanent posts to Holyhead. In the atmosphere of intrigue and cupidity that preceded the outbreak of civil war, it was impossible for Witherings to continue such a successful enterprise for long. In 1637 he lost control of the foreign posts and in 1640 of the inland section as well. It was said that whatever his successes in gaining revenue for the Crown, the postmasters had lost even more income from private letters, and Witherings himself made a fortune. In 1637 it was said that £60,000 was owed to the postmasters.[14]

In the period after the reign of Witherings, the running of the postal services became a subject of considerable litigation and political dispute. However, virtually all the postal service remained under the control of the Parliamentary forces during the civil war and in 1650 it was again put out to be 'farmed' by John Manley.[15] In 1653 the inland and foreign posts were again brought under joint control and in 1655 the Secretary of State John Thurloe, whose activities have already been mentioned, bought control of the system. The 1650s was a fertile period for the development of the postal service. In 1653 a packet service to Dublin and Waterford was initiated. In 1659 there was even a suggestion published in a pamphlet by one John Hill for a penny post run entirely by private enterprise. In 1657 an Act entitled 'Postage of England, Scotland and Ireland Settled' laid out the main lines of the postal system for the rest of the century. It set up a complete system for the British Isles, established a 'postmaster general' for the first time and re-established the monopoly for letter delivery and for post horses. This Act was retained in its essentials by a further measure passed after the Restoration.[16]

The pattern of post-roads used to convey letters developed in the mid-seventeenth century and continued until the advent of the railways in the nineteenth. The Great North Road went to Edinburgh, the West Road to Plymouth and later to Falmouth. There were also roads to Bristol, Dover and Yarmouth as well as the Chester Road which went on to Holyhead and thence from Dublin to Galway, Coleraine and Youghal. There were very few cross-posts giving direct connections between places on different main roads. Letters from one road to another had to pass through London and to pay postage via London.[17] A penny post was set up in London for a short time from 1680 to 1682 by a merchant called William Dockwra. He established a network of offices in the London area and promised to deliver letters there for a pre-paid penny. His activities met with opposition from porters who had formerly carried mail on a casual basis, and further difficulty came because of the lack of systematic numbering of streets. The network was ended by being pursued through the courts by James, Duke of York, who claimed Dockwra was infringing on his monopoly.[18] The penny post was then taken over by the Postmaster-General (Dockwra being Comptroller from 1696 to 1700) and survived as the London Post until 1855, completely separate from the general post. The separate postal traditions of London were thus begun in ways that often still survive. A cheap and efficient penny post, however, had to wait until 1840.

There were further innovations in the postal system of the late seventeenth century. The role of the postmaster general was reduced after the former Leveller John Wildman held the position for two years in the wake of the 'Glorious Revolution' of 1689. From then until 1823, except for short intervals, two people held the position in commission.[19] In Scotland, with which permanent postal communication had first been established in 1603, there was a separate Post Office for a time from 1695 to 1711. There was a similar arrangement for Ireland from 1784 to 1831, which was discontinued until the establishment of the Irish Free State in 1922.[20] In 1711 a new Act laid out the main lines of postal development until the reforms of 1837. It has been called the 'second charter of Post Office' following the legislation of 1657 and 1660.[21] This 1711 Act finally gave the monopoly on all inland posts to the postmaster-general, but continued the separate public penny post within ten miles of the London GPO. It also placed limits on the political activities of Post Office staff which are discussed in the next chapter.

The Post Office in the eighteenth century 'was not merely a branch of the revenue', it was also 'the centre of imperial communications . . . a propaganda and intelligence organ, serving as the government's mouthpiece, eyes and ears; and an important source of patronage, employing hundreds of officials, postmasters and sailors'.[22] In a period of rapid growth in industry and trade, the Post Office continued with little initiative to respond haphazardly to public agitation and to the activities of enterprising individuals in improving its service. In 1714 'surveyors' were first sent out permanently 'especially into the great manufacturing and distant parts', but it was only the development of by- and cross-posts in addition to the system running through London that led to an improvement in the facilities provided. This change was the work of Ralph Allen, Postmaster of Bath, who in 1719 worked out a scheme on these lines. In 1720 he was granted a contract to work the cross-posts, which was regularly renewed until his death in 1764. During his tenure he reorganised and extended the cross-posts and also improved the postal services on many of the main roads out of London. The Postmaster General viewed Allen's development of the cross-posts with favour because they increased the number of 'country letters', that is, letters which did not go through London. The average income from these country letters increased from £15,434 in the seven years before 1720 to £17,464 in 1727–34. By 1761 Allen claimed that he had dealt with 'the joint mischief of cheating the revenue and interrupting and obstructing the commerce'. When his contract was renewed for the last time in that year, the rent was still £6,000, but if receipts from country letters fell below £20,000, Allen was to reimburse the Post Office for the deficit. Allen's success was largely due to the strict supervision he exercised over postmasters and their accounts and to the intelligent use of postal correspondences between different towns. He went beyond being a mere 'farmer' of by- and cross-posts by improving the overall inland services of the Post Office in this period. Allen increased the income from an average of £177,492 in the period 1724–33 to £243,121 in 1754–63. However, he did this while obtaining a substantial personal fortune for himself, said to amount to as much as £500,000. Thus he became a powerful figure in the local government of Bath, with a substantial mansion where he entertained the most famous in the land, but he did little to increase the profits of the Post Office. While the income was increasing within the years mentioned, the proportion of expenditure to income rose from 46 per cent to 62 per cent and the profits actually fell from £96,002 to £87,911. Allen's tenure of power was thus not uniformly beneficial.[23]

While the conveyance of letters between towns was thus increased during the eighteenth century, there was not the same progress in delivery within towns. The London penny post, now under public control, was often praised. Daniel Defoe wrote in the 1720s of how

it is come also into so exquisite a management, that nothing can be more exact, and 'tis with the utmost safety and despatch, that letters are delivered at the remotest corner of the town, almost as soon as they could be sent by a messenger, and that from four, five, six to eight times a day.

Defoe also numbered amongst its advantages that it could 'employ so many poor people in the diligences of it', and boasted that none of the other great European cities had a similar service.[24] However, in the corrupt inefficient eighteenth-century administrative system with only three senior officials running the service, and with at least two of them often absentees, the service stagnated. It was at the initiative of a letter carrier, Edward Johnson, that the service was rationalised by reducing the number of offices and increasing the number of carriers. An Act of 1794 gave effect to his schemes and within two years the gross revenue of the service had been tripled to nearly £30,000, though at the expense of doing away with compulsory prepayment.[25] Elsewhere local deliveries were left to postmasters, who could do and charge as much as they liked. An Act of 1765 legalised penny posts 'for any city or town or the suburbs thereof' if the Post Office decided that the service was 'necessary and convenient'. The Act was but slowly put into effect, however. A penny post began in Dublin in 1773, and at Edinburgh a privately run system under Peter Williamson was allowed until it was taken over by the Edinburgh GPO in 1793. Further penny posts were established in 1793 in Manchester, Birmingham and Bristol. In 1774 in a number of towns, legal actions were initiated to enforce the free delivery of letters. An Act of 1801 allowed its expansion to any village asking for it to be delivered from the next post town. The postmasters general grudgingly thereafter admitted it in towns which demanded it, and from the 1820s onwards there was a rapid expansion of the local penny post. As late as 1772 there were letter carriers only in London, Edinburgh and Dublin. The local posts soon increased their numbers, as well as of sorters and clerks. In Sheffield, for example, where the penny post was introduced in 1817, it must soon have taxed the resources of the three letter carriers in the city.[26]

The expansion of trade and industry in the eighteenth century and the slow improvement in the road system made possible the development of the use of the horse-drawn coach. The mail coach of the 1780s was the first major technological change in the postal system since it began. It was adopted reluctantly, only after stage coaches had made possible a flourishing and illegal postal network which was quicker and safer than the old system of post-boys. The campaign for the introduction of mail coaches was led by John Palmer, an energetic theatre proprietor from Bath, who numbered among his achievements the breaking of strikes within his own profession. He does not seem to have been a competent administrator. He proposed a more effective form of work discipline for the post-boy, whom he described as an 'idle boy without character, mounted on a worn-out hack, who so far from being able to defend himself or escape from a robber . . . is more likely to be in league with him'. Palmer won the confidence of William Pitt who introduced his ideas after he became Prime Minister in 1793. He appointed Palmer Comptroller of the Posts, but he proved so unpopular that he had to be retired with a pension.[27]

The mail coaches were run on contract and maintained an average speed of up to nine miles an hour. They worked on a fixed time-table which still radiated from London. Business was arranged so that coaches left the GPO for the major post towns each evening – in the 1820s twenty coaches departed at 8 p.m. in a fixed order of precedence. They carried a few passengers as well as the mail, and extended the postal services to such towns as Liverpool and Leeds, which had not been well served in the past. The amount of legally carried mail grew rapidly and the income of the Post Office increased from less than £400,000 in 1782–3 to over £1,000,000 in 1798–9. Between the same years the profits of the postal system increased from £159,625 to £652,388. Not all of this growth can be attributed to the mail coach, since increases in rates and other factors were also important. However, there can be no doubt that the mail coach greatly improved the efficiency of the service, not least on the traditional post roads.

The era of the mail coach was a short one: within sixty years it 'was born, attained perfection and, alas, perished'. It gave way to the railway but had done much to capture the imagination of those looking back on it. The picturesquely named coaches and coaching inns, the gaily-coloured liveries and brightly burnished coach horns created a special world of their own, and the mail drivers and guards became 'a race of men by themselves', tough and convivial. One old coachman regretted the passing of an era 'afore reform and rails turned everything upside down, and men rode, as nature intended they should, on pikes [turnpikes], with smart and active cattle, and not by machinery like bags of cotton and hardware'.[28]

The eighteenth century also saw a great expansion in foreign posts. There was a privately run 'merchant strangers post' at least from 1514. This continued to be independent even though there was a royal appointee in charge from 1569, and from 1623 there was a 'Postmaster General for Foreign Parts'. Witherings was the first person to unite this position with control of the inland postal services. In 1633 it was decided 'in conformity with other nations' to establish 'packet boats at fit stages, to run day and night' from Dover to Calais.[29] Packet services in Ireland were established in 1653 and between Harwich and Holland in 1660. In 1689 a further service was started between Falmouth and Corruna in Spain, and during the eighteenth century Falmouth became the main package station and mail service to the West Indies, America and the Mediterranean. Boats on these routes were nearly always privately owned and run on contract for the packet service. The wars of the period created difficulties for the packets which were often heavily armed and could thus easily bully other ships and engage in a little private smuggling. Efforts to suppress the latter practice resulted in a mutiny and strike of sailors at Falmouth, which was suppressed with some vigour by the Admiralty authorities.[30]

The whole system of foreign mail ran at a considerable loss in the eighteenth century and thus was investigated by the Commissioners of Fees and Gratuities in 1788. The report of the Commissioners was so embarrassing that Pitt locked it in his desk for four years and it was not printed for a further twelve. They showed that the packet service had become 'an unbounded source of Expense and Peculation'. Those who profited included Anthony Todd, the Post Office Secretary who, besides receiving a commission of 2½ per cent on the whole expenditure of the packets at Dover, Harwich and Falmouth, also partly owned many of the ships and received numerous other emoluments. In order to remedy these abuses, the Commissioners recommended less arming of ships, and allowing them to jettison their cargo if necessary. They proposed reducing costs by ordering that boats under seizure should not be ransomed. Their deliberations also resulted in the order that nobody employed by the Post Office should have a financial interest in the packets.[31] In the same period a Ship Letter Act was passed putting an end to the futile efforts that had been devoted to preventing all private boats from carrying mail and fixing the rates for such carriage, increasing to twopence per letter the fees to masters of ships involved. At the same time a Ship Letter Officer was established. In 1827 the Falmouth packets were placed under Admiralty control, and in 1837 this was applied to the entire overseas mail service.[32]

POST OFFICE REFORM, 1835–40

The expanding postal services of the 1820s and 1830s were symbolised in 1829 by the movement of the General Post Office from Lombard Street to a new building just north of St Paul's Cathedral at St Martin's-le-Grand, surrounded by classical ionic porticoes and columns. This new building however housed a postal system that remained expensive and haphazard and an administration based on a system of patronage which could not keep pace with the demands of an expanding industrial society. The Post Office needed to change and like many other institutions of the period did so under the impact of social change and political agitation. The increasing political power of the commercial and industrial bourgeoisie lay behind the extension of the Parliamentary franchise in 1832 and the repeal of the Corn Laws in 1846. It was also instrumental in revolutionising the postal system. The period of the building of the railways in the 1830s and 1840s also witnessed a rapidly growing interest in popular education and political propaganda. The growth of a cheaper and more efficient postal service was part of the same process.

In the years after the Great Reform Act of 1832, Robert Wallace, a Glasgow merchant who represented Greenock following the extension of the franchise, began to campaign against the corruption and inefficiency of the Post Office. Basing himself on the 1788 Report and a further series of inquiries into postal revenue in 1829–30, Wallace attacked the inefficiency and inflated salary of Sir Francis Freeling, the aging Post Office Secretary, and asserted that his functions should be carried out by men 'bred up to business'. Between 1835 and 1838 a further ten reports were produced by commissioners appointed as a result of his efforts. They made numerous proposals to the Post Office and as a result of these, Wallace managed to initiate some important changes. In 1836 free tenders for mail coach contracts were allowed and in 1838 the money order office was nationalised. Its fees were then reduced and its business multiplied. The number of inland money orders increased from 55,000 in 1836 to an average of 7 million per annum from 1857 to 1861.[33] Wallace's campaign also did something to end the practice of 'franking'. This dated back for nearly 200 years and allowed MPs and members of the House of Lords to sign the outside of any letter which was then allowed to go free. Despite limitations in the practice from 1784 and its standardisation in 1837 there were still 6·6 million out of 82·5 million letters in 1839 sent by this method. In 1840 it was abolished except for official business.[34] In 1837 Wallace got a series of Acts through Parliament which generally standardised and improved the administration of the Post Office, but did nothing to fundamentally alter its practice and organisation.[35]

Important issues were raised in a pamphlet which also appeared in 1837 entitled *Post Office Reform: Its Importance and Practicability*, written by one Rowland Hill.[36] Hill was born in Kidderminster in 1795 and came from a remarkable family of Victorian social and educational reformers.[37] He was a founder member of the Society for the Diffusion of Useful Knowledge in 1827, and in 1835 was the secretary of a body that first proposed the colonisation of South Australia. In looking around for a new cause he alighted almost accidentally on postal reform. Like Palmer he came to the subject from outside, and also like Palmer, he made few friends within the postal service itself. Anthony Trollope, the surveyor and novelist, thought Hill 'entirely unfit to manage or arrange labour', and his activities as Post Office Secretary, described below in Chapter 4, make it clear that this was true.[38] Hill's plan nevertheless achieved so much fame and success that he is seen as one of the great Victorian benefactors when other critics and reformers of the postal system are forgotten. In his famous pamphlet, Hill pointed out that since postal rates had reached their maximum in 1812, the net postal income had hardly increased. Thus in 1815 it was £1,557,291 and in 1835 it was £1,540,300. This was despite the fact that the population had increased from 19·5 to 25·6 million in the same period. He thought that if rates were reduced then postage would increase. He found that the actual cost of taking a letter from London to Edinburgh was one-sixth of a penny, and asserted that 'the existing practice of regulating the amount of postage by the distance over which an inland letter was conveyed however plausible in appearance, had no foundation in principle'. He thus proposed a uniform rate of a penny for any inland letter weighing up to an ounce. Seeing how 'exceedingly tedious, inconvenient and consequently expensive' was the work of London letter carriers, Hill proposed the prepayment of letters, suggesting various methods of doing this, but eventually favouring the adhesive postage stamp.[39]

These proposals seized the popular imagination and soon a campaign of political agitation was undertaken on their behalf. Petitions to Parliament were organised from church organisations and mechanics institutes, a newspaper called *The Post Circular* was issued and a Mercantile Committee was set up. Wallace also arranged for a Parliamentary Select Committee.[40] The support of the commercial community, particularly the big banking houses, was a notable feature of the campaign for a penny post. Also of interest is the spirit of moral righteousness and the aims of social control that lay behind it, clearly indicated in the quotation given at the head of this chapter. The Select Committee was told by John Dunlop, a temperance advocate from Greenock, that 'one of the worst parts of the present system of heavy postage is, that it gradually estranges an absentee from home and family, and tends to engender a neglect of ties of blood'. Not only that, but a cheaper postage would prevent men having to 'go upon tramp' to search for work and would also 'satisfy the workmen's minds about the rate of wages in different parts of the country' and would thus put an end to 'excitement' and perhaps strikes. Hill himself hinted that it might even prevent the need for trade unions at all.[41]

Post Office officials remained steadfastly unconvinced by Hill's arguments. The Postmaster General, the Earl of Litchfield, said that 'of all the wild and visionary schemes which he had ever heard or read of, it was the most extraordinary'. Thus *The Times* could see the struggle for the penny post as 'the cause of the whole people of the United Kingdom against the small coterie of place holders in St. Martin's-le-Grand and its dependencies'.[42] The measure was finally agreed in Parliament in 1839 as the price of support by radical MPs for the failing Whig ministry of Lord Melbourne. A uniform inland postal rate of a penny for half-ounce letters was introduced from January 1840.[43]

It is important to point out, however, in distinction to most accounts of the matter, that those opposed to the measure were not knaves or fools in all cases. The old Secretary, Sir Francis Freeling, wrote shortly before his death in 1836 that 'to make the Post Office revenue as productive as possible was long ago impressed upon me by successive ministers as a duty which I was under a solemn obligation to discharge'. Many of Hill's associates were clear that they wanted the postal services to perform quite another function. Henry Warburton, the philosophical radical and MP for Bridport, whose role in securing the penny post was described as 'second to Rowland Hill alone', said that it was wrong for the Post Office to be 'treated as a mere matter of revenue' and it was right that the public should consider 'the primary object of its institution was to contribute to their convenience'. Hill himself despite a quotation on the title page of his pamphlet that revenue was 'not the primary consideration' remained less than honest about the effect his measure would have on Post Office income. In his pamphlet he said vaguely that 'reduction of postage to a considerable extent would produce an increase in revenue'. When the

Duke of Wellington said that a penny post would mean 'a sudden diminution in revenue', he replied categorically that 'the revenue would be more likely to gain than to suffer' from his proposals. Although most of the witnesses at the 1838 Select Committee had agreed that the number of letters would increase under the new arrangements, few shared the confident predictions, which Hill continued to voice, that the service would soon return to its former level of profitability.[44] Thus the profit fell rapidly from the £1·6 million that it had been in the three years before the introduction of the penny post to £0·5 million and did not again reach the 1840 figure until 1874. The figure for income of £2·3 million just before the change was however reached in 1851. The chief reason for the failure of Hill's predictions to come to fruition was that postal business did not increase at the rate he foretold. The increase in the first year in the number of letters delivered was only from 82·6 million in 1839 to 168·8 million in 1840. It is true that the numbers then rose very rapidly to 564 million letters in 1860, but even this figure was insufficient to reach the same profit. It was later calculated that a twopenny post might have enabled the profit to remain constant.[45]

NINETEENTH-CENTURY DEVELOPMENT

The Post Office in the era of the penny post became, despite itself and the predictions of its founder, a public service rather than a revenue-gathering department. The reasons for the comparative lack of prosperity in the nineteenth century cannot however be solely attributed to the failure of the predictions of Rowland Hill. The private railway companies which exercised a monopoly in carrying the mail overcharged and exploited the public postal service. The Post Office Secretary said in 1837 that the companies 'seem inclined to charge just as much as they please' and in later years there were complaints of their slowness and inefficiency. In 1855 it was calculated that carriage by rail cost 10d per mile and by any other method 2¼d. The 'railway interest' was one of the best organised nineteenth-century pressure groups with up to 130 MPs on the company boards to state their case. It was originally established to negotiate favourable terms for the carriage of mails and had many eloquent advocates, like Robert Stephenson, son of the famous inventor and entrepreneur. In 1856, the Inspector General of Mails showed that the railway companies charged at the very least 50 per cent more on the conveyance of mails than the coaching companies had done, and that this amounted to 300 per cent of their own running costs. By this means they obtained almost 4 per cent of their earnings from less than 0·2 per cent of the bulk that they carried.[46] The railway companies also exercised pressure for many years to prevent the Post Office from carrying parcels. Although there was a Postal Association agitating at least from 1851 for the introduction of a parcel post, it was only after pressure from the foreign countries who wanted reciprocal arrangements with Britain that a system was introduced here in 1883. Even then the railway companies insisted on having 55 per cent of the revenue, which was considerably more than their share in running it.[47]

The expansion of the overseas operations of the Post Office was also considerably inhibited by the pressure of private commercial interests. During the period from 1837 to 1860 when the Admiralty controlled the packet service, steamships were for the first time introduced. The big companies built their businesses with the help of enormous subsidies which were supposed to be partly based on the military and naval value of the ships. Thus Samuel Cunard was by 1846 charging £145,000 per annum for his transatlantic line and the Royal Mail Steamship Packet Company to the West Indies cost £240,000, although only £40,000 of its receipts actually came from carrying mails. The Peninsular and Oriental Steam Navigation Company – the P&O line – also began to develop services to the East. In 1853 a Select Committee found that the Admiralty was paying £825,000 a year for services on which the postage was about £480,000.[48] When the Post Office again took over the packet services in 1860, almost £850,000 was being paid for foreign and colonial contracts to shipping companies, severely limiting the returns on the service. In 1870 just over £1 million was paid to the shipping companies, including £450,000 to the P&O line alone. Successive postmasters general tried to confront the companies, but it was not easy to defeat them. In 1874 the West Indian service was put out to tender and it became 'almost self-sufficient'. In 1886 the costs on other Atlantic lines were reduced by threatening to send the mail in foreign ships to break the monopoly of the Cunard and White Star lines. As late as 1900, however, over £300,000 was still being paid out for these services. This represented a tiny fraction of the actual costs of postage.[49]

It was largely because of the enormous costs that the Post Office in the nineteenth century was reluctant to reduce the charges for international postage. In 1847 the American pacifist Elihu Burritt began his campaign in favour of Universal Penny Postage, which he ran in parallel with a League of Universal Brotherhood. *The Times* spoke favourably of his postage schemes as serving 'the greater and nobler principles of peace and good fellowship in the world'.[50] However, it was again only under pressure from foreign postal systems that the British agreed to change. In 1875, largely on the initiative of the Germans and the Americans, a Universal Postal Union was set up which fixed rates of 2½d per half ounce irrespective of distance, though this took some little time to introduce in Britain.

It was in the following period that a new postal reformer, John Henniker Heaton, put forward the aim of an Imperial Penny Postage which would, he said, give effect to a 'feeling in favour of closer union between the mother country and the colonies' and do something to stop 'crafty rivals' who wanted to 'replace us and our wares and our rule'. However, the Post Office remained opposed to such ideas and was only persuaded to introduce the Universal Postal Union rates within the Empire in 1892. Under the inspiration of the great bout of pro-Imperialist propaganda that surrounded Queen Victoria's Diamond Jubilee in 1897, the Canadians, who had never regarded their Post Office as a revenue-earning institution, introduced a penny rate on all foreign correspondence. In the following year there was an Imperial Postal Conference in London where a number of other parts of the Empire agreed to follow suit, so that eventually by 1911 there was a system of penny postage throughout virtually all the British Empire.[51] It had also only been as a result of Heaton's campaigns that the British Post Office adopted the Universal Postal Union rates. The Universal Postal Union at its various meetings improved and cheapened international postal communications.[52] A further step to universal penny postage came with the introduction of this facility with the United States in 1908.

Despite this slow and hesitant expansion of an international system of postal communication, the nineteenth-century inland postal system grew rapidly and in many important ways. The introduction of the penny post allowed all sorts of improvements in the systems of carrying the mails. The adhesive postage stamp allowed the easy and efficient prepayment of letters. Soon afterwards, people began to make letter boxes in their front doors, since prepayment, though it did not become universal, meant that letter carriers no longer needed to wait at the address for payment.[53] The practice of bellmen walking the streets to collect letters was discontinued in London in 1846, in Dublin in 1859 and other places in the following decade. This brought to an end what William Hazlitt described as 'a lively pleasant sound that rings clear through the length of many half-forgotten years'. In 1852 Anthony Trollope, then Postmaster of Jersey, adopted a continental practice of setting up a street pillar box at St Helier. Two years later six were set up in different parts of the centre of London. In 1856, fifty new boxes were constructed and the pillar boxes soon spread elsewhere.[54] From 1838 there were also Travelling Post Offices, or carriages on trains especially adapted so that sorting could be done in transit. Until 1860 this work was done by a special class of mail guards, but since that time sorting and postal grades have been involved.[55] Other changes in the 1850s included the introduction of postal districts in London – at first ten and later eight. The numbered subdivisions came in 1917. District offices also came to Liverpool in 1863 and eight postal districts began in Manchester in 1868.[56]

The penny post also brought with it changes in the type of mail carried. For one thing, gradual reductions in the rate allowed for a great increase in the number of letters. Thus, from 1871, up to an ounce could be carried for 1d with an extra ½d for each succeeding ounce up to twelve. By the period 1890–7 the average number of letters delivered each year was 1,796 million. After 1897 when the penny rate was allowed up to four ounces there were further increases to 3,477·8 million in 1913–14, or seventy-five letters per head of the population each year, as compared to three in the year before the introduction of the penny post.[57]

The service was improved in many ways. By 1859 it was said that 93 per cent of letters could be delivered free and in 1897 it was possible to announce that delivery could be guaranteed to any house in the United Kingdom.[58] Although the stamp on newspapers allowing them to go free was abolished in 1855, and they had to go by ordinary post from 1870, the numbers of newspapers sent still increased.[59] The sending of Christmas cards began in 1843 and it became a more widespread practice with the invention of cheap colour printing in the 1850s. From 1870 postcards could be sent, though up to 1894 they had to be specially provided by the Post Office. By the end of the century these included the increasingly popular picture postcards. Thus in the year up to March 1902, 445 million cards were delivered and in 1913 this had increased to 926 million.[60] Another new postal practice that followed the penny post was the registration of letters, ensuring that 'the temptation to dishonesty formerly affected to the servants of the Post Office [was] almost entirely abolished'. Begun in 1841, the registration system was cheapened in 1868 and there was a separate delivery arranged of letters so sent.[61] In 1848 a 'book post' was introduced and from 1904 this became a 'halfpenny post' for carrying printed documents of all kinds. By March 1914 the Postmaster General could report that in the previous year 1,172 million items had been carried in this way. By then the service had also been amalgamated with a separate inland 'pattern post' which existed from 1863 to 1871 and a 'sample post' of 1887–97, two arrangements which existed largely to avoid the susceptibilities of the railway companies, though as already mentioned, a parcel post system had been introduced in 1883.[62]

The nineteenth-century Post Office came to be seen as one of the great civilising influences of Victorian England. It also expanded from a small revenue-earning department of state to big business with an enormous turnover and a great number of employees. Although the postal revenue did take some time to recover from the impact of the penny post, when it did so there was a big increase. By 1880–1 the total income of the postal service was £7·0 million, and the profit £2·72 million. In 1900 these figures had risen to £13·78 million and £3·95 million respectively. In 1913–14 the postal services made a profit of £6·17 million and in 1918–19 £8·17 million.[63] In the same period the number of employees of the Post Office increased dramatically. In 1854, at the time of the first Postmaster General's report the total was a mere 21,574, including only 9,152 letter carriers, messengers and sorters. By 1880 this total had risen to 47,000 and by 1913–14 to 249,606 of whom 60,659 were women.[64]

This expansion was not simply the result of the growth of the postal services, but was also caused by the Post Office taking on a number of new functions, some of them in no way connected with communications. The money order department was used in 1861 to set up a Post Office Savings Bank. The original suggestion that the Post Office should handle small deposits was made as early as 1807. The measure was only introduced in 1861 when William Gladstone was Chancellor of the Exchequer and was part of the efforts of the Victorian governing classes to encourage thrift and self-help among the poor. Later the confidence of small savers grew in the facilities provided by the Post Office as against those provided by unreliable local banks. The Post Office Savings Bank was greatly expanded during the 1880s and 1890s when smaller deposits and other extended facilities were allowed. From 1905 'withdrawal on demand' for amounts up to £1 was introduced. By the end of 1913 there were over 9 million accounts with an average of £20 7s (£20 35) in each. Less successful were efforts to use the Post Office for insurance and annuity business following the Government Annuities Act of 1864. Although there was a small stream of business in the field, especially when it was brought in with the Savings Bank in 1882, the Post Office never seriously competed with the assurance societies and their canvassers.[65] Another new function adopted by the Post Office was the issuing of revenue licences. The revenue for dog licences was first collected in 1869 and soon afterwards guns, carriages and a number of other items were added to the list, as well as motor cars in 1902. Post Offices were also used to pay old age pensions after their introduction in 1908.[66] However, the most important extensions in the work of the nineteenth-century Post Office came not through expansion into these new fields, but through technological change in the field of communications itself.

TELEGRAPHS AND TELEPHONES

The sending of messages by means of electricity has greatly altered methods of communication for over a century now. It has also done much to change the character of Post Office work and the jobs of many of its employees.

Early methods of sending messages by telegraphy were developed in Britain and the United States in the 1830s and were used at first to help in the running of railways and mines. In 1846 what became known as the Electric and International Telegraph Company was set up by William Cooke, one of the original inventors, and John Lewis Ricardo, MP for Stoke and nephew of the great economist. This company, together with the British and Irish Magnetic, built up a network for the conveyance of public and private messages which by 1855 included a total of 600 stations and 8,500 miles of line, mostly on land leased from the permanent ways of railway companies. Rates charged were high – a shilling for twenty words up to fifty miles, increasing to five shillings over 150 miles. In 1860 and 1861 the London District Telegraph Company and the United Kingdom Telegraph Company entered the field. The latter organisation tried to charge lower fixed rates, but after a short phase of price cutting, oligopoly conditions returned to the industry with agreements between the companies for slightly reduced rates of a shilling up to 100 miles and two shillings beyond 200. By 1865 there were 16,000 miles of line sending 4·5 million messages.[67]

The telegraph companies, particularly the newer ones, were not very profitable and this was reflected in the difficulties they had in raising loans on the stock market. At the same time, the political and even military importance of the telegraph system began to be noted. As early as 1848 the government commandeered the system for a week at a cost of £300 to prevent Chartists from sending messages and to arrange for the deposition of troops and soldiers. In 1854 one progressive magazine asked: 'Is not telegraphic communication as much a function of Government as the conveyance of letters?' As a result of their high charges, extensive private powers and imputed inefficiency, the companies became 'exceptionally unpopular', so it seemed that there was 'no interest in the Kingdom . . . so cordially disliked by the press'.[68] Not only that, however, but many of those associated with the companies themselves came to favour public ownership. Thomas Allen, who had inventions in the field to his credit and was involved in the United Kingdom Company, favoured such a step in 1854, as also did J. L. Ricardo and a number of chambers of commerce. W. S. Jevons, one of the most distinguished economists of the day, and naturally an opponent of state intervention, nevertheless concluded that 'at present we have neither the advantages of monopoly nor those of free competition' and since the current situation was so unsatisfactory he 'would rather see that monopoly in the hand of the Government than that of a private company'.

In 1867 F. I. Scudamore, the energetic Receiver and Accountant General of the Post Office, was given the task of assessing whether the Post Office could run the telegraph system. He concluded that such an arrangement would be more efficient and described many methods whereby this could be put into practice. He summarised the case against the companies by asserting

that the existing charges for the transmission of messages are too high; that many places and districts are unprovided with facilities for telegraphic communication; that, in the great majority of places that are provided with telegraphic communication, the telegraphic office is inconveniently remote from the centre of business and population, and open too small a portion of the day.

Talk of a take-over and of the compensation that would follow soon solved the problems of the companies. For the London District it was found that 'shareholders are relieved of much anxiety' by the proposal since they could channel their compensation payment into forms of investment with a higher return. The older companies were in a position to pay much higher dividends and the value of their shares rose spectacularly. All of the companies withdrew whatever opposition they had initially expressed and were said to be 'jubilant' at terms which gave in to every demand they made.[69]

Thus it was that the Post Office, which had shown itself so well able to manage an increasing range of enterprises, took over the most advanced form of communication from private enterprise with little or no opposition even from the owners. It was certainly of some interest that in the year of the Second Reform Act, when the parliamentary franchise was for the first time extended to some working men, the state adopted an important new function. The process, however, did not go as smoothly as was anticipated. For one thing, although Scudamore had opposed taking over the whole of the system, it was soon found that, unless this was done, private interests would be able to retain control of the most lucrative parts. A number of extra parts of the system thus had to be bought. It was also discovered, after the original plans were discussed, that the government had to negotiate with the railway companies for the reversionary rights over the routes on which most of the telegraph lines were situated. The railway companies naturally drove a hard bargain, their claims being described by at least one postmaster general as 'preposterous'. Both they, and the newspapers, who had been enthusiastic supporters of nationalisation, were given special concessions in the use of the system, the latter being said to cost the Post Office as much as £400,000 per annum by 1901. Also, the telegraph companies did nothing to add to their capital stock or labour force in the final years when they were waiting to be taken over. Much new investment proved necessary at the time of the change and 2,400 new telegraphists had to be taken on as well as 1,000 messengers, almost doubling the labour force. Thus although the level of business increased in line with Scudamore's anticipations, the state telegraph system began with a burden of debt that it was never to shake off. The total cost of the take-over grew from Scudamore's original estimate of £2·5 to £6·6 million.[70]

Despite these financial burdens the Post Office ran the telegraph system cheaply and efficiently. A uniform rate of a shilling for twenty words was charged, including an increasing range of free deliveries. Within two years the number of offices open was almost doubled to 5,000 with 22,000 miles of line. By the year ending in March 1873, business had doubled since the state take-over began in 1870 to 15 million messages, and this figure had again doubled by 1885, when the sixpenny rate for telegrams was introduced. The Post Office showed no reluctance to introduce technical improvements. In 1873 the 'duplex' system for sending two messages on one line was introduced and in little over a decade 'quadruplex' and 'multiplex' systems followed. Various types of apparatus were tried, and the Morse 'sounder' system soon came into general use. In 1910, after much experiment with different systems, the Whetstone apparatus was introduced and from 1912 multiplex Baudot systems were widely used for continental communications. Other changes included a system of telegraphic money orders from 1889, the gradual reduction of the cost of deliveries and the increase in the range of areas covered.[71]

The Post Office also took over from the companies the development of submarine telegraph. The English Channel was first traversed in 1851, the Irish Sea in 1853 and the Atlantic Ocean in 1866. Nationalisation released capital to further such enterprises and soon there were lines which covered most of the British Empire including the Far East. By 1880 there were nine cables across the Atlantic and nearly 10,000 miles of line traversing the oceans of the whole world. A small Submarine Telegraph Company, set up in 1889, established links with European countries and was also taken over by the Post Office.[72] The Post Office also took up wireless telegraphy, having discovered its possibilities as early as 1884. By 1895 transmission without wires was used extensively in the case of breakdowns and between 1892 and 1902 a full system of communication between coast-guard stations and shore vessels was established. However, the exploitation of wireless telegraphy was too profitable to be left to public ownership, so most of the development of the system was left to Guglielmo Marconi, the Italian inventor, and his various commercial backers who soon built a virtual monopoly throughout the British Empire and North America. In 1904 a Wireless Telegraphy Act was passed, which meant that all equipment had to be licensed by the Post Office and by 1909 all British coastal stations had been bought up by the Post Office. The main work of developing the system was still left to Marconi's companies, and various leading Liberals became shareholders in them – a fact which caused a minor political scandal in 1912–13.[73]

The early forms of telegraph apparatus were simple enough to be operated by anybody who could read, but soon the development of morse code and of the complicated mechanisms involved in the new equipment caused the growth of a specialist class of operator. The companies were not prepared to pay much for this kind of skill, so they took on a new group that was just entering the labour market. These were young middle-class women, for whom there were few other openings, and who could be paid very little and closely supervised. By 1868 the companies employed a staff of 5,339 at an average wage of £40 per annum. This was a good deal below the average wage for 'clerical' work. As already mentioned the numbers employed by the telegraph service greatly increased at the time of nationalisation to a total of 9,000 in 1871 and over 11,000 in 1874. Although the telegraphists' skill was by no means a scarce one, it was inevitable that wages would increase, especially after the definite establishment of telegraph staff in 1872 and the setting up of a scheme of classification. The 1871 strike perhaps also helped. Furthermore, since the capital expenses were nearly all in the early period of the development of the system, it is also not surprising that wages became a very large constituent of its costs. In 1891 it was said that wages were 65 per cent of the total cost and by 1913–14 it was estimated that as much as 97 per cent of the total cost of the service was paid in wages, salaries and pensions. However, these figures were simply part of a wider problem for the telegraph service. In general it always had to have a very high proportion of working expenses to capital and in 1874–5 this had reached 86 per cent. The Select Committee of 1876 found that 'operational expenses' were too high, but it was difficult to see ways of solving this problem with the preliminary burden of debt, and with the expensive concessions to the press and the railway companies. In 1894, it was calculated that since the take-over by the state the excess of expenditure over income was only £1·79 million, though the accumulated deficiency was as much as £5·89. The plain fact was that although reduced charges – to as low as 6d for twelve words in 1885 – did increase the use of the service, they did not do so enough to allow the service to pay its way.[74] In any case, the telegraph was now faced with a rival so formidable that it was never really able to catch up with the problems it had first had to face at the time it was taken over by the Post Office.

It was some time before the telephone, which to a great extent replaced the telegraph as soon as it was satisfactorily organised, came under the complete control of the Post Office. This was partly because of a combination of private greed and *laissez-faire* dogmatism and partly for fear of making the same mistakes and ending up with some of the same burdens that bedevilled the telegraph system. The transmission of speech by electrical means first became practical with the invention in 1875 of the telephone by Alexander Graham Bell and with the various necessary subsidiaries that followed, notably the carbon transmitter by Edison in 1877 and the microphone by Hughes in 1878. In 1878 the Telephone Company was established to exploit Bell's inventions, and in 1879 an Edison Company was set up on the basis of the latter's discoveries. These two merged in 1880 as the United Telephone Company, later transformed into the National.

Although this new body was to dominate the system for some time, it lost in the courts to the Post Office. It was adjudged in 1880 that the 1869 Telegraph Act gave the Department control over the telephone system. There followed a period of uncertainty when the Post Office granted powers to private enterprise to develop various local and national networks, but usually with restrictions which weakened their powers of effective operation, notably their ability to erect wires and poles. The Post Office was hesitant about what to do, however. Although the chief officials, particularly Blackwood who was Secretary in the 1880s, were keen to go ahead, the political heads Fawcett and Manners were not. As late as 1887, Postmaster General Raikes declared that it was 'extremely doubtful whether there could be much public advantage' to be derived from a Manchester to London telephone link.[75]

Against this background of hesitancy by the Post Office and grievances of the companies about their inadequate powers, Postmaster General Fawcett in 1882 stated that not only would the Department now grant concessions to private enterprise on a more favourable basis, but that there would be 'free competition . . . amongst private companies and . . . of private companies against the Post Office', and that there was not 'the smallest chance that the Government would every buy up the rights of these companies'. In the meantime the Post Office had to show a profit on each individual exchange. In 1884 after further bitter complaints by the companies, the restrictions placed on them were further relaxed. The result of this was to allow private enterprise to control virtually the whole of the system, but never in a form that bore the slightest resemblance to free competition. By the time of the expiration of the patents in 1892, the National Company controlled all the important local companies, and even the Telephone Subscribers Protective Association. From the time when private enterprise was given its head 'every competing company' was 'absorbed by some existing company', until there was a complete monopoly.[76] By now too the National Company claim that the inefficiency of their service was caused by the restrictions placed on them was wearing thin, especially as they were demanding powers greater than those granted to any other private enterprise. At the same time, opinion favouring public ownership was increasing. In 1888 the Associated Chambers of Commerce declared themselves in support of such a step and in 1892 many voices were raised in its favour in a debate in the House of Commons. It is of interest to note that the main argument put forward against such a move at that time by the Postmaster General, Sir James Fergusson, was that the employees of any state enterprise were inevitably paid above the market price, so that costs of a Post Office run telephone system would be prohibitive. Fergusson later became a director of the National Company and was blamed for the frequent capitulation of the Post Office to the interests of the company.[77]

In 1892 the Government refused to grasp the nettle of public ownership, but tried to do something to alter the position of private monopoly. The Post Office refused to renew the contracts of the private companies, took over the trunk lines at an ultimate cost of £459,000 and confined the operations of private interests to areas where plant had already been established. Thus the Government took a permanent stake in the system itself and left the options open for a complete takeover.[78] Another proposal was now canvassed for running the service without putting it into the hands of the Post Office – control by municipal authorities. This was a period when many local authorities were first running gas, electricity and tramway enterprises, not without success. In 1898 a Select Committee found that the trunk services under public control were now the most advanced in Europe while the local services, run by private monopoly, were conspicuously behind. Once again, the Post Office was said to have too much on its plate, so £2 million was set aside for local authorities who wished to do so to set up services.[79]

The local authority alternative to Post Office control proved no more satisfactory than the various previous systems that had been tried. Few local authorities even considered such an enterprise and of those half dozen or so who did, only Hull found it possible to compete for more than a couple of years with the superior resources of the Company or the Post Office. The Glasgow Corporation set up a system in 1900 and was most tenacious in trying to keep it going. However, the Corporation could not afford to buy the most advanced equipment, and was unable to attract as many subscribers as the National Company, so was compelled to sell out to the Post Office in 1906. Brighton Corporation also sold its equipment to the Post Office in 1906. Tunbridge Wells in 1903 and Swansea in 1907 sold their already largely obsolete plant to the National Telephone Company. In Portsmouth, although the municipal system survived from 1904 to 1913 it never won more custom than the National Company, and after being taken over by the Post Office its plant only proved usable until 1916. Only the Hull Corporation found itself able to run a local service largely at a profit. In most cases, the area covered and the capital expenses incurred were too great for any local authority.[80]

After this the steps to Post Office control became almost inevitable. Efforts to stimulate competition between the National Company and the Post Office in London failed, so that there was soon complete interchange between the two systems and thus little serious argument in favour of allowing a private monopoly to survive. Within two years the Postmaster General reported increasing profitability of the system and in 1905 there was a further agreement about the provincial exchanges allowing the same interchange of services. In this period also the Post Office's arrangements were adopted throughout the system. Thus there were more call boxes, which the companies had seldom built, and the principle of 'measured service' for payment was introduced as opposed to special concessions to large subscribers. At the same time, the Post Office provided services to remote areas which could not possibly pay by themselves. It also connected subscribers internally, and set up the first automatic exchange. Thus there seemed little doubt that when the contracts of the Company expired for the second time in 1911, there was no serious reason to renew them. Furthermore, it was clear that the National Telephone Company was not in such a powerful position as the telegraph companies had been to enforce exorbitant compensation terms.

The total cost of the take-over, originally put forward as £21·9 million by the companies and as £9.4 by the Post Office, became on appeal £12·5 million. The

Postmaster General said in 1908 that it should be possible to get a 'moderate return on the capital expenditure' of the system and in the first year of the Post Office take-over a balance of £0·39 million was recorded against an expenditure of £5·39 million.[81] Thus the Post Office took over, more by default than by design, its most profitable and useful asset, which it continued to run with commercial success until 1981. Initially there were difficulties resulting from the failure of the companies or the local authorities to renew any of their capital equipment. Nevertheless, despite this and the shocks of war, it was possible in the 1920s to build up an automatic exchange system throughout the land in ways which were far superior to any private or municipal enterprise.

THE AGE OF EXPANSION

In the early part of the twentieth century the Post Office was established as one of the most unusual aspects both of state activity and of commercial and economic enterprise. It worked as a department of state, whose revenue and expenditure was part of the national budget and whose head was a member of the government. At the same time it was a largely successful and profitable commercial undertaking with a legal monopoly providing a service important parts of which were not in themselves profitable and would not have been provided in a free market. The Victorians saw this unique enterprise as part of the great civilising mission of the governing classes. Not only was it the 'powerful engine of civilisation' described by Rowland Hill, but Postmaster General Lord Stanley wrote in 1864 that 'the progress of the Post Office at once promotes and maintains the growth of commerce and education'.[82]

The success of the penny post, and the gradual acquisition of new functions by the Post Office into the twentieth century led to it being considered, despite all the complaints made about individual aspects of the service, as a more efficient way of dealing with such matters than private enterprise. The Northcote-Trevelyan Report in the 1850s was thought to have helped to create a civil service that was at the same time objective and efficient. The question of whether there were too many civil servants, or whether they were paid more than a 'market price' which could only have been determined where much fewer services were provided, troubled the dogmatic defenders of a 'free market' in the late nineteenth century. By that time few considered that the postal services could be organised in any other way. Thus even such a convinced defender of a market economy in a general sense as Alfred Marshall agreed that to suggest the running of the postal service by private enterprise 'would not be the act of a sane person'. None of the other agency services, notably the payment of pensions, could have been carried out as efficiently and in such a wide area by any other institution. The telephones, it was found after trying every other method, could work in no other way. Even the telegraphs in the hands of private enterprise could have provided only a narrow and inadequate service. There is little serious evidence of technological inertia in the Post Office. Despite all the losses in the telegraph system, every new innovation was tried and taken over. Another example was the use of motor transport, which was brought into the postal service after continuous experiment as soon as it became practicable. It could thus easily be argued by the early part of the twentieth century that even the new telecommunications sectors could most efficiently be carried out by the state.[83] The question of how all this affected the lives, numbers, attitudes and conditions of a substantial body of civil servants will be considered in the following chapters.

NOTES

1 Post Office *Report and Accounts*, 1979–80.
2 The best books on the history of the Post Office are Robinson (1948 and 1953); Hemmeon (1912); Joyce (1893) and Ellis (1958). Two good recent studies are Haldane (1971) and Austen (1978). See also Perry (1976). There is useful information in *Summary*, and in the PMG's Report for 1854. There is also much about the early history of the Post Office, together with many reprinted documents, in *Secret Committee*.
3 *Summary*, p. 5, including the quotation from the third continuation of the Chronicle of Croyland.
4 *Oxford English Dictionary*, VII (1933), p. 1,160 for an interesting account of the development of the term 'post', and Smith (1917), pp. 3–4, 6, for a clear statement of the early functions of posts. See also *Summary*, p. 5, and Housden (1903), p. 716.
5 Robinson (1953), p. 9. See also Coase (1955).
6 *Secret Committee*, pp. 95, 41; Foxell and Spafford (1952), pp. 7–8.
7 Firth (1898), pp. 530–1, 528; Birch (1742), VI, pp. 85–6.
8 Ashley (1947), pp. 284–7, 287–8; Turner (1918); Housden (1904); *Secret Committee*, pp. 112–13; Mather (1959), pp. 185–6, 228, 217–25; Tegg (1878), pp. 66–70; Lewins (1864), pp. 150–64. The legislation is in 9 Anne c.10, Section 40 (1711), 8 Edward VII, c.48 Section 56 (1908) and 1 & 2 Elizabeth II, c.36 Section 58 (1953). This is now replaced by the British Telecommunications Act (1981).
9 *Journals of the House of Commons*, VIII, (4 September 1660); *Calendar of Treasury Books* 1685–9, VIII i pp. 220, 226, VIII iii pp. 1, 513–7, 15 Car II c.14 (1663) and 1 Jac II c.12 (1685); Robinson (1948), pp. 53, 56; Hemmeon (1912), pp. 13ff.
10 For a full account of postal rates see Smith (1917), pp. 336–40 and also PMG First Report for 1854, p. 10; Robinson (1953), p. 15 and Marshall (1926), p. 144.
11 Housden (1903), p. 714; Walker (1938).
12 Printed in *Secret Committee*, pp. 32–3.
13 *CSPD* 1611–18, pp. 478, 562; 1623–5, p. 117 and 1627–8, p. 307. The much quoted 1628 petition is given in *Secret Committee*, p. 52, and summarised in *CSPD* 1628–9, p. 184. See also Housden (1906), p. 7; Hyde (1894), pp. 140ff. and Joyce (1893), pp. 15–16.
14 Clear (1935), p. 4; *Secret Committee*, pp. 55–7 for the 1635 documents; Joyce (1893), pp. 15–23.
15 The complicated struggles for control of the postal service from 1637 to 1653 are described in Hemmeon (1912), pp. 16–22, and Manley's appointment documents are in *Secret Committee*, p. 71. *CSPD* 1654, pp. 20–7, gives details of the settling of the farm on Manley and also some complaints from postmasters of rough treatment by him.
16 *CSPD* 1652–3, p. 312. The title page of Hill's pamphlet – a defence both of private enterprise and of the penny post – is reproduced in Staff (1964), p. 13. The 1657 Act is in *Secret Committee*, pp. 72–4, and the 1660 Act is 12 Car II, c.35.
17 This information is contained in a document reproduced in *SMLG* 8, 1898, under the title 'The Post Office in 1677' reprinted from 'The Book of Postage' in the Dartmouth Papers.
18 Staff (1964), pp. 160–7; Scott (1911), III, p. 45, for a good account of Dockwra's activities; Ward (1885), pp. 152–3, mentions possible efforts before 1680; *CSPD* 1697, pp. 543–4 and 1700–2, pp. 541–3 and *Calendar of Treasury Papers* 1697–1702, p. 537, reiterate the monopoly arguments against any local penny posts.
19 Ashley (1947), pp. 279, 282–9, 297; Ellis (1958), pp. 7, 9–19.
20 Bruce (1853), pp. 3–4. For the legislation see *Acts of the Parliament of Scotland*, IX, pp. 417–9, giving the 1695 Scottish Post Office Act and 9 Anne c.10, Section 2, which repeals these Scottish provisions. 23 & 24 Geo. III c.17 in *Statutes at Large Passed in the Parliaments Held in Ireland* (1786), pp. 552–72, establishes a Dublin GPO at the centre of a separate system. I Will IV c.8 re-established one Post Office for Great Britain and Ireland and 7 & 8 Will IV c.21 established a common postal rate. See also Haldane (1971).
21 9 Anne c.10; Robinson (1948), p. 98; Housden (1906), p. 13.
22 Ellis (1958), p. viii.
23 The much quoted 'Narrative of Mr. Allen's Transactions with the Government' of 2 December 1761 is published in Ralph Allen's *By, Way and Cross Road Posts* ed. A. M. Ogilvie (1897) and the quotations on surveyors and Allen's successes are to be found there. On the surveyors see Foxell and Spafford (1952), pp. 19–21. *Calendar of Treasury Papers* 1731–4, pp. 539–40, gives details of the profits made up to 1734 renewal, and 1739–41, pp. 449–50 on the 1741 renewal, including the undertaking to increase the regularity of the post. *Palmer Report*, pp. 144–51, gives Allen's 1761

contract and pp. 60–2 gives the revenue figures which were conveniently summarised in Ogilvie (1893a), p. 451 and tabulated in Ogilvie (1895). See also Ogilvie (1893b) and Hemmeon (1912), p. 37 for estimates of Allen's private fortune.

24 Defoe (1962), pp. 341–2; Robinson (1948), pp. 85–6 for some similar statements.

25 Joyce (1893), pp. 231, 302–7; 34 Geo. III c.17.

26 5 Geo. III c.25; 41 Geo. III c.7; Staff (1964), pp. 60–1, 178–88; Austen (1978), pp. 101ff.; Joyce (1893), pp. 197, 202; Buckley and Ward (1969), pp. 34ff.

27 *Summary* p. 8; Clear (1955), p. 15; *Palmer Report*, p. 101, quoting Palmer's original plan of 1786; 53 Geo. III c.157 (1813) for Palmer's grant.

28 Harris (1885), p. 243; Ogilvie (1895), pp. 407–8; Baines (1895b), p. 243; Hyde (1891), p. 70; Robinson (1948), pp. 242–3.

29 Housden (1906), pp. 739, 741; *Secret Committee*, pp. 45–7; *CSPD* 1631–3, pp. 521–2.

30 Robinson (1964), pp. 7, 27, 80–1, 151 and Norway (1895), especially pp. 197–221 on the strike.

31 Ellis (1958), p. 44; *Report of the Commissioners* in Tenth Report on the Post Office of 1788, in PP 1806, VII. On the delays see Binney (1958), p. 17.

32 On ship letters see *Summary*, pp. 48–9, Robinson (1964), p. 112 and Hemmeon (1912), p. 129.

33 See *Reports of the Commissioners* in PP 1829 XI and XII, and PP 1830 XIV. See also the ten *Reports of the Commissioners* in PP 1835 XLVIII, 1836 XXVIII, XXXVIII, 1837 XXXIV, i, 1837–8 XXXV. For the statement by Wallace see Robinson (1948), p. 251. For the statistics see *Summary*, pp. 102–3.

34 PMG 1st Report for 1854 pp. 14–15, 65; *3rd Report of Select Committee on Postage* in PP 1837–8 XX, i, p. 62; 1 Vic c.36 (1837) for the standardisation and 3 & 4 Vic c.96 (1840) for the new rates.

35 1 Vic c.32–6.

36 The first edition marked 'Private and Confidential' was published in January 1837 and was circulated among friends and public officials. The second edition, which appeared in February, is reprinted in *The Post Office Fifty Years Ago* (1887). There was a third edition in November, which was reprinted in 1838.

37 Hill and Hill (1880). See also Coase (1939).

38 Trollope (1923), p. 259. For similar statements about Hill's capacities as an administrator see *Hansard* II, 113, 890–5 (7 June 1850), 113 29–36 (19 July 1850), 114, 268–76 (10 February 1851).

39 Hill (1887), especially pp. 6, 18, 29 and Hill and Hill (1880), Vol. 1, p. 250.

40 On the petition see 'Post Office reform' in *Edinburgh Review*, 70, 1837, pp. 546–7. On the Mercantile Committee see Hill and Hill (1890), Vol. 1, p. 294. For a page of *The Post Circular* see Kay (1951), p. 112; PP 1837–8 XX i.

41 Second Report of Wallace Committee in PP 1837–8 XX, pp. 143, 216, 214; Hill and Hill (1890), Vol. 1, p. 309.

42 *Hansard* III, 38, 1464 (15 June 1837); *Times* (16 April 1839).

43 Hill (1887), p. 24; 2 & 3 Vic c.52 (1839), 3 & 4 Vic c.96 (1840).

44 Joyce (1893), p. 428; *DNB* LIX, p. 297, *Hansard* III, 49, 302 (12 July 1839); Hill (1887), p. 10; Hill and Hill (1890), Vol. 1, p. 354; Third Report of PP 1837–8 XX, p. 69; Hill (1841), p. 92, predicted the restoration of the 1839 net revenue in 1844.

45 Hemmeon (1912), pp. 245–50; PMG 60th Report for 1913–14, p. 13; Bronne (1858).

46 Alderman (1973), pp. 16, 232. Hill (1841), pp. 86–7, points out the expense of the early transition from mail coach to train, as also does PP 1837–8 XVI, p. 16. PP 1854 XI, p. iii, mentions complaints of inefficiency against the railway companies. See Smiles (1858), pp. 527–9, for Robert Stephenson's statement that the services of the railway companies 'entitle them to a large share of consideration and to a liberal compensation'. For a convincing refutation of this see PMG 2nd Report for 1855 pp. 14–16, 45–55 and *Hansard* III, 70, 412–3 (27 June 1843) where some staggering comparisons are made between the rates charged for posts and for other services by the railway companies.

47 Bagwell (1968), pp. 90–119; 45 & 46 Vic c.76 (1882): the Post Office (Parcels) Act; PMG 28th Report for 1881–2, pp. 2–3.

48 Robinson (1948), ch. 27; PP 1852–3 XCV.

49 23 Vic c.26 (1860); PMG 6th Report for 1859, pp. 53–5, 9th for 1862, p. 22, 17th for 1870, pp. 9, 30, 55th for 1908–9, pp. 52–3. On the successive efforts to reduce the subsidies see Robinson (1964) ch. 20, and for the examples quoted here, PMG 21st Report for 1874, p. 11 and Raikes (1898), pp. 257–66. See also PMG 51st Report for 1904–5, pp. 3–4.

50 Nortend (1880), pp. 32, 107; *Times* (26 June 1852).

51 PMG 38th Report for 1891–2, p. 8, 45th Report for 1898–9, p. 7, 52nd Report for 1905–6, p. 1, 57th Report for 1910–11, p. 3; Porter (1916), pp. 177, 178–82 and Robinson (1948), pp. 400–2.

For an example of official Post Office hostility see 'The Post Office and Mr. J. H. Heaton' in *SMLG* III (1893), where his efforts are attributed to a desire for 'self-advertisement', and his 'fundamental incapacity for the acquisition of facts and for sustained and logical arguments' is asserted.

52 The early history of the Universal Postal Union is given in Rolland (1901) and Sly (1927). See also *Times* (15 August 1891) on 'The history and constitution of the postal union' and Hatswell (1901). British reactions are recorded in PMG 21st Report for 1873, pp. 12–13 and 53rd Report for 1906–7, p. 4.

53 On the letter carriers see 18th Report for 1829 in PP 1829 XI, p. 74.

54 Hyde (1892); *Illustrated London News* (27 June 1846); Hazlett (1831), p. 186; Hatswell (1903); Trollope (1923), p. 258; PMG 2nd Report for 1855, p. 7.

55 *Summary*, pp. 44–6.

56 *Notes and Queries* 184 (1943), pp. 143–4; Robinson (1953), pp. 172–3, 238; PMG 2nd Report for 1855, pp. 9–10, 41–5, 12th Report for 1866, pp. 6–12, 15th Report for 1868, p. 6.

57 *Summary*, p. 11; PMG 60th Report for 1913–14, p. 31.

58 PMG 6th Report for 1859, p. 10 and 45th Report for 1897–8, pp. 2, 32–9.

59 Hemmeon (1912), p. 68; PMG 16th Report for 1869, pp. 3–4.

60 Bowie (1900), p. 36; PMG 16th Report for 1869, p. 5, 48th Report for 1901–2, p. 26, 60th Report for 1913–14, p. 1.

61 *B-H* (15 November 1862); *Summary*, pp. 26–32; PMG 14th Report for 1867, pp. 19–20.

62 *Summary*, pp. 13–16 and PMG 60th Report for 1913–14, p. 1. See also above p. 28.

63 PMG 57th Report for 1910–11, p. 109; PO Commercial Accounts for 1939–40, p. 11. See also Appendices 3 and 28–31 below.

64 PMG 1st Report for 1854, p. 20, 27th Report for 1880–1, p. 16, 60th Report for 1913–14, p. 25.

65 *Summary*, pp. 113–17; 24 Vic c.14 (1861); PMG 28th Report for 1881–2, pp. 8–9, 52nd Report for 1905–6, pp. 12–13 and 60th Report for 1913–14, p. 10. On insurance and annuities see PMG 12th Report for 1865, pp. 23–33, and 30th Report for 1883–4, pp. 10–11; also *Economist* (5 November 1881), p. 1,369, on the failure of the scheme.

66 *Summary*, p. 120; PMG 15th Report for 1868, p. 12, 17th Report for 1870, pp. 20–1, 49th Report for 1902–3, p. 93, 55th Report for 1908–9, p. 10.

67 Kieve (1973); PP 1867–8 XLI, pp. 43, 73–4. See also Perry (1981).

68 Kieve (1973), pp. 76–7; Mather (1953), pp. 49–52; Culley (1889), p. 215; 'The Electric Telegraph', *Quarterly Review*, 95 (1854), p. 151; *Economist* (11 April 1868), p. 412.

69 Scudamore's report in PP 1867–8 XLI, pp. 43, 73–4, gives full details of all the nationalisation schemes. For W. S. Jevons's view see (1866–7) and for the attitude of the companies, Kieve (1973), pp. 93, 148–9, 167, 169.

70 Special Report of the Select Committee on the Telegraph Bill (PP 1868–9 VI) pp. iii, 12; Lord John Manners in *Hansard* III, 331, 215–6 (17 March 1876); Meyer (1907), pp. 64, 80, 87; PP 1873 XXXIX for the terms of the railway companies and 31 & 32 Vic c.110 (1868) and 32 & 33 Vic c.73 (1869) for the legislation; Baines (1895a), Vol 2, pp. 27–8, 35 on the problems of the changeover. See also Preece (1901), p. 359, *Summary*, pp. 67, 77, PP 1867–8 XLI, p. 37 and PP 1873 VII, p. 95.

71 PMG 20th Report for 1873, p. 10, 25th Report for 1878–9; 26th Report for 1879–80, p. 16; 35th Report for 1888–9, pp. 12–13, 41st Report for 1894–5, pp. 33–8; 42nd Report for 1895–6, pp. 26–32; 55th Report for 1908–9, p. 15; 56th Report for 1909–10, p. 16 and 59th Report for 1912–13, p. 17. Preece (1901), p. 362. Baines (1895a), Vol. 2, p. 80.

72 Kieve (1973), pp. 15, 66, 104–18; Curran (1900).

73 PMG 48th Report for 1901–2, pp. 15–16 and 49th Report for 1902–3, pp. 18–19; Kieve (1973), pp. 243–5; 3 Edw. VII c.24 (Wireless Telegraphy Act 1904); Donaldson (1962).

74 Kieve (1973), pp. 32, 85–7, 185–90; Hemmeon (1912), p. 218; PMG 19th Report for 1872, p. 38; 21st Report for 1874, p. 38, and 60th Report for 1913–14, p. 124. PP 1876 XLII, p. 3; PP 1876 XIII; PMG 41st Report for 1894–5, pp. 33–8.

75 Baldwin (1925), pp. 11–12, 30, 38; Law Reports: Queen's Bench Division VI, p. 244; *The Telegraph and Telephone Journal* II (1916), p. 161 on a visit by Post Office officials to the first exchange in 1877 and *Times* (1 March 1878) on the registration of its existence; *Hansard* III, 319, 665 (16 August 1887), 212, 712 (17 July 1882) and 273, 1637 (12 August 1882). On Post Office policy in the period see PMG 28th Report for 1881–2, pp. 5–6 and Meyer (1901), pp. 20–1. See also Perry (1977).

76 For complaints on restrictions see *Times* (13 June 1884) and *Hansard* III, 288, 1052–68, with 1070–5 for promised modifications (22 May 1884). The changes are given in PMG 30th Report

for 1883–4, p. 6 and Baldwin (1925), pp. 570–1, and the subsequent situation in Hemmeon (1912), p. 223 and PP 1895 XIII, p. 9.

77   Baldwin (1925), p. 574; *Hansard* IV, 3, 166ff. (29 March 1892); 'The telephone scandal', *Saturday Review* (20 August 1898), p. 231.

78   PP 1892 XVII; PMG 38th Report for 1891–2, pp. 20, 79; 39th for 1892–3, p. 23 and 42nd for 1895–6, p. 16; 55 & 56 Vic c.59 (1892 Telegraph Act).

79   Baldwin (1925), pp. 353–7, 580–92; PP 1898 XII; 62 & 63 Vic c.38 (1899 Telegraph Act).

80   Meyer (1901), pp. 313–31; Baldwin (1925), pp. 357–80. See *Times* (7 September 1893) on the agitation in Glasgow and on the inevitability of national control. On various developments; PMG 51st Report for 1904–5, p. 20; 57th Report for 1910–11, p. 24 and 60th Report for 1913–14, p. 22.

81   PP 1905 VII; PMG 50th Report for 1903–4, pp. 23, 26, 91; 51st Report for 1904–5, pp. 22–3; 53rd Report for 1906–7, pp. 22, 24; 54th Report for 1907–8, pp. 24, 25; 59th Report for 1912–13, pp. 21, 23, 34. More typical local developments are described in Tupling (1978) and Earl (1978).

82   PMG 10th Report for 1863, p. 5.

83   Marshall in *Times* (6 April 1891); development of motorised services in PMG 50th Report for 1903–4, p. 3; 51st Report for 1904–5, pp. 2–3; 52nd Report for 1905–6, p. 49; for a defence of state enterprise in telecommunications see Lee (1913).

3 Post Office Workers in the Age of Expansion

> . . . there is no form of outside employment that could fairly and reasonably be compared with ours. But apart from that, we contend that the Postmaster-General has no right to fix his employees wages according to the standard of the open labour market – a standard which is not regulated by the necessities of the workers, but is forced by fierce competition down to the lowest subsistence point. The Postmaster-General has no competition to face. He can fix his own prices, and the public must deal with him whether they like those prices or not. He makes an immense annual profit, and therefore can afford to employ the pick of the working class and pay high wages. (Charles Durrant of the Fawcett Association)[1]

> No one can hope to get the British Civil Service into clear perspective unless he appreciates the extent to which its complex structure and its internal affairs are bound up with [an] infinity of gradings. (R. W. Rawlings, *The Civil Service and the People*, 1945, p. 21)

Perhaps the one thing that those who work in the Post Office always agree about is that their conditions and status are not what they used to be. Like the aristocracy and the middle class, Post Office workers always feel that they are in decline. The London postmen who were driven to strike action in 1890 looked back nostalgically to the days in the 1850s and before when they were 'letter carriers' in bright red uniforms, for all the world like army captains. Those who followed them in the 1930s and the 1980s bemoaned the decline of their status as well as their wages. Similarly, by 1890, London sorters and counter clerks regretted that their work had once been performed by people with top hats and high collars who could lay claim to the grand title of 'clerks of the minor establishment'. The telegraphists, from the time they joined the Post Office in 1870, felt the lack of proper recognition of their special skills. Increasingly in any case, all 'indoor' work was performed interchangeably by groups that came to be known as 'sorting clerks and telegraphists' or nowadays simply as 'postal officers'. None of these groups of workers, however, have yet utterly lost the feeling that they are part of a 'service', set off from those who only work for private capitalists, and playing their part in a system whose freemasonry only they can regulate.

As the employees of the Post Office moved out of the shadows of aristrocratic patronage to take on their respective roles in a modern bureaucratic machine, there was a long and complex evolution of their status and their relations with one another. Other chapters will take up the political and legal implications for the redress of their grievances. Here the chief concern is with the conditions and wages of those who worked in the Post Office during the period of its greatest expansion, from the mid-nineteenth century to the First World War.

NOT LIKE OTHER WORKERS

The legend put about by the authorities, MPs and professors of political economy during the nineteenth century was that those in public employment were protected from the vicissitudes of the private labour market and enjoyed privileges such as pensions, uniforms and Christmas boxes. The Post Office workers themselves, however, as they performed their specialised and repetitive tasks, took the view that their status was continually being undermined, their labours intensified and their rewards diminished.

It was only after 1800 that there were more than 1,000 people working for the Post Office. In 1792 the entire postal system of Manchester was conducted by an aged widow, together with her daughter and one letter carrier. About the same time, Edinburgh boasted three letter carriers and there were establishments of four at Bristol, Bath and Birmingham. As late as 1834 only 600 letter carriers were needed to cover all of London. The setting up of the penny post, the expansion of the communications system of the British Empire around the globe, and the acquisition by the Post Office of the telegraph and telephone system multiplied these figures by many hundreds.[2] A high proportion of the fetchers and carriers needed to keep nineteenth-century urban society in Britain on the move worked for the Post Office. So also did those who operated the telegraphs and telephones.

One of the great problems for those organising this enormous expansion was the inculcation of new and particular standards of work discipline. Those who in other circumstances were compelled to submit to the dictates of the factory hooter or the supervision of the gaffer had to learn the special standards of honesty and probity inculcated in the Victorian public service. However, it was a long struggle to transform the image of the dissolute and untrustworthy eighteenth-century post-boy into that of the respectable Post Office servant. Complaints about how it was done were loud and long.

The most dramatic of the early methods of enforcing discipline was capital punishment. From 1756, letter stealing was a capital crime and hangings for the offence were by no means uncommon. Accounts of the execution of individuals were circulated to postmasters, and in 1832 a 24-year-old letter carrier called John Barret was the last man to suffer in this way. The Postmaster General, after paying out the enormous sum of £137 to secure a conviction and to oppose any appeal, also secretly made contributions for the support of Barret's widow. The Post Office authorities opposed the abolition of this barbarity in 1833 on the grounds that without such a deterrent 'there can be no doubt that the losses will be increased to a frightful extent'. It is perhaps unnecessary to add that when the law was in fact changed in 1835, there was no perceptible increase in letter stealing.[3] Close supervision and draconian punishment nevertheless continued. There were frequent complaints from the postal workers about the 'rough, overhauling and inconsiderate manner' by which their honesty was subject to constant investigation, to a much greater extent than, say, bank clerks or commercial office workers. Long prison sentences for letter stealing were still common in 1889, a five-year sentence being considered normal, and 'dismissal on suspicion' a frequent event.[4]

Furthermore, Post Office workers were constantly under observation for the slightest sign of sloth or dishonesty. In Manchester in the 1850s, letter carriers were spied on by inspectors while doing their rounds, and in later years it was firmly believed to be 'a fact that peep-holes are made in halls and doors' so that the 'private lives and amusements of Post Office servants were carefully watched and entered in books'. Particular 'drivers' were attacked and even sketched in association journals and elsewhere. In 1909 recognition was withdrawn from the Irish Postal Clerks Association after a number of articles, including one suggesting that the postal superintendent of Belfast was better suited for the 'Governorship of a convict prison or a slave colony'. In another office in 1912 it was said that the staff objected to 'the constant nagging and constant hustling and shouting which is the rule'. Only the authorities were convinced that 'better control over the men' improved 'the general tone and morale in the service'. Another indication of the standards expected can be seen from the fact that from 1873 to 1888, 987 employees of the Department were dismissed for 'intemperance'.[5]

The authorities tried many other ways to make the workforce 'well disposed, industrious and respectable'.[6] They had an armoury of legal restraints not available to other employers and described in the next chapter, and they also tried to impose forms of regimentation that must have seemed familiar to the many ex-servicemen in the Post Office. Telegraph messengers were at one time compelled to do exercises and to march together in military formation. The provision of uniforms, and also of medical services and pensions, also began as means to enforce discipline. It was only much later that they were portrayed as special advantages of Post Office work, 'privileges' even.

The provision of special dress was proposed in 1792 by Postmasters General Lords Walsingham and Chesterfield in these terms:

> Security would be derived to the Public Correspondence if all our Letter Carriers were to have a uniform which would draw the public attention to their persons, and . . . it would occasion their being observed, either if they were loitering in Ale Houses when they ought to be delivering their letters, or if they were frequently seen in Pawn Brokers' shops . . .

Though the GPO letter carriers protested that this idea was 'a reflection on their honesty and even a disgrace', as well as exposing them to being robbed, the authorities managed to persuade them to don the new scarlet coats in 1793 with the argument that their Parisian equivalents were dressed in the same way without any particular harm coming to them. In 1834 Dublin and Edinburgh letter carriers were similarly attired, and by 1848 so also were porters and messengers. It was only in 1854 when the national and metropolitan forces were merged, that all sections of the outdoor force, in London at least, were provided not only with the scarlet coats, but also with trousers, in acknowledgement of the fact that the uniforms were to protect the wearers from the elements, and also to improve their appearance. They were still inadequate for these purposes. In 1859 the uniforms were attacked by one of their wearers as 'not only rubbish of the worst description, but the dress and workmanship are in every respect unsuitable for a twelve month's wear'. In response to complaints of this kind, it was agreed in 1860 to provide two suits a year, the colour of the coat being changed to blue, presumably making it easier to disappear into alehouses. By then uniforms were regarded as part of the special advantages of the job, and it was in response to agitation for better wages and conditions that rural letter carriers were provided with them in 1871. Telegraph messengers were also given uniforms at this time.

These teenagers posed a particular problem for the efforts of the authorities to impose a paternalistic discipline on them. There were complaints about 'the improper manner of wearing their caps' and 'the practice of wearing a curl or fringe in the front'. It was partly to put a stop to this that the shako caps with peaks at both back and front were introduced, and these became a familiar part of all outdoor uniforms in the period before the First World War. In 1910 a special departmental committee was set up to consider the great variety of uniforms by then in existence. The Committee reported that the original purpose of many uniforms was now forgotten, some of the higher grades even retaining the old scarlet coats of no apparent purpose. It divided uniforms into five types and made provision for separate protective clothing.[7]

The much-flaunted medical facilities were introduced into the Post Office after the 1855 cholera epidemic. They were not originally intended for the welfare of its employees at all, and were said to be motivated by 'economy as well as benevolence'. Those who benefited from them considered that their purpose was 'to prevent unsound constitutions entering the service', and the first Post Office medical officer claimed in 1862 that since his pre-entry examinations reduced the death rate from 15 to $6\cdot3$ per thousand, his ministrations were 'economical to the country by preventing absence from duty and unnecessarily early superannuation on the part of its employees; not to mention its action on malingerers'. Successive postmasters general also noted the effect of the facilities in preventing those under their charge from 'absenting themselves from duty on a false or insufficient plea of illness'. However, it was not possible for the doctors to operate entirely on that basis. As the Post Office pointed out in a letter to the Treasury in 1862:

> . . . the Medical Officers partake more of the character of a Medical Police, inasmuch as they act on behalf of the Department and not of its servants – their duty being in addition to the examination of Candidates, simply to visit Officers suspected of feigning or exaggerating illness. There, neither advice nor medicine is given.

Clearly, even the Treasury had to admit that there were occasions when employees of the department suffered from genuine illness, and it was in the interests of the service that they should be helped to recover. Some facilities were therefore provided, and this became one of the economic advantages constantly mentioned by the authorities in response to requests for improved conditions. It is not surprising, therefore, that in the 1890s, when there were 400 doctors retained by the Department, London sorters called for the abolition of the system, and its replacement by cash payments. The provincial postal clerks told the Hobhouse Committee in 1906 that the medical officer was simply 'an Official "whip"'. The postmen said they were simply 'a detective force', whose existence could not in any way be considered as one of the advantages of their jobs.[8]

The same general objection was never expressed to the non-contributory pensions which were provided from 1859 to all 'established' or permanently employed civil servants. In the Post Office, these had their origins in voluntary funds got up by the

London letter carriers and guaranteed for them by the authorities in 1833. In an era before any such general provision for old age, this was regarded as one of the special advantages of public sector employment always taken into account by the authorities in the determination of pay. Until comparatively recently, the superannuation that could normally be anticipated by civil servants has been regarded as 'one of the envies' of those in private employment, a special 'inducement to remain in the service of the state'.[9] By the early twentieth century, however, there was widespread agreement that 'the practical addition to pay' had 'in the past been overstated' and that pension rights should be set off against 'disadvantages attaching to service under the State, e.g. the limitations necessarily imposed upon freedom of action'. Superannuation was only a limited inducement for young entrants, but as the years went by it became 'an added incentive to good conduct', a 'disciplinary measure' for those with diminishing prospects of employment elsewhere. The Post Office Secretary himself in 1904 was 'inclined to regard the pension as being given primarily for the benefit of the employer and not the employee'. With the spread of pensions schemes to outside employment, anomalies in the state system grew more obvious. In 1909 after many years of campaigning, it was at last agreed that civil service pensions could be considered as 'deferred pay', to which widows and dependants were entitled.[10]

In the context of the nineteenth-century labour market the uniforms, the medical facilities and the pensions helped to create the stability and discipline necessary for the laborious and repetitive tasks that kept together a system whose like has never been seen since. By 1914 it was possible for one MP to marvel at 'the extraordinary efficiency of our postal system – how a person can receive a letter in the morning, reply to it, have an answer by six o'clock and send a reply to the letter which is delivered by half-past nine at night'. To carry on such a service required a great deal of back-breaking, irregular toil, often carried on under great pressure. One association leader explained in 1906 what happened:

> Post Office work is carried on at too great a rush. The public are allowed the maximum facilities for posting, with the result that letters are posted up to the latest possible moment before the mail goes, and the staff are worked at those times at too great a pressure.

Besides this pressure, Post Office workers often had to attend over very long periods of the day for a number of separate duties, to perform what amounted to compulsory overtime, or to work 'long and short duties' within separate weeks, or even separate days. Even after some improvements in this system, there were still many complaints. As late as 1906, only 628 established postmen in London could perform their day's work in one continuous period: 2,107 of them had to attend twice, 3,582 three times, and 679 four times. In 1873, there was a rush to the doors by the sorting force in London after the demand for two hours extra unpaid overtime. A similar 'riot' was initiated on Christmas Day 1886 by men who had been working continuously for twenty-four hours. Such appalling hours of work continued during the Christmas period until well into the twentieth century.[11] Even after overtime began to be paid at regular rates and many other improvements had come, it was still felt necessary in 1911 for the authorities to place guards in some parts of a London sorting office to compel people to work extra hours. A woman telegraphist told the Holt Enquiry in 1912 that the result of 'a great deal of speeding up' was 'that the staff is set one against the other', particularly on the allocation of overtime and split duties.[12]

The expansion of the rural postal system, boasted of in successive reports from the Postmaster General, was not achieved without considerable labour on the part of those who had to arrange and deliver the mail. In the 1840s and 1850s many cases could be quoted of rural messengers walking twenty-eight or even forty-five miles a day without respite and as late as 1891, twenty-one miles' walking was still required of rural postmen working close to London.[13] In this latter period, complaints about the pressure of their continuous labours on the telegraphists were frequently voiced and they certainly had a good case against 'long and short' duties and other erratic ways of arranging their work. It is not clear, however, though they often said so, that Post Office workers were particularly prone to phthisis and other wasting diseases. In fact, if only because of their preliminary selection they tended to be healthier than the rest of the population.[14] There was some agreement, however, about the existence of a condition known as 'telegraphists' cramp', which afflicted many of those who worked on morse sounders. In 1908 this was added to the schedule of industrial diseases and in 1911 a Departmental Committee made a number of recommendations about how people could work under less pressure and be less liable to its various manifestations ranging from mild discomfort to near paralysis.[15] The early telephonists did not seem to suffer from industrial diseases, but there was found to be room for a good deal of improvement in the design of their chairs, foot-rests and head gear.[16]

HIERARCHY

As the labour force of the Victorian Post Office expanded and multiplied there developed not only a wide range of new functions, but also a great profusion of new grades. The system of promotion by merit, one of the cornerstones of the re-organisation of the public service initiated in the 1850s, required an ordered hierarchy within which an individual could observe his progress. In the Post Office this hierarchy was not built as part of any rational plan. When new tasks presented themselves, the authorities normally dealt with them by the creation of temporary groups of workers such as 'boy sorters' or 'learners'. They continually added to the many thousands who remained on the fringes of the established labour force, and created a labyrinth of sub-groups with a complex set of relationships between the slightly superior and the slightly inferior. This system was essential in maintaining the system of subordination. Associations and unions always exercised pressure to simplify and rationalise the system, but they never broke down what W. E. Clery once described as the 'snobs' inferno' within the Post Office.[17]

The lowest caste was made up of the letter carriers, with a number of smaller related groups such as messengers, porters and labourers. The General Post letter carriers were regarded as aristocrats of a sort in the early nineteenth century, but as the system expanded they became the poorest section of the Post Office workforce. There was a big concentration of their numbers in London, especially after the merging of the national and metropolitan forces in 1855. Soon there were also large groups in the main towns with increasing numbers of rural messengers and letter carriers as the service expanded to every corner of the land. In 1883, when the parcel post was introduced, they all became 'postmen'. Except in the big London offices, they received their letters already divided into 'walks', after which they arranged and then delivered them. With the spread of universal education after 1870 more and more people were able to pass the simple tests of literacy and numeracy required to take up the work. By 1906, it was said that the examination was 'so elementary that scarcely anyone fails to pass it'. Increasingly, however, the available positions were closed to those who had not served an apprenticeship, either as telegraph messengers, or else in the army. One group of officials expressed the view in 1891 that the result of this was that 'the London postman of today is not what he used to be', particularly in comparison to the 'country lads' who had once provided the main source of recruits.[18]

The postmen themselves were also conscious of a decline in their status and rewards. They became more divided amongst themselves, and increasingly separated from the rest of the Post Office workforce. So it was that despite their reputation outside the service as happy extroverts, the letter carriers and postmen in the nineteenth century were often discontented, and prone to take up the most radical forms of agitation. The aristocrats of the 1830s and 1840s with their scarlet coats and superior airs increasingly felt themselves pushed down within the service into their own distinct and inferior world. Behind them stood an army of 'auxiliary', 'supplementary' and unestablished individuals ready to step into the shoes of any who brought down the wrath of the authorities, though in practice rarely obtaining the promotion they felt to be their due. Just above the letter carriers and postmen, an increasing number of intermediate groups, such as boy sorters and telegraph learners, separated them from the grades above, making it less and less likely that they would ever rise above the level at which they entered the service. In 1890, no London postmaster was prepared to say that the work of the sorters was more difficult or responsible than that performed by the postmen, and yet the sorters received much more pay. In public, the authorities maintained that the sorters needed greater 'intelligence and education' and though this seems to have often been the case in practice, there is little evidence of its necessity.[19] A profound resentment thus developed among those who were placed beneath the hierarchy of the service. 'Section after section', said one postman to the Tweedmouth Committee, 'begin, create privileges and draw up a ladder that others may not enter'.

The desire of postmen to be called 'Mr' may have 'caused some amusement among outside trade unionists', but it bore eloquent testimony to the need for recognition on the part of those who felt themselves to be outcasts within the service. This feeling lay behind the disastrous 'unification' campaign undertaken by the Postmen's Federation after 1906, when they put forward the demand for automatic access to the sorter grade. Although this was in essence recommended by the Bradford Committee in 1905, and was in effect carried through in the grade re-allocation of 1946, all that it did at the time was to provoke bitterness between the postmen and the sorters. The authorities naturally highlighted these divisions before the Hobhouse Enquiry in 1906 and the case of both grades thus went by default. Much earlier, letter carriers' leader William Booth had pointed to a more fruitful line of agitation: 'Unless there is some prospect of improving the position of the employed, dissatisfaction will always exist, no more or less in accordance with the amount of pay received.'[20] Thus it was that demands for higher wages were at the centre of every major agitation of letter carriers and postmen. These demands were complicated not only by the wide variation of pay within the Department, with all the difference in the world between a humble messenger in distant corners of Ireland or Scotland, and a first class man at the Chief Office in London. There also remained a number of increasingly resented survivals of the days of patronage, notably the much-discussed Christmas gratuities.

Conspicuous among other causes for discontent and resentment at the bottom of the Post Office hierarchy between 1872 and 1914 were 'good conduct stripes', pieces of braid sewn in a conspicuous place on uniforms and each carrying an increment of 6d (2½p) up to 1874 and thereafter of 1s (5p). They were first suggested by Postmaster General Monsell in 1872 in the wake of a strike of Huddersfield letter carriers and the announcement of the setting up of the first permanent union among their London counterparts. They were supposed to be awarded only for 'conspicuous good behaviour', at first only in central London, on a number of criteria, including that any wearer 'should not enrol himself in any society, the rules of which in the judgment of the Postmaster General, are opposed to the discipline of the service'. The letter carriers did not like the idea at first and a number of London men petitioned against it in 1874 on the grounds that it 'must of necessity result in a system of favouritism'. The authorities were happier with it, extending it throughout London at that time and to the entire country in the Fawcett revision of 1881, when stripes were also awarded to some of the minor grades in the engineering department.

By 1891, attitudes had changed and the Joyce Departmental Committee lamented that the stripes were no longer regarded as conveying any special distinction. This was something

> the men either cannot or will not understand. It has been explained to them over and over again, but to no purpose, they seem possessed with the idea – an idea the very name of the distinction is calculated to foster – that after the prescribed period of service, the condition of good conduct stripes being fulfilled one man is no less entitled to a good conduct badge than another. That they should have to wait for vacancies is to them unintelligible.

The postmen also argued that outsiders thought 'those who did not get them were badly conducted'. As a result of these criticisms, the limits on the numbers of first and second stripes that could be awarded were removed in October 1891, though the third stripe (and shilling) after fifteen years was still deemed a special distinction. In the face of further criticism, the Tweedmouth settlement of 1897 increased the numbers of stripes to six after thirty years, without any limit on their number. In the next period they went to other grades 'on no very settled plan' so that by the time of the Holt Report in 1912, they had come to be regarded as a normal addition to income from which only a tiny minority were excluded. As a result, there remained no serious arguments against their abolition. The payment that went with them was then consolidated into normal income.[21]

Above the level of postmen a number of other 'manipulative' grades grew up during the nineteenth century, not on the basis of any scheme for dealing with the new tasks that came with the expansion of the work of the Post Office, but from a series of *ad hoc* economy measures that were always designed to find people to perform tasks previously done for higher wages. In the mid-nineteenth century, one of the main purposes of the civil service reformers was to get rid of the large group of 'clerks' whose mode of entry was uncertain and whose functions were often minimal. From 1835 to 1851 the number of clerks in the London Post Office rose from 173 to 662 and the average annual wage fell from £172. 32 to £160. 72. The clerks in the provinces in the same period increased from 116 to 520 and their annual average wage from £68. 29 to £72. 90. The 1854 Elcho Report on the Post Office, whose members included both Stafford Northcote and C. P. Trevelyan, expressed the view that the 'work of sorting letters, which is now chiefly performed by clerks may, we think, be entrusted to members of the inferior establishment'. The Committee favoured a simple system of four grades of letter carriers and sorters with 'promotion by merit' between them. Postmaster General Canning feared that this might lower the tone of those doing the sorting, since the social class from which they were already recruited 'may be described as that which includes small tradesmen, farmers, attorneys' clerks . . . etc., very few of whom would send their sons to do the duty and wear the livery of letter carriers'. Another Post Office official feared the result of the sorters 'finding themselves as menials by all with whom they came in contact'. This was the essential aim of the reformers, so the sorter grade came into existence replacing the small group of 'sub-sorters' recruited from amongst the letter carriers. The former clerks were loud in their denunciations of a new system whereby

> the inducements to enter the service are not sufficient and the prospects for rising therein are too remote, thus deterring young men of respectability from soliciting appointments and compelling the introduction of 'labourers whose associates apart from the establishment are of a standard that makes their trustworthiness questionable.

The sorters began to be recruited quite independently of the letter carriers in 1864, and thereafter were separated from them by the appointment of young men to the junior grades and of women to the inferior duties. Most of the large group of specialist sorters were confined to London, though there were a few in Dublin. After they gave up aspiring to their old status as clerks, they began in the 1880s to campaign for equality with the newly-arrived telegraphists, with some success in terms of their wage levels. They also continued to regard themselves as socially superior, some of them in 1892 fearing that 'association with such bodies as the London Trades Council would be lowering us socially'. Amid their elevated and frustrated aspirations, the London sorters developed as an integrated group united by common problems and a definite *esprit de corps*. In the 1890s they built the most successful union in the Post Office.[22]

Another new task that came out of the mid-nineteenth century reorganisation of the Post Office was that of serving at counters, selling postage stamps, registering letters and so forth. This had been done by 'clerks' previously and still was at the Chief Office in London as late as 1879. From 1854, however, counter work was combined with sorting and from 1869 a specialised group of 'countermen' was recruited (together with some 'counterwomen') in London. After 1889, they also had to be qualified in telegraphy, then becoming known as 'counter clerks and tele-graphists' and continuing as a separate grade in the capital until the 1940s.[23]

Long before then a further complication had been introduced into the entire system with the arrival of the telegraphists in the Post Office in 1870. Their strike of 1871, described in Chapter 6, pp. 120–1ff. reflected in part the difficulties in integrating this new grouping in the Department service. Although a special scale was worked out for them by Scudamore in 1872, the telegraphists remained convinced that their skills were unrecognised, particularly by those on the postal side who were sent to supervise their work. At about the same time, in 1875, the Playfair Commission recommended the new system of civil service grades including a group of 'clerks of the second division' just below the top administration. The telegraphists then aspired to be members of this group and this was the main plank of their programme in the agitation that culminated in the formation of the Postal Telegraph Clerks Association in 1881. The authorities, however, had other ideas for dealing with telegraph work. They wanted to replace the few clerks who had formerly served local postmasters with a new group able to alternate between telegraphy, sorting and counter work. This usually involved reducing the status and pay of those who had previously performed part of the work and often proved impractical, especially in the larger offices.

As early as 1876, the authorities began to demand qualifications in both sorting and telegraphy in some of the smaller offices. The essential aim of the much-discussed 'Fawcett scheme' of 1881 was to continue this process at the expense of the telegraphists in the provinces. Thus they were told that they had 'not a shadow of a legal right' to their claim to be considered as clerks of the second division under the Playfair scheme. The main point was to expand the 'plan already in existence at several offices of amalgamating the postal and telegraph staff', by trying to ensure that 'all future entrants to the service, whether intended ultimately to be telegraph or sorting clerks, should be instructed in the elementary work of both branches'. Much confusion was caused in future years by the claim of the London sorters that the purpose of these proposals had been to elevate their pay and status to that of the telegraphists. In fact the main purpose was to reduce the telegraphists from the levels they secured after their strike in the settlement of 1872 and to merge them with the sorters and others.[24]

The main result of the Fawcett scheme was that the grade of 'sorting clerk and telegraphist' became standard outside London for the main groups of rank-and-file workers immediately above letter carriers and postmen. Despite all the efforts of the authorities, however, most Post Office workers at this level in practice remained solely on the postal or telegraph side. Thus although 'dual qualifications' for entry were introduced throughout the country in 1882, they had to be abandoned in forty-six of the larger offices within two years because of a shortage of candidates prepared to take up both parts of the work. By 1886 all the larger offices had separate postal and telegraph establishments. Only in very small offices was it necessary for people to rotate between the different tasks. In 1895, at the same time as the Tweedmouth deliberations, the Department set up a special committee to consider the whole problem, and this decided that the best thing to do was to make it necessary for every 'learner' from now on to be qualified in both branches, so that 'dual qualification' would eventually work its way through to the whole service. This was introduced through the provinces in 1896 and extended to London two years later. Every provincial telegraphist or sorter from then until 1946 was known as a 'sorting clerk and telegraphist'. In 1902 a further departmental investigation revealed that the system was not working properly in offices employing more than fifty people and in 1905 teenagers were again allowed to begin as 'learners' on the telegraph side alone. Amidst this confusion it was not surprising to hear one SC&T representative declare in 1906 that 'the great proportion of the staff scarcely know whether the particular office to which they are attached has or has not a dual system'. In London the 'dual' system was never implemented in any case, and specialist examinations for telegraphists were held right up to the First World War. In 1912, it was said that the SC&T grade, of whom there were by then 20,554 including 5,022 women, was

> employed in sorting, telegraphy and counter work . . . or a combination of these duties, according to the requirements of the office where he serves. All officers at all offices are liable to be called upon to perform any class of work, but in the largest offices ('divided' offices), where the duties are more arduous, specialisation in postal and telegraph work is necessary, and the duties are so arranged that one set of officers works in the sorting office and another in the telegraph instrument room.[25]

These shifts in the organisation of work in the Post Office help to explain the grievances and the divisions of the different sections of those in the workforce who aspired to the lost status and former conditions of the 'clerks'. It was mostly specialist telegraphists in London and the larger offices who set up and supported the 'Postal Telegraph Clerks Association' of 1881, together with those who served at counters. The main base of the 'UK Postal Clerks Association' of 1887 was provided by those in the smaller offices who combined these functions. Something of the feeling that lay behind the setting up of the first of these bodies can be gathered from the fervent applause that greeted the speaker who made the following statement at one of its preliminary meetings:

> They had frequently been compared with sorters – he objected to such comparisons . . . they denied us the title of clerks – nay, they even denied us the advantages of an ordinary artisan.

The telegraphists in this period considered that the work of sorting letters was beneath their dignity, 'only fit for messengers'. They said they were 'craftsmen' who 'took a pride in [their] work'. They were particularly bitter about their relative lack of access to promotion. This was largely the result of the way the work was organised, but to some extent the authorities gave in to the agitation and during the 1880s and 1890s created a new system of supervisors, inspectors and overseers. This further complicated the hierarchy and led to complaints from specialists in postal work that those on the telegraph side were getting more than their fair share of promotions.[26] The relative wages of those on the telegraph side definitely fell however, as the telegraph system became more of a financial liability to the Post Office and as the SC&T grade became more integrated. By 1906 they were thought in general to come from 'the better class of tradespeople' and the postmen 'from a rather lower stratum'. Though those who specialised in sorting 'to a considerable extent were drawn from the same class' as the postmen, they were thought by the authorities to possess the 'moral force' to supervise others, who themselves had 'a prejudice against employment on outdoor work of any kind' or generally against working with their hands. The provincial SC&Ts supported 'open' competition on the grounds that postmen were generally incapable of being promoted to do their work.[27]

The advances in technology of electrical communication brought other new groups into the service. The engineers, however skilled, who built and maintained the system were generally looked down upon by those who operated it. Besides being often paid by piece-work, they were usually unestablished and at times subject to instant dismissal. Those who ran the stores and factories were in a similar position. As the telephone system expanded, the number of those specialising in this side of the work of the Post Office also increased. From 1901 there was a grade of telephonists, consisting entirely of women, and in 1912, just before the National Telephone Company's system was finally taken over, there were 1,402 of them in London and 2,605 in the provinces.[28]

One other point about the evolution of grades in this period that should be made is to emphasise that London remained very much at the centre of the activities of the Post Office throughout, with concentrated groups in specialist grades to a much greater extent than elsewhere. Thus in 1878 of 45,947 established Post Office workers, 10,745 were in London, 5,919 of them at St Martin's-le-Grand. In 1912 there were 6,413 sorters in London as well as 2,918 telegraphists, including 950 women and 1,533 counter clerks and telegraphists, a majority of 863 being women. There were also in London the outdoor grades of porters and bagmen, of whom in 1912 there were respectively 1,646 and 110.[29] These specialist groups, concentrated in comparatively large numbers, were the focus of most of the early agitations described elsewhere in this book and the backbone of the early unions up to the time of the Tweedmouth Enquiry of 1895–7. Only when the associations grew and became accepted by the authorities did the balance then shift away from the capital.

A further dimension in the hierarchy of the Victorian Post Office was added by the increasing employment of women. The entry of sections of middle-class women into various para-medical, clerical and other professions was an important phenomenon of nineteenth-century social history throughout the industrial world.[30] Women were employed from the start by the telegraph companies, came with them into the Post Office and then gradually were employed on other work in the Department, particularly in the new specialist sections like the Savings Bank. In 1882, there were 321 women in clerical posts and 1,978 working as counter hands or telegraphists. By 1911 when most of the telephone system had been taken over 26,591 out of a total of 106,170 who worked for the Department were women.[31]

The 'respectable young ladies', 'largely recruited from the ranks of the lower middle class' were considered to have 'improved the tone of the whole staff'. The companies thought that because of some alleged affinity of telegraphy with domestic chores, 'the ladies make the best telegraph clerks'. They found them 'more trustworthy, more easily managed and . . . sooner satisfied at the lower wages'. When the system was taken over by the state it was thought to provide 'comparatively light and remunerative occupations for the daughters of Post Office officials'. The limited employment opportunities for women from that social background was such that when the first twelve positions of female counter clerks were advertised in 1872 the Civil Service Commission was mobbed with applicants. It was found 'surprising' to some 'how eagerly these posts at the Post Office at very moderate salaries are competed for', but right up to the First World War there was 'not a very wide field of employment for women with the wages found in the Post Office'. The authorities could thus pay much lower wages than they did to the men and could supervise women in ways that smacked of the most distasteful aspects of Victorian paternalism. After 1875 they could even dismiss them from the service for getting married. Because of the nature of the labour market, Scudamore considered that 'the wages which will draw male operators from an inferior class of the community will draw female operators from a superior class'. He also found women 'less disposed than men to combine for the purpose of extorting higher wages', a decided advantage from the point of view of a cheeseparing administrator.[32]

Unfortunately for the powers that be, however, the women did not remain so meek and mild for ever. As early as 1879, women clerks in the savings department petitioned for higher wages and in 1887 a number of them suffered disciplinary action for asking for an extra day's holiday. It became more obvious that the existence of one group more rigorously disciplined and poorly paid than another doing the same work was 'a source of evil to both sides by permanently lowering the rate of wages for all'. The differences persisted, however. From 1883 to 1893 there existed a class of women sorters only so the work could be performed more cheaply. The 'increase in the female staff at the expense of the male' coupled with the payment of lower wages for similar or identical duties was 'not only an injustice to the women concerned', but also 'a standing menace to the men, who rightly consider the presence of women as a blackleg class brings down wages and reduces their prospects of promotion. A sense of irritation and dissatisfaction is thus engendered between the two sexes'.[33]

These sources of friction only broke down slowly as the women employees of the Post Office began to join actively with their male colleagues in the associations. The first steps in this direction were slow and hesitant. One or two female delegates usually turned up to conferences of the PTCA and generally discussed such grievances as the desire to be known as 'Miss'. As late as 1897 the Tweedmouth Committee felt able to conclude that 'no considerable dissatisfaction existed as to their conditions of service', including their pay. None of the later inquiries got the same impression. Bradford and his colleagues were told by Mabel Hope that female telegraphists in London were obtaining a 'non-subsistence wage' and asked 'how can a woman in London maintain the respectable position demanded of her?' By this time it was said that a school mistress could earn more. The Hobhouse Committee in 1907 noticed that the wage differentials between women and men were becoming wider, especially higher up the scale. The answer of the authorities to all this was that the wages paid to women were not intended to maintain them, but simply to supplement the income of their parental households. There was a rule that women employees of the Post Office should live with parents or guardians, and though the Hobhouse Committee thought this essential to justify the level of wages paid, it never seems to have been enforced. A large proportion of the young women involved seem to have moved into the big cities and lived alone, often in 'half-charitable boarding houses'. One MP expressed the fear that as a result they might be 'exposed to certain difficulties'. However, though many of them might have had incomes to make them dependent on the Poor Law guardians, they were in fact compelled 'frequently to act' as guardians 'towards others'. Their subordination was reinforced by another rule which was enforced, the one that compelled them to leave the service when they married. It was sometimes said that the women did not want to price themselves out of their jobs by demands for equality, but eventually in 1913 the PTCA cut through all the enforced distinctions by boldly claiming the same pay and conditions for men and women.[34] It was not for a generation that this was even quite accepted as an aim, and not for forty years that it was achieved. However, the social realities and attitudes that lay behind the position of women within the Post Office labour force began to change as more and more female telephonists joined the service, and as many others performed a wide range of functions during the First World War.

One other group in the Post Office of this period who suffered discrimination were teenagers below 18, the age at which appointments to the main grades were normally made. In the 1860s there were 'boy clerks' and later also 'boy sorters'. The telegraph messengers were once the most familiar figures to those outside the service after the postmen. Most joined in the hope that they would eventually secure senior appointments. However, this became increasingly difficult especially after 1891 when the Joyce Committee recommended 'a rigorous weeding out' at the age of 16 and more positions were made exclusively available to members of the armed forces. More positions were also opened to outsiders in 1899. As a result ex-messengers usually only became postmen or sorters after enlisting for a time themselves. In 1909 and 1910 over 4,000 out of a total force of 14,000 were unceremoniously discharged without much hope of further employment.

Though there was never really anyone to speak for them, the fashionable concern with 'blind alley employment' for young people at the time led to the setting up of a Standing Committee on Boy Labour. In the years before 1914 this body planned the gradual absorption of the teenagers into the adult labour force by a number of measures of which the most important was the abolition of open competition for sorter and SC&T positions. 'Girl probationers' were also introduced for telegraphy. The associations did not see themselves as acting on behalf of the teenagers and opposed the ending of open competition on the rather insubstantial grounds that it made internal promotion between grades less likely. There were also complaints from local education authorities about the premature loss of some of their brighter pupils who wanted to pursue a Post Office career. The authorities argued that open competition had never really been intended for the lower manipulative grades in any case and that the quality of entrants was not much affected one way or the other. Other small groups of 'learners' were introduced after competitive examinations became normal in the provincial centres in 1893. The 'learners' were not even generally paid until 1905 and had to wait as long as six years for regular or guaranteed employment at the full rate. Only in 1932 was the class of learner finally abolished and standard 'probationary' periods created.[35] In 1947 the 'boy messenger' and 'girl probationer' grades disappeared also.

These teenagers, and especially the telegraph messengers, were always considered as a great disciplinary problem by the authorities. The involvement of some of their number in the famous male brothel in Cleveland Street frequented by members of the Royal Family which became notorious in 1889 must have caused some anxious moments at St Martin's-le-Grand. More usually, however, the concern of the authorities was to improve their appearance and prevent them from loitering in the streets. Special officers, usually ex-postmen, were allocated to keep them smart and to drill them, and the authorities also took an increasing interest in their education.[36]

From the 1890s onwards, under War Office pressure, increasing numbers of ex-soldiers were employed in the Post Office, some of them former messengers who at 16 failed further qualifying examinations. From 1897 half the vacancies for porters and postmen were allowed to ex-servicemen who took up all the positions open to them after the Boer War in 1902. Many boy messengers were thus displaced. The authorities were not entirely happy about the disciplinary record of former servicemen, notably their habit of 'liquidating' their army pensions in bouts of drunkenness, but generally they gave in to pressure from the military and the War Office. However, people recruited in this way were often paid considerably less than those who started in the Post Office. The associations rarely complained either, though one leader did tell the Holt Enquiry 'that ex-army men as a consequence of the army system of discipline were unsuited to the postal service'. By then, however, the authorities expressed themselves 'perfectly satisfied' with their ex-service subordinates.[37]

A 'closed' and complicated grade structure had thus come into existence by the early twentieth century. The system had one other important characteristic. There always remained at the fringes of the 'established' workforce a further group of the 'unestablished', often part-time and nearly always aspiring to permanent pensionable employment. Despite constant promises by the authorities to reduce the size of this group, it was always growing larger. In 1913 when 118,116 people held established positions in the Post Office, there were 122,018 who did not. By this time 'attempting to meet new needs with half measures' had brought about 'a partial abandonment of the "establishment" system'. Staff claims that people were kept unestablished to avoid paying them increases were not wide of the mark.[38] During the First World War the proportion of the unestablished grew larger still. They thus continued breathing down the necks of those who might imagine their jobs were quite safe, a reminder of expected disciplinary standards.

The complex and constantly changing hierarchy in the nineteenth-century Post Office had none of the visible simplicity aimed at by those who initiated the new system in the 1850s. When Northcote and Trevelyan argued for promotion by merit as an alternative to patronage, they saw it as a unique system whereby 'efficiency and economy may be combined'. However, any such aims became lost in a jungle of *ad hoc* sub-groups and a maze of special relationships between the superior and the slightly less so. There can be no question that the promotion system was cordially disliked by almost everybody who was subject to it, on the grounds that it made improvement for any individual into a 'lottery'. It was maintained that 'the advantage gained by the promotion of a meritorious junior officer before his time is more than counter-balanced by the injurious effects upon those who have been superseded'. A London sorter expressed in 1861 a view which seems to have been almost universal among them:

Merit, as Lord Palmerston said, is another name for favouritism and we find it so. Where a man can cook herring well, make a good cup of coffee, or can run an errand for a certain gentleman, or happens to marry into the family of some of the servants of the officials, these men get promotion while others are passed over.

Cases were always being quoted of people alleged to have obtained promotion without deserving it and then not being able to do the work involved. This is a typical example presented to the Holt Committee:

This gentleman who had been selected for exceptional merit to pass over 115 senior officers had eventually to be put back to his old place because he was unable to pass the qualifying examination. It was thought that his exceptional merit consisted of the fact that he had gone to lodge with the sister of a superintendent in the Birmingham Post Office and had had the good fortune to marry his landlady.[39]

Under pressure of this kind it is not surprising that the system of promotion by merit was never enforced in full. After its initial application it was revised at the

GPO in 1863 with a formula about 'seniority accompanied by competency and good conduct'. This was much preferred by senior clerks and surveyors like Anthony Trollope. 'There can be no standard,' said the novelist, 'by which the excellence of men can be judged, as is the weight of gold.' In later years, there was gradual change in attitudes on the part of the authorities. In the early part of the twentieth century it was said that the importance of seniority and merit were 'in varying proportions according to the importance of the promotion'. In 1912 it was said that the authorities did 'not pay so much attention to seniority as we did before, having had some experience of the evils which undue regard for seniority has caused'. These problems were thought to be particularly prevalent at the Central Telegraph Office in London where 'a great part of the evils' were 'due to the fact that for nearly 35 years promotion went mainly by seniority and the result was that the wrong men would get into superior positions and they very slowly die off because they have got nice fat jobs'.[40]

Thus, as the civil service grew so also opinions about how to improve their conditions changed. As the number of new grades increased and especially after the telegraphists came into the Post Office, each section aspired to the conditions of those immediately above them and individuals wanted promotion right to the top of the tree. John Newlands, Controller of the Central Telegraph Office in 1912, had entered the service as a boy messenger in 1870, but such cases were inevitably rare and promotion by seniority was almost universally preferred. 'It is a remarkable fact,' observed the Tweedmouth Committee, 'that almost every case that has come before us complained that they have not received a fair share of desirable appointments.'[41] These feelings were not necessarily caused by any particular capriciousness on the part of the authorities. They derived from the difficulty in adapting any promotions system to the exigencies of a rapidly expanding service. In particular, however, they were the inevitable outcome of the conceptions of those who remoulded the Victorian public service in the 1850s. By bringing into the state service the values of a society of isolated competitive individuals, they inevitably created discontented groups at the bottom of the heap. The agitations, the inquiries and the pressures from the associations introduced an element of rationality into the system of hierarchy, but they never drove out the jealousies and resentments that were essential to its very operation.

PAY

'Let no one go into the civil service in the hope of being highly paid or lightly worked', wrote one outsider in 1878, and he would certainly have secured the heart-felt agreement of letter carriers, sorters and telegraphists.[42] Not only did the Post Office workers have good grounds for considering their 'privileges' to be an empty mockery. They also complained bitterly about the lowness of their pay, and this grievance headed virtually every list they compiled during the nineteenth century. This was nearly always expressed initially in terms of comparisons with the grades above. After the sorters stopped wanting to be 'clerks', they became content with the title itself, but still aspired to the conditions of telegraphists. The telegraphists for their part aspired to the status and rewards of second division clerks, just as further down the scale the postmen compared themselves to the sorters. As hopes of improvement on this basis were gradually frustrated for one group after another, and as the allowances and perquisites of the patronage system faded away, then each group sought a higher and more systematically determined incremental scale.

However, the question remains of how well postal workers were paid before the 1920s, both compared to what they themselves had previously received and to what was obtained elsewhere. If complaints based on the first of these criteria were usually avoided, those based on the second were almost impossible to verify. There were always difficulties in making any sort of objective assessment. Thus gratuities and extra payments remained a substantial part of the payment of most public servants under the system of patronage which existed until the mid-nineteenth century re-organisation. For example, London letter carriers in the 1850s received special payments for early deliveries and the collection of letters. They also got gratuities of various kinds, which altogether often amounted to more than their fixed incomes. As a result they looked on proposals to standardise their wages with considerable suspicion. Christmas boxes could still be obtained by those directly serving the public. The authorities argued during every agitation that this represented a significant addition to income. Those who benefited from the efforts of commercial firms and householders to retain their goodwill were naturally reluctant to give up their rewards. However, they were never happy with the system. As early as 1846 one of the letter carriers at the GPO thought it 'a degradation to go about from house to house soliciting Christmas presents like the dustmen and the scavengers', and another said the return was 'not worth its value'. As the age of patronage gave way to one which aspired to standards of 'service', then the very idea of such a method of payment became less acceptable. By the time of the Holt Enquiry in 1912, the postmen expressed themselves 'against the "tipping" system', and for a principle not even then fully agreed 'of public servants serving the public being paid directly by the Government for services rendered'.[43]

Nor were these by any means the only complications in determining the level of income. Standard rates themselves were subject to almost every conceivable form of variation. In 1827 there were twenty-seven clerks in the Inland Section of the GPO doing sorting and they were paid on six different scales, receiving anything from £90 to £160 per annum. Letter carriers and messengers in the same period received as little as 10s 6d (52½p) a week, or as much as £1 3s (£1. 15) if they did some sorting. Local variations were even more striking. Thus in 1853 a letter carrier in London at the top of the lowest scale got £52 per annum, while his equivalent in Bodmin got £23, or as little as £10 in parts of Ireland. In 1856, when the first standard rates were agreed, there were seven different scales for letter carriers, from as low as 10s (50p) a week to as high as £1 10s (£1. 50), not to mention various subsidiary and temporary grades. (Very few people outside London earned more than 16s (80p) in any case.) In the 1890s when the average annual earnings of London postmen were well over £60 per annum, their 5,000 odd rural counterparts earned an average of £40 13s 6d (£40. 67). Frequent complaints were heard about the differences in wage rates within the shortest possible distances, with five separate scales in London as late as 1895. There was a particularly tenacious campaign by the postmen of Woolwich against their being excluded from the metropolitan area.[44]

By the end of the nineteenth century, the wages of postmen were usually comparable to those prevailing locally and the SC&Ts and other indoor grades had their wages determined by rough and ready criteria of the volume of work. The Hobhouse Committee in 1906 asked the Post Office to work out a system for determining wages which involved complicated but precise calculations based on the amount of business done by each office. This was applied to the different sections of the workforce and was further modified by the time of the Holt Enquiry six years later by taking into account figures for local variation in the cost of living which were collected by the Board of Trade. However, there were many complaints about the new system, not least because it was designed by the authorities. Workers in every town had arguments for being placed in a more favourable category. A particular grievance was that for a time the basis of the cost of living was calculated somewhat differently in Scotland from the rest of the United Kingdom. In deciding to leave this system more or less as it was in 1912, the Holt Committee expressed the view that 'no system perfectly logical and capable of hard and fast application can be devised', and 'it is very difficult to justify on the basis of differences of work alone, the drawing of the line between the classes at one point rather than another'.[45] Other differences between the pay of individuals derived from the sub-divisions within grades which existed until the 1890s, and from the steep incremental scales which remained a grievance until the 1970s.

For the superior and educated sorter, telegraphist or SC&T there was a constant struggle 'to maintain that degree of respectability to which his general surroundings entitle him'. This group might perhaps be said to be part of the 'labour aristocracy' standing between the skilled manual workers who set up the craft unions and the 'clerks' who did not show the same sense of labour solidarity. Letter carriers and postmen in the big cities could be located somewhere in the ill-defined 'great divide' between artisan and labourer. In 1860 London sorters complained that their rewards were 'scarcely more than those received by bricklayers' labourers', despite the fact that their work was 'of a highly responsible character, requiring probity, intelligence and a fair education'. A more objective survey of earnings of manual workers in 1867 placed even London letter carriers quite low down the list. They got less than instrument makers, engine drivers, printers, carpenters, bakers and most types of metal workers. They got about the same as chimney sweeps and miners. Those few groups who actually earned less included agricultural labourers, soldiers and most women. Provincial messengers and letter carriers were probably lower down the scale with an average of about £30 per annum in 1855 not placing them above agricultural labourers.[46]

A similar picture of comparative poverty emerges when one catches a glimpse of the living conditions of Post Office workers in the nineteenth century. One of the Department's own medical staff found on visiting the homes of those under his charge in 1855, 'rooms for the most part small, low, with very imperfect ventilation' and in many cases totally unfit for habitation. Their houses in general were found to be 'in a most insanitary condition, badly ventilated and over crowded'. It was also discovered that few of those recruited to the postal service were accustomed to the type of monotonous physical toil they were expected to perform, the majority coming from domestic service or shop work of various kinds. They were a good deal smaller than their modern counterparts. Their average age on recruitment in 1861 was 22, their height 5 feet 6½ inches and their weight 9 stone 6 pounds.

A number of pieces of evidence can be quoted to show that Post Office workers were not remarkably well off. One survey of London workers in the 1890s concluded that the advantages of being in the postal service could be attributed not to the wages but to the regularity of employment. Early in the twentieth century a close study of the wages and expenditure of a childless and teetotal London postman earning £1 12s (£1. 60) a week (£88 4s (£88. 20) per annum) found that he had nothing left for luxuries and concluded that in general 'the present financial position of the London postman is the same as it was fifty years ago'. In 1913 a younger postman in the provinces at £1 6s 6d (£1. 32½p) a week (£68 19s (£68. 90) per annum) was placed on a level just above those not in regular work.[47]

Beyond these general impressions, it is difficult to make an overall assessment of the wages paid to Post Office workers before the 1920s. The tables given in the appendices try to cover this as comprehensively as possible, though they can be taken at best only as indicating general trends. It was always possible during the nineteenth century, for reasons already explained, to quote examples of people doing work in the Post Office for which others had once been paid two, three or even four times as much.[48] If an effort is made to compare like with like and to describe some of the main trends, then the form and timing of the agitations described in later chapters can be explained.

The general trends of Post Office employment and wages may be set out as follows. Between 1835 and 1850 the size of the Post Office workforce was multiplied two and a half times. General money wages in this period were fairly static and so were those of the manipulative grades in the London Post Office. However, the rapid expansion of the system increased the numbers of clerks in the London area and reduced their average wage. Outside London, wages in the main urban centres, both among letter carriers and clerks, seem to have increased as new groups were attracted into the service. The average wage of the 844 provincial letter carriers in England and Wales in 1836 was £19. 01 and by 1850, 2,186 of them earned £22. 70 on average. Those in the rural areas did much worse. While Scottish provincial letter carriers between 1836 and 1850 increased in numbers from 34 to 424 their average wage fell from an average of £35. 54 to £15. 06. Those in the inferior grades in the Irish provinces increased in numbers from 83 to 521 between these same years, and their average wage fell from £19. 54 to £12. 38.[49]

In the period between about 1850 and 1880, the pattern of Post Office wages changed quite dramatically. Average wages outside London rose considerably, in line with the rising trend of wages in general, both real and nominal. Thus, according to one calculation of the average of letter carriers, sorters, stampers and messengers in the provinces, they got £30 per annum in 1855, £38 in 1863 and £58 in 1880. Although these aggregate figures no doubt conceal great variations, similar improvements were reflected also in the equivalent figures for provincial clerks between 1855 and 1880 of £68 to more than £90, and for postmasters of £100 to £160. In London the general picture was quite different. In the 1850s and 1860s, when both real wages and prices were rising quickly, the wages of London letter carriers remained constant in money terms. For the rapidly expanding ranks of sorters in London, even average money wages were falling fast in these years. This was the same period when many fringe benefits, particularly gratuities of various kinds, were being abolished. These trends do much to explain the sharp expressions of discontent during this period in London. Despite the various agitations, and the revisions of 1861 and later, the wages of London letter carriers do not seem to have risen as fast as those of most other workers during the 1860s and early 1870s. There is separate confirmation of this in a careful study of average earnings in 1872 undertaken by one of the service journals. This showed no real improvement since 1854.[50]

From the 1870s onwards it is clear that there was a general rise in the average wages of Post Office workers. In money terms they increased by between a quarter and a half up to the First World War and in real terms a good deal more than that. This improvement was particularly marked in the lower grades and was perceptibly more than for workers generally, especially when real wages in general were falling after 1900. The tables given in the appendices indicate these trends clearly enough, but they also reveal a number of interesting differences. There are many statements about these differences scattered through the pages of the evidence to the great inquiries on Post Office workers' conditions, and the authorities and separate groups made comparisons from dates and figures which suited best their own line of argument. In the 1880s and 1890s when the associations were first firmly established, the London sorters seem to have done quite a lot better than any other group. Thus, the postmen told the Tweedmouth Enquiry that between 1886 and 1896 while their weekly wage in London fell from £1. 33 to £1. 30, the sorters' increased from £1. 66 to £1. 81. According to figures provided by the authorities, between 1891 and 1903 the wages of sorters went up by 27 per cent and those of postmen by 7 per cent. These trends are also reflected in the figures in the appendices, though the calculation of averages may exaggerate them, since the number of postmen at the maximum was increasing.

The sorters themselves often denied that anything like this was happening and did produce some evidence that within these total figures, nearly all the benefit was derived by the more senior members. The figures in the Appendices also show clearly enough that the telegraphists did worse than the sorters. According to another official statement, the figures for average increases between 1885 and 1905 were 60 per cent for the sorters, 55 per cent for London male telegraphists, 13 per cent for female telegraphists and 19·5 per cent for postmen. The equivalent figures for male and female CC&Ts was 31·5 per cent and 26·25 per cent respectively. The relatively poor position of the telegraphists must partly have been the result of the economic weakness of their part of the service, but it also reflected the general narrowing of differentials that has been observed in the economy as a whole. The trend can be seen in the improvements in the comparative position of the postmen after the turn of the century, especially in the provinces. In this period certainly the Postmen's Federation took over from the Fawcett Association the role of the most effective of the organisations of Post Office workers.[51]

It would seem possible to conclude that Post Office workers did best in the period when they were building their associations and were able to exercise a sustained and increasing political influence. Their wages rose most in the years of the great public inquiries, more than in the early years of the penny post, and generally more than when an ordered system of bargaining was established after the First World War. It is instructive to make a comparison with conditions in the United States postal service, where real wages showed no significant increase between 1890 and 1914 and actually fell between 1903 and 1913 during the operation of the 'gag acts' when the lobbying of Congress was illegal.[52] British Post Office workers did much better when 'recognition' of their unions was only just being conceded, and when they were able to exercise continuous and public pressure on MPs and ministers, with the backing of increasingly powerful and effective organisations.

CRITERIA FOR PAY DETERMINATION

Though it would be possible to trace other trends from the appendices dealing with wages before 1920 and the sources on which they are based, this final section is devoted to a discussion of the particular and interesting question of how the wages earned by Post Office workers were determined in the era before the setting up of formal bargaining machinery.

As the civil service was gradually removed from the grip of the patronage system in the mid-nineteenth century, the complex and often arbitrary hierarchy developed in ways that have already been described. Behind all this, however, lay the basic principle set out as early as 1808 by the Select Committee on Public Expenditure.

> With regard to the salary and emoluments of each separate department, the public ought unquestionably to be served as cheaply as is consistent with being served with integrity and ability.

Twenty years later, it was thought that all that was necessary to go beyond this 'in order to determine the proper rates of salaries in Public Offices' was to make necessary comparisons with 'commercial and other establishments'. Northcote and Trevelyan considered that for the main groups of Post Office workers, it was 'of considerable importance to the public that salaries should be as moderate as the nature of their duties would justify'.[53] Constraints such as these were every bit as real in the nineteenth-century Post Office as they were for anybody who worked for private enterprise. A private employer who fears bankruptcy has a motive for keeping down wages, but so also has a Government that fears for its existence if it increases taxation. During the years from 1840 to 1920 the Post Office was a 'revenue earning department of state' – in other words it made profits as a form of direct taxation. The Treasury, the Parliamentary opposition and the electorate all exercised pressure to keep this revenue rolling in, and no government could ignore them. Of course, there were countervailing political influences also, as the associations increased the effectiveness of their lobbying, and won over sympathetic MPs.

At the same time as being subject to these competing political forces, the Post Office was not walled off from the market economy. Wage levels in the public service, and especially the timing and direction of changes, were clearly subject to many of the same influences as those operating in the economy as a whole. Whatever view was taken of 'outside comparisons' – and they were attacked from every side – they were never absent from the purview of those advocating or making changes. From the 1850s onwards, every agitation aimed at improvements for Post Office workers had a definite relationship to trends within the economy as a whole, both in terms of wages and business activity. The Postmaster General explained in 1873 of the letter carriers that in many

> parts of the country (more especially in the manufacturing and mining districts) owing to a general increase in the payment for labour, it has been found necessary, in order to procure and retain the services of men fully competent to carry on the business of the Department, to raise the wages.

When, after this, pressure for further improvements came from the letter carriers, forty vacancies were advertised, not because new workers were needed, but to discover whether 'their pay was a proper pay for such a kind of labour'. After 1,200 applications flooded in, the authorities were then in a position to argue that the letter carriers were being paid the rate for the job. In 1874, improvements were granted to other grades on the same basis of 'a general increase in the payment of labour'. In 1890 the Treasury expressed itself in agreement with such improvements for sorting clerks and telegraphists, as could be justified by the 'rise of wages in the open market'. Just over a decade later the Boer War brought about labour shortages that necessitated increases in the minimum rates for telegraphists in the chief provincial centres. Lewin Hill well summarised what was the general view of the authorities when he said that postmen should be paid at 'such rates as will secure an ample supply of persons well qualified for the work' and in 1906 the Secretary of the Scottish Post Office maintained that he was

> of opinion that the rates of pay current in other occupations ought most certainly to constitute a determining factor in governing the wages of those in the Post Office and when a comparison is made the balance will, I think, be found to be generally well in favour of the civil servant . . . I state with the utmost assurance that every vacancy in the Post Office could be filled many times over by fully qualified candidates . . .[54]

Purely market criteria were, however, modified in many ways within the Post Office. As the Chief Labour Correspondent of the Board of Trade told the Joyce Committee in 1891, it might be possible to offer a lower minimum wage, but 'it is a question of how far it is desirable for an important branch of the public service to take extreme advantage of [the] competition of unemployed labour for work'. Above the minimum, forces of competition in the labour market grew increasingly remote for those who acquired specialised skills. Accumulated pensions rights also placed them in different positions from those outside the service. Overlapping local labour markets also operated in a complicated way. Rural letter carriers had low wages in line with the agricultural labour force. Efforts made to set out the multifarious local rates in a systematic fashion from the 1850s onwards may have distorted local comparisons and by the 1890s the authorities were of the opinion that postmen were often earning a great deal more than was warranted by local conditions. On the other hand in London in 1904, it was very difficult to explain why it should be that 'the postman who delivers to 234 Old Ford Road received 4s [20p] less minimum than one who delivers to 232'. Similarly, the 'unit of work' criteria which were used in determining all local differences after 1906, bore no necessary relationship to the cost of living in particular areas, even if there might be said to be an element of 'accidental justice'.[55]

All of this, of course, assumes that there was, or is, a market value for wages which is capable of being objectively observed. However, it is necessary to agree with one major study of the matter that 'our knowledge . . . is somewhat vague', and furthermore that 'civil service pay can be related to the market rate (assuming the market rate to be known) only within a wide level of indeterminacy'.[56] This indeterminacy was the result of a large number of non-market factors which must now be considered.

The starting point for wages in the Post Office was the system of place and patronage which only gradually broke down during the nineteenth century and even operated in small ways into the early twentieth. It is true that it can be 'dangerous to exaggerate the role of custom in the wage structure of a fully industrial economy'. However, this structure was not formed in a void. It began as a modification or distortion of the pre-industrial wage hierarchy and only gradually came to approximate to the new pattern. Elements of precisely such a 'pre-industrial wage-hierarchy' persisted in the Post Office over a number of generations. Where once individual positions had been obtained through a network of family and interest, no rational system could be discovered in later years. Long after 1870 'wide variations existed in the pay that was given to similar men for the performance of similar work' and it could easily appear that levels of pay had been 'fixed arbitrarily'.[57]

The alternative to patronage initiated by the fathers of the Victorian state bureaucracy was the system of promotion by merit within fixed grades, which, if never attained, was always the ideal aimed at. The Post Office monopoly grew as a hierarchy with its own internal laws of motion – a sort of bureaucratic Newtonian solar system. Fawcett in the early 1880s was the only PMG who tried to argue for payment according to the amount of work performed and to claim that his settlement was 'based upon the intelligible principle of paying for work solely according to its quality'. In Fawcett's view letter carriers should receive more wages not because there were too few applicants for their jobs, but because 'wage rates were no longer adequate for the duties which they perform'. In fact payment was 'for status rather than actual work'. The Stanley settlement of 1905, for example, was expressed solely in terms of grade and age.[58]

Inevitably, as political pressures intensified and the workforce grew more organised, payment was made according to more explicit and systematic criteria. In the era which began with the Tweedmouth Enquiry in 1895, classes within grades were broken down and local differences were ranked into fixed 'classification'. As Sidney and Beatrice Webb pointed out at the time, one 'practically universal' result of trade union pressure was 'the insistence on payment according to some definite standard, uniform in application'. Such pressures have more recently been shown to narrow grade differentials as well as occupational and regional variations.[59]

The pressures to standardise were particularly strong for the Post Office in the era of the great public inquiries with much Parliamentary and other discussion. This period saw much effort to discover a plausible and agreed basis for wage determination. Whatever protestations are made to the contrary, such criteria always derive from comparisons. The real problem is to discover an agreed basis for them. 'External criteria', says one recent discussion of this subject, 'are essentially subjective . . . who . . . is perceived as being "in the same boat" and what determines this perception?' Serious problems derive in any case from the fact that 'effort, skill, responsibility and environment are mutually inconvertible'.[60] These problems lay at the basis of the tortuous discussions between the postal workers and the authorities about relevant comparisons which fill the pages of all the great inquiries. For the workers the main comparisons were made within the service and those who wanted to improve their situation sought either individual promotion or the moving up of their entire grade. In explaining to the Tweedmouth Enquiry why all their arguments about the need for improved wages were based on comparisons with the sorters, the Secretary of the Postmen's Federation hoped the Committee would

> be guided more by a desire to see contentment in a service where the 'market value' policy has for so long been tried and . . . given rise to a greater proportion of the abuses and anomalies that are still in existence.

Speaking to the same Committee, one of the London sorters expressed himself in opposition to

> a comparative statement of the relative emoluments or wages of skilled mechanics, such as carpenters and the like. Against such a comparison I wish to protest with all the powers I am possessed of . . . Our position is, to some extent unique . . . We ask that if any comparison is to be made with outside labour, it may be with the bank clerk who is paid for his honesty, or with the confidential clerk in the biggest and best of the mercantile houses.

Thus for all their protests, the sorters were drawn into comparisons. So also were the provincial postal clerks, who made unfavourable comparisons with pattern makers, plumbers, carpenters and brick-layers and in Ireland with masons, policemen and clerks at a Limerick bacon factory.

In later years international comparisons were introduced, at least in telegraphy. The authorities on the other hand selected their own examples, arguing that wages 'compare very favourably with the general rates of pay given in the commercial world to merchants' and lawyers' clerks and the like'. This argument was rejected by the Post Office workers on the grounds that if they 'found the people outside were getting less, even if it were less than they ought to get, they were bound to reduce the wages of Post Office servants'. The Holt Enquiry in 1911 was provided with ninety-eight pages of closely reasoned comparisons which led them to conclude that there was no basis for 'the proposition that Post Office servants suffer any disadvantage on the matter of wages as compared with persons engaged in other occupations'. Furthermore, they found 'no general agreement amongst the staff themselves as to the basis on which wages should be paid'.[61]

There were many other criteria for wage payment even more vague and more difficult to measure. A typical example can be found in the argument of one official about wage claims of 1804:

> It has been said formerly and by high Authority that if the Two Penny Post letter carriers were paid 'as labourers' it would be as much as could be Expected; but with all deference to that Authority; I am of opinion that the wages should be equal to the humble maintenance of a family.

The same official went on to argue for wages for letter carriers that were 'ample to enable them to maintain their rank in society, or support their families decently'. During the nineteenth century, when prices were considerably more stable than in our own, arguments based on the cost of living were not often heard. At a time when cost pressures were not always thought of as inevitably upwards, the Holt Committee discovered that

> the staff as a whole were reluctant to found their claims to increased wages mainly on the cost of living, not only because the claims put forward could not be justified by any actual increase in the cost of living, but also because the acceptance of this principle could involve a reduction of wages upon a fall in the cost of living.[62]

Instead, some sections of the staff argued for a rate of pay such that 'the ideal of family life' ought to be in the reach of everybody and that 'the present generation should be able to live in a better style than their grandfathers'. It was further maintained that Post Office workers ought to be able to aspire to the comforts of a 'refined middle class home'.[63] In the age of social surveys it was even argued that the less elevated versions of adequate living standards could be subject to objective verification. The postmen told the Bradford Committee that in deciding on

> a true economic basis upon which we might reasonably ask for our wages to be fixed, we came to the conclusion that the only course was, to take first of all a standard of physical efficiency and ask for local prices of general consumption.

The postmen worked out on this basis a minimum set of purchases which was described by Rowntree the social surveyor himself as not 'extravagant according to any reasonable standard'. By the time of the First World War it was agreed that all Post Office workers should have a minimum wage of at least a guinea (£1. 10) per week, and the PF argued with Postmaster General Samuel about whether anybody was actually receiving as little as that.[64] By that time the authorities had accepted a conception first put forward by the Bradford Committee and almost the only argument to survive from its deliberations, that they should 'draw a distinction in favour of the man who has reached an age when he might reasonably be expected to marry'. From the 1905 Stanley settlement it was also accepted that there should be some element of payment for responsibilities, though this cut across the aims taken up by the associations in the following period of getting equal pay for women.[65]

A further factor in the determination of wages was the economic position of the Post Office itself. It was sometimes argued on the postal side that the level of profitability might be taken into account and the point was, of course, frequently made in general propaganda about conditions. However, the telegraphists were of the opinion that 'profits and losses should make no difference' and on the whole, the authorities agreed with them in this period at least.[66] The argument that the Government should begin to set the pace in such matters generally grew more popular. As early as 1892 the Postmaster General is said to have declared 'that the market rate was not the standard by which any department or employer should be judged, and he was desirous that the Post Office should set an example to other employers of labour'. If Morley was not as good as his word, later in the 1890s Liberal MP and future PMG Sydney Buxton argued that the Post Office 'should set a good example to other employers of labour'. The associations themselves began to argue this systematically to the Bradford Enquiry in 1904 and by the time the MacDonnell Commission reported on the civil service as a whole just before the First World War it had become 'an accepted principle with all parties that Government should be a "model employer"'.[67] This statement was made at a time when the political influence of civil servants was at its height and future administrators were not to relish their position at the head of a wages race. The Tomlin Formula of 1931 was in effect the opposite of the 'model employer' argument, committing the Government to follow rather than to lead trends in the economy, and that worked out by Priestley in 1954 placed public servants above the average. The earlier view however was perhaps closer to more recent theory and practice of government in deciding wage levels according to their own opinion of what they ought to be.

NOTES

1 Bradford Evidence, p. 11.
2 The earliest figures are in PP 1828 XVI and isolated details in Joyce (1893), p. 292, Hyde (1891), p. 86, and Robinson (1948), p. 130.
3 The account of one such execution, though not of a Post Office employee, was extracted from the *Bath Herald*, 14 September 1811, and circulated by the GPO. Details of Barret's trial and various other efforts by the authorities to have letter carriers hanged are in POR 30E 101/1835 and copies of correspondence between Barret's widow and the Post Office were supplied by Mr J. Barber. See also Binden (1907), Carey (1897), and 5 & 6 Will IV c.81. *Post*, 10 June 1933, p. 510, gives another example.
4 *CSG* 20 June, 5 December 1863, 20 August 1864; *B-H* 8, 22 March 1873 for examples and discussions. *Money Market Review*, 31 January 1863, for the comparison with bank clerks and Raikes (1898), p. 310, on the mandatory five years.
5 *CSG* (28 March 1858); *Answers* (22 March 1890); *Toby* (8 May 1886); *Irish Postal and Telegraph Guardian* (December 1908); 'Withdrawal of recognition on account of articles in Association journals' (F 100); Hobhouse Evidence, p. 644; Holt Evidence, p. 698; *Blackfriars Magazine* (1889), p. 193.
6 PMG 5th Report for 1858, p. 40.
7 Uniform Clothing for Letter Carriers, 1792–1832 (POR 61/1); Committee on Uniform Clothing (1910), including historical information (POR 61/11); *CSG* (18 June 1859); Report on Telegraph Messengers' Appearance (1891) (POR 61/7); Postmen and Mail Cart Drivers' Uniforms (1895) (POR 61/2). See also Raynham and Calvert (1936), p. 37, 'RWH' (1915), *Post* (1950), p. 406; (1951), pp. 45–6, 69, 99 including illustrations.
8 Baines (1895a) Vol. I, pp. 250–2; *CSG* (21 November 1858); Lewis (1862), p. 585; PMG 50th Report for 1903–4, p. 29; POR 64/11; *Post* (15 October 1892); Hobhouse Evidence, pp. 147, 334, 325, 473, 552. For a later description see H. H. Bashford, *Post Office Medical Service* (1936) (POGP 31).
9 PP 1857 XXXV, p. 163; 22 Vic c.26 ii (1859); Walker (1961), p. 4.
10 Bradford Report, p. 19; Ridley Commission, p. 140, on inducements at entry; PMG 7th Report for 1860, p. 41; Hobhouse Evidence, p. 98; PP 1903 XXXIII, Sir George Murray in evidence to the Royal Commission on the Civil Service, p. 169. On the deferred pay campaign see Chapter 8 and on the subject in general Raphael (1964) and Rhodes (1965).
11 *Hansard* VI, 61, 1905 (30 April 1914); Hobhouse Evidence, p. 331 and appendices, p. 41; Swift (1929), pp. 91, 163; W. E. Loveday, 'Memoirs of an Edwardian postie', *Evening Standard* (23 December 1973); Tombs (1891).
12 Holt Evidence, pp. 286, 612.
13 *Essex Standard* (23 July 1850); *Times* (21 January 1845). The 1891 case is mentioned in Shepherd (1923), p. 191, and others are Hill (1876), pp. 46–7, *Times*, 30 May 1860 (22 miles), *Worcester News* 16 March 1865 (25) and *Daily Telegraph* 30 May 1865 (21).
14 Tweedmouth Evidence, pp. 158–66, where these claims were strongly questioned, and Bradford Evidence, pp. 198–9, 230–4, where they seem to be decisively refuted.
15 Report on Industrial Diseases, PP 1908 XXXV, p. 3, considered it 'beyond question . . . that the disease should be considered specific to the employment' and PP 1911 XLI put forward various suggestions for making people less liable to the condition and for helping those who got it. For an early account of the disease see *British Medical Journal*, 4 November 1882, where it is described by a Post Office doctor called E. Robinson, and for more details see Monell (1898).
16 Circular Instructions to the Post Office surveyors, heads of departments etc., are in PP 1911 L. See also Holt Evidence, pp. 1308–9, and *Telegraph Chronicle* (31 January 1913), pp. 65–6.
17 *Post* (25 July 1891).
18 Hobhouse Evidence, p. 638, Joyce Committee Report, p. 6 (POR 60/91).
19 POR 30E 1889/1891 VIII; Hobhouse Evidence, p. 47.
20 Tweedmouth Evidence, p. 503; Hobhouse Evidence, pp. 564ff. and p. 176ff. below on 'unification'; How We Began, p. 23; *B-H* (10 August 1872).
21 On their introduction, see below Chapter 6, p. 124. Full details and quotations are in POR 60/73 and 74, plus Joyce Committee Report, pp. 17–18. See also Holt Report, pp. 9–10.
22 The figures are calculated from those in PP 1852 XLIX. For a graphic account of the light workload and low entry requirements of pre-reform clerks see Trollope (1907), pp. 13ff. The Elcho Report is in PP 1854 XXVII and the interesting comments on various drafts are in POR

59/179. The sorters' laments are in *CSG*, 2 June 1860, and FA Minutes in (UCW) R VI/3, p. 368.

23 'Counter Clerks and Telegraphists. Origin and Method of Recruitment' (POR 57/12); Bradford Evidence, pp. 71–2.

24 The Fawcett Scheme is in PP 1881 LVII and the sorters' interpretation in Clery (1889). See also Chapter 6, p. 132.

25 These various inquiries and discussions are in POR 30E 5369/1881, 57/13, 63/5, 14 and 15 and the statement in *Information Supplied by the Secretary to the Post Office 1912* (to the Holt Enquiry), p. 125 (copy at POR 60/117), and also (UCW) F 029.4. The 1902 Report was printed in *The Telegraph Chronicle*, 27 December 1907.

26 Minutes of the Telegraphists Association in MC, undated, but probably June 1881; *Report of the Proceedings of the Telegraph Clerks* (Liverpool, 1881) pp. 36, 39–42; Matthison (1957), p. 97; Hobhouse Evidence, pp. 697–723 for supervisory grades; *Postal Journal* (1 May 1894) gives typical complaints that it is the postal side that suffers discrimination in matters of promotion, but the statistics collected in PP 1899 LXXVII seem to prove conclusively that there were fewest promotions among telegraphists.

27 Hobhouse Evidence, pp. 653, 638; *P&TR* (24 December 1914), p. 132.

28 Holt Evidence, p. 8, and Bealey (1976) *passim* on the engineers; *Information Supplied* (1912), pp. 125–6, 133–4 on the telephonists.

29 PMG 25th Report for 1898–9, p. 26 and *Information Supplied*, pp. 118ff.

30 There is a rapidly growing literature on this subject. For a useful account see Holcombe (1973), and for a good brief summary Davin (1973), pp. 7–9. For contemporary accounts see *Civil Service Magazine* (1901), p. 29, 1902, pp. 109ff, 1903, p. 210.

31 Bowie (1899); PMG 28th Report for 1881–2; Holcombe (1973), p. 212.

32 *Lady's Newspaper* (30 September 1854); 'Employment of women in the public service', *Quarterly Review* (1881), p. 188; PMG 18th Report for 1871, p. 13; *Standard* (5 December 1862); Rye (1859), p. 261; Bowie (1899), p. 51; M. Fawcett in *Atlantia Magazine* (1887–8), p. 175. Holt Evidence, p. 797; Martindale (1938), p. 147, on the marriage bar, and pp. 17–18 for Scudamore's memorandum, which is also in *Post* (1953), p. 671. There is some further (mostly published) material collected in the Fawcett papers in the Manchester City Archives (at M50/423) including efforts to rebut the view that 'young women' have 'a nervous dread of anything pertaining to calculations' and take twice as much sick leave.

33 Humphreys (1958), pp. 32–3; *B-H* (29 March 1873); Tweedmouth Evidence, p. 330; Morlay (1914), pp. 264–7.

34 *Post* (2 May 1891); Tweedmouth Report, p. 33; Bradford Evidence, pp. 68–71, 103; Hobhouse Evidence, pp. 31, 41, 274, Report, p. 28; Holt Evidence, pp. 798, 609, 547, 617, Report, pp. 75–6.

35 Martinuzzi (1952), pp. 59–60. Department Committee on Postmen (1891), p. 6 (POR 60/91); PP 1898 LVII (Post Office Estimates), Shepherd (1923), p. 200; Reports of the Standing Committee on Boy Labour in the Post Office in PP 1911 XXIX, PP 1913 XXXVIII, PP 1914 XLIV and PP 1914–16 XXXII. See also Hobhouse Evidence, pp. 312, 481–3; Holt Evidence, pp. 7, 248ff.; *Information Supplied*, pp. 124, 132; Bradford Evidence, p. 101; POR 50/12; Ammon (1911), an article in the *Daily Herald* (24 April 1912) on similar lines, and *Post* (1950), p. 102.

36 The full story of the hushed-up events of 1889 are revealed in two books published in 1976 by H. Montgomery Hyde and by L. Chester, D. Leitch and C. Simpson. Suspicion was first aroused by the fact that telegraph boys at St Martin's-le-Grand were in possession of far more money than their pay. See also Hobhouse Evidence, pp. 833–4, which may be a reference to the matter and p. 47 above on other problems.

37 Tweedmouth Evidence, p. 934; Holt Evidence, pp. 258, 494, 551–2, 600 and Report, p. 39; Hobhouse Evidence, p. 630.

38 PMG 59th Report for 1912–13; Shepherd (1923), pp. 105–6; Holt Report, p. 30.

39 Elcho Report, p. 9; *CSG* (15 January 1860); Minutes of Evidence taken before the Committee appointed to Inquire into the Internal Arrangements of the Circulation Department of the GPO (POR 30E 4801/1861), p. 50 and Holt Evidence, pp. 49–50. There is a full indictment of the system in 'Aliquis' (1868), pp. 4–5, 23ff.

40 POR 60/77, p. 27 and 30E 3849/1863; Hobhouse Evidence, p. 415; Holt Evidence, pp. 503, 1049.

41 Holt Evidence, p. 800; Tweedmouth Report, p. 10.

42 *Chambers Journal* (26 June 1878).

43 *Illustrated London News*, 6 June 1846, on the grievances arising from gratuities and the investigations in PP 1846 XLV, p. 46, for the quoted attitude. *CSG*, 5 February 1853, on

ambiguous attitudes to their abolition and Bradford Evidence, p. 151, for the later statement.

44 PP 1829 XI (Eighteenth Report on the Post Office Revenue), pp. 28–35; *Hansard* III, 124, 834–9 (1 March 1853) for the average figures and POR 30E 4472/1857 for the more detailed breakdown. The figures for the 1890s are in the tables in the appendices and those for the rural postmen are calculated from the Joyce Committee Report, p. 16 (POR 60/91). On variations in London and Woolwich see *PCE*, pp. 40, 653–4, and on the whole topic Hunt (1973), p. 352 and *passim*.

45 Hobhouse Report, pp. 31–2; Holt Report, pp. 41–3.

46 Tweedmouth Evidence, p. 351; Harrison (1973), pp. 47–8; 2 October 1860 and an unattributed cutting from the same period in MC; Baxter (1868), pp. 83–93; Martinuzzi (1952), p. 84.

47 PMG 2nd Report for 1855, p. 77; 4th Report for 1857, pp. 31, 69; 8th Report for 1861, p. 71; Baxter (1903), p. 12; Cruden (1904); Reeves (1913), p. 44.

48 For examples which ignore the evolution of grades see *Hansard* III, 168, 647 (22 July 1862), 181, 196 (23 February 1866) and 219, 1654 (15 July 1874).

49 The figures given here are derived from PP 1852 XLIX, given in full in Appendix 6; Martinuzzi (1952), pp. 22–4, and the conclusions from these sources and the other tables in the appendices. On the general position see Wood (1899), and Layton and Crowther (1938), p. 275 for this and later periods.

50 Martinuzzi (1952), pp. 82–5; Wood (1909); *Civilian* (10 August 1872).

51 Tweedmouth Evidence, p. 595; Hobhouse Evidence, pp. 15–17, 101, Appendices to the Evidence, p. 21. On relative wages in general see Knowles and Robertson (1951).

52 Douglas (1966), pp. 192–9, 378. See also Chapter 4, 87f.

53 PP 1828 V, pp. 17–18; PP 1854 XXVIII, p. 8.

54 PMG 19th Report for 1872, p. 15 (21st for 1874, p. 14, for a similar statement). On the 1873 market research see Ridley Commission, p. 394 and Swift (1929), p. 78. Treasury Letter 10948/90 dated 11 July 1890 is in (UCW) F 220 and the other points are in Bradford Evidence, pp. 85, 132, Joyce Committee Evidence, p. 122 (POR 60/91) and Hobhouse Evidence, p. 481.

55 Joyce Committee Evidence, p. 117; POR 30E 4472/1857; Tweedmouth Evidence, p. 742; Bradford Evidence, p. 160; Hobhouse Report, p. 31; Shepherd (1923), p. 97.

56 Routh (1952), p. 218.

57 Hobsbawm (1964), 'Custom, wages and workload in nineteenth century industry', p. 347; Routh (1952), p. 201; Hobhouse Report, p. 83.

58 Fawcett's settlement is in PP 1881 LVII, p. 2, and his arguments against the 'market' orientation of the Treasury in POR 60/15 (on which see also below, p. 130). Stanley's settlement is in PP 1905 XLIV, and the discussion that preceded it in POR 30E 6980/1905. On the criteria, Shepherd (1923), p. 128.

59 S. and B. Webb (1897), p. 279; Kerr (1957).

60 Hyman and Brough (1975), pp. 30, 41; Wootton (1962), p. 146.

61 PCE, p. 630; Tweedmouth Evidence, pp. 58, 314, 326, 440; Holt Evidence, p. 570; G. Stuart on NJC delegation to PMG, 18 December 1911 F 299.4; Holt Committee *Comparisons between Pay and Conditions of Employment of Post Office Servants and of Persons in Outside Employment* (1912) – copy at F 0299.4; Holt Report, p. 2.

62 POR 60/2, pp. 39–40; Holt Report, p. 3, though this ignores the Evidence (p. 153) of Stuart amongst others, that they would accept 'the fortunes of war' in the event of a fall in prices.

63 Holt Report, p. 3; Evidence, p. 640.

64 Bradford Evidence, pp. 149, 218; *Post* (1913), pp. 625–31.

65 Bradford Report, p. 21; POR 30E 6980/1905 XVIII; Holt Evidence, p. 611.

66 Holt Evidence, p. 554.

67 *Post* (17 December 1892), *Hansard* IV, 51, 349 (16 July 1897); *Post* (27 August 1904) and Holt Evidence, p. 1,257 for a similar view from the Engineering and Stores Association; MacDonald 4th Report, p. 83.

4 Public Servants and Trade Unionists: 1840–1920

The Postmaster General is determined no longer to tolerate a system of agitation which is got up by a few turbulent men and which tends to create a spirit of discontent and restlessness among the whole of the lower body of Post Office servants. With this view he forbids, on pain of dismissal, the holding by officers of the department of any meeting beyond the walls of the Post Office building for the discussion of official questions. (Minute of the Postmaster General of 12 March 1866[1])

The danger to the public service is urged in case the large voting powers of our civil servants should be used to influence Government action, – but this cannot be regarded otherwise than as a protection for government neglect rather than as a wall of defence against corrupt encroachments on public right, or attempts at indirectly controlling the Government in its management of the public service. (Lloyd Jones, *Chronicle*, Newcastle-on-Tyne, 30 June 1881)

Mr. Sydney Buxton desires to repeat the assurance that all servants of the Post Office have full liberty of making representations to the Postmaster General in regard to any matter which affects them. He is prepared frankly to recognise any duly-constituted Association or Federation of Postal Servants. He is willing to receive representations from the members or representatives of the Association if they be in the Service, or through its Secretary (whether he be a member of the Service or not) on matters relating to the Service as a whole, or matters affecting the class or classes of servants of which the Association is representative. (Post Office Circular, 1702, 18 February 1906)

In a very definite sense you are, for good or ill, the pioneers in an attempt to discover a new industrial philosophy – the philosophy of the economic relationship of the State and the Servants of the State, who are part of the State. (Fred Riley to the 1914 Founding Conference of the Postal and Telegraph Clerks Association, *Postal and Telegraph Record*, 18 February 1915, p. 289)

Until 1969 all those who worked for the Post Office were civil servants. This made them part of a unique system of rank and status, with its own special rules and standards. It also marked them off when they tried to improve their wages and conditions. In private industry it was only necessary to obtain the acceptance of the right to independent organisation and bargaining. In essence this was granted by the 1871 Trade Union Act. Public servants had to go beyond this and confront a panoply of legal, political and constitutional rules – they needed to challenge a part of the sovereignty of the state. The story of organised efforts to improve working conditions in the nineteenth-century Post Office is thus not only part of the development of trade unions, it also impinges on the evolution of Britain's modern state bureaucracy, and the definition of the position of individuals and groups within that structure. Post Office workers fought for the right to exercise industrial and political pressure at a time when the 'neutrality' of the civil service was becoming one of the most cherished of constitutional principles. They thus had to engage in a special sort of struggle not only for the right to act collectively, but also to do so independently of their individual position within the state machine. Their ultimate success was a small but essential part of the enlargement of political liberty.

In the previous chapter, the economic position of the nineteenth-century Post Office workers was considered, the value of their 'privileges', the justification for their attitude of superiority to the common herd, and the relationship of their wages and conditions to those in the labour market as a whole. The aim of this chapter is to go beyond the economic history of the Post Office workers before 1920 and to set out the development of their political and constitutional position.

With the building of a politically non-partisan bureaucratic state machine in the mid-Victorian period, the individual civil servant no longer considered that he owed his first obligation to a patron. Instead he was a servant of the state, the member of a 'profession' where 'the first obedience required is that of a workman to his work'.[2] As a result, those in authority within the public service 'continued right up to the First World War to consider mutual aid in seeking better conditions of service as a sign of ill-breeding not calculated to enhance their status as Civil Servants'.[3] There was in any case a genuine difficulty in negotiating with superiors who were ultimately responsible to members of the government. The employees of public revenue departments had the franchise restored to them by acts of Parliament passed in 1868 and 1874, but after this their right even to meet, and certainly to put pressure on MPs, was strongly questioned. If postal servants agitated in this way were they not 'buying favour' and undermining the independence of the legislature in the same way as in the bad old days of patronage? Thus, the earliest organisations of Post Office workers came up against political and constitutional questions that were closely connected with being able to bargain about wages and conditions. It was for the right to hold meetings, the right to petition Parliament and to put pressure on MPs that the first efforts of Post Office trade unionism were directed, the first 'martyrs' were created, and the general pattern of industrial relations within the public service ultimately determined.

Post Office workers became the pioneers of civil service trade unionism because their social status was closest to that group of workers who organised unions. At the same time, they had a more protracted and complicated struggle than other workers to secure the recognition of their right to organise. The peculiarities of their situation do much to explain the forms assumed by Post Office 'agitation', the discreet Parliamentary lobbying, the concentration around demands for inquiries and the advocacy for political action by organised labour. There were good reasons for Post Office workers to be among the first within the trade union movement to

actively support their own Parliamentary candidates. At the same time, their
organisations from the beginning had to confront more directly perhaps than many
others the 'right to manage' claimed by their employers who happened, in this case,
to be the state. This helps to explain the particular preoccupation of Post Office
trade unionists with enlarging the sphere within which they could bargain, and
their espousal at various times of radical views about how this sphere could be
expanded, from the guild socialist ideas of the early part of this century to the
'industrial democracy' advocated and practised in more recent years. It helps to
explain also why Post Office trade unionists embraced eagerly the promises for
'joint consultation' not only about wages and conditions, but also about the running
of the service itself which were put forward in the Whitley Committee reports of
1917. If the talk of 'joint control' was largely an illusion, the Whitley system did at
least provide a more efficient system of bargaining than Parliamentary questions
and lengthy public inquiries which had before then been accepted. Every step in the
regulation of industrial relations in the Post Office has been accompanied by
discussion about the rightful place of the workforce and its representatives. This
can be dated as far back as the right to hold meetings from the 1840s to the 1890s,
the recognition of the unions in 1906, and the setting up of the Whitley system in
1919. It goes as far forward as the setting up of new corporate forms in 1969 and
1981. It will perhaps always be the case that those who bargain with the state will
highlight questions of authority and control in industrial relations. It is the aim of
this chapter to explain how these matters were debated and decided in the Post
Office before 1920, to set out the political and legal problems involved and to
describe how eventually agreed bargaining machinery came to be established.

THE REGULATION OF PUBLIC SERVICE

The early years of the reign of Queen Victoria saw important changes in the status
of civil servants. In the 1830s sinecure offices were finally abolished.[4] Nevertheless,
the system of patronage, whereby ministers made appointments on the basis of
political friendship and family connection continued for some time later. Thus, in
1845, in order to appoint a letter carrier in Midlothian earning £25 a year, eight or
nine letters were written by two ministers. All such positions continued to be filled
after consultation with local MPs.[5] Following the Northcote-Trevelyan Report of
1853, and the related Elcho Report on the Post Office, patronage was gradually
eliminated in the selection of candidates for higher posts. In 1855 limited competition for vacancies began and in 1870 open competitions. These changes came
despite the opposition of Rowland Hill and other civil service chiefs.[6] However, the
appointment of sub-postmasters continued to be on the recommendation of local
MPs. Though ultimate power was put in the hands of the Postmaster General in
1895, it was only in 1907 that the new incumbent, overwhelmed with requests for
preferments to pay off political debts, asserted that 'the matter ought to be taken out
of the purview of politics altogether' and handed it over to the permanent officials of
the Department. In the United States the equivalent appointments remained under
the control of political parties as late as 1969.[7] In Britain complaints could still be
heard, at least until the First World War, about favouritism in the filling of some
civil service posts, 'jobbery' even, though this was not then thought to extend to the
lower reaches of the service.[8]

As the system of patronage faded away, postal workers did not immediately lose all sense of obligation to their superiors. Well after the independence of the individual letter carrier had been established it could still be said with justice that each one remained 'so identified with the government patronage that he himself becomes part and parcel of the great institution itself'.[9] This sense of dependence went along with the permanency of employment and 'privileges' which were also to some degree derived from the old patronage system. A continued respect for vested rights prevented dismissals for political reasons, so the 'spoils' system that became prevalent in the United States never developed in Britain.

It has been argued in the last chapter that the economic value of many of the privileges of public service was often overstated. They were in any case subject to a number of legal limitations. Thus, though permanency of employment was general, there was no absolute security of tenure. In an 1896 Court case it was decided that civil servants 'hold their appointment at the pleasure of the Crown' and in 1905 the Postmaster General, Lord Stanley, claimed to 'have full authority to appoint and remove such officers as I may think necessary'.[10] There is a right of appeal against such decisions to the Judicial Committee of the Privy Council, though this was an unusual and difficult business, which simply confirmed the discretion of the Crown.[11]

This legal position gave the superiors of a civil servant considerable authority over his work. The Treasury had full power to vary terms of employment as it thought fit by enforcing compulsory overtime and even by refusing to accept resignations, or compelling people to do work other than that for which they were engaged. Thus, when telegraphists tried to organise an overtime ban in 1898 against the Tweedmouth settlement, they were said not to be within their legal rights. Similarly, in reply to complaints about telegraphists being transferred to postal work in 1904, the Postmaster General said that 'all officers of the Department are expected loyally to perform any work required of them which they are capable of undertaking'.[12]

There has also always been a range of further restrictions of the legal rights of a civil servant. Thus he has had fewer means of redressing grievances against his employer through the Courts. Except in the case of the Workman's Compensation Act, he has had to apply for permission from the Home Office in order to sue the Crown. The state employee in Britain has no special protection such as is provided by the French *droit administratif*.[13] At the same time, civil servants are subject to the special restrictions of the Official Secrets Acts, the first of which was passed in 1889 and the most substantial in 1911, limiting their right to discuss their work with anybody. This was not necessarily a matter of military security, as could be seen from the famous case of the dismissal of Major Vernon from the Air Ministry in 1937.[14] Civil servants were also constrained from 1899 by the Prevention of Corruption Acts. They did have the special ability to ventilate their grievances through Parliament but, as will be seen, this was a right that had to be fought for.

Post Office workers have also faced some special problems as a result of their unique position as employees of a revenue department which was at the same time one of the largest commercial concerns in the land. The control exercised over its finances by the Treasury before the 1950s was such as to leave the Post Office with little initiative for independent action. The officials of the Treasury had to choose between various competing demands on the state's finances, not just those involving the grievances of ordinary employees of the Post Office, or other state servants. The traditional picture of the Treasury as continually mean and parsimonious may perhaps be over-simplified. However, there can be no serious doubt that it exercised a strong pressure against every wage increase for Post Office workers during the nineteenth century, and reduced virtually every improvement agreed within the Post Office itself.[15] A further political problem was that the Postmaster General was in many cases little interested in the day-to-day work of his Department, regarding his office as a stepping stone to something better, or else being incapable of altering the routines created by his permanent officials. Thus, in seven months from November 1922 to May 1923 there were four different postmasters general, although such figures as Henry Fawcett (1880–4), Cecil Raikes (1886–91) and Sidney Buxton (1906–10) did manage to introduce important changes, not least in the conditions of the employees of the Department.[16]

The particular position of the civil servant was not just a matter of the relative permanency of his employment and his political status. He was, at the same time, required to conform to a special code of conduct, both on and off duty. The nature of this code was in some measure defined in a Court case of 1928, *Ironmonger and Company v. Dyne*, when three employees of the Foreign Office had been using their official knowledge in speculative transactions in foreign currency for private profit. As a result a Board of Enquiry was set up of three leading civil servants who asserted that over and above the official rules and regulations about behaviour 'the Civil Service, like any other profession, has its unwritten code of ethics and conduct for which the most effective sanction lies in the public opinion of the Service itself'. The Board laid down a number of precepts which were later incorporated into the rules of all departments in a Treasury letter:

> The first duty of a Civil Servant is to give his individual allegiance to the State at all times and on all occasions when the State has a claim upon his services. With his private activities the State is, in general, not concerned so long as his conduct therein is not such as to bring discredit upon the Service of which he is a member. A Civil Servant is not to subordinate his duty to his private interests; but neither is he to put himself in a position where his duty and his interests conflict . . . It follows that there are spheres of activity legitimately open to the ordinary citizen in which the Civil Servant can play no part, or only a limited part . . . He is bound to maintain a proper reticence in discussing public affairs and, more particularly, those with which his own department is concerned. And lastly, his position clearly imposes upon him restrictions in matters of commerce and business from which the ordinary citizen is free.[17]

This statement of what the position was thought to be in the 1920s had a number of implications for the detailed conduct of all civil servants which had in the past been set out in specific regulations. Thus, there were certain restrictions with regard to patents, publications based on official records, bankruptcy, and the use of political or outside influence to support personal claims. Civil servants were precluded from accepting any post 'in the management of any Society or Company which would require their attendance at any time between the hours of 10 a.m. and 6 p.m.'. They were also forbidden to do anything which would impair their usefulness as civil servants or to engage in any occupation that might conflict with the interests of their department or with their position as public servants.[18]

Post Office workers have had in addition to these constraints on their behaviour as public servants a number of other regulations to govern their special functions. Thus, they were expressly prohibited from betting, being drunk or from engaging in additional occupations such as newspaper and parcel delivery work, those involving the receipt of money on deposit, or connected in any way with the sale of intoxicating liquor. They were forbidden to delay the Postal Service in any way, or to reveal or intercept the contents of telegrams. They were further prohibited from communicating with the newspapers on official matters.[19] There were also restrictions on the individual behaviour of Post Office workers, as can be seen in a number of instances. In 1895 a clerk was transferred from Sligo to Enniskillen for taking part in street preaching that aroused popular hostility. In this period two postmen at Oswestry were reprimanded when they were heard discussing politics in the street, and another at Bristol was threatened with the loss of an increment for failing to raise his hat to passers-by, though this was thought somewhat exceptional. In 1901 a postman was reprimanded for failing to salute a clergyman, and a temporary postman was dismissed in 1909 for singing carols in the street.[20] These cases show that well into the twentieth century, the Post Office authorities still sought to impose standards of behaviour on their subordinates which were not expected or enforced in private industry, and that such restrictions remained despite the progress of the staff associations.

THE POLITICS OF PUBLIC SERVICE

Beyond these limits on their personal behaviour, there were many other constraints on the activities of public servants. The two most important of these, for a long time confused, were the individual capacity to take political action, and the right to act collectively for any purpose whatever.[21]

These questions came up well before the end of the eighteenth century. In 1793 a number of wage increases were granted in the Post Office, largely it seems because of pressure from the clerks. Soon afterwards there were signs of incipient trade unionism in what was then the largest government department, when Tom Paine published his statement of the grievances of his former colleagues in the Excise Department. A series of co-ordinated petitions followed Paine's pamphlet and some substantial improvements were obtained in 1800. It was in connection with this agitation that the younger Pitt told the House of Commons that he would not countenance any petition to Parliament from the Excise officers who could only proceed by petitioning their own Commissioners.[22] This ruling was never fully enforced and in later years associations were often formed for special purposes. Thus, in 1845 a Civil Service Committee was established to secure the reform of the pensions system, though it did not survive the improvements that came with the 1859 Act. In the 1860s, a Central Committee representing some grades of Excise officers made a statement to the Commissioners of Inland Revenue which sought higher pay and an extensive re-organisation of the grades in the Excise branch. The various royal commissions on the civil service also encouraged combination. Both the Playfair Commission of 1874–5 and the Ridley Commission of 1886–90 received information from groups of civil servants acting on behalf of their colleagues. They also heard complaints about the existence of such pressure at all. They were obscure but often quite effective bodies with such titles as the Salaries Increase Movement and the Writers' Association whose activities were recorded from 1853 in the pages of the *Civil Service Gazette*. Robert Lowe, the Liberal politician who had previously been Chancellor of the Exchequer, told the Playfair Commission in regard to civil service 'writers' that on setting up the new system, the authorities had failed to foresee

> the danger of collecting a very large number of persons together, having friends all over the country, having a particular interest and that interest being to obtain better terms from the Government. I think we overlooked the political aspect of the question. Certain gentlemen have found it very expedient to make political capital out of the alleged grievances of these writers.

Though he was referring to one particular group, what he said could have applied to others as well. In accepting Fawcett's modified wages proposals of 1881, the Treasury expressed its determination to resist any such pressure. It was 'not prepared to acquiesce in any organised agitation which openly seeks to bring its extensive voting power to bear on the House of Commons against the Executive government responsible for conducting in detail the administration of the country'.[23]

Few employers agree willingly to bargain with their workforce, but resistance in the civil service came from a special set of circumstances and assumptions. In the mid-nineteenth century humble memorials submitted through departmental heads were considered the only legal means to secure the redress of grievances. The restriction on the political rights of public servants had their origins in a period when Parliament was trying to restrain the Crown from controlling it by distributing offices and pensions among its members. This culminated, after the 'Glorious Revolution' of 1688, with the exclusion of all offices of profit under the Crown from Parliament. However, later modification allowed the principal officers of state to sit there and later on officers in the army and navy and some others were added to the list.[24] Electioneering by state servants was forbidden by a measure of 1710, though until 1782 they retained the right to vote, constituting about 20 per cent of the electorate. When they were threatened with dismissal by both the main parties in an election if they did not vote for them, state servants were disenfranchised at their own request – thus laying the basis for their political independence.[25] Their situation changed, however, with the extension of the franchise in 1832 and 1867, and the Northcote-Trevelyan reforms. Some of the higher grades of Post Office employees, together with those from other departments, then combined for the restoration of their right to vote.[26] The desirability of this measure was by no means universally accepted and it was specifically excluded from the 1867 Reform Act with the agreement of both Government and Opposition. However, in 1868 Charles Monk, the MP for Gloucester, with the active support of some of those in the higher reaches of the service, secured the passing of a Revenue Officer's Disabilities Removal Bill and six years later also obtained the repeal of the Acts prohibiting revenue officers from taking part in the elections themselves. He could not, however, put an end to the ban on the officers of some departments sitting in Parliament, nor was he able to resist the pressure of both Gladstone and Northcote to exclude a clause which would have prevented the departments themselves from making regulations about the participation of their own employees in politics.[27] Thus, the Government was able to lay down limitations in its executive capacity to which it refused to give legislative definition.

Following further Parliamentary discussion on this matter a Treasury Minute was issued on 12 November 1884 taking a line that has since, with modification of detail, been generally adopted by governments. This said that civil servants 'should remain free to serve the Government of the day without necessarily exposing themselves to public charges of inconsistency and insincerity', through 'an unwritten, but operative law, rather than a new one'. The Treasury went on to say that a public servant adopted as a Parliamentary candidate should immediately resign.[28] On the eve of the 1885 General Election, Postmaster General Lord George Manners instructed his subordinates to 'maintain a certain service in political matters and not put themselves forward on one side or the other' by expressing their support for any candidate or acting as member of a campaign committee.[29]

In the following period a new range of elective positions was opened up, and a new set of arguments developed, about how Post Office workers and other civil servants could put pressure on elected representatives. When the 1888 Local Government Act set up new county councils, civil servants were forbidden from joining them, though they could serve on the less important district and parish councils. In 1891, the dismissal of W. B. Cheesman and William Clery of the Fawcett Association for lobbying Parliamentary candidates showed that there were definite limits within which the franchise could be exercised, though two years later Prime Minister Gladstone asserted that civil servants had the right to vote 'absolutely free from internal interference'. Conflicts continually arose in the following period. In 1902 Postmaster General Austen Chamberlain tried to prevent a postman from standing as a Labour candidate for the Swansea Town Council but was compelled to retreat after a campaign by the local Trades and Labour Council and various MPs. In 1904 an elected member of a Board of Guardians, which during that period administered the Poor Law, was 'refused leave to attend his duties'. Others were reprimanded for distributing election addresses, or for displaying election posters in their homes.[30]

In 1908 there occurred an incident which gave some national prominence to these conflicts. After two postmen had been elected as representatives of the Independent Labour Party on the Salford Borough Council, Postmaster General Buxton ruled not only that they could not take up their functions, but also that they could not address meetings on general political subjects. Whatever the regulations on such matters, it could by now easily be argued that they had not often been enforced. A local official of the PF argued that Gladstone's 1893 statement 'contradicts both regulation and custom', which were in any case 'antiquated' and 'ambiguous', and a local newspaper pointed to the sinister implications of a Liberal Minister preventing properly elected Labour men from taking up their functions. Furthermore, although the regulations prevented Post Office workers 'from helping to administer the present laws', it did not rule against efforts aimed 'to bring about a revolutionary change in society'. The *Civil Service Socialist* described Buxton's attitude as 'another illustration of the tyranny of bureaucratic collectivism'.[31] Faced with such pressure, and with illogical regulations which were almost impossible to enforce, Buxton felt compelled to retreat. He told the Cabinet that though it might be thought that Post Office workers were 'at present in possession of political power to a degree that may be regarded as a serious evil', nevertheless the current rules were 'futile as a check' and 'so far from curing the disease, they irritate'. He thought that if trade union officials were allowed to serve on elected bodies it would 'decrease their power for harm and unrest within the service'. On this basis it was announced in 1909 that

Post Office workers could serve on county and borough councils, except that 'any duties involved shall not conflict with the duties of the Department'.[32] After the First World War, the regulations were further changed, and in 1922 Post Office workers were allowed to canvass when out of uniform and soon a number of their leaders were to be found in Parliament.[33]

There was, however, a more fundamental problem than whether individual Post Office workers could be canvassers, or even candidates. This was what influence they could exercise when acting together on candidates or MPs. The legal limitation on the exercise of such pressure was for many years thought by some to be absolute. It was only after a protracted struggle that Post Office workers obtained the right to exercise political pressure. This was of considerable importance for their efforts to improve their wages and conditions.

In the 1860s the Treasury told civil servants that pressure for improved conditions exercised through MPs would be 'treated by them as an admission' of a case 'not good upon its merits'. In 1867 Post Office workers were told that they were forbidden from 'exercising political influence to obtain increases of salary or superannuation allowance'. Punishment would be inflicted, it was said, 'in every case where political influence is brought to bear in support of the applications'.[34] In the latter part of the nineteenth century, it came to be argued with increasing frequency that there were great political and constitutional dangers in the exercise of any kind of influence by state servants. Such pressure, it was said, could only be exercised in defiance of the proper machinery for decisions in departments of state and Parliament itself. The efforts of the Post Office workers to influence those with political power were seen not only as an attack on the constitution. They were even used as an argument against state economic enterprise of any kind.[35] Gladstone is said to have written that 'the organised attempt of servants of the state to use their political influence at the cost of the taxpayer is likely to become a serious danger', which would have to be dealt with by 'agreement between the two sides of the House'. He was against MPs taking up the cause of Post Office workers at all because this would 'inflame the minds of men who, though very competent in their duties were yet of humble station and naturally inclined, like other men, to believe that they were underpaid when they were told so'.[36]

Gladstone's great political opponent Benjamin Disraeli once said in his early radical days that 'any party who felt aggrieved by a public department could appeal to Parliament, including the department's employees'. However, such views were never heard from major political figures until well into the twentieth century. Thus after the Parliamentary franchise had been restored to civil servants in 1868, complaints were constantly heard in Parliament about the 'improper' pressures exercised by civil servants, especially from the Post Office, during and after elections. Thus in 1881 the telegraphists were condemned for using their votes 'for the furtherance of their own objects, although it was given to them to be exercised for the benefit of the community at large'. One minister, opposing the establishment of a Royal Commission on the grievances of postal servants in 1900, asserted that

> the House of Commons is the last body that ought to interfere in these questions of the employment of public servants . . . Already I think the pressure brought to bear on individual members by civil servants in their constituencies has become perfectly intolerable . . . and civil servants may depend upon it . . . that in the opinion of the great body of the Members of this House, they are taking a highly irregular course.

In the following year the Prime Minister opposed another call for a Royal Commission with the statement that since the House of Commons was 'omnipotent' the pressure brought upon it by civil servants placed 'the future of the public service . . . 'in peril'. Such pressure was also referred to as 'illicit' and simple 'blackmail'. The term 'dockyard Member' was used as one of derision, on the grounds presumably that it was reprehensible to be influenced by pressure from workers and not from normal business or party interests.[37] In one of the Australian states state servants were confined to their own special Parliamentary constituencies for a brief period. In the United States, feeling on the matter grew so strongly that all lobbying activities by civil servants were banned by Presidential decree from 1902 to 1912. Since then, however, in the absence of any other method, it has been the main bargaining instrument of Post Office workers. In France similar rules existed in the 1920s, but were broken with impunity.[38] These attitudes on the part of the legislators were the basis of the sharp opposition they expressed to the organisation of Post Office workers which aimed to improve their conditions by the main method that was in fact open to them – putting pressure on Parliament. Thus the TUC opposed all political restrictions on many occasions and thought the statement by Postmaster General Lord John Manners about the 1885 General Election was 'opposed to the liberty of the subject by depriving thousands of Britons of the right of citizenship'. Many similar statements emanated from the TUC in the following years and also from the Labour Party.[39]

BARGAINING WITH THE STATE – CONSTRAINTS BEFORE THE 1890s

These political, legal and constitutional constraints presented considerable problems to Post Office workers during their protracted struggle to win the right to negotiate about their wages and conditions. Between the 1840s and the 1870s, it was simply a matter of winning the right to meet in order to put together the memorials and to create enough publicity to get grievances examined. The much quoted regulation of 1866 given at the head of this chapter tried to keep agitation within the strictest limits, and it was used against each successive group of malcontents until 1890. By then, however, bigger issues were at stake. Post Office workers, like many others, were trying to set up their own permanent organisations. The telegraphists succeeded in doing so in 1881, and within a decade the other main grades had done the same. By that time the authorities had largely given up their efforts to extinguish, or at least to ignore, these bodies, and in 1906 'recognition' was the only logical step. The problem still remained of what the associations were to be allowed to do. Much of their most successful efforts were directed to lobbying Members of Parliament in the face of all the objections that have already been described. The great inquiries between 1897 and 1915 were the most conspicuous results of these policies. Forms of more direct bargaining began however as the regulations allowed the associations to discuss an increasing range of topics with the Postmaster General and his subordinates. A more ordered system of bargaining was clearly necessary and after many hesitations about the constitutional and other niceties involved, the First World War spurred on the setting up of arbitration machinery in 1916 and the adoption of the Whitley proposals two years later.

It is the aim of the rest of this chapter to show how the secret meetings in public houses in the City of London culminated in the setting up of a modern sophisticated system of collective bargaining. It was a lengthy process by which the problems already outlined were confronted and resolved, but it needs to be described as an essential background to many of the separate incidents described in succeeding chapters. More often than not the different generations forgot the experiences of those who had gone before them and repeated their mistakes. In defeating the limits placed upon them between the 1890s and the 1920s, Post Office workers charted a new course and established a set of norms in their relations with their employers which have in essence remained intact to this day.

The very early struggles, discussed in the next chapter, were nearly all around the efforts of a few hundred of those employed at the GPO to hold meetings in the area around St Martin's-le-Grand. In 1843 they were told that though they could not have meetings in the office 'no control would be exercised to their right to do so out of doors'. In 1857 they were forbidden from ventilating their grievances 'through the public'. By 1858 they were under attack for their failure to be 'open, manly and respectful' precisely for holding private meetings to get round this.

In the following decade, when a secret, if formal, organisation existed among the lower London grades, the authorities considered it necessary to keep a closer surveillance on what they were doing. This was the basis of the 1866 regulation which was often forgotten in later years, but it was periodically taken out of dusty pigeonholes to wave at those who had the temerity to set up meetings to organise petitions, demonstrations, and even unions. The authorities were eventually compelled to accept that meetings would at least take place. When Fawcett was Postmaster General in the early 1880s he asked every group to present their grievances, and so also did the Ridley Commission on the Civil Service in 1885. Local postmasters, depending on their disposition, would grant permission for meetings to consider the wording of memorials and the election of delegations.

By 1890 the London sorters were holding meetings in Post Office buildings which could not be fitted into any of the available rooms, so PMG Raikes issued a new regulation saying that such meetings could be held outside providing they were to be confined to Post Office workers, and enough notice was given to the authorities so they could send 'an official shorthand writer'. At a time when the victimisation of 'agitators' was by no means unknown, the presence of 'official reporters' was a source of considerable discontent, even when the regulation was modified to cover only meetings to which the press was admitted. Association conferences, starting with the PTCA in 1890, felt the need for great circumspection in the running and reporting of their proceedings as a result of the new regulation. However, as the range and size of meetings held by Post Office workers increased, the shorthand writers no longer appeared. In 1893 Gladstone announced an end to all restrictions on 'meetings of a political character, but relating to official questions'.[40] It was still some time before representatives of the authorities were welcomed at meetings of the workers.

Long before these changes, however, it had become obvious to sections of Post Office workers that mere meetings were by themselves insufficient. Thus in the early 1870s, the organisations of London letter carriers emerged from the shadows and tried to begin a 'Benefit Society'. Meanwhile, the newest group in the service set up a 'Telegraphists Association'. Though these efforts were outflanked and mercilessly smashed by the authorities, the same people set up the PTCA in 1881 and the Postmen's Federation in 1891. The Post Office Secretary prophesied in 1881 that the PTCA 'would launch the Department into a sea of turmoil and lawlessness'. This did not prove to be the case, since the Association did little to disturb anybody and, though the authorities eyed their activities with suspicion, they did not put a stop to them. According to one source, the reply to an application for an outside meeting as late as 1890 was as follows:

> Members of the Civil Service must remember that the public interest requires that their official action must be regulated by authority, just as much as that of Her Majesty's soldiers and sailors and the formation of any association intended to coerce those responsible for the administration to make concessions which in their judgment are not justified by the public interest, must be regarded as a most serious breach of discipline and dealt with accordingly.[41]

By this time, however, the associations had been given *de facto* recognition. Though PMG Raikes, during 1890, defeated the Postmen's Union, he at the same time received delegations from the leaders of the Fawcett Association. Soon afterwards, the Postmen's Federation was granted similar rights. Raikes insisted that he was not opposed to the existence of associations, but only to their being run by outsiders.[42]

FROM THE DISMISSALS OF 1892 TO 'RECOGNITION' IN 1906

In 1892, therefore, the Post Office associations were effectively recognised, though it was not until 1906 that this recognition was officially proclaimed and agreed. There was thus a period of some uncertainty during which the limits of an unproclaimed law were tried and tested. In the 1870s and 1880s, the initiative had been taken by the telegraphists, but now it was the London sorters who came to the fore.[43] In 1892 Sir James Ferguson, who followed Raikes as Postmaster General, refused to meet a delegation from the Fawcett Association to consider the settlement agreed by his predecessor and asserted that 'the reiteration of requests, which after full consideration have been refused, and still more, the objectionable tone adopted in this instance, is an abuse of the privileges of presenting memorials'.

A meeting of sorters on 11 May after considerable hesitation and against the opposition of Fawcett Association founder J. H. Williams, agreed that 'the time for Parliamentary action was now'. On 14 June, Ferguson told the House of Commons that efforts to extract promises from candidates in the forthcoming elections would be 'disloyal to the State' and would 'impair the purity of election'. The following day the sorters met again and agreed to a motion moved by W. E. Clery to go ahead with precisely such lobbying, though only to get promises of support for the setting up of a Parliamentary Committee of Inquiry. On 17 June the authorities issued a special *Post Office Circular* telling the Post Office workers 'that it would be improper for them, whether in combination or individually, to endeavour to extract promises from any candidate for election to the House of Commons with reference to their duties and pay'. On the following day Clery issued a counter notice saying that this did 'not affect the policy of the Association'. He explained that they were not asking about wages, but about the Committee of Inquiry. Ferguson explicitly attacked even this in Parliament, saying that even such a promise would 'prejudge the case' and was 'inconsistent with the duties of a public servant' as well as 'beyond his constitutional privileges'.

The sorters went on and extracted promises of support from at least fifty-six candidates. Ferguson, meanwhile, was almost defeated in his Manchester constituency by the Liberal journalist C. P. Scott and the Tory administration of which he was part lost the confidence of the electors. Nevertheless, since in those days ministries continued until Parliament actually voted them out, there was a short period during which Ferguson remained in office. He took the opportunity to dismiss both Clery and W. B. Cheesman, who had moved and seconded the original resolution and were now respectively Chairman and Secretary of the Fawcett Association, on the grounds of 'insubordination and defiance . . . subversive of all discipline'. The two martyrs were immediately given full-time posts by the Association, Clery at £2. 50 a week, and Cheesman at £2, a substantial increase for both of them.

The whole subject at this point became a *cause célèbre*, gaining widespread national publicity. On 26 July the Conservative *Daily Telegraph* said it was 'difficult to see' why asking about an Inquiry had been 'illegitimate', and on the following day the Liberal *Daily News* described Ferguson's action as 'high handed harshness'. When the new Liberal administration was announced in August, with Arnold Morley, a member of the well-known radical family, as PMG, furious pressure was put on him by the Fawcett Association, but he announced that he did not intend to reverse the decision of his predecessor. The feelings of ordinary Post Office workers about this can be gathered from the loud cheering that greeted Clery when he arrived at the Post Office sports meeting in Tufnell Park in North London on 13 September. Early the following year when he stood for FA chairman against Williams, who had disapproved of the policy on which his dismissal was based, Clery received 1,187 votes from the members against a mere 94 for Williams. If the Post Office had lost two sorters, the Fawcett Association had gained two officials. Clery was a capable publicist and Cheesman an efficient administrator, and soon they steered their colleagues into taking up more general questions connected with the conditions of the sorters.

The dismissals remained an issue that was taken up time after time over the following years, and the refusal of the authorities to negotiate with them rankled, as well as the Tweedmouth Committee's refusal to allow them to represent their members. In 1896 the authorities were prepared to consider reinstating Cheesman, but only if he made the most grovelling apology. In 1898, there was a full-scale Parliamentary debate where the call for reinstatement was defeated by 163 votes to 86. The action of the authorities was condemned each year at the TUC, and Clery seems to have had more success in persuading the Lord Chief Justice that his treatment was illegal. Clery continued to pursue his case for the rest of his life, even after he broke off his public links with the Fawcett Association in 1904, and even raised it with the 1924 Labour Government. It was not generally known that in 1907 the Liberal administration offered Cheesman the chance of an unestablished postmastership. By then his colleagues did not feel the need to accept such a compromise, even if they could have managed without their indispensable General Secretary.[44]

During the period from 1893 to 1895 when Arnold Morley was Postmaster General, continual efforts were made by the authorities, though with diminishing success, to hold fast the limits that had been placed by Raikes on organisation and recognition.[45] Not only did Morley refuse to consider the reinstatement of Clery and Cheesman. In February 1893 he stopped the increments of all the members of the Liverpool-based Executive of the UKPCA for the crime of making statements which, in his opinion, were untrue. For reasons which are not easy to understand, this incident won none of the same notoriety as many others from the same period. It was only a month later, in March 1893, that Morley refused to receive a delegation of telegraphists on the grounds that they had been elected from a mass meeting. In the following November he fined the Secretary of the Tracers' Association for submitting to him a resolution passed by a meeting, after advice from his officials that such a step 'should produce an excellent effect on other quarters'.[46] Morley refused, in July 1894, to consider a petition from the Postmen's Federation both on account of its 'informality' and also because it was 'signed by postmen in other towns and included matters with which London postmen have no concern'. He also refused to receive a delegation from the Fawcett Association, not simply on the grounds that they might include Clery and Cheesman, but also on the grounds that they might raise their case. However, he had to turn a blind eye to FA affiliation to the London Trades Council, and he did agree to meet a group of members on 28 May 1894.[47] Other changes were coming about as a result of pressure of various kinds. Discussions within the Cabinet resulted in Gladstone's statement on 28 August 1893 that 'as regards public meetings not of a political character, but relating to official questions, the Postmaster General has decided to withdraw the restrictions at present in force'. Under constant pressure from bodies in the Labour Movement and elsewhere, and the need to reply, Morley was compelled to make further concessions. Thus in March 1895, he admitted that he was now receiving delegations from unions, though he refused to acknowledge them as such. He even had to admit in the following May that there was no restriction on Post Office workers' associations affiliating to trades councils.[48]

By the end of his period of office as Postmaster General in 1895, Morley had been compelled to abandon the role of King Canute holding back the waves of agitation and got Herbert Joyce, one of the Post Office Secretaries, to say that there were 'no official regulations restricting the right of Post Office servants to combine or to meet, when not on duty, when and where they like'. He himself went further in a letter to J. A. Murray MacDonald, MP, in which he stated that they were also 'at liberty to invite Members of Parliament, or any other persons, to their meetings'. So he claimed 'All the privileges which trade unions enjoy and, in my opinion, rightly enjoy, are thus accorded to unions of postal officials'.[49]

Morley's successor the Duke of Norfolk tried to turn back this process. In 1896 and 1897 he refused to meet a number of delegations on the grounds that some of those constituting them did not suffer from the grievances of which they complained. Soon afterwards, however, the very setting up of the Tweedmouth Committee, the first public inquiry of its kind, implied that representative bodies were needed, and Tweedmouth himself commented in 1896 on 'how excellently well' the PF 'got up their case'. By February 1898, Sir Albert Rollitt, a Tory MP who had consistently supported the cause of the postal workers, was pointing out the advantages of recognising the associations.

My experience convinces me that in the Post Office, as elsewhere, these unions are frequently a restraining force . . . the difficulty is not so much with those who have responsible leaders, but rather with the unorganised, or rather disorganised labour.

In the same debate, Hanbury spoke for the Postmaster General, quoting with approval Morley's statement of 1895 about the rights of trade unionists. The limits which remained were made clear later in 1898, however, when the two Newcastle telegraphists were punished for statements made at a PTCA meeting.[50]

By now effective recognition was coming closer. There was an MP who described the Norfolk–Hanbury talks of 1897 as 'one of the most irregular proceedings that ever took place in this House', but despite the statements of the PMG that no 'bargain' was involved the talks were in effect a form of negotiation with the associations. For their own purposes, the authorities used transcripts of the proceedings from the association journals, so recently considered as subversive documents. In 1899 the Postmen's Federation presented a mammoth petition to Parliament asking for recognition, and in September of that year Norfolk announced that he would receive delegations from the associations. At the time this was described with some justice as 'practically conceding recognition' and it was later seen as the first acknowledgement of the 'official status' of the associations. While trying to deny that there had been any real change of policy, the Postmaster General now went so far as to allow time off from Post Office duties to members of a delegation from the National Joint Committee. There were still important limits on recognition, however. All submissions still had to be made through superior officers and postal workers could still, in theory, only raise matters with which they themselves were concerned. These restrictions were further modified by Austen Chamberlain during his brief period as Postmaster General in 1902–3. He agreed to discuss with delegations without restriction and accepted memorials directly sent to him. He also acknowledged communications from G. H. Stuart, who was at the time Secretary of the Postmen's Federation though no longer in the service.[51]

Between the time of the agitations that followed the publication of the Tweedmouth Report in 1897 and that of the Bradford Committee in 1904, there was thus a rapid growth in the acceptance of the organised efforts of the Post Office workers. When a delegation from the Postmen's Federation met Postmaster General Stanley in January 1905 to protest against his refusal to accept the verdict of the latest inquiry, J. C. Brown, Editor of the *Postman's Gazette*, suggested that 'it would have been better for the Postmaster General with his official advisers to meet periodically a delegation from our Society to discuss the grievances of those we represent and by such method arrive at a settlement'. If the authorities were not yet prepared to go as far as this they were soon ready to take new steps along this road.

The landslide victory of the Liberal Party in the General Election at the beginning of 1906 and the election for the first time of a distinct 'Labour' group of twenty-nine Members, meant that there was now an administration that was more inclined than its predecessors to admit the claims of trade unions. The new Postmaster General was Sydney Buxton, who had already said that he favoured the Department being a model employer, and who 'believed that the stronger and more responsible a trade union was made the more likely were the relations between the trade union men and the employer to be good and satisfactory'. He was thus a suitable person to make the definitive recognition statement in 1906. He said that 'the stronger and more representative the associations became the less would be the friction and the more easy it would be to arrive at a conclusion satisfactory to both sides'. Recognition was extended in 1907, when machinery was set up for local negotiation and appeals against its decisions. In 1910 Buxton's successor, Herbert Samuel, allowed negotiation on behalf of individuals in discipline cases, though not promotion.[52]

ASSOCIATION ACTIVITY BEFORE AND
AFTER 'RECOGNITION'

By this time the question for the authorities was not whether they were prepared to 'recognise' bodies which were daily growing more effective and powerful, but how these bodies could regulate their relations with employers who were also legislators. The severe limitations on the exercise of political pressure have already been described, and the attacks on their constitutional propriety. Any further consideration of the matter was constantly postponed by the inquiries into the Post Office on the argument that civil rights concerned the public service as a whole.[53] The MacDonnell Commission in 1913 at long last provided a forum for the consideration of the problem. Charles Ammon of the FA, speaking for the Civil Service Federation, argued for the right of unfettered political activity. The Commission concluded that although higher civil servants 'should be placed under the obligation to secure a proper reserve and reticence both in speech and writing in respect to political questions', for subordinate grades it would suffice to have a rule preventing them from using their official position to influence the outcome of elections. Although the Commission drew a distinction between civil servants acting collectively and as individuals, it failed to draw a similar difference between the exercise of collective rights for political or for trade union purposes, and thus lumped together the organisation of unions and the exercise of political pressure.[54] Its generally liberal recommendations were in any case by-passed by the outbreak of war.

After 1918 the arguments about political influence took on a different complexion, with the Whitley machinery taking some of the pressure away from Parliament. Nevertheless, 'civil rights' were not obtained in the way the unions had been asking for them, or as MacDonnell had recommended. Labour leaders showed the same curious concern for the 'neutrality' of the lowest grades of public servants and when they set up the Blanesborough Committee to consider this question in 1924, little substantial change was recommended.[55] The 1927 Trade Disputes Act created even greater restriction on political rights. Only after 1945 was the position at long last improved from the point of view of the civil servant.[56]

The great paradox was that the Post Office workers who as civil servants were subject to these large constraints on their political activities, nevertheless managed for a time to exercise a good deal of political influence. This was particularly the case in the period between the 1890s and the 1920s when the right of their associations to exist was gradually being acknowledged by the authorities and regular methods of bargaining had not yet developed. It was then that the National Joint Committee of Postal and Telegraph Unions built a formidable lobbying machine and it seemed to some that 'no agitation for Parliamentary action has been so vigorously, almost ruthlessly, pursued'. One of those involved later claimed that this 'pestering was our only chance' and he recalled how 'relays of devoted men and women' would spend hours on end waiting to lobby MPs. All the unions had their 'Parliamentary secretaries' in this period and Samuel Belderson performed this role on behalf of the telegraphists.

> Did a Member of Parliament, known or unknown to Belderson, get an office or an honour, or did his wife have a baby or his daughter get married, a nice little note came from the PTCA congratulating him – talk about casting bread on the water! Sammy buttered them!

Nor was it simply a matter of pressure on the House of Commons itself. Telegraphists were told in the 1900 General Election that 'Local branches should arrange interviews with both political parties; they should explain the grievances and try to obtain definite assurances. This is the only road to success'.[57]

It was under the impact of these methods that the great public inquiries after 1895 came into existence with forms and procedures increasingly favoured by the Post Office workers. Similar lobbying also got civil servants included in the worker's compensation legislation and eventually secured the principle that pensions would be considered as deferred pay in 1909. Between 1903 and 1914 there was thought to exist 'a tacit agreement between the workers and the Department that reference to a Select Committee would be in effect reference to arbitration'. However, the effects of such lobbying could be overstated. It was suspended altogether by the unions in 1907 while the Hobhouse Committee was meeting and it was comparatively rare for MPs to vote against their own party on questions of Post Office workers' conditions.[58] It was the very lack of success of these methods that inclined the workers to take their next step by themselves, sponsoring MPs. Clearly a working civil servant could not take on this role and there was also a problem about the relationship to the main parties. Despite these difficulties all leading associates supported the idea by 1900. Clery briefly became candidate for Deptford in 1902–3, essentially as a Liberal, and Stuart stood under the banner of the newly emerging Labour Party at York in 1906.

It was in the same period that objections to lobbying activity altogether grew more intense. Thus, during his brief spell as Postmaster General in 1902–3, Austen Chamberlain claimed that MPs 'not from one side of the House alone' came to him to seek 'protection in the discharge of their public duties against the pressure sought to be put upon them by the employees of the Post Office'. Two years later, as a General Election approached and a decisive shift in power was anticipated, pressure was increased. One association journal said they could obtain 'advantage from the political situation' by asking every MP opposed to a new inquiry 'to consider very seriously whether on this question he can afford to go into the wrong lobby'. Lord Stanley, the last Tory PMG for some time, asserted that the Post Office workers were

> abusing their rights as voters. It was nothing more or less than blackmail. It was nothing more or less than asking Members to purchase votes for themselves at the general election at the expense of the Public Exchequer . . . Some means should be devised whereby there should not be continual blood-sucking on the part of public servants.

This statement, especially the words 'blackmail' and 'blood-sucking', were vigorously attacked by Post Office workers and achieved considerable publicity as manifestations of anti-trade union prejudice. They figured in the address of the 1905 TUC President and even provided the refrain for a music hall song.[59] They also played a part in the defeat of Stanley in the 1906 General Election in the Westhoughton constituency which had previously been regarded as the preserve of his aristocratic family. Cheesman was sent by the NJC to campaign for his successful Lib–Lab opponent Tyson Wilson and told the electors that Stanley was 'a sweater, he was an enemy of trade unions, and would not allow combination among working men'.[60] During the election campaign he said he withdrew the word 'bloodsucker' but generally said he had 'nothing to reconsider or modify in my remarks'. After it was over he 'admitted using words which he now regretted and frankly withdrew', even if he had been right to resist the demands made on him.[61]

The 1906 General Election also brought in the Liberal administration that finally recognised the unions. From then until 1914 Select Committees of MPs were given the main responsibility for determining wages and conditions in the Post Office. For a time the Postmen's Federation wanted this to be formalised into regular reviews by Select Committees every five years. However, the MPs did not perform their task to anybody's satisfaction, as could be seen from the response to the Committees of Hobhouse and Holt. Increasing support for alternative methods was then heard. From 1906 civil servants began to advocate a Court of Appeals including MPs and civil service representatives, and in 1909 a Civil Service Court of Appeal Committee was set up with the support of the NJC to make propaganda for the idea. The proposal was subject to more objections of a constitutional sort than most possible alternatives, and, as a result, the Court of Appeals Committee provided only the basis for the broader Civil Service Federation set up in 1912. Meanwhile, other proposals were being put forward by those opposed to political pressures of all kinds who wanted to take the issue of civil servants' conditions outside the Parliamentary sphere altogether. Thus Austen Chamberlain agreed in 1909 that

> a tribunal could . . . be formed that would relieve [MPs] from direct or immediate responsibility for these matters; a tribunal in which public opinion would have confidence, and to which the Civil Servants could give a moral adhesion.

Similar views were expressed in this period by Lord Stanley and Henniker Heaton. Buxton argued for them in the Cabinet, but in practice continued to use Select Committees.[62]

The problem with the schemes put forward by the associations during this period was that they were always subject to constitutional objections about the threats they posed to Parliamentary sovereignty and ministerial responsibility. This helps to explain the diminishing enthusiasm of the Postmen's Federation for their idea of quinquennial reviews, and also the failure of efforts to secure an appeals board. Fewer objections of this sort could be made against the scheme argued by F. W. Jowett, Labour MP for Bradford, for the running of government departments by 'boards of control' representing both 'servants' and 'authorities'. In practice all that came from this was some representation of the associations on departmental committees. Before the setting up of the Holt Enquiry, the 'servants' were represented on the committee dealing with telegraphists cramp. However, the individual chosen did not have the support of the PTCA, and the report was ultimately repudiated. The Holt Committee in 1913 rejected any general right of the associations 'to nominate representatives on departmental committees', and complained that, despite recognition, the number of memorials and Parliamentary questions increased. The hostile reaction to the reports of both Hobhouse and Holt made it clear that there had to be a more generally accepted way of arranging things. David Lloyd George, who was at the time Chancellor of the Exchequer, said in 1913 that there was 'no worse body in the world for fixing a scale of wages than the House of Commons', and in 1914 the MacDonnell Commission on the Civil Service as a whole thought that there ought to be new machinery for the consideration of grievances. Although the Treasury did not support this, the problem was pushed back by the advent of war. It was nevertheless true, as Ramsey MacDonald put it in proposing the Gibb Enquiry to the Commons, that there was by then 'a general consensus of opinion in the House that to settle these questions either by commissions or by committees is not the best method'. Postmaster General Hobhouse agreed that they would have to create 'some authority standing between this House and the servants of the State'.[63]

The paradox of the Gibb Committee was that it was set up to reconsider, with staff representation, decisions made by a reputedly sovereign Parliament. Its very form, despite its limited role in actually making decisions, represented a major concession to the ideas put forward by Jowett and the associations before the war. This change allowed a further step to be taken in 1916, with the submission of the war bonus claims of the Post Office workers to arbitration, and the setting up of the Civil Service Conciliation and Arbitration Board early in the following year. Such a body would have been considered revolutionary less than a decade before, though feeling in the service now made it essential to stave off discontent. The Treasury was still not prepared to be bound by its decision, and the danger of this attitude was made clear by the further development of radical ideas among civil servants. As one association journal put it: 'There are Bolsheviks abroad and mild-mannered moderate men are gradually being coverted to their views . . . something more far-reaching than mere recognition will be demanded'.[64]

THE ADVENT OF WHITLEYISM, 1917-19

The solution to the historic political and legal problems of negotiating about civil service pay and conditions came in 1917 from an unexpected quarter. This was the Committee on Industrial Unrest which was set up under the Chairmanship of Liberal MP J. H. Whitley to resolve the great conflicts in engineering, mining and elsewhere. It proposed Joint Industrial Councils which, while not widely adopted elsewhere, provided a basis for a new industrial relations system in the public service. It is with an account of how this came about that this chapter will conclude.[65]

When Whitley's proposals for JICs were first published on 29 June 1917, they were sent to employers' organisations and unions, though not those in the public service.[66] However, it soon became obvious to some of the civil service union leaders that they were provided with an opportunity to argue again for something along the lines of an appeal board. The initiative probably came from the Civil Service Alliance, which had been set up by W. J. Brown and others after arguments about the regressive character of the recent bonus claims. Within four days of its appearance, the Alliance wrote to the Ministry of Labour asking if the Whitley Report applied to them. The Civil Service Federation immediately followed suit by asking the same question of the Treasury. In both cases the answer was no, but the unions could easily begin public propaganda to ask why the Government would not apply in its own sphere what was being recommended to others.[67]

In the meantime, matters had been proceeding within the NJC. Stuart Bunning prepared a memorandum in which he maintained 'that the general principle of the Report is in accordance with the desires of the organised Post Office Staff during the last four years'. He argued strongly that the proposals were 'not in addition to our present policy whatever that may be, but in substitution therefor', and to support them would involve 'abandoning the call for standing committees as well as many of the lobbying activities then undertaken'. A discussion in the NJC on the morning of the first big amalgamation meeting on 11 August 1917 revealed some difficulty because of the insistence of the Amalgamated Engineering and Stores Association, predecessors of the Post Office Engineering Union, on their 'craft' status. On this basis they wanted separate negotiating rights and this eventually led to the setting up of a separate Whitley Council altogether. However most of the other associations supported the idea of a National Joint Industrial Committee in the Post Office and agreed to campaign for it at the same time as proceeding to amalgamation.[68]

It seems that at about this point Stuart Bunning approached Whitley himself, and when the second report of his Committee appeared in October 1917 it stated quite explicitly that 'the expression "employers and workmen" in our reference covers State and Municipal authorities'. By the end of 1917 the Chancellor of the Exchequer had little alternative but to agree that the Government should be 'setting an example in this matter'. The Ministry of Labour also by now accepted this, and the Post Office authorities wrote privately to the Treasury that they could not see any difficulty in applying the Whitley report in their own case.[69]

Further progress was slow in the early part of 1918. The old problems of Treasury authority and Parliamentary control began to be discussed, and such new difficulties as the precise role of local machinery. The unions however were now convinced. When the PF and P&TCA Executives met on 23 February 1918, there were reservations about any compulsory arbitration element, but full support for the general principle. Other difficulties could be overcome, in the opinion of the NJC, if 'The constitution and functions of the National Council should be such that if the Treasury is to come in, it must do so as part of the National Council and not as a revising body'.

A number of MPs, notably Arnold Rowntree, began to exercise pressure on behalf of the proposals. The Civil Service Federation ran a meeting on 27 April representing 136,500 civil servants at which it was agreed that 'the principle of joint control has long since gone beyond the experimental state, and can be extended to the Civil Service immediately'. Following this meeting, a letter was sent to the Prime Minister demanding an interview and MPs were briefed on the widespread support for Whitley principles amongst all the Post Office associations. Numerous local meetings were held advocating the adoption of the system and MPs raised the matter on the Post Office estimates debate on 12 June.[70]

Following this pressure, the War Cabinet finally decided on 1 July to go ahead with a scheme, though only with consultative powers. This decision was announced in Parliament on 4 July, along with the setting up of an interdepartmental committee of Ministers to work out the details. This committee could only propose councils covering industrial workers and left the bigger problem of the administrative departments to a further committee, this time of heads of departments under the Chairmanship of Sir Thomas Heath, Joint Permanent Secretary to the Treasury. A delegation from the Civil Service Federation met the body on 14 November and proposed a network of committees with equal representation from both sides. The unions, including the NJC, spent the next few months busily constructing schemes for departmental committees with neutral chairmen. When the Heath report appeared on 7 March 1919, it proved a great disappointment. The Committee was prepared to concede that permanent officials 'like the General

Managers of Companies, are no doubt in theory employees, but in practice they exercise the functions and possess the attributes of employers'. However the Committee refused to draw the logical conclusion from this, maintaining that 'the control of the Minister must remain unimpaired', and that any joint bodies 'should be purely consultative'. Since it was also proposed to abolish the arbitration board and to restrict Parliamentary lobbying, the overall effect would have been to place civil servants in a worse position than before. This report, wrote Stuart Bunning later, 'looked like Whitley, smelt like Whitley, almost tasted like Whitley, but was not Whitley'.[71]

There followed a great meeting on 8 April 1919 in Caxton Hall between Chancellor of the Exchequer Austen Chamberlain and representatives of all the main civil service unions.[72] This meeting, which later became famous in the historical mythology of the service, presented many important tactical problems. Feeling was already strong as a result of the failure of the war bonus to keep up with the cost of living, and the desire for real change was widespread. However, the meeting contained representatives from every section of the service including some who had many sharp differences, and others whose views on many questions were quite unknown. This was the audience to which Chamberlain presented the Government's support for a version of the Whitley scheme which was now arousing the most profound disquiet. However it was feared that outright rejection might make matters worse still. Thus Stuart-Bunning addressed the conference in terms already agreed by the CSF, attacking Heath's document as 'an employers' report', and proposing only that a joint sub-committee should be set up to consider it. After F. J. Payne of the Society of Civil Servants had formally seconded, the psychological moment feared by the union leaders arrived. Would there be a breaking of ranks, or a maverick view expressed which could be seized upon by the authorities? Though Chamberlain appealed for more speakers none came, so he peremptorily expressed his agreement with Stuart-Bunning's proposal, which was carried unanimously, and a Committee with seventeen on each side was then set up. The common front which had been carefully forged by Stuart-Bunning ever since the evidence was presented to Heath's Committee, now existed right across the civil service.[73]

This common front was also successful in obtaining a favourable result from the Joint Committee set up after the April conference. The Committee, with Chairman Sir John Ramsey, First Controller of Establishments for the Treasury, and Vice Chairman Stuart-Bunning, broke down an initial wall of 'distrust and suspicion', and issued a report on 28 May 1919 conceding all the main points demanded by the associations. After accepting the principle of equal representation on a national Council, the following procedure was proposed:

> The decisions of the Council shall be arrived at by agreement between the two sides, shall be signed by the Chairman and Vice Chairman, shall be reported to the Cabinet, and thereupon shall become operative.

The report also spoke of the Council being involved in the 'determination of the general principles governing conditions of service', as opposed to the merely consultative role which had previously been envisaged.[74]

Why was it that in the end the War Cabinet and even the Treasury accepted this apparent diminution of their power? Before the Cabinet had agreed on 13 June it was pointed out by the Minister of Labour that in arriving at any conclusion the official side would be bound by the constraint that 'the Government will in fact have agreed to the decision being so taken before the matter is settled upon the National Council'. When Ramsey spoke to departmental heads, many of whom were hostile to the whole business, he threatened them with the possible consequences, including even the industrial unrest which was reaching a peak elsewhere at the time.

> Let me impress upon you that it is a very momentous departure. It is a complete break from the past. I hope and believe that if worked in the right spirit these Councils will succeed. I am perfectly sure that if they do not succeed, if after trial the system is found wanting, and does not satisfy the legitimate – I say 'legitimate' advisedly – aspirations of the staff and the reasonable hopes which they undoubtedly found upon it, we shall find ourselves embarked upon a sea of troubles far more stormy than we have had to navigate and we shall be in great danger and disaster.

The fears and qualifications on the official side were still expressed by Sir Austen Chamberlain at a further large representative meeting held at Caxton Hall on 3 July 1919. 'The Constitution which we establish', he said, 'is not like the laws of the Medes and Persians, and if experience shows it necessary it can be amended to meet any difficulties which may arise'. Despite all the qualifications, the National Whitley Council was able to hold its first meeting on 23 July 1919, and soon a network of departmental and other committees was in operation.[75]

The Whitley system provided at long last and after so many false starts and experiments, an agreed machinery for dealing with grievances in the public service. As recently as 1916 the Post Office Secretary had tried to disabuse a delegation from the NJC of 'the assumption that the wages of Post Office servants are settled by bargain or agreement with the Postmaster'. Now it could be said that 'future wage agreements will normally be the result of agreement between the Department and the staff'.[76] If Whitleyism provided a forum for dealing with the particular problems of bargaining in the public sector, it never quite worked in the ways that its founders envisaged. For one thing, 'Treasury Control' or government economic policy more generally were never entirely absent from considerations of wages and conditions in the public sector. For another, the National Whitley Council never quite operated as the ultimate decision-making body in the way that had been intended. Its sub-committees and the departmental bodies held more effective power and, in any case, the most important matters of wages and conditions came to be settled outside the Whitley structures themselves. There was always a resource beyond Whitley, either through the Arbitration Court defended so tenaciously by the unions during the 1920s, or later still through the industrial action that became normal at least in the 1960s.

However, in 1919, these were all matters for the future. For the moment, a new-found unity of civil servants in their associations and unions had compelled the Government to agree to a fixed form for dealing with their own industrial relations. This was the culmination of many generations of effort, and that for the moment was what was most important.

NOTES

1 Quoted in Swift (1929), p. 38.
2 Trollope (1861). It is wrongly claimed that the lecture is being reprinted for the first time in the 1938 edition; in fact it appears in substantially the same form in *Cornhill Magazine* III (1861) where it is indicated that it was originally a lecture delivered at the General Post Office on 4 January.
3 Gladden (1967), p. 127.
4 PP 1834 VI (The Report on Sinecure Offices) recommended this change. See also Cohen (1941), pp. 52–6.
5 Gash (1953), pp. 354–5; Richards (1963), p. 41.
6 Elcho Report and Northcote Trevelyan Report. For the orders in council indicating the changes see PP 1870 XIX (Civil Service Commissioners' Report). On Hill's opposition see PP 1854–5 XX (Re-organisation Papers), pp. 241–4.
7 Richards (1963), p. 56; *Hansard* IV, 1134 (19 February 1895), 159, 397 (21 June 1906) and 170, 640–1 (5 March 1907). See also Hanham (1960), pp. 76, 80–2 and on the United States, Siedman (1969).
8 'Member of Parliament', 'Plums for our friends' *London Magazine* (29 October 1912), pp. 230–4 and *Civilian* (23 November 1912). Moses (1914), p. 198, casts doubts even on the limited charges in these articles, though Hobhouse Evidence p. 310 shows that some believed them in 1906, at least for sub-postmasterships.
9 Rees (1866), p. 256.
10 *Hansard* IV, 142, 702 (8 March 1905). Mustoe (1932), p. 132, says 'The Crown has the power to dismiss at its pleasure'.
11 Mustoe (1932), pp. 132–3, described a case of Shenton *v.* Smith in 1895, though this seems to have been little known – see the report of a Special Sub-Committee presented to the Annual Meeting of the Civil Service Federation, 6 February 1915.
12 On the telegraphists in 1898 see below Chapter 7, and for the statement quoted *Hansard* IV, 135, 780 (6 June 1904). See also Emden (1923), pp. 20–4.
13 6 Ed. VII c.58, Section 9 (1906 Workman's Compensation Act). On the legal position in general see Dicey (1959), pp. 312ff. For some minor protections see Emden (1923), pp. 34–58, 62–3 and Mustoe (1932), pp. 60–74 which includes freedom from serving on juries and from certain aspects of the laws of libel and damages.
14 For examples see Thomas (1968), pp. 111–28 and Mustoe (1932), pp. 111–19.
15 See *Hansard* (HL), V 27, 90–7 (13 February 1917). There is a general discussion in Beveridge (1920), and more detail in Wright (1969), where it is argued that Treasury parsimony reflects more general Parliamentary and other political pressures. Whatever its origins, many examples of Treasury parsimony can be seen in succeeding chapters, for example over proposed improvements in 1851 (p. 104). Amongst other examples below see p. 110 (1860–1), 1872–3 (p. 125) and the Joyce Committee Report (referred to p. 151 n. 94 below).
16 For a typical example see Lascelles (1930) where the difficulties are described of 'a politician with no inside knowledge of a great business, to become master in his house in the few months in which he is studying PO methods'.
17 PP 1928 VII (Board of Enquiry Report), pp. 21–2.
18 Treasury Circular (8/77) of 11 August 1927, given in PP 1928 VII, p. 26. For a later account see MacKenzie and Grove (1957), pp. 149–52.
19 Mustoe (1932), p. 120 for the legislation at the time including 31 & 32 Vic c.48 (1868 Telegraph Act) and for the detailed rules *Postmasters' Manual* (1919), pp. 154–5, 167–71.
20 PP 1896 LXVIII; Hobhouse Evidence, pp. 610, 634; Smith (1931), p. 256.
21 There is a discussion of this distinction in PP 1948–9, pp. 26–7.
22 See POR 59/178 which includes the Tenth Report of the Parliamentary Commissioners of 1793, Paine (1772), Hughes (1936).
23 Playfair Report, p. 124; PP 1881 LVII (Fawcett Settlement), p. 2.
24 12–13 Will. III c.12, para 3 (the Act of Settlement). On the struggle between King and Parliament see Todd (1892) Vol I, p. 239 et seq. For a list of the exemptions see Anson (1922), pp. 101–5.
25 These restrictions are in 9 Anne c.10 para 44 and 22 Geo. III c.41, which, however, excluded revenue officers.
26 Swift (1929), pp. 41–6; Trollope (1861), pp. 24–6.

27 The Revenue Officers Disabilities Removal Acts are 31 & 32 Vic c.73 and 37 & 38 Vic c.22. For the debates see *Hansard* III, 192, 1533–8 (12 June 1868), 193, 390–401 (30 June 1868) and 219, 797–801 (1 June 1874). See also the Report on this in PP 1867–8 LVI.

28 For these and more details see Smith (1931), p. 236.

29 POC, 507, 3 November 1885.

30 Smith (1931), p. 237; *Post* (4 August 1894); *Hansard* IV, 16, 1218 (28 August 1893); Hobhouse Evidence, p. 608; R I/9; Martinuzzi (1952), pp. 182–4.

31 *PCH* (10 October 1908), p. 370; Martinuzzi (1952), pp. 182–4; *Civil Service Socialist* (1908), p. 129.

32 BL:BP 2/15(2) pp. 7, 6; *Hansard* V, 12, 1177–8 (28 October 1909); *Post* (1909), p. 449; Post Office, Information Supplied (to Holt, 1912), p. 110; *Postmasters' Manual* (1919) I, p. 175.

33 *Post* (11 November 1922); PP 1924–5 IX, pp. 8–9.

34 PP 1883 XXXVIII (Treasury Minutes); POC, 17 June 1867.

35 Meyer (1907), p. 96.

36 Heaton (1906), p. 571, *Hansard* III, 168, 676 (22 July 1862), 262, 141–2 (16 August 1881). For the context of these remarks see p. 111, below.

37 *Hansard* III, 111, 891 (7 June 1850); IV, 82, 226 (27 April 1900), 94, 1382 (7 June 1901), 139, 1619 (9 August 1904), 148, 1365 (6 June 1905).

38 Spero (1927), pp. 97–180 on the 'gag rules' and their operation and Doherty (1960) for an interesting account of the lobbying methods of American postal workers in more recent times. On France see White (ed.) *et al.* (1935), p. 143.

39 TUC 1885 Report, p. 40. For later examples see 1893 Report, p. 79; 1895 p. 56; 1897 pp. 52–3, 1898 p. 67; 1900 pp. 82–3; 1901 pp. 79–80; 1902 p. 74; 1904 pp. 121–2; 1907 p. 164; 1908 pp. 197–8; 1910 pp. 198–9; 1912 p. 238; 1913 p. 196; 1918 p. 174. The earlier motions are usually combined with calls for union recognition and the later ones asked for participation in elections. Judging from the debates, Post Office union leaders do not seem to have been satisfied that the TUC did much on their behalf. For Labour party motions see 1906 Report p. 57 and 1907 Report p. 61.

40 For details of these various agitations see Chapter 5. The regulations are in Swift (1929), p. 38, and POC, 787, 19 April 1890; 794, 21 May 1890. *Post*, 30 August 1930, gives a colourful account by W. E. Clery of the winning of the right to hold outside meetings and *Hansard* IV, 16, 1218 (28 August 1893) has Gladstone's statement removing the early restrictions.

41 Quoted in Humphreys (1958), p. 34, and Chambers (n.d.), p. 6, though this statement, for which no source is given, must be earlier, since Raikes, in February, agreed that 'associations for mutual benefit', 'could exist'.

42 POR 65/3, p. 98; *Hansard* III, 345, 718 (12 June 1890), 347, 6177 (23 July 1890). See also Chapter 6 below, especially p. 145.

43 The following account, including the quotations, is derived from *Post* (1892–3) and the FA Minutes for the same period in R IV/3 and Clery's detailed account (1892).

44 POR 65/4, pp. 255–70; *Hansard* IV, 1107–42 (18 February 1898); *Saturday Review* (30 June 1898); R VI/4, 14, 19 June, 10 July 1907, *Post* (1907), p. 239. See also R V/9, pp. 8ff.

45 There is a detailed account, with documents, at POR 65/3, pp. 125–208.

46 POR 65/3, pp. 139, 171; R V/9, p. 8.

47 POR 65/3, p. 127, 166–70, and *Verbatim Report* at MC 310.5.

48 POR 65/3, pp. 189, 199.

49 Swift (1929), p. 273, *Hansard* IV, 53, 1136 (18 February 1898).

50 *Hansard* IV, 53, 1120; Tweedmouth Evidence, p. 665.

51 R I/5; Murray (1927), p. 197; POR 65/4, pp. 305ff.

52 POR 60/32. On Buxton's earlier views see p. 62. The various statements are in POC, 1702, 18 February 1906, 1760, 19 March 1907 and 1930, 14 April 1910.

53 *Hansard* IV, 16, 1218 (28 August 1893), Hobhouse Report, p. 2.

54 MacDonald, 3rd Report, pp. 130–40, and MacDonald, 4th Report, pp. 95–100.

55 Labour's first Chancellor of the Exchequer, Philip Snowden, shows his continued espousal of the Civil Service 'mentality' in *Hansard* V, 169, 1018–9 (14 February 1924) though in 1919 the Labour Party's Advisory Committee on the Machinery of Government had supported the claim of the staff associations and even interviewed the Prime Minister on them on 18 August 1921. For the 1924 Enquiry see Cmd 2408.

56 For an account of subsequent events in the history of this matter see the report in PP 1952–3 XXII, pp. 3–4.

57 Shepherd (1923), p. 120; G. H. Stuart-Bunning in *Red Tape* (1931), p. 446; *Telegraph Chronicle* (1900), p. 50.
58 See also pp. 254ff. on deferred pay. Shepherd (1923), p. 124. Smith (1931), p. 123, shows that the highest number of MPs to vote against their party on Post Office conditions was 9, on 7 June 1901 and 6 May 1907.
59 *Hansard* IV, 121, 1023 (30 April 1903), TUC 1905 Report, p. 51.
60 *Bolton Evening News* (9 January 1906).
61 *ibid.* (28 November 1905); *Post* (1906), p. 435.
62 Hobhouse Evidence, pp. 613–4; *CSG* (24 March 1906); Humphreys (1958), pp. 67, 83; *PCH* (1909), pp. 336–8; *Hansard* V, 4, 232 (27 April 1909); BL: BP 2/15(3).
63 *PCH* (1908), pp. 120–1, 1910, pp. 373–4, 455; Holt Evidence, pp. 36, 352, Report, pp. 3–4; *PG* (1914), p. 384; *Hansard* IV, 63, 419 and 443 (30 April 1914). See MacDonald, 4th Report, pp. 85, 99.
64 *Aspirex* (June 1918).
65 Stack (1969) gives the fullest account. See also Parris (1973); White (1933), and Humphreys (1958), p. 78. These sources are supplemented in the account that follows by various volumes at R/V.
66 Humphreys (1958), pp. 94ff.; Armstrong (1969).
67 Brown (1943), p. 90.
68 R V/27, 29. See also Chapter 8 on the parallel amalgamation negotiations in the Post Office, pp. 261ff.
69 *CSG* 1920, p. 225; PP 1918 X (Ministry of Reconstruction Report), p. 6; Armstrong (1969), p. 137; Stack (1969), p. 289.
70 R V/29, 31; *P&TR* (2 May 1918), p. 415; R V/32; *Hansard* V, 106, 2240ff. (12 June 1918).
71 *Hansard* V, 107, 1850 (4 July 1918); R V/31; PP 1919 XI; *Post* (24 July 1943), p. 27.
72 *ibid.* and 7 August, p. 43, for Stuart-Bunning's own later account. See also *CSG* 1919, pp. 56–8.
73 Details of how this was done are to be found at R XXIII.
74 Armstrong (1969), p. 152; PP 1919 XI.
75 Stack (1969), p. 293; Armstrong (1969), p. 152; *CSG* 1919, p. 125.
76 *PG* 1916, p. 449; *P&TR* (24 April 1919), p. 202.

5 Sabbatarians and Sinners: 1840–1870

> We cannot persuade ourselves that things are well managed when a whole establishment is in that state of chronic disaffection which has for some time been characteristic of St. Martin's-le-Grand. It is not merely one man or one set of men, it is the entire body which is discontented, and which has been discontented for a long while past. Despite the risk of dismissal, the Post Office servants are perpetually agitating, remonstrating and memorialising their superiors. As soon as one disturbance has subsided another begins. The men have no confidence in their masters, and no satisfaction with their work. (*The Times* 12 September 1860)

> Everybody has heard of the loud and deep complaints of the London letter-carriers of the grinding oppression to which they are subjected, and their ineffectual struggle to obtain redress. In the provinces it is the same. The provincial post-offices are swarming with discontent and rebellious post-masters, post-office clerks, and letter-carriers; many of whom are not only overworked and underpaid, but have been duped out of their just and rightful claims. (*Money Market Review*, 31 January 1863)

It has sometimes been said that organised activity for the redress of grievances in the Post Office did not really begin until trade unions were properly established in the 1880s and 1890s. 'Organisation of postmen' in the words of one distinguished labour historian, 'was minimal in the nineteenth century'.[1] In other words, it has come to be held that all the numerous incidents so colourfully described more than eighty years ago in H. G. Swift's inimitable *History of Postal Agitation* did not amount to anything approximating to modern trade union activity. This view can no longer be justified. There is no reason to see the actions of workers to deal with their grievances as in some way unreal if they are not carried out by permanent and public organisations. Post Office workers in early Victorian England were not in a position to act like their modern counterparts. Nor was there any reason whatever why it should have occurred to them to try to improve their lot by electing full-time officials and putting them in a big office in London.

The fact is that at least from the time of the introduction of the penny post in 1840, those who worked in the Post Office were engaged in agitation about their grievances, which was not far from continuous and was certainly consistently organised. The quotations from the press given at the head of this chapter show that they made contemporaries well aware of this. The 'letter carriers' and sorters in the mid-nineteenth century did not live in a world where the methods and forms of modern trade unionism could in any way be assumed. The Post Office workers of those days were part of a public service only emerging from the days of 'influence' and patronage to something closer to modern forms of social organisation.

This context helps to explain the particular form taken by the first attempts by public servants to improve their conditions. It is certainly the case that long before trade unions were even thought of, the 'nineteenth century is full of examples of militant action by organisations of Civil Servants set up specifically to fight against cuts in pay and pensions'.[2] This action was first taken by those who worked for the Post Office, especially in London where they were most concentrated. Although there was no organisation in this period in the sense of a public body with continuous activity, this is not to say that efforts aimed at the improvement of conditions were merely spasmodic or 'informal'.

At first the postal workers turned to those who seemed most likely to be able to help them, looking in such unlikely directions as the Society for the Due Observance of the Lord's Day, the law courts, and even the columns of *The Times* newspaper. Increasingly, however, it grew clear that the Post Office workers would have to rely on their own efforts. In the 1840s there were instances of go-slow working aimed at putting pressure on the authorities, and by the mid-1850s there were secretive but nonetheless real bodies in existence that were able to put together memorials, to organise mass meetings, and even to produce a paper. The Post Office authorities responded with hostility to these developments, but they had to take increasing account of them. By the late 1850s, the authorities were compelled to take part in spasmodic negotiations with the leaders of the movement. By 1860 they had to run an inquiry into the conditions of the London letter carriers whose report remains to this day unpublished. Since then it can be said that improvements in wages and conditions have always been the result of pressure from the workforce. This chapter is devoted to an account of how these temporary and usually unacknowledged arrangements came about and developed.

THOMAS MITCHELL, ROBERT GRAPES AND THE FIRST BATTLES

The introduction of the penny post in 1840 brought heavier and more complex labours for all those who handled the increasing volume of mail that came with it. The stresses which were inevitable in any case were compounded by the overlordship of Rowland Hill, who placed the welfare of the workers very low on the list of priorities for the success of his postal reforms.

The first group to feel the effects of the introduction of the new system were the London letter receivers who performed some of the functions of modern subpostmasters. They submitted numerous individual petitions asking for higher fees to take account of their extra labours, and a number carried out their threat to cease working for the Post Office when they failed to obtain any improvements.[3]

More deep-felt and organised discontent soon manifested itself at the General Post Office in St Martin's-le-Grand. It is clear that secret meetings began there among the letter carriers and sub-sorters within months of the introduction of the penny post, and in 1842 a number of memorials were presented. These were rejected, but some early morning deliveries were abolished and small wage increases followed. However, discontent soon manifested itself further as the authorities tried to expand the workforce in ways which aroused the suspicions of those already in it. Thus a sub-sorter called Jonathan Roberts was suspended for refusing to train others to become sub-sorters. The authorities were alarmed to discover that his wages were then made up by his colleagues. They noted that the sub-sorters and letter carriers had 'a confederacy for the purpose of opposing, it is believed, as far as possible, all official management of which they may not entirely approve'. This 'confederacy' soon moved into further action. Early in June 1845, Robert Grapes, clearly leader of the clandestine organisation, launched a series of accusations against Federick Kelly, Chief Inspector of Letter Carriers, who earned a large income from producing a 'Directory of London Addresses' for which he rewarded 'favoured' letter carriers who helped him compile it. Grapes also approached the radical MP Thomas Duncombe, who took up the grievances of the postal workers in the House of Commons, not only in regard to Kelly and his Directory, but also on more general grounds that they were 'badly paid', 'made to do extra work for nothing' and 'reported and suspended often'. The Post Office was not prepared to consider these complaints seriously, and Duncombe's proposal for a Parliamentary inquiry was rejected.[4]

This did nothing to assuage the discontent of the postal workers. The General Post letter carriers asked for permission to hold a meeting, and it is interesting to notice that they received a reply in almost exactly the opposite sense to those that became normal in later years. The authorities said 'they could not have liberty to hold their meetings in the office, but no control would be exercised over the right they had to do so, out of doors'. Thus 130 letter carriers assembled at the Owen Glendower Tavern in Aldersgate Street near the GPO on 18 June 1845 to draw up a list of their grievances. The sub-sorters held two meetings in the following week at which they decided that their main demand should be for a 'higher rate of salary in the upper lists', in other words increases at or near the maximum. They issued some publicity and sent memorials to the authorities against the prevalence of payment by gratuities.[5] These efforts seem to have achieved very little, however, though secret meetings continued at which 'badly adjusted scales of salary' were discussed. The lack of any reply by the authorities produced a more militant response, 'anonymous placards . . . were stuck up in the newspaper-office, and so unwilling were the men to work on several occasions that it was with greatest difficulty the work was got through'. The London District letter carriers also held a meeting to which they invited the press on 31 July 1846, and drew up a memorial calling for 'a scale of wages proportionated to their respective daily duties and rising according to years of service'.[6]

The reaction of the authorities to all this was not to discuss the grievances which had been revealed, but to undertake an 'investigation' largely into the fact that discontent had been expressed at all. Although William Bokenham, President of the Inland Department, was supposed to consider the accusations against Kelly, in fact he worked closely with him, sending him copies of the evidence every day, and exonerating him of all the charges against him. Grapes and those who worked with him were accorded no such facilities. One of his main supporters, a sub-sorter called Thomas Mitchell, was suddenly dismissed while the investigation was still proceeding, allegedly for not providing sufficient excuse for absence during a serious illness. The real reason seems more likely to have been that he was just about to provide damning evidence of intimidation against him by Kelly as well as proof of how money being paid for substitutes was being allocated to Kelly and his supporters. The dismissal of Mitchell proved to be the only concrete result of the 'investigation', but after it was over the authorities watched carefully for any signs of the organisation that provoked it. When in July 1847 Grapes advised one of his fellows 'not to know too much' during further investigation into alleged dishonesty, he also was instantly dismissed. Despite the great complexity of this story, which the authorities seem to have been determined to keep obscure, there can be no doubt that Mitchell and Grapes lost their jobs because of their part in organising postal workers against the power of their employers. They can thus be called the first trade union martyrs in the history of the Post Office.[7] They were by no means the last.

A history of somewhat more attenuated 'insubordination' was reported during the 1840s from the Edinburgh office, the only other one in Britain of any size. The clerks and stampers petitioned continually for higher wages, generally without any result. They got the support of their local superiors, who agreed in 1845 that 'anything below £100 a year is utterly inadequate to maintain a person entirely in a respectable position in society'. Repeated requests were largely ignored in London, though there was a general revision of salaries in 1847.[8]

THE SUNDAY LABOUR CAMPAIGN: 1847–50

It was the failure of such methods as these that led the Post Office workers to consider new means of improving their conditions. Memorials had been ignored, meetings had proved ineffectual, and Parliamentary pressure had simply resulted in the victimisation of those who had organised it. It was this that caused them to search for allies among the highly respectable and frequently successful pressure group, the Society for the Due Observance of the Lord's Day. This organisation, one of the many offshoots of the crusading activities of evangelical protestantism, was set up in 1831 to prevent all forms of work and most forms of leisure on Sundays. It is known nowadays as the Lord's Day Observance Society.[9]

How the Post Office workers and the sabbatarians came together is not easy to discover precisely. We can assume that those who worked for the Post Office probably shared the indifference to organised religion prevalent in the urban working class. However, they sought the assistance of a group who drew attention to the intensity of their labour and demanded on their behalf at least one day's rest in seven. The Sabbatarians took up the cause of the postal workers with particular gusto because it gave them the opportunity, by asking that the Post Office set 'a high example to the whole nation', to break from their normal image as middle-class kill-joys determined to limit the pleasure of the poor. On this issue they could claim to be taking up the cause of the 'hard-worked, ill-paid, neglected and despised hive of industrious men who have had to withstand injustice, oppression and calumny'.[10] As early as 1835, Presbyterian Ministers in Scotland took the initiative to try to get Sunday posts abolished and they secured as a Parliamentary champion one Andrew Agnew, MP. In 1838 a carefully-orchestrated and widely publicised series of meetings and petitions prevented the introduction of Sunday deliveries in London. The sabbatarians won support not only from the postal workers, but also from those such as bankers from the City of London who did not want any disturbance to 'the quiet and domestic comfort they, their clerks and dependants had hitherto derived from the day of rest on Sunday'. The Postmaster General accepted this.[11] The Sabbatarians were also no doubt behind what was perhaps the first public expression of discontent in the Post Office outside London. In 1845, a group of letter carriers at Chippenham published a declaration explaining that Sunday working had 'become a real grievance, excluding, as it does the possibility of enjoying the Sabbath as a day of rest', and hence making them 'callous of all religious feelings, and . . . in danger of becoming both physically and mentally depraved'.[12]

The Lord's Day Society soon decided to become active on the issue, and in 1847 its most prominent member, Lord Ashley, already famous for his efforts to limit the hours of work in textile factories, managed to secure the abolition of all postal facilities on Sundays in Bath. The postal authorities responded to further pressure along the same lines by introducing more restrictions on postal business in provincial centres, including the closing of all money order facilities. To prevent the delay of an additional day in the conveyance of mails, the postal authorities proposed to make use of the services of twenty-five clerks at the GPO in sorting 'forward letters' – those going from one town to another through the capital.

This proposal to employ twenty-five men rapidly grew into an issue of national political importance, with the participation of all the leading political figures of the day, and with considerable behind-the-scenes activity on the part of the Sabbatarians. There were a number of reasons for the wide importance given to the issue. For one thing merchants in London feared that deliveries in the capital on Sunday would deprive them of a day of rest and end the existing delay in the diffusion of foreign trade information to their provincial competitors. Another important factor was the particularly inept handling of the problem by Rowland Hill, who thought that efforts to lighten the workload of those under his charge were part of a plot aimed against him personally by a 'cabal' of 'mutinous spirits'.[13]

It is difficult to ascertain the attitude of the postal workers themselves during the campaign. It was said that as soon as the proposed re-arrangements became known at St Martin's-le-Grand, 'a general thrill of astonishment and almost horror, pervaded the establishment', and immediately those involved 'banded together as one man, to resist the innovation by every means they can devise or adopt, short of absolute insubordination'. It is also possible that the GPO employees simply seized on this issue to draw attention to the increasing burden of their labours. Almost certainly for this reason they sent a delegation to Charles Blomfield, Bishop of London, well known for his sabbatarian views and his political influence.[14] The postal workers supported the alliance of Sabbatarians, city merchants and others who wanted to put an end to all Sunday labour in the Post Office, being content to hide behind such people when the risks of taking a more public role were considerable. There were those working at the GPO who found the sudden 'pretensions of piety' around them 'quite sickening', and it is hard to know how seriously to take the 'conscientious scruples' suddenly expressed by the clerks, sub-sorters and letter carriers. What was clearly genuine was their fear of 'an attempt on the part of the Post Office authorities to get seven days' work out of the men for six days' pay'. Furthermore, a public meeting of postal employees held at a chapel in Aldersgate Street on 5 October 1849 heard the condemnation of 'perpetual labour' and 'foreign habits' which would make postal workers 'demoralised and debauched'. Their concerns also come out in one of the many pieces of doggerel published at the time:

Work, work, work, morning noon and night,
Work, work, work, call you the labour light?
We ask one day in seven, always owed since time began
Sent by the love of heaven, in pity to toil-worn men.[15]

It was not long before the postal workers went beyond the composition of verses
in their efforts to resist the extra labour before it was due to be enforced on 28
October 1849. At first Hill was unable to obtain volunteers to perform the new
tasks and discussed the possibility of asking for them in other departments.
However, when the threat of the loss of promotion prospects was put about, enough
men were found in the Post Office. In the days that preceded the introduction of the
new arrangements Hill noticed 'symptoms of direct insubordination' and feared that
any false move would lead to the complete collapse of his scheme. Not only that,
but the more enthusiastic Sabbatarians were now advocating a cessation of all work
to show the authorities 'that there is One mightier than they whose commands you
reverence supremely'. However, even if strike action as a form of religious witness
did not find any support at St Martin's-le-Grand, on the first day the clerks had to
work 'some mischievous person' placed 'a 24 round ladder . . . in the path of the
letter omnibus'. Guards who refused to place bags on the carriages were instantly
dismissed, as also was a letter carrier named Hewlett who distributed leaflets
claiming that the introduction of a Sunday delivery was being contemplated.[16]
   It was at this stage that the whole business went out of the hands of the postal
workers and came under the control of the Sabbatarians and their middle-class
allies. This ultimately did little to serve the postal workers' interests because the
pressure groups over-reached themselves and were out-manoeuvred by the
Government. During the following months Hill made further concessions
abolishing all Sunday tasks at the GPO other than those concerned with 'forward'
letters, and making a number of similar changes in the provinces. By now it was
obvious to those like C. J. Vaughan, Headmaster of Harrow School, who 'tried to
take a *rational* view of the question', that the amount of Sunday labour in the Post
Office had in fact been much reduced.[17] The LDS, however, did not consider this
sufficient, arguing that 'a child could see that if the law of God is to be honoured . . .
the present system of sabbath profanation in our Post Office demands an immediate
and entire abolition'. To this end the Society organised with its usual efficiency.
Monster meetings were held, petitions distributed, and support obtained from
prominent religious figures of every variety including the Archbishop of
Canterbury and leaders of most of the dissenting sects. By 30 May 1850 over half a
million people had signed petitions for the complete abolition of Sunday postal
work and to everyone's surprise, including his own, Ashley got a motion through
the Commons to this effect by 93 votes to 69.[18]
   Whatever their role in obtaining this change, the postal workers were delighted
when it came, particularly outside London, where Sunday deliveries had until then
been general. On the first day it came into effect, 23 June 1850, they marched as a
body to church in both Manchester and Liverpool to express their gratitude to those
who had helped them. However, as perhaps was intended by the Government, the
extreme step of ending all postal activity for one day had such a dramatic effect that
very soon a major counter-offensive was under way. Meetings were organised
without delay by the proprietors of Sunday newspapers, which in those days were
usually sent by post, and as a result were particularly badly hit by the measure. The

newspaper proprietors attacked the postal workers for being able to 'dictate' to the authorities and the wider community with regard to what ought to be 'a public function exercised for the general benefit'. The anti-Sabbatarians did their own lobbying of Parliament, though because of the strength of respectable opinion ranged against them, the Government proceeded carefully, simply setting up a Commission of Inquiry. This reported in August and proposed that Sunday postal work should be resumed since 'whatever the amount of relief afforded to the servants of the Post Office there can be no doubt that it has been obtained at great sacrifices to the convenience of the public'. Thus on 1 September 1850 the previous position was restored.[19]

This episode was revealing in a number of ways. It showed that the postal workers, though their grievances were real enough, did not have the strength or the ability yet to fight on their own behalf. It also showed that however respectable were their allies and however well organised their pressure groups, they could not get far if they tried to abolish the kind of postal service that was generally considered necessary.

Nevertheless, the question of Sunday postal labour did not disappear after the events of 1850. Under the terms of the new arrangements it was still possible to stop deliveries in an area where receivers of six-sevenths of the letters agreed. In 1857 the Sabbatarians set up an organisation called the Working Men's Lord's Day Rest Association, and postal workers sometimes made contributions to this because of its work in organising petitions to stop their Sunday labours. In 1866 they themselves were forbidden to canvas for these petitions, though in 1871 the proportion of receivers of letters who had to sign them was reduced to two-thirds. In 1887, only the vote of a local authority was necessary for such a step, and in 1889 arrangements were made so that all Post Office workers could have off at least one Sunday in two. By this period, according to Swift, although postal workers continued to demand a complete cessation of Sunday postal work, they got little support, even from the clergy.[20] However, there seems to have been little protest when a limited postal delivery was introduced in London in 1899, and soon after the Postmaster General himself began to put pressure on local authorities to end Sunday deliveries. When all Sunday deliveries were eventually suspended during the First World War, the unions simply made representations that there should be no wage cuts as a result.[21] By this time, the issues which once had raised such high passion were long since forgotten. They were even more remote in 1976, when the Post Office itself, for reasons of economy, abolished Sunday collections, at first against the objections of postal workers and many outsiders.

CHRISTMAS BOXES AND THE LONDON REORGANISATION: 1852–6

The defeat of the Sunday labour agitation in 1850 drove underground efforts to improve conditions in the Post Office but did not bring such efforts to an end. During the next few years, various sections of postal workers reacted against those schemes of the authorities that they disliked. They were able to make their views felt in ways that clearly indicated a secret network of communication, and rudimentary organisation.

The first important issue came up within months of the defeat of the Sunday labour agitation, when the authorities announced their intention of forbidding the solicitation of Christmas gratuities. Strong opposition from the London letter carriers compelled the abandonment of the proposal for the capital by August 1852. A series of 500 petitions originating from the Manchester office and mostly worded identically, followed by letters to the press and Parliamentary discussion, resulted in the whole idea being abandoned by the authorities early in 1853. This was the first indication of any organised network beyond the capital.[22] It was probably the impetus created by the campaign that led to a meeting of 500 letter carriers, stampers and messengers in London on 29 May 1853. Overwork and low pay were the main grievances complained of, and a committee was elected to decide on methods to ameliorate them. In Liverpool memorials were organised by the lower grades, mainly about the fact that none of them could earn more than £1 a week. Open propaganda about low pay was so successful in Glasgow that local merchants organised a fund to supplement the wages of the letter carriers.[23]

Further discontent followed the merging of the London and General postal services in 1855. Letter collections were introduced at 10.00 p.m. and only after protests were extra allowances given for the work involved. More generally, those who worked for the old General Post Office felt that they were losing status and rewards to those in the new district offices. There was also a loss of status for former clerks who became specialist sorters. There were also changes in grade structure in the provinces after the mid-1850s, resulting in further problems. The Manchester letter carriers continued to be active. They had claims for higher wages accepted by the local postmaster and supported by John Bright, leading Liberal and local MP, but they were blocked by the Treasury.[24]

In the following period there were further indications of the survival of clandestine organisation among the workers in London. In 1856 meetings were arranged in different parts of the capital at which clerks and sorters as well as letter carriers aired their grievances. On 4 February a new memorial was presented. The authorities replied by condemning the 'highly discreditable character' of one of the meetings that had formulated the memorial. They argued that the Treasury and not the Post Office was responsible for cuts in extra duty pay and for the universally unpopular system of promotion by merit. The postal authorities also said that wage increases would only come with the ending of all meetings of the men, emphasising this point with the suspension of two letter carriers for a fortnight. This put an end to public agitation for two years. To forestall further publicity a new regulation was promulgated in 1857 saying that grievances could not be ventilated 'through the public', in other words by petitions to Parliament. To make matters more difficult such petitions had to be submitted first to controllers within the Post Office.[25]

THE 'GENERAL COMMISSION AGENT' AND 'THE PHALLANX'

The late 1850s saw some definite development in organised efforts by the London postal workers. In the summer of 1858 there was a general revival of trade union activity, notably in the building industry, and the Post Office was not exempt. This time the postal workers were able to exert enough pressure to compel the authorities to negotiate with them and even to make some nominal concessions. The establishment of a permanent form of organisation was advocated publicly for the first time, but there did not yet exist the necessary resolve to bring it about. At this time there seem to have been two bodies in London advocating the interests of the postal workers. One, which issued statements over the name of 'The General Commission Agent', simply published accounts of the grievances of the various groups. The other body, known as 'The Phallanx', may well have existed secretly at least since 1856, and went well beyond the expression of discontent.[26]

The agitation of this period began when the letter carriers felt enough confidence to defy the authorities by holding a meeting at a public house called *The Hole in the Wall* and there deciding that since the presentation of memorials had achieved so little, they should now try to approach the Postmaster General directly. They applied through William Bokenham, who was now described as the Controller of the Circulation Department. To their surprise they were granted an interview with the Postmaster General, Lord Colchester, on 28 July 1858.

The letter carriers were represented by John Carter of the GPO, Secretary of the Committee, William Small of the North West District Office, its Chairman, together with two others who spoke for the South Western and North Western offices. For the official side at first there was only Colchester and his private secretary. This meeting can probably rank as the first piece of public sector bargaining in the history of British industrial relations. The grievances of the London letter carriers were listened to sympathetically and outlined in some detail.

> The insufficiency of salary for the support and maintenance of respectability; the intolerable pressure of the combined duty of letter carrier and sorter; the injustice of compelling men already overtasked to perform the duties of sick absentees, and that without any remuneration, the addition of night collections, which, according to the [1854] Commissioners report ought to be paid for as extra duty, the pecuniary losses entailed in the reduction of salary and the abolition of perquisites; the multiplication of deliveries without extra payment of any sort, and the contemptuous and tyrannical bearing of certain superior officers towards the general body of letter carriers.

At this stage Bokenham was summoned by Colchester and expressed the view that there was some substance to a number of these complaints.[27] It must have seemed to many postal workers that this might make the beginning of a new era in their relations with the authorities. On 21 August about 1,000 London letter carriers, virtually the entire force, met at the Pathenium Hall in St Martin's Lane. Great confidence was expressed in Lord Colchester and only a letter carrier called George Padfield drew attention to the fact that nothing had actually been promised, expressing himself 'much dissatisfied'. These fears did not prove groundless. Having applied the velvet glove with one hand, the authorities now presented a mailed fist on the other. It was suddenly decided 'that order and discipline must be maintained among the large number of men in the service of the Post Office, even . . . by the infliction of heavy punishment'.[28]

The interview with Colchester stimulated new hopes. Lists of grievances were drawn up and a further series of memorials were submitted from the provincial centres, where there were complaints of even lower salaries and fewer promotion prospects. The authorities replied by getting some of the senior letter carriers to publicise the fact that they earned higher wages than those mentioned in the memorials, and granting them extra increments after they did so. On 18 September a meeting of the South Western District letter carriers was held at the *Blue Coat Boy* in Victoria Street, Westminster. Here the usual grievances about pay and promotion were retailed and discontent expressed at the delay of the Postmaster General in replying to the points made by the delegation of 28 July. The behaviour of some of the supervising officers was also referred to and it was on this that the authorities suddenly seized.[29]

On 29 September a statement described as 'a thunderbolt' was issued over the signature of Bokenham, though clearly it originated from Rowland Hill himself. This attacked the South West District meeting for its failure to be 'open, manly and respectful', asserted that pay and conditions were in many cases good, and that some progress had been made in their improvement. Furthermore, 'if any repetition shall take place of the improper acts mentioned above the Postmaster General, looking to the necessity of maintaining perfect discipline in so large a body of men, will reluctantly be obliged to suspend all progress of the kind'. These threats were backed by the dismissal of John Martin, a letter carrier of nine years' standing who had chaired the meeting together with the suspension of John Carter who was Secretary of the Committee that organised the delegation to the PMG, and of William James, who played a prominent part in the meeting. Two others had to work for a month without pay, two for a fortnight, and two more had their pay reduced. Well-organised efforts were made to obtain the re-instatement of Martin, and a delegation of MPs, clergymen and army officers pleaded with Lord Colchester on his behalf in November. Colchester was unmoved, and in the end collections were organised for Martin and his family. Soon similar pressure had to be exercised on behalf of Carter, who was also eventually dismissed.[30]

In the face of this, the letter carriers acted with greater circumspection. They placed the advocacy of their case in the hands of another respectable middle-class outsider, John Lilwall, Secretary of the Early Closing Association, a body which tried with the backing of some of the owners of the larger London stores to persuade them all to close on Saturday afternoons.[31] Lilwall did not however prove an effective advocate for the postal workers. Towards the end of 1858 a new scheme of wages was published for the London service. This was 'so miserable and so complicated' that it was difficult to assess its significance at first. Although it increased the rate of pay at the top of the lowest scale to £1 5s (£1. 25) it also greatly lengthened the period of service necessary to obtain this total, and made promotion beyond it even more remote than before. On average the new arrangement amounted to a wage cut, and in 1860 it was calculated that only 99 of the lower-grade postal workers in London earned more than £2 a week, with 1,592 getting £1 3s (£1. 15) or less.[32]

Despite all these disappointments, the new rates did provide increases for some and, together with the general introduction of superannuation in 1859, provided a definite answer to the agitation of the men. Although the confirmation of the victimisation of Carter and Martin led to calls for the setting up of a 'Letter Carriers Union', such a step had become impossible in 1859. Many were convinced that Lilwall's efforts had proved quite ineffective. The provincial postal clerks, who at this time earned as little as 80p a week (£41. 60 per annum) and never more than £1. 50 (£76) also tried to make their conditions known, but without effect.[33]

THE TIMES AND THE 1860 COMMISSION OF INQUIRY

The revival of agitation in the Post Office in 1860 can be attributed, as so often in this period, to a force completely outside the workers themselves and in this case beyond the Department and the public service. Perhaps because of personal contact, or a delegation of the type that initiated the 1849 sabbatarian campaign, a 'Special Correspondent' wrote in *The Times* of 29 and 30 March 1860 about the wages and conditions at St Martin's-le-Grand, attacking 'the whole system being treated more as a source of revenue to the Government than as a necessary public convenience, to the really proper working of which the ordinary considerations of profit and loss should be in great measure subordinate'. Conditions had not changed at the GPO since it was built in 1829 despite the enormous expansion of work there. Because profitability was 'the chief object pursued' there had developed a 'system of so far underpaying the hands employed as to make them quite fearless of dismissal and indifferent to doing their work properly'.[34]

These accusations produced a flurry of activity in the higher reaches of the Post Office administration.[35] The problem was complicated by the fact that the current Postmaster General, Lord Elgin, spent most of his time abroad and the real power was in any case held by Rowland Hill who was seriously ill. Only in August was a new and more active Postmaster General appointed in the person of Lord Stanley, and he still relied heavily on Hill. Even on his sick bed Hill was no friend of the postal workers, and he continued to act through his brother to prevent as far as possible any improvement in their conditions. These factors help to explain the somewhat capricious, but generally hostile actions of the authorities in dealing with the charges of *The Times* articles and in handling the organised agitation of the men.

Within days of the appearance of the original complaints in *The Times*, the authorities decided to set up an internal Committee of Inquiry, not to remedy the defects complained of, but to try to prove them 'inaccurate'. The membership of the Committee included William Bokenham, Frank Ives Scudamore and Anthony Trollope. Its establishment did not meet with the approval of the Hill family who tried to prevent it doing anything at all without their prior approval. The Committee was thus suspended for a time, but 'expectations' were 'so greatly influenced by the articles in *The Times*' that the authorities realised that some further positive steps would have to be taken. As a result the Committee was re-established in early May with two Treasury representatives added, and a notice was published on the 11th, informing the men that their grievances had been taken up and they now had the 'duty of abstaining from any proceedings tending to agitation'.[36]

Already, however, such agitation was well under way. All the main London grades produced their own memorials during April. In the case of the GPO letter carriers this took the form of a printed pamphlet complaining of 'a large amount of extra labour' and declaring 'the present system of driving, needlessly irritating and hurrying the men through their duties to be positively detrimental to the service and degrading and hurtful to the feelings of the men'. They asked for a wage increase on a scale from £1 3s (£1. 15) to £2 a week. The 231 GPO sorters made a number of similar complaints about promotion and pay. Much of the discontent at the Chief Office in any case arose from the continuing feeling of diminished status since merging with the London service five years before.[37] This feeling was particularly marked among the sorters, who held the first of a series of meetings to draw attention to the grievances of the postal workers in a school-room in Aldersgate Street. They complained not simply that they were being paid much less for work formerly done by clerks. They also said that they were allowed no proper method of taking up their grievances. As if to prove the truth of these complaints, the authorities tried to prevent a meeting of the letter carriers on 14 May by the interesting expedient of offering bribes to those who had called it. Seven hundred letter carriers nevertheless met in defiance of official obstruction and prohibition, the Chairman asserting that 'a whole people cannot be guilty of treason'. However, when a somewhat smaller meeting of letter carriers was held at a school-room near Farringdon Street specifically in opposition to the merging of the two postal systems, then the authorities felt able to dismiss four letter carriers – James Waller, Charles Cooper, James Shaw and William Clerk. At this point there was talk again of setting up a more permanent organisation that 'would inspire their tormentors with a little wholesome dread' and allay the danger that arose from 'the localisation of the agitation'.[38]

During these events the Committee of Inquiry proceeded with its work. It heard evidence from the leaders of the men, including some who were later dismissed. Thus, James Shaw told the Committee of a particular 'driver' who 'walked about making a great deal of noise, bellowing about the place'. Another letter carrier agreed that supervision was necessary, but maintained that they could manage better without 'a set of petty bees buzzing about', who would be better employed 'among the working class'. The sorters also argued their case to the Committee. Some of the officials of the Circulation Department were compelled to admit that sorting had lately grown 'very laborious', and many were now physically incapable of performing it. After listening to 116 witnesses, the Committee produced a Report on 21 July which concluded that the dissatisfaction expressed to them was 'not without reasonable cause'. They had also been convinced that 'the work of the men has been materially increased of late' so as 'to entail on them an amount of mental and physical labour which they could not reasonably be expected to endure'. The only important grievances of the men which the Committee was not prepared to consider sympathetically were those associated with the merging of the different postal systems. However, they recommended promotion by seniority and a number of significant wage increases, including £1 a week at the minimum for established letter carriers as well as guaranteed promotion to the higher classes. They expressed themselves in favour 'without hesitation' of a large increase in expenditure on the grounds that the men were 'as a rule underpaid'. They presented a series of powerful arguments in defence of this proposition:

The unpopularity of the service, the difficulty of inducing efficient men to enter it, the still greater difficulty of inducing them to remain in it, notwithstanding the advantages of continual employment and future pension, are of themselves proof of the correctness of this assertion. We find that dismissal for negligence or misconduct has to a great extent lost its force as a punishment and that the average length of service of letter carriers does not exceed ten years.[39]

These conclusions were vigorously opposed by the senior Post Office authorities, particularly by Rowland Hill, who was soon sufficiently recovered from his illness to assert that the very setting up of the Committee 'sins against every principle of subordination'.[40] As a result, the recommendations of the Committee were never enacted. Furthermore, the Report was never published, though its general outline was widely known. A meeting of letter carriers and sorters on 5 September called for its publication. Although this meeting showed that the men had not been cowed by the June dismissals, no concrete action was proposed.

The meeting was soon followed by a sudden outburst of discontent on the part of GPO auxiliary letter carriers. In August various suburban letter carriers had been induced to come and work at St Martin's-le-Grand at the rate of 10s (50p) a week for performing various tasks in the morning and afternoon. They were also offered regular extra morning work which would usually give them a total of 16s (80p). They also had, and this is probably what weighed with most of them, the chance of promotion on to the permanent establishment starting at 18s (90p). On 7 September these men were suddenly informed that their services were no longer required in the mornings and their pay would be reduced to the basic 10s (50p). The immediate reaction of the auxiliary letter carriers was to repair as a body to the magistrate's court at the Mansion House determined to sue the authorities for breach of contract. The magistrate agreed that they had a 'substantial grievance' since 'it was next to impossible for a man to maintain himself on 10s a week except under conditions of privation'. However, after consulting the postal authorities he concluded that there was no actual obligation to pay the full 18s. All he could advise, therefore, was the presentation of a respectful memorial to Postmaster General Stanley. Without the backing of effective organisation, there was little that such actions could achieve in the face of official intransigence.[41]

The appointment of Stanley as PMG at this time made it seem possible that there might be a fresh approach, so the auxiliaries merged their grievances with the general agitation. A fresh memorial was presented to the new PMG calling for the publication of the Departmental Report, and Stanley agreed to meet a delegation on 13 September 1860 from 'The Committee' to discuss it. The delegation consisted of the Committee's Chairman John Richmond, the Secretary Llewelyn Tilley, together with Henry Hines and Joseph Roseman. They 'impressed upon his Lordship the necessity of considering and adopting, as far as lay in his power, the recommendations contained in the Commission's Report, more especially that portion respecting the increases in pay'. Stanley did not seek to deny the rumours about the contents of the Commission's Report, but asserted that improvements had followed it on such matters as the design of uniforms and claimed that all other questions were being considered by the Cabinet.[42] This second place of direct bargaining in the history of the Post Office did not represent any consistent change of heart on the part of the authorities, but rather hesitation of a new man in the job who was waiting for Rowland Hill to recover from his illness before knowing what attitude to take.

The agitation continued in the later part of 1860. This was despite the dismissals that had taken place in June, and a published reminder from the authorities of the ban introduced three years earlier against them communicating their grievances 'through the public'. Thus at the end of 1860 efforts to compel those who received Christmas boxes to give them back to the Controller for redistribution were successfully resisted both in Liverpool and in London. It was taking a long time, however, to get a reply to earlier representations, and on 28 January 1861 the same delegation saw Stanley again to complain of this. In the meantime, the men were given some reason to hope for their views to be taken seriously by the fact that new rules about promotion were issued which promised to take seniority into account. Other groups began to take up their grievances also. The hard-pressed Post Office railway clerks whose spells of duty, according to one doctor, were 'sufficient to ruin the strongest constitution', submitted a memorial in May 1861.

In the meantime, there was further discontent at official procrastination. On 20 June 1861, a public meeting was held under the chairmanship of George Bowyer, MP, of London sorters, letter carriers, messengers and others. This meeting heard accusations (which were substantially true) that Rowland Hill was delaying further consideration of their claims. There were indications of further steps in organisation among the postal workers, with a report on its work being presented by 'The Committee'. There was also a proposal from 'The Committee' expressed through its Chairman, John Richmond, that there should be a petition to Parliament drawn up, in defiance of the official ban. This was agreed, as also was the proposal that the main demand put forward should be for a pay scale for all that began at £1 5s (£1. 25) and rose without interruption to £2. Bowyer well summarised the dilemma facing the postal workers. 'The men had grievances, but if they were quiet, some men said they had no grievances, whereas if they took a constitutional mode of obtaining redress, that of bringing their grievances before their superiors, they were guilty of insubordination.'[43]

After the meeting there were signs of increasing public support for the postal workers. One magazine run by Charles Dickens outlined their grievances in relation to both wages and the right to meet, and complimented them for 'pleading not striking'. Elsewhere it was reported that the London letter carriers were 'as near to a strike as it is possible for employees of a Government department to be'.[44]

THE 1861 SETTLEMENT AND ITS CONSEQUENCES

It was in the face of these indications of growing discontent that the authorities announced their response to the agitation. During the delay of almost a year and a half, the Post Office chiefs reduced the original proposals of the Committee of Enquiry, and then the Treasury reduced these still further. Each of the main groups was to be divided into two classes. A hundred first class sorters were to get from £2 to £2-10-0 (£2. 50) a week, and 450 in the second class £1-4-0 (£1. 20) to £1-18-0 (£1. 90). Sixty first class messengers and stampers would earn £1-8-0 (£1. 40) to £1-15-0 (£1. 75) and 204 in the second class £1-1-0 (£1. 05) to £1-7-0 (£1. 35). Three hundred and fifty first class letter carriers were to receive from £1-6-0 (£1. 30) to £1-10-0 (£1. 50) with 960 in the second class getting from £1 to £1-5-0 (£1. 25). There would also be a fluctuating number of letter carriers getting 18/- (90p) a week.[45]

The publication of these rates was followed almost immediately on 21 August by a meeting of London Post Office workers. Everybody expressed dissatisfaction, especially the letter carriers, who were alarmed at the reintroduction of classes within their grade, particularly when this came in association with 'promotion by merit', which was also proposed. In any case, the new arrangements would have the effect of leaving the great majority of letter carriers with the same £1-5-0 (£1. 25) they had received before. As for the sorters, although they now got more at the bottom of the scale, they were offered nothing whatever near the top, where most of them were. The formation of a now permanent group of auxiliary letter carriers was seen as a threat to conditions in general. The auxiliary men themselves complained that they would be unable to pick up any of the extras to which they had formerly had access.[46] Although much dissatisfaction clearly remained, the agitation diminished in the winter of 1861. This was no doubt in part because there were many who obtained some improvement, and also because it must have been difficult to see how to proceed when all the channels thought to be open had been explored.

However, the London 'Committee' remained active, now seeking new methods of putting pressure on Parliament. On 27 March 1862 a mass meeting was held at the Exeter Hall when members of 'The Committee' complained that whatever improvements had been secured 'the greatest evil of all – that which renders our life better – is still unrequited; there has been no satisfactory increase of pay'. It was claimed that the letter carriers were now receiving less than they had in the 1830s and 1840s.[47]

After this meeting the postal workers took the only step that now remained open to them. They drew up a petition to Parliament, and pressed MPs to take up their case. They denounced the 'trifling concessions' of the August award, claimed that the public service was suffering from low wages, and asserted that the rewards given to the auxiliaries threatened to bring 'needy and disaffected men' into the service. After some effort, Bowyer got a Commons debate on these questions on 22 July 1862. He called for the setting up of a Select Committee on the grievances of postal workers, asserting that the penny post system was 'based upon the principle that the Post Office ought to be regarded as a department of the public service and the question of revenue should be a matter of secondary consideration'. He further maintained that 'the efficiency of the public service . . . could not be attained unless the men were liberally paid'.

The reply to Bowyer was given by the Chancellor of the Exchequer, none other than William Gladstone. He said that those involved were men 'of humble station and naturally inclined, like other men, to believe they were underpaid when they were told so'. He implied that they were discontented only because they 'found a gentleman of ability and character' prepared to take up their case. This somewhat low estimate of the ability of postal workers to think for themselves was followed by the usual arguments about the fringe benefits they enjoyed, an assertion that policemen were paid even less, and a defence of the failure to publish the 1860 Report. Despite its inadequate arguments, this reply was too powerful for Bowyer, who was persuaded to withdraw his motion. Soon *The Times* reverted to type by publishing a ritual attack on the greed and presumption of postal workers.[48]

Within a week of this Parliamentary debate, a meeting of the lower classes of letter carriers took place in London. George Padfield, who was the Chairman, replied to Gladstone's argument by pointing out that low pay elsewhere was no argument for the pittance received by postal workers. Padfield said, in words which were echoed in virtually all meetings of postal workers in this period: 'The great question for us now is better pay, for I believe it is the duty of every man in the world to try and benefit the class to which he belongs'. The meeting had no concrete proposals on how to proceed in achieving these aims, though everybody agreed with one speaker who argued in favour of 'carrying on the agitation in a temperate manner and of maintaining a respectful attitude towards superior officers'.[49]

However moderate their demeanour, very little could be achieved by the letter carriers without action of some kind. Thus in the following December a further petition was drawn up, and on 23 February 1863 there was another interview with the Postmaster General. Stanley had clearly recovered from his earlier period of uncertainty. He told the delegation of letter carriers 'that it was no use urging our claims on him', because they had 'a very liberal scale of wages and plenty of men were to be had for the money'. He also told them that he 'highly disapproved' of their public meetings.[50]

After this further rebuff, the organisation of London letter carriers was inactive for a time. This was no doubt because no other method of agitation seemed open to them, and perhaps also because they were waiting to see the results of the efforts of other postal workers to improve their lot. The London postal clerks, who had previously set up a committee and submitted a memorial in 1860, re-established a rudimentary organisation in October 1862 and a fund. Their main grievance was inaccessibility to promotion and they held meetings on Post Office premises to ventilate it. They sent a delegation to see Stanley on 10 February 1863, just before the letter carriers, but also without any success.[51] The long-suffering travelling sorters also arranged a memorial and obtained some increases in pay, but only at the same time as a reduction in their allowances for the trips they made. They also met Stanley to complain, again without success.[52] There was also some agitation by the Birmingham letter carriers, which seems to have continued throughout the 1860s. Numerous memorials were presented, surveyors met delegations of the men and local publicity was given to their grievances. There was some co-operation with the sabbatarians, apparently with little effect. It was no doubt the result of such continuous pressure, however, that in 1872 the wages of Birmingham letter carriers were fixed at 18s (90p) to £1 5s (£1. 25) per week – rather higher than most of their provincial colleagues.[53]

THE LAST YEARS OF THE LONDON 'COMMITTEE': 1866–9

The main initiative for agitation by the Post Office workers remained in this period in the hands of the London men, especially the letter carriers. In the late 1860s, they again took up their grievances in the traditional way, through a semi-clandestine 'Committee', which however achieved little beyond the victimisation of those who organised it. After this, every agitation, whether successful or not, aimed to set up a permanent trade union organisation.

Although there was a lull in the London agitation during 1863 and 1864, 'The Committee' probably remained in existence. Thus there was no problem at all in calling together a new meeting on 24 November 1864 to draw up a new memorial for the Postmaster General, largely on pay. This was presented in the following January and in March Stanley replied that their remuneration had been 'finally settled' already. A meeting of letter carriers on 23 March 1865 elected a new committee to propose their next move. In November another meeting was held; a further memorial was drawn up, but this also was rejected. By now, however, prices had risen significantly since the previous settlement and, furthermore, 'nearly every other class of worker had an advance of wages' as a result of 'a general upheaval of trades throughout the country'. Thus, in January 1866, a new committee was elected, including sorters and stampers as well as letter carriers.[54]

In the following month the agitation inspired a Parliamentary question from future Postmaster General Henry Fawcett, to ask why their pay had not been increased. The reply, once again by Gladstone, simply referred to the scales fixed in 1861, and stated that people could still be found to do the work. At this point the authorities decided to retaliate. Not only did Stanley use the opportunity to promulgate the ban on outside meetings that was used against virtually every other claim for improvement for the next twenty-five years. He also dismissed from the service George Padfield, who had been a letter carrier in London for thirteen years, and prominent during this period in every agitation.[55] Nor was the punishment of Padfield an isolated incident. Similar treatment was meted out in the Scottish borders. Three messengers of Hawick in Roxburghshire were dismissed from the service in the following May for organising the circulation of memorials throughout the whole of Scotland. Their crime, according to the authorities, was that they acted 'collectively instead of individually'. They were called James Peterson, William Adamson and George Scott, and their respective weekly earnings were 14s 6d (72½p), 14s (70p) and 9s (45p). These were hardly princely sums even for 1866![56]

One result of all this was that postal workers became more secretive. It thus becomes more difficult to discover how they were organised in the next period. What is certain, however, is that they continued during 1867 to discuss how to proceed. Discontent was 'already too rife throughout the Service' for any abatement of the agitation, the workers throughout the land were securing 'increased pay and shorter hours' while 'the persistent course of the postal authorities has been in the opposite direction'.[57] On 1 August the London letter carriers, by means of one of their number who had a small printing press, produced the first issue of a paper called *The Postman*. This aimed to win the support of 'the true-hearted and tyrant hating masses of the population' to the cause not only of the letter carriers of London, but also of the provincial messengers, sorters and others.[58]

Just over a month later, on 9 September, 'an enthusiastic meeting of letter carriers' was held at St Martin's-le-Grand. On 16 December a group of respectable supporters was wheeled out for a public meeting at the Exeter Hall. The assemblage of course defied the official ban, so the only recorded speeches came from various members of the clergy who argued that postal workers were 'insufficiently paid' for those 'of such a high class, morally, religiously and educationally' and called for a 'special commission . . . to enquire into the statements of the men'.[59] The need for caution was reinforced by the dismissal soon afterwards of three clerks called Sager, Lucy and Witherton from the registered letter office. The charge against them was that they had shown 'the appearance of insubordination' by organising a memorial about their grievances.

Soon after this, the formation of a Liberal Government nurtured hopes that there might be a change of policy. A further petition was presented to Parliament, but without effect. Further discontent was provoked by the granting of some increases to a few senior letter carriers and to the senior officials of the Department. At this point 'The Committee' decided to issue a public statement exposing this and setting out the remaining demands including increased pay, better access to promotion and the abolition of Sunday work. This was issued over the name of James Johnson, Secretary of 'The Committee' in the name of a 'Post Office Employees Agitation Committee'. It was published in at least sixty-two different newspapers. The authorities could not afford to ignore this, and the new Liberal Postmaster General Lord Hartington showed himself no less repressive than his Conservative predecessors. James Johnson was summarily dismissed, on the grounds that his statement had been 'calculated to subvert all discipline and authority', and all the other members of 'The Committee' were told that they would suffer the same fate if they did anything to help him. An appeal on behalf of Johnson was signed by a number of London MPs, but he had to walk the streets for eight months looking for work and sustained only by £40 collected by his workmates.[60]

This event brought to an end one phase in the development of organisation and agitation among Post Office workers. The necessarily secretive methods of the Post Office had been supplemented by informal contacts, and organised by a series of 'committees' with various forms and titles, but clearly supported by those whom they represented. These methods had some achievements to their credit. There was the retention of Christmas boxes in 1853, the London improvements of 1861, and the relatively good position in Birmingham. However, all that the Post Office workers could do was to ask for improvements and protest when they were not granted. Every new agitation had its toll of dismissals, suspensions and loss of promotion prospects by those who took a prominent part. Clearly, better means had to be found.

The early 1870s saw a new spirit and new methods. The working-class movement as a whole grew more militant and more active. The postal workers were joined in 1870 by the telegraphists, who were not hidebound by civil service prejudices, and did not hold back from aggressive Parliamentary lobbying and even strike action. Thus in the next period both external and internal pressures acted to direct the Post Office workers to different more effective methods of confronting the authorities and improving their conditions.

NOTES

1 Bagwell (1974), p. 155; Swift (1929).
2 Ken Thomas of the Civil and Public Services Association in *The Times* (1 June 1976). Many such incidents from outside the Post Office in the nineteenth century are described in Humphreys (1958).
3 POR 30E 68TT/1841.
4 The investigation is in the various papers in PP 1846 XLV (p. 55 for the quotation) and *Hansard* III, 81 1319–72 (27 June 1845) is Duncombe's statement. The most coherent published summary is by G. H. Stuart-Bunning in *Post* (30 September 1944), pp. 360–1.
5 *Lloyd's Weekly London Newspaper* (20 July 1845); *Sentinal Weekly Newspaper* (28 December 1845). There is some additional material on these events in POR 30E 3150A/1848.
6 *John Bull* (16 May 1846); *Morning Chronicle* (1 August 1946). Other instances of 'insubordination' and the rest of the story up to the dismissal of Grapes can be traced in PP 1846 XLV. See PP 1847 LXII for the dismissal.
7 Other efforts to disentangle this complex story can be found in *PG* 1917, pp. 322–4, *Post* 1953, p. 645 and 1954, pp. 5, 37, 159 as well as in Martinuzzi (1952), pp. 34–45. The case for the men is further stated by Duncombe in *Hansard* III, 88, 955–61 (22 August 1846) and 94, 593–7 (20 July 1847).
8 PP 1852-3 XCV gives the Edinburgh memorials together with comments on them by the authorities (pp. 30–1 for the quotation). See also POR 60/10, *Postal and Telegraph Record*, 17 September 1914, p. 442, and *Post* 1951, pp. 203, 229.
9 The Minutes of the Society and its other records were kindly made available to me by the Secretary Mr H. J. W. Legerton. I have covered what follows in more detail in an unpublished paper called 'The failure of Victorian Sabbatarianism' (1977). Some contemporary sources are collected and printed in a series of articles by Smith (1955).
10 Granville (1850), p. 4; *Patriot* (22 October 1849).
11 On the Scottish campaign see Scott (1972), pp. 182–3 and Haldane (1971), p. 139. Details of how the London campaign was organised can be seen in the Lords Day Society Minutes II, pp. 208, 217–9 (26 October and 27 November 1838). Memorials from stockbrokers, bankers, lawyers and others are in PP 1839 XLVI and 1841 XXVI. See also PP 1837 L, pp. 303–5. The quotation is from a petition in MC.
12 LDS *Quarterly Publication*, July 1846.
13 *ibid.* January 1848; PP 1850 XX (Papers Respecting the Reduction of Sunday Labour), pp. 4, 26.
14 *Patriot* (7 October 1849); *Post Office Sabbath Slavery* (Flysheet of 29 September in MC); *Times* (9 October 1849).
15 Hill and Hill (1880) Vol. 2, p. 455; *Patriot* (1, 4, 8 October 1849); *Bell's Weekly Messenger* (10 and 24 November 1849). Swift (1929), pp. 16–18 is most inaccurate on these events.
16 Hill and Hill (1880), pp. 121–36; Clanricarde to Russell 24 October 1849 (POR 30/22/8B); *Bell's Weekly Messenger* (3 November 1849); *Patriot* (24 December 1849).
17 PP 1850 XX (Papers Respecting the Reduction of Sunday Labour), pp. 4–5, 13–18; Vaughan (1849), p. 4 (with original emphasis).
18 For details of the campaign see *Times* (9 October 1849, 18, 19 February 1850); *Patriot* (1 November 1849, 18 February 1850) and Alford (1850), p. 8. For the debate, *Hansard* III, 111, 466–85 (30 May 1850).
19 Lord's Day Society 19th Annual Report (1850), p. 21; *Illustrated London News* 29 June; 6, 13, 20, and 27 July; 10 August 1850; *Hansard* III, 112, 221–2 (24 June 1850); 326–27 (25 June); 1190–1917 (9 July) and 113, 1077–8 (15 August); PP 1850 XX (Report of the Commissioners). *Times* (11 July 1850) gives details of the political manoeuvring.
20 Working Men's Lord's Day Rest Association 9th Annual Report (1866) and *The Hardships of the Provincial Letter Carriers* (n.d.). *Birmingham Daily Post* (15 March 1865) for an example of co-operation between sabbatarians and postal workers. POC 2 April 1866 for details of the change. See also PP 1872 XVIII (Report on Sunday Labour); PP 1887 XII (Report from the Select Committee on Sunday Postal Labour) and Swift (1929), pp. 73–4.
21 Hosden (1899); *Express* (19 May 1907); *Postal and Telegraph Record* (15 March 1917).
22 *CSG* 19 and 26 February 1853; 4 September, 2 October 1858; *Hansard* III, 124, 841–51 (1 March 1853) and 126, 156–7 (21 March). The petitions are in PP 1852-3 XCV.
23 *CSG* 4 and 19 June 1853; 11 June on Liverpool and 12, 19 November on Glasgow.
24 On the Elcho re-organisation see Chapter 3, pp. 52. Developments in this period can be traced

in *CSG* (28 August 1858) and PMG 5th Report for 1858, pp. 72–4. On Manchester see POR 30E 4472/1857.

25 *CSG* (13 November 1855 and 13 April 1861).

26 Details of the activities of both can be found in *CSG*.

27 *CSG* (31 July 1858). There is also an account of the interview in the *Illustrated Times* of 14 August 1858, where it is said that Bokenham was 'repeatedly expressing his astonishment' at statements made by the delegation.

28 *CSG* (21 August 1858); PMG 6th Report for 1859, p. 39.

29 *CSG* (25 September 1858). Swift (1929), p. 35, refers to this meeting as if it was the only event of postal agitation in that year.

30 The 'thunderbolt' is in PMG 5th Report for 1858, pp. 40–1 and the disciplinary proceedings and what followed are described in *CSG*, 9, 30 October; 27 November; 4, 25 December 1858 and 14 May 1860.

31 On Lilwall and his movement see Whitaker (1973), pp. 49ff.

32 Lilwall's statements are in *CSG*, 16 October 1858 and later. The new scale is in PMG 5th Report for 1858, pp. 41–2 and the first reaction of those receiving it in *CSG*, 11 December 1858. *Times* (30 March 1860) assumed that the overall effect was to reduce wages, and Smee (1860) gives details.

33 Statements by early advocates of a Letter Carriers Union are in *CSG*, 11, 25 December 1858, on provincial clerks 5 February 1859 and on disappointment with Lilwall 23 June 1859.

34 UPW (1950) gives some further quotations from the *Times*, somewhat uncharacteristic then or since. A similarly sympathetic account is in *Fun*, 28 April 1866.

35 Details can be found in POR 30E 4801/1861, II. The papers there also give a full account of the Committee of Inquiry which followed, including its printed but unpublished evidence and report.

36 *ibid*, III, IV.

37 *ibid*, IV, and above, pp. 31, 104.

38 This account and all the quotations are in *CSG*, 12, 19 May, 9, 16 and 30 June 1860.

39 POR 30E 4801/1861 VIII: Minutes of Evidence taken before the Committee appointed to inquire into the Internal Arrangements of the Circulation Department of the GPO (1860), pp. 24, 23, 50, 188, 192, 240, and 277, and Report upon the Circulation Department of the General Post Office (21 July 1860), pp. 4, 8, 9 and 26.

40 From a letter of 21 February 1861 in the same file.

41 *CSG* (8, 15 September 1860). The incident was also reported in *The Times* of 12 September, where it provoked the outburst quoted at the head of the chapter.

42 *CSG* (29 September 1860).

43 *CSG* 22 September 1860, 2 February, 15, 22 June 1861. On the railway clerks, see the issues of 28 October and 22 June.

44 *All the Year Round* (13 July 1861) and *Saturday Review* (27 July 1861).

45 POR 30E 4801/1861 VIII for the details, including the negotiations between the Treasury and the Department. *Post* (5 May 1894) gives a slightly later version of the settlement.

46 *CSG* (24 August 1861).

47 *Standard* (31 March 1862).

48 *Hansard* III, 168, 672–80 (22 July 1862) for the debate and Chapter 4 p. 80 for another account of the significance of Gladstone's remarks. The attack on the postal workers is in *The Times* (25 July 1862), and there is another in the *Daily Telegraph* (10 November 1862).

49 *CSG* (2 August 1863).

50 *CSG* (13 December 1862, 28 February 1863).

51 For an account of organisation among the clerks in this period see *CSG*, 20 December 1862 and 14 February 1863. On later efforts among various other groups, 25 April, 9 May and 4 July 1863. Their provincial equivalents were less active, but had similar grievances; see *CSG*, 26 March and 13 August 1864, where a 'Union of Post Office Clerks' is advocated.

52 *CSG* (1, 8 April 1865).

53 There are numerous examples of this pressure in *CSG*, for example of 5 September 1863, 21, 28 January, 4 February, 25 November 1865, 2, 30 June, 7 July 1866, 5 October, 2 November 1867. See also Working Man Lord's Day Rest Association Eighth Annual Report (1866), p. 15; *Birmingham Daily News* (12 July 1871), where it is claimed that conditions are worse than in most other provincial centres and *Birmingham Daily Mail* (18 May 1872). POR 30E 3765/1872 gives details of the agitation of that year and the settlement that followed it.

54 *CSG* 30 January 1864 on a petition for Parliament and 23 July on the inactivity of the Committee. *B-H* 25 March 1865 on the March meeting, *CSG* 18 November 1865 on the November one; *B-H*

16 December 1865 on the general labour situation, 27 January 1866 for the fullest account of the January meeting. MC has a 'Circular Memorandum' of 22 April 1865 apparently in response, which claims various improvements since 1861, but all they seem to amount to is a slight increase in the number of sorters on the higher scale.

55 *Hansard* III, 181, 961–2 (23 February 1866); POC, 13 March 1866; *CSG* (21 April, 12 May 1866); Swift (1929), pp. 37–8. See also Chapter 4, p. 82, above. According to POR 65/3 pp. 11–12, written in 1905, Padfield later got his job back, and William Booth and another letter carrier were admonished.

56 *Hawick Advertiser* (9 June 1866).

57 *CSG* (7 August, 2 November 1867).

58 Swift (1929), p. 70. There is a copy of this first issue in BL, and *B-H* 14 September 1867 quotes a later one.

59 *B-H* (14 September 1867); *CSG* (21 December 1867).

60 *London Review* (29 February 1868); *CSG* 26 March 1868, 23 January, 13 February 1869; *B-H* 26 December 1868, gives the Agitation Committee statement. *Post* 22 January 1921, pp. 82–3, gives details on the dismissal of Johnson, and 30 April 1921, p. 435, gives a moving account by Johnson himself who was, amazingly, still alive over fifty years later and living in Luton.

6 Founding the Associations: 1870–1891

The Union is taking shape and form and must be crippled at any cost. (The Postmaster of Manchester to F. I. Scudamore, 20 November 1871, POR 30E 274/1872 II)

Every new adherent to Unionism is one more addition to the Army of Labour, and brings us one step nearer a State of Society when each shall work for all and all for each. (*Postman's Gazette* (first series), April 1890)

Is the Hon. Gentleman [PMG Raikes] aware that the ancient contention of the employers of this country was that they should settle their disputes with their workmen, without the interposition of the Secretary of a Trades Union? There were continually conflicts in consequence; but since the employers of Labour have taken the more common-sense plan for discussing these matters with the Secretary of the Union, there has been much peace. (Samuel Storey, MP for Sunderland, *Hansard* III, 345, 1139, 17 June 1890)

During the first thirty years of the penny post, from 1840 to 1870, when Post Office workers tried to improve their wages and conditions, they rarely even considered the possibility of setting up organisations with a continuous and public existence. As has been shown, during that period they ceaselessly publicised their complaints, drew up memorials, and approached MPs and many other possible patrons or supporters. They operated on the assumption that by these means they could achieve once and for all a settlement of their complaints. In the two decades following 1870, there was a different attitude. Every agitation now included the aim of setting up a stable and permanent association which could mobilise support, avoid persecution, and generally deal more effectively with the authorities. Between 1870 and 1891, all the methods of trade unionism were tried, including a number of strikes, and by the end of the period the forms of trade unionism had been adopted by all the main grades.

The Post Office workers changed their methods of pursuing their grievances partly because servile memorials and friendly MPs did not serve them well. However, they seem usually to have forgotten the mistakes, and even the successes, of their predecessors. What most induced them to change their ways was probably the force of outside example, the great struggles in the early 1870s by gas stokers, farm labourers and many others. They were no doubt also influenced by the beginning of the TUC in 1868 and the full legal recognition of trade unionism in 1871. When the trade union movement passed through a lean period in the late 1870s, Post Office agitation faltered also. After the successful dockers' strike of

1889, the London postmen tried to follow their example. The direction of agitation was also altered by the arrival in the service in 1870 of the telegraphists, who were uninhibited by the traditions of civil service decorum. It was their particular grievances that brought about the first strike in 1871, and led to the setting up of the first permanent association ten years later. Others soon followed their example.

THE ENTRY OF THE TELEGRAPHISTS AND THE FIRST STRIKE: 1870-1

The telegraphists did not fit easily into the Post Office structure and hierarchy when they first entered the service.[1] They had not been well treated when the companies were waiting for nationalisation, and they never considered that their high social status and special skills were recognised by those in authority who had formerly been in charge of postal matters. They were, thought Swift, 'often men of birth and education . . . an independent, Bohemian lot'.[2] They could also, in a unique way, communicate with one another while at work which meant, amongst other things, that their agitation did not need to centre on London. They were, however, just as much affected as their colleagues in the postal service by developments in trade unionism generally. As early as 1863, they showed their propensity to combine by establishing a Telegraph Clerks Provident Fund to which women were admitted on equal terms with men.

In 1866, efforts were made by employees of three of the companies in Manchester to set up a form of trade union organisation. A Central Committee was established by the Manchester offices for a Telegraph Clerks Association intended to cover the entire country, an arrangement common in the trade union movement in that period, and later used by the associations of telegraphists in the PTCA and UKPCA. A meeting took place on 13 October 1866 at which a number of offices were represented. The Secretary of one of the private companies at the time wrote that if he could discover who was running the Central Committee, he would have them dismissed and blacklisted. Two telegraph clerks, called Robey and Bradford, were in any case dismissed. The Central Committee and whatever organisation lay behind it then seems to have fizzled out. In later years there was a legend about a walk-out against an unpopular supervisor in this period, though the incident cannot be traced in the records of the time.[3]

During the next few years, the most important questions relating to the conditions of the telegraphists arose from the preparation of the nationalisation of 1870, and the way it was carried out. Inevitably this involved a degree of standardisation that was irksome for those who had worked for the companies. The financial problems of the system also led to a regime of cheeseparing that made F. I. Scudamore, architect of the new system as well as of the grading of the telegraphists, as unpopular in his way as Rowland Hill had been in previous generations.

Soon after nationalisation, memorials were presented asking for a fixed length of the working day, payment for overtime, and a scheme of grading to put telegraphists on the same footing as second division clerks. During the long period that followed without any reply, a group of Manchester telegraphists approached solicitors about whether they were likely to be covered by the Trade Union Bill then going through Parliament. Having decided that they would, they called a meeting for 21 October 1871, with a view to setting up a Union of Postal Telegraph Clerks on the same lines as in 1866.[4] The meeting was chaired by Frederick Heald, and the other moving spirits included T. W. Mulholland.

During the following month Scudamore began to receive reports from postmasters in various parts of the country of which the statement from the Postmaster of Manchester quoted at the head of the chapter is typical. More women were appointed at various offices, and the military authorities were contacted. These measures were aimed at providing blacklegs in the event of any possible strike action. In the meantime, messages between the different offices were intercepted by the authorities as they tried to unearth details of the growth of the organisation. They must have been alarmed at what they discovered. On 21 November, at Manchester, a telegraphist told his colleague in Liverpool during a lull in the transmission of normal messages: '130 in MR [Manchester] alone. Good general meeting this evening I heard . . . they can't do much to us now, we are too strong.'[5]

It was at this point that letters began to appear in the London *Standard* and elsewhere, partly referring to the great delay in setting the pay and status of telegraphists, and partly to disagreements alleged to be developing between Scudamore and his colleagues about the classification scheme he was preparing. On 7 December, Heald, Mulholland and others were summoned to the office of the Manchester telegraph supervisor and asked for details of the new organisation. They would say nothing. The supervisor then suspended nine of their number. At this point, as Heald later wrote, the other telegraphists

> flocked to our Committee rooms and determined to strike – not for better pay – not for less hours – but as a protest against the arbitrary action of the Department and in support of their elected Committee . . . We did not contemplate a strike, the blind fatuous policy of the Department caused it.

Two days later, 116 of them were out. After similarly provocative action by the authorities in other offices, including further suspensions and the threatened use of the notorious Master and Servant Act, about eighty men came out at Liverpool, sixty at Glasgow, and others at Bradford, Edinburgh, Dublin and Cork.[6]

Scudamore claimed that his actions so far were motivated by a desire to protect the inviolability of telegraph messages. This was soon thrown into question by his next action, delaying press telegrams out of Manchester on the night of the first suspensions giving news of the walk-out. Scudamore was vigorously denounced in the newspapers for this, and publicly reprimanded by the Postmaster General. He was nevertheless successful in his short-term purpose of depriving potential strikers of information about the causes of and support for the original walk-out.[7] As a result, although the strike remained solid in the original offices, it did not spread beyond them. In Dublin a group of women telegraphists who had not been expected to take any part, refused at any rate to work next to the group of soldier blacklegs sent to their office. However, this was the last incident to encourage the strikers. Nothing at all happened in London, and the Leeds telegraphists ignored appeals for support, even financial, being described as a result as 'damned measly skunks and naught else'. Although after appeals were issued to the trade union movement, and the strikers won the support of the TUC, local trade union officials thought telegraphists 'a species of nondescripts requiring careful handling'. In any case, the leaders of the month-old association, despite the accusations of the authorities, had never intended to organise a strike, and had neither the resources nor the resolve needed to do so now. Soon 219 were under notice of dismissal, including those who had originally been suspended. The strikers then began to appeal for their jobs back, and all who did so were successful, though many lost wages and promotion, and in some cases were 'exiled' to smaller offices or to London where they were subject to close supervision by unsympathetic colleagues.[8]

Although in the short term the strike was disastrous, it provided an impetus and a memory on which future action was based. In August 1872 a classification scheme was at long last introduced which set very low rates of pay, as little as £54 per annum in the provinces and £65 in London. Nothing of the claim for clerical status was conceded and a very divisive system of payment was put into effect.[9] Less than two years later, the telegraphists at the Liverpool office took the initiative in preparing evidence to the Playfair Committee on the Civil Service to support their claim for higher status. Though they collected lists of demands from all around the country, they resisted strong pressure from other areas to announce the establishment of a permanent organisation. When the evidence was not even heard, the entire movement fizzled out.[10]

During the rest of the 1870s, the telegraphists were caught in a loss-making system, overshadowed by the failure of their 1871 strike. However, if telegraphy was unprofitable in Britain, few if any networks elsewhere in the world were any more successful from that point of view. There is even some evidence that, on such measures of efficiency as the percentage of total expenditure of total revenue, the British system was actually improving in this period. In many cases, losses of the telegraph system were not particularly unpopular with those who benefited from the low tariffs, most notably the press. The pressure came for even lower charges, and they compounded the long-term loss making of the service after their introduction in 1885.[11]

THE BOOTH AGITATION AND THE WARRINGTON AND HUDDERSFIELD STRIKES: 1872–4

The next episode in Post Office agitation came from the postal side, and was characterised by an explicit adoption of the forms and methods of trade unionism. The extent to which the letter carriers and sorters in London paid attention to the activities of the much superior telegraphists is not easy to determine, but in the early 1870s they had plenty of other examples about them of new organisations that fought for and won the right to bargain with their employers. The London postal workers also had a remarkable leader in William Booth, a letter carrier at the Chief Office, who organised a campaign that won significant concessions from the authorities, pointing the way to even more effective methods to future generations. In Huddersfield, the letter carriers were rather less successful in expressing their resentment that during a time of boom in the surrounding factories, they were not able to receive any of the same benefits as their equivalents in private employment.

In May 1872, a meeting of London letter carriers and sorters agreed to set up the 'United Kingdom General Post Office and Telegraph Benefit Society'. Although this body never constituted more than a tiny proportion of the postal workforce, and did not include telegraphists at all, it nevertheless represented a pioneering effort to bring together Post Office workers as a whole on a permanent basis. The Benefit

Society for the first time tried to emulate the actions of trade unionists outside the
Post Office, and also sought their co-operation. It initiated what was by far the most
well organised and effective effort on behalf of those who worked for the Post Office
up to that time. Although Post Office workers retained many illusions about their
special status, it was becoming more obvious that their conditions bore an increasingly close relationship to those of other workers. In 1873 the Postmaster General
was compelled to grant wage increases 'owing to a general increase in the payment
for labour'. Thus it was becoming evident to many of those involved that 'had there
been no outside agency at work in addition to their own, such great results would
not have been achieved'.[12] Not only did postal workers discover the need to organise
themselves in a manner more akin to trade unionism, they also sought the assistance
of trade unionists outside the civil service. As they grew more powerful and
confident, their superiors in civil service and Government felt it necessary to assert
a countervailing authority. Conflict inevitably followed.

On 15 April 1870, Good Friday, there was a 'lecture' announced for the 'social
intercourse' of Post Office workers at the much frequented school-room in
Aldersgate Street. What was significant about this meeting was not so much the
circumlocution in its description, aimed to avoid the 1866 ban, as the presence of
Robert Applegarth, Secretary of the Amalgamated Society of Carpenters and
Joiners, at the time one of the best known trade unionists in the land. He spoke in
support of the right of his audience to 'meet in a calm, dignified and respectful
manner . . . in the same way that other men did', asserting that otherwise,
Government employees 'would be in a worse position than bricklayers labourers, or
agricultural labourers'. Both of these groups, who might have been thought to have
a lower social status than letter carriers or sorters, had recently compelled some of
their employers to bargain with them. Applegarth's introduction was followed by a
'lecture' from William Booth on the position of the letter carriers in which he
complained of their 'low pay, Sunday work and slow process of promotion'.[13]

It was some time before a further meeting along the same lines could be
organised, but relations with the trade union movement had nevertheless been
established. Later in 1870, as one success after another was recorded by the
organised efforts of other groups of workers, an appeal was issued through the trade
union movement complaining of 'the hardships of the letter carriers of England'.
These included the particularly low pay of auxiliaries, the heavy labours of rural
messengers, and the creation of the boy sorters grade. The Postmaster General, the
Marquis of Hartington, declared this rising tide of discontent to be 'pure invention',
and 'an aspersion on a well conducted class of public servants'.[14] Whatever the views
of those in authority, it was only a matter of months before the London letter
carriers were well enough organised to present a series of identically worded
petitions complaining that 'our present salaries are inadequate'. They called for an
increase of 10 per cent for all and the restoration of promotion by seniority. A series
of similar appeals followed from suburban and auxiliary letter carriers, and also
from some sorters.[15]

It was at this point that for the first time in the thirty-year history of agitation by
letter carriers the initiative shifted from London to the provinces. Strikes by miners,
agricultural workers and many others had forced up pay throughout the country,
especially in northern industrial areas. This naturally affected the poorer groups of
Post Office workers. In January 1872, fourteen auxiliary letter carriers at
Warrington went on strike to demand an increase in their weekly pay from 14s to

18s (70p to 90p).[16] However, they foolishly gave three days' notice of their intention to strike, giving the authorities time to dismiss them and to import blacklegs from London. Strikers lost their jobs, but those taken on to replace them were paid 16s (80p) and their demands were soon heard elsewhere. Also, a good deal more notice began to be taken of them. Thus when a memorial was soon afterwards submitted in Manchester, increases of 3s (15p) were granted at the lowest point on the scale, on a much less divisive basis than was usually the case in such arrangements.[17] However, it was at Huddersfield that there took place a much more dramatic dispute with more far-reaching results. The main cause of the Huddersfield strike was the provocative action of the authorities, but it clearly resulted from similar action by many other groups of workers in the same part of the country who had pushed wages and conditions to a much higher level than in the Post Office. The failure of the Huddersfield letter carriers to achieve the same results emphasised the distance that postal workers still had to travel in comparison to those with similar rewards but less authoritarian employers.[18]

On 8 May 1872, the fifteen town letter carriers of Huddersfield submitted a memorial asking for an increase in their wages from the 14–18s (70–90p) they currently earned. They said this placed them below 'the lowest of the workmen and artisan class'. In discussing this request, the authorities, both local and national, were prepared to admit privately that 'prices of almost every article to consumption have risen since the last application', and the wages of most comparable workers were increasing also. However, they turned down the request, along with a similar one from the eight rural and auxiliary men. They hoped that the price rises would only be temporary, and feared that a concession would mean that other claims from northern industrial towns 'could not long be resisted'.

On 28 May, the Huddersfield letter carriers held a meeting, reported in the local press, at which it was asserted that 'if their employers wished them to be honest and respectable, they must pay them wages which enabled them to sustain themselves as other men did'. The meeting also agreed to strike action, though only in the event of the victimisation of anybody who had participated in it. Against the strong advice of the local postmaster, the London authorities decided to prepare for any such event by sending a group of metropolitan letter carriers to Huddersfield. On 3 June the local postmaster discovered that the chief letter carrier, called Royston, had chaired the recent meeting and decided to suspend him. It was precisely at this moment that the potential blacklegs arrived from London, and this naturally alarmed the remaining Huddersfield men. Seeing the departure of Royston as a portent of how they themselves would be treated, they decided 'it would be more to our credit and honour to withdraw our services than to be dismissed forthwith'. Thus very early on the morning of 4 June, all the letter carriers went on strike. They issued a call to other workers for support, on the grounds that the imported men were already 'prepared to take our places . . .; we appeal to you, could you? would you? submit to such treatment'.

The local press, which was not particularly sympathetic to the strikers, reported that the blacklegs did not perform their jobs with much efficiency at first. However, the authorities were determined that those who walked out would never return, with the exception of an individual by the name of George Fawthorpe who provided information about the actions of his colleagues. Despite considerable difficulty in maintaining the postal service of Huddersfield for the rest of 1872, and the need to search for much more highly paid replacements as far afield as Ireland, none of the twenty-two strikers ever got their jobs back. The London blacklegs were still in Huddersfield in November, and the total proceedings cost the authorities not less than an additional £1,000. This was a high price to pay for temporary success in an effort to establish the principle of permanent subordination.

In London in the meantime, the men were proceeding with less militancy, though with just as much resolve. On 17 May 1872 the inaugural meeting of the Benefit Society took place at the Borough Road Congregational Church. The Secretary was Edward Hawkin, a letter carrier dismissed from the service during a previous agitation and the Executive included James Johnson, who had been similarly treated. Nominal posts were held by various sympathetic MPs like Charles Dilke and established trade union leaders like William Allan and George Potter.[19] The real moving spirit was William Booth, who visited the various offices in London and the provinces to gather support, under the watchful eye of the authorities.[20]

Initially, it was elected representatives of the various London offices who organised a memorial and a 'Committee' of their own numbers in the same form as in the 1860s. The authorities were prepared to accept this, and Postmaster General Monsell agreed to meet a delegation of the 'Committee' on 31 July 1872. Before the meeting took place, the authorities made a number of efforts to divide and rule the men. The beginning of the agitation had shown a 'fraternal feeling between the London letter carriers and letter sorters' which did not always exist, but the authorities steadfastly refused to allow any sorters into the delegation. Furthermore, they sought to dictate who should speak for the men by declining to meet Booth on account of his 'bad character'. This was in spite of a vote of 93 to 7 in his favour from his own office. Booth himself accepted the ruling philosophically, saying that as an 'agitator' he was already well used to having 'been removed from various offices . . . his home had been broken up and his pecuniary prospects sacrificed'. Nevertheless, he counselled moderation, advising against 'anything approaching to violence either in demeanour or action'.[21]

The meeting between Monsell and the 'Committee' showed that the authorities intended to play along the men. Thus the Postmaster General told the delegation that while it was his opinion 'you were really better off than most men in your position', nevertheless, he was prepared to look into their grievances in promotion and other matters. Furthermore, he said that he intended to introduce yet another divisive institution in the form of 'good conduct stripes', which would be granted to selected men after a long period of service without indiscipline. 'We want wages not stripes', shouted the men of the South Western District Office when they were offered them in November. 'Buttons and stripes won't feed our children. It's all favouritism.' The stripes were only accepted by being offered individually to those who were thus rewarded, and though later spread to the provinces they proved a fertile source of discontent until their abolition in 1914.[22]

When the postal authorities began to discuss among themselves the claims put forward in the memorials and the Monsell interviews, they were forced to agree that the cost of living as well as the wages of many other groups of workers had increased in the recent period. The London surveyor proposed major concessions 'in strict justice to the letter carriers and having regard to the state of the Labour Market', particularly because the demands so far had been couched in a 'most respectful and legitimate manner'. It was on this basis that the Postmaster General proposed to the Treasury a number of improvements for the London letter carriers, particularly a major modification in the 'break' in the middle of their wage scale. Even these modest proposals were rejected by the Treasury. This perhaps owed something to the rivalries of political leaders and civil servants, and also to the recent miscalculations which caused the losses after the nationalisation of the telegraph system. In any event there was bound to be further trouble when a notice appeared at the General Post Office on 21 January 1873 stating that, despite the promises Monsell had made to the delegation, the Treasury refused to agree to any improvements in the conditions of the letter carriers.[23]

Knowing the flood of anger and frustration which built up in every London district office as a result of this, the postal authorities continued to press hard for concessions from the Treasury. However, the Treasury officials grew increasingly intransigent, demanding more rigorous action against the organisers of discontent during the period of its inevitable growth. In defiance of official prohibition, public 'lectures' were organised by the men on 3 and 17 February 1873 addressed by well known trade union leaders who defended the rights of combination and advocated membership of the Benefit Society.[24] In the following period Booth and his associates organised a whole series of activities, including large and much publicised processions and meetings in Central London, as well as pressure on Parliament and on individual MPs.[25]

Continuing discontent was shown by the refusal of the sorters to perform any extra duties on 31 March. On this occasion the authorities retaliated by locking the doors, but they soon had to think of more subtle forms of counter-attack. The Benefit Society remained studiously moderate. Booth himself 'disavowed any intention on the part of the letter carriers to strike', and Hawkin asserted that they 'had always held entirely aloof from strikers, and do so now'. Nevertheless, they acted with the rest of the trade union movement, gaining support through their affiliation to the London Trades Council and taking part on 1 June in demonstrations against the Criminal Law Amendment Act, a measure restricting the effectiveness of trade union action. The Birmingham Trades Council was also persuaded to take up the grievances of postal workers with local MPs.[26] A big meeting on the GPO premises at St Martin's-le-Grand followed on 28 June. Despite increasingly desperate pleas from their opposite numbers at the Post Office, officials at the Treasury insisted on steps being taken to ban a meeting organised for 8 July by auxiliary and suburban men at the Western District Office. Later in the same month, they forced the disbandment of the committee of representatives from the various offices which had arranged the memorials and the delegation of the previous year.[27]

These actions of the postal authorities under Treasury pressure were their most ineffective to date. The enforced demise of the committee of representatives put the initiative for the organisation of any agitation entirely into the hands of the Benefit Society. The prohibition of even the most peaceful of meetings held with official permission in individual offices went beyond the restrictions of 1866 and, far from ending the agitation, simply created a new grievance. Meetings were held with MPs during July and, as there was a General Election, it proved possible to persuade a group of leading members of the Conservative opposition to make sympathetic noise, and even to arrange a Parliamentary debate on 28 July. The Cannon Street Hotel saw two enormous meetings of postal workers in the same period addressed by MPs, union leaders and other sympathisers. These meetings, on 16 July and 5 August, were held despite frantic efforts by the authorities to prevent them. They were preceded by processions in which men from all the main London offices participated. A further mass meeting was held at the Exeter Hall on 18 November, and in the following January of 1874 the grievances of postal workers were described to the meeting of the TUC by George Howell who was at that time its Secretary.[28]

How was it that despite this enormous build-up of support, the movement had collapsed by the end of 1874, with Booth left a disillusioned man with a debt of £35, and a number of sorters losing their jobs altogether? One factor was that either through fear of the consequences or else because of a feeling that they were above such things, only a small proportion of those who were eligible joined the Benefit Society. Despite all the big meetings in London, and the recruitment of members in Birmingham, Manchester and Liverpool, the Society could never claim a membership above 700, and only collected £388 in the first two years of its existence.[29] Another reason for the weakness of the Society lay in the limited reliability of its friends among the rich and powerful. Thus when a Tory administration replaced the Liberal one in 1874, the postal workers thought that something might come of the fact that the Conservatives had 'always shown a more liberal disposition towards the Civil Service than their opponents'. They were sorely disappointed. In Government Tory MPs suddenly became deaf to their pleas, and Parliamentary support evaporated. A conference organised on 29 April 1874 was attended by some twenty MPs near the Houses of Parliament. A group of MPs was lined up to meet the Postmaster General to demand a commission of inquiry. One of their number, the radical Roebuck, stepped out of line by asking a Parliamentary question on 4 May which allowed the Chancellor of the Exchequer to say that he had the entire matter in hand.[30]

This pre-empted further public discussion, though it was followed by the announcement of new rates of pay in the following month. These attempted at least in part to answer the agitation. They included the important concession of a minimum wage of £1 2s (£1. 10) a week for London letter carriers, thereafter rising at three-yearly intervals to £1 5s (£1. 25), £1 7s (£1. 35), £1 9s (£1. 45) and £1 10s (£1. 50). Auxiliary letter carriers were placed on a scale from 18s (90p) to £1 5s (£1. 25) and similar changes were announced for the sorters. The general effect of all this was to bring some improvement for the small groups at the minimum, but none at all for the vast majority at the top of the scale. The Benefit Society issued a leaflet pointing out that the main grievances had not been even considered:

> Will it give you in money more than about a tenth of what you have been asking for? Will it give you a clearly defined system of promotion? Will it abolish Sunday labour? No; most emphatically No.

A delegation from the Benefit Society told the London Trades Council that the authorities were determined to use the new rates to destroy their organisation. Thus the unpopular and divisive system of good conduct stripes was extended by promising them to individuals 'if they gave up the Society'. One of the men expressed the more general issues in this way:

> I will tell you what I think it is expected to do with its shilling on here and its two shillings there, with its nothing here and its nothing there, with its new name for this class and a little off the maximum of that class, it is admirably calculated to set the men one against the other as similar schemes have done in the past.

It was as a result of this that a significant proportion of the men were intimidated by such statements as the one which appeared in the high Tory *Globe* asserting that 'mutiny must be crushed out of the public service'. In any case, enough of them felt they had obtained something from what they were offered to organise a testimonial meeting for those who had led the agitation and to assume that that was an end to it.[31]

By this time the political and economic climate had completely changed. The farm workers, who had provided an inspiring example, were cowed and beaten after a number of lock-outs. Organisations of miners and others were smashed. 1875 saw the growth of unemployment and the beginning of a period known to contemporaries as 'the Great Depression'. This put the authorities in a position to act on the advice of the reactionary press. In September 1874 a clerk was suspended from the missing letter department allegedly for leaking information about his superior officers to the press. On 27 December all increments and promotions were stopped in the savings bank department until such time as whoever was responsible for similar leaks of 'gross and wanton aspersions on private character' either owned up or was revealed by one of his colleagues.[32] Soon afterwards five sorters were dismissed and a large number of others demoted in various ways allegedly for leaking information to the press, though this was denied by the newspapers involved.

What was really at issue now was the right of the men to complain about their conditions to anybody, even to one another. When they presented a memorial against the June settlement to the Controller of the Circulation Department in November, they were told that 'if they would not withdraw their demands, efforts would be made to obtain a cheaper class of labour'. A fortnight later the Postmaster General, Lord John Manners, replied in the same vein; not simply did he reject the claim, but he also demanded its immediate withdrawal. The former 'Tory radical' wrote privately:

I feel it incumbent upon me not only to oppose and check the spirit which the terms of this memorial and the course it has taken exhibit, but to evince, in some unmistakable manner, that I will not yield to clamour without reason what justice to the Public would withhold.

This was a return to the bad old days of Rowland Hill, and an indication of the real attitude of a Tory administration in which a certain ill-conceived confidence had been placed by the postal workers at the time of its formation.

What followed had something of the air of the trial of *Alice in Wonderland* about it, with 'Sentence first – verdict afterwards'. The sorters were forced to repudiate their memorial, and, having done so, were dismissed just the same. The five men who lost their jobs had all been active in the recent agitation, and despite the well organised efforts of MPs and others on their behalf, they were dubbed 'discontented and troublesome servants who had long been the source of great mischief to the Department'. The *Bee-Hive* newspaper, which had reported many cases of victimisation in comparable struggles elsewhere, considered the exercise of such arbitrary authority exceptional: 'never in any dispute which has occurred between master and servant has such an unmitigated act of tyranny been perpetrated'. It was not until 1878 that some of the suspended men were again allowed to do overtime working.[33] These measures intimidated the men in the London office for the next decade, but they were remembered in future generations as a spur to the building of a more effective organisation.

THE FAWCETT AGITATION AND THE FOUNDING
OF THE PTCA: 1880-2

It was in any case only a short time before the beginning of a new phase of agitation, this time by the telegraphists. As so often before, it was an inspiration quite outside the Post Office workers themselves that provided the first impetus for new efforts to improve their conditions. In this case it originated from Henry Fawcett, the blind Professor of Political Economy, who was appointed Postmaster General in the Liberal administration formed in April 1880. Though like all orthodox economists of his time, Fawcett was generally in favour of the operation of market forces in the determination of wages, he nevertheless had frequently shown sympathy with the claims of the Post Office workers, and said that he did not agree that their wages 'should be the lowest that would attract any class of physically capable persons. The end should be to have such a rate as would secure really efficient service by obviating discontent'.[34] In later years, a somewhat exaggerated view grew up of Fawcett's efforts to improve the lot of the Post Office workers, especially among London sorters. It was even said that he had a special agreement with Prime Minister Gladstone to allow him to reduce Post Office profits against increases in income tax.[35] His attitude was sufficiently different from his predecessors however to raise new expectations.

These expectations were first of all expressed by the Birmingham telegraphists, from whom a letter appeared in the *Civil Service Gazette* on 9 October 1880.[36] This initiated a flood of similar letters from every part of the country setting out grievances which telegraphists had been reluctant to express since the time of the 1871 strike. There was particular discontent about the plight of those stuck at the top of the third class grade with little chance of promotion. By the end of 1880, a number of clandestine local committees felt able to reveal their existence. Publicised meetings were held in most of the main centres which showed the deep-seated discontent which had existed for a decade. The Liverpool Committee which had drawn up a memorial of its own in the previous August, ran one meeting on 27 November and from this decided to set up a representative conference from all the areas. This meeting took place on 15–16 January 1881, and all the main offices, including London, were represented. Those present included leaders in the 1871 strike. It was agreed to re-formulate the claim to be regarded as second division clerks and to ask for higher salaries, fewer increments, increased payment for overtime and public holiday duties, as well as more leave and higher subsistence allowances when away from home. The meeting baulked at the idea of setting up a permanent organisation, but agreed to meet again to consider the possibility.[37] When a delegation got to see Fawcett on 15 March, the six-hour interview was of quite a different character from earlier meetings of this sort.[38] This time, the Postmaster General had taken the trouble to acquaint himself with the arguments being presented to him, and on many points he got the better of the delegation. This was really nothing to do with the large number of higher officials present, on whom the delegates blamed their own failure to present their case adequately. Thus Fawcett asked why so few telegraphists were prepared to be promoted to the positions of clerks when they aspired to their status, and why the pay of women was so much lower. The reply was that the clerks had their own case to make and the women also could 'take care of themselves'. Single male telegraphists, however, could not live on the wages they were getting.

The meeting between Fawcett and the delegation was followed by a period of continual meetings and lobbying by the telegraphists. Great emphasis was placed on the malevolence of the officials of the department as against Fawcett himself, and there was even talk in London of a ban on overtime. Feeling grew so intense that Fawcett came under strong pressure from the Post Office Secretary Sir John Tilley to make a public pronouncement. On 30 March 1881, he issued a *Post Office Circular* where he explained that he had met the delegation with a view to obtaining information from them, and took full responsibility for the tone of the reply to them. He warned against strike action of any sort while the reply was being considered.[39]

In June 1881 a reply to the delegation was promulgated.[40] This embodied a number of important concessions. Male telegraphists in the lowest provincial grade could get from £78 to £95 per annum and females from £60 to £68, an improvement on the Scudamore scales of 1872. In London now the maximum on the lowest class was £100 for males and £60 for females. There was also to be some limited overtime payment. This was the long remembered 'Fawcett scheme', comparatively generous to the telegraphist at the same time as trying to integrate them with the sorters below rather than with the clerks above, from whom they were finally and irrevocably cut off. The telegraphists did not consider themselves to have been well treated, particularly on this latter point. By 30 May Frederick Heald had arrived at the opinion that 'the necessity for a permanent association for the promotion of our interests is now recognised throughout the service'. A meeting of delegates in Liverpool on 17 July confirmed this to be true. It was agreed to take the historic step of establishing the Postal Telegraph Clerks Association with Liverpool as the 'centre'. The authorities discussed at first taking some action against this body, but eventually decided to leave well alone.[41]

The PTCA in its early years was a timid and conservative, not to say self-effacing organisation.[42] At first its rules were almost entirely concerned with the provision of friendly benefits so generous that the Association was often on the point of bankruptcy. Before 1885 it was not even possible to be a member without being part of the PTCA's insurance scheme and, after this, membership rose permanently to over 1,000. The main activity of local branches seems to have been to organise annual dinners at which toasts were drunk to Queen Victoria and the Postmaster General. The Association had no office and no full-time staff, and was run by a general secretary and central committee in Liverpool. In 1884–5 petitions for better pay for Sunday work were organised, but they were rejected by the authorities on the grounds that every such question had been settled for all time in 1881. There was some spasmodic official interference in the work of the PTCA. In 1883 one member was suspended and two had their wages cut for what amounted to association activity, and in 1885 two delegates were prevented from attending the annual conference. In 1888 the *Telegraph Service Gazette*, which supported the Association, was compelled to cease publication after being sued by the Post Office.[43] However, a certain level of official tolerance was shown by the fact that two early general secretaries, Thomas Morris and Joseph Scott, left their posts in 1886 and 1890 respectively on promotion to the grade of supervisor.

During the 1880s, telegraphists generally felt isolated and resentful, and were divided amongst themselves. Those few women who had helped found the PTCA soon dropped out. The London telegraphists, who did comparatively well out of the 1881 settlement, remained aloof. They considered themselves necessarily entitled to higher pay and opposed the Association's demand for an end to the classification of offices for differential rates of pay.[44] In relation to the rest of the service the telegraphists affected a tone of injured superiority. They resented in particular the increasing efforts of the authorities following the Fawcett Scheme to try to integrate them with the postal side, and to some extent slowed down this inevitable development. However, they did manage to win an increasing proportion of supervising appointments for themselves, and built a lobbying machine effective enough to ensure that their grievances were voiced with increasing frequency by MPs and in the press.

A number of other improvements in the conditions of Post Office workers also came during the period that Fawcett was Postmaster General. The sorters, apparently without any effort on their part, obtained a new improved wages scale of £2 to £2 10s (£2. 50) per week. Letter carriers from more parts of the country than ever before also submitted memorials to Fawcett, and a committee especially to draw them up was set up by provincial and junior letter carriers in London. This agitation did not develop further because of Fawcett's comparative success in wringing concessions from the Treasury.[45] This he did, not with the arguments of a political economist, but with those of a paternalist master. The Treasury view of course was that since civil servants were 'to a certain extent relieved from the competition to which all other classes are subject' they could not 'dictate' their wages. In any case, the only 'adequate test of wages is to be found in the consistency of the supply of respectable men who are fitted to discharge, and do discharge, their duties in a punctual and trustworthy manner'. Against this, Fawcett simply argued 'that of late years a Letter Carrier's duties and the conditions under which he performs them, have undergone considerable modification', with fewer gratuities, heavier weights to carry and longer hours of work. He also put forward with eloquence the case for the 'forgotten' rural letter carriers. The 'Fawcett settlement' announced towards the end of 1882 included improvements at every level, from the highest London scale going up from £1 3s (£1. 15) to £1 10s (£1. 50) to £1 4s (£1. 20) to £1 12s (£1. 60) and that at the lowest from £1 3s (£1. 15) to £1 4s (£1. 20) at the maximum, though the minimum remained 18s (90p). Letter carriers in Birmingham saw their scale rise from 18s (90p) to £1 1s (£1. 05) to £1 2s (£1. 10) to £1 8s (£1. 40) and those in Oxford went up from 16s (80p) to £1 1s (£1. 05) to 18s (90p) to £1 2s (£1. 10). This went hand in hand with the extension of the good conduct stripe system to the rural areas. In general, however, it was less generous than the improvements secured by the telegraphists and sorters.

THE RIDLEY AGITATION: 1887-8

If the improvements obtained by Fawcett for the letter carriers, as well as for the telegraphists, satisfied many of them for a time, it was not long before new reasons for agitation were found. The spark was provided only two years later, in December 1886, when the Ridley Royal Commission on the Civil Service asked for submissions from the postal workers. By this time Fawcett was dead and the Tories again in power wanted to review the civil service in the same way that Playfair, Northcote and Trevelyan had done for previous generations. The Post Office workers saw this as their chance, and the impetus provided eventually resulted in permanent union organisation being set up within four years by all the main bodies of Post Office workers.

The first result of the Ridley summons was a revival in the PTCA, as arrangements began to be made for the collection of evidence. There were stirrings also from the provincial postal clerks.[46] The postal clerks, though increasingly qualified for both postal work and telegraphy, usually specialised in sorting and counter work, especially in the larger 'divided' offices. On 21 January 1887 a meeting of representatives of this group was held in Liverpool, and it was agreed to set up the United Kingdom Postal Clerks Association, with George Lascelles as General Secretary. This was the second organisation of Post Office workers that can claim continuity down to the present day. The provincial postal clerks were more scattered than the specialists in telegraphy or the London sorters, so never built such a powerful organisation. At first their main demand was for extra pay for Sunday work, but they also wanted free access to the first class of their grade with uninterrupted pay scales from £52 to £100. The Association claimed responsibility for such minor improvements as better local work rotas, and appeared before the 1887 inquiry into Sunday labour. Such activities in their early years were the height of their ambition, and they were localised and comparatively ineffectual.

It was in response to the same call from the Ridley Commission that the postmen – for so the letter carriers were named since the introduction of the parcel post in 1883 – began to organise again.[47] On 11 April 1887 a conference was held in Bolton at which fourteen other northern offices were represented. A petition was drawn up to present to the Commission asking for higher pay and an end to the compulsion to deliver parcels. Nothing came of the suggestion that they should establish a Postmen's Provincial Association. As a result, the initiative remained in the hands of the London men as it had done in the past. However, it was not those at the Chief Office in St Martin's-le-Grand who were in the forefront. Their failure to respond to the rejection of series of memorials in 1886 brought about a new meeting on 23 July 1887 at Tolmer Square near Euston Station, close to the North Western District Office, but far from the scenes of earlier agitations. Twenty-three offices of London District and provincial postmen were represented. The meeting elected Tom Dredge from the North Western District as their Secretary and drew up a petition asking for higher wages and pensions, as well as improvements in uniforms and holidays. Dredge got in touch with his MP. He happened to be a Liberal in his 20s named H. L. W. Lawson, later known to history as Lord Burnham, proprietor of the *Daily Telegraph*, and Chairman of the Committee that set up standard salary scales for teachers.

The postmen got up another memorial and Lawson addressed a mass meeting of 1,000 of them on 13 August 1887. The Tory Postmaster General Raikes would not agree to see any postmen but did meet Lawson on 29 August and agreed to a number of very limited concessions. The most important was for a departmental inquiry into uniforms which eventually resulted in the provision of lighter summer suits. Following on the rejection of their main demands, the district and suburban men on 3 September agreed to set up a 'permanent committee' and the metropolitan auxiliaries held a large meeting of their own at about the same time.

The further growth of this agitation provoked a sharper reaction from Raikes in October, when the authorities refused to receive further representations from MPs or anybody else on behalf of the men. Dredge was also demoted to the second class. On 27 October Raikes told the district and suburban postmen that 'having due regard to the interests of the tax-payer' he would concede nothing. Undeterred, the Committee established in the summer now had an office, contacts outside London, and the grand title of 'The London and Provincial Postmen's Mutual Aid Society'. A further mass meeting was held on 11 February 1888 in defiance of official prohibition, and a new petition was presented. In April the postmen openly published the rules of their organisation, now styling it the 'United Kingdom Postmen's Benefit Association' and declaring that it aimed 'to establish and protect the general welfare of its members'. Unfortunately, it did not have the strength to do so and on 19 May 1888 Tom Dredge was dismissed. Soon afterwards, three of his colleagues were demoted for organising a petition in his support.[48]

THE BEGINNING OF THE FAWCETT ASSOCIATION: 1889-90

Before the end of 1887 the Ridley Commission had already announced that it was never going to get around to considering the Post Office at all. As a result both the PTCA and UKPCA declined from the peak of membership they obtained at the time when they were collecting evidence. They were soon both outpaced by the development of organisation among London sorters, a particularly integrated group with specialised knowledge shared by few others largely confined to London. There were about 2,500 sorters at the GPO, 1,000 at the various London district offices, 500 in the parcel post, and 150 in the travelling Post Office. These sorters built the most powerful of the early civil service associations, with a particularly remarkable set of leaders. Their grievances were publicised during 1886 in an East End Radical paper called *Toby* where individual supervisors were sketched and pilloried as 'drivers' and the call for an organised response went out.[49] It was at about this time that J. H. Williams, a particularly straight-laced teetotaller and Quaker working in the Foreign Branch, began to argue for an interpretation of the 1881 Fawcett Scheme that involved bringing the conditions of sorters up to those of telegraphists. This suggestion clearly captured the imagination of many sorters, and a large meeting was called on Post Office premises on 18 April 1889 at which the 'Fawcett Scheme Committee' was set up, with Williams as Secretary. The Treasurer was Harry Groves, another teetotaller and a Methodist Sunday School teacher.[50]

The authorities were in two minds as to whether to allow any meeting, and some of the officials wanted to discipline a young sorter called Clery whom they considered 'grossly disrespectful' for his statement that memorials were generally ignored. Raikes, however, thought it best to 'let this matter drop'. With trade unionism spreading like wildfire elsewhere, Raikes knew that it was more important to prevent the sorters from making 'common cause' with postmen, or anybody else, than to provoke a confrontation at this stage. He thus showed a 'leniency and indulgence' towards the sorters which contrasted with his treatment of other groups. He even interviewed Clery when his officials wanted to discipline him, and received delegations of the sorters' leaders while showing no 'recognition' of any kind to the associations.[51]

All this made it possible on 11 December for a large and enthusiastic meeting of sorters to agree explicitly to 'combine on trade-union principles'. On 8 February 1890 *The Post* appeared for the first time with Clery's name defiantly emblazoned on the masthead. After directly consulting Raikes, who agreed to 'postal servants forming associations for their mutual benefit', they held a meeting at the Memorial Hall, Farringdon Street, on 10 February at which the Fawcett Association was inaugurated. On 12 March a further mass meeting formulated the rules. The unusual title was less a tribute to the late PMG than an earnest that 'the very first thing we set ourselves to do' was 'to secure the fulfilment of that scheme'.[52] Raikes met a delegation of leaders of the newly formed Association at which he agreed to the 'luminous suggestion' of Clery that an independent committee of outsiders should consider the validity of the various interpretations of the Fawcett Scheme. This 'Luminous Committee' reported on 25 March 1890 against the sorters on every particular, as indeed they were bound to do if they considered the intentions of the author of the scheme. A mass meeting on 22 April fully confirmed a statement in *The Post* of 4 April that there was not a 'contented office or branch in the London area'. However, further delegations met Raikes on 3 and 6 June and put forward a number of new points on 'stagnation of promotion and low rates of pay' which the authorities agreed to consider.[53]

By the time of the postmen's strike in July, the Fawcett Association had few concrete achievements to its credit. It had nevertheless established, within limits, the right to hold outside public meetings and to publish its own magazine. However illusory the sorters' interpretation of the Fawcett Scheme, it had at least provided a rallying point. Though they had laid the basis for future gains, this was not just the result of their boldness or tactical flair. It was also because of the deliberate intention of the authorities to buy them off at the expense of the postmen and telegraphists.

THE TELEGRAPHISTS TAKE THE OFFENSIVE: 1890

While all this was happening, the other main groups had been building their strength. The PTCA which had declined from a peak of 2,125 members in 1887, revived in 1889, when they took up again the grievance of pay for Sunday labour and organised a series of Parliamentary questions on this and other matters.[54] Raikes insisted that there could be no concessions, but further agitation was soon stimulated by official over-reaction to efforts to ameliorate conditions in Cardiff.[55] The PTCA branch there managed to get support for their claim to be under-staffed from the local *Western Mail* which had itself experienced delays in the transmission of messages. The Cardiff telegraphists also tried to contact Raikes directly during a visit he paid to the area in December. This refusal to act through official superiors was the pretext for the transfer of a number of local activists, including the PTCA Secretary and his predecessor to other offices, in much the same way as after the 1871 strike. This time the publicity gave the PTCA a fillip it had not had since its foundation. At Cardiff itself the Association came into contact with mainstream trade unionism in the form of the Trades Council and, for the first time, attracted women into its ranks. Protest meetings, it was reported, 'gave an impulse to our movement' in every corner of the land. Perhaps most important of all, the London telegraphists abandoned the separate 'London Telegraph Clerks Association' they had set up in November and threw in their lot with the national organisation on 17 December, when they ran a meeting on the Cardiff exiles with Sir Edward Reid, MP for the town. Raikes was compelled to assert that the punishments were not intended as an attack on the PTCA of which he took 'no cognizance' nor would he take 'any steps against such associations on account of their membership'. This was recognition of a sort. The fact that it meant something was shown when, after protests, the Chairman and Secretary of the Liverpool PTCA were given promotions which they had previously been denied.[56]

Against the background of considerable publicity, a full-scale Parliamentary debate initiated by Earl Compton took place on 15 April 1890 on the motion that the grievances of London and provincial telegraphists required redress.[57] The usual questions of hours and wages were discussed, and there was a vote of 143 to 103 against the telegraphists, largely on party lines with Conservatives in the majority and Liberals and Irish Nationalists in the minority. In the week between this debate and the protest meeting of sorters about the 'Luminous Committee', Raikes republished a version of the 1866 rule that banned meetings outside Post Office premises. The authorities now had to be informed in advance of all such meetings, and could send a reporter. Only Post Office servants could be present. Since recent sorters' meetings at St Martin's-le-Grand had been so crowded as to constitute a danger to safety, these new regulations could hardly be seen as a gain.[58] Within a few days 'official reporters' appeared, amid protest, at conferences of the postal clerks and telegraphists. At the Eighth Annual Conference of the PTCA, which began on 31 May at Leicester, expansion could be shown despite the restrictions. There were now 5,000 members and two women were included among the London delegates. There was even one of the Cardiff exiles present, representing his new office. The most important grievance they discussed was compulsory overtime and there was even talk of refusing to do any. However, there was no concession from the authorities on this point.

It should not have been surprising that when the celebration of the penny post jubilee took place in telegraph offices, groans and silences greeted calls for cheering in every telegraph office. This action infuriated the authorities, but it was less this than the strength of the simultaneous agitation among postmen and the determination of the authorities to keep them separate that accounts for the comparatively favourable revision for telegraphists announced on 14 July. Increases included from £100 to £110 per annum for males at the top of the second class in London, and £1 12s (£1. 60) to £1 15s (£1. 75) in the provinces, with equivalent figures of £1 5s (£1. 25) to £1 10s (£1. 50) and £1 6s (£1. 30) to £1 8s (£1. 40) for women. These new rates, whatever their motives, were nevertheless a significant step forward for the telegraphists. However, since 'the prospects of the younger men were not by any means improved', in them 'lay the seed of another agitation'. Although the PTCA had come a long way since the 1880s, it remained timid and conservative. This was shown when L. H. Quin, one of the younger London leaders, was dismissed for protesting about the new rates of pay. The Association baulked from running a public meeting to present nearly £500 collected on his behalf after it had been banned by the authorities. Neither did the PTCA feel it had enough in common with the TUC or local trades councils to consider affiliation. Though the PTCA had been the pioneer association of Post Office workers, the wind of change was now blowing from elsewhere.[59]

THE POSTMEN'S UNION: 1889–90

The next episode of postal agitation, the setting up of the Postmen's Union, reached the history books of trade unionism, where it has always been portrayed as an inglorious, ill-led failure.[60] This interpretation is based on a retrospective view, and is to some extent coloured by special pleading. It ignores the substantial achievements of the Postmen's Union. They were the first in the Post Office to organise themselves independently, and showed the necessity to go far beyond the limits allowed by the authorities. To the Union must be attributed the substantial improvements obtained by the postmen in the early 1890s. It also indicated most of the forms of action that it was going to be necessary to pursue in the future. The Union faced great difficulties in dealing with determined employers with an almost unique capacity to divide and rule. Some of its problems may have been derived from the fact that it was organised by 'outside agitators', socialists and Marxists. Yet so also were the conspicuously successful match girls and dockers, as well as the gas workers. It might also be said that it concentrated too much on questions of Union recognition rather than on economic grievances, but this applied to many other new unions at the time. Above all it was not the Union or its leaders who forced the issue to a strike, but it was 'immediately and deliberately caused by the aggressive tactics of the higher officials'.[61] For all its weaknesses, and the victimisation that followed the strike, the Postmen's Union and its leaders hacked out a path along which has followed every subsequent generation of Post Office workers.

It is not surprising that after the 1888 victimisations, the postmen should look at the success of the match girls and others who were being organised by outsiders. They can hardly have been much encouraged in April 1889 to discover that their memorials of August 1887 were still being considered by the authorities.[62] Discussion about what to do next may well have taken place at a 'Grand Smoking Concert' held to raise money for Dredge in March 1889.[63] In the Summer of 1889 there took place the famous and successful struggle for the 'dockers tanner'. It was soon after this that W. A. Chambers, a journalist who knew Dredge, wrote in the *North London Press* of 28 September that 'the most significant labour movement' would now be 'the agitation among London postmen'. This had been initiated by a group of eighty-one of their number approaching Michael Henry, Secretary of the Labour Union, who had recently organised with success a group of coal porters.

To explain the background of this development, it is necessary to say something about the Labour Union, which flits somewhat uncertainly across the pages of the working class history of the time.[64] The Labour Union did not begin life as a trade union body of any sort, but as a political party consisting of former members of the Socialist League, which had split in 1884 from Britain's first avowedly Marxist party, the Social Democratic Federation. The Socialist League itself broke up in 1887–8, its most famous member William Morris turning to local activity, and some others taking up anarchism. A number of young workers under the influence of Frederick Engels, who was at the time spending his last years in London, set up a Labour Union. This group, whose most well known members were John Lincoln Mahon, A. K. Donald and Thomas Binning, published a statement in 1888 which explained that their aim was to set up 'an independent political party' of the workers. They described their aim as 'The Emancipation of Labour from the control of the monopolists and the realisation of a state based on co-operative principles in which workers will have all the wealth they create and idlers will have no place'. The Labour Union, one of many such bodies set up during that period of labour ferment, was eventually subsumed in 1892 into the London branch of the Independent Labour Party. What was distinctive about this body was that it took seriously its professed aim of 'improving the social condition of the people'.[65]

This was the group of 'outside agitators' approached by the postmen in the late summer of 1889. They had the advantage of many contacts in the world of journalism, not just in the *North London Press* already mentioned, but also in the radical London *Star* which was then in its heyday, and in its arch-rival the Unionist *Evening News* going through a brief, but temporary, period of approval of trade unionism. The *Daily Telegraph* also published information about what was going on, no doubt through the contacts built up with Lawson by Dredge. All this publicity meant that there was plenty of support for a meeting held in defiance of the authorities on 22 September at Camberwell Green, when about 300 postmen heard Mahon, and voted unanimously to support a union, though at first with secret membership. An individual by the name of E. S. Bull, an auxiliary postman from Finsbury Park, sent a full report to the authorities for which he was paid 3s (15p) 'expenses'. It was thought that 'the men as a Body are too well off to perpetrate the folly of striking', but Raikes asked for a close watch to be kept on the movement.[66]

On 24 September 1889 a meeting at the Central Democratic Club, Gray's Inn Road, headquarters of the Labour Union, announced the setting up of the Postmen's Union whose officials consisted entirely of outsiders, but included Tom Dredge. Fred Henderson was Chairman and Mahon Secretary. The new body declared itself to be 'all-embracing', calling on the sorters to join, and within a few days organised a number of local meetings and began to prepare new petitions to present to the authorities. The chief demand was for the same 6d an hour the dockers had obtained – which would have increased the postmen's minimum to well over £1 a week, with 2½d (1p) per hour extra for overtime. Speakers at the meetings emphasised the moderation of their aims and methods and explained the need 'for the organisation to be built up in secret until it is strong enough to defy' the 'shameful restriction' placed upon it. The Union would then be taken over entirely by the postmen themselves.[67]

It was at this point, within a few days of its foundation, that the Postmen's Union faced its first major problem in the form of an internal dispute. On 1 October Fred Henderson, one of the former Socialist League members, published a manifesto without consulting his colleagues. He retaliated to an attack on this action by sending a letter to the press which he also got Dredge and Chambers to sign, attacking the 'self-seeking men' who were running the Union, and claiming that they had 'attempted to make the Executive Committee into a mere sub-committee of [their] own political organisation'.[68] This squabble continued over the next few weeks. Nevertheless meetings were taking place throughout London, a magazine appeared, and Mahon, Binning and Donald were working hard to build the Union. They regarded Chambers as having put himself out of the organisation, Henderson was expelled, and within a few days Dredge publicly stated that his 'signature had been attached unwarrantably to the document' and continued to work with the others. There is no evidence that there was any substance in the charges put forward by Henderson, nor indeed that the dispute prevented support flowing into the Union. Thus on 20 October there was a demonstration of over 5,000 postmen in Hyde Park, and over the succeeding week-ends a number of successful assemblies were held in and around the London area. A meeting was held to mediate between the different sections of the Union leadership. It was attended by delegates who claimed to represent some 3,000 postmen.[69] Also present at the meeting were John Burns, late leader of the dock strike, Henry Champion, who was determined to stake his claim as leader of labour's political aspirations, and W. E. Clery, who did not want the sorters to be outflanked by this new organisation, but had no talents as a diplomat. These three vain, touchy men were inevitably unable to reconcile the contending groups when they were left to their own devices. In the meantime, it was agreed that the postmen's organisation should no longer be regarded as a sub-committee of the Labour Union and a number of postmen came on to the Executive.[70]

After this interlude the Union expanded rapidly. New branches were set up throughout the London area and contact was made with postmen in Newcastle, Leeds, Edinburgh, Glasgow and Liverpool. The *Postmen's Gazette* began to appear regularly, this first series finally running to eight issues.[71] During November and December, Mahon wrote to the authorities requesting recognition and various improvements. The reply, approved by Raikes himself, was that any such request would only be considered 'if it comes before him in a regular manner'. Mahon did actually get to meet Third Secretary Herbert Joyce on the recognition issue. No concessions were offered, but Mahon unfortunately did not have the imagination to make some capital out of the fact that it had taken place.

Meanwhile, the authorities began to make their own dispositions. Early in December an increase from 80 to 90p at the bottom of the lowest scale for London postmen was announced, together with the statement that the authorities would 'oppose all future claims for increases of wages to other classes of postmen'. The Union described this as a 'paltry concession' which could only provoke 'more discontent'. It was nevertheless able to argue with some justice that it was 'difficult to believe that this slight rise would have been granted had there been no union'.[72] At the end of the year Tom Dredge, whose reception at meetings showed him to be a popular figure, received his job back after signing a humiliating and much publicised declaration that his activities on behalf of his followers were 'forced upon me' by those who sought 'political and personal ends'.[73] In February there was a further tiny concession in the form of half pay for sick parcel postmen.

Meanwhile, the Union continued to expand. During March 1890 there was a general meeting that could report thirteen working postmen out of eighteen on the Executive, an interview with trade union MPs at the House of Commons, and a 'smoking concert' with an attendance of 250. The authorities, however, had another card to play. Although the Postmen's Union opened its membership to 'all workers in the Post Office from the telegraph boy to the district official', it was noted that 'feelings of class superiority, prevented the sorters from co-operating with other workers', and the leaders of the Fawcett Association did not in any case favour such an alliance. Officially inspired press reports spoke of the sorters as particularly 'respectable and intelligent men'. Such unusual flattery together with inherent feelings of superiority prevented any combined action by the Post Office workers at this time, thus limiting the gains that could be made by the postmen, or indeed any other group.[74] There were divisions also amongst the postmen themselves. While auxiliaries, juniors and parcel postmen joined in large numbers, those with long service and accumulated pension rights held back. Nevertheless, it was said in later years that the group with most to lose, the postmen at the East Central District Office, voted to join early in 1890.[75]

THE GROWTH OF CONFLICT: APRIL TO JULY 1890

By the late spring of 1890, the postmen had been able to hold meetings and publish their paper and had obtained a number of small concessions. However, they had not yet faced the full brunt of resistance from the authorities, who were quite determined to destroy any organisation led by outsiders. The postmen themselves were now certain that they needed outsiders to protect themselves from the sort of hounding to which they had always been subjected in the past. A confrontation was becoming inevitable. The leaders of the PU made another tactical error at this point when they declared that their quarrel with the authorities was 'entirely over the question of the right to meeting and combination'.[76] They knew very well that the political and legal pressures in a government department against such recognition were particularly strong. However, the problem had to be solved eventually, and there was nothing inevitable about the failure of the Postmen's Union itself.

In fact, for a time things went well. On 15 April there was the much publicised Parliamentary debate on the conditions of the telegraphists, and on 31 April groups of postmen marched behind bands to a general meeting just as they had done seventeen years before. On 4 May the Union unfurled a banner proclaiming 'Each for All and All for Each', and 800 postmen marched behind it to Hyde Park. They were part of London's first May Day demonstration, the biggest assemblage of organised workers the capital had seen since the days of the Chartists. Now that they had so manifestly joined the ranks of labour, it must have seemed to the postmen that they had it in their power to sweep all obstacles before them. Thus they decided to break new ground by a series of outdoor meetings and demonstrations. The Union considered that the new regulations for meetings recently granted to the sorters 'made combination impossible and meetings useless', and there were many who agreed with them.[77] Thus they aimed in quite a small way to extend the limits placed upon them by the authorities. The authorities for their part, however, were determined to resist, and this provoked the conflict that followed.

On 15 May 1890, while the high officials were celebrating the anniversary of the penny post in an orgy of self-congratulation, the postmen decided to mark the occasion by a march and an outdoor meeting at which they would give vent to their grievances. An official ban was proclaimed, and a series of processions was broken up by the police with considerable brutality, one group having to re-form eight times. Eventually, about 1,500 postmen got to Clerkenwell Green in the pouring rain to hear Mahon and James Keir Hardie demand on their behalf a share in the enormous profits made by the Post Office. The authorities replied by demanding an explanation from over a hundred postmen as to why they had been there at all. They found that 'the men . . . with few exceptions, claim their right as Citizens to be present'. They then decided to suspend thirty-one and remove the good conduct stripes of eight others.[78] What followed was described by the *Evening News* of 12 June in this way:

> As each victim appeared amongst his fellows he was loudly cheered. Last night at the Post Office, work was delayed and confused, the men obstinately refusing to take up the duties of the suspended ones. Inspectors and overseers lost control of their usually tractable subordinates, and at one moment there was imminent danger of the whole staff in a certain post-office turning out on strike. But the officers of the Postmen's Union had been prepared for all this and restored order.

The moderation of the union leaders at this point is significant and revealing. Although the work at St Martin's-le-Grand remained 'very much behind owing to the indignation of the men' the Union leaders protested with some justification that while 'termed vilely violent agitators . . . all the time they had to incite the men to keep quiet'. At a local meeting of 200 in East London on 13 June, Mahon said all financial loss would be made up by the Union, but he 'regretted the friction between officers and men'. Nevertheless, inspectors lurking in doorways as those attending the meeting went off, seized individuals and demanded their name and number. Still the Union reacted with moderation. Mahon assured the public that their aim was above all to peacefully 'educate public opinion as to their demands'.[79]

It did seem later in June as if these tactics were achieving some success. The Unionist *Evening News* was publishing full and sympathetic accounts of the activities of the Union. The doughty *Civil Service Gazette* which did not really approve of trade unions nevertheless thought Raikes the most unpopular Postmaster General ever. Hostile questions certainly faced him in Parliament and MPs themselves defied the official rules by attending Union meetings. The sorters too were beginning to pick themselves up from the disappointments of the 'Luminous Committee'. Raikes was even compelled before the end of June to meet a delegation from the Postmen's Union to discuss duty rotas at St Martin's-le-Grand, and to write directly to Mahon, even if only to reiterate his refusal to grant him recognition.

However, already the authorities were beginning to lash out in a way that inevitably caused bitterness. Two days after the rescinding of the 1866 rule about outside meetings, an outdoor meeting was held on Sunday 22 June at Finsbury Park in North London, an area where the Union was particularly strong. This meeting was peaceful and uneventful, but thirty people were suspended for attending it. As a result, feelings ran high by the time of a further meeting held in Hyde Park on the following Sunday 29 June. At least two overseers were recognised among the crowd and after the exchange of hard words and a few blows, these individuals had to be led off by the police. However understandable was such a reaction from men who had already had enough of official 'spying' on their meetings, Union leaders Mahon, Donald and Binning expended much effort in trying to restrain them, and the assembly broke up in good order.[80]

Feelings remained high during the following week when the authorities were preparing for further self-congratulatory junketing on Wednesday 2 July with a celebrity-packed Victorian extravaganza entitled a *converzatione* in the South Kensington Museum. On the Monday morning, 30 June, the overseer who had organised the Huddersfield blacklegging in 1872 was greeted with muffled booing at the Chief Office. On Wednesday morning a superintendent threatened to dismiss two men at the GPO, and the others only agreed to take out the post when this was rescinded. It was on the same evening that telegraphists in every office were supposed to cheer simultaneously in celebration of the penny post jubilee. They all refused to do so. Post Office officials must have been growing more and more worried. When the inevitable suspensions following the Hyde Park events began, the seven victims at the Chief Office were cheered to the echo. At this point it was said that after various pieces of informal go-slow working, 'the universal feeling among the men was to take action immediately by refusing in a solid body to go out with their evening deliveries'. Once again the postmen were held back from such a step by their leaders, though not before a meeting at the GPO on Friday evening had cheered an unfurled red flag and threatened further action if the suspended men did not get their jobs back.[81]

During the following week, relations grew more and more strained, but the leaders of the Union continually held the men back from being provoked into action. On Sunday 6 July, 400 postmen marched along the Thames Embankment as part of a procession to support a hospital charity. This was in defiance of an explicit prohibition from Raikes. On the following day, Monday 7 July, Mahon wrote once again to Raikes asking for the right to hold meetings, the lifting of the disciplinary measures, and recognition for the Union. The same evening there was a crowded meeting of about 1,000 Union members at Holborn Town Hall. Mahon wrote years later what can clearly be confirmed from reports at the time that 'a strike . . . was not urged by myself or anyone on the platform', even though 'the feeling was already at red-heat among the men'. There were some vague statements about strike action if the suspensions were not lifted, and it was asserted that the Executive was 'unable to continue a policy of forebearance, but had come to the conclusion that the men must either knuckle under to the Department or else must come out in the morning'. Despite this militant talk, which clearly reflected the mood in the ranks, the Union leaders brought in George Shipton of the London Trades Council to persuade the meeting to postpone further action for twelve days, during which time he would use his good offices in an effort to persuade the authorities to negotiate.[82] It may be that had the Union leaders been bolder, and begun to organise for and to call a strike at this point, then the outcome might have been different. However, they continued to put a misplaced faith in their ability to persuade the Post Office authorities to listen to their reasonable demands for recognition. The fact was that the strike which was now being constantly discussed was being prepared for only by the authorities, in whose hands the initiative remained over the following days.

THE LONDON POSTMEN'S STRIKE: JULY 1890

That particular Monday, 7 July 1890, must have been especially nerve-racking for those in Government, seeing as it did a remarkable coincidence of discontent in three parts of the state service. At the Wellington Barracks the second battalion of the Grenadier Guards refused without exception to go on parade, in protest against an unpopular officer. This dispute seems to have been settled without much fuss by moving other soldiers into the barracks and agreeing to an inquiry. Less peacefully settled was a more deep-going agitation amongst the Metropolitan policemen, aimed to secure the right to meet and to petition, as well as to obtain an assured pension. On that same Monday evening a small group of police strikers at Bow Street were violently charged by groups of 'loyalist' policemen on horseback. The strikers later admitted that they had been isolated, forced into premature action and then mercilessly smashed.[83] The postal authorities must have watched these events with some apprehension, but they clearly learnt something about the tactics to be pursued in dividing up the discontented.

On that Monday the postal authorities did two things.[84] They first demanded the presence of all postmen, including part-timers, early the following morning. This was not likely to have much effect after the men decided not to strike on the Monday evening, and the postmen lined up to sign on first thing on Tuesday morning without any trouble. However, much greater difficulty was caused by the other step taken by the authorities: the summoning of various auxiliaries who had been employed previously at Christmas and other periods of heavy mail. This step provoked considerable resentment, especially in the GPO at St Martin's-le-Grand, and at the recently opened massive sorting office at Mount Pleasant. At the Chief

Office, these 'strangers dressed in uniform' were driven from the building in the early morning and again in the afternoon. A stream of delegations from the men visited postal controller Tombs and eventually persuaded him to sign a statement acknowledging that the men had decided against strike action. The 'blacklegs' remained on the premises however. They were hidden behind screens, or in the cellar. A 'loyalist' from the Fawcett Association Executive which had also seen Tombs tried to assure the postmen that these people were not doing anybody else's work, but they were driven out of the building nevertheless. The sorters and postmen themselves cheered one another.

On the following day, Wednesday 9 July, tempers grew more heated. At Mount Pleasant there was some violence, particularly when the gates were locked. After they were opened, the 'blacklegs' were seen fleeing from the building 'without their hats'. The official report said they 'went into the street and disappeared'. Meanwhile at St Martin's-le-Grand sorting was still being carried out by the auxiliaries, and the men were only persuaded to take out their mail by a message sent in by Mahon about the victory won down the road at Mount Pleasant. Tombs later asserted that it was a show of police force that caused this result, and explained that at this point 'my desire was to avert a general turn-out' so that 'repression with a stronger hand could with better grace be applied'. If he had provoked a response at that point, he calculated 'at least two-thirds of the Postmen of London would have gone on strike'. At the same time he put in hand preparations 'for the morrow's early morning duty, which it was felt would be a turning point'.

First of all the postmen were cut off from possible sources of support. The telegraphists, who were seriously talking of an overtime ban, were persuaded by their champion, Earl Compton, to abandon any such action. With the sorters the position was more difficult. Monday night's meeting of postmen had been told that the Fawcett Association was in 'a state of collapse'. There may have been some justification for this statement, as a mass meeting of its members on the night of Wednesday 9 July clearly indicated. The discussion showed 'a considerable amount of difference of opinion', and 'scarcely a sentence was given utterance by any of the speakers which was not interrupted' by 'a suspicious minority'. Harry Groves was first of all able to report to the members that their latest representations had been 'favourably reported on by the Authorities' and sent to the Treasury. This clear effort to buy off any support they might give to the postmen was the result of a meeting with the Controller the previous evening. The meeting also expressed itself 'satisfied with the decision of the controller that we sorters shall not be compelled to do postman's duties', and was then persuaded by Clery, on this occasion showing uncharacteristic moderation, that 'whilst sympathising with the Postmen in their present position', their claim for Union recognition should be abandoned and they should negotiate with the Postmaster General 'through Ordinary Official routine'. The meeting was then addressed by one of a deputation of postmen and its attitude dramatically changed. After further discussion the meeting resolved 'by a large majority' that 'while recognising the services rendered by the Fawcett Association, pledges itself to join the Postman's Union at once'.[85]

This resolution was never, in the event, carried out, and the moderate attitudes of Clery, Groves and the other FA leaders were bitter memories for many years afterwards.[86] The likelihood of concessions now on their own demands clearly had an effect on the sorters. So also did a 'secret meeting' said to have taken place the same evening of more senior postmen, who determined not to support any strike. A mass meeting of postmen on the same evening at Clerkenwell Green at 9.30 p.m. did not explicitly plan for the strike that was now continually being discussed. It may well have been this very moderation that led the PU leaders to disaster. After Mahon had restrained the men in their now inevitable scuffles with 'spies', he spoke to them in terms which can only have created confusion. According to the *Pall Mall Gazette* reporter, 'somewhat contrary to expectation, Mr. Mahon recommended his hearers not to strike, as it would be illegal, and perhaps would end in punishment'. The *Evening News* reporter, on the other hand, heard him say that the Union 'was determined that no delivery of letters should take place in the morning', and that the members 'were on no account to commence work until they received orders'. What is certain is that in this confusion there was no clear call at the meeting for action of any kind, and that the authorities had a report of the indecision expressed at the meeting shortly after it ended. It was at that point that Tombs decided on mass sackings at once. He acted without consultation with Raikes, who was out of London. He sent Lewin Hill – at the time Principal Clerk – who had favoured such action from the start, to wake up Post Office Secretary Sir Arthur Blackwood in the middle of the night and together they sat up to prepare for the morning. It must have been about that time that *The Times* heard that a strike was expected, 'but in official quarters the opinion was strongly held last night that the men would have to yield owing to the lack of proper organisation'. This confidence was to prove well justified.

None of the leading officials of the Post Office slept that night. At about 3.00 a.m. Blackwood went to Mount Pleasant and after consulting those in charge there for over an hour, stood on one of the sorting tables to denounce those present for their 'crimes' of the previous day and to proclaim the dismissal of about a hundred of their number. The authorities knew that the next decisive stage would take place at St Martin's-le-Grand because the postmen had 'arranged to follow the lead of the City men'. Blackwood thus repaired rapidly to the GPO, where the postmen were just arriving for work. These comings and going were seen by a surprisingly large crowd of onlookers for that early hour. No less than 486 policemen were counted by one reporter in and around the building. The postmen as they went in said that they would not agree to work if the victimisations continued. Nevertheless, they did go in and began to prepare the letters for delivery. Mahon, who no doubt was less accustomed to such early rising than those who worked in the Post Office, was at this point 'unaccountably absent'. The men dismissed at Mount Pleasant thus decided on their own account to march to St Martin's-le-Grand. On their way they were joined by a few enthusiastic telegraph messengers. On arrival the crowd was confronted by the enormous force of policemen and were compelled to move away from the entrances to the building. As the postmen inside prepared their morning deliveries Blackwood heard that 'the main subject of conversation among them was whether the Department would replace the discharged men'. The postmen must have been subject to many competing emotions. Unlike the Mount Pleasant men outside, they were mostly holding permanent posts and had built up pension rights and good conduct stripes. They were preparing their loads under the eyes of enormous numbers of policemen, with the authorities breathing down the neck of every one of them. The blacklegs were manifestly waiting to step into the shoes of anyone who would not take out his mail. The authorities had carefully broken up and isolated them. The Union leaders had given them no decisive lead, and no guarantees of support. This indeed was what one newspaper described as 'the golden moment'. At 8.00 a.m. the first man picked up his mail bag, pushed past the 200 policemen in the corridor and walked out on to his round. Soon he was followed by others. 'The men were frightened. The hour had passed.' This was how one newspaper aptly put it. From then on the position of the dismissed men and their Union grew more and more difficult.

There was no violence, nor indeed a reaction of any kind, from the pickets when work got under way as usual at St Martin's-le-Grand. A few who refused to take out the mail were dismissed and joined the others outside. Together they marched to the smaller offices. At Leicester Square most of the unestablished men – sixty-five in all – walked out, and were instantly dismissed. The 'flying picket' added to its numbers at London Bridge, but at Waterloo they found that the parcel postmen had been padlocked in. Meanwhile, there was a stronger response in North London, where thirty-nine walked out at Holloway and twenty-nine at Finsbury Park. Altogether 106 people in that area came out. When the men at Whitechapel got the news from Mount Pleasant eighty-five of them 'set up a yell of defiance and marched out of the office'. They were replaced later in the day by auxiliaries who had to obtain military protection against the hostility of the local population. In all 435 men walked out that day. They joined twenty-two others already suspended for various incidents during the agitation. Only forty-four of this total ever got jobs in the Post Office again.

On that same Thursday evening, 10 July, the strikers met once again at Camberwell Green. They were tired out from their marching around all day, but Mahon told them that there would now be a 'general strike', 'until all demands are met', and told them to get home to bed so they could be ready to picket early next day. Here at last was some of the decisive leadership which had been so sadly lacking earlier in the week. The men assembled at four the next morning, and Mahon arrived forty minutes later with leaflets directed at those still working and headed *Who Would be a Rat?* Once again, however, the pickets were intimidated by an enormous force of police, especially in Whitechapel where there were some arrests. The day's work went ahead more or less normally. It was not even true, as Mahon claimed, that the postmen were getting the support of those City merchants who had shown sympathy to the dockers in the previous summer. Some of them were sending offers of help to the authorities. When on Thursday afternoon a 'conciliation' meeting was called by one of their number, it was taken over by a group who cheered Raikes for his efforts to smash the Union. At about the same time Raikes was receiving a delegation of EC postmen, including Charles Churchfield, who had written to him on the Monday before 'deprecating any extreme action'. The Postmaster General made certain that these discussions were widely reported, and concessions were offered on wages.[87] Another meeting took place with postmen from a number of London offices a fortnight later on 24 July at which Raikes offered rather less but clearly showed a willingness to negotiate, if not with the Union, then at least with the postmen themselves.[88]

Meanwhile on Friday 11 July, following the various walk-outs and dismissals, Mahon desperately sought help from elsewhere. He visited the home of John Burns at least twice during the day, but Burns, who had addressed a meeting of cabmen early that morning, knew a lost cause when he saw it, and referred Mahon to the London Trades Council.[89] By the evening there were signs of desperation, as postmen on their rounds were assaulted in the East End, while at the Whitechapel office eighty-three of the ninety-four men signed a pathetically servile petition asking for reinstatement. At Poplar, fifty men were said to have denounced Mahon and torn up their Union cards. The authorities were still in no mood for compromise, and the next morning *The Times* reported triumphantly that 'as the day progressed it became more and more evident that the neck of the movement was broken'. At the end of a difficult and at times worrying week, the City merchants, the newspaper editors and the Tory Cabinet ministers could again sleep easily in their beds. The power and majesty of such groups had been confirmed over the livelihoods of hundreds of postmen and their families, not to mention dozens of policemen.

This was not quite the end of the story for the men who had lost their jobs. Three hundred ex-postmen assembled at Holborn Town Hall on Saturday 12 July. Although there was a vote of confidence in the Union leaders, the dramatic fall in attendance from earlier in the week must have demoralised everybody, and only 100 could stir themselves to march from Hyde Park on the following day. The bitterness that inevitably followed was not just directed against Mahon. 'One who did not sign the petition' exclaimed in the *Star* on 18 July that 'the taint of their disgrace will cling to the men of the EC as long as the City is a name'. If this prophecy was not fulfilled, there must certainly have been some unquiet consciences for a time at St Martin's-le-Grand, and no doubt many who retained their jobs contributed to the distress fund to help those who did not.

Even the efforts to raise this money were plagued by bitterness and dissension. Later in the year Mark Burke, an auxiliary from Notting Hill who was the only one from his office to strike on 9 July, took over the administration of what was left of the fund, and hinted publicly at some peculation by Mahon. This was certainly untrue, and though the accounts had probably not been kept very efficiently, the real significance of the charges is that they reveal the sad demoralisation that had crept into an enterprise which had so recently been entered into with such high hopes.[90] Besides the few who got their jobs back, always after cringing apologies, the others threw themselves on the labour market as best they could. Burke ended as a tramway conductor in Richmond. The others campaigned at least for their pension rights into the 1920s.[91]

AFTERMATH OF THE STRIKE

For all the mismanagement and suffering that came with the 1890 strike, it nevertheless brought about a crucial change in the relations between the authorities and Post Office workers. In the short term, numerous concessions were granted to the telegraphists and the sorters in order to hold them back from making common cause with the postmen. In the long term, effective recognition of the right to organise had to be conceded, if only in an effort to ensure that similar trouble did not erupt again. There can be no doubt that Mahon and the strikers, whatever their errors and shortcomings, had ensured that relations with the authorities could never be the same again. Writing immediately afterwards, Controller Tombs drew the 'moral', 'that the memorials and petitions sent in by the men should be answered promptly', and 'any intended concession should be given quickly'.[92] It was not long before the authorities went well beyond this.

It is not fanciful to attribute the improvements granted in 1890 to sorters, telegraphists and provincial clerks, as much to the postmen as to the efforts of those directly concerned. The timing of the changes, to which a number of references have already been made, shows this clearly enough. Thus in March, an internal committee of inquiry was set up to investigate the conditions of sorting clerks and telegraphists, and proposed a large number of improvements in rates of pay. Further wage increases were granted to the telegraphists in July, and in November the sorters were in part rewarded for their co-operative attitude during the strike by being allowed now to earn up to £2 10s (£2. 50) and by important improvements in holidays and overtime.[93] The postmen themselves were not left out. The delegation from London offices that met Raikes on 24 July did more than simply establish the right for such meetings to take place at all. They also convinced Raikes that they should have boot allowances, of which he became a firm supporter. The strike was also followed by the most comprehensive inquiry into the conditions of the postman undertaken by the Department for thirty years. This Committee, under the chairmanship of William Joyce, was considering detailed evidence by November 1890, and on 17 July 1891 issued a Report which proposed major improvements for both London and provincial postmen. These included the abolition of separate classes within the grades, an allowance for boots and, for the first time, time-and-a-quarter payments for Sunday and other overtime. London suburban postmen also got increases at the top of their scales to £1 6s (£1. 30), £1 8s (£1. 40), £1 10s (£1. 50) and £1 12s (£1. 60).[94]

These improvements were certainly a response to the Postmen's Union, but they did not put an end to the grievances that created it. A protest meeting against the inadequacies of this settlement held by postmen at St Martin's-le-Grand on 15 August agreed to organise a meeting at which a national organisation would be established. This duly took place in September, when thirty-three representatives from London offices and thirty-eight from the provinces – many of them formerly active in the Postmen's Union – agreed to set up the Postmen's Federation with Charles Churchfield, of ECDO, as General Secretary. By December 1,000 London postmen could be assembled at a general meeting and in the following year a new *Postman's Gazette* was begun, and 4,000 were represented at the first annual conference. A Porters Mutual Aid Society was also flourishing in London before the end of 1891.[95] The favourable settlements also reinforced the position of the leaders of the already established associations of London sorters, telegraphists and provincial sorting clerks.

Thus it was that by the end of 1892, all the main groups of manual workers in the Post Office had set up organisations whose subsequent developments can be traced to the present day. The authorities were never again able to extinguish the organised expression of discontent, and the way was open to the development of effective trade unionism and formidable lobbying. There had been many people who laid their livelihood on the line to make this possible. Hawkin, Johnson and Booth of the London postal force had been prepared to stand against the stream in the 1870s. The telegraphists had not been intimidated by official victimisation in the 1870s and 1880s. However, the biggest contribution of all was made by those who suffered in 1890 in the course of a struggle to express their rights to independence. For a time many postmen tried to repudiate and to put the events of 1890 out of their minds. Resentment against the East Central District men, and of course against the sorters, was heard from time to time. It was not long, however, before there were those who were prepared to speak 'with pride of the incalculable good the union brought universally', and the Federation itself boldly asserted that

We cannot proceed . . . without paying a tribute of respect to the Postmen's Union, which undoubtedly paved the way for the establishment of our present stable and constitutional organisation. The pluck and methods of organisation displayed by members of the Postmen's Union are ever worthy of a place in our memory and doubly worthy to be recorded in a history or review of postmen's agitations.[96]

One of the founders of the UPW thirty years' later at the Eastern District office wrote that 'we have the men of 1890 to thank for the large measure of freedom and liberty enjoyed by the Post Office employee of to-day'.[97]

The postmen in 1890 might have found leaders who were more skilled – or luckier. They had looked to 'outsiders' because of the constraints that had been placed upon them. The lack of success of these 'outsiders' was to affect the character of Post Office trade unionism for many generations. Nevertheless, after the strike things were never the same again in the Post Office. The Union had taken a major step in breaking down mutual jealousies, at least amongst the postmen. Both sides were well aware that though the Union had been out-manoeuvred, it had been only one step away from a complete defiance of official rules. It had shown that internal division and petty repression need not prevail. For this reason every succeeding generation of public employees has walked in the footsteps of the Postmen's Union and the strikers of 1890.

NOTES

1 For more on the development of the telegraph system, see Chapter 2, p. 32f. and on the telegraphists Chapter 3, p. 52f.
2 Swift (1929), pp. 123–4.
3 These various incidents are mentioned in *B-H* (5 December 1863); printed circular of 21 November 1866 of the Telegraph Clerks Association and *Preamble and Rules* in UCW Records; Kieve (1973), pp. 185–6; Cully (1889), p. 215; POR 65/1.
4 This early history can be traced from an article about Frederick Heald in *The Telegraphist*, 1 December 1885, and from a letter of Heald dated 20 July 1902 with the rest of his correspondence in the MC, from which most of what follows is derived. Some of these documents are reproduced in 'The telegraphists' struggle in the 'Eighties' in *Post*, 30 December 1939, p. 344 and 13 January 1940, p. 5 and in 'The victimisation of Frederick Heald', *Post*, 29 June 1940, p. 355, 13 July 1940, p. 3, and 27 July 1940, p. 14. There are some press cuttings at R IV/22 and another account in Swift (1929), ch. XII.
5 All this and much more is to be found at POR 30E 274/1872, II, III, IV.
6 *ibid.*, V; Heald's correspondence, Swift (1929), p. 137. The press reports at R IV/22 give lower numbers for individual offices, but a higher overall total of 247. *Telegraph Chronicle*, 23 December 1908, p. 9, gives another coded telegram from this period, but 6, 20 January 1909, pp. 32, 54 record some dispute about its meaning.
7 POR 30E 274/1872 XIV–XX contains statements from press and PMG condemning the action of Scudamore. POR 35/308, p. 253, is a later effort to defend it.
8 *Freeman's Journal* (13 December 1871); 'BO' to Heald, 2 January 1872 (MC), POR 30E 274/1872 and *Telegraphist* (1 December 1885). Martinuzzi (1952), p. 105, says six or seven were dismissed but gives no source for this assertion. POR 35/308, p. 212, mentions a London clerk called Birchall who was 'allowed to resign' instead of being sacked, but Scudamore also argues that the suspensions and exiles are punishment enough.
9 Details in Swift (1929), pp. 144–6.
10 A printed circular was sent from Liverpool on 14 October 1874 asking other offices for details of pay and conditions and denying any intention of setting up a permanent organisation. A further circular of 30 November gives a long list of offices from which replies were received. Both are in UCW House.
11 Kieve (1973), pp. 185–94, for a full discussion of these matters. See also Chapters 2 and 9.
12 Chapter 3, p. 55, on the importance of outside comparisons, and for the quotations, PMG 19th Report for 1872, p. 15, and *B-H*, 10 January 1874.
13 For accounts of the meeting see Swift (1929), p. 48, *Times*, 16 April 1870, and *B-H*, 30 April 1870, and for protests against efforts to ban it, *CSG*, 30 April 1870 and *Hansard* III 200, 1815–6 (26 April 1870).
14 *B-H* 23 July, 6 August, 8, 29 October 1870.
15 The letter carriers memorials are all in PP 1873 XXXIX. For the sorters see *B-H*, 28 June 1872.
16 Details of the Warrington strike are at POR 35/308, pp. 239ff., 325ff., some of which is reprinted in Martin (1977) and *The British Mailcoach*, January 1979.
17 *B-H* (18 May 1872).
18 A full account of events at Huddersfield can be derived from the press cuttings, memoranda and other material in POR 30E, 7564/1872 and what follows is largely based on this. There is also information from the opposite point of view in *B-H* 31 May, 7, 14, 21 June 1872, and *Civilian*, 14 June 1872. Swift (1929), p. 84, mentions a strike in Hull, but he may be confusing the two towns on opposite sides of Yorkshire.
19 Swift (1929), p. 49; *B-H* June 1872 and 6 July 1872 for another early meeting.
20 Swift (1929), pp. 75–6, may exaggerate the extent of the surveillance, but POR 30E 8242/1873 VIII and XX makes it clear that it was no invention. A thick dossier on Booth records every single late attendance as well as many of his comings and goings, and a note of 30 April 1868 describes him as 'disrespectful and insubordinate in his manner towards his superiors'.
21 Swift (1929), p. 50; *B-H* 20, 27 July, 3 August 1872.
22 *Times*, 1 August 1872, and POR 30E 8242/1873 III for the interview and *Times*, 20 November, for the SWDO incident. For the history of 'good conduct stripes' see above p. 51.
23 Full details of the inter-departmental exchanges are in the POR files cited in notes 20 and 22, and summarised in POR 65/3, p. 267. Monsell, who was the first PMG in the Commons, was chided rather after the manner of a disobedient school boy. The general purport of the discussions was publicly known, as can be seen in *The Times*, 25 January and 25 February 1873.

24 *Times* (18 February 1873); *B-H* (1, 8, 15, 22 February 1873).

25 More detail can be found in Swift (1929), chs VI–IX, though his account is full of slight but tiresome inaccuracies. For example, on p. 69, he says that a postal worker wrote in the *Bee-Hive* under the pseudonym 'Silverstick'. No such name was ever used, though articles do appear signed by Hawkin, or else 'Owen Mason' or 'Frank Freeman'.

26 Swift (1929), p. 94 and *B-H* 5 April and 18 October 1873 on the sorters including a similar incident later in the year. The quotations and other statements are from *B-H* 21 December 1872, 8 February, 8 March, 5 April, 17 May, 7 June and 26 July 1873.

27 POR 30E 8242/1873 XXI and XXV.

28 *B-H*, 25 October 1873, on differences between the 'Committee' and the Benefit Society, and *Hansard* III 217, 1110ff. (28 July 1873) for the debate. Other developments can be traced in *B-H* for the period, and all the big meetings and demonstrations are reported widely in the press, e.g. *The Times*, 15 September 1873 and 12 February 1874, *London Journal*, 16 May 1874.

29 *B-H*, 28 March 1874, for finance and 1 August for membership, 16, 23 May for Booth's visits to Manchester and Liverpool, as well as news of the first (and apparently only) annual meeting. The Liverpool men were represented at some of the big London meetings, though by 'outsiders'. For Birmingham support for the society see *B-H* 27 February 1875. In Dublin and Edinburgh, where memorials were organised calling for parity with London, there seems to have been only the traditional form of meeting and committee without any contact with the Benefit Society (*B-H* 16, 30 August 1873).

30 *B-H* (31 January, 2, 9 May 1874) and *Hansard* III, 218, 1582–3 (4 May 1874).

31 The Benefit Society leaflet is in POR 30E 2735/1875 and the various speeches and testimonial meetings are reported in *B-H* 13 June, 1 August, 5, 19, 26 September 1874. *The Times*, 27 August, reports the delegation to the Trades Council.

32 *B-H* (26 September 1874); *Times* (1 January 1875).

33 POR 30E 2735/1875 for the details including the memoranda of Manners, which belie the tone of sweet reasonableness of his Commons statement that the men lost their jobs 'not for memorialising for an increase in pay, but because they allied themselves with professional agitators'. *The Times* of 26 November reprints the memorial, and on 24 December denies that it came from the sorters themselves. *B-H*, 13 February 1875, gives the view cited, and POC, 18 March 1875, the statement that anybody giving any information to the press is liable to 'instant dismissal'.

34 Stephen (1866), p. 443.

35 The statement about income tax is in *Hansard* V, 356, 1051 (1 August 1891) and other examples of later views in Hill (1909) and *Post* (26 August 1933), p. 166.

36 Swift (1929), pp. 148–54, gives details of what followed, which can also be traced in the various issues of *CSG*. In later years there was some controversy about which office had really initiated the agitation. While the first letter was from Birmingham, most of the subsequent initiatives came from Liverpool. In any case, the *Telegraph Chronicle*, 22 January 1909, p. 185, asserts what is evident from the *CSG*, that organisation was already under way before Fawcett became PMG.

37 *CSG* (22 January 1881) and *Report of the Proceedings of the Telegraph Clerks Held in Liverpool* (1881). Heald's correspondence in MC shows the efforts to draw up a unified list of grievances, and the other problems.

38 There is a verbatim manuscript account of the meeting taken by Miss Hoare in MC. *CSG*, 14 March 1881, reports that the delegation found it all 'decidedly unsatisfactory' and similar opinions are given in the issues of 26 March and 2 April.

39 *PG* 1917, p. 353; Stephen (1866), p. 442.

40 PP 1881 LVII for the 'Fawcett Scheme', which was to have a significance far beyond its original context – see e.g. Chapter 3, p. 53.

41 POR 65/3, pp. 57–64.

42 The details that follow are based on PTCA *Rules* (1881) and *Telegraphist* (1883–8), which did not at first identify itself with the Association. The General Secretary's reports for the period are in R IV/6 and there are also details in *Telegraph Service Gazette*, 8 June 1888 and *Telegraph Journal*, 2 June 1890. (The Central Committee Minutes for 1882–91 have found their way into MC.) A few delphic statements on this period are to be found in Hall (1902) and more detail in a series of articles by Helen Dixon in the *Telegraph Journal* beginning on 25 December 1908, though they contain a number of inaccuracies.

43 The telegraphists whose complaints were published were too frightened to go to court to repeat them, so the *Gazette* collapsed with a debt of £300.

44 *TSG* (25 February 1887).

45 On the sorters see Martinuzzi (1952), p. 112 and for the letter carriers, POR 60/15, 60/89 and R I/33.

46 *CSG* 4 December 1886 was the Ridley Summons and there is a copy at F 100 of the letter that called the first meeting of the UKPCA. *The Telegraphist*, 1 February 1887, gives details of its early history and there is a retrospective account in *Postal Journal*, August–December 1895. Swift (1929), pp. 228–39 has more details on the grievances of the provincial postal clerks which are also discussed in Chapter 8 below.

47 R I/33 has an account of the Bolton meeting and other relevant material, including the minutes of meetings held at the time in other London offices. Other details can be traced in Swift (1929), p. 194ff., *PTSG* in 1887, *PG* 1917, p. 370 and *The Tom Dredge Case* (1888). The effects of the campaign can be seen in *Hansard* III, 328, 1403 (16 July 1888) and official discussion on how to deal with it in POR 30E 18949/1891 I.

48 *PTSG* 1887–8, *Daily Telegraph*, 23 September 1890, and *Post*, 6 December 1952, on this phase. The Benefit Society Rules are at F 393.8.

49 *Post*, 19 February 1898, for the figures. *Toby*, 8, 15, 22 May 1886 for the articles and letters. Swift (1929), p. 161, claims there are similar articles in this period in a sensationalist paper called *Town Talk* and a local East End paper in cockney dialect called *The Rag*, but a careful search has failed to reveal anything.

50 On the Fawcett Scheme (PP 1881 LVII) see Clery (1889). Swift (1929), pp. 164ff., gives much detail on this agitation, in which he was an active participant. He is however unreliable on many particulars, and usually takes the side of Clery in the internal disputes of the movement.

51 POR 30E 300/1889 I; Raikes (1898), pp. 334–5, 338; Swift (1929), p. 220. *PSG* 19 April 1889 for the first meeting and *Post*, 23 August 1930, for the Raikes–Clery confrontation.

52 *Star*, 12 December 1889, gives a graphic account of the crowded December meeting and the discussions around the February one are preserved in R VI/I and recalled by Clery in *Post*, 30 August 1930. *Post*, 15 February 1890, gives Clery's statement on the name.

53 Full accounts of these meetings are in R VI/I from which the quotations are taken – see also *Evening News*, 18 June 1890. Clery's articles in the *Post* in 1930 give further details including a claim that he met Joyce the night before the report of the 'Luminous Committee' came out and was promised promotion if he gave up the agitation. Details of the subsequent demands are in Swift (1929), pp. 191–2.

54 *Telegraph Journal* (January 1890). The *Hansard* volumes of the period are full of Parliamentary questions about telegraphists' conditions.

55 *Departmental Tyranny at the Post Office: The Case for the Victimised Telegraphists* (Cardiff, 1890) contains all the early material starting with the *Western Mail* article of 22 August 1889. There is much more in the *Telegraph Journal*, 1 March 1890ff., and *Post*, 16 March 1940, p. 188, 30 March, p. 222, quotes some material now in MC.

56 *Telegraph Journal* (1 March 1890); *Daily Telegraph* (15 November 1889); *Cork Examiner* (13 March 1890); *Postal Journal* (November 1889).

57 *Hansard* III, 343, 581–602 (15 April 1890); *Telegraph Journal* (1 May 1890).

58 POC, 787, 19 April 1890.

59 *Telegraph Journal* May–November 1890; Swift (1929), p. 224. The quotation is in Hall (1902), p. 39. On Quin see R IV/22 and *Post*, 21 April 1934, where his death at the age of 66 is recorded. After his dismissal he became founder, proprietor and editor of the *Metal Bulletin*.

60 Swift (1929), pp. 194–213, sets out this basic view, which is in part designed to excuse the role of Clery and the sorters, which was not universally considered creditable. This is followed closely by Clegg, Fox and Thompson (1964), p. 216 and also by Thompson (1955), pp. 652–3, though he adds some further comments on the 'amateurish conduct of the affair' and the 'innate tendencies to intrigue' of the leaders of the Postmen's Union. *PG* 1914, pp. 51–2, reproduces a later statement of Lewin Hill and a number of articles in 1917 deal with the period. *Post*, January 1924, pp. 29–31 and 55–6, contains an account by Mahon himself. For the inner history of the PU most detail is to be found at POR 30E 300/1899.

61 *Post* (12 January 1924), p. 30.

62 *Hansard* III, 334, 1587 (4 April 1889).

63 The programme is in R IV/22.

64 Thompson (1955), pp. 615–6 and Pelling (1965), pp. 55, 58, 83, 110 where, for reasons unexplained, the Labour Union is identified with Hoxton in East London. There is some further information in BAR.

65 Thompson (1955), and Labour Union Manifesto (1888) at BAR 3/9.

66 POR 30E 300/1899 II. *Star*, 21 September, advertised the meeting in advance and gave a full

report on 23 September as also did the *Daily Telegraph* and other papers. Swift (1929), p. 200, gives the wrong date. Incidentally, Bull does not seem to have obtained the going rate for informers. According to the same Post Office file (XXVI) a total of £42 was paid for 'confidential services', including £15.75 for an unnamed 'Reporter', and £3.15 for Inspector Fox, manhandled at the Hyde Park meeting.

67 POR 30E 300/1899 III; *North London Press* (28 September); *Star*, 25, 27, 30 September, 1, 2, October.

68 *Daily Telegraph*, 1 October, has Henderson's Manifesto and 2 October what seems to be an officially inspired reply to it. The following protest is in *Evening News* (12 October 1889).

69 *Daily Telegraph*, 21, 28 October, 11 November, on the meetings which are also reported in the *Star*, where there is an account of the 31 October meeting given in most detail by Swift (1929), p. 202. A *Post Office Gazette*, 16 November 1889 (only issue), gave the membership as 1,400–1,500 and said that the internal dispute was having little effect. The *Illustrated Weekly News* of 26 October has a (not very inspired) picture of the 20 October demonstration, and on 2 November a rather cryptic account of the internal dispute.

70 Champion's continued hostility can be gathered from the piece in his paper *Labour Elector* (2 November 1889). Kent (1950) mentions the possibility that Burns might have become PU Secretary but concludes with justice that he was 'ill equipped for such a post'. Swift's (1929) account entirely reflects the view of Clery and is hardly credible knowing Clery's personality. This is the only source for the claim that Mahon would not work with Burns – he certainly sought his help later, when it was refused (see n. 89). After Swift's volume first appeared in 1900, Burns claimed he could provide 'other' information on what had happened – R VI/9, p. 263 – but there is no evidence of this in his papers (which are to be found in the British Library), or elsewhere. So it seems that it will never be possible to tell the full story of the involvement of Burns.

71 The BL has issues of this first *Postman's Gazette* for October, February and March and POR 30E 300/1899 V can add those for April and May as well as a final issue dated 19 July and numbered 8. BAR has issue 7. The details of meetings, delegations and contacts are taken from these.

72 *Star* (9 December 1889); Donald (1890), p. 13; *Illustrated Weekly News* (30 November 1889).

73 POC, 770, 31 December 1889 has the statement and *Postal Review*, 7 February 1890, a comment.

74 *Star* (22 February 1890); *Times* (11 February 1890).

75 *PG* 12 November 1892 and 1917, p. 385.

76 Mahon in *St. James' Gazette*, 1 July 1890. This paper also published on 26 June a strong attack on the 'professional agitators' leading the Union.

77 PU statement quoted in *The Times* of 20 June. *The Evening Dispatch* (Edinburgh) of 21 April considered that 'a more stringent system of coercion could hardly be designed', and similar sentiments were expressed by MPs in *Hansard* III, 342, 125–7 (6 March), 1270–2 (24 April), 4410–1, (25 April) and 345 *passim*. For more detail see Chapter 4, p.82.

78 These events are described in the *Evening News* and the *Star* for 17 May. The vigorous Parliamentary protests that followed them are in *Hansard* III, 344, 1281–3 (19 May) and the stern warnings and careful weeding out of individuals after that in POR 30E 300/1899 VII.

79 *Times* (20 June 1890), *Star* (16, 14 June), *Evening News* (14 June), *Nineteenth Century* (July 1890), p. 122. The authorities continually denied that there were any delays in deliveries (eg *Hansard* III, 345, 1363 – 19 June 1890) but London Controller Tombs later admitted them privately (POR 30E 300/1899 XX). *ibid.* XIX contains denials about the East London incident, though it is admitted that there were some officials involved in 'delicate' activities at the meeting.

80 *Evening News*, 23 June, describes the Finsbury Park meeting. Swift (1929), p. 206, gives the wrong date for the Hyde Park meeting which is described in all the papers on 30 June. The violence there was to some degree in the eye of the beholder as can be seen by contrasting the hostile account in *The Times* with the *Evening News* report which talks only of 'jostling' and notes the sympathy between policemen and postmen. That there certainly were 'official spies' present whose purpose was to prepare names for punishment is clear from POR 30E 300/1899 IX.

81 *Evening News*, 1–5 July for all this.

82 *ibid.*; *Times*, 7, 8 July; *PG*, 19 July. Mahon's letter is at POR 30E 300/1899 XI, and his later statement at *Post*, 12 January 1924, p. 30. The left-wing paper *Commonwealth* on 12 July says that the postponement of strike action at this point did not have the support of the men.

83 These events are in all the newspapers and there is an account of the policemen's agitation in Reynolds and Judge (1968), pp. 213–25.

84 The events of this and the following days are described in the daily press with the *Evening News* giving the fullest reports from the point of view of the men and *The Times* largely acting as a mouthpiece for the authorities. POR 30E 300/1899 XX has a retrospective account written by

Tombs from which the following quotations are taken. Another version, generally hostile to the Union, is in Price (1891), and this in turn seems to be the main source for the details given in the *Post Diary and Year Book* for 1922. *PG*, 1917, pp. 401–2 adds some further embellishments, not all of which seem plausible.

85 The Minutes of this meeting are in R VI/3, pp. 33–4, and the description in Price (1891), p. 347 and *Evening News*, 10 July. Martinuzzi (1952), pp. 127–8, underestimates the skill of the authorities by attributing the success of the sorters at this point to the moderation of Clery and the FA leaders.

86 See, for example, *Post*, 22 September 1906, pp. 634–5 containing a letter by E. J. Nevill which the *Postman's Gazette* refused to publish about the 9 July meeting, including reference to 'a secret meeting of a large number of letter-carriers' which is presumably the discussion of senior men who resolved not to strike.

87 *Hansard* III, 346, 1040 (7 July). The ECDO Committee represented the most aristocratic group of postmen, who stood to lose most by any punishment. It had decided to join the Union earlier in the year, but was now clearly worried by the talk of striking, and the authorities did everything to ease communication with them. See also *Daily Chronicle* (12 July) and *PG* (27 May 1893).

88 The fullest record of this is in *PG* 26 May 1906, pp. 309–14.

89 The letters left by Mahon are preserved in Burns's papers in the British Museum Additional Manuscripts 46289/121–3. On 11 July Mahon implores: 'Our men are a little inclined to lose heart . . . I wish you would come and help us. I think it is your duty to.' A week later he wrote pointing out that the London Trades Council mediation was offered only on condition the blacklegs were removed.

90 On these later stages see *ibid.*, 130, 271. The MC at 310.5 has some material, mostly financial, given by Mahon to the UPW in 1925, and a public exchange of letters between Mahon and Burke in December 1890.

91 On Burke there is a letter ın R VI/33 and POR 30E 300/1899 XX. The authorities carefully considered individual cases and only re-employed those who had played a very minor role. As late as 1918 they refused to restore seniority to the re-employed men. *Hansard* III, 349, 210–24 (28 November 1890) makes it clear that those dismissed included sorters who had approved of the Union, and people who had simply attended the earlier meetings. *ibid.* 751–2 (9 December) on the banning of collections for ex-colleagues.

92 POR 30E 300/1899 XX.

93 POR 60/90 for the report; Swift (1929), pp. 242–3 and Martinuzzi (1952), p. 131, for some details of the settlement. The overall effects can be gathered from the increases for 1890 and 1891 in wages tables given in Appendices 8 and 9, pp. 626–8 below.

94 *PG* 1906, pp. 309–14. The printed but unpublished report of the Joyce Committee, and a verbatim account of its evidence, is in POR 60/91, and there is some other material in POR 30E 189449/1899 and PP 1890–1 LXIII.

95 UPW 1950, pp. 14–15; *Evening News* (16 September 1892); *Post* (22 August, 19 September 1891, 30 January 1892).

96 *Post* 1906, pp. 643–5; *PG* 10 June, 12 November 1893, 1896, p. 570.

97 *Post* 28 February 1920, p. 200.

7 The Inquiries and After: 1895–1919

His Lordship tolls the knell of parting scheme;
Th' expectant crowd, disconsolate, melts away;
Th' elusive prospect fadeth like a dream,
And clouds enshroud the longed-for higher pay.

(Excerpts from an Elegy 13 January 1905
With Condolence to Thomas Gray, *The
Post*, 28 January 1905)

The one thing the Holt Committee will do with greater
success than anything mentioned in their Report will be to
hasten the uniting of all Postal Associations, and the at one
time wild improbability of an all-grade Postal Strike has
been brought into the realm of probability. (C. G.
Ammon, *The Post*, 12 September 1913)

During the two decades after 1895, public inquiries were the main means of altering
wages and conditions in the Post Office. This was a time when trade unions were
being built in private industry and agreed industrial relations procedures were
being established. The inquiries into the Post Office reflected the fact that
associations of Post Office workers had taken one step away from the system of
unquestioned authority in the public service, but were not yet at a point where they
were accepted as bargaining agencies able to negotiate agreements which would
then be observed. Great hopes were invested by Post Office workers in this means of
settling their grievances, but as the quotations above indicate, the results obtained
caused frustrations and disappointment not only with what was offered, but also
with the system itself. In the end new methods had to be found, and arbitration
machinery and Whitley councils were set up.

Long before the associations were built or there was the remotest chance of their
being recognised by the authorities, there had been inquiries within the Post Office
into the conditions of those who worked there. Thus in 1860 a group of officials
studied conditions at the General Post Office, and in 1890 the Joyce Committee
considered the grievances of disaffected postmen. However, these were secret
discussions by the 'benevolent despots' in charge of the service. Their proceedings
were never published, nor were many of their proposals ever implemented. In the
1890s, when the associations went into action, they had few methods of agitation
open to them beyond the meetings, petitions, bands and processions of former
generations. At the same time they were unable to deal directly with the authorities
about the details of their wages and conditions by methods that became normal in
later generations. The solution they devised was for persistent Parliamentary
lobbying centring around the demand for a full and public inquiry into all aspects of
their conditions.

There were important reasons why public inquiries, in various forms, came to the centre of Post Office agitation in the 1890s. For one thing, the call for an inquiry served to rally the scattered and divided ranks of Post Office workers. As they got together with increasing frequency to discuss their grievances, they grew more and more convinced that any independent and fair-minded outsider would inevitably take their part. On the other hand, those in authority within the Department, and Members of Parliament who transmitted pressure from constituents working for the Post Office, looked to this procedure as a method of putting an end to discontent once and for all. This was the background to the setting up of the four great inquiries of the period – the Inter-departmental Committee on Post Office Establishments under the Chairmanship of Lord Tweedmouth (1895–7), the Committee on Post Office Wages under Sir Edward Bradford (1903–4), the Select Committee on Post Office Servants under Charles Hobhouse (1906–7), and the Select Committee on Post Office Servants (Wages and Conditions of Employment) (1912–13) under R. D. Holt. There was also a committee to examine the issues arising out of the Report of 1912–13 under G. S. Gibb, which soon suspended its activities on account of the war.[1]

The proceedings of these various bodies showed that the agreement to set up an inquiry was by no means the solution to every problem. There were questions about who should do the inquiring, what they should inquire into, and what would be the effect of their recommendations. For the Post Office workers, it was a matter of trying to get any proceedings free from the pervasive influences of Treasury control and civil service cheeseparing, and to present their case in a way that was clear and without contradiction. The authorities, on the other hand, hoped to secure an outcome favourable from their point of view by the appointment of a group of senior civil servants chaired by a Liberal politician in the case of Tweedmouth. They then tried an 'outside' body of businessmen in the case of Bradford. The first of these provoked little but discontent in the workforce, and the second proved so unexpectedly favourable to their claims that its recommendations were never carried out. The inquiries under Hobhouse and Holt were Select Committees of MPs. Hobhouse reported in favour of some improvements for the lower grades, but left too many unsolved problems and a great deal of discontent. Holt undertook the most mountainous labours of all and published a report that was on the whole more favourable to the higher grades, but was hotly disputed by all. The problems of dis-entangling its recommendations were so complex that a new committee had to be set up to study it, which this time included representatives of the associations themselves. The advent of war caused the Gibb Committee to abandon its labours with some relief early in 1916. The war also led to the search for new and more satisfactory methods of resolving the grievances of Post Office workers and other public servants. This search began with the arbitration machinery and culminated in the setting up of the Whitley system.

The proceedings of these great inquiries and the results which flowed from them repay scrutiny more than half a century later. For one thing, the verbatim reports of the answers given to the questions put to Post Office workers and the authorities, speak to us down the generations of the aspirations and prejudices of both sides. They show the bonds and mutual jealousies within the workforce, and the attitudes of their superiors to conditions in the service. Furthermore, the inquiries represented a particular episode in the development of British industrial relations, and they brought their own important consequences. Their very proceedings acknowledged associations as representative organisations, indicated the need for more effective argument of the case of the Post Office workers, and showed clearly the ill consequences of disunity and mutual distrust. They thus played a major role in the strengthening of the associations, in making them work in a more professional manner, and in unifying their efforts. From the point of view of the authorities and the Government, they showed the impossibility of settling the grievances of large bodies of public employees by hiving them off to senior civil servants, or businessmen or, and this most especially, to committees of MPs. As the political pressures exercised by organised Post Office workers became more unified and effective, the inquiries grew less capable of arriving at any conclusion at all, and the need for a more fixed and satisfactory method of regulating industrial relations grew increasingly obvious. The failure of every alternative led to the acceptance of more 'normal' bargaining machinery in the form of Whitleyism, and eventually 'direct' negotiations.

TWEEDMOUTH: 1895–7

Though the demand for outside inquiry had been heard in Parliament as far back as 1845 and a Committee of MPs to consider the grievances of postal workers was suggested in 1867, the first widespread publicity for such a step was provided by Lord Compton's House of Commons motion on 15 April 1890 in support of the telegraphists. The demand gathered support from other sections of the Post Office workforce, and was at the centre of the events surrounding the dismissal of Clery and Cheesman in 1892 from the ranks of the London sorters. The preferred form for any inquiry was never quite clarified, though Keir Hardie advised the sorters against a cumbersome Royal Commission. By 1894, the postmen had joined in, and they even ran a joint meeting with the sorters centred around the demand.[2] During 1894 a series of delegations from MPs, the London Trades Council and others was organised, and eventually on 17 May 1895, Postmaster General Arnold Morley agreed to the establishment of an Inter-departmental Inquiry.[3]

When the personnel of the inquiry were announced, the Chairman proved to be Lord Tweedmouth, a leading Liberal politician who was just then completing a term as Lord Privy Seal in the outgoing administration. The other members were all leading civil servants. Sir Arthur Godley, Secretary of the India Office, was not greatly interested in the inquiry, and is said to have slept through most of it. Sir Francis Mowat represented the Treasury. H. Llewellyn Smith of the Board of Trade, in later years chief economic adviser to the Government, showed himself a rigid supporter of the principles of political economy, particularly of the determination of wages by the outside market. However, he was not unsympathetic to the Post Office workers. Last but not least was Spencer Walpole, Secretary to the Post Office, who was by far the most active member of the Committee and did all the things one might expect of someone acting as a judge in his own case. The associations and their members should have been warned of the problems by the make-up of the Committee, not to mention the terms of reference which maintained that the Post Office should 'continue to be conducted with a view to profit, as one of the Revenue yielding Departments'. The sorters were of the opinion that it was 'impossible to conceive that a Committee of Enquiry constituted as Mr. Morley suggests . . . can have the least sympathy with the claims that will be urged upon them'. However, most Post Office workers had such a profound conviction that right was on their side, that they simply could not conceive of an unfavourable outcome.[4]

The Tweedmouth Committee itself certainly went about its task with enthusiasm and industry. Its lengthy proceedings, held in Committee Room B of the House of Lords during 1895 and 1896, have been recorded for posterity in a positively luxurious profusion of detail, not only in the gigantic official 'blue book', but also in the journals of the associations and in the many special publications that they issued. The published verbatim account of the Enquiry's proceedings takes 1,152 double-columned pages and includes 15,772 questions and answers on virtually every possible aspect of work in the Post Office, together with a multiplicity of rejoinders and answers to the rejoinders.[5]

These pages reveal all the special snobberies and deeply felt resentments of those who found themselves trapped within an uncertain hierarchy from which they could not escape. Time after time the Committee heard complaints of 'discrimination', 'passing over', and 'favouritism'. They also heard much that reflected the mutual suspicions of postmen who wanted to be paid and treated like sorters, of sorters and counter clerks who thought they had a right to the rewards of the telegraphists, and of telegraphists who aspired to the status and conditions of the second division clerks. The sorters said they wished to be known as 'postal clerks', since 'a large proportion of their number have come from middle-class families and have been educated at fairly good schools'. From further down the scale came the bitter complaint that 'the official desire is that the postmen be called in the manner that convicts are called, i.e. number so-and-so, postman Walsh'. Nowhere outside the pages of the Tweedmouth Enquiry is it revealed more clearly how the progress of the Victorian Post Office was undermining the status of those who once held a more respected position in the community. As the service had expanded successive postmasters general had boasted in their reports of an increasing range of facilities provided. However, the Tweedmouth Committee had to admit what had long been obvious to those who worked there, 'that the Post Office has in the past increased the strain on its servants by its anxiety to afford the maximum of convenience to the public'.[6]

The Committee was appointed on 10 June 1895, first met on 24 June and finished hearing evidence a year later on 15 June. Its Report was completed on 15 December 1896, approved by the Treasury on 19 March 1897, and published on the following day. The very setting up of the Enquiry has been described with justice as 'one of the most momentous events in the history of postal trade unionism'.[7] The Committee refused to discuss 'civil rights', either in relation to trade union recognition or participation in political activity, nor would it hear evidence from Clery and Cheesman who were no longer working for the Post Office. Nevertheless, it was compelled to arrange its proceedings in such a way as to deal with representative bodies. Even if a certain fiction was maintained by questioning individuals about their personal employment history, it was not as 'typical examples', but as the representatives of organised groups that they spoke. The Enquiry not only strengthened the associations that already existed and stimulated contact between them, it also caused the setting up of many new organisations, for example among the sub-postmasters. Above all, both the proceedings and the results made obvious the necessity to further develop trade unionism in the Post Office in order to compete with the research facilities of the authorities and the arguments they had at their command.

The format of the Enquiry often had the effect of making the workers' representatives base their arguments on particular, exceptional cases. They frequently made generalisations from limited experience, or sometimes made assertions, notably on health matters, which could not be verified one way or the other. However, the authorities also made some errors of fact, and agreed to remedy a number of individual grievances during the course of the Enquiry itself. For example, they accepted that all work above forty-eight hours a week by travelling sorters should be considered as overtime. As proceedings unfolded, the views of the Committee developed, notably in a desire to break down and simplify the plethora of divisions and sub-grades in the service.

From the beginning of the Enquiry most of the grades resisted any comparison with outsiders, simply asserting that whatever they did was as valuable or as difficult as the tasks in the grade immediately above. If there was to be any outside comparison, it was always of a most elevated sort, for example between sorters and high-level 'confidential clerks'. More easily measurable were the 'split duties' of the sorters which they considered 'the greatest grievance under which they needed to labour'. Even here, however, it was difficult to arrive at an agreed and objective assessment. Thus while the Fawcett Association witnesses said that if their members attended only once a day it would cost the service £86,000, Jasper Badcock, who was Controller of the London Postal Service, put the figure at over £100,000 if all the repercussions were taken into account.[8]

The bewildering array of sub-groups within the service was made clear to the Committee from the evidence given on behalf of a series of small grades who performed tasks akin to sorters. Thus 'bagmen' who arranged bags of mail for the sorters had their claim to be placed on a level with sorters rejected. However, a wage increase, already recommended by Badcock and rejected by Walpole, was now agreed. The only grievance of the travelling sorters that was accepted, besides the one on overtime, was that punishments should be changed from extra duties to fines. The claim of sorters who did writing duties to be designated as a separate grade was also rejected, though the Committee did agree with the recent setting up of a new grade of 'sorter-tracers' from those who dealt with telegram dockets and other such documents, and who had had an association of their own since 1893. After the Committee had fought its way through this jungle of competing sub-groups it generally favoured greater standardisation. Where a new grade was set up, as in the case of the sorter-tracers, the reaction was less positive. W. E. Clery described this new arrangement as 'one of the greatest changes that have ever menaced our position'.[9]

Evidence on behalf of the telegraphists was presented quite efficiently by the PTCA, with representatives of the ten-year and five-year men, and the women. However, the telegraphists proved less convincing than most others, being particularly prone to vague and unsupportable statements – 'highly coloured' according to one spokesman of the authorities – about the intensity of their labours. They failed to convince anyone that their tasks were particularly demanding in a technical sense. The first witness on their behalf was Andrew Nicholson, Chairman of the London PTCA Branch, who, despite his opinion that 'the men at the Central Office ought really to be treated exceptionally', argued convincingly that the three separate classes within the telegraphist grade at the office did not perform functions that were substantially different. He claimed that when allowances were taken into account, many telegraphists were receiving less than sorters, though in his view they should be getting a great deal more. Comparisons were made with private cable companies where wages were higher. Walpole claimed that this disparity only existed because the companies needed to attract people from the comparative security of the Post Office. Charles Garland, London PTCA Secretary, gave evidence of pressure of work, resulting particularly from long and short duties on alternate days and weeks. There were also protests about the number of holidays that had to be taken outside the summer months.

The response to all this was given by Henry Fischer, Controller of the London Telegraph Office, who favoured the standardisation of the grade structure along the lines ultimately proposed by the Committee, particularly by further merging sorting and telegraph work. General complaints from the telegraphists with regard to health, holidays and pensions were largely ignored, and this despite a statement they got from the Professor of Civil Engineering at the Glasgow and West of Scotland Technical College;

> It is my firm belief that the telegraph service is distinguished to a marked degree from other branches in the Civil Service inasmuch as their physical labour is of an arduous and harassing nature and involves a constant physical strain.[10]

Women telegraphists got even less out of the Enquiry. Only two of them appeared as witnesses and only one of these had the temerity to ask for an increase in their extraordinarily low wages. The only point in the entire proceedings when Walpole told a witness 'I quite agree with you there' was to complaints about female telegraphists supervising men in London. The point, however, was insisted upon much more strongly by the authorities than by a male Association representative, who refused to accept that 'a man is capable of doing more work than a lady', and simply maintained that it was a matter of no particular group having a right to more than its fair share of promotions. On the question of their pay, the Association witnesses thought the women themselves would 'have something to say about that'. However, the women witnesses seem to have been too intimidated to make any impression. Thus there was no real reply given to the claims by the authorities that women were less efficient at some jobs, more frequently absent, and did not perform a number of duties, notably night-work. Thus the Report was able to arrive at the conclusion that:

> the evidence given seemed to indicate that no considerable dissatisfaction existed as to their conditions of service, and we are also assured by the Post Office authorities that there is a general absence of complaint from them, and that though their rates of pay are considerably lower than those for men, large numbers of women of good position and education are anxious to enter the Service.

A change in the labour market as well as in social attitudes was thus necessary before there could be progress from the point of view of women telegraphists.[11]

London 'Countermen', also represented by the PTCA, asked for the status of 'a cashier in a bank', and resented their title as more appropriate 'to employees in provision shops or grocery establishments whose work is not for one instant to be compared with ours'. The only response from the Committee was the proposal that they should be more closely integrated with the telegraphists.[12]

When the Enquiry went on to consider the provincial and general grades, they became less tolerant of repetition and internal rivalries. The case for the sorting clerks and telegraphists, led by Thomas Venables of the UKPCA, was particularly characterised by exaggerated and unverifiable propositions. Venables was compelled to admit that there was no way in which ultimate equity could be guaranteed for promotion as between the telegraph and postal sides. He was even drawn into a discussion of the relative merits of long and short duties as against split duties when he was advocating the abolition of both. There were some subjective comparisons with outside wages, and a few attacks on women for having undermined conditions in the service as a whole. James Green, an SC&T from Chesterfield, presented his evidence in a rather less restrictive spirit, referring to the great disparity of rewards for similar work throughout the service, attacking the wages paid to women as an example, and concluding that someone in his position could not 'be reasonably expected to maintain that degree of respectability . . . which his general surroundings entitle and require of him'. Replying on behalf of the authorities to all this and much more besides, Charles Kerry, the Postmaster of Stoke-on-Trent, asserted that 'the present rates of pay according to the market rate are sufficient', and 'compare very favourably with the rates of pay given in the commercial world to merchants' and lawyers' clerks and the like'. Such arguments were well calculated to appeal to all the principles of political economy and civil service cheeseparing. On disputed questions like the prevalence of people doing the work of the grade above, the Committee simply took the word of the authorities as against that of the association.[13]

The case for the postmen was generally well organised and presented, but suffered from the attacks made on others in the service. Charles Churchfield, Secretary of the Postmen's Federation, began well by asking for an increase in pay at the minimum from 19s (90p) to £1 4s (£1. 20). Few other witnesses even referred to the grievances of junior grades. Churchfield and the other witnesses went on to attack all non-service comparisons on the grounds that postmen were 'altogether a superior class to outside workers'. They resented the decline in their relative status since the letter carriers of earlier generations. They also compared themselves favourably with the sorters, claiming that the work of the postman was more arduous and equally as responsible. Other PF witnesses naturally were of the opinion that the work of the postmen 'cannot fairly be classified as unskilled labour', and that 'the so-called law of supply and demand' could not be said to apply to a postman who was unable to change his employer. Within the service, they argued, 'the difference between sorting clerks and postmen should be abolished, and the postmen and sorting clerks should be interchangeable'.

John Walsh of Liverpool said he would recommend the Committee 'to increase no salaries in the postal service except those of postmen'. Walsh was an eminently reportable witness who expressed himself vividly and colourfully, though more in terms of the mutterings that could no doubt often be heard when any group of postmen were gathered together than with evidence of a kind that might impress the Committee. He expressed all the resentments of those at the bottom of the hierarchy, asserting for example that new tests for sorters had been introduced 'in order to keep the postmen out', attacking the evidence of others, and at one point even being stopped by Walpole with the question: 'Is it necessary to your case that you should abuse your fellow officers or other classes?'. However, Walsh was not deterred, insisting that it was necessary to reduce the salaries of those higher up the service, since 'the clerk's comparative luxury, properly understood, is the cause of the postmen's misery'. In a final outburst, Walsh declared the promotion by merit system to be 'helotry' as a 'method of discipline'. No doubt statements such as these were cheered in many a postman's retiring room, but they rather obscured more substantial arguments about the weights postmen were forced to carry, the lack of payment for sorting duties, and a number of individual cases of hardship. Another Liverpool postman, Stephen Dowling, made a good case against split attendances and holiday arrangements, particularly on the capricious operation of the system, but again diminished the force of his argument by insisting that the sorters were always better treated.[14]

The next witness, D. S. Boston, a postman from Kentish Town, began by disagreeing with the spirit in which the Liverpool evidence had been presented. 'The London postmen do not complain', he said, 'of the high rate of any class in the Service. All that they complain of is that the channel is not open for them to rise to the same'. He argued that all split duties of eight hours should be done within twelve hours. Taking up the particularly unsatisfactory state of affairs on this matter in the Hampstead Office, he replied effectively to Walpole's claim that something was being done about this by saying that this had first been promised six years earlier. A similarly reasoned case was made out by Henry Wilson on behalf of those who served as auxiliary postmen for many years without getting established appointments. It was argued that such service should count towards pensions and allowances, and shown that in Glasgow virtually every established postman had to serve an apprenticeship as an auxiliary. Furthermore, although auxiliaries were normally supposed to pursue other occupations to supplement their meagre wages, examples were cited to prove that the extra duties imposed by the Post Office often made this impossible.

A series of witnesses then took up a number of particular grievances. G. H. Stuart argued that the parcel post should be separated from the letter post, though he was compelled to admit that this might be difficult to arrange outside the big cities. Punishments, which in London were in some measure standardised, could affect a postman for his entire working life. In the provinces they were uncertain and arbitrary. They were said to be inflicted for trade union activity, including writing articles in the *Postman's Gazette*. Rural postmen asked for a 16-mile limit on the distance they were to be expected to walk each day, and this was accepted by the Committee as an 'average', with eighteen as an 'absolute maximum'. The rural men also asked for the same rates of pay as those in towns, but this was rejected without serious discussion. Evidence was also heard about the medical services and the anomalies of the London zoning system. Postmen from the Chief Office complained about the call for the abolition of Christmas boxes, but were not well received by the Committee. Some other smaller groups also gave evidence, including an association of porters and labourers whose spokesman gloried under the name of Julius Caesar William Borgia.[15]

It was to this evidence of the postmen that the authorities felt it necessary to provide their most detailed rebuttal, with three major figures in the Post Office hierarchy appearing to give it. Jasper Badcock considered that there was no need for any changes at the bottom of the salary scale of a postman since there was 'no lack of applicants for postmen's places', though he did agree that 'the time he takes to reach the maximum is too long, and the increment ought to be increased'. Furthermore, in common with other London officials he considered 'a postman's duties are equal in importance to, and if anything more arduous than, those of a second class sorter'. He defended the payment of five different rates within London, though the Committee later reduced these to three. He claimed that efforts were being made already to prevent the total working period from exceeding twelve hours as recommended by the Joyce Committee in 1891, though there were certainly still exceptions. Badcock described the desire for separate parcel deliveries as a 'sentimental grievance', but conceded that 'a postman has not, as a matter of fact, a great chance of getting out of his own ranks'. He was prepared to make comparisons with the wages paid to London park-keepers to illustrate the advantages of postmen. He denied that people were losing promotion because of their trade union activity. On the other hand, he accepted that some of those associated with the erstwhile Postmen's Union had been described as 'generally unsatisfactory' in their reports.

Lewin Hill, Assistant Secretary and nephew of Sir Rowland, continued in the family tradition by taking up the grievances of the provincial postmen in a spirit that made one staff journal describe him as the 'most formidable antagonist to all the claims of the Postal working staff'. His opinion was that 'in all places we are paying more than the value of their labour', that as a result the postmen occupied a 'unique position', much better off than their European equivalents. He expressed his general attitude thus:

> My own view is that the time has come for telling the postmen, in common with the members of the rest of the manipulative staff, in answer to their demand for a general rise of wages, that the Department is satisfied that the wages already paid are in excess of the market value of their services; that this being so, no general addition to pay will be given, and that if the staff are dissatisfied, and can do better for themselves outside the Post Office, they are as they know, at perfect liberty to seek employment elsewhere.

Hill was opposed to any improvement on the grounds that it would simply lead to demands for more, denying that postmen would need recompense for the abolition of Christmas boxes, and even refusing to believe that any of them wanted to be promoted to the indoor grades. Herbert Joyce, another Secretary, took up on behalf of the Department a number of individual questions on punishments and promotions, accepting that some slight improvements had been introduced as a result of the points made in the earlier parts of the evidence.[16]

The PF replied to all of these arguments. They objected most strongly to outside comparisons and to any conception of 'market value'. Hill had shown that porters employed by railway companies earned less than postmen, but this was merely proof of 'what is a notorious fact, namely that the railway companies are among the worst sweating concerns in the country'. Churchfield argued against making such comparisons in the first place, not simply because only internal comparisons made any sense, but also because efforts to discover a 'market value' had already 'given rise to a greater proportion of the abuses and anomalies that are still in existence'. Though many of their witnesses had made errors of detail, the Federation for their part were able to correct a number of arguments from the Department on holidays, transfers and promotions within particular offices, and to assert that

> these errors in the rebutting evidence incidentally show that, notwithstanding their splendid machinery for gathering exact detail, the Departmental witnesses

are not above making mistakes sometimes. Small wonder, then, that our witnesses who had no access to the official records of Service unintentionally committed errors of detail.

The authorities were prepared to admit that they had a point.[17]

Besides considering the grievances of these main grades of Post Office workers and the groups immediately associated with them, the Tweedmouth Committee considered numerous smaller groups employed by the Post Office, especially those who immediately supervised postmen, telegraphists or sorters, and who found themselves suspended in an unsatisfactory and ill-defined limbo between the authorities and the rank and file. Typical of such groups were the London overseers, who had their own association, but presented their case with particular ineptitude, using statistics about sick absences which the authorities were able to turn against them and finding themselves in the end merged with the sorters beneath them rather than with the clerks and secretaries above.

The main witness on behalf of another tiny group of superior status called paperkeepers, who considered themselves the objects of particular discrimination, agreed with Lord Tweedmouth that the problem arose in part at least 'from the multiplication of these small classes'. London head postmen, who had had an association since 1892, also failed in their efforts to convince the authorities that they should be part of the administration. Similar claims from provincial telegraph and postal clerks were treated more sympathetically, though their numerous other grievances were generally ignored.[18]

The 921 head postmasters, who had set up an association in 1894 and could earn anything from £45 per annum to £1,000, wanted their own grading and promotion structure. This, however, brought them into conflict with the lower grades who wanted promotion to their posts. As for the sub-postmasters, of whom there were at the time 19,263 with only eighty-eight on the establishment, they were isolated and ill organised, and generally rebuffed with the argument that there were many others prepared to take their places. The only concession granted to them was an agreement to assess more often the amount of business in their individual offices for the purpose of determining their payment.

The Committee also heard the claims for a higher proportion of places to be made available to ex-soldiers. These were made by army officers who seem quite unaware of what qualifications might be necessary for Post Office work, or of the poor disciplinary record of ex-army men. The telegraph linesmen, predecessors of the modern Post Office engineers, also had had an association since 1886 reorganised especially for the Enquiry, and put forward their case for established employment, higher wages, and better promotion prospects. Most of the other groups like tube attendants, and provincial mechanics who did similar work, also had similar grievances. Adult messengers, who had not had a wage rise for thirty-four years managed to persuade the Committee it was time they did, though only in the lower part of the scale.[19]

The Committee devoted a considerable amount of time to considering the official rebuttal of these cases. For the London postal service, however, Badcock was prepared to admit that inspectors might be given more access to promotion and porters and labourers shorter incremental scales. W. H. Preece, Engineer in Chief of the Post Office, was compelled to agree to some of the more detailed points of those under his charge about overtime pay and allowances, but he would not admit their more general case. At one point he was stung to reply 'that these men want to have their cake and eat it'. As for Lewin Hill, he revealed clearly that the authorities had it in for the telegraphists, who had obtained improvements in 1872, 1878–9, 1881 and 1890 and whose wages and conditions were, according to him, 'to say the least quite sufficient to induce the right class of persons to enter the service, and once admitted to stay there'. He agreed with the efforts which had already begun to 'put the telegraphist and sorting clerk on an equality', and the Committee agreed with him. More ominously, they heard Badcock assert that the £115 per annum earned at the top of the first class of London telegraphists was 'adequate payment', without the added incentive of promotion to the grade of supervisor. Generally speaking, it was becoming clear during 1896 that the Post Office authorities and the Committee were coming into close agreement on the main questions of wages, as well as on other detailed matters such as cutting out allowances, and allowing some groups greater access to promotion.[20]

Thus it was that despite the magnitude and length of their labours, the proposals from the Committee were in the hands of the authorities by the end of 1896, and the Postmaster General almost at once expressed 'general agreement with the suggestions they make'. After some discussions with the Treasury which resulted in minor modifications, the proposals were published in March 1897, together with a chilling Treasury statement that they 'must be accepted as permanently satisfying all reasonable claims of the classes included'. The authorities asserted that the provisions would cost them £139,000 immediately, about 3 per cent of total revenue, and about £275,000 (over 6 per cent) in a full year. These figures were rather higher than those that had been privately calculated, and were hotly contested by the workers, who claimed that not more than £100,000 per annum was involved. As things worked out, this latter figure was more accurate. In any event, the recommendations could hardly be considered generous to the Post Office workers. Its complacency could be seen in the curt dismissal by the Report of many deep-felt complaints. Despite all the grievances about punishments and promotion brought before them, the Committee concluded that 'no case has been made out for want of care or vigilance by the heads of the Departments to prevent favouritism or undue severity on the part of its superior officers throughout the country'. On civil rights and pensions the sacrosanct practice of the whole service was defended. Nothing much beyond pious hopes for improvement was offered on such burning questions as split or long and short duties, on the timing of holidays and the numbers of auxiliaries and unestablished grades. The bitterly resented custom of the authorities in employing people on work proper to the grade above was described as 'a most salutary practice'.[21]

The Committee recommended, as the Department had long favoured, that sorters and telegraphists 'should be placed on a similar footing in relation to pay and service'. In addition they proposed, as the authorities also wanted, that there should be a special grade of telegraph supervisors, thus cutting off most ordinary telegraphists from promotion within the pay range from £160 a year to £190. This particularly unfavourable outcome for the telegraphists can be attributed not only to their failure to convince anybody that their work was particularly skilful or unhealthy, but also to the bitter reaction from the authorities to their years of successful lobbying, and most of all from the unprofitability of their side of the Post Office's business. Elsewhere, the Committee tried to lighten this blow by standar-disation of grades, and merging most allowances into wages. There was also a general aim of greater access to promotion combined with an 'efficiency bar'. An overtime rate of time and a quarter was also proposed, though this involved reductions in some cases, and the scales for provincial postmen were reduced from eight to five.[22]

THE STRUGGLE AGAINST THE TWEEDMOUTH REPORT

If the recommendations of Lord Tweedmouth and his Committee were to the satisfaction of its authors and the Post Office authorities, they provoked a bitterly hostile response from virtually everyone subject to them. Even the London sorters, who agreed that they had 'least cause to complain', said that 'only the fringes of our case' had been dealt with since demands on civil rights, a minimum wage, and many other matters had simply been ignored.[23] As for the postmen, their Controller said they had got less than he 'considered to be their due'. The PF ran a series of meetings expressing 'intense dissatisfaction'. As a result the authorities agreed not to ban the solicitation of Christmas boxes, a concession they were able to make without any cost to themselves.[24]

The most anguished reaction of all, naturally enough, came from the telegraphists.[25] On 24 March, less than a week after the publication of the Report, over 1,500 of them, including 200 women, assembled in London to be addressed by two MPs, together with their local Secretary Charles Garland who was cheered for fully two minutes when he spoke of possible 'unconstitutional action'. However, all that was actually done over the following weeks was to raise a 'voluntary levy' for 'combined and concerted action'. In London it was agreed to use this fund 'to protect all members who would suffer by over-zeal and indiscretion during the prosecution of the policy of the branch'. The regular 16th Annual Conference of the PTCA, which took place in Dublin early in May, reflected the same mood of militancy. The Association agreed to investigate the possibilities of Parliamentary representation, to support wage increases for women, and to fight the Report 'by all and every means in its power'. All hope for further progress was then centred on a delegation from the Central Telegraph Office, effectively the leadership of the London PTCA Branch, who met the Postmaster General the Duke of Norfolk, together with some of his officials, on 15 June. Although there was a full statement of the case against the Report, the *Telegraph Chronicle* described the whole proceedings as 'interviewing the sphinx', and said that the authorities 'left the vague and eerie impression of a hypnotic trance'.

There can be no doubt that a feeling of militancy and frustration grew among the telegraphists during June, especially in London, and this was reflected in a boycott of the refreshment department at the Central Telegraph Office. However, the need for a recall conference was now obvious, and it took place in London on 10 July. This meeting coincided with a crisis in the affairs of the Association. General Secretary Venables was replaced by C. E. Hall, and subscriptions were increased to 6d a quarter.[26] After a long session, including a late night meeting of London members, and much prevarication and buck-passing, the special Conference decided to ballot members on whether they would refuse to do overtime from Monday 26 July.

Considerable excitement followed during the week after the London Conference while the ballot was being taken. It grew increasingly clear that there was almost universal support for the proposed action, with 94 per cent voting for it at the Central Telegraph Office. Eventually 83 per cent of those who answered were in favour, this being 70 per cent of all male telegraphists. On Thursday 15 and Friday 16 July, the authorities met delegations of provincial and London metropolitan telegraphists and issued a Post Office Circular claiming that overtime was compulsory, and that in any case anybody refusing to do it would be dismissed. The same evening Sir Albert Rollit, the most consistent Parliamentary champion of the PTCA, managed to organise a debate on their behalf in the House of Commons. He warned of the 'chronic discontent' that had built up among the telegraphists since the publication of the Tweedmouth recommendations. He had a number of supporters. Captain Cecil Norris complained that 'insufficient consideration had been given to the evidence'. Sir Charles Dilke thought that the Report 'in a certain measure robbed Peter to pay Paul', and reported a widespread opinion that a 'sinister feeling lay behind' the newly established 'efficiency barrier'. Sidney Buxton, future Postmaster General, also spoke on behalf of the telegraphists. In the face of all this R. W. Hanbury, Financial Secretary to the Treasury and spokesman for the Post Office in the Commons, threatened the telegraphists with disenfranchisement if their agitation continued, but at the same time promised to meet the MPs to discuss the detailed points that they had raised.[27] This was the basis of the 'Norfolk–Hanbury conferences' that followed, perhaps the first real negotiations to take place in the history of the public service.

The authorities, who only seem to have heard about the telegraphists' ballot when they published their circular on 16 July, now began to take counter-measures. On Saturday 17th there was a remarkable incident at the Central Telegraph Office. Early in the morning Samuel Belderson, who was the Assistant Secretary of the London PTCA Branch, was held in a room for five hours and asked to repudiate his participation in 'an arrangement to obstruct and delay the transmission of public messages' by sending out the ballot form. Belderson stood firm on the principle that he was acting as a servant of the Association and he was tumultuously applauded when he appeared again among his fellows. In the end the authorities were compelled to resort to getting him to sign a statement that he had acted 'in ignorance of the latest decisions of the Postmaster General' on the matter of compulsory overtime.[28]

On Monday 19 July, the authorities tried another method of pressure by contacting Rollit to get him to persuade the telegraphists to call off any action. They threatened that otherwise the discussions proposed by Hanbury would not take place. The authorities later tried to deny that they played any part in this. Norfolk later told Rollit that 'we had nothing to do with what occurred between you and the Telegraphists. There was no bargain about it.' Fortunately for posterity, the authorities have preserved the records which indicate that this was a lie. The pressure thus exercised also proved effective. Although delays in the dispatch of telegrams were noticed in provincial newspapers, on the next day, Tuesday 20, Hall circularised PTCA branches recommending 'Members of this Association *not* to take any extreme step in regard to declining Overtime for the present, in order to allow time for the Department to state what proposals they are prepared to make'. On the same day a Post Office Circular appeared demanding 'practical evidence' that all talk of an overtime ban was at an end. A mass meeting of London members on the following evening. Wednesday 21, provided this. After some complaints about 'soft soap', it accepted an undertaking from Rollit that the forthcoming discussions with the authorities would consider 'any legitimate cause for complaint properly stated'. For the moment this appeared a great step forward. Belderson telegraphed Liverpool – 'We win all along line'.[29]

The 'Norfolk-Hanbury Conference' which followed on 28 July and the next five days provided 'almost a Gibertian sequel' to the mountainous labours of the Tweedmouth Committee. Nevertheless, it represented a step nearer formal bargaining procedures in the Post Office. Norfolk and Hanbury met various MPs who had taken part in the Parliamentary debate, together with their 'friends', who proved to be the leaders of the associations. The postmen and most of the smaller associations did not even know of the Conference until the last moment, and though the authorities told association leaders that 'the Department did not recognise our presence there', during part at least of the discussions they argued their case without MPs even being present. The issues considered were those that Tweedmouth had covered, together with the new ones arising out of the Report, such as the 'efficiency bar' and the loss of income due to the abolition of allowances.[30]

Though the verdict on a number of questions, particularly those affecting the sorters and postmen, was postponed, the main lines of the recommendations resulting from the Conference were produced in little over a week.[31] They were actually known to the London PTCA Branch on the evening of Monday 9 August, and were published the following day in a Post Office Circular. Although it was proposed to increase the number of telegraphists who did supervising duties, there was no concession at all on the reduction in the maximum earnings of those at the top of the ordinary scale. It was agreed to abolish the technical examinations for promotion, and there were some vague concessions about holidays.

The reaction of the telegraphists can be gathered from the telegram from Liverpool to London: 'Words fail to express our disgust at scandalous treatment. The cupidity of permanent officials only equalled by their affrontery in thus flouting our Parliamentary friends.' The authorities were well prepared for such a response. On 10 August, and for the rest of the week, they stationed a large number of policemen around the Central Telegraph Office in much the same way as they did in 1890 to confront the postmen. They not only leaked reports to the press that there were two people waiting to perform the job of anybody dismissed, they also published their own statement that they 'would hold every member of the service strictly responsible for the words he may use and the actions he may advise'.[32] These threats seem to have had their desired effect by the time the telegraphists met again on the Friday evening, 13 August. They still wanted 'a restoration of the old maximum of £190 per annum, £130 for juniors and £110 for all after ten years service', though they were nervous now about suggesting any new means for trying to obtain it. Rollit, who had acted to prevent militancy in the previous month, now told the London PTCA members that 'the final decision must be left to yourselves'. At the meeting itself it was left to Andrew Nicholson to express the bitter truth about the position of the telegraphists:

Were they prepared to strike? it was no use mincing matters . . . They had, in fact been out-generalled. What was done in London last July should have been decided upon in Belfast in May. (Cheers) But now they were handicapped – the time for action had gone by . . . overtime was steadily decreasing and they could not strike now.

He argued that further action now would be 'inadmissible and impolitic', and this was agreed.

The weakness of the telegraphists was now exposed, and the authorities proceeded to take full advantage of it. Although the PTCA was nominally led by the warring Liverpool 'Central Committee', it was the London members, most affected by the post-Tweedmouth grievances, who were expected to take action. When they failed to do so the entire agitation collapsed. At this point the authorities decided to dish out punishments.[33] Charles Garland, London PTCA Secretary, was hauled up for pointing out to the meeting on 13 August the possibility of strike action. He was excused after giving the explanation that he had simply said he or anybody else could leave the service if they did not like the conditions. The Secretary, Chairman, and two other members of the Newcastle Branch were punished by fines and reprimands for a motion at their meeting the same night saying they would support any overtime ban.[34] A meeting of PTCA 'District Centres' – representatives of all the main areas – was held in Liverpool on Saturday 21 August. The authorities were defied since they were not allowed to send in reporters and the various 'spies' they sent to hang around were treated with derision. This was small consolation for the fact that the Conference could only discuss such long-term methods of dealing with their deeply held grievances as Parliamentary representation. At the same time it was agreed to cover any monetary loss of the Newcastle men.[35]

The crisis had now passed. Early in 1898, a number of new and smaller concessions for the postmen and sorters were announced. However, the impossibility of any major initiative was indicated by the defeat inflicted on the Amalgamated Society of Engineers after the protracted lock-out later in the year. This had its effect in the Post Office, a fact which was acknowledged there. In appealing for support for the engineers in October 1897, the *Telegraph Chronicle* said that 'the failure of this battle will mean a serious weakening of every other union outside the Service, with corresponding restrictions and suppressions within'. If Post Office workers now to some degree identified themselves with the rest of their class, they also faced the same problems of an enormous campaign by employers, courts and press against their organisation and its aims. In the following September, the Duke of Norfolk put an effective stop to further agitation for the moment with these frosty words:

> I have declined, and I shall continue to decline, to allow decisions which have been considered by the Tweedmouth Committee, and which have been revised by Mr. Hanbury and myself, to be reopened. It is my belief that these decisions have been liberal, but whether they are liberal or not, it is for the interests of all parties that it should be understood that they are final.[36]

BRADFORD – THE BUSINESSMEN'S COMMITTEE: 1904–5

Following this major set-back the Post Office workers in the next period largely concentrated on consolidating their own forces and on obtaining an increasing measure of recognition for the associations from the authorities. The first hesitant efforts at co-ordinating the efforts of the associations can be dated to the period immediately after the Tweedmouth Report. Early in the new century, the first

Parliamentary candidates were also adopted from the ranks of the Post Office workers. This was perhaps the most distinct change of policy to follow the rejection of Tweedmouth's conclusions.[37]

This was also a period when the associations were particularly active and successful in lobbying those already inside Parliament. Every volume of *Hansard* Parliamentary Debates around that time is full of discussion about the conditions of Post Office workers, from the smallest grievance in the remotest part of Ireland to large-scale debates demanding new inquiries. On 18 February 1898 there was a full-dress debate centring around demands for recognition and civil rights, including the re-instatement of Clery and Cheesman, at which the friends of the Post Office workers were defeated by 163 votes to 86. A full-scale debate on the Queen's Speech was initiated in the following year by the Liberal–Labour MP W. C. Steadman, with spirited support from the Irish Nationalists. A reply from Hanbury attributed all grievances to Clery, who had been 'dismissed for agitation'. This time the call was for an inquiry made up of MPs, a proposition defeated by the narrower margin of 159 votes to 91. Less than five months later, there was another debate and a vote of 158 to 107. In April 1900, the demand for an inquiry was again discussed, and this time lost by 46 votes to 66. This margin showed the truth of the statement of one speaker that a number of Tory MPs were only just more afraid of the Government whips than of their Post Office worker constituents. In April 1901, the demand for a new inquiry was rejected by Austen Chamberlain, not simply on the grounds that nothing had changed since Tweedmouth reported, but also because any new discussion would result only in 'keeping the staff in a state of unrest'. There was another long debate on many Post Office grievances in the following June, and to the usual complaints about the constitutional impropriety of discussing such matters at all, John Burns proposed a permanent arrangement for the settlement of grievances. This time the call for an inquiry was only defeated by 128 votes to 103, and it was discussed again at length only three days later. Pressure continued during 1902, and yet another debate in April resulted in a vote of 150 to 110.[38]

If the margin of votes was moving against the Post Office workers, the political situation was developing in their favour. In the summer of 1902 a new Conservative administration under A. J. Balfour was formed which was in part aimed at holding back the threat of Labour advance and Liberal revival by some measure of social reform. A group of Conservative MPs became convinced that the Post Office workers were an appropriate group for favourable treatment, and on 26 March 1903 persuaded the new Postmaster General, Austen Chamberlain, to meet the London leadership of the PTCA in a form somewhat akin to the Norfolk–Hanbury discussions. Thus at the end of the following month, Chamberlain announced in Parliament that, although the Tweedmouth recommendations constituted 'a really fair and even generous settlement, nevertheless, the wages the postal servants receive are not in all respects satisfactory'. Thus while he was not prepared to set up any select committee, he would 'seek advice from men of practical and business experience' in an advisory committee on the wages paid to quite specific grades – postmen, sorters, telegraphists and sorting clerks and telegraphists. Their purpose would be to consider whether these wages were 'adequate', 'having regard to the conditions'.[39] Here at last was a response to the agitation, if not to the demands it had put forward, and when Chamberlain was followed as PMG by another Lord Stanley – the previous one had introduced the ban on meetings in 1866 – he agreed that the inquiry could go ahead in its original form.

The Post Office workers were suspicious from the very start, not only because of their bad experiences with Tweedmouth, but also because of the form of the inquiry, and the people who made it up. Although the workers might reasonably hope for something from Charles Booth, philanthropist and author of *Life and Labour of the People*, and Thomas Broderick of the Co-operative Wholesale Society, they had less reason to place confidence in R. Burbridge, Managing Director of Harrod's Stores, or in Samuel Fay of the Grand Central Railway, and especially not in Edward Bradford the Chairman, ex Chief Commissioner of the Metropolitan Police, who had broken the 1890 agitation that paralleled the one in the Post Office. The associations were also opposed to the idea of outside comparisons which was the main point made in the terms of reference. It is not surprising therefore that Charles Garland of the PTCA called it 'a bogus Committee', and the sorters said they could not 'regard any such inquiry as final'.[40] The paradox was that, of all the inquiries of the period, this was the one that proved itself most favourable to the claims of the Post Office workers.

The associations began by considering a total boycott of the inquiry, but in the end agreed that they would appear and not attack one another. It was said that they were still trying to out-do one another in their evidence, and there was a brief echo of the complaint about lack of promotion on the telegraph side, but nearly all the divisive statements came from within the grades, from small break-away groups like foreign branch sorters or Blackpool postmen who claimed the right to special treatment. One member of the PF Executive, E. M'Loughlen, also insisted on presenting a separate case for the rural men, but though he asked for a lower maximum, it was agreed that 'the real difference . . . was very slight'.[41] The evidence, which was covered in less than three months from November 1903 to February 1904, heard little of the verbal fireworks induced by a John Walsh or a Lewin Hill. It was remembered later by one of the witnesses as 'easily the least inquisitive committee that ever sat in the Department'. There was none of the same probing hostility from either side, and because of the terms of reference, none of the same burrowing into the smallest grievances of the most minor groups. The atmosphere was quite different from Tweedmouth's Committee:

> Questions were always intelligent, and that cannot be said of all the questions put in such inquiries, but they were very few and only called for concise answers. Witnesses came away with a feeling that much had been left unsaid.[42]

Because of this, the witnesses to the Bradford Enquiry presented their evidence clearly, concisely and without rancour. The four main associations were quite openly acknowledged and their representative character was never questioned. The first witnesses were a number of solid citizens from the Fawcett Association. They were all in their late 30s, and included a local councillor and others who could claim similar standing in the community. The only real complaint about the case they put forward came from one group of sorters who said that their representative had asked for too much at the maximum. Generally, they pointed to the deterioration of their conditions in comparison to those who did similar work in the middle of the nineteenth century, and to the strain of writing duties, travelling and dealing with foreign and registered mail. The PTCA and UKPCA, together with the Dual Workers Association from Ireland, went over a great deal of familiar ground on behalf of the telegraphists and SC&Ts. They attacked the 'breach of faith' in the

Tweedmouth settlement of their London maximum, and tried to take up the difficult question of promotion at a time when the postal and telegraph sides were being integrated. They also argued strongly for improved conditions for women, and for a new system for deciding on local wage variations. The postmen managed to boil down what they wanted to say to the statements of three witnesses, which generally amounted to a call for increased pay on the grounds of their great responsibilities and their inability to maintain themselves. The authorities, who presumably thought they had the result sewn up anyway, gave quite a perfunctory response to all this, denying that they had ever said London telegraphists could receive £190 per annum, saying that 'every effort is made' to avoid onerous or inconvenient duties and that their method of determining local wages by the level of business in fact reflected the cost of living.[43]

The evidence presented by the associations took up many issues which had long since been part of every list of grievances. The argument of the pressure and responsibility of their work was put forward by virtually every witness. The work of a London sorter, it was claimed, included

the technique, difficulty and intricacy of a skilled workman combined with the acumen of the clerk, geographical knowledge unique in itself and the intuition and capacity of an Inland Revenue Officer.

The result of pressure of work, said one sorter, was terrible:

My constitution was undermined. I was frequently on the sick list. The anxiety of trying to live on an insufficient wage is one of the most terrible hardships a young postal servant has to experience. When later on I undertook the responsibilities of married life I had often to go without food and sufficient clothing in order to meet family expenses such as periodical doctor's bills, rent etc.

The main response of the authorities to all this was simply to produce their Chief Medical Officer to state that in his opinion Post Office workers were not at all unhealthy in comparison with the rest of the population, and to assert that he, personally, had 'never seen a case of breakdown of health from nervous strain or other causes which owed [their] origin directly to the character of the work'. Another familiar line of argument was heard from every grade about their inaccessibility to promotion. The postmen said that above the age of 25 it was virtually unknown for one of their number to become an SC&T. The sorters said they 'had no possible chance of rising beyond the present maximum of sorter's pay'. The SC&Ts also resented their inability ever to become clerks.[44]

If the Bradford Committee heard many of these old complaints about conditions of work, they were given a new and generally much better worked out set of arguments when it came to their main business – the level of wages. Postmen, sorters and SC&Ts all gave some prominence, in a way which they had hardly done previously, to the need for improvements at the bottom of the various scales. They also called for higher maximums, usually in the form of greater promotion opportunities. W. W. Young, who led for the UKPCA, argued that 'the basis on which wages in private industry' was determined was not appropriate for the Post Office. The associations nevertheless proceeded to make the usual unfavourable comparisons with policemen, schoolmistresses and bank clerks. The association witnesses also all argued in general terms that they had a right to share in the increases in general wage rates which had been seen since the time of the Tweedmouth discussions. Thus the PTCA sought 'to base our claim for a higher wage upon the admitted increase in the cost of living since 1897'. The UKPCA asserted that there had been an 'increase in the market value of labour generally in the period 1893–1901'. For their part, the PF expressed the view that postmen 'have not had the advantage of the general increase in wages which have taken effect in other branches of labour' and were 'poorer than we were years ago, owing to the fact that rent and other commodities and the general standard of comfort have gone up'.[45]

There were two main arguments put forward by the associations in favour of wage increases: the idea of a 'marriageable age', and the call for local variations to be determined by the cost of living. This was the great age of social surveys, when it was optimistically believed that individual human physical needs could be precisely and scientifically determined. Charles Booth himself was a pioneer of such conceptions and some of the arguments were clearly designed to appeal to him. Thus, while the sorters spoke of their 'inability to reach a substantial salary at a reasonable age', the UKPCA argued in more detail that an SC&T, 'however abstemious and frugal he may be', did not earn at about the age of 25 'a sufficient wage on which he may be able to marry'. The Postmen's Federation extended these arguments with a number of statistical calculations of which the most striking was that the £1 1s 6d (£1. 07½) earned in a week by a young postman at the West Central District Office in Central London was 'about the sum which is spent on one London pauper'. The Federation also got Seebohm Rowntree, another pioneer of social surveys of the period, to write that a grocery list they had compiled, though above the level of bare subsistence, was not 'extravagant by any reasonable standard' but was nevertheless beyond the means of many postmen.

The workers also had a strong case, which could be subject to a form of statistical verification, about local variations in wages. The wages earned by postmen were supposed to accord to local variations in the cost of living, though there were numerous anomalies. The indoor grades were now supposed to have their salaries determined by the level of business at the office to which they were attached, and those who spoke for them to the Bradford Committee agreed that 'the disparity existing between the maximum at the larger offices is not justified by the corresponding difference in the duties performed, nor in the cost of living obtaining in the various towns'. As a result it was 'quite possible for two men to be rendering equal service and be governed by equal conditions, and yet receive a maximum wage varying by many shillings'. So it was argued that just as Tweedmouth had abolished classification within grades, Bradford ought to abolish it as between offices 'upon the same grounds, viz., that the work of sorting clerks and telegraphists is identical at all offices', variations to be based solely on cost of living criteria.[46]

What was astonishing about these arguments was not so much their novelty as the fact that they were accepted almost in their entirety by the Committee when it produced its Report in May 1904. It would not be expected that every small grievance put forward by the associations would be acknowledged, each proposed increase adopted in its entirety. However, it came as a considerable surprise to everyone to find that Bradford and his colleagues accepted the basic arguments of the workers. They began by complimenting the sorters on their 'very admirably drawn up' statements, and the postmen's representatives on 'the business-like and able way in which [they] discharged their responsible duties'. They went on to argue in defiance of their own terms of reference that there was no reason for them 'to obtain any specific evidence as to the rates of wages current in other occupations' since 'it is difficult to make any valid comparison between a National Postal Service and any form of private industrial employment, the conditions being necessarily so different'. Instead, according to Samuel Fay, they relied on 'the general knowledge individual members of the Committee possessed of wages throughout the country'. Nor were the advantages by any means of the sort normally claimed by the Post Office authorities. The benefits derived from pensions and other such rights had been 'overstated' and should be set off 'against the disadvantages attaching to service under the state, e.g., the limitations necessarily imposed upon freedom of action'. Even if there were many recruits there was 'widespread discontent', and 'a just claim for revision'. There should be equality as between indoor grades, and maximum wages for each of those on a common scale by the age of 26, 'when it might reasonably be expected that he would marry'. Local variations were to be determined largely on the basis of population.[47]

THE RESULTS OF BRADFORD

When the proposals of Bradford's Committee became known to the officials at Post Office Headquarters in St Martin's-le-Grand, they produced considerable alarm.[48] It was calculated that in a full year both SC&Ts and postmen would get well over £30,000 extra, and the entire package would cost £1,043,600, almost a third of the profit being earned at the time by the whole service. One of the leading officials wrote that the large improvements proposed 'apparently on the sole ground that there is widespread discontent . . . have set a premium on agitation'. For a time Postmaster General Stanley tried to suppress all news of what had been recommended, while an internal inquiry worked out a new set of recommendations which conceded some increases but cost a great deal less.

This new inquiry argued on general grounds against making major concessions:

It is undeniable that there is widespread agitation; and we conceive that such agitation is always likely to exist, however liberal and frequent may be the concessions granted, so long as it is made evident to the staff that, after short intervals of years, the agitation will result in a large expenditure of public money in their favour.

They also argued against the proposed standardisation of indoor grades on the grounds that

it has been found after 20 years experience, that all attempts to combine Postal and Telegraph work in London and at the large provincial offices have resulted in useless expenditure and impaired working.

These points were easy enough to make within St Martin's-le-Grand, but Stanley was faced with the unenviable task for arguing for them in public. After delaying his announcement for three months and timing it at the end of a Parliamentary session, Stanley told Parliament on 9 August that he would definitely not accept Bradford's

Report which had departed 'in many respects from the terms of reference', and 'if it were carried out it would involve a very heavy burden upon the tax payer'.

A number of frantic delegations from the associations followed, and in the following March of 1905, Stanley announced his response to all the discussions in a short statement which ignored most of the points made by Bradford and his colleagues and denied that there was any need for an improvement at the maximum or any change in the indoor grades. The one important concession, however, was an acceptance of the 'marriageable wage' argument put forward by the associations and accepted by Bradford. The result of this was that virtually every man of about the age of 25 got some improvement, but few women did, except at the minimum, and hardly any postmen, since they were predominantly older. The total cost of this settlement in a full year was claimed to be £373,300, and it represented the sole result of the deliberations of Bradford and his colleagues. It was described by one service journal as a 'monumental example of official ineptitude and bad faith'.[49]

It is of some interest to ask how the results of the Bradford deliberations proved so meagre. Nobody, least of all the staff associations, had expected the Bradford Committee to report in the way that it did. Its reasons for doing so remain obscure to this day. Some have argued that it was because the businessmen appointed were 'secretly favourable' to the men. It has also been claimed 'that the business men of the period were not in accord with the Conservative Government and that the report was designed to embarrass it'.[50] What seems much more likely is that the Committee, consisting entirely of outsiders, largely unaware of the complexities of public service snobberies and unaffected by the political jockeying that lay behind their appointment, produced recommendations that seemed to themselves both logical and fair. Just as the associations had gone to Tweedmouth blissfully unaware that there could be any reasonable case against them, so the authorities had approached the Bradford Committee convinced that little would be conceded. Thus their case went by default. Bradford and his colleagues showed their innocence in the minefield of civil service protocol by their scheme for the logical reorganisation of the indoor grades. The authorities had been trying with limited success to combine postal and telegraph work since the 1880s, and it was hardly likely that any outsider could exercise more effective pressure to the same end. The political naïvete of the Committee was shown by their refusal to make any outside comparisons. If they had really understood the public service, and aimed for their proposals to be carried out, they should have presented the case for them in terms of their original brief.

The other important factor was the attitude of the associations. When the Report first appeared, after much delay, on 15 July 1904, none of them expressed unqualified delight. The PTCA attacked the lack of improvements at the maximum, and particularly the refusal to acknowledge the 'breach of faith' on the reduction of the London maximum for telegraphists in 1897. The postmen were opposed to the use of population statistics for the determination of local pay differentials, rather than more precise cost-of-living criteria. They were particularly upset by a number of ill chosen phrases in the Report advocating the abolition of Christmas boxes without any accompanying compensation. As for the FA, though they thought the report 'an earnest attempt to meet our case', they did not accept the salary scales proposed for sorters who had formerly been postmen, nor the proposed new maximums.[51]

Within a few days a number of MPs had been approached, and by the beginning of October at least fifty local meetings had been held, often jointly by the different associations, to express these various objections to the Report. In later years it was argued that this campaign was 'probably the worst tactical blunder ever made by the societies' leaving it open to the authorities to ignore the Report altogether. It has been said that if the associations had argued for the acceptance of the Report as it stood, this would have placed the Government in such a difficult position that they would have been compelled to make substantial concessions. However, the associations did agree at the time for the acceptance of the Report, as far as it went. The postmen said it 'went a long way to meet the claim we put forward for a living wage'. Also the sorters called on the Postmaster General 'to adopt immediately the recommendations of the committee' which were described as 'the *Magna Carta* of the Postal Staff'.[52] Most later accounts have been wise after the event, but the fact is that the authorities had already decided what they were prepared to concede long before the Report was known. In any case, since the associations were not monolithic, there was bound to be a reaction from the postmen on Christmas boxes and from the senior telegraphists on promotion, whatever their leaders did. Not only is it difficult to see how the authorities could have been compelled to act differently, it also seems clear that the expressions of discontent even with what Bradford offered meant that further large concessions had to be made, both in the form of the recognition of the associations and the setting up of a new inquiry. The lobbying at the 1906 General Election compelled the new Liberal Postmaster General to accept the associations, as he may well have done in any case. He was also compelled to admit privately that 'it would seem almost hopeless (even if we desired) to resist the appointment of a Parliamentary Committee'.[53] Thus within months the unions had been strengthened and there was yet another forum for Post Office workers' grievances to be considered.

There are a number of other interesting points to be made about the reactions to the Bradford Report. The political context was a very special one in 1904–6, when a long period of Tory rule was drawing to a close, and members of every party were determined to show sympathy with the poor for purposes of the forthcoming elections. MPs were thus particularly active at this time in egging on the Post Office workers. It was the enormous pressure thus built up that made at least one major concession necessary once the Liberals came into Government in 1906. This proved to be the 'recognition' of the associations, though not the proposals of the Bradford Committee.

It is also significant that the most important tactical error of all was made by PMG Stanley himself in his famous 'blackmail' and 'blood sucking' remarks of 6 July 1905, described in Chapter 4. What was of particular importance about these remarks was not so much their novelty – such statements were made many times in Parliament since the 1890s, and even before – but the intense reaction they provoked. Not only did Stanley lose his seat in Parliament, but the grievances of the Post Office workers and their efforts to ameliorate them were brought right to the centre of the political stage. They have even been given as a factor in the Liberals' victory in the 1906 General Election.

In the circumstances it is important to recall that the rejection of the Bradford Report had important consequences for the associations themselves. The frustration and rage of the postmen was expressed in their withdrawal from the National Joint Committee and their formulation in 1905 of the disastrous claim for 'unification' with the sorters. Similar frustration was expressed by the sorters in their decision to withdraw from the TUC and Labour Party. 1905 was also a turning point for the PTCA who decided to change their previous practice and began to identify themselves for the first time with the wider trade union movement. It was in part at least a tribute to the efficiency of their lobbying activities over many years that in 1906 Parliament was feeling the pressure as never before, and the third of the great inquiries saw MPs themselves enter into the jungle of Post Office grade structures, payment systems and grievances.

HOBHOUSE – THE MPs TRY THEIR HAND: 1906–7

On 20 February 1906, exactly a week after he conceded 'recognition' to the associations, the new Postmaster General, Sydney Buxton, announced that he would set up a Select Committee of MPs. This came into existence on 20 March aiming

> to inquire into the wages and position of the principal classes of Post Office servants . . . and to report whether having regard to the conditions and prospects of their employment, and, so far as may be, to the standard rate of wages and the position of other classes of workers, the remuneration they receive is adequate or otherwise.

The careful vagueness on the thorny subject of outside comparisons was as much as the associations could have expected. The members of the Committee, including Charles Hobhouse, the Chairman, had often in the past expressed their sympathy with the Post Office workers. There were two trade unionists, John Ward of the Navvies Union who was Liberal MP for Stoke-on-Trent, and George Wardle from the Labour Party, as well as Claude Hay, a Conservative who had often advocated their cause, and an Irish Nationalist called John Meehan, also thought likely to be sympathetic. Much therefore was expected of the new Committee. The associations suspended their lobbying activities, reformulated their programmes, and prepared to present their evidence. They were quite prepared to accept the Departmental prohibition on making their case 'through the press'.[54]

The cases argued in front of Hobhouse and his colleagues took up 1,300 double-columned pages, with 22,516 questions, about one-third longer than Tweedmouth, the 'most laborious work' wrote Hobhouse in his diary, 'on which I was ever engaged'. Though many more smaller and superior grades were considered and a large number of additional statistical and tabular material was presented – some of it collected in a one-hundred-page appendix – the Committee managed to consider the evidence in less than nine months, from March to December 1906, and to present its Report in the following July. The question and answer format was on the whole more helpful to the official side, who were able to present their case as a whole and to 'correct or amplify the evidence given by other witnesses'.[55] The official case was made much easier, however, by divisions and differences between the different grades, which were mercilessly exposed by the authorities. This applied particularly to the case presented by the postmen, but also to disparaging comments against women by the telegraphists, and against virtually every inferior grade by the inspectors and supervisors.[56]

The Committee began, in what was by now the usual pattern, with the London sorters. They argued generally about the pressure under which they worked, asking for wage increases at both maximum and minimum, and for better access to promotion. They quoted Charles Booth and the economist Giffen from the minority Report of the 1894 Royal Commission on Labour to the effect that 'the minimum wages of any able-bodied adult man in public employment should, at any rate, be not less than 24s [£1. 20] a week'. Many younger sorters with wages well below this had to maintain themselves, and auxiliary sorters also relied on their earnings to a greater extent than they were supposed to. The postmen reported privately that the argument had been 'very tedious', and as a result 'failed miserably'. The separate case presented by the Foreign Section was also 'damaging to the ordinary Sorter's claim'. As a result of this, the official reply was most perfunctory, with one official maintaining that 'most Post Office servants have no politics and do not want any', and that 'the feeling of hostility that has been suggested by one or two of the speakers is not shared by the majority of the staff'. The Committee was largely convinced by this, and proposed little improvement for the main group of sorters beyond a slight increase at the minimum.

The sorter-tracers were treated somewhat more favourably, being allowed to join the lower parts of the sorter scale. Bagmen received some improvements during the course of the Enquiry itself, and afterwards a substantial increase in their scale from £1 4s (£1. 20) to £2 per week, up to £1 7s (£1. 35) to £2 5s (£2. 25). They did not, however, receive anything like the parity with the sorters that they claimed. Nor did the women sorters. The Committee agreed with the authorities that their work was simple, that they could live with 'friends and guardians', and that 'it would be undesirable to attract single women from the country by offers of higher pay'.[57]

The PTCA presented their case in a reasonably well organised way, though including the by now irrelevant harping back to the lost status of counter clerks, and with unprovable assertions about favouritism in promotion. Their proposal for automatic promotion to the overseer grade did arouse some interest, however. The women also put on a better show than in the past. Mabel Hope showed that 'no gain for the female staff as a whole accrued from the Stanley scheme'. She got one of the Committee to characterise the policy of the Department in relation to women as 'more economical than "respectable"'.

The UKPCA had a series of witnesses who presented the case more systematically for wage increases based on a rising cost of living and greater pressure of work, and argued about the problems of promotion when 'dual qualifications' on the telegraph and postal side were enforced. Lucy Witherington also spoke eloquently on behalf of the increasing numbers of women on the postal side:

A young woman sorting clerk and telegraphist cannot keep herself on her wage. It can only be done by the aid of semi-charitable institutions that were never supported for the benefit of the Department . . . the key-note of our contention is that *we are not* paid for the duties we perform. We have the same punishments and fines as the men, and we think this shows we are regarded as being equally responsible. Precisely the same work; implying the same capability . . . Equality we have on so many points, and yet the great disparity in wages . . .

Even if it was still thought impractical to advocate equal pay, this was the direction in which the argument was now moving. Evidence was also presented by the Association of Irish Post Office Clerks, generally with greater eloquence and exaggeration.[58]

The official replies concentrated on familiar issues. It was argued that the 'breach of faith' argument in relation to the telegraphists had been rejected by both Tweedmouth and Bradford. The refusal of the associations to make outside comparisons was also attacked, and all the assertions about favouritism in promotion were denied. Counter clerks did not work under particular pressure in 'ordinary circumstances', nor did the women telegraphists ever. The current grade system was defended and it was said that split duties were demanded only when absolutely necessary. The Secretary of the Scottish Post Office, E. P. W. Redford, expressed himself with particular vigour on the complaints about lack of promotion prospects:

> I believe that it is held by some of the witnesses that the majority of Post Office servants cannot look forward to more than a comparatively subordinate position in life. This is so with the majority in every sphere of life . . .[59]

In reaching its conclusions about these indoor manipulative grades, the Committee again largely accepted the official point of view. The 'breach of faith' argument on maximum pay for telegraphists was once again rejected, as also were all complaints about promotion. There were even said to be too many overseers in the cable room in London, and the general view was repeated that 'superior posts ought not to be created simply to make promotion'. Some improvements at the lower end of the scale for telegraphists in London were proposed, but nothing at all for counter clerks and telegraphists. There were some slight improvements at the bottom of the scale for the 600 female telephonists at that time employed by the Post Office in London. On the provincial SC&Ts, the Committee also largely accepted the views of the authorities. They proposed no change in the status of learners, and no improvements on overtime, split duties or promotion, accepting that the complaints from the telegraph side on this score were simply a result of declining demand for the services they provided.

Hobhouse and his colleagues did, however, propose one important change as a result of suggestions made both by the UKPCA and the Post Office authorities as well as on the basis of data provided for them by the Board of Trade. This was to take into account local variations in the cost of living in the calculation of various local wage rates.[60] They set out a new wages structure with five different scales. Though those at the bottom got nothing, there was some improvement for the 'five year men', and Hobhouse and his colleagues accepted the opinions of their predecessors about better pay at 'marriageable age'. The Committee picked on every difference between the PTCA and the UKPCA in their evidence, particularly their varied wage claims. They also quoted the statement by one of the UKPCA leaders that women were incapable of doing some of the work of serving at counters. They ignored such views as those expressed by Charles Garland of the PTCA that 'women do the work which they have to do as well as the men would perform the same work', and proposed only the most minimal pay increases for female SC&Ts. They also insisted on the reimposition of the ban on women working on Sundays, and receiving the overtime pay that went with it. They even refused any increase for virtually all the 1,300 provincial women telephonists, who were earning between 15s and £1 1s (75p–£1. 05).[61]

The weakness and internal inconsistency of the arguments presented to Hobhouse, as well as the dangers of the arguments from internal comparison, was nowhere better illustrated than in the case presented by the postmen. In an attempt to hide the divisions within their own ranks, and against the better judgement of their leaders, the main thrust of their case rested on making attacks on others. As a result nobody gained. The problem began with a resolution passed after the rejection of the Bradford recommendations at the 1905 Annual Conference of the PF. This proposed that 'the position of postmen throughout the United Kingdom be declared equal in status with that of sorting clerks, sorters and telegraphists, and that the clerical workers and supervisors be drawn from the combined force'. Even this was not enough for the postmen at the Chief Office at St Martin's-le-Grand, nor the East Central District Office, who did more sorting work than in other places, and insisted that they had a special case to present to the Committee. The PF leaders did not agree that there should be separate representation, and after a number of bitter exchanges, they expelled 700 postmen – virtually the entire membership at the ECDO. These men promptly set up the Central London Postmen's Association. They appeared separately before the Hobhouse Committee, though their witness was compelled to admit that he 'hardly differed at all' with the case as presented by the Federation, and what he said was largely ignored when the conclusions were announced. The CLPA remained in existence, though its conflict with the parent body diminished, until it joined in the setting up of the UPW in 1919. A further breakaway was avoided at Birmingham, where some of the postmen did work serving at counters, but another group was expelled at Crewe, where special privileges were claimed for work at the railway junction. In the end the Committee refused to listen to their case, and the new system for local wage determination they proposed actually reduced wages at the Crewe office.[62]

As a result of these experiences, the Federation leaders worked out a claim on which at least all the remaining postmen could agree, for equality with the sorters, and 'unification' of the postman, sorter and SC&T grade, in other words uninterrupted promotion from top to bottom of the manipulative grades. This, said Stuart, was 'one thing on which they were united', and the fact that they were also asking for more wages than the sorters were then getting was a tactical addition, because they were afraid 'that the demand would not be conceded'. The postmen's witnesses went to great lengths to show the Committee how much sorting they did. The Federation representative from the Chief Office put it like this:

> Since 1890 the position has entirely changed as regards wages, but not as regards duties, and now, as then, postmen will be found working side by side with sorters, doing identical work, subject to the same rules as to efficiency, and, owing to the stripe system, to even greater punishment in the case of failure.

A great deal of energy was devoted to proving this point, which in fact was hardly true outside the Central London area. Other Federation witnesses did take up the more substantial questions on wages, pensions, civil rights, good conduct stripes and so on.

The authorities had a field day in their replies. They argued, with some justice, that postmen only did 'the least important part of a sorting clerk's work', the SC&Ts being 'as a rule . . . much better educated', and thus best kept within their own system of promotion. Just as at the time of the 1854 reorganisation, it was argued that a common grading system of postmen and sorters 'would deter from entering the service the better-class men from whom the ranks of the sorting clerks are now recruited'. Some of the official witnesses argued that sorting was the most difficult of all work done in the Post Office, though this was later modified. Other official witnesses reiterated the view that postmen belonged to a 'somewhat rougher class', and the work of sorting letters 'requires a higher degree of intelligence, dexterity and continued application'. In fairness to the postmen it should be said that their arguments were based on a more logical method of organising the work, and the gulf between their tasks and those of the superior grades was probably less than in the 1850s. The eventual reorganisation of 1946 essentially embodied this 'unification'. However, 1906 was not the time for this to be argued, and they did not succeed in convincing the Committee that there was anything but an unbridgeable gulf in terms of 'responsibility and difficulty' between the postmen and those above them. The Committee did propose a reduction of the number of London zones from four to three, and of provincial classes from six to five, and some wage increases mostly at the maximum. They also advocated some other small improvements including the granting of good conduct stripes every four years after the first one, but put forward no change of any importance on promotion, supervising, Christmas gratuities, or the conditions of assistant and auxiliary postmen.[63] London postal porters, mail porters, tube attendants, night collectors and messengers also got little from the Committee except slight increases at the minimum.[64]

The Hobhouse Committee spent more than two months in taking evidence from a wide range of Post Office workers outside the ranks of handlers of post, telephones and telegraphs.[65] Their deliberations showed clearly that just as in previous generations, the various groups below the level of clerk had been expanded and elaborated. The current trend was for a great expansion in the plethora of grades whose function it was to supervise, oversee, superintend or inspect. At one point there was a groan from Hobhouse, not recorded in the published evidence, at yet another 'repetition of the importance of various supervising appointments'. The Committee derived some amusement at any rate from quizzing closely the representatives of these superior grades who had formerly been active in the rank-and-file associations, particularly C. E. Hall, formerly General Secretary of the PTCA and now an overseer who did not 'have to oversee anybody', and George Raby, former Chairman of the FA, now a postmaster. In general, the Committee tried to standardise these grades, and proposed a number of changes, especially in the London postal service, nearly always on the suggestion of the authorities. The central aim of all this was to re-establish a distinction which had to some extent been blurred between those who directly oversaw the manipulative grades and those who had little contact with them, being engaged largely on clerical duties. The Committee also considered the superior clerks themselves, and heard representatives from a 'London Postal Service Clerks Association', who had limited skill and experience in such representation and were 'very roughly handled', and of an 'Association of Women Clerks', who unconvincingly concentrated on the grievances of individual classes within the grade. For these groups the Committee aimed generally to ensure 'the severance, as far as possible, of clerical from other duties'.

The sub-postmasters, who had been organised since the time of Tweedmouth, presented a much more carefully argued case that their non-Post Office business tended to fall off, and that the many applicants for their positions had 'not the slightest idea what was expected', nor of the precise system whereby their salaries were determined. The sub-postmasters convinced the Committee by these arguments of the need 'to get rid of a system which was at once distasteful to the Sub-postmasters, and unsatisfactory, laborious and expensive to the Department', by asking the authorities to work out a new system for the determination of payment based on weights assigned to numbers of letters received, telegrams delivered and so forth. This became the basis not only for the remuneration of scale payment sub-postmasters in subsequent generations but to some degree also of the rank-and-file grades as well. The sub-postmasters were profoundly discontented both with the system itself and with its results, which involved lower rewards for a great many of their members. Postmasters as usual claimed their own special scale, but got very little when the authorities argued that their salaries had increased by 28·5 per cent since 1886.

The Hobhouse Committee was the first to consider seriously the grievances of the rapidly expanding and increasingly important groups of engineers, maintenance mechanics and storekeepers who kept going the telegraph and telephone system. The Committee 'found considerable difficulty in disentangling the one from the other' amongst these groups, 'so great [was] the interdependence and overlapping of employment'. The linesmen, mechanics and others could not in most cases lay claim to the advantages of civil service employment. They were often paid by piece-work and also frequently discharged when there was no work for them to do. One of the witnesses argued that

> the great prevalence of un-established labour, or so-called 'Temporary Hands con-tinuously employed', has operated against the success and efficiency of the Engineering and Stores Departments for the past two or three decades. It has lowered the status of the Department generally, and has been the means of bringing down the wages of certain classes to such a point as to prevent a decent existence.

In reply to this the official witnesses argued that these were 'employees whose skill can be carried on to the open market', that they were getting 'above the general market value', and that their 'numbers must fluctuate largely with the fluctuations of the work'. They were not strictly comparable to those in outside employment doing similar work. In some cases at least this was because the unions who organised them outside the service would not recruit people who did piece-work. The Department in any case showed it 'was never inclined to give the workers advantages over outside workers where direct comparisons could be made'. However increasing numbers from such groups were becoming permanent employees of the Department. The only significant change proposed by the Committee for this group was that 'tradesmen' could be paid at local union rates, an arrangement never carried out, according to the Post Office, because those involved preferred the protection of public employment.

Besides taking up the grievances of every group of more than a hundred Post Office workers, and working out new guidelines for the determination of local wage differentials, the Hobhouse Committee also made a few general points. They paid a good deal of attention to the conditions in a number of offices, accepting some of the complaints from the staff on this score, but attributing most of the faults to the ill organised way in which changes were carried out in re-building or repairing buildings because of uncertainty about the division of responsibility as between the Board of Works and the Post Office itself. The Committee largely took the part of the Post Office in these matters, arguing that it should be responsible for its own buildings, and also that general inspection and re-decorating should be carried out more frequently than had been the case until then.

They also heard from the medical officers themselves about their grievances, of which the most important was having their efficiency tested at the age of 60. The Committee was not, however, inclined to regard such complaints with much sympathy, especially after they extracted from the Chief Medical Officer of the Department, D. A. H. Wilson, the information that although he was supposed to be full time in this post at £1,100 per annum, he also got £80 working for the Civil Service Supply Association, and £50 from the Civil Service Co-operative Society. Though Dr Wilson promised to work harder in inspecting buildings, and claimed to have started doing so while the Committee was in progress, they nevertheless considered his multifarious appointments to be 'improper'. They also proposed that more Post Office workers should come under the ministrations of his service. On 'risk allowances' for counter losses, which had been partly abolished after Tweedmouth, they recommended that these should now lapse altogether, though the staff generally did not favour this, especially as the authorities refused to recognise their own insurance schemes.[66]

REACTIONS TO HOBHOUSE

Despite all the confidence that the staff had placed in it, the acceptance by the Hobhouse Committee of the official view on risk allowances was fairly typical of their general conclusions. It applied also to their new method of calculating local differentials, which in practice proved even more complex than originally proposed. To give it effect there had to be twelve levels of classification, and some new entrants got less than before. The general effect of the numerous new wage scales was to quicken the rate of promotion at the lower end. Of substantial improvements, however, there were none.

The reaction to the Report on the part of the Post Office workers was generally one of impotent rage. For the UKPCA it was 'a colossal disappointment'. The postmen, whose entire case was repudiated, condemned it as 'one of the most cruel and cowardly documents' on Post Office conditions ever issued. They ran a special conference at which there was much letting off of steam, and a Chairman, who expressed their disillusionment with the 'people's representatives'. The sorters spoke of 'disappointment and disgust . . . deeper rooted and more intense than ever before', and Cheesman complained that London telegraphists at the maximum could now get more than his members. He also said he had 'documentary proof' that the Report had followed the lines proposed by the Department. There was little need for such evidence when the Committee openly admitted following the official scheme on the classification of sub-offices. The greater problem was how to deal with this. One solution proposed to the PF was for the Union 'to organise and propagate the principles of Socialism for the direct purpose of bringing about a system of society whereby our just deserts shall be recognised'. A more immediate aim was proposed by the PTCA, which had generally stood aloof from the back-biting in the evidence. It called for 'cool heads and clear brains'. Its members understood more clearly than anybody else how conflicting claims had allowed the Committee to accept the only consistent view of the matter, the one presented by the authorities.[67]

The associations did not feel able to do anything other than protest as the Report was implemented during 1907 and 1908. They attacked the MPs, especially the two trade unionists who had been on the Committee. They lobbied the Parliamentary debates where it was discussed. They argued amongst themselves on the respective merits of utter rejection and compromise.[68] Generally, however, they learnt the hardest lesson, which was the need for greater unity of effort, underlined by the success of the deferred pay movement in 1909. The sorters and postmen dropped their differences enough for the latter to rejoin the NJC in 1910. The PTCA and UKPCA began to work more closely together. After some further discussions, the associations agreed in 1910 to abandon their efforts against Hobhouse and to campaign together for another select committee.

At first their efforts had very little effect. The 1911 Post Office estimates debate heard an unusual lack of concern for the welfare of the staff, and one journal said that 'the sting has apparently been taken out of Postal grievances'. The entire industrial atmosphere changed in the autumn, particularly as a result of the strike on the railways. Postmen were immediately involved by the refusal of some of their number to do the work at stations of those on strike and this was agreed by the Postmaster General. *The Post* concluded that it had become clear 'that the present methods of Postal trade unionism are unproductive of substantial results'. Before the end of the year association leaders even told one of the mass meetings that 'we will not stop short at constitutional action' in pursuit of a new inquiry. By then large numbers of mass meetings had taken place, Postmaster General Herbert Samuel had seen representatives of the National Joint Committee on 28 September 1911 and had himself agreed in October to the idea of a new inquiry. He had some difficulty in persuading the Cabinet to accept this. On 7 December the *Daily Express* said 'Will there be a postal strike by Christmas? This is the question which is being discussed by thousands of postmen, sorters, telegraphists and sub-postmasters.' On 11 December it was announced that the Cabinet had agreed to the setting up of a Select Committee and this was eventually done in the following April of 1912.[69]

THE HOLT SELECT COMMITTEE: 1912-13

The nine members of this body were appointed to consider

> the wages and other Conditions of Employment of the principal classes of the Post Office Servants, of the unestablished Sub-Postmasters, and of such other smaller classes as the Committee may think necessary; and having regard to the conditions and prospects of their employment, and, as far as may be, the standard rate of wages and the position of other classes of workers, to report what alterations, if any, are desirable.

The phrase 'as far as may be' clearly embodied a compromise on the different views about wage determination, and it was difficult in the end to go beyond its studied vagueness. For the moment, however, matters seemed to be arranged to suit the associations. Holt and his colleagues met in the same Committee Room 15 of the Palace of Westminster as had Tweedmouth, a place 'lofty and somewhat sombre, with high windows', with glimpses of the Thames, Big Ben and St Thomas's Hospital. The representative character of the associations was no longer in question, and leaders of the National Joint Committee could not only attend, but also prompted the witnesses.[70]

The Select Committee itself consisted largely of new MPs. One member was William Tyson Wilson who had defeated Stanley in 1906 in the famous Westhoughton election, who tried to feed questions to the witnesses on behalf of the workers, though with limited success. The Chairman was Richard Durning Holt, Liberal MP for Hexham, a Liverpool shipowner who was determined to make his mark on the service. Others included James Arthur Dawes, a Liberal solicitor from Walworth, who occasionally brought proceedings to life with bad-tempered questions, sometimes directed at Holt himself. The Committee was much more aggressive than its predecessors, and even had a number of sharp and open disagreements within its own ranks.

Once again there were more words spoken, pages written and documents collected than ever before. There was over twice as much evidence as Tweedmouth, and a third more than Hobhouse. This time there were 33,695 questions on 1,774 pages besides many reproduced documents, indexes and so on, taking altogether almost four whole volumes of the Parliamentary Papers for the year. There was also much supporting material including the full texts of the various submissions, like the very useful *Post Office Information* supplied by the authorities.[71] Despite all this profusion of detail, the Holt Committee decided that it could reconsider anything discussed by its predecessors, and they considered evidence even from the smallest and most unrepresentative individuals unless what they said was purely of local interest. It is not surprising that Holt took eighteen months to get through the work, much longer than his predecessors.

The Holt Committee was much more aggressive than those that had gone before. It relied to a great extent on cross-examination, which, as FA members were told, placed 'great responsibility on the representative who, through an insufficient grasp of his case or an attack of nerves, might fail'. In general, despite a failure to get a common programme on every question, those sent by the major associations, with the help of their 'mutual attitude' agreement, presented their evidence with competence, and refused to be drawn into invidious comparisons. Thus Ammon and Mulholland spoke for the National Joint Committee on general questions relating to consultation, overtime and pension rights. When Ammon appeared on behalf of the sorters themselves, he argued that all promotion should be through their own grade, and thus cut off the postmen from some of their promotion opportunities. Nevertheless, he refused to describe their work as 'inferior'.

On detailed points of special pleading like the classification of particular sub-offices, the Committee 'relentlessly' pursued the 'weakest cases'. Edith Howse did find a way to stop the merciless probing of the Committee in its tracks with the words 'the experts said the "Titanic" could not sink; but she did'. Much the worst treatment was meted out to witnesses like J. Frampton of the Central London Postmen's Association, who persisted in the 'unification' arguments left over from Hobhouse. The chairman attacked his 'long and involved statement' and ridiculed his claim for £4 10s (£4. 50) a week for a seven-and-a-half hour day, an increase of many hundreds percent, far in excess of the demands of the Postmen's Federation. Others were heard who clearly represented nobody but themselves. W. J. Chuter of Virginia Water, a non-union postman, presented himself in full uniform complete with five good conduct stripes to argue rather unconvincingly that the cost of living was higher outside the big towns. R. Ingham appeared on behalf of a small body known as the Writers Association – secessionists from the Fawcett Association. They were London sorters and overseers who did some clerical work and claimed clerical status. They had some justification in the argument that the Hobhouse Committee had intended to raise their status, but according to Stuart, special pleading on the importance of their work was treated as a 'burlesque' by the MPs. A similar lack of tolerance was accorded to arguments about special status from groups like tracers and sorters.[72]

Nor did the representatives of the authorities get away lightly from the Committee. They were sceptical of Sir Alexander King, Secretary of the Post Office, when he claimed that supervisors were intimidated by the associations. Nor were they much impressed by the sixty-four 'surprise visits' carried out by the Medical Officer in five years to 1,500 Post Office buildings. The Second Secretary, Edward Crabb, who was before the Committee for days on end, was treated with limited respect. He seemed ignorant of many aspects of Post Office work, unable to understand some of the questions, and generally floundered on such complicated matters as good conduct stripes. As for Christmas gratuities, he denied that they were taken into account in fixing the wages of postmen, though it was easy to quote many cases when increases were refused because of their existence. Crabb also denied that there was a small error in the figures provided by the authorities that the PF managed to discover, and was criticised by the Committee for rejecting PF evidence without having an alternative to offer. Stuart's verdict was that Crabb

> failed to impress the Committee. The one good point he was able to make against us was destroyed by the inaccuracy of his own figures and the contradictions of his statement, while his general attitude of pronouncing strongly against us and evading any favourable reply, even when the facts were against him, left an unpleasant taste in the mouths of some of the Committee.

King was clearly stung by the attacks he provoked from the staff. When he reappeared as a witness in December 1912, he felt compelled to make a special statement denying that 'administrative and supervising officers', were 'actuated by a deliberate desire to withhold from the staff their reasonable rights and privileges'.[73]

The indoor manipulative grades[74] also generally presented their case with greater skill than in the past, the PTCA and UKPCA only producing two witnesses each. However, the inconsistencies which remained were mercilessly exposed by the Committee. The PTCA claimed rather more on the maximum for SC&Ts. Unlike the UKPCA they also asked for equal pay for women, and based their claim entirely on increased value of work. The PTCA naturally placed greater stress on the value of the work performed by telegraphists, and also called for the abolition of the overseers class, and of the efficiency bar. William Ash did reasonably well under cross-questioning, and Mary Hickey argued competently, asserting that 'pay is not given because of responsibilities'. For the UKPCA, George Middleton put forward an interesting case on the social expectations of those he represented. However, he became confused on the question of carrying seniority in promotion, and his colleague Lynes would not admit that telegraphy was more demanding than sorting.

All of this was much less damaging than the evidence of W. A. Haxby, a 'blackleg witness', who attacked the PTCA for calling for promotion by seniority, for being affiliated to the Labour Party and for publishing the names of non-members in Liverpool. Haxby was really concerned with the more substantial claim for the implementation of the Hobhouse recommendation that technical qualifications for overseers should be abolished. J. Normalie of the Association of Irish Post Office

Clerks was even worse. He made a string of unsubstantiated allegations, starting with the view that women were lowering the standard of work, and culminating with the claim that there was religious bias in promotion policy which Holt described as 'an absolutely unfounded slander'.[75] Another AIPOC witness attacked the women, as well as those who worked on the edges of the larger towns.

The official reply to all this was lengthy, but clear and largely successful in convincing the Committee. It made the usual comparisons between telegraph and sorting work, largely to the detriment of the former, denying that the losses made in telegraphy had any effect on pay. It went on to claim that the demands of the PTCA would cost £2 million, which the Post Office Secretary expressed as 2d on income tax. The claims of the UKPCA were said to cost £825,600. Such calculations had rarely proved very accurate in the past, but they were widely accepted in the absence of opposite arguments from the associations. The only significant point on which the Committee got the better of King was in showing that the number of special duties at the Central Telegraph Office meant that the old system of grades had in effect been restored. Another line of questioning that made Stuart 'despair of Parliamentary friends' was undertaken by Tyson Wilson when he tried to argue that a number of women had been wrongly placed on the established list. The Irish case was largely dealt with by simple denials, though it was possible to explain exceptionally poor prospects of promotion by the persistence of patronage in Dublin until 1897.

Despite the fact that the case of the bulk of the Post Office labour force was covered between May and November of 1912, Holt and his Committee spent until the following May considering many others. The supervising grades did not get off lightly in their numerous inflated claims about their own importance. Dawes told one of them, 'I look upon [this] statement as absolutely an attempt to mislead the Committee'. Holt ridiculed the overseers who wanted to be called 'supervisors', since this was simply a replacement of the English by the Latin form, and could just as well be replaced by the Greek, which would give them the title of bishops. As for the clerks, Dawes told one of them that 'It would be of great assistance to me if in your statement you came down to the level of a Select Committee of the House of Commons'. A less elevated tone was adopted by two former 'agitators' who appeared before the Committee. E. L. Hilton, a superintendent at the Central Telegraph Office, accepted the now historic claim that the overseer grade should be abolished and telegraphists allowed to go straight to the maximum. Michael O'Toole, a founder of the PTCA and now Controller of the Dublin Telegraph Department, refuted some of the more ill advised charges of his subordinates, but refused to comment on the level of their pay.

Others who did badly before the Committee included officials who did not themselves seem aware of the differences between the various supervising grades, women sorters and clerks who stuck to their guns on equal pay, and representatives of the Engineering and Stores Association, who could not make up their minds whether they were prepared to have their wages determined by the cost of living. The E&SA was more effective in arguing that Hobhouse's reorganisation proposals had not been properly carried out, and that as they became more integrated into the Department comparisons with outside Post Office work grew less relevant. Charlie Jeremy, the *Journal* Editor, argued well against piece-work, and drew from Holt the astonishing statement that 'speeding-up is a good thing in itself'. Stuart thought 'their case was so good that even poor advocacy did not spoil it', and because 'they were tremendously in earnest they quite impressed the Committee with the reality of their grievances'.[76]

The Holt Committee was the first to make a serious inquiry into the conditions of telephonists, and Edith Howse made her career as a trade union leader on the basis of her answers on the matter. In particular, she used a report by an outside business-man printed in a paper called *The Organiser* in June 1912, which dealt with complaints of a sort later to be very common:

> There is . . . a widespread popular impression that telephone operators spend a good portion of their time chatting to one another and otherwise frivolling. This is grotesquely absurd . . . the telephone operator's time is filled almost to the human limit by the 'load' of calls placed upon her by the management.

Miss Howse's famous answer about experts being wrong on the *Titanic* was in reply to a claim that experts said they could deal with 220 calls in an hour.

The official case against this part of the evidence did not go well, especially as there was apparently nobody who understood the complexities of the case that had been presented. King was unable to explain why superior grades worked shorter hours in London, and his Assistant Secretary, L. T. Horne, got himself tied in knots in explaining why night telephone operators were unestablished. It was, he said, to attract older men, and yet the age maximum was 35. Holt thought the matter had best be dropped 'unless the Post Office have something better to say'. Horne also contradicted himself by denying that telephonists were unhealthy and then saying they needed frequent medical checks. He was compelled to agree that his statement might 'mislead the Committee'. William Slingo, Engineer-in-Chief, obviously knew a great deal more about the technical side of telegraphy than he did about his subordinates, and he had nothing to say about grievances on promotion, or on how frequently unestablished linesmen were discharged from the service. He had to agree with Dawes that tables compiled on this were 'not a bit of good to us'. The Controller of Stores, George Morgan, did better in arguing that many who worked under him were happy with piece-work, but less so in explaining exactly why they should have to remain unestablished.

The Committee made little effort to disentangle the complexities of the scale payment system for sub-postmasters which had been proposed by Hobhouse, but left it to the Department itself to denounce as unworkable the criteria they them-selves had devised. Nor did Holt and his Committee display much interest in the usual claims of the postmasters for their own internal system of promotion, especially as the authorities said they were overpaid in any case. The postmasters said they were not 'deterred from doing their work by the action of associations of employees', but thought they had insufficient redress in the event of unjust attack. Even less impressive were the witnesses on behalf of the Amalgamated Society of Telephone Employees, who had just come into the civil service with the nationalisa-tion of the telephones, and who had many genuine grievances. They heaped so much praise on the National Telephone Company that Dawes was driven to wonder 'why any subscriber should have gone to the Post Office at all'. In fact this was hyperbole rather than argument and the official side was able to quote a letter by ASTE General Secretary Jeffreys from 1909 making statements about the relative merits of the Post Office and the Company 'almost diametrically opposite to those given in evidence'. The Society also made claims for inflated wage increases which were ridiculed by Holt. Other more reasonable arguments did not go down well either, even though promises had not been kept that people could retain the advantages of their previous employment when joining the civil service, and women had done particularly badly in the transfer. The Committee also seems to have accepted the official view that inflated wage scales had been agreed by the Company in 1910 in the full knowledge that 'they would never have to pay the maximum'.[77]

The Holt Committee finished its public hearing on 1 May 1913, and, despite the inordinate length and detail of its labours, managed to produce by the following August a bulky Report which summarised its proceedings and made numerous recommendations. It seems to have been written almost entirely by Holt himself. For all its great length and apparently comprehensive coverage, not to mention the hostile and aggressive questioning which had preceded its birth, it changed much less than its predecessors. In practice Holt showed a marked preference for officially received opinions of the way things ought to be done.

The Report began well enough by asserting that, as a general principle, the cost of living ought to be taken into account in the determination of wages, and that it had risen by $11 \cdot 3$ per cent since the last settlement in 1905. It also put forward 'the ideal of family life' as one which should be considered in wage determination. However, when the details were scrutinised, it became clear that there was little on wages for the average Post Office worker in these newly enunciated principles, beyond a few increases at the maximum in the higher grades. The women, about whom so much had been said, got virtually nothing. Small points were conceded like individual representation on promotion decisions, and greater inspection of buildings. Meal reliefs were to be allowed to everybody, but only in their own time. This meant an increase in hours of work for most people, and an introduction of the 'net hours' system prevalent in private industry, but until that time avoided in the Post Office. This change in meal relief arrangements was never introduced. Further modification in breaks and in long and short attendances was not envisaged since 'it is impossible to provide reasonable convenience to the public at a reasonable expense by a regular staff working regular hours'. On other general questions there were small concessions such as a half-day holiday, though there was no change proposed on major grievances like the disappearance of open competition, since 'it is doubtful whether in aggregate there was much difference between officers recruited by the two methods', nor on the horrifying complexities of the Hobhouse classification system, since 'no system perfectly logical and capable of hard and fast application can be devised'.

For the individual grades there were some improvements, mostly for the better off. Good conduct stripes were abolished as desired, and the money consolidated into wages. However, since only about 5 per cent of those entitled to the stripes were not receiving the money in any case, this concession did not amount to much. On every other point to do with postmen, the Committee largely accepted the official view. They did not like Christmas boxes, but thought that since there could be no compensation in the event of their abolition, they would have to be left as they were. Similarly, while the Committee noted, with regret, the increase in the numbers of unestablished postmen, they did not propose any real change. All they said was that increasing the numbers of auxiliary postmen should not be 'treated as a back door method of entrance to the establishment', and that assistant postmen should not be compelled to remain in this position for more than a year.

The complaints of the SC&Ts, London sorters, CC&Ts and others, were outlined in the Report in considerable detail, including the claim for equal pay for women. Once again, however, most of these points were ignored in the recommendations. Thus it was said that 'complaints made of the learner system do not appear to be well founded', and there was nothing wrong in this case with 'paying small or even nominal wages'. London telephonists were offered nothing at all. As to restrictions on the right to transfer between offices, the Committee expressed its approval 'of the present practice of the Post Office'. On allocation of duties between the various grades, the special Norton Committee had allowed them to leave that matter altogether, though they did recommend the setting up of a separate establishment for wireless staff. The improvements proposed for some of the smaller London classes such as porters, bagmen and tube attendants were not inconsiderable, though none got the equality with higher grades that they asked for. Bagmen, for example, went from a scale of £1 7s (£1. 35) to £2 5s (£2. 25) up to £1 10s (£1. 50) to £2 8s (£2. 40). Some women telephonists got wage increases and a system of establishment for night telephonists was initiated, though not many people benefited at the time.

The Committee's proposals for the higher grades were more radical. They wanted the supervision of boy messengers to be by postmen paid special allowances, and thought that similar grades in the provinces such as 'acting head postmen' should be drawn from the ranks of the postmen, with the supervision of SC&Ts kept quite separate. There were few economic benefits to any individuals from these organisational changes. An even more significant change was proposed in relation to 'writing duties', for which the Committee thought 'rotation' had not been 'uniformly unsuccessful'. Instead, they proposed the setting up of a new grade of 'clerical assistants', first, second and third class, and the more rigid definition of what writing duties were left to lower grades. Thus they anticipated the setting up of a separate clerical establishment after the First World War. The most important change from the point of view of the engineers was the granting of establishment to a certain number of the more skilled, and there were also some marginal changes such as travelling allowances for electric light and factory staff, as well as a mess room for the first time at the Post Office stores. The Committee showed greater generosity to the 457 charwomen employed by the Post Office. The Treasury had refused to increase their wages above the 4d an hour they currently received, but the Committee thought they should get 4½d, and 5d after five years. There was little change of significance proposed for the sub-postmasters, or postmasters, except that some of the poorer postmasters should go onto the scale payment system. In the final section of the Report, covering the grievances of the former employees of the National Telephone Company, the policies of the Department in the transfer were described as 'remarkably liberal' – a typical and final confirmation of the general attitude of the Committee to the arguments that had been presented to them.[78]

REACTIONS TO THE HOLT REPORT

Philip Snowden, who was then a Labour MP, expressed himself as 'completely bewildered' by the Report and thought that it 'could not have succeeded better if it had been deliberately drawn up so as to be incomprehensible'. The Postmaster General announced his intention of giving it 'careful consideration'.[79] However the workers themselves soon showed they were in little doubt about its meaning. 'Mails were delayed; telegraphic typewriters dropped mysteriously from the top to the bottom of high buildings'.[80] The association leaders proceeded, however, with great circumspection, not wishing to repeat the blunders they thought they had made in the wake of the Bradford Report, nor yet to reject the various minor improvements promised by Holt. 'Experience has shown', wrote Ammon of the FA, 'that where wild and extravagant language may, for the fleeting moment, please the crowd, if it cannot be backed by action equally forceful, the reaction is disastrous to the enemy.' However, there was little sign that the available alternatives were much use either. The NJC met at Matlock and on 22 August published a statement characterising the Report as 'an insult to the intelligence of the Post Office employees'. It could not, they asserted, be considered 'as a proper verdict on their just and moderate claims'. The Government was called upon to 'take immediate steps to deal with an acute and dangerous situation'. However, no such steps were proposed to the Post Office workers themselves. During August the UKPCA and PTCA argued against any negotiations, though they both later changed. A general meeting of London sorters called on the FA Executive 'to decline to enter into any negotiations', and to demand instead only pay increases in line with the cost of living. On 20 September a special Conference of the Postmen's Federation voted in favour of a 'strike policy' by 549 votes to 175, and agreed to set up a 'defence fund'. These were policies they had rejected at their Annual Conference only three months earlier. However, no actual strike action was proposed, and Stuart made sure that the Conference also agreed to further meetings with the authorities. Stuart had not only to convince his own members, he had to get a majority in the NJC by getting the PTCA and UKPCA, then on the point of amalgamating, to vote separately for the proposition. The FA members were also brought into line by being persuaded that negotiations were the only possible form of action.[81]

From the point of view of the associations, one important effect of the Report was that it caused discontent amongst all the larger grades. The proposals for the clerical grades made it possible to see a 'definite antagonism between the higher officials and the rank and file' in its main outlines. On seeing the proposals even the supervisors shared in 'the feeling of disgust with which it has been received throughout the service', and concluded that they 'had enough of these ill-assorted bodies, selected who knows why or how'.[82]

On 23 September the authorities issued a statement which claimed that the proposals as they stood would cost them £1 million. This figure was multiplied by ten times for the purpose of cartoons in *Punch* and provoked *The Times* into a trenchant statement of class war asserting that in the event of any strike there would be a dozen blacklegs ready to take any position, and 'not a glimmer of public sympathy'. The magazine *Truth* showed a greater preparedness to withdraw mis-representations, and the Oxford students' *Varsity* even produced a sympathetic account of conditions at the local office. None of this affected the Post Office workers one way or the other and there was an immediate movement towards much closer working by their associations. After the announcement of ballot results in September, the merging of the PTCA and UKPCA proceeded apace. A meeting representing all the associations held in Caxton Hall, Westminster, on 27 October heard Stuart say that the Report 'brought home the need for the closest possible amalgamation to everybody in the service', and it was proposed that even the supervisors, and perhaps some day the Post Office secretary himself, should be included in such unification. However, the achievements of the Committee set up to pursue these aims were in the short term limited.[83] By now the main demand initiated by the engineers put forward at meetings of all sections throughout the country was for a complete rejection of Holt's proposals and an across-the-board pay increase of 15 per cent.

The policy of negotiating with the Postmaster General on the Report, foisted by Stuart on many unwilling colleagues, did not prove a success. The main problem was, as the telegraphists had discovered in 1897, that there was a great deal of talk of strike action in the association journals and at the meetings, but no serious attempt to prepare for it, or still less to carry it out. When the first NJC delegation met PMG Samuel on 4 November 1913 this point was pushed home. Samuel began by warning that a strike would not be treated in the same way as in private industry, and Stuart was driven to retort that 'if that statement had been made to an outside Trade Union, it would have fetched them out in a week'. These preliminaries set the tone for a series of bad-tempered exchanges between Samuel and Stuart which constituted the rest of the discussion. Although it was agreed that the negotiations would remain 'confidential', readers of the *Postman's Gazette* were assured that their outcome 'may be said to be nil'.

At a further meeting a fortnight later on 19 November, Samuel announced that the increase to 'net hours' proposed in the Report would not be introduced, though neither would the half-holiday for all. Furthermore, anyone getting less than £1 15s (£1. 75) in London or £1 10s (£1. 50) outside would get an immediate incremental increase. Stuart acknowledged that 'the Government have made some very considerable concessions', a phrase not much liked by his colleagues. The rest of the interview consisted largely of similarly bad-tempered exchanges about strike action that had characterised the first one.

Stuart argued that the threats from the authorities in late October were a 'tactical blunder'. In fact they served to diffuse some of the agitation. A third discussion with Samuel on 11 December was even less efficacious with Stuart claiming with some justice 'that the Government does intend to reduce our real wages'. The Postmaster General replied that they 'were unable to grant the incessant demands that were being made on the public Treasury' and rejected the 15 per cent claim out of hand. The only concrete point discussed was how many Post Office workers were earning less than £1 a week. The authorities claimed that this was less than 1 per cent of the total, and they would mostly get more when the Report was implemented. A further meeting of the joint Executives was held on 16 December and this did not come up with any new proposals for action. A strike ballot was rejected, and further intense Parliamentary lobbying was proposed. In January it was agreed that the postmen should also meet the Postmaster General again.

By February 1914 some of the Holt proposals were already enacted. Samuel had now retired as Postmaster General and had been replaced by the same Charles Hobhouse who had been responsible for the earlier Select Committee report. Hobhouse was a much less significant political figure than Samuel, and showed a much less certain touch in handling what remained of the agitation against Holt's Report. When he met a delegation from the Postmen's Federation on 16 March he refused to discuss the wages provisions of the Report on the grounds that they had already been decided by the Cabinet. The postmen stormed out with the words 'thank you for not having heard us'. The Department issued what it considered to be a final word on most aspects of the Report on 3 April. Though this involved wage increases for almost everybody, dissatisfaction remained intense, and lobbying activity, particularly of MPs, was taken up with gusto.[84]

When at last the Holt Report was discussed in the House of Commons on 30 April, it was met during the course of a seven-hour debate with a barrage of abuse such as can but rarely have been accorded to a Committee set up by the House itself. This can be partly explained by the comparative inexperience of the Members of the time. The Liberals, who had been in office for eight years, were weak in Parliamentary terms. They had survived two narrowly fought General Elections in 1910 only with the support of the Irish Nationalists, to whom they were in the process of granting Home Rule, and of the Labour Party, who asked for little in return. The Conservatives used the Holt Report as an opportunity to show an unaccustomed concern for the grievances of the Post Office workers. Their real purpose was to weaken and possibly even to defeat the Government. The Report thus found few defenders, even the new Postmaster General expressing some reservations, and announcing that a minimum wage of £1 2s (£1. 10) per week would be introduced, hardly likely to affect many people if the figures recently produced by the Department itself were to be believed. Only Holt himself defended the Report. Patrick Brady, Irish Nationalist MP for a Dublin constituency and another of the Members, wondered whether he should not have produced a minority statement. The debate was adjourned until 10 June when the Report induced a further barrage of abuse. This time, the Liberals had arranged a way out for themselves. They got Labour leader Ramsey MacDonald in the debate to take up a proposal initiated by Stuart for an outside Committee including representatives of the associations to reconsider the Report. This had already been agreed on behalf of the NJC by Stuart who considered that through its establishment 'postal workers have won the most astonishing victory ever known'. It certainly saved the Government. The Tories were left raging with frustration and calling MacDonald a 'bonnet', which is defined as 'a thing or person used to put a good face on underhand proceedings'.[85] The Post Office workers for their part now had yet another new form of negotiating procedure with which to contend.

THE GIBB COMMITTEE: 1914–17

The joint body which was set up consisted of Stuart and Young elected by the NJC for the associations, King for the Post Office, and Roland Wilkins for the Treasury. Sir George Gibb, a railway company executive, was Chairman. This Committee was far more important for what it was than for what it decided. Its very existence indicated representation of the workforce in pronouncements about their conditions. Its proceedings were first of all interrupted by the outbreak of war in August 1914, after which association leaders agreed to cease agitating for improved conditions for their members. Before the end of the year the demise of the Gibb Committee was accepted and it was soon agreed to abandon it altogether, in order to give a clear run for the arbitration machinery set up during 1917. The two reports issued by Gibb and his colleagues[86] were limited to the consideration of some problems arising out of the application of the Holt proposals, such as the position of some who might lose out by the timing of the abolition of good conduct stripes, or the changes in acting lists and substitution. The effects were generally beneficial to small groups of the staff, but they were very rapidly overshadowed by the much greater results of the advent of war.

POST OFFICE WORKERS IN THE FIRST WORLD WAR

The most immediate effect of the outbreak of war in August 1914 was the rapid depletion of the Post Office workforce. Before the end of 1914 over 28,000 men volunteered for the armed forces, and many more followed later as conscripts. In the middle of 1915, 25 per cent of the membership of the FA was in the armed forces. By June 1918 73,000 people had been released for war service from the Post Office and a workforce of 144,500 men and 32,000 women was replaced by one of 78,000 men and 79,000 women.[87] The Prime Minister promised that all civil servants could return to their jobs, so the departing workers were replaced by 'temporaries', from 1915 including women. As the melancholy lists of dead and missing mounted up in Post Office Circulars and staff journals, it became clear that many of these people need not be so temporary after all.

The beginning of war meant that all the excitement of the struggle against the Holt Report was soon forgotten. At first the association leaders responded with full bellicose ferocity to appeals for patriotism. Post Office workers were told that 'the British home, the Empire, nay, the whole fabric of civilisation, is in grave jeopardy', and that 'it behoves every young man who is physically fit and capable of bearing arms to rise to the occasion'. Stuart appeared on a joint recruiting platform with officials from the Department at St Martin's-le-Grand on 25 October 1915, though not without protests from the Federation. He and other leaders were also involved jointly with the authorities in a 'Post Office Relief Fund', collecting charitable donations for those who had enlisted.[88] Despite rapidly rising prices, union leaders in the Post Office as elsewhere agreed to abstain in the early period of the war from seeking higher wages for their members. As a result, they concentrated on other questions such as separation allowances for the wives of soldiers. There was also the problem of the curtailment and general disruption of the communications system arising out of the war itself. Offices were generally open for shorter periods, and deliveries drastically curtailed. There were increased and generally more onerous duties for those remaining in the services. 'Since the War commenced', wrote the *Postman's Gazette* before the end of 1915, 'postmen's duties have worsened, split attendance increased, staff lessened, men taken off walks to make room for women, and in some cases the whole of the established staff transferred'.[89] In such circumstances there was a good deal of overtime working, though at first nothing like enough to make up for falling real wages. Some effort was also directed against the curtailment of postal facilities on Sundays in the provinces, and similar cuts.[90]

However, many of the most important problems arose from the position of the 'temporaries', and the effect they were likely to have on the wages and conditions of the permanent staff. At first most of the associations looked askance at the new arrivals, and most did not even admit them to membership. However, the Postmen's Federation, whose membership fell from 44,000 to 34,000 in the opening period of the war, despite constant appeals to those who remained to maintain the contributions of their departed colleagues, soon took up the cause of 'temporaries' and recruited them, as also did the Engineering and Stores Association. Stuart still found it necessary to attack some local branches who thought themselves 'too superior to accept the temporary men and women as members', though this was only in a minority of cases. Elsewhere branches called for equal pay for women, but the Executive thought this went too far.[91] On 11 November 1914, a delegation from the NJC and the War Emergency Workers National Committee –

representing the main leaders of TUC and Labour Party – met PMG Hobhouse
and obtained an increase from the £1 4s (£1. 20) originally paid to London 'temporaries' to £1 6s (£1. 30) or £1 8s (£1. 40). Wages paid to these temporaries
remained 'woefully insufficient' as well as 'not based on any established Post Office
principle', with rates more according to what local postmasters thought the market
would bear than with the usual classification criteria. As a result pressure was
marked both through national labour organisations and local trades councils.[92]

The most important question in relation to the 'temporaries' was the same as in
many outside industries – whether the 'dilution' of the workforce was going to be
permanent. 'Unskilled and underpaid labour', as one staff journal pointed out, 'is
always a serious menace to Trade Unionism'. In the face of some pressure, the
Postmaster General was prepared to give an undertaking similar to the one that
applied in outside industry, saying that he had

> no intention of replacing permanent employees by casual labour, or of deter-
> mining questions as to employment after the War by reference to decisions
> arrived at in consequence of war requirements and necessities.

Nevertheless, as association leaders pointed out in an interview in 1915, it was
impossible to know what conditions it was that were being restored with the same
precision as was the case in outside industry, where more formal rules and bargaining might apply.[93] For the moment, however, the undertaking seemed reasonable enough.

It was not very long, however, before the burning question for all Post Office
workers became the falling value of their pay. Prices rose rapidly, especially in the
opening months of the war, living standards fell, and the Government compelled
some private employers to accept compulsory settlement of disputes. Before very
long local branches were calling on leaders of the Post Office workers 'to take action
for an immediate increase in wages'. As a result of this pressure, a claim for a wage
increase was formulated by the NJC on 1 March 1915.[94] This called for a 'bonus'
to be paid up to six months after the end of the war of 4s (20p) a week for those
earning up to £2, 3s (15p) for those earning up to £2 15s (£2. 75), and 2s (10p) for
those on up to £210 per annum. This was a very moderate claim, much less than the
already observed rise in prices, and asking for nothing on overtime pay or superannuation. It also diminished higher up the scale, but discriminated against women
by asking only 2s (10p) for all of them. This was against the stated policy of the
P&TCA, though it got their support.[95] The temporaries, it was proposed, should
'participate' in any improvements. Because of its generally progressive and partial
nature, some of the superior grades not even being involved for 'patriotic' reasons,
the claim itself occasioned more than its fair share of anomalies which built up
difficulties for the future. Even more significant, though hardly noticed at that time,
was that this was the first claim ever submitted that was based on cost-of-living
criteria alone. Also of considerable long-term significance was the fact that all other
means of approach besides 'delegations', in other words direct negotiations, were
rejected. A conscious decision was taken not to pursue the claim though Parliamentary questions, or even the Gibb Committee.

For some weeks the Treasury refused to even consider any increase. Soon there
were signs of escalating unrest in outside industry and with bellicose language from
association leaders to match. There was support from such quarters as the novelist

Arnold Bennett, who described Hobhouse as 'hopelessly prejudiced, stupid and ill-informed' as well as manifesting an attitude 'responsible for a great deal of the class-friction that had recently been developing'. The PF Executive unanimously voted against proposing strike action to the membership, only on the grounds that they could not guarantee support from the telegraphists. The authorities were compelled to make a response. They faced a problem in deciding precisely how to do so. They could have gone for the creation of some new 'inquiry' by civil servants, MPs, or outsiders, but this did not seem likely to be efficacious. Thus on 28 April they announced their willingness to go to arbitration. The first person they approached to act in this capacity, Lord Wrenbury (a former judge), refused to do so on the grounds that the Government would not agree in advance to accept his ruling. Eventually, Sir James Woodhouse, who when an MP had been involved in the Norfolk–Hanbury discussions, agreed to act.

On 21 June 1915 Woodhouse met delegations from the NJC and the authorities. Stuart stated the case with admirable brevity, showing steep increases both in the cost of living and in the wages of other public servants. Woodhouse published his findings very soon after on 8 July, awarding 3s (15p) to those on £2 or less, 2s (10p) to those on £2 to £3 and nothing to those above. Women were to get half of this, and temporaries, all in the first category, were to be treated as such. Increases in the superannuation allowance were also proposed. 'On the whole', said *The Post*, 'the disposition of the service seems to be to take it and be thankful'. However the Treasury was inclined to delay, and pressure had to be put on through Labour leader Arthur Henderson who was then in the Government. Treasury agreement to the general principle was eventually secured in September, and the payment was back-dated to 1 March.[96]

A number of delegations from the NJC met the PMG during the next period on the reduction of postal facilities and other such general issues. One of these, from the postmen demanding equal pay for women, was met with a statement from Postmaster General Pease that the women only got 'found money'. This was described by the PF as being on a par with Stanley's infamous statement about 'bloodsuckers'.[97] As prices continued to rise, and wages in outside industry went up in parallel, demands for similar improvements came from Post Office workers. In June 1916, the PF Conference called for a further 'war bonus' of 5s (25p) across the board, including women, and this was immediately submitted through the NJC, and won general support throughout the civil service. Dubery of the FA explained to the Postmaster General that the claim was 'based on the cost of living primarily'. The NJC was also prepared to accept a purely temporary increase.[98]

In September, a reply to the claim was published. This offered marginal increases on the previous award, ignoring the claim for equality. Details are set out in Appendix 11, p. 631, and it was said that the increases would end with the war. This was a step back on the previous statement. It was therefore described as 'perhaps the biggest insult that any Postmaster General has inflicted upon his staff'. In view of the real increases being achieved elsewhere and the continuing shortage of labour, 'trouble at the PO' was predicted. On 5 October the NJC wrote proposing arbitration. Numerous mass meetings were held, some of which expressed considerable dissatisfaction at the line of the NJC and further delegations. The PMG maintained that his hands were tied because the civil service as a whole was involved. It was clear that some new method of settling matters would have to be agreed. Thus a new piece of machinery was agreed on 2 November 1916. At the same time the Government agreed to a number of insistent demands from the labour movement, including rationing of foodstuffs.

THE CONCILIATION AND ARBITRATION BOARD: 1916

The Conciliation and Arbitration Board for Government Employees was set up by resolution of the War Cabinet in December 1916, and published its first awards in the following May. It was under the Chairmanship of Sir William Collins, Liberal MP for Derby, who was replaced in July 1918 by F. Gore-Brown, a well known barrister, and included also Harry Gosling of the Lightermen's Union and National Transport Workers Federation, and A. K. Butterworth of the North-Eastern Railway, who was replaced by Sir Robert Turnbull at the end of 1918. Its very setting up involved 'introducing an entirely new principle into the public service and overriding the Treasury as the ultimate and final authority'. In the Post Office as elsewhere, the Board discovered that many disputes 'were frankly differences between the Treasury on the one hand and claimants and their department on the other'. Proceedings were more informal than in the earlier inquiries into Post Office workers' conditions and conspicuously briefer.[99]

After discussions lasting a matter of hours, the arbitration board granted increases of wages greater than anything that had been secured by all the earlier inquiries put together. Until 1919 all the main changes in Post Office workers' wages, and for the civil service as a whole, were negotiated by reference to it. Even though it fitted in somewhat awkwardly to the Whitley machinery that was set up thereafter and to the rigid cost-of-living ladder that then evolved, it became a popular body with most civil servants, and government efforts to abolish it were defeated in the mid-1920s.

The very first claim submitted to the Board came from the National Joint Committee for the Post Office workers in March 1916. Most of the details can be gathered from the table given in Appendix 11. However, it should be noted that an equal increase was claimed for, but not granted to, women. Also, for the first time a claim was submitted for those earning above £3 a week for 8s (40p) extra, and they got 5s (25p), or 3s 6d (17½p) at higher levels. For juveniles below 18, an extra 50 per cent was asked and an extra 4s (20p) secured.[100] For all its inadequacies, the postal and telegraph clerks thought it 'a real attempt to lessen the hardship imposed on postal servants by the increased cost of living'. The temporaries submitted a separate claim but this was simply absorbed into it, giving them about half what they asked for. This could do little but provoke discontent, not least because it was not supposed to come into effect until 1 January 1917.

The usual protests were made against this settlement, and the Parliamentary debate on the Post Office estimates in that year largely concentrated on it.[101] Prices continued to rise rapidly, so it was hardly surprising that a new claim for a war bonus was submitted in November before the previous one had time to come into effect. This time it was submitted through the Civil Service Federation. It asked for a complete across-the-board increase of 15s (75p) for everybody earning up to £500 a year. The Treasury was not now opposing the principle of the war bonus, but was denying that prices were still rising as fast as earlier in the war. The decision of the Arbitration Board was a combination of splitting the difference and maintaining the inequalities that already existed. Table 7.1 shows what was secured in some detail not given in Appendix 11.

Table 7.1

	Men	Women	Juveniles	Temporaries
Up to £2 pw (£104 pa)	14s (70p)	9s (45p)	7s (35p)	6s 6d (32½p)
£2–£3 pw (£156 pa)	13s (65p)	8s 6d (42½p)	6s 6d (32½p)	6s (30p)
£156–250 pa	15% (£34 min.)	10%		
£250–350 pa	12% (£37. 50 min.)	8%		
£350+ pa	10%	6⅔%		

These increases were granted as from 17 December 1917. They did represent some improvement, though how tenuous was shown by the refusal of the Board to allow them to be consolidated into wages. In fact they remained a long way behind the increases in prices that had taken place since the beginning of the war. Retail prices had doubled, and money wages elsewhere had gone up more than that. Few in the public service or Post Office were earning above 35 per cent in money terms more than what they had earned at the beginning of the war.[102]

In this situation it is hardly surprising that the Post Office associations, and those in the rest of the public service who had now become their close allies, put relentless and continuing pressure on the Arbitration Board. On 17 December 1917, temporary Post Office employees were awarded 6s (30p) extra each week for men, 4s (20p) for women and 2s 6d (12½p) for juveniles, over and above what had been obtained in previous settlements. In March 1918, the Board rejected a startling new claim submitted by the PF for equality between temporary postmen and post-women and their permanent colleagues. Details of the settlement following this claim, as well as subsequent changes, are given in Appendix 12, p. 632. In May 1919 a wide range of improvements was granted to the temporary grades, including temporary sorters, SC&Ts and CC&Ts. This consolidated their bonuses into earnings, gave them overtime pay, and generally put their conditions within striking distance of the rates obtained by their permanent colleagues. By this time, the basis for this carefully preserved distinction was breaking down, but there had also been general increases for the permanent grades in July 1918, and then again in March and November of the following year. The most important details of these are summarised in the table given in Appendix 11. These show clearly how the better paid grades gradually made up the disadvantages they had suffered in earlier settle-ments, and how the inferior position of women was maintained against all efforts to weaken it in the claims which were submitted. There was some talk about, though not much evidence of, 'a rank and file movement' among women against the decisions of the Board. Some even wanted to go on strike. The regressive nature of these later settlements was particularly galling to those who set the pace in the earlier ones, and after the last of them, the postmen thought it 'a most miserable award' which would 'have the effect of largely adding to the numbers of our members who feel that the [arbitration] board has outlived its original purpose'. They called for completely new machinery, both on the union and official sides.[103]

CONCLUSION

Well before the end of 1919, the entire method of settling disputes in the public sector was thrown into the melting pot. The very acceptance of arbitration as early as 1915 had put paid to many of the old shibboleths about Treasury control. The exigencies of war forced many decisions which were seen as arising from special circumstances, and were expected to be only temporary in their application. However, they could not then be forgotten when the next discussion took place. Thus when claims were referred back to the parties by the Arbitration Board, the fact that more or less normal industrial relations bargaining was taking place could not be obscured. Settlements between most temporary grades and the Post Office were arranged in this way in the middle of 1918, and this was not forgotten when subsequent claims were submitted. Also during the war, the careful complexities of the Hobhouse and Holt provincial classification schemes were undermined with the stroke of an official pen, and the new simplified systems could not then be brushed aside after the end of the war.

If it became more obvious that things could never be the same again in civil service bargaining, there was no pre-conceived plan for what a new system might be like. One major factor was that because of the rigidities and delays in the systems that already existed for civil servants, their real improvements had kept well behind those in outside industry, who in many cases may actually have benefited from wartime inflation. There can be no doubt that the real living standards of Post Office workers fell during the wartime period. The post-Holt discontent, which had been so abruptly brought to an end by the outbreak of war, expressed itself with increasing ferocity as the war went on. Not only did Post Office workers in common with other sections of organised workers grow more militant in the latter part of the war. As Ammon asserted in 1913 in the statement given at the head of this Chapter, their discontent had already led them to seek new ways of resolving their grievances. The unification of trade union effort is described in the next chapter. At the end of Chapter 4 an account has been given of how the new Whitley machinery evolved and came to be accepted. There were then many new problems and new procedures. The UPW came into existence in 1919 with a general wage claim for the consolidation of bonus payments and for an increase besides. There were similar moves from elsewhere in the civil service.

Before going on in other chapters to describe how this new system worked out, it is well to remember that the trade unionists who went into the Whitley system at the end of the war did so on the basis of the many experiences which have been described in this chapter. They had been through the great public inquiries, the select committees, the lobbying, and the somewhat less spectacular arbitration machinery of the wartime period. This chapter has described in some detail the special experiences under this complex and unusual method of settling disputes, both because they are of interest in themselves, and also because they helped to mould the conceptions and attitudes of subsequent generations.

NOTES

1 The proceedings and reports of these Committees are to be found in the following volumes of Parliamentary Papers: 1897 XLIV (Tweedmouth); 1904 XXXIII (Bradford); 1906 XII and 1907 VII (Hobhouse); 1912–13 IX and 1913 X–XIII (Holt); 1914–16 XXXII and 1916 XIV (Gibb). They are referred to for the rest of this chapter simply by the names of their respective chairmen.

2 On the earlier examples see Chapter 5, pp. 99, 113 and on Compton's Motion p. 138. A similar motion proposed on 17 April 1891 was defeated by 163 votes to 93 (*Hansard* III, 352, 851–92) and further such demands on 16 September 1893 were withdrawn, though Arnold Morley, the new PMG, was 'very indistinctly heard' (*Hansard* IV, 17, 1453–4, 1456–67). The telegraphists supported the call for 'an independent enquiry' – see *Statement of the Male Portion of the Provincial Clerks* (1893). Similar statements for the sorters are in *Post*, 17 June and 7 October 1893, and 15 December 1894 reports the joint meeting with the postmen addressed by Keir Hardie. *Post*, 18 July 1892, argues for a Select Committee of MPs.

3 *Post*, 1 September 1894, for one such delegation of MPs, and *Hansard* IV, 33, 1446–86 (17 May 1895) for agreement to establish the inquiry.

4 Tweedmouth Report, p. 4, on the terms of reference. *Post*, 1 June 1895, for reservations on the constitution of the Committee and *PJ* October 1895 for an attack on this attitude. The PTCA asked at first for the right to nominate their own representatives – see *Summary of the Claims of the PTCA* (1900), pp. 35–6.

5 Besides PP 1897 XLIV, see the PF's PCE, the London Postal Overseers Association *The Case of the London Overseers*, and the Postal Telegraph Linesmen's Association *Verbatim Report*, though the two latter largely reproduce the official version.

6 Evidence, pp. 110, 19, 503; Report, p. 6.

7 Smith (1931), p. 47.

8 Evidence, pp. 58, 2, 103, 1058, 1068.

9 Evidence, pp. 124–7, 134, 98–9, 114–5 and Report, p. 15. On the 'sorter-tracers' see Evidence, pp. 445–63, 473–7, 1,110–2 and for Clery's comment *Post*, 10 October 1895.

10 These various arguments, including the quotations, are in Evidence, pp. 264, 138, 260, 144, 162, 321, 267–8, 158, 162 and 1,101, and in Report, pp. 10–11, 13–14. For more details see PTCA, *The Telegraph Service* (n.d. 1894?) giving a number of statements favourable to their case by MPs and the press, and on the general evolution of the grades, see above, Chapter 3, pp. 52–5.

11 Tweedmouth Evidence, pp. 360, 156–7, 177–81, 264, 266, 274; Report, p. 33.

12 Evidence, pp. 189, 211, 267ff.; Report, pp. 10–11; Chapter 3, p. 52.

13 Evidence, pp. 296–8, 305–6, 314–5, 336–7, 351–2, 389–91, 440, 443.

14 PCE, pp. 35ff. and Evidence, pp. 477ff. with quotations from pp. 485, 484, 492, and pp. 496–518 for Walsh and 519–31 for Dowling. In later years Walsh was remembered as someone who though doing some 'mischief' was 'a great pioneer', a 'sincere eloquent and able man'. See also Jackson (1958), p. 518. He wrote a short book published in Glasgow in 1897 called *Eternally Onward*, which is a strange mixture of semi-socialist and semi-religious mysticism from someone who seems to have had doubts about both socialism and religion.

15 Evidence, pp. 531, 536–66 on the auxiliaries; 566–76 on parcels; 578–95 on punishments; 620–41 and Report, p. 24, on rural postmen; Evidence, pp. 680–701 on porters and labourers and 701–13 on the others. A London Postal Porters Association was set up in July 1895 with the active encouragement of the FA (*Post*, 20 July 1895).

16 Evidence, pp. 717, 718; Report, p. 21; Evidence, pp. 722, 723, 726, 731, 742, 744–5, 746, 758, 772–84. *Post*, 6 June 1896, for the verdict on Hill. POR 30E, 5827/1897 XIII makes it clear that most London postmasters considered the duties and responsibilities of postmen at least as arduous, if not more so, than sorters. Badcock, however, did not consider postmen outside London could be paid so much because they did no sorting.

17 PCE 635, 630, 637; Evidence, p. 1,124.

18 Evidence, pp. 230, 834, 463–8, 840–6; Report, pp. 16, 26–8.

19 Smith (1931), p. 40; Evidence, pp. 785–813, 991–4 on postmasters, pp. 813–30 on sub-postmasters, pp. 861–7, 934–5 and 1,043–9 on ex-soldiers, pp. 867–80 and Bealey (1976), pp. 34ff. on the linesmen, pp. 899–913 on the other engineers and pp. 922–5, 934–42, 1,005–8 on the adult messengers.

20 Evidence, pp. 925ff., with quotations on pp. 1,086, 953, 971, 1,088.

21 POR 30E 5827/1897 XIV, XIX and *passim*; POC, 1190, 26 March 1897; *Post*, 1933, p. 52 for the associations' calculation; Report, pp. 5, 6, 8, 9.

22 Report, p. 10 and *passim*.

23 *Post* (7 August 1897). (The sorters' general meeting to consider the report was however a 'comparative failure' with only a few hundred present and little enthusiasm for Parliamentary representation – *ibid.*, 17 April.)

24 PF, *Report of the Mass Meeting of Postmen . . . 25 March 1897*, p. 5; POR 30E 5827/1897 XIII; *PG* 1897, *passim*.

25 Material on the actions of the telegraphists in 1897 is in R IV/22 and *Telegraph Chronicle* from which the following quotations are taken. R IV/5 contains many of the relevant PTCA circulars.

26 A verbatim account of the Conference is preserved at R IV/10. The dispute between Venables and the Liverpool men was a complex one, exacerbated by his failure to prepare any action against the Tweedmouth Report, but also deriving from the decision taken the previous year that he and his deputy should be *ex-officio* members of the Central Committee regardless of whether they had support in Liverpool. On finance, the Central Committee wanted the increase to be 3d a week.

27 *Hansard* VI, 51 325ff. (16 July 1897).

28 POR 30E 3067/1897 IX. There is an account of these events by Belderson himself in R IV/22 and a further version in *Daily Mail*, 19 July. This paper was sympathetic to the telegraphists at this time and published full accounts of the agitation. On 17 July it attacked the 'policy of provocation' by the authorities. For a very different view see *The Times*, 22 July.

29 POR 30E 3067/1897 XII; R IV/5, 77 (with original emphasis); *Telegraph Chronicle*, 23 July 1897, pp. 254ff. *Yorkshire Post*, 21 July 1897, claims delays were caused by the agitators, but the authorities denied this – see *Morning Leader*, 6 August 1897.

30 *Post*, 7 August 1897, and other service journals for details. POR 60/25 has a full transcript, and see 30E 3067/1897 XVII for other information.

31 What follows is from the *Telegraph Chronicle* unless otherwise stated. Press cuttings in R IV/7 add little.

32 Details of the police and other dispositions of the authorities can be gathered from POR 30E 3067/1897 XXXV.

33 Swift's account (1929), pp. 292–4, though written less than three years later, confuses the chronology at this point, putting the punishments before the 'conference', thus obscuring the timing of the authorities. POR 30E 3067/1897 XVI shows that it was decided not to punish a telegraphist whose letter to the *Yorkshire Post* appeared on 21 July.

34 POC 1218, 1219, 18 and 19 August, give for the original meeting on 3 April details of these incidents. The *NT Telegraph Flashes*, April 1897, and *Telegraph Chronicle* of 3 September give a different view. The Secretary at Newcastle insisted on associating himself with the motion, even though his name did not appear in the 'incriminating' newspaper report. The mover and seconder 'confessed' and thus got away with reprimand. The *Manchester Guardian*, 23 August, said all this showed it was time the PTCA was properly recognised.

35 Besides the *Telegraph Chronicle*, see also R IV/22.

36 PMG 44th Report for 1897–8, pp. 77–8.

37 For full details see Chapters 4 and 8.

38 *Hansard* IV, 53, 1107–46 (18 February 1898); 66, 1523–62 (20 February 1899); 72, 99–128 (1 June 1899); 82, 199–244 (27 April 1900); 92, 1325 (25 April 1901); 94, 1358–99 (7 June 1901) and 1562ff. (10 June 1901); 106, 705–48 (18 April 1902).

39 *Telegraph Chronicle*, 27 March 1903, pp. 173ff.; *Hansard* IV, 121, 1020–8 (30 April 1903); Bradford Report, p. 3.

40 *Leicester Evening News* (10 September 1903); *Post* (29 October 1903).

41 Bradford Evidence, pp. 77, 65–8, 235–7, 240–2, 138–42; R I/10, 29–30 July 1904.

42 G. H. Stuart-Bunning in *Post*, 1933, p. 213.

43 Evidence *passim*, especially pp. 235, 61, 97, 178, 182, 184.

44 Evidence, pp. 19, 38, 198, 153, 21, 128.

45 Evidence, pp. 148, 14, 131 (minimum pay), 129, 163, 103, 56, 120 (comparisons), 106, 120, 162 (general increases).

46 Evidence, pp. 28, 133, 218, 97, 104, 168–9.

47 Report, pp. 7, 17, 19–21ff.; *Times* (25 August 1904).

48 Details in POR 30E 6980/1905, and *Telegraph Chronicle*, 4 November 1904, p. 218, shows some inside knowledge of its proceedings. Unfortunately the proceedings of the Enquiry itself have not been preserved to cast light on how the Committee arrived at its unexpected recommendations.

49 POR 30E 6980/1905, XIV XVI; *Post*, 12 January 1905, for one of the delegations. *Hansard* IV, 139, 1600–1638 (9 August 1904) for the debate, bitter on both sides, followed by a vote, 172–87; PMG 15th Report for 1903–4, p. 28; PP 1905 XLIV; Hobhouse Evidence, pp. 267, 274; *Telegraph Chronicle*, 5 May 1905, p. 245.

50 Martinuzzi (1952), p. 169; Smith (1931), p. 71.
51 These arguments were put forward in specially produced pamphlets, one by the PTCA called *Statement Respecting the Report of the Committee on Post Office Wages*, dated 23 July 1904, the PF's *Statement of Our Views on the Report*, 4 August, given in *PG* 1904, pp. 459–60; and the FA's undated *Report of the Committee on Post Office Wages as it affects Members of the Fawcett Association*.
52 Stuart-Bunning in *Post*, 1933, p. 228, a view repeated in UPW (1950), p. 31, and Martinuzzi (1952), p. 174. For the quotations see *PG*, 1904, p. 412, *Post*, 8 October 1904, and POR 60/32.
53 Memo from Buxton to Cabinet in the BL at BP 2/15 (2).
54 *Hansard* IV, 152, 216 (20 February 1906); Hobhouse Report, p. 1; Smith (1931), p. 80; POC 1711, 17 April 1906.
55 David (1977), p. 59. This latter comment is in the interesting *Secretary's Report* (PFSR), Vol. 1, p. 81; collected by the PF while the Committee was sitting, mostly written by Stuart.
56 Besides the examples quoted below, see also Evidence, p. 114, for sorters against postmen, p. 744 for rivalries on promotion, and for the usual differences between telegraph and postal sides, pp. 290, 306ff.
57 Evidence, pp. 62, 70, 117, 286, 168ff., 240, 229, and Report, pp. 14–23. PFSR Vol. 1, pp. 8, 11.
58 Evidence, pp. 260, 307, 309, 274, 284, 321ff., 368–70 (with original emphasis), 373ff.
59 Evidence, pp. 411ff., 443, 469, 472, 481, 483.
60 Evidence, pp. 510ff., appendix, pp. 28–35.
61 Report, pp. 23–41; Evidence, pp. 341, 522, 257.
62 For details see *PG*, 1905, p. 218, R I/13. PFSR, *Post*, 1933, pp. 324–5 and Evidence, pp. 614–21. The CLPA evidence reprinted as a pamphlet is in MC 310.6. *Central London Review*, March 1907, p. 84, says the Crewe expellees set up their own association. See also Chapter 8 for the CLPA, below pp. 245–6.
63 PF EC Minutes, 18 March 1906 (R I/13), see also R I/14. Evidence, pp. 551–696, especially pp. 564, 634, 638, 646, 662, 667; Report, pp. 41–8. On attitudes in 1854 see above, Chapter 3, pp. 69–70, n. 22.
64 Evidence, pp. 697–735; Report, pp. 49–51.
65 This and what follows is covered in the Evidence, pp. 736–1,286 and Report, pp. 51–95. For quotations see Evidence, pp. 808, 1,209, 1,284 and the comments in PFSR Vol. 1, pp. 60, 66, and Martinuzzi (1952), p. 202. For more detail, Neale (1913), pp. 122–5 and 141–54 and Bealey (1976). Stuart PFSR Vol. 1, p. 91) thought the engineers 'spoiled a good case, by over-elaboration, and sticking to superficial distinctions'.
66 Evidence, pp. 490–5, 1,053–62, 1,244–9, 1,289–300; Report, pp. 4–6, 12–14. An internal committee (POR 30E 29074/1908) also considered the case of smaller grades like paperkeepers and some night telephonists.
67 *PCH* 1907, p. 332; *PG* 1907, pp. 373, 411, 432; *Post* (24 August 1907); *Daily Express* (26 July 1907); *Telegraph Chronicle*, 23 August 1907, p. 237, 6 September. R V/33 shows that Cheesman did obtain, perhaps from a telegraphist who handled it, a telegram said to show that the Department knew about the Report before it was published. Hobhouse denied this, and Buxton said it referred to quite other matters. In any case there were many other reasons beyond direct collusion for Hobhouse to accept the views of the Department.
68 *Hansard* IV, 192, 1111–1215 (16 July 1908), and V, 4, 187–306 (27 April 1909). For some of the discussion see FA Minutes for 12 February 1908 at R VI/14, *PG* 1908, pp. 558–60 and *PCH* 1907, p. 289.
69 Details of the national campaign and delegations are given in Smith (1931), p. 101, Martinuzzi (1952), pp. 227ff. and *Labour Leader* (20 February 1912). See also *Post* 1911, pp. 224, 347, 346, 495; R V/2, pp. 64ff.; *PG* 1911, pp. 99ff., 442ff., and *Hansard* V, 32, 1571–2 (7 December 1911).
70 *Engineering and Stores Journal*, January 1913, p. 39.
71 The evidence submitted by the associations was usually even fuller than the version given in the published reports – some of it was duplicated or printed separately, and some published in association journals. There is another mimeographed *Report* on each day's proceedings by Stuart at F299.4. This is bound but without pagination, so subsequent quotations are given with related evidence.
72 *PG* 1912, p. 73; *Post* 1912, p. 337; Holt Evidence, pp. 33–75, 255, 286, 1,307, 239, 296, 301–27.
73 Evidence, pp. 378, 412, 450, 453, 474, 742.
74 Evidence, pp. 540–839, especially pp. 588–9, 611, 640, 685, 779–80, 791–2. *PCH* 1912, pp. 690, 714, contains complaints that the evidence was too complex, and *Post* 1912, p. 705, that the complexity of telegraphy had been emphasised as against sorting.

75 Normalie was later compelled to withdraw what he said – see POC, 2102, 6 May 1913.

76 Evidence, pp. 938, 918, 921, 1,092, 1,250. For more detail in the E&SA case see Bealey (1976), pp. 105–8.

77 Evidence, pp. 1,373, 1,464, 1,458, 1,490, 1,495, 1,602, 1,645, 1,680, 1,756–7.

78 Holt Report, especially pp. 37, 40, 42, 61, 88, 89, 192, 193.

79 *Scottish Co-operator* (3 October 1913); POC 2117, 19 August 1913.

80 At least according to the POEU *Journal* for 1928, p. 221.

81 *Post* 1913, pp. 489, 511, 565ff.; *PCH* 1913, pp. 484, 551; *PG* 1913, pp. 548, 552. The Matlock and subsequent NJC meetings are recorded at R V/13. Postmaster General Samuel seems to have forgotten all these statements when he came to write his *Memoirs* (1945) which claimed (p. 78) that 'legitimate grievances' were 'remedied' and there was 'a general revision of inadequate rates of pay'. This was not how it appeared at the time.

82 *Civilian*, 30 August 1913, p. 297; *Supervising*, September 1913, pp. 158, 157.

83 *Times* (23 September 1913); *Truth* 1, 29 October 1913, p. 613; *PCH* 1913, p. 629, 1914, pp. 1–6. For more details on the steps to amalgamation see below p. 260.

84 There are verbatim accounts of the various meetings at R V/11, 15 and F 299.4. See also *PG* 1913, pp. 622, 644, 636, 694, 1914, p. 64; *Telegraph Chronicle* (10 December 1913), POC, 2131, 25 November 1913.

85 R V/15; *PG* 1914, pp. 150–2, 411; POC, 2151, 3 April 1914; *Hansard* V, 61, 1887–2000 (30 April 1914) and 63, 319–450 (10 June 1914). The definition is from the *Oxford English Dictionary* and a later account is to be found in the POEU *Journal*, 1928, p. 222.

86 They are in PP 1914–16 XXXII and 1916 XIV.

87 Figures in *Post*, 1915, p. 226 and PP 1918 XVI.

88 *Post* 1914, p. 432; *PG* 1914, p. 519 for the recruitment campaign and for protests, p. 543, 1915 pp. 317, 444 and R I/26, 25 April 1915, p. 12 – a vote on the PF Executive of 10–6 against Post Office army recruitment.

89 *PG* 1915, p. 574. See *Post* 1915, p. 145, for other complaints.

90 See above Chapter 5, p. 103.

91 *PG* 1915, p. 43; R I/26, 24 October 1915, p. 9, 27, 22 October 1916, pp. 3–6.

92 *Post* 1914, p. 401; *PG* 1915, p. 98.

93 *Hansard* V 71, 746 (28 April 1915); *PG* 1915, p. 310.

94 *PG* 1915, pp. 93, 100; R V/19; Smith (1931), p. 133.

95 The NJC Minutes of 1 March 1915 (in R V/19) show that this was only agreed by 7 votes to 6. For a protest see *P&TR*, 11 March 1915, pp. 532–3.

96 *Post* 1915, pp. 196, 294; *P&TR*, 15 July 1915, gives a similar verdict on the offer; *PG* 1915, pp. 400, 437 also discusses it. See POC, 2248 of September 1915 for the details also set out in Appendix 11, p. 631, and F 600 for details on Woodhouse's appointment.

97 *PG* 1916, p. 268.

98 R V/21, 11 July 1916, p. 5 and *PG* 1916, p. 416 for the discussions. POC, 2413, 19 September 1916, for the settlement.

99 Collins (1919). The Report of the Conciliation and Arbitration Board (PP 1918 VII), p. 7, gives the quotations and Gosling (1927), pp. 217–9, adds a little. *PG* 1917, p. 371, R I/27, 17 September 1916, V/26 and 27 outline some typical discussions.

100 *P&TR*, 10 May 1917, p. 8, for the quotation. See also Civil Service Arbitration Board, *Awards and Agreements May 1917 to August 1919* and F 0.074.

101 *Hansard* V, 94, 78–125 (5 June 1917). R V/25.

102 R V/24 for the negotiations. For the general increases see Layton and Crowther (1938). Routh (1954) puts the increases gained by civil servants somewhat higher.

103 *P&TR*, 26 September 1918, p. 161, 20 February 1919, p. 117; *PG* 26 September 1918, p. 376.

8 From Association to Union: 1891–1920

By a consistent and energetic policy, and by improved organisation, the Fawcett Association has come to be recognised by public men and the Press as the organised voice of the London Sorting Staff, and its action is watched with interest and sympathy by an increasing circle of friends whose position in public life enables them to render material assistance to the work we are endeavouring to effect. To give our action a greater probability of success, and to strengthen our hands, it is desirable that you, if not already a member, should at once join the Association as an expression of sympathy with its work, and as a method of affording that financial aid which is so desirable a considera- tion to any movement. If there is no branch at your office, may we suggest the advisability of opening one – for the value of unity, of strength and combination, which alone can improve even conditions of local official life. (Letter to London sorters from the Fawcett Association, June 1893. (UCW) R VI/3, p. 312)

The Postmen's Federation is the advanced and permanent form that has resulted from [the] efforts of many capable men, who are willing to sacrifice themselves, if necessary, for the good of their brother officers. (J. K. Christie, 'Paul Provan, Postman, A Tale of Temptation and Tyranny', in *PG*, 1897, p. 271)

No man who has studied the history of the Postal Tele- graph movement can fail to have been struck by the fact that every concession made by the Department has been given reluctantly and with a grudging hand. Despite the whole of the long period which has elapsed since the Postal Telegraph Clerks' Association was established in 1881, there has scarcely been one occasion upon which the chiefs of the Post Office voluntarily conceded anything whatever for the benefit of the rank and file. Every revision without exception has been forced from the Department after stormy agitation more or less prolonged. (*Telegraph Chronicle*, 4 August 1899, p. 53)

The organisations that first broke through all the legal and economic impediments to improving wages and conditions in the Post Office, that arranged the appearance at the great inquiries and first obtained recognition from the authorities, were extraordinarily puny by modern standards. Though they built a large membership among the main sections of the Post Office workforce and carried out an enormous range of activities of every kind, they did so with conspicuously low membership dues, and without any serious effort to set up a professional machinery. It is almost impossible to conceive today, looking through the enormous range of publications of that period, with periodicals and pamphlets for almost every grade, and considering the lobbying, deputations and organising work that went on, that virtually all of this was carried out by people who had already done a full day's work in the Post Office, including split or irregular duties. The Fawcett Association acquired two full-time officials against its will in 1892, the postmen took on a full-time Parliamentary candidate in 1902 and the amalgamated telegraphists and postal clerks two officials in 1914. Yet with small offices scattered throughout the country, the four major organisations, and a number of smaller ones, secured major gains for their members and were in a position to unite by 1919 to create the powerful Union of Post Office Workers.

Post Office trade unionism of this period took on its particular organisational form because the associations began without any certain or approved role. In 1890 the active spirits amongst the postmen were dismissed and in 1892 the two leaders of the sorters also lost their jobs. Succeeding generations were reluctant to place their interests in the hands of outsiders, and it would have created difficulties in any case because before 1906 the authorities would not negotiate with such people. During that period there was no way of knowing whether the associations had any kind of guaranteed or regular future. One of those who ran a branch of the Postmen's Federation in the 1890s was 'shadowed, persecuted and refused extra duty', and in another branch a member felt 'compelled to withdraw from the Secretaryship, owing to the tyrannical manner in which I have been treated'. This is not to mention the fact that the UKPCA was almost destroyed in 1893, when the entire Executive was compelled to resign their positions by Postmaster General Morley. There were many other individual cases of victimisation.[1] With such a tenuous existence over so long a period, it was not surprising that the Post Office associations had none of the top-heavy structure that characterised many of the other unions that first began in the 1880s and 1890s. Later tepid syndicalist and guild socialist theories created the opinion that leaders should not be allowed to be too powerful in any case. However, these were imposed upon habits of thought and action that had already been formed.

Previous chapters have described the early years of the Postal Telegraph Clerks Association after its foundation in 1881, the United Kingdom Postal Clerks Association after 1887 and the formation of the Fawcett Association and Postmen's Federation between 1888 and 1891. In Chapter 7 the main activities of these bodies has been set out. The purpose of this chapter is to describe the organisation, internal life and the gradual coming together of these and a number of smaller bodies. The setting up of organisations of sorters and postmen in the late 1880s and early 1890s was part of the surge of 'new unionism' which left few sections of the working class unaffected. The rhythms of Post Office trade unionism were somewhat different from those in outside industry, depending less on the trade cycle than on the Parliamentary session and the possibilities of applying political pressure, and membership and activity increasing up to and immediately after the various inquiries. Unlike many other unions set up during the 'new unionist' upsurge, Post Office workers were in a position to maintain a continuity of activity, an increasing strength and a level of influence within their industry. It is the aim of the rest of this chapter to describe and explain this.

THE FAWCETT ASSOCIATION – PACEMAKERS OF THE 1890s

Although the Postal Telegraph Clerks Association and the United Kingdom Postal Clerks Association were already well established before the period covered in this chapter, and although the Postmen's Federation soon became the largest organisation in the service, it was the London sorters who provided in the 1890s the most dynamic and successful of the main Post Office associations.

The circumstances of the setting up of the Fawcett Association have been described in Chapter 5, and in Chapter 4 something has been said of how it acquired two full-time officers in 1892.[2] Even beyond its peculiar name, the Fawcett Association had a number of special features as a trade union. It consisted entirely of educated, articulate people who worked closely with one another and had a great deal of opportunity to discuss their grievances together. The sorters thought themselves at 'the hub of the Postal universe' and the authorities considered that they possessed 'a general education and intelligence which are, if anything, somewhat superior to the requirements of the work'.[3] London sorters were voluble in their complaints, touchy about their status and capable of a high level of solidarity. They developed their cohesion slowly.

At first the different groups at the Chief Office, who dominated the Association in the early years, had to agree to work together. The rivalries between Williams and Clery in 1891–2 were not just clashes of personality and policy. They also reflected the difference between the 'aristocrats' of the Foreign Letter Branch, and Clery's colleagues in the Registered Letter Section. Cheesman became Secretary in March 1892 in part at least because, as a Western District man, he was aloof from these divisions. In later years, as the postal system was decentralised, the Chief Office became less pre-eminent, and the Inland Section was moved from St Martin's-le-Grand to Mount Pleasant. This led to conflicts along different lines. Thus the Chief Office men demanded to be placed on the same seniority lists as those in the district offices, who now had much greater access to promotion. In April 1905, the Central Committee ruled against the Chief Office men, who included such prominent members as E. J. Nevill, for putting forward this policy at all. Gradually, however, the rest of the force were won over to the equity of 'unification' of the lists. In 1907 a 'plebiscite' returned a narrow majority against it, but another poll in 1909 showed a similar majority in the opposite direction. After careful negotiations with the authorities, it was eventually agreed, during 1910, that a third of district promotions should be reserved for Chief Office men, and the FA leadership weathered the inevitable storm of abusive letters and two emergency general meetings.[4]

Other internal conflicts in the FA were dealt with more easily. Thus in 1898, the Registered Letter Branch was compelled to withdraw a petition which was against the general policy of the Association, and in 1907, Robert Farrell, who was a prominent member, resigned from the Association together with a number of his supporters rather than accept the line of the general body of members against a special grade for sorters on writing duties.[5] Against sectional protests that preceded all the inquiries, and their own frequent internal disputes, the Association leaders gradually broke down the divisions of interest within the London sorting force.

The figures given in Appendix 14, p. 634 show that, though the Fawcett Association was small by the standards of some of the major unions, it managed unlike many others to retain a stable membership throughout the period. A number of other interesting trends lie behind the overall figures. At the beginning of 1898, when the Fawcett Association was at the height of its influence, it had 2,198 members. The 1,758 members at the Chief Office constituted 67 per cent of what was possible there. The district offices had 960 members, or 78 per cent of their sorters. If the smaller numbers at the Parcel Post and Travelling Post Office are included, the Fawcett Association had 3,107 out of 4,622 possible members in London – 67 per cent. By 1911, these figures had risen to 4,956 out of 5,981, or 83 per cent of possible membership, and the table in Appendix 14 shows that in the last period of the Fawcett Association's existence this had risen to 95 per cent, almost as much as could be expected without compulsion. However, all wartime association membership figures in the Post Office are somewhat artificial, since they often include members in the armed forces who had built up large arrears, and in the case of the Fawcett Association exclude temporary grades who were actually doing the work.[6]

By this time the predominance of the Chief Office had long since disappeared, as also had the small groups of members at the Dublin Chief Office and in Belfast and Oldham. The Dublin Branch, which was originally set up by Clery in 1890, was characterised by occasional bursts of activity, but was frequently struck off the list of branches for failure to pay more than a nominal amount to the central funds, and eventually abandoned altogether in 1903 to the Irish Association of Post Office Clerks. Any argument for other provincial sorting clerks and telegraphists being in the Fawcett Association soon became impossible to sustain, with two associations catering for their interests. Thus when a small group of SC&Ts who specialised in sorting at East Dereham in Norfolk applied to join in 1902, they were simply referred to the UKPCA. Among other peripheral groups was a small number of women sorters, whose association was set up in 1904 and was 'affiliated' to the Fawcett Association until 1915. These women did some clerical duties, seem to have held only one meeting a year and had extremely low membership dues. Under the leadership of Rose Smith-Rose from 1911 they devoted much energy to dramatic productions and concerts. In later years they did some negotiating, and during the war changed their name to the Association of Civil Service Sorting Assistants. They were then actively involved in most of the joint civil service activities and eventually, in 1933, with Miss Smith-Rose finally retiring, were merged to the Civil Service Clerical Association. This was the logical place for them to go by then, since changes in civil service grading made sure of their claim to be considered now as a general Treasury 'clerical' class rather than an inferior Post Office manipulative grade.[7] When the 'Postal Bagmen's Association' was set up in 1906, it was 'affiliated' for a year but this was not continued as the main aim of the Association was for an equality with the sorters of which the latter did not approve.[8]

The structure and internal life of the Fawcett Association reflected the close integration of the working lives of its members, as well as their volubility. It operated essentially on the principles of 'primitive democracy'.[9] There was not even a proper branch structure until 1892, and it was not until some years later that the branches in the separate offices seem to have developed any kind of life of their own. This was primarily because the sovereign power in the Fawcett Association was in the hands of general meetings of members. All members could attend these assemblies. The annual meetings normally took place on two evenings in February or March, and were supplemented by special meetings to consider particular grievances or internal crises. They were nearly always attended by between 1,000 and 2,000 members. Though clearly such meetings could not initiate details of policy, they nevertheless exercised a decisive influence over the affairs of the Association. Fawcett Association leaders grew increasingly unhappy about having policies decided in this assembly, but their only serious effort to set up a conference with a delegate structure was defeated in 1912 by a vote of 1,302 to 1,062.[10]

The main decisions about the running of the Fawcett Association were made through its Central Committee, a body elected by the branches, with one representative for every 200 members. This, boasted Clery,

> was a more democratic body than the Council of any other Trade Union. Every man in it was elected in open competition for the honour of doing very arduous work, and received no pay, save the consciousness of duty done to their fellows.

This was a large and well attended body, and when its total membership reached nearly 80 in 1910, its constitution was slightly modified, but it still had around 50 to every meeting. At first it was only supposed to meet quarterly, but it gradually met more often, and after 1903, when the provision of substitutes was made easier, it normally conducted its business on every second Wednesday afternoon. The Central Committee was much given to setting up sub-committees, but, though its power over the individual branches was absolute, it occasionally submitted thorny and decisive questions, such as the dispute over the internal unification of promotion lists, to 'plebiscites'. These polls usually ended in close votes between about three-quarters of the members, making it possible to urge either way for the propositions originally advanced. The Central Committee elected from its own ranks four members who, together with the officers, constituted the Executive. Most matters were considered first by the Executive, but it could take no decisions involving finance, and generally does not seem to have had a predominant voice up to the time of an unsuccessful attempt in 1907 to abolish it altogether as 'pernicious to the democratic policy as well as a menace to the fundamental principles of the Association'.[11]

The officers of the Association included a registrar responsible for compiling lists of members, a treasurer and three trustees, as well as the editor of *The Post*. There was an organising secretary from 1895 to 1904, and an assistant secretary to deal with the friendly society activities which grew more important after 1910. Officers were subject to re-election at the annual meetings and occasionally the incumbents lost their positions. One who did not was W. B. Cheesman, who was full-time Secretary from 1893 until amalgamation in 1919. He began on the maximum salary for the sorter grade, and in 1905 he was given the wages then being claimed for an overseer, to which position he would no doubt by then have been promoted, and also the conditions being claimed for the grade, including a full month's holiday. In 1906 a pension scheme was set up for him, and in the following year it was decided not to allow him to accept a sub-postmastership as a compromise on re-instatement. Thereafter, efforts to get him back in the service were made with diminishing enthusiasm, though it remained on the platform of the Association. Cheesman was methodical and hard-working, but he clearly did not dominate the proceedings of the Association. A survey of his work-load in 1908 showed that he put in fifty-seven hours a week, a great deal of this on purely routine activity such as typing agendas and addressing envelopes.[12] Clery, who was paid as full-time Chairman between 1893 and 1903, must have done a great deal less work than this, but he did much to mould and change the policies of the Association. It was Clery who initiated the turn to the TUC and the London Trades Council. It was he who first published a journal openly identified with the Fawcett Association, ran outside meetings, appealed to MPs and even suggested that they should support an MP of their own. The Fawcett Association was never quite the same after Clery's traumatic removal in 1903.

Before and after the important watershed in 1903, the Fawcett Association existed with a minimum of official apparatus. An office was first rented in 1893 at a cost of 5s (25p) per week at Pye Corner in Giltspur Street, a stone's throw from St Martin's-le-Grand. This was to give the dismissed agitators a base. The office was moved in 1895 to 11 Bartholomew Close, and in 1901, as if to symbolise the diminishing importance of the Chief Office, the Fawcett Association Headquarters went nearer Mount Pleasant to 49 Gray's Inn Road. Two years later they were finally settled nearby at 55 Doughty Street, where they stayed until the amalgamation. These offices were used to hold committee meetings and to store the records, but apparently for little else besides. In the early period Cheesman was only available to visitors from 2 to 4 in the afternoon, though he must have been there for meetings most evenings. He had little secretarial help, except for a time from a Miss Stevens, with whom he quarrelled. The Fawcett Association took the unusual step of submitting its rules in 1893 to the Registrar General of Friendly Societies. It retained a solicitor called Wareham after 1898, yet it did not possess a typewriter until 1898, a duplicator was only procured in 1899, a telephone in 1905 and a filing cabinet in 1911.[13]

The financial details given in Appendix 14 show part of the reason for this limited apparatus. Membership dues were very low, with only 6d (2½p) paid at first. This later went up on a sliding scale according to income, from 6d to 1s (5p) to 1s 6d (7½p). The largest item of expenditure for the FA was the free circulation of *The Post*. This was originally undertaken in 1892 when the authorities banned its open sale. Much of the rest of the money was spent on officers' salaries and on substitution expenses. Though there were two auditors elected from the members, effective financial control was exercised through rigorous questioning of the smallest items of expenditure at the annual meetings. Before 1910 it did not occur to anybody to consider investing any surplus funds at more than the 1 per cent they obtained from a current bank account.[14] Only a few years later was this taken at all seriously with the purchase of some war bonds.

Friendly society functions were never important for the Fawcett Association. Though statements about friendly benefits were written into the rules, from the start the members never showed much interest in them. A voluntary Mutual Aid branch operated between 1900 and 1907 but its membership never exceeded 700. In 1907 a contributory system for sickness and death benefits was agreed, including for a time pension provision. Like many other such schemes, this proved more generous in its payments than in its subscriptions, and it soon became a drain on the main funds of the Association. After various modifications, a special Central Committee sub-committee concluded, in 1914, that the whole business was 'an encumbrance on the finances without offering very substantial benefits to the members'. It was recommended that 'the Association should revert to its former position as a Trade Union only', and this was agreed at the 1915 Annual Meeting.[15]

The relative power and shifting relationships of the leaders, the ordinary members and the Central Committee of the FA, depended to a great extent on the personalities involved and the particular issues that arose. Some incidents in the history of the Fawcett Association can help to illustrate them.

In October 1899, after the appearance of a letter in *The Post*, a special general meeting of members was called which expressed its disapproval at the expenditure of £200 on Swift's *History of Postal Agitation*. The worst thing about this was said to be that it was undertaken by the officers behind the backs of the Central Committee. This expression of disapproval felt by the members about their leaders was given a great deal of prominence in *The Post*. As a result, a 'Supervisory Committee' was set up by the Central Committee to approve the contents of each issue of the journal. Previously the editor had had sole discretion. D. Griffiths, who occupied this position at the time, had only been elected the previous August. He considered that he derived his authority from the membership, and immediately came into sharp conflict with the Supervisory Committee. The issue of *The Post* for 11 September 1899 appeared with black spaces and asterisks, and included a leader entitled 'A Few Words on the Ethics of Postal Journalism'. Griffiths was immediately suspended by the Central Committee, and at a Special General Meeting of 5 December it was agreed that the Central Committee was responsible for the contents of the journal. This was not the end of the story, however. Clery took over as temporary Editor early in 1900 only after a close vote, and when a permanent replacement was to be chosen early in the following year. Ammon, who had been 'recommended' by the Central Committee, was nevertheless rejected by the members and Charles Durrant, who had objected to any recommendation being made, became Editor.[16]

Other events illustrated that ultimate authority remained in the hands of the members, notably the decision to disaffiliate from the TUC and the Labour Party. This was taken when a 'plebiscite' held in 1908 showed 1,163 to 1,489 against affiliation to the Labour Party, and 1,593 to 1,520 against the TUC. At the same time the members voted by 1,809 to 1,305 in favour of remaining in the United Government Workers Federation. These disaffiliations were opposed by all the leaders of the Fawcett Association, and in November they called a Special General Meeting in an effort to reverse them. This Meeting brought down the wrath of the members. Those present were told that the very calling of a meeting militated against 'the democratic principle that members should dictate the policy'. The decision to disaffiliate, they said, had been 'brushed aside by the Committee as readily as the Bradford Report had been brushed aside by the PMG'. The assembled members went on to pass a motion condemning the entire leadership. All the officers other than Cheesman then resigned and sought re-election. This they secured, though in the case of Chairman Nevill and Editor Ammon, there were substantial votes against them. Pemberton, who led the opposition at the General Meeting, was elected NJC delegate.[17]

Besides casting an interesting light on the balance of forces within the Fawcett Association, the issues of this controversy also show how far the Association had departed from the thrusting, progressive policies of its early years. In Clery's day, the Fawcett Association had not simply been the pioneer of canvassing Parliamentary candidates, it had also been the first in 1893 to affiliate to the London Trades Council, and Clery at one time used to sign proudly its initials after his name. In 1894 the Trades Council ran a Committee of Enquiry into Civil Servants' Conditions, and in 1895 Clery was part of a delegation that met the Chancellor of the Exchequer on the conditions of public employees. In 1897 Cheesman joined the Trades Council Executive, in which capacity he chaired a meeting in defence of the locked-out engineers. The Fawcett Association also made a spectacular entry to the TUC with Clery's trip to Belfast in 1893 and his vitriolic disagreement with John Burns on the floor of the Congress at Norwich in the following year.[18] Clery was also behind the setting up of the United Government Workers Federation in 1895, though the Fawcett Association dominated this and remained the only Post Office affiliate.

Almost from the time of its foundation, the Fawcett Association probed the possibility of becoming more effective by having an MP of its own. From the mid-1890s to 1903 there was a continual and complicated discussion within the Association on how such an aim could be achieved. Clery was sent to the Labour Electoral Congress of 1893 and 1895, but remained throughout his career a convinced Liberal. He supported Liberal candidates in elections, and discussed the possibility of standing for a number of local Liberal Associations, whilst rejecting a similar approach from Keir Hardie about an ILP seat in Glasgow. The Fawcett Association's protest meeting against the Tweedmouth report agreed to the principle of direct Parliamentary representation and this was confirmed in a poll of members by 1,052 votes to 795. The Central Committee adopted this policy at its meeting on 25 October 1897 and, in the following February, agreed by 24 votes to 6 that any such candidate should be independent of the Conservative and Liberal parties, who 'have denied and still deny us the Right of Combination and Civil Liberty'. This policy was far ahead of any of the other Post Office associations at the time, including the postmen.[19]

In the following August of 1898, it was announced that Cheesman had been adopted by the United Government Workers Federation as Parliamentary candidate for Epping. There was much complex jockeying behind this move. In the following year Cheesman announced that he was standing as a 'Labour and Liberal' candidate with the support of the local Liberal Association. This was against his own inclinations, but he justified it on the grounds that 'an independent platform is at present impossible'. Clery agreed this change of front with delight, but Swift thought the entire enterprise was becoming 'a Pandora's box out of which it seems all kind of evil will spring, leaving not even hope at the bottom'. The general view was that there was not much chance of a Liberal winning the seat in any case. So in 1900, the members voted by 1,580 to 711 against devoting any money to this purpose. As a result, Cheesman did not stand in the 1900 General Election.[20]

The Fawcett Association remained committed to a policy of Parliamentary representation, if not to any particular method of securing it. It never had a simple 'Lib-Lab' position, but a series of policies which reflected the complicated break for a Post Office association from the older forms of Parliamentary lobbying to the new ideas of independent action that were at the time developing in the labour movement as a whole. For civil servants this change was a peculiar and difficult one. Thus the Fawcett Association was affiliated to the National Democratic League, a short-lived organisation of left-wing journalists and trade unionists which aimed to create a party separate from the Liberals but including those outside the working-class movement. Cheesman, on the other hand, as his own candidature showed, was by inclination an orthodox supporter of the Labour Representation Committee, and he served on its Executive Committee from 1902 to 1903. In later years Cheesman said that he quarrelled with MacDonald over the secret electoral pact with the Liberals. It was Clery's position that was unusual. He told the 1903 Labour Representation Committee Conference 'that a Liberal Association, or a Tory, or any other body of men on earth prepared to accept the constitution' ought to be allowed to affiliate. When he was adopted as Parliamentary candidate for Deptford in April 1902, he worked with the local Liberal Party but also got the endorsement of the Labour Representation Committee. This was partly the result of a peculiar local position where the Trades Council and Liberal Party were closely identified.[21] The ignominious collapse of Clery's candidature in less than a year was a result of Clery's debts and financial dealings and his break from the Association. This was not just a great blow for Clery, but also for the Fawcett Association and its policies. The withdrawal from national policies by the Fawcett Association which followed in 1908 resulted from disappointment with what had been achieved rather than any reversion to older attitudes. Relations with the postmen became so bad that all that could be done in the next few years about the various candidatures of Stuart was to address hostile questions to him through the columns of the *Post*. These same columns were opened for a time to Frank Goldstone, Labour MP for Sunderland from 1910 to 1918 and later General Secretary of the National Union of Teachers. As in many other matters, the war changed attitudes radically and at the beginning of 1918, the members voted by 2,213 to 646 in favour of financing Parliamentary representation on an independent basis. Later in the year they supported Ammon's candidature in North Camberwell, though he had already been adopted through the local ILP.[22]

There can be no doubt that the Fawcett Association was never the same again after it had dispensed with the services of Clery. After 1903 where others led, they followed. Though the sorters in the various London offices resolved their differences, they often did so by accentuating their disagreements with the other grades, particularly the postmen. Rivalries came to a head after 1901, when the sorters began to demand that all promotions to the position of overseer should be reserved for them. The postmen said that this made the sorters into 'the greedy boys, the "Jack Horners" of the service', and attacked them with some justice as 'a sort of buffer between the Department and the postmen's claim'. The same tensions persisted in London into the 1940s, and are discussed in Chapter 10.[23]

Disagreements between postmen and sorters came to a head with the 'unification' policies presented by the postmen to the Hobhouse Enquiry and described in detail in Chapter 7. The sorters brought their righteous indignation against 'blacklegging' before other sections of the trade union movement, but they obtained little satisfaction from the TUC. They brought their campaigns for the implementation of the Bradford Committee's proposals and against those of Hobhouse to all the labour movement bodies they could find, but the Labour Party had only limited power to act on their behalf. It was the disappointment that followed this rather than any particular change of political attitude that led the 1908 Annual General Meeting to decide to withdraw from the London Trades Council. The meeting considered the Trades Council unable 'to protect and promote the interests of the trade unionists of the metropolis'. A similar feeling lay behind their decision to leave the TUC and Labour Party. The movement against identification with the TUC was to some extent derived from older feelings of exclusiveness. As one member told the 1908 Annual Meeting:

with all due respect to trade unionists, they did not come up to the standard of postal servants with regard to pay, and they desired to raise themselves higher and not get down.

However, there were new sentiments stirring also. In 1910 when the issue was discussed further, another member attacked the prominent Labour MP Philip Snowden for his boast that he could 'play politics sensibly', and expressed a view that was by then becoming common in the working-class movement as a whole:

> Though the Labour members realised that the interests of the Conservatives and the Liberals were diametrically opposed to those of the workers, yet they found the Labour Party . . . just as much against the liberty of the workers as any other Party.

When the matter was discussed in later years, there were many who objected on the grounds that 'the Labour Party is merely part and parcel of the Liberal Party', and when the Editor of *The Post* asked for views on the matter, he noticed that 'the whole of the objection' he got 'came from those to whom the Labour Party is too mild a body'.[24] London sorters were by now too closely identified with the rest of the trade union movement to maintain their old isolation and superior airs. In 1912, affiliation to the TUC was again agreed, and in 1916 they went back to the London Trades Council. The return to the Labour Party in 1918 inevitably followed.

Another interesting reflection of the complex and competing attitudes of the London sorters could be seen in the way the policies of the syndicalist movement were reflected within their ranks. In April 1911, with the agreement of other officers, Fawcett Association's Chairman Neville, took an action for libel against a paper called *The Industrialist* which had attacked his attitude to tests for sorters and his conduct as an acting overseer. The paper, which showed a close knowledge of the workings of the Inland Branch Sorting Office and of 'the inner life and work of the Association', was on the fringe of the syndicalist movement itself, rejecting conventional trade unions altogether. That this current of opinion gained support among this group of workers is interesting in itself. The leadership's reply was not unexpected. 'Questionable innuendoes and objectionable insinuations', it was said, 'have been hurled at them by a small but excessively vocal section of disgruntled extremists within our ranks.' However, as the court case dragged on, largely because the syndicalists had no money to pay costs or likely fines, the members became unhappy about the way things were going. Nearly 100 of them resigned in protest, and a special meeting of the Inland Branch had to be held to explain the actions of the leadership.[25]

This paradoxical mixture of attitudes could be seen in the Fawcett Association during the war years. By June 1915, about a quarter of the members had joined the armed forces, and a few more did so when conscription was introduced in the following year. The sorters would not accept that the temporary replacements were capable of doing the work to anything like the proper standard. The 'temporaries' were of course nearly all women, and the Fawcett Association leadership refused to believe that they were in any way obliged to look after their interests. In fact, they considered

> that the introduction of the opposite sex is by far the most serious menace that the

war has at present brought to the London Sorters, and shoulder not be proceeded with until every other means, including restriction of public service, has been tried and found wanting. It is our opinion, and one in which everyone who knows the London postal service will concur, that a complete sorter's duty is not a fit employment for women . . .

There was, of course, a genuine and partly fulfilled fear in all this that 'if women are to take the cleaner and lighter type of work from the men, the result on the male staff can only be deplorable'.

While the Fawcett Association continued to take this view of the employment of women, they grew more radical on the question of the war itself. Harry Dubery, Editor of *The Post*, spoke out against the war at the 1915 TUC, and though he felt constrained to tell members that he was not necessarily speaking for them, no serious protest followed. There were protests, however, as the wage claims became more necessary and more frequent, but less and less efficacious. At a General Meeting in November 1916, there was talk of 'the wretched display of weakness we had on the part of our leaders'. Later on, as new negotiations developed thick and fast, there was less dissatisfaction on economic questions, but more on general political ones. This more radical temper could be seen from the vote at the 1918 Annual General Meeting following a similar line in the P&TCA for peace by negotiations. There were even some who wanted the entire war condemned as a manifestation of the ills of capitalism. When Dubery resigned as Editor later in the year, partly to work with an outfit known as the National Alliance of Employers and Employed, he now had been by-passed by a group on the Central Committee whom he thought 'extremely vocal and apparently powerful in the country at the moment' who were against any conciliation with employers. When the General Meeting held on 7 October 1918 to change the rules so as to affiliate with the Labour Party took place, the only speaker who stood up to oppose them found himself completely isolated: 'I am very sorry my supporters are not here; I thought that I was leader of the patriotic party in the Association, but I cannot find them'.[26]

These various incidents in the history of the Fawcett Association help to illustrate the curious ambivalence of its attitudes during the course of its journey into the mainstream of the labour movement. The London sorters were part of the breed of clerks with starched collars who moved to the respectable late Victorian terraced houses in Holloway and Clapham. Yet they were pioneer trade unionists within the civil service and also the very first to turn to the wider labour movement. For all their genteel pretensions and their location on the social penumbra between the middle and working classes, they came to identify their interests with the postmen and with other workers in the public service and elsewhere. Clery exaggerated when he told the 1893 TUC that though the sorters were 'an exclusive snobbish lot', they 'had no greater aspiration than to be recognised as working men'. However, they increasingly came to see it as in their interests to be regarded as bona fide trade unionists. The same Fawcett Association that won assistance from Keir Hardie and Karl Marx's daughter Eleanor, also mourned the passing of Queen Victoria and William Ewart Gladstone.[27] The sorters aspired to some of the standards of respectability of generations they had almost forgotten when they agreed that working on Sundays was an issue 'of principle and politics'. They addressed one another not as 'brother' or 'comrade' as other trade unionists did, but as 'Mr', and also expected to be addressed in this way by the authorities. They started an 'association' named after a Postmaster General. Nevertheless, they spoke more and more often of 'trade union principles', they attacked the postmen nor as inferior mortals but as 'blacklegs', and they identified themselves increasingly with the main trends of opinion within the trade union movement as a whole.[28]

These changes in attitude reflected themselves in the personalities of the leaders of the Association. Men like Williams and Groves, who set it up, were later remembered as 'staid men of the Sunday School Superintendent type'.[29] The second generation of the Association's leaders were more often than not socialists of the more idealist variety. Thus Robert Farrell was a Councillor and a member of the Independent Labour Party, Harry Dubery was on the ILP National Administration Council and author of *London for Socialism*, and Isaac Ray was active in the Civil Service Socialist Society. Charles Ammon, who was the dominant figure in the Fawcett Association in its later years, combined both sides. He was an active Methodist and lay preacher as well as a candidate for the ILP with a long career ahead of him in Labour politics. It was these men who provided the ethos and the leadership in the Fawcett Association, even if their followers did not share all their opinions.

One other perhaps surprising aspect of the lives of Fawcett Association members was the extraordinary range of social activities opened up to them by their employment and their Association. The authorities were the inspiration behind such bodies as the Rowland Hill Benevolent Fund and the Post Office Relief Fund, and some sorters must have been kept busy in meetings and social activities organised through them. The Fawcett Association itself took over the organisation of the Post Office Sports Day, and was actively involved in numerous 'dinners', 'smoking concerts' and other forms of social activity which must have filled the lives of many people.[30] This is not to mention the Fawcett Association 'Debating Society' set up in 1897 and the Fawcett Association's 'Carnival' attended in 1898 by 1,500 people. The Association was also involved in collective and social activities through affiliation from 1894 to the Hospital Saturday Movement which raised money for voluntary hospitals, and from 1903 to the Workmen's Early Trains Movement.

All of these activities must have made conscientious Fawcett Association members identify themselves with one another as much as with the Post Office as an institution. It must also have associated them with the postmen, telegraphists and engineers who worked with them, as well as with the trade union and labour movement. If conservatism , snobbery and inertia made the Fawcett Association a less effective instrument of the Post Office workers after 1903 than it had been before, then increasing fellow-feeling within the service provided the basis for greater unity of thought and effort after the Fawcett Association was no more.

THE POSTMEN'S FEDERATION

The organisation of postmen emerged and developed somewhat differently from the sorters. Coming out from under the shadow of the defeat of the 1890 strike, they very slowly took on the predominant weight within Post Office trade unionism merited by their size. The Postmen's Federation was set up by the superior postmen from the Chief Office, of which the first General Secretary, Charles Churchfield, was a typical example, under the patronage of the Fawcett Association. It took almost a decade for them to align themselves with other trade unionists, but when they did they became pioneers of many aspects of Post Office agitation. James Brown ran the most informative journal in the service for twenty years, and the postmen took practical, though not successful, steps to secure the direct Parliamentary representation of which others only talked. While showing the same reluctance as other associations in the Post Office to take on full-time officials, the postmen had in Stuart a leader whose voice became dominant in association matters from about the time he adopted the title of General Secretary in 1911, and who steered the Postmen's Federation through the last of the great inquiries, the war and the amalgamation. In the end it was the Postmen's Federation, and not only from weight of numbers, that played the largest role in moulding the form and constitution of the Union of Post Office Workers.

The use of the term 'Federation' in the name of this organisation did not have any special significance at first beyond an effort to distinguish the new organisation from its predecessors. It was, and remained, 'always a union and not a federation'.[31] The scattered membership gave more life to local branches than was often the case in other trade unions, and this was particularly true in larger urban centres. In Manchester and Brighton, where branches eventually had their own discussions with local postmasters and surveyors, they also had an active social life with their own publications, sick benefit societies and holiday clubs.[32] There was great variation in influence and activity, as can be judged from Table 8.1 showing the amount paid in 1906 by members to their PF branches. In all cases this included 2s (10p) national affiliation fee, and in some cases payments to the Mutual Benefit Society.

Table 8.1

Number of Branches	Amount paid by Members
20	Below 4s (20p)
41	From 4s to 5s (25p)
39	From 5s to 6s (30p)
81	From 6s to 7s (35p)
5	From 7s to 8s (40p)
39	From 8s to 9s (45p)
1	9s 8d (48p)

If branches were often rich and influential, district committees were rarely so. Efforts were made from 1903 to group branches in this way, and a number of elaborate and hotly contested schemes were proposed. However, they never covered the whole country, and were almost entirely concerned with organising weaker branches and representing them at conferences. Most local branches 'evinced little interest' in schemes for district development and national leaders like Stuart were in any case of the opinion that 'the powers of these councils must necessarily be limited'. In 1911 only twenty-nine of the eighty-nine proposed bodies were in existence and a more permissive system was adopted.[33]

Local bodies of the Postmen's Federation were not given much power under the rules, but neither were the national leaders or officials. Subscriptions to the national office were only 1s (5p) per member per year at first, and still remained low at 3s (15p) in 1902 when a full-time Parliamentary candidate first had to be paid. After constant appeals from their leaders, members agreed to pay nationally 2s 6d (12½p) in 1910, and despite all the effects of wartime inflation, again to increase this only to 3s 6d (17½p) in 1919, the final year of the Federation's existence. This meagre income was supplemented by poorly supported levies, one in 1909–10 raised £806 (less than 6d (2½p) per member) and others during the war had similar limited effect.

On such a shoe-string budget, virtually all the work of the Federation, including the production of the *Gazette* and the discussion of long-term policy, had to be carried out by men who also did a full day's work delivering letters. Only in 1897 was a clerk employed at the Central Office, and in 1900 there was one appointed for the Mutual Benefit Society. The *Gazette* operated independently with its own full-time staff and finance, largely self-supporting. When James Brown was Editor in 1896–1916 it was published in Glasgow, in all but eight years of its existence. The other chief positions of the Federation moved around the country with the holders. From 1900 to 1910, when MacLaren was Secretary, the organisation was largely run from Glasgow. By 1914, when small offices were rented separately for the *Gazette*, the Mutual Benefit Society, the General Secretary and the General Treasurer, Stuart grew exasperated:

> The work of the Postmen's Federation is done badly. It will always be unless members of the Society realise that a trades organisation, like any other business, requires working on a business footing. At present the Federation has three separate and distinct offices, one in London, one in Glasgow and one in Swansea, and a more foolish, inefficient and wasteful system could not be devised by mortal man.[34]

Whatever the Postmen's Federation officers and Executive felt about this extraordinary system, the membership and their representatives showed time and again that they approved of it. Nothing indicated more clearly the attitude of active members than the barrage of questions that greeted the insubstantial balance sheets presented to every conference. Brown complained that the questions were 'frivolous, and in some cases vexatious', but they continued. Conference delegates insisted on having auditors from among their own ranks, even after 1900 when they sought professional advice. One of the early PF leaders 'trusted they would not treat their representatives any worse than other labouring men treated theirs', but this advice was never followed. Leaders complained of 'the continual captious and ill-timed criticisms which are for ever arising from this or that district office in the London area'. The most complicated section of the rule books restricted the provisions and travelling expenses of the Federation's officers, and conferences refused time after time to set up any kind of full-time leadership.[35]

The origins of this attitude can obviously be traced to the fears of professional outsiders who were thought to have misled the Postmen's Union in 1890. Later, however, a distrust of the leaders and a determination not to allow them to leave the ranks of the postmen became an abiding attitude within the Federation. Thus a point of view that began as a mark of cautious conservatism later became associated with radical, semi-syndicalist notions to be found elsewhere in Post Office trade unionism.

The earlier attitudes can best be seen in the case of H. M. Wilson, who was elected General Secretary in 1896. On taking up his office late in the following year, he came under strong pressure to attend various local meetings and in order to do so, he falsified his entry in the casual leave book at his office. An overseer got to find out about it, and Wilson was immediately dismissed. This punishment was undoubtedly excessive and indicated that PF leaders had still, as the *Gazette* put it, to be 'like Caesar's wife, above suspicion'. However, since Wilson had become an 'outsider', he could not now hold elected office in the Federation. Wilson then agreed to resign, and Churchfield resumed his previous office as General Secretary. By 'private arrangement' at first, Wilson became his secretary and drew his salary. Few postmen who expressed themselves on the matter did not sympathise with Wilson, but most agreed with one branch secretary that 'it is necessary and essential that we should have a General Secretary whose interests in the service are identical with ours'. The members voted by 5,114 to 4,060 against making him 'outside' Secretary. At the 1898 Conference it was agreed 'that in every case where the Department deals with a man as Mr. Wilson has been dealt with, his comrades all came to his support'. They did so, and Wilson was confirmed as full-time clerical assistant to the General Secretary at £100 per annum. This was more, but not much more, than most postmen got. Thereafter Wilson became a shadowy figure without influence on the Federation's affairs. In 1904 he was given organising work to do, and in 1909 retired on a pension.[36]

When Stuart was elected full-time Parliamentary Secretary in 1902 at a salary of £150 per annum, this was so that he would be an MP. Brown thought it obvious that 'the majority will agree with us in not allowing Mr. Stuart, or any other person who is not a postman, to VOTE in our affairs'. He failed to get into Parliament and little provision was made for him in the rules. In large measure, because of the force of his personality, he increasingly assumed the role of the Federation's main leader and representative. In 1909, he threatened to resign if he did not receive an increase in pay, maintaining that 'he had worked twelve hours a day including Sundays, for the last four or five years'. His pay then went up from £200 to £230, and in 1913 to £300, about three times the wage of the best paid postman. In 1917 this was further increased to £450. From 1911, Stuart was described as the General Secretary, partly because it was thought he might be prevented from standing for Parliament by the Osborne judgement. In fact, this had long since been a more accurate description of the functions he performed.[37] When Alfred Harris was invalided out of the service in 1907, he was not allowed to remain General Treasurer even though he had filled the position efficiently for fifteen years. One of those who argued against Harris being allowed to do anything other than office work 'wherever possible' was the youthful William Bowen, who thought that 'by increasing the number of officers outside the service, they would reduce the control of the Executive over them'.[38]

From Churchfield onward, every officer argued that 'so long as we conducted our business without outsiders', then 'we must expect that [it] would never be properly done'. The members, however, time after time expressed their opposition to 'placing the Federation under the control of autocrats' and against any 'disposition to build up a system of big salaries; to create offices for the benefit of individual members instead of for the good of the Federation'. John Walsh told the 1907 Conference that full-time officers 'would become the masters instead of the servants of their society'. During the following year determined efforts were made to convince the members that 'we cannot expect to have Trade Unionism on the cheap', and it was maintained that

the Societies whose membership is largest, and who have accumulated the largest funds, are those who have been able to secure and maintain for their members the highest rate of wages, the shortest hours and the best conditions of work.

A Special Committee set up by the 1908 Conference from outside the Executive, reported in the following year that as a result of the extremely low national contributions, 'there is little or no cohesion between branches and headquarters and, as at present constituted, there can be no combined action emanating from the Central Office'. Postmen's Federation members paid to their Head Office each year the sum of 1s 11d (9½p), as compared to 11s 2d (56p) in the National Amalgamated Union of Labour, 11s (55p) in the Gas Workers and General Labourers, 10s (50p) in the Amalgamated Union of Co-operative Employees, not to mention much more in many craft unions. Yet a proposal to increase the contribution in the Postmen's Federation to 7s (35p) was lost by 386 votes to 197, and much modified proposals for just one full-time officer were also defeated in 1911.

Only the shocks of the war and the pressures of the forthcoming amalgamation led to any modification of this position in the last year and a half of the existence of the Federation. During that period the Organising Secretary was allowed to go full time, three further Parliamentary candidates were elected, though not immediately withdrawn from the service, and the membership paid 3s 6d (17½p) each to the National Office. In the final months the main functions of the Postmen's Federation were concentrated in Parliament Mansions, Victoria, where Stuart had been since 1906. 'The time for cheap trade unionism', it was once again announced, 'was past', but many of these traditions were carried forward into the early Union of Post Office Workers.[39]

The Postmen's Federation was begun in a mass meeting at the Chief Office which elected the first Executive Committee on 21 September 1891. Early in 1892 the links with the Fawcett Association were broken and the new organisation began to bring in people from the district offices, and then those from outside London, at first mostly former branches of the Postmen's Union. By the time of the 1st Annual Conference in September 1892 the majority of the fifteen Executive members were from outside London. There were some who thought that 'the management as vested in the Executive Committee men had worked smoothly and satisfactorily'.[40] It was only in 1897 that complaints about a 'London bias' in the Tweedmouth evidence led to the abolition of separate provision for London representation. The East Central District Office Branch never fitted into the Federation, collapsing altogether in 1896 and providing the basis in 1906 for the break-away Central London Postmen's Association. Memories of the 1890 strike remained strong at the Eastern District Office, and as late as 1897 there were only three members there. Postmen from the London offices did not dominate the Federation, especially during the period when it was run from Glasgow. However, London concerns constantly broke into Federation affairs. The disastrous 'unification' policy for postmen and sorters agreed by the Federation was attacked as 'incompatible with our past history as a united society' because it was really a policy for London, the only place where sorters and postmen worked closely together. Even after the abandonment of 'unification', a London versus provinces tension still lay very much beneath the surface, as could be seen from a lengthy Executive discussion in 1911 about how London men were 'disloyal' for running a meeting of their own in anticipation of the appointment of the Holt Enquiry.[41]

From about 1897, however, the Executive usually managed to bring together the competing interests at least of all postmen. On the other hand, since the Executive only met four times a year, and consisted almost entirely of working postmen, it could not become powerful or effective. Before 1907, association leaders could not even obtain more than ten days of 'special leave' to perform their business, so most meetings had to be held on holidays and week-ends.[42] After that, when twenty days were allowed, Executive meetings became major events in the life of the Federation, moving round the country and co-ordinated with local branch activities and recruitment campaigns. The meetings by then had also come to consist entirely of the consideration of the minutes of the permanent sub-committees which carried out the main business of the Federation. Much the most important of these was the Parliamentary Committee which after 1911 was called the General Purposes Committee. In the days of limited lobbying activity, this Committee was mainly run by London members, though when Direct Parliamentary Representation was adopted as Postmen's Federation policy in 1902, the Committee came to consist of the main leaders of the Federation. It spent the vast majority of its funds, £2,301 out of £3,650 in 1903–4 for example, and a new Executive member in 1900 soon came to realise that 'almost the whole work of the Society was done by the Parliamentary Committee, who simply reported the results to the Executive quarterly meetings'.[43] The Committee also had a full-time convenor from 1902 in the person of Stuart, so that when committees of inquiry were not in existence, it took up individual cases, legal and industrial.

The *Gazette* was also run by a sub-committee charged with its management, and in the early period responsible for more money than the Federation itself, and also for a larger staff. Within the general instruction of avoiding 'political and religious subjects', the Editor and his committee were largely left to their own devices. No serious conflict resulted, though John Walsh's eccentric articles about metaphysics had to be stopped in 1892 after objections from religious members, and there were occasional protests about articles and features before 1914 which advocated socialism. There was some sharper controversy in 1913 when John Brown wrote in the post-Holt period that 'all this talk of striking at this juncture without long and careful preparation is nothing short of criminal folly'. A reprimand from the Executive for this observation was only avoided by the casting vote of the Chairman.[44] However, this was as nothing compared to the controversy which was continually stirred by the 'Branch Notes'. There were constant complaints on the one side about their tedious parochialism, and from the other about any delay in their appearance. However, they were deliberately maintained because local activists wanted them and national leaders thought they helped to develop loyalty to the organisation as a whole. They still caused no end of trouble. Thus in 1908, the Federation had to apologise to the Postmaster of Halifax about the charge that he had 'driven two popular officials to early graves'. In 1911, the PF was obliged to settle out of court after being sued by a medical practitioner in Hackney who worked for the Post Office and who, according to an article in the *Gazette*, had to be 'brought to his senses' and compelled 'to treat the men properly'.[45] Efforts to relieve the pressure of space by publishing weekly instead of fortnightly were constantly rejected by the members when they appeared in all the reorganisation schemes, and the publication in 1902 of a magazine called the *Postal Mentor*, largely designed for the same purpose, was a financial disaster.[46] The *Gazette* remained successful, however, and long after it pioneered verbatim reports of the Tweedmouth proceedings, it contained accounts, somewhat dense and detailed by today's standards, of all the items of general interest to postmen.

PF finances, under the control of another Executive sub-committee and scrutinised in every detail by the members, were uncomplicated in the extreme. Another sub-committee and an officer also were put in charge of the Mutual Benefit Society, which began in 1895, and was much the most successful of all such schemes run by the Post Office associations. In its first form, members had to contribute ½d entrance fee, and then 1d or more depending on length of membership for each 'call' to a member who died or honourably left the service. In 1896 a 'widowers' branch ('C') was set up, and in 1902 the rising scale of contributions was abolished and a 'B' branch was set up for those who were prepared to pay slightly more. The scheme was popular and in 1898 it was claimed, probably with only limited justification, 'that 50 per cent of the members of some branches have only joined the Federation because of the Mutual Benefit Society'. By 1908, there were 16,000 people in the 'A' class, 5,000 in the 'B', and 3,000 in the 'C'. These figures rose as high as 20,826, 9,053 and 6,254 respectively in 1914, despite the advent of state insurance of various kinds. The 'call system', which also existed in the 'Northampton' Society and elsewhere, inevitably produced vested interests among members as they moved closer to acquiring the rewards for all the levies they had paid. Because there were thus never funds in existence to cover even a small proportion of possible claims, it was admitted that 'ordinary actuarial lines . . . were not applicable to our society'. All efforts to deal with this by instituting a system of regular contributions were resisted. They were rejected at PF annual conferences in 1907, 1909, 1911 and 1914. The Mutual Benefit Society limped on, despite even the special problems of the wartime period, as an important, though somewhat separate, part of the life of the Federation.[47]

The position and tasks of the national leaders of the Postmen's Federation constantly changed. At the beginning the only officers were the General Treasurer (Alfred Harris from 1892 to 1907) and Charles Churchfield who, as General Secretary, was also responsible until 1896 for the production of the *Gazette*. Despite his onerous duties, the General Treasurer received only £30 per annum at first, increased to £50 in 1898 with £10 for the office rent, £52 in 1903 and £75 in 1914. In 1919, immediately before amalgamation, this was suddenly made a full-time post at £200 per annum. When Churchfield stopped acting as Editor of the *Gazette* in 1896 his salary was reduced from £75 to £52. This General Secretary's honorarium was increased again to £75 in 1910 in acknowledgement of the fact that at least some of his earnings as a postman were lost. The same function and salary were taken over in 1911 by Tom Robinson, who was known as Organising Secretary from 1911 until his death in 1919. He was paid £100 per annum in 1916 and £300 in 1919. Robinson's title was misleading since he performed organising functions not in the usual sense of recruiting members, but in the sense of getting together the Executive and its sub-committees and arranging the work at Headquarters. The reason for this has already been mentioned – the peculiar position of Stuart. Stuart was a full-time 'Parliamentary Secretary' in 1902, and by 1911 when he started being called 'General Secretary', was already spokesman for the Federation, and performed other important functions such as the task of taking up individual cases. Brown was paid £75 for editing the *Gazette*, and this was increased by an annual rate of £10 to £120 after 1913. On his promotion in 1916, Brown handed over to the only other holder of the position, H. J. Lincoln. From the time the Mutual Benefit Society was set up in 1895, its Secretary also had an important position, receiving at first only £15, this sum gradually increasing to £52 from 1902, £75 from 1914 and

£100 in 1919. William Bowen held this position from 1910. As in the Union of Post Office Workers, the Postmen's Federation chairman was not considered to be an officer of the Society. The Executive elected one of its own number to serve as chairman, and until 1909 local branches nominated one of their number to officiate at annual conferences.

Sovereign power in the Postmen's Federation rested with annual conferences which met for three or four days. In the early years these were particularly badly organised, with ill conceived agendas, local chairmen unable to control the 'stars' of the movement, amendments constantly raised at the last moment, and often with little decided about wages and conditions. The 1897 Conference was considered by Brown to have been

> undoubtedly, a lamentable waste of time . . . Matters of minor importance were debated with a fulsomeness that was discreditable in view of the broader issues set out for decision, and the result was that great principles were slurred over, or the debate upon them closed after too brief a discussion.

The Postal Telegraph Clerks Association Conference, in contrast, was thought to be 'as decorous as a Quaker meeting'.[48] In later years there was a Standing Orders Committee and devices to cut down debate such as voting on the entire national programme so as to exclude detailed amendments. Members could arrive at decisions if they put their minds to it, as they showed when the Special Conference held in April 1906 in Manchester worked out details of the 'unification' policies for the Hobhouse Select Committee.[49] After 1900 'referenda' were also held on contentious issues, though less often than in the Fawcett Association, and the conferences themselves developed a routine that made them more effective as decision-making bodies.

With such a weak centre throughout most of its history, the precise location of power and authority was always difficult to determine. Thus in 1903, E. McLoughlin, the previous year's Executive Chairman, insisted on giving evidence to the Bradford Committee against the explicit instructions of the Executive, but without any disciplinary action taken against him. In 1909, the leadership attacked branches who submitted separate protests against the Hobhouse Report, but in the following year branches representing 25 per cent of the membership conducted their own campaign against split holidays.[50] In these cases, it was difficult to see whence authority within the Federation was derived, and how decisions could be arrived at and enforced.

For all this ramshackle structure, however, the Postmen's Federation was the best run of the main Post Office associations, with a steady flow of internal communication and well kept records, including eventually printed verbatim Executive minutes. The leaders of the Federation did not exercise anything of the same authority that they do in the modern Union of Post Office Workers. Thus most of them, including the General Secretary, were opposed to the major change of policy in 1906 in the 'unification campaign', but they were overruled by the Executive and also by the Special Conference. In later years Stuart built a predominant position, despite, or perhaps because of, his lack of any power under the rules. He initiated most of the main lines of policy including the case presented to the Holt Select Committee, the wartime claims and the ultimate acceptance of Whitleyism. This authority was not undermined in the final months of the existence of the

Postmen's Federation when its members accepted the need for full-time officials.

PF members were generally more isolated from one another than those in other Post Office associations, and it was difficult to organise regular general meetings of branches or any district organisation. The postmen were very much outsiders within the National Joint Committee even before they left it altogether in 1906. Their sense of distinctness from the higher grades grew in later years. Thus, though Churchfield was allowed to remain a member after his promotion, promoted grades such as lobby officers and assistant head postmen were eventually compelled to set up their own associations.[51] On the other hand, though postmen did at times look up with jealousy at the sorters and telegraphists, they did not usually adopt an attitude of superiority to those in inferior grades. Auxiliaries were welcomed into membership on condition that they were prepared to acquire permanent positions, and a special department was set up by the Federation to find them jobs. In 1909, when there were 35,441 members they included 2,027 auxiliaries, 1,282 assistant postmen and 632 who were unestablished. A National Union of Auxiliary Postmen was set up at that time in Croydon, which claimed to be 'non-political' and to be trying to improve the conditions of the grade without abolishing it. This brought about an intensification of recruitment efforts by the Postmen's Federation, which seems only to have been necessary in the Croydon area.[52] In 1911, when a similar break-away was threatened, it was decided to abandon an earlier decision and recruit adult messengers and labourers. Eventually, in 1916, even teenage telegraph messengers could join. By then, the war had brought great problems for the recruitment policy. In 1917, though the official membership including temporaries was 54,411, so many people were away on military service that subscriptions were only actually paid by 31,051. In the following years the respective figures were 38,699 out of 65,078 and 41,228 out of 61,910. In this situation it is not surprising that the Postmen's Federation, in contrast to the FA and P&TCA, was open to the temporary grades, and spread its net as widely as possible in the period immediately before amalgamation.[53]

Though at the bottom of the scale within the Post Office, the Postmen's Federation in its early years went to great lengths not to appear as other trade unions. The actions of the authorities helped to mould this attitude. At the first meeting of the Brighton Branch in 1893, 'a superintendent hiding in a doorway carefully noted the names of each postman as he saw him enter'. A few years later Postmen's Federation members were told that they

> should be careful not to let anyone get the idea that the Federation consists of men who are of careless habits and discontented natures . . . Show your superior officers that belonging to our Society does not make you any worse, but, on the contrary tends to increase your respect for yourself and your position, and makes you perform your duties in, if possible, a more careful manner than ever. Don't attempt to work antagonistic to them [sic]. Claim their sympathy, which you can do justly, for our aspirations are pure and our claims legitimate. Invite them occasionally to your social gatherings.

This approach to the authorities marked the activities of the Postmen's Federation in its early years, despite brave assertions that 'petitioning, begging and praying have been cast off once and for all'.[54]

In fact, this was about all the PF did in the years before the Tweedmouth

Enquiry. The Federation concentrated, as late as 1899, on presenting big national petitions on the question of recognition. Such activities helped to unify the aspirations of scattered groups of postmen, but did little to improve their conditions. They were either ignored or rejected by the authorities. Even after the Tweedmouth Report in 1897, the Executive felt able to propose nothing beyond 'petitioning periodically'. At the same time John Walsh described efforts to obtain Parliamentary representation as 'a mythical and most foolish proposition' and it was defeated at the Conference by a large majority.[55] The dismissal of General Secretary Wilson at the end of 1897 reinforced some earlier tendencies to caution. However, the frustrating outcome of the Norfolk–Hanbury discussions early in the following year and the example of the sorters made the postmen look to new methods. They co-operated with the other associations and began to take part in the more active Parliamentary lobbying. By the middle of 1898 the PF Executive was convinced that they needed to try and get an MP of their own, and in the following year persuaded the Conference to support this. The members took longer to be won over. In 1899 they rejected the proposal for Parliamentary representation by 4,484 votes to 3,199 in a 35 per cent poll. There was agreement in the following year, however, to affiliate to the TUC, and in 1902 after a ten-hour discussion the Annual Conference elected Stuart to be their Parliamentary candidate.[56]

From 1903 the Federation pursued the aim of getting Stuart into Parliament as 'a consistent and central part of their policy'. From the time of its adoption up to the war, four such efforts were unsuccessfully made. The details are set out in Appendix 23. These statistics, however, say little about the shifting relationship of political forces involved. Stuart was first adopted in 1903 by the Labour Representation Committee at York, a two-Member constituency then held by the Conservatives and a place where the secret pact between Labour and Liberal leaders was supposed to operate to elect one of each. The alliance did not do much to help Stuart in the 1906 General Election. Although he said nothing about the Postmen's Federation in his election manifesto, or indeed anything at all with which a Liberal could have disagreed, over 2,000 Liberals gave their two votes to the official Liberal candidate rather than one each to him and to Stuart. One factor in this was thought to have been a message of support obtained by the Liberals from Will Crooks, who in 1903 had won Woolwich as a Labour man with Liberal support. The result was that the official Liberal, Greenwood, came top of the poll, and was elected together with a Tory, and Stuart came ignominiously last.[57]

The position in the next contest was even more complicated – a by-election in Dundee in 1908. Here Stuart agreed to stand before the Liberals had put forward a separate candidate. Winston Churchill, who was at the time a member of the Liberal Government as President of the Board of Trade was then adopted. After this, Stuart received little or no help from the Labour leaders including Ramsay MacDonald. This may partly have been because of divisions between Scottish and English Labour Party supporters, but was presumably also because of the secret agreement with the Liberals.[58] In the following year Stuart was adopted for Eccles, a constituency previously fought by Ben Tillett and thought to be winnable. Once again, the Liberals got a statement from Stephen Walsh, Miners' leader and MP for neighbouring Ince, in support of the Liberal candidate, and this was thought to have been decisive in getting the miners to vote for the Liberals in the General Election of January 1910. A certain distrust for 'carpetbaggers' may also have played a part.[59]

Later in 1910, before the second General Election of that year, Stuart was adopted in West Wolverhampton, a constituency which had been held by Labour from 1906 to the January poll. Stuart was anxious not to make the same mistake again, so he made inquiries about how likely he was to win from a number of people including the Liberal agent. As a result he decided that it would be a mistake to again commit the PF to the necessary trouble and expense, so withdrew shortly before the poll. This led to accusations both from the Independent Labour Party and from some members of the Federation about 'certain discussions with leading Liberals' which Stuart rebuffed fairly easily. More difficult for him, however, was to answer the charge from one PF member that 'from beginning to end, thanks to the action of the Labour Party with which they were affiliated, their Parliamentary candidate policy had been a fiasco'.[60]

After eight years of the Parliamentary representation policy, it was difficult to see what had been achieved. Stuart had gone about the task with gusto, continually examining constituencies to be fought and then actively campaigning when they had been chosen. He was under attack from both sides on the question of his independence from the Liberals. He had not made his position clear in the York contest, though in the end this did not help him much. However, as the policy developed, the postmen like other Post Office workers became disenchanted with lobbying the traditional ruling parties, and began to identify themselves increasingly with the political as well as the industrial wing of the labour movement. By 1910 there were even doubts about whether they could lobby Conservative MPs at all, and one leader of the Federation asserted that their identification with Labour was now so close that

> For good or evil they had thrown in their lot with that Party, and it was too late to go back to that policy which had been in existence ten or twelve years ago. Had it not been for the birth of the Labour Party, their position would have been what it was fifteen or sixteen years ago – they would still have been wandering in the wilderness.

In 1918 every single member was exhorted to 'VOTE FOR LABOUR CANDIDATES AND HELP LABOUR FIGHT CAPITALISM'.[61]

One other particular problem faced by the PF in its electoral policies was that they were particularly sensitive to legal restrictions on their right to use money for electoral purposes. The successful case of Osborne against the Amalgamated Society of Railway Servants in 1909 apparently made such activities illegal for all trade unions. In 1910 the Federation got its own 'postal Osborne' by the name of Thomas Wight. This Dundee postman sued the Federation with funds provided by an outfit known as the 'Anti-Socialist Union' in an effort to stop all electoral activities. The Federation was able to claim justifiably that they did not insist on any pledge from candidates, but they refrained for two years from paying any money to the Labour Party.[62] Later on, Stuart went out of his way to tell the 1914 Federation Conference that they 'had no control over his politics' and were 'not at liberty to tell me what I shall do or not do on political matters'.[63] Whatever its constitutional correctness, this was not the spirit in which the original candidature was conceived.

By 1914, in any case, the question of Parliamentary representation did not loom so large either for Stuart himself or for the Federation. As the only full-time officer,

Stuart naturally had a great deal to do after recognition was secured in 1906. Thus he attended and summarised the Hobhouse Select Committee sittings every day. His complaints about his workload have already been mentioned. In the years after 1903 the postmen discovered that there were other ways in which they could aim at the amelioration of their grievances besides getting an MP. The aim was not abandoned, however. Stuart once again stood early in 1914 for North-West Durham and again lost. This time there could be no real excuse about Labour support, with Keir Hardie canvassing for him for five days and support also from Stephen Walsh and all the prominent Labour leaders. The seat had been held by L. A. Atherley Jones, son of the famous Chartist Ernest Jones, in the Liberal interest and it was said that the substantial Irish population there supported his successor. *The Times*, however, thought that the result was 'chiefly interesting for the strength of the Labour poll' which should 'be a growing force in all elections now'.[64]

By the time of the 1918 General Election, the policy of Parliamentary representation was not just the policy of Stuart or of the Postmen's Federation. The 1918 Annual Conference decided to put up three further candidates. Both the PF and the P&TCA had candidates, and Ammon of the FA also stood under the auspices of the Independent Labour Party in Camberwell. There were two other postmen who stood locally without trade union sponsorship. All nine of these were firmly Labour candidates, and all failed to be elected in the 'coupon' General Election arranged in an atmosphere of chauvinist hysteria partly directed against the working-class movement.

It is possible to trace the stages of the transformation of the cautious 'federationists' of 1892 to the unquestioning pillar of the mainstream of the Labour movement in 1918. In the early period, the PF eschewed altogether even the appearance of trade unionism. In 1893 members were told 'that the time had not arrived for the Federation to affiliate to Trades Councils' and in the following year they decided to take part in May Day activities only as a 'non-political demonstration as citizens'. The need to look further afield for support became obvious after the failure of the Norfolk–Hanbury talks in 1899 to obtain what they wanted. TUC affiliation in 1900 was soon followed by the adoption of a Parliamentary representation policy and affiliation to the Labour Party. In 1904, fifty-nine branches were affiliated to trade councils and the *Gazette* encouraged more to do so. By 1905 it was agreed that

A Trade Union stands in the same relation to an individual as a Trades Council does to a Trades Union, and if an individual believes in joining a Trades Union he cannot logically oppose the affiliation of his Trades Union to a Trades Council.[65]

The affiliation of local branches to trades councils and also to local Labour Parties had by this time become common if not universal.

The rejection of the Bradford Report in 1905, and the failure to secure any effective aid on this matter from outside, was the beginning of a less expansive, more inward-looking period in Post Office trade unionism. Just as the London sorters decided at that time to cut themselves off from the rest of the trade union movement, so postmen reacted by cutting themselves from other sections of Post Office workers. This was a period when all the resentments within the Post Office hierarchy expressed themselves most sharply. The Fawcett Association had since at least 1901 demanded that all promotion to supervisory positions in London, including those over postmen, should be in the hands of sorters. The postmen's reply was the so-called 'unification' campaign initiated at the 1905 Conference, confirmed at the Manchester Special Conference of 1906 and presented to the Hobhouse Committee in 1907. It represented a spirit of defiant isolation by the postmen. Cheesman, on behalf of the London sorters, said

> no self respecting Trades Union could stand by and see its members black-legged by another society claiming to be a Trades Union and joining in the advantages of the Trade Union movement generally without an effort to stop such encroachments.

When the case came before the TUC Parliamentary Committee early in 1906, Young of the UKPCA stated quite justifiably that the postmen 'had offered to do work at a lower rate than the clerks were receiving', since they could hardly claim the same pay without doubling and tripling their wages. The TUC was quite unable to reconcile the differences. The feeling that lay behind the entire episode is clarified by this entry in the 'Branch Notes' in the *Postman's Gazette* from Paddington:

> We have observed with a considerable amount of amusement the strenuous efforts of the local branch of the Fawcett Association to obtain for its own use the retiring-room officially designated for postmen. That the postmen should have a kitchen better than the one allocated to the aristocrats of Labour was a contingency too awful to contemplate, and therefore strong protest was made by them, the result being defeat most humiliating. Efforts of this description bring to light the hollowness of the sorters' professed friendship, and the agitation against our so-called 'black-legging' methods.[66]

The disastrous results of attitudes such as these, and the divisions which flowed from them, were nowhere more clear than in the unexpectedly unfavourable outcome of the Hobhouse deliberations in 1908. This led to the restoration of links between the postmen and other sections of Post Office workers, to such an extent that by the time of the Holt Enquiry, the postmen declared themselves to be against any promotion at lower rates of pay. It also led to a final break from the old attitudes of exclusiveness from the rest of the trade union movement, particularly in the Postmen's Federation. The Federation was then accepted as a legitimate and even necessary part both of the working-class movement and the Post Office service. In 1904 its Conference was visited by Postmaster General Stanley, and his successor Buxton was there in 1906 and 1909. Post Office secretaries were present in 1909 and 1911. After recognition in 1906, they were much more like other trade unionists meeting the authorities in the same way as others negotiated with employers. The 'labour unrest' of the summer of 1911 was the turning point in this process. The strike of railwaymen in August could not be ignored by postmen, who often carried mail into stations and could well have been employed to then carry them into trains for blackleg drivers. After some Manchester postmen refused to do any such thing, Stuart went and told the Post Office Secretary 'that if the Department insisted on using the men as strike breakers they would be bound to take them out'. Though some Postmen's Federation Executive members baulked at this threat they did endorse an editorial statement that

The policy of the Postmen's Federation is still a 'non-strike' one but the question of postmen being called upon to act as strike-breakers can only lead to one result, and that is our refusal to do the work.

Correspondence columns in the *Gazette* in the next few weeks showed a clear weight of opinion in the Federation in support of this action, the only criticism being that it did not go far enough.[67]

As indicated in the previous chapter, these events had a decisive effect on the campaign that forced the setting up of the Holt Enquiry. It also compelled the postmen finally and decisively into the arms of the mainstream trade union and labour movement. By 1917, it was the conventional wisdom within the Federation 'that the betterment of their conditions of existence depends upon organised labour being sufficiently strong to compel the Government to deal with their demands'. In the Wight case they tried to make out that they were a 'Civil Service Benefit Society'. Fortunately, this description was not tested legally, and it was soon abandoned. Brown asked later, 'if we are not a Trade Union then what are we?', and by 1913, they were claiming to be 'the largest Union in the country'.[68]

The recognition and the inquiries brought about another change of importance, and this was in the range of the Federation's activities. Before about 1906 comparatively simple questions of wages, promotion and conditions of work were all that came up in any meeting of the Postmen's Federation. After that, recruitment to the service and other matters relating to the long-term organisation of the Department were discussed in increasingly frequent exchanges of letters and deputations to the Postmaster General and his subordinates. Although in 1913 an attack on a possible Post Office secretary was considered insubordinate by the authorities and led to the partial withdrawal of recognition, in fact such questions were coming up more and more often. Representation on Departmental committees, at one time an impossible demand, was conceded in effect by the Gibb Committee.[69] The rallying call 'colour service to count', in other words military service to be added in the calculation of pensions, was taken up by the Federation after at least two separate organisations had been set up specifically to campaign for it. The two outside bodies united in 1913 and attacked the PF for dealing with something they thought outside its competence.[70] This process further developed during the war when postmen complained about having to work harder, not simply because there were fewer of them, but also because the arrangements made by the authorities were inefficient and unlikely to produce the desired result. In 1917 the *Gazette* boldly denied that the new system of numbering within the London postal districts would, as was claimed, 'save labour and money required for War purposes'.[71]

The war did not simply widen the scope and aims of the Postmen's Federation and the membership to include 'temporaries', women and others. It also saw changes in the internal life of the Federation that would have been inconceivable less than a decade before. Bowen, Lincoln, Robinson and Wallace were withdrawn from the service to work as full-time officers, a step which would have scandalised the pioneers. The aims of industrial unionism became the received opinion within the PF, leading to a new stage in Post Office trade unionism in 1919. Changes came fast in 1917–19, but their direction came logically from many previous discussions and developments.

THE POSTAL CLERKS

The United Kingdom Postal Clerks Association was the weakest of the four main Post Office associations.[72] Its origins in the 1887 Ridley agitation have been described elsewhere, and it remained rather localised in North-West England even in its later years. It was set up by George Lascelles, revived by George Landsberry and run later by Ernest Lea. Though because of the weakness of their Association they tended to be favourably disposed to joint action, these leaders were considered ultra-conservative even in the Post Office. The reaction against their methods in the Manchester Branch produced a band of rebels who remained a thorn in the side of Post Office union leaders well after amalgamation.

The UKPCA organised those in the provincial offices on the postal side, mainly sorting and serving at counters. Though in the larger 'divided' offices there was a clear distinction between postal and telegraph work, this broke down in the smaller 'undivided' offices. Thus though at times it was hard to see any difference from the Postal Telegraph Clerks Association in the main centres there were definite divisions of interests between postal clerks and telegraphists on promotion, hours of work and other matters.[73] Though official efforts to break down the distinction were resisted, increasing numbers of entrants were qualified in both postal and telegraph work, even in the divided offices. By 1914, therefore, the basis for separation from the Postal Telegraph Clerks Association had been sufficiently eroded for the two organisations to be amalgamated into the Postal and Telegraph Clerks Association.

Outside the large offices, the provincial clerks worked in quite small and isolated groups. They were never integrated in the same way as the London sorters, and the weakness of their Association reflected this. They belonged to a social layer with certain pretensions to gentility, and this often held them back from effective concerted action such as supporting Parliamentary candidates in the way that the postmen did. They began in the shadow of the Postal Telegraph Clerks Association and always remained behind the other associations, at times even dependent on them. This caused them usually to push harder for joint action and this was their small but distinctive contribution to the amalgamation that was ultimately achieved.

The Liverpool-based Executive Committee described in Chapter 6 had few achievements to its credit when it collapsed altogether in February 1893. This was after all its members were suspended for accusing the authorities of 'maladministration' in a petition to Postmaster General Morley. The original leaders, including the founding Secretary George Lascelles, then resigned and were subject to punishment for the rest of their Post Office careers.[74] For two years the Association was run by Paul Casey, also a Liverpool sorting clerk. Casey does not seem to have been particularly efficient or conscientious, and the Manchester members called a Conference in June 1895 at which he could only present a balance sheet containing an income of £36 since 1892, with £30 going on his salary and a balance of 3s 6d (17½p). At this Conference Manchester was made the 'centre' of the Association, with George Landsberry as Secretary and all the members of the Executive from then until 1907 drawn from this 'headquarters office' and the surrounding towns.[75]

It was some time before the United Kingdom Postal Clerks Association got a proper journal. At first it sought a corner in some of the commercially produced papers on the fringe of the association movement, including the *Telegraph*

Chronicle, which collapsed in 1893. In 1892 there was also a *Post Office Journal* (*Postal Journal* from 1893) under the proprietorship of one Alpheus J. Kendrick who also ran a small stationery and printing business in Liverpool. Some leaders of the Association, notably Lascelles, seem themselves to have had some financial interest in the venture. It was generally dull and not very well informed on Post Office affairs, only identifying itself with the UKPCA in 1895. It also got into trouble with the *Postman's Gazette*, whose verbatim account of the Tweedmouth evidence was reproduced by Kendrick. In 1897 the Association leaders decided it was time they took over the *Journal* themselves. There was some disagreement with Kendrick over suitable terms, so in September 1898 they set up their own *Postal Clerks Herald* in rivalry with the *Journal* which collapsed in the following March.[76] Even then, however, their troubles were not over. The *Herald* almost disappeared in the early months with the defection of its advertising manager and was only rescued from oblivion by a timely visit to Glasgow to make use of the advice and practical experience of James Brown of the *Postman's Gazette*. Over the next few years the *Herald* still lost money. Between 1898 and 1903 it borrowed £219 from the United Kingdom Postal Clerks Association's general account, and was said to be 'crippling the funds' of the Association. However, the resurgence of membership following the Bradford Report made it possible to go fortnightly in 1905. From then on the *Herald*, if not the most inspired in the service, paid its way and discussed more intelligently than most such issues as the grievances of clerks at small offices and Post Office administration and finance.[77]

The organisation of the UKPCA itself was not complicated. It never had full-time officials, and the possibility was hardly even considered. The Association only went so far as employing a typist in the last two or three years of its existence. There is little sign that the finances could have run to more than this with subscriptions only 9d (4p) until 1899, then 1s 3d (6p), 2s (10p) in 1901 and 3s (15p) in 1903. The Executive based in Manchester from 1895 to 1907 met fairly frequently as required. When Leo Brodie from Glasgow did much to revive membership from 1899 to 1901 as Organising Secretary, he did so without ever attending the Executive at all. Effective decisions seem often to have been made by the Manchester officers who from 1898 met in one another's houses as the misnamed 'Finance and Emergency Committee'. Even after a National Executive was set up in 1908, this Committee continued to act 'practically as an executive body'.[78] Other sub-committees then included one to run the *Herald* and another called the 'Permanent Evidence Committee' to which some more long-term questions were referred.

The system of running the organisation from one head office was later thought to have been 'best of its time', but it meant that there was little effective central control.[79] Thus the Sheffield Branch in its early years seems to have paid little attention to the national organisation except when it was electing conference delegates. Negotiations were conducted with the local postmaster, MPs were approached and attitudes struck with but limited reference to the national movement. The Liverpool Branch remained weak after 1895, but still carried on its own work. The Manchester Branches had to conduct what were considered to be national activities of the movement through discussions with their own local postmaster, and retained a certain amount of independence afterwards. In 1908 when power had gone from their hands, they were found expelling members who requested overtime, without the approval of the Executive who did not feel able to take a line on such a matter.[80] A small group of officers made most of the national decisions, approaching the inquiries and later also the authorities. Most conferences seem to have been like the one in 1902, 'quiet but earnest', and internal conflict within the Association was minimal. In 1905 W. W. Young resigned from the Executive because a statement he made in a delegation that Post Office profits should be given to the staff was repudiated. In 1907 he resigned from activity altogether in disgust at the Association's rejection of work through the Labour Party. In 1910, Albert Lynes, an Executive member from Liverpool, also resigned rather than accept the policy of allowing sorters to be recruited from the ranks of telegraph messengers. In the discussion that followed it was said that 'should the history of the Association ever be written in all its completeness, we are afraid many men would be weighed and found wanting'.[81]

This weakness, however, was less a result of the particular personalities of the United Kingdom Postal Clerks Association leaders than the situation of their constituents. The postal clerks stood half way between the rank-and-file postmen and the superior telegraphists, overseers and clerks. Though they sought the aid of the Postmen's Federation to keep the *Herald* going, they carefully guarded the position of their grade from any inroads from below. Thus they always talked of 'open competition' and opposed the promotion of any numbers of postmen to the grade of SC&T or to any expansion in the work performed by the postmen themselves. The postmen were bitter about this, as one of them indicated in 1894:

> You petitioned for a higher examination for persons entering the Postal Service, evidently to prevent Postmen entering the Postal Clerks' class, and the heads of the Department, eager to seize every opportunity to silence the aspirations of the Postmen and play class against class, raised the barrier against us – raised the wall an additional six feet or so; showing clearly that not any elevation, but an exclusion, was the object.

The UKPCA nevertheless continued to oppose 'closed' entry, and snobbishly claimed that the postmen would never get promotion on any form of open competition. When the Hobhouse Committee recommended some rationalisation of responsibility between the grades, the improved prospects for the postmen became the 'question of the hour' for the UKPCA, entirely dominating their 1908 Conference. The 'encroachment of Postmen, at Postmen's rates of pay, upon the duties of sorting clerks' made it 'absolutely evident that the Department are bent on giving full rein to this trade union runaway'. This was the main subject of their first major deputation to the Postmaster General in 1910, and their appearance in 1912 before the Norton Departmental Committee on the allocation of sorting duties. Norton rationalised the already existing practice, though he could not cause the underlying conflicts to vanish.[82]

The UKPCA found it necessary to keep their distance not only from the postmen, but also from the London sorters. Though Lascelles was in communication with Williams and Clery very early on, his Association soon expressed hostility to the abrasive tactics of Clery in the early 1890s. At that time the FA had not decided to confine its recruitment to London. By the time it presented its Tweedmouth evidence, it became a matter of faith for the UKPCA 'that an Association having its executive in London, cannot fully or fairly represent sorting clerks, e.g. in provincial offices'. Later, however, when the distinction between the London and provincial associations was defined and accepted, relations grew more friendly, with proposals in 1902 for the merging of the two associations or at least of their publications, and with an assumed similarity of status thereafter.[83]

Relations with the telegraphists were more difficult to resolve, though in later years there were said to have been contacts from the very start. Although there were frequent statements about the comparative lack of promotion on the postal side, many questioned the basis for having two different associations. A proposal to aim for a merger was withdrawn at the 1898 Conference in the face of arguments about conflict in promotion prospects. The post-Tweedmouth militancy of the PTCA did something to change this attitude: 'our sympathies, our efforts, our aims are with the Telegraphists', said the UKPCA at their Conference. A more tolerant spirit was the outcome of the early NJC meetings, and in 1902, after discussions on the problems of recruitment, lists of branches were exchanged and an agreement made to maintain the status quo in those individual offices at which either association already had members. In 1907 it was possible through the NJC to appoint an arbitrator, George Kelly MP, to obtain agreement that telephonists should be in the PTCA, and in the following year to revise the agreement to include the recruitment of new members. There proved to be an increasing number of issues on which the two associations could co-operate, notably on the downgrading of certain sub-offices and the consequent reduction in the numbers of sorting clerks and telegraphists. The road was opened for the amalgamation eventually achieved in 1913 and described later.[84]

Though looking down disdainfully at the postmen below, the postal clerks argued that they should have overseers in their organisation because

the line of demarcation between many of the duties is of such a haphazard kind that it is not always possible to tell where a worker ends and a supervisor begins to be responsible.[85]

The UKPCA also agreed more fervently than the others that no 'violation of official discipline' was involved in their activities and decreed that the 'due subordination required by the Service shall not be interfered with'. Their leaders hotly contested that any 'antagonism to supervision exists and is fostered', repudiating branches which were disciplined as a result of attacks on their immediate superiors.[86]

There was always something of the small businessman about the postal clerks. The commercial entanglements of their own journal have already been mentioned, and a number of UKPCA leaders seem also to have been involved in another of Kendrick's ventures known as the Post Office Employees Mutual Guarantee Association Ltd, which was wound up after the Tweedmouth Committee recommended an end to the payment of bonds as a guarantee against counter losses. On the other hand, the UKPCA never established any of the mutual benefit schemes popular amongst most of their Post Office colleagues. Such an effort, it was said, would be 'bad in principle, it is the introduction of a Foreign element, and it would only give rise to whimpering that some person or persons at the fountain head were making a good thing out of it'.[87] Clearly, some of the earlier experiences still rankled.

It was in part at least an element of social aloofness that led to the constantly reiterated opposition of UKPCA members to working through the Labour Party. In 1901, however, they agreed to affiliate to the TUC, a policy never subsequently questioned. In 1902 the Association adopted a policy of Direct Parliamentary Representation, and supported Clery until the collapse of his candidature. Thereafter, the question of Labour Party affiliation was hotly contested in the Association. Most of the leaders supported the idea, and it was carried at the 1905 Conference by 56 votes to 12. A lengthy discussion followed in the columns of the *Postal Clerks Herald* characterised by bad-tempered interventions from members outside the leadership on the lines of

> how utterly useless it is to attempt to argue with individuals who contend (or pretend) that the only possible road to progress with the United Kingdom Postal Clerks Association is by virtue of Socialism.

The members then voted by 1,587 to 1,445 against affiliation, a view emphasised after much further discussion by 3,324 against 1,366 at the end of 1906. Efforts to bring up the matter again were treated with hostility at subsequent conferences, and the funds accumulated to give effect to the policies were later used in solving the more general financial problems of the Association. The last straw came for some of the socialist-inclined leaders when the 1910 Conference most illogically on a close vote declared the UKPCA to be 'non-political'. This was changed in 1912 to 'non-party political'.[88]

For all their narrow provincialism, however, the UKPCA did make some contribution to the development of Post Office trade unionism. Perhaps the most famous incident in its history concerned the case of one Archibald Dick, a member in Glasgow. In 1907, Mr Dick fell in love with a Miss Minty, an attitude of which Miss Minty's father vigorously disapproved. Mr Minty went to the lengths of writing to Postmaster General Buxton, who got Dick transferred to Manchester at the bottom of his incremental scale without giving any reason. This raised many important issues of Post Office employment and its regulation. What was the correct machinery for individual discipline? Why were charges not given in writing as advocated by the Tweedmouth Committee? Above all, what had the private life of a Post Office employee got to do with its disciplinary procedures? The rights of associations to make representations in individual cases had not yet been conceded, but the Association took it up with vigour. It even showed a brief moment of militancy by refusing at one point an invitation to discuss the general problem with Buxton until such time as the particular case was satisfactorily settled. Mr Dick himself had an exemplary work record both in Glasgow and in Manchester. Even if his pursuit of Miss Minty had produced some unpleasantness, it was difficult to see what concern this was of the Post Office authorities. As the case grew more celebrated, it began to be taken up in the press and in Parliament. Delegations of Labour MPs in particular were put off by the authorities with hints of deeper scandal than could be revealed. There were in fact no such scandals, and the authorities were compelled to retreat as the truth came out. The Conservative MP, William Joynson-Hicks, got a full Parliamentary debate on the matter in April 1909, and the Postmaster General promised to review it. Eventually, on 19 June, he admitted that the punishment was 'excessive', and transferred Dick back to Glasgow, though he apparently still lost some seniority. Dick himself wrote that the UKPCA's leaders 'have come forward on my behalf with a courage that has filled me with surprise and admiration' and the Manchester Branch ran a farewell concert describing the outcome as 'the triumph of love'.[89]

The Dick case was perhaps the only event in the history of the UKPCA that brought it national headlines, but they did manage to expose the authorities and their methods and to compel the granting of further measures of recognition, in allowing individual cases to be taken up. The clerks left their mark on the Post Office trade unionism in two other interesting ways. They were the first to take up the desire for self-improvement by their members and to support and advocate the aims of the Workers Educational Association.[90] Furthermore, it was they who first took a serious interest in extending the range and functions of the Post Office itself, what they called their 'constructive policy'. In 1910 they called for the extension of the facilities provided by the Post Office Savings Bank, and in the following year for increased insurance facilities and a postal cheque system. The Executive ran a campaign on these questions in the following period, and despite some opposition both from the authorities and from some members that they should take up such issues at all, took it to the TUC in 1911 and 1912, and thence to delegations to the Postmaster General. Later there were favourable references to 'the Craft Guild System of Control' as 'the panacea for which we are seeking'. If little of substance was achieved by all this, the postal clerks at least showed that it was possible to broaden the horizons of trade unionism in ways that had some significance for the future.[91]

There were other ways also in which the limited, blinkered attitudes of the postal clerks in the early period broke down. They adopted a hostile attitude to the women members they recruited at first, and from 1896 to 1898 excluded them from membership altogether. The proportion of women on the postal side was much less than in telegraphy, but the threat involved in leaving them unorganised was obvious, so they were re-admitted.[92] They necessarily remained a small section of the membership, and efforts to encourage their participation were held back by the hostile attitudes often taken by local branches. However, the national leadership on the whole encouraged women to join and in 1908 Lucy Withringham was appointed women's organiser.

At the 1909 Conference, there was an interesting debate on the issue. The Liverpool Branch proposed 'the substitution of male for female labour' on 'returned letter and counter duties in class 1 offices' on the grounds of the 'large proportion of late and night duty which is incidental to Postal work in large towns'. Male speakers argued that women were taking over the easier duties and claimed 'that the female Telephonists were gradually being transferred to duties on the Postal side'. For all their individual prejudices, the postal clerks were shamed out of the attitude each of them might have taken individually. Cartwright of Leicester pointed out the alternatives that were being offered:

He dared say some of them had sisters, as well as wives. It had been demonstrated that the night duty was an exceedingly arduous one. How many men would care to see their sisters plodding home after a midnight duty in the Sorting Office? But what was the alternative to female labour in the Post Office? Were women to be thrown out of employment altogether?

After other arguments combining chivalry and economic necessity, Lucy Withringham herself was more aggressive. She attacked the men, saying that 'women were now on the labour market and had come to stay'. She said that women were reluctant to join the Association because they thought the men 'would turn them out of the offices tomorrow if they got the opportunity'. She attacked male 'short-sightedness and selfishness' and said they would get full civil and economic rights whether they liked it or not. After this, there was little that could be done except to refer the matter to the Executive.

The Executive tried to adopt an attitude of compromise. After surveying the attitudes of various unions, they drew a conclusion not entirely warranted by the evidence that there had been 'a total disappearance of the old spirit of opposition and jealousy to the employment of women by the New Trades Unionism'. They agreed to discourage local opposition to the women because

> Any antagonism on the part of the men members of our Association would tend to drive women into the ranks of unorganised labour, which would always prove a menace to our organisation, as well as leaving them to the mercy of the employer.

On the other hand, they agreed to discuss with the authorities the proposition that 'the proportion of Women's Labour to that of men shall be definite at each office' and never seized the nettle to the extent of demanding equal pay for equal work as the telegraphists did at the Holt Enquiry. In setting out the UKPCA's policy the women's organiser said that although they thought 'that the women's claim for absolute equality should be unreservedly conceded',

> after carefully considering the whole position, we agree that the disparity in the remuneration of the two classes as laid down in the Association programme, should be recognised as long as women are departmentally prevented from performing the work of the Post Office on the same conditions as men.[93]

If this uneasy compromise on the position of women was all that the UKPCA could finally produce, it did at least mark a change from their attitude fifteen years earlier. Very soon, however, they were to be overwhelmed by changes in ideas much more radical and thoroughgoing than anything dreamed of in the early period. As with the postmen, the turning point was the transport strikes of 1911, and the activities around the Holt Enquiry. Before the merger had been effected with the telegraphists, the 1912 UKPCA Conference saw some extraordinary scenes, unprecedented in its history. The Manchester delegates, including Arthur O'Donnell and William Owen, both later prominent in the affairs of the UPW, vigorously attacked the Executive on almost every question. They chided 'lack of progressive ideas', its alleged domination by the delegates from the small offices and particularly its failure to agree that they had the right to strike. Owen reflected a feeling that went well beyond the postal clerks when he asserted that 'every Trade Union in the country has been misled by its Executive during the past two years'. The mood in 1913 represented an even bigger break from the attitudes of the past. This time the Conference itself contemptuously rejected a statement partly in line with Middleton's Holt evidence on 'the rightful claim of Postal Clerks to be regarded as members of the middle class', and instead decided that they wanted 'a closer connection with the general Trades Union activities' and affirmed 'the right of workers to share in the determination of working conditions'. Furthermore, the Conference rejected by 83 to 61 'the view that as Civil Servants we have no right to withdraw our labour in order to enforce our demands', a decision greeted by noisy scenes of rejoicing and the singing of the *Marseillaise*.

Later in 1913 the mood became more militant, sharper still, and at the Special Joint Conference with the PTCA on 6 December 1913 calls for one Post Office union were strongly supported. It was agreed to enter into compacts with the National Union of Railwaymen, the Miners' Federation and the Transport Workers Federation. The rejection of a call for strike action by 85 to 83 led to charges of vote-rigging and to a walk-out in which O'Donnell and Craig Walker of the United Kingdom Postal Clerks Association were prominent.[94]

These expressions of anger and frustration among the most quiescent and conservative section of Post Office workers showed something of the new spirit which lay behind the first of the amalgamations, and which laid the basis for the formation of the Union of Post Office Workers. The last issues of the *Postal Clerks Herald* in 1913 and early 1914 were very different from the first ones fifteen years earlier. On 23 December 1912, it was reported, 150 SC&Ts at Liverpool walked off their sorting jobs and demanded to see the Postmaster about some of their work being handed over to postmen. Though they dispersed fairly easily, the anger beneath the surface was made manifest. During the Christmas rush of 1913, 150 temporary sorters at Glasgow went on strike against low wages and bullying supervision. Though they were not UKPCA members, the *Herald* thought them 'reasonable citizens claiming a living wage', and said on their return that they would never again be so badly treated even if their wages were still too low. It is not surprising that members were told in the same period that the Miners' Federation was a 'wonderful body', 'employing a host of fully-occupied organisers' and with conference delegates who 'don't bother to discuss problems from the employers point of view' and instead spent their time 'discussing ways and means of enforcing their demands'.[95] If postal clerks were not quite in that position yet, they at least wanted to be, and aimed to set up their new organisation in 1914 in a very different spirit from that of their forebears.

THE TELEGRAPHISTS

The fourth and last of the main organisations of Post Office workers before the First World War was the Postal Telegraph Clerks Association. This body organised telegraphists and those on the telegraph side in undivided offices as well as London counter clerks and telegraphists. In its final years it also included telephonists. The PTCA's origins as a little known benevolent society have already been traced, and its volatile response in the post-Tweedmouth period has been described.[96] The sharp militancy of 1871 and 1897 and the pioneering of the 1880s did not make the PTCA the most conspicuous or dynamic of the associations in later years.[97] This was partly because of its peculiarly inefficient forms of organisation, as well as the economic weakness of the telegraph service. However, the telegraphists became the Parliamentary lobbyists, and by the time of the Holt Enquiry had built up a record as defenders of the interests of women employees of the Post Office.

Unlike the UKPCA, the PTCA had large numbers of members concentrated in London, both at the Central Telegraph Office and serving at counters in district offices. There was always rivalry between the London and provincial members, exacerbated by the fact that until 1907, the Association was run by a 'Central Committee' based in Liverpool. Efforts to set up a form of national leadership were constantly proposed by the London branches. The Special London Conference of 1897 agreed that 'the time has arrived when the Executive should be placed on a more representative basis', but although the matter was discussed – usually at great length and with some bitterness – at each succeeding conference, it took a decade for it to be resolved. The locally based Central Committee, which could, in theory, have moved to the town of another general secretary, was considered by some to be 'both democratic and representative, in the truest and broadest sense' as well as 'decidedly more efficient, and only costs a trifle against the expenditure of hundreds of pounds' on any possible alternative. Its opponents argued that the Liverpool Committee was secretive and unrepresentative. After numerous conference debates, a committee of five was set up by the 1903 Conference and divided into a majority of three and a minority of two. The 'provincial' minority would not condemn the Central Committee for only presenting edited versions of their recent minutes, but they did agree with the London members to the proposal for a Central Executive. This scheme was presented to the members after the 1904 Conference. The members supported it by 2,120 votes to 1,568. This result was considered indecisive, because only a minority of total membership had voted in favour. In 1907, the Liverpool Committee itself proposed the change on the grounds that official recognition made the old system unworkable. A National Committee was set up by the 1907 Conference and this ran the Association during its last seven years. During this period the National Committee operated increasingly like the Postmen's Federation with the same reliance on sub-committees and the same four or five meetings a year. Its meetings were also moved around the country and linked with efforts to recruit more members.[98]

For its entire history, the source of authority within the Postal Telegraph Clerks Association was uncertain. 'District centres' were set up in the 1880s. They were strong branches which organised others and were supposed to reflect their opinions. Special conferences of these 'district centres' were held to express the views of ordinary members in 1887, 1895 and 1897, and in later years they were circularised by the Central Committee on all important questions. In 1893 it was admitted that they were 'rather slow . . . to ascertain the opinions of staffs'. The 1903 inquiry found that they often did not reply at all, whilst members at the smaller offices complained that in any case their views were not represented by these methods. The 'district centres' were abolished in 1908. By that time a 'small offices committee' with its own secretary set up in 1896 had long since faded away. The local branches, especially in the big cities, remained strong enough, some with incomes running into hundreds of pounds and with printed annual reports as comprehensive as any local trades council.[99] The division of authority within the PTCA was further complicated by the existence in 1895 of a Parliamentary Committee of London members, responsible to the Central Committee or Executive, but performing independently many of the important lobbying activities of the Association, especially when Samuel Belderson ran it between 1899 and 1908. The Committee helped to provide a focus for the activities of London telegraphists and an alternative to a break-away 'Metropolitan Postal Telegraph Clerks Association' discussed in 1899. As it grew more effective, provincial members became less suspicious of their London colleagues and worked through it also.[100]

The Association's journals provided yet another separate focus within the PTCA structure. During the 1880s the *Telegraphist* and *Telegraph Service Gazette* had vied for the loyalty of members, but after 1889 the Association worked successively with the *Telegraph Journal* and *Telegraph Chronicle* run respectively by A. W. Morris (who quarrelled with the Association over control and expenditure) and by John

Gennings, an ex-telegraphist who later became head of the Central News Agency. Gennings worked amicably with the leading figures of the Association from 1893, and his independence had definite advantages:

> . . . as the Telegraph Chronicle is an independent journal neither owned or controlled by the Postal Telegraph Clerks Association, not by any members of that organisation, the Postmaster General cannot apply Russian methods of controversy to its Editor.

However, the members grew more suspicious of Gennings's position in later years, suggesting that he was making money at their expense, so that in 1913, when amalgamation with the United Kingdom Postal Clerks Association was being consummated, a change in the status of the journal was already under discussion.[101] The stolid twice-monthly *Chronicle* can hardly have been very exciting, even to those whose somewhat parochial concerns were outlined in its pages. The PTCA therefore published separately much material setting out its policies, including substantial pamphlets like *Telegraph Troubles* in 1898 by Charles Garland and *The Case for the Telegraph Clerks* in 1903 by J. M. Robertson, a professional writer. The Association also published numerous pamphlets setting out sectional cases, and short general statements like the one on *Telegraph Cramp* in 1907, a short history by the General Secretary in 1902 and *Our Association: A Brief History of its Development, Achievements and Objects* in 1913.

The idiosyncratic constitution of the Postal Telegraph Clerks Association meant that it possessed few national figures of authority. The Liverpool-based general secretaries did not derive their position from the membership as a whole. This was made clear when Venables was driven from office in 1897 despite the virtually unanimous support of a National Conference. General Secretary McKinney in 1902 exhorted the London branches to withdraw a circular urging support for direct Parliamentary representation, but he could do little to enforce his will.[102] After 1894 there were also Liverpool-based assistant general secretaries who in all cases succeeded to the position after the promotion of previous incumbents. It was only in 1910 when the National Executive had been set up that a full-time clerk would be appointed in the small Liverpool office and the possibility of a full-time general secretary could be discussed. Members had already begun to feel some bitterness against 'long processions of promoted General Secretaries passing into the Overseers' class, and promoted over the heads of men of equal ability and very much longer service'.[103] Besides the Parliamentary secretaries, the general secretaries and their deputies were the only figures with national authority. Such important leaders as Charles Garland, probably the best known member in the wider world, and William Davis, best known in the other associations, held no national office in the PTCA and instead derived their authority from their own branches in London and their relationship with outside activities like the sanatorium movement and the National Joint Council.

With little to spend money on, the Postal Telegraph Clerks Association naturally had few financial problems. Its subscriptions were always the highest among the Post Office associations, even without the insurance element which predominated in the early period. At first members paid ½d per week (11p per annum) outside the insurance scheme and in 1885 this was reduced to 1s (5p) per annum. The subscription was doubled to 6d per quarter (10p per annum) in 1897 and further increased to 6d a month (30p per annum) in the following year. There were two other interesting aspects to the finances of the Association. First, from 1899, after a conference when 'considerable tension was found to exist between London and the provinces and a split was occasionally threatened', the London branches were allowed to retain 50 per cent of their subscriptions, as opposed to 33⅓ per cent for the rest of the country. After the setting up of the National Executive this arrangement was clearly unnecessary and from 1910 all branches were allowed to retain 45 per cent though the amount actually collected locally varied a great deal. The second interesting feature of PTCA finance was the practice initiated by General Secretary Morris of investing the reserves, and by 1913 a large portfolio of stock was held in local authorities and railway companies, as well as in the Mersey Docks and Harbour Board.[104] After 1888 when it was no longer considered necessary 'to seek protection behind the shattered garb of cheap philanthropy', the insurance branch diminished in importance. However, the scheme still provided 'a benefit out of proportion to the subscription, and in 1897 on actuarial advice the death benefit was reduced from £21 to £18. In later years, as the founders gradually died off and had their benefits paid, few new people joined the scheme, and it ceased to be of any significance as a service to members. It was wound up altogether in 1910, and the remaining funds paid to the 211 survivors.[105]

By this time the Association had worked out a number of more effective methods of looking after the interests of its members. The telegraphists became the most persistent of Parliamentary lobbyists, a fact which infuriated opponents of their 'interference' in all aspects of Parliamentary activity from elections to questions and debates. It was through contacts developed in the earliest period that they got Lord Compton to initiate the historic Commons Debate of 1890 on their grievances, and it was they who first began to put pressure on candidates in the 1892 General Election by issuing an unsigned circular bemoaning their lack of promotion prospects. The PTCA's Parliamentary Committee, which began work in 1895, became increasingly effective. On the precedent of the 1890 Cardiff case, the Association managed to get a great deal of publicity in later years for grievances at Bristol where, as Davis later put it, the Postmaster General found the administration 'in a very bad way', though 'he was by no means certain that our people were blameless'. By 1904 it was possible to claim that the Committee was responsible during the course of a year for no less than seventy-five Parliamentary questions, not to mention the setting up of the Bradford Committee. By this time not only was there close contact with many MPs of all parties, but the Parliamentary Committee was itself consulted by outsiders about conditions within the Post Office. Some matters were taken up by MPs without going to Parliament at all and in 1905 Belderson contacted Long, a member of the Cabinet, about the failure of many of their petitions to get through to the proper authorities.[106]

During the 1906 General Election, the Parliamentary Committee was at the height of its powers and organised an intervention of almost military precision, with numerous local interviews and carefully researched lists of 'pledge breakers' and those who refused to give precise promises about future voting. This type of activity was less important after the granting of official recognition in 1906 and particularly after the publication of the Hobhouse Report in 1908, when 'looseness of talk' by Parliamentary Secretary Belderson as well as the comparatively favourable treatment of London members meant that some of the London–provincial tensions again came to the surface. In 1913 it was agreed, against the strong opposition of the

London members, that since its lobbying activities were now 'practically defunct', all such work should be concentrated in the hands of a full-time general secretary. The negotiations with the UKPCA meant that this proposal was never carried out and the Parliamentary Committee and its secretary continued in the amalgamated society, though more directly under the control of the Executive, and was even proposed in the UPW amalgamation.[107]

As a result of their comparatively effective lobbying, the telegraphists were the least interested in direct Parliamentary representation. As early as 1895 they had found difficulty in getting some MPs who had promised to support them to act on their behalf, so the proposal to run a candidate was first put forward. The idea was agreed in principle in 1898 following the Tweedmouth Report. However, little was done to carry this out in the following period. There was a 'voluntary fund' set up in 1899 on the personal initiative of Thomas McKinney, and two inconclusive 'referenda' were run in 1902 and 1903, the latter returning 2,928 in favour of the running of an MP, and 1,428 against. Even this did not seem mandate enough to proceed when some members continued to be 'surprised to see with what determination this policy of direct representation is pursued on the part of prominent members of the Association' without, apparently, much enthusiasm from elsewhere. Some PTCA leaders continued to advocate the idea, though many members preferred more traditional methods of lobbying and using official recognition as well as of Parliamentary select committees. However, the PTCA did affiliate to the Labour Representation Committee in 1902. This does not seem to have greatly affected its activities for the next twelve years, and £331 that had been collected to stand an MP was eventually handed over to the UPW in 1930.[108]

The telegraphists were always to some degree 'outsiders' within the Post Office structure. They always argued in favour of open competition for their positions. All members agreed that 'it requires greater knowledge and superior qualifications to be an efficient telegraphist than to be a mere sorter', and that they were 'members of a skilled craft combining education with special training and yet we are far behind large masses of men who have no education and very little skill'.[109] By always claiming the right to more promotions on the telegraph side, they naturally came into conflict with the sorters, notably in the Bradford and Holt inquiries.[110] They were initially not keen on organising permanent co-operation with the other Post Office associations. One branch exhorted the 1899 Conference to 'Remember you are Telegraph Clerks in conference, and act accordingly. No federation.' Despite this, the same Conference decided to affiliate to the TUC, against threats of secession and a statement that 'they were not boiler-makers, but employees belonging to the finest Civil Service in the world'. The PTCA delegates looked to the TUC in later years to support them in their grievances, and in a few cases local branches, at Liverpool and Southampton at least, were also active in trades councils.[111]

Within the service, the PTCA also took the initiative in the deferred pay campaign and in the Sanatorium Movement, and outside it played some part in defence of the principles of free trade against attacks upon it by Joseph Chamberlain and others. The PTCA was much less enthusiastic than the postal clerks about the possibilities for expanding the service. Though there were occasional calls for cheaper telegrams, members 'objected to the Association funds being expended' to give publicity to such arguments, and thought that since some prominent businessmen had said they were against the idea 'how can an insignificant body like the

PTCA hope to convert the public?'[112] The position on membership in Ireland where the 'Dual Workers' Association', later the Association of Irish Post Office Clerks, began to take over their members, caused the PTCA some concern.[113] However, the basis for difference with the postal clerks diminished over the years and by the time of the Holt Enquiry it had been possible to agree that telephonists should be in the Postal Telegraph Clerks Association. Except on promotion, there was little basis for hostility now, so there was only mild opposition to the amalgamation discussions which were initiated in 1911.[114]

By this time the PTCA had made two other interesting contributions to Post Office trade unionism. First, it took up seriously the question of the health of its members. This did not just apply to the special problem of telegraphists' cramp, on which the Association campaigned with some success,[115] but also to cures for tuberculosis, in which Charles Garland took a particular interest. Starting from a resolution at the 1903 PTCA Conference, the issue was taken up with other associations, with the authorities and with various outside supporters including members of the medical profession and even of the royal family. Before the end of 1903 a Post Office branch of the 'National Association for the Establishment and Maintenance of Sanatoriums for Workers suffering from Tuberculosis' was set up in co-operation with the well established Hospital Saturday Fund. The Post Office authorities agreed to allow subscription by deduction from wages, and a year later over 30,000 had joined the scheme. A sanatorium was opened at Benenden in Kent in 1907, and within six months forty-two patients were admitted. This continued to be run by the National Sanatorium Association and was used by the Post Office Sanatorium Association. The 1911 National Insurance Act diminished the usefulness of the project, and after wartime inflation and a major fire in Benenden in 1924 had taken their toll, there were complaints about mismanagement. However, there was also frequent and continuing praise for a service which continues to the present day.[116]

Another special PTCA initiative was an attempt to expel or otherwise discipline workers who performed overtime. However, it was not successful. The Manchester Branch found difficulty in taking up the question in 1906 because of the diversity of opinion among the staff 'as well as the willingness of some members to accept overtime under any conditions'. In 1906 the Glasgow Branch also tried to move the expulsion of three such malefactors and in 1908 the Executive agreed to expel a number of members who worked at special events at below the agreed rate. Such unapproved activity continued, however, and it was reported that in London in 1910 some members hung about in the evenings like 'casual labour' at a 'factory' hoping to get overtime.[117]

The PTCA had one other characteristic of considerable importance, and this was its high proportion of women members, at least in its later period. Though there were always a great number of women telegraphists, there were few women members in the early PTCA and virtually none outside London. The unfriendly attitude of male telegraphists to their female colleagues was in part at least a result of deliberate efforts by the authorities to introduce a group who were given lower wages and easier working hours. However, in 1893 a motion from Swansea asking for women to be confined to one-fifth of the operating force was withdrawn when the London branches threatened to secede if it was passed. In the following year when women were granted marriage gratuities, the credit was claimed by Garland and Nicolson on behalf of the London PTCA. The PTCA branches in London also supported women protesting against having to work evenings, and women were very much involved in the eruption of militancy which followed the issuing of the Tweedmouth Report.[118]

In the years after Tweedmouth, women disappeared almost entirely from the activities of the PTCA, and some of them became active opponents of the Association, though without any serious proposals for alternative ways of improving their conditions. This was not altogether surprising in the face of a resolution at the 1899 Annual Conference opposing the employment of women altogether. Although the resolution was much modified, in the following year not a single woman attended the Conference. In 1902, the Conference agreed to take up the conditions of telephonists just coming into the Post Office, who were then all women. At the same Conference, both women present argued against equal pay and one of them

> thought it no more reasonable to expect the Department to pay women the same wages as men as it was to expect the rates of pay to be the same in King's Lynn and London . . . A uniform rate sounded well in theory, and, while much of the work was no doubt identical in character and equal in efficiency, they had to recognise that other distinctions, for example, hours of duty and other matters . . . made the claim for equal wages of the sexes unreasonable.

After this, women began to join again, and the question of whether they should affiliate to the Women's Trade Union League was discussed with some fervour, opposition mostly coming from the women themselves, but being eventually agreed in 1906.[119] The women now felt they could state their claims with reasonable frankness:

> They did not wish to say or do anything which would interfere with the claims of the men, which they recognised were just and reasonable, but they did think that the claims of the women had been overlooked.

Thereafter it could not be said that they were ignored by the PTCA. By 1908, when 2,916 or exactly 30 per cent of the membership were women and a record nineteen of them attended the Annual Conference, it was agreed that three of them should join the Executive. In 1910 it was agreed by 52 votes to 15 to affirm

> the principle that where other conditions of employment are equal, wages should also be equal, irrespective of sex; and this demand be an essential to the PTCA programme.

This policy was reasserted in 1912 and argued without any qualification to the Holt Committee of that year.[120]

The Holt Committee did not feel able to assent to such a radical proposal, and this was greeted with a most ferocious reaction at the Extraordinary Joint Conference of the PTCA and UKPCA held on 6 December 1913. Not only was there resentment against Holt and the Department, but also against the leadership of the associations for their weak-kneed attitude. Most remarkable of all was the call for militant action in alliance with railwaymen and miners from the representatives of this most quiescent group among the most exclusive and educated section of the trade union movement, personified by Mabel Hope of the PTCA. The Executive, she said, had

thrown over all that has been won in the past by the labour of those who have
gone before you . . . I for one will do my best to press forward the spirit of this
resolution – pushing it if necessary against the members of the two Executive
Committees. I will uphold this policy until such time as it becomes a victorious
policy. I am unconcerned whether or not the two Associations accept it. I am here
to fight for the rank and file.[121]

With such strong feelings abroad, it was to be expected that the first great amalgamation of Post Office trade unions would be invested with high hopes. There were
only five years of the most exceptional conditions in which these hopes could be
tested.

THE POSTAL AND TELEGRAPH CLERKS ASSOCIATION:
1914–19

The special conditions of wartime and the lack of any tradition of decisive and
unified action presented the Postal and Telegraph Clerks Association with considerable difficulties. Many of its leaders went off to the forces and its full-time officers,
increasing from two to six during its existence, did not have great influence. Its lack
of any real activity early in the war and its exclusion of temporaries until it was
nearly over, meant that the P&TCA never had the dynamic, all-inclusive character
that was once hoped for. Its main contribution to Post Office trade unionism was
perhaps the discussions it began on such questions as the effect of technical change
and on forms of bargaining and 'control' of the public service. On major matters of
wages and conditions, it largely followed the postmen and the other members of the
NJC.

In the early months of the war, the P&TCA Executive was paralysed into
inactivity. The *Record* described the war as 'a terrible calamity' and never
trumpeted the bellicose sentiments of Stuart and some other Post Office union
leaders. The rapid departure of members for the armed forces threw the Association
into confusion. They regarded the 'temporaries' – often married women who had
previously been established telegraphists or postal clerks – with horror. In the very
early stages of the war members were told not to do 'systematic overtime' to fulfil
the tasks of those who had left, but then overtime was encouraged in order to reduce
the numbers of new arrivals. By November 1914, the Executive felt compelled to
accept into the Post Office – though not into the Association – those 'genuinely
unemployed of the sex normally doing the work'. Even this policy could not last
long with 3,000 from the grades covered by the Association already in the armed
forces. Hostility to the newcomers did not arise from any particular restrictive
spirit, or even from opposition to women. It represented the continuation of a
traditional opposition to a cheese-paring Department who paid people less for doing
the same work. Thus the P&TCA was only putting forward the old policy
presented to the Holt Enquiry and on many previous occasions, that everyone
working in the Post Office should have an established, permanent position.[122]

It is not surprising that complaints were soon expressed against 'the total lack of
initiative shown by the Executive Council in the present crisis'. Nevertheless a vote
of 8,039 to 3,668 was recorded in favour of the cancellation of the 1915 Annual
Conference. During that year there was no change in the pre-war policies of the

Association, and inevitable difficulties followed. Thus Olive Johnson, who was a Branch Secretary in London, instructed day telephonists to refuse night duties in line with traditional policy even though as Acting Supervisor she was supposed to recruit people for such work. There was some division even within the Association about where Miss Johnson's primary loyalty should lie, but the Executive could not 'admit the contention of the Department that "acting" in a supervisory capacity in any grade should preclude Association officials from active participation in Trade Union work.' However, the Department never conceded the point. Nor did it retreat on an even sharper dispute with the Postmaster of Nottingham who was ill disposed towards the P&TCA and particularly its local Secretary A. E. Bools and whose regime was described in the *Record* as 'Government by tyranny'. The authorities went so far as to allow a local inquiry into the local administration in January 1916 in which the staff were represented by Stuart Bunning. He concluded his case with the statement that 'Mr. Telford is no longer fit to be Postmaster of Nottingham'.[123] It was progress of a sort that such statements could be made, but it could not yet be expected that they would have a great effect.

Early in 1916, a poll was again taken on the abandonment of the Annual Conference, and it was agreed by 7,999 to 7,048. This produced considerable discontent and an active revolt which led to the calling of a 'conference of branches' from Liverpool, and the movement was supported by Treasurer James Hunter, Organising Secretary Fred Richardson and by Alfred Lynes. Faced with this revolt, the Executive agreed by 9 votes to 8 to call a Conference in Leeds in July, though not without attacking the 'internal disloyalty' of some of its members, who all resigned but were all soon re-elected.[124] Neither this Conference, nor the one which followed in May 1917, reflected a substantial change in the policies or attitudes of the Association. After two sharp debates it was decided not to admit the temporaries. On the latter occasion, one speaker said they 'should recognise that the temporary workers were their enemies' and the proposition was lost by 189 votes to 162. By this time the Association could not be said to be catering for all those working in the sorting clerk and telegraphist and related grades, and its position was becoming more difficult to defend. There were some signs of change. Thus the 1916 Conference voted for peace by negotiations though it also expressed support for the Allied cause. In 1917, the pre-war strike policy was also re-affirmed.[125]

These changes in policy did not develop without opposition, particularly from those in the armed forces, who wrote to the *Record* in large numbers dissenting from the 'peace resolution' of the Association and also from its agreed policy to cater for the 'Civil Service interests' of conscientious objectors. One 'infantryman' wrote in pointing out that most of these protests came from Royal Engineers and others away from the front line:

> I have had nineteen months in the trenches and that is more than enough. I say, therefore, let us end this terrible business, here and now, if possible.

The isolation of members in the forces was also shown by the fact that they campaigned to some extent independently on their particular grievances, such as allowances for those in the Special Services. Those in the armed services were also radicalised by their experiences. It was said that every voting paper from servicemen which arrived after the close of the poll in 1919 favoured amalgamation, and also that they did much to contribute to the spirit of the final Annual Conference when delegates 'were not prepared to pay undue attention to the point of view of the Executive Committee on important matters of policy'.[126]

The war also presented important problems for those who remained in the Post Office. For the first time, telegraphists had to face the consequences of technical changes. The first introduction of key boards for telegraphy made the Post Office authorities consider the creation of a new inferior grade of female 'typists'. The P&TCA expressed opposition, and a Special Committee under the Chairmanship of Sir Archibald Williamson, MP, agreed that 'the balance of advantage is against the creation of a special class of typist telegraphist at the present time'. The *Record* could now certainly claim that 'the trade union position is saved', but could not fail to confront the results of other technical changes and the report of a further committee later in the war that the old methods of Wheatstone working would soon be superseded by high-speed 'Multiplex' apparatus.[127] Though the continued primacy of telegraphy over the telephones was assumed by the Executive, they nevertheless began to take up the grievances of telephonists more seriously than in the past. They not only protested about telephonists being compelled to work through air raids, but also took up the notable disparity of their wages and conditions from those who had been longer in the service. The 1919 Conference agreed to organise a strike ballot if demands for improvements were not met.[128]

This vote typified much of the spirit of Post Office trade unionism in the last two years before the setting up of the Union of Post Office Workers. There had been militant talk after the Holt Report in 1913 and on some occasions in the early part of the war. The *Record* condemned in 1915 the 'surrender of trade union rights by erstwhile leaders of the Labour Movement' who had arrived at understandings with the Government. Later in the war radical attitudes became predominant. There was stormy applause at the 1917 Conference for a resolution supporting the (February) Russian Revolution. From that time, the officials of the Association began to produce articles and leaflets on 'The Forward Policy' of the P&TCA arguing for strike action, for working more closely with the Labour Party and the Triple Alliance, and for strengthening the Association by higher membership fees. Mary Herring agreed that the new desire of women members 'to take a more prominent part in Association activities' compelled the men into 'a belated discovery that the "cheap labour menace" consists of an army of women very ready, given training and encouragement, to work out their own salvation'. She also drew some conclusions of a sort becoming predominant in Association discussion:

> The attainment of real official recognition, which in turn shall widen out into a system of Joint Control is the most urgent work of the moment for the Association. By this means the deplorable ignorance of Headquarters will be eliminated, and a possibility will be opened for real harmonious relations with the Department . . .[129]

This statement showed how the Association by 1917 was again taking up the threads of the policies and attitudes set out at the time of its foundation three years earlier. In 1914 the Founding Conference passed by 219 votes to 171 a resolution which called for 'the extension of the principle of Official Recognition leading up to partnership with the State in the management and control of the Postal Service'. One delegate exclaimed that 'it would seem as if they were at a meeting of the Social Democratic Federation or of some Syndicalist Society', but he was in a clear minority. The notion of 'democratic control' was argued strongly during the course of the war as an alternative to the way 'in which the rights of the Staff and the interests of the public are frequently overlooked in an endeavour to create commercial profit'. This was argued at the TUC and elsewhere and became part of the discussion on Whitleyism in 1918. The smallest steps in wartime consultation are highlighted:

> The praiseworthy action of our Controller in asking District Postmasters to consult local representatives of the Association on the subject of air-raid precautions contains the germ from which we hope joint control will grow. This simple action has already had a profound effect. It has, at one stroke, greatly increased the importance of the District Secretary.

The changing attitude of the authorities was shown by the fact that, also before the end of 1917, the Postmaster General agreed to see a delegation from the P&TCA on the 'development' of the Post Office, particularly the extension of its banking, an issue on which the old UKPCA had been forbidden even to make propaganda as recently as 1910.[130]

During its last two years the P&TCA witnessed a positive seething of discussion on all the questions facing Post Office and public sector trade unionism in general. After a brief retirement from the NJC during 1917, the Association enthusiastically took up the cause of amalgamation. The only serious opposition at the 1918 Conference came from those who thought they could not sink their differences with the supervisors. By then, Sidney Webb and the Fabian Research Department had taken up the expansion of postal cheque facilities as one of the main planks in their policy of 'How to Pay for the War'. General Secretary Newlove had been at Oxford at the time that G. D. H. Cole first put forward his ideas about 'guild socialism' and these ideas served to present a solution for all the old problems of control and industrial relations. In July 1916, Editor George Middleton was an enthusiastic participant in a series of discussions held between labour leaders and middle-class sympathisers on 'The Reorganisation of Industry', and was particularly struck by the ideas of A. E. Zimmern on 'a scheme for enabling Postal Associations to take a real part in shaping the conditions of work for postal servants'. By the end of 1917, a full discussion was in progress about the significance of the Whitley proposals. They were alternatively defended against charges from the National Guilds League that they were merely attempts to increase the control of the employers, and attacked as 'merely attempts to side track Labour in its struggle to supplant the Capitalists'. Early in 1918, G. D. H. Cole addressed Postal and Telegraph Clerks Association district organisers on the 'widespread demand by organised labour for a large, if not dominant, share in the control of industry'. A year later Cole addressed a similar meeting, and he had then come to this interesting view of the Whitley report:

> As applied to private industry, I don't think it was a ha'path of good to anybody, because it did not give you anything you hadn't got. It only gave you recognition. But as far as the public services were concerned, it was possible to take hold of it and use it to bring about a certain measure of control by the organised staff.[131]

By this time the Government was under strong pressure, not least from the P&TCA, to apply the Whitley proposals to its own employees, and the process whereby this came about is described at the end of Chapter 4. For the P&TCA the Whitley campaign went alongside a general radicalisation. Thus the temporaries were at last admitted during 1918. The Manchester Branch, though not the Executive, supported a strike of temporaries. Affiliation to the Labour Party was agreed by 11,215 to 1,277, a margin which would have astonished many of the pioneers. The 1918 Annual Conference heard a rousing speech from Labour Leader Arthur Henderson about a 'people's peace'. This new spirit could be seen clearly not simply in the enthusiastically undertaken amalgamation negotiations, but also in the sentiments frequently expressed in the letter columns of the *Record*. Here is a typical example:

A careful examination of the results of a strong trade union with a reliable strike fund proves conclusively that there is no other way for any class of workers, to obtain decent conditions of labour and a living wage. The sooner the Association pulls itself together the better it will be for our members. We have dallied too long over the matter.

The nature of the new spirit was underlined by the letter that appeared in one of the final issues of the *Record* which condemned all strikes as 'detrimental to the interests of the nation as a whole'. The writer, whose identity was explained in an editorial note, was none other than George Landsberry who had revived and re-built the UKPCA after its initial collapse in 1895. Times, however, were now much changed.[132]

Despite the thrusting, radical ideas of its later period, it is clear that the P&TCA was not a well run organisation. For all his Oxford training, Newlove was not a success as General Secretary, though the main reason for this seems to have been the serious illness from which he suffered after August 1917. He moved his office from Liverpool to Paternoster Row in the City of London in the early months of the Association. There were complaints soon after about his office management and later charges of general 'inefficiency'. Stuart-Bunning thought that these charges may have been the result of disappointment from the 'Liverpool gang' about not having their nominee Larsen elected General Secretary. It was originally agreed that Newlove would resign in the middle of 1917, but for reasons now difficult to discover, he hung on until 1919, and was paid his salary until the end of 1920. He took part in the amalgamation negotiations but consulted Riley on any matter of importance. Albert Lynes was elected his successor at the 1919 Conference, but never served because the postmen could not agree to taking him out of the service at a late stage in the amalgamation negotiations. In these circumstances, it is not surprising that Stuart Bunning found the General Secretary 'little in evidence' at the 1918 Conference.[133]

These problems meant that *Record* Editor George Middleton, who continued to be based in Manchester, was the main spokesman for the Association. He ran a journal which well combined the minutiae of Post Office life with discussion on some of the broader questions with which they were then confronted. Middleton was often in a minority on such questions as the admission of temporary workers, which he favoured long before it was accepted.

These full-timers worked with an Executive Committee with a total of twenty members, including Frederick Riley as Chairman up to 1918, James Hunter as Treasurer, H. R. Young as Parliamentary Secretary and Fred Richardson, later

Lord Mayor of Liverpool, as Organising Secretary. The Executive Committee met three or four times a year, mostly operating through an increasingly complex network of sub-committees, up to fourteen of them by the middle of 1918. The Parliamentary Committee of London leaders taken over from the PTCA worked until the amalgamation mostly on individual cases.[134] There were fewer deputations to the authorities and indeed very little for the Executive to do in the early part of the war. Gradually, however, its tasks increased. About 2,000 women telephonists finally came over in 1916 from the ASTE along with two extra women on the Executive. A full-time woman organiser was then elected at the 1916 Conference, and this was Edith Howse, who remained based in her home town of Manchester. A number of other important changes were made in the last four months. As a result of the 1918 vote in favour of Labour Party affiliation, a policy much discussed but never seriously adopted by the P&TCA's predecessors was suddenly taken up with a will. Middleton was approached by a number of constituency Labour Parties and eventually adopted at Altrincham. Walter Baker, who was now the Parliamentary Secretary, was adopted in Harborough, Leicestershire, Fred Riley in Leicester South and Horace Nobbs at Heywood. There was at one stage the idea of challenging the Postmaster General to dismiss them, but the General Election came so quickly at the end of 1918, that for fear that their candidatures would have been declared invalid, they resigned from the service in any case.[135] After their defeat, all three were integrated into the work of the Association with Nobbs as Treasurer and Organising Secretary, Riley as Acting General Secretary and Baker as full-time Parliamentary Secretary. These carried over with 'vested interests' into the amalgamation and, together with George Middleton and Edith Howse, took five of the eleven full-time officerships in the newly formed UPW. Thus it was not only in the realm of ideas that the postal clerks and telegraphists took a predominant weight within the newly formed Union.

ENGINEERS AND OTHERS

By the time the UPW was being set up in 1919, there existed a large number of other associations of Post Office workers besides the three major organisations whose development has been traced. Most of these have been mentioned already in Chapter 7, but now some account should be given of how they fitted into the constellation of organisations in 1919, a few joining the amalgamation and a number of others going off to grow in their own way.

There were seven smaller bodies which joined the UPW in 1920, all of them representing particular London grades.[136] The most important of them was the Central London Postmen's Association, whose origins in a breakaway from the Postmen's Federation at the East Central District Office during the preparation of the Hobhouse evidence have been described in Chapter 7. The CLPA represented the oldest and most 'aristocratic' section of postmen. They had once 'set the pace in postal agitation', and looked back nostalgically to the days before trade union recognition in the Post Office 'when matters requiring departmental redress were dealt with by an officially recognised committee elected by the general body of men'. However, they soon began to emphasise their credentials as trade unionists. Thus, though they also ran a gratuity branch, they claimed that 'the CLPA rests on a Trade Union basis, pure and simple, whilst the Postmen's Federation relies on the basis of a mutual benefit society, which is bound to have a weakening effect on agitation'. Furthermore, as the Central London Postmen's Association rules were submitted to the Registrar General of Friendly Societies, each member was 'a legal trade unionist, which is more than any *federated* postman can claim'. They were active in such labour movement bodies as the National Association for the Extension of Workmen's Trains and the London District Right to Work Council. In the early years they continued to attack the Postmen's Federation with some venom, taking a particular dislike to G. H. Stuart, its General Secretary, who they claimed had 'succeeded in establishing a dictatorship unheard of in the trade union world'. In 1908 they decided to try and recruit members from outside the Chief Office, and set up a branch at the South West District Office, but this cannot have been large, since the total membership only went up from 938 in 1907 to 946 in 1909. By 1912, when they submitted the now discredited 'unification' arguments to the Holt Enquiry, a number of members were calling for merger talks with the Postmen's Federation. Though it took longer for the differences to be resolved, during the war the Federation actually proposed their admission to the National Joint Committee, and the placing of their leaders on the platform of the Amalgamation Conference of September 1919.[137]

The most important of the other associations based in the capital was the London Postal Porters Association. There were nearly 2,000 porters in the London postal service, virtually all of them ex-servicemen, and a small minority could hope to be promoted to the rank of established postmen or sorters. They first set up an Association in July 1895, which claimed up to 500 members, ran a mutual benefit scheme and brought out a *Postal Porters Journal*. They presented a case to the Tweedmouth Enquiry but achieved very little from it, and the organisation seems to have collapsed when the General Secretary, Tommy Sanders, left the service in 1900. It was, however, revived in November 1902 (in the hall of a Ballet School near the site of Goodge Street underground station) and began a monthly paper called *Postal Porter* which became *Postal Advocate* in 1905. The Secretary for most of the rest of the Association's life was W. H. Manning of the Inland Section. The porters needed their own association because they were not accepted by any of the other grades. They had an excellent case to make against their extremely low wages – a maximum of £1 10s (£1. 50) per week from 1881 to 1911 – and few had promotion prospects. There was less to be said of their claim to do almost the same work as sorters. The Postal Porters Association was run, like the Fawcett Association, by an Annual General Meeting and a large Executive Committee, meeting monthly and representing one member in twenty-five. In 1907 the membership was 1,155, which was said to be over 80 per cent of possible, and in 1919 1,500 was claimed, though a good few hundred of these were 'honorary members' serving in the forces. At one stage the postal porters expressed some sympathy for the dissidents of the CLPA, but their Association pushed for closer unity. They refused to join a federation of smaller associates set up in 1909 by the sorter-tracers, and affiliated in 1916 to the National Joint Committee. They opposed the federation scheme in 1919. The members then voted solidly to join the Union of Post Office Workers.[138] Promoted members set up a 'Head Porters Association' in 1909 and this claimed 135 members at the Holt Enquiry, being 'affiliated' to the London Postal Porters Association until 1914. The HPA was reconstructed in 1917, and went into the Federation of Supervisory Associations set up soon after.[139]

The other London grades were smaller still. The bagmen, a grade created in

1881, sorted out the bags in some of the London sorting offices, had an association from January 1906 which was 'affiliated' to the Fawcett Association for its first year, but withdrew because the Fawcett Association could not accept their claims to equality with sorters. By 1912 they were recruited entirely from the ranks of the messengers, and in 1919 came into the UPW with 110 members.[140]

The Tracers Association organised a grade which was created in 1875 in the Accountant General's Department to record and find telegrams after they had been sent. Their Association was set up in 1892, three years before they were declared redundant as a grade. Nevertheless, they remained a lively and inventive group, affiliating to the London Trades Council in 1894 and getting Keir Hardie to ask Parliamentary questions on their behalf during the same period. They later affiliated to the United Government Workers Federation, and brought in 100 members to the foundation of the UPW, when they formed their own branch.[141]

Quite distinct from the tracers were the sorter-tracers, a grade which was set up during the Tweedmouth deliberations in 1896. They spent half their day working as sorters and the other half as tracers. The reason for this was to allow the reduction in the numbers of split attendances necessary for the other grades. They also set up a Sorter Tracer Association in 1904, and started a periodical in June 1905 called *The Review* which continued for the rest of their existence. They were refused affiliation to the Fawcett Association because of the hostility of the tracers. By 1908 the Sorter Tracers Association had 303 members which was claimed to be 98 per cent of possible. However, they soon lost more than a third of these to the sorter grade in the post-Hobhouse settlement. This proved rather favourable to their claim for equality with the sorters by allowing them the option of becoming sorters, or, if they remained in their old grade, of going up the same incremental scale as the sorters, except for the final three rungs. However, there were many aspects of their conditions still to be considered, and when Postmaster General Samuel met their representatives on 25 July 1910, he thought he had 'spent more hours over the Sorter Tracers than any other class in the Post Office service, there being so many complicated questions arising'. These complications further increased when there was some re-allocation of duties during the war. The unfortunate remark by postman Frank Johnson of the UPW Executive that as a redundant class they had nothing to do but draw their money, seems to have been enough of a blow to their dignity to hold them back from the UPW amalgamation until the beginning of 1926. They then voted unanimously to come in and join a branch along with their old rivals, the tracers.

Writing in the final issue of their *Review*, their last chairman said he hoped that 'posterity' would not 'conclude that they were always an insular self-satisfied lot'. Looking back many years later, there seems no reason to draw this conclusion of the Sorter Tracers Association. The sorter-tracers had separate interests which were not catered for at the time by any of the other associations. It was only their failure to get reasonable financial terms for affiliation to the National Joint Committee that led their Secretary George Holyoake to initiate at the end of 1910 a Post Office Servants Federation with the support of bagmen, the adult messengers and the Central London Postmen's Association. The STA also ran a memorable mass meeting during the pre-Holt agitation on 3 October 1911. It was addressed by no less than two MPs as well as James MacDonald of the London Trades Council, and 'ended with undescribable enthusiasm'. Once the question of contributions was settled, they left the Federation to the adult messengers, the breakaway CLPA and the auxiliary postmen.[142]

Another small London association which tended to keep apart from the others before the amalgamation was the Tube Staff Association, set up in November 1903 and organising tube attendants and night collectors at the Central Telegraph Office. They brought another branch of 120 members and a balance of £13 into the UPW.[143]

These special organisations of London grades – a few also had some members in Dublin – were not hostile to the larger grade associations and mostly came into the amalgamation without serious regrets. A number of other organisations existed for special reasons. The Women Sorters Association, for example, was also a London body and consisted of women doing specialised tasks in some of the smaller offices. They were 'affiliated' to the Fawcett Association up to 1919, and the role of their indefatigable Secretary Rose Smith-Rose has been mentioned earlier in the chapter. During the war they took on the title of Post Office sorting assistants and recruited those temporaries refused by the Fawcett Association. They did not join the amalgamation and worked briefly with the sorter-tracers in a short-lived National Federation of Post Office Societies set up in 1920, and later in the various civil service federations.[144]

Irish sorting clerks and telegraphists also set up their own Dual Workers Association in 1900, since the UKPCA had only spasmodically recruited members in Ireland. By 1904, as the Association of Irish Post Office Clerks, they adopted a nationalist stance and began to recruit those on the telegraph side. The Postal Telegraph Clerks Association tried to counter this and returned some members, especially among Northern Protestants. However, the Irish Association could claim to organise 75 per cent of the grade in 1912. The Association of Irish Post Office Clerks had its recognition withdrawn briefly in 1909 for some intemperate words against a supervisor and showed neither skill nor success in presenting evidence to the Holt Enquiry. The Association protested about the dismissal of some of its members for being involved in the 1916 nationalist rising, and in later years took part in a number of strikes in support of national independence. When this aim was eventually achieved it united with other Post Office grades to set up the Irish Postal Workers Union in 1922.[145]

Two other small break-away organisations deserve mention. The National Union of Auxiliary Postmen was set up in February 1910 by a Croydon auxiliary called Thomas Easthope, and recruited about 500 members, mostly around the Croydon area. Its main *raison d'être* was opposition to that plank in the Postmen's Federation platform which called for the abolition of the auxiliary grade altogether. They appeared before the Holt Enquiry and though never recognised by the authorities, were represented in the wartime amalgamation negotiations.[146] They seem to have disappeared by the time of the amalgamation itself. Another break-away was the Post Office Writers Association set up in March 1908 by London sorters who did writing duties to campaign for the implementation of their interpretation of a paragraph of the Hobhouse Report referring to the creation of a separate grade of 'writing assistants'. They claimed 107 members when giving evidence to the Holt Enquiry but they had to admit that a greater number of members of the Fawcett Association had the same grievances.[147]

A much larger organisation which presented evidence to the Holt Enquiry was the Amalgamated Society of Telephone Employees. Under the private companies this had brought together in 1909 the National Association of Telephone Operators (set up in 1904) and the National Society of Telephone Employees (1906). It was not organised by the same method as Post Office unions and included supervisors and telephonists as well as engineers. Negotiations with the other associations were not easy for the ASTE, which by 1914 had 14,500 members, more than 80 per cent of the ex-employees of the Company. In 1915, after Postmaster General Samuel recommended, not for the first time, that they should fit in with the ways of the Post Office, they suddenly tried to recruit telephonists from the P&TCA. This having failed, they agreed to transfer most of their members to an amalgamation with the Engineering and Stores Association which became the Amalgamated Engineering and Stores Association. As mentioned elsewhere, about 1,500 of their members also came into the P&TCA where two positions were reserved on the Executive, and a full-time organiser was elected to cover telephonists.[148]

Also of considerable importance among the manipulative Post Office workers were the various organisations which eventually became the Post Office Engineering Union. No account need be given in this book of this history which has been fully written by Frank Bealey and published in 1976. The engineers in the early years had many problems about establishment and the outside comparisons of their wages which were quite different from postmen, sorting clerks or tele-graphists. Like most others, the linesmen began to organise to present their case to the Ridley Commission in 1886, but a more stable Linesmen and Mechanics Association had to wait until 1896. The name was changed to the Engineering and Stores Association in 1901. This body appeared before all the inquiries and was involved in most of the other joint activities with the other associations including affiliation to the NJC and support for the Labour Party. Though strong supporters of amalgamation before the war, the amalgamation with the telephonists in 1915 seems to have altered their attitude and they then became more interested in emphasising their 'craft' skills. The Amalgamated Engineering and Stores Associa-tion of 1916 became the Post Office Engineering Union in 1918 with the inclusion of some supervising grades. Despite occasional differences beginning in 1920 with the separate setting up of Whitley machinery, the POEU has since usually worked harmoniously with the UPW.[149]

One other important group of manipulative workers who should be mentioned are those temporary employees of the Post Office who were compelled by the attitude of the P&TCA and the FA to form their own organisations during the First World War. The Post Office Sorting Assistants – formerly Women Sorters Associa-tion – has already been referred to, but this only recruited in certain offices in London. Of greater importance was the Temporary Sorters Association set up at a meeting on 9 March 1915 of 100 temporary sorters in the Chandos Hall in London under the Chairmanship of G. H. Stuart-Bunning, after the Fawcett Association had refused to recruit them. By November, they began to produce a monthly printed journal, to recruit in all the main London offices, and to appeal for women to join. At the first Annual General Meeting held in London on 2 April 1916 it was agreed 'that all temporary employees in the London area not eligible to join any existing organisation be accepted as members of the TSA'. In practice this only seems to have added London porters and a few cleaners to their numbers. The postmen joined the PF, and the few temporary telegraphists joined nothing at all. However, they then became the Temporary Postal Workers Association, and changed the name of their journal to the *Temporary Postal Workers Gazette* which came out almost every month until September 1920.[150] Outside London, the temporary SC&Ts were slower in getting organised and a National Association of

Temporary Postal Employees was not set up until Easter 1917 with L. Musgrove from Newcastle-on-Tyne as General Secretary. For a time there was also an organisation in Glasgow known variously as the Temporary Employees Association and the Temporary Workers Association. This won the support of the Glasgow Trades Council, though not of the Postmen's Federation, for a strike call in October 1916, and seems to have disappeared with the dismissal from the service in the following June of its Secretary R. G. Murray, who was a temporary postman.[151]

At about the same time the other two organisations of temporaries made some attempt to amalgamate. They failed to do so perhaps because the London subscriptions were always double those in the provinces, but they did agree to share their magazine and to set up a Joint Committee. The Joint Committee assumed some importance during the arbitration proceedings of 1918 and 1919, and it could claim to represent 15,000 people. Differences with the NJC caused delays in the first of the arbitration claims, so the temporaries worked more closely with their permanent colleagues after that. Most of the early leaders of the London-based Temporary Postal Workers Association were soon conscripted into the army, unless they were too old like Ernest Rebbeck, Editor of the journal and General Secretary from April 1917. He, like many other leaders, had a long career in other trade unions behind him, in his case as a member of the London Society of Compositors for twenty-five years. The proportion and number of women members increased rapidly during the war, but few of them took leading positions. While the provincial NATPE held a series of annual conferences, the TPWA was organised in the same way as the Fawcett Association, and held five annual general meetings at which its officers were elected. Rose Smith-Rose and her sorting assistants helped the TPWA and so did Stuart-Bunning of the Postmen's Federation. The Fawcett Association, on the other hand, with the conspicuous and individual exception of Alfred Watson, remained hostile throughout. The permanent sorters had good reason to fear for their conditions when the anti-union press began to claim that their work was being done just as well by people who were paid a great deal less. The temporaries themselves had good reason to feel indignant when the writer of some local notes in *The Post* of 27 July 1917 described one of their members as 'more of a nuisance than he is worth'. Editor Dubery was compelled, in the circumstances, to chide his members and ask them to 'condemn the system of which both temporary and staff members are unwilling victims'.[152] As for the periodic crises of conscience and eventual decision to accept the temporaries by the P&TCA, the provincial association was not impressed. General Secretary Musgrove of the NATPE 'ridiculed the idea of either their willingness or ability to fight the good fight' on their behalf, and the *Gazette* maintained with some justice that the P&TCA 'decision to admit temporary workers to membership was not influenced by a sympathetic desire to help or to study their interests in any way'. Rather, it was said to be an attempt to grab their money and make their policies compatible with the PF pending amalgamation.[153] The temporaries got their own back in the final period of their existence by accusations of 'poaching', extending even to the early months of the UPW, which in all conscience could not be contested.

Despite these divisions, the two associations of temporary workers served the interests of their members with some success. They were recognised early on by the Postmaster General and negotiated on many smaller questions before getting increasing amounts out of the arbitration proceedings in the latter part of the war. A notable victory in 1919 got them overtime pay. By then, Whitleyism meant that 'the temporary staff had no alternative but to follow the established people'.[154] As their numbers were rapidly diminishing at this point they soon disappeared, but they could claim, with justice, to have brought some more 'trade union spirit' into the Post Office, showing almost as clearly as the Holt Report had done the perils of narrow self-interest. As outsiders, they also displayed a more critical attitude to Post Office officials. They were less easily taken in by 'a revival of the press-gang' in the form of army recruitment encouraged by the authorities, nor were they prepared to 'trust the employers . . . and the rest of it', when the post-war Whitley schemes were discussed.[155] However, in 1920 they were gone as suddenly as they had arrived five years before.

Of more permanent importance, but also of much great complexity, were the asssociations devoted to the interests of the supervising and higher grades. Despite the comprehensive coverage which is aimed at in this book, it is impossible to deal with every one of the fourteen associations of supervisors, and the thirteen other organisations of various kinds listed in Appendix 25. A number of these have been mentioned in accounts of the inquiries in Chapter 7, and the Head Porters Association has already been described in this chapter. Nowhere in the Post Office was the sense of exclusive rank and status more pronounced than amongst such grades as these. Some small associations such as those for the assistant head postmen or the inspectors of tracing covered people promoted from the lower grades and doing work little different from those immediately below them in the hierarchy. Some were specialised groups within the telephone and telegraph service, often recruited separately for their technical knowledge and somewhat isolated from the various associations which are chiefly described in this book. A few others, however, have a history which merits a brief reference.[156]

As always, the story begins in London. There were a number of overseers in the Fawcett Association, many of these formerly active members while they were sorters. As late as 1907, the FA and UKPCA refused on instructions from the authorities to drop their overseer members. However, an Overseers' Association was founded in 1894 and presented evidence to the Tweedmouth and subsequent inquiries. As the London Superintending Officers Association, now including also assistant superintendents, it was strong enough in October 1911 to begin producing a small monthly printed journal called *Supervising*. This opened with greetings for the Postmaster General and went on to record how they got 'nothing' from the Holt Report, and later how they held back from claiming anything at all in the early period of the war.[157]

The provincial supervising grades had set up a Postal Telegraph and Telephone Controlling Officers Association in 1906 and this also began to produce a rather more substantial magazine in 1911 with the title *Controlling Officers Journal*. In 1912, 2,071 members were claimed including 1,270 overseers and 492 among various types of superintendents. In the same spirit as their London equivalents, the controlling officers modestly expressed their aim as 'the improvement of positions of each Supervising class, to conserve their rights, and make practical suggestions for the development and efficient working of the service'.[158]

The supervisors felt themselves particularly exposed to abuse from their many superiors and inferiors. One of their leaders expressed the problem in this way:

When a man in the Post Office became a head postman, an overseer, or super-intendent, he was neither fish, fowl, nor good red herring. One did not know where he was from the stand-point of the class war. He was something betwixt and between.

For their own part, the supervisors regarded themselves as under attack from both sides. The junior clerk was an 'Office Boy, puffed up with conceit' and the 'position of the Overseer is, in every respect, superior'. The overseer was 'a scapegoat for every sin of omission and commission', and on the 'frontier line' between the higher officials and the manipulative grades and 'if there is any trouble at all with the rank and file the overseers have the worst of it'.[159] Their associations retained a somewhat ambiguous role very much in the shadow of the larger rank-and-file associations. As they were reminded by Stuart Bunning in 1917, they benefited from the work of the rank and file Associations, rarely, if ever, made any acknowledgement of that work, [and] did not contribute towards its expense'. This became increasingly clear as these associations were taken over by former leaders of the rank and file. During the First World War, McKinney performed the same job of General Secretary for the Controlling Officers Association that he had done for the PTCA a decade before, and Edwin Nevill was Chairman of the London Overseers Association as he had been of the FA. When Dubery visited the 1919 Annual General Meeting of the London Association he reported that 'there were so many familiar faces, I am still wondering whether it is not a meeting of the old Fawcett Association'.[160]

Under these influences the supervisors naturally began to consider more unified forms of organisation. In the first flush of anger at the Holt Report, London postal superintending officers even voted to join the National Joint Committee, but a referendum put a stop to that. In 1914, however, approaches were made from the London Association to the controlling officers with a view to amalgamation. However, once the plan was worked out the Londoners rejected it, and decided to go instead for a Federation. In May 1916 a Federation was set up and it was joined soon by the Telegraph Supervisors, the Telephone Supervisors, the Society of Post Office Engineering Inspectors and another Association of Superintendents from the smaller provincial offices. At this point the negotiations became involved with those larger manipulative associations and with the short-lived support by the London sorters for a federation rather than an amalgamation scheme. After a series of complicated manoeuvres described below, the Federation of Supervising Officers remained as the only survivor of the short-lived scheme stopping short of unity of the associations. At the same time, Harry Dubery left the editorship of *The Post* and the Fawcett Association in 1918 to work full time for the shady National Alliance of Employers and Employed as well as for the Federation. Though some of the supervisors favoured joining the amalgamation, most did not, and it was probable in any case that the manipulative grades would not have had them.[161] This organisation worked reasonably satisfactorily as a Federation until after the Second World War. When Dubery retired in 1921 he was replaced as full-time Secretary until 1942 by H. E. R. Alefounder, formerly of the P&TCA. Amongst the chairmen were William Davis from 1921 to 1923, and from 1928 to 1931 Don Grant, one-time Organising Secretary of the UKPCA. It was only in 1951 that the London Postal Superintending Officers Association and the Controlling Officers Association finally merged with the Telegraph Supervisors to form a body known as the Association of Post Office Controlling Officers. It was this body that became in 1968 the Post Office Management Staffs' Association and in 1981 the Communication Managers Association.[162]

Further up the Post Office hierarchy, most of the various grades of clerks and assistants to surveyors and others had their own associations by the First World War, usually working only through annual meetings. Much the most important of these was the Women Clerks Association which could claim 1,865 members in 1912 and tried to negotiate behind the backs of the inferior grades in 1915 with the Gibb Committee.[163] There was also a Head Postmasters Association which existed from 1894, continually protested their loyalty to the Department, and argued in front of all the main inquiries for their own closed system of promotion. They finally merged in 1912 with the Postal Controllers and Postmasters to form a Senior Postal Staff Association.[164] Outside the Department altogether was the Sub-Postmasters Federation which was founded in Wakefield in 1897 and began a journal in 1902. It associated itself closely with other sections of Post Office workers, affiliating to the NJC in 1908 and having its own life and achievements which can be traced to the present day.[165]

THE LONG ROAD TO UNITY: 1890–1920

In all the welter of Post Office grades and sub-divisions there were voices raised, at least from the 1890s, for joint action and eventually for amalgamation. It is the aim of this section to describe some of these forms of combined activity, and to say something of the National Joint Committee, originally established in 1897, and from 1912 the organiser of an increasingly successful combination which laid the basis for the UPW in 1919.

All the earliest and most ambitious schemes for joint activity and even unification came from Clery and the Fawcett Association. Immediately after his dismissal from the service in 1892, Clery proposed the setting up of a Civil Service Federation. The PTCA thought this much too ambitious, but was prepared to discuss it and to support a joint petition. When Clery met General Secretary Venables in Liverpool on his way to the TUC in the following year, the idea of a Federation was rejected along with Parliamentary representation because of the 'conflicting interests' involved. Clery also managed to get a joint meeting with the UKPCA in Liverpool, but they were at the time going through a major internal crisis which made it difficult for them to do anything at all. Rivalry between the two provincial clerks' associations made agreement in any case unlikely. Nevertheless, Cheesman found the Edinburgh PTCA Branch 'fully alive to the mutual advantages that could accrue from such amalgamation, but Liverpool blocks the way'. Little interest in such matters could be expected either from the early leaders of the Postmen's Federation, who were hostile to sorters and telegraphists in general, and to Clery in particular.[166]

It was James Keir Hardie in 1894 who suggested the first properly co-ordinated action of the associations by persuading them to campaign jointly for a public inquiry into their conditions. As a result, a joint public meeting of 1,500 was held on 8 December 1894, with the participation of the London sorters and postmen together with the Tracers Association, to demand a Royal Commission on their grievances. This was said to mark 'a new era of postal agitation' and in January a 'Parliamentary Committee' was set up by the three associations for joint action on a number of topics including pensions and civil rights. On 18 February 1895 the Committee ran a delegation to the House of Commons, and a week later it was decided to begin a 'Postal Services Federation'. Despite friendly approaches, the

PTCA and UKPCA stood aloof from this body, and the postmen soon left it because of Clery's insistence that lobbying should continue during the 1895 General Election. Clery himself attributed the eventual establishment of the Tweedmouth Committee to its activities.[167]

It was the failure of this venture that caused the Fawcett Association to look to other public servants outside the Post Office and to join them on 17 August 1895 to set up a United Government Workers Federation. This body, which was dominated by the Fawcett Association, and was to some extent its creature, campaigned for minimum wages for government employees and those working on government contracts. After the Tweedmouth Report it became the proposed medium for efforts at Parliamentary representation. However the tiny organisations that made it up, such as the Labour Protection League representing dockyard workers and women bookfolders, meant that it was able to report only limited achievements in practice. At the time of its 3rd Annual Conference in 1898 it was said to be 'scarcely yet off the stocks', yet it continued after the foundation of the UPW, mainly serving the interests of its smaller affiliates.[168]

Less ambitious efforts at combined action were taken in the 1890s for particular ends. Thus a joint delegation of London sorters and telegraphists met representatives of the Midland Railway Company in 1892 to try to persuade them to grant excursion tickets to Post Office workers outside the holiday season. When this failed a body known as the Postal and Telegraph Employees Railway Movement was set up in 1893. This was run by William Davis at the PTCA and members of the Fawcett Association. The Railway Movement achieved its aims, and was wound up in 1901, having provided an example of continued and concerted action.[169]

Leading on from such efforts was the more successful and well known campaign known as the Deferred Pay Movement.[170] This body aimed to get civil service pensions paid to widows and dependants of those who died before retirement by allowing superannuation to be considered as 'deferred pay' rather than as a grant to an individual. Discussed by the PTCA as early as 1888, and initiated by them in 1897, the Movement was really based on earlier models like the campaign of the 1860s for the franchise for revenue officers. It was dominated by higher civil servants from the War Office and the Admiralty, though a few prominent Post Office associationists were also involved. Many of them were suspicious of their main Parliamentary champion, A. H. Aylmer Morton, Tory MP for Deptford and a strong opponent of the aims of Post Office trade unionism. The postmen on one occasion withdrew because of a refusal to allow representation to reflect their numbers. There were often complaints at its gentlemanly discretion, its refusal to 'take more active measures', and some thought it 'sought too much to evade publicity which is the life and soul of their movement'. In 1904 the NJC discussed leaving it altogether.[171] Despite all these criticisms at the time, it was eventually successful at least in establishing the principle of 'deferred pay' and so was later seen as a model of quiet and effective lobbying.

After its inaugural meeting in 1897 the Deferred Pay Campaign collected the signatures of 50,000 civil servants in support of its aims which were presented in the following year. In 1900 they got 335 MPs to support the setting up of a Royal Commission on the superannuation system, and this came about in 1902, reporting in the following year. It proposed some improvements in the form of a reduction in the amount of the pension from one-sixtieth to one-eightieth of income per year in return for twelve months' pay for the dependants of those who died before receiving it. The associations were prepared to accept this as an instalment, providing the bonus was increased to one-and-a-half years' pay. Nothing then happened for some months. A delegation met Chancellor of the Exchequer Austen Chamberlain in May 1905, and he was not prepared to agree to anything without a measure of general opinion in the civil service. A poll was then taken in which three questions were answered as follows:

For an 18-month bonus – 41,393
For a 12-month bonus – 28,559
For the current system – 12,916

The majority had naturally opted for the most favourable system, but the three-question referendum had been sufficiently ambiguous in its result to provide the Treasury with an excuse for refusing to introduce any change.

By now the issue was being taken up more widely in the civil service. Local joint committees were set up and the main Post Office associations became active again in the campaign, with the Postmen's Federation collecting most towards the 'appeals' on which it was largely financed. When the Liberals came to power, another delegation met Chancellor of the Exchequer Asquith on 5 July 1906 and he played on the ambiguity of the poll result as well as the unwillingness of service representatives to accept lower rates if the actuarial calculations they demanded showed them to be necessary. After this refusal, the Campaign then organised a further poll in 1907 on the Royal Commission scheme and 75,857 voted for it (including 52,589 in the Post Office), with 20,264 against (7,224 from the Post Office). A further meeting was then arranged with heads of department who were of course themselves affected and they, including Post Office Secretary Babington Smith, exercised some pressure on behalf of the Royal Commission scheme. This was eventually incorporated into the Superannuation Act of 1909 (9 Edward VII, 10). Women, the majority of whom had voted against the scheme in the 1907 poll because they had no guarantee that any dependants would get a gratuity on their behalf, were excluded, and so were others who failed a fairly vigorous medical test.

The Deferred Pay Committee was finally wound up in 1910 with large 'testimonials' being presented to its leaders including £500 to H. Rolfe of the War Office who had been Secretary since 1897, £70 to H. Rowbottom of the PF and £60 to William Davis of the PTCA, both of whom had served on the Committee. These were presented by Postmaster General Buxton in June 1910, and there was a farewell dinner in the following December.[172] These junketings emphasised the role of top officials in the campaign and a general air of co-operation which did not characterise other joint efforts of the period.

By this time, for most Post Office workers such joint efforts were now being undertaken by their National Joint Committee. This body, however, had had a protracted and difficult gestation which goes a long way to illustrate the difficulties of industrial unionism in the Post Office.

The feeling of bitter disappointment following the Tweedmouth proposals provided a pretext for a meeting, on the initiative of the postal clerks, of the four main Post Office associations on 11 December 1897.[173] Here it was agreed that they all supported a fairly comprehensive programme including a Parliamentary Select Committee into their grievances and official recognition. Some other points on classification of offices and on night duty and holidays were agreed at the meeting, though the PTCA representatives said they could not be bound by them. The meeting also passed the first of the much quoted 'mutual attitude' resolutions whereby the associations agreed that in the event of 'taking action on any point of a national programme where it is necessary to bring in comparisons having reference to conditions of employment affecting other organisations in the Post Service', they should meet to arrange the exclusion of 'any odious matter'. The 1897 Conference also agreed to set up an 'Amalgamated Postal Federation', which in 1902 assumed the more accurate title of 'National Joint Committee of Postal and Telegraph Employees'. In the early period the four main associations, together with the Engineering and Stores Association, were affiliated, and they each sent three representatives with equal affiliation fees and voting rights. The main inspirer and guiding light of the NJC was William Davis of the PTCA, Secretary in the early stages and Chairman from 1902 to 1914.[174]

'Some future historian of Postal agitation', predicted Charles Garland in 1902, would see the early meetings of this body as 'the beginning of the most important era of our movement'. H. G. Swift, completing the first edition of his *History* at the time of the Second Conference held in Derby in 1899, also thought 'an epoch in postal history' was about to begin.[175] This, however, was not to be. The Derby Conference, for all the surface cordiality and compromise, showed that serious divisions still existed. Delegates from the four main associations could of course agree about recognition, civil rights, and re-instatement for Cheesman and Clery. However, when it came to more immediate questions, they discovered much less accord. Thus they were unable to produce any figure for a minimum wage because the postmen said £1 4s (£1. 20) per week was too ambitious, when many of their own members got less than £1. Nor could the PF accept the aim, which they also considered utopian, of the abolition of all split duties, though a compromise was agreed calling for improvements. The postmen's own policy of direct Parliamentary representation was only approved by 183 votes to 127, and a motion calling for support for independent candidates had to be withdrawn. The FA agreed to a single journal only in parallel with those that already existed.[176] The next NJC Conference – in London in 1902 – was even less successful. The PF failed in its efforts to condemn the FA for trying to reserve all London overseers' positions for sorters. The *Postman's Gazette* concluded that 'the grievances of the postmen's class are real and genuine, and we do not need a Postal Congress to advertise them'. 'It is high time', said a correspondent to the *Telegraph Chronicle* soon after, that 'the joint movement bubble was burst'. The PTCA delegates thought the London meeting 'only moderately successful' and lacking in 'that cohesion in the movement so very necessary to ensure success'.[177]

In the period up to 1911, the role of the NJC was limited by the divisions between grades and associations.[178] In 1901 the PF demanded the expulsion of the FA on the London promotions question. When the others refused to accept this, the postmen decided to remain affiliated solely to campaign for a Select Committee of Inquiry. In 1903, the postmen also refused to submit their Bradford evidence to the other associations in advance, or to discuss their Parliamentary lobbying activity with the NJC's own Parliamentary Committee.[179] By 1905 these divisions had boiled over into the Postmen's Federation campaign for 'unification' of the grades and they left the NJC altogether without bothering to give others the satisfaction of expelling them. There followed a very lean period for Post Office trade unionists, where despite the official recognition of new associations and the setting up at last of the

Hobhouse Select Committee, little or nothing was gained. Frustration at this was reflected in internecine conflict. The sorters and the UKPCA tried to arraign the PF before the TUC Parliamentary Committee. For their part the TUC leaders refused to take sides in what they described, quite wrongly, as a 'demarcation dispute'. In the discussions, the FA could with some justice take the role of the injured party, but the postmen brought up all the old resentments about the deterioration of their relative position and even the failure of the sorters to support them in the 1890 strike.[180] It is not surprising that the NJC should in this period be described as 'simply a quarterly discussion society'. It was with some difficulty that Davis managed to persuade the 1907 PTCA Conference to shelve a motion for disaffiliation. Stuart told Davis at the time that 'the present NJC is in my opinion both a nuisance and a danger'.[181]

However, by this time already some new ideas were blowing through Post Office trade unionism. Disunity was seen as the main cause of the disastrous proceedings and report of the Hobhouse Select Committee. In January 1906, W. C. Steadman, trade union leader and MP, arranged a meeting between leaders of the FA, UKPCA and Engineering and Stores Association to discuss Parliamentary representation. In 1907 the FA and UKPCA resumed their amalgamation discussions somewhat more seriously than they had undertaken them on the earlier occasion in 1902. The leaders of these two associations, who essentially organised the same people in London and the provinces and had no possible competing interests, agreed in March 1907 to a scheme for a 'National Union of Post Office Clerks', with a full-time secretary, who presumably would have been Cheesman. A plebiscite was held within the UKPCA on the scheme, and though there was a majority in its favour, only 59 per cent of the members voted, and only 1,902, or 35 per cent of the total, registered their support. The FA considered that this showed 'it may fairly be assumed that the members of the United Kingdom Postal Clerks Association are not yet ready for amalgamation', and the matter was 'dropped for the present'.[182]

After this failure, it was time for the National Joint Committee to take an initiative. Thus during 1908, the NJC-affiliated associations – 'refugees' as Millard of the UKPCA put it, 'from the earthquake created by the [Hobhouse] Parliamentary Committee' – put resolutions through their 1908 Annual Conference calling for a special NJC Conference on 'the extension of the principle of common working' and amalgamation.[183] This meeting duly took place at the end of August in Matlock Bath, agreed a large number of common aims, even on wage claims, and established a special sub-committee which set out a scheme for a National Federation. The sub-postmasters, whose post-Holt radicalisation involved them joining the NJC, thought the idea was to see that the NJC 'should have the functions of an Executive Committee on all matters which by the decision of the affiliated associations are accepted as of common interest'. However, because of the attitude in particular of the PTCA it was decided in 1910 that it was not possible to proceed any further on this basis.[184]

The NJC up to this time was not generally regarded as much of a success. If viewed from the point of view of the lofty aims of amalgamation, this was perhaps the case. However, it was 'more a deliberative and consultative body', and Davis was quite justified in arguing that it constituted 'the best form of union they had up to the present time', with some achievements to its credit.[185] In the first place, through a Parliamentary Committee which worked in co-operation with the PTCA's own Parliamentary Committee, it developed a machinery for lobbying. Many of the numerous Parliamentary questions about Post Office workers' conditions in the period came through the contacts and efforts of Davis. When Cecil Norton made an effective intervention in the 1905 Estimates Debate, he told Davis 'that if I succeeded in stating your case satisfactorily, it was in great measure due to the admirable brief furnished to me by you', a document which had all the features it should have, being short, clear and comprehensive. The NJC also played a role in the deferred pay and workmen's compensation issues. The other success of the NJC in this period was that despite the frequent and well-publicised divisions, it did actually manage to settle the dispute between the UKPCA and the PTCA in 1907 by the appointment of an arbitrator. When the Irish clerks refused to accept a similar method of settling their dispute with the PTCA in 1908, they had to disaffiliate. The NJC never had the authority to settle such disputes, but it did allow them to be aired.[186] The most important achievement of the NJC before 1911 was that it kept alive the idea that there could be unity between the competing grades, and thus made it possible to operate quite differently during its last nine years.

The bitter lessons of the differences expressed before the Hobhouse Enquiry forced the associations to consider their attitudes. Cheesman put it as follows:

> The greatest lesson of this experience is, undoubtedly, the power of united action
> . . . The petty jealousies between the classes should be buried for ever, and the whole postal force stand as one man for the good of each and all. The policy of the Department in the past has been to set class against class, well knowing that internecine strife enables them to govern in their own sweet way which ever tends to the cheapening of labour at the expense of the staff.

This was a lesson that had painfully been learnt, but the NJC provided the machinery for applying the lesson. Millard said that the NJC in 1909 'never looked out upon such wide possibilities for good as is the case to-day'. Following this, there was a full discussion on questions of policy, including the carefully formulated demand for a Standing Committee of the House of Commons and, eventually, a full-blooded scheme for the reorganisation of the service including a new hierarchy for promotions. Though neither of these ideas came to much, the general change of mood was indicated by the return in 1910 of the prodigals of the PF, despite continuing differences on policy.[187]

Internal divisions were also broken down by the emergence of what was known at this time as the International Federation of Postal and Telegraph Servants. This came at the initiative of the French Post Office unions, whose strike in 1909 had been followed with considerable interest and sympathy in Britain. Though a few delegations had gone from the PTCA to the equivalent French unions before this, the main French Postal Workers conferences in Lyons in 1909 and again in Marseilles in 1910 were attended by a number of foreign delegates. The result was a meeting in Paris on 6–7 June 1911 which included delegates from the FA, PF and PTCA and agreed to set up a permanent organisation with a Secretariat which came under the leadership of Felix Koch of Switzerland, and also included Stuart. Some information about comparative conditions was published and a second meeting held in London on 25–6 June 1914. The German delegates were legally forbidden from affiliation, but attended as observers. Vague resolutions about international solidarity and against restrictions on civil liberties were ineffectually passed. Attendance of union representatives at meetings of the Universal Postal Union were also proposed. The outbreak of war put a stop to any further activity and Koch died of influenza in 1917.[188]

The war also interrupted the widespread transformation of attitudes amongst British Post Office workers which had followed the transport strikes in the summer of 1911.[189] After the postmen in many areas showed solidarity with striking railmen, their leaders began to express the view that 'we ought not to let present opportunities pass without making an effort to gain something for postal servants'. Delegates at an emergency meeting of the NJC following this exhortation expressed hesitation about acting without a long process of internal consultation. However, the mood of the members in a series of mass meetings that followed pushed the NJC leaders into acting in an unprecedented manner. Thus for the first time the associations acting jointly through the NJC organised the agitation that led to the Holt Enquiry. They jointly agreed the evidence presented to it, and the enormous lobbying effort following it, which compelled the Government to set up the Gibb Committee. Throughout this the Post Office associations operated with a co-ordination they had never shown in the past. The NJC was thus transformed during the last nine years of its existence into an instrument which did have a significant role as a representative and organiser of the diverse grades and their associations.

The negotiations before, during and after the Holt Enquiry have been outlined in Chapter 7. What should be noted here was that the machinery involved was very different from any of the previous inquiries, the whole campaign being run through the NJC, with special meetings of the combined executives of affiliated organisations on three occasions in these years at important turning points. This unity of effort was not achieved without some bitter debate and a number of walk-outs, notably by the UKPCA. However, a unified strategy evolved. Furthermore, none of the affiliates now considered themselves powerful enough to negotiate alone with select committees, postmasters general or MPs, except on their own special problems. In all of this G. H. Stuart, though nominally only Secretary of the Parliamentary Committee, was the dominating figure, leading all the delegations, initiating most of the main lines of policy and clearly in control of most of the changes. By 1915 the NJC's position had become such that its authority was completely accepted on the war bonus agitation, and it also played a major role in the merging of the Engineering and Stores Association with most of the ASTE.

The changed position of the NJC was such that it was also able to get agreement with the P&TCA on the recruitment of telephonists from the ASTE, after strongly condemning both sides for disruption and procrastination in the negotiations.[190] It was the NJC which negotiated all the bonus claims during the war, and elected two members to the Gibb Committee who reported back to it. It was also the NJC that discussed and agreed to the establishment of Whitley councils in the Post Office.[191]

However, it was a long and difficult business before the disunity of the sectional associations could be broken down. Although joint evidence was presented to the Holt Committee, there was no agreement about a general scheme for reorganisation. When protests against the conclusions of Holt developed, there was no common policy about what to do. Although the telegraphists and postal clerks talked about strike action, they refused to take the simple step of organising a ballot of their members on the issue. The militant talk of 1911 and 1913 in the NJC in practice came to nothing. The setting up of the Gibb Committee as a re-run of Holt owed less to the particular skills of the Post Office associates than to the peculiarities of the political situation.[192] These experiences once again compelled the asociations to consider closer co-operation, and they did so with greater seriousness than before.

While the Holt campaign had been going on, unity was consummated between the telegraphists and the postal clerks. Following the failure of the earlier negotiations with the Fawcett Association and the settlement of a number of demarcation disputes, the UKPCA approached the PTCA for unity discussions after their Annual Conference of 1910. By the early part of 1911 a complete scheme for a 'Postal and Telegraph Clerks Association' was outlined, with most of the main features of the organisation eventually set up. The most important difference was that only one officer was to be withdrawn from the service. These proposals were accepted in most of their details by both Executives in September 1911, but an outbreak of local demarcation disputes and objections to some of the statements contained in the preliminary Holt evidence of the UKPCA meant that the entire process was abandoned in September 1912.[193] The uselessness of working separately became clear in the Holt evidence of the two organisations presented in the following month, so the PTCA soon took the initiative for the talks to be resumed. The polls which were held in July 1913 of which the results are given in Appendix 24, showed that the only remaining opposition was within the UKPCA, where some reservations about Labour Party affiliation were still being expressed. However, the two Executives met on 20 August during the Matlock Bath meetings which first discussed strategy against the Holt Report. Soon there was agreement to use PTCA rules but to defer Labour Party affiliation. Nearly all the main tactical questions in relation to the Holt Report were then discussed and agreed between the Joint Executives, including the efforts to postpone the strike ballot. By 23 September, at the height of the post-Holt agitation, it was possible to hold a Joint Conference in Liverpool to finalise most of the details. A further Joint Conference in Leicester on 6 December heard bitter condemnation of association leaders for their weak reaction to the Holt Report. However, nobody now questioned the amalgamation itself and at the beginning of 1914 the Postal and Telegraph Clerks Association finally came into existence.[194]

By this time, serious amalgamation efforts had come from other directions. On the basis of a motion passed at the PF Conference, Stuart called a meeting at the Caxton Hall, London, on 27 October 1913 of fourteen societies including the National Union of Auxiliary Postmen, the CLPA, the ASTE and the Engineering and Stores Association.[195]

The only disagreement at this meeting was about whether supervisors and overseers should be invited to further discussions and it was agreed that they should, by 31 votes to 6. There was no disagreement about the need for amalgamation, and a number of speakers emphasised that it was not just the Holt Report that made this necessary. The Conference elected a Committee which reported to a further meeting on 15 December. This agreed to the constitution of a 'Postal Workers Association' (the word 'union' being consciously avoided), with seven full-time officers and an office in London. The Conference rejected the view of Brown from the PF that there were too many paid officers, and also the efforts of the UKPCA to allow for greater grade autonomy. However, Brown managed to persuade the PF Executive to reject the scheme by 8 votes to 7 as 'undemocratic', and although this decision was condemned later in the year by the Annual Conference, this particular initiative thus came to an end.

Two further developments showed that united action was still very much in the air. The first was the setting up in 1912 of a Civil Service Federation which presented evidence through Ammon to the MacDonnell Commission. The Post Office workers were affiliated through the NJC, and the affiliates from other departments were predominantly from unestablished grades. The Federation worked out a programme initiated by the NJC for five-yearly select committees into the conditions of civil servants, and did some lobbying on the question of superannuation. However, its weight was not much greater than the NJC itself, especially after some of the clerical grades broke away to form the Civil Service Alliance, so it trailed behind on the wartime bonus claims, and it disappeared in the reorganisations at the end of the war.[196]

More hopeful from the point of view of the Post Office associations was that despite the collapse of the proposals discussed at the Caxton Hall meetings, negotiations began in June 1914 between the P&TCA and the FA. However, this discussion was dogged by the reluctance of the P&TCA to take on any obligation for Cheesman and Clery, and by the insistence of the FA on separate union machinery for London sorters. It petered out in the summer of 1915.[197]

Whatever the result of such discussions, the war was now compelling the associations to work together more closely than ever. The campaigns on the war bonus, and the delays in securing any real increase in wages, compelled association leaders to consider again new and more effective methods of organisation. This time the solutions proposed were more diverse and the negotiations more complicated than before. When the second of the bonus claims was going through in the summer of 1916, the P&TCA proposed a joint meeting with the PF, FA and AE&SA which took place on 20 November. This discussed a scheme for amalgamation not very different from the one eventually achieved. The main opponents were now the AE&SA who wanted a federal scheme and delayed further discussion. The meeting of the Sub-Committee which followed on 4 February 1917 was not a success. Stuart-Bunning decided to take the opportunity to object to a paragraph in the *Postal and Telegraph Record* which revealed some detail of confidential NJC discussions with the Arbitration Board. A further meeting on 19 April showed that differences between the associations were growing more acute. The AE&SA had decided that it would not go further than an increase in the powers of the NJC. For its part, the Fawcett Association declared itself to be in favour of a federal scheme. Richardson of the P&TCA wrote privately that what lay behind this was for the AE&SA 'a case of officeholders afraid of their jobs' and for the Fawcett Association a fear that Ammon would lose his predominant position. The P&TCA itself approached the postmen and it announced itself prepared to discuss the possibility of amalgamation with anyone.[198]

At this point the initiative was taken through the NJC. The decision was taken on 4 May 1917 to call a Conference of as many societies as possible to discuss the variety of schemes now in existence. It was also agreed to reorganise the NJC, to abolish the somewhat cumbersome arrangement of having a separate Parliamentary secretary, and to appoint Stuart-Bunning as the authoritative Secretary with an office and a clerk. This step was clearly aimed at allowing Stuart-Bunning to negotiate the amalgamation, though he said privately to Newlove that he thought the prospects for amalgamation were now bleak. However, before he could do anything at all, Newlove and his colleagues on 3 June suddenly decided to walk out of the NJC. Though the P&TCA leaders were unhappy in any case that there had been so much discussion short of amalgamation, the issue on which they walked out was quite a different one. They objected to the suspension of the Gibb Committee and argued with some justice that such decisions would only have been taken in the past with the agreement of all NJC affiliates. They were not in any way prepared to accept the argument from Stuart-Bunning that the past achievements of the NJC 'were won by most people shutting their eyes to the decisions of Annual Conferences and Executives'.

The defection of the P&TCA brought about the bitterest flurry of inter-association charges since the postmen's 'unification' campaign of 1906, spiced this time with personal animosity between George Middleton and Stuart-Bunning. An editorial appeared in the *Postman's Gazette* headed 'Ichabod! Ichabod!' (clearly penned by Stuart-Bunning) which attacked the 'black record' of the P&TCA from the time of the fight against Holt, their acquiescence on the inequality of women in the first war bonus claim and their 'wrecking Amalgamation' by 'sheer stupidity' both in the recent negotiations and before. 'No society is less respected by the Post Office' charged the editorial, and Middleton felt compelled to reply in hurt but not particularly effective terms.[199]

This extraordinary exchange did not provide a very propitious atmosphere for the largest Conference yet of representatives of Post Office associations, which took place in the Caxton Hall on 11 August 1917, a meeting which one participant thought 'remarkable for the number of delegates who spoke at great length and said practically nothing'.[200] The meeting was the most representative that had yet been held, with people from no less than thirty-seven associations present including many from supervisory and clerical grades. However, it proved disastrous from the point of view of amalgamation, with the smaller societies and special interests predominating. The view of many such marginal groups was expressed by Thomas Easthope of the auxiliary postmen who spoke of 'the fear that the official of the smaller societies will be swallowed up' and a spokesman for 200 male supervisors at the Central Telegraph Office who were 'not prepared to sacrifice our autonomy'. Bowen of the PF made an eloquent plea that 'so long as we were willing and desirous in ourselves to preserve and accentuate the differences which prevail in the P.O., so long will the P.O. take advantage of them'. Stuart-Bunning pointed out that organisations like his own had already broken down many sub-divisions that had existed before. The smaller bodies represented did not share these sentiments and since voting was by society, it was their view that predominated. Thus the Conference agreed by 18 to 4 with the proposal of R. W. Slack of the Supervising Officers' Joint Committee to 'two or more federations . . . with a working arrangement'. Even a motion calling on those who wanted to amalgamate to go ahead was defeated. A committee was set up which worked out a scheme for three different federations, manipulative, supervisory and clerical, with a Federal Council, which was approved at a further meeting in Caxton Hall on 11 December.

By the time of this second meeting, however, matters had moved very fast, and relations between the societies had changed dramatically. Not only were the smaller societies determined to maintain their identity but the AE&SA, despite earlier support for amalgamation, now said that their members 'stand in a special position by reason of their craft and the peculiar nature of their working conditions'.[201] The FA declared the Federation proposals to be 'an excellent scheme' and soon Harry Dubery, *Post* Editor, was its provisional full-time Secretary. Although the first full meeting on 23 March could announce 41,000 in the Federation, it was now tiny and unrepresentative.[202] The postmen and the P&TCA never participated in the federation scheme at first because they wanted to defend the NJC. Eventually, the

Fawcett Association was also compelled to withdraw, and all that was left was a Federation of Supervising Officers with Dubery until 1921 at its head. In some ways this was just as well, because there would certainly have been strong objections to including supervisors in any amalgamation. The AE&SA also formed a Federation with some of the superior grades on the engineering side later in 1918, remained isolated from the rest of the service and changed its name to the Post Office Engineering Union in June 1919.[203]

Two days after the big Caxton Hall meeting of 11 August 1917 Stuart-Bunning decided that it was necessary to make a new approach on behalf of the Postmen's Federation to the P&TCA, despite his recent public polemic against its leaders. Stuart-Bunning was concerned not only to resist a federation scheme which was designed to swamp the large societies at the expense of small sectional bodies. He also wanted to develop an effective instrument which could act in a possible Whitley Council scheme in the civil service. For their part, the P&TCA was the only organisation still unequivocally committed to amalgamation and they decided quite independently that their sole option now was 'to approach the PF with an urgent appeal for them to consider the importance of early amalgamation with us'. Within a short period Stuart-Bunning found there to be 'no question as to the desire of the Postal and Telegraph Association to amalgamate with us'. It was in this spirit that agreement was reached on 13 September at a meeting of two sub-committees held in Matlock. Only two members of the P&TCA leadership were opposed to alliance with the postmen – Charles Mulholland who soon afterwards withdrew from the Post Office, and the Treasurer J. F. Hunter who took promotion in 1919 and eventually retired in 1938 as Assistant Postmaster of Leeds. For the rest, Mabel Bray expressed herself 'agreeably surprised' at the lack of serious reservations about a scheme which now included many features eventually agreed. There were to be eight or nine full-time officers, a London Headquarters, a weekly journal and a separate Mutual Benefit Society based on the PF's.

On 27 October 1917 a joint meeting of PF and P&TCA Executives was held in Birmingham. This was described in the *Postman's Gazette* as 'a red letter day in the annals of Postal Trade Unionism'. However, although 'joint working' began on the first day of 1918 there were many details still to settle. There was a good deal of argument about the likely role and respective salaries of the full-time officials of the new body, some of which derived from the decisions which remained within the P&TCA. It was also difficult to bring together the varied means of working of the two organisations. The P&TCA opposed the system of sub-committees which ran the PF, but were strongly in favour of maintaining a Parliamentary Committee so that they could continue 'to use Parliament on every occasion in order to continually harass and worry the Post Office'. Other problems concerned the certainty of increased subscriptions, difficult in particular for smaller bodies like the Central London Postman's Association, Messengers Association, London Postal Porters and the Sorting Assistants, who were already expressing a desire to join. The smaller organisations were also unlikely to fit in with the reserved Executive places then being proposed.[204]

The next meeting of joint Executives, held in Matlock on 12 January 1918, was not a success.[205] The P&TCA strongly attacked the proposals for complete centralisation being put forward by the PF. In particular they objected to the idea of all subscriptions being sent to the Central Office, and Riley considered that 'local autonomy', with strong branches, 'had been the key to the success of our Society'.

Herbert Parker of the P&TCA, who was personally opposed to amalgamation, went further:

> I am afraid myself that a result of amalgamation – I had the same fear when the PTCA and the UKPCA amalgamated – may be the creation of so large a body as to have tendency to less effectiveness in its real work in the Department. You get tremendous offices with a large number of clerks, and instead of conducting your warfare with the Department as you should be doing, you are eternally managing or mismanaging your own affairs.

Thus spoke some older traditions in Post Office trade unions and amongst P&TCA leaders. Parker grew so worried that he began to discuss behind the scenes with Stuart-Bunning about what needed to be done to prevent the two organisations from drifting apart.

By the time the joint Executives met again on 23 February 1918, there was full agreement that a common attitude needed to be taken to the Whitley proposals and a greater propensity to compromise on other matters. It was now accepted that there would be a combined system of district councils and district organisers, and that about a quarter of subscriptions could be retained by branches. Thus by the time of the second meeting of the proposed federation held at the end of March the PF and P&TCA were in a position to announce the outline of their amalgamation scheme and interim joint working arrangements. Already on 16 March J. M. McGriffith of the Fawcett Association Central Committee approached Newlove of the P&TCA for discussions. Within smaller organisations like the Telephone Provincial Clerical and Contract Officers Association there were arguments raging about whether they should continue to support the Federation.[206]

Meanwhile, the P&TCA and PF negotiations were proceeding. A further joint Executive meeting on 4 May agreed to continue the campaign for Whitley councils in the civil service. Disagreements between the two organisations were now narrowed down to the PF's desire to be more generous with officers' pensions, and its refusal to agree to married women being officers. Though the views of the postmen generally predominated on these points, there was some further delay before they were put into effect. This was partly because it was not thought possible to proceed until the end of the war, and partly because the P&TCA Conference in May insisted on passing a number of modifications to the proposed scheme, mainly on the position of the officers. This did not prove acceptable to the negotiators and a further Special Conference was held in November at which the original scheme was passed unamended. Already there were schemes for joint work in operation in some branches, and by January 1919 both organisations were in a position to organise ballots for their members.[207]

At this point the FA, pushed hard by Charles Ammon, approached the others for discussions, which began on 23 April. They asked for a separate London District Council for Sorters and two reserved seats on the proposed Executive. These proposals were promptly accepted. The FA remained, however, the junior partners in the amalgamation and were not in a position to get their candidate Ammon proposed as Deputy General Secretary or Editor. Ammon only became Organising Secretary and Cheesman, who was due to retire soon, was one of the assistant secretaries. The other full-time positions ended with four from the PF and six from the P&TCA. The first Executive only slightly reduced this imbalance with ten lay members from the PF and seven from the P&TCA together with the two reserved places for the FA.[208]

Once the amalgamation ballots had been successfully completed during the summer, a Joint Conference of the three societies took place on 18–20 September 1919 in the Central Hall, Westminster, and the amalgamation was confirmed.[209] The Central London Postmen's Association was also represented even though it still existed as a separate organisation. Most of the main points which had been agreed between the Executives of the three organisations were accepted, but there were some important changes agreed. Following from the arguments about local financial autonomy, the Conference agreed that 'branches shall be empowered to collect and retain any additional subscriptions that may be required for local trade union purposes'. Also the Conference agreed to a rate of representation at future conferences of the amalgamated society which made it certain that they would be enormous assemblies of over 1,000 members. This persists to the present day in the UCW allowing for the representation of a wide range of the Union's members.

One interesting aspect of the amalgamation was the position acquired by G. H. Stuart-Bunning. As the first Post Office worker deliberately taken out of the service in 1902 and as by far the most experienced and clear-headed negotiator he had become the dominant figure in Post Office trade unionism for at least the last ten years before the setting up of the Union of Post Office Workers. He had led all the major deputations before and after the Holt Report and the negotiations and arbitration proceedings during the war. He had also initiated all the main lines of Association policy including the reaction to the Holt Report, the setting up of the Gibb Committee, the campaign for Whitley councils and, of course, the amalgamation itself. Thus on 29 November 1917 Middleton wrote to Parker on the position: 'Everyone speaks of the General Secretaryship as synonymous with S-B, and it is taken for granted by the PF that he will be an agreed nominee for that position'. However, this did not come about and the reasons bear some discussion. The fact was that, for all his dominating personality, Stuart-Bunning did not suffer fools gladly. In the words of one of his civil service trade union colleagues many years later: 'his great capacity was marred by a great lack of generosity'.

Even besides this he had had a number of important disagreements during 1918 and 1919 with his colleagues in the PF leadership. He thought some of the later claims to the Arbitration Board were discriminating in favour of the better off. He signed an official report about the employment of ex-servicemen which seemed virtually certain to undermine conditions in the service, and was repudiated by all the other members of the PF Executive as well as the NJC. He disagreed with the claim for shorter hours that was formulated in 1919, since he thought it would lead to a loss of jobs. He then resigned his positions both as Secretary of the NJC and of the PF, and refused to stand as secretary of the amalgamated society, claiming that he was quite out of sympathy with its likely policies. Stuart-Bunning's arrogance had made him many enemies, and it was only by 29 votes to 13 that the joint Executives agreed to propose that he should be kept on at a fee of £200 per annum in an 'advisory capacity'. Just what this involved was never clear, though it was perhaps a device to allow him to remain a member of the TUC Parliamentary Committee, of which he had just been elected President. However, the amalgamation Conference refused to accept Stuart-Bunning's new role, some delegates hinting at the 'mystery' behind his position and the possibility that he had a number of other lucrative jobs lined up. His 'advisory' role was rejected by 956 votes to 607 and in a dramatic flourish at the end of the Conference, where his advocacy of the amalgamation scheme was dominant, he responded to a vote of thanks in this way:

> forgive me if I remind you of a little custom they had in Italy in mediaeval times, which is sometimes practiced in the present day, of inviting a man to dinner and poisoning him or stabbing him to get rid of him by some convenient means. Then afterwards to absolve the conscience of the people who did it they used to raise glorious monuments to his memory. Your vote of thanks reminds me of that custom. You gave me a vote of thanks yesterday when you decided that I was no longer fit to hold any part in your movement . . .

At this, the amalgamation Conference broke up in confusion and silence with one delegate shouting 'now cheer him'.[210]

The amalgamation brought into question not just the position of Stuart-Bunning but also of the NJC. During the war it had begun to adopt a dominant role which would have been inconceivable a decade before. It co-ordinated all the main wage claims and negotiations with the authorities on more minor questions. It provided the predominant weight within the Civil Service Federation which spoke for a large proportion of the entire public sector. From 1916 it even organised the intervention of postal workers' leaders at the TUC. In the past their delegations had mainly contented themselves with getting resolutions passed supporting their own rights to decent wages and conditions. The role now grew much more important. In 1916 Ammon was delegate to the American Federation of Labor Conference in the United States and in 1918–19 Stuart-Bunning was TUC President, negotiating on labour conditions with the Versailles peace makers. The work of the NJC in 1918 and 1919 increased dramatically and it began to consider even quite minor matters of Post Office conditions. However, once the amalgamation was under way it became obvious that one of the traditional problems would be intensified. Bowen told the NJC meeting in late July 1919:

> I cannot see how it is possible for the Amalgamated Society, with its huge membership, to come here with a small representation and run the risk of being outvoted by the representatives of the smaller societies on almost everything connected with their policy.

Given this, there seemed little further to say. A number of the smaller societies joined the UPW, and the NJC wound itself up on 15 January 1920 with a few words from Cheesman, its only surviving founder.[211]

This was the end of an era for Post Office trade unionism. Joint work had been necessary at a time when joint organisation was impossible. There were other ways in which common attitudes had been moulded, and the final section of this chapter will describe them.

THE GREGARIOUS POST OFFICE WORKER

In order to complete this account of two generations of Post Office trade unionists, a brief account must be given of some of the numerous other forms of association which existed within the Post Office in the same period. The ranks and grades of hierarchy were cut across in the early part of this century not simply by the efforts of the associations but also by an enormous range of charitable, insurance and political activity which existed the length and breadth of the service. These go a long way to explain the marked changes in the attitudes and aspirations of ordinary Post Office workers that have been referred to many times in this chapter, and go some way to forming the character of life and work in the Post Office in later generations.

There has already been reason to refer to the close links between the members of the Fawcett Association and the numerous sporting and other social activities in which they engaged.[212] However, even the list given there reflects only the smallest part of the many social activities that existed in the Post Office. Some of these were charitable institutions, often initiated by the authorities themselves. The most well known of these was, and is, the Rowland Hill Benevolent Fund set up in 1882 with the money left over from what had been collected for the erection of the statue to Rowland Hill at St Martin's-le-Grand. This fund provides for distress among Post Office workers or their dependants. After complaints about its remoteness from many Post Office workers, the associations were allowed, in 1910, to nominate representatives on its governing body.[213] Another charitable organisation which still exists was founded in 1870. This is the Post Office Orphan Homes Benevolent Institution, looking after the children of those in the London Postal Service. The growing role of the associations was indicated by the fact that the Post Office Sanatorium Movement, which a high proportion of the workforce joined, was initiated by the PTCA, supported by the authorities, and run mostly by union leaders. It later became the Civil Service Sanatorium Society.[214] The unions also took a close interest in the Post Office Relief Fund, set up during the First World War by a Committee whose 'democratic character' was shown by its inclusion both of the wife of the Postmaster General and various association leaders.[215] These are but examples of numerous other charitable bodies that existed in the Post Office.[216] There were others of a more directly utilitarian character like the Civil Service Supply Association set up in 1873 for the purchase of wholesale goods, or the Post Office Employees Mutual Guarantee Association, wound up in 1909 after making regular payments over the years and providing a handsome final payment to its members.[217]

There was another form of association of even greater importance to Post Office workers in the days of Victorian self-help, and these were the Benevolent or Insurance Societies, which did much to bring together Post Office workers from different offices and grades in the period when associations were first built. The first and most well known of these was the United Kingdom Postal and Telegraph Benevolent Society, set up in 1875 by established rank-and-file members of all sections of the service in the town of Northampton, by which name it was normally thereafter known. It aimed to provide small grants to widows, dependants or nominees of members when they died, and at first did this by means of a 'call' system, or levy of 1d on every member at the time of each death.[218] Despite the initial suspicion of the authorities, the 'Northampton's' founder John Asher managed to get the approval of Postmaster General Manners and within a year there were over 2,000 members. In 1881 a 'Widowers Branch' was added, and in 1899 a 'gratuity branch' by means of which payments could be made in the event of retirement from the service. As the membership by now had reached nearly 20,000 and the 'call' system had become impractical, a small reserve fund was initiated in 1903 with a partial system of fixed weekly contributions in 1906.[219]

The 'Northampton' proved so popular that a number of similar institutions were soon set up. In 1877 there began a Post Office Insurance Society which had insurance and gratuity branches and was based on regular but rather higher contributions. This was sometimes known as 'the Sammy Small' after its secretary in the early years and later secretaries included A. J. Mosedale of the FA and J. L. A. Cartwright, who was perhaps related to the UKPCA founder of the same name. The 'Sammy Small' was almost entirely dominated by leading members of the Post Office associations. Stuart was Chairman for many years, with Buckland, Lincoln and other PF leaders playing a conspicuous role. It also became the largest society with over 36,000 members in 1908, and seems to have been the only one to register under the Friendly Societies' Act in the early period.[220] The refusal of either of these societies to admit unestablished Post Office workers, despite a campaign led by H. M. Wilson of the PF, resulted in the setting up in 1894 of the 'Amalgamated Postal and Telegraph Benefit Society', sometimes known as 'the Wandsworth'. By 1909 this had just under 15,500 members, a full range of benefits and a rather lower average age than the others, a fact which probably saved it from some of the same problems.[221] There was also a Civil Service Insurance Society set up in 1890 which organised life insurance through the major companies,[222] as well as a number of Approved Societies set up under the 1911 National Insurance Act.

These Societies provided benefits for Post Office workers and brought together many of the association leaders, but they did so on a basis which often provoked bitter and complicated controversy. From the very start the 'Northampton' was subject to suspicion. When the PTCA was being set up in 1881, it began its own gratuity section because it was considered 'entirely problematical whether the new entrants into the establishment will join the Northampton Association in such numbers as will keep the benefits up to the present scale' since at the start many 'old men, too old indeed to join an ordinary Insurance or Burial Club entered the Northampton' without any medical tests. In later years it was thought that the call system would save 'an institution which has no actuarial basis, and which, if the laws of political economy were not so uncertain and unreliable in their action, would have died a violent and ignoble death years ago'. Further attacks followed as the Society moved closer to the point when people would begin to get less out than they had put in. In 1902 it was described as a 'combination of indiscriminate charity with un-assured Insurance and irresponsible Patronage'.[223] Criticisms of this kind led to series of changes of rule in 1906 and again in 1909 which introduced a combination of weekly subscriptions and the call system which essentially meant, as was inevitable eventually, that older members would now receive less than they had paid. An actuarial report in 1913 led to further changes being proposed at the 1914 General Meeting. A court case was organised against the Society which found that the earlier alterations of rule had not been made according to the proper form, so after a great deal more money was paid out, the recommended changes were introduced at a stormy meeting in June 1916 chaired by J. C. Brown.[224]

The passion provoked by these events spilt out into the pages of the association journals. An ill conceived defence of the old order was organised by George Lascelles, founder of UKPCA. A similar dispute broke out in the Post Office Insurance Society following another unfavourable actuarial report, but after one conference refused to act on these recommendations, another special one had to be called to do so from 1918.[225] The development of National Health Insurance, old age pensions and other welfare benefits gave these benefit societies a different significance in later years in the eyes of ordinary Post Office workers. Some have continued to use them, however, and they continue unobtrusively to this day, filling a small corner in Post Office life. The 'Northampton' wisely registered under the Friendly Societies Act in 1921. In 1931 it announced its willingness to merge with similar societies and in 1937–8 united with the 'Wandsworth' as the United Kingdom Civil Service Benefit Society.

Though these organisations and societies certainly involved very large numbers of Post Office workers, there were some others which had smaller membership but greater influence on the associations. During the nineteenth century the sabbatarian movement was of some importance for Post Office workers, and much has been made in earlier chapters of this. It is hard to discover, however, if many Post Office workers were actively involved in the various sabbatarian organisations, other than on a purely trade union basis. There was, however, a more active General Post Office Temperance Society in existence from 1877.[226] The founding President was Arthur Blackwood, later Post Office Secretary, a devout evangelical Protestant who specialised in distributing religious tracts to the sorters and postmen at St Martin's-le-Grand. In 1890, the year he organised the smashing of the postmen's strike, he produced his own tract called 'For the Good of Service', which recruited a number of other Post Office workers to the temperance crusade. In 1899, it was later said, there were as many as 8,400 members, but this was its zenith. In 1904 it only claimed 3,237 and this had fallen to 400 in the 1930s when the Post Office Total Abstinence Society was only producing a duplicated magazine. However, its well-wishers still included Samuel Belderson who set up the PTCA together with the aged J. H. Williams, and Charles Ammon, MP, founders of the FA.[227] Another significant nineteenth-century institution in which some Post Office workers were involved was the volunteer movement, and the 24th Middlesex Volunteers were also known as the Post Office Rifles. A number of members fought in the Boer War, and G. H. Stuart was an active member.

During the decades covered in this chapter very different attitudes from those involved in joining organisations such as these began to emerge. The generation of Williams and Belderson, the gentlemanly lobbyists, was replaced by one which included socialists, syndicalists and those who responded to all the changes in feeling and attitude sweeping the trade union world. For reasons outlined in detail in Chapter 4, and elsewhere, Post Office workers had to think more deeply than some others about how it was possible to negotiate the improvement of wages. In all the sections of this chapter a radically changed attitude from active members in 1911 and again after 1918 has been traced in some detail. The effect of the contact with electoral politics and with the TUC and Labour Party has been mentioned. There were also some special influences at work within the Post Office itself.

The role of Marxists in setting up the Postmen's Union of 1890 has been described elsewhere, but this was repudiated and usually forgotten later. The Fawcett Association's founder, E. J. Nevill, was involved in the socialist movement and acted with William Morris, though it is difficult to trace much of this in Nevill's trade union conduct. However, there was a small but persistent left wing within the Post Office workforce of some importance for the early UPW, and something should be said about this. In 1894 a number of FA members who were in the newly formed Independent Labour Party ran a meeting at the Fawcett Association Headquarters which set up a Postal Socialist League.[228] There was a similar organisation at the East Central District Office with 120 members and another at the Central Telegraph Office called the 'Pioneer Socialist Society'. These two merged in 1906 as the Post Office Socialist Society and in 1908 united with a number of other local bodies to form the 'Civil Service Socialist Society'.[229]

A number of Conservative MPs asked Parliamentary questions about this body and attributed various sinister motives to its founders. They need not have worried. In reply to questions from the Postmaster General, they said they were 'educational' and 'non-political', and in fact they carried on their existence quietly without much direct or immediate effect on official life or trade unionism. However, the CSSS did have important long-term effects. The first Editor of its journal was J. G. Newlove, and amongst its provincial correspondents were John Craven from Hull, Arthur O'Donnell from Manchester and J. Craig Walker from Leeds. There were 900 at a meeting in February 1908 addressed by Victor Grayson, the MP recently elected to Parliament as a 'Socialist', and H. M. Hyndman of the Social Democratic Federation. In 1908 a circulation of 2,000 was claimed for the *Civil Service Socialist*. If these developments did not provoke the street fighting prophesied by Conservative MPs, they did have a significant effect on many future union leaders, who seem to have predominated in the Society. In the early period the Society mostly concerned itself with abstract discussions in support of socialism, but after about 1910 when Newlove went on to Ruskin College, it grew more interested in the theories of the syndicalist movement, at that time widely discussed among sections of younger trade unionists. The syndicalists within the FA, whose conflict with authority had been described already, were a fringe group of limited influence. However, those involved in the Civil Service Socialist Society were of much greater importance. John Craven moved the first motion calling for 'popular control' of the 'Postal Telegraph Service' at the April 1913 PTCA Conference, which then became the policy of the time. Mabel Hope, who wrote regularly in the journal, was a witness for the women of the Central Telegraph Office to both Hobhouse and Holt Committees. Craig Walker and O'Donnell were both active in the UKPCA and were later leaders of the UPW. These three led the walk-out at the December 1913 Joint Conference of the PTCA and UKPCA which discussed but rejected strike action against the Holt Report. If militant industrial policies were of limited importance for the immediate future, Guild Socialism became a policy which Newlove campaigned for on his return to be General Secretary of the P&TCA in 1914, with the support of G. D. H. Cole who taught it to him in Oxford.[230]

The generation that set up the Union of Post Office Workers was fired with the attitudes that derived from all the pre-war discussions in the working-class movement. How far they had travelled can be seen from the remoteness of the spirit that informed this message of the founder of the United Kingdom Postal Clerks' Association, George Lascelles, to the 1897 Conference:

Nothing could be more detrimental to their cause than to adopt the questionable policy of mechanics etc., who in order to secure a share of increased profits of their trade were prepared to bring temporary misery to thousands of lives. Our profession is not a fluctuating one, and we cannot transfer our services from one employer to another, therefore they should forever banish all talk of strikes in any shape or form as outside the region of practical politics.

Such was not the attitude of the postmen in Salford who refused to deliver circulars in 1909 or of the temporary employees in Glasgow who struck with the support of the Trades Council in 1916.[231]

While these were isolated incidents, they showed changing attitudes, making the postmen refuse to do the work of railwaymen in 1911 and again in 1919, when the UPW first came into existence. The effects of the Holt agitation and the First World War were to create a different breed of Post Office worker from the ladies and gentlemen who had set up the associations in earlier generations. There was talk before the war against 'the old men with their old-fashioned methods hampering Postmen's Federation', and preventing 'any progress whatever'. Afterwards it was said:

> The Post Office will find the men and women of to-day are very different beings to those they dealt with five or six years ago. The order of things has changed, the worker is no longer content to drag out a bare existence, knowledge has come to them of their power, and with this has also come a determination to have their rights.

Yet there were some things that had not changed. In 1919 Bowen explained why the Executive of the Postmen's Federation refused to take up the case of a postman who had been dismissed for living with a married postwoman. 'The point is whether this man has conducted himself decently, he accepted the conditions of service in the Post Office, and he ought to uphold its standards of morals'.[232] Clearly, in all the changing attitudes of these years, there were some things that had not changed.

NOTES

1 *PG* 1896, p. 658, 4 February 1893. Other cases are outlined in an interesting document in R V/9, prepared for submission to the Holt Enquiry.
2 The chief material on the FA is in R VI (which largely consists of Minutes of Committees and General Meetings) and *Post*, 1890–1919.
3 *Post* 1912, p. 433; Hobhouse Evidence, p. 193.
4 R VI/13, 14 April 1905, for the beginning of the dispute. The rest can be traced through the minute books and *Post*, especially 1907, p. 429 for the first 'plebiscite', 1909, p. 223, for the second, and 1910, pp. 313ff. and 1911, pp. 98–9 for the negotiations with the authorities. The letter columns of the *Post* (eg 1909, pp. 166, 324) do much to illuminate the competing interests involved.
5 R VI/8, p. 84, /9, p. 9, and /14, 18 March 1908. See also pp. 248 below.
6 *Post*, 13 February 1898, 1911 p. 61, 1914, p. 443, and UPW 1920 AR, p. 30. Full details are given in Appendix 14, p. 634.
7 R VI/20, pp. 137–40, /10, p. 166; *Post*, 4 November 1933, p. 368; *Red Tape*, October 1933, pp. 17–24.
8 *Post* 1906, p. 85, 1907, pp. 85–6, 104–5 on the bagmen.
9 Copies of the 1900 and 1913 FA Rules are in R VI/22, as well as a document called *Officers' Duties, Accounts etc.* R IV/11 has the 1904 rules and VI/4 contains details of the discussion at the time of their adoption. For some of the more important of subsequent changes see *Post*, 1 January 1898, 30 January 1904, 1910 pp. 64–6 and 460–3 for the version of that time.
10 *Post* 1912, p. 251.
11 *Post*, 9 December 1899 and 1910, pp. 64, 66, 75–6 and 99; R VI/14, 11 September 1907; *Post* 1910, p. 461.
12 R VI/14, June–July 1907, 7 September 1908.
13 R VI/9, pp. 3,428, /16, 20 September 1911.
14 For the discussion on the return on funds, see *Post* 1910, pp. 69–70.
15 R VI/16, 5 February 1913; *Post*, 12 May 1900, 1914 pp. 422–3, 1915, pp. 97–8.
16 R VI/3, p. 165, on the 1891 position of the Editor being accountable only to the members and /9, p. 179, on responsibility to the Central Committee in 1900. The controversy can be traced in the latter volume in R and in *Post* from 16 September 1899 on.
17 *Post* 1908, especially pp. 262, 497ff.
18 Burns attacked Clery's outside interests largely, it seems, in an effort to cast doubt on the *bona fides* of any of his opponents. Clery's challenge to a public debate was not taken up (*Post*, 15 September, 3 November 1894).
19 R VI/3, p. 303, /7, p. 210 on the early congresses. On Clery's proposed candidatures see *Post*, 3 September 1898 (Walworth in 1893) and R VI/7, p. 248 (Glasgow in 1895). For the 1897 events, *Post* 5 June, 17 July, and R VI/8, p. 272.
20 R VI/9, *Post* 24 June, 1 April 1899 and 9 June 1900.
21 LRC 1903 Report, pp. 15, 26; *Post*, February 1936, p. 87; Thompson (1967), p. 243.
22 See Clinton (1983), and *Post* 1918, p. 52.
23 *PG* 1901, p. 347.
24 R VI/14, 13 March 1907; *Post* 1908, p. 86, 1910, pp. 90, 89, 1913, pp. 578, 369.
25 Holton (1976), pp. 44–5 for the Industrialist League, and *Industrialist*, September 1909 and February 1910, for the offending articles. See also *Post* 1911, pp. 291, 270 for the quotations, 160, 264 for the court case, and 379 for the special meeting.
26 *Post* 1915, pp. 226, 214, 361ff., 1916, p. 353, 1918, pp. 281, 353.
27 *Post* (18 September 1893). For various references to the personalities, see R VI/8, pp. 303, *Post*, 2 February 1895, 28 May 1898, 16 February 1901.
28 R VI/10, p. 190, /20, p. 65.
29 G. H. Stuart-Bunning in *Red Tape*, April 1931, p. 445.
30 *Post*, 4 January 1896, for one of countless examples.
31 The rules were first published in 1896 and came out in most later years as part of the membership card. There are copies of most of them in R I/33 and in MC. The files at RI consist largely of the minutes of the PF Executive. *PG* is the fullest service journal up to the war, with a considerable range of local notes, usually of limited interest. PG 1918, p. 1, on the title.
32 *PG* 1901, p. 284, for the history of the Manchester Branch which can also be traced in *The Postman* and its successors. For Brighton see Paul (1924) and for the table R I/13, 20 October 1906, pp. 38–9.

33 *PG* 1903, pp. 143–4, for the scheme and R I/10, 20 January 1905 and /9, 22 October 1904 for the comments. *PG* 1911, pp. 172, 297 gives the later position.
34 Rule Books give subscription details, and other points are in R I/5, p. 55, /7, 10–11 October 1902; *PG* 1909, p. 461, 1910, p. 187, 1914, p. 249.
35 *PG* 1901, p. 251, 1896, p. 594, 1904, p. 266.
36 *PG* 1897, p. 553, 1898, pp. 182, 375, 373, 406 and 1904, p. 348. See also R I/2.
37 *PG* 1903, p. 150, 1909, pp. 317–21, 1911, p. 305, R I/18.
38 *PG* 1907, p. 293, R I/16, 15 August 1907, pp. 8–11, 15.
39 *PG* 1897, p. 449, 1907, pp. 87–93, 293–7, 1908, pp. 297–9, 436–7, 1907, pp. 150ff., 308ff., 1918, p. 363; R I/13, 20 October 1906, p. 59.
40 R I/1, 20 October 1892.
41 *PG* 1905, p. 171; R I/21, 28 October 1911, pp. 29–48.
42 There was a long campaign on this question, in particular by the PF, and it was the first major concession after recognition. Hobhouse Report, p. 7; POC, 1782, 13 August 1907.
43 *PG* 1904, p. 261; R I/20, 12 February 1910, p. 18.
44 *PG* June, July and August 1892, 1916, p. 61, 1913, p. 705 and R I/25, 6 January 1914, pp. 17–24.
45 *PG* 1908, pp. 454, 541, 1909, p. 619, 1911, p. 857 and R I/21, 15 April 1911.
46 R I/16, 19 October 1907, pp. 8–9 and /9, 22 July 1904, p. 14, /7, 11 October 1902.
47 *PG* 1898, p. 374, 1908, pp. 140–1; R I/16, 18 January 1907, p. 36, 5 August 1907. See pp. 267f. for non-trade-union benefit schemes.
48 *PG* 1897, p. 460, 1902, p. 115.
49 R I/14 is a verbatim report of the special conference.
50 R I/6, 26 June 1903; *PG* 1903, pp. 309–11, 1908, pp. 192–3, 1909, p. 216.
51 *PG* 1909, p. 201; R I/11, 20 January 1905, /13, 27 April 1906, p. 7, on the promoted groups and attitudes to them.
52 *PG* 1897, pp. 254, 264; R I/20, 22 July 1910, p. 2, /33 for a NUAP leaflet. See p. 248 and below, n.146.
53 R I/18, 22 October 1909, p. 28, /21, 27 October 1911; *PG* 1916, p. 270, 1917, p. 157, 1918, p. 182, 1919, p. 166.
54 Paul (1924), p. 11; PF, *Explanatory Pamphlet concerning the Postmen's Federation* (Glasgow, 1900), pp. 5, 7; *PG* (18 March 1893).
55 *PG* 1897, pp. 423, 441.
56 *PG* 1898, pp. 198, 214, 1902, pp. 252ff.; R I/2.
57 *PG* 1906, p. 76. The election address is in R IV/23 and some other points in Poirier (1958), pp. 263, 267, and *Civil Service Magazine*, 1903, p. 137.
58 *PG* 1908, pp. 219, 232–3, 291–5; Labour Party 1909 Report, pp. 61–2.
59 *PG* 1910, p. 86.
60 *PG* 1911, pp. 286–9; *Labour Leader*, 2 December 1910, p. 763 on 'Knavish Tricks'.
61 R I/20, 22 July 1910, pp. 5–11; *PG* 1918, p. 386.
62 *PG* 1911, pp. 558–60, 572; R I/21, 28 October 1911, 1/33, for efforts by Stuart to prevent the Dundee Branch expelling Wight, and some inconclusive information reflecting on his motives.
63 *PG* 1914, p. 355.
64 For discussions on NW Durham, including the legal difficulties of contesting it, see R I/17, 6 December 1906 and /25, 4 January 1914, pp. 1–4. For the campaign, *PG* 1914, pp. 60–1, and the quotation *Times*, 2 February 1914.
65 *PG* 11 November 1893, 14 April 1894, 1904, p. 419, 1905, pp. 1–2, 57.
66 Some details of these disputes can be found in F 299.3 and PFCE I, pp. 78–9, with the other quotation in *PG* 1907, p. 368.
67 R I/21, 20 August 1911, *PG* 1911, pp. 442ff., 1913, p. 313, 1917, p. 152.
68 *PG* 1917, p. 152; R I/23, 25 April 1913, pp. 13–14, 4 July 1913, p. 2.
69 *PG* 1913, p. 376 and R I/23, 25 July 1913, p. 14.
70 Relations were often strained with these other associations, partly because of doubts about the justice of the claim itself and partly because the ex-servicemen often denied the right of the PF to take up the issue of all – F 229.3, R I/21, 31 May 1911, p. 5, and /17 *passim*. See also *The Campaigner*, February 1918.
71 Chapter 7, p. 191, and *PG* 1917, p. 88.
72 See above, Chapter 6, p. 131. UKPCA records in R II do not include even a complete set of Executive minutes and no rule books have been discovered, nor records of any kind before 1894. The 1897 Minute Book is in MC. See also Lascelles (1936), pp. 464–5.
73 Holt Evidence, p. 620, sets out the differences.

74 This incident was rarely referred to later, though *PJ* 20 August 1893 and December, 1895, p. 122, say something about it. The *Post Office Journal* of the period doubtless contains more, but I have not located any copies.
75 R II/2 for the Conference. *PJ* October 1895, p. 56, implies peculation on the part of Casey, though *PJ* January 1896, p. 216, shows that some members thought he was badly treated.
76 Lascelles outlines most of this in *PJ* July 1898, pp. 782–3, and other details are in R II/2 and /4 and *PG* 1896, pp. 518–9. According to W. J. Davis in *Post*, 16 September 1933, p. 233, Kendrick tried to persuade the NJC to take over the *Journal*.
77 R II/4; *PCH* March 1903, p. 139.
78 *PCH* 1910, p. 241; R II/3 and 5.
79 *PCH* 1907, p. 53.
80 R II/1 and /9, Sheffield Branch minutes, and /6 for Liverpool. *PCH* 1908, p. 222.
81 *PCH* February 1902, p. 128, May 1905, pp. 292–3, 1907, pp. 101–2, 1910, p. 597, 1911, p. 30.
82 *PJ* June 1894, September 1895, p. 41, *PCH* 1908, p. 180, 1910, pp. 141ff., 1912, pp. 156ff.
83 *PJ* 1895, pp. 59, 75, 172, 211 and May 1895, p. 292 for the quotation. R II/7, pp. 14–15, 40–1, 207 for the merger discussions, though the reasons for their collapse, probably related to the internal problems of the FA over Clery, are not clear.
84 *PJ* January 1895, p. 238, August 1897, p. 590, August 1898, p. 301; R II/4, p. 200; *PCH* 1907, p. 346, 1909, p. 99, 1912, pp. 193–4, 255, 1913, pp. 223, 251, 269.
85 *PCH* 1908, pp. 166–7, 1909, pp. 96, 500–1.
86 *PJ* February 1896, p. 244; *PCH* 1909, p. 501, 1912, pp. 259, 746.
87 *PCH* February 1899; R II/4, p. 124.
88 *PCH* 1901, pp. 335–6, 1902, p. 122, May 1905, p. 304, November 1905, p. 38, February 1906, p. 150, December 1906, p. 556, 1911, pp. 231–3, 1910, p. 212, 1912, p. 198.
89 *PCH* 1909 *passim* especially pp. 334, 335 and *Hansard* V, 4, 220ff. (27 April 1909). See also *Post*, 6 October 1923, p. 313.
90 *PCH* 1909, pp. 353ff., 1910, pp. 2–3.
91 *PCH* 1910, pp. 193ff., 1911, pp. 807, 229–30, 326, 1912, pp. 200, 1913, pp. 217ff., 521; TUC 1912 Report, pp. 254–6, 1913 Report, p. 83. In R II/12 there is a copy of a pamphlet (Crossley, n.d. 1911?) dealing with the postal cheque and transfer system. For the delegations see POR 6636/1911.
92 *PJ* 1896, p. 295, 1898, p. 802.
93 *PCH* 1909, pp. 183–5, 205–6, 1910, pp. 114–8. Reynolds (1910), p. 3 in R II/12. See also Chapter 6 p. 129.
94 *PCH* 1912, pp. 125–7, 227, 262, 1913, pp. 180–3, 209; R II/11. The 1913 Conference is also discussed on pp. 260.
95 *PCH* 1913, pp. 10–11, 26–7, 575, 1914, p. 3.
96 See above Chapter 6, pp. 128–30 and Chapter 7, pp. 163–4.
97 The PTCA records at R IV are rather fuller than for the UKPCA. There are also two minute books in MC at the time of writing for 1882–91 and for 1904–7. Besides Hall (1902) there is a series of historical articles by Helen Dixon in *Telegraph Chronicle*, 1908–10, but they do not go beyond 1895. There is also a brief retrospect by William Davis in the issue of 24 October 1913, p. 181.
98 *TC* 2 January 1903, p. 51, 15 January 1904, pp. 88ff., 4 November 1904, p. 199, 3 May 1907, pp. 67ff. The proceedings of the 1903 Committee are preserved in R IV/15.
99 R IV/8, 15 February 1893; *TC* 15 March 1904, p. 192. R IV/11, 14 and 21 have a number of annual reports, all from big cities.
100 R IV/22 and below.
101 *Supervising* 1931, pp. 258–9; *TC* 2 June 1905, p. 21, 15 April 1910, p. 64, 25 April 1913, pp. 217, 242; R IV/8 for the Morris affair.
102 R IV/10 and above, Chapter 7, p. 163, R IV/23.
103 *TC* 15 April 1910, pp. 48, 58.
104 *TC* 27 May 1898, p. 199, 15 April 1910, p. 57, 14 March 1913, p. 144.
105 Hall (1902), p. 33; R IV/5, 66; *TC* 3 March 1911, p. 245.
106 The 1892 'Promotions in the Postal Telegraph Service' circular is in MC 310.5 and R IV/5.34. PTCA *The Case of the Bristol Telegraphists* (1906 or 7) together with the comments of Davis are in R IV/23. See also R IV/24, *TC* 11 March 1904, p. 171 and 5 May 1905, p. 264.
107 R IV/8, 13 February 1895; *TC* 9 February 1906, pp. 118–9, 14 March 1913, p. 142, 25 April 1913, pp. 219ff. R IV/24 contains material reflecting the Committee's activities, including election leaflets from 1906 which they clearly inspired, and evidence of active help for Thomas Bayley and other favourable MPs.

108 *TC* 17 January 1902, pp. 65–6, 11 October 1901, p. 186, 13 March 1903, p. 147, 11 September 1903, p. 129, 20 December 1901, p. 36. Blair (1905) in R IV/14 and F 112.1. See also *Post*, 4 May 1929, p. 386.

109 R IV/5, 12; *TC* 10 May 1895, p. 937; R IV/10, Vol. 1, p. 26.

110 *TC* 15 February 1904, p. 139, 5 February 1909, p. 211, and pp. 168, 184 above.

111 *TC* 9 June 1899, pp. 231, 241, 13 February 1914, pp. 87–8.

112 *TC* 18 December 1908, p. 49, 23 March 1906, pp. 186–7.

113 *TC* 11 March 1906, pp. 186–7, 8 April 1904, p. 213, 16 September 1910, p. 5. See also 3 February 1909, p. 211 for an altercation with the FA.

114 *TC* 8 February 1911, p. 209, 28 April 1911, pp. 93, 112.

115 See Chapter 3, p. 49 and the short pamphlet on *Telegraphist Cramp* in R IV/23.

116 *The Lancet*, 22 July, 6 July, 14 September 1901; R IV/14 and /21 and XX; *TC* 13 March 1903, pp. 168–9, 20 January 1904, p. 118, 23 September 1904, p. 176, 7 April 1905, pp. 215–6, 1 December 1905, pp. 22ff., November 1907, pp. 70ff., 29 March 1912, pp. 31, 47–8; *P&TR* 13 April 1914, p. 328. Garland (1912).

117 R IV/11; *TC* 27 July 1906, p. 202, 17 April 1908, p. 49, 18 February 1910, p. 218.

118 *PG* 1918, p. 18; *TC* 31 January 1896, pp. 1,313–4, 28 February, p. 1,312, 3 September 1897, p. 336, Chapter 7, pp. 157, 163.

119 *TC* 18 January 1901, pp. 48–9, 6 June 1902, p. 13, 9 June 1899, pp. 236–8, 14 March 1902, pp. 149–50, 158, 16 December 1904, p. 43, 21 April 1905, p. 234, 23 March 1906, p. 6.

120 *TC* 21 April 1905, p. 323, 17 April 1908, p. 48, 15 April 1910, p. 56; Holt Evidence, p. 306.

121 R II/10, pp. 47–8. More on Mabel Hope on p. 270.

122 *P&TR* 6 August 1914, p. 302, 29 October 1914, p. 570, 5 November 1914, p. 596, 31 December 1914, p. 152, 7 January 1915, p. 171; R III/17, 14 November 1914, p. 9; P&TCA *Casual Labour in the Post Office* (n.d. 1914?) in R III/5.

123 *P&TR* 17 December 1911, p. 111, 14 January 1915, p. 189, 3 June 1915, p. 63, 7 October 1915, p. 432, 24 June 1915, p. 136; R III/17, 5 June 1915, p. 7. On Nottingham, R III/5 and *P&TR* 1 July 1915, pp. 144–6.

124 *P&TR* 9 March 1916, p. 349, 27 April 1916, p. 499, R III/7, 11 May 1916, pp. 8–9.

125 *P&TR* 20 July 1916, 17 and 24 May 1917.

126 *P&TR* 10 August 1916, pp. 278ff., 14 September 1916, p. 362, 14 February 1918, p. 232, 9 January 1919, p. 65, 6 February 1919, p. 100, 25 September 1919, p. 135, 15 May 1919, p. 230.

127 Edwards (1917); *P&TR* 29 July 1915, pp. 229, 221, 1 February 1917, p. 210.

128 R III/18, 25 January 1917, p. 13; *P&TR* 22 May 1919, p. 244.

129 *P&TR* 26 August 1915, p. 310, 24 May 1917, p. 49. The 'Forward Policy' leaflets are in the *Record* also, though some are in R III/15 and all, together with the quoted statement, are bound in the BL at WP 5372.

130 *PCH* 1914, p. 253; *P&TR* 2 September 1915, p. 330, 23 September 1915, p. 390, 9 August 1917, p. 235, 8 November 1917, p. 8.

131 *P&TR* 16 May 1918, p. 4, 3 August 1916, p. 264, 27 July 1916, pp. 242–3, 11 October 1917, p. 372, 17 January 1918, p. 162, 31 January 1918, pp. 196ff., 6 February 1919, pp. 98ff.

132 *P&TR* 8 August 1918, pp. 105–6, 28 February 1918, p. 263, 4 July 1918, p. 65, 16 May 1918, pp. 9–10, 3 April 1919, p. 172, 16 October 1919, p. 247.

133 There is clearly more to be said on this matter than can be discovered in R III/17, 28 January 1916, p. 4, /18, 24 August 1916, p. 20, /10, 1 June 1917, p. 8, /11, 22 November 1918, 5 June 1919; *PG* 1918, p. 164 and a letter of 30 October 1917 in R V/23, and 22 November 1917 in R XIII/5. See also R XIII/7.

134 There are four volumes of EC minutes which I have put at R III/17, 18, 10 and 11. The Organising Committee minutes for 1916–19 are at III/4.

135 *P&TR* 20 July 1916, p. 225, 4 July 1918, p. 65.

136 There are some lists in F 139 and Appendix 25, p. 646 below.

137 *Central London Review* July 1906, June 1911, July 1909 and *passim*.

138 This account is based on copies of *The Postal Advocate* in the BL and the material at R XV. See also R I/28, 26 October 1917 and *Post*, 22 May 1920, pp. 488, 5 November 1927, p. 358.

139 *Postal Advocate, passim*.

140 *Post* 1906, p. 85, 1907, pp. 85–6, 104–5; Holt Evidence, 122 and above. The *Central London Review* contains some reports for the Bagmen's Association.

141 *PG* (20 July 1895); *Post*, 21 February 1920, p. 156; *Tracers Budget*, 1894; *Tracers Chronicle*, 1900 and 1901.

142 Posterity has some reason to be grateful to the STA for remembering to send every issue of The

Review from June 1905 to January 1926 to the BL, and all quotations are taken from this. See also Chapter 7, p. 156 and *Postal Advocate*, March 1913, where another small association is severely reminded of the difference between tracers and sorter-tracers.

143 *CSG* 1903, p. 74; *Post*, 13 June 1920, p. 565; *Central London Review (October 1911)*.
144 *Post* 1916, p. 210; The *Review* (June 1920).
145 *TC* 19 February 1909, pp. 223–4, 30 April 1909, p. 74; *P&TR* 16 August 1917, p. 237; *Post*, 11 March 1950, p. 86.
146 Holt Evidence, p. 233, R I/21, 27 October 1911, p. 8, I/33 for a recruitment leaflet.
147 Holt Evidence, p. 296.
148 Above, p. 245. The full story of the ASTE and its predecessors is given in Bealey (1976), chs 3 and 4. See also *PG* 1915, p. 401 and *P&TR*, 19 August 1915, p. 286, 10 February 1916, p. 271.
149 See Chapter 10 below.
150 *TSA Gazette* from November 1915 continued as *Temporary Postal Workers Gazette* from June 1916 is almost the only source on both London and provincial organisations.
151 R I/27, 22 October 1916, p. 28; *P&TR* 27 September 1917, p. 337.
152 See particularly *TPWG*, February and July 1917.
153 *TPWG* (June and July 1918).
154 *TPWG* (September 1920).
155 *TPWG* (September 1916, January 1919).
156 There is very little history before 1916 but some interesting statistics in Federation of Post Office Supervising Officers, *21 Years of Achievement* (1939).
157 R V/3, 11 May 1907; *Supervising* (August 1913, April 1915).
158 *Controlling Officers Journal* (July 1912).
159 *PG* 1913, p. 615; *Supervising* (August 1913); *COJ* (May 1915); Tweedmouth Evidence, p. 220.
160 *COJ* (May 1917); *Supervising* (March 1919).
161 *Supervising* (June 1919). See above on some attitudes to supervisors, and below on the 1916 negotiations.
162 There are some points on this later history in Hodgson (1947) and Seaton (1963).
163 Stuart-Bunning tells the story in the POEU *Journal*, 21 September 1928.
164 See Chapter 7, p. 161; *PG* 1918, p. 65, and *The Postmaster* 1907–9 in the BL.
165 There is plenty on this in Neale (1913), and a little in NFSPM (1935). There is an excellent analysis by Brown (1963).
166 The FA minutes in R VI/8 cover most of this, but see also VI/3, pp. 357, 362, VI/10, p. 165; *Post*, 2 September 1893, 6 January 1894, and *Telegraph Journal*, 15 September 1892.
167 *PG* and *Post* for these events. In June 1895 the Federation refused to delegate Clery to the Labour Electoral Congress (R VI/7, p. 240). On the PF, see R I/1, 5 July 1895.
168 *Post* 7, 21 September 1895, 1 January 1898; UGWF *Rules* (1895); *PJ* October 1895 attacks the Federation as a creature of Clery, but *Post* 1908, p. 218, was still putting forward its advantages. The BL has the *Government Workers Advocate* from 1911 to 1916.
169 *Pall Mall Gazette* (4 February 1892); *Post*, 4 February 1892, 19 August 1899 and 18 January 1902; *PCH* January 1900, p. 73. For efforts to revive it which seem to have come to nothing, see R VI/20, p. 386.
170 There is a file of material on this collected by Davis which I have placed at R V/34 and a pamphlet entitled *History of the Civil Servants Deferred Pay Movement 1896–1906* (mostly consisting of various petitions submitted) at R IV/11, summarised in the STA *Review*, January 1907. See also Smith (1931), pp. 92–5, *PG* 1918, pp. 97–8 and *Post*, 25 August 1923, pp. 181–3. These sources contain slightly different results for the polls of 1903 and 1907.
171 R I/9, 23 October 1904, p. 19, R VI/9, p. 269; *PG* 1899, p. 473; R V/3, 14 May 1904.
172 *Civilian* (18 June, 26 November 1910).
173 *PJ* 1897, p. 654 and R II/2, 9 November 1897 for the initiative and R V/33 for the meeting.
174 For some early meetings see *Post* 5 March, 28 May 1898; *PG* 1898, pp. 261, 268.
175 *Post* 1902, p. 335; Swift (1929), p. 300.
176 *Post* (14 October 1899); *PG* 1899, pp. 470ff.
177 *PG* 1902, p. 414; *TC* 7 November 1902, p. 222, 13 March 1903, p. 155.
178 The Minutes for 1901–12 are in R V/2 and 3.
179 R V/3, 5 September 1903 and I/8, 30 January, 16 October 1903. See also I/10, 29 January 1904, p. 24 and *PG* 1904, p. 564, for further opposition to the NJC in the PF.
180 R V/34 has something on the meeting with the TUC. See also TUC 1907 Report, pp. 95–7, 163–4, *PCH* 1906, pp. 410–12 and 536–8, *PG* 1906, p. 616.
181 *TC* 28 February 1906, p. 146, 3 May 1907, pp. 72ff. (where the seconder of the disaffiliation resolution was J. G. Newlove); R V/33 (letter of 22 February 1907).

182 *PCH* 1907, pp. 143–4; *Post* 1907, pp. 421, 425; R VI/14, 15 January 1907. See also above, pp. 228–9 for other inter-association relations in this period.
183 *PCH* 1909, pp. 518, 69.
184 There is a verbatim account of the Matlock proceedings in R V/1 and the document it published is in *TC* 19 February 1909, pp. 221–2. Later material from the sub-committee is in V/33.
185 R V/25, 4 May 1917, p. 21; *TC* 3 May 1907, p. 74.
186 R V/34, /3, 11 May 1907, 1 September 1908; *TC* 14 October 1910, pp. 48–9.
187 *Post* 1909, p. 43; *PCH* 1909, p. 519; *Post* 1910, pp. 399–401; R V/2, 24 September 1910.
188 F 600; *PG* 1911, p. 344, 1914, p. 420.
189 R V/2 on this and what follows. R V/9 has Stuart's letter of 21 August advocating the full meeting.
190 R V/19 and /21; Bealey (1976), pp. 111ff.
191 This is recorded in voluminous detail in the minute books in R V, which include verbatim reports of all meetings and much else besides.
192 R V/7 for the scheme, *PCH* 1912, p. 36 and R IV/17, p. 127 for hostility and /13, 10, 11, 15 on the meetings of 1913–14.
193 R IV/17 pp. 27, 103, 169, 183; *PCH* 1911, pp. 163, 450, 512, 1912, pp. 175, 604–5.
194 R IV/17 pp. 211, 243ff.; *PCH* 1913, pp. 546ff.; R II/10.
195 *PG* 1913, pp. 336–7, 612ff., 1914, pp. 1ff., 97ff., 380 for this and subsequent events. The verbatim minutes are in R I/25 and reproduced in the *Gazette*, though not the bitter discussion at the next meeting when Stuart was accused of rushing the scheme because he wanted to be general secretary. See also R XIII/2.
196 R V/13 and 21; *Post* 1913, p. 312, 1915, p. 357; *PCH* 1913, p. 357, 1915, p. 43; *PG* 1915, p. 452.
197 R III/2 and XIII/2.
198 R III/2 for all this, *P&TR* 4 January 1917, p. 141, for the offending paragraph, and R XIII/7, 21 April 1917, for the quotation.
199 R V/25 and XIII/7; *PG* 1917, pp. 175, 216, 249; *Post* 1917, p. 219; *P&TR* 5 July 1917, p. 146, 12 July, p. 160.
200 R V/35 and XIII/3 for a verbatim account (of this and the subsequent meeting), *P&TR* 16 August 1917, p. 238, for a summary, and STA *Review*, September 1917, for the verdict.
201 AE&SA *Journal*, November 1917, p. 169; *P&TR* 6 December 1917, p. 66.
202 *Post* 1917, pp. 397–401, 1918, pp. 100, 114.
203 Bealey (1976), pp. 134ff., POEU *Journal* (July 1919).
204 R XIII/5, 6, 7; V/23, 24, 29; I/28; *PG* 1917, p. 360.
205 These and subsequent discussions are given in detail in R V/29, 30, 31, 32, 33, and in I/29 and XIII/4 and 5.
206 *PG* 1918, pp. 88, 30; *P&TR* 18 April 1918, p. 372; R XIII/7.
207 *P&TR* 16 May 1918, pp. 13ff., 28 November 1918, pp. 17ff.
208 R I/30; R V/33, R XIII/5.
209 There are full accounts in *PG*, *Post* and *P&TR*.
210 R XIII/5; Brown (1943), p. 94; R I/30, 2 March 1919; *PG* 1919, pp. 315, 347, 350; V/33.
211 R V/33, 24 July 1919, 15 January 1920.
212 Above, p. 208.
213 *Central London Review* (June 1907); *PCH* 1910, p. 437.
214 Above, p. 244.
215 *Postal Advocate* (September 1914).
216 Some are listed in F 393.8.
217 *Chambers Journal* (9 February 1878); *The Postmaster* (August 1909); *PJ* 1897, pp. 457, 497, 523.
218 I am grateful to Mr F. L. Lucas, Secretary and Treasurer of the United Kingdom Civil Service Benefit Society, for some of the information in this paragraph and those following. The original rules of the 'Northampton' are in F 393.8 and a useful history up to that time in *PG* 1908, pp. 1–2. A brief account of all the main Societies is in *Controlling Officers Journal*, June 1912.
219 *Post* 1903, p. 231; *TC* 18 May 1906, p. 16.
220 *PCH* 1908, p. 390, 1913, p. 547; *PG* 1917, p. 148.
221 *PG* 1907, pp. 355–7; *Postal Advocate*, January 1909; *PCH* 1913, p. 547.
222 *TC* 19 November 1906, pp. 45–6. This still exists.
223 Letter to Heald on 30 May 1881 in MC, *SMLG*, 1899, p. 304; *Civil Service Magazine* (June 1902). See also *ibid.*, September, October 1902; *Post* 1902, pp. 132, 166.
224 *PG* 1914, p. 306, 1915, p. 568; *P&TR* 9 March 1916, p. 355, 15 June 1916, p. 123; *Supervising* (May 1914).
225 *PG* 1917, pp. 89, 105, 153; *P&TR* 1 March 1917, p. 277, 22 March 1917, p. 330, 10 May 1917, p. 1, 13 December 1917, p. 93.

226 There is a slightly apologetic account of this by Belderson in *TC* 22 December 1899, and a run of an erratically produced and titled periodical in the BL for the period 1904–39.

227 PO, *Temperance Pioneer* (May 1905); Post Office Total Abstinence Society *Bulletin* (January 1933, January 1934).

228 *Post* (1 September, 6 October 1894).

229 *Civil Service Socialist* (February 1908–March 1915).

230 *TC* 25 April 1913, p. 215; R II/10; *Post* 1914, p. 241; *PG* 1915, p. 445. See also below, Chapter 11.

231 *PJ* 1897, p. 615; R I/18, 5 February 1909, I/27, 22 October 1915. Above pp. 239–40.

232 *PG* 1913, p. 547, 1919, p. 376, R I/29, 4 May 1919.

9 From Service to Business: The Post Office since 1920

We believe that the community as a whole requires the Post Office to continue along the lines of putting social service before profit. (Post Office Staff Associations, *Control and Organisation of the Post Office*, 1932, p. 15)

The Post Office has many social obligations. But the existence of the objectives does not mean that the Post Office should be run primarily as a vast social service without regard to the economic facts of life . . . The Post Office . . . must be free to use the criteria applied in the world of commerce for gauging efficiency: it must be free to innovate and develop as a business seeking to meet and anticipate its customers' demands. (*Status of the Post Office*, Cmnd 989, March 1960, p. 3)

Everyone knows how to run the Post Office except the Postmaster General and those who run the Post Office. (Ernest Marples, *Hansard* V, 579, 633, 5 December 1957)

In the years from the great reforms of 1840 to the outbreak of war in 1914, the Post Office was an expanding, self-confident and prosperous institution, a golden island of public enterprise in a surrounding sea of private capitalism. The First World War began the process whereby all the familiar landmarks of the service have been swept away one by one. Slowly at first, but with increasing rapidity in the past thirty years, the world has seen the passing away of the great centralised Victorian bureaucratic machine, where the Postmaster General and his Secretary sent out much of the post and all of the 'surveyors' – or regional administrators – from under the shadow of St Paul's Cathedral. In the final years of its existence as a unified institution, the Post Office took on the characteristics of a modern corporate enterprise, including all the paraphernalia of self-conscious management techniques, with specialists in every field from public relations to accountancy and from forward planning to industrial bargaining, to say nothing of practitioners in the burgeoning technologies of communications.

It was immediately after the First World War that familiar characteristics of the Post Office system began to disappear. Wartime price inflation swept away the once sacrosanct penny post in 1918. In 1919–20, the Department for the first time in its history announced a deficit of expenditure over income. Soon afterwards the complex system of telephone tariffs was overhauled. The 1920s and 1930s heard the first serious criticisms for over a century of the organisational structure of the Post Office. The Bridgeman Enquiry of 1932 responded to these criticisms by initiating the first hesitant steps in the direction of a modern business enterprise, including

some elements of decentralisation and the effort to direct at least part of the profit
from the coffers of the Treasury to long-term projects and planning. Change came
slowly, however. The Second World War accelerated the process of administrative
decentralisation, but it also saw a return to the systematic use of the Post Office's
charges as a form of taxation.

Thus it was that by the mid-1950s the Bridgeman recommendation for limited
autonomy had not actually come into effect, and there still remained the same
political control and the same lack of long-term planning. By then, however, the
Post Office had ceased to occupy the same predominant position within the public
sector. A number of other economic activities had been nationalised, and they were
run in such a way that they were expected to make a profit and plan for long-term
capital development without the day-to-day political control that remained in the
Post Office. There were other important changes in the 1950s and 1960s which also
affected traditional methods and values. For one thing, the inflationary pressures of
the period of the great boom forced up costs at the same time that political pressures
kept prices down. Thus it became increasingly difficult for the postal system to
record the same level of profit that had been normal in the past. Furthermore, from
1956 onwards the telecommunications side of the Post Office began to outpace the
postal side. Reversing the pattern of eight decades, the telecommunications system
took in a larger income and, taking advantage of unprecedented rates of technological improvement, grew apart from the more labour-intensive and less
technically advanced postal system. This led to the first serious efforts to organise
the finances of the Post Office with a view to long-term planning which could,
amongst other things, stimulate and make use of technological innovation in a
period of economic growth. During the same period as the first serious efforts to
mechanise postal sorting and the introduction of Subscriber Trunk Dialling, the
Post Office took its first real steps in the direction of financial independence, in 1955
and 1960. The White Paper of 1960, setting out the second stage in this process, is
quoted at the head of the chapter as a characteristic statement of the changing
philosophy of the Post Office, a break from the once familiar concerns of service to
the community, setting out the predominant aims and attitudes of a modern
corporate commercial enterprise.

Seen in this historical context, the revolutionary developments in the public
communication system since the mid-1960s flow logically from the problems
discussed since the Bridgeman Report in 1932 and from the solutions proposed
since the late 1940s. The creation of the Post Office Corporation in 1969 and the
particular form it took was but one expression of the extraordinary faith in
corporate management and planned economic and technological growth of the
Labour Government of that period. It represented what by then had become the
conventional wisdom about how to deal with the postal and telecommunications
services, and with the technical innovation necessary to maintain and develop them.
These changes did not take place without being accompanied by what had now also
become a normal method of dealing with economic crisis, the restriction of expenditure in the public sector. The new corporate structure in the early 1970s was subject
to restrictions not only on its investment plans but also on its financial and pricing
policy in such a way as to provoke a crisis both of labour and capital the like of
which had not been seen before, nor has yet been seen since.

It will be for historians of the future to see in context the ever-accelerating technological innovations and rising labour productivity in telecommunications and the

final break-up of the Post Office in 1981, followed by steps to hand over some activities to private capital. However inadvisable these latter steps may be said to be, and however tied to the idiosyncratic dogmas of a particular Conservative administration, there can be no doubt that they flow historically from the gradual drawing apart, at least since the 1950s, of the two major parts of the Post Office, in finance, in management and in form. Nor is there anything new in the restrictions being placed at the time of writing on investment in and development of the communications system as part of an effort to deal with short-term economic problems. Even the 'privatisation' of parts of the system is not without precedent. Such steps were not only advocated fifty years ago by Lord Wolmer and other Conservatives, they were in part carried out by the effective subsidies given to the private shipping companies in the nineteenth century, and the 'ring' of telecommunications suppliers which operated between the 1920s and the 1970s.

However, it is not possible from the vantage point of the early 1980s to predict which of these seeds will grow and which will be trampled underfoot. What can be said with confidence is that when the time comes to set out the developments following from the creation of separate corporations for posts and telecommunications, it will be necessary to describe a world of which even our immediate predecessors can have very little conception. If Rowland Hill had lived to be 150, he would have found many common problems to discuss with Sir Evelyn Murray, the last Secretary of the Post Office until 1934, and with his Postmaster General, Sir Kingsley Wood. However, if Murray and Wood were alive today, they would see some of the same buildings they once knew, but they would hardly recognise the uses to which they were being put, and the problems being discussed within them. The aim of this chapter is to set out some of the details of the vanishing world of the last two or three generations in the Post Office, as a necessary description of the environment of the many millions of men and women whose activities played a familiar and necessary part in the pattern of national life.[1]

THE BEGINNINGS OF UNCERTAINTY: 1918-22

The opening of the First World War in 1914 saw the first period of sustained inflation in the economy as a whole for just under a century. During the four years of war, prices approximately doubled, and though this was thought of at the time as temporary and abnormal it was never reversed. Some of the results both of the fact of price inflation and of attitudes towards it are outlined in the chapters that deal with wage negotiations. During the war the Post Office refused to increase postal charges on the grounds that this would mean 'a tax on communication and the abandonment of the Penny Post which had been maintained for seventy-five years'. The system of postal tariffs was still seen as an achievement of peace and the model for such arrangements throughout the world.[2] The same did not apply to telephones, however, and the provincial rate for a local call was doubled from 1d in 1915, while in London it went up from 2d to 3d.

None of this could prevent the first serious crisis in the finance of the Post Office for more than a century. In April 1920, a deficit of over £1 million was recorded for the previous financial year, and by April 1921 the deficit had risen to £6·7 million. In the face of this, the Post Office authorities were compelled to abandon the basic inland charge of 1d a letter. The price was increased to 1½d on 3 June 1918, and temporarily ½d more from the first day of 1920 to 29 May 1922, by which time a surplus had again been reached. This 1½d remained the basic inland rate for eighteen years, when another war-time increase (to 2½d in 1940) remained unchanged until as late as 1957. The abandonment of the penny post in 1918 after seventy-eight years was seen at the time as having a significance well beyond the communications system. 'The European War', one commentator said nostalgically in 1924, 'interfered with this as with most other good things'.[3] In later years there was occasional talk of restoring the penny post, but it never came to anything. Nor were the numbers of daily deliveries in the main cities ever increased again above three or four to the luxurious profusion of the past.

It is important to make the point that the end of the penny post did not come about because the postal system itself was losing money, but because of the losses which were being sustained on the telecommunications side. In the financial year 1919–20, a total loss of £8·4 million was recorded on this side of the service, including £4·7 million on the telephone system. Efforts to improve the finances of the telegraphs concentrated first of all on tariff increases. The rate for inland telegrams had stood at 6d (2½p) for twelve words and ½d (0·21p) per word above since 1885. In 1915 the rate for twelve words was increased to 9d (3·75p), and on 1 September 1920 this was further increased to 1s (5p) for twelve words and 1d (0·42p) for each extra word. Various accompanying charges included increases for press and for night telegraph letters. The system itself was also changed in an important way by the introduction in 1921 of telegraph delivery by 'walks' instead of taking out individual messages as they arrived. As well as reducing the service, this also reduced the number of telegraph messengers to 800.[4] For the workforce an even more important change in telegraphy was the replacement in the following years of the old morse and Baudot systems by teleprinters. The first teleprinter was introduced into Britain by Creed in 1921, and in the following year began to be used in the Post Office, and other such rationalisations as the closing down of less busy circuits were also introduced. At the same time, some public effort was made to defend the system against its more ignorant critics.[5]

In the immediate post-war period the greatest public attention was, however, directed at the telephones. In 1920 the Department ran an internal inquiry into telephone rates to consider the mounting deficits. The increased tariffs recommended by this body were then considered by a House of Commons Select Committee under the chairmanship of Sir Edward Coates which was given the task of 'placing the Telephone Service on a remunerative basis'. The Select Committee could not resist the usual view that 'in many instances there is undoubted ground for complaint' or that the charges were 'inefficient and unbusinesslike'. Nevertheless they came to exactly the same conclusions as the internal inquiry, that the flat charges should not continue nor any revision of it, but instead that every call should be charged.[6] From 1 April 1921 therefore there was an increase to 3d for all local calls (the level they were in London already) and there were comparable increases in trunk calls. One result of this was an immediate fall in the number of telephones, a public outcry led by various commercial interests and the appointment of yet another Select Committee, this time under Evelyn Cecil, which reported in March 1922.[7] Not for the last time, the Select Committee heard the complaints of local telephone managers against being subject to the authority of those on the postal side. So instead of dealing with such problems as those deriving from being financed from year to year, the Select Committee thought all the problems could be resolved by administrative change, concluding

> that the re-organisation of the telephone administration on more commercial lines is the fundamental requirement for efficient development, and that if it is carried out wisely it will prove a solution of most of the failings which have been disclosed. They accordingly recommend the separation of the telegraph and telephone department on the one hand from that of the mails on the other . . . The disappearance of the office of surveyors from the telegraph and telephone department should follow, and the evidence has disclosed their position in regard to district managers to be often that of a fifth wheel to the coach.

However desirable these changes were thought to be at the time, nothing was done to put them into effect. The political situation was too uncertain over the following months, with a rapid succession of governments and postmasters general, for there to be what amounted to a major Departmental reorganisation. Post Office Secretary Sir Evelyn Murray, who opposed changes of the sort proposed by the Select Committee, was clearly in a good position to prevent them from occurring. The UPW for its part thought the proposals 'preconceived' and considered that there would be 'very great difficulty' in putting them into effect.[8] All things considered, as most parts of the system began to turn in a profit again, it was hardly surprising that there was no significant change for some years.

THE LONG DECLINE OF THE TELEGRAPH

Before going on to consider the period of the late 1920s and early 1930s when pressure for change in the Post Office was more intense and successful, it is worth saying more about the somewhat separate problems of the inland telegraph service.

In the 1920s, inland telegraph traffic continued to decline and to lose money, as it had always done. In November 1927, therefore, Postmaster General Mitchell Thompson set up a committee of three outside businessmen 'to examine the possibility of effecting substantial economies'.[9] The Chairman of this little group was Sir Samuel Hardman Lever, a director of Dunlop Rubber and of the *Daily Mail*, and the other two were Sir Harry McGowan, President of Imperial Chemical Industries, and Lord Ashfield, also director of numerous large companies. The Committee decided that the price increases of 1921 had not been responsible for the continuing decline in demand and profits, though they did conclude that the low tariff policy since 1885 had been a major cause of the persistent indebtedness of the past. They considered that the origins of the problems of the 1920s 'were to be found partly in trade depression, but mainly in the competition of the Telephone Service'. The Committee attached much of the blame to the telegraphists. They attacked promotion by seniority and asserted that many of the older telegraphists refused to come to terms with the new technology, deliberately changing to non-operational duties instead of mastering the new techniques of the teleprinter. The Committee advocated fewer supervisors, but also more girl probationers performing a wider range of duties at lower wages. They also proposed to reduce the ability of telegraphists to appeal against disciplinary decisions. These methods of dealing with the workforce were much the most concrete of ideas of Hardman Lever and his colleagues. They showed even less imagination in their proposals for differential pricing through the day, and for the abolition of press rates and inland charges to the Irish Republic.

In the circumstances it was hardly surprising that the UPW took the view that 'a more outrageous document was never produced' and considered what it called 'the attack on the staff' to be 'mean and spiteful', revealing 'in all its ugly nakedness, the real spirit of the capitalist employer'. The Union lobbied the Post Office management against the proposals, and the authorities for their part seem to have made little effort to give effect to them.[10]

One at least of the Hardman Lever proposals did not raise much controversy, and this was the idea of sending a group of Post Office officials to the United States to look at the more profitable system in operation there. Such a group went for three months towards the end of 1929 under the Chairmanship of Leon Simon, who was later Director of Post Office Telegraphs and Telephones.[11] This team discovered that the two US companies, the Postal Telegraph Company and the Western Union, both banned independent trade unions, the latter allowing a 'company union'. They also found that 'a very high standard of qualification' was demanded from the operators and a system of 'merit awards' was further used to induce discipline. There were some other important differences from Britain:

> The American Telegraph Companies, as commercial concerns, do not interpret so strictly as the British Post Office the obligation to treat all sections of the public alike, and are not bound to the same extent to study the interests of the most remote districts. They are thus able to concentrate on the provision of a high-grade service for business telegrams between large centres of population. They have, moreover, been able to develop the telegraph service as a separate business, and have not had to dovetail it into an organisation carrying on other activities. They have also the advantage of a considerable degree of elasticity in the handling of their staffs. They can make remuneration more or less proportionate to merit, can restrict annual leave to the less busy periods of the year, and so forth.

Fortunately for industrial relations in the British Post Office, the Simon Committee did not advocate the immediate transplantation of these conditions. They did however propose a series of changes of which the most important included the more rapid abandonment of out-of-date apparatus, greater specialisation amongst staff, open competition for male telegraphists, more centralised supervision and efforts to advertise the service, including the introduction of greetings telegrams.

Nearly all of these proposals were carried out during the next few years, eventually with the co-operation of the UPW. The Union's initial response was to deny that Simon was 'an unbiased witness', and to complain with justice that 'official policy has been to advertise continually the "loss" on the telegraphs, and to attempt to meet the annual deficit by cutting down costs'.[12] Nevertheless the management soon showed that they intended going about dealing with the problems of the telegraph service with somewhat greater forcefulness than in the past. They quickly moved ahead with the abandonment of obsolescent equipment, and persuaded UPW leaders and members to accept the consequences of this through such means as early retirement and the recruitment of new female staff to operate the tele-printers. At two special UPW conferences in 1930 and 1931, UPW members, who felt they had little alternative, adopted what was perhaps a surprisingly accommo-dating attitude. The delegates would not however accept the advice of their leaders by agreeing to measures of rates of output for disciplinary purposes. Nor would they accept any increase in the hourly output of telegrams from 60 to 80. By the late 1930s, however, they had been compelled to accept even that, along with a degree of co-operation with the changing technology and organisation of the service that has largely continued without interruption until the present time.[13]

For reasons discussed in more detail later, the Bridgeman Enquiry in 1932 did not propose any radical change in the organisation of the telegraphs, though they thought that they 'should in due course be merged with the Telephone Service'. Noting that it was 'in the unfortunate position of lying between the upper and nether millstones of an expanding Telephone Service and a Postal organisation' that could deliver throughout the British Isles within a day, Bridgeman and his colleagues could do little but acknowledge an irreversible trend.[14] Major efforts were made from 1935 onwards to expand the telegram service.[15] The most important of these was the reduction in the tariff to 6d (2½p) for up to twelve words. This increased the traffic and reduced the deficit. The earliest efforts were also made at an advertising campaign to popularise the service. The message of this campaign was that the telegram could be used to convey a great deal more than bad news, or fish prices. One typical ditty from the advertising ran as follows:

> Sing a song of sixpence
> Sixpence for a wire!
> Nine good words for sixpence
> All you can desire!

The greetings telegram also did much to expand the scope of the service after 1935. The particular problems of the war also allowed greater use to be made of the telegram service. Special facilities for evacuees and other such schemes allowed an expansion of traffic, even when the rate for nine words doubled to 1s (5p) in 1943, and while greetings telegrams were suspended from 1943 to 1950.

The long-term decline of the telegram service was resumed after 1945.[16] The post-war grade reorganisation and the raising of the school-leaving age to 15 resulted in 1947 in the disappearance of the once familiar boy messengers and girl probationers. This led not simply to the removal of 'telegraph boys' from the streets and young girls from the offices, but also to a sharp increase in the costs of each telegram – from 11d each (4·8p) to 3s 4d (16·6p). A boy messenger in London in 1939 received 19s (95p) per week at his maximum in return for the prospect of a job in the Post Office. The junior postman who delivered the same telegram in 1953 would have received £3 5s (£3. 25). At the same time, however, the introduction between 1949 and 1952 of automatic switching between circuits resulted in a rapid fall in the workforce, by as much as 6 per cent in one financial year, 1950–1, and by about 39 per cent between 1953 and 1958.[17]

Nevertheless, the decline of the service continued apace. The 64·1 million telegrams delivered in 1945–6 fell to 35 million in 1952–3 and to 19 million in 1956–7. Increasing prices did little to recoup the inevitable losses – they may well have intensified them. In 1951 the standard charge increased by 50 per cent to 1s 6d (7½p) for nine words, in 1954 it doubled to 3s (15p), and in 1963 the charge was once again increased to 5s (25p) for twelve words. By then the use of the service was rapidly giving way to telex and telephone. In 1935 two businesses out of three used telegrams, in 1951 it was half and by 1958 it was nearer a third.[18]

In 1957, when the number of telegrams delivered fell below 20 million for the first time, Postmaster General Marples set up an inquiry under Sir Leonard Sinclair, the Chairman of Esso Petroleum, which also included former TUC Chairman William Beard and F. W. Paish, Professor of Economics at the London School of Economics.[19] The Committee found that the deficit of the service was now about the same size as its income and that business traffic was about 20 per cent of what it had been before 1939. It set out the dilemmas that followed from this:

> We think that the telegram can be regarded to-day as of only marginal importance in the business community and the position as regards social traffic is not dissimilar . . . since so much telegraph traffic appears to be essential or open to transmission by other means, we have considered whether it is justifiable to continue the present inland public service.

However, the Committee decided that it was desirable to retain the inland telegram system. This was partly because there was a residual public service provided by the 200,000 'life and death messages' still being sent – about 1 per cent of the total. Sinclair's Committee quoted with approval the Central Office of Information survey of the previous year in maintaining the need for a service that 'concerns no one very often, but many people very occasionally, and which, when it does concern them, matters much to them'. If Postmaster General Marples accepted this general conclusion and agreed to expansion of greetings telegrams, he did not accept the proposal to alter the structure of the tariffs to include a fixed charge plus a relatively low addition for each word. In fact there was no further increase in charges until as late as April 1963. Nor did Marples do anything about those other two longstanding drains on the system, the special rates for press and for railways. The press rates virtually fell into disuse with the increasing use of private wires and telex, and the railway privileges were finally abolished in 1967.

In the meantime, the Sinclair Report did lead to a new set of internal joint discussions which continued the traditions of co-operation first established thirty years before. In May 1959 a joint management–union committee was established to 'consider what changes can be made to increase the efficiency of the Inland Telegraph Service'.[20] Efforts were made to improve the efficiency and productivity of the service by phased redundancies, better lay-out of offices, improved interchange with telex and telephone systems, larger intervals between deliveries, and a higher age limit for those doing the deliveries. None of these measures, however, could prevent the continuing decline of the inland telegram. By 1967 the Select Committee on Nationalised Industries found that the inland system now contributed little more than 0·5 per cent to the telecommunications income of the Post Office, £3·6 million out of £404 million. Tariff policies of various sorts as well as numerous other measures had made it impossible to escape the fact that this was 'a dying service' that 'cannot be made to pay'. Its continued existence could 'only be justified on social grounds'.[21] In 1968 the Prices and Incomes Board suggested that it 'should be treated as a social service and financed by means of an Exchequer grant' or else abolished altogether, with special provision being made for 'life and death' messages. For a time at least one Cabinet minister thought it had been agreed to abolish the service altogether.[22]

During the 1970s, the decline of telegraph traffic continued at much the same rate as before and the problem continued to be discussed with few new suggestions coming from any quarter. In 1972 a new union–management committee resulted in more attractive greetings telegrams, and some other measures. In 1977, the Carter Review Committee set out the problems of the system as if nobody had ever thought of them before, once again asserting that its abolition would have to be considered, with the special twist that the 'life and death' messages should be dealt with by an outside agency.[23] Further discussions in the late 1970s took place when the rate of decline showed some tendency to diminish. The result has been yet another scheme to save the service, this time much reduced and merged with the overseas telegraph system. In presenting this to the members in 1980, the Union's Executive wrote that 'in the long history of the Telegraph Service' this could be 'probably the last major report that the Union will be putting to its members'.[24] With fewer than one UCW member in 200 now concerned in any way with telegraphy, and with a level of output that is daily subject to ever more intense competition, there can be little doubt that we are seeing the life of the service fading away. A separate service finally disappeared in 1982. Yet it would be sad not to remember that these events came to pass almost exactly a century after the most thrusting, active and technologically advanced section of Post Office workers had set up its first permanent trade union organisation.

SOME OTHER TELECOMMUNICATIONS

Before resuming the account of the general development of the Post Office, a few words should be added on other aspects of the service which are somewhat apart from its more general problems.

The overseas telegraph system began in the mid-nineteenth century, traversed the Pacific Ocean by 1902 and spread wider and wider afield with each succeeding year. The policy of the Post Office was to run cables itself to the continent of Europe, but to subsidise private concerns to do so elsewhere.[25] In 1903 Marconi showed that it was possible to transmit and receive radio messages across the Atlantic without wires, and his company became the chief of a number of others who built up an international wireless and cable service. By 1927, however, a conference of the British Government and its various imperial allies expressed concern over the lack of central control in a system of such military and strategic importance. There was also talk of 'reckless mismanagement' in the Marconi Company. In 1934, therefore, the various companies were merged into what became known as Cable and Wireless Ltd. Opponents of nationalisation thought such a system of state-organised private industry was 'a model that should be followed in the case of an internal telegraph and telephone'. The UPW and others pressed the case for nationalisation.[26] In 1938 the Government took over some shares in the company and in 1946 finally nationalised it. *The Times* pointed out at the time that such a step would probably also have been taken by a Conservative Government. The UPW nevertheless approved the step, though not of the setting up of a public utility company outside the Post Office.[27] The state-run company developed a network of submarine cables which have been superseded by the development of communication satellites since 1965. Despite occasional and sensationalised commercial lapses, Cable and Wireless Ltd was until the 1980s a successful and profitable international enterprise.[28]

The operation of the overseas telegraph service itself remained in the hands of the

Post Office. This has been highly centralised and has involved a small number of operators.[29] It has not suffered the same dramatic decline as the inland system, with traffic remaining more or less constant from the 1950s to the 1970s until it too began to suffer from competition. It is a symptom of the decline of both sides of the system that the 'final solution' being prepared for the 1980s was the merging of inland and international systems.

The Post Office has throughout the period had responsibility for a number of other aspects of electrical communication, in most cases involving very limited numbers of staff. For seventy years, from the time of the 1904 Wireless Telegraph Act, the Post Office had powers of regulation in relation to the broadcasting system, now passed over to the Home Office. This involved high political drama of various sorts, but little of economic importance, and nothing at all from the point of view of the workforce.[30] The development of various forms of wireless telegraphy can be dated from the much publicised ship-to-shore messages which resulted in the capture of the unfortunate Dr Crippin in 1910, to a point where more than half a million such messages were transmitted in 1938–9. In 1926 the Post Office opened a wireless beam station at Rugby largely for wireless telegraphy, and this later became involved in wireless telephony, in the days before the pace of technological change was likely to render obsolete almost any reference that could be made in these pages to contemporary developments in this field.

FORCES FOR CHANGE: 1923–32

The Post Office went back into profit in the financial year that ended in 1923, and did not again record an overall loss for more than thirty years. During this period it remained a government department with finances decided from year to year and then handed over to the public exchequer. However, this was a system subject to increasing criticism and ultimately to fundamental change.

The sources of criticism of the Post Office administration during the 1920s were many and varied. A system of outside consultation was initiated by Postmaster General Samuel as early as 1913 in the form of local telegraph and telephone committees, which were set up by chambers of commerce or of trade, or, in their absence, by local authorities. In 1921 Postmaster General Kellaway, under pressure from the Federation of British Industries, set up a national body known as the Post Office Advisory Committee. These were the direct ancestors of bodies that still operate under somewhat different titles but, though they may have affected particular details of the running of the service, they did not have much overall influence. By the early 1930s, the national Council was hardly meeting at all.

More effective were probably those pressure groups representing commercial interests and calling for the development of the telephone system. Various efforts from before the First World War were brought together in 1924 to form the Telephone Development Association, a body described as being 'composed of manufacturers and suppliers of telephone plant in its widest sense'. It generally called for more telephones, and attacked Treasury control as inhibiting such development. The UPW generally supported its activities but looked with some suspicion at people whose first concern was by no means the welfare of the workforce.[31] Another source of pressure for the development of the system came from the economic schemes being put forward in the late 1920s by the Liberal Party. Their

1929 electoral statement, entitled *We Can Conquer Unemployment*, in which the economist J. M. Keynes, amongst others, had a hand, advocated greatly increased investment in the telephone as part of a general programme for economic recovery. The UPW did not look with great enthusiasm at a scheme which saw the telephone service 'as an adjunct to the labour exchange', but in any case the economic arguments behind such notions had little chance of success in the political circumstances of the period.[32]

Much the most well known and effective pressure on the Post Office was associated with the name of Lord Wolmer, who was Conservative Assistant Postmaster General from 1924 to 1928, and then set himself up as a successor of Rowland Hill and Henniker Heaton in the role of a great Post Office reformer. Wolmer's campaign reflected to some extent the pressure which can always be heard from big business and Conservative politicians against public enterprise, particularly during periods of economic recession. However, he spoke with some knowledge in favour of an 'authority free from political or Treasury control', and argued for the curious solution of a single 'Public Utility Company' with private shareholdings.[33] Wolmer also played up to some of the ignorant prejudice that periodically fills newspapers with stories of letters delayed and undelivered, phone calls unconnected and so forth. There were fewer deliveries than had been the case in the main towns before 1914, and more pressure on an under-capitalised telephone system. However, these were not the fault of public enterprise as such. Nor were those leading the attack on the Post Office as disinterested as they sometimes claimed.[34]

Wolmer's career as a critic began in January 1928 while he was still Assistant Postmaster General. He made some remarks at a private meeting which were picked up by the *Daily Express* to the effect 'that if the Post Office was managed by private enterprise it would be a more efficient and economical service'. The UPW and others thought that this might be the end of Wolmer's political career but Prime Minister Baldwin let it pass with the ferocious rebuke that 'when he has attained years of discretion he will speak with that caution which characterises every one of our utterances'. Wolmer was at the time 40 years of age![35] He kept his position until the second Labour Government took over in June 1929 and then contributed to *The Times* a series of articles attacking the inefficiency and bureaucratic outlook of the Post Office. Even while he could not forbear to notice the cloven hoof of the profit-maker behind these arguments, George Middleton of the UPW was compelled to admit to being 'in the unfortunate position of having to confess that Lord Wolmer's allegations that the bureaucracy of the Department is not infrequently a barrier to progress, are not without good foundation'. Citing other examples of the refusal to advertise and to expand its facilities, Middleton expressed the hope that Wolmer's campaign might 'lead to a demand for a more enterprising administration'.[36]

However, soon afterwards Middleton and his chief colleagues, who were at the time all Members of Parliament, were confronted with a Commons Debate on whether there should be an inquiry to see if any or all of the services 'should be transferred to an ad hoc public corporation'. All the UPW leaders were opposed to any suggestion of such a form of organisation, and felt compelled to launch into a somewhat more well informed and forceful defence of the Post Office than could be mustered by Postmaster General Lees-Smith. Middleton was not unaware of the paradox when he said 'I find myself in an extremely difficult position for the moment of defending where I have been accustomed to attack'.[37]

The House of Commons Debate clearly indicated that much of the criticism of the Post Office was based on a combination of ignorance of its operations and malevolence against public enterprise of any sort. During 1931, however, other more powerful forces began pushing for reorganisation. The Tomlin Commission reported on the civil service generally and expressed the view 'that the time has come for a review of the question of whether the organisation of the Post Office is framed too much on the lines appropriate to Departments generally'. Though Tomlin and his colleagues were trying to avoid taking a decision themselves, there was clearly some basis for their argument that the particular problems of a revenue-earning public enterprise were such that 'a Special Committee or Commission should be appointed to enquire into Post Office organisation'.[38] Later in the year other voices were added to those putting forward such demands. Clement Attlee, though not at the time as important a figure as he was subsequently to become, became convinced during his six-month tenure of the office of Postmaster General in 1931, that change was overdue. He was frustrated by the 'autocratic rule of Sir Evelyn Murray which he considered the result of over-centralisation'. He called for an end to Treasury control and 'the detailed interference of Parliament'.[39]

It is hardly surprising that at this point the UPW's leaders, though naturally taking account of Atlee's views, grew increasingly frustrated at the rain of criticism coming down on the Post Office. In November the recently elected Editor, Francis Andrews, allowed to be published in the *Post* an article under the unedifying title 'Is there a nigger in the woodpile?'. This suggested a link between Wolmer's campaign and the fact that his father the Earl of Selbourne was a director of the Telegraph Construction Company. A threatened libel suit followed, and the Union was advised that the only way out of it was an abject apology, which soon appeared.[40] In the meantime, however, for whatever reason, Wolmer succeeded in getting 320 MPs in the new Conservative-dominated Parliament to sign a petition to the Prime Minister calling for an inquiry.[41] The new Postmaster General, Kingsley Wood, determined to make his political mark, finally gave in to the pressure and soon a Committee of Enquiry was under way.

BRIDGEMAN AND AFTER

The three-man Committee of Enquiry carried out its work within the first eight months of 1932.[42] Its members were Lord Bridgeman, landowner and Tory politician, Lord Plender who was prominent in the world of accountancy and a regular member of many similar inquiries, and Sir John Cadman, well known engineering consultant and former Professor of Petroleum Technology at Birmingham University. This team could well be expected to respond to the pressures of the business community, but what was most remarkable about their recommendations was that, despite the great barrage of criticism of the Post Office, they did not propose any thoroughgoing change.

In looking at the Bridgeman Report in the context of the arguments that had produced it, there is no obvious reason why the Committee should find 'that in general the standard of efficiency shown by the Post Office in the performance of its duties is very satisfactory'. Postmaster General Wood had every justification in commending the 'remarkable efficiency' of the staff discovered by the Committee, and UPW General Secretary Bowen was quite correct to assert that they 'rejected the main case of the critics'.[43] In fact the most radical changes they proposed were the development of a more powerful regional structure and limiting the amount that needed to be paid to the Treasury. Bridgeman and his colleagues did not express any support for taking the Post Office away from the control of a Government Department. Nor did they see any grounds for separating telecommunications, or some part of it, from the Post Office.

It has recently been suggested that this perhaps unexpected caution on the part of Bridgeman and his colleagues was less a result of the merits of the case than of a number of particular circumstances.[44] It has been said that the intrigues of Wood and the Chancellor of the Exchequer Neville Chamberlain to hold on respectively to the political base of a large department of state and to the revenues it earned influenced the terms of reference and the outcome of the Enquiry. It has been argued that the great variation in the points of view of the opponents of the system was used to obstruct new ideas, and that the clear need to break up the functions of the Post Office were inhibited by organisational inertia and the power of the mandarins at St Martins-le-Grand who misunderstood and did little to stimulate technical change.

It would seem, however, that though there is something to be said for seeing the limits to change within the inertia generated in one of the largest bureaucracies in the world, it is simply to read history backwards to argue that there was a strong case as perceived at the time for the break-up of the Post Office, or for some such arrangement as the setting up of a public corporation for the telegraph and/or telephone operations. Thus although in 1928 the Hardman–Lever Committee, as already indicated, had called for the break-up of the system, there were very few who supported this. In commenting on the proposal *The Times* cited it as the opinion of MPs that 'it is quite impossible to separate the telegraph branch from other services and saddle it with a deficit'.[45] Furthermore, even Wolmer himself had been hard put to it to find a means of breaking away from the postal system anything more than the more minor functions performed by the Post Office.[46] His scheme for denationalisation was simply not practical politics. The very existence of the grade of sorting clerk and telegraphist and the rotation of work between the different functions made any reorganisation of the system very difficult. The Bridgeman Committee was well aware of this:

> Separation presents formidable practical difficulties in regard to Buildings, Staff and Plant. The Telegraph and Telephones are at present worked to a large extent in the same buildings and by the same staff as the Mails Services . . . Under present circumstances in all but the larger offices, the counter staff now deal indiscriminately with all natures of business, and in all the smaller towns the sorting and telegraph operating staff are combined . . . No man can serve two masters, and the appointment of separate staffs would entail large additional expense and would result in two separate organisations, neither of which would be carrying a full load.
>
> The separation of Telephones from Mails and Telegraphs is also open to grave objections. Plant is largely identical and interchangeable.

The same case was put forward by Wood himself during this period:

> It has sometimes been suggested that the Post Office has come to embrace a

greater variety of businesses than can efficiently be placed under a single control. The experience of recent years, during which the dovetailing of Post Office services has been scientifically studied, does not support this view. From the use of the same engineering staff and, to an increasing extent, of the same lines for telegraph and telephone traffic, the interweaving of telegraph and the telephone facilities and the provision of joint garages for the motor vehicles employed in different branches, to the housing of a variety of services in single Post Office buildings and the employment on night duty in some of the smaller offices of one officer to perform telegraph, telephone and sorting duties, the economics of combined service, and its convenience to the public, appear increasingly to outweigh its possible disadvantages.[47]

Thus it was that in the given circumstances of the early 1930s, it was these arguments that won the day, and it is anachronistic to imagine that more thorough-going institutional change was possible. This is not to deny that there were significant changes following the Bridgeman recommendations, which were substantially adopted. Thus an important step was taken away from the traditional system of financial and political control. The arrangement of sending the entire revenue to the Treasury each year was abandoned in favour of the payment of a fixed amount. An ultimately irrevocable step had been taken away from the old system, even if it was a long time before it was replaced by a new one. Thus Bridgeman proposed that £11·5 million per annum of the profit should be paid in full to the Treasury and 50 per cent of all earned above that should be retained. This was however proposed at a time when the actual surplus was under £11 million and the amount to be paid had to be reduced in practice to £10·75 million.[48] This allowed the Post Office to build up a small capital account which had reached £3 million by 1938. However, the trend of profits then went down, and the fund was expected to go into deficit by 1940.[49] The outbreak of war however was once more used to induce the Post Office to take up again a frankly tax gathering function.

Prices were pushed up, and all the resulting increases of revenue were once again paid directly to the Treasury. The standard letter charge went up in May 1940 from 1½d to 2½d, and the surplus reached a record of almost £40 million in 1944–5. It was not to be until 1955 that the financial principles enunciated by Bridgeman were finally brought into effect.

The main lines of administrative change proposed by Bridgeman did however come into existence rather more quickly. The setting up of a 'functional board' to run the Post Office was intended as a measure to bring the main elements of its work, particularly on the telecommunications side, into the top decision-making body. The all-powerful Secretary Sir Evelyn Murray, who was more than just a symbol of the over-centralised non-technical system, was moved from the job after twenty years to the Department of Customs and Excise. The new office of Director General was taken over by the somewhat less forbidding figure of Sir Donald Banks from 1934–6, and for the decade after 1936 by Sir Thomas Gardiner. Both of these men were regarded as Post Office specialists rather than 'generalist' mandarins.

The most important change proposed by Bridgeman and subsequently put into effect was the decentralisation of the service. The old structure, whereby any decision of importance, including all operational questions, went through the Secretariat, was abandoned. The 'fan' structure was to be replaced by one that could more easily be represented as a 'family tree'. Decentralisation was to be 'carried to the lowest possible level consistent with the efficiency of the service'. Thus the central 'functional board', though covering all the activities of the Department, was limited to general points of policy. Detailed administration was to be carried out by a new regional organisation. Here the old 'surveyors' were to be replaced by 'Regional Directors' who should be 'the repository of the widest possible powers'.[50] Below that level, the postmasters were no longer to have powers on the telephone side, a change which seems to have had few opponents.[51]

The new regional organisational structure was not built with great urgency. A Scottish Region centred in Edinburgh began in March 1936, along with one for North-East England based in Leeds. Later in 1936 the London Postal Region followed and in April 1938 a separate London Telecommunications Region began. In 1939 a North-Western Region based in Manchester was set up, and a sub-region in Northern Ireland. Steps were also taken to separate local telephone areas from the postal system. The outbreak of war accelerated the process, so that further regional structures were set up in 1940 in the Home Counties, the Midlands and the South West.

By 1950 an inquiry including Post Office officials and union leaders found that the new system was 'working with reasonable smoothness'.[52] This Committee recommended further decentralisation and steps in the separation of telecommunications from posts. Attitudes on such matters were beginning to change, however. UPW General Secretary Geddes thought that the separation of the two services could be 'misunderstood and misapplied'. Douglas Coward, who was the POEU General Secretary at the time, did not have any such reservations. By 1954 the future POEU General Secretary won support for the view that the telecommunications section should be able 'to stand on its own feet', though his Union was not finally committed to separating the functions of the Department for some time. By then the telecommunications side of the Post Office had become the leading sector. As it grew more expensive and profitable, resentment increased against having anything to do with those on the postal side.[53] A further internal committee considered from 1959 to 1962 'whether the functions of the engineering and tele-communications staff are well adapted to a fully automatic system'.[54] This Committee heard further talk of separation of postal and telephone administration from the POEU and the Post Office Executives, but opposition from the traffic managers. As a result no further major administrative change was proposed.

During the decades when the process initiated by Bridgeman was extended to the setting up of a public corporation, and finally to the splitting asunder of the two sides of the Post Office, many of the old characteristics remained. In the late 1970s there was still talk 'of the great range of decisions which go up to the central Board' and of the need for 'a greater delegation of power to local operating units'.[55] Clearly some of the historical roots of the organisational structure of the service had not yet been cut out, despite all the efforts to do so.

THE POST OFFICE IN THE 1930s

The great wave of criticism that brought about the Bridgeman Enquiry was succeeded by a period when the Post Office made a much more conscious effort than ever before to advertise its successes and its many new services. As early as 1931,

Attlee set up a Telephone Publicity Committee, and during his six months as Postmaster General he also brought in Sir Stephen Tallents from the Empire Marketing Board and sought the advice of outside businessmen about methods of publicity. 'Reticence', wrote PMG Wood in 1934 when he set up a fully fledged Public Relations Department, 'was once the policy of the Post Office', but its 'declared policy' now aimed 'to take the public into its confidence and enlist the co-operation of the customer'. The effect of this could be seen in this unsolicited testimonial from one national newspaper in 1938: 'The praise of the Post Office is nowadays in everybody's mouth; its efficiency, its enterprise, its alertness and responsiveness, its courtesy and humanity.'[56]

The efforts to 'sell' the Post Office during this period went well beyond drawing attention to the flagging telegraph service. A wide range of posters and other forms of publicity was employed to encourage the use of all its facilities. 'Brighter Post Office weeks' were inaugurated. Particular efforts were devoted to persuading people to post earlier in the day. Forty-seven 'Green Papers' were published between 1933 and 1939 to explain aspects of the work of the Department in a popular way. A newly designed and bright *Post Office Magazine* replaced the rather staid *St Martin's-le-Grand* and the *Telephone and Telegraph Journal.*[57] Perhaps most interesting of all was the famous Post Office Film Unit. This began with the take-over in 1933 of the library of films which had been amassed by the defunct British Empire Marketing Board. In such productions as *Night Mail, Telephone Workers* and *Cable Ship* the Unit not only increased public knowledge of the services provided, but also made a major contribution to the development of the documentary cinema, associated in particular with the name of John Grierson. With the employment of such distinguished skills as those of Benjamin Britten and W. H. Auden, who was ever again to hear the Post Office advertised in such eloquent terms as these?[58]

> This is the night mail crossing the border,
> Bringing the cheque and the postal order,
> Letters for the rich, letters for the poor,
> The shop at the corner and the girl next door . . .
>
> They continue their dreams,
> But shall wake soon and long for letters,
> And none will hear the Postman's knock
> Without a quickening of the heart,
> For who can bear to feel himself forgotten?

The 1930s also saw important developments in the telephone system, most notably the spread of automatic telephones.[59] The first automatic exchange was opened in Epsom in 1912, but twelve years later there were only twenty-two such exchanges. Despite the economic depression the number of automatic exchanges grew to 300 in 1930 and to 2,000 in 1937, covering nearly half of the subscribers in the country. By 1950, 70 per cent of telephones and 83 per cent of local calls were automatic, though the same rate of conversion did not continue, and the last manual exchange did not disappear until 1977. For the operators this development meant some redundancies. However, the numbers fell much less than might have been expected, partly because the numbers of telephones increased dramatically and telephonists were still needed for trunk calls and to assist callers. There were also arrangements made for what nowadays would be called redeployment, particularly for supervisors.[60]

The advent of the dial telephone did much to develop the systems and alter the perceptions of the customers. It created the basic designs which have become familiar down to our day. There were some who retained 'fond memories' of the 'hello girls'. More generally it was agreed by the 1940s that there was something to be said for the move away from having to speak 'into a hole in a varnished wooden box' to an exchange where all that could be heard was 'the clamour of innumerable voices' and then to 'a ruffled and an enormously distant squeak that you dimly recognised as your correspondent'. Even the modern manual exchange had become 'not much more than a sedate whispering gallery' with 'tiny glow lamps twinkling in and out'.[61]

Nor were these by any means the only improvements in the telephone facilities provided during this period. In 1929 'personal calls' were first introduced, in 1934 transferred charges calls, in 1936 the famous 'speaking clock' and in 1937 the first '999' emergency call system was started in London. Such services, and many others, have now become so much a part of the system that it is difficult to conceive how important they were in their day as developments of marketing and publicity, an answer to the critics from Wolmer onwards that a nationalised industry was incapable of displaying any imagination. Another interesting trend was in tariff alterations, including reductions for various services. Thus in October 1934 there were reductions in exchange line rentals and cheap trunk calls were introduced from 7 p.m. to 5 a.m., a period later extended. This latter change did not meet with unqualified delight from the staff, but they did show definite efforts to expand and improve the service.[62] There were important developments on the postal side during this period. The large numbers of collections and deliveries that had been common in Victorian times, at least in the major cities, were reduced. As late as 1943, however, there were still four deliveries a day in London. It was only in the 1960s that the provision of a continually operating postal system was overtaken by developments in electronic forms of communication. During the 1920s and 1930s there were many important improvements in methods of postal delivery. The small numbers of motor vehicles that had been used before 1914 were transformed into a great fleet covering most postal operations in the main cities by the 1920s. Another improvement in the passage of mails came through the Post Office underground railway, which opened in 1927, linking major stations north of the Thames from the Eastern District Office in Whitechapel to the main line station at Paddington.[63] The use of the aeroplane created the possibility of a world-wide and uniform service as well as improvements within Britain itself. This was initially seen as somewhat apart from the rest of the postal system, air mails were integrated into the normal system after 1936 without special post boxes or payments, and aeroplanes were also used to reach the more remote corners of the British Isles.

The 1930s also saw the first serious efforts to improve the productivity of postal operations by mechanical methods of sorting. In 1933 there came into use in Holland a machine known as the 'Transorma'.[64] This worked by letters going on a belt past an operator who tapped a number into a keyboard which then conveyed the letter to one of about 250 boxes. The machine, inevitably dubbed the 'robot sorter' in the press, was introduced as an experiment in the Brighton Sorting Office in October 1935. This followed a considerable amount of discussion with the

UPW. The Union forced the Post Office to employ postmen and sorting clerks and telegraphists rather than underpaid women, as was the case in Holland. They also agreed to people working the machines forty minutes on and twenty off, as against the sixty to fifteen in Holland. These conditions on the operation of the machine came not simply because of the negotiating skill on the Union side, but also because of the marked reluctance of the Post Office staff at Brighton to volunteer for duties which seemed distinctly onerous in comparison to team work on manual sorting, or the less relentless duties in serving at counters.

The 'Transorma' experiment did not prove a success. Some of this was the result of particular problems with the staff. The wartime 'temporaries' were paid allowances on a somewhat different basis from normal staff and efforts to set up a uniform system of payment collapsed in 1954. Later still the small group of members who could operate the machines had a vested interest in its continuance rather than the restoration of manual methods of sorting. These were, however, by no means the most important reasons for the problems of the 'Transorma'. For one thing, its initial installation involved the complete rebuilding of the Sorting Office. Thereafter the letters that came out of it were not properly 'faced', and so caused difficulties at a later point in their progress. In 1955, when the Post Office management surveyed the failure of efforts to get a standardised payments system, they admitted that the machines ran 'at a loss compared to the manual system', this being 'because the staff savings arising from their use are more than offset by the running costs of the machines'. They were finally abandoned in 1968 after a protracted period when the operators tried to put off the event until another mechanical sorting system could be employed. By then the 'Transorma' had become an anachronism, perhaps symbolising the extraordinary difficulties that always face those trying to improve the productivity of postal work.

THE LAST YEARS OF THE MILCH COW: 1939-55

This was to prove to be the final period during which the Treasury took over the profits of the Post Office each year after the manner of a milch cow, or at least it had been so described by Post Office reformers as far back as Henniker Heaton in the 1880s. These were also the last years when day-to-day political control of the Post Office resided in Parliament, and detailed administration was in the hands of the Postmaster General. As already indicated, the outbreak of war resulted in the collapse of the first efforts that had been made in the direction of financial autonomy for the Post Office. A new pricing policy also resulted in record profits to which the telephones for the first time made a significant contribution. The same system was retained in what were said to be the exceptional circumstances of the ten years after the end of the war in 1945, though by then inflationary pressures made it more difficult to adjust prices at such a rate as to maintain or increase the amounts paid to the Treasury.

The war did at least bring about the extension of one of the principles of the Bridgeman Report, and that was decentralisation. The entire country was covered by regional organisations during 1940, and at the same time the Headquarters' officials were sent to Harrogate and most of the money order staff to Morecambe. There were many strains to the system during the rest of the war, starting with the use of postal orders as legal tender for the first three months and continuing with falling traffic, shortage of manpower and the destruction of a great deal of property. For all that, the Post Office is generally thought to have maintained its part in the communication system at an exemplary level of efficiency throughout the war.[65]

A remarkable level of service was maintained in wartime. Daily deliveries were only reduced from four to three in London in 1943, and one delivery a day was organised to every unit of the armed forces. Though the traffic fell by about 25 per cent, such special tasks as the issue of ration books kept up the level of activity on the postal side. The penny post centenary was celebrated in melancholy manner in May 1940 by putting up the standard charge to 2½d, and telephone tariffs were also increased. This was partly at least in an effort to discourage use of the telephone during the war, and advertising was also issued to the same end.

In June 1940 the Battersea Branch office was destroyed by a bomb, but letters were delivered the next day in the area. On 29 December 1940 the historic Central Telegraph Office at St Martin's-le-Grand, which handled a quarter of the traffic in the country, was also destroyed. Within thirty-six hours alternative facilities were in operation on the same site. There were many similar achievements elsewhere, notably at the massive Mount Pleasant Sorting Office, which was also badly damaged. There were even some innovations in the services provided, such as the sending of 'airgraphs' – microfilmed air letters – from 1941 to 1945.

The decade after 1945 saw the restoration of many of the services discontinued by war.[66] The 'all up' rate for air mail, for example, was restored by 1948, at least for Europe. In the following year the travelling post offices on the railways, suspended during the war between the main towns, were restored. In 1951 the first use of the aeroplane for inland mail was announced. Labour shortages in the post-war period resulted in the restoration of war-time delivery restrictions in the main towns in 1948. However, by 1951 it was possible to announce late collections at around 8 p.m. in 900 centres. In the same period the telephone system expanded more rapidly than ever before with new investment, above £20 million, for the first time in 1947–8. In September 1949, a special ceremony saw the five millionth telephone handed over by PMG Wilfred Paling at a farmhouse in Kent. In 1950 it was claimed that Britain had the highest rate of growth of automatic telephone exchanges, and the confidence felt in the period can still be seen in the construction of buildings to house these exchanges in what were then the most up-to-date architectural styles at Newmarket and at Kelvin House just behind St Pancras Town Hall.

However, the level of investment, particularly in telecommunications, was still thought to be insufficient. There was, as one commentator has since put it, a 'capital and labour famine'. A Parliamentary Select Committee in 1950 proposed few measures that would be taken to deal with this, within the given financial arrangements. The shortage of labour and the effects of the economic downturn made it impossible to suggest how to keep up with the demand for telephones and to fill the spare capacity of the producers. As the first hesitant efforts began in 1951 to make prices match mounting costs, the UPW at least became convinced that 'Rowland Hill is Dead'.[67] By the early 1950s inflationary pressures and the changing structure of the service began to reduce its profits. As the appendices indicate, the main reason for this was the failure of the postal system to grow and the increasing problems of such services as parcels. In 1954, the same year as the large increases in the telegram tariff already referred to, parcel post rates were increased at all weights, and these prices crept up year by year. By 1 January 1956 even the once sacrosanct letter post finally went up by 25 per cent to 4d, though only for weights above two ounces.

CHANGE UNDER THE TORIES: 1955-64

In part because of the decline in profits from the Post Office, in part also because of new concepts of corporate management in an expanded public sector, the principles enumerated by Bridgeman were finally and irreversibly applied to Post Office finance in 1955-6.[68] Though the Treasury retained powers over the payment of wages and some other matters, a fixed sum of £5 million was to be paid to the Treasury, and three-year investment plans were to be worked out on the telecommunication side. 1956 not only marked the first step in cutting the historic link between the Post Office and the Treasury, it was also the first year that the income from the postal business was exceeded by that of telecommunications. This initiated a period of unparalleled technological growth in this field which, despite hiccups caused by trade recession and government policy, has continued apace up to the present day. In 1955, the Priestley Report on the Civil Service was also published establishing in its principle of 'fair comparison' the basis for bargaining about wages. This was to have an effect on Post Office affairs such that one commentator said of the Priestley Report and the 1955 White Paper setting out the changed financial relationships that 'the fates of the two documents were inexplicably linked'.[69]

Before setting out the detail of these changes, it is necessary to say something of the economic and political context in which they occurred. The post-1945 nationalisations resulted not only in increasing state intervention in the economy, but also in a phase of economic management outside the classically conceived free market price mechanism. From the point of view of efforts at general state intervention, the period after 1947 has been described as one that witnessed the 'demise of planning' and the 1950s as being 'extraordinarily tranquil for the most part'.[70] At the same time, the British economy went through a phase of unprecedented economic growth, cutting across periods of 'stop-go' in which government action played a part. There was a trend to increased state intervention, publicly promoted welfare services and broad political consensus. There were even discussions on what were known as 'the problems of affluence'. The historically unprecedented rates of inflation also caused greater consideration of corporate planning strategy in such matters as pricing policy. It is of interest to notice that the first discussions amongst orthodox 'neo-classical' economists about 'marginal cost pricing' often referred to postal and telecommunication services, and the first application of views about how to price different bits of the same service was to the Post Office.[71] For the first time discussion, both amongst outside commentators and those responsible for the services themselves, went beyond a simple consideration of overall surplus or deficit and long-term capital investment to deal with the losses of parcels as against letters and with variable tariffs between domestic and commercial users of the telephone.

A number of developments during the long period of Conservative Government from 1951 to 1964 were of considerable importance for the Post Office. In the early 1950s the so-called 'Butskell' period, named after Labour Chancellor Gaitskell and Tory successor Butler, was characterised by greater state regulation of the economy than had been normal in the past. From 1955 onwards there was a growing support for government management of the booms and slumps in the economy and an acceptance of some of the principles which had been enunciated by John Maynard Keynes. The boom, partly government induced, which preceded the General Election of 1959, allowed Tory Prime Minister MacMillan to win on the slogan 'you never had it so good'. The collapse of this boom resulted in widespread pressure from the business community and elsewhere, for a refinement of the means of economic planning. This policy was taken up and developed by the Wilson Labour administration after 1964. It has been said of the change of government in 1951 that 'an economic history could present a coherent picture of government policy without mentioning a change of government in order to explain what happened'.[72] The same can certainly be said of the change of government in 1964. Although the new government had its own policies in many fields, in matters of economic planning there was a clear continuity of policy before and after. Nowhere can this be seen more clearly than in the Post Office.

The attitudes to the Post Office are perhaps best symbolised in the characters of the last Tory holders of the office of Postmaster General. The ninth Earl De La Warr, who held the position from 1951 to 1955 was perhaps typical of the traditional aristocrat who had been assigned to it in the nineteenth century. Charles Hill, the 'radio doctor' who held the position from 1955 to 1957 was rather less typical. The last two PMGs were most definitely from the non-patrician wing of the Tory Party. Ernest Marples, from 1957–9, was one of the most prominent and, one might almost say, abrasive politicians of his day. He was succeeded up to 1964 by Reginald Bevins, who like Marples did not attend university, and who was also a self-made businessman from Merseyside. It was this rather special set of politicians who officiated over the development of a new system of Post Office administration and finance.

The first financial year when the Post Office was due to pay only £5 million of its profits to the Treasury was the one ending in April 1956. This proved to be unfortunate. In September 1957 there was a major international financial panic which included a balance of payments crisis in Britain and policies of retrenchment by the Government. Amongst other things, public investment was curbed, though not enough for Chancellor of the Exchequer Thorneycroft, who resigned along with two of his colleagues in January 1958.[73] These events had a considerable effect in the Post Office. The three-year development plan, which had been part of the new budgetary arrangements, was abandoned. Following this, in April 1957, the Post Office turned in its first deficit for thirty-five years. This was blamed by the Post Office management on post-Priestley wage awards, though in fact they were only able to attribute £22·7 million out of £52·9 million increased expenditure on this. The overall loss of over £3 million was made up of £1·5 million on the telegraphs, £1·7 million on the posts, with a very small surplus on the telephone side. It is also of some interest to notice that in this same loss-making year, the inland letter service turned in a healthy profit of £9 million and the parcel service an overall loss of £3·2 million.[74] This pattern of financial results dominated discussion on likely solutions for many years after.

These developments were the essential background of the drive to economy and efficiency in the Post Office in the years from 1957 to 1964 under the rule of Marples and Bevins. 'The public', wrote Bevins later, 'did not understand why when we were making millions we should go for higher prices.' The rationale for this was supposed to be efforts 'towards bringing the charges for individual services into fair relationship with the cost of these services'.[75] However, such a policy was by no means consistently carried out. In October 1957 it was the inland letter service, profitable in itself, which saw its first increase in prices since 1940, with the basic rate for inland letters going up from 2½d to 3d. Since the ensuing fall in traffic was only 1 per cent, a considerable temptation was created to resort to similar measures in the future. Prices on the telephone side could however be simplified and to some extent reduced as a result of the large investment programme in automatic telephones and Subscriber Trunk Dialling.[76]

After the Queen made the first STD call in Bristol in December 1958, the telephone system underwent unprecedented expansion. The overall growth can be seen from the figures given in Appendices 27 and 31. In 1960, there was a rapidly expanding demand and shorter waiting lists while the number of subscribers to manual exchanges fell below a million for the first time. In September 1960 some trunk telephone charges were actually reduced, and early in the following year it was possible to boast that with over 8 million telephones, the UK had more than anyone else outside the United States.[77] The UPW was involved in the changes which inevitably flowed from this. Thus Assistant Secretary Nan Whitelaw visited the United States in November 1958 as part of a team headed by the Director of Inland Telecommunications, F. I. Ray. One result was the announcement in March 1959 of a 'Friendly Telephone Policy'.[78] This combined something like boy scout exhortations with a faith in the new technology and methods of commercial enterprise. It is worth quoting a statement issued to staff at the time which gives something of the flavour:

1 For any great enterprise objectives must be clearly stated and widely understood.

2 The aim and purpose of the telephone service is not only to serve but to please the customer. Everything must be subordinated and surrendered to that aim.

3 Scientific advances are making possible the most sweeping and radical changes in telephone history. These match the electronic age in which we live. Much will always remain to be done but technically our course is charted for years ahead.

4 Scientific progress by itself is not enough. What really counts is the spirit of the men and women behind the machines. Machines must be servants not masters.

5 Our telephone service must be a personal service to meet the customer's wishes. We must study their wishes all the time; we must then satisfy them by a service which is courteous, pleasing and speedy.

6 To that end all our thinking, training, procedures and organisation will be directed – in every department at every level. And we must act boldly. We must not be paralysed by precedent or inhibited by fear of error. If we try and fail, we shall be forgiven. If we do not try, we shall be condemned – and rightly so.

7 But success will elude us unless we are a united, determined and dedicated team with management and staff moving in harmony.

8 Finally, we must never forget we are a monopoly. We do not face the challenge of competition. So we inherit special responsibilities to the community. We must not fail them. Let our purpose be to give the finest and most courteous service in the world. And let it be seen that we have this daily sense of purpose.

Nor were these the only changes in the telephone service in the period.[79] The award-winning and now familiar design of kiosks came with the STD system.

Telephone calls at the cheaper rates could be made after 6 p.m. from July 1958, and all day Sunday in July 1960. In 1959 the first experiments of the 'freephone' service were undertaken. In the next year or two improvements in marketing were introduced, such as allowing the use of credit card numbers in making calls. Following the Central Office of Information Survey on the telegraph service in 1957, and the Sinclair Committee Report of the following year, the Post Office began its own market research activities on the telephone side and encouraged local managers to take part in them. Efforts to improve the postal side of operations during this period included the introduction of a 'model' Post Office at Kingsway in London's West End in September 1958, providing the best facilities then available, the standardisation of letter boxes, and the abolition of specialised Post Office counters. A general expansion of the service was confirmed by the fact that for the first time in 1959–60, 10,000 million letters were sent within one year.

These developments took place during the 1959 Election boom, a period of 'go' soon to be followed by one of 'stop'. During 1960 there occurred what has been described as a 'Brighton Revolution' when a conference of the Federation of British Industries, then the main employers' organisation, called for greater government planning for economic growth.[80] At the same time, a long-term look at public expenditure undertaken by Lord Plowden and eventually published in July 1961 indicated a new set of attitudes on these matters.[81] Although accepting continued Parliamentary control, Plowden and his colleagues emphasised what they saw as the need for managerial professionalism. Appealing for five-year planning cycles of expenditure to match resources, they argued that throughout the public sector recent experience had shown 'that short-term "economy campaigns" and "stop–go" are damaging to the real effectiveness of the control of public expenditure'. At almost the same time, efforts were made to set out more general and rational criteria for the running of nationalised industries.[82] These enterprises should, it was said, 'pay their way' and plan their capital projects over periods of five years in order to do this. Targets for returns on capital were also advocated, and also pricing policies that allowed different services to cover their costs.

These discussions played a role in changing the economic policies of the Conservative Government, but they took place against the background of a deteriorating economy. A growing balance of payments deficit during 1961 was followed by a period of recession when unemployment rose to what was then considered an unacceptable level of almost a million. It was in the face of this that Tory Chancellor Selwyn Lloyd announced a series of economic measures on 25 July 1961, including a 'wage pause' and reductions in public spending.[83] On 'planning' he even announced that he was 'not frightened of the word'. The first timid effort to set up a machinery for this was the replacement of the Council on Productivity, Prices and Incomes of 1957 by the more effective National Incomes Commission in 1961. To this in 1962 was added the National Economic Development Council, which aimed to allow government, unions and employers to discuss long-term economic strategy.

These developments affected the Post Office in almost every possible way. Not only did the 'wage pause' lead to a great deal of strife between unions and management. During 1961, the financial arrangements of the Department were again revised.[84] A new Post Office Act was passed which increased its financial independence and aimed to bring about greater efficiency along the lines advocated by Plowden. The basic aim of the change, according to the White Paper that set it out, was to make the Post Office 'innovate and develop as a business seeking to meet and anticipate its customers'. Thus instead of the old system whereby estimates and appropriation accounts were discussed each year in Parliament, new profit and loss accounts were supposed to reflect more accurately real income and expenditure, including service to other government departments. Although the Postmaster General still had to present an annual report to Parliament, and although the Treasury retained control over staff pay and conditions and large-scale investment, many more day-to-day decisions were supposed to be placed in the hands of the Post Office management. The decisions in practice had to be taken within narrow constraints. Thus although the 1956-7 deficit was not repeated in the years immediately following, the £20·9 million surplus that was reached in 1959-60 still represented only 5 per cent of expenditure and about 2·5 per cent of assets employed. The major reason for this was the restrictions on investment that the Treasury continued to impose, which meant that despite all the technical innovations in the communications in the late 1950s, levels of investment only went up from £82·3 million in 1955-6 to £93·9 million in 1959-60. In the latter year this represented a return on capital of 7·8 per cent, though when the £6·2 million on the postal side was added, the overall return went up to 8·6 per cent. This clearly indicated the necessity for a new approach to Post Office financial arrangements, which was set out in this way:[85]

A public enterprise carries, of course, social obligations which rule out a precisely equal performance. But a concern like the Post Office, with capital requirements of some £100 million annually, can hardly be said to be paying its way unless it provides a return not too remote from that in the private sector, and one which will enable it to plough back a satisfactory proportion of its own capital. These conditions appear to call for a return on capital at any rate not less than 8 per cent.

During the period when Bevins was Postmaster General in the early 1960s, sustained efforts were made to keep the return on capital above 8 per cent, successful only in 1960-1, and to push up levels of investment, where much greater improvements could be reported.[86] The unhappy effects of these efforts on industrial relations in the Post Office are described elsewhere. For the moment it should be noted that the Postmaster General was faced with other problems also. In a period of economic downturn, the level of increase in business was not maintained. Profits began to fall again in 1961-3 though the final year of Tory rule saw them again at record levels. However, this result was achieved entirely from the expansion of telecommunications. On the postal side there was an extensive advertising campaign initiated in May 1963 on the slogan 'Someone somewhere wants a letter from you'. This was abandoned at the end of 1964 after costing £467,000 when it came up against a historically unprecedented and apparently intractable set of problems.

One new problem for the postal system in the late 1950s and early 1960s was an acute shortage of labour in the larger cities. This had important effects on Post Office working and wage patterns.[87] There was an increase in the level of overtime working which had considerable effects on earnings levels and bargaining patterns. There were also the first serious efforts at technical improvement on the postal side since the ill-fated 'Transorma' machine had been introduced in the 1930s. It was still a long time before the new machines had much effect on labour productivity.

This was not because of lack of co-operation from the UPW, which had a policy from 1956 of supporting technical innovation in return for shorter hours.[88] It was much more because of the considerable difficulty in constructing systems that could out-pace the dexterity of human eye and memory.

As early as 1955 a parcel-sorting machine constructed by the Sovex Company on principles similar to the 'Transorma' came into widespread use. An experimental machine for sorting letters introduced at Bath in the same year was not a success.[89] In 1957 electronic letter sorting started at Southampton and efforts began to be made to develop machines for facing letters. At the same time a more general system involving the use of postcodes began to be developed, initially to great publicity, but for a long time with limited effect.[90] In 1959 more serious efforts with the use of postcodes in the Norwich area were started and a mechanised sorting office was opened at Leeds. In 1961–2 machines were introduced at the South-Eastern District Office in London, and at Liverpool and Glasgow, which allowed the separation of letters from packets, faced letters the same way and franked them.

It was not an easy task to make such innovations as this affect the efficiency and profitability of the postal system. For one thing, there are considerable difficulties in improving productivity in sorting when only parts of the system operate on a mechanised basis. In any case, the most difficult problems in the postal system were not in the letter service at all but in the parcel post.[91] It had been the competition of the railways which had delayed the original introduction of the parcel post to as late as 1883. In 1935 there had been reductions in charges which had arrested the decline in traffic. After 1945 there was no significant increase in traffic and prices were frequently increased to compensate for shortfalls in income. From 1960 efforts were made to rationalise the system, and the Post Office and Treasury came to agree that there were no 'social obligations' involved in a service largely used by commerce. Serious efforts were made to centralise and rationalise the system starting with an experiment in East Anglia in 1963 and culminating in a programme introduced in 1967 to reduce the number of parcel sorting depots from 1,400 to thirty-five. These schemes, which had the support of the UPW, resulted in the parcel service making a profit in 1967–8, the first time since separate figures were published in 1957.[92] This happy position did not continue into the 1970s however when problems of pricing and growing competition from the outside significantly reduced traffic and brought in its train a further set of losses.[93] By the mid-1970s the Post Office Board even contemplated abandoning the service altogether, but pressure from the UPW amongst other things led to its retention, and an invigorated marketing policy has in the early 1980s again pushed up the traffic in advance of the centenary of the service in 1983.

In the early 1960s the problems of the postal system remained acute, as mounting losses showed. The main solution attempted was to increase prices and this was done for virtually all categories of mail except the standard inland letter. Other efforts included the standardisation of Post Office buildings and counters, the opening of a Philatelic Bureau and the issuing of sets of colourful stamps. It was later claimed soon after the inland postal rate was increased by 25 per cent from 3d to 4d in 1965 that the long-term problems of the postal system had been suppressed and ignored.[94] The problems were in any case marked by the fact that there was 'much greater scope for increasing productivity by the introduction of new inventions and approved techniques' in telecommunications, and increasing investment went into this. This was a period of the expansion of Subscriber Trunk

Dialling, and the first long-term planning of telephones symbolised perhaps by the new Post Office Tower dominating the North London skyline. Waiting lists were reduced and the most ambitious of long-term plans were eventually fulfilled.[95] In 1962 it was possible to report the first demonstrations of data transmission, and a new experimental satellite communication centre was opened at Goonhilly Down in Cornwall, not far from the spot where Marconi had transmitted radio signals across the Atlantic. These developments presented hope for the future and made it possible to say that the Post Office had become

> a Ministry of Communications, a science-based enterprise on the threshold of a new era of expansion and improvement made possible by new inventions and the application of new techniques which are changing the art and shape of communications.[96]

THE POST OFFICE UNDER LABOUR: 1964–70

It was against the background of this technological change that the balance of Post Office activity in the mid-1960s shifted decisively into telecommunications. The new marvels of economic communication that appeared every year were but particular manifestations of the general expansion of high technology industry, when a new generation of scientific technique brought with it a phase of economic growth unparalleled before or since. The 'white heat' of the 'scientific revolution' promised by Harold Wilson before his election as Labour Prime Minister in 1964 has long since dimmed and disappeared. Nevertheless, such phrases did accord with contemporary perceptions of economic reality, as well as with conventionally approved solutions to the economic problems of the time. They certainly had considerable effects on the Post Office.[97]

If, as has already been emphasised, the 1964 Labour Government did not suddenly invent economic planning, or a passion for administrative reform and advanced management technique, it did develop these ideas to the highest point they were to attain. Though the Conservatives initiated the National Economic Development Council in 1961, it was Labour who expanded the concept through the ill-fated 'National Plan' of 1964. If the Tories had tried the National Incomes Commission in 1962, it was Labour who developed the larger and more pervasive National Board for Prices and Incomes in 1965. The Tories commissioned the Plowden Report of 1961, which argued for managerial efficiency in the public sector. It was the Labour administration that set up the Fulton Committee of 1966–8, with its sustained attack on 'the philosophy of the amateur', and its call for technical experts and 'skilled managers' to run the civil service.[98] Since the 1960s the great reforms of what were regarded as a turning point in the history of the civil service have increasingly been brought into question. The professional managers are said not to have been produced by the Civil Service College, and in 1981 the Civil Service Department, the most important of the Fulton-initiated reforms, was finally abolished.[99] Yet the importance of these developments at the time should not be underestimated, nor their role as part of 'the widely held belief in the 1960s that performance could be improved by structural reform'.[100] The all-pervasive character of the optimistic notions of those days should not be forgotten by those compelled to live through times that have made them more cynical and more sad.

The changes in the Post Office after 1964 should be seen in the context of this same exaggerated faith in the efficiency of the technological innovation and administrative reform. The Post Office had some basis for such optimism. As is well known, the exaggerated growth forecasts of the 1965 National Plan were not in general attained, interrupted as they were by the July 1966 sterling crisis and the measures that followed. Although the Post Office was affected by the same interruptions, overall investment levels went up from £187·3 million in 1964–5 to £459·8 million in 1970–1. This was 44 per cent above the £319·3 million figure set out in the National Plan, a good increase even allowing for a rate of inflation of approximately 30 per cent.[101]

The mid 1960s was also the first period of steadily rising prices in the Post Office. The much discussed 25 per cent increase in the basic inland postal rate in 1965 gave the postal service a three-year run of profits between 1964 and 1967, the only such set from 1955 to 1976. During the same period improvements in segregating and facing machines were introduced and the National Postal Museum was opened. The postcode system was also expanded and in September 1968 the two-tier postal system was introduced, mainly as a method of rationalising the deployment of labour through the working day.[102] The further 20 per cent increase in inland letter rates introduced at the same time did not have the same effect in pushing up profits. Progress in telecommunications continued to cover for this, and the extraordinary growth of this part of the system was symbolised by the opening of the Post Office Tower in 1966. Another manifestation of the expanding telephone system came in the abandonment of the old names of the exchanges and their replacement by all-number dials. There were some who regretted the loss of once-familiar words:[103]

> Must we forever say goodbye to you
> Poetic KEAts and WORdsworth – BYRon too?
> Majestic ELGar stirling IVAnhoe,
> Immortal DICkens, GIBbon (the scholars woe) . . .?

and so on, until . . .

> Time marches on and calls us to pursue;
> To-morrow to fresh dials and systems new!

In this period also the Bulk Supply Agreements with the private telecommunications suppliers, which had existed since the 1930s, could now be shown to have restricted the growth of the system and its ability to export. As a result they were essentially brought to an end in 1967 by Postmaster General Short.[104]

Short's predecessor Benn had been responsible also for a number of measures aimed to expand the services provided by the Post Office. As well as increasing the activities of the Savings Bank, Benn finally consummated what had long been the earnest desire of Post Office trade unionists by announcing in July 1965 the setting up of the National Giro. After some false starts and early difficulties this has become a part of the whole service.[105] Even this, however, did not prove to be the last of the important changes of this period. For the 1960s saw a process of rationalisation and administrative changes which brought the biggest upheaval in the Post Office since the 1830s.

The first changes came in the sphere of consultative machinery. The setting up of local telephone committees in 1911 has been mentioned already.[106] The Bridgeman Report in 1932 recommended the strengthening of the National Advisory Committee[107] and in 1933 it was reconstituted to include Charles Craig, General Secretary of the National Union of Railwaymen and John Cliffe, at the time an official of the Transport and General Workers Union, but later a member of the London Passenger Transport Board. In 1945 Bowen, who had retired as General Secretary of the UPW, joined. Meanwhile the local committees were revamped to cover all aspects of the work of the Post Office and they remain, largely representative of commercial interests, in that form to this day. The National Advisory Committee does not seem to have been a great success. It only met a dozen or so times between 1955 and 1965. It had fallen into desuetude altogether in 1965 when Postmaster General Benn decided to set up a Post Office Users National Council which aimed

> to represent at national level the interests of the users of Post Office services, to ensure the existence of adequate consultative arrangements at local level; to receive proposals from the Postmaster General, and to make recommendations to him about the services.

The new national body consisted largely of representatives of the local organisations and was given more power under the 1969 Act to be consulted on major changes in Post Office policy. Under the chairmanship initially of E. D. Kamm from ICI and later of Lord Peddie, formerly of the Co-operative Wholesale Society, who before his death in April 1978 had made the Users Council very much bear his imprint, POUNC took up its responsibilities with enthusiasm, and certainly with greater effect than similar bodies in other nationalised industries. However, as the emergence of such outside groups as the Mail Users Association showed, it did not serve all the interests for which it was intended.[108]

Another new institution founded during this period with even more publicity was the Economic Development Council ('little Neddy') for the Post Office. First established in March 1966, this was seen as yet another development of national economic planning, the first EDC dealing exclusively with the public sector.[109] This issued a flurry of reports on such vital issues as the problem of forecasting demand and the structure of telephone tariffs, where it advocated change to make trunk calls cheaper.[110] It also discussed and supported the two-tier system of postal charging. However, the shocks created by restrictions on public expenditure, rivalry between the various parts of the service, and union disquiet about involvement in the whole enterprise, resulted in the collapse of the EDC, which did not survive incorporation.

Another part of the effort to plan and develop the Post Office was the appointment in 1965 by Postmaster General Benn of the McKinsey management consultant firm to perform a full-scale inquiry into the workings of the Department. McKinsey's began by drawing attention to what were considered to be 'forces which tended to inhibit management from seeking change', including 'Parliamentary control', 'a lack of definition of specific end-results', 'the absence of a major incentive which would award the innovator and the risk taker' and finally 'the inevitable inertia resulting from lengthening and drawn-out joint consultations before any change is implemented'. A good number of specific changes came from the McKinsey study. They included the appointment in November 1965 of a Deputy Director on the Telecommunications side, and after that of a Planning

Branch within the postal service. The Post Office began to set out some specific goals for management, such as a scheme for profit improvement in head post-masters' areas. McKinsey also influenced the efforts which began to be made in 1967 to predict likely influences on future postal business and to rationalise sorting office methods and counter duties. It was also said that the administrative separation of the three parts of the service that evolved up to the incorporation of 1969 came from McKinsey.[111] However, no final McKinsey Report ever appeared. The reason for this is alleged to have been that the Prime Minister Harold Wilson, under pressure from the UPW and elsewhere, resisted the creation of a separate telecommunications corporation. However, he was unable to resist the pressure now growing for incorporating the Post Office as a whole and taking it out of the direct ambit of government.[112]

The beginning of discussion on this process, though not necessarily the decision itself, began through the Select Committee on Nationalised Industries, which deliberated through 1966 and reported early in the following year.[113] This aimed to provide as comprehensive a survey of the Post Office as had Bridgeman in 1932. If the Select Committee did not initiate so many changes as Bridgeman it certainly reflected the fact that they were taking place, and produced a report and evidence taking account of a wide range of opinions and attitudes of the time. All of the main problems of postal mechanisation and profitability as well as telecommunication development were outlined from the point of view of management and unions. For the first time Post Office Director General Sir Edward German was able to go beyond expressing his approval of the growth of independence following the changes of management and finance in 1955 and 1961 and to assert that there was 'a growing realisation that the problems facing the two services are so very different' and that 'possibly a good case could be made for separation'.[114] For their part, the unions representing various grades in telecommunications were moving to call for incorporation of the service. The UPW had come to favour a unified corporation, but the non-engineering unions as a whole favoured the continued existence of the Department of State.[115] Although the new system was decided as the discussions went on, the Select Committee also considered more detailed questions of development, accountability and pricing policy, the first time that such matters had been discussed so publicly and so systematically.

The Select Committee's Report set out what had by then become the conventional wisdom on the running of the Post Office. It assumed the necessity of a change in status, and was particularly trenchant on pricing policy which it asserted had been determined in the past by political expediency rather than economic rationality. It thought the 1966 postal increases had been 'still disappointingly limited' and advocated the further development of forward planning. It asserted that on the telecommunications side 'the present tariff structure has grown up in a haphazard manner' with charges too low for rentals and local calls and too high for long distance. It also definitely asserted that 'each section of the service should be priced so that revenues cover the cost', though admitting that some elements of social provision had to be assumed at least on the postal side.[116]

The 1967 Report in many ways reflected the transition from the era of seeing the Post Office as a public service to one when it became simply 'a business' almost without qualification. In the same period of transition from department of state to public corporation, the Post Office also faced a period of particularly rapid price rises combined with general government pressures on the finances of the public sector. In November 1967 a new White Paper built on the financial arrangements which had previously been set out in 1961.[117] More emphasis was now placed on each part of an enterprise paying for itself, and it was proposed that the Post Office should aim at an overall rate of return of 8 per cent. This was later divided into 8·5 per cent for telecommunications and 2 per cent for posts. The Prices and Incomes Board considered this along with a new proposed set of increases in charges, and published a Report early in 1968.[118] The Board made the most thorough analysis yet published of Post Office forecasting and pricing policy. It argued for the refinement of forecasting methods and tariffs based on a more thorough application of what was known as marginal cost pricing. In other words, separate individual services were supposed to pay for themselves. In the meantime, however, the Board did not propose anything significantly different from what the Post Office itself wanted. It supported the two-tier postal system and the price increases involved in that, and proposed very small modifications in the telephone charge increases.[119]

By now, however, the Post Office was well launched on its reorganisation as a public corporation. Announced on 3 August 1966 by the Postmaster General Edward Short, this was a step which can be said to have flowed logically from the reforms of the previous decade, but its progress illuminated a number of important changes which had taken place in attitudes over the years.[120] Perhaps most surprising of all was the change on the part of the UPW. Though always in the past passionately opposed to the public corporation as such, its spokesmen now came to the view that its role as a 'political football' had become untenable and it would be best 'taken out of this arena so its staff could get on with the jobs'. Within four years of the new arrangements and despite the crippling strike of 1971, the Union's Deputy General Secretary thought that

the conclusion must be reached that a Business type organisation such as the Corporation provides is more suitable to the needs of the Post Office organisation on the basis of a Government Department.[121]

On the management side in the Post Office there was no apparent reluctance to accept the new arrangements. This allowed them to develop a new range of regional and other organisations aiming to respond to the McKinsey complaints about 'under management'. There was also the strong bait of greater administrative independence and a diminution of the day-to-day political control which had long been said to hamper their work. For certain Conservative politicians the change made it possible to argue for separation of the postal and telecommunication sides of the service, usually now linked with a weakening of the monopoly and handing over of sections of the service to private enterprise.[122]

The new organisation did develop the trend towards separation of posts and tele-communication which had been implicit for more than a decade.[123] The new Post Office Board was small and functional, not reflecting, for example, as in most similar bodies, the interests of consumers. The Postmaster General was replaced by a Minister of Posts and Telecommunications with fewer powers and also with fewer day-to-day responsibilities for the running of the service. To compensate for this, annual reports were still to be presented to Parliament, and the role of the Users Council was emphasised. Corporate status did not basically alter the financing of the Post Office, which had to be provided internally to produce the same general targets as other nationalised industries. On the question which was only then becoming of significance the Government's White Paper took the same view as the Select Committee had a few months earlier:[124]

> Posts and Telecommunications are vast businesses in themselves, with different characteristics and meeting different needs. But they have been run jointly by the Post Office in the past and are complementary in some respects and interdependent in others . . . There are thus real advantages in the continued overall direction of . . . affairs by a single body.

The transition from government department to public corporation was eased by this means. However, during the course of the transition local and regional organisations of the two sides of the Post Office were developed independently and the proportion of common service functions on a national level was reduced, so that the ultimate separation became more likely.

FROM INCORPORATION TO CLEAVAGE: 1969–81

There can be no question but that the final twelve years of existence of the unified Post Office saw by far the most continuous and tumultuous set of changes in its entire period of existence.[125] There was first of all the 'vast labour' involved in the actual transition to corporate status.[126] At the same time, despite a waning faith during the 1970s in the efficiency of administrative change, the Post Office nevertheless saw development in its form, its financing and its functioning greater than at any previous time. Writing at the time of the break-up of an institution which has existed for many centuries, it is not easy to assess which events of its last decade have long-term significance. However, some indication can be given of what appears now to be important in the light of the historical experience that has been considered.

One major point will no doubt continue to be valid, even after two completely separate corporations come to look at their own particular problems, and it is this. However much the Post Office and its successors move away from the old forms of finance and organisation, the decisive role of government influencing levels of profit, prices and wages has by no means been abandoned. The accounts of the postal and telecommunications services are no longer subject to Parliamentary scrutiny each year, nor do the profits revert to the Treasury. Yet all the significant developments in the system remain tied to changes in government economic policies in ways which are even more overpowering than before. When the Corporation had been in existence for little over a year, its first Chairman, Lord Hall, was sacked over disagreements on such questions, and this may well have been behind Sir William Barlow's premature retirement in 1980. The economic policies of the Conservative administration of the early 1970s were the direct cause of the record deficits and reduced investment levels that followed, and the different attitudes of the Labour administration failed at first to limit the rapid wage and price increases of 1975. Once again, at the time of writing, the so-called 'cash limits' of the administration of Margaret Thatcher, hold back the development of postal and telecommunications systems in ways which are no different in kind or effect from the Treasury book-keeping of the 1950s leading to the starvation of investment, or indeed from the decades of the 'milch cow' when profits were used to replenish the

Treasury coffers. At all times economic and financial pressures from outside the system, mediated through government, have influenced its development quite independently of its own needs and momentum. Even handing over sections to private capital may not alter this as much as some people imagine.

If the Post Office in the 1970s can be said to have been dominated by one influence above all others, that would no doubt be said to be the historically unprecedented price increases, particularly in the middle of the decade. The period was punctuated with three major points of crisis – the 1971 UPW strike, the 1975 financial collapse, and the inability of sections of the postal service to carry out their obligations in 1979. Throughout these years, unprecedented technological development and profound external economic crisis created long-term problems for the Post Office which were accompanied by a level of public criticism at least as great as in the 1830s and the 1920s.

The new Post Office administration did not mince its words about its preliminary problems:[127]

> the Board took over a postal service which was running at a loss, a telecommunications service which faced explosive growth at a time when contractors were falling well behind in providing new equipment, a National Giro which had made a disappointing start, and some under-developed opportunities for improving service efficiency and profitability. Labour relations, though traditionally good on the whole, were deteriorating, partly because of uncertainties among the staff about the implications of reorganisation and change . . . Furthermore, both sophisticated and lay criticism had sharpened against the GPO and had, indeed, become acrimonious.

The 1971 strike which followed was not simply a result of the strains of the transition to incorporation, the uncertainty felt by the workforce and the disappointed expectations that followed the chance. It also derived more particularly from government attempts to impose restrictions on the wages of a group who were in any case touchy and frustrated. This was but one aspect of the economic policies of a Tory Government in the early 1970s attempting to deal in its own particular way with record levels of inflation.

During each of the first three years of the 1970s, the retail price index went up by 8 per cent per annum. In 1973 this increased to 12 per cent, in 1974 to almost 20 per cent and in 1975 to a peak of 23½ per cent, including monthly increases of 4 per cent in both April and May of that year.[128] It was not simply these facts but the efforts of the Conservative Government to deal with them which dominated the affairs of the Post Office in the early 1970s. From the beginning the Government showed itself willing to be persuaded to keep down charges. Increases in postal rates were first of all delayed under pressure from the Post Office Users National Council from September 1970 to February 1971, thus losing the postal service £30 million. The deficit then began to climb. In July 1971 the Post Office was persuaded, it was said, by 'political private arm twisting' to support the initiative of the Confederation of British Industries by agreeing to keep price rises down to 5 per cent.[129] Over the following period of mounting deficits, the Government was eventually persuaded to agree to subsidise the losses on behalf of its prices policy. However, the losses rapidly mounted, eventually reaching the extraordinary figure of £308 million in 1974–5. This had all kinds of serious long-term consequences, however attractive it appeared to consumers in the short term. As the Post Office Users National Council pointed out at the time this could only be achieved by a policy of 'under pricing' which[130]

> can lead to artificial stimulation of demand in some areas, and will inevitably generate serious criticism of the Post Office when eventually prices are put back to a realistic level.

Nor were the policies on Post Office prices by any means the only way that major problems were stored up in the early 1970s. Thus the efforts to keep down wages did not end with the 1971 confrontation, and in fact proved more successful than in outside private industry. The inevitable result of this was an increase in the already existing labour shortage to 10 per cent of what was thought necessary overall, and more than that in such places as London and Birmingham. The failure of the Post Office to deliver many millions of cards posted for Christmas 1972 was but one consequence. By 1974 it was clear that the service was deteriorating more generally, with less than 90 per cent of first class letters now being delivered the next day, and the Post Office Board was able to quote numerous other examples of the unpleasant results of 'the unparalleled shortages of Postmen and Telephonists'. The Board also issued a statement unprecedented in the entire history of the Post Office, which must have had every Post Office administration since Francis Freeling and Rowland Hill turning in their graves. They went so far as to express their sympathy for[131]

> the deep sense of unfairness and disquiet amongst Post Office staff who felt their pay had fallen seriously behind the general level of pay for similar work done elsewhere.

Some of the other developments of these years have much more of a feeling of *déjà vu* about them. This applies in particular to the Government decision of December 1973 to enforce a 20 per cent reduction in capital spending.[132] Though brought down to 13 per cent in 1975, this proved difficult to enforce and had disastrous consequences for the maintenance and development of the service. In particular it indicated that the much-vaunted independence of the new corporation was as illusory as it had ever been for the Department of State. The same factors lay behind the extraordinary story of the Post Office Pension Fund, where problems derived from the lack of serious provision for managing such enormous sums ever since they were cut loose from the Treasury in 1961. Even though a contributory element was introduced with incorporation, its real financial position was apparently never questioned or discussed. Rates of inflation then caught up with nominal investment of the Fund in government stock, allowing outsiders to blame anybody and everybody for subsequent problems and making it possible for the Government to avoid its real responsibilities. Currently, as the splitting of the Fund is being discussed, a general principle of paying for it year by year has evolved.[133]

The consequences of the very high inflation of the early 1970s affected the Post Office in many other important ways. Thus in 1975 the new Labour Government decided to return to economic pricing. Wages were improved and with them recruitment of staff and the services they provided. During the course of the year the price of first class inland mail was almost doubled, in two steps from 4½p to 8½p. Increases in telephone charges on a similar scale resulted in disconnections being greater than the demand for new connections. Nevertheless, it was quite possible for the Post Office management to assert in the following year that 'critics who prophesied that services had been priced out of the market were proved to be wrong', as profit levels came back into the black even for the postal system other than parcels.[134]

As had been prophesied by everyone including the Prices and Incomes Board, these inevitable price increases convinced the ignorant – and the malevolent – that there was something terribly wrong with the Post Office. During 1975 the Select Committee on Nationalised Industries considered the letter service, but, like its predecessor a decade before, was overtaken by events and confined itself to generalities while welcoming the newly constituted outside inquiry under the chairmanship of Charles Carter, Vice Chancellor of the University of Lancaster.[135] As public disquiet against the price increases built up during the year, the Conservative opposition took the opportunity not simply to call for the second major inquiry into the Post Office but also to attack the monopoly, the unions and public enterprise generally.[136] The Labour administration therefore initially resisted the inquiry, but was soon compelled to give in to the somewhat separate set of pressures from the Post Office Users National Council for 'a programme of immediate and lasting reductions in costs', without 'cuts in basic services', and as a necessary step in this direction, a 'full and wide ranging enquiry'.[137]

The Carter Enquiry and Report cannot yet be said in any sense to be matters of history.[138] At the time of writing, legislation to give effect to some of its proposals has only recently been enacted. The Report involved a great deal more than simply the splitting up of the Post Office, which was in any case the logic of the history of the last twenty-five years. It also provided the pretext for the development of more sophisticated forms of forecasting and measuring the performance of the Post Office, as well as a serious attempt to look at the financing of the system beyond the simple criteria of profit and loss which had so clearly failed to measure anything important during the crisis years of the mid-1970s. However, if the measure of 'short-run marginal cost pricing' is to be the main means whereby decisions are made about costs and tariffs, it will never simply be as a 'business' that the entire system will survive. It must certainly be said that the Carter Report, of all the documents about the Post Office produced during its long history, is perhaps the most difficult to read or to understand. It is also conspicuously innocent of that very history, assuming that such problems as profitability and work organisation never existed before 1975 and that the solution can be found in greater vigour of management technique quite apart from the economic and political context. If the gruff no-nonsense tone of Carter and his colleagues means that they cannot be accused of the naïve optimism of a Tony Benn or a Rowland Hill, it does nevertheless conceal other preconceptions which may not be true. Like Charles Dickens's Mr Gradgrind they assume that more and more facts, this time about Post Office performance, will, when collected, allow the solution to problems which may themselves be no less intractable for being described and quantified.

However, it will only be after much more water has flowed under many more bridges that it will be possible to see these developments in their historical context. It will then not be considered surprising that the Government of the day hesitated to carry out Carter's recommendations at a time when it was attempting to alter the structure of Post Office government through the 'industrial democracy' experiment.[139] If this experiment could be seen in some quarters as the fulfilment of the dreams of the old guild socialists, it could also be seen as a last effort to plan the communications system generally in terms of social needs. Others were arguing at the same time that the 'Council on Post Office and Telecommunications Affairs' advocated in the earlier Report as an advisory body should be utilised as a means whereby decisions could be taken in relation to the economy as a whole as they affected employment, planning and growth.[140] The possibility of more refined methods of looking at the public sector in terms of economic rationality and efficiency was further developed.[141]

This all came to a sudden stop in 1979. The serious deterioration in the postal services during the summer of that year produced a new chorus of abuse against the Post Office and its employees, but also some constructive suggestions about changes of technology and organisation.[142] The change of Government of the same year brought with it not simply a new commitment to the break-up of the old Post Office, but also a propensity to question the need for public provision of its services.

At the time of writing in the early 1980s yet another wave of institutional change is sweeping through the system. Many of the organisational changes advocated by Carter are being carried out, and there can be no question of their long-term significance. More doubt must however be cast on whether the ill-thought-out and dogmatic efforts currently being made to hand over sections of the Post Office to private enterprise will prove either practical or enduring. Amidst technological changes that continually expand the scope of telecommunications and lead some to doubt whether the postal system can survive as it has been, an abiding and over-riding problem will undoubtedly persist – the tension between public enterprise and government. Amidst current discontents this problem will inevitably remain, and differences will always exist on planning and investment decisions between those who look to the development of the communication system and those who have wider political interests. It is hardly necessary to be reminded of this when of the first three chairmen of the unified Post Office, one was dismissed and one is thought to have resigned precisely over arguments on long-term investment plans. As for the other, he issued scarcely-veiled attacks on the 'formidable' powers still wielded by government.[143] Thus it is that where once was written 'Treasury control' there now appears some such phrase as 'cash limits' or 'lower public spending'. In all cases the effect is the same. A general agency, acting for good or ill through government, over-rides those who attempt to develop the posts and telecommunications systems themselves. This influence may be eternal. It certainly dominates the history of the past sixty years, and will continue to do so.

THE UNION AND CHANGE IN THE POST OFFICE

There is no particular reason why a trade union should be for or against technical or organisational change initiated by those who employ the members it represents. There is no necessary correlation between such changes and the welfare of the workforce. So a union may sometimes be in favour of change, and sometimes against, depending on its likely effect. A number of examples have been quoted during the course of this chapter showing the UPW co-operating with change on some occasions and on others opposing it. It is not always certain that from either point of view it has necessarily served the interests of its members.

One thing that has usually happened is that whenever the Post Office as a whole has been under attack, the workforce in general and the unions in particular have always been imputed a share of the blame. This was the case from the time of the criticisms launched by Lord Wolmer in the late 1920s to the abrasive intervention of Reginald Bevins in the early 1960s and the attacks on the letter service in the late 1970s. Such developments have been known to drive unions and management into one another's arms, and the Parliamentary debates from 1930 which have already been quoted provide a good example of this.

Union members have often seen themselves as proponents of the expansion of the facilities of the Post Office. The most well known example of this was the campaign for the postal cheque system initiated by the United Kingdom Postal Clerks Association in 1910, taken up by the TUC and rejected by the Post Office authorities.[144] The idea was taken up notably by the Fabian Society and was also continued by the UPW. A number of delegations met the management in the 1920s, but an outside inquiry rejected it in 1928.[145] The UPW continued to advocate it, notably through J. Craig Walker who was the Chairman in 1930.[146] The eventual establishment of the Giro system after 1965 cannot simply be attributed to the trade unions, but the planting of its seed and its early development certainly can.

Nor were they by any means the only ideas for the development of the Post Office which emanated from the Union side. As early as 1921 it was said that

the formation of the 'UPW' . . . represented an important step, not only towards the idea of a Union inclusive of the whole industry, but also towards the more conscious adoption of a policy of using the power and knowledge of the Union to increase and develop the efficiency of the Post Office as a form of national service.

The resources of the Union were used not simply to propose reorganisation of the service but also to advocate in the mid-1920s the freeing of the service from Treasury control and the use of all profits for investment in ways that did not come into effect for thirty years. The Union also proposed in 1930, before such things were seriously considered by the authorities, 'an extended and sustained publicity campaign', brighter facilities, an extension of the parcel post and special express delivery services.[147]

The UPW and the other unions on the non-engineering Whitley Council reacted angrily against the pre-Bridgeman campaign of criticism against the Post Office. They opposed all talk of handing over the services provided to a public utility company or to private enterprise.[148] Their preliminary response to the main proposals of Bridgeman was also negative, but more cautious. Early in 1935 the UPW expressed the view that 'large regions would not tend to the public advantage', but was prepared to accept a 'truly experimental scheme'.[149] During most of 1935 and 1936, the UPW Executive's discussion on the new regional structure largely centred on the access to promotion to posts which had been moved to regional offices. It was members of the Controlling Officers Association who lost the jobs, but after considerable discussion with the CSCA most of the posts in the end were open to manipulative grades and very few supervisory posts were lost in the district offices.[150] By the beginning of 1937 it was becoming clear that most of the fears the Union had expressed in the new structure had been proved unfounded and General Secretary Hodgson told the Executive that amongst the officers there was a general agreement that while decentralisation has produced no violent changes from the system that was in operation before the Bridgeman Report, there is evidence of a certain relaxation of the stiffness which existed under the former system. Every opportunity had been conceded by the Regional Directors for frank discussion on all subjects.

The first two of the regional directors had already visited the Union's Headquarters and had been quite prepared to discuss matters where the Union had no formal rights. Thus when further regions began to be established in 1938, the Union expressed reservations about the speed with which they were introduced but did not seriously oppose them.[151] It is interesting to note that all of these changes took place through Union Headquarters, and although some Union members wanted the growth of regional structures and support for regional Whitley councils, this was strongly resisted by the Union's leaders and ultimately defeated.[152]

After the war, there were still members of the Union who opposed the regional structure, but they were easily overruled by the leadership. General Secretary Geddes, as already indicated, was involved in a review of the system in 1950.[153] Besides the major reorganisation of grades during this period, the Union was also involved in discussions about the reduction of postal deliveries in London and the large cities, and the longer opening of offices. The conflict between management aims and workforce aspirations was clearly shown in the bitter arguments about earlier deliveries, later collections and the increase in split attendances. In London at least there were even hints of possible secession from the Union.[154] Such a resolution of the problem was pre-empted by the manpower shortage of 1947, which forced the abandonment of many later deliveries and so great a reduction in split attendances that large compensation could be granted for what remained.[155]

On more particular questions of technical change, the Union never presented a blank wall of opposition. This applied almost throughout its history on the problems of the telegraph system. The Union could hardly have been expected to find much to favour in the Hardman–Lever Report of 1928 since it largely blamed the members for the problems of the service. It did however acquiesce, after the visit by Simon and his colleagues to the United States, in the changes, including the introduction of new technology, which followed after 1930. On the telephone side, the fact that the introduction of automatic working did not greatly reduce the workforce may have had the effect of increasing union propensity to co-operate with technical change.

Attitudes did not change quickly, however. The Union did agree to take part in the Post Office Joint Productivity Committee when it was set up in 1949.[156] There were difficulties in its early years caused in part by the proposed inclusion of secessionists and in part by Union resistance to regional machinery. In 1950, the Union refused to take part in the Anglo–American Productivity Committee despite strong pressure from the TUC, and there was a good deal of internal dissension including a narrow vote at the Annual Conference about accepting a productivity handout in 1952.[157] In general, discussion was more concerned with changing manpower deployment resulting from technical change. The important 1956 Conference decision about accepting such change in return for the reduction of hours has already been referred to, and the consequences can be seen in the participation of the Union in another visit to the United States in 1959, this time to look at the telephone system, and in discussions that same year on the future of the telegraph service.[158] Similarly, the Union co-operated with postal mechanisation schemes of this period. Ron Smith was a member of the Director General's Forward Policy Group on Postal Mechanisation in the late 1950s, and the Union's journal frequently and favourably commented upon the various developments in postal mechanisation in the period. On the other hand, the Union remained unconvinced by a scheme doggedly argued by Edwin Wells and his Postal Reform League for mail sent after midday to be cheaper and slower – something not far from the two-tier system eventually adopted in 1968.[159]

In more recent years, the Union has still tended to remain conservative on matters of organisational change, but has been closely involved in developments of tele-graphy, automatic telephones and sorting machinery. It actively co-operated with large-scale reorganisation aimed to preserve the parcel service and more recently initiated a full consideration to the likely long-term effects of further technological change.[160] It is hardly to be wondered at, however, that it remains opposed to further organisational change based on reducing the facilities provided and putting an end once and for all to all elements of service in posts and telecommunications.

NOTES

1 Despite the importance of the subject the secondary literature on which this chapter has been based is necessarily very limited. The best accounts remain Robinson (1948 and 1953) though they grow thinner on the more recent period. Two useful accounts from inside the service are Murray (1927) and Crutchley (1938). For the more recent period, see Pitt (1980), by far the fullest account of the matter, and Corby (1979) which unfortunately only deals with the most recent period. Also of interest are the officially produced *The Post Office 1934*, *The Post Office 1950*, *The Post Office 1951*, as well as the forty-seven 'Green Papers' on various subjects produced in 1933–9.
2 Staff (1964), p. 150 and Smith (1917), *passim*.
3 Saxon Mills (1924), p. 101.
4 Kieve (1973), pp. 250, 290.
5 *Post*, 12 February 1921, p. 152, is a good example.
6 Select Committee on Telephone Charges in PP 1920 XXVII.
7 Select Committee on the Telephone Service in PP 1921 VII and 1922 VI.
8 Pitt (1980), p. 57; *Post*, 6 May 1922, p. 437, 17 June 1922, pp. 605–7.
9 Committee on the Inland Telegraph Service in PP 1928 XII.
10 *Post*, 31 March 1928, p. 276, 21 April, pp. 342ff.
11 A copy of the February 1929 *Report and Recommendations* is at F 430.6 and a list of the main proposals is in *Post*, 16 March 1929, pp. 242–3. For further details see POR M 70/1929.
12 *Post*, 15 December 1928, p. 472.
13 Most of this is in UPW (1933) in other material at F 530.7 and in *Post*, 5 April 1930, October–December 1931, 1938 CS pp. 89–94 and ECM 18–19/12/29, 457 and 12–14/4/38, 231–2.
14 See Bridgeman Report PP 1931-2 XII, p. 11 and Post Office Accounts 1936-7, p. 7.
15 There is much material on this at F 530.
16 *ibid.* on this and most of what follows.
17 PO *Commercial Accounts* 1949-50, p. 7, 1950-1, p. 8, 1954-5, p. 9; Sinclair Report.
18 Kieve (1973), p. 263 and Central Office of Information (1957).
19 Sinclair Report (1958).
20 Details at F 503.7.
21 PP 1966–7 XVII, Vol. I, pp. 133, 214.
22 PP 1967-8 XXVII, p. 49; Crossman (1976), p. 727.
23 PP 1976-7 XXXIX, p. 93. For a useful summary see Bowyer (1978).
24 *Post*, 26 September 1980, p. 5.
25 Post Office (1911), pp. 78ff., gives details. See also Brown (1928).
26 *Times* (16 March 1927); *Daily Express* (21 November 1928), and more generally F 552.4.
27 *Times* (10 November 1945); *Post*, 10 March 1945, pp. 365–6.
28 PP 1975-6 XXXV.
29 Details of how it worked at the time are to be found in Murray (1927), ch. VI.
30 Murray (1927), pp. 115ff.; Reith (1949), pp. 104–6 and Bevins (1965), pp. 88ff. for two of the political dramas relating to the establishment of the BBC and of the ITA.
31 Pitt (1980), p. 45; F 544.7. See Telephone Development Association (1931). The body, which still exists, changed its name to the Telecommunication Engineering and Manufacturing Association in the 1950s. For a UPW discussion see ECM 22–24/10/30, 78–9.
32 Pitt (1980), p. 48; F 540.
33 A full statement of his ideas is contained in Wolmer (1932), whose title of course consciously echoed Rowland Hill.
34 A defence of the Service against its more ignorant attacks is Tallack (1928).
35 Wolmer (1932), pp. 19–20; *Post*, 21 January 1928, p. 43.
36 *Times* (30 September–2 October 1929); *Post*, 12 October 1929, p. 290.
37 *Hansard* V, 235, 508–70 (12 February 1930).
38 PP 1930-1 X (Tomlin Report), pp. 64, 63.
39 Attlee (n.d. 1954?) pp. 86–7; *Post*, 24 October 1931, pp. 368–9 and *New Statesman* (7 November 1931).
40 *Post*, 21 November 1931, p. 472, 2 January 1932, p. 2; ECM 17/12/31, 133.
41 It is given in Wolmer (1932), pp. 23–5. See also POR 33/4451.
42 PP 1931 2 XII (Bridgeman Report).
43 *ibid.*, p. 17; POC, 3177, 24 August 1932; *Labour Magazine* (February 1933).
44 By Pitt (1980), especially ch. 4.

45 *Times* (28 May 1928).
46 See his book pp. 156ff.
47 Bridgeman Report (PP 1931-2 XII), p. 19; *The Post Office 1934*, p. 8.
48 For clear accounts of how the system worked see Crutchley (1938), pp. 220ff. and Robinson (1953), pp. 277-8.
49 Estimates in Cmnd 3869 (PP 1938-9 VII).
50 These quotations from the (internal) Gardiner Committee whose purpose was to decide on the implementation of these proposals. Details at POR 33/5029 are summarised in Pitt (1980), p. 84.
51 *Post*, 18 April 1931, p. 380.
52 Post Office (1950), Vol. 1. p. 12.
53 Bealey (1976), pp. 322-3; *The Review* (January 1954); Pitt (1980), pp. 114ff.
54 Details in Pitt (1980), pp. 116ff. The report was submitted to the Director General in 1962.
55 Carter Committee Report (1977) PP 1976-7 XXXIX, pp. 9, 10.
56 Attlee (n.d. 1954?), p. 86; *The Post Office in 1934*, pp. 10-11; *Observer* (4 December 1938).
57 Robinson (1948), p. 435, (1953), p. 257. Crutchley (1938) describes these developments from the point of view of the man who succeeded Tallents as Director of Publicity in 1935.
58 Auden (1977), pp. 290-2.
59 On this see Gillett (1936); Belgrave (1937), Glenfield (1938).
60 Details at F 547.2 including Report of the Departmental Whitley Council of April 1935.
61 *Evening Standard* (6 April 1931); Hay (1946), p. 53.
62 Details of these changes are taken from the annual Post Office *Commercial Accounts* which came out each year from 1920-1 until 1938-9. See also Chapter 12.
63 Carter (1937).
64 Details on 'Transorma' are at F 527.1 and quotations unless otherwise stated are from there. There is also a large file on the subject in the UCW Postal Department.
65 See, for example, Hay (1946) and Robinson (1953), ch. 20.
66 The period from the 1940s to the 1960s is hardly covered in the secondary literature, except for his particular preoccupations by Pitt. On the immediate post-war period the sources used are two publications of the Post Office called *Post Office 1950. A Review of the Year's Activities*, and *Post Office 1951. A Review of Post Office Activities*, and the Commercial Accounts and Reports.
67 Pitt (1980), p. 103; PP 1950 IV, p. iii and *passim*; *Post*, 5 May 1951, p. 147.
68 The new system is set out in PP 1955-6 XXVI. See also Horsfield (1956).
69 Priestley Report, pp. 23-9; Pitt (1980), p. 125.
70 These phrases are from Smith (1979), pp. 109, 119, a useful survey of the whole subject.
71 Ruggles (1949-50), and Hazlewood (1950-1).
72 Harris (1972), p. 135.
73 See Dow (1970), pp. 95ff.
74 Post Office, Commercial Accounts and Report for 1956-57.
75 Bevins (1965), p. 74; Post Office Report and Accounts for 1957-8, p. 15.
76 PP 1957-8 XXIV, Full Automation of the Telephone System.
77 Post Office Report and Accounts 1959-60, p. 7, Post Office Report and Accounts 1960-1, p. 10.
78 Post Office (1959); Post Office Report and Accounts 1958-9; *Post*, 14 March 1959, pp. 199ff.
79 The developments set out in this paragraph can be traced in the Post Office Reports of the period.
80 Brittan (1971), pp. 241-3; Budd (1978), p. 94.
81 PP 1960-1 XX.
82 PP 1960-1 XXVII.
83 *Hansard* V, 645, 218ff. (25 July 1961).
84 PP 1959-60 XXVII, PP 1960-1 XXVII (Post Office Act 1961). There is a useful summary in PP 1966-7 XVII, pp. 367ff.
85 Post Office Report and Accounts 1959-60, p. 4.
86 This statement is based on the published figures from the Post Office though the entire matter is something of a statistical minefield as can be seen from the rather different interpretation of another set of figures from this period given in Bealey (1976), p. 331, and repeated in Pitt (1980), p. 141.
87 See, for example, Post Office Report and Accounts 1960-1, p. 20, and Report and Accounts 1961-2, p. 15.
88 *Post*, 7 July 1956, pp. 396ff.
89 *Post*, 27 October 1956, pp. 611-14.
90 *Daily Mail* (30 January 1958); Post Office Report and Accounts for 1958-9, p. 6, for claims that foreigners were flocking in to see the innovations.

91 Details on this and what follows are to be found at F 520.2.
92 PP 1966–7 XVII, I, p. 596; *Guardian* (6 December 1967); *Post,* 17 February 1968, p. 4.
93 Corby (1979), pp. 222ff.; PP 1976–7 XXXIX, p. 83.
94 On all this see Post Office Reports 1961–5, Bevins (1965) and A. W. Benn in *Hansard* V, 716, 1966 (22 July 1965).
95 Post Office Report and Accounts 1962–3, p. 32; PP 1963–4 XXVI.
96 Post Office Report and Accounts 1964–5, p. 7.
97 For the classic statement see Labour Party 1963 Conference Report, p. 140, and for a typical example see 'The Future of the Post Office' in Benn (1965), pp. 137–40.
98 PP 1967–8 XVIII, especially pp. 104–6.
99 *Daily Telegraph* (19 April 1980); *Guardian* (19 June 1980); *Times* (14 August 1980).
100 Brown and Steel (1979), p. 47. For a trenchant account of the attack on Fulton see Kellner and Crowther Hunt (1980), especially chs 3 and 4.
101 PP 1964–5 XXX, II, pp. 220–4. Pitt (1980), p. 144 cites the cuts and quotes the proposed increase in overall output, but does not refer to the actual outcome.
102 These developments can be traced from the Post Office Annual Reports and from Jenkins (1980), pp. 102ff., a somewhat uncritical but reliable account.
103 This is from a leaflet issued at the time by the Post Office Joint Production Council.
104 *Hansard* V, 761, 316–7 (WA) (28 March 1968); Pitt (1980), pp. 146–7.
105 There is a full account of the genesis and early history of the Giro in Davies (1973) and something on its subsequent development in National Giro (1977). See also *Hansard* V, 716, 1633ff. (21 July 1965) and PP 1964–5 XXX (Cmnd 2751).
106 See above, p. 288 and F 550.
107 Bridgeman Report (PP 1931–2 XII), pp. 40–1.
108 Besides the annual reports and publications, see also Benn (1966); Post Office Act 1969, 14, and PP 1976–7 XXXIX (Cmnd 6850), p. 44.
109 F 200.3(a); Pitt (1980), pp. 148–9.
110 *Newsletter* of the EDC for the Post Office, July 1969.
111 PP 1966–7 XVII, I, p. 48, II pp. 554–6, PP 1967–8 XXVII (Cmnd 3574), pp. 15–16; Post Office Report and Accounts for Six Months ending 31 March 1970, p. 2.
112 Bealey (1976), p. 371.
113 There is a summary of some aspects of the Report in Pitt (1980), pp. 151–3 and Bealey (1976), pp. 371–2.
114 Report I pp. 31, 34.
115 Report II pp. 95–128, 603–15.
116 Report I *passim.* Quotes all on pp. 208–18.
117 PP 1967–8 XXXIX. See also n. 82 above.
118 PP 1967–8 XXVII (Cmnd 3574). See also Fels (1972), p. 228. It is interesting to notice that the PIB calculations for staff costs are given as 74·4% for posts and 47·1% for telecommunications in 1966–7. The equivalent figures (based on income not expenditure) which I have calculated are respectively 67·2% and 52·3%.
119 The Post Office did pay some attention to the report, as can be seen from Report and Accounts 1967–8, p. 6.
120 *Hansard* V, 733, 467–72 (3 August 1966). PP 1966–7 LIX, Post Office Report and Accounts 1967–8, p. 5.
121 Denis Hobden in *Hansard* V, 773, 96 (11 November 1968) and Stagg (1973), p. 37.
122 *Hansard* V, 773, 49–58 (11 November 1968) Paul Bryan.
123 Post Office Act 1969, ch. 48. See also Post Office (1967).
124 PP 1966–7 LIX, p. 8.
125 Pitt unfortunately says very little on the period after incorporation, though Corby (1979) presents a good deal of detail on the postal service from his own point of view.
126 Baker (1976), p. 67.
127 Post Office Report and Accounts March 1970, pp. 2–3.
128 Figures in the Department of Employment *Gazette,* March 1976.
129 This phrase is taken from an interesting but undated UPW document headed 'The Postal Service' and kept at F 520.3. See also Post Office (1972), p. 8.
130 PP 1973–4 XIV, p. 6.
131 Post Office Report and Accounts 1973–4, pp. 15, 18.
132 *ibid.,* p. 12.
133 Corby (1979), pp. 155–63; PP 1976–7 XXXIX (Cmnd 6850), pp. 112–17; Hird (1980).

134 Post Office (1976), pp. 6–7.
135 Second Report on Nationalised Industries, PP 1975–6 XXXIV.
136 *Hansard* V, 895, 1342–1410 (15 July 1975).
137 PP 1974–5 XXX, p. 14. See also POUNC (1975).
138 PP 1976–7 XXXIX (Cmnd 6850 and Cmnd 6954). See also the well thought out and useful UPW evidence (UPW1976).
139 (PP) 1977–8 (Cmnd 7292).
140 PP 1976–7 XXXIX (Cmnd 6850), pp. 60–3; Cripps and Godley (1978).
141 National Economic Development Office (1976); (PP) 1977–8 (Cmnd 7131).
142 (PP) 1979–80, Monopolies and Mergers Commission.
143 Ryland (1971), p. 10.
144 Chapter 8, p. 231 and for more detail Davies (1973), pp. 69ff.
145 See 'The Development of the Post Office' in Webb (1916); PP 1928 XII, *Postal Cheque System*.
146 See *Post*, 30 March 1929, pp. 280–2 and 9 May 1931, p. 442.
147 *New Statesman*, 7 May 1921, p. 124; ECM 16–18/7/24, 31–2, 15–17/4/25, 216–9, 22–24/10/30, 75–6.
148 See *The Post Office. Organisation and Control* published by the Post Office Staff Associations, from which a representative quotation is given at the head of the chapter.
149 ECM 9–11/4/35, 183, 184.
150 The Executive Minutes are full of discussions on these matters – see especially ECM 17–19/7/35, 42–4, 62/3/35, 155–78, 3/4/35, 179–83, 15–17/7/35, 49–58, 12–14/4/38, 245–8.
151 ECM 20–22/1/37, 155, 28–29/4/39, 219–21.
152 ECM 12–14/3/38, 247–8, *Post* 1939, CS pp. 59–63.
153 ECM 7/12/47, 840. See above, p. 293 and n. 52.
154 *Post*, 13 April 1946, pp. 200–3; ECM 11/10/45, 88ff., 24–26/4/46, 451–5, 28–30/1/47, 783, 795–6, 813–4.
155 ECM 7/3/47, 849–58, 20/3/47, 861–74.
156 ECM 19/1–17/2/49, 640, 659–61, 29/3/49, 688–90, 20/4–4/5/49, 697.
157 ECM 26–28/7/49, 43–9, 18–20/10/49, 111–13, 21–22/3/50, 291–3, 17–18/4/50, 309, 317, 320 20/6/52, 11; *Post*, 5 November 1949, pp. 551–2, 21 June 1952, pp. 24–6.
158 See above, pp. 286, 300, 303.
159 *Post*, 29 March 1959, pp. 238–9, 15 August 1959, pp. 388–9, 6 February 1960, p. 171; Wells (1930); ECM 12–14/7/44, 52, 14–16/2/45, 288, 18–20/10/49, 100, 107–8.
160 Walsh, Moulton-Abbot and Senker (1980) and UCW Executive (1980).

10   The State of the Union

> I am also proud to belong to such an organisation as this because it gives me a feeling of confidence in my fellow-worker. I know he is thinking of me as I am thinking of him, and we should stand by one another. The more this feeling is cultivated the better it will be not only for the worker, but for the community whom we serve. (Victor G. Smith on 'Why I am Proud to be a member of the UPW' in *Post*, 9 September 1922, p. 245)

Boy messenger Smith was by no means the only member who felt his position had been strengthened by the setting up of one Union of Post Office Workers from the divided ranks of the manipulative staff. Most of the main grades now had one organisation with a National Office and an authoritative full-time leadership who could negotiate through agreed procedures with their employers. For more than sixty years after its foundation, there were few significant changes in the rules and structure of the Union of Post Office Workers. The most conspicuous feature retained by the Union throughout these years was the democratic tradition inherited from its predecessors and which in many important ways is alive to the present day. The annual conferences of the 1980s may be somewhat more ordered than their predecessors but they have not yet lost a fire and brimstone that echoes the general meetings of the Fawcett Association and the tumultuous gatherings of the Postal Telegraph Clerks Association of a century ago. The UPW retained all the rules, in their essence, for the election of their officers and the continual re-election of their Executive Committee, which still makes them unique amongst those unions coming from the civil service. The paradox has been that the Union retains not only democratic traditions but also a marked level of centralisation which, over the years, has been accompanied by increasing professionalisation and authority from the leadership.

The basic form and structure of the UPW was inherited almost directly from the Postmen's Federation, and can be easily stated. The Union's officers were elected by the members for life. They were the general secretary and his assistant (or deputy from 1948), assistant secretaries, together with a treasurer, organising secretary and editor. At first there were three organising secretaries, but this was reduced within a few years to one. The initial three assistant secretaries within sixty years increased to eight. The lay members are represented by an Executive whose most senior member becomes chairman for one year, and members express their views at annual and special conferences. Delegates come from branches which also send members to district committees. Within this simple and largely unchanged structure there have been a number of interesting alterations over the years, and it is the aim of the first part of this chapter to set these out in detail. There will then be a description of the welfare and educational activities of the Union and, finally, an account of the important problem of 'secessionism'.[1]

THE UNION AND ITS MEMBERS

All the main indoor and outdoor manipulative non-engineering grades have always been eligible to join the UPW in their various forms and titles – postmen, postmen higher grade, SC&Ts, CC&Ts, telephonists, sorters, P&TOs, postal officers and so on. Amongst intermediate grades, head postmen were included up to 1938, and again after 1955 when the title became redundant. Supervising postmen and SC&Ts were included between 1934 and 1948 and some other smaller groups like exchange attendants and liftmen in 1930, firemen and porters in 1944, overseas telegraph operators and Post Office domestics in 1955, and catering grades and Tower attendants in 1969. The Executive Committee has always had the power to recruit from such other groups as it thinks fit, though this never seems to have led to any dispute with organisations catering for engineering or management grades. Provision was also made since the beginning of the war for the admission of temporary grades, though at first without continuity of membership. Since 1958 provision has been made for members becoming Parliamentary candidates to retain their membership. District councils since 1923 could admit people to honorary membership, and branches could do so since 1930. In more recent years such members have been able to serve in a representative capacity for the Union. Since 1931 there has also been a 'Roll of Merit' largely made up of retired Union leaders.

One interesting way in which UPW membership application changed in 1965, following the internal battle of the previous year, has been in the obligation to sign a printed form undertaking not to 'resort to the Courts' on any disciplinary questions 'unless and until I have followed the provisions of the Rules dealing with the determination of such disputes'. Of more general significance has been the spread since that time of check-off systems of payment culminating in the agreement with the Post Office in July 1976 for compulsory union membership. This has put an end to the constant calls from the time of the foundation of the Union for negotiated benefits to be confined to members only, a policy which the Post Office never showed any inclination to accept. It was taken up with some enthusiasm by the Union just before the war, and again in 1948, and in the mid-1950s. On a number of occasions, most notably in 1949, 1955 and 1956, conferences condemned the Executive for lack of progress on the demand, though it is difficult to see what could have been done to compel an employer to discriminate within the workforce in this way.[2] The call for a closed shop was vigorously opposed by General Secretary Geddes in the late 1940s, at a time when the Union was contesting with secessionists for sole rights to negotiate. Compulsory membership in the form of a post-entry closed shop first became Union policy in 1964, and finally came into effect on 5 July 1976.[3]

These compulsory membership arrangements may well in the future give a different meaning to another issue of importance for the Union – the power to accept and expel. This has always in the past gone from individual branches to the Executive which, ever since 1958, could exclude any member considered 'not a fit and proper person for membership'. Before the 1970s the power of expulsion was used very sparingly indeed. There has always been an appeal to annual conference, which has only been used in rare instances – and in one case at least (that of Ron Beak in 1970) the Executive recommendation for expulsion was overthrown. In another case, in 1933, the Executive refused to accept the expulsion of Miss Taylor from the Hitchin Branch, apparently as part of an effort by her male branch officials to get her off desirable money order duties. The Executive expressed the view that there were 'lapses on both sides' and this seems to have been accepted. In a similar case at Dumfries in 1943 a member called J. G. Clarke individually negotiated better duties. The local branch refused to accept the Executive's instruction to readmit him to membership and would not collect his subscriptions. Nor were they impressed when Clarke threatened to sue them, on the grounds that anyone 'who will not observe the decisions of membership and violates constitutions' had 'no right in law or anywhere else'. Faced with this, the Executive seems to have accepted the local view. On the other hand, they fully supported at the same time the expulsion of T. Asnett of the Edinburgh Postal Branch who discussed with secessionists his charge that the local Branch Secretary had negotiated himself more Sunday overtime duties. Similarly, in 1949, the Executive did not hesitate to expel G. Roberts of the Sutton Indoor Branch who had got a question asked in Parliament about the campaign to get clerical status for the new P&TO grade, a policy which the secessionists accused the Union of pursuing with less than enthusiasm. Roberts was certainly in breach of the rule and made little effort to redeem himself by telling the Executive:

> Cordially I consider that Post Office Trade Unionism has NEVER been so impotent as now. It has fallen greatly since the days of Bill Bowen, when it WAS a Trade Union and NOT regarded as ballast for the TUC and the Labour Government. Mr. Geddes writes to the 'Evening Standard' saying what the Union proposes to do . . . what does it do?????? fall asleep again.[4]

Since 1958 there have been complicated rules about appeals against expulsion and since 1969 there have been provisions for suspension of members and for the operation of a disciplinary committee of the Executive. A more detailed code was placed in the rule book in 1973 following the large-scale expulsions of those who reneged on their obligations during the 1971 strike.

Until recent years, subscriptions in the UPW were very low. They have always been on a sliding scale of some sort and until 1948 were 5d (2p) for those on the highest wages (up to £1. 50 per week initially, but £1. 75 after 1928, and for all full-timers after 1944). During the same period a second class of member (initially those on £1 to £1. 50, but later £1. 25 to £1. 75) paid 4d, and a third class was created paying 3d, with a fourth class at 2d. Since 1944 this has been simplified to two tiers: full, originally at 5d, and part-time or junior at 3d. Increases have been fairly continuous since then, getting to 3s (15p) and 1s 6d (7½p) at the time of decimalisation in 1971. It was only in the 1976 Rule Book that provision was made for automatic increases, and the rate was tied to 1 per cent of the lowest grade, initially a cleaner and later on the main catering scale. This had reached 52p for full-time adults by 1980. Membership subscriptions have gone up in recent years more quickly than the rate of inflation, but from a very low starting point. Deduction of subscriptions at source was strongly advocated from the Manchester Amalgamated Branch since the 1930s when it was strongly opposed by Union leaders. *Post* Editor Francis Andrews declared that 'he was against having the bosses' side of the table collecting Union subscriptions'.[5] In 1946 the Manchester Branch set up a 'holiday club' whose little-concealed purpose was to collect subscriptions as members were paid. Eventually the principle was accepted by the Union's Executive and was negotiated in 1966 without dissent. A related rule unchanged since 1920 has been to allow expulsion of members who default on their subscriptions for two months. Since 1930 this period did not need to be continuous and since 1966, the powers of the Executive Council to deal with the matter were increased.

The organisation of branches was a rather simple business. Before the 1950s, the only important provision in the rules was that members in small offices could form district branches. The various grades were encouraged to form amalgamated branches and many did, especially in the large cities. The Liverpool and Manchester branches were in a position to see that 'each grade or sector has its own machinery in connection with its own particular business'. Some amalgamations did break down, however, and as a result the numbers of branches showed some tendency to increase – from 1,216 in 1930 to 1,258 in 1946, when there were 775 amalgamated branches, about 62 per cent with 319 covering outdoor grades, 112 indoor, twenty-nine indoor postal and twenty-three indoor postal and telegraphs. In 1958 there were still complaints originating from the Bristol Branch about 'the continued drift to set up grade branches' and the fact that some of the old divisions persisted, especially in London.[6] The splitting of the businesses in 1981 may well alter attitudes on this, as on other matters.

In some ways local branches of the Union have had a good deal of power and autonomy, though there has been a definite trend to more professional management since the 1940s and to more central control since the 1960s. Branches have always been able to retain a good proportion of the subscriptions they collect. In the original Rule Book they were able to keep 4s 7d (23p) per annum, or 21 per cent, on the highest levels of contributions. By 1958 this had risen to 11s 8d (58p), just under 25 per cent, and the 1980 Rule Book brought this up to 30 per cent. Some of the larger branches seem to be keeping up to 40 per cent of all they collected in the past, building up very large reserves.

The running of local branch finance has never been easy. This is illustrated in the case of the amalgamated Branch at the East Central District Office in London in the late 1920s. Here the Treasurer, with a membership of up to 2,600, dealt with £5–6,000 each year in four different funds, working every afternoon and every evening of the week and all day on Sunday. The holiday fund of the branch was about £400 short and its Secretary was expelled from the Union. The Treasurer was expelled also, even though there was 'no suggestion' that he had 'misappropriated any of the money' and 'the amount of work he had to do . . . was too big a job for any one man to do in his spare time'. Other officers of the Branch said 'his greatest crime' was that 'he trusted other people too much'. Nevertheless, the Executive would not rescind his expulsion, and despite efforts to subdivide the work of the Branch, difficulties seem to have persisted for some time.[7] It is interesting to notice that when the Secretary of the Exeter Outdoor Branch in 1946 defaulted on sending £12 from the sick fund, the members retained confidence in their local official rather than in the Executive who tried to discipline him. They resented in particular the extraordinary and unwelcome attentions of the Investigation Branch of the Post Office.[8]

As the years went by, efforts were made to keep greater control over such problems. From 1944 audited accounts of each branch had to be sent to the General Treasurer. From 1964 much fuller provision was made for separate accounts and outside auditors for larger branches. Since 1965 much more power has been given to the Executive to deal with the affairs of local branches on how they should run their accounts and much else. Within these limits, branch officials have been given increasing powers. In 1931, they were recognised as 'the normal channel of local communication between the Department and a recognised association on matters affecting the interests of the staff'. In 1943 some effort was made to ensure that branch secretaries had time to perform their functions during working hours, and the level of such activity has gradually increased until it became enshrined in legislation in the 1970s.[9]

One other important aspect of the functioning of local branches of the Union lies in their ability to communicate with one another other than through Head Office. In 1958 George Woodcock of the TUC wrote that such rules were 'uncommon', and the UPW did not in fact have one such until 1966. A 'small offices committee' representing branches thought to have their own special interests functioned in the mid-1930s, though without the approval of the Executive. The Executive was also unhappy about the efforts of individual branches to organise pre-conference discussions. Though they could not always stop it, General Secretary Geddes got them to do so in 1945 when the Manchester Branch tried to organise opposition to the re-allocation agreement.[10] Generally speaking, co-ordinated activity by branches has not provided a focus of opposition to the Union's leaders. This has come, in so far as it has manifested itself, in the vigorous traditions of individual offices and grades. It has been seen most notably in London, which even had its own peculiar grades until the 1940s and which gave birth to all the effective secessions from the Union before that time. Without ever threatening to leave the Union a number of other branches have also had a powerful internal life on occasion bringing them into conflict with the centre. The most persistent example of this has been the Manchester Branch, continually critical of the Union's leaders since before the foundation of the UPW itself, but London branches have tended to take on this role more recently, particularly through the postmen's section of the London District Council. More typically, local branches have increased in power and authority over particular matters such as the allocation of overtime and more desirable duties. This has only led to a conflict of authority within the Union when the Post Office management has negotiated on a national level to change customs and practices which have developed locally. There remain many other matters, including social activities, on which local branches maintain a vigorous independent life. This applies to the powerful amalgamated branches in the big cities and in the London district offices, though the diminishing continuity of membership between the 1940s and 1970s has reduced knowledge of branch traditions. Some of the smaller provincial branches have nevertheless developed real traditions which are recognised and respected. The continuation of a vigorous branch life is also shown in the many hundreds of local periodicals which continue to appear. The *MR View*, incorporating the old Manchester telegraphic abbreviation, is perhaps the best known, but there is also the *St Mungo* from Glasgow and many many more.[11]

Going beyond the level of groups of branches, the Union as long ago as 1919 thought in terms of negotiating machinery at regional level, but before the 1980s this had only developed in the London area. Although the Bridgeman Report in 1932 created regional management machinery, until recent years there was little call to deal with industrial relations matters there.[12] Nevertheless, there has always been a district structure. The Union at its foundation took over the district committees of the Postmen's Federation and the district organisers of the P&TCA. In the early years there were a number of arguments about their powers and functions. In 1920 it was agreed that smaller branches could be represented through them at annual conference, though this was sometimes attacked as undemocratic. In 1922 the Executive proposed fixed forms of representation and also special arrangements for four sectional councils in London – postmen, sorters, other indoor grades, and porters.[13] In April 1923 the Post Office asserted that it 'could be wrong in principle and inconvenient in practice' for them to give any recognition to the DCs, and the Executive put forward some further constitutional changes. However, Craig Walker at the Executive still thought they suffered because 'they had absolutely no authority', and one DC Secretary said they were 'left hanging, like the coffin of Mahomet, between Heaven and earth – based on nothing'. Their meetings were said to be 'flat stale and unprofitable and represent an absolute waste of money'. The Executive tried to make some improvements in 1924, but they seem to have had little effect.[14]

In the 1920s and 1930s the Scottish and London District Councils, for whom special provision is made to this day in the Rule Book, were by far the most important. Covering much wider and integrated areas with larger membership than others, they performed important functions in propaganda and organisation. The London body retained some of its pre-amalgamation bargaining functions and was also known to put pressure on the Executive. The special London structure, with sub-committees for different grades equivalent to those on the Executive and at Union Conferences, continued initially to oppose the secessionists but has been maintained since their disappearance. During the war an Outer London District Committee was added, but this functioned somewhat differently because the grades were more closely integrated in the branch structure.[15] Efforts to stimulate similar arrangements elsewhere in the 1930s did not succeed.[16]

Further efforts were made in the post-war period to regularise district council machinery, though one such scheme was rejected in 1946 on the grounds that it gave too much power to the Executive. Nevertheless steps were taken to merge the posts of organiser and secretary and a model constitution was agreed. This gave the district councils power to 'consolidate branches, and to assist them in their work', though without the ability 'to interfere with [their] internal affairs'. The district councils were also given the task of informing members 'of trade union activities and policy' and encouraging branches 'to link up with the general trade union and Labour movement'.[17] The district councils were further streamlined and standardised in 1958, with district organisers and their committees being given a not insignificant role in education and organisation. Outside London and Scotland they continued under the direct control of the Executive with very limited powers. This system and tradition will no doubt change in the 1980s with the reorganisation of the postal and telecommunications systems.

THE OFFICER CORPS

The basic structure of the UPW's leadership remained virtually unchanged during the entire period of sixty years when the Union operated under that name. There was always a group of officers directly elected for life and nineteen members of an Executive elected at the annual conference. Only in the 1981 reorganisation was the number of EC members increased to twenty-two. The power and standing of 'lay' Executive members have increased over the years. They have seldom lost their positions once elected, and nearly all full-time officers have served an apprenticeship as members of the Executive. It is interesting to notice that when the rule was introduced in 1935 to make it necessary for aspirants for office at this level or above to have the support of their own branches, this was opposed by the General Secretary.[18] It has occasionally had some significance since that time. Elections for the Executive have always gone back to the annual conference with casual vacancies filled by the next highest candidates. Officers' elections have also normally gone to the annual conference where they emerge from the same card votes as any other decision there. The proposal that this should be replaced by a ballot vote of members was defeated in 1927, though since 1966 provision was made for branch ballot votes in the event of vacancies arising between conferences.[19] The Executive and officers elected in this manner have always had the main power and responsibility for running the Union.

The chief officer of the UPW has always been its General Secretary. He has had in every rule book the responsibility of dealing with 'all general matters', and specific duties of preparing and diffusing information on the Union's work were added in the 1930s. He has since 1965 been defined as the principal negotiating executive and administrative officer. The five holders of this position between 1920 and 1982 were each in their different ways dominating and powerful personalities. W. J. Bowen, the first General Secretary, and Tom Jackson, the most recent, were the only two to have worked as postmen. Bill Bowen's skills lay in steering the Union through a period when economic depression threatened the livelihood of the members, the 1927 Trade Disputes Act threatened their status as a Union, and the secessionists threatened its very existence. Bowen's successor Tom Hodgson showed a level of intellectual grasp and negotiating skill perhaps exceeded only by Stuart-Bunning of the Postmen's Federation, but suffered from serious illness for much of the term of his office. Charles Geddes led the Union from 1944 to 1956 in the era of tough union bosses of the ilk of Arthur Deakin of the Transport and General Workers. He did not suffer fools gladly, still less so his opponents. By sheer force of personality he probably dominated all aspects of the affairs of the Union to a greater extent than any other holder of the office. His two successors, Ron Smith and Tom Jackson, have had to cope with a world of instant media coverage and rapid change both in the constitution of the Post Office and in the form of negotiations they have had to conduct. To the epoch of Ron Smith in the late 1950s can be dated the creation of a more streamlined and professional organisation, and to Tom Jackson from the mid-1960s to the early 1980s can be attributed a particular skill in projecting the Union and its policies within the labour world as well as in society more generally. His successor Alan Tuffin originated in the P&TO grade and will no doubt have made his mark for the historians of later generations.

The post originally entitled assistant general secretary was changed to deputy general secretary in 1947. The responsibility to 'keep the records of the Union' and to 'collate statistical and general information' was passed over to the general secretary in 1930, but the role of the office has since been enhanced by allowing its holder to deputise for the general secretary since 1947 and 'to carry his full authority wherever necessary' since 1965. Of the eight holders of this position before 1982, only Charles Geddes and Alan Tuffin later became general secretary. But all the others have had an important part to play, with Walter Baker, for example, setting up the Research Department before his period as MP in Bristol East between 1923 and his death in 1930. His successor James Paterson often had to perform important functions during the illnesses of Hodgson, and later successors including Lionel Andrews and Norman Stagg have played a very significant role in the life of the Union.

The officer originally called 'Treasurer and Mutual Benefit Society Secretary' had his designation changed to general treasurer in 1927. Since 1923 he has had to present a quarterly statement, since 1930 he has had to present it to the Executive and until 1958 he had to publish it in the Union journal. In the 1953 Rule Book he took over from the organising secretary the obligation to compile a list of members. More recent holders of the office have also been involved in the management of the Union's own staff and Headquarters.

The role of organising secretary has traditionally been concerned with recruitment, with the work of district committees and with the educational work of the Union. There were originally three people in this post, who were supposed to divide the country between them. However, H. J. Lincoln resigned in February 1921 following the burning of some financial records at the old office of the Postmen's Federation in the Edgware Road.[20] Charles Ammon did not involve himself in day-to-day organising work between the time that he was elected to Parliament in February 1922 and his retirement in 1928. In any case his interests were largely on the educational side of the job, so he left Horace Nobbs to do most of the actual organising.[21] Thus in practice it was the rather unassuming Nobbs who maintained and built up the Union's membership after the first few traumatic months. He also had the help of Edith Howse, who was at first described as Womens Organiser, and she did publish details of membership amongst women. In fact she worked on behalf of the telephonists as an Assistant Secretary, and this was acknowledged in her title from 1930. In 1940 the name of the office was changed to Assistant Secretary (Telephones).[22] The other assistant secretaries at first all dealt with particular sections of the Union membership, including W. B. Cheesman who acted on behalf of the London sorters until his retirement at the end of 1920.[23] Fred Riley then took over general responsibility for indoor grades and Harry Wallace for outdoor grades. Wallace also had responsibility for the Union's General Purposes Committee. Since 1947 there has been an assistant secretary dealing with legal and medical matters, and in 1953 a further assistant secretary was added to cover postmen higher grade and grade revisions, making a total of five. To those have been added another to help with the tasks of the general secretary since 1969, an extra telephonist since 1970 and another to deal with telecommunications in 1980, making a total of eight.

The workload of all these officers has increased a good deal over the years. The position of editor in particular was thought even before anybody did it to be 'a two day a week job', and George Middleton seems to have managed it very easily during his periods as an MP from 1922–4 and 1929–30. In fact most of the work seems to have been done by his full-time assistant, Allen Skinner, and following Middleton's retirement there was strong support for the idea of handing over the work to the Assistant General Secretary. Also there was a good deal of support from Union branches for Skinner himself taking over the job, but the 1931 Annual Conference decided that as an employee of the Union he could not stand.[24] The same principle applied to Alfred Seaton, who was at the time Personal· Assistant to General Secretary Bowen, in his effort to stand as assistant general secretary. Francis Andrews, a telegraphist from Birmingham, took over as Editor in 1931 and for the next fifteen years produced a magazine of some note in the annals of trade union journalism. These were characterised by Andrews's high-flown 'literary' editorials, by his passionate advocacy of workers' control, and by the excellent cartoons of Arthur Hagg. As well as this, Andrews frequently published his own verses in *The Post*. Though perhaps a little sentimental for modern taste, they added a certain style and charm to the life of the Union. When UPW House was opened in 1937, Andrews penned some lines which are typical of his style, though more specific as to content than usual.[25]

> This house of ours do we dedicate
> To the freedom our labouring fathers won,
> To Harvest, Food, and the simple thing
> And to all free men beneath the sun.
>
> Ours are the hand and brain that set
> The pattern of speech from town to town,
> Till the words of the Earth are a living net,
> And the thought of the Earth declared and known.

In more recent years the Union's magazine has become perhaps more conventional. It has remained more literate and informative than many other such productions, adopting a magazine format in the mid-1950s, with pictures and shorter articles, and going over to newspaper format in 1967. Since 1963 more routine matters had been covered in a regularly produced *Branch Officials Bulletin.*

As already mentioned, Ammon and Middleton were both Labour MPs in the mid-1920s. Walter Baker, the Assistant General Secretary, was MP for Bristol East from 1923 until his death in 1930. He was joined in the 1929 Parliament not only by Middleton but also by General Secretary Bowen. This made it possible to speak to a wider audience about the grievances of members, to have greater access to those responsible for their wages and conditions and even to defend the Post Office against its critics. However, their position did create some problems in the running of the Union. From 1922 onwards, the Union had the arrangement of paying MPs who were officers 50 per cent of their salary and having a fairly formalised system of substitution. Thus Hodgson acted for Bowen as 'Assistant General Secretary' during his two years in Parliament. Nevertheless some disquiet was expressed during this period, Francis Andrews even claiming that the Union 'was fast passing to a position of government by clerks'. The Union did survive the experience and even the bad feeling created by Middleton's sudden departure at the beginning of 1931 to become First Church Estates Commissioner.[26] However after 1931 none of the Union's officers again became MPs. This was formalised in the Rule Book of 1949 preventing the general secretary from taking on such a role, a ban extended to all the officers in 1955. From 1948 officers who took other full-time positions were also deemed to have forfeited their pension rights.

The officers were elected in the UPW until they reach the age of 55 or 60, though the first Executive Committee only defeated the proposal for annual re-election by 14 votes to 8.[27] Elections were always held at Conference until the mid-1960s when a system of postal balloting was introduced for periods between conferences. Within this there had been changes in the position of officers in the Union, and this can be illustrated in particular from the many discussions about their salaries and conditions.[28]

The original eleven full-time officers were given £420 per annum, with £520 for the general secretary and £470 for his assistant.[29] The question of something comparable to the cost of living bonus payable to the members was ruled out of order at the May 1920 Annual Conference and again at the Executive in July 1920. Increases were nevertheless introduced on this basis bringing the salary levels up to £528, £601 and £674 respectively.[30] The May 1921 Conference was the first of many which condemned the manner of arriving at this decision, though not the payments themselves. The Conference was not able to find a permanent basis for deciding such matters, nor was the Executive in 1923 when a discussion broke down over the issue of substitution allowances.[31] Later that year some bitter feeling was expressed within the Executive about the terms on which loans for houses for Edith Howse and Horace Nobbs had been granted. Though this issue was taken up by one of the Manchester branches, nothing more was involved than favourable terms to aid moving to London.[32]

None of this did anything to alter the position of officers who were not earning much more than their best paid members. Thus in February 1925 General Secretary Bowen asked the Executive for an improvement in the bonus rate on grounds of 'high prices' and the fact that 'the work performed is daily increasing in value and responsibility'. The Executive agreed to pay a cost-of-living bonus on full salary and for this was again roundly condemned by the 1925 Conference. A Special Committee of lay members of the Union was set up to consider the matter including the Executive's chief critics Arthur O'Donnell and Walter Owen from Manchester. As before, the Conference agreed to pay the extra money in any case.[33]

In January 1926 the Special Committee produced a report which was to dominate discussions of the matter over the next thirty years. It clearly echoed many of the negotiations in which the Union itself was involved.[34] On the claim for a general wage increase for the officers which had been submitted by Bowen, the Committee concluded that his main argument about the cost of living increasing was clearly incorrect since prices were much lower in 1925 than they had been in 1919. As for increasing responsibilities, the Committee 'were unable to find any evidence that the officers, with the possible exception of the General Secretary, are in any way overburdened with work'. Further, they could see no reason for comparison with other trade unions since this would mean 'UPW salaries would be determined by some other body', a clear reflection of the Union's objection to 'outside comparisons'. The Committee then went on to consider general criteria on which a claim could be based:

We believe that the trade unionist is prepared to pay an adequate salary to an officer, to make provision for those belonging to him, and to give him the best possible working conditions; but he is not prepared to pay a salary which would lift the officer on to a far higher plane of life than that on which he previously existed. The view is common that very high salaries may, and do, lift the officer on to a plane of life where the whole outlook is changed; where he no longer feels the pressure of economic circumstances, and, as a consequence, not seldom fails to appreciate the hardships suffered by the rank and file. Your committee do not wish to discuss this view, but we know no good reason why a man's standard of life should be greatly raised on his becoming a trade union official.

The trade-union movement does not *hire* service: it aims to reward service, so that those who devote themselves to the movement shall not suffer hardships or be forced to make undue sacrifice. The rank and file wages, which prior to his appointment, was the measure of his standard of life, does, however, invariably mean hardship, and it may be assumed that the trade union leaders, crippled and worried by the narrow limitations of a rank and file wage, could not give the constant and devoted services which his work demands.

Somewhere, then, between the low plane of the rank and file wage and high plane of a much superior standard of life lies the just remuneration of the trade union leader.

The Committee then considered the highest salary paid to Union members, who were London sorters, and this was £273 per annum. Together with the claim that was being made for them, this would come to £325. Allowing for the further expenses of an officer, £400 seemed reasonable.

This salary has been arrived at not by considering what the Union can or cannot pay, not by considering what other unions pay, not by considering what our officers are 'worth' to the Union, nor a valuation of the quality and quantity of the work they do. It is the result of the application of the principles accepted by us and set out in the early part of the report.

The Committee saw no reason why the Editor should get extra money, and anyway Middleton was not occupied full-time in producing *The Post*. He should therefore be given some other duties. In considering the General Treasurer, it was proposed that his salary as Mutual Benefit Society Secretary should be paid to the Union. It was also proposed that, in view of his many extra duties, the General Secretary should be paid £575. It further asserted that these rates should not be subject to any deduction or addition on account of ' "cost of living" decreases or increases'. It was thought that officers who were MPs should get half their salary as was already the practice. The Committee also considered the £300 received by Middleton as Chairman of the staff side of the National Whitley Council and the £100 received by Bowen as Chairman of the Departmental Whitley Council staff side. They thought that nobody receiving more than £400 from the Union should get this money, but left it for the Conference to decide. The Committee also recommended changes in the pension arrangements.

A long, confused, and interesting discussion of these matters took place at the 1926 Conference held in the month after the General Strike.[35] The views of the Executive, which were hostile to the report on every particular, were heavily defeated by the Conference, and new lower wage scales were introduced. New appointees to officers were to be at the new rates recommended by the Special Committee, though the old officers were to continue as before.

A number of efforts were made, usually amid considerable acrimony, to restore these salary reductions. Such efforts were defeated in 1927 and 1928, including a proposal, originating from Bowen, for arbitration.[36] At the 1929 Conference, a motion was carried to bring the General Secretary's salary back to £675, and that of the other officers to £520, thus restoring most of the reductions that had come in the wake of the 1926 report. A motion to this effect was carried by 878 votes to 559.[37] The Manchester Branch as usual took the lead in attacking this decision, and at a special meeting of members on 19 May 1929 declared it to be unconstitutional. They did not however attack the decision itself and, after some hesitation, the Executive decided to pay the increase and incorporated this into the new Rule Book.[38] The matter was finally resolved at the 1930 Conference where the view taken by the Executive was confirmed by 941 votes to 796.[39]

There was one further bitter debate at the 1931 Conference. There were calls for an investigation of the pension entitlement of officers. This came up in particular as a result of the sudden decision of George Middleton to retire early in 1931 to take on the job of Church Estates Commissioner. He had received a grant of £2,000 in lieu of his pension rights. One local branch published a leaflet that claimed he had already been supplementing his income as a UPW officer by money he obtained as an MP, for his role in the National Whitley Council, and also as Chairman of the Civil Service Housing Association. Once again the 1931 Conference decided not to go back on decisions previously made, but it was agreed that officers taking up other paid employment in future could forfeit their pension rights.[40]

By the mid 1930s some confusion had developed, with various officers paid according to rates decided at different times. Both Executive and Conference took the view in 1935–6 that this anomaly would be resolved as new people were elected.[41] However in 1936 it was discovered, for reasons not entirely clear in the light of all that had been decided, that the differential between Tom Hodgson, the new General Secretary, and his brother officers was not as wide as had been envisaged in 1926. The 1938 Conference made a new set of decisions putting the General Secretary on £620, less than his predecessor had sometimes obtained. The rest were all to have £520, the maximum they were then obtaining. This came about with a good deal less acrimony than had occurred in the past.[42]

There were two major discussions on the salaries of the officers during the Second World War. Just before the 1941 Conference, when the officers had granted a cost-of-living bonus to the Headquarters staff, they applied for such an increase themselves, on a temporary basis, not pensionable, at 15s (75p) per week. There was considerable discussion on the matter at the EC, with Geddes asking this question:

> If it was not a fact that the Dunoon [i.e. 1926] Report was no longer the policy of the Union, that it disappeared when, by decision of Conference, the salaries of the officers were altered from those laid down in the Dunoon Report, and therefore it had no relevance to the issue?

It was clear from the discussion that this view was not widely held, but nevertheless the Executive agreed, by 10 votes to 7, to submit the claim to the Conference. The claim itself was accepted by the Conference, but 'a number of delegates indicated a desire to have recorded that they protested against the manner in which the matter was presented'. Arthur O'Donnell expressed a disquiet that revived some older memories:

> It took them months to get an increase of five shillings for a man on £3 per week, but Conference could decide in five minutes to give an increase of fifteen shillings to men on £500 per year. The question of officers' salaries had always been mishandled. Was it fair play that they were not given adequate notice?

Once again, however, the Conference condemned the manner by which the Executive had arrived at the decision, but gave the increase 'with a good heart', and then after refusing a proposal from Hodgson to postpone the implementation of the decision for a year, passed a unanimous vote of confidence in the officers.[43] A new effort was made in 1944 to increase the salaries on the initiative of a local branch and on the grounds of comparison with other union leaders. Hodgson himself spoke at the Conference against it, arguing that the principle of the 1926 report was 'as sound to-day as ever it was' and that 'the work of the officers of the Union was in the word "service" and not in salary'. The proposed revision was therefore defeated.[44]

After the war, the atmosphere in which the salaries of the officers were discussed went through considerable change. In 1946 the Executive and Conference agreed to increase the salary of the General Secretary to £750, 10·5 per cent more than the £678. 50 he had received since 1941. All the others got £650, bringing them up by 12·4 per cent from the £578. 50 they had been receiving. These increases were justified as a reward for the latest improvements secured for the members, and even the traditional opposition from the Manchester Branch was muted.[45]

Further developments between 1948 and 1950 gradually altered the position. At the Executive Charles Geddes argued, as he had done long before he was General Secretary, that the 'service' principles of the 1926 Report had been superseded, and had long since ceased to be observed. It was some time before this was agreed.[46] In 1949, for example, despite clear evidence that the UPW leaders received much lower salaries than leaders of virtually every other union, the Executive decided by 12 votes to 9 to stick to the old criteria. After the Conference of that year a sub-committee of lay members of the Executive consisting of Ernest Mercer, Jimmie Murphy and Handel Edwards came to the view that though the old criteria had not been in operation for a long time, service should still be the primary criteria and 'officers' salaries should not be related to the rise and fall in the wages received by the rank and file members'. The sub-committee also arrived at the view that the cost of living should not be 'the governing factor in determining officers' salaries', and that 'due weight' would need to be given to the 'generous scope of the present pension scheme'. Despite all this, they nevertheless proposed a large increase to £900 for the General Secretary, (20 per cent more), £760 for his Deputy and £730 for the other officers (17 and 12 per cent respectively). The 1950 Conference how-ever further increased this to £1,000 (33⅓ per cent) and £800 (23 per cent) respec-tively on the proposal of the Cardiff Branch, these figures still being said to be 'not high enough to encourage careerists'.[47]

Two years later at the 1952 Annual Conference, the Executive proposed an increase based on the civil service pay agreement then applying to the members, of 10 per cent on the first £500 and 5 per cent thereafter. The Belfast Amalgamated Branch argued against this on the grounds that it would encourage careerists and instead proposed 12½ per cent above the maximum on the London P&TO grade. General Secretary Geddes spoke bitterly against this:

> The UPW was notorious, and he used the word deliberately and without offence, as the worst Trade Union employers in the Civil Service, and it was a fact that the officers' salaries of the Union did not compare in any way whatsoever with the salaries paid by other Civil Service Trade Unions.

Geddes said the mover wanted to go back to the 1926 criteria. The Belfast amend-ment was defeated and another, from Cheltenham, agreeing to an increase of 12½ per cent (about twice the EC proposal) was carried.[48]

This was the last discussion where a serious attempt was made to compare the position of the Union's leaders with those of its members. From now on comparisons began to be made with other trade union leaders, and with those in management with whom they negotiated. This is significant not only in indicating the more elevated position of the Union leaders, but also in indicating the widespread application of the new bargaining criteria from the Priestley period. It took some time for such comparisons to be accepted, however.

During 1954, some newspapers published articles drawing attention to the poor wages and conditions of British trade union leaders, notably in comparison with their counterparts in the United States.[49] In October 1954 the UPW officers argued that this applied with particular force to them, especially in the light of comparisons with Post Office management and other civil service unions. Thus it was not difficult to show

> that the General Secretary of the Union receives a salary lower than the Head Postmaster of Haslemere. He is, of course, paid a much lower salary than any officials with whom any Union Officer has to negotiate. In the view of the officers any reasonable assessment, from the value of work point of view, would clearly place all the officers well above the salaries paid to most of the Head Postmasters in this country.

The Executive decided to consider these arguments by setting up another sub-committee, this time consisting of Jimmy Murphy, Norman Stagg, Fred Moss, Jim Brennan and John Currie. This body by no means accepted the arguments of the officers. In particular, it rejected comparisons with management and also argued that if the salaries of other civil service union leaders were compared with those of their members, then UPW officers did not come out too badly. They also pointed to the favourable superannuation terms and set forward a set of criteria not very different from the 1926 Report, including service combined with an adequate wage.[50]

The discussion between the officers and the Executive sub-committee dragged on into 1955.[51] Although there was never really any agreement on the criteria to be used, particularly on what was described as the 'no strings attached' policy of the 1950 Conference, the argument was in practice resolved by the officers getting what they asked for, but for reasons other than those they put forward. The salaries were to go up by almost 15 per cent for the General Secretary to £1,290, by 25 per cent for his Deputy to £1,132 and by 15 per cent to £1,032 for the rest. In the end the Executive agreed to this with one dissentient. The 1955 Annual Conference assented after a low-key discussion in which Geddes expressed himself 'embarrassed' at having to discuss the matter at all. The only delegate who spoke strongly against the rise was not keen about having to explain it to the members and thought he would now 'rather describe the General Secretary as a prosperous banker than a poor boy'. In Geddes's final year as General Secretary in 1956–7 a further 15 per cent increase was granted based on cost of living criteria. There was no controversy at the Conference this time, though there was some at the Executive because of comparisons that were made with Headquarters staff. A further sub-committee also proposed that the lay members of the Executive's Finance Committee should each December make recommendations to the January meeting of the Executive.[52]

The new General Secretary Ron Smith then initiated a new discussion with the Executive following the 1957 Annual Conference. Yet another sub-committee was set up, this time consisting of Harry Burnett, Philip Dielhenn, John Gault, Tom

Jackson and A. R. T. Mash.[53] Ron Smith argued particularly strongly for some form of outside comparison. Valid comparisons could not easily be found, however, particularly with the union leaders, whose functions and powers could be very different from those in the UPW. Early in February 1958 discussions and meetings took place between the sub-committee and the officers which were now seen as closely equivalent to normal trade union bargaining according to the methods and arguments then general. The sub-committee worked out figures based on an average of comparable unions, and the officers maintained that these did not take into account such items as perquisites and allowances of which there were few in the UPW. The sub-committee then slightly increased the offer to 11 per cent, giving £1,700 to the General Secretary, 9 per cent to his Deputy to £1,500, and 7 per cent or £1,260 for the rest. At the 1957 Annual Conference, much higher increases were proposed by a delegate from Wallington on the grounds that the earnings of the Union's leaders were 'shocking' and that 'these posts would never be filled in outside private enterprise at the salary offered . . . He discounted the argument that high salaries would attract careerists by saying that the Conference would deal with them in the right way.' His amendment however was not accepted. Another interesting point was made by C. R. Morris of Manchester Amalgamated Branch who argued that the delegates had a right to more information on details of the comparisons being made. The Conference however prepared to accept the recommendations without further discussion. This was in spite of a running argument at the Conference between Smith and some London members which to some degree coloured the debate.

After the 1958 Annual Conference the Executive reverted to the procedure of referring the matter to the lay financial committee members who recommended a 3½ per cent cost-of-living increase which did not prove contentious enough to reach the floor of the 1959 Conference.[54] The same procedure decided on a nil increase in the following year for what were vaguely described as 'economic factors'.[55] Under the same procedure a 4 per cent cost-of-living increase was agreed in December 1960, but it was back-dated for eleven months. Smith now proposed that the sub-committee should reconsider the basis of the comparisons which had been worked out in the 1957–8 discussions.[56] This was much easier said than done. A series of sharp discussions and close votes ensued during the course of which Tom Jackson, as one of the members of the sub-committee, announced his intention of moving rule changes 'to prevent officers voting on their own salary conditions'.[57]

The sub-committee did, however, get round to considering some new criteria for determining the wages of the officers in the early part of 1961.[58] They favoured in particular comparisons with officers in other civil service unions. They discovered that in larger unions the officers earned more, that pay was often related to what the members got, and the UPW certainly paid a good deal less than the average. Taking account of such other factors as better superannuation and Outer London weighting, they arrived at a series of massive increases: 35 per cent for the General Secretary, bringing him to £2,961 per annum, 20 per cent for his Deputy at £2,264, and £1,740 for the rest, an increase of 9 per cent. The General Secretary agreed that comparisons had to go well beyond other civil service unions, but did not come up with a better figure.

When it came to the 1961 Annual Conference, the 4 per cent cost-of-living increase already proposed was agreed. It was also accepted that discussion about the best form of fair comparison would continue.[59] This had still not been resolved, however, in time for the 1962 Conference, when there was nevertheless a lengthy discussion. On behalf of the Executive, Tom Jackson agreed to a further 4 per cent cost-of-living increase, explaining that this had been arrived at without pressure from the officers themselves, simply as part of the normal annual review. Some delegates wanted a freeze, but they were dismissed as using the same arguments as Tory Chancellor Selwyn Lloyd. Numerous other amendments were defeated including some that called for higher increases. In the end the 4 per cent increase was accepted, bringing the salaries up to £2,390, £2,050 and £1,740 respectively.[60]

It was in 1963–4 that a new set of principles for determining the pay of the officers was finally agreed. Early in 1963 the usual sub-committee agreed to a 4 per cent cost-of-living increase backdated to April 1962 on the grounds that this was what the membership had secured.[61] This new argument was agreed without discussion at the 1963 Annual Conference, and the Executive was instructed to

> review ways and means whereby it would be possible to make economic adjustments to officers' salaries concurrently with the adjustment of wages and salaries of the membership following an economic pay award.

Soon afterwards a formula was worked out to give concrete expression to these principles. By this it was decided that

(a) The salaries of General Officers shall be adjudged at the same time, by the same percentage, and having the same operative date as every other economic pay adjustment made for the Postman class at maximum.

(b) The General Officers shall have the entitlement of a 'fair comparisons' settlement in the same year as Postmen have the opportunity.

This was substantially accepted at the 1963 Annual Conference.[62] The Conference also heard an interesting exchange when one delegate proposed linking the increase to the Ministry of Labour cost-of-living index in an effort, as he said, to 'get rid of the misconception that General Officers should be treated the same as them'. Smith replied to this saying that though the officers would have their salaries reviewed at the same time as postmen, it would be as trade union officers that changes would be made. He also agreed with the movers of the amendment when they

> wanted to take the whole thing out of the area of Annual Conference, out of the area of the frankly embarrassing situation of discussing one's pay in a public atmosphere of public headlines as they had done for so many years in the UPW.

From 1964–6 these further small increases were agreed based on the cost-of-living increases secured for the members.[63] In 1965 a new step was taken to work out a more general solution on the determination of officers' salaries, which succeeded in resolving the matter, at least until the present time. This was the setting up of an 'outside' committee of experts which deliberated until shortly after the 1966 Annual Conference. The Chairman was Lesley Williams, General Secretary of the Society of Civil Servants, and the other two members were Ted Fletcher of Associated Industrial Consultants Ltd, and H. D. Hughes, Principal of Ruskin College.[64] Their report compared UPW salaries with those paid by various other civil service unions. They noticed that pension provisions were considerably more generous than in the other unions, where they were mostly based on civil service practice. Pay scales rather than fixed salaries were recommended at a level of £2,950×£175–£3,300, £2,400×£100–£2,700, and £1,800×£75–£2,175. It was suggested that London weighting should be added to these scales (£85 for Inner London), thus embodying increases of well over 20 per cent. A final suggestion was as follows:

> All major Civil Service unions have linked the pay of their officers with a convenient Civil Service grade. This does not necessarily reflect equivalent responsibilities but is a convenient link for pay purposes . . . Both the Union and the officers know where they stand and frequent discussion on pay of individuals is avoided. The UPW may wish to consider whether a convenient linkage of the new scales with the Executive or Head Postmaster scales would offer a similar advantage.

The Executive's Finance Committee was prepared to accept this, though not without some doubts.

> It would not be true to say that the committee unreservedly accepts the findings and conclusions of the Enquiry Committee, in fact there are a number of points on which the Committee have doubts and reservations, not least of which is the amount of money involved.

However, since the exercise had been carried out on the lines recommended by Conference, the Committee thought it should be accepted.[65] The Executive then dropped the incremental scales, deferred the difficult questions of the pay link and pensions, and set out a series of figures which were put to the 1967 Conference. As a result the General Secretary's salary went up by 29 per cent to £3,352, his Deputy by 23 per cent to £2,747 and the Assistant Secretaries by 15 per cent to £2,180. It is a measure of how much attitudes in the Union to such matters had changed that the only dissension at the 1967 Annual Conference was over whether the timing of the new scales should take account of the wage freeze which the Union would not accept for its own members. In the event, it did not.[66]

From 1964 onwards annual increases for the officers had become the norm, and this continued after the 1966 Williams Report. It took much longer however to break the link between the timing and extent of the change and the rate paid to postmen, such as had been recommended by the Committee. One delay was caused by the movement outside the civil service. Nevertheless the principle of comparison with management grades, which was found to obtain in most other civil service unions, was in fact brought into effect in 1972. The Conference in that year agreed without serious dissension to tie the General Secretary's salary to that of the Post Office senior management grade which would be the postmaster of a large town such as Leeds. It was also agreed to decide on the other officers not by tying them to any particular grade, but by maintaining what had since 1954 become the traditional differentiation, 80 per cent for the Deputy General Secretary and 65 per cent for the other officers.[67] As a result of this, changes in officers' salaries have become simply a technical matter for the Finance Committee, and have ceased to involve any great controversy. The only difficulties have been created by anomalies arising from various government incomes policies, particularly as they affect higher incomes. In this of course the officers have suffered many of the same problems as the members they represent.

There are other aspects of the conditions of officers about which something could also be said. As already mentioned, they have traditionally benefited from excellent superannuation arrangements, though these have been modified over the years. The original Rule Book in 1920 allowed for compulsory retirement at 55, a lump sum equivalent to a year's salary and two-thirds of salary thereafter. There was also provision that women officers should resign on marriage, from 1923 with the equivalent of the Post Office's marriage gratuity. This provision, which was never put into effect, continued as late as 1964. From 1931 officers could remain until they were 60, but all pension rights were forfeit if they took up other paid employment. In 1944 this latter point was modified to give 'absolute discretion' to the Conference on those who retired early. A number of important changes followed the 1949 Civil Service Superannuation Act and were introduced at the 1951 Conference. The main effect of these was to reduce the liability of the Union in respect of officers who already had civil service pensions.[68] From 1954 widows were given the right to one-third of pensions and from 1956 special provision was made for officers who became MPs. The setting up of the Post Office Corporation brought about further changes which brought the officers' pensions outside the civil service, providing for a sliding scale of pensions based on length of service. This came into effect for those elected after November 1968.[69]

These changes in the conditions of the officers of the Union have been described in detail not simply because they have loomed large in the internal life of the Union and provided a major item at many of the Union's conferences. They have also been worth tracing in this way as an illustration of a number of important aspects in relations between the UPW's leaders and its rank and file. The one thing which is very clear is the long persistence of the traditions of the pre-amalgamation associations, and in particular the power of 'lay' members represented either on the Executive or at Conference. In part because of the particular concerns and attitudes of this section of public service workers, all of the pre-UPW organisations were reluctant to take their leaders out of full-time employment in the Post Office. The Fawcett Association only got permanent leaders because of their dismissal for trade union activity in 1892, and it was not until 1902 that the Postmen's Federation took Stuart out of the service so that he could stand for Parliament. Until long after the foundation of the UPW, those who were elected by the members to serve in a full-time capacity were expected to serve on conditions only a little different from those whom they represented. As the saga of the salaries issue in the Union shows, it was only in the 1950s that the UPW was prepared to consider the development of a full-time professional group to govern their affairs. This change went hand in hand with the development at local level in larger branches and district councils of many officials who, although Post Office employees, work virtually full time on Union affairs. It remains notable that, even when this had come to be accepted without serious question in the 1970s, the UPW still had a conspicuously small corps of full-time officers. These officers were subject to a degree of accountability unknown in other unions that were or had been in the civil service, and rare in other unions of any kind. All this did not prevent the domination of powerful figures, from G. H. Stuart-Bunning to Charles Geddes and Tom Jackson, but it did place important constraints on them all.

THE EXECUTIVE COMMITTEE

From the first to the thirty-second editions of the Rule Book, the Union's Executive has consisted of nineteen lay members together with the officers. In the early years, seats were reserved for the three major parts of the amalgamation – four each from the PF and the P&TCA and two from the Fawcett Association. Though at first intended to be only temporary, this arrangement continued until 1933 in an effort to placate the indoor postal grades, who in any case were represented to a much higher proportion than their numbers by the mid-1920s. An effort to create a regional basis of representation was agreed by the 1977 Annual Conference, but it was not found practical to implement it, and in any case it was discovered that Executive members since 1933 had come from a wide range of offices, though the big cities and especially London tended to predominate.[70]

The functions and powers of the Executive in the very first Rule Book were briefly set out. The Executive carried out 'the ordinary duties of a board of management between the Conferences of the Union'. There was particular reference to disputes with branches, to financial matters, and to the conduct of the Union's journal. It was not until 1948 that significant new powers were added – to consult Union delegates to TUC and Labour Party conferences, and to interpret ambiguities in Union policy. Although the powers of the Executive grew in the following period it was only in the 1965 Rule Book that they were codified in a form which has continued into the 1980s. There were new powers set out in relation to financial matters including the pensions of officers; legal proceedings involving the Union; the authorisation of agreements; control of subordinate bodies and their relationship to the employer including industrial action; the enforcement of rules and exercises of disciplinary powers; the approval of appointments within the Union; and the control and organisation of branches.

The internal functioning of the Executive has always been simple. Until 1958 there was provision for regular quarterly meetings, and thereafter for them to be held monthly. The Union chairman has always been annually elected directly by the Executive Committee after each annual conference, and has in practice always been the most senior member of the Executive. Virtually all the officers of the Union have acted in this capacity at an earlier stage in their career. Though the rule book to this day says little about the duties of the chairman beyond presiding at Conference, chairmen in fact have also presided at Executive meetings and have been seen in a general sense as representing the members in the major policy decisions and negotiations of the Union. On occasions, the exercise of these responsibilities has brought chairmen into conflict with the officers, particularly when they have tried to exercise some influence over the work of the officers themselves. One such dispute in 1940 led to a clearer definition of the powers of the chairman and agreement that 'he should be freely consulted by the General Secretary of the Union on all important questions' and that 'he should take his place as Chairman on all deputations appointed by the Executive Committee or by the request of a Committee'. Between 1941 and 1965 the chairman was also a member of all *ad hoc* and statutory committees, though without necessarily presiding.[71] One important function of the other Executive members has always been that of substituting for the general officers during periods of sickness and holidays. The exercise of this function has on occasions led to discussions about those entitled to perform it, and to changing regulations about how they should be paid. The difficulty of substituting for MPs has already been mentioned, and there were also problems when General Secretary Hodgson was seriously ill, or when in 1944 Assistant Secretary Marjorie Peake was dying of cancer without being aware of the fact.[72] Generally speaking, however, the exercise of the function of substitute has worked smoothly and has often served to prepare future holders of officers' positions.

Ever since the Union was first set up, the Executive has operated through a series of functional sub-committees whose membership is largely determined by seniority. A General Purposes Committee of officers and six Executive members has considered all matters coming before the Executive, though usually detailed points rather than matters of general policy. Other sub-committees originally covered finance, organisation, Parliamentary work and the Mutual Benefit Society. The latter sub-committee, later covering the Assurance and Endowment Society, eventually consisted of three members added to the Committee of Management. The Parliamentary Committee from 1932 dealt with legal and medical matters, and from 1958 a Legal and Medical Committee replaced it. In order that the Executive members should deal with the general work of organisation there was a conscious policy at the beginning not to have sub-committees for grades.[73] Only in 1953 were they set up to deal respectively with telecommunications grades, with those doing indoor postal work, and with postmen and PHGs. The exact coverage has varied with developments in the grading structure. Since 1965 there has also been a Discipline Committee.

One of the most critically-minded members of the Executive was Arthur O'Donnell. Eighteen months before his resignation in 1931 on account of its ineffectiveness he wrote an interesting article on its functioning.[74] He accepted that to the ordinary member the Executive appeared 'a dull and slow crowd if not actually reactionary'. He considered that the reason for this was that decisions were the results of 'a compromise of half a dozen or more different opinions'. Members of the Executive had to specialise because of the amount of paperwork and the complexity of the issues, and some spoke for the particular interests of women, smaller offices and so forth. Nevertheless, 'the majority of the problems affect all grades', but a certain sensitivity to the problems of amalgamation was clear:

> Only to mention 'grade' in the dullest of discussions is like an alarm; everybody sits up, and becomes intently and almost suspiciously watchful; not, mark you, to put grade against grade, but not to be behind-hand in seeing that justice is done to every grade.

This concern with the welfare of others did not display itself on every occasion nor was the Executive always 'a fervent guardian of the democratic rights of the membership'. However, a reading of the minutes does bear out at least two of O'Donnell's other observations. First, there have never really been any permanent 'rebels' on the Executive, as there have been in other unions, but mostly shifting alliances which have varied according to the issues. Secondly, there was no 'dominating personality' in the way that was not unknown elsewhere:

> We all defer to Bowen a little, as the man who has to fill in all the details of our rough propositions, but the 'GS' is often meeting fiery opposition. Be it said that he replies with, at least, equal vigour. On the occasions when the vote goes against his wishes, 'Bill's' face is a study, but he's a good-natured chap, and soon recovers.

It must be said, however, that Bowen normally got his way on these occasions, and Geddes did so even more frequently. There were some occasions when the officers operated as a group with opposition from a large section of the Executive. This happened during the 1932 wage negotiations, when unsuccessful efforts were made to get a formal prohibition of officers voting at all. It is interesting to note though that when the settlement was eventually at issue on the Executive, the officers did not in fact vote. There was some similar dispute in 1958 on the issue of officers' salaries, though this was settled without great difficulty.[75] Separate 'unofficial' meetings of officers were abandoned in the mid-1960s.

An important point about the UPW Executive was that it had a good deal more authority than similar bodies in other unions. Since the UPW always had few full-time officials, the annually elected members of the Executive have had important functions to perform, and they have increased over the years. Since it has been unusual for those once elected to lose their positions, Executive members have become something very near to full-time officials, subject to annual re-election. They have arrived at the peculiar position of being paid by the employers but acting on behalf of the members. Their remaining 'lay' status is still attributable to the deep-going but perhaps now forgotten suspicions of the Union's founders to 'outsiders' who might be remote from the problems of the members.

Between 1919 and 1958, the Executive Committee's proceedings are recorded in verbatim minutes which, despite considerable repetition and frequent obscurity, can be used to consider the main decisions and the methods of arriving at them. Since 1958 there have been separate volumes of 'Associated Documents' and no recording of speeches. Thus for the more recent period, it is a good deal more difficult to discover how decisions were made within the UPW and why.

CONFERENCES

Voluminous records also exist for the enormous, garrulous and at times chaotic conferences of the UPW. To this day, the annual and special conferences of the UCW echo something of the tumultuous meetings of letter carriers, sorters and telegraphists that first established trade unionism in the Post Office during the nineteenth century. Nowadays there is a professional leadership, more clearly defined and powerful, and there are detailed rules of order and debate. However, Union conferences are still democratic gatherings where the platform does not always have things as it would wish, and a genuine clash of views can and does frequently take place. Conferences have not taken every important decision for the Union, nor have their decisions always been clear and enforceable. They have, however, provided the most important forums for discussion, and the point of ultimate appeal on every major question.

The basic pattern of the UPW's annual conference did not vary throughout its entire history. With the sole exception of 1926, they were held in the first week of May. In the year of the General Strike the delegates could not get to Dunoon until June. In another traumatic year for the Union – 1971 – the Annual Conference was a somewhat truncated affair, and later in the year a special conference was necessary to take major decisions following the Hardman Report. Such special conferences, once rare, have become regular in the life of the Union, dealing with important questions affecting the whole Union or particular sections of the membership.

At the annual conferences, as they were in the UPW, the chief discussions and decisions were heard in the main conference hall. There were also 'sectional' conferences, to deal with questions facing particular groups of members. Their decisions were always subject to ratification at the 'main' conference, though in practice they were rarely questioned. In 1952 there was a good deal of discussion about the role of the sectional conferences, partly as a result of an incident where one group of delegates voted in more than one of them and partly because of demands from secessionists that they should be given a good deal more power. The result was that after 1953 the delegates from different grades were clearly defined by their voting cards.[76] The power of the UPW conferences did not change, at least on paper, though their form did. Before 1953 they were divided simply into 'indoor' and 'outdoor' grades. After that there were three separate conferences. One of these has always been for postmen and PHGs. One of the others at first was for inland telegraphists and telephonists, to which were added all the other telecommunication grades in 1973. The other sectional conference included those doing counter and clerical work, and was confined to them after 1973. New conditions in 1982 have increased the power and independence of separate conferences dealing with posts and telecommunications, but this will no doubt lead to new attitudes and traditions.

Branches have always been allowed up to ten delegates. Until 1965 they only had to have 901 members for this, though thereafter they have had to have 3,251. Since 1923 smaller branches could be represented through district committees. Annual conferences have always considered reports from the officers as a major item, particularly one from the General Secretary which has grown over the years into a formidable document on the work of the Union, whose headings were set out in the 1976 Rule Book. The number of motions and amendments per branch or district committee has been limited to three each since 1927, though there is nowadays provision for emergency motions also. Since 1930 it has been decreed that 'Conference decisions shall be binding on all members'. There has always been a system of card voting, including for the important matters of the Union's officers and Executive and for representatives at such bodies as the Labour Party, TUC and PTTI. Before 1927 and after 1945 only half of such delegations could be officers.

The rules of order at UPW conferences have been frequent matters of debate and modification. There have often been complaints that conferences have not been efficient instruments for reflecting or deciding policy. They have often been castigated for their great size and condemned as 'wasteful of time and costly of money'. One delegate to the 1932 Annual Conference went further:

Several hundred delegates are transported to some outlandish watering-place, invariably somewhere expensive to get to, and left there for a week. The majority never open their mouths, although a number of earnest young men and women – who have learned how to cure the world's evils by zealous attendance at evening classes – endeavour to obtain as much space in the printed report as possible. Many of the delegates seem to be 'on the make', while the others sit and hopefully wait for the session to end. A vast number of strange ideas, mainly regarding the uniforms of the outdoor grades, are discussed, and this section of the heavy and important labours of the conference is not overlooked by the 'bright' Press, which then has a fine opportunity of poking fun at the Union and the Postal Service . . .

This jaundiced view was by no means universally supported and many others thought that despite the drawbacks, no better means had been devised.[77] The procedure was frequently modified in an attempt to make sure all the business was covered. As early as 1924 efforts were made to keep down the number of motions submitted and to cover the officers' reports better by increasing the notice that had to be given to modify them.[78] Further changes in 1929 increased the sectional conferences to one day and tried to improve the skill and continuity of the Standing Orders Committee by allowing members to be elected in the same way as the Executive.[79] Yet more changes in 1931 included restrictions in the practice of referring back sections of the officers' reports, agreed only narrowly by the Executive, and efforts to reduce the amount of discussion on the reports of the Standing Orders Committee.[80] The 1936 Conference appointed a sub-committee to consider the matter again and further modifications were proposed on such matters as the time allocated to the Chairman's opening speech and to fraternal speakers, though an effort to alter the method of card voting was not agreed.[81]

After 1945 conferences grew larger and more complex, and increasing amounts of business remained undone. An Executive sub-committee in 1947 proposed new procedures which included a great deal more effort to composite resolutions and the placing of motions against sections of the officers' reports, as well as reducing the number of times branches and individuals could speak. This was withdrawn as inadequate and a new series of proposals was accepted in 1948 which added a fairly rigid timetable and attempted to resolve some of the questions on reports through correspondence in advance.[82] Despite all these efforts however, the business was never completed, and a new set of major revisions was proposed by the Executive in 1957 and substantially passed at the Conference that year. The most important change was that 'the review of the year's work by the General Officers and the Executive Council shall proceed concurrently with the formulation of new policies'. All new policies were to be in special reports and resolutions. This led to the form of the conference agenda pad familiar to delegates today.[83] Amongst many other important changes since that time have been the introduction in the 1966 Rule Book of a system of three levels of priority to the business. This has served to ensure that important items have not been passed over, as happened in the past. Since 1969 there has been a carefully conceived time-table for the submission of business and since 1970 triennial rule revisions conferences.[84] One consequence of these changes has been to increase significantly the powers of the Standing Orders Committee, whose members have been elected from the conference since 1930. Their decisions are frequently challenged, but seldom over-turned.

FINANCE

The UPW's rule books have included a number of other important rules which impinge on the life of the Union, particularly in connection with industrial and political action and finance.

Something of the history of the rules for industrial action in the Union are set out in Chapters 12 and 13. The strike ballot and levy were agreed in 1920 and abandoned in 1921 for reasons outlined elsewhere. The rule about the strike fund remained suspended until it was restored by a vote of 82,094–21,305 in its favour in 1947.[85] However, there was no strike fund until 1965. In 1961 the proposal to initiate one was defeated though it was agreed that the Executive could call a strike without a ballot.[86] In 1965 the Union agreed to set up a Special Defence Fund, which continues in existence until the present day.[87] Rules to do with political activity hardly changed during the history of the UPW, though they were inoperative from 1927 to 1945 (when the political fund became a sick benefit scheme). They have allowed the Union to give financial support to those competing for public office and to finance meetings and literature aimed at furthering various political objectives. Provision has also been made for members who object to such activities to withdraw their contributions towards them.

The finance of the Union, though its scale has increased, operated with virtually no change throughout its entire history. Banking has always been with the Co-operative Wholesale Society, and since 1944 provision has been made for most cash reserves to be invested which has largely been in practice in a portfolio of government stocks. One rule which appears in the 1920 Rule Book and with only drafting changes in 1980 reads as follows:

> The Annual Conference shall determine how, when and to what extent the funds of the union shall be used, but should occasion arise requiring, in the opinion of the Executive Council, an expenditure not provided for in decisions of Conference, their approval shall be a sufficient authority to the officers of the Union for such expenditure.

Although the main decisions about policy are taken at conferences, details of finance are decided by the general treasurer and the Finance Committee. This has been done within the constraints about the level of expenses which have naturally varied over the years. There has also been provision for the Executive to consider what up to 1927 were described as 'trade appeals' and thereafter 'such financial appeals as may be consistent with the aims of the Union'. There has always been provision for the funds of the Union to be audited both by professional accountants and by two lay members. The 'members' auditors' have in the past had some influence on overall financial policy, but nowadays are mostly concerned to see that detailed items keep within the rules. During the special circumstances that followed the 1971 Industrial Relations Act, the rule book set up a category of protected funds. Since the Act has disappeared the Union's property and assets have been entrusted to trustees appointed by the Executive Committee.

Table 10.1

		1921	1934	1947	1957	1966	1977
Annual conference	£	4,414	3,272	11,598	21,983	34,793	170,880
	%	6·4	5·0	9·5	9·0	5·3	4·5
Executive committees	£	2,714	2,313	4,292	7,402	11,197	54,257
	%	3·9	3·2	3·5	3·0	1·8	1·4
District and organising	£	4,516	3,009	18,018	25,704	48,993	366,206
	%	6·6	4·2	14·7	10·5	7·8	9·6
Affiliations	£	492	44	3,878	5,174	20,091	40,323
	%	0·7	0·1	3·2	2·1	3·2	1·1
HQ and salaries	£	25,818	29,339	38,052	85,351	163,480	734,773
	%	37·6	41·1	31·1	34·8	26·0	19·3
Total expenditure	£	68,734	41,359	122,527	245,098	628,946	3,809,554

It is of interest to notice that amidst all the changes in the life of the Union, the basic pattern of expenditure has not changed enormously. This can be seen from Table 10.1 which takes the main items in typical years chosen at random including the interesting trend of the reduction of the proportion of income spent on central services. Some of this may derive from variations in the methods of calculating the figures. Since 1955 the rule book has also made provision for some funds to be made available 'to render assistance to our colleagues in the colonial and the international trade union movement'. The amount started at 1s (5p) per member, and is now 1/52 of the annual class 'A' contribution.

HEADQUARTERS

The first Headquarters of the UPW was at 43 Cromwell Road in South Kensington, at the corner of Queensbury Place, opposite the Natural History Museum.[88] The Union had originally tried to secure something in the vicinity of the old offices of the Postmen's Federation at Parliament Mansions in Victoria, but it was soon found that offices could be secured on far better terms a little further out, and the striking romanesque building was bought from the Commissionaires for the Exhibition of 1851 at a sum of £7,500. It had twenty rooms and a large kitchen in the basement behind a fine façade which was not permitted under the terms of the purchase to display any indication of its function.[89] The pale green walls and marble fireplaces dominated the vast rooms where the main work of the Union was carried on. 'The brooding spirit of another age' appeared to one visitor in 1931 to hover over the place, 'the age of crinolines, top-hats and side whiskers'. The General Secretary was discovered 'in a Pickwickian attitude, with his back to a massive fireplace, in the solid setting of a Victorian dining room'.[90]

Such premises might have been suitable for a trade union first trying to establish itself in the twentieth century. However, by 1934 it was clear that the UPW had outgrown it, and the Executive began to consider what to do. There was at first some suggestion that the Union might be decentralised following the changes in Post Office administration, as indeed some of the leading officials discussed again in the 1950s. However, in practice the same pattern was simply moved elsewhere. After rejecting a number of sites in central London including Empire House in St Martin's-le-Grand, immediately opposite the General Post Office, the Executive came to the view that the Union would best be served by a purpose-built premises in South London 'where development is proceeding, but not yet at a stage where the cost of a freehold site is excessive'. The site eventually secured was one housing the old Headquarters of the Amalgamated Union of Building Trade Workers, who had built new premises next door.[91] The Cromwell Road house was not eventually sold until well into 1938, when it went for £5,000 to a property company acting on behalf of a firm of solicitors. This was a loss of £2,500 in a very depressed property market. Meanwhile a total of £35,783 was spent on the new site (£5,000) and building (£26,483). This was begun on 5 August 1936 and formally opened on 16 July 1937 in a ceremony attended by leaders of the main civil service unions and Ernest Bevin, at the time General Secretary of the Transport and General Workers Union.

The new building was not as elegant as its predecessor. However, it is situated at the bottom of Crescent Grove, one of the finest Regency terraces in London.[92] The Union now owns one house in that small private estate, and its isolation has long since been taken away by a large council estate on the opposite side of Crescent Lane. The original two-storey building was utilitarian in the manner of the period of its construction, with long corridors leading to the offices of the various departments and an impressive 'Board Room' with a Roll of Merit recording the names of the pioneers and main leaders of the Union.[93] It has served the Union with reasonable efficiency over the years, though expansion in membership and activities since the 1940s has brought about various expansions, of which the most important has been the construction of an additional floor on the top of the building, opened in 1976. As the fiftieth anniversary of the building approaches, some departments are being outhoused in a nearby building owned by another trade union, though it seems likely that the building which was at first proposed as 'Bowen House' but became instead 'UPW House' and now 'UCW House' will continue with similar functions for generations to come.

The work of the Headquarters has always been divided into the same departments as other aspects of the work of the Union, organised by officers and Executive sub-committees. There have always been Finance, Editorial and Organising Departments, the latter also dealing with the Union's education. At times there has been some discussion about the better co-ordination, or even merging, of these two functions, but many do have some distinct aspects. There has also been since the 1920s a department to deal with the overall responsibilities of the general secretary and his assistant or deputy and a Legal and Medical Department since the 1950s. There have always been departments dealing with particular grades along the same lines as the officers. At first they were 'Indoor', 'Outdoor' and 'Telephones', but these have evolved into a clearer division between 'posts' and 'telecommunications' in the more recent period.

Another department worthy of more detailed description is the Research Department, often called in the early period the 'Information and Statistical Department'.[94] This seems to have been the first such in a trade union. It was originally set up in May 1920 by Walter Baker, the first Assistant General Secretary, who had been associated with the Fabian (later Labour) Research Department. He got Walter Milne-Bailey, a Cambridge graduate, to come and take over the 'compilation of statistics, information and records for the use of the Union'. Milne-Bailey left in March 1922 to set up the joint TUC/Labour Party Research Department, and later published *Trade Union Documents* (1929) and *Trade Unions and the State* (1931). G. Grant McKenzie held the position until 1926 when he went off to become successively Secretary of the Labour Party Research Department, Personal Assistant to Clement Attlee, Press Officer to the British Embassy in Washington and to the Electricity Board. McKenzie was in turn replaced in 1926 by Edgar Hardcastle, a graduate of the London School of Economics, who had formerly worked for the National Union of Agricultural Workers and the International Federation of Trade Unions. Hardcastle remained for thirty-five years and was eventually replaced in 1967 by the present incumbent, E. A. Geaney, the first holder of the post with a background in the Union. In the early period a large proportion of the efforts of the Department were devoted to storing and cataloguing records according to a system invented by Milne-Bailey and broadly in use to this day. The services of the Department were utilised during the early period in particular by Baker and the Union's other MPs. This caused some resentment elsewhere in the Union, and even led to calls for the Department's abolition. From about the time of the 1927 arbitration proceedings, the efficiency of its efforts became more evident, and during the period after 1931 when the Union had no MPs the Research Department became involved in all the major questions of the day, from the Bridgeman Enquiry to the 1937 arbitration. After 1945 the Union's MPs had to look elsewhere for their information needs, especially as the preparation of wage claims turned into an annual event and the method of bargaining by outside comparison involved the compilation of detailed information from many sources. This has continued until the present day to be the largest single task of the Department, though it still compiles information more generally relevant to trade unionism and the postal and telecommunication systems, and acts as a store of the Union's records. Since the 1960s the Department has been able to make use of graduate assistants and to replace most of the mounds of paper that once filled it with microfiche and the equipment that goes with it.

Considering the size of the Union, and the low number of elected officials, the UPW's full-time Headquarters staff has not been large. In 1923 there were forty-one clerical employees working at Cromwell Road, together with seven domestics and four temporaries. At about the time of the move to Clapham there were forty-eight clerical staff and eight domestics. These numbers had gone up by 1981 to 100 clerical and eighteen domestics, roughly in line with the increase in the size of membership. Outside the research officer who has always been in a somewhat special position, most of the 'chief clerks' and 'personal assistants' have been recruited from the ranks of activists in the Union itself. Thus Alfred Seaton, who acted as Personal Assistant to Bowen from 1926 to 1935, was Chairman of the Union in 1924, and Harry Mottershead, who acted in a similar capacity for Harry Wallace before his death in 1926, had been the first Chairman of the Union. Other members of the Headquarters staff have at least since 1935 claimed the right to apply for such positions, though they have nearly always been obtained by members of the Union. This has occasionally led to personality clashes resulting in at least one case in the return of one former branch secretary to the Post Office.[95]

On the whole, however, relations between Union officials and their staff have been satisfactory. The staff have always been organised by the union once known as the National Union of Clerks and nowadays as the Association of Professional Executive, Clerical and Computer Staffs (APEX). From the start the branch has tended to operate somewhat independently of the parent union. At no stage would there have been strong disagreement with what Bowen said in 1921:

> No one can allege that the staff was over-worked or under-paid, or that the Union was either unreasonable or ungenerous. They would compare in this respect most favourably with other unions.[96]

In 1923 a Joint Staff Council was set up, but this collapsed two years later when the staff withdrew after arguments on a number of issues including the appointment of senior staff and the delay in settling a wage claim. It is interesting to note that when the Joint Committee was eventually re-established in 1942, the Executive, like the Treasury for the Union's members, reserved the power to take unilateral action. In the meantime there had been a major settlement of the early wage claim made at a Conference held early in 1926 between clerical unions representing staffs employed by unions and the unions themselves. This agreed to pay £3. 50 per week at 21, rising to £5. 50, which was £1. 25 more than was currently being paid in the UPW.[97] It took seven further years to set up a superannuation fund. When discussions began in 1926, the staff refused to consider a contributory scheme, but the Union's officers insisted that they could not afford any other sort.[98] It took a protracted discussion from 1929 to 1933 to get a scheme off the ground. During the course of this, the staff agreed to a 2½ per cent contribution from wages, and the Executive to various forms of lump-sum payment which they had at first resisted. Although the eventual scheme was generous enough, it was accepted by the staff only 'under duress' and after they had been given a certain amount of control over the trust fund.[99] Amongst UPW staff in later years the view persisted that the settlement was on the whole very satisfactory, though only in 1981 was it extended to all sections of the staff. There was also a story that one of the conferences had been lobbied on the issue, though there is no account of this in the written records.

After the early 1930s there do not seem to have been any further serious disputes between the Union and its employees. Wages and conditions do seem to have remained somewhat better than for comparable work elsewhere. A further wage agreement was, for example, reached in 1938.[100] There was somewhat more difficulty about the desire of the officers to upgrade some of the senior staff and there was some dispute during 1941 about whether F. C. Woods, former member of the UPW Executive and General Secretary of the Clerical and Administrative Workers Union, should be able to negotiate directly on a matter. In 1949 there was some further disagreement around efforts to reduce the amount of overtime being worked and to mechanise the Union's accounts.[101]

Many aspects of the internal life and organisation of the UPW can be attributed to the particular personalities involved. Thus it has been said that General Secretaries Geddes and Smith were somewhat more involved in handling their staff than were their predecessors or successors. Similarly, the attitudes of the various editors of the *Post* have clearly played some part in moulding the life of the Union. However, the last word on this matter must be left to one of the old leaders of the P&TCA, N. A. Larsen, who expressed this view not long before the move to the new Headquarters in 1937.[102]

It is one of the penalties of our progress towards greater and more efficient trade union machinery that personalities become less significant – in our national work at least. On my rare visits to Cromwell Road I always feel that there, as at the General Post Office itself, the machinery works, if not independently of the man that controls it, at least without being greatly affected by any but the strongest personality. It was not always so. In the early days almost everything depended upon the character of our leaders.

It must be said that since the move to Clapham and the development of more refined forms of industrial bargaining and modern office technology, the machine has grown even more. The 'personalities' have not disappeared by any means, but the ability of the machine to fuel itself without any particular individual has increased over the years.

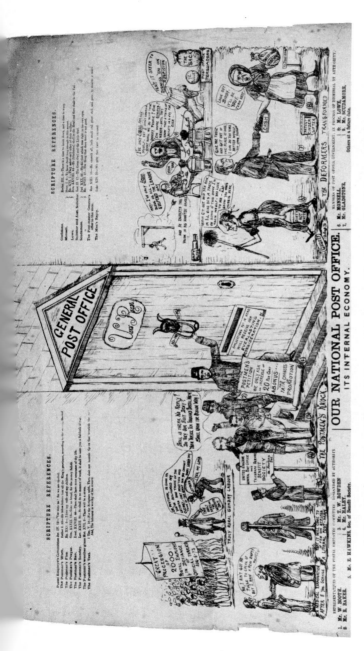

1 'Our National Post Office. Its Internal Economy' by 'Gagef', 13 August 1873

This cartoon, published during the first (unsuccessful) efforts to set up a permanent trade union among London letter carriers, illustrates almost every grievance put forward in the period. There are references to prohibitions of meetings, to Sunday labour, and protests against the operation of the system of medical examinations and 'good conduct stripes'. The main leaders of the 'Benefit Society' clearly do not expect to achieve much by the traditional methods of presenting petitions. On the left, Postmaster General Monsell is (accurately) portrayed as a person of limited political power, and Prime Minister Gladstone is seen handing over the profits of the Post Office to Chancellor of the Exchequer Robert Lowe for any purpose other than the welfare of Post Office workers. On the top right of the picture are various Post Office officials, notably Frank Ives Scudamore (who had recently been in conflict with the telegraphists following the take-over of the service) rejecting claims and dispensing punishments with the support of the press. See Chapter 6.

(From the Morten Collection in the Bruce Castle Museum)

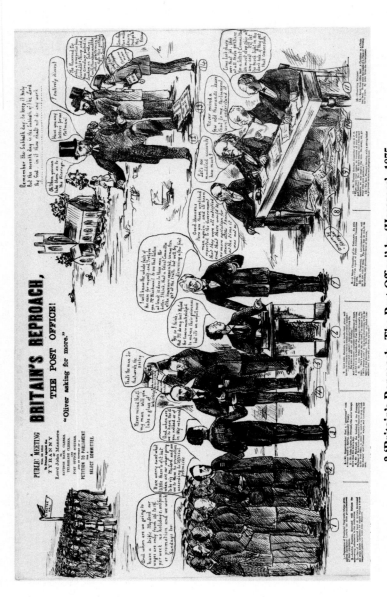

2 'Britain's Reproach. The Post Office!' by 'Hassgees', 1875

This cartoon is from a period when the sorters in London were trying to obtain a Select Committee to look into their grievances. It refers to some of the same grievances, but attacks (somewhat unfairly) the letter carriers whose own efforts had been defeated two years earlier. Various supervisors and high officials are again attacked, including Scudamore (who is not named) and S. M. Blackwood, the ex-Grenadier Guard, evangelical and temperance advocate who had been introduced as a 'financial secretary' to shake up the Post Office administration of Sir John Tilley, whom he later replaced. Postmaster General Lord John Manners is also pilloried for his efforts to crush any form of independent action among the sorters. See Chapter 6.
(This picture, which never seems to have been reprinted since its original publication, is in the British Library Reference Division at 1881 c 3 (94).)

N.B.—THE POSTAGE ON THIS NUMBER IS ONE PENNY.

POSTMAN'S ✳ ✳

Published Fortnightly
FOR THE
Postmen's Federation.

GAZETTE.

Copyright.]

[Entered at Stationers' Hall.

VOL. V.—No. 9.]   MARCH 14, 1896.   [PRICE TWOPENCE.

SKETCH OF THE COMMITTEE AT WORK

On Thursday, the 28th February, 1896.

EXPLANATION.

The occupant of the Witness Chair is Mr. F. Baker, of Gloucester, in course of his examination on the Rural Postmen's Grievances.

The gentleman on the left, in the back ground, is R. Bruce, Esq., the Secretary to the Commissioners.

The three gentlemen on the right, in the corner, are Lewin Hill, Esq., Principal Surveyor in the Secretary's Office ; — Verner, Esq., Mails Contract Department ; and a Clerk from the Secretary's Office.

3 The Tweedmouth Enquiry at work, February 1896

The first of the great inquiries into the grievances of Post Office workers, campaigned for over many years, was set up in June 1895 and presided over by Lord Tweedmouth. On 28 February 1896, Frank Baker of the Postmen's Federation presented the case for rural postmen. See Chapter 7.
(From the *Postman's Gazette*, 14 March 1896)

LORD STANLEY AND THE POST OFFICE

West Houghton is a constituency chiefly composed of workers.

It should be represented by a man who is at least capable of showing some practical sympathy with working men, but your present Member has shown himself to be entirely out of sympathy with those employed under him in the Post Office.

Among the Voters in West Houghton are very many Trades Unionists.

Should the constituency be represented by a man who desires to smash Trades Unionism? NO!!!

Lord Stanley's conduct as head of the Post Office shows that he detests Trades Unionism, and has no sympathy with working men.

He refuses to even consider letters written by a duly elected officer of the Postman's Trade Union.

He punished a man for simply signing a respectful petition in his capacity as a Trades Union Secretary, and refused to reconsider his decision.

He absolutely declines to discuss matters with the men except upon his own terms and subject to his own conditions.

He will not consent to an arbitration between himself and the Postal Employees, and after appointing a Committee himself—will not accept its verdict.

He called the men under him "Bloodsuckers" and "Blackmailers" because they asked him to consider their claims, but at the same time threatened them with severe punishment if they dared to criticise his actions.

He boasts that he has levelled up the wages of the Rural Postman to those of the Town Postmen, but the truth is that in many cases that he has reduced the wages of the Town Postmen to the level of the Rural Postmen.

For years before Lord Stanley's rule, no full-time Postman in Great Britain received less than 16/- per week. Little as this is, Lord Stanley thought it too much, and in some places the Postmen are now to receive only 15/- per week. Yet Lord Stanley says he has sought to benefit the lower paid workers in the Post Office.

This is how he has done it.

Lord Stanley says postmen receive pensions. He ought to add that there are loopholes in the Pension Acts which frequently deprive men of their justly-earned rights, and he refuses to do anything to amend them.

He also refused to compensate the widow of a man who died through the excessive nature of his work, as certified by a coroner's jury.

When pressed, he gave her—from public money—a charitable grant of a few pounds.

He could not be sued for Compensation as the Workmen's Compensation Act does not apply to Post Office Workers, so we appeal to you.

The man who deals thus unjustly by his servants, will deal unfairly with Labour generally, and should not be elected as a representative of a Labour Constituency.

Lord Stanley was absent from the House of Commons in 1904 and 1905, when the Trades Disputes Bill was being considered; in 1902 he voted against workmen's funds being safeguarded from the effect of judge-made law.

When the Workmen's Compensation Act was being discussed he voted for every proposal to render it of less benefit, and against every one making it of more benefit to the worker.

Voters of West Houghton! does Lord Stanley represent you and your wishes in these acts for which he is directly responsible? If not, vote for the Labour Candidate,

W. T. WILSON.

4 'Lord Stanley and the Post Office', 1906

This leaflet was given out in the General Election at Westhaughton, and was directed against the Postmaster General who called the workers 'bloodsuckers' and 'blackmailers'. It was part of a successful effort to unseat him, and to replace him by a candidate who represented working men more faithfully. See Chapter 4.

(Copy in UCW Archives at R VIII/23)

POSTMAN'S ✳ ✳ GAZETTE.

Published Fortnightly
FOR THE
Postmen's Federation.

Copyright.]

[Entered at Stationers' Hall.

VOL. XX. No. 18.]   SEPTEMBER 9, 1911.   [PRICE ONE PENNY.

THE RAILWAY STRIKE.

The Postman—" I may not be able to help you, comrade, but when you strike I'll not be one to ' break ' you."

5 The Railway Strike, 1911

This cartoon indicates the growing identification between Post Office workers and the wider trade union movement in this period. (Note the 'shako' cap, part of the postmen's uniform until the 1930s.)
(*Postman's Gazette*, 9 September 1911)

William Booth (1840–1907) leader of the London letter carriers from 1866 until he left the Post Office in 1874, after unsuccessful efforts to initiate a permanent organisation. (*Postman's Gazette*, 14 March 1908)

William Edward Clery (1861–1931) sorter, union leader, playwright, author and actor–manager. Inspired the Fawcett Association and the policies for which he was dismissed from the Post Office in 1892. This brilliant but erratic Irishman served as Chairman of the FA, but departed in unhappy circumstances in 1903. (*Post*, 23 December 1899)

Wallace Bligh Cheesman (1865–1947), founder of the Fawcett Association, dismissed with Clery in 1892. Then General Secretary until 1919, after which he was for a year Assistant Secretary of the UPW. (*Post*, 15 February 1896)

George Harold Stuart (1880–1947) (known as *Stuart Bunning* from 1915), the dominant figure in Post Office trade unionism in the generation before the UPW. From 1902 he was Parliamentary Secretary, and then General Secretary of the Postmen's Federation, and was disappointed not to take the same role in the UPW, which he played no small part in founding. (*Postal Clerks' Herald*, 14 December 1912)

7 Post Office Association leaders in August 1913

This picture was taken at the Matlock meeting of the National Joint
Committee which considered what to do about the Holt Report. On the top
row it includes (left) *Albert Lynes* of the UKPCA, later Secretary of the
Liverpool Amalgamated branch; (2nd left) *Walter Owen*, also of the PCA,
one of the 'Manchester rebels', and later Secretary of the Amalgamated
branch there; (3rd left) *Harry Duberry*, at this time *Post* Editor; (5th left)
J. Clancy, also of the Fawcett Association, but later the principal inspirer of
the secessionist National Federation; (6th left) *W. E. Rose* of the Engineering
and Stores Association at a time when this predecessor of the POEU was
prepared to work closely with the other unions. On the front row starting
from the left is *George Middleton*, editor of the *Postal Clerks' Herald*, and
from 1920 to 1930 of the *Post* during much of which time he was also a
Labour MP; (2nd left) *G. H. Stuart*; (3rd left) *J. C. Brown*, editor of
Postman's Gazette 1896–1915, and at this time Chairman of the NJC.
(*Postal Clerks' Herald*, 6 September 1913)

43 Cromwell Road, opposite the
Natural History Museum in
South Kensington, and
occupied by the UPW from
1920 to 1937.
(*Post*, 13 October 1927)

UPW House, Crescent Lane,
Clapham, London SW4,
purpose-built next door to the
building workers' union
nowadays known as UCATT,
and occupied since 1937.
Shown here is the main part of
the building before the extra
floor was added in the 1970s.
(UPW, *Your Union
Headquarters*)

9 Two early problems for the UPW

'Whitley Polemics' – an indication of how civil service trade unionists felt they were achieving very little from the new negotiating machinery in the inter-war period.
(*Red Tape*, January 1924)

WHITLEY POLEMICS

Sympathetic Person: "You seem to have got very much the worst of it."
Dishevelled One: "Not at all; not at all. I got my own back."
Sympathetic Person: "How?"
Dishevelled One: "I 'Registered Disagreement.'"

'The Garden of Reorganisation' – secessionist counter clerks and telegraphists are told that their interests are not being served by the UPW scheme to allow better promotion prospects for postmen.
(*Postal Telegraph*, 15 February 1924)

THE GARDEN OF REORGANISATION.

Mr. U. P. DOUBLEYOU : "Excuse me, Sir, if you stay with me, I'll lead you up the garden."

10 The PMG discovers the Black Peg! by Arthur Hagg

One of Hagg's many witty cartoons from the 1930s. This refers to the unsuccessful efforts of the Postmaster General (Kingsley Wood) to get women telephonists in London to take on evening duties.
(*Post*, 1 April 1933)

11 'Look Pleasant Please' by Arthur Hagg

This cartoon cleverly combines references to early efforts to improve Post Office publicity with the refusal of the Post Office to grant any wage increases at all. Note Hagg's four stock characters of male counter clerk or sorter, female telephonist or telegraphist, postman, and the telegraph boy. Note also the reference to early 'talkies'. The Post Office Film Unit proved a great success, but the Post Office workers did not get their increase until 1938!

(*Post*, 14 October 1933)

John William Bowen (1876–1965), first General Secretary, 1919–36. A postman from near Swansea, from 1910 was Secretary of the PF Mutual Benefit Society. He proved effective at maintaining the organisation in a difficult period, though without the flair that Stuart Bunning might have shown.
(*Post*, 2 May 1936)

Charles J. Geddes (1897–1983) General Secretary, 1944–57, telegraphist, TUC President in 1954 and peer in 1958. A tough anti-Communist union boss from a period when this was the norm.

Ronald George Smith (1915–   ) From a Post Office family, a postman and later a sorter, as General Secretary from 1957–66 took the Union into pay research and the 1964 strike.

Tom Jackson (1925–   ) Postman and later PHG in Leeds. Rose to prominence as a critic of Geddes, and as General Secretary from 1966 to 1982 became one of the most well-known figures in the trade union movement, leading the UPW out of the civil service and through the great conflict of 1971.

13 The UPW Executive in 1955
This picture, taken at the Douglas Annual Conference, includes most of those who led the Union from the mid-1930s to the early 1980s, including many who chaired the Union. They are:

Top row (l to r): Phillip Dielhenn; Jimmie Murphy; John McKane; A. R. T. Mash, Organising Secretary 1964–76; Norman Stagg, Editor from 1956 and Deputy General Secretary 1967–80; Fred Moss, General Treasurer 1962–81; John Currie, Indoor Secretary 1956–69.

Middle row: Sid Franklin; Ron Smith, General Treasurer from 1953 and General Secretary 1957–66; Jimmie Gault; Les Sayles; E. V. W. Marshall, Assistant Secretary Legal and Medical 1957–73; Tom Jackson, Assistant Secretary Outdoor 1955–65; G. Handel Edwards, Legal and Medical Secretary 1951–7; Chris Stennet, Outdoor Secretary from 1964 and General Secretary 1966–82; G. F. S. Fathers; Sam Hyde-Price.
Front Row: Les Morgan, Assistant Secretary Outdoor 1955–65; G. Handel Edwards, Legal and Medical Secretary 1951–7; Chris Stennet, Outdoor Secretary 1949–55; Nan Whitelaw, Telephones Assistant Secretary 1954–69; Charles Geddes, Assistant General Secretary from 1941, and General Secretary 1954–66; James Brennan; Richard Hayward, Assistant Secretary Legal and Medical from 1947 and Deputy General Secretary to 1955, later on PO Board; Harry Randall, Organising Secretary 1940–55 and Labour MP; Lionel Andrews, Assistant Secretary Indoor from 1952 and Deputy General Secretary 1956–67; Danny Brown, Assistant Secretary 1953–75; Ernest Mercer, Editor in 1954 and General Treasurer 1956–63.
(UCW Research Department)

14 Union leaders go to negotiate at the time of the 1961 Work to Rule

A. R. T. Mash, Ron Smith, Nan Whitelaw, Lionel Andrews, Les Morgan and Danny Brown go to the General Post Office to protest about the 'pay pause' of Selwyn Lloyd, encouraged by their members.
(*Post*, 28 October 1961)

15 Unofficial strike pickets in 1964

These pickets stand in King Edward Street close to the old General Post
Office on the day after a large and lively demonstration of postmen, the first
such for many decades, expressed their disapproval of what was offered them
in negotiations by Postmaster General Bevins. The one-day official strike
came a few days later on 16 July.
(*Observer*, 12 July 1964)

16 The 1971 Strike

One group of strikers always given prominence in the Hyde Park demonstrations each week at the end of the 'Ho Chi Minh Trail'. (UCW Editorial Department)

SERVICES TO MEMBERS

In the earliest years of the Postal Telegraph Clerks Association, and to some extent also the Postmen's Federation, insurance and other welfare provision loomed very large indeed. Right down to the present day, the Union continues to provide such services. It has sometimes been argued, notably by secessionists in the inter-war period, that these facilities play a significant role in securing and maintaining the loyalty of ordinary members of the Union. However, there is little evidence to bear out this contention.

The Union has always retained the services of outside medical experts to look after the health of members. Bowen argued for 'the utility to trade unions of appointing medical officers', and it was later agreed that 'he would be able to assist members in entering hospitals for treatment and would insist and see that they were securing every attention. He would also be able to recommend suitable local men when required.' The first medical adviser, who retained this position until his death in 1956, was H. B. Morgan who served in a similar capacity for the TUC and other unions and was also a Labout MP from 1940–55.[103] The functions of this post have altered somewhat in a period when individual medical facilities which prevailed outside the Union and the Post Office have improved.

Of more general significance for the members was the Mutual Benefit Society. This had originally been set up by the Postmen's Federation in 1895, and was taken over by the UPW.[104] The problems which arose from the 'call system' of continual levies have been described. They inevitably came to a head as large numbers of members reached retiring age and the incentives were reduced for new members to join. By the late 1920s, the system faced collapse, though the members meeting in 1927 refused to change the basis of the Society. Bowen, who had managed the Society before being UPW General Secretary, said it had always been 'far too generous' and he had proposed changes as far back as 1914. On the Executive, John Houlihan expressed this view:

> The call system could not be put on a sound financial basis, and it was always a drawback to recruitment that a call society could not guarantee any specific sum as benefit. When the MBS started it was certainly necessary in those days, long before the advent of National Health Insurance. The average young man today visualised something above the amount he would get from the MBS.[105]

The Executive tried to get actuarial advice on the Society, but found it would be too expensive to alter the basis of its operation. Instead, it argued for a sliding scale of contribution and benefit. These proposals, which maintained the basic call system but reduced the benefits of membership, were accepted in 1930 and immediately resulted in the ending of new recruitment and the withdrawal of many previous members. Following this a general inquiry was set up at the 1931 Conference and the immediate result was a further loss of members.[106] During the eighteen months up to 1932 membership fell from 14,858 in the 'A' grade to 7,067; from 9,115 in the 'B' grade to 4,096, and from 7,039 to 3,176 in the widower's grade.[107] All this was in spite of constant efforts of the Central Secretary and UPW Treasurer William Lockyer to convince people of the old arguments that benefits went up with numbers of members and that they themselves had some control over the situation.[108] Eventually, a meeting held during the 1932 Conference agreed to abandon the call system and to set up a more soundly based insurance and savings system against the eventualities of retirement, widowhood and accidents. Though some of the older members shared the small reserve fund that had been built up, there was still a good deal of resentment at the change, and continuing resignations.[109]

However, the Society then began to consolidate and to build up membership again on the new basis. In 1937 the name was changed to 'The UPW Assurance and Endowment Society' and it has since provided a service to a minority of UPW members. Amongst changes since that time have been increases in benefits in 1963 and another change of name in 1975 to 'UPW Insurance Society'. This was an indication of the growing importance of such matters as motor insurance, and the wide and increasing range of facilities now provided. Nevertheless, the same general services envisaged by the founders before the end of the last century still exist in the form of endowment policies and savings and insurance schemes of various sorts.[110]

One other form of cover provided more generally to the members has been the sick benefit scheme. This was originally introduced in 1928 in order to use up the section of members' contributions which had formerly been devoted to political purposes.[111] It did not work easily or without controversy. Until 1937 its provisions were decided from year to year. It was gradually extended from its original stipulation that it would make up the half pay of established officers for six months and the difference between Post Office sick pay and National Insurance levels for unestablished members after thirteen weeks. The scheme was not at first based on any estimate of its likely cost, or effect. Organising Secretary Horace Nobbs said in October 1928 that 'the number of members that I could definitely say have joined as a result of the half-pay scheme are comparatively few'. Executive members sometimes expressed the view that it was 'damping down the trade-union principle of the Union', and particularly as expenditure increased during the war 'there were some members of the [Executive] Council who would not hesitate to get rid of the scheme altogether' because they had to 'make up their mind whether the UPW was a Trade Union or a Sick and Dividend Society'. The officers of the Union also worried from the start that the scheme might become 'a vested interest, and the Union would be committed to a liability it could not face'. Gradually over the years, as the members drew increasing benefits, it became 'like the old MBS . . . not on an actuarial basis [but it] lent itself to improvements without any regard to the result on finance'.[112]

Nevertheless, the scheme was gradually improved during the 1930s, despite the disquiet in some quarters about the disproportionate amount going to unestablished members. From 1928 to 1939 about £10,000 a year was spent on payments, this being around 14 per cent of the Union's expenditure. From July 1940 temporary members were able to obtain the benefits, and from July 1942, part-time temporaries. Since such members were much less catered for by other types of insurance, they derived a great deal of benefit from the Union's scheme. Expenditure on it rose dramatically to an average of £21,000 during 1940–4, about 25 per cent of the Union's income.[113] As a result, the 1945 Conference agreed to drastic reductions in the benefits, making it possible to obtain them for only nine weeks in the year for established grades and six weeks for all others.[114] As a result of this, expenditure fell rapidly, to £7,204 by 1952, 4·8 per cent of income. Despite a slight improvement in the entitlement of part-time temporaries in 1953, the expenditure continued to fall to around 4·1 per cent of income in 1969 at £29,581.[115] By then benefits from other sources including National Insurance as well as concessions obtained from the Post Office meant that the scheme also had considerably diminished importance for the membership. Nowadays a small *ex gratia* payment to widows or next of kin is also allowed.

The Union has also throughout its history taken up individual cases of accidents at work, legal difficulties and so forth. In the early years such matters were under the control of the assistant general secretary, but since 1947 there has been a separate Legal and Medical Department dealing in particular with accidents at work, and various related matters.

EDUCATION

Although it would be possible to set out other services the Union has provided to members and how they have changed, it is on the matter of the education given to members that the Union has made a particular contribution. It is also possible through looking in more detail at the UPW's educational policies to trace some significant changes in the Union's aspirations and activities.[116] Thus the UPW has a longer history of active participation in trade union education than virtually all other unions. In the days when those providing trade union education were divided into warring factions, the UPW was the largest union to support those who believed that trade union education did not need to be 'independent' of established ideas and educational institutions. The general 'liberal' education provided on this basis then came under attack within the Union, whose educational activities developed towards 'training' of members in union administration and negotiation.

At the time of the foundation of the UPW in 1920, education provision for trade unionists was seen in terms of 'evangelical humanism' where various organisations aimed 'to create an understanding of society and its workings, not to inculcate technical skills'. Trade union leaders did not have 'any other conception of trade union education than education for citizenship in general'.[117] These concepts were common to all the various organisations. In 1899 Ruskin College had been set up to provide residential courses in the social sciences and from 1903 the Workers Educational Association classes in a somewhat wider range of the humanities. Students at Ruskin in 1909 went on strike and demanded education independent of the universities and based on the trade union and labour movement. They set up a Central Labour College, various local colleges, and the Plebs League that argued in favour of their policies.

For a time there was great rivalry between these two sections of the movement, and the 'independent' wing had the wider support of the trade unions, especially in mining and railways.[118] In 1921 the WEA set up the Workers Educational Trade Union Committee (WETUC), largely as a response to critics from the National Council of Labour Colleges who denied their independence from those outside the working-class movement who financed them. The UPW was the second union to join the WETUC, and defended it as an organisation 'composed wholly of trade unions and those unions supply the whole of its own income'.[119] UPW leaders were strong and active supporters of the WEA, with one officer usually on its national committee, Organising Secretary Horace Nobbs acting for many years as Chairman of its Standing Orders Committee. Affiliation continued throughout the period of the Trade Disputes Act since it was adjudged not to be 'political'.[120] UPW leaders argued against those of their members who wanted a '*biased* and frankly *partial* education movement' and favoured 'broadening instead of narrowing knowledge'. As late as 1951, when disputes between the different wings of the working-class educational movement were said to have 'become absurd and meaningless', the Union's leaders thought they 'should not make any concession' to the National Council of Labour Colleges even to the extent of running joint classes.[121] The UPW also provided a high proportion of WETUC and WEA students.

During the 1920s and 1930s the UPW arranged through the WETUC to remit the fees of students who attended WEA classes. From 1922–9, 4,350 members, well over 500 a year, benefited from this. In association with the WETUC, union members also attended week-end schools with members of the Railways Clerks Association and Iron and Steel Trades Confederation. Tutors on the general economic and political subjects covered included G. D. H. Cole, Barbara Wooton, R. H. Tawney, Bertrand Russell and W. H. Marwick, one of the few full-time tutors. Between 1926 and 1939, 4,276 UPW members attended summer schools on similar lines run by the WETUC, and from 1929 others attended one-day schools. In 1928 the Union began to organise correspondence courses through Ruskin College and with the help of the WETUC. These were initially designed to deal with topics similar to those covered by the schools, but it was soon found that the most popular courses offered were those in English composition and grammar. It is of interest to note that in this early period a survey of those taking these courses shows that the majority were SC&TS and there were as many sorters as postmen.[122] In 1929 correspondence courses for branch officials began, and these soon became popular also. By the mid-1930s over 250 members were taking correspondence courses each year, about a third each taking courses in English or for branch officers. In 1945 the Union itself took over the running of courses on its work, and during the 1950s an average of 162 people took them each year, when they were taught to express themselves, run meetings, negotiate, keep accounts, and other matters 'of vital importance to branch officials and those who are interested in Union work sufficiently to equip themselves'.[123] In the same period a gradually diminishing number of UPW members, from as many as 228 in 1951 to as few as seventy in 1958, were taking correspondence courses through the WETUC in such topics as English language and literature, government, philosophy, psychology and economics.

From 1930 the Union also began to run its own week-end schools for younger members. In 1938, 308 boys and ninety-four girls attended these schools.[124] By then they generally included one topic of general interest such as the international situation or the history of the working-class movement studied with an academic lecturer, followed by a discussion on the work of the Union usually led by a member of the Executive.

The values and attitudes on which these activities were based are of some interest. In the early years UPW leaders considered that even in the face of a comparatively limited demand, the education provided by the Union should be based on the broadest principles. They considered that 'industrial freedom for the workers will be through the efforts of well-informed unionists' and that 'the cultivation and discipline of the mind' was a valuable aim in itself. They wanted to ensure that 'the intellectual heritage handed down to the nation through centuries of struggle' would come to 'men and women who had left school too soon'. This was seen in the general context of the work of the Union where it was 'more and more necessary for individual members to be fully equipped with social and economic knowledge in the development of their trade union work and in the extension of their experience'. The general subjects in the correspondence courses were defended as 'almost essential, or at any rate of considerable service to anyone who desires to take his or her place other than nominally either in local political movements or in any other form of Labour or trade union activity'. General social and economic questions predominated among those covered and they were often taken up in a tropical way. In 1926 members discussed the mining industry and currency problems, in 1929 rationalisation and slumps, and in 1939 subjects connected with international affairs. When complaints were made that such studies were irrelevant to the work of the Union, one rank-and-file member said he 'thought that the push and pull of economic powers that was dragging them towards war was a fact to be understood by every worker' and others spoke of the need for such courses to 'defend democracy'.[125]

However, these views did not go unchallenged. In the mid-1930s there was a sustained campaign against them led by Arthur O'Donnell and his Manchester Branch. In 1934 O'Donnell argued for less 'education' and more 'training' which would be 'calculated to produce in increasing numbers men and women well-versed in the aims and methods of the UPW and the structure and method of Post Office administration'. It was said that the correspondence courses for branch officers dealt 'with the form, rather than with the matter, of Branch Officers' work', and that week-end and day schools were 'a waste of time so far as increasing the effectiveness of Union representatives or engaging the serious interest of our younger members is concerned'. It was claimed that those trained as branch officers did not take up union positions and that 'the men taking courses in logic, philosophy and so forth were not coming into their branch offices'. At the 1935 Annual Conference, the Manchester Branch proposed training courses along the lines argued by O'Donnell, with cash rewards for those who completed them successfully. As a result the Executive undertook a full review of the educational policies of the Union, found the suggested innovations 'impracticable', and said 'that the work done, both specialised union work and that which is more general, benefits the Organisation to a great extent and must also benefit the members taking advantage of what is offered'. At the 1936 Conference the views of the Executive won support, but O'Donnell said he had not expected 'to do more than break the ground and sow the seed for the future'.[126] He had indeed succeeded in doing this.

In the meantime, however, the courses provided by the Union were by no means as remote from the ordinary preoccupations of members as was sometimes claimed. Not only was the economic and social state of the world considered to be relevant to Union work, but many of the topics covered actually dealt in a general way with the day-to-day activities of members. Thus a discussion under the title 'What are We to Expect in the Present Industrial Organisation and its Tendencies?' was largely about the efficacy of Whitleyism, and week-end schools in the early years included discussions on trade union organisation, how technical change was affecting telephonists and policies of the Union like 'workers' control'. There was even something on trade union law and how to run meetings and recruit new members.

Despite this, it is clear that in general there was a gradual movement away from the liberal values practised in the early years and towards an education more closely tailored to helping members in their ordinary Union work. The correspondence courses for branch officials and the courses arranged by district councils were indications of this trend before 1939, and the courses provided by the TUC in which the Union participated showed an increasing concentration on training trade unionists in professional skills. During the war, the Union's own education provision moved dramatically in the same direction. From 1942 resources were concentrated on week-end schools run by Union leaders. Though at first they dealt with such topics as 'Man in Society' and 'How Public Opinion is Formed', they soon began to move away from this and to concentrate almost exclusively on the work of the Union. From 1945, therefore, these schools were largely devoted to this topic and were run by the Union's officers. In 1949 members of the Post Office management began to attend, and thereafter a number of schools were run each year and divided into advanced and primary, based on Union experience rather than age. By now it had become clear 'that 80 per cent of the educational work of the Union is directed towards improved branch efficiency; the encouragement of young members and the stabilising of branch membership etc'.[127] By 1955 the syllabus for the 'primary' school covered the organisation and work of the Union, bargaining procedures and the work of the Union's MPs in Parliament. The 'advanced' schools covered similarly practical topics, but also touched on international trade union organisation and workers' education. By the late 1950s about 150 members of the Union were attending three of these schools each year, together in all cases with representatives of the management.

The Union has also itself run, through its district councils, schools 'devoted to purely UPW business'. From 1934–9 these schools were run in conjunction with regular meetings, and dealt with the Whitley system and the work of the Union's branches and Headquarters. They were resumed on a regular basis from 1950–5 when it was said that they had 'the primary purpose of helping along the newer branch officers, through absorbing the experience of others'. Since then they have simply served as an opportunity for a leader of the Union to address district councils on some aspect of his or her work. By 1959 they were said to be leading to more continuity in the work of local branches.[128]

Besides educating its members through its own efforts and jointly with the WETUC, the UPW has sent its members to the educational activities organised by other working-class bodies. Between 1929 and 1935 Union members attended summer schools run by the TUC and 'confined to subjects of immediate and practical importance to those concerned in the day-to-day work of the Trade Union Movement'.[129] Lack of demand led to their abandonment between 1936 and 1941, after which their popularity increased. After the war the TUC also began to run summer schools on the same lines for women and for younger trade unionists. The UPW usually sent two or three people each year to such schools, and similarly to those run by Scottish TUC and the Labour Party. However, despite the small numbers – 211 from all unions in 1955 – there were interesting developments in the subject matter covered. For the first time in the period after 1947, the TUC provided opportunities to trade union officials to cover such topics as operational research, work study and management techniques. UPW members in this period began to study 'Trade Union participation in efforts to improve technical efficiency, time and motion study technique, job evaluation and Trade Unions and scientific management', and 'to gain a grounding in industrial administration'.[130] The range and scope of such courses increased with the opening of Congress House and its Training College in 1957, and by the time of the merging of the WETUC and the NCLC in 1964 under the auspices of the TUC, much educational work had already become centralised under its wing.

The UPW has generally been reluctant to send people to long residential courses, on the grounds that it was not 'right for the Union to spend money on individuals as such'.[131] Although residential scholarships were frequently advertised by the Union, it was only with the utmost difficulty that members could even get loans to finance such courses. Ruskin College was regularly supported by donations, however, and some branches in South West England contributed to a scholarship to allow a member to attend University College, Exeter, during the 1930s. Members won various other awards, including in one case from the TUC in 1928 to attend Balliol College, Oxford. By the late 1940s members were regularly winning awards to attend Ruskin College, Hillcroft College for Working Women and the Trade Union Studies Course at the London School of Economics. For a short period in the early 1950s the Union even financed people to attend this latter course as well as others to attend two other residential colleges – Newbattle Abbey and Coleg Harlech. Although two subsequent officers of the Union benefited from this, it was difficult to justify the expenditure on the grounds of its return to the Union, and it was abandoned in 1953. As if to confirm the fears that existed, one member, who won a scholarship from other sources to attend Hillcroft College in 1957, spoke of getting out of the 'blind alley' of her job as a telephonist and taking up 'welfare work'.[132] Arguments about expense also limited the amount of educational activity abroad. However, in the post-war period it became common for members of the Executive to attend schools run by such bodies as the International Confederation of Free Trade Unions and the European Productivity Agency. In 1954 rank-and-file members comprised nearly all of a party of twenty-four that visited Western Germany as guests of the Deutsche Postgewerkschaft.

One other important aspect of the education provided by the UPW was to build loyalty to the trade union and its policies. Thus one student at a 1947 School was brought to the 'realisation that we, as individuals have a definite role in the UPW framework', and another was made 'to value my trade union more'. Leaders of the Union 'decided that here, as in all else, the trade union should be a rallying point; that here membership should mean one more phase of comradeship, one more endeavour outside the workshop, sweetening and helping the life inside'.[133] Considerable emphasis was placed at the Union's schools on social activities such as rambles, visits to theatres and historical monuments as well as sports and games. Students often spoke about this aspect of their education, and it is clear that it did something to inculcate an *esprit de corps*, an identification with companions and fellows as well as with the organisation that encompassed them. Thus one student could describe a school as 'one of the most enjoyable weeks of my life', and the officer responsible for organising another said: 'The motto of the school was "play hard and work hard", and it is no exaggeration to say that this was lived up to'. The schools also played a role in breaking up grade snobbery and attacking the secessionists. At the 1949 Youth Schools some students learnt this lesson. 'The advantages of an amalgamated trade union were made obvious by comparing the progress of the UPW with non-amalgamated organisations which have been operating in the different grades.' At other schools members learnt that 'it matters not what our grades are, but how we can best help each other', and were taught 'the folly of grade and office rivalry'. One member of the Executive thought that with proper training of the rank and file, 'he was sure that ultimately the secessionists would fade away'.[134]

The schools were increasingly used from the 1940s and 1950s to bridge the 'gap between Headquarters and the Branches'. Members learned 'how very hard our Executive Officers worked, – and, what is more saw a great deal of their problems'. One UPW student at a TUC summer school in 1948 reported an 'overriding impression of disappointment' at the failure to criticise union leaders or to consider 'a relationship within industry differing from the existing master-and-man concept'. Increasingly however, the very form of the education given moved away from discussing such questions at all, concentrating on the techniques of bargaining, and UPW schools had representatives of management along to explain their point of view. By the time that trade union education more generally came to be centralised under the wing of the TUC in the 1960s it had come to be seen as a 'powerful instrument for welding the loyalty of full-time officials and rank and file trade unionists'.[135]

Through the education provided by the UPW efforts were also made to inculcate the members with a loyalty to the wider working-class movement. In the 1930s there were complaints that some of the courses were providing aspirants to promotion 'with cheap facilities for their purpose'. Efforts were therefore made to introduce 'a definite labour bias' and to explain the reasons for the Union's affiliation to the Labour Party and TUC. Through contact with other trade unionists in educational activity members were reminded of 'the application [on] the Trade Union movement generally and industrially' of their activities.[136]

With the great expansion of trade union education facilities in the 1970s and the subsidisation of much of it from the outside, there has been more activity at less expense for the Union in recent years. In 1924 the Union spent £854 educating its members – about 2·2d (1p) per head. In 1952 the figure was £5,000, about 3p per member, higher than any union except the Civil Service Clerical Association. In 1958 this had risen to £15,020, almost 21·9d (9p) per member. This was at a time when the average expenditure on education was about 4d (1·5p) per member, and only one union (the Draughtsmen) paid out more than the UPW. More recent figures had been somewhat lower – at £1,736 or 0·9p per member in 1967 and £126,455 or 0·6p per member in 1979.[137] The active participation of the Union in the WEA and in the regional machinery of the WETUC has been reduced. During most of the 1920s and 1930s the Union paid for between 300 and 700 students every year to attend every class, an average of about 350 to attend week-end schools, and 200 to do Ruskin College Correspondence courses after they started in 1927. The members involved in TUC summer schools and residential courses were much smaller. Then, in 1929, 436 members had the remissions for classes, 266 attended week-end schools, forty-one went to WETUC summer schools and 283 went through Ruskin College correspondence courses, a total of 985. This corresponds to 1,133 involved in courses of every sort in 1958 and 800 in those centrally organised in 1979, though local branches then participated in a good number of others. The more recent expansion of the UPW's educational programme involved the acquisition of even more specialised technical knowledge than before, particularly in such fields as health and safety and pensions where detailed expertise is of considerable importance to Union members.

THE SECESSIONISTS – ORIGINS AND EARLY HISTORY

In any description of the organisation and ethos of Post Office trade unionism from the 1920s to the 1970s it is inevitable that the issue of breakaway organisations will loom very large indeed. The existence of such organisations on the engineering side of Post Office trade unionism has been described in a well known study.[138] Fissiparous tendencies in other parts of Post Office trade unionism can be traced from its very origins to the present day, and similar trends could no doubt be discovered in any British trade union aiming to cover a major section of an entire industry. This was of particular significance in the Post Office, and the organisations which broke away from the UPW and attempted to serve the interests of various sections of the workforce had a major influence on the attitudes and activities of Post Office trade unionism.

This is not a subject that lends itself to dispassionate and objective discussion. Virtually all of the sources for its study reflect a prejudiced, not to say abusive attitude. Claims and counter-claims are continuously made about the size of organisations and their achievements which are in nearly all cases exaggerated or, at worst, downright inaccurate.[139] Although it is not difficult to understand the feelings of those who believed themselves to be swallowed up in the coils of an all-pervasive trade union bureaucracy, it is not so easy to sympathise with the long-forgotten snobberies of those performing one set of Post Office duties as against others. On the other hand, it cannot be taken to be self-evident that the lack of orderliness in bargaining procedures that resulted from rival organisations representing the same group of workers necessarily served them ill, however much they may have irked the main Union and the employers. This point had particular application to the male night telephonists who had a rival body to the UPW for over forty years and whose general conditions – for whatever reason – improved remarkably throughout that period. It must also be emphasised that, however obscure and reactionary the attitudes of secessionists may seem to those looking back from an enlightened vantage point decades later, they certainly had support among those they claimed to represent. A large proportion of London sorters and counter clerks, a significant number of postmen, and a probable majority of male night telephonists did support organisations that expressed a good deal of hostility to the UPW. Many of the charges they made against the Union were ridiculous and untrue, but the fact remains that during the entire existence of two important London grades, and for almost the whole period when there were significant numbers of night telephonists, the secessionists were seen by large numbers of Post Office workers as representing their interests more faithfully than the larger UPW. This is quite apart from the question of whether the existence of breakaway bodies actually benefited the grades themselves or Post Office workers as a whole. The identification with secessionism was most complete and long-lasting from the night telephonists, who in any case had problems and attitudes that put them somewhat apart from other members of the Union. Most London counter clerks probably supported their Association rather than the Union, and a significant proportion of London sorters certainly remained faithful to the Guild of Sorters until their grade was finally abolished in 1947.

Each of these groups had the important characteristic that they were closely integrated and specialised sections of the workforce. The same can also be said of the two other small breakaway bodies which operated during this period as the Government Overseas Cable and Wireless Operators Association, formed in 1924, and the Northern Ireland Postal Clerks Association which emerged in 1922 from the confusion of political change and the somewhat different pattern of trade union organisation that had always existed in Ireland. Efforts to organise secessionist bodies amongst grades who worked in various offices in different parts of the country did not prove a success, as can be seen from the moves in this direction amongst provincial SC&Ts in the 1920s and 1930s, amongst postmen from 1930–44, and from the failure of the effort to set up a National Association of Postal and Telegraph Officers after 1947. The breakaways only had a real life and effectiveness when they organised a clearly defined group which could contrast itself with the rest of the UPW's grades.

Most of the pre-amalgamation associates had suffered from breakaways of one sort or another, which have generally been referred to in Chapter 8. In all cases they came from groups within grades who felt they had a right to special treatment. This applied in particular to the Central London Postmen's Association which was an important part of the 1920 amalgamation and whose traditions at least were behind the establishment of the Postmen's Association by City of London Postmen in 1930. The Fawcett Association also had their own breakaway group after 1908 amongst sorters who qualified to do writing duties. Though they provided what was in effect a pressure group on the main organisation, it is perhaps not surprising to find that Robert Farrell, a sorter at the South East District Office who led this movement, identified himself with the Sorters Guild of the 1920s. There was also some hint of a breakaway among London telegraphists in 1914 reflecting some of the older tensions which had long affected the PTCA, but secession was avoided.

A series of rapid developments both of attitude and organisation can be traced in Post Office trade unionism from the time sharp disappointments were expressed in 1912–13 at the results of the Holt Select Committee until the amalgamation agreed in 1919. Many younger trade unionists, including those in the Post Office, were affected by the propaganda of syndicalists and others in favour of the closer co-operation of different sections of workers and the formation of unions to cover entire industries. Many of those who worked in the Post Office, especially if they had served in the armed forces or belonged to superior grades, were remote from such changing attitudes. One group of secessionists claimed that while they had been 'immersed in blood and mud' during the First World War, those who remained behind 'were deceived by the fantastic promises of unscrupulous politicians'. Another group expressed their real remoteness from decisions about trade union amalgamation which they found it almost impossible to understand.[140]

Many were still in the Army, many had just left it, all had, during the War absorbed an entirely new set of ideas, wholly inapplicable to post-war life, when they found themselves suddenly confronted with the necessity of making a momentous (but, happily, not irrevocable) decision before they had time or the opportunity to adjust their mentality to the new conditions.

Although it is argued in Chapter 12 that the importance of opposition to the strike policy of the UPW was exaggerated, there is no doubt that this played some part, along with a general feeling of remoteness from the new bureaucratic machine based in Cromwell Road. The great improvements secured in 1920 were described in later less happy years as 'a mere pittance obtained by the Union, through secret negotiations'. Suspicion of new forms of organisation was hardly surprising within a Union whose constituent parts had in the past hardly employed full-time officials at all. There were inevitably those who thought that 'permanent officials of the UPW are getting out of touch with the needs and requisites of postal life'. 'Amalgamation', it was said, 'benefited a few leaders at the expense of their colleagues'. The consequences of these feelings were thus expressed by James Clancy, a leading figure among the early secessionists:[141]

> The way of amalgamation will never be. The centre of authority is too remote; the individual or the office is shut out from the real motive power, and the knowledge of what is taking place becomes a closed book; and, where knowledge ceases, interest ends.

Particular grades came to the view that their interests were not represented within an amalgamated organisation. 'Is not the Union', asked one London group, 'mainly composed of men who realise that if the CC&Ts were given their due they would get less'? Later they were even more explicit:

> From the point of view of the CC&T grade, it cannot be said that the UPW is a democratic organisation. All the CC&Ts in that body may desire a certain thing, and yet it be denied them.[142]

Differences between generations and suspicions of militancy and bureaucratic remoteness were not in themselves enough to explain the initial impetus behind the setting up of secessionist organisations. What was also important were the traditions of London particularism expressed especially by the indoor London grades. This is a typical statement from a Federation leaflet in 1923:

> What Sorters won for Sorters through the Fawcett Association, Sorters can equally well accomplish for Sorters through the Sorters Guild and the National Federation.

The Fawcett Association in particular had entered the amalgamation negotiations very late, and right until the end many of its leaders had favoured a looser form of association with the other organisations than actually developed. Wallace Cheesman only worked in the UPW over the first few months and Charles Ammon became much more concerned with wider questions in the Labour movement. There was no doubt a genuine desire amongst sorters to maintain the particular traditions of their past organisation from their noisy general meetings and their access to the highest Post Office authorities. It was an effort by sorters at the Western Central District Office to set up a separate branch that provoked one of their number, Joseph Shesgreen, into booking Terry's Theatre in the Strand for the meeting that actually set up the Federation on 23 January 1921.[143] The unyielding attitude of the UPW Executive on the issue of separate branches, however understandable, was clearly a major factor in encouraging secessionism. In any case the Executive did soon afterwards feel compelled to set up a special District Council to cover the indoor grades, an arrangement which continued for the entire history of the UPW.[144]

There was one over-riding question which helps to account for the establishment of the Guild of Postal Sorters on 13 July 1921 and its subsequent stability until it was finally disbanded on 31 July 1948. 'In the whole course of its existence', said the

Postal Telegraph towards the end of that period, 'the Guild has had one major problem, the problem of PROMOTION'.[145] Behind this lay a great deal of fear, and, it must also be said, a certain amount of snobbery, directed against postmen. The ill advised and ultimately abandoned scheme discussed in the UPW in 1923–4 to reorganise the grades was seen as a threat to the special position of the sorters, and the Federation in the early years continually reiterated the utterly unfounded claim that the Union had asked for 'equality' between sorters and postmen. In the meantime, they put on pressure against the arrangement which had existed in London since 1898 that the position of overseer could be secured either by sorters or postmen. These were allocated on a strict quota of one in three or four in the various offices with 382 going to sorters and 136 going to postmen. The sorters objected strongly to the fact that postmen usually got these promotions at a lower age than they did, and some of those who got them might, in the past, have failed the test to enter their grade. They argued that there were other avenues of promotion open to postmen, so that all the positions should be reserved for them. After considering the question for over a year, the Post Office management produced a scheme in July 1924 which effectively conceded the sorters' claim by proposing to reserve 120 extra posts for sorters, leaving only sixteen for the postmen. This was accepted both by the Sorters Guild and by the Sorters' Grade Council in the UPW. The London Postmen's District Council objected, however, and the UPW engaged in two further years of negotiation which eventually resulted in the number of promotions available to sorters being reduced to eighty-nine, a solution accepted neither by the Union nor by the Guild.[146]

The promotions issue was a good example of the effects of directly competing interests between the grades. Although the Union had tried to increase the number of posts available, the solution in the end pleased nobody. This competition between grades generally proved to be the logic of secessionism in the 1920s and 1930s, though it may well have improved the situation of some of them. It was certainly reflected in the way they organisationally developed.

The establishment of the National Federation of Postal and Telegraph Clerks in January 1921 was, as has been indicated, a direct result of grievances about union organisation by certain London sorters. Its officials were nearly all from this grade, together with one or two counter clerks. The aim of the Federation at first was to co-ordinate the work of four 'autonomous' guilds covering sorters, CC&Ts, SC&Ts and telegraphists. Telephonists were at first quite explicitly omitted, since, according to one Federation member, they 'included so many young girls who had not reached years of discretion'.[147] The title 'Guild' was perhaps an unlikely one for those who denounced the Union's policy of 'Workers' Control' in the Post Office as tantamount to support for Soviet rule, and the Union got Guild Socialist G. D. H. Cole to say that the title had nothing to do with him.[148]

From the very beginning it was maintained that each Guild was 'autonomous' i.e. it manages its own domestic affairs in its own way, without the veto of the Federation Executive or the interference of any constituent grade of the Federation'.[149] As a result the function of the Federation itself was never entirely clear, though it provided a focus for the recognition of SC&T dissidents in scattered provincial offices and for the establishment of an organisation of night telephonists in 1928. Its last conference took place in 1932, and soon afterwards it disappeared.[150] To all intents and purposes thereafter the Federation became the Guild of Sorters. The magazine the *Postal Telegraphist* was taken over by the sorters, as also was the Headquarters in Russell Square in Bloomsbury, until it was destroyed in an air raid in December 1940.

THE GUILD OF POSTAL SORTERS: 1921–47

The Sorters Guild was and remained the strongest constituent of the original Federation. It was established 'amid scenes of old time enthusiasm' on 13 July 1921.[151] The most important demands it articulated have been described. It had a strong base amongst 7,700 or so London sorters, all male, in the major London offices. Within a year in April 1922 it claimed 3,310 members and thereafter published the details shown in Table 10.2.

Table 10.2

Year*	Sorters Guild membership	Sorters Guild subscription (£)
1922	3,223	2,789
1923	3,136	2,706
1924	3,354	2,681
1925	3,407	na
1926	3,386	2,786
1927	3,287	2,781
1928	3,182	2,675
1929	3,022	2,532
1930	na	2,386
1931	na	2,052
1932	na	1,481
1933	na	1,410
1934	3,011	1,425
1935	3,037	1,420
1936	2,998	1,391
1937	3,056	1,324
1938	3,058	1,325
1939	3,004	1,206
1940	2,832	1,090
1941	2,762	1,006
1942	2,692	1,025
1943	2,619	928
1944	2,564	870
1945	2,776	779
1946	2,443	893
1947		638

*In most cases this refers to 31 December.

The figures for the war-time period are explained by the fact that the Guild continued to count those of its members who served in the forces and at the same time refused to admit the temporaries who were doing their work. In general, the UPW in the 1920s claimed to have about 10 per cent more members among sorters than the Guild, 3,635 in 1922, 3,778 in 1925 when the Guild was at its peak, gradually climbing to 4,656 in 1934 and 6,169 in 1940. It should be pointed out that these figures were disputed on both sides, though it is probably fair to conclude that until the war, the Guild organised about 40 per cent of sorters and the Union perhaps 50 per cent.

The Guild of Sorters was able to obtain recognition for negotiating purposes from the management in individual offices in November 1921 and for general questions relating to the grade from February 1923. This level of recognition continued until the end of 1947, during all the rest of the existence of the sorter grade. The Guild always claimed that it wanted to 'resurrect the ideals and aims of the Fawcett Association', and in some senses it did keep alive that very particular *esprit de corps* which characterised the London sorters since the 1880s.[152] The Guild continued to campaign for what amounted to the historic claim of the Fawcett Association by asking for equality with the clerical grades. It did this at the 1927 and 1938 arbitration negotiations.[153] It could also claim to be the first organisation in the Post Office to set up a half-pay scheme, which was imitated not only by other secessionist bodies, but later by the UPW itself. However, the position of sorters did not greatly improve during the last years of their existence as a grade, and it is perhaps not surprising that the Guild did not grow again after the mid-1920s.

It is very difficult to judge whether the policies and existence of the Guild of Sorters served the interests of those whom they tried to represent. It may have given them some self-esteem and they were certainly able to claim that they 'made the indoor grades, and especially the Sorters . . . respected and feared in UPW circles'.[154] Yet it cannot be said that all its policies were efficacious. They asked without success for the restoration of open competition for recruitment to sorters (it having been abolished in 1911 to give better opportunities to postmen). At the same time they claimed for themselves exclusive access to the grade of overseer, and in fact its abolition and merging into their own grade. This latter aim could be condemned by the UPW as much as anyone else as 'cheapening' the work of others, and certainly showed a level of blinkered self-interest which was an inevitable result of their particular preoccupations. They grew more feeble in the 1940s when they refused to admit temporary sorters to the Guild. When the long-expected reallocation of work between grades was negotiated in 1945, they were more concerned to expand their possibilities of promotion than to question the scheme itself.[155]

Following the setting up of the new grade structure, the management withdrew recognition from the Sorters Guild at the end of 1947 except with respect to those people who elected to remain in the old grade. On 8 April 1948, a final general meeting was held at which it was agreed to disband the Guild, and members were urged to join the newly-emerging National Association of Postal and Telegraph Officers. After more than twenty years of claims to be non-political it comes as something of a shock to find on the back of the last issue of the Guild's journal the advice

To regain your Personal Freedom and Good Standard of Life – Join the Conservative Party.

It is only fair to the Guild to point out that such sentiments had not been normal in its publications in the past, though they had at times associated themselves with some Conservative MPs who were not generally noted as friends of trade unionism. They also became involved in a body known as the Federation of Independent Trade Unions, which brought together those who remained outside the TUC.[156]

THE ASSOCIATION OF COUNTER CLERKS

The second major constituent of the original National Federation of Postal and Telegraph Clerks came from the grade of counter clerk and telegraphist, a group special to London of whom there were about 2,100 in the mid-1920s, 60 per cent of them being women. A 'Guild of Counter Clerks and Telegraphists' was initiated at a meeting held at the YMCA in Tottenham Court Road on 22 March 1922 with C. F. Bishop of the Eastern District Office as Secretary.[157] In the following April, 520 members were claimed and by 1925 recognition was secured in a number of London districts. However, in March 1924 a quite separate group of CC&Ts, most of whom broke away from the UPW, set up an Association of Counter Clerks. They maintained that at the UPW Conference in the following May, a wage claim was modified by the votes of delegates from other grades. The already established Guild called for 'autonomy not isolation' by continuing affiliation with the Federation, but the Association won more support and full recognition in March 1926. In the following May the Guild was disbanded and its original founders went over to the new body. Bishop became Editor of the *Counter Clerk*.[158]

It is not difficult to understand the reason why the counter clerks wanted to organise themselves apart from the other grades, especially the sorters. Like the other indoor postal grades they argued for 'the status, conditions and salary obtaining in the Clerical Grades of the Civil Service'. However, their case for this was peculiar. Those who worked at the counters were generally acknowledged to be best 'in a position to successfully argue a claim for increased remuneration from the stand-point of "value of work"', and this proved to be the case in practice.[159] This led them on to the view that they had 'nothing in common' with the other grades 'from a working stand-point' and to complain that within the UPW 'the value of counter work was belittled in favour of sorting'. Furthermore, on matters of promotion within the London area, they were in direct competition with the sorters and thought it necessary to argue quite independently for what they considered to be their rights.[160] Like the sorters, they wanted open entry to their grade, as had obtained before 1906, though with a proportion of places for boy telegraphists. However, women had always had more open entry and after 1936 the Post Office began again to advertise positions publicly.[161]

Unlike the sorters, the counter clerks did not have a tradition of independent organisation, so their Association did not in practice operate as anything other than a large trade union branch. Counter clerks were more isolated at work, and even though the majority were women, men dominated the affairs of the Association. (The ACC argued like the UPW in general terms for equal pay, but also wanted more men in the grade.)[162] There can be no doubt that for a long period the Association organised the larger proportion of the grade. Privately, the UPW admitted that though 1,255 CC&Ts had joined from the P&TCA, in 1924 UPW membership in the grade was 856 and at the beginning of 1926 this had fallen to 807. At the same time the ACC claim of 950 was thought roughly accurate and they had the majority in most London districts. ACC membership rose to 1,107 at the end of 1926 and to 1,028 at the end of 1927 when the Union only claimed 736. In 1930 the ACC claimed double the number of CC&Ts that were in the UPW. They claimed 1,306 early in 1937 when the UPW figure was 1,083, and 1,476 against 1,095 two years later at the beginning of 1939. ACC membership was said to be 'the highest ever' at 1,500 in 1943, though this included people serving in the forces. Only in 1945, when the ACC claim fell to 1,141, did the Union dare to claim more, at 1,398.[163]

Though they clearly organised a significant proportion of the members of the grade, the ACC on the whole was somewhat amateurish. Their claims for improved wages and conditions were inflated and ill-conceived. Their efforts to achieve 'upgrading', or equality with clerical grades, were presented to almost every possible tribunal including the Bridgeman and Tomlin Enquiries, and time after time to the Post Office itself. These representations had no effect whatever. The ACC never took its claims to the Arbitration Court independently of the Union, as the Guild of Sorters did on one occasion without success in 1926, and as the Guild of Telephonists did very frequently.[164] The fact remains however, that, for all the arguments about exaggerated claims and so forth, the CC&Ts did best of all out of the 1927 settlement. The reason for this may well have been that the employers were inclined to accept the 'value of work' from a small group rather than outside comparisons that would cost them more. It nevertheless made it possible for the ACC to throw back the Union's arguments with some heavy irony:

> We find that our *incomplete and exaggerated* claim obtained for the men a larger increase on the maximum than has been gained since 1890, and that the women's maximum has been increased by 2s (10p) a week . . . If the meagre result obtained in our case was really due to mismanagement and exaggeration of values, to what does the UPW ascribe the more meagre results obtained in the claims presented wholly by them?[165]

Whatever the justice of this argument, there can be no doubt that it appealed to a large proportion of the grade. In 1937 the CC&Ts actually got the lowest percentage increase, and thereafter the secessionists grew weaker.

The male counter clerks who ran the ACC were educated, respectable and conservative. They reprinted the well known article 'On being Bourgeois' which took pleasure in this 'term of reproach' and said that 'the *bourgeois* understands the art of living much better than anyone else'. They held their early meetings at the Irish Club on the Charing Cross Road, a location later described as 'grim and uninviting', and later moved to the nearby YMCA.[166] There is little evidence of internal controversy within the ACC, though clearly there were some problems created by their insistence on being non-political. Thus they opposed the 1927 Trade Disputes Act, and also condemned the UPW for campaigning against it. A series of articles favourable to the Soviet Union appeared in their journal in 1932, causing some objections. When the war came, they lost their earlier impetus. They objected rather impotently to the employment of part-time and temporary people on counter duties, and could not do much to affect the earnings of their members at a time when all the negotiations took place for the civil service as a whole through machinery in which they could play no part.[167] When the reorganisation that led to the abolition of their separate grade took place in 1945–6, they thought the new P&TO grade would mostly get the clerical status they had always been claiming. However they did not sign the agreement because ex-members of their grade would still have to compete with sorters for promotion.[168] The last General Meeting of the Association was held on 27 February 1947 following the withdrawal of recognition, and members were encouraged to join the new NAPTO.

TELEGRAPHISTS

The original National Federation of Postal and Telegraph Clerks in 1921 was supposed to include two other 'guilds'. The first of these was the Guild of Telegraphists, which was set up in November 1921. Only in London was there a grade separately described as telegraphists, and in 1927 there were about 2,850 of them with 1,507 in the UPW. By this time, although the Guild of Telegraphists issued a Seventh Annual Report and had membership subscriptions of £254, there is no evidence that it had more than a few dozen members, and it had faded away by 1933 without having secured any form of recognition.[169] There had always been separatist tendencies among London telegraphists, but the continual decline in demand for their services, and the technical changes that altered out of all recognition the work they had to do, meant that it was very difficult for them to argue their case alone. The small group of them who believed that they could, broke away from the UPW in 1924 to form the Government Overseas Cable and Wireless Operators Association. At the time it recruited amongst a total workforce of 400, but this later increased. They secured recognition in 1929 and submitted a wage claim in the following year. They continued to exist into the 1950s and after unsuccessful efforts to join the Association of Scientific Workers they had recognition withdrawn in 1958.[170] Throughout their existence they remained weak and ill organised, though they clearly had a good number of problems to set them apart from other UPW members.

There are said to have been other breakaway movements in the Cable Room in the 1940s. For a brief period in the early 1960s the overseas telegraphists also formed their own organisation, but in the end they too found that the UPW served them better.[171]

SC&Ts

The fourth and last of the bodies that were supposed to constitute the 1921 Federation was the Guild of Sorting Clerks and Telegraphists. When set up in May 1922 this claimed 2,091 members and these were said to be largely concentrated in the smaller offices.[172] This body, which does not seem to have had any links with the pre-amalgamation associations, had as its main demand parity with the London CC&Ts. The potential members were much more scattered than their London equivalents and Horace Nobbs was certain from the start that the problems of organising them were such that 'amalgamation was assured'. In April 1925 the SC&T Guild obtained the right to make local representation and by the beginning of 1927 had secured this at eighty-three offices where they were able to prove 40 per cent membership. A vicious battle, office by office, was fought over the next period to win members. Horace Nobbs put it thus:

I think it would be correct to say that hardly an office in the country is escaping an avalanche of leaflets, some argumentative, some of them scurrilous. I wish I could say that these are not having any effect, but I am afraid they are.

The SC&T Guild grew so that by the time of its sixth Annual Conference in 1927, fifty-six delegates were present.[173] However, there was certainly some justification in the Union arguing that if they had recognition in eighty odd offices, there were at least 1,200 offices where they had not. In the meantime, there was a significant further development. At its 1930 Conference, the majority of the SC&T Guild decided to break away from the Federation. This was in part at least because the recent adhesion of the telephonists 'resulted in a form of organisation differing little from the Union'.[174] From then on there was a Guild for SC&Ts inside the Federation and another outside. The Post Office authorities immediately withdrew recognition from all those outside the Federation and all recognition to either side was withdrawn by Postmaster General Attlee in May 1931. The two bodies apparently settled their differences in the latter part of 1932, though by this time the Federation had virtually ceased to exist. The Union calculated the 'outsiders' at this time to have 1,340 members and they in turn said the insiders had 200. In 1936 the Union's calculations put the SC&T Guild membership at 760, and without recognition at any local office it soon afterwards faded away. It was however alleged to have been involved in the establishment of NAPTO in 1946 and contributed £5 10s (£5. 50) to its initial launch.[175]

Local recognition for provincial SC&Ts was retained for one small group by the Northern Ireland Postal Clerks Association (known as 'the NIPs') which was founded in December 1922, obtained local recognition in 1927, and appeared before the Arbitration Tribunal in 1927 and 1938. It continued the traditions of the old 'Dual Workers Association' from 1900 and then identified itself with the secessionist bodies of a later generation. It published a *Gazette* which was still appearing during the Second World War, by which time the Union seems to have had at least as many members in the SC&T grade in Northern Ireland. The Northern Irish Association suffered the same loss of recognition as its London counterparts following the 1947 grade reorganisation and was only allowed to represent individuals in the redundant grades thereafter, but did not formally cease to exist until as late as April 1954.[176]

POSTMEN

One other secessionist body whose formation and development can be entirely attributed to the others was originally set up by postmen of the East Central District Office at the Chief Office in St Martin's-le-Grand in the City of London.[177] A sick pay fund set up amongst the postmen there in 1929 allowed meetings that heard the ventilation of some of the old grievances against superior grades and no doubt also the revival of some memories of the Central London Postmen's Association which had claimed direct access to sorter status. On 30 May 1930, forty-seven postmen at the Chief Office who had not apparently previously been in the UPW transformed the sick pay organisation into a 'Postmen's Association'. Their slogan 'equal pay for equal work' embodied a claim for parity with the sorters.[178] By September, the Association was able to bring out a journal called '*Postmen's Alarm*', and soon afterwards began to recruit members at other London offices, particularly in the Northern , South Eastern and Paddington districts. The name was changed to the London Postmen's Association in November 1931. During 1933 it was decided to extend the scope of the Association both by including auxiliary and temporary grades and also by setting up branches outside London. To the demand for equality with the London sorters was added a demand for equality between provincial postmen and SC&Ts. In September 1933 the name was again changed to the National Association of Postmen and the periodical to the *Postmen's Journal*. In May 1934 an office was opened at 9 Highbury Terrace in North London, where it remained until the Association was finally wound up in 1944.

The fundamental impetus behind this secessionist body was the feeling that postmen were losing out to the next grades above them. The first issue of their journal took up an old theme which was frequently repeated:

> To-day, the work of the postman and sorter is so interwoven, that it is impossible to discern a dividing line, especially in the larger offices . . . The poor old postman for the last ten years has gradually been losing ground, especially in London.

The postmen naturally felt the opposite way to the sorters about the vexed question of access to promotion. How could the UPW, with its own sorter members 'resist this claim of the Federation' regarding overseerships?'[179] It is interesting to see the views expressed by at least one postman who left the Union late in 1930:

> After an association extending over 30 years, with the UPW & PF I am bound to realise that the Postmen's grade is being exploited in the interests of the Sorters leaving me no option but to support the Association that will fight for the Postman's interests, untrammelled by any other grades.

The logical outcome of this of course was to question the existence of the sorters grade, and to find that the UPW could not give justice to any postman's claim without casting grave doubts on the necessity of maintaining 'A Sorter's grade' at all.[180] Not only did the secessionists demand their automatic right to promotion and superior work and status. They also attacked the traditional claim for integration of the porters grade into their own, as well as the educational tests demanded of ex-servicemen who wanted to become postmen.[181] Although attitudes of this sort did flow from direct rivalry between the grades, nevertheless a certain fellow feeling developed amongst the secessionists and it was in the end asserted that everyone stood to benefit.[182]

> A claim made by postmen for equality with sorters and SC&Ts, for example, is an added urge for the sorters and SC&Ts to bring to fruition their own claims for equality with the clerical classes.

During the period after the NAP was set up as a national body, membership rose to a peak probably around the middle of 1934. The highest membership figure claimed by the NAP was 3,354 in 1934, and the highest income from affiliations was in the year ending in the following August. On the basis of the income from affiliations the Union privately calculated the membership during the 1930s as follows:[183]

1934 – 2,146
1935 – 2,447
1936 – 1,886
1937 – 1,298
1938 – 1,680
1939 – 1,530
1940 – 1,180

These figures, which seem likely to be substantially accurate, were from a time when there were around 51,000 in the established postman's grade of whom over 45,000 were claimed for the UPW, together with up to 19,000 auxiliaries of whom about 8,000 were in the Union. There can be no doubt, however, that the initial impetus following the setting up of the NAP did appeal to some sections of postmen. Real branches existed in 1934 in Manchester, Liverpool, Preston, Sheffield and Nottingham as well as in a number of the London offices. Like the other secessionist bodies, the NAP had a half-pay scheme and it started a postmen drivers' protection scheme in October 1935 before the Union did.[184]

However the NAP suffered severely from its inability to get recognition of any kind. Its leaders did not have experience of trade union administration even at branch level, and they became so convinced by their own rhetoric against the Union that even the employment of a temporary clerk became a matter of controversy. Their amateurish approach was shown to its worst effect when they finally set up a meeting with some MPs at the House of Commons on 17 June 1936. Although a good number of MPs attended, they gave only the most perfunctory attention to the vague statements on membership and rushed off when a division bell rang in the middle of the discussion.[185] After this the Association did not recover any further enthusiasm and its membership declined. In 1937 a wage claim was formulated which was 'duly submitted to the Postmaster General but could not be entertained on the score that we as an Association were an unrecognised body'.[186] The Association had to content itself with watching the UPW arguing in front of the Arbitration Tribunal. The Association also suffered from a number of damaging internal rows. In September 1936 the General Secretary had to attend a meeting of the Western District Office Branch to oppose a resolution to disband it. The 1938 Conference heard an argument about the size of the Executive and in 1939 there was an even sharper debate about the refusal of the Executive to publish membership figures despite a Conference resolution instructing them to do so. A further dispute in 1941 meant that the Branch at the East Central District Office which had set up the Association refused for a time to send any finance to the Headquarters.[187]

The argument for a separate organisation of postmen was much weaker than that for the other grades. The NAP had many of the same forms of jealousy and the narrow-mindedness of the other secessionist bodies without the snobbery. Although resolutely 'non-political' like all the others it was nevertheless capable of publishing sentiments such as these:

> Militant Trade Unionism is a thing of the past, the triple alliance is dead – killed by its leaders, and the workers have been betrayed on both the industrial and political field . . .
> Amalgamated Trade Unions of to-day have ceased to function except as glorified state clerks and collecting agencies for party funds. Leaders who used to live for the working class now live *on* them, send their sons and daughters to college and many into Society. The whole thing has become commercialised, and Trade Union Leadership is taken up as a career just as any other profession.

It is interesting to notice that the Communist Party, despite the fact that it supported breakaway unions at the time the Postmen's Association was set up, nevertheless said that postmen should remain in the UPW, and later characterised the NAP as a 'scab union'.[188]

Thus the NAP had no clearly defined set of ideas or function and it is not surprising that from 1935 onwards it was in decline. This was exacerbated during the war, and when finally the decision was taken to close down on 23 May 1944, the Association claimed only 781 members. R. S. Young, who was General Secretary for most of its existence, was compelled to be frank with his members:[189]

The stark truth must be faced that after 11 years as a National Association for Postmen we have failed to attract the vast majority of our grade into joining our ranks . . . No Association or Society can continue to function without the moral and financial support of the people they desire to represent. Frankly we must admit that we have neither. The majority of the postmen grade are to be found in the UPW . . .

Postmen had clearly and decisively shown that they preferred an amalgamated organisation to look after their interests and for this reason the NAP failed.

NAPTO AND THE RECOGNITION ISSUE AFTER 1947

This was by no means the end of the story of secessionism for the UPW. Besides the National Guild of Telephonists, whose story is somewhat apart from the others, there was another attempt to set up a special organisation by those of the basic white collar P&TO grade which came into existence in 1946. There were about 21,000 in this grade following the reorganisation of that year, engaged largely in writing and counter duties. For the first time there were no special arrangements in London. While the changes were going through, a joint meeting was held in May 1946 in London between representatives of the ACC, the Guild of Postal Sorters and the Northern Ireland Postal Clerks Association. The Guild of SC&Ts was represented by Cliff Leak who had for some years been Chairman of the UPW in Leeds but felt particularly disgruntled at the grade reorganisation. There were also representatives of the National Guild of Telephonists and of the Government Overseas Cable & Wireless Operators Association. At this meeting it was decided to set up a National Association of Postal and Telegraph Officers.[190] This was eventually started on 1 March 1947 and the obligatory journal first appeared in the following month.

The General Secretary of the new body for its six or so years of existence was A. F. Williams from South East London, but a number of other leaders came from outside London, including William Heap from Preston who was Chairman for most of that time. NAPTO continued the traditions of the successful London grade organisations and won more support in the provinces than the old Guild of SC&Ts. It was probably also much more widely known than its various predecessors, and conducted a much more successful Parliamentary campaign than before. However, it did not have that same integration and that same clear set of grievances as did its successful predecessors. It tried to argue that the UPW refused to claim clerical status for their grade but this clearly was not true. It tried to make disparaging comments about the new postmen higher grade, but this seems to have fallen largely on deaf ears. At its peak in July 1949 it claimed 4,765 members and this was only just over 20 per cent of those in the grade, at a time when the Union's membership in the grade was 13,760, well over 60 per cent.

NAPTO failed not only for lack of a clear rallying point against the Union, but also because it never got recognition of the sort that its various predecessors had secured. In the 1920s trade union recognition for individual offices and grades was granted without a great deal of difficulty since it was not very different from what had happened before. By the 1940s and 1950s the preference of both employers and unions was for more ordered structures. Secessionist organisations thus had less chance of success.

When the new grades were set up in 1946 the UPW tried to get sole recognition for all of those it covered, including night telephonists, where it certainly did not have a majority of organised members. This claim, which was quite inaccurately decried by the secessionists as a demand for the closed shop, was received sympathetically by the Labour administration who did gradually withdraw recognition from the old grade associations, though not from the National Guild of Telephonists. This was done on the basis of what came to be known as the 'Listowel formula' set out in a letter addressed to the Union on 30 December 1946.[191] It was this letter that allowed the London grade associations to negotiate for their redundant members only, withdraw the right of the Northern Ireland Postal Clerks Association to negotiate for any but individuals, and continued to recognise the National Guild of Telephonists and Government Overseas Cable & Wireless Operators Association. However, the Postmaster General tried to establish some general criteria for such claims in the future by setting out what was said to have been past practice.

> He sees no reason at present for departing from the policy hitherto pursued of considering a request for recognition from an Association if it can show that it has in membership at least 40% of the organised staff of the grade or grades concerned.

To this he added a three-year period before such claims could be reconsidered, and the new stipulation that it would only then be withdrawn if the membership fell below 33⅓ per cent of organised staff. As a matter of fact this was not an accurate account of the criteria that had been employed in the past. As has been seen, the Post Office authorities in the mid 1920s had been prepared to recognise unions that had 40 per cent members at individual offices. The Listowel formula was soon described as having general application in the civil service. It was set out as such in a publication of 1949 on *Staff Relations in the Civil Service* published by the Treasury. Its effect was to make it much more difficult for a newly founded secessionist organisation to establish itself, and in fact there were no further successful rivals to the UPW.

However, one other effect of the 'Listowel formula' was to make it clear that the UPW could not claim recognition for an individual grade if it did not command the allegiance of a large proportion of those within it. For this reason, since the night telephonists were regarded as a separate grade, the National Guild of Telephonists was able to continue. At the same time, the possibility of recognition was opened for the Engineering Officers (Telecommunications) Association (EO(T)A), which broke away from the POEU in 1945 and organised a significant proportion of one grade.[192] However, the withdrawal of the 'local recognition' variation was a blow to NAPTO which was thus unable to carry out any functions at individual offices in preparation for general recognition as its predecessors had in the 1920s. Its claim for recognition as a national body on the grounds that it covered

40 per cent of those organised in the grade was submitted late in 1948 and rejected in the following March.[193] Although it argued that the Union's membership claims were inflated, the Post Office was not inclined to enter into an argument of that sort, so NAPTO gradually declined thereafter until it finally took the decision to disband late in 1953.

In the late 1940s and early 1950s, the issue of recognition of trade unions in the Post Office secured more publicity than it had since the days of William Clery and Sidney Buxton. This was in part because of the skill for publicity displayed by the secessionists, particularly of EO(T)A who had the foresight to employ the services of W. J. Brown, ex-General Secretary of CSCA and then a maverick independent MP for Rugby. At the same time there was an attempt by some of the 'non-political' trade unions to organise and they set up an anti-TUC 'Independent Federation of Trade Unions' in June 1946. The major British newspapers were going through one of their periodic phases of blaming all the economic ills of the nation on the trade unions, and this theme was taken up by some Conservative politicians in attacking the major Post Office trade unions. No less than sixty-three Parliamentary questions were asked on the topic between 1948 and 1954, and there were also some major debates.[194]

During 1949, the UPW forced the pace on the matter by renewing its claim for sole recognition, an issue on which it met the Postmaster General on 29 September. It soon became clear that the attitudes of the authorities were changing, particularly after Ness Edwards became Postmaster General in February 1950. As a former trade unionist in coal mining, Edwards could not be expected to have anything but a deep antipathy for breakaway trade unionism which in his own industry had on occasion been deliberately fostered by some employers. The Labour Government at the time was very much concerned to develop good relations with the established trade unions and their leaders as part of an attempt to confront the serious economic crisis that faced them. No doubt the Postmaster General also came under the influence of his namesake John Edwards, who besides being a powerful and effective backbench MP was also former General Secretary of the POEU. For all of these reasons, Ness Edwards showed a scarcely concealed hostility to all the break-away organisations, including those which could probably have secured recognition under the Listowel formula. Thus he told the House of Commons on 17 May 1950 that he was not going to settle the problem simply on membership figures:[195]

Questions of recognition in the Post Office are not in my judgement, suitable for settlement by reference to any automatic formula. Each case must be considered individually, and in any arrangement which may be made it will be one of my principal objectives to assure that the interests of the staff are safeguarded.

There were none to ask the question as to whether in their circumstances the cause of equity was best served by an employer who took it upon himself to define such further criteria for recognition as 'the general working relationship in the Post Office'.[196] The whole topic was further complicated by the fact that Edwards insisted he was not really going back on Listowel's ruling, and that in any case he was simply doing what he vaguely asserted Lord Wolmer had done in the past.[197]

The Postmaster General made it clear what his attitude was, whatever the rights and wrongs of the matter, when he spoke to his 'fellow trade unionists' at the UPW Conference on 25 May 1950 and asserted that having seen 'far too many little unions speaking for narrow little interests' in mining he was 'not going to offer rewards to dissident elements'.[198] Furthermore, when the Conservatives soon afterwards initiated a full-scale debate on trade union recognition, he made it clear that his ruling was based not simply on objective criteria. In particular he referred to the way that through NAPTO he was 'abused by a counter clerk in a public conference in the most shameful manner', and how they encouraged 'a spirit of indiscipline and in some cases a spirit of sabotage'. As a result of 'a vendetta between various members of staff ' cases of discourtesy could not be dealt with, and registered letters were even lost.[199] These extraordinary statements led to a good deal of further Parliamentary discussion and to letters in the columns of *The Times*. At first Edwards tried to reply to questioning by claiming that his examples were only hypothetical. He was to some extent rescued by the UPW's MP Harry Wallace who showed that continued debate was serving nobody's interests.[200] Another effort to resolve the problems was in a meeting on 30 October 1950 of representatives of all the main unions, but this achieved very little.[201] Eventually in February 1951 Edwards decided to set up a special committee to examine the problem of recognition of new staff associations within the field of existing recognised associations and to advise on general policy and outstanding claims.[202]

This inquiry under the chairmanship of Lord Terrington, a lawyer who had also been a leading civil servant and industrial arbitrator, was made up of Lincoln Evans, General Secretary of the Iron and Steel Trades Confederation, Florence Handcock, Chief Womens Officer of the Transport and General Workers Union, John Boyd, Vice-President of the Ship Building Employers Federation and Harold Farrer, President of the Wool Employers Association. Its proceedings extended over the period of the 1951 General Election and the return of a Conservative Government and it eventually published its Report in February 1952.[203] This provided little comfort for the secessionists. They considered the 'principle of non-duplication of recognition as a sound one' and went on to support 'trade union discipline' for which reason 'we think it would be wrong to place official facilities at the disposal of the unrecognised associations' to help them organise. Since it merely provided an incentive to secessionists, the Committee was strongly of the view that the Listowel formula should be abolished. It also considered that it was bad policy to reintroduce local recognition as a preliminary to national recognition. Although the Committee did not necessarily support one union for the entire Post Office, it did urge joint talks between the various secessionist bodies and the unions from which they had seceded.

These proposals clearly favoured the established unions and only the secessionists already recognised would have much hope under them. W. J. Brown waxed somewhat grandiloquently that it could have been 'drafted by a Committee of a Nazi Party concerned with the setting up of a Nazi Labour Front'. However exaggerated this statement there was certainly some basis in the view that 'from now on, it is the Post Office and not the Post Office Servants which will determine the structure of trade unionism in the Post Office'. Leonard White, who was Brown's successor as CSCA General Secretary, agreed that the Report was in danger of creating '"House Unions" whose continued existence as officially recognised negotiating bodies must always be at the will and pleasure of the employer'. There clearly was some justice in this, though White later pointed out that it should in no way be regarded as support by him of secessionism.[204]

In view of the activities of Conservative MPs in the previous period the

Terrington Report clearly placed the new Postmaster General Earl De la Warr in some difficulty. The Conservative Government never said they accepted the Terrington Report, but in effect they were ultimately compelled to carry it out. Earl De la Warr began by consulting the various interested organisations. On 27 May 1952 he met NAPTO together with EO(T)A.[205] NAPTO General Secretary A. F. Williams drew attention to 'the Conservative Party Election Manifesto which had stressed absolute freedom of choice in trade unionism', and asserted quite correctly that 'it was virtually impossible for any of the present claimants to achieve recognition under the conditions proposed by the Committee'. Earl De la Warr also met a delegation from the Whitley Council staff side on 5 June, at which Charles Geddes of the UPW told him that he 'found it difficult to see any grounds on which rejection of the Committee's advice could even be contemplated'. Representatives of the supervisory grades were even more alarmed at the possibility in that event of new secessions.[206]

On 25 June 1952 the Postmaster General expressed himself as 'not willing to improve the recommendations of the Report', asserting with some justice that there would be 'serious danger' in his taking a decision on such a matter. He considered it 'most desirable that a dispute of this sort should be settled by the staff themselves'.[207] The very next day Geddes tried to initiate discussion both with NAPTO and with the National Guild of Telephonists. Similar discussions were held between POEU and its breakaway bodies.

Geddes told the Postmaster General on 3 July that very different concepts of trade unionism were at stake. Nevertheless, there was now pressure on everybody to agree to joint discussions. The UPW's General Secretary told his Executive that they would need to 'be handled with the greatest care and delicacy', and that they for their part had to be prepared to make significant concessions. This was not only because they had to attempt to resolve the differences of the past, but also because in the event of failure, the Union was going to have to confront again the recognition issue and it would then be important to have shown a constructive attitude. Such an attitude was not shown by the National Guild of Telephonists. They were not prepared to consider the possibility of amalgamation, even after a Post Office official told them that they were mistaken in their belief that the Terrington Report had nothing to do with them. On that basis the Union was not prepared to negotiate with them.[208] NAPTO's attitude was quite different, and they had a lot less to lose since they had not yet secured recognition in any form. A lengthy series of discussions took place between NAPTO and the Union between August 1952 and March 1953 presided over by Ernest Green, former General Secretary of the WEA.[209]

The general tone of these discussions was a good deal more constructive than many such had been in the past. The UPW was at the time in the process of reorganising its sectional conferences and was prepared to think in terms of expanding their scope, though not to the extent of allowing them to decide on general matters of wages and promotions. The Union was able to argue that the decisions of sectional conferences in practice were rarely challenged, and that there had never been opposition when amalgamated branches split up. The greatest differences in the end related to the extent to which the problems of particular grades could be considered independently of one another within a united organisation. The Union thought this could be done only 'where there were no repercussions on other grades and where there is no overlapping interest'. For NAPTO on the other hand 'questions of pay based on value of work, status, recruitment and training should properly be discussed by the sectional conference concerned'. Perhaps surprisingly, it was agreed in February 1953 to approach the Post Office management on this matter. On 23 March two senior officials, T. Daish and G. R. Parsons, announced an adjudication which stated that a particular sectional conference should only consider matters in which members of a grade or grades catered for by another sectional conference have either no interest at all or only marginal interest. This formulation proved quite acceptable to the UPW's Executive, but not to NAPTO.

These talks had clearly been undertaken in good faith on both sides but eventually they collapsed for the same reasons that had manifested themselves ever since 1921. The fact was that some Post Office workers simply refused to accept that they did not have quite separate interests from those of their fellows. The talks between the POEU and EO(T)A also collapsed. After all this the Conservative Postmaster General announced a decision on recognition which, paradoxically in view of all that had happened, 'did not differ in any significant way from those made by the Labour Postmaster General'.[210] Both the POEU and UPW had shown themselves prepared to make significant constitutional changes. The Postmaster General was therefore not prepared to recognise either EO(T)A or NAPTO. On 31 July 1953 there was a somewhat bizarre Parliamentary Debate on the issue. Conservative backbenchers attacked the Government for breaking from previously stated policy, while Labour members supported the Government's policy as logical and just. Nor was this the only paradox. Assistant Postmaster General L. D. Gammans asserted that the decision was justified as serving 'the interests of the men concerned', a verdict which was hardly for him to decide.

Whatever the rights and wrongs of the matter, this soon put an end to the post-1945 breakaway trade unions in the Post Office. NAPTO apparently decided to disband early in 1954[211] and EO(T)A later in the same year. However, by far the strongest of all the secessions from the UPW remained alive and well for another two decades or more.

THE NATIONAL GUILD OF TELEPHONISTS

A number of references have already been made to the National Guild of Telephonists and in particular to its establishment in 1929 as part of the National Federation of Postal and Telegraph Clerks.[212] Like the sorters and the counter clerks, male night telephonists had a separate set of grievances and interests. They were badly paid and expanding in numbers and responsibilities. They had a clearly defined set of grievances and a pattern of working hours that set them apart not only from other Post Office employees, but even from the working population as a whole. There were only about 1,300 night telephonists at the time of the 1927 arbitration proceedings, but their numbers increased to over ten times that number before the introduction of subscriber trunk dialling began in the late 1950s. Throughout this period, more night telephonists were members of the National Guild of Telephonists than of the UPW.

The Guild had one attribute which set it somewhat apart from other secessionists and this was a leader of some stature in the person of Edgar Lansbury, nephew of the Labour politician George Lansbury who was for a time Party leader, Edgar Lansbury was a member of the UPW's Executive from 1921 to 1929, during which time he was an enthusiastic supporter both of the strike policy and of guild socialism. He went with his members at a time when they showed a hostility to women in the Union, with particular reference to the Assistant Secretary Edith Howse. Lansbury thereafter steered them away from some of the restrictive attitudes that might have been expected to go with this. As opposed to the other secessionists, Lansbury expressed a set of attitudes more akin to those of other union leaders and well to the left of many of them.[213] The strength of the NGT was also sustained by the fact that the position of members of the Guild improved substantially over the years. Before the 1927 arbitration a night telephonist in inner London on the maximum received £2. 15 a week basic wage compared to £2. 30 obtained by a postman. By 1938 they were equal at £3. 75 and after 1946 the night telephonists went ahead, by as much as 14 per cent for a time in 1955 when they were earning £6. 55. It is not easy to judge the extent to which these improvements can be attributed to the existence of a separate organisation, and it is perhaps to be expected that both Union and Guild should claim they were responsible for them. However, they clearly helped to maintain the Guild's support.

A significant group of male night telephonists only came into existence with the expansion of the system after the First World War. In 1920 those doing this work began to secure full-time established posts. There were a few night telephonists in the P&TCA and a separate branch was set up for them in London a few months before the amalgamation. They immediately formulated a demand for equality with the SC&T grade, and also for shorter working hours and longer leave.[214] On all aspects of their conditions, the night telephonists throughout the 1920s remained in a conspicuously worse position than most other Union members.

Despite the position of Lansbury on the Executive, the London night telephonists never seem to have been content with the services provided by the Union. In 1924 they are said to have approached the Workers Union for discussion, and by 1927 a large proportion of them were not paying their subscriptions to the UPW. The Union's Executive launched an investigation into this which was followed by a series of organisational disputes bearing some resemblance to those that had led to the formation of the National Federation of Postal and Telegraph Clerks in 1921. The night telephonists branch responded to the investigation of their poor subscription payments with the demand that their affairs should no longer be handled by Edith Howse and that they should be given the power to negotiate quite independently. They also wanted to set up a new branch at the GPO. The Union's Executive was prepared to concede the last of these points, and for a time even persuaded Lansbury to withdraw his proffered resignation. However, the branch members were determined to pursue their independence, persuaded Lansbury again to pull out of the UPW, and on 5 March 1928 set themselves up as a new 'Guild' within the Federation. By the following September they secured recognition on the basis of a London membership of around 1,000. They then began recruiting outside London and in May 1929 they obtained recognition, jointly with the UPW, in respect of all night telephonists and call office attendants. In 1934 they were recognised in Northern Ireland also.[215] They retained this recognition until 1970.

In its early years the National Guild of Telephonists was a small rather amateurish organisation without any full-time officials. By the outbreak of the Second World War its membership had risen to 3,344. It always tried to recruit women telephonists, claiming to have as many as 3,245 of them in 1950. However they were probably all part-timers and in any case only a tiny proportion of the

21,724 women telephonists in the Union at the time. The Guild never secured any recognition for its women members. Nor did it get very far with its efforts to recruit telephonists outside the Post Office.[216]

The issue that gave some life to the Guild in the early period was the efforts of Post Office management to employ women in London after eight o'clock in the evening. Both Union and Guild campaigned hard against this, asserting that the women themselves were against it, and no doubt it was thought to have a deleterious impact on the norms of domestic organisation. At any rate, the Union ran a big meeting of women to protest against the proposals in February 1936. However, the Guild constantly claimed that the Union pursued the issue with less than enthusiasm, and when eventually it agreed to the payment of special allowances to women who worked in the evenings, this was described by the Guild as 'a bad blunder'.[217]

During the 1930s the Guild submitted a series of general wage claims, always by comparisons with various grades who got more than they did. In 1931 they presented a claim that their wages should 'not be less than that recognised for the main indoor grades'. This was as ill timed as the claim of the Union at the same time for 10s (50p) increases for all, and achieved just as little. Soon after this, both Union and Guild went to the Arbitration Court to seek time-and-a-half payment for Sunday working. This was rejected, along with both wage claims. In 1934 the Guild again went to arbitration, this time alone, again claimed parity with the SC&T grade, and again got nothing. In 1938 both Guild and Union were together at the Arbitration Court and some improvements were secured. By this time the Guild was claiming sole recognition in respect of night telephonists. This was however not easy to sustain in the face of the Union's assertion that it had 3,345 male telephonist members at the end of 1939, exactly one member more than the Guild.[218]

It was in the war period and immediately afterwards that the Guild of Telephonists grew into something more than a body of marginal significance, especially after the substantial improvements obtained by night telephonists in 1946. Its claimed membership rose as high as 4,832 in 1943 including 3,035 full-time males, and in October 1946 it was able to show itself to have 4,712 fully paid up male members to a special check carried out by the management. In October 1945 the Guild was also able to take Edgar Lansbury away from being London Secretary and make him full-time General Secretary. In 1948 Roy Damerell was taken on as full-time Assistant General Secretary and in the same year the Guild's Office was moved out of Lansbury's house initially to Kensington High Street and in 1951 to 72 Queen's Road, Croydon, where it thereafter remained. In the following years the Guild was able to negotiate actual changes in wages and conditions in ways which had not really been possible in the pre-war period, and it developed a life of its own and something of an *esprit de corps* that made many people forget the distant disputes in which it had its origins.

Lansbury retired in 1951, though he remained President until his death in 1960. He was replaced as General Secretary by Roy Damerell until he in turn went in 1956 to become an industrial relations adviser to the colonial government in Kenya. J. E. Barnfield was then General Secretary until 1966 when he was replaced by Jim Fitzgerald who had been a major figure in the Guild since becoming National Chairman in 1952 and Assistant General Secretary in 1957. The issues on which the Guild maintained and sustained itself in the years after 1945 are not always easy to determine. The post-war grade reorganisation did not affect the telephonists directly, but did involve some alterations of duties mainly to cut out part-timers and to start some night duties as early as four o'clock in the afternoon. Though the Guild had long since been compelled to abandon its efforts to prevent women from working in the evening, it refused to accept any new adjustment of working hours. It then berated the UPW for negotiating a compromise with the Post Office.[219] However, during the course of the post-war reallocation, the night telephonists for the first time got higher wages than postmen, and they secured a better settlement than most other grades as a result of the 1949 arbitration discussions. The rapid expansion of the system during this same period without significant technical change meant that the number of night telephonists increased, and their numbers were kept up by the expansion of the cheap rate period during the 1950s and 1960s.

It is easy to sense a growing strength and self-confidence from the Guild during the post-war period. The NGT had no difficulty in rebuffing what it described as the Union's 'impudent' claim for sole recognition in 1946. On 1 December 1947 there was a public debate between the general secretaries of the Union and Guild, Charles Geddes and Edgar Lansbury, with Ron Smith of the UPW in the Chair. Faced with what seems to have been a largely hostile audience, Geddes was not at his best. He was in any case not in an easy position in having to explain the perfectly good reasons why the Union did not demand so much for the night telephonists as did the Guild. He resorted instead to sharp attacks on Lansbury for personal ambition and on Guild members for being duped by him. To this Lansbury simply replied that he did the best he could for his members.[220] The Guild was strong enough to refuse serious discussions with the Union about reunification following the Terrington Report in 1952, when all the other secessionist bodies were destroyed. Its membership went up from a total of 6,000 in 1945 to 7,004 male members a year later and 9,100 by the end of 1948. In 1950 it claimed its highest total of 11,554 male telephonists, and this figure fluctuated from 9,000 to 11,000 from then until 1965. During this period the Union never claimed more than half that number among night telephonists, though it always had far more among the women. The total number of night telephonists (including part-timers) in the 1950s and 1960s fell slowly from around 18,000 in 1951 to just below 16,000 twenty years later.

During these years the Guild was able to develop a life of its own which established it as a body in its own right, quite apart from the particular factors that had brought it to birth. It ran its own insurance scheme, including a sick fund set up in 1944, and a mutual aid fund which continued with a call system right into the 1960s. The Guild even ran an education programme in the form of a number of schools for branch officials from 1962 onwards. It also supported with increasing intensity the separation of posts from telecommunications though without much argument or detail. However, the thing that kept the Guild in business was its continuing ability to negotiate about wages and conditions. It is not possible to make an objective judgement of the effects of having two organisations advocating the claims of the same set of people. Nevertheless the fact was that the relative position of the night telephonists did improve from 1946 onwards. There was clearly an argument to be made that the existence of the Guild helped to bring this about.

This is not to say that the efforts at national negotiation by the Guild were conspicuously successful. They only achieved anything in their forays to the civil service Arbitration Court when they were also 'in the field' with the Union, and when the Post Office was considering a wide range of other grades. It must be said that besides the improvements that came with the 1946 reorganisation, night telephonists also did conspicuously well in the 1949 wage settlement, getting an increase of 16s (80p) a week at the maximum when others got only 6s (30p). The breakdown of provincial differentiation in 1951 also benefited many night telephonists, though in this they were treated no differently from other Post Office workers. In all these negotiations, the Guild continually claimed credit for improvements which they had not obtained, and attacked all claims which fell below their own. In 1951 they submitted a claim after the Union and were only informed about it after it had been agreed by the National Whitley Council. The Union then said that the Guild had nothing to do with the settlement, and was sued by Guild General Secretary Damerell on the grounds that this was a reflection on his competence. Honour was saved on both sides when the Union denied it had intended any such reflection.[221]

In the mid-1950s the Guild moved away from its old form of comparisons by arguing that the relativities achieved in 1949, particularly between day and night telephonists, should be maintained. Thus when in 1956 the UPW got a 13s (65p) increase at the maximum for the women and nothing for men, the Guild strongly argued for a restoration of the previous difference. This was not accepted by the Post Office.[222] This form of argument changed after the 1955 Priestley Royal Commission on Civil Service Pay. At the time both Guild and Union submitted claims for improvement based on the value of work, entirely without success.

The first agreement on equal pay in 1955 and the various technical improvements culminating in the beginnings of STD had important effects on the work of telephonists. Ultimately, the division between day and night telephonists broke down altogether. At first however the Guild argued that only men would be able to do the increasingly specialist work. Nevertheless from 1957 women were able to work up to 11 p.m. A further set of changes involving special allowances for night work was introduced in 1961. The response of the Guild was simply to go to the Arbitration Court to get the allowance improved.[223]

In the new atmosphere in the 1960s, the Guild reflected in almost the same way as the Union the emergence of greater militancy. Because of the position of its members, the Guild was also able to gain some improvements from productivity bargaining. The Guild after protesting about the Union's attitude signed a three-year agreement for annual rises of 5 per cent in 1964, but this was overtaken by the wage freeze of July 1966.

In the meantime, pressure began to build up for the Guild to settle its differences with the Union. This centred in particular on the Guild's continual and always unsuccessful attempts to get recognition for women. The peak figure for women members they had given in 1950 was never attained again and they rarely published details thereafter. In 1962 they said they had 2,476 women members at a time when the Union had 30,019 women telephonists. In 1963 the Guild set up a Women's Recognition Advisory Council which continued the fruitless campaign until 1970.[224]

In 1960 Postmaster General Bevins responded to one of the Guild's forays on women's recognition with pressure for a meeting with the Union. This took place in the following year but to little effect.[225] In 1965, Postmaster General Benn, when faced with the same problem, took a more energetic initiative. Conciliation talks were arranged with H. D. Hughes of Ruskin College playing the role of inter-mediary. The UPW Executive decided to suspend its steady stream of propaganda against the Guild and to take a very conciliatory attitude. A scheme was worked out by July 1966 roughly similar to what had been discussed with other groups of seces-sionists, including the right to separate branches and separate voting cards at sectional conferences. It was also agreed to take on to the UPW's staff the Guild's full-time officials Jim Fitzgerald and S. Roberton.[226] Pressure in the Guild to refuse to accept any change was very strong and the announcement of the imminence of a public corporation held out the hope of a completely independent trade union organisation for telecommunications. On this basis although the 1967 Annual Conference of the UPW unanimously accepted all the concessions, the Guild decided that it would soldier on.[227] In one further desperate effort UPW General Secretary Tom Jackson and Deputy General Secretary Norman Stagg met the Guild Executive on 18 October 1967 and even went so far as to offer them a seat on the Post Office Joint Trade Union Council 'as a token of good will in the hope we would grow to know each other better and perhaps amalgamate in the long run'. Once again this was rejected and the propaganda war between the two organisations was resumed with a venom rare even over the previous forty years.[228]

In June 1969 further discussion was initiated first of all by the new Managing Director of the Post Office Corporation William Ryland. Over the following months the Guild met the new management of the Post Office Corporation in an attempt to persuade them to accept their proposals for a rationalised structure of the Post Office trade unions. Management were clearly not in a position to accept any such thing, though they were able to hint that they would withdraw recognition from the NGT.[229] The Union then put forward a series of yet more conciliatory proposals. In addition to all the things in the Hughes package of 1966, the Union offered to take on Fitzgerald as an Assistant Secretary, with Roberton as his Personal Assistant. It was even proposed that two further members of the NGT Executive should have places reserved for them on the Executive of the UPW. These were accepted by the leaders of the Guild and presented to the members early in 1970 with the advice of John Donne that 'no man is an island'. Two generations of divisive propaganda could not be so easily washed away and in April 1970 it was announced that Guild members had voted by 4,163 to 2,132 against these proposals. On 1 May Ryland said that the major proposals had been 'statesman-like, forward looking, and entirely in the best interests of the Telephonist Grade'. He therefore ordered the withdrawal of recognition on 1 September 1970.[230]

All that remained was the position of Fitzgerald and Roberton. The former was taken on as Assistant Secretary of the Council of Post Office Unions, and the latter worked on telephone matters in UPW House. The diminishing members who remained faithful to the Guild were able to argue that a combination of Union and employers had come together to defeat a small group. In the peculiar legal and industrial situation of the early 1970s, they were able to pursue this argument through the courts.[231] First of all the Guild changed its name to the Telecommuni-cations Staff Association, and may have recruited a few of those who objected to going on strike in 1971. It then tried to use the machinery of the 1971 Industrial Relations Act to force the Post Office to grant it recognition. After the UPW Executive decided to defy the trade union boycott on Industrial Relations Act machinery to deal with this, the claims of the TSA were not upheld either by the Industrial Relations Court or the Commission on Industrial Relations. They did get some eccentric endorsement for their efforts from Lord Denning and the Court of Appeal during 1973, but this was ultimately overthrown by the House of Lords in 1974.[232] For the moment this was the end of secessionism for the UPW.

One final aspect of the demise of the National Guild of Telephonists should be noted. The separate grade of male night telephonist finally passed away during the 1970s, and with it the basis for the existence of such an organisation. Although UPW membership among night telephonists following the collapse of the Guild and the TSA rose to as high as 13,884 at the end of 1976, by the end of 1980 this figure had fallen to 2,853. Technological, social and other developments had thus finally put an end to the basis on which this particular body had existed more rapidly and more completely than all the arguments of two generations.

CONCLUSIONS

Readers unfamiliar with the development of trade unionism in the Post Office will perhaps be surprised at the scale of the attention that has been devoted to those who tried to break from and defeat the Union of Post Office Workers. This is justified not so much by the numbers involved and by the need to set out some of the complexity of the issues. It is also because of the substantial effect that the secessionists had on almost all aspects of trade union activity between 1921 and 1971, and because this is a subject that allows a good deal of light to be cast on the structural problems of a union which aims at a substantial industry-wide coverage, and also at the specific grievances of particular groups of Union members and Post Office workers.

The passions aroused on both sides as a result of secessionism have been outlined, and numerous other examples could be quoted. There were those on both sides who expressed alarm at the tone and effect of such expressions. On the one side lay the particular pride and jealousies of those whose life and work was bound up with particular skills. On the other side was the whole existence of a united organisation with loyalties and values that transcended any particular circumstances.

The almost unbridgeable gap that existed can be seen from the almost inevitable failure of every effort to resolve the differences made over the years. The discussions, often recorded at inordinate length, show a level of mutual hostility rendering negotiations of any kind extraordinarily difficult. Thus in 1923, pressure from Postmaster General Neville Chamberlain made the Union take the initiative for discussion whose terms the Federation would not even accept. In 1924 negotiations initiated by rank-and-file members on both sides took place under the chairmanship of Sir George Hulme of the London County Council. The Federation insisted on massive changes in the Union's constitution to allow virtually no powers at all to its Executive Council, and broke off negotiations before they could be completed. In 1929 the Society of Civil Servants, to which the Federation was until that time affiliated, took the initiative for further discussions and the Union was prepared now to consider expanding the functions of its Executive sub-committees, but again the talks broke down.[233] The various talks in the post-war period nearly all had the same dismal results.

In the end it was not possible for such discussions to conclude in compromise. Either the Union should be an amalgamated industrial union covering workers of various sorts and conditions, or else it would be a loose federation such as even the secessionists themselves could not sustain. The UPW retained its centralised character and its somewhat staid and orthodox image in part because a large proportion of dissent and criticism, at least until 1970, came from sources such as these. In the 1980s and later, it will no doubt be possible for changes in policy and organisation to be made without the constant need for members to look over their shoulders at outsiders whose very purpose is to attack all that they do.

The secessionists had an effect not only on Union structure but also on bargaining. The temporary collapse of the Post Office Whitley Council between 1929 and 1932 is described on pp. 452ff. In London, Whitley organisation was never restored while the secessionists continued to exist. There was, however, a so-called Extra-Whitley Committee in London for 1933 through which the secessionists were at least informed about what had been decided elsewhere, and were perhaps able to have some effect on the decisions.

However, for the vast majority of Post Office workers in the grades covered by the Union, the main events of their trade union life were expressed through the Union of Post Office Workers. This is of course not to say that all members spent all their lives thinking about the Union and its policies, and as a result it is hardly surprising that they are not always clear about the policies and attitudes voted for by their representatives.[234] However, when ordinary members are consulted about their attitudes, for example to Labour Party affiliation, they are not necessarily found to be behindhand. In 1920 and in 1947 they agreed by substantial majorities to Labour Party affiliation, even though a sociologist at a comparatively peaceful time in the development of the Union discovered uncertainty on this point.[235] In the big industrial battles between the 1960s and 1971 only a tiny minority failed to rally to the Union, and a very good proportion of those who did, complained that their leaders had not gone far enough.

The fact is that, however desirable it may for trade union activity to consist of continual mass meetings, it does not do so. As a result the actual aspirations of trade unionism are expressed independently of the lives of the members. The trade union machine, the activists and the professional bureaucracy, have the task of reconciling the aspirations of a large number of diverse groups. They will not always do so to their liking, nor will they necessarily serve their best interests, however much they try to do so. The activists and the professionals inevitably develop a life of their own, and a set of attitudes that puts them apart from those whose lives are not centred on trade unionism. Yet theirs will be the expression of the trade union as it comes into contact with the ordinary uninvolved member.

The early parts of this chapter have been concerned to describe the development of the organisation of the UPW. Particular detail was given on discussion about the pay of the officers as an illustration of a major aspect of the life of the Union and the changing role of its professional leadership. The education policies of the Union before the recent period were also detailed as a further reflection of changed aspirations and attitudes. It is hoped that all other significant aspects of organisation and internal life have also been outlined. The aim in the following chapter will be to locate the UPW in the trade union movement and the wider world.

NOTES

1 The main sources on the organisation of the Union are the rule books of which there were thirty-two editions between 1920 and 1980, with many discussions at executive and annual conference meetings. Dates given in this chapter refer to the dates when the rules were changed, not necessarily precisely the same as when they were enforced.

2 *Post* 1939, CS p. 55, 1939, pp. 9, 70, 152; 1948 Agenda p. 162, *Post* 1949, pp. 87, 130, 16 July 1949, p. 4, 16 July 1955, p. 6, 1956, p. 379.

3 *Post*, 24 May 1952, p. 298, 1975, CS p. 11, 5 May 1976, pp. 1–2; UPW (1969).

4 On these incidents see ECM 17–20/10/33, 70–1, 23–25/1/34, 91–3, 27–29/7/43, 24, 29–31, 27–29/10/43, 121, 124, 18–20/4/44, 322, 335–6; GPC Minutes, 27/4/44 p. 5; ECM 18–20/10/49, 100–1, 108.

5 *Post* 1939, CS pp. 44–5; ECM 28–30/10/41, 81–4.

6 *Post*, 3 December 1932, p. 450, 5 July 1958, p. 408; ECM 29/8/46, 634–41.

7 ECM 24–26/1/45, 202–3 on branch reserves. On the ECDO case see ECM 12/1/28, 68–73, 25–27/4/28, 151–3, 18–20/7/28, 34–5, 16–18/10/28, 45, 23–25/1/29, 76.

8 ECM 23–31/7/46, 548, 598, 29/10–1/11/46, 660, 679–80, 28–30/1/47, 785, 796, 15–17/3/47, 885, 902–3.

9 *Post*, 6 June 1931, p. 538; POC, 3126, 2 September 1931; ECM 27–29/7/43, 35, 57–9, 27–29/10/43, 128, 142–4.

10 *The Listener* (20 January 1958); ECM 24–26/1/33, 145–7, 22–24/11/45, 218–24.

11 On local journals see *Post*, 15 July 1922, p. 38, 4 April 1941, p. 97, 11 September 1954, pp. 515–6, 9 October pp. 563–4, and the series of local branches in *Post*, 26 November 1921, p. 497 (Manchester T&T), 10 December 1921, p. 549 (Inland Section), 4 February 1922, p. 101 (Birmingham Postmen). For a good branch history see Reading Amalgamated Branch *50th Anniversary/Jubilee Souvenir Edition* (Reading 1969), and *Post*, 17 December 1932, pp. 492–3.

12 ECM 17–20/10/33, 41–4, 23–25/1/34, 85–6.

13 ECM 30–31/3/20, 9–10, 23–5, *Post*, 10 April 1920, pp. 349–52, 18 February 1922, p. 152, 4 May 1922, pp. 343–5.

14 ECM 18–20/4/23, 269, 17–19/1/23, 159; *Post*, 11 March 1922, p. 247, 8 November 1924, p. 370; ECM 13–14/12/23, 129–32, *Post*, 15 March 1924, pp. 253–4.

15 ECM 28–30/7/42, 33–5; 28/10/–5/11/47, 123–9, 27–30/1/48, 245–51.

16 ECM 16–18/10/34, 56–60.

17 ECM 18–24/10/45, 144–55; *Post*, 16 March 1946, p. 162, 22 June 1946, p. 41, 21 June 1947, pp. 28–30, 6 March 1948, p. 29; ECM 27–29/7/48, 451.

18 *Post*, CS for 1935, pp. 43–4.

19 *Post*, 11 June 1927, pp. 565–8, 17 December 1966, pp. 373–4.

20 ECM 26/2/21, 6ff., 13–16/4/21, 2.

21 *Post*, 2 June 1928, p. 502.

22 ECM 20–22/1/22, 74–5, 28–30/10/41, 121–2.

23 *Post*, 26 December 1919, p. 450, 21 May 1921, p. 491; ECM 8/12/20, 12–13.

24 Baker to Riley in R XIII/5, 18 November 1917. ECM 8/1/31, 113–7, 21–23/1/31, 134, 146–50. *Post*, 7 March 1931, p. 228, 16 May 1931, pp. 460–5, 476–7.

25 This is an extract from a piece called 'Dedication' in *Post*, 24 July 1937, p. 62. Collections were published in 1915, 1921 and 1928 and others included *Seed Time and Harvest and Other Poems* (Manchester 1931). *The Orchard and Other Poems* (1943), *The Sow's Ear* (1944), *Forth Alone and Other Poems 1945–53* (n.d.), *Remembered and Other Poems 1953–58* (n.d.). See also *Daily Herald*, 10 August 1921, for an attack on their quality and *Post*, 20 August 1921, p. 166 for a defence.

26 ECM 12/6/29, 12–14, 17–19/7/29, 38–40, 22–24/10/29, 85, 22–24/1/30, 141–2, 8/1/31, 113–7, 21–23/1/31, 134.

27 ECM 8–10/1/20, 8–9. The developments after 1981 are not discussed here.

28 A separate OSF was formerly in the possession of the Research Officer. It is summarised in Clinton (1974).

29 OSF, *Officers' Salaries. Summaries of Discussions etc*, 7 June 1955, and *Report on Interpretation of Decisions Referring to the Allocation of Bonus to Officers' Salaries*, February 1925; *Postal and Telegraph Record* (18 April 1918); *PG* 27 April 1918.

30 ECM 13/17/20, 58 and memorandum dated 30 June 1920 submitted to the EC, of which there is a copy in OSF.

31 *Post*, 19 February 1921, p. 189, 21 May 1921, pp. 491–2, 28 May 1921, p. 532, OSF, *Report of Officers' Salaries Sub-Committee* 16 February 1923, and ECM 21/2/23, 196–7.

32 ECM 18–20/5/23, 26–8, 17–19/10/23, 90–1, 14–16/10/25, 46, 49, 18–19/3/26, 89.

33 Bowen's memo of 29 January in OSF and the discussions in ECM 10/2/25, 163, and *Post*, 30 May 1925, pp. 446, 459–60.

34 *Post*, 6 March 1926, pp. 204–8, 13 March 1926, pp. 226–8, 20 March 1926, pp. 245–8. The report also reached the anti-trade union press – see *The Patriot*, 15 April 1926, pp. 356–7.

35 *Post*, 19 June 1926, pp. 456–68, 26 June 1926, pp. 483, 485, 488.

36 *Post*, 5 March 1927, p. 228, 28 May 1927, p. 508, 11 June 1927, p. 578; ECM 8/2/28, 110–1; *Post*, 2 June 1928, pp. 504–5, 9 June 1928, p. 514.

37 *Post*, 8 June 1929, pp. 511–15.

38 *MR View*, May 1929 Supplement, June 1929, pp. 3–5. ECM 12/6/29, 6–8, 18/7/29, 38; 1930 Rule Book, pp. 23–4, 1927 Rule Book, p. 20.

39 *Post*, 24 May 1930, pp. 516–19.

40 *Post*, 11 April 1931, pp. 355–6, 16 May 1931, pp. 465–7, 472, 6 June 1931, p. 563; Willesden Branch UPW – *Mr. George Middleton MP . . . a few vital facts* (copy in OSF); 1932 Annual Conference Report, pp. 243–4.

41 ECM 17/10/35, 76–81, 24/1/36, 140–4; *Post* 1936, CS pp. 8–10.

42 *Post*, 6 March 1937, pp. 237–8, 1937 CS pp. 27–9, 50–3; Geddes (1937); *Post*, 26 February 1938, p. 186.

43 ECM 29/4/41, 255, 20/4/41, 263–7, *Post*, 14 June 1941, pp. 24–5.

44 *Post*, 24 June 1944, p. 23.

45 OSF, *Memorandum on Consolidation of Salaries of Officials*, 21 January 1946; ECM 26/1/46, 304–7, 30/1/1946, 329; *Post*, 9 March 1946, p. 53.

46 ECM 30/1/48, 307, 20/2/48, 1A–6A, 2/2/49, 679–82, 17/2/49, 685. There are various documents relevant to these discussions in OSF.

47 ECM 20/10/49, 174, 30/1/50, 269–70, 22/3/50, 294–7, 18/4/50, 334–5; OSF, *Officers' Salaries*, 3 January 1950; *Post*, 1 July 1950, pp. 20–1.

48 *Post*, 12 April 1952, pp. 232–3, 21 June, p. 32; ECM 17/1/52, 174–5.

49 'Union chiefs underpaid. Large funds but low salaries', *Sunday Times* (23 May 1954); 'He's got his PC, CH, CBE – but is he *PAID* enough?' *Sunday Express* (13 June 1954). See also 'The Labour scene, financial problems of unions and party. II. Penalty of unattractive salary' in *The Times* (30 August 1955).

50 OSF, *Officers' Salaries and the Cost of Living Index 1920–1954*, 7 October 1954, Memorandum on Officers' Salaries (M41/17/54) of 20 October 1954, and ECM 21/10/54, 181–3.

51 The various memoranda during the Executive discussion are in OSF and the rest of the story is in ECM 7/1/55, 198–200, 18/1/55, 46 and *Post*, 29 January 1955, p. 146, 9 April, p. 280, 16 July, pp. 27–9, 13 August, p. 470.

52 ECM 17/7/56, 88, 9/8/56, 117–18, 214–16. *Post*, 2 February 1957, p. 136, 6 July, p. 424.

53 The documentation of this discussion and what follows is especially extensive, particularly in OSF. See also ECM 29/10/57, 220, 274, 3/1/58, 454, 482–3, 4–5/2/58, 563–7 and 27/2/58, 579; *Post*, 22 February 1958, p. 217, 19 April, p. 301, 5 July, p. 407.

54 ECM 29/1/59, 145 and AD (EC 42/59) dated 23 January; *Post*, 21 February 1959, p. 157, 29 August, p. 426, 23 January 1960, p. 40.

55 ECM 27/1/60, 126; AD (EC 577/59(F)): Report of a Special Meeting of the Finance Committee on 18 December 1959, pp. 1,383–4.

56 ECM 15/12/60, 200–1.

57 OSF, *Review of Officers' Salaries*, 21 January 1961 (EC 32/61); ECM 1/2/61, 254–5, 9/2/61, 258. Two (unsigned) letters in OSF claim that the percentage calculations in the report are in error.

58 All this can be traced from documents in OSF.

59 *Post*, 27 January 1961, p. 422, 25 February 1961, p. 206. Report of 1961 Conference, p. 16.

60 ECM 26/10/61, 114–15, 14/12/61, 168–70, 24/1/62, 207–8; AD (EC 620/61): Review of Officers' Salaries, 9 December 1961; (EC 635/61): Report on Officers' Salaries, 21 December 1961; *Post*, 10 February 1962, p. 2, 9 June, pp. 308–9; 1962 Conference Report, pp. 3–6.

61 ECM 31/1/63, 161, 23/2/63, 162, AD p. 823 (EC 54/63); *Post*, 23 February 1963, p. 162; 1963 Conference Report, p. 3.

62 *Principles to Govern Economic Adjustments of General Officers' Salaries*, 21 November 1963 (OSF and EC 557/63 (F)); ECM 27/11/63, 66–7; 1964 Conference Agenda, p. 43, Report, pp. 8–9 and *Post*, 13 June 1964, p. 371.

63 *Officers' Salaries*, 30 July 1964 (EC 417/64); *Post*, 23 January 1965, p. 27; 1965 Annual Conference Report, p. 8; ECM 24/6/65, 7; 1966 Conference Agenda, p. 2; Minutes, p. 1; *Post*, 25 June 1966, p. 146.

64 *Officers' Salaries*, 29 June 1966 (EC 349/66) in AD. (Although there is some material relating to this and what follows in OSF, the best source in general is the Minutes and AD of the Executive.)

65 ECM 30/6/66, 11; AD (EC 659/66 (F)) *Officers' Salaries* 16 December 1966 and *Finance Committee: Special Meeting* (EC 665/66 (F)), 16 December 1966.

66 ECM 29/12/66, 70–2; *Officers' Salaries* 20 January 1967 (EC 46/67 (F)) and ECM 26/1/67, 85–6. *Post* (Special Issue), 24 March 1967, pp. 2–8, 24 June 1967, p. 7.

67 *Post*, 18 March 1972, pp. 10–11, 29 July, pp. 7–8.

68 *Post*, 10 March 1951, p. 76, 14 July, pp. 270–1.

69 *Post*, 8 April 1970, pp. 14–17, 22 July, p. 16.

70 ECM 14/11/47, 224–6; *Post*, 19 June 1948, pp. 2–3.

71 ECM 15–16/10/40, 115–18, 23/5/41, 13–15, 25–26/7/41, 65, 28–30/10/41, 123.

72 ECM 7/5/37, 1–2, 4/6/37, 11–12, 13–15/10/37, 80, 90–1, 18/8/42, 80–97. On Marjorie Peake see ECM 24–26/10/44, 73–4, 9/11/44, 141, 30/11/44, 157–62, 24–26/1/45, 177.

73 ECM 3–6/10/19, 28.

74 The article on 'The UPW Executive Council: Its work and needs' is in *MR View*, July 1930. On the resignation see Chapter 12, p. 479.

75 ECM 18/6/32, 28, 28/6/32, 36. Chapter 12, p. 526f below.

76 ECM 20/2/53, 271; *Post*, 14 February 1953, p. 143.

77 *Post*, 8 November 1924, p. 370, 21 May 1932, p. 508, 4 June 1932, p. 548.

78 *Post*, 15 March 1924, pp. 254–5, 16 May 1925, p. 406; ECM 22–24/1/24, 173–4.

79 *Post*, 2 March 1929, p. 191, 25 May, p. 464.

80 ECM 5/6/31, 11, 27/11/31, 124–6.

81 ECM 15–17/7/36, 66–7, 13–15/4/36, 115; *Post*, 27 February 1937, pp. 195–6, CS pp. 49–52.

82 ECM 7/2/47, 840–5, 28/10–5/11/47, 203–7; *Post*, 21 June 1947, p. 30, 19 June 1948, pp. 45–7.

83 *Post*, 2 February 1957, pp. 133–6, 16 February, p. 165, 13 April, p. 288, 6 July, pp. 424–6, 22 February 1958, pp. 195–6.

84 1969 Conference Report, pp. 262ff.

85 *Post*, 21 June 1947, pp. 44–5, 6 March 1948, pp. 12, 58. 19 June 1948, pp. 33–4.

86 *Post*, 10 June 1961, pp. 365–9.

87 *Post*, 27 March 1965, p. 273, 19 June, pp. 436–7.

88 For a general description see Suthers (1932).

89 ECM 3–5/10/19, 50, 12–13/19, 9, 25/2/20, 10–11, 8–9/5/20, 21, 88–9.

90 John Craven in *Post*, 24 January 1931, p. 68.

91 ECM 16–18/10/34, 54–5, 9–11/4/35, 159–61, 26/4/35, 199–200, 3–4/5/35, 202–4, 17–19/7/35, 15–19, 15–17/10/35, 49–51.

92 For details see Hobhouse (1967).

93 See *Your Union Headquarters* (n.d. 1963?)

94 See 'Notes on the Research Department', 26 February 1960, at F 110.5, and other documents there.

95 See, for example, ECM 1/8/44, 70–2, 9/11/44, 137–41, 14–16/2/45, 288–91, 24–26/4/45, 350–5.

96 ECM 20–22/1/21, 6.

97 ECM 21–22/11/19, 15–17, 15–17/4/28, 200–3, 213–14, 14–16/10/25, 52, 57–8, 2–4/2/26, 81–2, 18/8/42, 84–6, 15–17/4/42, 235.

98 ECM 13–15/4/25, 107–8, 119, 19–21/10/26, 33–4, 16–19/2/27, 57–8.

99 ECM 22–24/1/30, 138–41, 14–16/4/31, 177–8, 5/6/31, 12–13, 10–13/11/31, 97–8, 20–22/1/32, 171–5, 20–22/7/32, 58.

100 ECM 18–21/1/38, 198–204, 12–14/4/38, 248–50, 6–8/7/38, 45, 4–6/10/38, 104, 25–27/1/39, 163–4.

101 ECM 17–19/7/40, 63–70, 14–15/12/49, 175–90.

102 *Post*, 17 February 1934, p. 147.

103 GPC Minutes, 18 June 1920, p. 2, 18 August 1920, p. 2.

104 See above, Chapter 8, p. 218.

105 ECM 22–24/10/29, 86–8.

106 Details of this can be found in *The Post*, see e.g. 15 February 1930, p. 142, 21 November 1931, p. 495, 9 January, p. 24.

107 ECM 19–21/4/32, 236–7 and 18–20/10/32, 100 give these and other figures.

108 *Post*, 20 June 1931, p. 608, 16 July 1932, p. 57.

109 *Post*, 19 November 1932, p. 415; ECM 20–22/7/32, 54–6, 11–13/4/33, 176–7.

110 There is some information on this at F 109. See also *Post*, 29 November 1980, p. 5.

111 See *Post*, 3 March 1928, pp. 196–7 and ECM 18–20/7/28, 13–17 for its original form and early

working. Some further details are at F 393.1 and the main changes can be traced in successive rule books.

112 ECM 16–18/10/28, 46, 22–24/10/29, 67, 24–26/1/45, 182, 22–24/1/30, 125, 24–26/1/45, 183.
113 These trends and figures can be traced in *Post*, 26 June 1943, p. 170 and ECM 24–26/1/45.
114 *Post*, 3 March 1945, p. 52, 26 May, p. 13.
115 *Post*, 31 January 1953, p. 126, 4 July 1969, p. 9.
116 The following section is based in part on Clinton (1975).
117 Simon (1965), p. 307; Raybould, 'Changes in trade union education' in Raybould (1959), p. 32; Corfield (1969), p. 167.
118 Something of the flavour of these battles can be gathered from Craik (1964) and Miller (1977).
119 *Post*, 9 September 1922, p. 253.
120 Stocks (1953), p. 153.
121 *London Post*, February 1922, p. 86 (original emphasis); TUC 1923 Report, p. 260; Waller (1956), p. 29; ECM 6–7/11/51, 56.
122 This is from a list of early students in ECM 16–18/10/28, 47–8, though the sample is small.
123 *Post*, 6 July 1957, p. 443.
124 Corfield (1969), pp. 68–9.
125 *Post*, 12 June 1920, p. 564, 23 April 1932, p. 413, 19 March 1939, p. 274; ECM 24–26/1/33, 149, 22/2/36, 165; *Post* 1938, CS p. 40, 3 December 1938, p. 670.
126 *MR View*, February 1934, p. 20, April 1935, p. 3, June 1936, p. 13, July 1936, p. 8; *Post* 1936, CS p. 50, and 22 February 1936, p. 165; *MR View*, June 1936, p. 12.
127 ECM 28/7/49, 67.
128 ECM 19–21/10/26, 41; *Post*, 31 January 1953, p. 113 and 24 January 1959, p. 121.
129 *Post*, 18 April 1931, p. 384.
130 Peers (1958), pp. 165–7; TUC, *Developments of Educational Series for Trade Unionists. Notes and Suggestions* (1953); ECM 16–17/1/51, 170, 19/4/51, 245–6.
131 *Post* 1938, CS p. 61.
132 *Post*, 25 January 1958, p. 163.
133 *Post*, 19 September 1948, p. 582, 22 January 1947, p. 373 and 23 February.
134 *Post*, 2 December 1949, p. 595, 10 October 1953, p. 371, 20 October 1951, p. 442; ECM 24–26/4/46, 417.
135 ECM 24–26/7/45, 22; *Post*, 18 December 1954, p. 707, 23 October 1947, p. 435; Corfield (1969), p. 159. These points are argued and illustrated more fully in Clinton (1975).
136 *MR View*, June 1936, p. 12; ECM 17–20/10/33, 46, 23–25/1/35, 128; *Post*, 14 October 1948, p. 327, 1936 CS p. 50.
137 The UPW figures are derived from the annual reports of the General Treasurer and the other points from Roberts (1956), p. 338, Peers (1958), p. 158, and Clegg and Adams (1959), p. 70.
138 Lerner (1961), pp. 144–86.
139 The Union's files at 130, 133 and 100 contain a good deal, as indeed do *The Post* and the Executive Committee Minutes where in some periods there are references to 'secessionists' on virtually every page. These include much of the secessionists' own material, and there is some more at the Modern Records Centre in the University of Warwick. The chief secessionist periodicals are *PT, CC* and *The Telephonist*. The Postmen's Association/National Association of Postmen produced *PA* and *PJ*, and the National Association of Postal and Telegraph Officers, *P&TO*. All of these are in UCW House. The *SC&T*, said to be produced by the SC&T Guild in the 1920s and 1930s has, on the other hand, not been found. The Northern Ireland Postal Clerks also produced a *Gazette*.
140 *The Case for the Sorters' Guild* (n.d. 1932?) at F 133.6 and Guild of SC&Ts, *The Case for the Federation* (n.d. 1925?), p. 5.
141 *PT* 15 November 1922, 16 April 1928, 1 January 1924.
142 *PT* 1 December 1924, *CC* July 1926.
143 See Chapter 12, p. 464 below on this.
144 *PT* 1 February 1928, p. 37, article by J. Glanyon 'Joes Shesgreen'.
145 *PT* July 1941, p. 103, in an interesting article on 'Guild history, past and present'.
146 *PT* 16 April 1923, p. 170, 1 August 1924, p. 328, 1 May 1928, p. 169. See also Sorters Guild, *Some Questions Answered*, pp. 4–5 (at F 133.5).
147 *PT* 15 June 1922, p. 179. For the continuation of the policy of not allowing those below the grade of SC&T to join see *PT* 16 June 1924, pp. 254–6, and for its abandonment see 15 June 1927, p. 257, 1 November 1927, p. 394, 1 June 1928, p. 207.
148 *CC* July 1928, p. 167.

149 *PT* 16 January 1928, p. 19.
150 *PT* June 1932. Further details at F 133.
151 *PT* August 1921.
152 *PT* January 1941.
153 *PT* 15 July 1926, pp. 133–4.
154 *PT* 1 June 1922, p. 161.
155 *PT* April 1945, pp. 41ff.
156 *PT* July 1948, June 1947, p. 63, December 1947, pp. 134ff.
157 *PT* 15 April 1922, p. 101, 15 February 1923, p. 71.
158 *PT* 15 April 1924, p. 168, 1 May 1925, p. 168, 15 May 1925, p. 204; *CC* March 1927, p. 52, 30 September 1927, p. 203.
159 *CC* October 1924.
160 *CC* March 1925, February 1925.
161 *CC* 15 June 1928, p. 144, February/March 1944, p. 17.
162 *CC* April 1937, p. 81, December 1933, p. 276.
163 There is some discussion and comment on these figures at F 133.1 and in *CC* December 1930, p. 313, March 1943. UPW figures are taken from the annual reports of the Organising Secretary.
164 *CC* February 1934, pp. 24–45, August 1935, p. 155 on the 'upgrading' claim. UPW, *Secessionism, its Futility and Failure* (n.d. 1953?), p. 51.
165 *CC* 30 August 1927, pp. 189–90.
166 *CC* December 1936, p. 341, January 1942, p. 10.
167 *CC* November 1940, p. 252, March 1943, p. 43, November 1941, p. 153.
168 *CC* March 1946, p. 57.
169 *PT* 1 August 1928, pp. 284–5, 15 August 1928, p. 305, 15 December 1932, pp. 286–8.
170 *CC* February 1930, p. 50; *PT* 15 March 1928, p. 103, *Postal Telegraph* September–October 1952 and other material at F 100. *Post*, February–April 1953, contains some interesting letters on the Association.
171 Details scattered through F 100, and for some other details see ECM AD 1961–2, p. 2,288ff., summarising much up to that time.
172 Details on this and what follows are mostly in F 133–4. *SC&T* does not seem to have survived. For the structure and the quotations see ECM 8–9/1/25, 126, 15–17/4/25, 17.
173 *PT* 1 February 1923, p. 37, 15 June 1927; ECM 13–15/4/26, 109.
174 *SC&T* May 1930, given at F 131.
175 *Post*, 30 May 1931, p. 525 and *PT* July 1932, p. 150. There is an interesting account of a Guild meeting in Leeds in January 1936 at F 133.6, and later references in *P&TO* March 1948, p. 135, and March 1949, p. 40.
176 F 133.9; *PT* 15 January 1924, p. 25, September 1942, p. 117, giving quotations from the *Gazette*. The details of the later period are taken from Marsh and Ryan (1980), p. 177.
177 *PA* September 1930–August 1933 and *PJb* September 1933–June 1944 seem complete at the BL. There are rather fewer copies at the UCW but a good file of material at F 133.6.
178 Details at F 133.6.
179 *PA* November 1930, January 1931.
180 There are some manuscript resignation letters at F 133.6. *PA* July 1931, *PJb* September 1936.
181 *PA* September 1930, July 1931.
182 National Association of Postmen, *The NAP Case in Black and White* (n.d. 1937?), p. 6.
183 Details at F 133.9.
184 *PJb* October 1935.
185 *PJb* July 1936, and a private account at F 133.6.
186 *PJb* October 1937, June 1938.
187 *PJb* September 1936, June 1938, June 1939. The ECDO dispute is in F 133.6.
188 *PJb* July 1934. One early undated cutting at F 133.6 and a later one from *Daily Worker* (6 July 1935).
189 *PJb* March–April 1944.
190 *PT* June 1946, p. 76, July 1946, p. 86. *P&TO* March 1948, p. 135. The UCW's *P&TO* file is fairly complete and there is some additional material at F 133.2 and at F 100.
191 Given on the first page of the *Post* volume for 1947.
192 On this see Lerner (1961), pp. 157ff.
193 *P&TO* February, May 1949.
194 The questions are listed at F 100.
195 The formula is in a letter (at F 100) to the UPW dated 3 January 1950 but its publication was

delayed by the General Election – *Hansard* V, 475, 1187–94 (17 May 1950).
196 A letter in the POEU *Journal*, September 1950, makes this point.
197 *Hansard* V, 477, 708 (6 July 1950).
198 *Post*, 8 June 1950, p. 229.
199 *Hansard* V, 477, 708–9 (6 July 1950).
200 *Hansard* V, 477, 1327–9 (12 July 1950).
201 F 100 has details.
202 *Hansard* V, 484, 90–1 (WA) (15 February 1950).
203 Many of the submissions including a 187-page document of the UPW are at F 100. See also PP 1951–2 XVIII, Report of PO Reorganisation Committee.
204 *Engineering Officer* (June and April/May 1952).
205 NAPTO *Special News Letter*, 30 May 1952 (at F 100).
206 Notes on this meeting are also at F 100.
207 *Hansard* V, 502, 2242 (25 June 1952).
208 *The Telephonist* (February 1953).
209 Details of this and what follows are at F 100. A verbatim account of the UPW/NAPTO disussions is to be found in *Post*, 20 June 1953, and even more details at F 100. There is a summary in *P&TO*, April 1953.
210 Lerner (1961), p. 181; *Hansard* V, 518, 1542–6 (30 July 1953), 1748–68 (31 July).
211 ECM 21–27/4/54, 305. A letter to UPW branches on 2 February 1954 at F 133.2 says the decision had been taken, but this is the only record that could be found.
212 The main sources are at F 133.7 and in *The Telephonist*. There is some material at the Modern Records Centre in Warwick, mainly annual conference agendas 1958–70 deposited by the last General Secretary J. Fitzgerald (MSS–90).
213 In *The Telephonist*, January 1953, Lansbury wrote that 'prominent Trade Union leaders have forsaken their historic role in defending the workers interests and they are now the Governors'. The first Chairman, J. E. Dearnley, withdrew in 1933 to become a Labour Party Branch Secretary (See *PT* June 1933).
214 Early issues of *The Telephonist* give an account of the pre-history of the Guild. The issue for September 1966 has a useful article by A. L. Fraser, 'The night telephonists and the Guild'.
215 *PT* 2 January, 15 March, 15 May 1928; F 137.7.
216 *Telephonist*, February 1954, p. 9, refers to efforts to get 'non-industrial status' in other government departments, but they did not amount to much.
217 *Telephonist*, May, June 1930, May 1938, p. 38; *Post*, 21 April 1934, pp. 344–5, 16 February 1935, p. 138, 21 December 1935, pp. 477–82.
218 *Telephonist*, December 1929, February, April 1934, May 1938, p. 15.
219 *Telephonist* (December 1946); *Post*, 9 November 1946, pp. 591–7.
220 *Telephonist* (January 1948); *Post*, 20 December 1947, p. 400. A verbatim report of these discussions is said to have been published.
221 *Telephonist* (August 1954); *Post*, 16 February 1952, p. 127. See also *Manchester Guardian* and *Times* (6 July 1954).
222 *Telephonist* (May 1956).
223 *Telephonist*, September 1968, pp. 14–15, gives the Guild's version.
224 *Telephonist* (September 1963).
225 *Post*, 10 August 1961, p. 469.
226 For details on all this see F 133.7 and ECM AD 67/66(G); *Telephonist*, February 1967.
227 *BOB*, 16 July 1967, 286.
228 Details are in ECM AD 686/67. *Telephonist*, September 1969, contains particularly vitriolic material. See also *Post*, 13 January 1968, p. 8.
229 *Telephonist* (November 1969).
230 For an account of this see the printed Special Report of the 1970 UPW Conference at F 133.7.
231 Full details at F 133.
232 *Times*, 12 May 1973, 10 March 1973, 17 October 1974.
233 For a brief (and not objective) summary of these discussions see UPW, *Secessionism its Futility and Failure* (1953), pp. 70ff. Verbatim reports from 1924 are at F 131.5 and the others are given in *The Post*.
234 This is a major point in Moran (1974).
235 Moran (1974), pp. 53–4; *Post*, 15 May 1920, p. 468, 21 December 1946, p. 678. See also F 106.5.

11 The UPW and its World

Amid the hunger, strike and picket, speech,
Street corner, soap-box, drab committee-room,
I see the long light span the salmon reach,
The shaft fall headlong through the beeches' gloom.
Francis Andrews, 'The Union' in *The Sow's Ear* (1944)

The aim of this chapter is to add to the accounts which are given elsewhere of the day-to-day activities of the Union and its structure, a description of its attitudes in relation to the labour movement and the wider world, and to say something of how its leaders and active members responded to the general political and economic problems which they had to confront.

In earlier chapters some effort has been made to trace in detail the process whereby various disparate groups of Post Office workers set up permanent organisations, and then came to see themselves as having common interests. In the course of this process, from the 1880s to the 1920s, they entered the ambit of the wider trade union movement and came to share the common aspirations of that movement, including support for labour representation in Parliament. They retained these loyalties even during the period from 1927 to 1946 when they were legally debarred from affiliation to the outside labour world, and they have developed their role within the movement ever since. Much detail has been given elsewhere of the legal and economic consequences of the fact that Post Office workers were civil servants and for many decades by far the largest group of manual workers in the public sector. This meant that they developed a particular set of attitudes towards their own industry and the state service as a whole which can be encompassed in such phrases as 'workers' control' and 'industrial democracy'. It also meant that they had a particular attitude to bargaining which went well beyond the political lobbying of pre-amalgamation days, but yet never quite cut loose from it. The ordered relationships of the set of institutions that went with the Whitley system have predisposed the UPW and its leaders to look to corporate planning and incomes policies as a means of serving the interests of the members, despite the many problems that followed.

This chapter is an attempt to illustrate and explain these attitudes of the Union, with particular reference initially to its Guild Socialist traditions. There is some description also of the attitude of the union to strikes, to its women members and to some other matters that help to explain what sort of a Union it has been. There will also be an account of the role of the Union in the TUC and Labour Party and some reference to the Postal Telegraph and Telephone International.

THE GUILD SOCIALIST TRADITION

It is not difficult to trace the various personal influences and general political discussions that led to the adoption of the policy of 'partnership with the state' in the management and control of the Postal Service by the Postal and Telegraph Clerks

Association and later by the UPW.[1] It is however important to stress that the adoption of this policy by the UPW was part of its efforts to resolve some of the problems that arose from the industrial relations experience of its active members and leaders. It is of some interest to trace the means whereby the distinctive policy of the UPW was developed and maintained in the Post Office and the trade union movement right into the 1960s and beyond.

The one person who can probably be said to have initiated this movement was John Newlove who was Secretary of the London and Home Counties District of the PTCA at the time he went to Ruskin College in 1908. He was at this time also Editor of the *Civil Service Socialist* and came under the influence of G. D. H. Cole, Oxford don and Guild Socialist.[2] When the Postal and Telegraph Clerks Association was set up in 1914 with Newlove as General Secretary, its programme boldly stated that it aimed at nothing less than 'the control, in conjunction with all Postal Associations, of the Post Office undertaking'. Details are given in Chapter 8 of how these ideas were then developed, and adopted in particular by George Middleton, first Editor of the UPW's *Post*. Similar ideas were enthusiastically taken up by Francis Andrews who followed him as Editor in 1931 and by Jim Chalmers who succeeded him in 1945.[3]

Guild Socialism was one of a series of new theories which came out of the socialist movement in the period preceding the First World War.[4] It derived from a number of influences. It began with appeals to return to medieval forms of social organisation coming from people who never considered themselves socialists of any sort and later became admirers of the 'corporate state' of Mussolini, and of Hitler's Germany. However, beyond providing some initial impetus these people did nothing to develop the 'guild idea'.[5] Another stream that came to make this movement was represented in the literary-philosophical notions of A. R. Orage and his circle. Orage dabbled in a number of anti-establishment ideas ranging from Fabianism to theosophy and later became a supporter of the 'social credit' theories of Major Douglas which were also discussed in the UPW in the 1930s.[6] Initially, however, he provided a medium through the magazine *The New Age*, which he ran from 1907, to transform the somewhat impotent arts-and-crafts notions of A. J. Penty into the more hard-headed sort of doctrines set out by S. G. Hobson. His writings influenced young activists like Francis Andrews, at the time a local official in the Birmingham PTCA. Another of the influences on the formation of Guild Socialism was the pre-First World War movement against state control and the extension of government. This was associated in particular with the name of Hilaire Belloc and outlined in *The Servile State* which was published as a book in 1912. Another influence was syndicalism which had the support of many younger and active trade unionists, who believed that by the amalgamation of all unions in each industry and widespread strike action it would be possible for the working class to develop institutions that would replace the capitalist system.

The Guild Socialists themselves absorbed these various influences and began to argue their case just before the outbreak of the First World War.[7] It was largely developed by a group of middle-class intellectuals led by G. D. H. Cole and William Mellor. They favoured industries being run by managements elected by those who worked in them. The National Guilds League, established in 1915, said it aimed at 'the abolition of the wage-system and the establishment of self-government in industry through a system of National Guilds working in conjunction with the state'. The call for its first conference said

A new interpretation of both socialism and trade unionism is the message of Guild Socialism, which aims at reconciling national ownership of the means of production with Trade Union control, the needs of organised producers with the joint demands of the organised consumers.[8]

In the following period, J. G. Newlove, now General Secretary of the P&TCA, became an active member of the Executive Committee of the National Guilds League and of its Trade Union Committee. George Middleton, Editor of the P&TCA's *Record*, later joined the Executive and became an extremely active proponent of guild principles. Middleton argued with some enthusiasm that 'self-government' was one of 'the objects of the newer trade unionism'. He maintained that 'more state nationalisation' was 'bound up with bureaucracy, red tape and incompetent management' which would not arise if industries were run by guilds which guaranteed employment and negotiated with the state acting on behalf of consumers. A first step was for unions to be set up in each industry consisting of 'every employee, regardless of grade, from the managers downwards'. (Such a structure had not got much support in recent trade union amalgamation negotiations in the Post Office.) This step would allow managers and foremen to be elected and they would become 'the servants of the people engaged in a particular industry'.[9] These arguments were constantly heard within the P&TCA, and its leaders at the time of the amalgamation were said to be 'all National Guildsmen', 'definitely committed to the control policy'. The 1917 TUC heard such ideas not only from Edith Howse, but also from George Ammon of the FA who advocated 'something along the lines – if one might use the phrase – of guild socialism'.[10] On the basis of such support the National Guilds League published in 1919 a scheme for *Workers Control in the Post Office*. This drew attention to the fact that efforts aimed at the expansion of the facilities provided by the Post Office had been rejected by the management. An all-inclusive union could be set up to secure such aims by sharing control of the service with the state. Cole himself commended the P&TCA as being 'the first union to make a public and open demand for joint control'.[11]

Such argument as this carried on into the newly amalgamated UPW. The first object given in the first Rule Book was 'joint management of the Post Office in conjunction with representatives of the state'. Although this was not much discussed at the 1920 Annual Conference in Morecambe, an evening fringe meeting was held to argue the case. During the year it was argued among the members, and the 1921 Edinburgh Annual Conference adopted an explicit Guild Socialist policy which was returned as a plank in the union's programme until as late as 1960:[12] 'The organisation of Post Office workers into a comprehensive industrial union with a view to the service being ultimately conducted and managed as a national guild'.

During the early part of 1921 the Union's first Research Officer devoted himself to producing a widely circulated pamphlet, which he first of all discussed in some detail with G. D. H. and Margaret Cole, about how guild principles could be applied in the Post Office. It is interesting to notice that the case was argued to a large extent in terms of the improvements it could bring about for those who worked there.[13] Two years later the union's second Research Officer Grant MacKenzie argued for a new sort of control that went beyond this to ensure that 'the whole system of industry is altered from top to bottom'.[14] General Secretary Bowen involved himself during the same period in discussion with colleagues abroad about changes in the control of their postal and telecommunications systems, and early issues of *The Post* contained a number of articles about how to go about obtaining such control in Britain. Cole, Hobson and others contributed to these discussions.[15]

However, soon afterwards the policy ceased to be a live issue in the Union. This was for a number of reasons. For one thing, it was quite clear, as G. D. H. Cole put it, that despite all the talk in the Union about control 'there is a long way to go for the UPW even in discovering what it wants, to say nothing of getting it'. There was also a good deal of confusion about the real significance of Whitleyism. There was certainly an illusion abroad 'that it either was, or could lead to, control'. Some Union members felt that they might perhaps 'be able to use Whitleyism . . . as an easy evolutionary road to workers' control'.[16] Following the great enthusiasm which came about as a result of the amalgamation, the advent of the economic depression in the winter of 1920–1, the establishment of secessionist organisations and the collapse of the strike policy in the following months, there was a much more sober mood in the ranks of the Union and its leadership. Bowen in particular became much more concerned with short-term economic issues and with preserving the amalgamation than with any more general and long-term aims.

Nevertheless, the adoption of the Guild Socialist policy was not without effect on the Union. It continued to provide an inspiration for those Union leaders, and Francis Andrews was by no means the only one, who sought ideals in trade unionism beyond the satisfaction of immediate economic demands. It provided an impetus for efforts to extend the scope of bargaining. These began to bear fruit only in 1951 when Postmaster General Ness Edwards first agreed to regular discussions with the Unions on matters to do with the service itself, quite apart from wages and conditions within it.[17] During the same period the labour movement in general and the TUC in particular came to accept the views championed most notably by Herbert Morrison that the best way to run nationalised industries was through largely autonomous public corporations. Until the late 1940s the UPW argued strongly against such forms of organisation, particularly on the grounds that they excluded representatives of the workforce from any share of control.[18] These arguments seem to have been virtually forgotten when the time came in the 1960s for the Post Office itself to become a public corporation. By then, however, there was a new phase of discussion about 'participation' and 'industrial democracy' in which the Union, with all its traditions, was in a good position to take part.

From its very beginning the UPW maintained that 'the control of industry by the workers should be an integral principle of state ownership of industry'.[19] In the 1920s and 1930s, Francis Andrews in particular continued to make propaganda for such ideas, though to little effect. Others however argued that it was not easy for the Union to take away control from a Post Office bureaucracy which had defeated all efforts by politicians to do so. On the other hand during the 1930s Guild Socialism came to be seen as an alternative solution to the economic crisis, preferable to the moderate policies pursued by the trade union leaders since the General Strike. Nevertheless, when the 1930 UPW Conference told the Executive to consider how to go about achieving control jointly with the Post Office authorities, they were not keen on pursuing the matter. All they proposed was that the Post Office Whitley Council would be restored.[20] The discussions which led to the Bridgeman Enquiry and reorganisation of the Post Office also led the Union to refine its arguments. Some members expressed themselves opposed to 'socialism (on the instalment plan)', in other words, control shared between Union and management. Nevertheless the Executive produced a report for the 1933 Conference which envisaged the Post Office being run by a joint board which was half state nominees and half Union members, with a politically appointed Postmaster General in the chair.[21]

The development of this set of ideas within the UPW was very much part of a ferment of discussions within the labour movement at the time of the economic and political collapse of 1931. Some of the old Guild Socialists such as Hobson argued now for new political institutions. He wanted a 'House of Industry' nominated by employers and labour to replace the House of Lords and won some support for this idea in the trade union movement.[22] Following the collapse of the second Labour Government in 1931 and the departure of MacDonald and Snowden to the 'National Government', there was a strong move to the left in the Labour Party. The 1932 Conference adopted the policy of nationalisation of the banks.[23] For some even this was insufficient, and they broke away in the Independent Labour Party. Among their number was Francis Andrews.

Meanwhile, Cole and Mellor began to take up some of their old ideas through discussions with some of the main union leaders. They ran a number of discussions in April and May 1933. In the course of these Bowen explained opposition to public corporations, expressed an interest in the House of Industry idea and set out the recently adopted policies of the Union. Andrews explained that joint control was only what should happen 'at first'.[24] He also described the concept as 'post-revolutionary' and at the same time doing nothing to interfere with the supremacy of Parliament. A pamphlet was produced through the auspices of the New Fabian Research Bureau supported by Bowen and a number of other major union leaders which strongly attacked public corporations and called for workers' control in the management of nationalised industries.[25]

One other aspect of the intellectual ferment of that period worth more than a passing reference was the movement known as 'Social Credit'. This had some impact within the UPW, if only because it had a tireless propagandist in the person of J. W. Coward, Secretary of the Newcastle Postal Branch, who got some local support and conference discussion on the matter.[26] The theory, which was invented by Major C. H. Douglas, a Canadian engineer, took the view that by the creation of a single state bank – though not by altering the structure of the ownership of industry – it would be possible to issue credits to all members of the community which they could then spend or invest. One variant of the theory heard in the UPW was that within nationalised industries it would then be possible to distribute the profits to those who worked there. The idea attracted Andrews for a time, and Research Officer Hardcastle had to go to considerable trouble including consultations with well known banker Reginald McKenna and the economist J. M. Keynes to find arguments to disprove it. Although Douglas appeared before the prestigious MacMillan Committee on the financial system in 1931, his views were not taken seriously by McKenna who believed banks could only issue credits against debts and by Keynes who said they were simply inflationary. For some UPW members however they appeared a possible way out of economic depression and poverty. As early as 1920 Bowen wrote to Orage for details, and in 1933 almost every issue of *The Post* was full of abtruse articles and letters for and against the theories of Douglas. The Executive felt constrained to consider an 'open letter' advocating support for Social Credit and signed by members of the Newcastle Branch.[27] The Douglasites even took to maintaining that campaigns for higher wages were a waste of time when all could be resolved by adjusting the credit system.

Within a year or two this particular bubble had burst. Its comparative strength within the UPW reflects both the search for a simple solution to a horrifying economic cataclysm and the comparative remoteness of the Union in the period from some mainstream ideas in the labour movement. In 1938 Hobson expressed his disappointment at the UPW's arguments in the Arbitration Court, which he thought would not have been necessary had the Union been able to obtain the setting up of a guild that could make the basic financial decisions.[28]

However, the Union's policy was by no means forgotten, even though there were those who considered it inadequate to call for joint control rather than full workers' control.[29] At the 1941 Conference, against the advice of General Secretary Hodgson, a special Executive Sub-Committee was set up to consider the implementation of the 'joint management' plank of the union's programme. The report which was produced reflected a further modification of the traditional arguments not only by accepting Whitleyism as a step towards control but also by explicitly recognising that a joint 'National Administrative Council' should still 'receive from Parliament such orders as the House may approve'. At the Conference a full-dress debate agreed to go ahead with a further educational campaign, though not with immediate implementation of the policy.[30] The policy was then discussed in almost every issue of *The Post* and at numerous district council and educational meetings. One Executive member, Bob Cyples, was reprimanded by his colleagues for telling the London District Committee 'A' that 'the report gave no political lead; it aimed at merely extending the present Whitley machinery, and it leant towards guild socialism the value of which he doubted'.[31] Other unions were also approached, as well as the TUC. Articles appeared in other trade union journals including the National Union of Railwaymen's *Railway Review, The Review* of the Society of Post Office Engineering Inspectors and the *Monthly Journal* of the Amalgamated Engineering Union, expressing interest and support. A Conference of Post Office unions on workers control was held at UPW House on 24 March 1944, which revealed significant differences of approach. Propaganda was directed at trades councils and other sections of the labour movement with particular reference to the Union's objections to public corporations which one Executive member, Jenny Duncan, described as part of 'the present dangerous tendencies towards Fascism'.[32]

In the latter part of the war the issue of 'workers control' was discussed at inordinate length in *The Post*. There were lengthy descriptions of how it might work in the Post Office and heated arguments were conducted for and against. This in part reflected the preoccupations of the Editor but also a general desire for discussion on the likely shape of post-war society. It must be admitted that Union attitudes on the matter were usually somewhat imprecise, and at times verged on the myopic. Thus George Lascelles, first General Secretary of the old UKPCA, wrote in 1943 objecting to the political implications of the idea and said he thought it all 'smells too much like the corporate state of Mussolini'. The reply to this was characterised more by bad temper than reasoned argument. There was a similar unreasoning reply to George Williams, soon thereafter and for many years Central Secretary of the Manchester Branch. He said that the policy was received 'politely, with respect, but not with noticeable interest'. He complained that there was 'so little tangible about it' and in any case 'it seems fairly obvious that no capitalist government would agree to Workers' Control, or even to an EC Report which would be any use to the staff'. Future General Secretary Ron Smith largely ignored these points in a somewhat abusive reply. An anonymous writer who supported the policy was more honest about its meaning:

> Is not the attitude of most of us to-day a willingness to hold to certain vague utopian aspirations; a preference for not giving any clear definition, a refusal to relate them to present policy?

The Manchester Branch Chairman pointed out that there was still no means to achieve the policy and that grade rivalries meant there was still no real unity, not to mention a single industrial union. In response, the young S. A. R. Seaton maintained that this was just dissent for its own sake. By the 1944 Conference an effort to abandon the policy altogether was only lost by 1,089 votes to 1,154.[33]

While these discussions were going on in public, privately not everyone took them as seriously as Francis Andrews. Thus in January 1944 Andrews and his sub-committee tried to get the Executive to set up a 'League for the advocacy of Guild Socialist principles in Industry' and to begin to argue for wages on the basis of need rather than work done. In pushing for the rejection of this Charles Geddes expressed 'his view that the average member was far more interested in, for example, classification than Workers' Control, and in wage policy'. Doubts were also expressed by Andrews himself about how much support he was getting for his efforts. They nevertheless continued. The Union's case was put by delegation to the TUC Economic Committee in April 1945. George Woodcock, on behalf of the TUC, expressed opposition to detailed Parliamentary control, and said there was little support for 50 per cent trade union representation on the boards of nationalised industries amongst other unions.[34]

The Union nevertheless took up its policy with a will in the post-war period. The scheme for a National Administrative Council in the Post Office was agreed at the staff side of the Post Office Whitley Council in July 1945, but few other unions showed the same enthusiasm as the UPW in pursuing it. The POEU in particular dragged its heels. In February 1946 the workers control sub-committee again met the TUC Economic Committee, but again without any effect. TUC General Secretary Vincent Tewson in particular thought that the experience of the Union strengthened the arguments against Parliamentary control and that 'it was too early to judge or condemn public corporations'.[35] At the 1947 TUC George Douglas and George Stevens put forward arguments for 'Joint Administrative Boards in Nationalised Industries' which were remitted to the General Council. A further meeting with the General Council Economic Committee failed to reach any agreement about this and the Union again submitted its scheme to the 1948 TUC. By now, however, discussion with the POEU had gone much further and they submitted amendments, accepted by the General Council and the Congress, calling for a 'National Advisory Council' in nationalised industries rather than an 'Administrative Council'. By the beginning of 1949 some steps along these lines were accepted in the Post Office. The result was informal and irregular meetings agreed by Postmaster General Ness Edwards in June 1951 and continued by his Conservative successor.[36]

In the 1950s, the Union continued to argue its line with the TUC and Labour Party, and to push its policy of a Joint Administrative Board amongst Post Office unions. A full debate took place at the UPW's 1954 Annual Conference. The Executive proposed a scheme under which trade union members on the Board would not be mandated, and decisions would be made by agreement between the two sides. It is interesting to notice that all but one of the delegates who unsuccessfully tried to have these changes abrogated as a reversal of the principles set out in 1942 subsequently became officers of the Union. They were Harry Burnett, Kim McKinlay, Norman Stagg and Maurice Styles.[37] Further efforts to push the policy through the Post Office Whitley Council again encountered the resistance of virtually all the other unions with the interesting exception of the controlling officers. New propaganda was issued to explain the Union's view and it was frequently mentioned in the following years, though little was done about it. After some hesitation, it was decided in 1960 to begin to press again, particularly in the Labour Party, for the traditional policies of the Union.[38]

By this time the context in which the arguments were taking place altered somewhat. Following the election of the Labour Government in 1964, the question of 'industrial democracy' came to the centre of discussions about policy. The Labour Government largely failed in its efforts at economic direction through the Industrial Reorganisation Corporation. It got even less from its efforts to secure planning agreements and a new discussion began in the labour movement about new forms of control and organisation of industry.[39] The Donovan Royal Commission on Trade Unions and Employers Associations 1965–8 discussed possible representation on management boards and in May 1966 the Labour Party National Executive set up a Working Party on Industrial Democracy chaired by Jack Jones, soon to become the General Secretary of the Transport and General Workers Union. At the 1967 Labour Party Conference a resolution was passed which welcomed this development and called for legislation to 'provide for trade union participation in management'. Among the most enthusiastic supporters of the resolution was Norman Stagg of the UPW who attacked 'joint consultation' as inadequate and asserted that

the role of a trade union in a socialist society is . . . constructive in the sense that our concern with industrial efficiency is no less than that of management.

The 1968 Party Conference accepted a report calling for the extension of trade union bargaining functions and trade union participation in the management of the public sector.[40]

Although such ideas were gradually gaining support from some sectors of the labour movement, they were not yet accepted by the Labour Government. During the period when the Post Office was being turned into a public corporation after 1966, there were calls from the UPW for workers' representation on the new Post Office Board. Postmaster General John Stonehouse rejected this with the argument that management was a specialist, technical function in which ordinary workers could not take part.[41] However, this view, so frequently heard in the past, was now being overtaken by new ideas about dealing with the problems of a corporate economy. As the price for accepting various forms of wage restraint Jack Jones and other union leaders asked for 'trade union representatives on the Management Boards of all nationalised undertakings and other public authorities'. A resolution to this effect was agreed at the 1968 Congress, in a clear reversal of the traditional TUC attitude.[42] Another important straw in the wind was the introduction of worker-directors on to the regional boards in the steel industry in 1967. It is of some interest to note that the main architect of this scheme was Ron Smith, who joined the British Steel Board from the UPW, and was thus placed in a position to carry out some of the schemes he had advocated in the Union twenty years and more earlier.[43]

It was during the period of Conservative rule from 1971–4 that the new approach of the trade unions was finalised. Not simply did they reject the industrial relations legislation of the Government, but they also called to an increasing extent for the expansion of trade union powers and for various forms of trade union participation in management. Thus at the 1972 TUC it was Bryan Stanley of the POEU who called for a study of 'how workers in the public sector can play a greater and more decisive role in the running of their industries'. A lengthy document was passed which called for power to be taken away from shareholders and autonomous boards and diffused to the workers' representatives, who should make up 50 per cent of the board. In welcoming a revised version of the scheme in 1974 Norman Stagg told the TUC how the UPW had always opposed Morrisonian concepts of nationalisation and emphasised one point about workers' representatives on boards:

> A trade union representative must always be responsible to the members he represents. He must be elected by those members and be responsible and account-able to them. If those members elect him, those members can dismiss him.

Similarly, the 1973 Labour Party Conference called for 50 per cent trade union representation on the boards of nationalised industries.[44]

This was the background to the final emergence of the 'industrial democracy experiment' in the Post Office in the late 1970s. It began with a commitment in the Labour Party Election Manifesto of October 1974 to 'introduce new legislation to help forward our plans for a radical extension of industrial democracy in both private and public sectors'. The Labour Government in practice did not press ahead with carrying out this promise, and may well not have done so had it not been for the fortuitous passage over some of its Parliamentary hurdles of a Private Members' Bill on these lines proposed by Giles Radice. As a result of a further series of manoeuvres, the fullest expression of the policies so recently developed by the TUC was to be found in the majority Report of the Enquiry set up under the chairman-ship of Lord Bullock which reported in January 1977. The proposals for worker-directors on a unified board with an agreed number of independents (the so-called $2x + y$ formula) was greeted with an extraordinary level of abuse from press, Parlia-ment and private industrialists.[45] Whether or not this document will be seen as an historic starting point for future generations, it certainly initiated very little for its own. Before the entire issue becomes lost in myth and legend, it is well to recall that doubts and hesitations about Bullock were not confined to opponents of the trade union movement. The miners traditionally opposed what Arthur Scargill described as 'the castration of the Trade Union movement', and from diverse political stances both engineers and electricians also expressed opposition to trade unions taking on quasi-management functions. Thus the TUC shortly before Bullock was published agreed to oppose 'any form of participation that would tend to weaken trade union independence'.[46]

Bullock's Report, however, only applied to private industry. From the point of view of the development of 'industrial democracy', things were supposed to be different in nationalised industry.[47] Before the 1974 elections, the UPW had already worked out a scheme for 50 per cent trade union representation on a 'supervisory board' in the Post Office. By January 1975 a joint scheme with the POEU along these lines was published, and in the following December this was presented to Secretary of State for Industry Tony Benn. Benn expressed support and joint discussions then began. These took some time to settle, in part because of the problems of negotiating the details. The delay was also because the Carter Committee set up in November 1975 and reporting eventually in 1977 was strongly opposed to any such departure from commercial norms involved in having trade unionists on the Board. Despite this, on 16 July 1976 a tripartite meeting was set up at which unions, Post Office management and Government were represented. The unions set out their scheme, though with some qualifications from the CPSA. William Ryland, Post Office Chairman, spoke with somewhat less enthusiasm. However, the Minister of State for Industry Gerald Kaufman described it as 'an historic occasion' and told the other two parties to work out a scheme by September.

Agreement on the form of the new Post Office Board did not prove easy. Post Office management was never prepared to accept 50 per cent trade union representation, but an independently evolved version of the Bullock $2x + y$ formula allowed 'independents' to be appointed, providing both sides accepted them. Later the operation of Labour's pact with the Liberals resulted in the inclusion of additional 'consumers' representatives'. On the question of whether the chairman was to be adjudged part of the management team there was an agreement worthy of Solomon. In his role as chief executive he was regarded as part of management, but when acting as chairman he was regarded as independent. The unions also abandoned their position of calling for a two-tier board and replaced them with proposals propounded by the majority of Lord Bullock's Committee. This allowed for a separate 'management board' of the executives themselves which proved in practice able to take significant decisions. In February 1977 agreement was achieved on these points and discussion began on local machinery. On 4 May 1977 a second 'tripartite' meeting endorsed the scheme. Later in the month it went through the UPW Conference in the face of a good deal of opposition which included the first root-and-branch disagreement with the entire concept ever expressed at a UPW Conference.[48]

It did not prove easy to decide on the precise character of union representatives. Within the UPW two members were elected who were both 'non negotiating' officers – Fred Moss, the General Treasurer and Ivan Rowley, the Organising Secretary. Although they reported back on their activities to the Executive and to conferences, they were not in any direct sense mandated. In practice the biggest problem for the unions in the final stage of the discussion was the balance of representation between the smaller unions. This was eventually resolved by allowing the powerful CPSA to have the seat it wanted and for the Post Office Management Staff Association to be seen as representing a constituency that included the Society of Civil and Public Servants, and the Society of Post Office Engineers as sharing representation with the telecommunications controlling officers and the sub-postmasters. The net result had the interesting parallel with the old National Whitley Council staff side where the smaller associations had a very much heavier representation than their relative numbers would allow. Thus there were two board members for the UPW, two from the POEU which covered well over 75 per cent of the workforce and three others from CPSA, POMSA and SPOE, far higher than their relative numbers in the workforce.

The same pattern of representation and powers was followed in regional boards and joint area policy committees.[49] The experiment for the national board began in January 1978 and was unceremoniously ended two years later at the behest of a

Conservative Government with a rigid and doctrinal opposition to all erosion of management prerogatives, with the support of Post Office executives equally hostile to any such change. The experiment in relation to the national board is hardly yet a matter of history and the local structures continue at the time of writing. It is possible to say that many of the pioneers of the ideas of industrial democracy within the UPW and its predecessors would have recognised the problems which came up during the period when the unions contributed a significant proportion of the members of the Post Office Board. However, it is unlikely that they would have accepted the results. For one thing, those who in the past allowed for less than 100 per cent union representation never spoke of less than 50 per cent. For another, the fact that in practice the Management Board actively excluded the main board from a share of the power confirmed the criticisms of the two-tier conceptions the Union developed in later years. One point, however, which perhaps only became clear during the final period of the experiment was the relative powerlessness of the Board itself, which had a 'reactive rather than an initiatory role'. One of the surveys of the experiment put it as follows:

> The union's demand for representation at the Board was based on the desire to be involved at the early stage in policy formulation. It does not seem that the Post Office Board has permitted such involvement to any significant degree, for reasons related to the union nominees' very presence on the Board, but also to less contingent reasons related to the structure of the Post Office and the nature of its activities.[50]

One other aspect of the matter which might have surprised early proponents of industrial democracy was the relative lack of controversy within the unions about the constitutional position of their representatives. Ivan Rowley and Fred Moss were subject to a good deal of questioning at annual conferences of the UPW and some said they had gone beyond their role as union representatives, for example by supporting the restoration of Sunday posts. On the other hand it was said that Union representatives took too much of an interest in industrial relations matters on the Board. They were not, however, generally thought to have gone beyond their mandate, and though many reservations were expressed, the 1980 UPW Conference voted to continue what was left of the experiment.[51]

Two teams of researchers were charged with investigating respectively the results of the national and local experiments. They came to broadly similar conclusions. They described how the unions have sought to fulfil the highest ideals, but were prepared to modify these ideals in practice and to accept the limited successes that were achieved. The management, on the other hand, hoped for little and generally considered themselves to have achieved even less. Sir William Barlow, who was Chairman of the Post Office Board throughout the period of the experiment, was well known to be entirely hostile. While it was found that on the Board 'each group's primary emphasis was upon influencing the postures and decisions of the other',[52] in the end there was something of a dialogue of the deaf. The greatest paradox was that the new corporate managers were largely recruited from private industry, while the trade unionists normally had a good deal more experience of the Post Office. In the end it might have been this that would have surprised most of all the Post Office administrators of the distant days of Francis Freeling or Rowland Hill, or Evelyn Murray.

It is not possible in the early 1980s to see whether this experiment will have long-term significance, and in any case the local experiments still continue at the time of writing. It is, however, certain that the scope of things to be bargained about between management and unions has expanded over the years, and that the 'workers' control' concepts of the UPW, whether or not they will ultimately achieve their large ideals, will have made a contribution to this. In the end it is difficult to disagree with the view of one commentator:

History suggests that the movements for industrial democracy well up every so often, only to founder on the four rocks of conceptual ambiguity, trade union and official Labour ambivalence, employer hostility and rank-and-file apathy.[53]

If this is a little simplified it nevertheless contains a good deal of truth. In the long term, whatever the fate of the experiments of the late 1970s, there can be no doubt that the issue will 'well up' again in some form or another in new times and new circumstances.

STRIKES AND THE UPW BEFORE 1926

Another subject which gave the UPW its special character in relation to the rest of the trade union movement and helped to establish its particular identity, lay in its attitude to strikes. Their particular legal and constitutional problems are described in Chapter 4 and they resulted in the view that they were not as other trade unionists in matters connected with industrial action. This led not simply to the abandonment of the UPW's own strike policy in 1921, a step whose considerable effect is set out in Chapter 12, but also to doubts and hesitations of the very question of the legality of striking in the 1930s and 1970s. The problem did not simply arise when it was a matter of industrial action by the Union itself.

The earliest form in which this question presented itself was in the attitude of Post Office trade unionists to strikes elsewhere, especially in transport.[54] As early as 1911 there was an example of trade union solidarity with embattled railwaymen when Postmen's Federation Secretary Stuart got a circular issued to all surveyors and postmasters instructing 'all postmen going to stations with, or for, parcel mails that only the usual work should be done by them'. The *Postman's Gazette* letter columns over the following weeks made it clear that there was strong support within the Federation for this stand.[55]

At its very birth the UPW was confronted with a series of events that recalled this precedent. On 18 September 1919 there was the amalgamation conference that set up the UPW. A week later on 26 September there began the first ever national strike initiated by a trade union leadership, called by the National Union of Railwaymen. The leaders of the week-old UPW were soon actively involved in a struggle which was seen at the time as a decisive test of trade union strength.[56] The day the strike began a delegation from the Union met officials at the GPO who agreed that they would not have to handle mail diverted from the railways. On Monday 29 September a further meeting was held with Post Office Secretary Murray when he said he would still ask for volunteers to handle diverted mail. The Executive therefore issued instructions 'that members must not volunteer for other work than strictly Post Office duties'.[57] A conference of union leaders met on 1

October and set up a delegation including Bowen that negotiated with the Government and ultimately settled the strike. Meanwhile the very first meeting of the amalgamated UPW Executive beginning on 3 October was dominated by the strike. A new set of instructions was worked out to clarify what work members could now do. Riley expressed an interesting view:

> The Murray at Headquarters this week was a very different Murray from the one we have seen before. It may be that he is afraid of the situation and to be honest with ourselves, I think we too were in great measure afraid of it. It is no use burking the facts.

The Union's leaders were not inclined to advocate strike action by their own members, but this did not decide everything. The veteran Cheesman attacked a public statement by Ammon that the Union was 'neutral', but did not go any further. Canavan thought they 'should still go on bluffing to a large extent' and it was agreed to organise a strike ballot as part of this policy. Bowen's statement showed the tensions of the time.

> It is quite easy to say that the position as we found it to-day is one that may easily lead to revolution. But that is beside the point. What we ourselves are particularly concerned with at the moment is how far we can stave off revolution in order to have a more suitable opportunity to fight the workers' cause.

However it did not come to this, and the Union needed to take no further steps after the strike was settled the following day. The main reaction of branches after this was to attack the Executive for not having gone far enough.[58]

Later industrial disputes on the railways always had a direct effect on Post Office workers. The ASLEF strike of May–June 1955 closed down the parcel service and considerably reduced overtime payments for UPW members. Strikes by the NUR during the 1970s elicited support from the UPW, though in 1975 after some heart searching, the Executive agreed to allow members to handle mail that had been brought by outside contractors.[59]

In the first few months of its existence, the Union was also involved in industrial action by its own members and others. Thus 24 April 1924 saw a brief strike of members in Manchester during the wage negotiations, an action of which a number of Executive members 'heartily approved'.[60] In the same month Irish members of the Union who participated in a general strike for the release of political prisoners were told that 'the decision must rest with the individual' on whether to support it or not. Later in the year some Executive members thought their colleagues were wilfully turning their backs on the action of British troops in the Irish war of independence. 'If they were sincere', they were asked 'why had they been so silent as regards Ireland? Women and children were being hunted down by British soldiers and their houses burned to the ground, the people having to be on the fields at night time. Yet [they] remained silent.'[61] However, before much longer the independence of part of Ireland was recognised and the members there went to form their own union.

Union leaders were also very much involved in the Council of Action which was set up to include various wings of the movement in August 1920 to co-ordinate 'direct action' against any British intervention in the war against the Soviet Union.

When the UPW Executive discussed the issue on 7 August, Harry Wallace reflected a general mood when he said that Labour could not 'effectively' oppose the war in Parliament, so 'direct action' would be needed and the issue was sufficiently important to justify 'even unconstitutional methods'. He thought the Union would have to be prepared 'to bring its workers out on strike on this question'. Most Executive members were of the opinion that even if as few as 30 per cent of the membership would support a strike they should go ahead. Fred Riley thought that they could not 'call out women who know practically nothing about the question and have no training in international problems' but most agreed with Mabel Bray that

> although they no doubt included in their membership many young women who did not follow international questions, yet she was sure on the question of peace or war they would all do their best to stop another European war . . . She was confident that more than 30% of their members would come out.

Thus the Executive agreed to support whatever action was decided by the trade union movement generally.[62]

Two days after the Executive meeting on 9 August a decision was taken by trade union and Labour Party leaders to set up the Council of Action and Bowen became a member. A delegation met Prime Minister Lloyd George on 11 August and on the 13th a national conference called for 'direct action' in the event of war. Within the UPW a manifesto was issued calling on workers to support all opposition to 'this abominable and senseless war' and many members contributed to a fund to help the cause.[63] However the strike did not take place because the British Army did not intervene in the war and the Council of Action faded away by the end of the year. There was some opposition to the stand taken by the Executive from Brighton members and amongst Swansea telephonists for example. However, much more typical of attitudes expressed in the Union was a resolution for the Manchester Joint Committee which

> pledges itself whole-heartedly to support any action the Executive Committee may decide to take in conjunction with the organised forces of labour to prevent the Government from pursuing its atrocious policy, in its efforts to crush Russia, and thereby arresting the progress of the workers of Europe.

Although the issue was exploited by some of the 'superior' grades in London, an effort to repudiate what the Executive had done received virtually no support at the 1921 Annual Conference.[64]

The turning point for the Union's attitudes to such generalised strike calls was 15 March 1921, the day known then and since in the labour movement as 'Black Friday'. The miners who were threatened with wage cuts were promised support from their partners in the 'Triple Alliance' – railway workers and engineers. Before they were left to fight alone, UPW leaders had a good deal of discussion about what they could best do to help them.[65] On 8 April they secured the now usual assurance that they would not be compelled to do the work of others in the event of a strike. There was some argument about the likely effect of keeping open telegraph and telephone lines, but on the whole this was likely to help the workers' cause. A good deal of formal negotiation took place with the POEU on these points. Co-operation and support was agreed, though generally in the vaguest terms. A co-ordinating committee was set up, but it never needed to meet when the action supporting the miners was called off. Nevertheless it was agreed to send £1,800 immediately to help the miners, despite objections from the Union's trustees. Over £7,000 was eventually collected by Union members for the locked-out and defeated miners.[66]

By now the Union's own attitude and role had changed. The mood induced by the collapse of the trade union movement on 'Black Friday' was no doubt a factor in the collapse of the UPW's own strike policy later in 1921. Nevertheless, it was firm in its attitude for the next threat of generalised action on 31 May 1925 promising support for the miners in the same terms as before.[67] This time the Government capitulated and agreed to subsidise the miners on 'Red Friday'. Later in the year the Union gave very active support to a strike of telegraphists at the Marconi Company against sackings.[68] The Union was also involved in the latter part of 1925 in the 'Civil Service Defence Campaign' which was strongly supported by the members.

THE GENERAL STRIKE AND THE TRADE DISPUTES ACT

When the issue was finally joined between miners and Conservative Government in the General Strike of May 1926, the UPW was naturally concerned.[69] Bowen was a member of the General Council and as such was charged with publicity during the period when trade union members came out on strike in support of the miners. Though there was never any serious possibility of UPW members coming out on strike, the Union was very much involved. Its staff and facilities were heavily used by the General Council during the course of the dispute, and up to ten members of the Union's staff were working there by the end. The initial disappearance of rail services and the large-scale disruption of road transport severely affected the Postal Service during the dispute, and placed increased pressure on telephone and telegraph operators.

From the beginning within the UPW there was an Emergency Committee of London Executive members and officers, and there was also a joint committee with the POEU and the controlling officers, though the latter showed less than enthusiasm for the strike and had withdrawn before it was over.[70] Representatives of the three unions met Post Office Secretary Murray, who gave what amounted to the same guarantees as on previous occasions, saying that people would not be called upon to do additional work. However, he refused to undertake not to ask for volunteers, and he said that arrangements would be under constant review. A series of meetings between unions and management over the following days confirmed the willingness of the authorities to avoid trouble by sticking to these arrangements.

Except in one place where a small group was talked out of it, there is no evidence of volunteering of any sort amongst Union members. At least one member of the secessionist National Federation of Postal and Telegraph Clerks at Portsmouth helped in the transport of mails and some supervisors may also have done so. The problem of strike-breaking in telecommunications was more difficult, however, and telegraphists found it difficult to avoid having to deal with messages which would normally have been handled by striking railway clerks. There was some talk in the Union of trying to distinguish between various messages, and the Postmaster General had powers to do this as well. Neither side pursued this. The authorities employed blacklegs to transport mail, though not in Post Office vans, but they seem to have gone to some trouble to keep them quite apart from the rest of the workforce. In at least one case blackleg drivers in London were ejected from the North Western District Office refreshment bar.[71] When a blackleg van was interfered with by strikers in the street outside the South Eastern District Office, postmen refused to move it and the police had to be called to do so.

The attitude of the Union and its members was almost entirely sympathetic to the miners. George Middleton said that it was 'the duty of all trade unionists to stand by them and to make whatever sacrifices are demanded for the fight'.[72] The strong support of the members for this is shown by the centrally collected contributions of more than £25,000 to the miners' relief fund as well as numerous local contributions. The Union's central funds added £5,800. Bowen went to some trouble to monitor membership attitudes during the dispute. Chairman W. T. Wood visited London branches every day, and written reports were sent in from over 200 branches, which were accurately summarised by Bowen as indicating 'very strong support for the policy of the EC and deep sympathy for all those on strike'. A small body of critics opposed the strike and a few of them left the Union over it, many of these apparently being female telephonists. The 3,000 or so members lost during the year can only partly be attributed to this, and in any case they were soon made up, as can be seen from the membership figures given in Appendix 35, p. 667.[73] A rather larger minority, who did not leave the Union, thought the Executive too timid and considered that they should have been on strike, though Union leaders and the TUC opposed this throughout. One commentator has noticed the extent to which enthusiasm increased within the Union during the course of the strike, and far more common at the end among ordinary members were doubts about the TUC's 'conduct of the withdrawal of the General Strike'. Even though Bowen thought 'unconditional surrender' was 'by no means an accurate expression', Middleton said 'that the circumstances of the termination of the General Strike have come as a profound disappointment to trade unionists, strikers and non-strikers'. The Executive itself only narrowly defeated a resolution demanding an explanation from the General Council. By the time it came to the Union's postponed Annual Conference in June, although there was unanimous support for what the UPW's own Executive had done there was a resolution from one of the branches at London's South Western District Office repudiating 'the ignominious surrender of the General Council' and calling 'for its immediate resignation'. It was, however, lost.[74]

Outside the Union matters were different. The controlling officers withdrew from their joint committee with the UPW during the course of the strike. Those representing more elevated grades still on the 'Joint Consultative Committee' of the National Whitley Council withdrew on the pretext of a circular calling on them not to volunteer for strike-breaking. Details of this are given on p. 449 below, but numerically they were a very small minority. However, opponents of the strike had some vociferous allies in the House of Commons and Fleet Street, and they launched an almost daily campaign of vituperation aimed in particular at the full-time officials of civil service trade unions.

At the same time as the Post Office authorities were submitting claims to the Arbitration Court for wage reductions, a series of editorials in the *Daily Telegraph* and Parliamentary questions centred on an attack on civil service trade unionism in general and on the UPW in particular.[75] The main theme of this was that 'outsiders' were interfering in the affairs of civil servants. This is why particular fire was directed against full-time officials on the Whitley Council and on the circular that had been published during the dispute over Middleton's name. There was some amusement to be derived perhaps from the charmingly dotty statements of a certain Lieutenant Colonel Dalrymple White who spoke of 'a paper called "The Post" in favour of revolutionary doctrines'. However, a more serious theme of the attacks consisted in calls for the granting of recognition from the breakaway Federation and even its withdrawal from the Union. It is interesting to notice that the Federation itself did not directly attack the General Strike, but simply its leadership. It told Post Office workers that the TUC had 'deserted the miners, and may yet desert YOU', and asked Post Office workers whether they wanted such officials 'who have made a hash of their own affairs, to meddle in Postal affairs?'[76] Such statements do not seem to have had a great effect on UPW members but they did help to gain approval from the Post Office authorities.

The campaign of vituperation directed against civil service trade unions culminated in the legislation announced on 3 August 1926 by Chancellor of the Exchequer Winston Churchill, eventually taking the form of the Trade Disputes Act of 1927. This legislation was directed not only against any 'strike designed or calculated to coerce the Government either directly or by inflicting hardship on the community', whatever that may mean. The fifth clause of the Act confined the membership of civil service trade unionists to bodies including only other civil servants and prevented them from affiliating to any organisation 'which is not confined to persons employed by or under the Government or any federation comprising such organisations'.[77] These stipulations were explained by the Conservative Government as a method of putting an end to divided loyalties in the public service. Civil service trade unionists themselves saw them as an attack on their democratic rights, and on their ability to improve their conditions.

There was some disagreement inside the Union and the civil service generally about how best to prevent this legislation from being passed. W. J. Brown of the CSCA favoured a noisy publicity campaign.[78] UPW General Secretary Bowen initially 'deprecated too much publicity and demonstrations' and placed all his hopes on a deputation that saw Chancellor of the Exchequer Churchill on 1 April 1927.[79] Lobbying of this sort had often been successful in the past, but it achieved nothing on this occasion. Special local organisations in Parliamentary constituencies advocated by Brown were set up. There was a widespread publicity campaign and a revival of *The British Worker* published by the TUC during the General Strike. However, none of this prevented the Bill from passing either. Bowen certainly did not mince his words when addressing his last TUC in 1927:[80]

We have been especially attacked and dealt with in the Trade Disputes Act, a mean reprisal upon the whole of the movement and upon what the Government seems to conceive to have been the weakest link in the Trade Union chain . . . We are told we must not associate with workers outside the Service because we are kidded into the belief that we are not as other people are. We have no delusions about that, my friends. If we had at all, the Postmaster-General would have dissipated any views of that kind when we had to face his representatives quite recently before the Industrial Court. While we had one representative of the Government dissociating us from the workers outside, we had another, for his own purpose, definitely associating us with them. If our wages are to be related to the wages paid outside we have a right to say that we shall stand four-square with other workers to maintain our standard of living.

The UPW was compelled to disaffiliate from the Labour Party in July 1927 and from the TUC at the end of the year. It also had to leave the Postal Telegraph and Telephone International, though not the Workers Educational Association for the odd reason that it was 'apolitical'.

THE UPW AND THE LABOUR PARTY

Before going on to consider the effects of the Trade Disputes Act, something should be said of the Union's activities as part of the wider labour movement before the Act was passed. This was a period which saw the culmination of many years of the efforts of the Union's predecessors in relation to the Labour Party.

It was in the early 1920s that all the efforts to get a Post Office trade union leader into Parliament finally succeeded. Such efforts can be dated back at least as far as Clery's disastrous candidature at Greenwich in 1902, to Stuart's many subsequent efforts to get elected and to the many failures in the 1918 General Election. At long last there was a success in a by-election in February 1922 when Charles Ammon was returned as Member of Parliament for North Camberwell. He had long been a leader of the Fawcett Association and remained Organising Secretary of the UPW until 1928. He was soon joined by Walter Baker, the Union's Assistant General Secretary, who was MP for East Bristol from 1922 until his death in 1930, and by *Post* editor George Middleton who also became a Member of Parliament in the 1922 General Election, remained until November 1924 and was subsequently re-elected in 1929. General Secretary Bowen stood for Newport a number of times, initially at a by-election in 1922 which played an important part in the collapse of the post-war Conservative–Liberal coalition. Local issues from which Bowen was somewhat remote and a scurrilous attack on his alleged support for pacifists in the civil service characterised this campaign.[81] He was, however, never successful in that seat, but was when he stood in Crewe, for which he was MP from 1929 to 1931. The 1929 General Election saw not only the election of Bowen and the re-election of Baker, Middleton and Ammon. There was also success for Outdoor Secretary Harry Wallace at East Walthamstow, of Indoor Secretary Fred Riley at Stockton on Tees, where he defeated Harold MacMillan, and of the Union's Medical Adviser Dr H. B. Morgan at Camberwell North East. Thus in the 1929 Parliament that supported the second minority Labour Government there were five MPs who were officers of the UPW, and two others closely associated with the Union. All of them subsequently lost their seats in the 1931 débâcle, though Ammon was returned in 1935, and Wallace eventually in 1945.

In view of all the hopes that had been invested in the existence of 'Postal MPs' by the pioneers of Post Office trade unionism, it might have been expected that they would serve to greatly increase the power and effectiveness of the UPW. They cannot be said in practice to have done so. For one thing, like other unions, the UPW was 'unable to define clearly what they expect MPs to do', and in the end they often became preoccupied with matters quite outside the Union's ambit including the affairs of their constituents. In general it could be found that 'expectations of party loyalty take precedence over union loyalty'.[82] Generally speaking, the UPW had exercised no control over its MPs, and when it came to conflicts of loyalty between the Union and its interests and the tactical or strategic perspectives of the Parliamentary Labour Party, the Union's MPs were far more likely to choose the latter.

This is not to say of course that the Union's MPs could not perform a number of limited but important functions on behalf of the members. Naturally they were able to put pressure on ministers during negotiations, to take up individual grievances in ways which had often been done by others in the past, and to show a good deal more knowledge about the affairs of the Post Office than many of those given charge of its administration. The UPW's MPs themselves found it necessary of course to defend their Union against baseless and vindictive charges, as Ammon did with some skill during the period between the General Strike and the passing of the Trade Disputes Act. They also found themselves in the not entirely comfortable position of arguing in defence of the employers of their members, if only against some of the more ignorant and obscurantist criticism that was often to be heard from the Conservative benches in the period of the second Labour Government.

The biggest problems came however when there was a possible division of loyalty between the Union and the Parliamentary Party. The most famous example of this occurred in February 1931 when Bowen led the Union's MPs in voting in favour of the setting up of the May Committee which aimed at limiting government expenditure and was likely to bring about wage cuts for government employees. W. J. Brown of the CSCA voted against the measure.[83] It was this incident probably more than any other that led one left-wing delegate to address the 1931 UPW Annual Conference as follows:

> He believed that the party machinery had such a grip of their representatives in common with the representatives of other working-class bodies, that they could not move. They were tied, and, unless they were prepared to risk ostracism and to become outcasts, and that was a dubious advantage, they could not function for them in the House of Commons . . . What they had was a machinery, a bureaucracy of trade union officials with vested interests, and the machine had got them, and the rank and file had to fight for their own salvation.

This judgement might seem harsh, but one Executive member John Wallace was little less so in asserting that though there had been gains from Parliamentary representation, 'Riley maybe got lost in the corridors or the lounges' so little had been heard of him. Neither was he much encouraged by the sight of those Union MPs who did speak 'not on behalf of the membership, but aiding the then PMG to defend the service from attacks by so-called private enterprise'.[84]

There were many aspects of the Union's relationships with prospective and actual MPs which proved difficult to resolve. In the first place, financial arrangements were often a problem. The Union's members voted in 1920 by 49,559 to 5,772 to set up the political fund, and in the period up to 1927 the number who opted out of it was negligible.[85] The Union's 1922 Annual Conference agreed that its MPs would receive half their salaries. In 1924 there was some discussion about how the money paid out to constituencies was being spent and the Executive tried to ensure that its 'political contribution' was 'distinct from the financing of everyday routine of propaganda and organising activities' of the local organisations. It refused to finance local elections or to pay more than 80 per cent of election expenses, though some local constituencies objected even to this. At Bristol East in particular the Union's General Secretary and General Treasurer had to visit the constituency party to explain why the Union could not keep up the level of subsidy being demanded for what was essentially a safe seat.[86] The arrangements made were roughly in line with those later decided at the 1933 Hastings Conference of the Labour party, which fixed levels of payment for maintenance of constituency parties, though not for elections.[87] The position of the Union's MPs was also complicated, particularly when they came to decide what call they had on the resources of the Union itself. In 1925–6 Ammon and Baker were utilising the services of two full-time typists at Cromwell Road, but the Executive was not prepared to allow the extensive use of the Research Department.[88]

In general, however, the MPs grew remote from the affairs of the UPW, certainly the day-to-day work of Headquarters. Some of the Union's leaders worried about what might happen to them if they went into Parliament and then were defeated. Horace Nobbs, who stood in 1918, withdrew in 1921 from being a candidate as a result of these fears and actually carried out the job of Organising Secretary which nominally was also held by Ammon.[89] Nobbs preferred to remain an officer of the Union. Others came back without difficulty including Bowen and Wallace, who both stood again without success in 1935. However, the experience of 1929–31 resulted in a new rule in 1932 that officers could only become MPs with the sanction of the Executive. This was not however easy to operate. When Ammon resumed his position as MP in 1935, he was no longer directly linked to the Union. In 1944, when he went to the House of Lords, the Executive considered standing General Secretary Tom Hodgson for his seat, though it seems to have been expected that he would then retire from the Union. Nevertheless, the feeling in the UPW that North Camberwell was in some sense 'their' seat was not shared by the local party and when they began to show more preference for a local candidate, Hodgson withdrew.[90]

By this time the Union had long since been subject to the influence of the 1927 Trade Disputes Act. It seems likely that the same developments in relations between the Union and its MPs and candidates might have occurred without the Act. However, in the short term the passage immediately created problems about the financing of the Union's Parliamentary efforts. Money was already being sent to five constituencies that were being contested, and agents were being paid at Crewe and East Walthamstow. Appeals were issued in *The Post* for contributions, which did not go unnoticed by those ill disposed to the Union. On 7 May 1929 a Conservative MP asked whether this was legal and the Postmaster General replied that since appeals were only being issued in the names of candidates it was quite admissible.[91] Three days later the 'Bowen Trust' was set up. This was largely a means of channelling money from the Union to the support of its Parliamentary candidates. The £12,853 in the political fund was moved in this way, and some Union members, up to around 3,000, subscribed a further £500 or so by early 1930.

However, with five of the Union's leaders as MPs in the Parliament of 1929–31, the fund was by no means adequate to provide half their salaries, together with various secretarial and other facilities. Early in 1930 the payment of the MPs had to be suspended, and new arrangements were initiated by the establishment of the Direct Parliamentary Representation Society with local 'centres' organised by UPW branches and with annual meetings held at UPW conferences.[92] Initially this had some success. Membership rose to 7,614 in October 1930 and to 9,577 in the following March. However, the Society soon thereafter began to decline, to as low as 2,509 in 1934 and to 2,795 in 1943. This was despite continual exhortations to members, including support from Ernest Bevin and others. Eventually the payment of agents had to be suspended and it was only possible to support Williams and Randall in the 1945 General Election.

It has been argued that the low level of support for the Direct Parliamentary Representation Society was an indication of the apathy of UPW members on such matters. When the Society was finally disbanded in 1948 it was acknowledged 'that the Society did not achieve all it set out to accomplish' and UPW members should have been able 'to join and work to a far greater extent'.[93] However there were quite a few other reasons why the members might fail to support the Society. For one thing, there was a good deal of disillusionment amongst them not only with the failure and collapse of the 1929–31 Labour Government but more specifically with the complete inability of the Union's MPs to exercise successful pressure on it. This applied not least on the very issue of the restrictions on the political activity of the Union. Furthermore, there always remained some doubt about the legality of the activities of the Direct Parliamentary Representation Society. Thus the Union's officers were not nominally members, it being largely run by Executive members who were 'Crown Servants'. The nominated officers were always members of Headquarters staff. This further factor discouraged members who were less committed to the Union, or less convinced of the efficiency of Parliamentary activity, from involvement in the DPRS.

Problems of legality continued to worry the UPW leaders, particularly after the failure of the war-time campaign to defy the Trade Disputes Act. Following the collapse of Hodgson's efforts to take over at Camberwell from Ammon in 1944, the Executive again considered the matter of regularising such candidatures and it was agreed that the Executive itself should elect up to two officers as candidates, they should remain officers while MPs with half salaries, and that they should receive clerical help from the Union. It was eventually agreed to support Harry Randall at Clitheroe and W. R. Williams at Heston, with Wallace at East Walthamstow standing independently of the Union from which he was shortly to retire.[94] Though all three of these were soon afterwards returned in the 1945 General Election, it was nevertheless decided to expunge from the records any further reference to the new arrangements agreed in October 1944. Details of the support given to various candidatures in 1945 cannot now easily be traced because they were not included in the printed minutes. It was ironic that the Union was seeking to engage in the most constitutional of activities in some secrecy and under the threat of legal action. Nevertheless legal opinion did confirm that a case might have been made against the DPRS since it was entirely under the control of the Union's Executive and effectively subsidised from its general funds.

These fears were laid to rest in 1946 by the repeal of the Trade Disputes Act. The Union members voted by 42,729 to 13,611 to restore the political fund on the same basis as before 1927 and delegates immediately started to attend conferences of the Labour Party again.[95] It also became possible to consider again the matter of the Union's relations with its MPs. In October 1945 there were efforts to get an extra officer appointed to replace the MPs, and in the following January the Executive narrowly refused to support the candidature of Lockyer, who was due to retire as General Treasurer, for a seat at Preston.[96] The Union continued to support its officers Williams and Randall, who remained in control of their respective departments, though only able to attend for less than one-third of the days of the year.[97] Funds were supplied by the Union to the Parliamentary constituencies of its officers, and to its former officer Harry Wallace at East Walthamstow. This last was the only one of the three seats retained in the 1950 General Election, though Williams was returned for Droylsden in 1951.

By this time it was becoming clearer that the direct representation of the Union by having its officers in Parliament was not working in the way that had been envisaged. For one thing, being an officer had become much more time-consuming than had been the case twenty years before. Bargaining had become a somewhat more continuous, not to say technical, business, particularly in the wake of the Priestley Report in 1955. It is thus not surprising that from 1949 the General Secretary was not allowed to be an MP, and from 1955 none of the officers at all. In 1956 the position was regularised, with agreement that there should be a Parliamentary panel of six. In 1962 this was again altered to increase the power of the Executive in examining those who joined the panel. There was some suggestion that the aim of this was to keep off those who were 'left of centre', but the Conference argued that it was not easy to exercise the Union's influence in this way.[98] From the time that Harry Randall retired as Organising Secretary of the UPW in 1955 (though he remained MP for Gateshead West until 1970) none of the central leaders of the Union have been on the panel. Some of those on the panel have not even been on the Union's Executive.

To this day the UCW continues to finance a small number of candidates and to run the panel whose names are submitted to various seats. Sponsored MPs always take up questions of interest to the Union members, and have been very actively involved indeed in dealing with the various changes in the status of the Post Office service since the 1950s. W. R. Williams acted as 'shadow' Postmaster General from 1960 until his death in 1963. Charles Morris, his successor in the seat at Manchester Openshaw, and a former Executive member of the Union, became Parliamentary Private Secretary to the Postmaster General in 1964–6 before going on to various other positions. In general it must be said that the role of these sponsored MPs, though important in some ways, is not of central significance to the major industrial activities of the Union. They go beyond what sympathetic MPs like H. L. W. Lawson and George Bowyer did in the 1880s and 1890s, but not a great deal.

The Union's contribution to the Labour Party more generally, to its political and organisational development, has not been great. Charles Ammon was on the National Executive Committee from 1921–6, and Lionel Andrews briefly in the mid-1960s. Delegates have attended the conferences and frequently spoken up to 1927 and since 1947. They have argued for the specific policies of the Union, notably on 'industrial democracy', but it cannot be said that in general they have made a major or distinctive contribution to the Labour Party programme and policy. In this of course they were not greatly different from most other trade unions. The same might also be said of the UPW's tendency to support the 'platform' within the Labour Party. However this has never been an uncomplicated business. As is made clear elsewhere, Geddes was a strong supporter of the prevailing anti-Communist orthodoxy of the early 1950s, a supporter of German rearmament and opponent of Aneurin Bevan. However, their views by no means went without challenge. Thus in 1954 the Executive only agreed by 17 votes to 10 to support Gaitskell against Bevan for Party Treasurer.[99] Support for German rearmament by UPW delegations to TUC and Labour Party in 1954 unleashed a good deal of controversy within the Union. One correspondent to *The Post* attacked

the undemocratic decision of the Executive Council. Trade unions came into existence because of the desire of men to end the oligarchical powers of the capitalist, and it is with a somewhat sardonic eye that I observe the hierarchy of the Trade Union movement indulging in these very practices which brought them into existence.

Another member noted that the Union's vote could have swung the issue either way.

It seems to me that if my views are to be adequately represented at the Labour Party Conference, I shall have no alternative but to cease paying my political levy, in order that my vote in the block carried by the union delegation is not cancelling out my local party vote.

These correspondents were J. McKinlay of the Metropolitan Branch and T. Jackson from Leeds.

At the Union's Conference in 1955, there was a lengthy debate before the view of the delegation was endorsed. Nevertheless, in 1955 the Union delegates voted against the platform on the issue of whether the Deputy Leader should be on the National Executive, and also against the official line on the control of profits and prices. Again there was a good deal of debate within the Union following the 1959 General Election defeat of Labour. A correspondence in *The Post* largely reflected the view that this was because 'we were more anxious for power than for socialism'. Perhaps surprisingly, however, the Union endorsed the abortive efforts of Gaitskell to drop the commitment to public ownership from the Labour Party constitution. They also generally supported him on the issues of defence and disarmament, though not without considerable debate and strongly supported opposition.[100] Thus, though it is possible to quote leaders of the UPW of various generations on the manipulation of the bloc vote and on its application in support of the labour movement's establishment, this has not always been as clear and straightforward as some commentators have suggested. A full examination of this matter, however, is beyond the scope of this book.

UPW AND TUC BEFORE THE TRADE DISPUTES ACT

The Union has always taken an active role in the TUC ever since the first period of its affiliation from 1920–7. It elected delegates to all the congresses of the period who spoke on a number of issues, and Bowen was on the General Council from 1921. Although the UPW cannot be said to have been at the centre of affairs in the TUC itself, the fact that it was affiliated did play a part in the development of the Union during the period.[101]

The pre-amalgamation associations had been affiliated to the TUC for some years. The Fawcett Association joined in 1893, though it disaffiliated briefly in 1908–11 for reasons explained in Chapter 8. The PTCA affiliated in 1899, the Postmen's Federation in 1900 and the UKPCA in 1901. In 1916 G. H. Stuart-Bunning joined what was then called the Parliamentary Committee and in 1919 he was Congress President. Before the foundation of the UPW, and to some extent afterwards, Post Office trade union delegates often confined their intervention to matters of direct interest to themselves. Thus they consistently took up the restriction of their 'civil rights', by which they meant their ability to engage in political and electoral activity. After years of agitation on this matter, the 1924 Labour Government set up the Blanesburgh Committee of Enquiry which proposed no serious change. Bowen was a member of the TUC–Labour Party Committee which tried to put further pressure on the Conservative Government on this issue, but this was abandoned in the changed atmosphere that followed the General Strike.[102] The Union used the TUC as a means for their campaign to expand the functions of the Post Office, particularly by the adoption of the postal cheque system.[103] The Union was also in a position to take up from its own experience the inadequacies of the Ministry of Labour cost-of-living index as a measure of working-class living standards. This view later became a commonplace in TUC statements on the matter.[104]

The UPW delegates at the TUC supported the strengthening of its organisation. They voted for the setting up of the General Council as a stronger co-ordinating body in 1921, and increasing the power of the TUC to become involved in industrial disputes. The UPW also took up with enthusiasm the TUC's efforts in the period to encourage union amalgamations though these had little effect in the Post Office. The 1925 Congress took a number of militant decisions including the adoption for the first time of a programme known as the Industrial Workers Charter. Bowen commended these decisions 'as showing a real and practical determination to make progress', despite being castigated in the press as steps 'to red and rank socialism'. The Union also supported the increased powers taken by the General Council in advance of the General Strike.[105]

There were two particular issues taken up by the UPW in this period which are of some interest. One was the consistent opposition of the Union to the existence of a separate women's group on the General Council. This view was strongly argued a number of times by Edith Howse, though Bowen did not agree with it. She got a resolution on the agenda of the 1925 Congress. She argued against the women's group especially on the grounds that it was simply a means for some of the larger unions of getting people on to the General Council, having failed herself on a number of occasions to do so. In 1925 the arrangement was defended with the argument that without it women would not get on to the General Council at all.[106]

The other issue in which the Union took a particular interest was trade union education. In 1921 Charles Ammon supported the consolidation of all working-class educational activity under the TUC so that 'we shall equip ourselves for that larger share in the machinery of government which all of us recognise is coming very rapidly for the workers'. Bowen became actively involved in the discussions that followed this. He put forward the usual UPW arguments against what was called 'independent working class education' on the grounds that he favoured 'broadening instead of narrowing knowledge'. When an appeal was launched to take over a house called Easton Lodge for such activities, Bowen strongly supported 'a workers university'. Other delegates were not so convinced however and one of them suggested 'that the Labour Movement is not going to be saved by the kind of people produced at such places'. The scheme was referred back to the General Council and soon afterwards sank without trace.[107]

All such discussion was put to an end by the Trade Disputes Act. Despite all the protests already described, the Union was compelled on 31 December 1927 to withdraw its affiliation and to remain for the next twenty years outside the TUC.

THE UPW UNDER THE TRADE DISPUTES ACT: 1927-46

It is not easy to measure the effect of this legislation, which was bitterly resented, on the development of the UPW. Particularly up to the 1938 arbitration settlement, these were hard times for Post Office workers, and no doubt this would have been the case whatever their affiliations. However, there can be no doubt that the lack of contact with other sections of the working class movement isolated the Union and reduced confidence in its ability to serve the interests of the members. The frustration involved eventually led to war-time efforts to defy the law in ways which are unique in the history of the Union.

Some contacts with the TUC were maintained. The Chairman and Secretary of the Union normally attended the congress each year as visitors. TUC General Secretary Walter Citrine attended the 1928 UPW Annual Conference and each conference from 1932 to 1936. It is of some interest to notice what he said and how he was received. Up to 1935 he was very warmly applauded by the delegates as a representative of a wider movement to which they remained loyal despite their exclusion. The 1935 Conference Chairman Ernest Dunster said this:

> They wanted their people to realise that there was something more in declaring themselves trade unionists than that their attention should be wholly concerned with their own particular domestic affairs.

Citrine in turn normally gave a general account of the development of the trade union movement and of international politics, with particular reference to the growth of 'dictatorship'. In 1934 he expressed his general philosophy of trade unionism in this way:

> He knew that there was a current opinion in 'uninstructed Trade Union circles' that the act of conducting negotiations with employers consisted in the main in the possession of a rather stentorian voice and a capacity for banging the table in their presence. He had not found, in his experience of twenty years, that that was entirely efficacious . . . these were days when Trade Unions required to put before employers arguments not merely of a humanitarian character, but arguments supported by facts and statistics, and of a technical character too.[108]

However it was Citrine's reception at the 1936 UPW Conference that was particularly memorable. He came immediately after his acceptance of a knighthood from the 'National' Government, a step which was deeply unpopular among active trade unionists. There were protests against him being received at all, not only on general political grounds from left-wing delegates but also from the somewhat less predictable Arthur O'Donnell, full-time Secretary of the Manchester Amalgamated Branch. O'Donnell was not, he said,

> a Left Winger, but he did welcome the sign of protest from the Conference, which he regarded as healthy and of happy augury for the union . . . Whether the reference back was carried or not, there was bound to be an unpleasant and painful scene, because he knew from his own branch that they would not be prepared to sit in the hall and listen to Sir Walter Citrine.

Jenny Duncan said that despite claims

that they might be insulting Sir Walter Citrine, but what about Sir Walter Citrine insulting the workers. (Cheers). When he did speak, they should all rise up and leave the hall, and leave him with the Executive Council and the titled people on the platform.

A very narrow card vote of 1,080 to 910 agreed to hear Sir Walter, and this is how his initial reception was described in the official report:

On Sir Walter Citrine rising to speak, many delegates left the hall, but he was received with rousing cheers from those who remained . . . He deplored more than any words could convey that any incidents could have arisen which could be magnified into any semblance of friction. Had he consulted his own feelings only he would not have been there. He had come because he prided himself that there was a sense of fairness and inherent decency on the part of men and women who refused to condemn any man unheard. (Cheers). He thanked those of them who without any canvass for him, were good enough by their majority vote to confirm the decision of their Executive Council that he should come. He came there for them and not the others . . . those who were most loud in their affirmation of the necessity for preserving democratic institutions and democratic methods were the first to try to establish the principle of dictatorship.[109]

It is perhaps not surprising that after 1936, Sir Walter never again found time to attend UPW conferences, though invited on a number of occasions. TUC chairmen did attend a few times in his place. The temper of the delegates on this matter showed that however much they were kept separate from the rest of the trade union movement, they nevertheless shared many of the same passions.

Nor were UPW visitors to the TUC in this period always happy with what they found. W. T. Leicester thought the 1929 Congress 'quiet', with 'debates falling below the standard of former years' and John Coyne was not much impressed in 1932 at the 'deathly silence' that characterised the debate on the General Council's Report which has 'lost all trace of criticism and challenge'. Nor was he happy at the refusal to meet a delegation of hunger marchers as a result of which 'not one of us left the hall without the bourgeois feeling conferred by police protection!' Others spoke of the 'almost solid mass of middle-aged officials' engaged in 'an extraordinary spectacle of futility' and Charles Smallwood in 1935 thought Citrine's arguments for purging Communists from the trades councils not 'so successful' as 'on some of the other debates'. The Union's Executive was also unhappy about war-time restrictions on the right to strike, but the matter was not pursued.[110]

Generally speaking, however, the Union visitors identified themselves with many aspects of the development of TUC policy. They favoured the closer discussion with employers' representatives that followed the General Strike. After one visit Hodgson commended the purge of Communists from the trades councils as a fight against 'civil war methods at home'. In particular, Union visitors linked resolutions calling for the forty-hour week with their own efforts to pursue this aim within the Post Office. It may well be that the 1931 Congress discussion had an important influence on making the Union take up this issue.[111]

By far the greatest interest by UPW visitors was shown in the issue of industrial democracy and this manifested itself in various forms at almost every congress. Union visitors seized on statements that seemed to be in line with UPW policies. Thus Roland Bishop was impressed by the call of 1931 TUC President Arthur Hayday for 'the workers, through their unions' to be 'definitely associated with administration and policy' in the nationalised industries. In the following year the General Council published a report which on the whole favoured Morrisonian concepts of nationalisation, without any union participation in management. This was attacked from the floor of the Congress and a very vague motion calling for the reorganisation of industry was in the end passed. The only card vote at the 1933 Congress was on the same issue when the General Council's report was carried on a narrow vote, against a resolution calling 'as a statutory right, that 50% of the representation on Managerial Committees shall be accorded to workers' nominees'. However, a resolution calling for trade union representation on the boards of nationalised industries was passed at the 1933 TUC, so that in 1934 the same general resolution went through without dissent. A writer in *The Post* found this very encouraging:

> It indicates a steady growth of support for Workers' Control. Labour's recent flirtation with Public Utility Corporations seems to be reaching the cooling-off stage, and, if I read the signs right, the star of real Workers' Control is quietly and steadily rising in the trade union sky.[112]

During the war period, the Union stepped back from this optimistic view, expressing reservations that co-operation with the war was an instalment of workers' control. In particular Ernest Bevin's phrase 'self government in industry' made one UPW commentator unhappy. 'The people who conceived that phrase used it to indicate the application of Workers' Control, but it is not altogether clear what Mr. Bevin had in mind'. George Morris was afraid that some discussions about workshop committees showed the need for the Union 'to drive home the importance of Workers' Control, and the dangers that will arise from the extension of national ownership without such control'.[113]

In a number of ways the UPW generally was a much less assertive and self-confident body in the two decades that followed the General Strike. One interesting manifestation of this was in a private discussion in 1932–4 about the legality of strikes in the civil service between General Secretary Bowen and a legal writer called N. E. Mustoe.[114] Mustoe was generally of the opinion that on the basis of somewhat antiquated legal decisions about public servants who failed to take up their duties, civil servants had no legal right to strike at all. He also had the view that since the civil service was not a 'trade or industry', then the various immunities that applied to strikers elsewhere did not help civil servants. By the same token the general ban on strikes in the 1927 legislation did not apply to the civil service either. Bowen felt compelled to concur with this, but after surveying various examples from the past of how the Post Office authorities had reacted he concluded that

> they seem to have handled strikes or threatened strikes in much the same manner as any other employer, varying their reaction according to the widespread nature of the discontent, and according to the seriousness of the inconvenience a strike might cause.

It is of interest to notice that the question of the legality of strike action was not raised in the strikes that took place even in the 1870s. It certainly was not in question in 1890, and on all the various occasions when the Post Office workers reacted to other disputes in subsequent years. By the time the issues discussed in the early 1930s came to be tested in practice, the legal and political situation was very different. The major strikes in the Post Office between 1962 and 1971, both before and after incorporation, were not attacked on the grounds of their illegality, though of course they were for other reasons. It was the new atmosphere of attacks on trade unionism more generally in the late 1970s that brought the issue full circle, and brought the legality of strike action again to the centre of consideration. This phase, however, has in no sense yet gone into history.

In the 1930s, however, the Union continued to be faced with legislation that was seen as weakening its ability to act on behalf of its members, and which led to some of the most well published and significant events in its development. Efforts to repeal or to defeat the Trade Disputes Act were continuous throughout its existence.[115] Resolutions were passed virtually every year at the UPW Conference, at the TUC and elsewhere. Initially it was hoped that the 1929 Labour Government would simply repeal the measure. A good deal of complicated lobbying took place before a Bill to repeal the Act was introduced in October 1930. However, the Labour Government relied on the support of the Liberals for a majority. The Liberals managed in February 1931 to secure an amendment banning all strikes that 'adversely affected the interests of the community'. This would certainly have made the position even worse than it was under the Act, so in April the new Bill was withdrawn.[116]

As the years went by, the Government became increasingly dilatory in its reaction to protests and the Union's activists grew increasingly frustrated. One delegate at the 1936 UPW Annual Conference was afraid that the Union 'was beginning to forget all about Clause 5, and to be a mutual admiration society rather than a fighting union'. Three years later the Union's Chairman J. P. Riley was even more pessimistic about the long-term consequences of the measure. He began by looking back to the pre-amalgamation associations.[117]

We were recognised as part and parcel of the Workers' Movement. We played our part right well. It would be interesting to study the Conference Agendas of those years, or even of our own Union from 1920 to 1927, in order to compare them today with what is a purely domestic agenda paper to a respectable House Union.

It seems that the Youth of today accepts Clause V as inevitable, and is content with wage claims from a purely Post Office or, shall I say, Civil Service viewpoint – with, one must admit, the definite improvements in conditions through Union action. The appeals today seem limited to obtaining concessions within eight hours of Post Office duty through local agreements and Whitleyism.

These feelings of frustration were reflected in the increasingly intense efforts by the UPW and its allies on the Civil Service National Whitley Council staff side to do something to get the legislation repealed. In 1936 the Union began to put pressure on the Labour Party to guarantee a specific undertaking to repeal the legislation, and following discussions between Hodgson and Arthur Greenwood of the National Executive in the following year this was obtained. In 1937 the TUC began to press for the Prime Minister Neville Chamberlain to meet them on the issue and a delegation led by Ernest Bevin eventually did so on 24 February 1939. Although Chamberlain agreed that things had changed since 1927, he was not prepared to promise anything. After a good deal more pressure behind the scenes a TUC General Council delegation again met Chamberlain on 7 March 1940. Now Chamberlain at least was more definite. He 'stated that the amending legislation would be highly controversial and such legislation in war-time was impractical'. In reply the General Council issued a statement which concluded 'that the retention of this Act upon the statute book was a mockery of the ideals for which they were fighting'.[118]

The months that followed these statements saw continuous and frustratingly unsuccessful agitation against the Act. For the leaders of the trade union movement as a whole, this was an issue which embodied what they hoped would provide a break from all the old repressive attitudes of the Tories in relation to the unions, in return for the co-operation they readily offered in pursuit of the war. For the UPW even more, the continued ban on their association with the rest of the movement weakened their ability to take part in general decisions which affected the lives of all their members. The repeal of the Act as a whole, and for the UPW particularly Clause V banning their affiliations, became a symbol of all that they were fighting for. Every war-time conference of TUC and Union echoed with comparisons between the Trade Disputes Act and the legislation of fascist Italy and Germany. Feeling grew so intense that by 1943 for the first and only time in its history on the issue of affiliation, the UPW was prepared to defy the law.

Yet, for all that, the legislation remained on the statute book at the end of the war, enforced in its full rigour. The reason for this is to be sought in the political alliances of the war-time period. The formation of the Coalition Government in May 1940 soon put into the Cabinet not only the same Arthur Greenwood who had promised to get the repeal into Labour's programme, but also the same Ernest Bevin who had campaigned volubly against the Act on many occasions. Yet Greenwood and Bevin found that the question of the Trade Disputes Act went down their list of priorities. In November 1940, soon after becoming Minister of Labour, Bevin promised to get the matter discussed, but when a joint Labour Party/TUC delegation met Prime Minister Churchill in the following February he reiterated the view that such matters could not be dealt with in war-time. The same result came when the TUC met Churchill in April. Little more was achieved by a National Whitley Council delegation to Bevin at about the same time. The TUC began at this time to take the first forms of unilateral action by inviting the UPW to send representatives to some of its sub-committees.[119]

By the middle of 1941 nothing at all had been achieved from all the efforts made. There was a suggestion – perhaps from Labour members of the Government – that the unions should now abandon the campaign for the repeal of the entire Act and concentrate instead on the points that restricted the activities of local and national public servants, clauses V and VI. At first the TUC approved this and Hodgson said it would be better 'to improve the position of the Trade Union world generally'. Under pressure from the Parliamentary Labour Party TUC leaders decided, however, to lobby for these more limited aims.[120] They met people from the Conservative Party organisation where the response was found to be 'entirely negative'.[121] Nothing was achieved at a similar meeting with the Liberal Party on 12 February 1942. After numerous further delays, Prime Minister Churchill told the TUC in June that 'the matter should not be pressed, particularly at this crucial period in the war'. Further efforts to put pressure on individual ministers, including Labour ones, came to nothing.[122]

By now members of the Union were growing restive. The hectic and almost continuous negotiations on the bonus during 1942, the long hours of overtime and general difficulties of working in the war, increased the feeling in the Union that it was time for more drastic action. At the Annual Conference in May 1942 one delegate said 'that members should take the matter into their own hands' by associating with the outside trade union movement. Soon afterwards, John Moohan was suggesting on the Executive that they should 'consider instructing the branches to affiliate to local Trade Councils and to challenge the Government on the issue there'.[123] Such affiliations had not been unknown in the past, and by April 1943 Citrine said that if UPW branches wanted to affiliate the General Council 'would not feel justified in prohibiting the Trades Council from accepting the affiliation'. During the next period UPW branches began affiliating to trades councils and in many cases playing an active part in their affairs. By the end of 1944, more than half the branches in London had such affiliations, and a total of 321 representing 121,421 members were so affiliated.

This was a form of defiance which was difficult for those in authority to deal with, and nothing was ever done about it. However, it soon became obvious at numerous meetings of UPW branches early in 1943 that there existed 'the unmistakable desire of the members of the Union to press forward on this issue'. At the Executive meeting in April the proposal to go ahead with affiliation regardless of the consequences was only lost by one vote, but it was already clear that the Conference Agenda 'showed no other item in which so much interest was demonstrated as in the one of Civil Rights'. When it came to the Conference General Secretary Tom Hodgson caught the general mood:

There comes a time in the affairs of men when one could not act under discipline imposed, especially when it was of an oppressive character. It behoved self-respecting men and women to demonstrate defiance.

This defiance was reflected in a motion from the floor of the Conference which called not simply for the widest participation in the working-class movement, but also for the Union to act by ignoring the 1927 Trade Disputes Act and asking the TUC to accept the Union's affiliation. The General Secretary said he accepted this as 'strictly in line with their policy' and it was carried 'with one dissentient'.[124]

This decision catapulted the UPW into national prominence probably greater than anything it had obtained before that time. Its action was met with abuse often based on ignorance. Thus when *The Times* said it was 'a hasty and ill-considered action', this was presumably because it knew nothing of sixteen years of agitation and delay. Perhaps more surprising was the opposition from Labour Party leaders, including those outside the Government, who showed an ill-concealed hostility to the Union pursuing the issue in war-time, and refused to express any support for its action.[125] However, the application for affiliation was certainly popular with many UPW members, including a great number of those serving in the forces. One of these expressed a very commonly held view when he said that for him 'the struggle against Fascism and Clause V are one'.[126]

Before the Union could do anything further, a group of leaders of other civil service unions arranged to meet Churchill on 3 August 1943. They included White of the CSCA, Edwards of the POEU and Houghton of the Inland Revenue Staff Federation. Although they regarded themselves in some sense as mediators, Hodgson considered their intervention to be 'amateurish bungling', and all they got from Churchill was the declaration 'that someone must climb down'.[127] This delegation, whose precise starting point had probably more to do with differences within the National staff side than with opposition to what the UPW was trying to do, heralded a flurry of further activity. TUC General Secretary Citrine immediately went to see Labour leader Clement Attlee who was at the time Deputy Prime Minister. Speaking apparently for himself and also for Morrison and Bevin, the other Labour Cabinet members, Attlee said 'that he and his colleagues were prepared to carry out the provisions of the Act on the Civil Service', and the entire question raised 'the position of Labour Ministers in the Cabinet'. He 'realised that this might lead to a break up of the whole show'. He also said, perhaps more surprisingly, that he had definite legal opinion that trades council affiliation was not illegal.[128]

The War Cabinet was thus determined not to be defied, and won the support of its Labour members for this position. On 12 August a statement was issued by the Treasury in these terms:[129]

The Union of Post Office Workers have made application for affiliation to the Trades Union Congress. It is understood that the application will be considered at the forthcoming conference in September.

It is important that members of the Service should recognise in advance the position in which they would be placed if an association of which they are members were affiliated to the TUC. The effect of the law is as follows. If an association of which established civil servants are members becomes so affiliated the result follows that the warning contemplated in the Act must be given to every established civil servant who is a member of the association. If at the end of one month, thereafter, that established civil servant has not resigned his membership of the association, he automatically becomes, in the words of the Act, 'disqualified from being a member of the Civil Service'. This has the effect that he loses his established position, and that all his accumulated pension rights are forfeited. It is the Government's duty to state this position clearly and the duty of the Civil Service organisations to bring it to the notice of their members.

These naked threats naturally produced a rapid reaction. On 13 August, the day after they were issued, the Union's Executive met TUC leaders and then discussed the position themselves. They were faced with a crisis in the affairs of the Union which had some parallels to the 1921 position over the strike levy.[130] Some of the same elements were present including the secessionists, who had already been running meetings and stepping up recruitment efforts. This time, however, the doubts and hesitations of members were not simply about exercising their power as trade unionists. The threat to their pensions and jobs was something much more fundamental. As a result only one Executive member, George Douglas, 'deplored the defeatist attitude' of the meeting and wanted to go ahead with the application. However, a more representative view was expressed by Dick Ruth who said that 'the union was faced with the greatest crisis of its history unless it retreated'. It was agreed that the 'application for affiliation to the TUC be deferred for the time being'.

Before this decision was revealed to Union members, or to the world at large, there was an interesting interlude.[131] On 19 August the TUC General Council expressed itself prepared to go ahead with the application whatever the view of the Union, or indeed of the law. The General Council met the Parliamentary Labour Party which refused to discuss the issue and called on the Union to withdraw the application. The UPW Executive heard that the statements of Churchill at this stage were more favourable to the Union than those of Attlee, and publicised its retreat on the 20th. A circular was sent out to branches explaining the decision and so ensuring members of 'information from a source which enables it confidently to say' that there would be no action on trades council affiliations. The public position was that there had not been a withdrawal at all, but the matter had been placed in the hands of a Joint Committee of TUC, Labour Party and Parliamentary Labour Party. At the TUC in September the actions were unanimously endorsed.[132]

Later in the war further efforts were directed towards the repeal of the legislation. Propaganda if anything was intensified, and the UPW for example made contact with every other trade union before the 1944 Congress. After a secret session there the new UPW General Secretary Charles Geddes told his Executive that 'there had been a slackening of the fight on the part of the General Council'. Nor was the Labour Party forthcoming, refusing to make it a central plank in the election campaign which was now soon expected. Geddes even felt constrained to pledge that civil service union leaders would not join the General Council after affiliation, on the grounds that there were those who considered this the sole motive for the campaign.[133] Civil service unions co-operated nationally and locally in further activities increasingly directed to political lobbying. In March 1945 Churchill replied at the end of a long series of delays that the Conservative Party would not support any modification of the law. Finally the issue could only be resolved by the election of the first majority Labour Government later in the year. The King's Speech on 15 August 1945 announced the repeal of the Act which Prime Minister Attlee said 'had to a large extent poisoned the industrial life of this country'. A simple repeal of the entire measure finally reached the statute book on 22 May 1946 as the 1946 Trade Disputes and Trade Union Act.[134]

UPW AND TUC SINCE 1946

The re-entry of the UPW and other civil service trade unionists into the wider trade union movement began as soon as the repeal of the Act was announced. Since then, UPW delegations were sent to Congress each year and to many other activities. The four UPW general secretaries of this period served on the General Council. Charles Geddes occupied an important position especially during his period as President in 1954-5. Ron Smith was also on the General Council, and his successor Tom Jackson played a major role when he too joined it in 1967, taking his turn as President in 1978-9. He has been succeeded by Alan Tuffin.

Between the late 1940s and early 1980s, there were some questions on which the Union had a distinctive position within the TUC. It was normally in a minority in arguing, as it continued to do in the 1950s, for direct trade union representation on the boards of nationalised industries. If the Union did not persuade the majority of the delegates to its point of view on this, it did at least hold back the TUC from a complete espousal of the principles of Morrisonian nationalisation. It had less effect, however, in one particularly distinctive view that it put in the late 1960s, when it failed to get support for its resolutions opposing British Summer Time.[135]

Generally speaking, the UPW has tended to vote with the majority of unions in the TUC on the main issues of policy. This has applied particularly during the periods when general secretaries Geddes and Jackson were themselves major figures in the TUC establishment, playing a role in moulding these policies. UPW leaders also tended to support the main lines of TUC policy on wages. This has applied in particular to the various forms of wage restraint exercised by Labour governments, though not those of the Conservatives. The Union's own bargaining preoccupations, notably in the mid-1960s and in 1971, had to some extent served to modify its attitudes.

Over the years since 1946, the Union has participated in many aspects of the work of the TUC. It continued to be involved in its educational activities, which seem to have grown more popular with the members after the war than before it.[136] The Union has also regularly sent delegates to the Women's TUC Conference, even when it was difficult to do so in the 1950s because these meetings clashed with the Union's own conference. They have not always been uncritical observers of proceedings there. The delegates at the 1950 Conference found the attitude of TUC General Secretary Vincent Tewson 'rather pontifical', and in the following year Nan Whitelaw and Winifred Rowe thought there were too many formalities and 'too little time left for full discussion on resolutions'. In 1956 Kim McKinlay unsuccessfully moved a resolution aimed at improving the recruitment of women to trade unions. Two years later she was arguing within the Union against the existence of a separate women's conference.[137] Although delegates have attended since that time, this has generally speaking been the Union's attitude. Delegates have also been sent to conferences of non-manual workers organised by the TUC, though they do not seem to have found much to interest Post Office workers there, and the Union did not object to the ending of these conferences after 1975.[138]

UPW delegations to the congresses themselves have always been half officers and half lay members. The constraints on them once sent have been limited. When Charles Geddes was asked by Fred Moss and Kim McKinlay at the 1952 Union Conference to give details of how he had voted, he described this as 'an absolutely impossible proposal' and considered that it was unacceptable that 'conference might instruct TUC delegates on the way they should vote'. Efforts to refer back the report of the delegation for lack of information were defeated at both EC and Conference in 1953, and again in 1954. Reference to successful efforts to alter the votes on German rearmament have been made, and in 1955 on the initiative of Norman Stagg, the Executive began to consider the agendas in advance. In 1958 General Secretary Ron Smith was prepared to accept criticism about the failure to publish details of how the Union's delegation had voted. In practice, however, it is clear that the main decisions are made by the delegates themselves.[139]

On the major political issues of these years the UPW, particularly in the period of Geddes, reinforced the predominant TUC views. Geddes was very much a product of the style of trade union leadership in the late 1940s and 1950s, the era of those such as Arthur Deakin of the Transport and General Workers, Tom Williamson of the General and Municipal Workers and Lincoln Evans of the Iron and Steel Federation. This was a generation of tough union bosses, anti-Communist to a man and prepared to throw around their weight and their block votes to enforce their opinions. On some such matters the UPW went further than others, for example being generally prepared to accept the anti-Communist purge of the civil service in 1948, though the TUC itself wanted greater safeguards.[140] Geddes himself went further than this and in his report to the 1949 UPW Conference spoke sneeringly of 'so-called progressives' whose aim it was, he said, to 'seek to gain control or, where that fails, destroy the Trade Union of which they claim to be the most loyal members'. Some Union members objected to this and one at least thought that 'under the guise of combating the Communist menace [which was hardly significant within the UPW] Mr. Geddes was, in fact, trying to stifle discussion'. The Conference delegates did not repudiate the statement of Geddes, but neither would they agree to a ban on Communists holding office, such as obtained in some other unions at this period.[141] Geddes also generally supported the setting up of the anti-Communist International Confederation of Free Trade unions, and on this he was not challenged at Union conferences.[142]

The UPW also distributed a good deal of the material coming out from the TUC in this period with such titles as *The Tactics of Disruption* and *Defend Democracy*, and agreed with the General Council about the need to purge CP members from the Glasgow and London trades councils in the early 1950s. There was a time when the simple statement from Charles Geddes that 'those who adhered to a particular resolution wittingly or unwittingly supported the policies of the Communist Party', was said to be enough to defeat it. The need for anti-Communist vigilance was also emphasised by Ron Smith. Geddes wrote a glowing report of one TUC publication entitled *The TUC and Communism*, and this was the main item in *The Post* for 26 March 1955. He told UPW members that 'every trade unionist should be an anti-Communist' and said that those members who objected to this were simply retailing Communist propaganda. Geddes rounded in particular on J. R. Lawlor, a Communist Party member, who was at the time Secretary of one of the West Central District Office branches. Geddes claimed that Lawlor was motivated by political considerations rather than the welfare of his members. Lawlor was defended in his turn by his branch members and went on in later years to become an Assistant Secretary of the Union. So much had times changed that when he died eighteen years later, he received a glowing tribute from Geddes's successor Tom Jackson. Two other UPW officers have also been CP members. Internal discussion has long since revealed strong opposition within the UPW to the 'official' line on such issues as German rearmament and unilateralism. The Union also strongly opposed the British invasion of the Suez Canal in 1956. Gradually attitudes changed on industrial matters also.[143]

The same strongly anti-Communist ideas were fiercely expressed by Geddes when he was TUC President. Soon after taking up his position in September 1954, he wrote a newspaper article expressing his view of the achievements of the TUC:

No organisation in the world has played a more important part in saving the Western World from the menace of International Communism. Old women of both sexes who sit in hotel lounges and swear at the TUC should remember this. It was the TUC which prevented Communism from spreading in Great Britain in the post-war years and is largely responsible for the steady decline in the influence which the Communist Party of Great Britain exercises among the workers today.

It is interesting to note that Geddes was also a strong and early supporter of the European Economic Community, largely, it would seem, for political reasons.[144]

Although, as indicated elsewhere, Geddes did not always have things his own way
on such matters, he was in favour of the expulsions from the Labour Party of
Aneurin Bevan and others in 1955 for their opposition to German rearmament. He
justified this in a speech to trade unionists in Manchester in March 1955, which
was much attacked in the press at the time:[145]

I believe every man has a right to his conscience, but when personal conscience
interferes with the good of the party, then personal conscience must give way to
the party.

In keeping with this disciplinarian view Geddes also spoke out against unofficial
strikes of all kinds, and advocated the strongest methods of dealing with them.[146]

> The problem must be resolved by the trade unions and employers stating publicly
> that they will refuse to recognise or deal with the leaders of an unofficial strike.
> The trade unions should amend their rules giving the executive body power to
> expel immediately the leaders of such strikes.

Some of the same stern attitudes are to be found in the issues of economic policy
which were debated in the late 1940s and early 1950s. The issue of loyalty to the
post-war Labour Government was one which helped to induce some of the violent
feelings whose expressions have been quoted. This loyalty was severely tested when
the Labour Government from 1948 onwards was attempting to hold down wage
increases.[147] Following the devaluation of the pound on 18 September 1949, TUC
leaders met Chancellor of the Exchequer Sir Stafford Cripps who persuaded them
to circularise affiliated unions in favour of 'rigorous restraint on all wages, salaries
and dividends'. At a special conference of Executives held on the following 12
January, the UPW supported the line of the TUC. This did not meet with
universal approval within the Union, nor on its Executive, though it was eventually
agreed on a narrow vote. A further resolution, however, agreed to reiterate the 1948
UPW Conference decision to opposite all wage freezes, and this was agreed against
Geddes's advice.[148] However, at the Congress meeting in the following September it
was decided 'to abandon any further policy of wage restraint', and it was largely for
this reason that the General Council's report was rejected. Efforts at the 1951 UPW
Conference by Fred Moss of the Metropolitan District and others to challenge the
fact that the UPW had supported the General Council were brushed aside by
Geddes and lost.[149] On economic matters with a less direct effect on his members,
Geddes supported a moderate line without so much internal criticism. This applied
to the discussions on nationalisation at Labour Party and TUC following the
election of the Conservatives in 1951. Geddes's speech to the 1953 TUC was afterwards remembered as presenting a case to '"go slow" on nationalisation' that was
clear, eloquent and effective.[150]

In the period following the collapse of the Labour Government's wages policy in
1951, there was a good deal of discussion about alternative economic policies in the
trade union movement. An interest in ordered and co-ordinated wage bargaining
among leaders of Post Office trade unionism is something that goes back a long way,
certainly before the foundation of the UPW. Geddes was at the centre of the discussion of such matters in the 1950s. For one thing, he favoured a stronger role for the
TUC in being able to intervene in industrial disputes, partly in order to enforce a

form of centralised discipline.[151] During his period as President, the Economic Committee of the TUC worked out what was known as 'the Geddes Plan'. This included many elements which were to become commonplace in the discussions of the National Economic Development Council and corporate planning machinery a decade later. Instead of annual wage claims, it was argued, there should be joint reviews with employers of production, prices and other factors. This, said one commentator, 'would mean much closer links between all unions, and much more central control over economic planning'. In a speech outlining his ideas in October 1956, Geddes explained the thinking behind them:

> What I cannot understand is, if the trade union movement and its spokesmen demand a controlled economy, whether they believe that you can succeed by having a trade union movement, which is, after all, at present like a series of guerrilla groups in the jungle . . .
> If we, the workers, persist in claiming that the only way we can improve our standards is by increased wages, we shall, in fact, inevitably reduce our standards because sooner or later we shall be overtaken by our own policy.[152]

Such ideas were to be a great deal more important for the future than they proved at the time. The development of greater industrial militancy initiated by the railway strike of May–June 1955 and culminating perhaps in the London bus strike of 1958 helped to create a less conciliatory climate. The 1956 TUC unanimously rejected wage restraint, and by 1961 Geddes's successor Ron Smith moved on behalf of the General Council a resolution protesting about the Selwyn Lloyd pay pause, against which UPW members themselves were to take action in the following January.[153]

If the Union's interests by the early 1960s had shifted away from planning the economy as a whole, they did take up in that period a theme which has also gone deep into the long-term preoccupations of the leaders of Post Office trade unionism. This has been the matter of the organisation of the TUC itself. As a pioneer industrial union, the UPW has always been interested in the greater co-ordinating of trade union effort. The 1962 UPW Annual Conference passed a motion from the Leeds No. 1 Branch of the Union saying that the TUC should go beyond being a talking shop. This initiated the long-remembered discussion at the Congress later in the year introduced by Ron Smith and taken up in the following years on the general structure of the trade union movement.[154] If these discussions did not achieve much that seemed tangible at the time, they led to an atmosphere which undoubtedly caused a good deal more centralised direction of trade union effort, in particular against the Labour Government's restrictions on trade union activity in its document *In Place of Strife*, and also in the opposition to the industrial relations policies of the Conservative Government of the early 1970s.

The same two questions of the co-ordination of efforts in the trade union movement and the centralisation of economic decision-making have remained at the centre of the UPW's intervention at the TUC in recent decades. In taking up again in 1969 the issue of TUC structure, General Secretary Tom Jackson reminded the delegates that this was part of a discussion the UPW had initiated in 1963. This led to further discussions in the General Council and at Congress in 1970–1.[155] In practice, however, discussion was held up by the traumatic events following the 1971 Industrial Relations Act and the efforts of the TUC to organise defiance of it. The UPW in general supported this line, though it is of interest to notice that it voted against some of the suspensions of unions who co-operated with the Act agreed at the 1972 and 1973 Congress. Since the Union's own interests were affected, Norman Stagg also spoke strongly against a resolution which proposed suspension of all those 'using any of the facilities of the Act'. For reasons explained elsewhere, the Union did go to the Industrial Relations Court to counter the claims of the secessionist National Guild of Telephonists.[156]

On matters of incomes policy more generally, the UPW in 1970–4 and subsequently after 1979 opposed all Conservative efforts in this direction. However, the Union has consistently supported the various efforts at planning wages which have taken place under Labour governments. Thus General Secretary Tom Jackson spoke at the 1967 TUC in favour of a 'high-wage, high-efficiency policy', and put his weight behind the voluntary efforts at wage vetting subsequently made through the TUC in 1968. The UPW also supported the voluntary policy agreed at the 1975 TUC, including the £6 flat rate increase policy initiated by Jack Jones of the Transport and General Workers' Union. [157] In 1976 the Union discussed opposition to any form of return to unfettered free collective bargaining. However, the TUC delegation was eventually prepared to accept the somewhat vaguer formulation which was carried that year, presenting conditions for a return to free collective bargaining.

There are other issues which could be mentioned from more recent years, but it will be a little time yet before it is possible to see them in any historical context. One thing that is certain however is that there has been a great transformation from the days when W. E. Clery was looked at in the 1890s as something of an oddity amongst other trade unionists at the TUC, and also from the days when the Union had to separate itself from its fellows from 1927 to 1946. There are many millions of other trade unionists now in the public sector along with the UCW and there are many more who organise large sections of non-manual workers. The UCW of the 1980s is very much more integrated into the wider trade union movement than was the Fawcett Association of the 1890s or the UPW of the 1920s. Yet Clery and Bowen would surely have recognised the same continuing preoccupation with the centralisation of trade union decisions, and with an attitude towards agreed bargaining methods that goes deep into the consciousness of those who have for many generations now been dealing with the state.

SOME MINORITIES

There can be no doubt that those who have not been white, male and above about 30 have normally been at a considerable disadvantage within the UPW. Although a good number of members, perhaps up to a third at times, have been women, they have at no time played a commensurate role in the affairs of the Union. This is discussed in more detail below. It should also be mentioned that in the late 1920s there was some discussion about setting up a 'women's auxiliary' such as existed in railway workers' unions and in the National Association of Letter Carriers in the United States. This seems to have been directed at the wives of active members, but never came to anything. There was support also for setting up youth sections, and this was agreed at the 1939 Annual Conference. Although this form of organisation seems to have had some importance within the large London Metropolitan Branch, it did not survive for long, and was only vaguely remembered in the mid-1950s as a possible example to be followed.[158]

The first Rule Book of the Union of Communication Workers included in the objects of the Union, the pursuit of 'racial and sexual equality between and for all members of the union at all levels of the Post Office and the union'. The inclusion of such aims in the Union's Rule Book might perhaps have been a matter of controversy in the past. Occasionally UPW members have advocated policies of racial discrimination, but they have never obtained serious support.[159] At one time a member of the Union propounded in the letter columns of *The Post* his opposition to 'the pollution of the white race by all those black people who are coming over here'. He also professed himself 'not interested in the human element or the trade union angle' on the matter.[160] It is perhaps not surprising that such views did not endear themselves to active Union members, though it cannot be claimed that Post Office workers have been immune from their influence. The Executive has at times taken a lead against manifestations of racialism, and in 1958 strongly supported the stand taken by the TUC against attacks on the black community in Nottingham and Notting Hill,

> recognising the valuable and important contribution that coloured members of the Union are making in the work of the Post Office, and calls upon all its members to fight against all forms of racial discrimination and intolerance wherever this may arise.

A similar position was taken by the Union publicly in the 1970s, notably when in September 1976 General Secretary Tom Jackson made a Labour Party Political Broadcast directed against racialism. Some extreme right-wing organisations have recruited members among UPW grades and occasionally, as in 1978, it has been said that they have got finance from Union members. However, their impact in the Union as a whole has not been significant.[161] In recent years a number of black members have begun to play a prominent role in the affairs of the Union. It can be anticipated that when the Union's history comes to be written in later generations, it will be possible to say much more about the role and participation of black people in the workforce and the Union.

WOMEN AND THE UPW

There is already a much longer history behind the particular position of women in the Union of Post Office Workers. There have been many occasions in previous chapters to record the events in their employment in the Post Office, the development of their inferior status, and the effect this had on the pre-amalgamation associations.[162] Thus women came from the telegraph companies into the Post Office in 1870, when their services were commended because they were 'less disposed than men to combine for the purpose of extorting higher wages'. They were recruited from 1874 into the Returned Letter Branch and from 1875 into the Savings Bank. At this time they were seen as displaced gentlefolk, who a generation earlier might have been governesses and provided the models for the novels of the Brontë sisters. In the late nineteenth century there was a great mechanisation of office skills, particularly through the introduction of the typewriter and also the telephone. This increased the numbers and reduced the social status of those who worked with these new machines, who were usually women. It was even argued at the Post Office Enquiries that telegraphy in particular was 'women's work' through some alleged affinity with needlework. By the time the UPW was set up, women constituted an important part of the poorer section of the workforce, integrated with the others by a complex network of subordination.

The most important characteristic of the situation of women in the Post Office during the first century they were there was the fact that they received lower wages for doing the same work. Women Post Office workers had their own pay scales and conditions, and usually were in their own separate workgroups with their own supervision, in part at least in response to pressure from those who considered that there was some undefined 'moral' threat in mixing the sexes at work. Women normally performed specialised tasks and duties which were considered more onerous and less desirable. It gradually came to be assumed from the 1870s that they would cease work on marriage and this 'marriage bar' had become a formalised system when 'marriage gratuities' were introduced in 1894. Those few women who stayed in the Post Office for long could never attain a higher status than was involved in supervising their younger sisters. They took on all the alleged characteristics of the 'old maid', acting as reactionary 'mother' to perhaps '200 emancipated modern misses', attacking their every smallest infraction of the regulations, and disapproving both of their membership of unions and of other such 'abominations as short skirts, bobbed hair, low necks and powdered noses'.[163] By about 1920, therefore, these older women had the responsibility of shepherding the great mass of women Post Office workers, usually girls up to their mid-20s who were supposed to look on the Post Office as a transition from their position as dutiful daughters to wives and mothers. These young women mostly lived in the houses of their parents and were considered to be in the process of searching for marriage partners. In the big cities they often seem to have sought hostel-type accommodation.

The inferior status and work accorded to the women in the Post Office and their position as temporary employees on lower wages naturally had its effect on Post Office trade unionism. As has been shown in earlier chapters, they were not admitted into the ranks of the London sorters and were never recruited to the Fawcett Association. The Postmen's Federation did however accept them as temporary members during the First World War. There were always some women in the provincial offices, usually working as telegraphists within the grade of SC&T. From the 1890s they joined the UKPCA, though they were actually excluded from membership of this body from 1896 to 1898, and there was some resentment from the men as they began to do postal work. Meanwhile some women served at counters in London and a good many of them worked as telegraphists. They provided some members and a few conference delegates in the PTCA. However they had so little impact that the Tweedmouth Committee in 1898 felt able to conclude that 'no considerable dissatisfaction existed as to their conditions of service'.[164] Women telegraphists played a large part in the expressions of discontent that followed the publication of the Report of Lord Tweedmouth, and no later account of Post Office grievances could take the same attitude.

First, however, the women had to establish their position in the associations. The 1896 Conference of the PTCA rejected a resolution calling for equal pay and women delegates spoke against it in 1902. In later years it was said that fear of the adoption of such a policy drove the women away from the associations for a time.[165] During the period of the great inquiries it became clear that divisions and differences of all kinds only led to disaster. In 1908 Lucy Withrington became women's organiser of the UKPCA and was instrumental not only in getting women into the Association but also in persuading the men that they would not serve their own interests by seeking to restrict work functions of the women, or to exclude them from doing work on the postal side. Eventually they were demanding equality for those who did the same work. The PTCA by 1910 was in a position to agree unambiguously to equal pay as part of their programme, and this was presented to the Holt Enquiry in 1912. During the First World War women, including married ones, came to the Post Office workforce in larger numbers than ever before. In 1916 the P&TCA appointed Edith Howse as the first full-time women's organiser, and by the end of the war the National Joint Committee as a whole argued for equal pay.

By the time the UPW was founded, therefore, half a century of experience dictated the attitude of the Union. There was never any doubt about the centrality of the equal pay demand, and this was part of the Union's programme throughout its existence. The importance of this was often pointed out to the membership, as this article in *The Post* in 1933 made clear: [166]

> The principle is whether in any grade two scales of payment are to be made. The difference between the payments is due not to the differing value of the work, but to the systematic depressing of the standard of the more highly paid staff by the continuous introduction of those who are prepared to take a lower wage. The claim for equal payment without equivocation or fiddling adjustments, demands to be met on broad grounds of principle. No Trade Union would tolerate two sets of pay in an industry, even if the particular details of the work demanded were selected to bolster up the differentiation, if the sex question did not obtrude. It is clear, therefore, that the state, as a settled policy definitely does employ women because they are cheap, and the results are bad for everyone concerned.

It is certain that the Union did not pursue the aim of equality with continuous and unabated energy. However, the same could have been said of such other demands in its programme as workers' control in the Post Office, or for that matter higher wages. There were times when the equal pay demand was deliberately used by the authorities to argue that claims were utterly unrealistic or to delay general increases. This happened in some of the bonus negotiations during the Second World War. At times, Union conferences voted to give less emphasis to the demand. This happened in 1924, though there was some confusion introduced when the question of equality between telegraphists and telephonists was also mentioned. [167]

It needs to be said that until the 1960s at least, the demand for equal payment of men and women was perceived by all concerned as a general goal only likely to be secured in the distant future, at the same time, perhaps, as the ending of the classification of offices for pay purposes, or the abolition of incremental scales. Thus when, for example, the claim for equal pay was dropped during the negotiations that ended in the 1927 Arbitration Court, this was a defeat for the Union's members, but so also was the general retreat that had to be made in the claim as a whole in the face of the Post Office's claims for wage cuts. In any case, the authorities always used the argument that equality was a matter for general government policy which they could not change. [168]

So long as women received lower pay, then they would always cheapen the jobs of everybody when the Post Office tried to employ them on extra duties. This happened when the extra employment of women in the Cable Room in the early

1920s was said to be 'destructive to the morals of the union'. It happened also when the authorities in the 1930s extended the hours of work of women telephonists after the introduction of cheap evening calls. There is no evidence that it has been possible to discover that any section of the workforce supported this change. The secessionist National Guild of Telephonists was able to portray the issue as largely one of women against men, but the Union mobilised large numbers of women in opposition.[169]

Some of the same issues arose on the extension of teleprinter work to women telegraphists from the 1920s onwards. Women also came to be employed in some offices on postal work as a direct effort to keep down costs. The Union therefore began to argue for the 'correct proportion of men and women' on telegraph and other work. General Secretary Geddes who himself came from the Central Telegraph Office at a time when women were replacing men on the new teleprinters, argued strongly for this. Elsewhere head offices were being downgraded to district offices and women given duties for which men had formerly been paid more.[170] This was the background of the resolution passed at the 1935 Union Conference attacking 'the growing and disproportionate predominance of women in divided and amalgamated offices', moved on behalf of the Executive by the future General Secretary Tom Hodgson. Some of the terms in which the matter was discussed can only be described as ugly and unpleasant. W. R. Williams spoke of how Hitler and Mussolini had shown that a nation could not 'afford to despise its male population' and Hodgson of 'a nigger working two hours a day for one coconut'. Behind this, however, lay the fact that no men had been appointed in Belfast and Edinburgh since 1922 or in Liverpool since 1927 to the telegraph service. Men who had trained on telegraphy were compelled to take up postal work. These changes were being initiated, as Hodgson pointed out, by the same authorities who refused to move to equal pay and 'exploited women's employment every day'. He was, however, quite unable to answer a point made by Miss Saunders of Reading:

> She did not delight at all in the disproportionate ratio of women to men; it was entirely wrong; but the blame for it lay to a great extent with the Union itself. She did not want to be ultra-critical but they must remember that for years there had been artificial segregation in small and large offices of men and women. There had been barriers set up against women, and it was said that they must not do writing and other duties to which they thought they had a claim. Women are thus placed in a position where they were to a certain extent inferior, and could not be regarded by their Union colleagues or by the Department as equal.[171]

The fact was that women in the UPW had to resist attitudes which had their origins far outside the trade union movement. It was Union members, however, who re-enforced the baleful influence of the most reactionary prejudices not simply by arguing that women needed before anything to look after homes and children, but also by accepting that they occupied a subordinate role at work itself. Thus in 1920, General Secretary Bowen told the Executive that women should perform tasks thought less desirable because there existed 'a large volume of duties that the men do not like and will not do if they can avoid them'. 'Neither do the women like them', retorted Mabel Bray, but Bowen still thought 'it is work that women do better than men'. On the indoor side, the most desirable work was thought to be writing duty rather than sorting or working at the counter, where the hours were more regular and the tasks more interesting. Women were systematically excluded from this duty and when Jennie Duncan tried to get this policy reversed at the 1939 Conference, no male delegates spoke in support. It is not surprising that she found 'the tone of the conference more in keeping with a Fascist organisation than a working-class Trade Union'. In particular she said that the 'excuse that we must await the granting of equal pay for equal work' was indefensible.[172]

It needed a good deal of social change to transform the attitudes that were being attacked by Jennie Duncan, and their results. To bring this about within the UPW necessitated strong argument from women members themselves, some of it necessarily laced with heavy sarcasm:

'Do women in the Post Office want equal pay with men?' 'No, oh dear, No!' 'Why not?' 'Oh well, for one thing, we aren't quite equal, *really*, are we? It would be silly to pretend we are, don't you think? Of course it's true that we do quite well when we are put on the same work and that on the telegraph circuit we often "whack 'em"; and when we were allowed in the sorting office we had a reputation for high-speed working. But the men never liked it very much; they said we were fools, and seemed to think high-speed sorting done by girls ought to be punishable by death! Seriously, though, we couldn't claim equality, because we don't do night duty. What do you say – the men are paid for it? Well, yes, that's true. But you know it wouldn't be fair to draw the same wage as a man with a wife and family – although it must be admitted he married to please himself, not me. Oh yes, they *do* say we are cheap labour and a constant drag on them so long as we are working for lower wages; but we try to be as decent as we can, and generally efface ourselves, so they can't really grumble at us. We never clamour for writing duties, or, in fact, for any of the "senior" duties. Don't we *want* them? Well, I haven't thought about it much, but I think it would be nice to have something to work up to – better than this everlasting slogging and stagnating on uninteresting manipulative duties, and waiting for something to turn up to take us out of it. And if we don't marry and leave? Oh, well, I hadn't thought about that either . . .' 'Is there any reason for claiming the same wages as a man?' 'Well, yes, it does rather seem so. But, I say, men wouldn't RESPECT us so much if we did the same duties and received the same wages, would they? They would say we were apeing them, and that a pretended equality had turned us into monstrosities. What's that – I think a show of inferiority makes men respect me. Hum . . .'

Some were inclined to blame the Union's leaders but another comment from a woman member in this period urged the women to take the issues up themselves:

It is astounding that my experience in a big branch shows that, although at the Committee and the General Meetings, women are invariably in the majority, yet the men nearly always decide the policy. We cannot blame them for that, even if we wanted to; and we don't. The fault, if any, lies in the fact that we will not speak, and so frequently seem content to be led, rather than attempting to give a lead.[173]

It was to be many years before these attitudes were changed and throughout the period the issue of unequal pay remained at the centre of concern. Although the

1919 Sex Disqualification (Removal) Act contained the provision that 'a person shall not be disqualified by sex on marriage from the exercise of any public function', it did little to alter the basic problem. In 1924 the National Whitley Council official side ruled that unequal pay was not a matter for negotiations and the staff side began their own separate agitation on the issue.[174] The need for an overall political consideration of the issue was frequently given as an excuse in many negotiations with government departments during the next thirty years. It became virtually a standard reply from Chancellors of the Exchequer that the economic problems they were currently dealing with – whatever they happened to be – were so grave as to preclude consideration of such a major change.[175]

The demand for equal pay continued to be taken up at various times during the 1920s and 1930s. It was certainly part of the UPW's 1920 wage claim, though it was dropped in 1927. There were many other issues with regard to women's inequality that needed to be considered also.[176] At times equal pay seemed so difficult to achieve that male UPW leaders saw as an alternative 'child endowment' or family allowances.[177] During the period the most comprehensive consideration of the issues was by the Tomlin Royal Commission on the Civil Service which reported in 1931. Partly because the unions themselves were unable to present a consistent position, Tomlin and his colleagues provided a good excuse for subsequent official inaction by failing to agree about the marriage bar and equal pay. They did however popularise the phrase 'fair field and no favours' which then became a rallying cry. They also advocated common means of entry and promotion, even while doubting whether it was 'possible to introduce aggregation' for 'Post Office manipulative staff '. The special Whitley Council Committee on women's questions drew up lists of grades reserved for one sex and tried to encourage aggregation of men and women within them. In the Post Office similar lists were drawn up and common entry encouraged for some of the higher posts.[178]

In the mid-1930s general propaganda for equality was put forward by the UPW and other civil service unions. In *The Post* there were articles that consciously condemned the proposition that 'Women's Place is in the Home' on the grounds that this was 'to condemn her unthinkingly to a prison of four walls'. Full publicity was also given to various efforts of the National Whitley Council. The CSCA perhaps discussed the issue more extensively in the period and also more imaginatively, as can be seen from one contribution to their journal:

> I was young when I joined the Branch Committee.
> And full of ideas – which was rather a pity,
> For they looked surprised and said to me,
> *'The Clerical Assistant makes the tea'!*
> But I vowed I wouldn't remain so meek
> Shouted 'equal pay' and 'the five-day week'
> But they only smiled saying, 'let it be'
> *'The Clerical Assistant makes the tea'!*[179]

It was propaganda such as this that began to have an effect, and on 2 April 1936 the Government was defeated in a Parliamentary vote on equal pay for common civil service classes. This was, however, soon afterwards reversed by being turned into an issue of confidence. As a result of such pressure, the Treasury came to accept that the level of inequality in wages would have to be reduced. In 1937 the National

Whitley Council negotiated that as a general rule women should get 80 per cent on the maximum, and this matter came into the UPW 1938 arbitration discussions. In fact it seems in most cases to have been nearer 75 per cent, though women CC&Ts got 77·5 per cent of the male wage.[180]

It was the advent of war in 1939 that was followed by perhaps the biggest changes in the situation of women in the civil service and the Post Office. Although women did all the jobs normally done by men as sorters, counter clerks and postmen, they continued to do so at inferior wages and conditions and on a 'temporary' basis. This provided a new impetus for demands for equal pay. In 1944 the House of Commons went so far as to vote for 'the rate for the job' in education, and it was soon after this that a Royal Commission on Equal Pay was appointed, eventually reporting in 1946.[181] The Union presented to the Royal Commission the general view that equal pay should only be obtained on the basis of women doing the same jobs as men, including working at night. It was possible for Charles Geddes to assert that the UPW was not 'for equality between men and women' but for 'equal pay for equal work irrespective of sex'. The problem would not, however, be resolved so easily. In practice the Post Office authorities argued for the same thing when they spoke against 'interfering in the existing wage structures', and this was essentially the view that prevailed at the Royal Commission. However, three women members of the Commission, including Anne Loughlin, General Secretary of the National Union of Tailors and Garment Workers, presented the view that equal pay should be mandatory for all kinds of work.[182]

The reality of the attitude of the Union and its leaders and members became clear when they had to confront the actual employment of women in the Post Office during the war. Although there was no exclusion of women from the Union in 1939, as had been the case in 1914 in all but the Postmen's Federation, there was considerable concern about women doing driving and carrying work. The call for equal pay for such was described as a 'shibboleth' at one Executive meeting in October 1939, and the issue was avoided by dealing with the employment of women as a purely temporary phenomenon. When women on the Executive in October 1940 tried to get the Union to negotiate on the rate following the job, they were defeated by 8 votes to 6, and in the following April the Executive agreed to take up the conditions of temporary workers but not on the basis of equal pay. The Union never agreed that women could obtain those supervisory posts from which they had been excluded before the war, nor that unestablished women should get equal pay in any circumstances.[183]

There seems to have been some change in the attitude of the Union leadership from about the middle of the war. Thus in 1943 the Executive negotiated extra money for women doing evening work, in defiance of the usual argument that this would price the women out of the work altogether. After this the Executive began to take up the issue of sexual equality more seriously, particularly as a result of the prompting of two of its members, Jennie Duncan and Winifred Rowe. The issue of equal pay was taken up in Parliament by the National Whitley Council staff side, mostly through W. J. Brown, formerly one of its leading members and then MP for Rugby. Jennie Duncan and others were unhappy that only 'common classes' were considered for equal pay in the civil service, which would help only about 20 per cent of UPW women members.[184] This pressure clearly played a part in allowing the Royal Commission on Equal Pay to be established.

The employment of large numbers of women during the war had a profound effect on one aspect of women's subordination at work, and this was the marriage bar. The bar always served to underpin the basic assumptions about women's employment – that each woman was only there to supplement the income of one household until she had to set up another. It was supported 'under present industrial conditions' by the majority of the UPW Executive in 1921.[185] The existence of the marriage gratuity which provided a 'dowry' at the end of employment helped to reinforce the bar. This was especially the case in the 1920s and 1930s when the mass slaughter of the First World War was said to have reduced the numbers of available husbands, and the 'marriage gratuity' made civil service women into more attractive wives. It was this that was adduced as the explanation for a vote of 3,537 to 1,396 in the CSCA in 1930 of women members in favour of the marriage bar and the lack of any serious campaign against it at the time of the Tomlin Royal Commission.[186]

However, during the 1930s attitudes began to change. Thus a number of leaders of the CSCA strongly encouraged discussion of why the marriage bar should be abolished, though they allowed E. N. Gladden, the well known writer on civil service affairs, to argue for it on the grounds of 'Social Health before Equality'. A further ballot in the CSCA was only postponed by the outbreak of war and meanwhile one UPW Executive member George Morris argued that the marriage bar 'however applied, constitutes a civil disability for women as a sex'.[187] The marriage bar was abolished for teachers in 1944 and also at the BBC. In 1944 the CSCA, who represented most women civil servants, finally voted against the system and the National Whitley Council staff side took up a campaign against it. A National Whitley Council Joint Committee including Charles Geddes and Winifred Rowe considered the matter without making any definite decision, and in October 1946 the Labour Government finally grasped the nettle and abolished the marriage bar for the entire civil service.[188]

The attitude of the UPW as a whole to the marriage bar at this point was to support its retention. When the Executive discussed the matter in April 1944 James Chalmers thought it 'a tricky question' and said that the abolition 'would worsen the prospects of the single woman'. There was a vote of 11 to 10 against taking a stand and the Annual Conference of that year voted down by 144 to 441 a resolution that it was 'an unjust inteference in the private life of an employee and should be abolished'. After this the Executive continued to defend the system with arguments such as the defence of unmarried women and redundant grades. Women members of the Executive objected to this and so also did the Metropolitan Branch of the Union which organised many women telephonists. The 1946 and 1947 Union conferences also refused to condemn the marriage bar and its defence was part of the reallocation of grades negotiations of the period. General Secretary Charles Geddes told the delegates that 'privately he thought they were right' to adopt this position.[189]

This remained the attitude of the UPW up to the time of a well-publicised discussion within the Union which took place in 1953 and 1954.[190] At the 1953 Annual Conference there was a motion which argued as follows:

In view of the rising unemployment figures and the consequential effect on the careers of single women, conference instructs the EC to seek agreement to the reimplementing of the marriage bar in the Post Office.

The resolution was proposed by Miss Moir from the Edinburgh Female Telegraphs

Branch who argued that married women were losing their 'dowry' in the form of the marriage gratuity by getting established positions, and that these women were preventing the promotion of their more junior female colleagues. It was supported by two other women with similar arguments, but opposed by Julia Benton and Jennie Duncan, who said they had never expressed opposition to postmen's wives doing other jobs.

The passing of this resolution caused a mild sensation both within the Union and in the trade union world. Efforts were made later in the 1953 Conference to have the issue reopened, but they were ruled out of order from the chair. A number of articles appeared in *The Post* later in the year attacking it, including one from a young activist in the Leeds Branch called Tom Jackson who made the interesting point that it was not the unemployment argument that actually got the resolution passed but phrases that reminded the delegates of what women's proper role and behaviour was thought to be – for example 'women dressed like bookies' wives' and 'armsful of early morning children'. The Union got no support whatever from other civil service unions for its policy, and little sympathy even from the Post Office. At the 1954 Annual Conference therefore General Secretary Charles Geddes asked the Conference to agree 'that the prohibition of the employment of married women in industry is contrary to the general policy of the Trade Union movement' and consequently they should rescind their motion of the previous year. He told the delegates that the previous year they 'perhaps had not taken into consideration all the factors' and taken a decision that 'had been to go back on the progressive thought which had been part of union policy for years'. Whatever the truth of this claim, the Conference agreed to revoke its previous decision.

This was not quite the end of the story of the UPW and the marriage bar. The same 1954 Conference, the only one in the entire history of the Union to take a decision against its application to the members, did not agree to pass a resolution against its application to the UPW's own staff. In fact it was only at this time that married women were allowed to work on the staff of the Union itself. It took even longer for the UPW to get round to abolishing the marriage bar for its own officers. In 1955 the Executive recommended its retention and this was confirmed at the Conference. In 1956, 1957 and 1958 resolutions to put an end to the practice were defeated. The issue was kept off the agenda on a number of later occasions and even when the Executive finally got round to proposing a change in 1964, they still wanted women to declare their marital status before standing for office. There was even some opposition from the floor.[191] However, this did not come about when eventually 'Kim' McKinlay was elected UPW Assistant Secretary in 1969, the first married woman officer in the history of Post Office trade unionism.

Even then, however, the issue of equal pay for members of the Union had not finally been resolved. UPW policy was always of course in support of this, and the Union played some part in the Whitley Council staff side campaign that followed the post-war Royal Commission Report. This did not prove easy. Delegations met Labour chancellors Cripps and Gaitskell in February 1948 and January 1951 only to be told that the state of the economy would not allow it. The UPW's 1949 Conference agreed to refer back a section of the Report on the basis that the leadership had given in too easily as a result. However in 1950 it would not accept a scheme for women to go on to the same incremental scales as men as a step in the right direction. At the same time, the Union supported publicly and with enthusiasm continued efforts to put pressure on the Government to give equal pay to its own employees.[192] As the economic position improved in the early 1950s, then it was possible for the civil service unions to argue their case with increasing effectiveness. On 16 May 1952 a motion was passed in the House of Commons calling on the Government to announce when equal pay would be introduced in the public service. A series of deputations to Chancellor of the Exchequer R. A. Butler, various mass meetings and publicity campaigns followed. Eventually, in his budget speech of April 1954, Butler announced that the matter should be discussed through the National Whitley Council and in January 1955 he agreed to the implementation of equal pay through a series of steps culminating on 1 January 1961.

The period of the introduction of equal pay involved a great deal of complicated discussion and negotiation for the UPW. The central problem in these discussions was whether women could get equal pay when they did not have precisely the same conditions of work. It is of interest to notice that in contrast to such discussions in earlier generations, a great deal less was heard about family responsibilities and the like, and a great deal more about the organisation of work itself. It remained the predominant view within the Union until the 1970s that certain tasks, particularly those performed by postmen and PHGs, were proper to men. The employment of women in these grades was said by one member in 1951 to be 'an insidious form of labour dilution; a potential threat to the union's solidarity and a direct threat to wages and working conditions'. Thus it was that during the negotiations on equal pay the primary consideration of the Union was 'to preserve those two grades as wholly male grades'. This remained the UPW view as late as 1973 when the old arguments about dilution and the cheapening of work did not apply, and soon such discrimination became illegal.[193] This attitude did not apply to the P&TO grade where women had traditionally been doing most of the same work as men. Thus in 1954 the Union was arguing for 'aggregation of all posts, integrated establishments and a common seniority list'. Although this was at a time when the number of women candidates by open competition was a good deal less than for the posts reserved for them, nevertheless it was possible for this to change.[194]

The greatest problems in the implementation of equal pay were in the telephonist and telegraphist grades where traditionally identical work had not been done. Women had worked during the day and not usually even after 6 p.m., especially when there was an agreement phasing out part-timers in 1946. Male night telephonists had generally shown little inclination to transfer their duties to days and a poll of branches in 1948 voted 104 to 28 against such a change. In 1955 an agreement was negotiated with the Post Office whereby women already in the service could decide to stay on the same duties at 95 per cent of the pay. They could get equal pay if they decided to become liable to all the duties men did, including night work. At the 1955 Conference there was fierce argument on these issues, with many women arguing for full equality without the 95 per cent option. In the end the telephonists' delegates agreed to it by 558 to 158 and the telegraphists by 256 to 13.[195] This agreement was not a success since men were not prepared to volunteer for days and few women at first volunteered for nights. In 1960 the 95 per cent scale was abolished for telephonists and separate 'day' and 'night' rotas introduced with allowances for the latter. Since 1975 there has been no distinction between men and women in the fulfilment of these duties except by tradition.

This was by no means the end of the issue of the subordination of women. As the 1973 discussion showed, the UPW did not accept the full implications of equal pay until it was about to be thrust upon them legally and politically. The separate wage rates disappeared in the 1960s and the separate duty rotas gradually in the 1970s. Now that there are women sorting letters and working telephone exchanges at night there is not the same basis for prejudice as before. There are certainly still battles to be won on the issues of participation of women in the Union and ensuring that their interests are served in postal and telecommunications systems. But these will be matters for historians of later generations.

THE UPW AND OTHER UNIONS

While it has been the main purpose of this chapter to make some points on the role of the UPW in the wider trade union movement and in particular matters which distinguished it from other similar bodies, a few words must finally be said about the Union's relationship to two other sets of trade unions, allied organisations in Britain and internationally.

The establishment of the Postal Telegraph and Telephone International from a number of meetings held before the First World War by European unions of postal and telecommunication workers following the 1910 postmen's strike in France has been referred to in Chapter 8.[196] As has also been indicated, what organisation there was largely disappeared under the impact of the First World War and the death in 1917 of the first Secretary Felix Koch. The same European organisations reconstituted the PTTI after a series of meetings culminating in the first post-war World Congress in Milan in October 1920. Ludwig Maier of Austria became the Secretary until his death in 1933, when he was followed by Franz Rohner of Switzerland who was succeeded in 1940 by Fritz Gmür. Stefan Nedzynski followed in 1965. W. J. Bowen of the UPW was President from the re-establishment until 1949, and Charles Geddes succeeded him until 1957. There were ten meetings in European cities in the inter-war period, including one in 1928 in London. They discussed general political matters and questions of interest to workers in the industry. The International's affiliations diminished during these years. In 1925 the Italians withdrew following on the fascist seizure of power and for similar reasons they lost the Germans in 1933 and in 1934 the Czechs and Austrians. The parallel disaffiliation of the UPW after 1927 was constantly compared to these. Despite very restrictive interpretations of the Trade Disputes Act by the Registrar of Friendly Societies the Union, having first cleared their legality, continued to provide payments for the PTTI under the innocuous heading of 'Books and papers of the Research Department', and Bowen officiated at the meetings working from an office at UPW House after his retirement from UPW leadership in 1936.

During the Second World War the PTTI Secretariat continued to exist, but its only function was to help refugees. It was re-established at a Conference held in London in September 1946.[197] Since then the PTTI has expanded. Unions from the United States and Canada affiliated by 1950. Its first Inter-American regional conference was held at Mexico City in 1957 and its first Asian Conference in Tokyo in 1959. As its affiliations have expanded around the globe so also have its activities. Thus in 1958 A. R. T. Mash of the UPW spent ten weeks in the Caribbean helping to organise various unions there and in 1963 General Secretary Ron Smith went to Argentina in an effort to act on behalf of a union whose recognition had been withdrawn and whose officials had been dismissed. Educational activities, in which

UPW Deputy General Secretary Norman Stagg played a conspicuous part, were also expanded from the 1960s.

The PTTI has over the years discussed and surveyed conditions of postal and telecommunication workers over the world. In the 1920s issues such as industrial democracy and the position of women were discussed. Since the 1950s the largest discussion has been on the impact of new technology. Surveys and discussions undertaken through the PTTI have provided background for discussions and negotiations in the British Post Office. For example, before the issue of the deduction of Union contributions from pay was taken up with the Post Office in 1959, the practice of other countries was studied through the PTTI.[198] Perhaps more important has been the re-enforcement provided for some of the general political attitudes of the Union's leaders, especially in the late 1940s. Thus the 1920 Milan Congress passed, with only the Swiss and Germans dissenting, a motion 'protesting with all energy against capitalism and militarism as the cause of war'. The Congress also protested against the blockade against Russia and against the terror launched against supporters of the former socialist government in Hungary. The UPW actively participated in a boycott campaign against the Hungarian regime, one of whose victims was the former Secretary of the Hungarian Postal Workers' Union, Oscar Levai.[199]

It should be said that such general political attitudes were not common in later years in the PTTI. Thus the 1922 and 1924 congresses decided against the affiliation of the postal and telegraph workers from the Soviet Union. After the Second World War, it seemed that this separation might end and negotiations were in train in 1943 for the PTTI to become part of the all-inclusive World Federation of Trade Unions. The Union's Executive agreed by 18 votes to 1 that efforts should now be made to involve the Russians. The onset of Cold War followed however and the PTTI, against some objections within the UPW, fully supported the anti-Communist International Confederation of Free Trade Unions set up at the end of 1949.[200] These events helped to mould some of the political attitudes of Charles Geddes and others referred to earlier in the chapter. One result of this has been that the International has had no contact with postal and telecommunication workers in the Communist world.

None of this has prevented the PTTI from supporting their colleagues who are on strike or who have faced imprisonment and other forms of repression on account of trade union activity. Political statements of the PTTI have often been in the form of generalised support for democracy and liberty. One occasion when for the UPW such declarations went beyond this was in the temporary boycott of messages to South Africa initiated by the PTTI in January 1977. This was carried out in the face of ferocious opposition from various anti-trade union bodies culminating in a legal judgement by Lord Denning and his Court of Appeal. This in turn resulted in the abandonment of the action by the Union. It has not been often that the PTTI's advice has received such publicity in Britain and affected ordinary members of the UPW so directly.

Within the British Post Office, relations between the UPW and other trade unions have more often than not been characterised by considerable distance and mild cordiality. Occasionally there have been arguments with other organisations covering other Post Office grades, and sometimes leap-frogging negotiations, but there has been none of the same bitterness that has been known in other industries. A number of these bodies have been run by those formerly active in the UPW and its predecessors. Thus G. H. Stuart-Bunning ran the Sub-Postmasters Federation for a time in the 1920s and even tried to propose amalgamation. UPW leaders would not agree until the position of the sub-postmasters' own employees was clarified.[201] The Union has made various attempts to organise sub-office assistants but has rarely recruited more than a tiny number of them, and has not been recognised as acting on their behalf.

The unions organising management staff within the Post Office, particularly what was once the Association of Controlling Officers and is now the Communication Managers Association, have naturally had closer contact with the UPW. Henry Alefounder was on the UPW Executive in its first year, and was then General Secretary of the Controlling Officers from 1921 until 1942. He was followed from 1942 to 1960 by Eric Hodgson who had worked as a clerk at UPW House, and by Sid Seaton, formerly on the UPW Executive, and then by Frank Pratt who had performed a similar function to Hodgson. His successor, R. J. Cowley, was also active in the UPW. Given the fact that members of the Controlling Officers and CMA usually supervise the work of UPW members, relations have been comparatively cordial. There have been occasional arguments, such as when in 1929 the Controlling Officers' Conference complained about a deterioration in the standard of recruitment to the Post Office. In 1939 London counter clerks even proposed a merger of the two organisations. This however was largely to emphasise their superior status and does not seem to have been taken seriously.[202]

The largest of the other Post Office unions is the Post Office Engineering Union. This was a comparatively weak and insignificant body at the time it withdrew from the amalgamation discussions in 1919, somewhat unexpectedly and with arguments about their 'craft' status which applied only to some of them. Relations were not broken off however and a Joint Committee considered some matters of mutual concern.[203] What was not often realised in later years was that the amalgamation discussions were resumed in 1929 on the initiative of the UPW. This was at a time when both organisations were threatened with secessionism and the reassertion of grade rivalries generally. Discussions were chaired by Walter Citrine of the TUC and POEU leaders visited the UPW Executive in July 1930. For its part the UPW put forward a series of proposals along the lines of what had been argued by its constituent bodies in 1919. It agreed to extend the system of Executive reservations and sectional conferences and to allow no less than three sub-committees of the Executive to cover parts of the POEU. The leaders of the POEU and some sections of its membership appear to have been well disposed towards this, but it was never thought that there would be a majority for amalgamation amongst the engineers. The POEU Conference in 1926 had rejected amalgamation and their 1930 Conference discussion concerned the reorganisation of the Union itself rather than amalgamation with the UPW. The atmosphere changed in 1931 when some work was transferred at the Central Telegraph Office from mechanics to telegraphists. Although the mechanics were secessionists from the POEU, Bowen thought that 'this was no argument against the fact that the union had broken a trade union principle'. As for the POEU, its General Secretary C. H. Smith was quoted as follows: 'Your craft has gone. Mere girls can do your job. It is time mechanics come into their own. The work is ours.'[204] This was not a sentiment conducive to further amalgamation talks, and they collapsed without trace.

The matter of closer working or co-operation with the POEU has been taken up on a number of occasions since that time. The POEU has gone from about one-fifth the size of the UPW to about half, and was largely made up of people who worked in what by the 1950s became the larger and more profitable section of the Post Office – telecommunications. In 1945 the UPW again approached the POEU for discussions which took place in April 1946. Although the UPW still wanted to propose amalgamation, the POEU would not consider it. John Edwards, POEU General Secretary, used the same arguments as his predecessors had twenty-five years earlier in asserting that they had little in common with the UPW, and really 'a closer affinity to engineers than anyone else'. Nevertheless, the UPW pressed for co-operation. A Joint Committee was eventually set up in January 1947. This dealt with some general political matters over the following period and encouraged local co-operation despite 'some "sticky" questions on which the two organisations are bound to have differing interests and points of view'.[205] The two unions tended to grow further apart in the 1950s, especially when the POEU argued in favour of the separation of posts and telecommunications.[206] It has since advocated trade union organisation that reflects this.

The UPW has nevertheless continued to press for greater unity of efforts amongst all unions covering posts and telecommunications. In 1963 it made further proposals in this direction. Early in 1967 when incorporation was being discussed, General Secretary Tom Jackson urged discussion on 'One Big Union' for the Post Office. However, the Union's members, like their predecessors in 1919, did not favour working with representatives of those who supervised them, and other Post Office unions were not prepared to go beyond arrangements for joint workings.[207] A Council of Post Office Unions nevertheless came into existence during the period when there was one Post Office corporation. As a result, for the first time since 1919, a national joint body acted on behalf of the main unions in posts and tele-communications. It did not however have anything like the comprehensive powers and activities of the National Joint Committee before and after the First World War. COPOU's scope resembled more the Whitley Council activities of the 1920s and 1930s, covering not the main wage negotiations, but some general issues such as leave, superannuation and London weighting.[208] Its usefulness came to be questioned even within the UPW, and efforts to get more substantial co-operation with the POEU following from a joint Executive meeting early in 1972 did not achieve much either.[209]

The setting up of two separate corporations in 1981 has meant that COPOU no longer has a function to perform and it has been closed down. In the flurry of discussion that surrounded this, the forces ranged against unity of trade union effort in posts and telecommunications seem likely to prevail in any new arrangement that may emerge. This has caused some unhappiness in the UCW. During 1981 General Secretary Tom Jackson noted that the old grade rivalries of the UPW and its predecessors had gone. No group was now 'continually defending [its] personal self interest and there is recognition of the greater good.' Nevertheless, the old calls of unity and amalgamation were no longer to be heard. 'Perhaps we now have a whole generation of activists', he concluded sadly, 'who knew or care nothing about safeguarding the future of P&T trades unionism.'[210] Truly, many of the hopes of the UPW pioneers will be thrown into reverse if this continues, and the UCW may have to turn out in quite new and unexpected directions if it is to serve the interests of its members and strengthen the organisation that supports them. The Post Office Unions' Committee began in 1982 and seems likely to have a comparatively limited role.

WHAT SORT OF UNION?

In some ways this situation in the 1980s has brought trade unionism amongst postal and telecommunication workers full circle. It was the gradual breakdown of grade rivalries in the early years of this century that made it possible by 1919 to set up the Union of Post Office Workers. Divisions between grades still plagued the Union in its early years, but were largely overcome in the 1940s and disappeared in the 1970s. Disunity also took generations to overcome for the modern POEU and CMA. Yet the attitudes indicated in the relations between these bodies in the past might become less important in the future as they look out into a different world where they are no longer confined within the old boundaries of civil service and Post Office.

This chapter has been concerned to describe and bring out some of the special characteristics that went to make one of the great industrial unions created in that extraordinary period of creative trade union activity after the First World War. Perhaps the most significant aspect of this were the attitudes to control of industry and industrial bargaining that have been described under the heading of 'Guild Socialist Tradition'. The long experience of state employment and the intellectual influences acting on Post Office Union leaders in the years after 1911 helped them dictate a set of ideas, at times submerged, which nevertheless came very much to the surface in the 1970s, to be submerged again, though probably not for good.

Another major theme had been to trace the break from civil service protocol to full-blooded modern trade union conceptions. Again an important stage was marked by the pre-1914 labour unrest which affected Post Office trade unionists, no matter how remote from industrial militancy they were themselves. They had built by the 1920s a history of participation in the wider labour movement which has been described. They continued, against all the difficulties, to look towards the Labour Party and the TUC. Although they did not come out in the 1926 General Strike, they suffered its consequences in being cut off from their affiliations for twenty years. This caused so much bitter opposition from UPW leaders and activists that they went to the brink of defying the law during the war. After 1946, however, the UPW was able to play its full part in the wider labour and trade union movement in ways which have been outlined. The 'Guild Socialist tradition' shows that this has not been in some simple way to the 'left' or the 'right', as might perhaps at first be thought. The Union's attitudes to such matters as incomes policy and trade union organisation do not derive from simple philosophical notions either. They come much more from specific efforts to confront the problems of industrial bargaining and to find clear solutions. Nor can the consistently unequal position of women members of the UPW be explained in some simple way, though it certainly derived from a bundle of social attitudes coming from well beyond trade unionism and the Post Office. On this matter as on many others, the Union has been compelled to make and to accept changes. UCW members have entered the 1980s with a working environment and a Union altering perhaps more rapidly than ever before. They will not be able to escape from ideas and attitudes formed over a number of generations. However, they will perhaps be convinced more than any of their predecessors that their ideas and their ways of doing things will not be, like the laws of the Medes and Persians, fixed for all time.

NOTES

1 There is some relevant material in the Cole Collection in the Library of Nuffield College Oxford, particularly in the boxes at B 3/3/E, B 3/5/B and B 3/5/E. There is also some at UCW F 580. See also above, Chapter 8, on the P&TCA.

2 Cole says in Chalmers, Mikardo and Cole (1949), p. 25, he was someone 'whom I knew well', and who 'had a great deal to do with bringing the Guild idea prominently before his members!'

3 Besides numerous references in *The Post*, Andrews set out his ideas in his inimitable way in a pamphlet (Andrews, 1946).

4 The literature on the guild socialism is extensive, especially in the writings of G. D. H. and Margaret Cole. Later in life Margaret Cole wrote a vivid sketch of 'Guild Socialism and the Labour Research Department' in Briggs and Saville (1971), a volume which also contains the so-called 'Strorrington Document' of 1914, a preliminary statement of the principles of the movement and a piece by F. Matthews on 'The building guilds'. Besides works by and about G.D.H. Cole and S. G. Hobson, see Reckitt and Bechhofer (1918, 1920), Carpenter (1922) and Glass (1966).

5 See Penty (1906). His anti-socialist views are given in (1919), pp. 6, 77–102, and support for Mussolini in (1937), p. 50. Admiring comments from the extreme right are in Murikes (1937) and Kiernan (1941), pp. 33–6.

6 Carpenter (1922), pp. 100–1, 126–8, 190–2; Orage (1936); Hobson (1938), p. 139. See also pp. 392ff.

7 Hobson (1914).

8 Cole Collection B 3/5/B.

9 Middleton (1919).

10 *P&TR*, 8 March 1917, 23 October 1919. Goodrich (1920), p. 15; TUC 1917 Report, pp. 351–2.

11 Cole (1920), p. 162. See also Hobson (1920), p. 314.

12 Middleton (1921); *Post*, 15 January 1921, p. 58, 28 May 1921, p. 536.

13 Milne-Bailey (1921). For criticism of an earlier draft of G. D. H. and Margaret Cole see F 580.

14 G. Mackenzie, 'Industrial Control', memorandum of 21 February 1923 at F 783.

15 *Guild Socialist* February 1923 and May 1923 describes such meetings. See also J. W. Bowen, Report on 'Control of Industry' in Second Congress of the PTTI at Berlin, August 1922, and Cole (1921), pp. 418–19.

16 *Guild Socialist* (December 1922); *Post*, 30 April 1921, p. 422. In a paper at F 784 Bowen rejected Whitleyism as 'foreign' to Guild Socialism.

17 Details of the early meetings are at F 580.

18 See UPW (1945).

19 ECM 30–31/3/20, 6, 12.

20 George Morris initiated a discussion on 'Is workers' control in the Post Office still desirable?', *Post*, 21 September 1929, p. 224. Andrews replied in 28 September, p. 249, and in 22 November 1930, p. 466, 14 December, p. 488, with a further attack on the problem on 25 January 1931, p. 72. See also *Post*, 19 October 1939, p. 321, 26 October, p. 327, 9 November, p. 378; ECM 21–23/1/31, 139–41.

21 *London Post*, August 1932, p. 126; *Post*, 11 February 1933, pp. 144–6, 1933 CS, p. 47. For a sympathetic summary of the new policy see Morris (1934).

22 Hobson (1931 and 1938), pp. 244ff. For some examples of support for the idea see Clinton (1977a), p. 169.

23 Labour Party 1932 Report, p. 194.

24 Details in Cole Collection B 3/3/E, Box 7, Folder 97. There is some complementary material at F 783 on these discussions from which the latter quotation is taken.

25 Cole and Mellor (1933).

26 There is a thick file at F 800.2.

27 *NT & District Post* (August 1933).

28 Hobson (1938), p. 260.

29 *Post*, 26 August 1939, p. 164, 9 September, p. 216, 21 October, p. 263.

30 *Post*, 4 June 1941, p. 21, 7 March 1942, p. 5, 27 June 1942, pp. 5–7.

31 *London Post*, January 1943, p. 5; ECM 20–22/1/43 265–70; *Post*, 29 May 1943, p. 6.

32 *Post*, 23 May 1943, pp. 6–7, 10 July 1943, p. 6, 11 December 1943, pp. 181–2; *Railway Review* (16 June 1944); AEU *Monthly Journal* (January 1944); ECM 13–15/4/43, 383. There is a separately printed report of the March 1944 Conference at F 580.

33 *Post*, 1 May 1943, pp. 416–17, 21 August 1943, pp. 59–60, 4 September, p. 77, 2 October, p. 110, 30 October, p. 132, 24 June 1944, p. 21.
34 ECM 19–21/1/44, 283–5, 12–14/7/44, 49–51, 14–16/2/45, 241–4, 24–26/4/45, 373–5.
35 ECM 24–26/7/45, 47, 49, 18–24/10/45, 183, 191–3, 24–26/4/46, 466, 469–70.
36 UPW (1947); TUC 1947 Report, pp. 519–24, 1948 Report, pp. 378–84; ECM 27–29/6/48, 499–501, 29/3/49, 690–6, and F 580.
37 *Post*, 11 April 1953, p. 242, 4 July, p. 48, 6 March 1954, p. 186, 3 July, pp. 31–3; UPW (1953a).
38 *Post*, 28 January 1956, pp. 136–8, 24 January 1959, p. 35, 23 January 1960, p. 45. UPW (1957a).
39 These developments are outlined in Elliott (1978), pp. 205ff.
40 Labour Party 1967 Report, pp. 253, 258, 1968 Report, pp. 154ff., 344ff.
41 *Post*, 24 June 1967, p. 10; *Times* (5 August 1968).
42 TUC 1968 Report, pp. 531–40.
43 At least two accounts of this experiment have appeared. (All worker-directors, including one who has served on the main board are selected by management rather than elected by unions or workforce.) See Brannen *et al.* (1976) and Bank and Jones (1977).
44 TUC 1972 Report, p. 503, 1973 Report, pp. 292ff., 521ff., 1974 Report, pp. 384ff., 548. Labour Party 1973 Report, p. 178.
45 Elliott (1978), pp. 215ff. Bullock Report, PP 1976–7 XVI, cmnd 6706.
46 *A Debate on Workers Control* (Institute for Workers Control, 1978); TUC 1976 Report, p. 547. See also 1975 Report, p. 540, for a similar point.
47 This brief account is largely based on material at F 580. See also Gnanapragasm (1980) and Batstone, Ferner and Terry (1980), and Snell, Taylor and Wedderburn (1980). For another view see 'Post Office participation fraud', *The Leveller*, April 1978, which however contains some inaccuracies.
48 *Post*, 1 April 1977, containing 'Special report on industrial democracy within the Post Office' and 30 June 1977, pp. 28–30, giving the Conference debate.
49 The structure is clearly set out in Stagg (1978).
50 Batstone *et al.* (1980), pp. III 12, III 31.
51 *Post*, 22 July 1978, pp. 11ff., 31 July 1979, pp. 15ff., 30 June 1980, p. ii.
52 Batstone *et al.* (1980), p. VI, 1.
53 Forester (1980).
54 See Clinton (1976a) for much more detail on what follows.
55 *PG*, 26 August 1911, p. 442, and all the issues for September. Stuart (Bunning) later recalled these events in *Post*, 6 May 1933, pp. 404, 406.
56 Most details are in a 'Memorandum on Negotiations with Secretariat in connection with Railway Strike' at F 353, and Transport Workers Federation *Report*.
57 ECM 3–7/10/19, 4 and *passim* for what follows including quotations.
58 ECM 3–7/10/19, 57–9; *Post*, 22 May 1920, pp. 495–6.
59 Details at F 717.1.
60 ECM 8–9/5/20, 16–19.
61 ECM 8–9/5/20, 5–8, 15–16/10/20, 73.
62 ECM 7/8/20, 16–18.
63 *Post*, 21 August 1920, pp. 155–6.
64 *The Manchester Postman* (August 1920); *Post*, 21 May 1921, p. 493. See also the letter columns of *The Post*, August–October 1920.
65 GPC Minutes, 8 April 1921; ECM 13–16/4/21.
66 *Post*, 3 September 1921, p. 211, 9 July 1921, p. 36.
67 ECM 30/7/25.
68 *Post*, 14 November 1925, p. 946; F 353.
69 See Clinton (1976b). Much the same material is covered in the very useful Adams (1977) which also has a little from Post Office Records. Almost all the relevant material is now at F 353.2, but there is a little also at F 748.3.
70 Minutes of all these meetings are in ECM.
71 *Hansard* V, 196, 1962–3, 197, 357.
72 *Post*, 1 May 1926, p. 362.
73 Adams (1977), pp. 70–2 for a fuller analysis.
74 Adams (1977), p. 48; Scottish Midland and West Highland UPW District Council Minutes for 26 June 1926; *Post*, 22 May 1926, pp. 374, 380, 12 June, p. 441; ECM 29–31/5/26, 135–6, 17/5/26.
75 These are to be found particularly in *Hansard* V, 196 and 197 and are summarised in detail in Clinton (1976b), pp. 29ff.

76   *PT* 15 June 1926, p. 205.
77   Trade Disputes and Trade Unions Act, 1927, 17 & 18 Geo V, ch. 22.
78   Adams (1977), pp. 75ff., confirmed for example by the rather defensive tone of the editorial in *Post*, 2 April 1927, p. 308. See also F 060.6(a).
79   ECM 19–21/10/26, 31.
80   TUC 1927 Report, p. 419.
81   Ramsden in Cook and Ramsden (1973). Some of the leaflets of the campaign are at F 122.5.
82   Muller (1977), pp. 144, 189. The points made here are generally in line with Muller's analysis, though he does not pursue the point about UPW MPs being able to confront their nominal employer in a way that other union MPs could not normally do.
83   See Chapter 12 below, pp. 476–7.
84   *Post*, 23 May 1931, p. 506; *DPR News* (December 1931). (One of the few surviving copies of this journal kept at F 112.1.)
85   *Post*, 3 June 1920, p. 13; F 112.
86   ECM 16–18/7/24, 38–9, 14–16/10/24, 82, 14–16/10/25, 41–2, 19–21/10/26, 34–5.
87   Muller (1977), p. 55; Labour Party 1933 Report, pp. 36–7.
88   ECM 14–16/10/25, 44–5, 2–4/2/26, 64–7.
89   ECM 16–17/4/21, 19–22.
90   ECM 5/1/44, 215–18, 29/2/44, 308.
91   Details on this and what follows are at F 112 and F 112.1.
92   ECM 3/5/30, 208, 15–16/4/30, 198. F 112.1.
93   Moran (1974), p. 91; *Post*, 13 March 1948, p. 118.
94   ECM 7/6/44, 11, 12–14/7/44, 54–5, 24–26/10/44, 132–6, 9/11/44, 141–2.
95   ECM 4/11/47, 219, 21–23/4/48, 350, 363–6.
96   ECM 22/8/45, 71–4, 9/1/46, 225–30.
97   ECM 27–29/6/48, 480ff.
98   1962 Conference Agenda, p. 53, Report, p. 6; *Post*, 10 February 1962, pp. 8–9, 25 January 1964, p. 29. See also F 112.
99   Harrison (1960); ECM 17/9/54, 88.
100 *Post*, 25 September 1954, p. 558, 9 October, p. 579, 4 June 1955, pp. 367–8, 14 November 1959, p. 621, 11 June 1960, pp. 452ff., 9 July, pp. 350ff.
101 I have written two detailed chronologies on 'The UPW and the TUC 1920–1945' and 'UPW and TUC since 1945'. For the TUC more generally see Roberts (1958), Lovell and Roberts (1968) and Martin (1980).
102 TUC 1923 Report, pp. 389–90, 1925 Report, pp. 497–8, 1926 Report, pp. 283–7; Blanesborough Report, PP 1924–5, IX cmd 2408.
103 TUC 1926 Report, pp. 481–3.
104 TUC 1921 Report, pp. 217–18.
105 *Post*, 4 March 1922, pp. 199–200, 13 September 1924, pp. 202–4, 10 April 1926, p. 294.
106 TUC 1922 Report, pp. 108, 288–91, 306–7, 1923 Report, p. 317, 1924 Report, pp. 310–1, 1925 Report, pp. 507–9; ECM 8/5/25, 230, 15/5/25, 16–17.
107 TUC 1921 Report, pp. 362–3, 1923 Report, p. 260, 1926 Report, p. 355, 353.
108 *Post* 1935, CS p. 29, 1934, CS p. 41.
109 *Post* 1936, CS pp. 21–3. For Citirine's own account of these events see his (1976), p. 320.
110 *Post*, 21 September 1929, p. 222, 17 September 1932, p. 233, 24 September 1932, p. 251, 21 September 1935, p. 222; ECM 24–26/10/44, 95–6.
111 *Post*, 15 September 1928, pp. 197–202, 10 October 1936, p. 291, 22 September 1934, p. 228, 19 September 1931, p. 254.
112 *Post*, 19 September 1931, p. 254. TUC 1932 Report, pp. 219–20, 390–400; Labour Party 1933 Report, pp. 205ff.; TUC 1933 Report, pp. 371ff.; *Post*, 23 September 1933, p. 254.
113 *Post*, 6 September 1941, pp. 74, 77, 18 September 1943, pp. 85–6, 29 September 1945, p. 284.
114 The documents are at F 353. Bowen submitted some corrections to Mustoe (1932).
115 See F 050.6.
116 For a fuller account see Allen (1960), pp. 248–9, and for UPW reaction *Post*, 31 January 1931, p. 82, 28 March 1931, p. 298 and ECM 21–23/1/31, 131.
117 *Post* 1936, CS p. 7, 1939, CS p. 4.
118 TUC 1939 Report, pp. 243–4; *Post*, 18 March 1939, p. 241; TUC 1940 Report, pp. 207–8.
119 ECM 15–16/10/40, 98.
120 *Post*, 14 June 1941, p. 5; ECM 29–30/4/41, 270, 25/3/41, 7; TUC 1941 Report, pp. 334–41.
121 TUC 1942 Report, p. 53.

122 *Post*, 27 June 1942, p. 8; ECM 28–20/7/42, 53.
123 See Clinton (1977), pp. 169–70 and ECM 29/4–1/5/43, 396–7.
124 *Post*, 6 March 1943, p. 5; ECM 29/4–1/5/43, 396–8; *Post*, 29 May 1943, pp. 11–12.
125 Labour Party 1943 Report, pp. 153–4, 213. There are copies of hostile letters on this point from Hodgson and Citrine at F 050.0.
126 *Post*, 24 July 1943, p. 28 and most of the letter columns of the period.
127 *Post*, 21 August 1943, p. 55; ECM 13/8/43, 81.
128 All this is from a memorandum by Citrine contained in a report of the 13 August meeting at F 050.5.
129 Reproduced in POC, 3775, 18 August 1943.
130 ECM 13/8/43. On 1921 see pp. 462f.
131 Reported in ECM 19–20/8/43. See also Allen (1960), p. 261.
132 TUC 1943 Report, pp. 227–31.
133 TUC 1944 Report, p. 220; ECM 24–26/10/44, 96–7.
134 TUC 1945 Report, pp. 206–7; *Hansard* V, 413, 56 & 112 (15 August 1945); 9 & 10 Geo VI, ch. 52.
135 TUC 1953 Report, pp. 397–400, 1968 Report, pp. 449–52, 1969 Report, pp. 646–8.
136 ECM 25–26/7/50, 65.
137 ECM 5–6/7/50, 23, 6–7/11/51, 84, 17/7/56, 60, 27/11/58, 104 with AD and GPC Minutes 9 September and 16 October 1958.
138 ECM 15–17/1/52, 165, AD 478/58(G), 959.
139 *Post*, 21 June 1952, p. 15, 4 July 1953, p. 25; ECM 15–17/10/52, 158–60, 20–21/7/54, 79–80, 12–14/7/55, 98, 22/8/55, 101–3; *Post*, 5 July 1958, p. 438; ECM AD 372/63(G) 16 August 1963.
140 ECM 22/3/48, 325–7; TUC 1948 Report, pp. 532–8. See also *Post*, 5 June 1948, pp. 231–3, 19 June, p. 25, 25 September, p. 385, 20 November, p. 472.
141 *Post*, 29 January 1949, pp. 6–8, 16 July 1949, pp. 3–4, 16. For another protest see ECM 19/1/49, 641–2, 661.
142 TUC 1952 Report, p. 354; *Post*, 22 November 1952, p. 567, 21 June 1952, p. 45, 11 January 1958, p. 1.
143 *Post*, 21 May 1955, p. 357, 29 September 1973, p. 1, 10 November 1956, p. 625, 11 January 1958, pp. 1–2, 10 June 1961, pp. 397–9.
144 *Reynolds News* (12 September 1954); TUC, *Industrial News for the Use of the Press*, 28 January 1955.
145 *Manchester Guardian* (21 March 1955); *Daily Mirror* and *Daily Telegraph* (22 March). For a rebuttal of 'the recent attack on Mr. Bevan by the right wing of the Labour Party' by Tom Jackson see *Post*, 23 April 1955, p. 319.
146 'How to Check the WILDCAT STRIKERS' in *Evening News*, 29 June 1955.
147 Details at F 771.
148 *Post*, 1 July 1950, pp. 8–9.
149 TUC 1950 Report, pp. 467–73; *Post*, 21 October 1950, pp. 393–6; 14 July 1951, p. 270.
150 TUC 1953 Report, pp. 383ff., 475ff.
151 *Post*, 8 October 1955, p. 551.
152 *News Chronicle* (24 September 1956); *Financial Times* (23 October 1956).
153 *Post*, 29 September 1956, pp. 549–51; TUC 1961 Report, pp. 579–82.
154 *Post*, 9 June 1962, p. 317; TUC 1962 Report, pp. 294ff., 1963 Report, pp. 315ff., 1964 Report, pp. 374ff. See also Paynter (1970), p. 98.
155 TUC 1969 Report, pp. 481ff., 1970 Report, pp. 509ff., 550ff.; *Post*, 26 September 1970, p. 4.
156 TUC 1972 Report, p. 437. The Report of the Delegates (EC 808/72) is at F 771.2. See also Chapter 10, p. 379.
157 TUC 1967 Report, pp. 542–3; *Post*, 9 March 1969, p. 1; ECM 16/2/68, 122; F 771.2.
158 ECM 16–19/2/27, 53–4, 7/5/27, 92–3, 5–7/7/39, 20–3, 15–16/10/40, 85; *Post*, 19 January 1957, p. 41.
159 ECM 26–28/7/49, 7, 18–20/10/49, 10–13/1/50, 213.
160 *Post*, 7 May 1955, p. 336. See also *Post*, 5 March 1955, p. 237 for another expression of his views, and a number of letter columns of the period, largely hostile.
161 *Post*, 11 October 1958, p. 584, 11 October 1976, pp. 6–7 and other issues before and after; Eaton and Gill (1981), p. 271.
162 See, for example, pp. 55ff., 185, 231–3ff. The general background is set out in Evans (1934) and Martindale (1938) which unfortunately have not found successors.
163 *Post* (24 September 1927).

164 Tweedmouth Report, p. 33.
165 See above, Chapter 8, p. 239 and *Post*, 13 July 1933, p. 35.
166 *ibid.*
167 *Post*, 24 May 1924, p. 502.
168 Boston (1980), p. 168, weakens her powerful indictment of the UPW and other unions by failing to take account of this point.
169 On the Cable Room see ECM 21–22/2/23, 208 and *Post*, 29 July 1922, p. 104, and on evening duties for telephonists, plate 10 and p. 376.
170 For discussion on these matters see ECM 23–25/1/35, 137, 9–11/3/35, 174–5.
171 Boston (1980), p. 169; *Post* 1935 CS pp. 66–9.
172 ECM 8–15/1/20, 40, 42; *Post* 1939 CS p. 109, 15 July 1939, p. 44.
173 Ward (1924), p. 432; Pease (1939), p. 6. See also *Post*, 13 March 1937, p. 258, for the best letter of a series discussing where real responsibility lies.
174 ECM 9–12/2/25, 181–3; *Post*, 27 December 1924, p. 507, 26 February 1927, p. 188.
175 'Equal pay in the civil service. A short history of the campaign', *Whitley Bulletin*, April 1955, pp. 65–70.
176 For two lists see Herring (1921), pp. 120ff., and (1922), pp. 370ff.
177 Morris (1924), p. 632.
178 *Whitley Bulletin*, May 1934; ECM 23–25/1/35, 153, 1–2/5/37, 214.
179 *Post*, 12 January 1935, p. 34; ECM 15–17/10/35, 41; *Red Tape*, November 1937, p. 108.
180 ECM 15–17/10/35, 72, 2/4/37, 168–9, 13–15/7/37, 42, 13–15/10/37, 108, 114, 116–17, 18–21/1/38, 166, 173–5.
181 Lewenhak (1977), pp. 247–8; Royal Commission on Equal Pay Report in PP 1945–6 XI.
182 ECM 6/6/48, 8–14, 24–26/7/45, 30, 43 and 29/1–1/11/46, 675 for the quotation.
183 ECM 10–13/10/39, 109–10, 23–25/4/40, 225, 28–30/7/42, 62–3, 46–9.
184 ECM 27–29/7/43, 47–9, 27–29/1/43, 180–1, 19–21/1/44, 266–8.
185 ECM 19–20/10/21, 70–3.
186 Wigham (1980), p. 124; ECM 19–20/3/30, 169–71.
187 *Red Tape*, April 1938, p. 473, and a number of other articles in that period; *Post*, 29 July 1939, p. 84.
188 Wigham (1980), p. 125; *Post*, 8 June 1946, pp. 336ff., 26 October, pp. 565ff.
189 ECM 18–20/4/44, 348–50, 29/10–1/11/46, 693–4, 735–6; *Post*, 24 June 1944, p. 15, 22 June 1946, pp. 39–40, 21 June 1947, pp. 16–17.
190 Boston (1980), p. 253. *Post*, 6 June 1953, p. 253, 4 July, pp. 45–6, 50, 3 July 1954, pp. 43–4. For comments see *Post*, 6 June 1953, p. 359, 24 October, p. 539 (including the quotation), 7 November, p. 616.
191 *Post*, 5 March 1955, p. 214, 7 June 1958, p. 346, 25 January 1964, p. 119, 13 June 1964, p. 410.
192 *Post*, 16 July 1949, p. 9, 1 July 1950, pp. 17–18, 28 July 1951, p. 329, 2 January 1954, p. 14.
193 *Post*, 5 May 1951, p. 166, 9 April 1955, p. 278, August 1973, p. 40, 1976 CS p. 7 for a final, unsuccessful effort to reassert this view, described by Tom Jackson as 'the last dying kick of a dinosaur'.
194 *Post*, 28 August 1954, p. 484, 29 January 1955, p. 103.
195 UPW, Special Report on Equal Pay (Telephonists and Telegraphists) (1956); *Post*, 4 June 1944, p. 370, 16 February 1957, pp. 165ff. See also F 026.2.
196 See above, p. 258; PTTI (1951); 'The story of the PTTI', *PTTI Studies* (1973); Gmür (1959); PTTI (1963). See also *Post*, 6 August 1932, p. 110.
197 *Post* (28 September 1946).
198 *Post*, 24 January 1959, p. 34.
199 ECM 20–22/1/21, 57–60.
200 ECM 18–24/10/45, 193–7, 21–23/4/48, 412–14.
201 ECM 8–9/5/20, 12–14.
202 *Supervising* (15 September 1929); ECM 22–24/10/29, 76–7, 10–13/10/39, 96–7.
203 Above, Chapter 8, p. 262, and ECM 3–6/10/19, 44–5, 79, 16–18/7/24, 30.
204 Bealey (1976), pp. 188ff.; ECM 23–5/7/30, 42–58, 19–21/11/32, 228, 232–3.
205 ECM 24–26/7/45, 29, 9–11/5/46, 477–80, 28–30/1/47, 795; *Post*, 22 February 1958, p. 197.
206 Bealey (1976), p. 321; *Post*, 13 December 1958, p. 669.
207 *Post*, 18 May 1963, pp. 309–14, 11 March 1967; 1967 Conference Report, p. 12.
208 F 139.1.
209 *Post*, March 1973, 31 March 1972.
210 Jackson (1981), p. 3.

12 Bargaining under Whitleyism, in Depression and War: 1920–45

> The record of work done by Whitley Committees in the few years they have been at work is nothing to be ashamed of when regard is had to the fact that not a single section of Government servants was prepared to use, even as a last resort, the ordinary fighting weapons of outside bodies of workers. There have been failures on the Whitley Councils, but there have been successes. Success is a relative term. When an army is fighting a hard battle it sometimes wins a success by holding its own ground. (George Middleton, MP, *Post*, 19 September 1925, p. 776)

> Since 1921 we have been steadily losing ground. Arithmetic has been used to prove us wrong. Sophistry has been tried to keep us quiet; but the lower the index fell, the clearer became the bareness of our larder, the stinginess of our standards of life. We declare, quietly but with unswerving conviction, that we have had enough of it. (Editorial in *Post*, 10 October 1931, p. 309)

> We are satisfied . . . that broad general comparisons between classes in the service and outside occupations are possible and should be made . . . In effecting such comparisons the State should take the long view. Civil Service remuneration should reflect what may be described as the long term trend, both in wage levels and in the economic conditions of the country. (Tomlin Royal Commission, 1931, PP 1930–1, X, p. 85)

The first two and a half decades of the Whitley system of bargaining in the civil service did not fulfil the high hopes that were placed in it when it came into existence, along with the Union of Post Office Workers, in 1919.[1] Although the Whitley system in the civil service regularised the method whereby Post Office workers bargained about their wages and conditions and resolved the age-old problem of who should bargain with whom, it did not by any means provide the only machinery for the resolution of industrial relations disputes. The cost-of-living bonus which dominated all discussion on civil service pay from 1920 to 1934, and again during the Second World War, was negotiated by the National Whitley Council, as also were such important matters as the level of inequality in the pay of women. However, the major wage claims of the UPW in the inter-war years were decided outside the Whitley machinery, either by the direct negotiations that took place in 1920 and 1934, or else by arbitration, as in 1927 and 1938. Even after

1939, when the bonus system was decided through the National Whitley Council, many important matters still went to arbitration.

The reason for the disillusionment and despair expressed in *The Post* editorial quoted at the head of the chapter was not so much the machinery of bargaining, but rather the bargains themselves. No form of negotiations in the 1920s and 1930s could overcome the realities of economic depression and pressures on the public sector which took the form of using the Post Office as a means of raising revenue for the Government. For all of these reasons, the advent of Whitleyism did not inaugurate a period of great improvement in the wages and conditions of civil servants. Still less did it bring about any measure of 'workers' control', or consultation of any sort with the workforce about the running of the service. Indeed, had it not been for the particular circumstances of the cost-of-living agreement for the civil service which was negotiated in 1920, it is doubtful whether any serious improvement in the conditions of those subject to it could be attributed to Whitleyism during its first two decades.

The first section of this chapter is devoted to describing some of the problems and difficulties of the Whitley structure in its first twenty-five years, in the civil service generally and in the Post Office in particular. The main arguments in public sector bargaining in this period are then outlined, and the rest of the chapter will be devoted to describing the major negotiations that affected Post Office workers in this period.

THE LIMITS OF WHITLEYISM

When the new arrangements first began there was some basis to marvel at how 'the Whitley system has taken root and developed an extraordinarily complex structure in the short space of two years' with committees in every department and a network of local bodies also. Even W. J. Brown, most critical-minded of service leaders, thought the new system was likely to provide a real basis for the settlement of grievances.[2]

For Whitleyism, as for any other method of public sector bargaining, the first problem was the old one of coming to terms with the ultimate authority of the state. When the National Whitley Council was set up, the staff side thought it had won a great victory by the formula that once the Council's agreement was reported, it should 'then become operative'. In practice, however, it soon became clear that the official side was never independent of government policy and did not intend to give away any of its ultimate authority. A special committee of the National Council was compelled in October 1921 to the conclusion that though the authorities aimed

> to make the fullest use of Whitley procedure, the Government has not surrendered, and cannot surrender, its liberty of action in the exercise of its authority and the discharge of its responsibilities in the public interest.

It had already become clear how this would work in practice. In 1921 all those with incomes above £500 per annum lost their war bonus as a result of one of the first of many Government economy campaigns. This 'Supercut' showed clearly that a determined administration could do what it liked, without even going through the motions of using the Whitley machinery. The Industrial Court, despite being an outside authority, accepted in 1925 the right of the Government in the case to take unilateral action. Replying to protests against the 'Supercut' two years later, Chancellor of the Exchequer Winston Churchill sharply maintained that the authorities could not 'surrender their liberty to take such action as may appear to them in any case to be required in the public interest'.[3]

There were nevertheless some constraints on the Government. It could be argued that the 'Supercut' case concerned only a small group, said to be outside the system in any case, and less prepared than others to go beyond protest against the treatment they received. It could also be said that, on certain questions at least, 'the Cabinet had in fact surrendered its final judgment' to the arbitration machinery. For this reason, the staff side remained very much attached to arbitration, even though the Whitley system had been envisaged by its founders as replacing it. Thus, the Civil Service Arbitration Board took on a new role under Whitleyism as a final resort in the event of disagreement. The Board was less used under the new arrangements – the number of cases it considered falling dramatically from ninety-nine between May 1917 and July 1919 to nineteen between August 1919 and July 1921. Nevertheless, arbitration was still considered necessary. The first Official Side Secretary of the National Council expressed it in this way:

> When it is clear that agreement cannot be reached, the question passes from the realm of Whitleyism and we are where we were before the establishment of Whitley Councils. If the disagreement is in regard to wages, the normal course is for the staff to apply to the Arbitration Board. The establishment of Whitley Councils, therefore, has not affected constitutionally, the position of the Arbitration Board.

Despite this, the 1921 Geddes Committee on public expenditure, as part of its efforts to reduce Government spending, recommended the abolition of the Board. This was clearly less because of the cost of running the Board – a mere £1,886 per annum – than because it could 'authorise expenditure without the authority of the Chancellor of the Exchequer', which the Whitley Council machinery could not. The Conservative Chancellor of the Exchequer, Sir Robert Horne, in any case convinced himself that the Board could not co-exist with Whitleyism and in February 1922 announced its abolition, along with the placing of MPs on the official side of the main Whitley Council.[4]

This was followed by a campaign of surprising scope and intensity for the re-establishment of arbitration machinery, run through the National Whitley Council staff side, and a body specially set up by the union leaders and called the Civil Service Joint Defence Committee. The enthusiasm with which this cause was taken up can be attributed to a determination to erect a barrier against Treasury efforts to limit public spending at a time when efforts to cut Government expenditure were taking on the character of a political crusade. For the UPW there was an additional reason to support the Arbitration Board, since working through it gave them more ability to deal with questions of pay without direct consultation with weaker and smaller unions.[5] The campaign had the support of all sections of civil service trade unionism, and the leadership of a number of old hands at Parliamentary lobbying. An exception was Stuart-Bunning, still Staff Side Chairman, but increasingly out of sympathy with the aspirations of his colleagues. The campaign's success owed much to the fact that it was conducted during a period of exceptional political uncertainty, with no less than three general elections and five separate administrations in the space of little over two years from 1922–4.

The first statement in defence of the Arbitration Board was published in April 1922, and union leaders then organised a series of lobbying activities aimed at putting pressure on Ministers, MPs and Parliamentary candidates. On 15 May, a delegation met the Chancellor of the Exchequer, and on the following day a meeting of over forty MPs was organised. On 27 July Charles Ammon of the UPW, then a newly elected MP, managed to get a Parliamentary Debate on the issue in which only members of the Government defended its decision and they with 'unexpected weakness'. During the November 1922 General Election virtually all the candidates were approached, and a total of 415 expressed their support for arbitration machinery though there was a fear within the UPW that some of them favoured compulsion. Following the defeat of the new Conservative administration on 10 April 1923 on another civil service issue – starting pay of ex-servicemen – the Government felt compelled to capitulate on this also, so on 4 May Chancellor of the Exchequer Stanley Baldwin told the National staff side that the arbitration machinery would be restored.[6] Protracted negotiations followed, with the staff side favouring a special body with a chairman agreed by both sides, but having to settle eventually for the use of the machinery of the Industrial Court, set up under the 1919 Act, to provide a chairman. The other two arbitrators were to be a nominee of the Treasury, and one from the Ministry of Labour, in effect someone with the confidence of the union side. The scope of the Industrial Court was greater than its predecessor since it could go beyond considering demands for increases in wages and could pronounce on 'weekly hours of work and leave', as well as bonuses and other extra payments.[7] When the new arrangement came into effect it was said that 'subject to the overriding authority of Parliament, the Government would regard themselves as bound by the awards of the Court'. However, as already mentioned, the Court made it clear in its consideration of the 'Supercut' case in 1925, that it regarded itself as bound by the policies of the Government. The staff side therefore aimed to weaken this link by getting the tribunal formally separated from the Industrial Court. This was done in 1936, though Sir Harold Morris was Chairman from 1926 and retained that position until 1942.[8]

It is not easy to measure the results of this system, as against any possible alternatives. Certainly there always remained a suspicion that the Industrial Court 'whilst ostensibly impartial' was 'really a piece of Government machinery'. However, Post Office trade union members and other civil servants often expressed confidence in its objectivity.[9] In any case it became a major public forum for the settlement of the grievances and claims of civil servants, and provided a buffer between the unions and the Treasury which was accepted by both sides. The Arbitration Tribunal thus heard many of the same arguments and performed some of the same functions as the pre-1914 bodies from Tweedmouth to Holt. After 1939, more of the major issues went into the Whitley machinery itself, and the Pay Research Unit in the 1950s provided a more sophisticated form of outside reference. Increasing government pressure since the 1960s has thus not essentially raised any new issues.

Besides the external constraints on Whitleyism, there were also inevitable problems for the staff side caused by the diversity of interests and grades which were represented. To get all the nuances of caste difference represented on any committee, however large, was no easy task. The Post Office unions in general and the UPW in particular, always had to accept that on the National Whitley Council those in higher grades and smaller organisations were allowed much greater representation than their comparative strength would suggest. This made less difference in practice than at first seemed likely, particularly as the National Whitley Council itself became an increasingly formal body, simply registering the decisions made by sub-committees and informal contacts. Many major negotiations were conducted through bodies nominally entitled 'Bonus' or 'Cost of Living' sub-committee, but in fact consisting of the leaders of the main unions meeting their principal opposite numbers from the Treasury and government departments. Sometimes this led to protests from those bodies which got excluded, as the Institution of Professional Civil Servants was during the 1932 negotiations on bonus consolidation.[10]

The differences of attitude between the various constituents of the staff side did have at least one important consequence during this period. This occurred when the following circular was issued by George Middleton of the UPW on behalf of the General Purposes Committee of the National Whitley Council on 3 May 1926, the first day of the General Strike:[11]

That advice be given to all civil servants not to volunteer to perform during the crisis any work other than their own normal duties, and to report to the Headquarters of their organisations (through local Branches) any attempt to cause them to perform any work outside their normal class or grade.

This advice, issued, as Middleton later put it, 'almost as a matter of course' with the purpose of 'advising civil servants what their position was in an industrial dispute', was based on a number of precedents. It was taken up by Tory MPs to attack trade unionism in the civil service, including the participation of any full-time officials in Whitleyism, to support the breakaway union Federation in the Post Office, and to call for legislation against civil service trade unions even more draconian than was eventually passed as the 1927 Trade Disputes Act.[12] The General Purposes Committee was described in one national newspaper as

to all intents and purposes a Socialist organisation, which is manipulated by the wilder trade unionists of the Minority Movement, who seek to reduce Great Britain to the miserable plight of Russia in order to add to their own private importance and to become her despots.

One somewhat more rational service journal expressed the view that 'Personal acquaintance with these alleged firebrands would reveal the fact that a hide-bound conservatism is their commonest characteristic'.[13] The most serious result of all this from the point of view of Whitleyism was that it provided a pretext for the withdrawal from the National Whitley Council staff side on 5 July 1926 of the Joint Consultative Committee of higher civil servants, which included the Society of Civil Servants, the Association of First Division Civil Servants, the Civil Service Legal Society and the Association of His Majesty's Inspectors of Taxes. This schism took from the National staff side the four members representing the fewest people, who in any case considered themselves to have quite separate problems and dealt independently until after 1945 with the official side. Some desultory efforts were made before that to get them back, though the UPW in particular was not keen on pursuing them. The Institution of Professional Civil Servants remained loyal, and the Society of Civil Servants was indirectly represented from 1930 through its affiliation to the Confederation.[14]

This was by no means the end of dissention, and in later years the 1920s were seen as a time when 'some cynics declared that the only thing that kept the Staff Side together was the Cost of Living Bonus'.[15] As indicated later, the issue just as frequently threatened to drive them apart. There were great difficulties in reconciling the diverse interests of manipulative and clerical grades, the former represented by the 'Post Office Group' of the UPW and the POEU, and the latter particularly by the CSCA and W. J. Brown. These divisions were at the centre of many of the disputes described in the following pages, even though they were more often attributed to Brown's abrasive personality, or his breaches of the confidentiality of meetings.[16]

Many problems in the Whitley machinery derived from individual unions having to surrender some of their authority. Bowen set this out to the UPW Executive in 1932:

> On matters of common interest an endeavour had always to be made to obtain a common policy on the Staff Side. If the decision of the [UPW] EC conflicted with other members of the Staff Side, it would be subject to vote. If the Union's policy were defeated, then they would have to adopt the policy of the Staff Side.

However, this was not as difficult as it sounded, as Bowen's successor Hodgson pointed out eight years later when he told the Executive

> that the Union's long experience on the Staff Side showed that the Union could get pretty much what it wanted from the Staff Side. It was a wrong assumption to go along on every question in the belief that, if they wished, the remainder of the Staff Side could do down the lower-paid grades.[17]

This was not because the UPW got its way in every case, though no effective decision could be taken by the staff side if there was strong opposition from any of its major constituents. As a matter of fact, despite the many dissensions outlined in this chapter, the National Whitley Council staff side operated as a comparatively effective trade union confederation, particularly after 1939.

The National Whitley Council as a whole, however, did not decide many of the major problems facing the civil service before the 1940s, as George Middleton explained in 1930:[18]

> We have never regarded the Whitley system as a substitute for trade unionism. It was at best an instrument for the handling of those problems which, in the interests of both sides, must necessarily be disposed of as they arise. Whitleyism at the best is analogous to the negotiations and pourparlers that have to be undertaken by the combatants even on the field of battle. In regard to the differences between employers and employed where the issues are fundamental and arise from totally irreconcilable points of view, Whitleyism can be of little or no service. In such cases it must finally become a test of fighting power of the respective sides.

Thus at about the same time the Staff Side Chairman complained that 'full and definite powers tend not to be given to the official sides of the National and Departmental Councils to enable the Whitley system to function in the manner in which it was intended'. He pointed out how much was being decided outside the machinery itself and the difficulties of staff side representatives in getting time off to attend meetings. It later became the conventional wisdom that the first year or two was a 'golden age' after which 'there was hardly anything constructive done'. From then and until 1939 it was said that 'the Staff Side say what they like, but the Official Side do what they like'.[19]

'Whatever Whitleyism was', it became clear within months of its beginning, 'it was never "control", though undoubtedly it was put forward to satisfy the demand.' Before the system was two years old, UPW General Secretary Bowen regarded the 'control' it gave not in terms of the participation of the workforce in decision-making, but more as an increase in their responsibilities making them consider 'the question of output', 'improving methods' and even 'discipline'. When the advent of war in 1939 'brought the Staff Side to a position of effectiveness, responsibility and power it had never achieved before', this happened because the workforce was prepared to accept poorer conditions and wage increases a good way behind prices.[20] When the UPW again began to take up the demand on workers' control at this time, Whitleyism was not seen as having much to do with it. Nevertheless there can be no doubt that the scope of Whitley discussions was expanded during the war to carry such questions as 'development and status' which had previously been taboo. As a result the war period was later seen as a golden age for the development of civil service industrial relations because many of the expectations of the staff side representatives were fulfilled.

The Whitley Council covering the non-engineering part of the Post Office had many difficulties before the 1940s. It was said in 1943 that 'conditions have appeared to be against its highest fulfilment'.[21] Besides having two separate Whitley Councils at departmental level, the Post Office also saw a greater gulf than elsewhere between those who made up the official side and the Post Office. It was said that many higher officials would not accept that there was anything 'to differentiate the Whitley system from ordinary deputations from Associations to Departmental Heads'. In particular it seems to have been generally agreed that 'the known sentiments of Sir Evelyn Murray', who remained Post Office Secretary until 1934, were inimical to the new arrangements. Murray's frequent absences from meetings provided a source of complaint. Although Bowen could perceive in the early period 'a thaw of the old official iciness', this did not prevent the feeling that meetings were 'merely a statement met by a decision', nor did it prevent complaints about 'secret diplomacy'. Often decisions were made by the authorities without reference to the official machinery at all. Thus in 1925, hours of business at many offices were extended and Sunday services abolished without any reference to the Whitley Committees. Requests from the staff for access to acting and promotion lists were treated as a nuisance by busy local officials. Increasingly the system was considered to be 'under a cloud' and it was thought only 'outside the more formal framework of Whitleyism that greater progress has been made'. In 1927 George Middleton went so far as to assert that

Whitleyism is nationally and departmentally little more than machinery for enabling official decisions to be translated into action without the administration being incommoded and inconvenienced by having to fight the postal unions.

Even Stuart-Bunning, who could be seen as father of the system, admitted that some officials did not take it very seriously, and thought the National Council was encumbered by having to deal with the Treasury classes.[22] There were sometimes greater achievements at local level. Thus in Birmingham in 1927 the local committees stopped, at least for a time, the employment of women in branch offices, and in other places Christmas arrangements and training were amicably settled by the Whitley machinery. Work rotas, especially on the telephone side, could also be satisfactorily dealt with in this way. However, it was on a local level that it was most difficult to argue that a 'Whitley Council is not a periodic deputation from the staff', and it seemed to many staff side representatives that little was being achieved in the meetings that did take place. One participant expressed it in 1925 in this way:

> If we think for a moment of the type of item which appears on the average Local Whitley Committee's agenda we will find it difficult to prevent ourselves reaching the conclusion that the bulk of items could be much more expeditiously and satisfactorily dealt with through the machinery of the local branch of the UPW, and that the balance do not merit that the time of intelligent men and women should be wasted on them.

Complaints were also heard from the official side about the restricted outlook of the local bodies and their 'grandmotherly protection' of very little indeed.[23]

The most intractable problem for Post Office Whitleyism during this period was staff side representation. From the beginning the UPW was at a disadvantage in terms of its representation as compared to the other organisations. Thus on the Post Office Manipulative Whitley Council in 1928, when the UPW had over 90,000 members, representing a majority of those covered, it had only eight representatives, as against sixteen from all the other associations. The UPW was prepared to tolerate this, partly because most important discussions went through subcommittees, and it was rare for any vote on the National Council to reflect the different interests of the various unions. The one question where this did happen was on the representation of the breakaway National Federation of Postal and Telegraph Clerks. From the time of its foundation in 1921, the Federation sought representation within the Whitley machinery. In 1923, when the UPW, with the support of other unions, refused to allow the Federation to join the staff side of the London Postal Services Whitley Committee, the official side withdrew. This action, described by 'a disinterested service journal' as 'ill advised and precipitous' put an end to the London Whitley system for two decades, and set out the battle lines for a conflict that was soon to threaten the system more generally.[24] The efforts of the Federation to gain representation on the National Post Office Whitley Council received a fillip in the changed atmosphere after the General Strike. It was then, for reasons which remain to this day 'not wholly clear', that the staff side became 'determined to force the issue'.[25] It was easy for the UPW to quote from as far back as July 1919 a statement by the then Chancellor of the Exchequer that 'the staff must choose its own representatives', and that 'the allocation of seats on the Staff Side of Whitley bodies is a matter for the staff and not the Official Sides'.[26] Nevertheless, Post Office Secretary Sir Evelyn Murray asserted in December 1926 that although representation was 'primarily a matter for the Staff Side themselves to determine', he thought that 'when a question arose as to how far the Staff Side were really fully representative, the Official Side was bound to concern themselves in the matter'. The Society of Civil Servants and other bodies representing higher grades were now very much out of sympathy with the main unions, so took the decision to line up on the official side on this issue. In November 1928 the official side proposed to add representatives of the Guild of Postal Sorters and the Association of SC&Ts on to the Post Office Manipulative Whitley Council. The UPW Annual Conference in the following May passed by the surprisingly narrow majority of 977 to 828 a resolution which attacked the official side proposals as 'designed to undermine the constitutional rights of the Staff Side to determine its own form of representation', and instructed the Executive 'to decline to agree to the proposal'. When the staff side agreed to the official proposal by 14 to 10, the UPW, with the support of the CSCA, refused to attend any of the meetings at which the decision was effected. Then the official side in July 1928 suspended the National Council, together with all local office committees, though some of the sub-committees stayed in existence, mainly to deal with the clerical grades.[27] There was naturally much discussion at the time about the rights and wrongs of these proceedings. There can be little doubt that the UPW had constitutional right on their side, and they did after all represent far more people than those who voted against them, and certainly more than those who had seceded from their ranks. It is also clear that the same Conservative administration that had dealt with the General Strike and forced through the Trade Disputes Act, was prepared to give in to its reactionary backbenchers who supported the secessionists as 'good', or in other words less effective, trade unionists. However, the narrowness of the vote at the UPW Annual Conference showed that the intransigent attitude of Bowen and the leadership did not have universal support, and their very rigidity made it difficult to see how changes could ever be brought about within the machinery, however unrepresentative it became.

This position could not be allowed to continue, however. On 24 June 1930 the members of the disbanded staff side met and, at the bidding of the Civil Service Clerical Association, decided to try to take a further initiative on the matter. This was not only because the then Labour Government was thought more likely to be sympathetic to the established organisations, but also because negotiations with the Federation seemed at the time to be near the point of possible unity. When eventually an interview with Postmaster General Attlee took place on 2 July 1931, the UPW was at least able to claim that they had agreed to the latest unity proposals, and it was the Federation that had rejected them. When the management replied on 21 August, they said that any new Post Office Whitley Council could not cover the grades of sorters, CC&Ts and night telephonists, nor would it be possible to reconstitute the machinery in London. These proposals were accepted by the UPW and the other bodies previously on the staff side, survived a change of government from Labour to 'National', and resulted in a reconstituted Post Office Whitley Council resuming operations on 24 May 1932.[28]

At this first meeting of the reconstructed Council, Bowen expressed the hope that there would be no more 'reserve on the part of the Official Side' or 'reluctance to put down matters for discussion'. In a somewhat frosty reply Sir Evelyn Murray retorted that there were many matters when 'the staff interest was not the predominant interest' but of course 'Mr. Bowen's remarks would be borne in mind and considered in connection with each question as it arose'.[29] So, as might be expected, little changed. During the years up to the Second World War there is little sign of any major development in the functioning of Whitleyism in the Post Office. The retirement of Murray in 1934 and the reorganisation of the administration of the service in the following period led to protests about the lack of Whitley organisation within the new regional structure, but does not seem to have made any difference.

One major problem which should be mentioned in making such judgements as these lies in the nature of the records left by Whitley bodies of nearly all kinds. The minutes, reports, and even the National staff side's *Whitley Bulletin* are normally couched in such vague and oracular terms that any general judgement or measure of change is very difficult to make. It is not surprising that in the best account of the system, contained in Henry Parris's *Staff Relations in the Civil Service* of 1973, most of the general judgements, and all the vivid phrases and accounts, derive from interviews conducted by the author with those who were active in the system. Though most of Parris's general judgements have been followed in this account, there are great dangers in the type of evidence he uses. It is well known that old men forget, and select from their memories. Thus when Dr Parris quotes former UPW General Secretary Geddes as asserting that 'I used to use my local Whitley a very, very, great deal as the only way in which you could force . . . the Official Side to talk to you', he does not mention that the Central Telegraph Office of the 1930s, to which reference is made, was by no means typical of the Post Office or the civil service.[30] It had an integrated well established and well educated workforce quite different from ordinary local offices with divisions of interest between different types of SC&Ts and postmen, not to mention very different local managements. Thus at Birmingham in 1934–5, the SC&Ts demanded their right to be represented on the local Whitley Committee, and they refused even to discuss this with representatives of other grades. Bowen himself was compelled to come down and agree to their demands, under the threat that otherwise they would join a secessionist organisation.[31]

The National Whitley Council for the non-engineering part of the Post Office also had its difficulties. Looking through the minutes and annual reports, one is struck not only by the triviality of a number of the issues raised, but also with the inordinate length of time spent in discussing them, sometimes extending over many years. Thus the staff side opposition to retaining people beyond the age of 60 was raised as early as 1920, repeatedly referred to sub-committees and studied and surveyed, until at the end of 1925 the official side said in essence that they would continue to retain people as they found it convenient. Naturally enough, 'The Staff Side intimated their dissatisfaction with the attitude of the Official Side'. There was little left for them to do but register disagreement with the decision taken.[32] Naturally there were no cases where the official side registered their disagreement with the decision of a Whitley Council at any level. However, there were smaller but nonetheless important decisions reached by Whitley Committees on a departmental and local level in the Post Office. If during the first period of the National Post Office Committee, the writing duties agreement was thought to be its only important decision, in later years there were some smaller victories. Thus a small grade like the tracers could have a detailed consideration of their problems, and pressure could be placed on management on such matters as education for new entrants, promotion, the conditions of those acting for higher grades, and, particularly important at a local level, work rotas, extra duties and overtime arrangements. From the mid-1930s it was even possible to gain concessions on such important questions as the superannuation rights of part-timers.[33]

It is essential to emphasise that the problems of Whitleyism in the civil service during its first two-and-a-half decades are only in part attributable to the particular difficulties of developing bargaining machinery in the public sector. The main reason why Post Office workers and other civil servants did not get as much as they might have hoped out of the system after the very early period was much more to do with world economic depression, mass unemployment and the comparative weakness of the trade union movement as a whole. Before describing in more detail how this worked out, it is worth summarising the main negotiations of the period and the arguments and issues they encompassed.

ISSUES IN POST OFFICE AND PUBLIC SECTOR BARGAINING: 1919–45

Before the First World War most industrial relations bargaining took place in terms which assumed that each bargain would settle matters for all time. Such was the case with the Tweedmouth Post Office Settlement of 1897. After 1945, the relations between management and workforces have usually been conducted in ways which assumed frequent change. The period covered in this chapter represented the transition between these two sets of assumptions, and the arrangements that flowed from them. Between 1920 and 1945 it was assumed on both sides of industry that wages and conditions would alter over time. Such changes were thought likely to be infrequent and only on the basis of large alterations in external conditions. This is why during the inter-war period, though the story of Post Office wage bargaining will seem in some ways familiar to the modern reader, for all its slowness and the confusion of the arguments, it will also echo some of the older ways of looking at things that have been set out in previous chapters.

The early post-war negotiations in the Post Office and civil service generally took place at a time when the government, like all other employers of labour, was fearful of the new found strength of the trade unions and prepared to make major concessions. This was why the cost-of-living bonus granted to all civil servants in 1920 was generally considered to have benefited them, especially if they were, like UPW members, on lower levels of pay. Under the system which began on 1 March 1920, those whose basic scales gave them £1 15s (£1. 75) per annum received an additional 130 per cent. Those earning up to £200 per annum received a further 60 per cent on the remainder of their income, and those earning between £200 and £500 received a further 45 per cent on the last part of their income.[34] These percentages were then varied in line with changes in the cost-of-living index compiled by the Ministry of Labour, at the rate of 1/26 for every five points change in the index. Changes were normally expressed as a percentage of basic earnings in 1914. For the first years of the scheme as the table given in Appendix 40, p. 681 shows, these arrangements resulted in some increases. These were, however, wiped out by the end of 1921 as prices began to fall, remaining well below the original level for the rest of the 1920s, and though arrested on two occasions in its last period, the index fell to very much below the original figure at the time when consolidation into basic income began to be discussed. While it is certainly true that prices in general were falling, and many wages in outside industries may well have been falling to a greater extent, civil servants in general and Post Office workers in particular felt that the reductions involved particularly serious attacks on their real earnings. They argued that the Ministry of Labour index did not take account of their more genteel middle-class standards of expenditure. They did succeed in persuading the Labour administration of 1929 to lessen the impact of the one scheduled bonus drop, but the entire issue then became embroiled in the protracted consolidation negotiations which are described in their due place below, beginning on page 480.

Within this system there were also still sets of general wage claims and negotiations with the Post Office which developed according to their own dynamic. The first of these, the claim set out in 1919 and resolved in the following year, was undertaken at a time when the new Union was self-confident and prepared to undertake militant action. Although, as will be seen, the settlement was not thought to be extraordinarily generous at the time, it nevertheless achieved more than for all the rest of the period covered by this chapter.

During the years of the cost-of-living bonus in the civil service, the position of the trade union movement in general, and of the UPW in particular, grew weaker. The abandonment of the strike policy in 1921 and the setting up of the secessionist associations weakened the position of the Post Office workers *vis à vis* their employers. The long and sorry story of the UPW claim that began in 1922 and culminated with minimal improvements in the Arbitration Court in 1927 reflected this very clearly. As will be seen, the Union was reluctantly compelled in 1925 to talk of 'outside comparisons' as an argument for improvement, and the Postmaster General was able to argue initially that this provided no basis for increases at all. Following the defeat of the General Strike in 1926, he then felt in a position to actually argue for wage reductions. Though the Arbitration Tribunal handed out very few of these, on the basis of a principle it described as 'fair relativity' it only granted the smallest increase to some grades.

If the Union was prepared to swallow this in the circumstances of 1927, it did not remain passive during the next seven years, which were dominated by the protracted ending of the cost-of-living bonus system. It was partly to try to discover an answer to this thorny problem that the Tomlin Royal Commission deliberated from 1929 to 1931. The Royal Commission's proposals for consolidating the bonus were not, as we shall see, accepted by either side, and avoided advocating any change at all on such important questions as the classification of office in the Post Office and the marriage bar.[35] However, it did discuss and formulate the proposed basis for determining civil service wages which is quoted at the head of this chapter. Even if this at the time was rejected by the Union side, it had become the basis of arguments about wages in the public service by 1945.

In the meantime the abortive wage claim put forward by the UPW in 1931 used more traditional arguments. 'Wages of Post Office Workers', it was said in support of the claim, 'must be fixed according to a civilised standard of life, and not in comparison with some stages of industry which are still but little removed from barbarism.' The new element that came into this set of negotiations was the point, frequently made in Union discussion at this time, that the workers should share in the profits being earned by the Post Office. To this view PMG Wood replied:

It would be fallacious to regard the produce of this tax as a ground for increasing wages, just as it would be fallacious to propose a reduction in wages in the event of the Chancellor of the Exchequer finding it practicable to remit the tax.

The Union's answer was in effect that productivity had improved, with profits going up more than the wages of the workforce, which were 54 per cent of expenditure in 1925–6 and 47 per cent in 1929–30. The same arguments were heard in a well publicised Parliamentary Debate of 1933, whose details are set out on page 482 below.[36]

These themes were present in all the main negotiations of the 1930s described in this chapter. Attitudes and arguments were only slowly changed after the point in February 1932 when the 'National' Government announced its endorsement of the Tomlin formula quoted at the head of this chapter 'that the remuneration of the various classes should be fixed and revised from time to time by reference to outside wage limits'.[37] This was seen at the time as simply the traditional government argument, and rejected by the unions on this basis. However, there was much less talk now of the 'privileges' of government employment at a time when pensions and paid holidays were becoming much more general in outside industry. Furthermore, the unions were now thinking in terms of accepting at least some of the Tomlin argument. At the National Whitley Council staff side some thought that there ought to be something to be said for wage claims on the basis of price rises, if not of wages earned elsewhere. Within the UPW it was even admitted that certain specific comparisons with jobs outside the Post Office might be possible.[38]

However, this was not the main argument put forward for the UPW wage claim of 1937. As will be seen, the cost-of-living argument was quite decisively rejected by the UPW, and this resulted in particularly sharp disagreement with other civil servants. The main argument used by the Union was that the value of the work of all sections of Post Office workers had increased since 1927. However, although the Union was not prepared to argue about long-term trends in wages and economic conditions, it was nevertheless prepared to make comparisons with outside wage rates because there were some grounds for the view that 'outside pay has moved upwards while manipulative pay has fallen'. During the arbitration proceedings General Secretary Hodgson was able to make telling points against the outside comparisons quoted by management. However, although the Tribunal argued very vaguely that it had taken into account every possibility, it was asserted by the UPW's Chairman in 1939 'that the award is closely related to, if not solely based on, the conditions in outside industry'.[39]

During the war period, as shall be seen, civil service negotiations followed much more closely the rhythm in outside industry and were directly affected by settlements there. UPW Executive Member Richard Ruth said in 1942 that 'the basis of the Staff Side [bonus] claim had been put on the Tomlin formula', and outside comparison was the main argument for the 1943 claim.[40] By then, as will be seen, the Government had moved on to a completely new set of arguments which have a familiar ring to modern ears.

THE CLAIM AND NEGOTIATIONS OF 1919–21

This claim was formulated during the amalgamation negotiations and aimed to use all the strength of the newly unified organisation for a large general wage increase, a reduction in incremental scales, and greater equality of pay between different parts of the country and between men and women. It was negotiated at a time when general working-class militancy remained high before the onset of deep recession and unemployment, and when the Union was still in the first flush of its early enthusiasm, with a strike policy and a leadership with radical attitudes on many questions. Yet if the formulation and negotiation of the claim are examined, it becomes clear that not everything hoped for was achieved. Many of the original aims were modified before they even got to the stage of negotiations, during which management was allowed to seize the initiative and further reduce the modified aspirations of the Union. Nevertheless, especially when the cost-of-living index is taken into account, a great deal more was obtained for the members than would have been possible in the changed economic climate of a few months later. As a result the settlement of 1920 was recalled with some nostalgia by Post Office workers over the decades that followed.[41]

The original claim was formulated in the most general terms at the Amalgamation Conference in August 1919. Further progress was held up by the last of the war bonus awards on 11 November 1919, and it was decided to channel disappointment about this into a claim negotiated directly with the Department. Middleton said 'they should try to get by negotiations what they had failed to secure from the Arbitration Board'. The Wages Sub-committee of the Executive then formulated the claim with a general proposal that incremental scales should not be above fifteen steps, against up to twenty-six then in existence, that London scales should be reduced from three to one and those in the provinces from five to two. The Sub-committee proposed a general minimum at 18 years of age of £1 5s (£1. 25) per week for London (as against 19s (95p)) –a 32 per cent increase – £1 3s (£1. 15) in larger provincial offices (against 18s (90p)) – 28 per cent, and £1 1s (£1. 05) in the smaller offices (against 15–17s (75–85p)) – 24 to 40 per cent. For most of the smaller grades it was proposed to demand the equality they had always asked – porters with postmen, tracers with sorters and so forth. For the women it was proposed to ask £1 less on the maximum, the Sub-committee being of the opinion that 'the present was not an opportune time' for demanding either equality or the same level of increase for all members.

It is an interesting comment on the state of mind of Post Office workers as well as many others that many members of the UPW Executive regarded these rather large claims as hopelessly timid, when they came to consider them on 21 November 1919. Canavan thought 'it was time to get rid of the scale business altogether' and though others were not prepared to go as far as that Baker was of the opinion that the mere reduction to fifteen steps 'could cause the gravest possible dissatisfaction to the work of their members over 30 years of age'. 'It did not matter' said Buckland 'what it cost it was a question of justice'. It was agreed to ask for ten steps, and also for two classifications only – London and the provinces – as well as equal pay for men and women. It was further agreed to ask on behalf of the night telephonists for equality with SC&Ts rather than postmen. Edith Howse summed up the general attitude by arguing that they should insist on 'a proper wage' so that 'we would get the proper staff and conditions could be improved'.

This general line was repudiated by Bowen, Baker and the rest of the Wages Sub-committee when they returned to the Executive on 12 December. They came up with the proposal for a 10s (50p) increase for all based on comparisons with the August 1914 cost-of-living figures. This attempted to be not altogether regressive, but also to avoid the more fundamental issues of equal pay and classification. As Bowen argued, this was

> not because they did not realise the full force of those claims but because they felt that when an attempt was made to homologate particular ideas and tack them into a wage claim it simply meant deferring the whole question for a considerable time.

Bowen further argued that some parts of what they were putting forward were simply impossible – thus some postmen would get a 230 per cent increase and many others more than 100 per cent. 'Such a position', he maintained, would 'give them no chance of arguing with the Department. They must be practical and put forward a claim which they could establish by argument.' Riley argued that 'the general political situation' should make them cautious.

This view was strongly attacked by other Executive members, particularly those from the indoor grades. Larsen said:

> It was the duty of the EC to carry out the wishes of the members as expressed, and not to consider whether or not the time was opportune, whether they could be well supported by the PMG, or whether they would enlist public sympathy.

Mabel Bray made a prophetic point on the classification and equal pay issues: 'If the time was not now opportune for pressing these matters forward, she feared it never would be'. Horace Nobbs thought that if they did not pursue the classification issue 'they would lose their small office membership'. 'Our members', said Nobbs, against Bowen's protestations that they had to be 'practical', 'think that they have a chance of getting such things.' Bowen replied that in that case 'we must educate them . . . it is no use putting forward unreasonable claims'. A combination of the officers and the outdoor men, who stood to lose less from the claim in its new form, secured its passing by 16 votes to 10, though fears of sectionalism in the Union led to these figures being suppressed in *The Post* along with the main arguments of the debate.[42]

The claim in its new form was now submitted to the Post Office and meetings took place on 14 January and 3 February 1920 between Bowen, Baker and Mottershead for the Union and Murray and Rover for the authorities. From the start the authorities took the initiative. They said the question of the cost-of-living claim was in the Whitley machinery, and hinted at concessions if the same thing was done with the issues of classification and minimum rates. As for the separate issue of a general increase, they proposed a sub-committee, which the Union's representatives rejected. During February the Union Executive reluctantly agreed to defer the cost-of-living issue, while publicising its willingness to strike on the issue. At the same time it accepted the proposed joint sub-committee after Murray told them that he had Treasury sanction to consider the 10s claim and to backdate it to 1 January. This could then be seen, as Middleton put it to the Executive on 25 February, as 'a bit on account'.

In the next stage of the negotiations, which directly involved a representative of the Treasury, the authorities made some concessions on the classification issue – agreeing to reduce the rates in London from three to two, and in the provinces from five to three. Lengthy discussions on 17 and 18 March 1920 forced the Union representatives into the position of considering these tiny concessions in isolation from the overall claim. At further discussions on 24 March, which the Treasury representative did not even bother to attend, the official side ignored the proposal to expand London for wage purposes beyond the postal area and also the fact that sections of the indoor force in London were already on one scale and so stood to lose in the new proposals. The official side then compounded the frustration of the Union's representatives by raising the issues of outside comparisons and subsistence standards, clearly more relevant to the overall claim, which, on their insistence, had been hived off elsewhere.

No further progress could be reported to the Executive meeting on 30–31 March, which had to content itself with sending two telegrams of protest to the Prime Minister before engaging in a desultory discussion on rumoured offers. The real offer came in the first week of April and proposed a few increases, mostly concentrated on the lower end of the scale. For example, a provincial SC&T at 21 would get an increase from £1 3s to £1 8s per week (£59. 80 p.a. to £72. 80, about 22 per cent more) and the equivalent postmen would go up from £1 2s to £1 6s (£52. 20 to £67. 60 – nearly 30 per cent). Increases were proposed for the first fifteen of the nineteen steps on the indoor scales, though only for nine out of fourteen or more for postmen. There was no way the UPW leaders could accept such extraordinarily divisive proposals, and they made this clear at a meeting on 8 April, further repudiating the outside comparisons on which they were supposed to be based. The Post Office replied the next day by offering 2s (10p) per week across the board for everyone, with 1s (5p) more on the maximum for some. It was also proposed to abolish the postmen's 'boot allowance' which had been invented by PMG Raikes in the 1890s and consolidate it into a payment of 6d (2½p) per week. A more substantial improvement was offered in the proposal to extend the London scale to the entire postal area.

When the UPW Executive met on 10 April, Baker thought that 'this would certainly not be satisfactory to our members in any shape or form', particularly because older members were still being offered very little. However, although this attitude was supported in a unanimous vote, Bowen pointed out that members in smaller offices stood to gain a lot by the reclassification scheme. 'Did ever a negotiating committee', he asked, 'get precisely what it asked for?' Against this argument there were only six dissentients on the classification proposals, and the 2s increase was also agreed 'as an instalment of their claim'. This tendency to compromise by the Union's leaders was arrested by a large meeting of members which took place on the following Sunday 11 April in the Albert Hall. The size, militancy and enthusiasm of this assembly was remembered for more than a generation, and served to fortify leadership when the next meeting with the authorities took place on 15 April.[43] Although the UPW representatives said they were prepared to compromise on the 10s (50p) per week claim, they expressed themselves unwilling to go below 7s (35p). The authorities, who seem also to have been impressed by the Albert Hall meeting, agreed to go off and discuss this with the Treasury.

A new factor now entered into the situation which decisively moved the balance towards compromise. This was the separate negotiations on the cost-of-living bonus in the Whitley Council, where during the following week the official side announced its willingness to accept 130 per cent of pre-war wage rates as a basis for the sliding bonus, as well as equality for women, at least on this offer. The Post Office authorities on 27 April then increased their offer to 3s (15p) on the maximum for male outdoor grades, 2s (10p) for women and 2s 6d (12½p) for the indoor grades. Though the two sides were now getting close to what was eventually agreed, the Executive meeting on 30 April did not show much inclination to accept these latest figures. Postmen Canavan said that 'not one of the things they regarded as essential had been carried', and telephonist Edith Howse argued that some of her people seemed likely to lose the advantages they had gained in 1918. This combination meant that the Executive rejected this offer by 18 votes to 5, though it was agreed by 17 to 12 to continue negotiations. Bowen once again argued that Executive members had to be 'practical' and that the 'Post Office was now giving out 25/- [£1. 25] to all classes' if the cost-of-living bonus was taken into account. This was not necessarily as enormous as it sounds, because prices had increased by more than 100 per cent since the rates had been set on which the increases were based. Some Executive members argued that increases being offered were now large enough to make militant action unlikely. However, at the Newton Street Sorting Office in Manchester on 24 April, the incident of 'Canavan's Whistle' showed a different attitude. At this signal from the local Executive member the entire staff walked out for half an hour.[44] This expression of discontent was less a reaction to the latest offer, than to a lack of information about it. A motion from the Manchester Branch itself was described by Bowen as 'typical of many others'. It expressed

> indignation at the unwarrantable action of the EC of the UPW in constantly withholding information from the membership regarding wages negotiations, and demanding that not less than 10/- should be accepted from the Department, and claiming a strike ballot in the event of a refusal.

After some further informal discussion the Department increased its offer to 3s 6d (17½p) for all male staff and 2s 6d (12½p) for all women. Even if a long way short of the original claim, this represented a substantial increase for everyone and was accepted by the Executive with only four dissentients, and by the Morecambe UPW Conference on 11 May by a majority of 1,447 to 195.[45]

This was by no means the end of the story. Many more weeks of negotiations followed, and it was six months before the entire issue was agreed. There were numerous details to be settled, especially for the smaller grades. The Union, for example, could not agree the Department's claim that the tracers were 'overpaid'; but had to accept a lesser increase for them of 2s (10p) on the maximum. There was also a hard fight for the auxiliary grades, and for the boy messengers. At the Executive meeting on 22 July, Larsen argued that it was a fundamental issue of principle that boy messengers should receive the same wage at the same age as postmen, and that there were also strong arguments against the 'docket system', a form of piece-work whereby the messengers were paid, up to a certain maximum, on the numbers of telegrams delivered. Another issue was the position of the caretaker-operators, who looked after remote exchanges and did some telephone operating. It was only after some haggling that the right of the UPW to negotiate on their behalf was even accepted.

When the Executive met on 7 August, these and numerous other subsidiary questions were still at issue with the authorities. By now the industrial situation was different from the point earlier in the year when the authorities had been prepared to make continual concessions, and the 'Hands off Russia' crisis, which led a few days later to the setting up of the Council of Action by the whole trade union movement, also cast a shadow of uncertainty over any detailed negotiations. Wallace thought it 'desirable in view of the critical position of affairs in outside industry to come to a final settlement as rapidly as possible'. Middleton said that because of the delays, 'the restiveness of the members was increasing rapidly' and Bowen agreed that the delays were making them 'the laughing stock of the trade union world'. However, the Executive was not easily convinced. It was eventually agreed to accept the offers on the main grades, but there was a vote of 15 to 13 to defer the case of the auxiliary postmen. After much heart-searching it was agreed to continue to try to get shorter hours rather than higher wages for night telephonists. Compromises were accepted on 11 August on most of these points, a little more being secured for the auxiliary postmen and night telephonists. As for the boy messengers, it was eventually agreed that when they were 20 they could get what postmen got at 18 in return for the final abolition of the 'docket system'. Though this only affected a minority of the messengers, it was later portrayed as one of the great victories of the negotiations.[46]

In many of the discussions on the smaller grades, which continued well into 1921, a definite hardening of attitude by the authorities can be clearly detected, reflecting not only the diminishing strength of the labour movement, but also the financial problems of the Post Office, and the increasing pressures on public expenditure of all kinds. Thus on 12 April 1921, the Post Office authorities rejected their own favourite argument for outside comparisons by refusing to pay wireless operators as much as their counterparts received in the Marconi Company on the grounds that 'the present time was a most inopportune one owing to the financial condition of the country'. Nor were they prepared to pay ex-servicemen who became postmen the rate for their age. When the authorities put forward a scale payment system for the caretaker-operators, taking into account rent, attendance, the amount of cleaning done and so forth, one Executive member told his colleagues on 20 January 1921 that 'the Department . . . did not intend to improve their wages and were only making tools of them to reintroduce the unit system'. It was however eventually accepted in the following September 'under protest'. By the time it came to the very last group of all – the three basket makers employed by the Department – they got no rise at all. Later in 1921 the authorities reduced the meal relief time of night telephonists from fifty minutes down to thirty. In the light of subsequent events, Bowen was hardly wise to attack Edgar Lansbury for 'abusing his position on the Executive Council' by raising this issue. The industrial world by 1921 was a very different one from two years before when the big claim had been initiated.

Despite the difficulties and disappointments, the negotiations had not been a failure. Both the Union and the authorities had to make tactical decisions in the new sort of battle involved in direct negotiations. If the management showed greater skill when the negotiations began, the UPW members and their leaders pushed all the harder as they proceeded. When taken in conjunction with the cost-of-living bonus arranged through the Whitley machinery, Post Office workers probably gained more in 1920 than they were again in a position to secure before the 1950s. For all the frustrations that were felt at the time, these early months of the UPW were seen with some justice in later years as a golden era of unity, militancy and achievement.

THE ABANDONMENT OF THE STRIKE POLICY, 1921

There can be no doubt that the aftermath of the 1920 negotiations marked an important watershed in the attitudes and activities of the UPW. There had been an enormous transformation of approach from the pre-1914 differential lobbying and appeals to 'middle class values'. By the end of the First World War there was a much more militant posture, and talk of 'direct action', 'workers' control' and much besides. Yet for many members this change had taken place too quickly. With the onset of large-scale unemployment in the winter of 1920, and the defeat of the Triple Alliance of miners, railwaymen and engineers in March 1921, then the atmosphere changed rapidly. Within the UPW a mood of doubt, hesitation and disunity amongst both members and leaders was reflected in the abandonment of the strike policy. Whatever the justification for this step, it cannot be said to have enhanced the ability of the Union to act on behalf of the members.

Support for a strike policy had been agreed by the PF in 1912 and by the P&TCA in 1916. The Amalgamation Conference of September 1919 agreed 'by a large majority . . . that the strike policy be a plank in the programme of the new amalgamated society', so that it would then 'become an effective fighting force'.[47] At the Union Executive's second ever meeting steps were taken to get credits from the Co-operative Bank in the event of a strike, and for the Labour Research Department to handle publicity as it had done with conspicuous success during the railwaymen's strike of the previous October. At the Annual Conference in June 1920 it was agreed to hold a referendum on a levy of 6d (2½p) per week to set up a fund. Amongst those now speaking against the policy were Edgar Lansbury who said that his night telephonists were too poor to afford this.[48] Nevertheless the Union was still using the threat to implement this policy not only on the wage negotiations which have already been described, but on a number of other issues also. Thus in June Bowen informed the PMG that the Union was taking part in a 'trade union boycott of Hungary' in protest against the barbarous 'white terror' that had followed the overthrow of the left-wing Government there. It is interesting to notice that the PMG replied not that such action was illegal, but merely that it was ineffective, and more could be achieved through diplomatic channels. The Union was also actively involved in supporting the Council of Action set up in August by the TUC and other labour leaders to organise 'direct action' in the event of war against the Soviet Union.[49]

The time was passing now not only for the kind of political concessions that these steps secured, but also for the economic concessions of the sort which had been commonplace in 1919. Unemployment was increasing, militancy was abating, and doubts and hesitations were growing in the working-class movement. Union members were being lost to the dole queue, and those remaining at work displayed much less confidence than before. As plans went ahead in 1920 to ballot Union members on the strike levy, the improvements in their conditions already described were being granted to one section of the membership after another, and Bowen privately advocated that the whole idea should be indefinitely dropped. At first few others shared his fears. Research Officer Milne Bailey, normally noted for his caution, wrote a paper enthusiastically outlining the gains made by other sections of workers through strike action. Union leaders addressed numerous local meetings expressing support for the strike policy and the pages of *The Post* were full of such statements. Later in the year 107,049 ballot papers were issued setting out the conference resolution and asking the question: 'Are you in favour of the adoption of the strike policy with the contribution stated above?' To this 48,157 members replied 'yes' and 35,411 'no'. Taking account of the probable over-estimate of the size of the membership, this was about an 80 per cent poll with at least 57 per cent of the total membership in support of the policy.

When the Executive met in early December, Ammon argued that implementation of the policy should be postponed because members would refuse to pay the extra money. Nevertheless it was agreed to go ahead on collecting from 1 January 1922. Very soon members were found to be refusing to pay. In Leeds it was said that 129 out of 627 members on the telecommunication side would not do so, and fifty out of 265 on the postal side. Lansbury, who still favoured postponement, said he 'did not believe that there was a real feeling against the strike policy. The opposition was to the increased subscription.' After further heart-searching the Executive agreed to visit the offending branches.[50] However, the situation was soon transformed by a development apparently not anticipated by the UPW leadership. A meeting of 800 London sorters on 23 January at Terry's Theatre, from which Bowen was turned away, voted by 303 to 132 to set up a 'National Federation of Postal and Telegraph Clerks'.[51]

The new organisation reflected the views of what might be termed a 'silent minority' within the UPW. Post Office trade unionism had changed very rapidly over the past four or five years, especially in London. There can be no doubt that there were many who resented these changes, especially amongst London sorters, who had themselves had a vigorous organisation of their own with a high level of membership participation. Furthermore, they had been brought very late into the amalgamation discussion. The straight-laced sorters of the old school still looked down on the postmen and other grades, and had not been carried through with the same enthusiasm to the more radical attitudes of the post-war period. It is important to notice however that they did not actually object to the strike policy. As their preliminary 'Manifesto' put it:[52]

> We of the Federation do not recoil with horror from the forging of that weapon; but we view with consternation the fact that, in the decision to use it, all the juvenile and unestablished grades will have an equal voice with those of long established service, to whom a failure of a Postal strike would prove a tragedy impossible to depict in words.

The setting up of the Federation hit the UPW leadership like a bombshell, and the existence of this breakaway body and its successors was to have an inordinate effect on the policies of the UPW right through until the 1970s. In 1921 the new organisation, which was supposed to include all grades other than postmen and telephonists, provided a way out for some of those who did not wish to be bound by the decisions of the amalgamated organisation. During April Union leaders held secret meetings with branch officials of the London sorters and telegraphists who expressed the opinion that 40 per cent of their membership would soon be lost to the Federation, but that 'should the strike policy be withdrawn the other Organisation would wither away immediately'.[53] In the Eastern District Office, it was reported that of 251 members only seventy-eight were paying the levy and 129 had joined the Federation. At the Western Parcels Office seventy of seventy-seven members had also joined the new organisation. The Executive, assisted by local officers, issued leaflets appealing to sorters at various district offices and also to telephonists to abide by the democratic decisions of the Union. However, delegates from the South Western District Office Branch were excluded from the 1921 Annual Conference on the grounds that they refused to be bound by any such decisions.

The May 1921 Annual Conference in Edinburgh gave decisive support to the strike policy by 1,123 votes to 334.[54] Middleton expressed the spirit of desperate zeal with which this decision was reached:

> The Union of Post Office Workers, when it came into being eighteen months ago, told the trade union and industrial world that it was a trade union capable of

taking its place in the front line of the working class movement. Now they were debating whether they should throw over the only weapon the worker had – the control of their own power. They had been reminded – and the people who expressed this view were more dangerous than their open enemies – that the membership might come down to 20,000 or 30,000. He did not think it would; he believed they could depend at least on the 50,000 workers who voted in favour of the Strike Policy. But, even though the figure could come to 20,000, let them have a UPW of 20,000 knowing that they were conscious of their demands and able to fight for them.

However, despite the size of the vote and the fact that the monthly membership figures reported to the Executive began to show an upturn in March, the Union's leaders were not in reality prepared to contemplate a reduction of membership on anything like that scale. They were influenced by a number of factors. One was the gloomy prospect for the whole trade union movement. On 21 March 1921 – 'Black Friday' – the leaders of the railwaymen and transport workers refused to come to the aid of the miners who were threatened with wage cuts following the de-nationalisation of the mines. A bitter lock-out followed and on 1 July the miners were compelled to accept the owners' terms. While this was going on, the Federation began to bring out a regular printed periodical and to win members outside London. Entire UPW branches went over to the Federation in Sunderland and Scunthorpe, and at Wrexham all the indoor staff did so. In March, June and September 1921, the sharp fall in the cost-of-living index produced its first, and by far its largest, reductions in money wages for UPW members, as much as £1 a week in many cases.

Faced with all these problems, the Executive decided, at a special meeting on 21 September, on the proposal of Bowen and by a vote of 11 to 10, to suspend the strike levy. They voted by 10 votes to 9 against holding a special conference on the issue. A number of branches sent in resolutions supporting this decision, though reaction in the large branches in the big cities was very hostile indeed. The letter columns of *The Post* showed a distinct majority of the active members against the Executive's decision. The Manchester Branch, amongst many others, expressed the opinion, which clearly had some substance, that the Executive's action was 'unconstitutional'.[55] The Federation rejoiced in these divisions, declared that the UPW was 'the laughing stock of Great Britain', and called on all those who were 'tired of communist clowning and Bolshevik Buffoonery' to come and join them. The opposite attitude was displayed when Bowen attended the 800-strong AGM of the Manchester Branch in January 1922, and received a very hostile reception for his role in the abandonment of the strike policy. However, those who opposed the change in line were much more likely to remain loyal to the Union than those who supported it. By the time the whole matter came to be considered at the Cheltenham Annual Conference in May 1922, a vote of censure on the Executive was defeated by 1,188 votes to 377.[56] By this time the whole matter had become an embarrassment to Union leaders and members. The money which had been collected was kept in an 'emergency fund' and used for recruitment purposes in the 1930s.

These events were of considerable importance for the future development of the UPW. It cannot be denied that the Executive exceeded its powers in abandoning the strike policy in the face of a clear mandate from the Annual Conference. Nevertheless, they were able to maintain that they acted in the best interests of the members by arresting a massive decline in membership. However, some at least of this fall would have taken place in any case. All unions suffered a decline in this period, in most cases not fully recovered until after the Second World War. Some of the decline can also be attributed to inflated figures put out at the time of the amalgamation. Furthermore, detailed figures submitted to the Executive showed that the general decline ceased after March 1921. The Executive cannot be blamed for its fears that the Federation could win widespread support for its appeals to the old sectional prejudices. However, had they been less obsessed by the secessionists, and continued their uncompromising stand on the strike policy, there can be little doubt that the fall in membership would have been a great deal less than that envisaged by Middleton at the 1921 Conference. This was not the last time pre-occupation with secessionism was to cloud the judgement of the UPW's leaders.

However profound the grievances of those who left the Union, it cannot be argued either that the setting up of the Federation served the interests of Post Office workers or that they benefited from the abandonment of the strike policy, however necessary it was to defend the Union against the secessionists. These events of 1921 left the workforce and their representative institutions divided and weakened in dealing with the Post Office management during the difficult years that followed.

THE SECOND WAGE CLAIM: 1922-7

The story of the second wage claim presented by the UPW and the negotiations which followed it will inevitably seem extraordinary to anyone used to the claims and negotiations of more recent times. Not only were the discussions exceedingly protracted by modern standards, but they were the only negotiations in the modern history of the Post Office where the management actually sought, and to some extent obtained, reductions in money wages. The eventual settlement of the claim by the Arbitration Court in 1927 was effected not through negotiation which had taken effect in 1920-1, but with the forms of appeal to outside authority as had taken place in the years before 1914. During the lengthy discussions on this claim, the hopes raised by the first Labour Government and the setbacks suffered after the defeat of the General Strike in 1926 had a great influence on the course of events. The abandonment of the strike policy, and the general atmosphere of defeat and despondency after 1926, not to mention the decline in prices and wages, meant that the Union was prepared in the end to settle for what in other times and other places would not even have provided a starting point for negotiation.

The claim itself had its origins in a resolution at the same 1922 Cheltenham Annual Conference that had confirmed the abandonment of the strike policy. The Conference left it up to the Executive to formulate a new wage claim, a task they undertook with a conspicuous lack of urgency.[57] The main problem for the Union was that with prices falling and unemployment rising, and with Post Office workers to some extent protected from these phenomena by the cost-of-living bonus and their comparative security of employment, it was difficult to present any general arguments for a substantial wage increase. In preliminary discussions, London CC&Ts argued that their counter work had grown more difficult, night telephonists wanted equality with the SC&T grade, and the few printers who worked for the Post Office said that their pay had fallen 25 per cent behind what was paid outside.[58] When the Executive discussed the matter early in 1923, Bowen tried to get them at least to drop the claim for equal pay for women, but was defeated by 12 votes to 10. Because of the wild statements of the Federation, one Executive member thought all they could do was 'to make a wage claim such as individual sections demanded whatever the prospect of success'. It was then that they hit on the idea of a scheme to reorganise the grades – the only way a general claim could be formulated with arguments about intensity of work and benefit to all concerned.[59]

It took some time to get together a reorganisation scheme, and it proved an unmitigated disaster from every point of view.[60] Though the May 1923 Annual Conference approved the idea, the authorities announced in September that they would not discuss it. A detailed scheme came out the following January, and it consisted essentially of placing all the main grades as 'Post Office Clerks' with a few minor grades like labourers as 'Post Office Assistants'. This in some ways resembled the sort of demand that the Postmen's Federation had advocated before 1914, and was widely seen by the indoor grades as an attempt to improve the condition of postmen at their expense. This feeling provided a fertile recruiting ground for the Federation, and at both Colchester and Shrewsbury it was said that all SC&Ts resigned from the UPW because of it. One Executive member said that many members now held the view – which was of course quite false – 'that the Postmen were dominating the reorganisation scheme, and they were thought to be a majority on the EC, and they would force their views on the other members'. Bowen pointed to the obvious conclusion: 'If the Report is adopted, unfortunately, as far as we are all concerned, we are told that there will be a very large number of secessionists. Some secessions had already taken place.' A Special Conference considered the scheme on 28–29 February 1924 and heard some bitter differences expressed, with Executive members lining up with their own grades. Thus Riley, Middleton and Mary Herring spoke against it on behalf of the indoor grades from which they came, and postman Buckland supported it. Bowen said afterwards that 'we had sectionalism pure and simple'. He made a preliminary presentation in favour of the scheme and then 'saw the blocks of people who were sitting silent' and 'seemed likely to disappear for good'. In his summing up, whilst attacking the scheme's opponents, he advocated its rejection and this was agreed by 1,033 votes to 632. The entire proposal, which had provided striking testimony of the fragility of the four-year-old amalgamation, was then buried for good.[61]

During the unfolding of this sorry tale, the election of the first Labour Government provided some hope that the Union's claims might now be more sympathetically considered. There was further delay in proceeding when negotiations with the Federation made it seem possible that the outstanding differences might be resolved. When this did not happen, the Union decided to give priority to the question of starting pay for ex-servicemen – the claim that military service should count in the calculation of incremental scales, and an important issue for large numbers who were receiving lower wages than others of the same age who had not served in the armed forces. However, even such a comparatively straightforward question as this did not elicit a favourable response from the Labour Administration. During the negotiations it was thought that perhaps a direct approach to Prime Minister Ramsay MacDonald might achieve something since 'the bonds were much closer than would be the case under any other regime'. Ultimately, they felt 'practically forced', as Middleton put it, and with very little gained 'in the prevailing circumstances, to agree to whatever conditions were proposed to get the starting pay question settled'.[62]

When the Executive discussed the general wage claim again following the reorganisation fiasco, much of their proceedings were dominated by the unsuccessful efforts to come to terms with the breakaway Federation. A £1 10s (£1. 50) per week (£78 p.a.) minimum wage was discussed but this was not thought likely to be popular. Neither was the idea which came from Tom Hodgson that they should take 'due regard to the actualities of the economic situation' by claiming only a £250 maximum. This clearly was against the spirit of the Conference resolutions. Harry Mottershead said that they were taking this attitude simply from 'the Union's distinct fear of the Federation'. 'It was time', he went on, that 'the Union took its courage with its own hands and told everyone that the time for fancy claims had ceased'. There was little evidence of support for such a view from the membership, however, and it was defeated on the Executive by 14 votes to 5. With some fear that they might soon be dealing with an even less sympathetic Conservative Postmaster General, the Union submitted a detailed claim for increases and reduced numbers of incremental steps for every grade on 23 October 1924.[63]

The campaign for the claim was launched with a series of local meetings in December 1924.[64] If it was easy enough to rally the members in favour of a wage increase, it was naturally more difficult to persuade the management. The main argument put forward in the opening salvo was that 'dissatisfaction with the present rates of pay exists throughout the service' and that 'the proposals were not submitted as a valuation of work, but to bring the remuneration more into relation with outside conditions'. However, since wages were showing little sign of rising elsewhere, the only way this view could be sustained was by outside comparisons of the sort that had been put to Tweedmouth, which sounded more like special pleading than rational argument. The reply of the Post Office Secretary on 15 December pointed to the very vague arguments that were presented for the claim and alleged that it would cost £6–9·5 million. Whatever the truth of this, there was certainly something in his assertion that they had not made 'at least a *prima facie* case for the revision of scales which were settled by agreement in 1920'.

Early in 1925, the Executive considered what to do next. There was agreement that they could not make outside comparisons of the sort that would 'lead in all probability to a call by the Department for a fluctuation in rates of pay according to the state of the outside labour market'. This could adversely affect such groups as wireless operators, who performed work exactly comparable to outsiders. There were other particular problems for the Executive. For one thing 'an unofficial committee' was campaigning for the London rate to be paid up to twelve miles from Charing Cross. The night telephonists were an even more difficult problem. They persisted in their desire for parity with SC&Ts, though in fact they were getting less than postmen and their claim was actually rejected by the annual conference. A delegation met the Executive to argue that the original claim was essential 'to absorb the whole of the redundancy that would be created in 1926' by the introduction of semi-automatic exchanges in London. The Executive remained unmoved by this none-too-convincing argument, and thus built up resentment amongst this group.[65]

There was pressure however for more general progress, and a letter was sent to the new Conservative Postmaster General, Sir W. Mitchell Thompson, on 8 January 1925, arguing that the 1920 settlement was not intended to be final, and in part was only catching up on what should have been obtained as long ago as 1905. The reply on 10 February was stark and unyielding:

The fact that the Post Office staff desire that their standard of living should be raised cannot be accepted as warranting the reassessment of their wages on a basis which has no recognisable relation to the general level of wages or the economic condition of the country . . .

The Postmaster General's position is that wages of the Post Office staff are at present, in general, commensurate with the duties they are required to perform, and no evidence has been adduced by your Union which offers any grounds for modifying that view.

The letter also made it clear that the authorities had no intention of conducting direct negotiations in the same way as they had in 1920. It was suggested that the gulf between the two sides was so wide that it would be best to submit the matter to the recently re-established Arbitration Board, which was already considering a claim from the supervisory grades. Further appeals from the Union for direct discussions were rejected by a management which reiterated its view that the entire claim appeared 'to be wholly unreasonable and to rest upon no economic basis whatever'.

Despite this, the Union leaders insisted on meeting the Postmaster General in a delegation on 11 March 1925. They argued for increases with phrases from the Bradford and Holt reports about the need for 'contentment' and the 'ideal of family life'. They were on firmer ground in maintaining that the cost of living had risen faster than wages since 1905, and especially since 1914. They were prepared to discuss the question of the value of their work, but not any comparison with outside employment. In reply, the Postmaster General maintained that it was impossible to fix wages 'without regard to conditions in outside industry', and though the state 'aimed at being among the best employers . . . it must have reasonable regard to the economic conditions of the country and the standard of values in other industries'. After this, all the UPW Annual Conference in Colwyn Bay in May 1925 could do was to attack the Postmaster General for 'the rejection of the elementary principle of collective bargaining'.[66]

The next move by the Union was to arrange for a delegation from the General Council of the TUC to meet Mitchell Thompson on 16 June 1925 largely to try to convince him of the need for direct negotiations. Alonso Swales of the Engineers and the builder George Hicks were at a loss to understand the attitude of the Postmaster General who said 'he was not speaking as an employer' . . . 'but as a representative of the State'. To seasoned trade unionists, insistence on outside comparisons and on the sanctity of the 1920 settlement sounded no different from any ordinary employer refusing to grant a wage claim. Mitchell Thompson grew exasperated:

It was all very well to talk about bargaining, but he assumed that when Mr. Bowen came forward and made a statement that an additional six or nine million wage bill was absolutely essential he was perfectly honest in thinking that the claim was well warranted. Mr. Bowen must also do him the honour of assuming that when he said that he thought the claim was preposterous, he was equally honest. Between these two positions, there was really no possibility of bargaining.

In correspondence following these discussions the Post Office insisted on the need to consider 'the rates payable in other industries' before there could be any direct negotiations, and the TUC reply said that any employer could say this 'as a justification for not participating in negotiations'. These exchanges led to some hints from the Union side that they might be prepared to consider outside comparisons in particular ways. This was argued by the Union's MPs Ammon and Baker in the House of Commons Debate on the estimates on 20 July 1925, and in September the TUC wrote saying the UPW was prepared to accept outside comparisons 'as a factor and a factor only'. The reply from the Post Office was that this had to mean 'the wages paid for manipulative work in industry generally'. This would have made it hard to argue for improvements, so the Executive accepted the inevitable after a 'somewhat prolonged' discussion in February 1926 and agreed to go to arbitration.[67]

These exchanges took place in the highly-charged atmosphere that began with 'Red Friday' in July 1925, when the Government was compelled to retain its subsidy in order to keep up the wages of miners, and ended with the General Strike of May 1926, whose defeat led to wage cuts for miners and other workers. During the General Strike, PMG Mitchell Thompson had been Chief Civil Commissioner in overall charge of strike-breaking. It was just before this conflict that the UPW finally sent off its claim to the Arbitration Court. The question of equal pay for women had to be excluded on the grounds that this was a general matter of policy outside the competence of the Court. The Union was however allowed to argue for a proposal to reduce area classifications for wage levels from five (two London and three provincial) to two (one London and one provincial), to allow people to enter the service up to the age point at 24 and to argue for various increases, the most important of which can be seen on the table in Appendix 38. The official reply on 21 May 1926, a week after the end of the General Strike, was 'that the Postmaster General proposes shortly to submit to the Court a counter-claim for reduction of scales in certain classes'. To this bombshell it was now the turn of the UPW to respond that no prima facie case had been made out for it. Details of the official proposals are also set out in Appendix 38.

The hearing of the Arbitration Court on these issues began on 10 January 1927, in the Middlesex Guildhall, later moving to the Headquarters of the Civil Service Commission at Burlington House.[68] The Court's Chairman was Harold Morris, KC, Recorder of Folkestone and Liberal MP for East Bristol in 1922–3 where he had been defeated by the UPW's Walter Baker. The other members were former miners' leader Frank Hodges, and James McKie Bryce who had a career as Secretary of various employers' organisations. The proceedings of the Court had many echoes of the Tweedmouth tribunal and other inquiries of the past. There were two major differences, however. Discussions were somewhat more informal and, more importantly, the case presented for the workers was much better organised, if not necessarily more potent in the circumstances.

In preparing its case, the UPW went to some trouble to collect material on the individual income and expenditure of its members. The returns showed that although many members had well above average wages, few said they had any money left for entertainment or drinking, or for holidays except very occasionally.[69] The case of the Union was therefore presented on 'the principle of maintenance', of setting up an adequate standard of living, and making that the basis of the claim. This argument, which had been given some scientific basis in the work of Seebohm Rowntree, had been used with devastating effect, though in a somewhat different context, by Ernest Bevin in putting forward the case of the dockers before the Shaw

Enquiry in 1920.[70] It had the great advantage from the point of view of the UPW that it reconciled the competing claims of the various grades, avoided the thorny subject of job evaluation and in no way relied on outside comparisons which might well have gone against them. The Union thus began its case by asserting that 'the proper remuneration of and good conditions of the staff' should be 'the first cost' on the Post Office and efforts to secure this could not be characterised as 'making the taxpayer pay'. Quoting the Bradford Report on the need for 'contentment' and Holt on 'the ideal of family life', the Union went on to argue that the state should be a 'model employer' offering 'the highest and best standards' to employees who needed to maintain 'a definite status in the community'. There were some references to 'an increase in the value of work', at least in counter duties and by telephonists. Much effort was expended to show that the dietary standard necessary for a reasonable life, as defined by Rowntree, could only be obtained by those at the top of the scale. The case for a reduction of the five area classifications determining levels of pay was argued with details of numerous anomalies. After a brief nod in the direction of the original call for equal pay for men and women, the Union then tried to show that the Post Office counter-claim would in many cases reduce real wages below the standards of 1914, and in some cases even below what was secured in the Tweedmouth settlement of 1897.

The Union's case continued with submissions on behalf of individual grades. A number of examples were given in an effort to show the additional burdens of London sorters, though in truth it was hard to maintain that their position had greatly changed since the time of Tweedmouth. The counter clerks were able to provide a more convincing list of additional tasks they had been given since the days of the Holt Report, and went on to make the usual comparisons with elementary school teachers and clerks working for banks and local authorities. For those doing telegraph work, the case largely rested on the numerous types of technical equipment then in use, though there was some exaggeration in the argument that different skills were involved in the operation of the triplex and quadruplex Baudot systems. For telephonists, their 'services to the community, and the important part they play in the commercial and social well-being of the country' were emphasised. The Union even quoted the Chairman of the Manchester Chamber of Commerce about the value of the telephone service during the recent General Strike, 'especially to those organisations engaged upon essential services in the interest of the public generally'. The strain on telephonists' health was also described. For postmen, porters, boy messengers and the smaller grades, the skill and arduousness of their duties were the main – virtually the only – argument put forward for higher remuneration.

E. Raven, Second Secretary, presented the case for the Post Office. He argued for reductions for young entrants and at the maximum of most scales on the general ground of outside comparisons:

> In the present position of the national finances, the Government feel it more than ever indefensible that their own employees should be raised to the position of a privileged class with a wage level which would be unattainable in an industry subject to ordinary economic conditions.

He pointed to a number of measures that had made life easier for various grades, for example the introduction of postal district numbers in London which had simplified the tasks of sorters. Postmen in 1912 performed split attendance in 88 per cent of cases in London and 43 per cent in provinces. These figures had been reduced respectively to 17 per cent and 13 per cent, with nobody now making three attendances. Since 1922 the outdoor force also had a system of meal reliefs. Raven expressed himself prepared to merge the provincial Class I and London rates, but in no other way to alter area pay differentials. More generally he was against 'the idea that wages in the Post Office should be revised in order that the standard of life of the various grades might be progressively increased'. It was, said Raven, 'the opinion of the Postmaster General' that any 'upward movement had gone too far', and the taxpayer should not have to finance further improvements in the standard of living of Post Office workers.[71]

To this Bowen was able to reply effectively that all improvements had come as a result of agitation and that the Post Office seemed to want to be an 'average' rather than a model employer. Although the management had attacked their use of Rowntree's family budgets, they had not presented any alternative. Nor could they deny that there were still many split duties and unsocial hours.

When it came to lengthy presentation of cases to the Court, the workers' case was generally hampered by the arguments put by the secessionist organisations, which tended to be exaggerated and inaccurate. However, the management side did not really present any serious arguments for their claims for reduction, and did not get the Court very interested in the question of outside comparisons. The workers' representatives, including the secessionists, were much more successful in capturing the imagination of the Court's members on details of the work they did by concentrating on the general 'intensity of labour' case that they wanted to emphasise. Bowen also achieved some success in getting the Deputy Director of Statistics at the Ministry of Labour, E. C. Ramsbottom, to agree that cost-of-living figures could be used to prove almost anything.

The Guild of Sorters was able to present the main case for their grade, claiming the rate for clerical officers (£1 10s 8d (£1. 53) × 18 to £4 15s 6d (£4. 77¼)) (30/8 × 18 to 95/6) which was about a 50 per cent increase. They considered themselves 'manipulative workers' only in the same sense as pianists or surgeons, and argued that the Ministry of Labour cost-of-living index did not apply to people of their elevated status. The case presented for the sorters by Hodgson of the UPW, who had not himself belonged to that grade, lacked the same panache, though it was somewhat more realistic. The authorities found it easy to ignore this when they rebuffed the more preposterous claims of the Guild.

The Association of Counter Clerks General Secretary F. J. Marshall argued the case for this grade with some exaggeration, though Hodgson for the UPW presented some inaccurate and dated worksheets. There were some heated exchanges on the position of sub-office assistants, not least because of the difficulty of deciding who should represent them. On telegraph work, it was easy for the authorities to argue that the new machines had actually made the work easier, and the diminishing use of the morse sounder had reduced the likelihood of cramp.

The general case of the SC&Ts for equality with the clerical grades was described by Raven as 'preposterous and ridiculous', and he was even able to cite publications from the Union side to the effect that sorting work in the provinces had grown easier in recent years.[72] In response, it was nevertheless possible to show the complexities both of the work and of the classification system for determining local wages. In response to claims for improvements for postmen because of complex and additional duties, Raven replied that all their indoor duties were 'simple in character, called for no other qualification than those of honesty, trustworthiness and ordinary intelligence, and could be performed efficiently after a few days by the ordinary new entrant'.[73] He claimed that the only significant change in the work of postmen since the Holt Enquiry of 1912 was the introduction of motor transport, and special allowances were paid for that.

After some similar exchanges on the smaller grades, both sides summed up, Raven concentrating on the general fall in prices and wages and Bowen on inter-grade comparisons. Unlike its many predecessors, this inquiry ended with praise from Bowen for the personal qualities of his main opponent and with these words from Raven himself:

> The atmosphere of the proceedings throughout had been altogether different from the atmosphere which had prevailed at previous inquiries into cases connected with the Post Office staff, and it indicated very substantial progress towards the establishment of better relations between the staff of the Post Office and the administration, a progress for which Mr. Bowen himself was entitled to no small share of the credit.

With this, the Court went off to consider the findings.[74]

The award of the Court was announced on 11 August 1927.[75] It was certainly not over-generous to the Post Office workers. One important aspect of its provisions was to pay more at the maximum to CC&Ts than to telegraphists and more to them in turn than to sorters, who were in fact given nothing at all. Nor were postmen in inner London, but some outside got a little, and the SC&Ts generally got small improvements. The only real response to management calls for reductions was around the bottom end of the main scales, and these were restored by around the age of 20. In defiance of an earlier- promise by the Chairman of the Court, management delayed back-dating the new rates until 1 August.

The arguments given by the Court for its decisions were, to say the least, vague and fragmentary. After giving it as their opinion that since 1920 wages in the Post Office had fallen in the same general measure as in outside industry, they asserted

> that the broad principle which should be followed in determining the pay of Post Office Servants is that of the maintenance of a fair relativity as between their wages and those in outside industry as a whole and as between the various classes within the Postal Service, with due regard to the adequacy of the payment for the work done and the responsibilities undertaken.

They were a little more precise on outside comparisons which they thought 'cannot in themselves be conclusive'. However, they did not consider that either side had made a case 'to warrant any substantial change in the settlement arrived at in 1920'. They avoided the thorny question of classification of offices altogether, though agreeing that the criteria on which they were based were anomalous and outdated. The even thornier question of equal pay for women was also ignored. Other important matters such as trip allowances were simply postponed.

Naturally, there were bitter complaints from the Union about this judgement. Even the London counter clerks who had done best said that 'as far as our grade is concerned, Arbitration has come to an untimely end'. Middleton went so far as to express his 'doubts of the capacity of the Industrial Court to discharge properly the functions assigned to it with regard to Civil Service affairs'. Nevertheless, he said that what had been set out was 'binding on the Government as an employer and must be accepted by the Union'. After this, there was what can only be called a deafening silence in the Union on the whole question. The discussion at the relevant Executive meeting was, to say the least, perfunctory.[76] The experience of the miners in being starved back to work a year before was no doubt a bitter warning for all Union members. The enforcement of the Trade Disputes Act in those same weeks no doubt also diminished the will to fight. It would seem that many Union members thought they had come out of their negotiations well enough in the circumstances.

A number of other issues left over from the negotiations dragged on over succeeding months. The first was a claim for a 50 per cent increase in all allowances. Here the management conceded quite large improvements for supervising – for example, those for female telephonists went up from 3–5s (15–25p) to 4–6s (20–30p). However, Bowen found it 'embarrassing' that similar concessions were not made to night telephonists, and no doubt there was an element of calculation on the part of management in that. Also, they did not concede anything new to motor drivers, and were less generous to the telegraphists, whose general position was under discussion.[77] On efforts to improve subsistence allowances, negotiations took a different pattern. Here the management offered rather smaller improvements in line with what had been granted to other civil service grades. Thus an SC&T who had to work away from home would get in a week £15 16s 2½d (£15. 81) as against £10 18s (£10. 90). In July 1932 the UPW Executive decided by 13 to 7 to go to the Arbitration Court to try to get an improvement on these rates, but 'changed circumstances' made them reverse this decision in November, and accept what had been offered.[78]

The inevitably divisive issue of classification of offices also figured in this period. The claims of individual offices for higher classification were negotiated through the 1920s by a special Joint Committee. The Arbitration Board refused to recommend any changes in 1927. A number of branches then grew dissatisfied with the vigour with which their cases were being pursued, though Bowen said privately that many branches had no real case under the rules. A number of branches held a special conference of their own early in 1930, which Bowen attended. After this it was agreed to submit the whole case for the abolition of the classification of offices for pay purposes to the Royal Commission, much to the chagrin of the Controlling Officers Association. The Union had a good case in arguing that local variations in the cost of living were diminishing, and there were numerous anomalies. However, the Tomlin Commission simply ducked the issue, and the Union had to return to negotiating individual cases, a position that persisted until after the Second World War.[79]

THE FALLING BONUS: 1928–31

The rapidly falling prices after March 1927 soon affected the cost-of-living bonus in such a way that money earnings were continually being reduced. This now became much the biggest pay issue throughout the civil service. Elsewhere such bonuses were being consolidated into income, often at levels that could no longer be argued as the Ministry of Labour index continued to fall. Since the proportion of the bonus in total income was greater on lower levels of income, the UPW tended to be more wedded to the system than those in better paid grades. Consolidation was always a gamble against the likely future level of prices, and UPW leaders were more cautious about abandoning the bonus than those from some of the other civil service unions. Efforts to get unity and an 'All-service Programme' were to some degree put back by these factors, though by the end of negotiations extending over many years, the Whitley Council staff side was compelled to work in a cohesive manner.[80]

All early initiatives towards consolidation of the bonus came from the management side. In 1927, while the UPW wage arbitration proceedings were still going on, the Treasury proposed that changes should take place less frequently. After considering it, the staff side decided to leave well alone.[81] In September 1928 the official side now proposed full consolidation at a level of 67½ per cent above the 1914 wage figure, which was about the level of the index as it then stood and around that which a number of local authority and other employees had recently accepted.[82] Consideration of this offer was bedevilled by the fact that the mercurial W. J. Brown of the CSCA decided it would benefit his members and other civil servants, despite the fact that this was a time when it stood at its lowest level since 1920. Though it may now look different in retrospect, there was no reason in 1927 to believe that prices would not again rise, and it was impossible to see that this level of the index would not be reached again until after war broke out in 1939. Thus although Brown and the CSCA wanted to go for immediate consolidation, Bowen was completely opposed: 'He had no hesitation in saying that the Civil Service Cost of Living Bonus Scheme was easily the best in the country and they should, therefore, consider only the possible conditions and consequences of any alteration'. Brown then started pushing for a complete renegotiation of the agreement, and Bowen, with the support of the higher grade Institution of Professional Civil Servants, proposed consolidation at 70 per cent above the 1914 figure rather than 67½ per cent. The arguments around Brown's radical and risky proposals reached such a pitch that the normally mild-mannered Bowen felt compelled to walk out of the meeting. When it resumed, another of the UPW's representatives, Craig Walker, said 'there was little call' from UPW members for any change.[83]

At this point Brown chose to launch a blistering public attack on his staff side colleagues for their lack of boldness and their failure to present any real alternative to what was being proposed by the management. The response of Bowen and his colleagues was not so much to defend their position – though there were perfectly good arguments in favour of it – as to attack Brown for revealing disagreements within the staff side. After lengthy discussion the staff side then produced proposals on which everyone could agree. These included a minimum adult wage of £3 10s (£3. 50) a week, more than £1 above what was being earned by a postman of 21 at the time. There was also a call for full bonus for those on the higher levels of pay, including those who had received nothing since the 1921 'Supercut'. Although the official side agreed to set up a joint committee on these claims, it is hardly surprising that by the middle of 1929 this had simply decided to 'register disagreement'.[84]

Matters were now changed by the results of the 1929 General Election. For one thing, Bowen, together with a number of other UPW leaders, was now in Parliament, as was W. J. Brown. The new Chancellor of the Exchequer, Philip Snowden, had in the past expressed himself opposed to the bonus system, but he absolved himself from having to take any decision on the matter by setting up a

Royal Commission under the chairmanship of Lord Tomlin to discuss the bonus and other contentious questions. However, after meeting a delegation of the National Whitley Council staff side on 16 July 1929, Snowden announced that the currently ruling figure of 70 per cent would continue, even though by then it should have fallen to 65 per cent. The evidence presented to the Royal Commission by the staff side essentially argued that this position should continue for good.[85]

As the Royal Commission received its evidence, and the general economic position grew increasingly difficult during 1930, the hard-pressed minority Labour Government showed itself less and less willing to make any special consideration of the case of civil servants. Nevertheless, the 70 per cent figure was retained in March 1930, and in September, when it should have fallen to 60, it was only reduced to 65. On the UPW Executive this was described as 'a success' while it was admitted that 'there will be some feeling of disappointment in the Civil Service that there was any reduction at all'.[86]

Bowen and his colleagues in the UPW were inclined to leave it at that, Brown and the CSCA again wanted to make a great deal more noise. Thus although Bowen ensured that the staff side did not sponsor a public campaign against the bonus drop, a letter of protest was nevertheless sent to Snowden and a large mass meeting was held by the CSCA at the Central Hall on 4 September on the demand for full consolidation at 70 per cent.[87] Snowden's reply was rather dusty. He

> rejects that his generous concession, which involves a very large addition to the taxpayers' burden for the benefit of the Civil Service, should have been received in such a spirit of ingratitude.

The staff side replied that it had not been 'a spirit of ingratitude that dictated our protest, but of profound disappointment' that the system was still continuing. Privately, staff side leaders admitted that they were losing the propaganda war, and tried to emphasise the case of the lower paid. Snowden was 'too busy' to meet them before the end of 1930, though with the index steadily falling, he agreed to do so on 19 January 1931. After listening to the usual attacks on the basis of the index and pleas for the lower paid, Snowden pointed out that they had made no reference to the economic crisis which was causing widespread wage cuts and unemployment of over 2 million. He then announced his decision:

> The industrial and economic depression was far more severe than when he made the concession in regard to the bonus and it was impossible to disregard the storm outside. He was not proposing, though great pressure had been put on him to do so, that the pay of the Civil Service should be reduced, but the Cabinet had decided after a full review of all the circumstances, that the Cost of Living Bonus Agreement must be strictly adhered to.[88]

This soon resulted in a drop of the index to its lowest level yet of 55 on 1 March, and to its lowest ever of 50 on 1 September 1931, developments naturally viewed with some consternation by civil servants. The bonus was now effectively being used as a method of wage cutting for civil servants generally in the absence of the more direct cuts soon introduced for teachers, members of the armed forces and others. The UPW was still inclined to proceed carefully, and *The Post* opined that the bonus system 'stands as a bulwark against demands for cuts until it is raised by consent'. The CSCA began a campaign of demonstrations and meetings. The staff side was compelled to allow various groups to go their own way, and rejected all the more radical approaches. In Parliament Brown voted on 11 February, with twenty others, against the setting up of the May Economy Committee and on 26 February was suspended from the House during a debate on the bonus.[89]

During February 1931, it became clear that feeling was growing within the UPW on the issue, and there were indications from the membership of the desire for a more vigorous policy. In reporting a meeting of 600 workers from Mount Pleasant on 12 February, *The Post* agreed that the members present were 'not easily convinced of the dangers of open revolt in the House of Commons' by the Union's MPs. A demonstration at the Albert Hall of UPW members on 24 February showed considerable strength of feeling, but also heard of Bowen's cautious approach. From within Parliament he was using some of the old methods of political pressure which had served Post Office workers well enough in the past. On 23 February, Snowden met a delegation from the liaison committee between Labour MPs and the Cabinet, and Bowen himself met Snowden on a number of occasions. No doubt many members were more impressed by Brown's activities, but in the end nothing moved the Government. On 1 March the bonus dropped from 65 to 55, and wages fell accordingly.[90]

CRISIS AND MILITANCY: 1931–2

The bonus issue continued to cause seething discontent for the rest of 1931. After some hesitation, the UPW leadership decided to campaign for consolidation of the bonus at the figure of 70. In July the Tomlin Commission proposed consolidation essentially at 55, but on 1 September the rate fell to 50.[91] This level, which was to persist until July 1934, brought discontent to a level which was to have considerable consequences for the UPW.

Already the UPW leadership had decided to try to deal with the entire problem by a different means altogether. After the March bonus drop, Bowen proposed at the UPW Executive that they should put in a wage claim. This should be for 10s (50p) across the board, and should be based not on the outside comparisons so frequently utilised by the authorities and soon to be sanctified by Tomlin, nor yet on 'subsistence' arguments which had been used in the 1927 discussions. Instead the high profits of the Post Office, increasing by 15·76 per cent from 1925 to 1930, were to be compared to the much smaller increase of 3·65 per cent in staffing. It was a productivity argument, or so it might have been put in later years, buttressed by some references to low pay for the worse off sections. It had little hope of getting very far, and members expressed the view at the 1931 Annual Conference that it was unlikely to achieve anything in the current economic climate without a strike policy.[92] However the claim did at least provide a clear and straightforward policy against all the uncertainties and frustrations surrounding the bonus.

On 6 August 1931, a UPW delegation met Clement Attlee during his brief period as Postmaster General, and presented the claim. Attlee was in a position to be friendly enough, but he was no doubt more preoccupied with the cuts in public spending and the political crisis which was to lead within the month to the collapse of the Government. It was followed on 24 August by the so-called 'National' Government including MacDonald, Snowden and other former Labour leaders, which was even less likely to be favourable to the claims of public servants. In October this new Government engineered an overwhelming electoral victory as a result of which, amongst other things, all MPs from the UPW and other civil service unions lost their seats.

After the Tomlin Report appeared in July, the National staff side decided to campaign not only against the general proposal for outside comparisons, but also on a number of more detailed points, of which the most important was the consolidation of the bonus at 55. The strongest feeling of all was provoked by the bonus drop to 50 on 1 September. Even before it happened, the staff side had a rather bad-tempered meeting with Chancellor Snowden. Once the drop came, more militant attitudes prevailed, a number of enormous meetings took place and within the Post Office there was the first disciplinary action for trade union activity for over twenty years.[93]

The dilemma facing UPW and other union leaders is evident from a number of discussions at this time. Bowen thought 'the greater their argument against the fall in the bonus the more there was danger that the recommendation of the Royal Commission on the bonus might be applied'. Though others argued that 'to remind the members of the virtues of the 1920 agreement would be to court misunderstanding', nevertheless, Bowen 'thought it was dangerous to lead the membership to believe that it was possible to succeed' in abolishing it on some such basis as consolidation at 70. In the absence of any serious alternative, he thought it was probably safest to stick to the 1920 agreement.[94] Nevertheless, there were pressures for more positive action. During October there were large numbers of demonstrations in every part of the country protesting against the bonus drops, though not offering any very clear alternative.[95]

In Manchester meanwhile a general meeting of the members on 11 October 1931 rejected the report of Central Secretary Bert Hamnett on the grounds that not enough was being done to improve their wages. The meeting demanded 'immediate and definite action' from the Executive of the Union. In the meantime, the members decided themselves to begin to 'withdraw goodwill'. This involved such measures as sorters refusing to hurry along certain kinds of mail usually given priority, and postmen not using their own bicycles. After warning the members not 'to do anything for which the Department can get you', O'Donnell and Wallace went off to the Executive Meeting on 14 October. O'Donnell said there that the members 'did not think the 10s flat rate increase worth pursuing', but they did want action on the bonus and he proposed a general and 'immediate withdrawal of goodwill'. 'There was a spirit amongst the membership at the present time', in his view, 'which rightly organised could win public attention'. Although no decision was taken at this point the mood was shown by the fact that, in the absence of Bowen, a resolution aimed to separate the UPW's bonus campaign from the rest of the National staff side was only lost on the casting vote of the Chairman.[96]

By early November the Manchester action was beginning to cause some delays in the post and publicity for the discontent that existed. At a meeting in the retiring room on 5 November, O'Donnell and Wallace warned the members not to get themselves in trouble by going too far. Meanwhile at the top of the Union, with Bowen now fully back in harness after the shattering Election defeat of himself and the Labour Party, there was a different attitude. On 4 November Bowen persuaded the General Purposes Committee to withdraw all talk of action, and to embark instead on 'the further education of the membership'. At the Executive meeting beginning on the 10th, strong and differing feelings within the Union were reflected. Bowen said that many members must have 'voted for the very things the Union was fighting against'. Arthur Winyard however drew the opposite conclusion from the Election results asserting that 'the present Government would be ruthless, and that unless the workers did some definite action they would find that in a comparatively short time trade unionism in Britain would be converted into a kind of fascist organisation'. There was a vote of 7 against 17 for a revival of the strike policy. The Manchester Executive members Wallace and O'Donnell argued for a 'withdrawal of goodwill' at least in the larger offices. However, all that Bowen and the majority of the Executive were prepared to agree to was a survey of opinion in the larger offices. On 11 November, O'Donnell and Wallace announced their resignation on this issue and 'on account of the shiftless policy of the Executive generally'. They later explained that this had been precipitated because

> the Executive Council, with one or two exceptions, had no faith in the membership. The one great excuse for inaction was that the membership 'would let you down': that they would not support a strong lead. If we ourselves had such a low conception of the spirit and courage of the membership . . . we would not seek to serve for one moment in any local or national capacity.[97]

On 16 November Bowen met the new Postmaster General Kingsley Wood who warned him that disciplinary action would be taken against malefactors. Two days later Bowen embarked on his tour of large offices where he found limited support for action. However, on 20 November the authorities announced the suspension of O'Donnell and Wallace. This bombshell was soon followed by others. A young SC&T called Kane was next suspended for taking part in the action, but so also was Hamnett, this for what he had said at the special Union Conference on the telegraph service. The new National Government had brought back nineteenth-century attitudes with a vengeance! This posed delicate problems for the Union leadership. Although Bowen was prepared to call for reinstatement at mass meetings, internally there was talk of 'disloyalty' and Bowen said they 'did not want to put themselves in a position of condoning everything Manchester had done'. Nevertheless, the Union leaders protested to the authorities and pressed them not to end the suspensions but to set up a joint inquiry into what had happened.[98] The authorities justified their treatment of Hamnett with reference to the recent agreement on the reorganisation of branch secretaries which left each one 'responsible for the propriety of his conduct'. However the authorities were on very weak ground in this case and were eventually compelled to withdraw even the 'serious offence' notice contained in his record.[99] They were not prepared to be so lenient on the others, however. Following a discussion with a delegation of Union leaders on 8 December, the authorities announced on the 10th the dismissal of O'Donnell, the transfer of Wallace to Nottingham with probation and the loss of an increment, and the loss of an increment for Kane.

The authorities never went back on their decisions, though the issue rumbled on for some years. Local branches agreed to make up the loss of income of Wallace and Kane, and the Manchester Branch appointed O'Donnell at an income of £200 per annum as full-time Branch Secretary. This was a figure he insisted upon, and must have been a good deal less than he had been paid as an SC&T. Bowen tried with limited success to raise his dismissal in Parliament. The TUC General Council was reluctant to help because they 'always found it difficult to condone what was done by local bodies against Executive Council policies'. In following years the issue became concentrated on the question of the failure of the Manchester management to recognise O'Donnell as 'a suitable person to make representation on behalf of the staff'. As a result of his dismissal there was even some question as to whether he could attend conferences, occasions he was not inclined to miss, usually to berate the Union's leaders. His case for recognition was strong, and he even won the support of the newspapers who had been in favour of his dismissal in the first place. Eventually, in 1939, the authorities conceded that he could meet them in all circumstances except in the workplaces. By then his income had risen to £260 and £312 per annum – more than an SC&T, but less than the Union's central leaders.[100] O'Donnell, who eventually retired in 1945, was the only officially designated full-time local official in the entire history of the UPW.

Two days before the original Manchester suspensions, on 17 November 1931, the newly appointed Postmaster General Kingsley Wood met a delegation from the Union on the 10s wages claim. Chairman Roland Bishop was nothing if not frank:

> We have been accused of sitting on a safety valve and have to confess to doing so. We have been accused of failure to give a lead. Our lead has been to follow the channels of legitimate representation.

Wood sympathised with the 'difficulties of the leaders of the Union' and defended the cost-of-living index. Following the disciplinary action in Manchester, the authorities wrote on 14 January 1932 rejecting the wage claim in its entirety:

> Sir Kingsley Wood has no desire to dispute the statement made by the deputation that a considerable amount of hardship exists amongst the lower paid Post Office staff at the present time, and he would have been very glad if it had been possible, with due regard to the state of the National finances, to take some steps to alleviate the position. He regrets, however, that after full examination of the case he finds it impossible to concede any part of the Union's claim.

Bowen thought this 'entirely different in tone to replies received on previous occasions' but this did not prevent Wood from reiterating his refusal in reply to a further delegation on 4 February.[101]

THE END OF THE COST-OF-LIVING BONUS: 1932–4

The complex and protracted negotiations on the end of the bonus took place at a time when, after the drop of September 1931, civil service wages would never again be lower. The negotiations were complicated both by the constant fear that prices would begin to rise again eventually, and by the fact that they were actually falling. Thus the continued operation of the bonus would have led to even lower wages than were actually obtained, and uncertainty and divisions still characterised the staff side approach. The operation of the system allowed 'economy cuts' to be made in the wages of postal workers and many others in September 1931, and divisions and differences, as well as falling prices, allowed the maintenance of these rates until 1934. It was only in July 1935 that the levels paid before September 1931 finally returned.

Before the end of 1931, National Whitley Council staff side leaders met large groups of MPs and Neville Chamberlain, the new Chancellor of the Exchequer. On 22 February 1932, Chamberlain announced consolidation at 50, which was what they were then getting. After some hesitation, the staff side decided to oppose consolidation at this point, arguing for the continued operation of the 1920 agreement and running a public campaign on the issue.[102] Perhaps surprisingly, this campaign even won some sympathy from the high Tory *Morning Post* and *The Times*. The former expressed itself thus:[103]

> An essential condition for an efficient Civil Service is that it should be adequately paid, and there is much to be said for the view that the existing emoluments, and any likely to be proposed under a consolidated system, are in many cases on the small side.

During the summer of 1932, prices again began to fall and it became increasingly clear that if the 1920 agreement continued, then wages would fall again in September. It was in these circumstances that Sir Warren Fisher and Sir Horace Wilson, respectively Head of the civil service and Chairman of the official side, met a small group from the National staff side on 19 May 1932, and proposed consolidation in March 1933 on the basis of the current figure. Although the staff side rejected this, they became increasingly obsessed by the fact that the figures published each month were showing with increasing certainty that the average figure would drop in September. On 14 June 1932 the official side presented a new set of proposals, somewhat more favourable, to continue at 50, and to leave consolidation until March 1934, providing the figure kept between 30 and 60. The staff side discussions following this offer reflected the real dilemma it posed. The non-Post Office section seemed prepared to accept it, though without being seen to be doing so. Within the UPW, there were some who still thought it best to carry on with the 1920 agreement, though Bowen considered that this was now out of the question. There were others who wanted to stick out for the Tomlin proposals. However, with the figure for the index at its lowest ever level of 36 in May and June, and the inevitability by September of a substantial drop under the then existing arrangements, support grew for the acceptance of the official proposals. The Executive of the Institution of Professional Civil Servants accepted it unanimously, and that of the Civil Service Clerical Association did so against the advice of General Secretary Brown. Within the UPW, Bowen circularised the branches with the view that this was the best they could get for the moment, and said that it would be all up for grabs again two years later in 1934. On this basis 311 of the 325 branches within the UPW expressing an opinion counselled acceptance. On 7 July 1932, after all the hesitations, the National staff side finally voted for acceptance.[104]

THE WAGE CLAIM AGAIN: 1932–3

During this temporary consolidation period, Bowen proposed in October 1932 that it might 'prove profitable' to take up the 10s across-the-board wage claim again. PMG Wood, however, proved a great deal less forthcoming than he had done in earlier discussion, and only agreed with some reluctance to meet a delegation on 7

February 1933. Amid all the usual talk about the difficulties caused by the economic situation, Wood said he had 'not forgotten' the poorer paid and would be prepared to take up their position in the future. There were delicate problems for the Union in pursuing a wage claim covering only part of the membership, and though the Executive rejected the idea, it received the support of around a third of delegates at the 1933 Annual Conference. The Conference also decided against mass lobbying in favour of more traditional methods of Parliamentary pressure. A further delegation met Wood on 11 July, and he was even in a position to put them off with the argument that the Conference delegates had been 'by no means unanimous that it was wise or desirable to put forward such a claim at the present time'.[105]

The Union leaders also managed to get their claim raised in Parliament during the Summer of 1933. All the old arguments were heard. Former PMG Attlee, on 30 May from the opposition Labour benches said that the Post Office profit was 'swollen by reductions in wages'. Wood was able to quote Arthur O'Donnell to the effect that to talk of 'the surplus in relation to wages is to pursue a false train'. Stafford Cripps replied that O'Donnell was not arguing for lower wages. The vote on this occasion was 280 to 37 for the Government. There was a similar discussion on 24 June, and another on 24 July when Labour leader George Lansbury argued that 'the Post Office's profits should just be used for giving a decent standard of life to the people who carry on the industry'. Assistant Postmaster General Sir Ernest Bennett replied that they were still sympathetic, but could do nothing. He included the statement *Tempora mutantur, et nos mutamur in illis* – times change and we with them. *The Post* cartoonist was able to respond with one of his wittiest about 'small change' and 'no change', but for the moment that was all.[106]

Well before the end of 1933, civil service trade unionists began to discuss what would happen about the bonus consolidation that was due on 1 March 1934. The members were receiving about 50 per cent above the 1914 figure, and the index figure was climbing only very slowly to that level – it was 43 at the end of the year. With an eventual rise in prices always expected, it was difficult to know what to do for the best. The CSCA reflected the mood of hesitation by arguing for continuing the present arrangement at 55. The UPW argued for a permanent settlement at 60, Bowen cheerfully admitting that this involved a reversal of policy. However his staff side colleagues were not prepared to accept this without a number of qualifications, and by 4 January 1934 a lengthy claim was worked out, including compensation for those earning from £91. 25 to £200 per annum, for the full amount of the bonus, restoration of the 1921 'Supercut' on the higher incomes, and equal pay for women. Joint mass meetings were organised throughout the country on this programme, in which the UPW and its lower paid members were particularly well represented.[107]

This comprehensive programme may have served to unify the staff side. However it did not impress the official side. They replied in some detail on 2 March, showing the great cost of the proposals. They argued for the validity of the Ministry of Labour cost-of-living index, at least for the purpose of measuring levels of change since 1914. The official side even disputed the figure of a $13 \cdot 7$ per cent fall in money wages produced by the Statistical Bureau which had recently been set up by some of the staff side unions. This figure had been obtained by taking the median in certain grades, and not a real average. Reiterating that the average rate above 1914 for 1933 had been 40 per cent, they proposed to consolidate from 1 March 1934 at the then current figure of 50.[108] Bowen and some others were in favour of accepting this, but the UPW Executive and the majority on the staff side favoured continuing to push for the original claim. As it turned out, this probably did gain a little. MPs were lobbied, large public meetings held throughout the country, and on 17 April 1934 Chancellor of the Exchequer Neville Chamberlain announced in his budget speech a restoration of half the drop of 1931, in other words consolidation at 52½ from November 1934.[109] The staff side continued to press for the figure of 55, a position agreed for example at the 1934 UPW Conference, against protests that it did not go far enough. The official side was not however prepared to budge during 1934, and a number of bad-tempered meetings and eventual registering of disagreement took place within the Whitley machinery.[110] The 55 figure for consolidation was eventually achieved in July 1935, no doubt in part because of the improved economic situation, and perhaps also as part of an effort to win the support of civil servants in the General Election of November 1935. By then the index figure itself was creeping up. It was over 50 by the end of 1936, 60 a year later, and an average of 56 during 1938. The arguments for higher wages could then be put forward on a new basis.

THE 1934 WAGE CLAIM – LITTLE VENTURED, LITTLE GAINED

The 1934 claim was first pursued when the consolidation settlement seemed inevitable. It began as an attempt to take up some of the same points as in the general claim argued since 1931. It continued in the first serious direct negotiations with the Post Office since 1920, but ended with simply 'rounding up' some of the improvements in consolidation. In the circumstances, it is difficult to see that much more could have been achieved.

The claim had its origins in a rather vague resolution passed at the UPW's Annual Conference in May 1934 asking for improvements on grounds of 'hardship'.[111] This was sent to the new Director General, Donald Banks. He replied on 10 July that much had already been secured by the consolidation. He agreed however that some details of that settlement might require modification 'particularly in the case of lower paid staff'. This response did not greatly please the UPW Executive, since it offered improvement to very few. Nevertheless they elected a delegation to meet Banks to argue with him that there were 'weaknesses' in 'several of the wage scales and rates'. Not much was expected of the delegation, as was shown by Ruth's advice to it that 'if in negotiations they were committed to some form of discrimination, he would prefer it if they kept it to themselves'. The expectations of the members were, however, being aroused, and they sent in resolutions drawing attention to such issues as the vagueness of the claim, and its failure to demand anything for women members.[112]

However, it soon began to look as if some progress was being made. On 14 October editorials appeared in both the Labour *Daily Herald* and in the Tory *Daily Express* supporting the claims of lower paid Post Office workers. It was also clear that Postmaster General Wood, as part of his extensive political ambitions, wanted to appear as a friend of the Post Office workers. However, he wanted to do this at the minimum of expense, and management tactics became clear in a series of 'informal' meetings in August and September, where the Union's delegation was manoeuvred into discussion on such minor matters as bringing auxiliary workers into the permanent force. At the October Executive meeting Charles Geddes, no doubt reflecting the feelings of better paid members, described the actions of the Union delegation with some exaggeration as 'a betrayal': 'while the way they were adopting was the easy way' he said, 'it was not the right way'. When the offer finally evolved during November the management cleverly gave it simultaneously to the UPW and the secessionist bodies, placing the onus of acceptance on the Union and compelling them to arrive at a decision more quickly than many of its leaders wanted. Although there were improvements for unestablished classes and auxiliaries and small increases at a number of points on the established scale, Bowen was compelled to admit that 'the task of the Negotiating Committee had been difficult, and the result not spectacular'. Executive members described the offer variously as 'mean and despicable', 'miserly', and much else besides. They voted to reject it by 14 to 3. However, opponents of the offer had very little to propose by way of alternative, so that all that could be decided was to return to the negotiations to propose comparatively slight modifications.[113]

At the second of two further meetings with management, Deputy Director Gardiner was not able to offer 'the slightest hope that anything at all was possible with regard to the amendment of scales'. In fact, out of the approximately 420 points on various scales, 37 had been reduced. At the next UPW Executive meeting on 5 December rejection was lost by 11 to 9, and the negotiators returned with a mandate to try and get some more for the lower paid groups. However, nothing more changed. On 10 December Bowen wrote accepting the inevitable, and Wood presented the settlement in Parliament on 13 December as a great improvement for the poorer paid. This was not the view of the poorer paid themselves, as one UPW district committee put it: 'the benefits to be received have been very much exaggerated'. Nevertheless, there was a widespread feeling within the Union 'that every effort was made on our behalf'. A characteristic statement in a local Union journal was that they should be 'thankful for small mercies'. Despite the strong statements in the secessionist journals that nothing had been achieved, this view received only a handful of votes at the UPW's 1935 Annual Conference.[114] Though this was not a period of good wages and conditions in the Post Office, there was a great deal less discontent than three or four years earlier. Thus the negotiations about the consolidation of allowances, mostly for the technical qualifications of telegraphists, roused little passion even amongst those affected.[115]

THE FORTY-HOUR WEEK CLAIM: 1935-7

This claim represented some effort to get an overall improvement in the conditions of Union members without making another wage claim. During this period, the Trades Union Congress began to interest itself in the general policy of reducing hours in order to relieve unemployment. In 1931, the forty-hour week was adopted as TUC policy and in 1935 it was secured as a 'convention' of the International Labour Organisation. Efforts were made over the following years to get the 'National' Government to adopt the policy, but without success.[116] In the meantime, the UPW began to discuss the forty-hour week. It was adopted as the policy of the UPW in 1933 and discussed inconclusively with PMG Wood in 1934. In 1935 the Whitley Council staff side began to argue for a five-day week. At the Union's Conference in May of that year the delegates agreed, against some reluctance from Bowen, to approach the Post Office authorities again on the demand for a forty-hour, five-day week so they could 'set an example to outside industry'.[117]

Negotiations on the claim extended over the next few years, and despite a certain amount of propaganda effort by the Union, and some very minor improvements, the forty-hour demand finally collapsed into the wage claim launched in 1937. The first efforts centred on TUC General Secretary Citrine, who expressed the view that as long as 'a reduction of the working week did not involve wages', the Government would do nothing. Eventually a delegation met the Postmaster General in March 1936. Despite a densely argued and complex case, with numerous international and other comparisons, he refused to discuss anything except slight improvements on irksome attendances, meal reliefs and night duty allowances.[118] During 1936, the Union launched into a general propaganda campaign for the forty-hour week, circularising MPs and others and running a lengthy series of public meetings on the issue. It took until April 1936 to obtain a reply from the Post Office, wherein it was claimed that only forty-three, or even forty-two hours were actually worked and that a nominal forty-hour week would really be thirty-five. By then UPW Executive members were prepared to agree in private that members were more interested in the new wage claim than in whatever improvements could be obtained on unsocial hours and meal reliefs. Discussions dragged on into 1938, by which time it was clear that the Post Office authorities were prepared to concede very little. There was some desultory talk of taking the matter to the Arbitration Court.[119] By then, however, the Union was well launched into discussions at the Court on more substantial matters.

THE WAGE CLAIM AT THE ARBITRATION TRIBUNAL, 1938

These negotiations, which culminated in lengthy hearings of the Civil Service Arbitration Tribunal in the somewhat incongruous surroundings of the head-quarters of Methodism at Central Hall Westminster, were the most important discussions of Post Office wages since 1927, and secured the greatest improvements since 1920. Although the form of the proceedings echoed the great inquiries of the past, there were important differences also. The most obvious one was the way in which the Union's leaders were able to win much of the argument by an informed eloquence backed by a depth of research, going well beyond the special pleading of the past. The results of the arbitration could be seen as the triumph of Hodgson's period as General Secretary and of the more practised oratory of Harry Wallace. They also owed much to the research of Edgar Hardcastle. Nor was the Union's success simply a result of its own efforts. These were negotiations conducted in the full glare of national publicity, and inevitably linked to the aspirations and achieve-ments of other sections of workers. They took place at a time when the shadow of mass unemployment was lifting, and wage levels generally had begun to rise. Post Office workers had extracted themselves from the cost-of-living bonus system at a time that had not proved particularly beneficial to them, and there was certainly now a case for the improvements that had since been enjoyed by many others.

The claim, which began to be discussed within the UPW leadership before the end of 1936, was submitted in September 1937 and in December it went to the Arbitration Tribunal. After some further delays, the Court began public hearings of the case on 23 May 1938, and then went through forty-three days of evidence and discussion, finally coming to an end on 7 November. The settlement was announced in December, and backdated to October. Discussion on certain aspects of its implementation continued well into 1939 and beyond. Very broadly, people at most points on most scales got increases of 6–8 per cent against a claim of around 15 per cent. This was generally regarded as a successful outcome for the Union and its members.[120]

Discussion on a possible wage claim began among UPW leaders somewhat slowly and secretively towards the end of 1936. In the following March, the barest outline of a claim had been worked out by an Executive sub-committee and was published, against the objections of General Secretary Tom Hodgson, in *The Post*. At the same time, Post Office Director General Sir Thomas Gardiner was saying in private discussion that if the claim was delayed, it would be dealt with all the more quickly through arbitration. By now, however, there were twenty-four resolutions on the Union's Conference's order paper calling for substantial wage increases, and a mass meeting at the Holborn Empire on 18 April 1937 clearly showed that the expectations of the members were rising.[121] By the time of the Annual Conference in May, a lengthy debate was necessary. The delegates accepted the general motions of the Executive subject to the important proviso that the old efforts to achieve 'relativity' with other civil service grades should be abandoned. With this qualification, the views put forward by Hodgson were accepted.[122]

> They wanted authority not to present a wage claim that might be regarded as a long-term programme, but a wage claim they could regard as practical for immediate presentation, capable of being argued in the light of present-day circumstances, with the object of claiming as much money as possible for every member of the Union of all grades, male and female.

Over the next few months, a great deal of energy was devoted to formulating the claim before it was eventually presented. Women in grades also including men could not be discussed, since the level of their inequality was being independently assessed by a sub-committee of the National Whitley Council, and the eventual settlement would incorporate its decisions. Smaller grades were to be similarly dealt with, so the only groups of women directly discussed were 16,650 telephonists, 1,200 girl probationers and 950 cleaners. The 'realism' of the claim was established by its lack of any reference to classification of wages by areas and by the minimal efforts to reduce that other important inequity, the incremental scales. Despite all the talk of poverty of the youthful members of the Union, the general tendency of the figures eventually presented was to claim less for those at the lower end of the scales. Thus only 11 per cent was asked for the youngest provincial postmen in the smallest offices, when 17 per cent was asked for those at the maximum.

Many special interests also asserted themselves in the formulation of the claim. Thus a figure of 30 per cent at the maximum was proposed for postmen in inner London, whereas their provincial equivalents were only thought worthy of 16 or 17 per cent. However, as Gardiner himself admitted, there were special circumstances where the London postmen did a great deal of sorting work. There were also special arguments in favour of the conspicuously underpaid London porters, for whom 41 per cent was demanded at the maximum to give them equality with postmen.

There were quite different reasons for the particular demands put forward on behalf of the London counter clerks and telegraphists, telephonists and sorters. Here the 1937 claim was aimed to recreate the equality between these grades which had existed from the 1897 Tweedmouth settlement and was ended in the 1927 Arbitration Court award. This could only be done by making a very high claim (about 23 per cent at the maximum) for the sorters, rather high for the telegraphists (19 per cent) and about average for the CC&Ts (15 per cent). In part at least the demands of the secessionist bodies influenced the level of these claims. In general the Union's rivals asked for nothing at all at the bottom of the scales and for much longer incremental scales rising to very high levels indeed. As Appendix 39 shows, the Guild of Sorters wanted 26 per cent at the maximum, and the Association of Counter Clerks 33 per cent. However, even they were outdone by the Guild of Telephonists, who demanded 43 per cent at the maximum. The Union, no doubt to some extent in response, put forward a scale that went up to over 30 per cent of the one then prevailing. Besides excluding the interests of women because of the separate Whitley discussion, no special emphasis was placed on the low wages of SC&Ts in smaller offices, with the argument that the classification issue was also quite separate. Beyond the exceptions noted, a general principle of asking for 15 per cent at the various points on all scales was agreed by the UPW Executive and an approximate differentiation of 15 per cent between London and the provinces was also accepted, again subject to the particular considerations for the London postmen.[123]

Before the arguments in favour of these figures could be marshalled, there occurred a series of events without which no major negotiations of the period would have been complete – a row with W. J. Brown and the Civil Service Clerical Association. At its Conference in May 1937, the CSCA had decided to press for a general wage claim for all civil servants based on the increases in the cost of living since the consolidation of 1934. The case for attempting to improve conditions with such arguments was by no means self-evident. For one thing, it was not thought inevitable that prices would continue to rise, and in any case there would be all the usual arguments about the difficulty of finding a scientific basis for cost-of-living calculations. A general claim would also diminish the arguments that could be put forward from the UPW about the effects of technical change on the work of its members. Thus although Brown got the support of a majority on the National Whitley Council staff side for a cost-of-living claim, he did not persuade those representing most of its constituents, and he was defeated by 18 votes to 4 in his proposal to get the staff side to proceed in any case. He then responded characteristically by publishing tendentious accounts of the staff side proceedings and vigorous denunciations of the UPW's leaders for their alleged weakness on this and many other questions. The CSCA ran a public meeting on 30 November to which all Post Office workers were invited. Brown wrote a pamphlet, *To Postal Workers*, which combined a reasoned defence of the cost-of-living basis with unflattering comparisons between the recent achievements of his organisation and the UPW. A number of UPW members indicated their support for Brown's arguments. They can hardly have been greatly inspired by Hodgson's riposte in a pamphlet entitled *Mr. Brown's Fallacies Revealed*, which attacked the CSCA for downgrading the work of its members.[124]

If this unhappy episode served any purpose, it was to emphasise that the rising cost of living would not be the main argument in favour of increasing wages in the Post Office. The letter setting out the claim, dated 6 September 1937, concentrated on the argument that the value of work had greatly increased since 1927, and discussions with Director General Gardiner in October added the point that the wealth both of the Post Office itself and of the nation as a whole was increasing. The reaction of the authorities was to say that, though all this was little different from the 10s claim a few years earlier and would cost £5–6 million, they nevertheless might be prepared to offer some increases on the maxima along with the shortening of scales. The UPW Executive was inclined to accept this as a starting-point for discussions, and on 18 November sent copies of the new scales they had in mind to the Post Office. It took less than a fortnight for the Post Office to reply that so vast a claim 'does not furnish a useful basis for negotiation'. After this, reference went ahead to the Arbitration Tribunal. The claim was published, and on 12 December UPW members rallied in the Albert Hall.[125]

In the five long months before the arbitration proceedings actually opened, the air was full of alarm and rumour. It took until 11 March to get agreed terms of reference and until 23 May until proceedings actually began. During this time the authorities agreed to separate discussions on the smaller grades and to maintaining the relative position of the women. One difficulty was that the secessionist bodies began to claim that secret bargains were being struck in these discussions. The Guild of Postal Sorters had some reason to be aggrieved since they had already been well advanced in their own negotiations, only to have them referred to the Tribunal. However, Gardiner had done something to stir up bad feeling, perhaps unconsciously, by comparing the work of the sorters unfavourably with the other grades, including the postmen. UPW leaders did not make any secret deals, but they were placed in a difficult position. This helps to explain the somewhat inflated claims made on behalf of the London grades, and the complaints from London postmen that their special position was insufficiently acknowledged. From within the Union as a whole, the strongest criticism of the claim was its failure to ask for more at the minima. However the voice of those on the lowest pay was not always loudest, and within the Executive Geddes led a group who argued for more at the maxima. Hodgson managed to sweep aside all such reservations when he rose from his sick bed to an eloquent defence of his line at the Annual Conference in early May 1938, and to an even more eloquent presentation of it to the Tribunal later in the month. Nothing but approval and strong support was then heard from the members.[126]

The Arbitration Tribunal met on the stage of the 2,600-seat Central Hall, with numerous spectators coming and going.[127] They included, so the story goes, a deaf old lady who thought a religious service was taking place. The tone of the proceedings was relaxed and affable. The Chairman, Sir Harold Morris, was a veteran from the 1927 proceedings, and from many other such discussions. He succeeded in showing an undiminishing and enthusiastic interest in the minutiae of Post Office work throughout the entire proceedings, and at times even to inject a note of humour. He thought it 'an awful blow' that there were regulations 'preventing the sending of pink-coloured quinine to Aden'. A similar interest was shown by the second member of the Board, J. J. Mallon, who was Warden of Toynbee Hall and active in such bodies as the WEA and League of Nations Union. The third somewhat less active member was Herbert Parkes, an iron and steel employer and well known as an employers' representative on arbitration bodies.

The Tribunal worked as follows. The UPW presented the general case first and then the details for individual grades. The pattern was for the Union to present its case, followed by a Post Office representative and then the Union's reply. There were also interjections throughout from both sides, and at the end of every section Hodgson gave a detailed riposte on the outside comparisons provided by the Post

Office. This form of discussion gave the advantage to the Union, who not only had an 'extra bite on the cherry' at each stage, but also continually placed the authorities on the defensive. Thus John Coyne was able to condemn the 'Jekyll and Hyde-like attitude' of management. They wrote in their own publicity on counter clerks that 'no other servant of the Department, and very few people in other walks of life, have so many and varied services to perform'. Yet before the Tribunal they could only talk of their simple mechanical tasks, their limited need for knowledge and their 'unoccupied time'.

Generally speaking, the Union case was better prepared and its leaders were much more eloquent before what amounted to a public meeting. At one point the Assistant Director General T. H. Boyd had to ask for his nervousness to be taken into account because he was 'not as practised a public speaker as Mr. Hodgson'. It was Hodgson who got headlines in the press for his account of the 'raking and scraping and enforced economy' of his youth as an SC&T in Newcastle. Wallace grabbed some publicity by asserting 'that it might be a good thing if employers did get six months for underpaying their workers'. John Coyne brought out the case of the counter clerks vividly by providing a book with the 150 stamps with which they had to be familiar. When telephone controller J. Y. Bell felt able to assert 'that from my personal observations the Girl Probationers are a much more cheerful, happy set of souls than might be gathered from the observations of Miss Howse', Edith Howse herself responded that 'in five or six years they will be sorry they are there'. The successes of the management in those arguments were much rarer. Against the Union showing how many people had left the Coventry office for higher wages outside, they were able to produce a letter from someone who tried to return.[128]

The main burden of the argument presented by the Union was that their work was more valuable in 1938 than it had been in 1927 in terms of output, productivity and technical difficulty. However, they began by presenting a very wide range of argument about the poverty of the membership, the generally rising level of wages and prices, and the rises in National Income and the wealth of the Post Office. As always, it was easier to show how such poverty was manifested amongst younger members and they even found an office where staff made collections to buy mid-day meals for boy messengers. However, scientific accounts of subsistence levels could also be quoted once again to show how Post Office workers more generally were falling behind. It was not difficult to produce wage indices to show that no Post Office grades were receiving the increases being secured elsewhere. The Union tended to quote special cases where wages had risen a lot, like the Co-operative Societies, or good local authorities. The management was much harder put to it to find cases arguing in the opposite direction, like the notoriously oppressive railway companies. Because of the overall economic situation, the Union was more prepared than in previous discussions to talk in terms of the 'fair relativity' of the rates in outside industry that had been referred to in the 1927 Arbitration judgement. However, there was still little serious attempt to compare tasks and earnings. It is true that more valid comparisons could perhaps be made between counter work and the duties of bank clerks than had once been the case, but there was rather less serious purpose served by dragging up old references to elementary school teachers from the Tweedmouth Enquiry. One important aspect of outside comparisons had however changed. There were now increasing numbers outside the civil service who enjoyed paid holidays, pensions and the other 'privileges' which had been supposed in the past to allow public servants to exist on lower wages. All that was left was the ancient argument from the management about security of employment, and the equally ancient riposte about the discipline which this allowed them to exercise.

However, the central argument in all the welter of discussion and invective was about value of work, levels of output and productivity. From the beginning Hodgson maintained that though his members needed higher wages regardless of the state of the enterprise for which they worked, 'nevertheless the flourishing financial position of the Post Office has an important bearing on the Union's claim'. The rising number of letters and telegrams delivered, telephone calls connected, postal orders and licences issued, combined with the increased income and profits made the case that Post Office workers were providing more value and merited greater rewards. For the counter clerks, the sorters and postmen, the range of their knowledge and the arduousness of their tasks were outlined day after day in excruciating detail. For the telegraphists and the telephonists, technological change had made their work more valuable. Most telegraphists were said to be able to use the old morse sounder instruments as well as the modern teleprinters, and the advent of automatic exchanges was moving telephonists beyond the routine duties of placing pegs in holes.

The general reply of the authorities to all this was that 'the character and value of the work of the members of the manipulative classes, taken as a whole have not appreciated since 1927, but rather the reverse'. Furthermore, 'the vast proportion of the increase is in straight-forward types of business like the handling of letters and telephone calls, and has been met by appropriate increases of staff'. To all the great detail about the complexity of the work of inland sorters, Boyd replied that it was

> a comparatively simple operation, the main requirements being a certain manual dexterity and a knowledge of British county geography. Both these qualities can be acquired by any person of average intelligence, and reasonable efficiency is acquired after training, the period of which is about a month.

The management argued that technological changes had made Post Office work easier. Thus it was said that 'developments in telegraphy had done much to simplify the work of telegraphists', and that 'even though the apparatus is more complicated, the operator's duty is simpler'. 'Telegraphists cramp' would now disappear, and training could be successfully completed within five months. It was also maintained that telegraphy had 'now become an occupation primarily suitable for women'. (The management did not trouble to present any psychological or social arguments for this, any more than they had considered it necessary to go beyond vague talk of 'manual dexterity' when arguing in the 1890s that an earlier generation of completely different instruments had also been especially suitable for women. The fact is that their aim was to resolve the problems of a loss-making service by paying lower wages.) As for the telephonists, their work was generally 'light and simple', was becoming easier still with the advent of automatic working, and there were many applicants to do it.[129]

A number of other major questions recurred in the detailed discussion of duties performed and the statistics about wages earned. One is the persistence of what nowadays would be termed unsocial hours. The Union's case for the SC&Ts put it like this: 'The uncertainty and variation of hours of attendance have adverse effects on the staff. Domestic arrangements cannot be regularised, nor social life enjoyed with any certainty.' This was besides the irregular, varied and split attendances.

Even the authorities themselves had to admit that 53 per cent of provincial postmen still had two attendances and 6 per cent had three. Another grievance that came up in various contexts concerned access to promotion. Here the management was compelled to present a number of arguments along the lines that every poor person has a right to enter the Ritz. When management asked why so few London postmen applied for supervisory posts, the reply was that they would gain very little financially as a result. The UPW had excluded itself from making such comparisons with other grades as part of its general approach.

Such constraints did not of course apply to the UPW's rivals in the organisation of sections of the staff. Thus, the Northern Ireland Post Office Clerks Association, whose representatives the Tribunal heard at the Royal Court of Justice in Belfast in September 1938, at the height of the Munich crisis, brought up the old claim for 'clerical status'. They also called for the abolition of classification of offices, though all their offices outside Belfast and Derry were in Class III. Generally, they said much the same as the UPW, however, and Hodgson considered that 'huge chunks of the Union evidence had been lifted and embodied in their case'.[130] The case of the Guild of Telephonists was, however, very different from that of the Union, when it was heard back in London on 17–21 October. Edgar Lansbury being ill, the main case had to be presented at short notice by G. L. Robinson, the Guild's President. He made a number of gross errors, like presenting a sheaf of papers without any explanation, and doggedly refusing even to discuss outside comparisons. The Tribunal members went so far as to refer to 'amateurs who do not know how to present cases'. However, Robinson does seem to have been more successful than Edith Howse in making the system of logging various kinds of calls on 'tickets' sound very demanding. He clearly did not do his case any harm, since the night telephonists, along with the London postmen, were the only people to get as much as 9 per cent at the maximum from the Tribunal.

Considerably less effective was the case presented by E. L. Thomsett for the Association of Counter Clerks from 24 October to 3 November. Not only did the terms of reference have to be altered, but on one or two detailed points they were tripped up, including the hoary argument of comparisons with bank clerks. However, Thomsett was able to argue that he had spoken as a working CC&T (unlike Coyne) for seven hours as opposed to two-and-a-half and for much higher salary scales. Unlike the Guild of Telephonists, the ACC was prepared to make comparisons with outside work, though only with the most elevated senior clerks.[131] In the event, the CC&Ts got the lowest percentage increase, around 6. The Guild of Postal Sorters, for whom G. H. Taylor spoke on 3–7 November, no doubt relying on some of the experience of the Fawcett Association, were a great deal more successful in presenting a more well conceived and detailed case. This helped them to achieve a slightly higher percentage increase than the counter clerks, though the differential between the London grades was nevertheless maintained.

THE 1938 AWARD – A 'TRIUMPH FOR THE UNION'

When the verdict of the Tribunal was announced in December, there was great rejoicing at UPW House. Hodgson, it is recalled, danced with delight on hearing it. He immediately expressed the view that though the award 'falls far short of the standard aimed at in the Union's wage claim', it was nevertheless 'a triumph for the

Union'. If further consideration of the figures somewhat modified this rapture, nevertheless rejoicing at the increases secured after so many years of rejection and disappointment was general throughout the membership. Congratulations flowed into UPW House not only from numerous branches of the Union but also from the TUC and other unions. TUC General Secretary Vincent Tewson commended 'the magnificent work which has been performed on behalf of your membership' and Ernest Bevin of the Transport and General Workers wrote that 'your members have every right to be proud of the service they have received'.[132]

However, the generally justified feeling of triumph and achievement could not obscure some small but important problems. For one thing, the small percentage increase on the very low wages of unestablished grades did not bring them up to a standard that prevented considerable discontent. A cleaner in Central London for example got £2 15s (£2. 75) a week at his maximum, which was less than the London indoor grades got at 24, or postmen at 26. Cleaners and other unestablished grades like porters and liftmen expressed considerable discontent at the settlement, and soon another, separate, claim was put on their behalf. The Union refused to accept a Post Office offer made in 1940 which gave these grades 8–10 per cent on their minimum and 4–6 per cent on their maximum. Though the Union took this case to the Arbitration Court in 1941, they achieved only the most insignificant modification of the Post Office offer, since similarly low wages were paid by other employers, including other government departments.[133]

Another issue coming directly out of the 1938 award went back to the Tribunal and was dealt with to the considerably greater satisfaction of Union members. The Post Office proposed to take two years to move those affected from the maxima of the old rates to the new ones, whereas the Union argued that the Tribunal award meant this should be done within twelve months. On this dispute the Tribunal found in February 1940 entirely in favour of the Union, and added for good measure some improvements for those approaching the top of the scales.[134] By this time, many new problems were facing the members, in comparison to which these faded into insignificance.

POST OFFICE BARGAINING AND WAGES IN THE SECOND WORLD WAR – THE BONUS

The First World War had fundamentally altered the forms of public sector bargaining in Britain through the introduction of arbitration machinery and Whitleyism. The Second World War saw fewer changes in the formal structure of bargaining, but many more in its focus and the terms of its argument. The hesitant move towards wage negotiation by outside comparison and the 'Tomlin formula' which the UPW leaders had made in the 1938 arbitration proceedings became the central trade union argument for increasing wages in war-time. The timing and extent of wage settlements in engineering, mining and elsewhere was the major plank of the case for improvements put forward jointly by all civil service unions during the war period. Yet just as the union side began to accept what had historically been the main management argument about how their wages should be determined, their masters also began to strike a new attitude. Suddenly, and with little warning or precedent, national economic planning for war was combined with a more centralised and systematic attitude to public sector wages. Amidst efforts to control the movement of labour and the outbreak of strikes, the Coalition Government also introduced in July 1941 a White Paper which constituted the first government statement of the need for wage restraint in order to halt the 'wages and prices spiral'.[135] Not for the last time, it was on its own employees that the government first attempted to impose 'restraint' and 'sacrifice'.

The war-time administrations initially wheeled out the Tomlin formula to argue that civil service wages should be determined not by price levels, but by outside settlements, which were at the time trailing behind the cost of living. When the level of outside settlements began to move up, the government's argument against increasing the wages of its employees then became the 'general policy in regard to wages and prices'. As Post Office workers and other civil servants came to pay increasing regard to what was being obtained by miners and engineers, their employers began to argue that these groups and not public servants were 'exceptional', earning special privileges. Truly the whole argument had come full circle![136]

Thus the form and course of war-time wage bargaining in the public sector cannot simply be attributed to a greater willingness to co-operate in the face of a foreign enemy, though undoubtedly this was a factor. There was also a deliberate government policy to induce greater co-operation and a definite effort to keep down the wages of civil servants. On the whole this was successful. Prices rose by around 25 per cent between the beginning of the war in September 1939 and May 1941, and thereafter remained fairly stable until 1948. Civil servants secured a number of increases in the 'bonus' by which their basic wage rates were regulated in this period. However, their pay did not catch up with the 25 per cent inflation rate until as late as November 1945. During the course of this lengthy period, a number of changes can be seen in the organisation of bargaining, in the arguments used about it as well as in some other aspect of wages, particularly for the temporary grades.

From the beginning of the war, those in government showed themselves determined not to repeat the errors they had made in 1914. In the very earliest weeks, one UPW member noticed the difference:

> The outstanding fact is the way the leaders of the Trade Union Movement have been taken into the confidence of the Government. There is nowadays no economic issue upon which the Government would dream of taking action without consultation beforehand with the executives of the trade unions concerned.

By May 1940, the leaders of the Labour Party and of the largest union in the land, Clement Attlee and Ernest Bevin, were members of Winston Churchill's War Cabinet. For UPW members there was the startling appearance at the May 1940 Annual Conference of Assistant Director General T. H. Boyd, their great adversary from the 1938 arbitration proceedings, who made this extraordinary statement:

> They at Headquarters recognised and approved of all Trade Unionism stood for. If they seemed at times to act contrary to that sentiment, it might be because time did not permit of consultation or it might have been because of a slip-up. He had to confess to two or three since the war began, and he had not been ashamed to do so. What he wanted to say was that, if there should be anything in that direction, it was never deliberate or of malice aforethought.

This was a remarkably conciliatory statement, not to say self-abasing, even if it was followed by talk of 'economic staffing' and the need 'to accept sacrifices'.[137]

This exaggerated effort at winning over the organised working-class movement had a considerable effect within the civil service. Not only were doors opened for the leaders of the TUC and the unions within it, but the National Whitley Council found itself able to deal with the authorities much more comprehensively than ever before. This is not to say that the Whitley machinery itself was strengthened. The National Whitley Council only met once during the entire war, on May Day 1941, for a somewhat abortive discussion about general staffing levels. Nor were the important matters even discussed in the Emergency sub-committees and other formal bodies. The major questions were decided, sometimes with limited consultation, by bodies such as the Cost of Living Sub-committee, which had little nominal power, but through which the leaders of the main civil service unions negotiated directly with the Treasury on the main questions facing their members. These procedures were sometimes attacked as cumbersome and undemocratic,[138] but it is difficult to see how else it was possible to reconcile the competing interests involved. It did certainly have the effect of enhancing the position of such leaders as Albert Day of the Society of Civil Servants, Chairman of the staff side and also of Bill Brown and later Len White of the CSCA, and of Hodgson and Geddes of the UPW.

In the opening weeks of the war, when price inflation set off at as brisk a pace as it had in 1914, many private employers and local authorities immediately agreed to increases in the form of a 'war bonus'. For the civil servants, with their own particular experience of the operation of a 'bonus' system during the period of falling prices in the late 1920s and early 1930s, it seemed possible that there might need to be a different way of settling their grievances. After all, the great majority of them as recently as 1937 had expressed 'a deeply rooted disinclination to take any step which would again tie the remuneration of Civil Servants to the official Cost-of-Living Index figure'. Against the single voice of W. J. Brown, they had decided that any pay claim based on rising prices would be 'unwise and against the best interests of Civil Servants'.[139] A Cost-of-Living Sub-committee of the National staff side spent the next two years in desultory discussion about a possible alternative to the Ministry of Labour index, but had not managed to arrive at any satisfactory conclusions by the beginning of the war.

However, once the war began the need immediately presented itself to save civil servants from the effect of increases in the cost of living, with the Ministry of Labour index during September 1939 going up from 55 per cent above August 1914 levels to 65 per cent above, and rising by 1 January to 75 per cent above. This was the background to the astonishingly limited heart-searching which led to the formulation of a claim by a National Staff Side Sub-committee including UPW Assistant General Secretary Paterson for a bonus system based on the much maligned Ministry of Labour index. The plan was for there to be quarterly changes by 5 per cent steps up to £208 per annum incomes, and with 50 per cent compensation above that.[140] Before the scheme was a fortnight old, a delegation from the staff side presented it to the Chancellor of the Exchequer Sir John Simon. This meeting showed clearly the willingness of the Government at the highest level to discuss with union leaders, but beyond this it was not a success. For one thing Simon said that he though the claim was 'premature', though he might be prepared to consider increasing wages in the future if prices continued to rise. At this point W. J. Brown said, in an intervention privately described by his staff side colleagues as 'disastrous' and 'inexcusable', that they would waive all claims providing prices did not go up by more than 25 per cent. Hodgson of the UPW and Edwards of the POEU tried to rescue the position by telling Simon that they represented members more closely equivalent to those outside who had received increases.

In the end this was what mattered. Despite the grim war news during 1940, with the collapse of armies throughout Western Europe in the face of advancing German forces and the retreat of the British Army from Dunkirk in June, those who remained behind did not feel able to surrender their standard of living. The pages of the *Post* during 1940 are full of accounts of large meetings calling for a cost-of-living increase, and this was negotiated by the National Whitley Council staff side during April. The negotiations were remarkable not simply for the fact that they were taking place at all, but also because they were conducted directly between the staff side and the Treasury. [141] Although the Treasury insisted that they were not prepared to grant full compensation for the cost of living, they did agree to quite large concessions during the course of negotiations, going up from increases of 4s (20p) for those on up to £4 10s (£4. 50) per week, to the figures which can be seen in Appendix 41. They also during the negotiations conceded equality of increase for women and granted something to those under 18. This package was presented to the Cost-of-Living Committee of the Whitley Council staff side on 10 May 1940, the day of the invasion of Belgium and Holland and the collapse of the Chamberlain Government. These were certainly exceptional circumstances, and most people were prepared to accept the lack of proper consultation within the Whitley machinery in return for the improved offer and a quick settlement. Afterwards W. J. Brown expressed the general view. 'The Staff Side was not equipped with the same power as industrial leaders, and it was remarkable that they had managed to obtain almost the same results with less power.' Feeling was not quite unanimous, however, as was shown by the large vote at the UPW Conference on 23 May 1940 for an immediate effort to secure full compensation for the cost-of-living increases. [142] The authorities followed with a surprisingly large increase of around 10 per cent for the temporary grades, an issue discussed more fully below.

It was by means of increasing the bonus that civil service union leaders tried to improve the wages of their members during the rest of the war. None of the later negotiations went anything like as smoothly as this first set. Problems arose immediately with the new claim initiated later in 1940, which was followed by acrimony and division of almost every conceivable kind. [143] The main concern in the preliminary discussions was from unions outside the Post Office and the manipulative grades who wanted the maximum at which the bonus was paid raised from £4 15s (£4. 75) per week to £7 per week. However, those representing the lower grades insisted on a more comprehensive claim which was rejected in its entirety by the official side at meetings in August and September 1940. Eventually the staff side met the new Chancellor and former Postmaster General Sir Kingsley Wood on 27 November, and he refused to consider any increase except possibly in the ceiling. This threw the staff side into considerable confusion, as was perhaps the intention. There was pressure on the one hand from those representing the better paid to concentrate on the level at which the bonus should be paid, and on the other hand – particularly within the UPW – for a claim to improve the lot of the lower paid. After a series of acrimonious meetings, the staff side in January 1941 put together a proposal which seemed destined to get the worst of all possible worlds by claiming both a higher ceiling and increase in the main bonus of 125 per cent, from 4s (20p) to 9s (45p). The authorities then muddied the waters by agreeing to put up the ceiling and at the same time offering more to the men than the women, 3s 6d (17½p) and 3s (15p) respectively. The new climate in the service and the fact that there were now very large numbers of women likely to be subject to the increase meant that the staff side could not accept this. Nor could they do so when the official side increased the offer on 21 February to 10s (50p) for men – more than they had asked for – but only 8s (40p) for the women. The final bitter blow was that the official side at the beginning of March not simply forced through the settlement without agreement, but actually reduced the amount they had previously offered to the women.

This new payment set the pattern for all subsequent settlements, and the form of the settlement did at least have the advantage from the staff side point of view that the issue could be taken up again immediately. During the summer of 1941, when the Government's calls for wage restraint were being issued, the question of increasing the level of pay at which the bonus was obtained came up. This did not affect the UPW very much, except to ensure that when the matter went to the Arbitration Tribunal during August, the general question of the level of the bonus itself could not be put into the melting pot. In fact the settlement gave a bonus to those earning £250–500 per annum at 50 per cent of the rate of their more poorly paid colleagues. There could be little done to hide the disappointment, even of those who got something from this settlement.[144]

This was very soon followed early in 1942 by pressure within the UPW for a new general wage claim, and it was with some difficulty that the Union's leaders were able to persuade the membership that it was preferable to continue to negotiate these matters in harness with their civil service colleagues. The claim which was eventually put forward was for 16s (80p) bonus for people currently on 10s (50p) and 7s 6d (37½p), with 6s (30p) for those earning £500–800 per annum. The first Treasury offer could not have been more calculated to split the ranks of the staff side. They offered 13s 6d and 10s (67½p and 50p), but only to those earning up to £175 per annum. However, the UPW and other lower paid groups did not break ranks, and eventually these rates were proposed for those on higher pay also. This was accepted with numerous reservations, including objection to the rigid 80 per cent proportion that was now being forced on the women, the fact that the cost-of-living principle had now been abandoned altogether, and the pitifully low increase for juveniles.[145] This latter issue was fought out with particular bitterness later in 1942, with the official side offering to pay more to both boys and girls if the principle of unequal pay was acknowledged. After numerous disagreements within the National Whitley Council, UPW General Secretary Hodgson expressed his view in January 1942 from what had occurred that[146]

> so long as the Union hung on to sex equality on a side issue of this kind they would lose all the time. The Treasury had won handsomely and he regarded the settlement as a very bad one indeed.

Already, however, there was strong pressure from within the UPW to proceed on a new claim.[147] On 28 November 1942 a rather premature notice in the General Secretary's column in the *Post* announced that further improvements were already being sought. This claim was not even formulated until the end of January 1943 and not agreed by the staff side until 12 March. It was for 10s (50p) per week more on the bonus for all earning up to £250 per annum, as well as commensurate amounts for those earning more than that. The main argument for the increase rested on what had been secured elsewhere. After the staff side met the Treasury on 16 April, the UPW Conference on 3 May passed a resolution protesting about the delay in securing what they had been promised the November before.[148] Though the delay was not as great as it seemed, the UPW negotiators were now keener to settle. However, they could not accept the offer made by the Treasury on 14 May of an increase of 1s 6d (7½p) on the bonus, hardly a serious response to a claim for 10s (50p). This led to charges from the staff side, clearly justified, that the Treasury was now trying to get away from the Tomlin formula by claiming that increases gained in outside industry were all exceptional. Their response, possibly another attempt to create divisions, was at first to offer 1s 6d (7½p) on the bonus to everyone earning up to £750 per annum. The unions again stuck together and 3s 6d (17½p) (around 25 per cent) was offered before the end of May to those on up to £250 per annum. A delegation again met the Chancellor on 31 May to argue that this was not enough. They were treated to 'a dissertation for 7½ minutes on the vicious spiral, wage rates and inflation'. If the UPW leaders were not much impressed by this, they were more convinced by the argument that the offer was more or less in line with some recent outside settlements, and they agreed to accept it. However, some other staff side members were under less pressure than the UPW to settle quickly and it was agreed that individual associations could now go for modifications if they wished.[149]

It was a much more favourable settlement than this on the railways that immediately followed which caused the staff side to jointly and immediately put forward a new claim of £1 for everyone. Though some sections of the staff side feared that this was premature, it was possible as soon as 29 September for staff side Chairman Day to tell Sir Alan Barlow, the Chief Treasury negotiator, that 'the comment of many Civil Servants was that the Official Side had swindled the Staff Side and that the latter were simpletons'. Although Sir Alan naturally tried to rebut such a suggestion, he nevertheless offered a good deal of what was being asked, as Appendix 41 shows. There were drawbacks, however, from the staff point of view. The position of the juveniles was not greatly improved, the 80 per cent rule for women was now rigidly established, and it was agreed that there would be no modification for a further year.[150]

However, prices in the latter part of the war did not continue to rise, nor did the level of wage settlements in industry generally. The result was that the last two modifications in the bonus, the increases of 1 November 1944 and the consolidation twelve months later, were not accompanied by any of the same excitement as were the earlier claims. There were no contentious meetings of the staff side, no resolutions of protest from individual unions and branches, indeed, little heated discussions of any kind. The 1944 negotiations, on a claim for an increase of 6s (30p) for the men were rewarded with 4s (20p). The same total, as always, was asked for the women and the original offer of 1s 6d (7½p) was pushed up to 3s (15p). This once again put them at almost exactly 80 per cent of the male total.[151] The 1945 negotiations were overshadowed by the grade changes in the Post Office and elsewhere. This time the Treasury quoted the part of the Tomlin formula about revisions not having to be too frequent. Consolidation was therefore finally agreed on the second day of 1946.[152]

OTHER WAR-TIME WAGES ISSUES

A number of other important issues on wages were handled in direct negotiations between the UPW and the Department. There was a protracted discussion about allowances which lasted for most of the first part of the war. The separate claims on the pay of the temporary grades were also of importance initially, though they were generally subsumed into the general wages issues discussed in the UPW during the latter part of the war. It is to these developments that the final section of this chapter is devoted.

Efforts to get improvements on the allowances, mostly for temporary supervising, technical qualifications, and knowledge of languages began as far back as 1938. However, few issues were more divisive within the Union, and a grand scheme worked out by the officers was rejected by the Executive in November 1939. A general 15 per cent increase was eventually claimed and presented in April 1941. The discussion dragged on well into 1942 when one EC member claimed with some justice 'that the Union had submitted a case to the Post Office with absolutely no argument behind it'. The problem was that it was almost impossible to present any general argument, and the particular arguments were virtually all too complex and technical for what might be gained from them. Nevertheless, the Post Office management were prepared to be very forthcoming, no doubt because little expenditure was involved. In the end an average increase of 20 per cent agreed during 1942 and 1943 was more than was originally claimed, though less than prices had risen in the meantime. A complex discussion on subsistence allowances continued into 1944.[153] These negotiations can hardly be described as an outstanding success for the Union, though despite the difficulties something had been achieved.

Of much greater importance were wage claims presented on behalf of temporary workers. Those performing the tasks of soldiers absent in the war were mostly women, generally in their 20s, and paid initially on short incremental scales at or near the lowest points earned by their permanent colleagues. There was never any hesitation in the UPW, as there had been amongst most of the Union's predecessors during the First World War, that they should recruit and represent the temporaries. Although there was some difficulty in reconciling their aspirations with those of other Union members, such problems occurred all the time in the UPW. The difference with the temporaries perhaps was that their interests were invariably placed second to those of the permanent members. There were two major negotiations conducted on their behalf, and described in succeeding paragraphs. The first was in 1941, when a general wage claim resulted in the lengthening of incremental scales. Though this was not in line with the general policy of the Union, it did bring the temporaries nearer to 'the rate for the job'. A second settlement in 1943 put them on scales that were identical with their permanent colleagues.

In the first Christmas of the war, the Union put in a claim for 2d (0·83p) per hour for casuals – an increase of about 14 per cent. The Post Office granted ½d (0·2p, or 3·5 per cent), in London only.[154] A similarly negative attitude was shown to a more general claim proposed for temporary employees of around 10 per cent up to the fourth and fifth point of the adult incremental scale, which was about 85–90 per cent of the maximum.[155] Early in 1940, the Union began to push the issue to the Arbitration Tribunal. In July, after negotiations in outside industry had secured some further increases, the management proposed an increase of 5s (25p) per week on a slightly extended incremental scale. This represented an increase of 8–10 per cent on the rates already received. There was a good deal of opposition to accepting it, with 8 votes against 14 on the Executive, and a majority at the 1941 Annual Conference referring it back.[156] Similar improvements were obtained later in the year for the permanent but unestablished grades of male cleaners, doorkeepers and liftmen, though the more general problem of getting them established had to be postponed until the end of the war.[157]

At the 1941 UPW Conference, the strong feeling of the new temporary members manifested itself, not only in the rejection of the 1940 settlement, but also in statements about their 'dire circumstances' and about the fact that people of the same age were getting less than half the wages for the same work. Hodgson did succeed in getting a motion withdrawn which called for the 'rate for the job' with the argument that this would be 'a menace to the established staff'. However it was clear that a new approach was necessary.[158] The Executive worked out a claim for which the main argument was the one heard at the Conference – that the temporaries were doing essentially the same work as their permanent colleagues. They claimed an increase of up to 12 per cent on their much shorter incremental scales. This would bring them to the maximum at the age of 23 or 24, at which point seven or eight incremental steps remained for their permanent colleagues. Since the principle of equal pay was also embodied in the claim, this involved asking up to 24 per cent for the women. This claim was submitted on 5 August 1941, and entirely rejected on 9 October, not only on the grounds that equal pay was out of the question, but more generally because the last settlement was so recent.

A limited amount of further pressure from the Union produced a surprisingly comprehensive reply from the management. They proposed a set of somewhat longer incremental scales, paying less to males at the lower levels but going up to somewhat more than the Union was demanding at around the age of 28. For women, who were of course the vast majority of those involved, this would mean increases at every point on the scale, though not equal pay. For younger men, if there were any such, it would actually mean wage cuts. This offer naturally caused considerable difficulty for the Union, but, on the grounds that few people if any would actually get lower wages, the officers agreed to it in principle and negotiated some improvement, notably one extra incremental step. When this finally came to the Union's Executive on 5 December 1941, they had an ultimatum to accept or reject on that day, or there could be no backdating to 1 November. The Executive naturally found much to object to in the proposals, particularly in the lack of equal pay and the lengthening of the incremental scales. They decided to reject them by 15 to 8, but then voted by 12 to 11 against going to the Arbitration Court on the issue, and finally agreed by 17 to 8 to go back to the Post Office simply to discuss 'anomalies at the starting points'. Since it was generally agreed that nobody would be affected by these anomalies, this meant in practice accepting the latest Post Office proposals. Although the Executive accepted the offer as a *fait accompli* in January 1942, there had been many breaches of principle in the settlement and it was natural that branches continued to express their dissatisfaction with it.[159]

At the 1942 Annual Conference, the wages of the temporary grades were inevitably a major talking point.[160] A complete rejection of the recent settlement was not agreed, mainly because Geddes raised the spectre of temporary grades actually earning more. Nevertheless, a very critical resolution was passed for equal pay for women, and the adult rate for all at 21. The Union's officers tried to get this embodied in the current bonus claim, but the Executive would not agree. They did, however, manage to persuade them not to put forward the very costly claim the Conference had agreed, but instead a set of incremental scales much the same as the permanent grades to about three or four steps below the maximum. There were some problems derived from such issues as demanding equal pay for the different grades of telephonists, but in the end this was what was submitted to the Post Office in December 1942.[161]

The course of negotiations during 1943 followed a somewhat similar pattern to those of 1941. The Post Office first of all entirely rejected the claim. The Union then began to discuss putting the claim to arbitration, a course agreed at the 1943 Annual Conference. However, after further delay, the Post Office made a set of proposals on 4 August, which put the temporaries on exactly the same rates as their permanent colleagues. The Union was disappointed that this meant even longer incremental scales, but in practice it gave everyone an increase, so was accepted by the Executive by 13 votes to 9.[162] This settlement now meant that the pay of temporaries was subsumed into general discussions about wages and the bonus for the rest of the war.

Following this, there was an attempt to set out a comprehensive policy on wages which in the end, however, came to very little, for reasons which can easily be seen. The need for a comprehensive policy was set out in a resolution put forward to the Executive by George Douglas just before the 1943 Annual Conference, 'in view of the multifarious claims on wages issues affecting every section of the UPW'. A rather low-level Executive Sub-committee, without any officers or outdoor men, was set up. It considered also a resolution passed at the 1943 Conference calling for much shorter incremental scales, to get to the maximum in about five steps by the age of 25.[163] Despite the opportunity presented for a comprehensive discussion of wage policy, the Sub-committee could see little that was likely to be achieved by a general claim before the end of the war and simply put forward the claim on incremental scales originally proposed. This went to the Post Office in February 1944 and was rejected in March.[164]

The 1944 Annual Conference again proposed efforts to achieve an 'early increase in the basic pay of established and unestablished grades'. However, the new General Secretary Charles Geddes in October persuaded the Executive that 'despite the argument that the sovereignty of Conference cannot be opposed, the resolution was impossible of implementation at the present'. This was because it could not be argued that the quality of work had been improved in recent years, and outside comparisons could only be made with those doing more overtime working than Post Office workers were prepared to tolerate. Later in 1944, Geddes again persuaded his Executive to withdraw the claim on reduced increments, which by then was on its way to the Arbitration Court. This was done on the basis that the Post Office scheme to reorganise the grades was being postponed by this discussion, and would put as much if not more money in the pockets of the members.[165]

The Wages Sub-committee now became a more powerful body including the main officers of the Union, and its main function was to negotiate the new grade structure in which Post Office workers were to be placed in the new and very different post-war world.

NOTES

1 This conclusion largely coincides with the view put forward in Parris (1973). A more rose-tinted but detailed account can be found in White (1933), and a positively rhapsodic view in Callaghan (1953).
2 Macrae-Gibson (1922), p. 6; Brown (1921), p. 18.
3 See above p. 92, n. 60; Gladden (1943), p. 25; Parris (1973), p. 33; *Hansard* V, 203, 2186 (17 March 1927).
4 White (1933), p. 28; Parris (1973), p. 106; PP 1922 IX (Geddes Report), pp. 67–8; *Hansard* V, 150, 1910 (22 February 1922).
5 See Parris (1973), pp. 70–1.
6 *Post*, 29 April 1922, p. 426, 2 June 1923, pp. 586–7, 19 January 1924, pp. 44–5 and virtually any other issue in that period. *WB*, April 1922, p. 11, May 1922, p. 19, January 1923, p. 85, May 1923, p. 17; *Hansard* V, 157, 719–88 (27 July 1922), 162, 1145–76 (10 April 1923); ECM 17–19/1/23, 155–7, 12–13/3/23, 219–20, 30–31/5/23, 10–15, 3/5/24, 233–4.
7 *WB*, March 1925, pp. 5–6; ECM 16–18/7/24, 48–9, 8–9/1/25, 122–3; *Post*, 14 March 1925, p. 227.
8 White (1933), p. 107; *WB*, April 1927, p. 13, December 1936, p. 73.
9 The first view is expressed by Middleton (1928), p. 276. A more favourable opinion can be found in Brown (1943), p. 190.
10 NWC (SS) Minutes, 7 July 1932, p. 46; *Times* (30 June 1932).
11 F 748.3.
12 *New Civilian*, 21 July 1926, p. 48; *Hansard* V, 196, 1971–2 (14 June 1926), 2475 (17 June), 197, 22 (21 June), 198, 28–9 (12 July).
13 *Daily Mail* (5 August 1926); *New Civilian*, 7 July 1926, p. 1, 14 July, p. 22.
14 NWC (SS) Minutes for 1928, p. 75, for 1930, p. 24.
15 ECM 18–24/10/45, 177.
16 A notable example was during the course of the 1931 negotiations with the Chancellor of the Exchequer, described below.
17 ECM 25/2/32, 182, 23–25/4/40, 209.
18 *Post*, 1 November 1930, p. 390.
19 *WB*, July 1929, p. 40; *Post*, 11 February 1950, p. 45; Parris (1973), pp. 36, 37.
20 Parris (1973), pp. 58–62; *Post*, 13 June 1931, p. 584, 9 December 1922, p. 522; ECM 18–24/10/45, 177.
21 Gladden (1943), p. 38.
22 These statements and quotations can be found in *Post*, 7 November 1925, pp. 922, 923, 9 December 1922, p. 520, 25 December 1920, p. 521, 26 September 1925, p. 800, 10 October 1925, p. 840, 17 December 1927, p. 468, 28 June 1930, p. 636.
23 *Post*, 12 November 1927, p. 381, 6 August 1921, p. 125, 10 January 1925, p. 26, 3 January 1925, p. 6, 17 December 1927, p. 464.
24 White (1933), p. 75; *Civilian*, 23 June 1923, p. 197.
25 White (1933), pp. 76ff. for a full account.
26 Smith (1931), pp. 198–9, gives these and other examples. See also White (1933), p. 81.
27 *Post*, 12 February 1927, p. 152, 19 May 1928, p. 440, 25 August 1928, p. 142.
28 ECM 23–25/7/30, 33–5, 10/2/30, 109, 10–13/11/31, 77–8, 19–21/4/32, 250–3; *Post*, 15 August 1931, pp. 134–5.
29 *Post*, 2 July 1932, pp. 16–17.
30 Parris (1973), p. 180.
31 ECM 16–18/10/34, 66–7, 75, 86; 23–25/1/35, 135–6, 146; 9–11/4/35, 166–7, 174.
32 *Post*, 1 April 1922, p. 325, 6 February 1926, p. 112, and 10 March 1928, p. 202 for yet more complaints from the staff side on the issue. *MR View*, July 1932, for a thorough critique.
33 *WB*, July 1935, p. 36, November 1935, p. 81.
34 For details of the scale see *Post*, 12 June 1920, pp. 562–3, and POC, 2515, 25 May 1920, reproduced in *Post*, 5 June 1920, p. 542.
35 PP 1930–1 X (Tomlin Report), pp. 63, 125.
36 *Post*, 15 August 1931, p. 126, 13 February 1932, p. 140.
37 ECM 25/2/32, 181.
38 NWC (SS) Minutes, 22 February 1932; ECM 25/2/32, 182–3.
39 *Post*, 4 June 1938, p. 500, 2 July, p. 457, 6 May 1939, p. 400. Civil Service Arbitration Tribunal Award (HMSO 1939), p. 18.

40 ECM 23/6/42, 18, 20–22/1/43, 250–1.
41 Besides *Post* and ECM there is a full file of these negotiations at F 372. The following quotations are from the relevant ECM unless otherwise stated.
42 See *Post*, 10 April 1920, p. 349.
43 *Post*, 17 April 1920, pp. 372–3, 20 March 1943, p. 71; F 372 has Bowen's speech.
44 *Post*, 1 May 1920, pp. 413, 420. There are said to be papers on this at F 353.1 but they have disappeared.
45 *Post*, 22 May 1920, p. 481.
46 Wallace (1925).
47 *P&TR*, 2 October 1919, p. 220. F 114 has papers on what follows.
48 *Post*, 29 May 1920, pp. 512–20.
49 *Post*, 17 July 1920, p. 52, 21 August 1920, p. 131.
50 ECM 8–9/12/20, 20/1/22, 19ff.
51 The only account of this meeting seems to be in *Post*, 29 January 1921, p. 109 – hardly an impartial source. For a fuller and more general account see Chapter 10, 359f.
52 *PT* March 1921.
53 ECM 13–16/4/21, 26ff.; F 114.
54 *Post*, 21 May 1921, pp. 503ff.
55 ECM 21/9/21, 48; *Post*, 8 October 1921, p. 321, 15 October, p. 343; *MR View*, September 1921.
56 *PT* October 1921, pp. 125–8; *MR View*, February 1922; *Post*, 20 May 1922, pp. 498ff.
57 *Post*, 20 May 1922, pp. 497–8; ECM 17–19/1/23, 177–81, 12–13/3/23, 229–39.
58 There is a file in the UCW Research Department covering these discussions, but kept apart from the main filing system.
59 ECM 17–19/1/23, 177–81, 12–13/3/23, 229–39.
60 The proceedings of the Executive Sub-committee with related material is kept at R XXI.
61 ECM 30–31/5/23, 12, 13–14/12/23, 128–9, 22–24/1/24, 140–4, 27/2/24, 178–8, 7/3/24, 184–5, 189. R XXI/2 for the Special Conference.
62 ECM 19–20/6/24, 5–7, 16–18/7/24, 31, 40, 42, 14–16/10/24, 53–5.
63 ECM 7/3/24, 185–9, 3/4/24, 195–201, 19–20/6/24, 14–17, 14–16/10/24, 61–3. Details of the claim itself, and of some of the discussions around it, are to be found in a large bound volume published by the UPW (1927). Quotations from correspondence, reports of delegations and detailed figures in the following account come from this source.
64 *Post*, 6 December 1924, p. 452.
65 ECM 8–9/1/25, 104–110, 9–12/2/25, 150ff., 171–2.
66 Most of this is in UPW (1927), pp. 376ff. See also ECM 15–17/4/25, 208–10, 8/5/25, 223, and *Post*, 23 May 1925, p. 438.
67 ECM 14–16/10/25, 57, 2–4/2/26, 69, 76–7; *Post*, 11 July 1925, p. 582.
68 The Union's case is set out in detail in UPW (1927), while that of the Post Office is set out more briefly in *Information Supplied by the Post Office* (January 1927). The *Post* volumes for 1927 give detailed accounts of the Tribunal's proceedings.
69 This file was formerly at R.
70 Seebohm Rowntree (1918); Bullock (1960), Vol. I, p. 129.
71 These statements are given in *Post*, 22 January 1927, pp. 64ff.
72 *Post*, 9 April 1927, p. 334.
73 *Post*, 28 May 1927, p. 520.
74 *Post*, 18 June 1927, p. 613.
75 Given in *Post*, 20 August 1927, pp. 127ff. See also POC, 2924, 18 November 1927.
76 *CC*, 30 August 1927, p. 185; *Post*, 20 August 1927, p. 136; ECM 11–14/10/27, 26–8.
77 ECM 17–19/7/29, 22–4, 15–16/4/30, 183–4, 189, 22–24/10/30, 74–5.
78 ECM 22–24/10/30, 72, 22–24/7/31, 21, 26–9, 10–13/11/31, 72, 77.
79 ECM 12/6/29, 9, 18–19/12/29, 107–10, 22–24/1/30, 130–2, 19–20/3/30, 157–9; PP 1930–1 X (Tomlin Report), pp. 61–2.
80 *WB*, February 1928, for the 'All-Service Campaign' and its programme.
81 NWC (SS) Minutes for 1927, pp. 35ff., 43ff.; ECM 11–14/10/27, 50.
82 Details in a document at F 373.3. NWC (SS) Minutes for this period give some details on the discussions that followed, though they clearly avoid recording some others.
83 NWC (SS) Minutes, 5 July, 13 September, 27 September 1928; ECM 16–18/10/28, 51–4.
84 *Red Tape*, October 1928; NWC (SS) Minutes, 12 October 1928; ECM 16–18/10/28, 52–4; *Post*, 20 April 1929 and 27 July 1929.
85 *WB*, July 1929; *Post*, 3 August 1929, p. 81; ECM 22–24/10/29, 83–4, 19–20/3/30, 106–8. There is a copy of the staff side evidence at F 373.5.

86 *Post*, 15 March 1930, pp. 260–2, 26 July 1930, p. 89; ECM 23–25/7/30, 39–40.
87 NWC (SS) Minutes for 6 June 1930; *Red Tape*, October 1930, pp. 15ff.; *Post*, 30 August 1930, p. 189, 13 September 1930, p. 236.
88 *WB*, September 1930, January, February 1931; NWC (SS) Minutes, 12 September 1930, pp. 75–6.
89 *Post*, 7 February 1931, p. 120; *Red Tape*, March 1931; NWC (SS) Minutes, 5 February 1931, pp. 5ff., 10 March, pp. 10ff.
90 *Post*, 21 February 1931, p. 183, 7 March 1931, p. 242, 14 March, pp. 254–5.
91 ECM 26/3/31, 160–1; *Post*, 30 May 1931, p. 517; PP 1930–1 X (Tomlin Report), pp. 99ff.
92 ECM 26–27/6/30, 10ff. on earlier arguments, ECM 2/5/31, 194 for later ones, put forward in a document by Bowen kept at F 372.5. See also *Post*, 23 May 1931, pp. 503ff., 13 June 1931, p. 580 for the claim and 2 July 1949, pp. 393–4 for a later account.
93 NWC (SS) Minutes, 30 July, 21 September 1931; *Post*, 1 August 1931, pp. 100–1.
94 This interesting discussion is in the UPW GPC Minutes, 17 September 1931.
95 See for example *Post*, 31 October, p. 394, *Red Tape*, November 1931.
96 The details of what happened were later reported by Hamnett in ECM 27/11/31. Quotations are in ECM 14–15/10/31, 54, 58ff. See also *MR View*, December 1931, and F 353.3.
97 UPW GPC Minutes, 4 November 1931; ECM 10–13/11/31, 85–9; *Post*, 30 January 1932, p. 84; *MR View*, December 1931, p. 16.
98 ECM 27/11/31, 107ff.; *Post*, 5 December 1931, pp. 545–6; ECM 17/12/31.
99 POC, 2 September 1931, p. 356; ECM 19–21/4/32, 224ff.
100 *MR View*, January 1932, p. 15; F 050.6 and ECM 20–22/1/32, 160, 30/4/32, 269–73; *Manchester Guardian* (24 March 1932); ECM 22–24/7/32, 45–7, 6–8/7/38, 11–13, 25–27/1/39, 118, 134, 18–20/4/39, 174.
101 *Post*, 28 November 1931, pp. 516ff., 23 January 1932, p. 68; ECM 20–22/1/32; *Post*, 13 February 1932, pp. 140–1, 27 February, pp. 220–1.
102 *Post*, 12 December 1931, p. 560; ECM 25/2/32, 181ff.; NWC (SS) Minutes, 29 February, 3 March 1932.
103 *Morning Post* (13 April); *Times* (19 April 1932).
104 ECM 26/5/32, 3ff., 18/6/32, 23ff., 28/6/32; NWC (SS) Minutes, 30 June, 7 July 1932; *WB* (July 1932); *Manchester Guardian* (30 June 1932).
105 ECM 18–20/10/32, 116–17; *Post*, 24 December 1932, p. 504, 21 January 1933, p. 44, 25 February 1933, pp. 176ff.; ECM 11–13/4/33, 165, 9, 187–8; *Post*, 1933 Supplement, pp. 11ff.; *Post*, 22 July 1933, pp. 64, 66.
106 *Hansard* V, 278, 1808, 1833–54 (30 May 1933), 279, 705–15 (20 June 1933), 280, 2293, 2301 (24 July 1933). The quotation is from Harrison (1577), p. 99 and the cartoon in *Post*, 5 August 1933, p. 103.
107 ECM 6/12/33, 73ff., 3/1/34, 107ff.; WC (SS) Minutes, 7 December, 18 December 1933, 4 January 1934; *WB*, February, March 1934, pp. 88–9. For the meetings see *Red Tape*, December 1933, pp. 149ff. and January 1934, pp. 215–16; *Post*, 16 December 1933, pp. 487ff.
108 The document is given in ECM 9/3/34, 113ff.
109 ECM 9/3/34, 116ff., 10–12/4/34, 134, 139, 144. *Post*, vol. 29, *passim* for the meetings. *Red Tape*, April 1934, p. 420 and *WB*, April 1934, p. 40 for the last stage of the negotiations, WC (SS) Minutes, 14 March 1934, for their attitude. *Post*, 28 April 1934, p. 360 for the Chancellor's statement.
110 ECM 4–5/4/34, 147–8, 16/6/34, 22/6/34, 21; *WB*, August 1934, pp. 41, 43; NWC Minutes, 29 June 1934.
111 Most of the main details are in a *Post* Supplement published in December 1934, though not always bound in with the volume for that part of the year. There is a little material at F 372.6. But most of the interesting discussion is in ECM, which, however, gives only a most general account of the negotiations themselves.
112 ECM 11–13/7/34, 77ff.; UPW GPC Minutes, 8 August 1934.
113 ECM 16–18/10/34, 70, 20/11/34, 91ff.
114 ECM 4–5/12/34, 111ff.; *Post*, 22 December 1974, p. 584; POC, 3301, 14 December 1934. The opinions given are in ECM 7–11/4/35, 190; F 372.6 and *Post*, 1935 CS, pp. 9–11. Later issues of *Post* reveal further opposition.
115 ECM 15–17/10/35, 67–8; *Post*, 21 March 1936, pp. 246ff.
116 TUC 1931 Report, pp. 327ff., 1932 Report, p. 222, 1933 Report, pp. 159ff., 243ff., 1935 Report, pp. 160ff., 314ff., 1936 Report, pp. 340ff.
117 *Post*, 20 July 1935, p. 52, 28 March 1936, p. 265, 16 February 1935, p. 154, 9 March 1935, p. 220, 16 March 1935, p. 236, 30 March 1935, p. 291, 1935 CS, p. 50.

118 ECM 17–19/7/35, 44, 15–17/4/36, 192ff.; *Post*, 28 March 1936, pp. 265ff., 4 April 1936, pp. 289ff.

119 *Post*, CS 1937, p. 12, 24 April 1937, p. 384, 19 June 1937, p. 544, 4 December 1937, p. 448, ECM 2/4/37, 167–8, 30/4–1/5/37, 230ff., 4/5/37, 3ff., 1/9/37, 81, 18–21/4/38, 164, 12–14/4/38, 219, 226.

120 The files of papers in the Union's Research Department (at 372.7) on the 1938 proceedings rise about four feet from the floor. They include verbatim summaries, reports of sub-committees, background papers, plus newspaper cuttings, and much else besides. The Union produced a printed *Wage Claim and Evidence* (1938) and very detailed accounts of the Tribunal in *The Post*. The Union's files at 133 contain information including verbatim accounts of the secessionists' submissions, and there is more at 372.7 together with propaganda against them. Material submitted by the Post Office is also at 372.7, as well as in the verbatim proceedings and summaries. The tribunal's awards were printed both with respect to the UPW and the secessionists.

121 *Post*, 6 March 1937, pp. 228, 215–16, 24 April 1937, pp. 381ff.; ECM 20–21/1/37, 163–4, 4/4/37.

122 *Post*, 1937 CS, p. 29.

123 ECM 13–15/7/37, 45–59, 1/9/37, 61ff.

124 NWC (SS) Minutes, 2 September, 4 November, 2/6 December 1937; *Red Tape*, September 1937, p. 994, November, pp. 103ff., December, pp. 197–8; *Post*, 27 November 1937, pp. 428, 442, 4 December, p. 463, 18 December, p. 106. The two pamphlets are at F 080.4.

125 ECM 13–15/10/37, 104–6, 12/11/37, 7/12/37; *Post*, 23 October, pp. 321–4, 18 December 1937, pp. 496–8.

126 For this see ECM 1938 *passim* and *Post*, 1938 CS, pp. 18–26.

127 Most – though not all – of the verbatim reports are in the UCW files, and all those of the secessionist organisations. However, very full summaries of the former are given in *The Post*, and the ACC printed a report of its own participation.

128 All this is to be found in vols 37 and 38 of *The Post*.

129 The quotations on the management case are in *Post*, 11 June 1938, p. 530, 2 July 1938, pp. 14, 60–1, 1 October 1938, p. 452.

130 ECM 4–6/10/38, 81.

131 See *Mets Journal* November 1938 and *CC*, December 1938, pp. 301ff. The ACC published a verbatim account of its own evidence, which, according to the UPW, excluded the worst of its gaffes.

132 *Post*, 23 December 1938, p. 725, 31 December, p. 741, 28 January 1939, p. 74, and *passim*.

133 *Post*, 21 January 1939, pp. 63ff., 26 July 1941, p. 29, 7 March 1942, pp. 3–4; ECM 15–16/10/40, 87, 22–27/1/41, 150, 8–10/4/41, 228.

134 *Post*, 30 December 1939, pp. 340–2, 13 January 1940, pp. 13–14, 27 January, pp. 29–34, 10 February, p. 54.

135 The White Paper in PP 1940–1 VIII is given in full in *Post*, 9 September 1941, p. 79, together with a TUC statement repudiating it.

136 NWC (SS) Minutes, 26 June 1942; ECM 21/5/43, 9–11 gives an interesting memorandum by Albert Day discussing these issues.

137 *Post*, 13 January 1940, p. 4, 1 June 1940, p. 312.

138 NWC (SS) Minutes, 6 August 1942, for accusations about 'a dishonest and disgraceful position' by those responsible for conducting negotiations and *Post*, 29 May 1943, pp. 8–11 for a resolution at the UPW Conference questioning that this was the best way to proceed.

139 *Post*, 18 December 1937, p. 500. See also above.

140 Details on this and what follows in ECM 23–25/4/40, 202ff., and NWC (SS) Minutes. Some UPW Executive members thought the scheme represented 'the lower-paid grades being used as window dressing to bolster up the rest of the Civil Service' but the majority were prepared to accept it for the sake of unity with their trade union colleagues.

141 Full details are given in NWC (SS) Minutes.

142 *ibid.*, 15 May 1940, p. 8; *Post*, 1940 CS, p. 20.

143 Very full details of this are given in the NWC (SS) Minutes, supplemented by ECM.

144 ECM 3/5/41, 205–9, 29–30/4/41, 269; *WB*, September 1941, pp. 51–3. There is a detailed defence of the settlement in *Post*, 20 September 1941, p. 87.

145 Besides the SS Minutes, see ECM 23/6/42 and 28–30/7/42. Also an account by Hodgson in *Post*, 8 August 1942, pp. 39–40.

146 ECM 20–22/1/43, 248.

147 The chronology of these negotiations (and of the previous ones) is given in some detail as a result of the row caused by delays in ECM 22–29/7/43, 72–8.

148 *Post*, 29 May 1943, pp. 8–11.
149 ECM 2/6/43, 13; NWC (SS) Minutes, especially for 3 June.
150 NWC (SS) Minutes, 5 August, 2 September, 17 October 1943.
151 For these negotiations, see NWC (SS) Minutes, 23 November 1944 and ECM 9/11/44, 144–5.
152 Most of the details are in ECM 22–24/11/45.
153 This story can be traced in ECM 3/11/39, 135–43, 24/11/39, 150–7, 22–27/1/41, 157–8, 8/1/42, 143, 13–15/4/43, 345, 14–15/5/42, 246, 27–29/10/43, 159, 11–13/5/44, 306–7.
154 ECM 24/11/39, 145ff.; *Post*, 17 February 1940, pp. 189–90. At F 377 there are some press cuttings indicating successful efforts to publicise the grievances of the casuals.
155 ECM 17–19/7/40, 41–7; *Post*, 20 April 1940, p. 267, 24 August 1940, p. xvii, 14 June 1941, p. 4.
156 ECM 15–16/10/40, 87, 22–27/11/41, 176–8.
157 *Post*, 14 June 1941, pp. 4, 25.
158 *Post*, 1 November 1941, p. 135. The main course of the negotiations that followed is given in ECM 5/12/41.
159 ECM 27–29/1/42, 170, 178–82, 15–17/4/42, 216.
160 *Post*, 30 May, pp. 148–9 and 27 June 1942, pp. 9–12.
161 ECM 10/6/42, 7–9, 11–13/11/42, 157–72, 1/12/42, 187–98; *Post* (12 December 1942).
162 ECM 20–22/1/43, 236–54, 19–20/8/43, 95–105; *Post*, 20 May 1943, p. 3, 4 September, pp. 70–2.
163 ECM 29/4–1/5/43, 393–4; *Post*, 29 May 1943, p. 21.
164 ECM 27–29/10/43, 165–80; *Post*, 14 April 1944, p. 6.
165 *Post*, 24 June 1944, p. 23; ECM 24–26/10/44, 126–9, 28/12/44, 171–5.

13 Bargaining in the Great Boom and after: 1945–1971

> We think that a correct balance will be achieved if the primary principle of Civil Service pay is fair comparison with the current remuneration of outside staffs employed in broadly comparable work, taking account of differences in other conditions of service. (Priestley, Royal Commission on the Civil Service, November 1955, Cmd 9613, p. 25)

> . . . the Executive Council had made its call to our members. The choice before us is to accept that which we know in our hearts to be completely unjust, or to show our determination to fight for what we believe to be right. (Tom Jackson, *No Alternative: The Claim of the Union of Post Office Workers*, January 1971)

The development in industrial relations and bargaining in the years between the Second World War and the break-up of the Post Office in the early 1980s are a good deal more tortuous and complex than in all the years that have previously been covered. In order to devote as much attention to the details of the bargaining in these years as has been possible for all the periods covered in earlier chapters, it would be necessary to write another volume at least as long as this one. This is both because of the much more rapid pace of bargaining, with the 'annual round' becoming the norm for the first time in the 1950s, and also because of the complexity of the issues and arguments in comparison with earlier periods.

This is not to say that the discussions about wages and conditions in the Post Office in more recent years have thrown up any totally new concepts and arguments fundamentally different from those described in earlier chapters. Many of the same pressures have continued to bear down on Post Office pay. Where once there was a profit to be used as part of taxation, the same 'good housekeeping' came to be enforced by means of economic planning and wage restraint. Furthermore, the same arguments about the best means for deciding on Post Office pay were heard as in previous generations, even if they have sometimes been argued in a different way.

The major period of general discussion and internal change in the Post Office in the early 1930s had coincided with the enunciation of the 'Tomlin formula' for public sector wage determination by the general trend of outside wages. Similarly, when in the mid-1950s Post Office finances were for the first time given some independence from governmental decision, the 'Priestley formula' quoted at the head of the chapter attempted to give a scientific, or at least objective, means of making such comparisons. Although the Priestley formula contained that element of 'outside comparison' which the unions had disliked since the nineteenth century, it also spoke of the state's 'categorical obligation to remunerate its employees fairly' which sounded something like the old call for the state to be a 'model employer'.

The Priestley formula and the Civil Service Pay Research Unit set up to enforce it corresponded in a number of ways to the semi-automatic ways of making bargaining decisions which had been discussed by civil service trade unionists at least as far back as the years before the First World War. There had been many efforts to discover a clear and effective machinery for such bargaining. However, it was no easy matter to discover valid and agreed 'outside comparisons'. Post Office workers had warned Lord Tweedmouth of this as long ago as 1897!

Nor were these inherent difficulties the only reasons for the fact that the Priestley formula did not provide the ultimate solution to generations of trade union effort. The mid-1950s began the movement of the Post Office from the leisurely world of a revenue-earning department of state to the tougher commercial values of the Post Office Corporation and its successors. From the mid-1950s also can be dated a change in the means of conducting industrial relations when, after a break of thirty years, the weapons of confrontation were again wielded by both sides. Various government attempts to control incomes, prices and investment policy combined in the Post Office to produce, particularly in the years from 1962 to 1971, a new period of wage determination by industrial confrontation. This in turn affected the character of Post Office trade unionism. If the UPW's leaders did not lose their taste for tidy bargaining patterns and their skills as political lobbyists, they were nevertheless compelled to become much more trade unionists like the others, needing and utilising their industrial muscle. This had profound effects on the policy, organisation and internal life of the UPW.

In this process the 1971 national strike was a traumatic watershed. After it was over, UPW members broke with the language and concepts of a previous age. They were no longer part of 'the service', 'Post Office people' in serried ranks who sought redress from 'the authorities'. The hard commercial attitudes of the 1970s and 1980s have turned the modern UCW members into 'employees' with an organisation that has had to rely on industrial strength. This would certainly not have been recognised by those who set up the Post Office trade unions a century ago and operated in the period of the inquiries, or under the old Whitley system. It would even have seemed strange to those who built the UPW in the long years when it had no strike policy, and had to rely on the force of rational argument applied to the formulae of Tomlin and Priestley. It has finally, and after the passing of so many generations, transcended most of the snobberies and separateness of the past, and transformed those who work for the Post Office and its successors into trade unionists recognisable within the movement as a whole. Perhaps past generations would have been surprised at this, but they would surely have recognised that this was in the end the logic of what they had built, for all the legal and political veils that once obscured it.

Many of the events of the history of industrial relations in the Post Office since 1945 have been determined by the great re-allocation of grades which took place immediately at the end of the war. These were soon followed by wage negotiations in 1946 and 1947. A period of greater restrictions on wages came next, so that settlements were made in 1949 and 1951 in the Arbitration Court, the latter including a claim on provincial differentiation. In 1952 there was a settlement through the National Whitley Council and the negotiated settlement of 1954 began the period of annual wage rounds whose arguments were dictated by the 1955 Priestley Report. By the time of the 1962 negotiations, a new period of industrial action was brought about by Conservative efforts to freeze wages, a phase that continued during Labour governments in the 1960s and culminated in the 1971 strike. Since then the annual negotiations have been directly conducted in a somewhat more tranquil atmosphere. It is this basic outline that will now be set out in more detail in this chapter and the one that follows.

THE RE-ALLOCATION AGREEMENT OF 1946

This was the only systematic attempt in the entire history of the Post Office to set out a structure of grades organised around their various functions, their modes of recruitment and their roads to promotion. It overturned the historic system of grading on the postal side. It abolished all the specialist London grades of sorters and counter clerks, and their provincial equivalents the sorting clerks and tele-graphists. It set up the new postmen higher grade performing superior sorting office duties in every part of the country, and the grade of postal and telegraph officer largely responsible for counter duties and for some writing work. It could hardly be expected that these changes, and numerous smaller ones that accompanied them, would be introduced without any friction. Nevertheless, considering the great difficulties over the allocation of such duties in the past, they went through with surprising smoothness. The most important reason for this was clearly the generosity of the Post Office authorities in building substantial improvements of wages into the scheme, rising to as high as 10 per cent or more for those near the maximum rates of pay.

The main issues in the 1946 re-allocation agreement went back at least to the latter part of the nineteenth century when the tasks of the indoor postal grades were finally standardised. Letter carriers had become postmen in 1883 and the standard dual qualification for other postal work had been recognised by the creation of the provincial grade of sorting clerk and telegraphist. The larger the town the more likely were those in this grade to specialise in telegraphy sorting or counter work, and in London itself there were separate grades for each of these three tasks. Postmen, however, were not simply deliverers of letters. Particularly in London, they had always been involved at various parts of the process of sorting letters, including the more complicated inward sorting. From the 1890s at least, the Post Office authorities always aimed to extend the amount of sorting done by postmen. This was only standardised in 1946.

Before the Tweedmouth deliberations in 1897, extra duties performed by post-men were paid by a complex set of *ad hoc* and local arrangements which the Committee's Report served to sweep away.[1] Lord Tweedmouth nevertheless noted that more sorting work was done in London by postmen and expressed the view that this should be done elsewhere. To some extent this happened and in Belfast and Hull in 1902, for example, some inward primary sorting was given to postmen. After allowances began to be paid for such work in Cardiff and Hull in 1906, the UKPCA, representing the provincial SC&Ts, protested that their position was being eroded. They evinced a number of statements from Postmaster General Buxton to the effect that postmen would never be given sorting duties full time and most of the inward sorting would always be retained by the SC&Ts. The postmen nevertheless began to claim the right of automatic promotion to perform all sorting office duties, and this was the basis of the divisive and unsuccessful 'unification' case presented by the Postmen's Federation to the Hobhouse Committee in 1908. The authorities wanted to standardise sorting office arrangements, at least for the provinces, and in 1911 set up a Committee under the chairmanship of Assistant Postmaster General Cecil Norton. This issued a report in January 1912 which provided the basis for all discussion on the matter for the next thirty-five years. Its proposals to further expand the sorting office duties of postmen were, however, interrupted by the war, as also were the recommendations of the Holt Committee in 1913 that similar arrangements should apply in London.

During the First World War the allocation of duties in sorting offices was to some extent frozen, but after it was over, the authorities continued to press for the expansion of the duties of postmen. In 1921 the work of outward sorting was greatly altered by the agreement to introduce a standard 48-box fitting, half the size of many previously in use and considerably simplifying the tasks involved. Nevertheless, it took six years for a Joint Committee of UPW and official side to consider the allocation of sorting duties during the 1920s. This was not only because of the problems resulting from the UPW's own ill-fated reorganisation scheme of 1923–4, but also because of the difficulty in reconciling the various interests in order to arrive at an agreement. This did not prove possible, and when the Joint Committee reported this in 1928, the UPW Conference clearly showed support for the view that members should not be allocated 'superior' duties without getting higher pay.[2] Despite this, the Post Office authorities went ahead in a piecemeal way in doing what they had always wanted. In 1929 the management put about 100 postmen in the Inland Section on facing, stamping and primary sorting, in defiance of the Union. By the end of 1932, over 200 provincial head offices had seen some form of reorganisation, though it was said that this had only led to a net loss of seventy-one SC&Ts and twenty-two extra postmen, together with various allowances to others.[3]

The fact was that the Union's Executive found it extremely difficult to come to a decision on these matters because of the likely conflict of interest between the grades. In 1936, the authorities indicated that they were going to introduce some further changes in London. By this time there were only sorters in eight of the 113 London offices, but the Union leaders were worried that any further agreement to expand the tasks of postmen would be seized on by the secessionist organisations. They agreed to try to work out a scheme of their own, but were pre-empted by official proposals presented in May 1937. These would have allowed postmen to do virtually all forms of sorting except foreign mail. A good deal of bitterness followed because of the secrecy in which negotiations were conducted. Union leaders were keen to maintain this, and the Guild of Sorters were bound by secrecy also.[4] However, the entire issue was shelved when everyone went to the Arbitration Court at the time on the major claim, and it was formally buried with the outbreak of war.

When the UPW Executive in 1943 considered the wide range of wage claims before it, it again decided to seize the nettle of grade reallocation and worked out a new scheme for postal and telecommunication officers divided into two grades. Virtually all the main sorting and operational duties would have been in the hands of the superior of these grades, whose form bore some resemblance to the ideas which had been rejected by the Union in 1924. Though agreed by the Executive, these proposals were not put any further to the test, since the authorities issued a new general scheme on 24 January 1945.[5]

The essence of these proposals was not greatly modified during the course of the protracted negotiations which followed its first statement.[6] It went to the Annual Conference of the Union in May 1945 and to a special conference in November. It

was finally signed on 30 April 1946, accepted by the 1946 Annual Conference, and
came into effect on 1 June. The most important changes were the duties of the
postmen which were expanded to take in a number of sorting office duties formerly
only done in London, such as private box sorting and bagging inland correspondence. At the same time other grades such as porters and tube attendants were
absorbed into the postman grade. All the superior sorting office duties were to be
done by an entirely new grade called postmen higher grade, who were to be
uniformed but normally confined to sorting offices. The PHG, which was nation-
wide, had some resemblance to the old London sorter grade, but with the important
difference that the normal means of entry was now from the ranks of postmen. At
first it was expected that postmen themselves would be recruited from the ranks of
ex-servicemen and boy messengers. The latter source soon dried up because of the
raising of the school-leaving age and the abolition altogether of the grade of boy
messenger in October 1947. Although some leeway was allowed for particular
pressures and special circumstances, all counter and writing work was in future to
be done by another entirely new grade known as postal and telegraph officers. After
initially being made up from the old London CC&T grade (which they most closely
resembled) and from SC&Ts and sorters, the new P&TOs were expected to be
recruited from outside by open competition and to have the most immediate access
to higher positions in supervising and administration. There was also to be some
effort to separate out the work of telegraphy to the telegraphist's grade, though a
Post Office proposal for a new group of male night telegraphists disappeared during
the negotiations.

These general proposals, which naturally contained a good deal of complicated
small print, seem to have been generally accepted by the mass of UPW members.
The 1945 Annual Conference heard Ron Smith on behalf of the London District
Council argue that they could not agree to such major modifications without
hearing the views of those who were still in the forces. However, an overall rejection
of the scheme only received 144 conference votes against 461. Similar arguments
were heard at the November special conference combined with the more general
argument that the desire for larger wage increases was being bought off by
superiors' duties, but again the scheme survived, this time by a card vote of 1,717
against 681. Ernest Mercer, who was a sorter in the Inland Section and later became
General Treasurer of the Union, spoke at the 1946 Annual Conference for many ex-
servicemen who felt unhappy and to some extent betrayed by the changes they
discovered on their return to the Post Office. By then, however, there was little they
could do to prevent the new system from coming into operation.[7] In October 1945 a
move on the Executive by George Douglas to have the entire scheme rejected was
defeated by 8 votes against 14.[8]

Besides the large wage increases which have already been mentioned, the scheme
also brought significant improvements in wages through changes in office classifications. A new Class II included all outer London and larger provincial offices, and
102 officers were raised to this level from Class III, while thirteen went from Class
II to Class I. Another important improvement secured after the negotiations was the
granting of established status to a number of smaller grades such as cleaners and
liftmen who had not previously had access to it.[9] However, not all the gains sought
by Union leaders at this time were secured. The Union argued for equal pay for
women and equal access to the P&TO grade. The authorities were not prepared to
accept any of this and in any case the Executive maintained that the old arrange-

ment of not allowing women access to the better writing duties should continue. Women on the Executive were also worried by the fact that, along with these negotiations the Union was agreeing to reorganise telephone duties so that male night telephonists could now begin as early as 4 p.m. Other issues which came up during the negotiations naturally included questions about the rights of those coming from the old grades, and efforts to get more access to the P&TO grade for postmen. Generally speaking, however, the whole matter was settled with surprising ease.[10] The Post Office workforce was launched into the new period organised for work as their superiors had wanted them to be since the nineteenth century, and which they themselves now accepted as inevitable.

WAGE NEGOTIATIONS BEFORE PRIESTLEY: 1947-55

During these years wages were improved by almost every available method, including direct negotiations, reference to the Arbitration Court, and discussion on the National Whitley Council. By the time the Priestley Report set out the new basis for wage determination, the annual wage round had just been established.

The high expectations that followed the war were reflected in a series of claims formulated before the re-allocation discussions had finished. A claim for a forty-hour, five-day week was presented in December 1946, and argued largely on the basis of special disabilities of Post Office workers with their difficult hours of attendances, and by comparisons with at least the best of outside employers.[11] Discussions on this were complicated by the fact that the 'net' working week was thought to be forty-two to forty-three hours, though nominally it had been forty-eight since the 1890s. Furthermore, the issue became entangled with the Government's general exhortations to improve productivity. Thus when Postmaster General Lord Listowel replied to the claim on 3 March 1947, he said that shorter hours could only be considered 'if it can be shown by the Union to lead to an increase of over-all output without additional manpower'. The POEU had in fact managed to obtain some improvements on that basis and Geddes persuaded the UPW to argue for similar reductions in hours in combination with discussions around a Joint Production Committee. It did not prove any easier to get a response to this than it had done to the similar claim in the 1930s, and it soon became lost in the wage claim. The 1950 Union Conference insisted on the matter being nevertheless pursued, and the official side replied early in 1951 that it would not discuss it in view of the continuing deterioration in the economic situation.[12] There, for the moment, this matter rested.

The immediate post-war period had already built up a particular expectation for wage improvements long before the re-allocation agreement had been concluded. Two particular issues which were felt not to have been satisfactorily resolved by re-allocation were embodied in claims submitted in February and March 1947.[13] First of all, increases were claimed on the maximum for the new P&TOs of around 9 per cent. The abolition of separate rates for sub-office postmen was also demanded. Two more general issues were submitted on 21 April 1947. The effort to shorten incremental scales, which had begun three years earlier, was taken up again when it was asked that maximum pay should be achieved at the age of 25. (It was then usual at about 32.) The second part of this claim was for a general increase in line with the rise in the cost-of-living index since 1938. In April Geddes wrote to the authorities pointing out that the index had now gone up by 65 per cent and the earnings of none of the grades had gone up so much – postmen at head offices got 55 per cent more, P&TOs compared to their earlier equivalents got 48 per cent if men, and 57 per cent if women. Although male telephonists got 61 per cent more than in 1938, women telephonists got only 48 per cent more.

When this was considered at the 1947 Annual Conference, the claim was very considerably increased. A £5 minimum at 21 was demanded, involving a considerable increase of more than 30 per cent for postmen in the larger offices, with 21 per cent for P&TOs. It was also proposed to reduce the incremental steps from 13 to 5 and to increase all maximum rates by £1, this representing an increase of anything from 20 per cent upwards. Though the Executive refused to add equal pay for women and the abolition of classification of offices for pay purposes, it was still a formidable list. Geddes thought it could be argued directly with the Post Office, and compared to general outside trends under the Tomlin formula. He thought that likely high settlements outside and the general labour shortage could result in securing a good deal of what they were asking.[14] However, very soon the whole context in which the discussions could develop was changing. A rapidly deteriorating balance of payments position was exacerbated by inflationary pressures at home, and in a major debate in Parliament on 6 August 1947, Prime Minister Attlee appealed 'to workers in all industries and employers not to press at this time for increases in wages, or changes in conditions that would have a similar effect'.[15]

It was against this background that the Postmaster General, Wilfred Paling, and all the leading officials of the Department met the entire UPW Executive on 15 October 1947 to appeal to them to abandon the claim altogether. The Union leaders replied, as they were bound to do, that they simply could not accept this.[16] The feeling of the membership was clearly indicated as the meeting was going on by the numbers of (unsolicited) telegrams delivered to the meeting, insisting on a firm stand by the Executive. In the press the issue was seen as a test of wills both of Government and trade unions generally. It was to confirm the resolution of UPW members that ballot papers on the restoration of the strike fund were sent out at this point. The Executive also decided, on the proposal of Dick Hayward, to set up a sub-committee to consider 'the withdrawal of good will'. At Weston-Super-Mare there was a brief strike on 13 October which seems to have been largely occasioned by resentment against the actions of the local postmaster, but no doubt reflected a general mood of militancy.[17]

Faced with this, the Postmaster General met a further delegation on 28 October and announced his willingness to negotiate. The following day, a full case against the Union's submission was put forward. In particular the official side denied that outside wages had risen to the extent claimed by the Union, and made some other calculations to show that Post Office wages since 1938 had gone up by not 56 per cent but 59 per cent. They also maintained that the claim would cost £15·5 million – well over half of the profit earned in the previous year. On the basis of their interpretation of the arguments provided by the Union, the Post Office was prepared to consider increases at the lower end of the scale, tapering off to nothing at the top. In the case of one grade, cleaners, they offered the alternative of fewer incremental steps and no increase at the maximum, or of a smaller increase at the maximum. The negotiator reported this to the Executive, but did not see any purpose in discussing what was regarded by Geddes as simply 'the preliminary skirmish'.

The rest of the discussion was completed with some speed, to a great extent no doubt because Union leaders feared that they would be caught up in the gathering economic crisis. By 3 November, the Union's Executive was able to consider a comprehensive set of proposals from the official side which was a good deal more than their preliminary offer. Scales were shortened by two steps and increases were now proposed at all points and all grades. The increases were still a good deal greater at the lower ends of the scales. For example, London postmen at 22 could receive 102 per cent more than they had done in 1938, but if transferred from the old to the new maximum, the increase was only 60 per cent. The P&TO and PHG grades did not do quite so well compared to their pre-war equivalents, with London PHGs getting 56 per cent more at the maximum than sorters, and 60 per cent more than SC&Ts in the larger provincial offices. Women generally went up somewhat more, with 34 per cent for London telegraphists at the maximum, compared to 31 per cent for men. However, as usual the male telephonists did better, 67 per cent ahead of 1938 in London compared to 56 per cent for the women, and 73 per cent against 54 per cent in the larger provincial offices. Most of this seemed reasonable enough. However there was one part in the package which presented some difficulty and this was the proposal that there should be no further claims for two years.

The Union's Executive on 3 November 1947 accepted that some of their arguments had been defeated and were not prepared to reject the entire package. Only the question of the two-year delay was opposed without qualification, and there was some case for arguing that this was in breach of the Tomlin formula which the offer was supposed to reflect. If there were to be significant changes in wage patterns elsewhere, would this not then entitle them to further consideration? Therefore the Executive agreed to the two-year formula only if in that period there was 'no substantial rise in prices or in the percentage increase in wage rates in outside industry'. They also agreed to changes in relation to boy messengers and girl probationers which amounted to the complete absorption of these grades into the ranks of postmen and telephonists.[18] The official side accepted most of what the Union was now arguing, including full assimilation of the new scales. They abandoned the two-year stipulation though Geddes thought this was because of fears about 'the interpretation that might be placed upon it by outside industry'. They accepted better rates for juveniles but would not budge on the date of the settlement, which the Union had been trying to get back-dated. Speaking to the Executive on 4 November, Geddes argued that this should now be recommended to a special conference of the Union, and this was agreed by 17 votes to 10. Geddes thought that although there was a strong opposition to any compromise, especially in London, this would not win the majority, particularly as the membership would not have received anything at all by the time of any special conference.

The special conference met in Blackpool on 27–28 November 1947.[19] The mood of the membership was again confirmed by the result of the strike ballot which showed 82,094 in favour and 21,305 against a strike policy. There was a fiery discussion with large numbers of opponents to the settlement from offices such as Glasgow and ECDO. Although there was much these speakers could say about the poverty of Post Office workers and the justification of the original claim, there was little they could propose in terms of new tactics or new negotiations. The possibility of going to arbitration was heavily rejected by 2,283 votes to 150. A lengthy and eloquent address from Geddes agreed that there was still much to do to improve conditions, but said that there was no other means to get more. He won a narrow majority for acceptance of the settlement – 1,619 against 1,167.

In the circumstances, this settlement was seen as a good one, attributed by at least one other civil service trade union leader to the superior political clout of the UPW.[20] Some Conservative MPs saw it as an indication of a weakening resolve by the Government to enforce wage restrictions. The effect of the 1946 re-allocation and the 1947 agreement were summarised as follows:

> These two revisions balance each other. The 1946 revision gave most benefit at the maximum, whilst the 1947 revision gave most benefit in the middle ranges 21–30.
> The aggregate effect of the two revisions taken together is that there has been a fairly evenly distributed increase of about 20 per cent throughout the scales; but rather above average in the middle ranges.

Since these increases had been obtained over a period when the Retail Price Index had only gone up by 11 per cent, there could at last be seen some restoration of much that had been lost before the 1938 settlement.

The atmosphere in which wage negotiations were conducted over the remaining period of Labour Government from 1948 until 1951 was quite different. The Government was faced with international economic crisis which led amongst other things to the devaluation of the pound in September 1949. During this whole period, there was continual pressure on wages, particularly through joint discussion between Government and union leaders. There was sometimes a tone of fierce loyalty to 'our' Government by union leaders who had for generations looked forward to a majority Labour administration. In February 1948 a White Paper was published which asserted that 'until more goods and services are available for the home market, there is no justification for any general increase of industrial money incomes'. In particular it said that the Government itself would 'observe these principles in any negotiations in which they are directly concerned'.[21] Amidst a good deal of talk about the need to limit profits and dividends, the freeze was in general accepted by the TUC General Council. However they added many qualifications including the maintenance of differentials and adjustments for 'workers whose incomes fell below a reasonable standard of subsistence', or pushed up output or were in under-manned enterprises. This was accepted at a meeting of TUC affiliated executives held on 24 March 1948. Though the UPW Executive had agreed by 16 votes to 6 to support the TUC line, this was heavily defeated at the Union's Annual Conference held six weeks later by 1,953 votes to 557. The Conference nevertheless agreed to accept a wage freeze in the event of prices being cut by 10 per cent. In line with this the Conference passed a series of resolutions calling for wage increases including general improvements for P&TOs and PHGs based on value of work and increases for the remaining unestablished grades, plus parity between telephonists and telegraphists. The Conference also passed a resolution demanding that maximum be paid at the age of 25 to all grades.[22]

This 1948 wage claim proceeded a good deal more slowly than its predecessors. The Executive was in any case faced with a problem in dealing with a set of resolutions on wages which General Secretary Geddes privately asserted to be 'inconsistent and outrageous'.[23] In part at least they proceeded because of fears of what the secessionists might do. It was decided at any rate to go ahead immediately with the claim for maximum pay at 25. This was submitted on 8 June 1948 and rejected out of hand by the administration on 2 July. The reply maintained that no arguments had been presented for changes in the incremental scales so soon, and there was no basis for such improvements under the Government's White Paper.[24] Despite continued misgivings on the part of Geddes, the Union's Executive decided to put forward a comprehensive claim of which the most conspicuous other feature was a demand for an extra 12½ per cent on the maximum. This was sent to the Post Office on 20 October.

On 6 December 1948 there was a meeting between leading officials of the Post Office and thirteen members of the Union's Executive. The claims were presented by the Union's various officers. There was much less reference to percentage changes since 1938 and direct outside comparisons, though recent increases in the Retail Price Index were mentioned. Much more was said about the dissatisfaction in various grades. This did not impress the authorities who again replied on 10 January 1949 with a comprehensive rejection of the claim. Then, as had been widely expected from the start, the entire matter was put into the hands of the Civil Service Arbitration Tribunal.

The 1949 arbitration hearings took much less the form of set-piece battles than had those of 1938 and 1927, or their various predecessors. There was some dispute initially about the terms of reference, and the Union succeeded in keeping the discussion away from precise scales such as was advocated by the Post Office. The claim went to the Arbitration Court on 27 April and, to the amazement of the Union expecting a discussion on the scale of 1938, proceedings were completed on the following day. It is perhaps even more astonishing that the tribunal felt able to present an award on the last day of May.[25] The Union's case included value of work statements about the various grades, but concentrated also on generally relating the claim to the February 1948 White Paper on Incomes and in claiming that the economic situation generally, as well as wage increases in particular, indicated that it was time for a further improvement. Geddes performed with some skill in picking at comparisons that served the interests of the members. The Tribunal's award did not alter the incremental scales in any way, but gave increases at every point, generally lower on higher incomes. The amounts obtained varied from around 4–6 per cent, and were accepted with virtually no controversy within the Union itself.

There was at this point a delay in formulating any further wage claims. One reason for this was that there had been other improvements. For example, members benefited from a review of allowances which had come through at the end of 1948 and had involved a wide range of increases of up to 20 per cent back-dated to June 1947.[26] In 1949 delegates were prepared to be more tolerant about wage restrictions. Thus the 1949 Annual Conference rejected a resolution against the Government's White Paper on Incomes and also refused to go ahead on getting the same maximum pay for PHGs as for redundant sorters. The Conference, however, agreed to campaign through Labour Party and TUC for limits on prices and profits.[27]

Generally speaking, the Union continued to support the Government during 1949. Following the devaluation of the pound in September there were some further efforts by the Government to keep down wages. The Union supported the line put by the General Council to a conference of union executives on 12 January 1950, asking them 'to reconsider existing wage claims and sliding-scale arrangements with a view to holding agreed wage rates stable', at least while there was no major increase in prices.[28] This was the high point in co-operation between unions and Government on wage restraint. There was talk of the setting up of national wage bargaining machinery to cover all industries and the co-ordination of claims and settlements, linked in with rather more vague proposals about prices and profits. It was at this time also that the Union began to participate in a new Post Office Productivity Committee.

Soon, however, all such efforts at co-operation were lost in a flood of trade union opposition caused by the accumulated resentment about the restraint in the previous period and the growing inflation that developed during 1950. Increasing numbers of unions put in substantial claims, and in June the TUC General Council issued a statement calling for 'greater flexibility of wage movements in the future'. However, even this was not enough for the September Congress, which rejected wage restraint altogether.[29] A similar change of mood was evident among civil service trade unionists generally. On 16 March 1950, the National Whitley Council staff side (despite the UPW's dissent) wrote to the Prime Minister saying that while it did not question the Government's policy in general, there was nevertheless 'a widespread belief among Civil Servants of all grades that the Government's policy of wage restraint is being applied more severely to them than to other workers'. The letter referred in particular to the apparent pressure from Government on the decisions of the Arbitration Court. After a reply on 2 May, Prime Minister Attlee agreed to meet a delegation on 27 May. Although there was little concrete result, the unions did give publicity to their fears and thought they then detected a general modification of attitude on the official side.[30]

In the meantime, the mood of the May 1950 Annual Conference of the UPW was quite different from its predecessors. As already mentioned, the Conference decided to pursue the forty-hour week claim. This was not all, however. The Conference narrowly accepted the TUC delegation's support for the economic policies of the General Council, it rejected wage freezing in general, and passed resolutions demanding a 10s (50p) per week increase for all and a £5 minimum wage at 21. Some demands were not agreed, including equal pay for women, but the Executive now had a clear mandate to proceed.[31] There was some delay in presenting the claim, in part so that evidence could be collected about the expenditure patterns of members, and also so that some other settlements and inflation figures could be taken into account. It was intended to base the claim entirely on the Tomlin formula and outside comparisons, placing particular emphasis on Government statements about helping the lower paid, which had been made in discussions about recent settlements. The UPW claim was presented to the Post Office Director General on 28 December 1950.

It was now the turn of the official side to delay proceedings. The first discussions were held on 16 February 1951 and the first offer did not come until April. This largely ignored the claim, particularly for a better minimum wage and shorter incremental scales. It offered increases for women up to 20 in London of 3s (15p) per week, and 4s (20p) to all others. Somewhat more was offered to London PHGs and cleaners, at least near the top of the scale. There was also a proposal to reduce the number of wage levels outside London to two. On the same day that this offer was made, though before it was known to the members, there began a movement of unofficial industrial action in support of the claim. At midnight on Tuesday 17 April, a work to rule began at the West Central and Eastern District offices in London.[32] The spread of such action, which was a new departure in the history of the UPW, dominated the rest of the negotiations. The management offer was soon rejected by branches representing 91,200 members and accepted only by those with

7,000. By 25 April the Executive decided to refer the entire question to arbitration.[33]

However, this was not good enough for large numbers of members, especially in London, who wanted more drastic action. On 24 April the London District Council recommended a work to rule and ban on overtime throughout the capital from May Day, a week later. On 25 April, members walked out of Mount Pleasant sorting office to express their support for this demand, and on Sunday 29 April such action began at Leeds. Although the London District Council was persuaded to call off its recommendation for slower working, a mass meeting of Mount Pleasant workers decided, on 2 May, to continue, and there was sporadic action in some other district offices. On 3 May, a mass meeting at Central Hall Westminster saw General Secretary Charles Geddes facing a very hostile reception from 8,000 members. He was unable to speak for fully twenty minutes, and when he did, could only promise action of the vaguest sort. Les Morgan, Secretary of the LDC, who had called off the work to rule, was not able to speak at all.[34]

It was against this background that the UPW leaders urged haste on the official side. The Arbitration Court proceeded with even greater expedition. It met on 16 May 1951 and after by far the swiftest consideration of a general Post Office claim, issued its award in less than a week, on 21 May.

The award was backdated to 1 January and constituted a good deal more than the original Post Office offer. In general, adult men got 8s (40p) per week extra, women 6s 6d (35p) and juveniles 4s (20p). This meant that a postmen at the maximum in the larger offices had an increase from £5 17s (£5. 85) to £6 5s (£6. 25), or 6·8 per cent. For postmen at the smallest (Class III) offices the full claim was proposed – 10s (50p) a week more, though postwomen only got 8s (40p). This increase gave all adult male members of the Union the £5 per week demanded and opened the way to the provincial differentiation revision which the Tribunal thought should now be considered. This was directly negotiated later in the year, with the number of classifications now reduced from four to three and with some further consequent increases coming in on 1 January 1951. For example, the provincial postman in the smallest offices now got on to his maximum two years earlier at the age of 27, when he got £6 11s (£6. 55) a week, this being a further 4·8 per cent increase.[35] There was also a separate set of negotiations for cable room telegraphists complicated by the fact that the secessionist Government Overseas Cable and Wireless Association submitted an identical claim. There were also particular grievances about the lack of progress since nationalisation that led to a good deal of pressure being placed on the UPW Executive. The Arbitration Court on 8 March 1951 granted increases of 5–6s (25–30p), roughly comparable to what had been obtained elsewhere.[36]

The year 1951 saw a number of interesting developments in civil service pay bargaining. Within the UPW there was a good deal of discussion on this topic following the Union's May 1951 Annual Conference. General Secretary Geddes was the architect of a report which envisaged an automatic method of settling pay and conditions in the Post Office, and was agreed at a special conference of the Union held in November of that year.[37] Geddes argued for an extension of the Tomlin formula about outside comparisons to the agreed adjustment of wages in line with the wages index published by the Ministry of Labour. This would only be readjusted after intervals of three years. It would not, however, preclude separate claims based on value of work. This scheme represented a last attempt from the Union side to use the experience gained in the Government/Union discussions of

1948 and afterwards to set up an ordered system of bargaining for the public sector. It was a clear product of the years before industrial confrontation in the public sector, and also before the annual wage round came into existence and the Priestley criteria tried to combine regular reviews with value of work criteria.

These ideas and the discussions that surrounded them had some short-term impact. In the latter part of 1951, the National Whitley Council staff side argued for an increase for all civil servants based on the general increase in wages over the past twelve months of just under 10 per cent. Lesser amounts were claimed for those earning more than £500 per annum, which did not include many UPW members. Though the official side refused to be bound by any general formula and the UPW was reluctant to be bound by arguments other than those based on the wages index, the staff side case was accepted almost in its entirety and a 10 per cent pay 'addition' was agreed at all points up to £500 per annum, and dated from 1 January 1952.[38] Though apparently seen at first as something like the routine 'bonus' arrangement and therefore only 'temporary', this increase was consolidated with all civil servants' incomes within a year. It was to prove the only general civil service increase negotiated in this way before the days of pay research.

The election of a Conservative Government in October 1951 did something to alter the atmosphere in which bargaining was conducted. For a time the new Government chose to concentrate on financial and monetary methods of managing the economy. There followed a period of four or five years when it interfered a good deal less than the Labour administration had done in public sector pay negotiations. The rate of inflation fell somewhat from the levels of 1951 and the manpower shortage was reduced during a period of full employment. Thus until 1955 a more peaceful atmosphere prevailed. There were various further plans put forward during this period for general methods of settling wages, some of them argued by UPW General Secretary Geddes. A scheme for a 'Wages Council' to organise general wage bargaining covering the entire economy was associated with the name of Douglas Houghton, at this time from the Inland Revenue Staff Federation. When this was discussed within the UPW it was attacked by one young activist called Norman Stagg as likely to sap the strength of the unions. It was supported by another young member, Tom Jackson, on the grounds that it could be a step to planning and socialism.[39]

None of this came to pass during this period, however. Nor were wages automatically settled in the Post Office. Some improvements were secured at the end of 1951 for Postmen Higher Grade, whose relative position had not been accepted by the Union at the time of re-allocation in 1946. There were also parallel negotiations for redundant grades which continued well into 1952.[40] There were protracted negotiations also on a general value of work claim which went in following the November 1951 special wages conference of the UPW. After a series of delays, this did not eventually find its way to the Arbitration Court until the end of 1952, where a claim on behalf of the cleaners was comprehensively rejected on a majority vote. The Union then turned to a general 7 per cent claim for the National Whitley Council staff side based on the increase of wages over the previous year. The Treasury refused to accept this form of negotiation. This left the UPW on its own, and the Union negotiated with the Post Office during January 1953. The Union claimed 6 per cent, based on the wages index over the previous twelve months, and secured between 5 and 6 per cent on all grades – 7s (35p) for men, 6s (30p) for women and 3s 6d (17½p) for those under 21.[41]

By the time it came to the UPW Conference in May 1953 there was still a good deal of discontent on pay. For one thing, the POEU had achieved greater increases by going to the Arbitration Court and making comparisons with outside grades. For another, the value of work claims of the various grades had secured nothing after more than a year and a half. Furthermore, all efforts of the unions to set up general civil service wage bargaining had collapsed. The UPW Executive therefore proposed to the May 1953 Conference that they should proceed with the value of work claims which it expected would go to Arbitration Court. After a protracted debate the Conference decided to go ahead with this, instead of any general wage claim.[42] The negotiations which followed these claims were naturally complex. They included a large survey of local prices by ninety-six local UPW branches. Many national firms were contacted in an effort to argue for greater standardisation of the provincial rates, which had not been done before. Details were worked out to show that the recent series of percentage increases had been particularly hard for those in the middle and on the bottom of the scales. A long series of value of work claims went to the Arbitration Court and were considered in the spring and summer of 1954.[43]

The decisions handed down from the Arbitration Court to these claims of the UPW grades in 1954 did a great deal to intensify discontent in the Post Office and to weaken respect for the established methods of resolving differences. Some grades obtained a little. Thus female telephonists had their London maximum increased by about 10 per cent from £6 12s a week (£6. 60) to £7 5s (£7. 25). However PHGs only got about 5 per cent from £8 14s (£8. 70) on the London maximum to £9 4s (£9. 20). On the other hand postmen and male telephonists got nothing at all. For the male telephonists the Union got the Ministry of Labour to agree to re-submit the claim. There were similar discussions about the postmen's claim, but in the meantime considerable discontent again arose in London. The Parcels Branch and the London District Council again called for go-slow working. General Secretary Geddes seems to have kept this down to a minimum with a series of letters which proved more efficacious than his ill-fated direct confrontation three years earlier. He narrowly survived (by 1,592 to 1,329) a vote on this issue at the May 1954 Annual Conference. There was even more discontent from the P&TO grade, despite an offer to them of an increase of around 10 per cent on the London maximum, from £9 4s to £10 2s (£9. 20 to £10. 10). The Union Headquarters received 249 telegrams and thirteen letters on this, the vast majority calling for rejection, and some for strike action. 'A few', reported Geddes with horror, 'even called for the resignation of the General Secretary!'. A ballot of P&TO members was held and the result announced in August. The Arbitration Court award was rejected by 14,050 votes to 2,214 and the call for a strike ballot was agreed by 9,427 to 6,556.[44]

The result of all this was that despite all the contemporary meetings of the Priestley Royal Commission, the UPW Executive had to retrieve something for the members by working out an overall wage claim based on the increases in wages and prices over the past year.[45] On 6 July 1954 a new claim for a general 6 per cent increase was presented to the Post Office based on increases in the wages index and the disturbances in relativities caused by the somewhat variable decisions of the Arbitration Court. Geddes had some direct discussions with Postmaster General Earl De La Warr on 10 August where there seems to have been an effort to subsume the matter with the Priestley Royal Commission. There was also an argument put forward by the Earl that the Union was simply refusing to accept arbitration decisions that they did not agree with. Although there was clearly some truth in this, the official side was probably just as concerned as the Union leaders at the clear expressions of discontent now coming from the members. For example, a meeting run by the London postmen's District Council on 10 September got 3,000 members to vote for a strike ballot.[46] Direct negotiations were conducted during September and by 6 October the Union had pushed up a low original offer to as much as 10s (50p) for postmen, 9s (45p) for male telephonists with good increases for all those going on to new scales. There was a further complication in November when the Union tried to get a further increase, on the grounds that the National Whitley Council had negotiated something more. The Post Office resisted this, and a special conference of the Union held in Bournemouth on 22–3 November 1954 was prepared to accept the October offer. General Secretary Geddes, the current TUC President, was then at the height of his powers and managed to persuade a very sober-sounding conference to accept what was being offered by 2,050 votes to 866. New *Post* Editor Ernest Mercer asserted that this indicated that now 'the General Secretary was perfectly in tune with the membership'.[47]

Before the Priestley Report finally appeared in November 1955, there was yet another set of negotiations. The Annual Conference in May 1955 passed a resolution calling for a general increase to keep up with the Ministry of Labour wages index. This was agreed, against the advice of the General Secretary, at the proposal of new Executive member Tom Jackson, who was dressed down on his arrival at the Executive for the presumption that the Union should ask for increases every year. This claim was for about 7 per cent and went to the Arbitration Court on 3 August. An increase of roughly 5 per cent was granted on the following day. The Post Office tried vainly to resist on the grounds that it was too soon since the last settlement and everything should be left to the Royal Commission. It is of interest to note another point made by the UPW. It said that since the POEU got a slightly higher increase on its last submission to arbitration, they should 'catch up' with this. This argument was rejected by the tribunal.[48] During the course of 1956, the Union also negotiated some increases for postmen near the top of the scale. Increases of 7 per cent were also obtained for cleaners based on what had been obtained in other civil service departments.[49]

THE PRIESTLEY ROYAL COMMISSION: 1955–6

The years 1955 and 1956 saw major changes in patterns of Post Office bargaining. There were many reasons for this. The period of post-war uncertainty and economic strain had given way to one where the economy was growing, inflation was rising and labour was no longer in short supply. In May 1955 a new Conservative Government had been elected, increasing its majority from 17 to 60, and taking the first hesitant steps to forms of economic control and management. The pre-election boom gave way to an autumn budget in 1955 to deal with the 'overheating' of the economy and eventually to the setting up of the Council of Prices, Productivity and Incomes in 1957. This was to be the first of many such bodies. As was discussed in some detail in Chapter 9, an important facet of this general change in economic organisation was the first step in the freeing of the Post Office from direct Treasury control and the setting up of separate and long-term targets for growth and performance.

These were not the only factors affecting the decisions about wages and conditions in the Post Office in 1955. At the same time the trade unions began to cast aside the constraints they had been under since 1926 and to act in a way that had not been seen for almost two decades. In January 1955, the Government granted an increase to members of the National Union of Railwaymen following an inquiry. One result was a strike for the restoration of differentials called by ASLEF in the following May – the first such national dispute since the General Strike. Meanwhile, within the civil service itself, including the Post Office, an utterly new atmosphere of wage bargaining had developed since 1951. It was then that the National Whitley Council staff side first negotiated on behalf of the entire civil service and reached the 'pay addition' agreement which came into effect on 1 January 1952. Over the following months wage claims were taken with bewildering frequency to the Treasury, the Arbitration Court and the Post Office authorities. Another central bargain was struck in 1954 and there were more negotiations in 1955 with the UPW taking part in ways which have been described in previous paragraphs. Trade Union leaders like Charles Geddes, who had been brought up in the 1930s and 1940s, found it difficult to come to terms with a new and different world where prices and wages rose rapidly, and negotiations took place at a pace which was positively frenetic in comparison to the past. A new generation of leaders took over at the 1956 Conference of the UPW. Charles Geddes was replaced as General Secretary by Ron Smith, and his new Deputy was Lionel Andrews. Ernest Mercer became Treasurer and Albert Sampson replaced Henry Randall, MP, as Organising Secretary. Norman Stagg became Editor of *The Post*.

This new UPW team had to face a new set of criteria for Post Office finance and a new (or perhaps revived) set of arguments about wages. The Priestley Royal Commission was set up by Chancellor of the Exchequer R. A. Butler, with the argument that such discussions, like those of MacDonnell in 1912 and of Tomlin in 1931, needed to be held every twenty years or so. Although Priestley was to produce some new machinery for negotiations, the actual discussion on which this was based, varied a good deal from many similar exchanges in the past.

Priestley and his colleagues were given the major task of considering 'whether any changes are desirable in the principles that should govern pay', and also whether there should be changes in the pay scales themselves and in hours of work, holidays and superannuation.[50] On most of the specific points the unions advocated improvements and the authorities opposed them. The Commission accepted general arguments for shorter hours and proposed steps in the direction of a five-day week. They would not accept the case argued by the associations for non-established pay to count for superannuation purposes. On the general argument about wages, the fundamental dispute, simplified and shorn of all its less essential aspects, was a very old one, going back in the Post Office at least to the 1890s. As had always been the case, the staff side, the unions and the workforce generally argued that conditions in the civil service and Post Office were entirely unique and should be determined by strictly internal criteria, perhaps allied to such standards as what a good employer might pay. The authorities on the other hand argued for wages to be determined by comparison with outside wage trends and work. On the whole, it was this latter view that convinced the Royal Commission and resulted in the new machinery being set up in the wake of its Report.

This is to oversimplify the extensive and complex discussions that preceded and followed the Report of the Royal Commission. The UPW took its submissions very

seriously indeed, with considerable discussion on the Executive, and a special
conference in December 1953 where delegates argued in detail on all the main
points in the Union's evidence.[51] The Union argued that the Royal Commission
Report should not present a basis for a wages determination applying to workers as
a whole, but that there should be unfettered negotiations for the Government's own
employees. The basic criteria should 'be determined as the result of an assessment
of the value of the workers (or group of workers) to the industry in which they are
employed'. There should also be a comparison with 'the purchasing power of other
workers' and the changes in their levels of wages. Most of the UPW's statement was
taken up with a detailed refutation, grade by grade, of the possibility of making
outside comparisons. Particularly telling on this was a list of all the outside comparisons that had ever been made by the Post Office authorities since the 1890s. It
was possible to list many hundreds of such comparisons which had come and gone
since the distant days of the Tweedmouth Enquiry. The Union set out a series of
claims for each grade based on the value of their work. On leave and hours of work
they simply argued for the same as the rest of the civil service. On overtime they
wanted to be paid at time-and-a-half with double-time on holidays, and on superannuation they put forward the traditional demand for service in the armed forces to
count as a qualification on the principle of deferred pay.

The same basic arguments were put forward by other unions to the Royal
Commission, even though it was not possible to agree to a joint general submission.
The Institution of Professional Civil Servants, for example, argued a quite different
set of difficulties in relation to external comparisons, because although there were
many more people doing similar jobs to government scientists, they were doing so
in quite a different environment. The joint negotiations through the National
Whitley Council were, it was said, the best means of maintaining internal
relativities. The POEU argued most vigorously of all against external comparisons
of any kind and for what was, even then, the old-fashioned concept of 'a living wage'
combined with considerations of the skill of their members and the differentials
between them. The Association of First Division Civil Servants on the other hand
was prepared to consider combining outside comparison with changes in internal
relativities through a complex formula for marking changes at various dates worked
out by R. G. D. Allen, Professor of Statistics at the London School of Economics.

The Treasury also repeated arguments which had by then become almost classic,
even if few of those involved seemed aware of this. They said that payment should
be such as to attract enough people to do the work. There were two important
challenges to this line of argument in the early 1950s in comparison to the past. In
the first place, there were serious labour shortages in some parts of the civil service.
The establishment of postmen was under strength in Coventry and some other big
cities, and skilled scientists were difficult to recruit in certain departments. It was
possible for the UPW to argue that postmen were not as easily recruited as before
the war, so that the age of entry had had to be increased. The Union also pointed
out that the recruits by open competition to the P&TO grade were not at the educational level hoped for by the Post Office. Secondly, the arguments against the
efficacy of the 'privileges' of superannuation and permanent employment were no
longer as before. It could now be said that there were superannuation schemes as
good, if not better, outside the service. Furthermore, the lure of secure employment
no longer had the same importance as in earlier years.

The Report produced by Sir Raymond Priestley and his colleagues was a clear, coherent and well argued document. It repays careful study as a good indication of the attitude of mind of intelligent and thoughtful students of the problems of public sector bargaining at a point of economic boom and rising wages, when new bargaining techniques were being considered. Also the direct interference of the Government itself in the decisions made was not yet considered to be an over-whelming problem. As already stated, and as already set out in the quotation at the head of the chapter, the Royal Commission came down fundamentally on the side of the Treasury, the authorities, or, as they were beginning to be called, 'the employers'. They argued that outside comparisons should be the fundamental determinant of wages and conditions. However, they did not do so without con-siderable qualification. They argued that 'internal relativities' had to be 'the secondary principle' in arriving at any agreement. Furthermore they argued against the old 'model employer' argument of the unions saying that this would mean that 'Civil Service pay negotiations would become involved with political issues', a point which has rarely worried governments when they have been exercising pressure against rising wages. Nevertheless they accepted that the civil service should be a 'good employer', and while this was 'not necessarily the one who offers the highest rates of pay', it should 'compare well with the generality of employers', and the service should 'pay somewhat above the average'.[52]

One other feature of the Priestley Report which marks it out in its period is its belief in the possibility of finding a scientific and rational means of setting wages and conditions in the civil service and elsewhere. Priestley himself was particularly enthusiastic about 'the new science of job evaluation' which he thought could provide an agreed and effective means of arriving at settlements. He even persuaded Charles Geddes of the UPW and Stanley Mayne of the Institution of Professional Civil Servants to agree that it was worth giving it further consideration.[53] Priestley and his colleagues linked such developments with a neutral arbiter which could make objective judgements, and this took the form of the Civil Service Pay Research Unit. The ideas and methods they proposed were to become very much part of the new industrial relations techniques of the 1960s and 1970s, though usually associated then with incomes policies in ways that Priestley did not consider.[54] In some ways this was the industrial relations equivalent of the belief in scientific management and rational technique which lay behind the changes in Post Office administration in the period 1965–68 and characterised also in the attitudes of the Fulton Committee on the Civil Service in 1966–8. These issues were set out in more detail in Chapter 9.

The Priestley Royal Commission made recommendations on a number of other more specific matters to do with civil service wages and conditions. Most of those that related to the Post Office were not particularly satisfactory to the UPW. The Royal Commission did not think hours of work should be changed, nor that there was a case for granting clerical status to P&TOs. It also thought the issues of new wage scales for these and other grades was beyond its competence. It did propose, as already mentioned, reductions in working hours in general, the rationalisation of provincial differentiation on the lines proposed by the Treasury at the time, and the counting of non-established service towards pay scales in ways being proposed by the associations.

It is perhaps not surprising that the initial reaction of most of the unions to the Royal Commission Report was a combination of hostility and bewilderment. The Institution of Professional Civil Servants described it as 'a bad document' and the

CSCA journal spoke of 'puzzled, plaintive, angry buzzing' among its members.[55] The UPW was even more uncertain than the other bodies since fewer specific recommendations actually applied to them. The Executive made inquiries to clarify that they were subject to the new formula. They could not but admit to 'profound disappointment' at this, and thought their difficulties in accepting it likely to be 'almost insuperable'. Nevertheless, they were not in a position 'to reject the formula of fair comparison in favour of the Tomlin formula', as this seemed to be the only available alternative.[56]

Faced with this, the Government and National Whitley Council official side adopted a tactical approach which proved extremely effective. First of all, they announced acceptance of the Report, including many aspects which were very beneficial to civil servants. They then launched into immediate and very detailed discussions with the union leaders in which they pointed out the many advantages that could accrue to their members. Finally, they insisted that all of this would have to be seen as a 'package' to be accepted or rejected as a whole. On working hours, the official side showed it proposed to move even more quickly than the Royal Commission advocated to a normal five-day week, and to accept a forty-two-hour week in London and forty-four in the provinces. It also agreed to the improvement of leave allowance for some people and to improvements in the new provincial differentiation scheme. With this went acceptance of what was to be known as the Civil Service Pay Research Unit. By 10 April 1956 it was possible for this to be presented as the agreed position of the National Whitley Council. It then went through the conferences of the unions. The UPW meeting in Margate did not publish its proceedings on this point, but the Executive accepted that they might as well try their luck with the Pay Research Unit as they had in the past with the Arbitration Court. Members attempting to improve their wages found this acceptable, so that by June 1956 all the civil service unions were able to accept the main outlines of what had been decided.[57]

FROM THE POST-PRIESTLEY 'PACKAGE' TO THE 'PAY PAUSE': 1957–61

As has been emphasised, the Priestley Report brought about considerable changes in the public sector of industrial relations. One of its main effects on the bargains in which the UPW was involved, was to turn discussion away from the Arbitration Court and to bring it more closely in line with the rest of the National Whitley Council staff side. The first 'job evaluation' claims soon went through the Pay Research Unit and involved a new set of arguments about outside comparisons such as had often been eschewed by the UPW in the past. However, this was only to prove a temporary phase. Claims were settled through the Whitley Council machinery in 1957 and 1958, and there were some other separate agreements of importance. As it turned out, this was only a prelude to efforts to freeze wages and consequent industrial confrontation that lasted for more than a decade.

Arising directly out of the post-Priestley discussions, a general 7 per cent claim was presented for the entire civil service early in 1956.[58] Although the official side first tried to postpone consideration of this until 'outside' negotiations 'had been completed', they did eventually agree to a further 'pay supplement' from 1 April 1956. This was in addition to what had been negotiated on 1 July 1954 and 1 July

1955. The increases pushed up wage rates by 6s (30p) at the bottom of the scale to 14s (70p) at the top, in all cases around 3–4 per cent.

From 1 July 1957, further increases were paid to UPW grades on the basis of two quite separate sets of negotiations. The first of these derived from the beginning of the Civil Service Pay Research Unit in October 1955. The Union attached great importance to being first in using the Unit, and hoped that it would provide a solution to such long-term problems as the call for 'clerical status' for P&TOs. However, the settling of wages and conditions by this means proved a good deal more complicated than had perhaps been envisaged, and rather different. The Pay Research Unit's very first report – on P&TOs – took until 18 February 1957, and the second one, on postmen, until 11 April. There had to be not only the long and complicated splitting up of jobs into components and going into considerable detail on possible comparisons. The comparisons made began with the time-honoured special pleading from both sides, and ended with actual figures based on the arguments in the Royal Commission. One important aspect of the negotiations was that since the comparisons were confidential, the basis on which the final decision was made could not be revealed to those who were actually being paid at the new rates.

By the time of the May 1957 UPW Annual Conference, the Executive was in a position to present to the delegates a full 'package' of proposals, including changes in hours and increases in wages for all the grades. Though the members had to decide whether to accept or reject the package as a whole, it contained many attractive features. For one thing, it increased the holidays of postmen from two weeks to three, the first such change since the Tweedmouth settlement of 1897. Hours of work were also reduced, for postmen to forty-four net, for P&TOs from forty-eight to forty-four gross and for PHGs and others to forty-six gross. These standardised figures helped to bring about further efforts to improve hours of work over the following period. Another feature of the 'package' was that after many years of effort, the P&TOs obtained equality with clerical officers. They got 11 per cent more at the maximum, though it took four extra years to get it. Their scale was still three years shorter than the clerical officers. Amongst other increases, male telephonists in London got an extra 11s (55p) at the maximum, nearly 6 per cent, PHGs got 16s 6d (82½p) which was 7 per cent, and postmen got 8s 6d (42½p), 4 per cent. The 1957 Conference accepted this without any great opposition, and it received 2,676 votes against 255.[59]

The 1957 'package' agreement was the most important one of the post-Priestley period. It was described with some justice by the 1958 Conference chairman as having 'provided for greater changes than those which took place under re-allocation in 1946'.[60] The 'package' resolved some disputes that went back further still. The call for shorter hours of work, though often raised, had not been seriously negotiated for sixty years, and efforts to obtain clerical status went back at least to the 1870s. These were the most significant changes in wages and conditions secured since the war and they set the scene for a series of further pay negotiations involving many groups of civil servants beyond the Post Office.

Between 1957 and 1961 there were three sets of central pay increases negotiated by the National Whitley Council staff side for the civil service as a whole. The first of these came soon after the 1957 'package' agreement and involved a general increase payable from 1 July of that year. As a result a male P&TO in London secured an extra 5 per cent and a postman got 10s (50p), slightly more than that. By the end of 1957 therefore significant increases had been secured, though it took a little longer for the next increases to be secured in early 1959, backdated to 1 December 1958. They were of roughly the same order. The third and last of these increases came after prolonged negotiations during 1960 and were paid from 1 January 1961. It was for a general 4 per cent increase for all. By the beginning of 1961, therefore, it was possible for UPW General Secretary Ron Smith to talk of 'ten tremendous years' from the early 1950s during which time the rate of pay of London postmen at the maximum had increased by 70 per cent, P&TOs by 83 per cent, and with the advent of equal pay, by 130 per cent for women. Female telephonists earned 114 per cent more.[61] This was during a period when the Retail Price Index went up by somewhat less than 50 per cent, and wage rates of manual workers generally by under 70 per cent.

Even if Ron Smith's dates and figures were a little selective, it is not unfair to conclude that considerable improvements in wage rates had taken place. When taken in conjunction with changes in provincial differentiation and with equal pay, there were certainly considerable improvements for Post Office workers during the 1950s. However, as Ron Smith himself pointed out in the same 1961 New Year message, and as many subsequent correspondents to *The Post* made clear, there were large numbers of Union members who were not content with what was being achieved. Eventually after 1961 the irresistible force of UPW discontent met the immovable object of government incomes policy. Before that, however, the UPW itself changed a good deal, between the time of the 1957 'package' agreement and the reductions of hours in 1960–1. As a result of many isolated actions and better arguments, the Union was becoming something different from what it had been.

When the post-Priestley package agreement was being implemented in April 1958 there was a good deal of discontent, especially in London. There was go-slow working in offices at West Central, East Central and the Mount Pleasant. The 'package' was supposed to put a stop to short unofficial tea-breaks which had been normal. There were delays in mail in Central London and some work was transferred to Birmingham for a while. Local negotiations apparently restored the local practices, though the 1958 Conference condemned what had been a minority action.[62] However, this was by no means the last such dispute in London sorting offices.

It was during negotiations for shorter hours that further trouble developed. Abortive efforts to secure a shorter working week had been taken up in 1935–7 in a very lean period for the Union, and similar efforts in 1945–51 have been referred to earlier. The Priestley Royal Commission made some significant points on the issue. It argued that though the five-day week was now becoming common in outside industry, this was not applicable to the more protracted attendances necessary in the Post Office. The Union nevertheless submitted a general claim to the Post Office in July 1956 for work to be arranged in a forty-four-hour, five-day week. The case was to some extent argued by outside comparisons, but mainly on the hardship to Post Office workers.[63] As already indicated, some of these arguments led to improvements in the 'package' agreement of 1957.

The 1958 UPW Annual Conference decided to proceed further on a general claim for a forty-four-hour week for all those in the Union. The main thrust of the argument for this claim was that there had been general improvements in productivity as a result of Union co-operation. The advent of Subscriber Trunk Dialling and the spread of mechanical sorting meant that Union members had a good case to argue. In fact the only response from the Post Office on 9 April 1959 was that the matter had been resolved in the package agreement. This reply was described by the General Secretary, Ron Smith, as 'perhaps the most disappointing the Union had ever received' and was followed by a 'storm of protest' from members. Later in 1959 two meetings were held with the Post Office, and on the suggestion of the Union, special joint sub-committees were established early in the following year.[64]

However, these lengthy negotiations did not proceed without the expression of a good deal of strong feeling on the part of the members. Over and above the issues themselves, the expression of this discontent was of considerable significance in the development of attitudes in the UPW. At its October 1959 meeting the London District Council protested about the delay in the negotiations and a decision was taken to hold a meeting of members on the issue on 25 November at the Central Hall, Westminster. On 20 November, General Secretary Ron Smith was invited to attend, and he said he would submit this to his Executive. The Executive eventually decided by 16 votes to 5 that the action of the LDC was out of order. The meeting had taken place and 2,700 members reacted with considerable enthusiasm to calls for the preparation of strike action, for shorter hours and for the issue to be pursued generally with greater vigour. Speakers included Kim McKinlay, who was then Secretary of one of the London sectional committees, and Fred Moss, Secretary at the time of another and Chairman of the Union as a whole. Dick Lawlor, Communist Party member and prominent militant in London, said that those in leadership 'had to be prepared to meet the occasional challenge of the membership'. He announced that there would be a demonstration the next day from Clapham Common to the Union's Headquarters. Over 1,000 members attended this and handed in a petition.[65]

The response of most of the Union's leaders to all this was very hostile. The Executive decided that the demonstration was against Union rules though Ron Smith accepted the petition. *Post* Editor Norman Stagg wrote a lengthy editorial in the issue of 12 December 1959 under the heading 'No Room for Wreckers'. He attacked those who directed their efforts against the Union's Executive rather than against the Post Office. He particularly objected to banners reading 'Smithie – Stop Dragging Your Feet' and 'Has the UPW been taken over by a Little Mouse?' – a reference to Ron Smith's absence from the Central Hall meeting. More generally, Stagg set out a classic view about trade union bargaining:

> how can any Trade Union Official negotiate with confidence in an atmosphere punctuated by boos and jeers? And who stands to profit when the link between our Headquarters organisation and our Branches is weakened?

He also set out the steps which had been taken in the negotiations and pointed out how well informed the Communist *Daily Worker* had been about the demonstrations.

The letter columns of *The Post* in the following weeks were full of various opinions about this. Most were hostile to the views expressed by Norman Stagg. A 'Conservative Trade Unionist' thought that the leadership might 'be more enlightened than to resort to digging the "Communist skeleton" out of the family cupboard'. Other writers pointed out that the LDC had cancelled a further demonstration at St Martin's-le-Grand at the behest of the Executive. H. J. Jones of the London Parcels Service summarised the opposite general view to the one put forward by Norman Stagg:

Take note that to-day, trade unions are losing membership, in my opinion due to the extreme right-wing attitude being adopted by most trade union leaders. Too keen upon taking a defensive attitude, they take great pains to educate us to the art of compromise, which they claim to be modern negotiation. Compromise after compromise, till eventually they have nothing other than their consciences to compromise.[66]

In a 'Postscript to A Controversy' the General Secretary Ron Smith, in *The Post* of 27 February 1960, concentrated on a defence of Norman Stagg's editorship on the reasonable grounds that he had allowed a large volume of criticism of his own views to be published. He emphasised his view that no branch or district council

is entitled to take action by 'Mass Meeting', 'Members Meeting', Protest Marches, demonstration or the like, which have as their purpose, expressed or otherwise, to influence the determination of policy or the course of negotiation.

He argued strongly for the sovereignty of Annual Conference as the body to which the Executive Council is responsible and accountable, so that the Executive Council had 'the responsibility for the policy and conduct of Union affairs between Annual Conferences'.

The issue of hours of work itself was not settled without a good deal of further difficulty. Three separate sub-committees were set up to negotiate the issue nationally and a special conference was held in October 1960. This accepted the proposal for a forty-four-hour gross week for telephonists and telegraphists, involving small but significant practical improvements. The postal side would not accept a gross working week of forty-five hours for postmen and forty-four for PHGs.[67] Following this, a poll of the membership narrowly rejected the Post Office offer by 36,478 to 35,990. The Post Office again refused to improve the offer and a further poll considered a number of alternatives, the largest number – 59,055 – now voting to accept the Post Office offer, though 21,096 favoured industrial action and 10,552 another conference. At the conference itself a card vote narrowly accepted the offer by 1,493 to 1,378.[68] A much later general claim on hours in 1974 was to lead to some further internal dissension but by then it could be linked to reductions in postal deliveries which were taking place in any case.[69]

SOME TRENDS IN THE 1950s AND 1960s

The controversy surrounding the issue of shorter hours, especially in 1959, is of interest as an example of the sort of argument that will take place as long as there is trade unionism. It is a vivid illustration of the fact – pointed out by Ron Smith and Norman Stagg – that 'unofficial action' of the sort that was becoming increasingly common in the trade union movement as a whole also had an effect on the UPW. As part of the trade union movement, UPW members now expected a good deal more from negotiations a good deal more quickly than they had twenty or even ten years earlier. It is also of interest to see the new way in which dissent and disagreement was now being expressed within the UPW. Before the First World War such disagreements in Post Office trade unions might have been expressed in rivalry between grades and associations. In the period before the Second World War they might crystallise around breakaway organisations, especially in London. From the 1950s dissent was expressed much more within the Union, through the established machinery of conferences and branch and district meetings, though not always without bitter battles and clashes of constitutional authority. It is of interest also that the centre of dissent within the UPW, which had in earlier generations been firmly located in Manchester, had now shifted to the capital city itself. There was always London particularism in the Post Office. However not since the telegraphists threatened to go on strike in 1897 had it been the centre of trade union militancy in the service. Fifty years later it became so again.

It is also of some interest to note that the focus of this particular dispute was one which had rarely before been a major issue in the Union – hours of work. This arose from the fact that the length of time actually worked assumed much greater importance at a time when labour shortage dominated the calculations of the Post Office and overtime working assumed much greater significance. The labour shortage affected many aspects of working for the Post Office during the period of the great boom from the 1950s to the 1970s.[70] Thus, for example, there were problems of recruiting to the P&TO grade by limited competition within the Post Office, in part because of the narrowing of differentials in actual earnings from those in 'lower' grades who would make up their pay in overtime working. The Post Office found it increasingly difficult to insist on the minimum educational qualifications they wanted in the early post-war period for those who came into the job from the outside. For telephonists, one important consequence of labour shortage was the effect it had on the advent of equal pay. The agreement of 1956 had allowed women to obtain equal pay if they opted to do the full range of duties. Only about 25 per cent of women in practice did so, and even those who accepted 95 per cent of the full rate were not happy to work in the evenings. Thus at the end of 1959 there had to be a further agreement allowing the 95 per cent optants to work during days only. This exacerbated the division between men and women telephonists for at least another decade. Finally, the labour shortage affected postmen and PHGs by greatly expanding the level of overtime working, especially in the big cities. This increased the amount of bargaining that had to take place on a local level and helped to exacerbate disputes of the sort that have been described.

The period of the great boom also saw standardisation and improvement in a number of other aspects of the working lives of Post Office workers. These included such ancient matters as counter losses, uniforms, provincial differentiation and incremental scales. They also included the resolution of the historical claim to 'clerical status' for those who worked in counters and telegraph offices. Before going on to discuss the battles of the 1960s, something should be said about these changes, all tending in the direction of great standardisation and uniformity.

One important agreement in 1951 concerned what happened about losses incurred by those serving at Post Office counters.[71] Before 1897 there had been risk allowances, at least in London, and these were then abolished in opposition to the wishes of the staff associations. The unions began to argue against the system of deducting losses from wages, at least over 5 per cent of the total. Though various experiments had been undertaken in suspending the 5 per cent rule between 1925 and 1928, these simply led to disagreements about why more losses were then reported. In 1951 a Joint Study Group nevertheless proposed that the 5 per cent rule should go, all losses should be borne, and discipline should be tightened in other ways, particularly by deferring the increments of those persistently losing money. There had also been a system of counting gains against losses and then paying them to Post Office charities which was to be suspended. At the same time there were important improvements in disciplinary procedures on late attendance, allowing lateness of under five minutes to be disregarded for disciplinary purposes, with a standard system of wage deduction thereafter. These proposals simplified procedures and improved the position of those working at counters. It was accepted by UPW members with the sole proviso that people should be able to appeal against the loss of increments. There was more resistance to the reassessment of the value of work at counters for the purpose of allocating staff, though change had to come there also.[72]

Nor were these the only forms of standardisation to affect Post Office workers during the 1950s. A very old question was finally resolved by a settlement of 1956 about rotation between counter and writing duties. In 1948 following re-allocation a general right to access to such duties was conceded. Only in 1956 however were all P&TOs after a certain qualifying period able to undertake writing duties.[73] Another large-scale joint discussion in the period brought about the first full-scale overhaul of Post Office uniforms since 1910, with a new generation of dress and styles.[74] Other forms of standardisation in the period involved the breaking down of the inequities of many generations. Details are given elsewhere of the processes whereby the inequalities between men and women were diminished by the abolition of the marriage bar in 1946 and the equal pay agreement of 1954, eventually brought into effect in 1961.

Another historic change in the 1950s was in provincial differentiation. The old system of classification of offices according to size and level of business was to some extent based on local differences in wage rates that existed during the nineteenth century. In the Post Office the variations were a potent source of discontent and division at least from the time of the Tweedmouth discussions in the 1890s. Hobhouse in 1908 had tried to set out a complex method of deciding local differentiation by population size and level of business, but this was not a success. In the inter-war period there were constant efforts to get the classifications of individual offices improved. By the 1930s there were five separate rates in the Post Office – with three different provincial classifications and two in London. In 1951 a new scheme was worked out with the Treasury which made outer London and larger provincial towns identical, and merged classes II and III. It also brought the rates of pay much closer – the outer London/provincial rate being about 2 per cent below London, and the provincial rate about 5 per cent below that. Further efforts to reduce these differences were largely made by the joint action of civil service unions, and eventually in 1958 a new agreement was reached which by 1962 broke down the old system altogether into a 'London' and national rate. There was some talk in the UPW soon after this of getting higher rates in some of the provincial centres, but this was rejected as impractical. In the 1970s there was a trend for the London addition to increase along with the size of the area in which it was paid, but this was of much more limited importance than the old classification system.[75]

One other major field for standardisation in wage payments was in incremental scales. Complaints about the length of time it took to reach the maximum rate of pay were sometimes made in the days when claims were based on 'family wage' arguments. In the 1950s and 1960s the number of steps was reduced in various negotiations. Thus postmen reached their maximum at the age of 28 instead of 30 in 1947, at 26 in 1950 and at 25 following the 1957 'package' agreement. The 1959

UPW Conference adopted a comprehensive programme on the issue and in 1960 and 1962 attacked the Executive for pursuing it with insufficient vigour. There was some argument about whether its inclusion was part of the reason for the unsatisfactory outcome of the postmen's 1963 negotiations.[76] It was not until after Post Office workers left the civil service in 1969 that there was major change in this. Following the 1971 strike and Court of Enquiry the incremental scale system finally broke down and lower pay went only to probationary groups, or those under 18.

Another issue tending to standardisation in this period was the claim for 'clerical status' of the new grade of postal and telegraph officers, or at least for equality with the clerical officers grade. This was a demand of a sort which went back to the very origins of trade unionism in the Post Office, and it lay behind the establishment of the Postal Telegraph Clerks Association in 1881. Sixty or seventy years later the demand had a somewhat different content. By then the term clerk had perhaps a less elevated connotation and there was a large proletariat of clerical officers within the civil service, largely organised in what was then known as the Civil Service Clerical Association. When the new postal and telegraph officer grade was created in the Post Office to do the work at the counters and in the writing rooms, they became a large group of people requiring a fair standard of education and a good deal of accumulated skill. In the discussions with the Post Office over the re-allocation agreement that created the new grade, the Union never accepted the new rates of pay. So there was the basis for protracted efforts to improve the position of the P&TOs by calling for parity with clerical officers. This campaign on behalf of just over 10 per cent of UPW members, with a weight of a great deal more than those numbers might indicate, owed something to the existence of secessionism among this grade, and inevitably came into conflict with those representing the clerical officers with whom comparisons were made.[77]

The demand for 'clerical status' for P&TOs was at first opposed by the UPW leadership, and defeated at conferences. General Secretary Geddes argued strongly that more could be done for P&TOs by putting forward a quite independent set of demands. Another objection, never openly argued, was that the creation of a common grade could have led to further problems in the field of trade union organisation, possibly including secession to the CSCA. One publicly stated argument was that by tying a Post Office grade to people in other departments, they would diminish the capacity of the Union to negotiate on their behalf. As George Douglas put it, the argument was

> really whether or not the UPW shall build up its own standards (including wages and hours), assess its own responsibilities and value its own work, or accept the standards of another grade which is just as dissatisfied with their standards as we are with ours.[78]

There were some ways in which the conditions of clerical officers were inferior to those of P&TOs. For one thing, they had less access to promotion, though this only mattered for a minority. Furthermore, they were most likely to be transferred to other parts of the country. Finally, much of the work done by P&TOs – the Post Office claimed as much as 40 per cent – was of a routine character such as was done by the lower grade of clerical assistant elsewhere. Nobody wanted to pursue this comparison.

On the other hand, members of the Union were able to take up the call for 'clerical status' as a rallying cry. The secessionists of NAPTO certainly won support with it. It was possible to argue with justice that many P&TOs left the Post Office for lower wages and more regular, week-day, hours of work. The 40 per cent figure for routine duties was disputed, as also was the range of promotion open to P&TOs.[79] The call for equality thus still provided a focus of considerable importance.

As a matter of fact, the P&TO grade in the settlement of May 1949 was at most points ahead of the clerical officers, especially in London. When the arbitration tribunal early in 1951 granted further increases to the CSCA members, there were inevitably demands within the Union for further increases. The UPW began to talk about 'relativities' with the clerical grade and this produced a good deal of back-biting between the Union and the CSCA.[80] This goes some way to explaining the lack of enthusiasm in the UPW for the general wage negotiations of the civil service as a whole during those years. It also helps to account for the particular strength of feeling amongst members of the P&TO grade about the failure of their value of work claim in the Arbitration Court in 1954, and the diminishing confidence of the UPW in the Arbitration Court thereafter. The 1957 'package' secured essentially the same scale for the two grades, and the assumption that the clerical officers would be 3 per cent ahead. Subsequent settlements preserved this relationship until August 1960, when the Post Office agreed with the UPW to 'alignment' of the two grades. The only difference was that, as had become traditional, the CO scale was slightly longer.[81] This led to another visit to the Arbitration Court by the clerical officers who got their extra 3 per cent in June 1961.

Thus although the 1960 agreement essentially secured the 'clerical status' for which the very first Post Office trade unionists had campaigned a century earlier, this was by no means the end of the story. For one thing the 'pay pause' of Selwyn Lloyd in July 1961 began the era of incomes policies during which the context of negotiations changed. The press began to take up 'leap-frogging' between different groups as an example of the kind of process leading to the inflation that Selwyn Lloyd's policies were supposed to prevent.[82] Furthermore, the move away from the civil service in the mid-1960s and the general shortage of recruits in this period meant that those in the P&TO grade began to think in quite different terms when it came to deciding how their wages should be determined. In a complete reversal of the position a decade and a half earlier, the P&TO members pushed against the Union leadership, and the Conference eventually agreed in 1965 to campaign to break from the alignment with the clerical grade. Behind this lay increasing discontent especially with the length of incremental scales and increasing duties brought about by the philatelic bureau and the Giro.[83] These points went in the last of the UPW submissions to the Pay Research Unit in 1968. Although some pay increases were secured, these were not thought altogether satisfactory for the P&TOs. However, the departure from the civil service then put the entire problem in a new context.

One other aspect of bargaining in this period to which some reference was made in Chapter 9 was the co-operation of the Union with technical change in the Post Office. As early as 1949 the Union supported a Joint Productivity Committee in the Post Office, set up to improve efficiency and productivity at a time of economic crisis. At first some members of the Union opposed the idea, but Geddes won majority support for it. In later years the Joint Production Council became part of the general efforts to exhort members to co-operate with technical and other such changes.[84] A network of local joint productivity committees still existed in the early 1970s, covering about a third of the branches of the Union where small concessions were secured from management in return for small payments to refreshment and sporting clubs. By then, however, the issue of productivity bargaining was posed in the very different context of incomes policy.

Some emphasis has been placed in Chapter 9 on the role of the Union in the discussion of general technological change. Besides the general factors already mentioned that predisposed Union members at times to display a loyalty to Government and Post Office, there were particular problems in the continuous and irreversible decline in the telegraph system. After a series of anguished discussions, the delegates felt compelled to agree at the 1954 Annual Conference that they could only accept the inevitable.[85]

> It will be seen that notwithstanding the enormous amount of time, thought and energy directed by so many people to the future of the Telegraph Service, there has emerged no single suggestion or combination of suggestions possessed of sufficient potential impact to seriously avert the decline of traffic on an acceptable economic basis.
>
> The Executive Committee continued, therefore, to be guided in its considera-tion of the whole problem by the inevitability of the decline and its duty to protect the interests of its members, those remaining in the service and those made redundant by any developments, either political or mechanical.

This meant negotiating redundancies, though all those involved were given the possibility of taking up other jobs in the Post Office. It was those developments and the discussions on technological change outlined in Chapter 9 that 'allowed the spirit of helpfulness latent in the telephone staff to find easier expression'. It was in this context that Postmaster General Marples spoke in 1957 of 'Post Office trade unions' as 'absolutely first-rate'.[86] This was the view of a particular period, and would not have been said at other times. It was not much longer before industrial relations were so transformed in the Post Office that many such matters were seen very differently indeed by all concerned.

CONFRONTATION UNDER THE TORIES: 1961–4

In Chapter 9 some effort was made to place the development of the Post Office in the 1960s in the context of new efforts at corporate planning in the British economy. One important manifestation of government economic planning was in the field of wages. Of course there had been attempts in the late 1940s to limit pay increases in order to deal with economic crisis. There had almost always been talk of the need for 'retrenchment' and the limitation of rewards in the civil service and the public sector generally. The 1960s, however, saw in a much more systematic and general way government attempts to plan for the incomes of all including its own employees. This initiated a new era for the Post Office worker as for all others in the public sector where government policy became the first and often the predominant factor in discussions about wages. This affected the contours of bargaining in the Post Office in many ways. It led to direct bargaining and industrial confrontation of a sort quite without precedent in the history of the Post Office, but which will undoubtedly mould the conceptions of those who will have to deal with these problems in generations still to come.

The issue began for the UPW at its May 1960 Conference with a resolution agreed by 2,829 to 203 for the Executive to 'prepare a claim for an increase in wages'. This was effectively secured in the 4 per cent increase centrally negotiated from 1 January 1961. Following this, the National Whitley Council made an agreement for a quinquennial cycle of pay research and annual discussion of central pay based on changes in the Ministry of Labour Wage Rates Index, which would begin each year in November. This was presented to the UPW's membership by General Secretary Ron Smith, as a means of bringing 'common-sense and stability into future pay negotiations'. The 1961 Annual Conference, which proved to be one of the most militant in the history of the Union, rejected it. The Conference decided on a series of narrow votes which reflected real changes of attitude 'that future policy on wages shall be based on all relevant factors, e.g. cost-of-living and industrial strength'. The same Conference reinforced this by voting to allow the Executive to call a strike without submitting the matter to a poll of members. It also agreed to submit a claim for a general wage increase for all grades.[87]

The UPW's claim was submitted on 27 July 1961, by which time it had been overtaken by events elsewhere. Two days earlier the Conservative Chancellor of the Exchequer, Selwyn Lloyd, had promulgated a 'pay pause' for all civil servants. All the plans of orderly negotiations in the Post Office disappeared when confronted by these efforts to fly in the face of previously agreed bargaining arrangements. Post Office workers were placed in the front line not only for all workers who wanted higher wages, but also in defence of agreements whereby such matters could be discussed at all. 'Why pick on us?' asked General Secretary Ron Smith. The answer, as he expressed it, was that Post Office workers were 'deliberately selected as an example for outside workers to follow'. At a mass protest meeting of 3,500 civil servants at the Central Hall Westminster on 30 August, particular indignation was expressed by civil service union leaders at the fact that the Government was proposing to decide itself on the date and application of awards from the Arbitration Board. Ron Smith told the meeting that this attack on industrial relations institutions that were now 40 years old was 'gambling on the sense of responsibility of the members and leaders of Trade Unions'. A resolution making the same point was proposed by Ron Smith at the September TUC and carried unanimously.[88]

Thus it was that in 1961 after three decades during which it had been possible to ignore it, the ultimate question of public sector bargaining was being posed. What would happen if the Government simply took action on its own account? The answer, so often hypothetical in the past, now rested in the hands of the Post Office workers.

On 9 October 1961 the UPW's claim was again discussed at the Post Office, and on 17 November it was comprehensively rejected. The entire UPW Executive then met Postmaster General Bevins on 30 November. He expressed himself bound by the 'pay pause' and said the Union should wait for the latest pay research exercises, which were due in the middle of the following year. After what the Government had said, the Union could not now, as would have been normal in the past, go to the Arbitration Board. For the first time in the history of the UPW, the only alternative now open to the Executive Committee was to call some form of industrial action.

A special sub-committee of the Union's EC spent November discussing the best form of action, and Executive members visited all fifty-nine district councils. On 4

December the Executive decided that members should 'withdraw their individual good will and work to rule' from 1 January 1962. On 28 December, 6,000 members at the Albert Hall heard TUC General Secretary George Woodcock denounce the Government and its policies, declaring that the UPW was now in the forefront of fighting them.[89]

The work to rule began on the first day of 1962. It was not, Union leaders insisted, a 'go slow', but it certainly delayed the service, especially on the postal side. PHGs checked every bag during sorting, and postmen drivers observed all traffic regulations about speed and parking. Such actions slowed the mail by the observation of rules that were not normally adhered to rigidly in practice. Other delays perhaps came with over enthusiasm. Some letters were not delivered because addresses were incomplete, and others were turned over to check that they should not be going at the rate for unsealed correspondence. Soon millions of letters were piling up in London, and many were not getting through to smaller offices. This first national action involving the UPW secured a good deal more publicity than might perhaps have been the case in later years, and it was one of the first industrial disputes to be given widespread television coverage. Sympathy for the Union was strong, and one Gallup poll published during the work to rule showed that 48 per cent of those questioned supported the UPW, and only 23 per cent were for the Government.

On 7 January, the position was described by Ron Smith in this way:

The Post Office has now resorted to the most unprecedented measures it has ever had to use in normal times. Customers are being appealed to not to use our Service, temporary staff are being recruited through the country, special trains and vans hired, collections and deliveries of mails cancelled, excessive compulsory overtime offered, and mails are being re-directed to an extraordinary degree. The readiness with which the Post Office is meeting these additional heavy costs is in strange contrast with its unwillingness to even negotiate with us.

Private reports received by the Executive indicated that although there was some hesitation in small rural branches and amongst telephonists, the vast majority of the membership was supporting the work to rule with enthusiasm and many members, particularly in London, wanted to extend it into an overtime ban. These views were reflected in an Executive meeting on 11 January, where Fred Moss proposed that 'we shall instruct our members not to volunteer for overtime' from 14 January. However the Executive decided to present the face of sweet reason to the world by writing to the Postmaster General agreeing to call off the work to rule if he would begin unconditional negotiations leading, if necessary, to 'an unfettered Arbitration Court or even an independent arbiter'.[90]

On 12 January, the Postmaster General gave his initial response to this, in which he simply repeated that he would be bound by pay research. Ron Smith could only reply that the Union still wanted unfettered negotiations on its claim. On 16 January, Postmaster General Bevins again wrote offering to refer the claim to arbitration. He said he would agree to any award, though without backdating. At its meeting on the following day, the Union's Executive accepted that this represented a step forward, particularly when taken in conjunction with a statement following a long Cabinet meeting that the Arbitration Court would be restored. However, Bevins continued to talk in public of refusing to negotiate on terms dictated by the

Union, and many branches were calling for a definite money offer. The Executive on 17 January agreed to continue the work to rule, including a refusal to undertake voluntary overtime. Again it refused to go further and to endorse a call for a ban on compulsory overtime because this might lead to dismissals. By 23 January, Bevins admitted that an extra £250,000 had been paid in overtime and £750,000 lost by delays in the service and other results of the action. However he thought this was 'really a row of beans compared with the damage to the national economy that my submission to pressure might involve'.[91]

As the work to rule went into its third week, it was reported that many district councils were now calling for further action. A survey of branches showed only a minority opposed to a ban on compulsory overtime. Only thirteen branches in the entire country had refused to participate in the work to rule. At a further Executive meeting on 25 January it was possible to point to indications of support for the Post Office workers in public opinion polls. Statements from the Postmaster General became more conciliatory. A letter on 31 January from Bevins insisted that talks could now go ahead on the assumption that the 'pause' would end on 31 March. Though this did not go so far as his statement on 29 January that he was 'seeking means by which normal relations can be restored', it was enough for Ron Smith to propose to a meeting of the Executive on 31 January to call off the work to rule to allow further negotiations. This was not easily accepted by the EC. Eight members (against 19) voted to demand further assurances and if necessary then to go on to a ban on overtime. The recommendation to return to normal working was carried by only 15 to 12. The members seem to have accepted this with little dissent. There was discontent in London because work was not re-routed to them. An angry meeting of the LDC '3' on 2 February threatened to continue the work to rule and the issue persisted into April. There was some unofficial industrial action at the Western District Office at one stage in defiance both of Assistant Secretary Les Morgan and Assistant District Organiser J. R. Lawlor, because the district postmaster tried to arrange new duties on terms which varied from those before the work to rule.[92]

Negotiations on the Union's original claim resumed with a meeting between UPW leaders and Postmaster General Bevins on 8 February 1962 and with his officials a fortnight later. Bevins wanted to discuss in terms of the return to a period of a 2–2½ per cent 'guiding light' which was supposed to begin in April. He suggested proceeding either through pay research surveys, the central civil service claim or the Arbitration Court. The Union rejected the surveys as taking too long, the central claim as ineffective, and the Arbitration Court since this was now tainted by government interference. Ron Smith and his colleagues made it clear that they wanted a general increase to get Post Office workers up to the level of increases elsewhere. A major part of the argument was the general shortage of recruits to the service, shown for example in the lack of entrants to limited competitions. Negotiations dragged on into March without the Post Office making any offer and with various settlements elsewhere eroding efforts to enforce the pay pause, including those for electricity supply and road haulage workers. After further pressure from the Union side and a further meeting with the Postmaster General, a reply was received on 22 March that direct negotiations would be resumed on the understanding that no increases from pay research would be paid until the beginning of the following year, 1963. This was seen as a step forward, and on 29 March a claim for a 7½ per cent increase for all grades (other than P&TOs who were linked in with the central civil service claim) was submitted. At a further meeting on 6 April, the Post Office responded to this claim with an offer of 2 per cent. This was rejected out of hand.[93]

This 2 per cent figure was in line with the 'guiding light' on wage increases which the Government was now trying to impose. The central civil service pay claim of 5½ per cent had met with a similar response, 2½ per cent, and had been similarly rejected. Both the National staff side and the UPW Executive at its meeting on 9 April 1962 decided to resort to arbitration. The decision to go to arbitration was only taken on the casting vote of the Chairman against another proposal to ballot the members on whether they wanted to do this or take strike action. The Executive Committee also registered a strong protest

> at what it considers to be a graceless repudiation of the Union's goodwill efforts in restoring a negotiation atmosphere, which this paltry and derisory final offer has now completely destroyed.

The Executive explained its decision to go to the Arbitration Court by asserting that a strike would be 'challenging the government of the day' and would not be capable of defeating its policies. Though there was some opposition at the May Annual Conference to the line agreed by the Executive, the submission to the Arbitration Court nevertheless went ahead.[94] The Union's case was presented to the Arbitration Court on 4 June, with the main argument being the overall increases in general wage rates since the Priestley Report in 1956. It is of interest to note that the major argument presented by the Post Office was one which had never really figured before in such discussions. This was that the increase would contribute to the general level of inflation.[95]

The decision of the Tribunal announced at the end of June was to offer 4 per cent from 1 April to the Union members. This was nearer their claim than the offer of the Post Office and was well above the 2½ per cent put forward by the Government. It was generally considered a success for the Union and an exoneration of the tribunal and of those leaders who had 'placed their hopes in a judgement of independent minds at a critical stage in our Union's history'.[96] Along with a similar increase obtained for P&TOs through the central civil service claim, this certainly represented a major breach in the efforts of the Conservative Government to hold down wages. However, it did not yet mean that wages in the Post Office were going up to the same extent as elsewhere, or in line with the cost of living.

There was no way therefore that things could easily be resolved in 1963 when the Pay Research Unit reports began to be discussed. A 3 per cent increase was obtained in the early part of the year through the National Whitley Council for civil service common grades and this effected the P&TOs as well as cleaners and radio operators. Some grades secured increases through direct negotiations following pay research reports, and this included telegraphists and overseas telegraphists, the latter getting a good settlement because of recruitment problems.[97] As discussion went ahead on other grades covered by pay research it became increasingly clear that agreement was not going to be secured through direct negotiations. The enormous PRU reports on postmen and telephonists from 1962 did not lead to any magic formula. On 23 April 1963, General Secretary Smith told the Director General that 'the Post Office needed to get away from the rigid attitude of thinking that median tables were a substitute for negotiation or a realistic policy on wages'.

Yet it was precisely such calculations which were supposed to be at the centre of the pay research system. In the following month it was Ron Smith's turn to defend the arrangement to the Union's Annual Conference. In a debate described at the time as 'one of the all time "greats" of Conference', he defended pay research from its critics declaring that it was the Post Office and not the Pay Research Unit that was to blame and that the discussions 'gave us the opportunity of turning Post Office comparisons into *fair* comparisons'. The most telling argument was that there was no real alternative, and the Conference accepted this. However it also agreed that another arbitration reference was inevitable, and this followed in July.[98]

The discussions at the Arbitration Court in June 1963 again indicated that the pay research exercise by no means presented a simple solution. The Post Office was in fact offering only very small increases on the lower part of the scales, and the Union was claiming around 6 per cent increases on maxima attained at 23 instead of 25. This last point came out of a number of comparisons and so also did the main argument presented by Ron Smith on behalf of the postmen that the outside comparisons 'do not take into account the versatility expected of Postmen'. Similarly for the telephonists, the main argument presented was that they had co-operated with technical change and then become more skilled. The result was a great disappointment. Although the Arbitration Tribunal accepted that there should be increases of some sort at every point on the scales, there was no reduction of the scales and increases of the order 2 per cent for postmen. (Postmen higher grade got increases in line with this soon after.) The telephonists did get the incremental scale reduced by one step but maximum pay on the national scale only went up from £12 6s 6d (£12. 32½) to £12 10s (£12. 50). This was immediately described as 'a bitter disappointment' by Ron Smith. He wrote of how the discussions on pay research had shown the difficulties of deciding on who were good employers. They had discovered what had not been immediately obvious before, that in practice pay rates were less determined by the kind of work done than by the area or enterprise in which they were being earned. One consolation at least was that the Tribunal had rejected the arguments of the Post Office and given an award of some sort.[99]

The dissatisfaction within the UPW in the latter part of 1963 reflected a widespread feeling in the trade union movement as a whole during the closing months of the long period of Conservative Government. Although the Union had generally expressed support for the economic planning efforts of the Government in this period, and Ron Smith himself had joined the National Economic Development Council, they did not support restriction on incomes. The September 1963 TUC condemned all forms of incomes restraint and the UPW's journal declared 'NIX to NIC' – the National Incomes Commission which the Government hoped would go hand in hand with the National Economic Development Council.[100] At the end of the year the Union leadership produced another 'Special Report on Wages Policy', and this was discussed at a special conference in Blackpool on 24–5 February 1964.

By the time the conference took place there had been a number of other developments. Further central pay negotiations between the National staff side and the Chancellor of the Exchequer, Reginald Maudling, had resulted in a long-term pay offer of the sort which had been rejected by the 1961 UPW Conference. This 'contract pay' was for a 3 per cent increase for 1 January 1964, and 3½ per cent on 1 January 1965 and 1 January 1966. This offer affected P&TOs as well as such smaller grades as cleaners and radio operators. It did not include separate negotiations on hours of work, expected to go to the Arbitration Court, and it did not exclude separate pay research exercises. It was ratified on 6 February and when it came to the Special Wages Conference, this was accepted. However, as already outlined, the P&TO grade members within the Union had now taken steps to get out of the system altogether.

For the postmen and PHGs whose wages were tied to theirs, the issue was coming to a head. On 23 December 1963 a formal 'claim for a substantial and immediate improvement in the pay of Postmen and Postmen Higher Grade' was submitted to the Post Office. The main argument presented was direct comparison with outside manufacturing wages and 'an unjustifiably rigid interpretation of pay research'. At meetings with the Post Office on 15 and 23 January there was no indication of any acceptance of these arguments and instead the same four-year 'contract' was offered as had been negotiated by the National Whitley Council staff side. The rejection of this was fully endorsed at the Special Wages Conference in February, along with a general view that they should be 'extremely reserved in the use of the Civil Service Pay Unit for so long as the present rigidity of approach exists in the Post Office Administration'.[101]

Following this the Union tried to get negotiations going at the highest level. On 13 February the Post Office agreed to increase its offer to 4 per cent, but this was rejected. On 11 March a delegation met Chancellor Maudling and PMG Bevins. Maudling replied two days later advocating a visit to the Arbitration Court. The experience of the 1961 pay pause and after meant that this was no longer considered an option, so the Executive on 13 March 1964 for the first time in the history of the Union agreed to take strike action. Postmen and PHGs were to come out on 16 April, and it was decided thereafter to ban overtime. The only dispute within the Executive at this point was how soon to announce the strike decision. A series of further discussions with Maudling followed in late March and early April. The Union pushed for an independent inquiry into the interpretation of part of the Priestley Report and the Government tried to get the whole matter referred to the Arbitration Tribunal. 'All the stale arguments about comparability were repeated', wrote PMG Bevins later, 'until I felt physically sick'.[102] Eventually, on 9 April, the UPW Executive announced its strike plans for 16 April. On 13 April the Chancellor capitulated and agreed to set up a Special Committee, so that on the following day the strike was called off, at least for the moment. At the Albert Hall 7,000 members were told they had won a victory.

The Committee on the Pay of Postmen under the chairmanship of A. L. Armitage, who had been President of Queens College Cambridge since 1958, did not prove a success.[103] Other members of the Committee included Victor Feather, at the time Assistant General Secretary of the TUC, and two members of the Priestley Commission Barbara Wootton and Willis Jackson. They were charged in particular with interpreting Clause 664 of the Priestley Report which referred specifically to the problems of making outside comparisons for postmen:

> For example, the duties of the postmen consist mainly of collection, delivery and sorting. Many outside workers are employed on duties of the same broad type, though we are not aware of any work containing the precise combination that goes to make up the postman's job. But we think that any such comparisons may well have to be supplemented by more general comparisons on the lines indicated by the Union of Post Office Workers, namely by looking at the skill, initiative and responsibility required for the work of these grades and for broadly similar tasks

outside the Service. While we agree with the Post Office that this sort of comparison is always 'a very broad business', we think that every effort should be made . . . to make it as close as possible.

The basic problem arose from the fact that there were very few people outside the Post Office who did the same work as postmen. There could not really therefore be direct functional comparisons in the way that Priestley envisaged. This was why the Union wanted the comparison to be as broad as possible, preferably with manufacturing wages as a whole. It was the failure of the wages of postmen to keep up with these general increases that was behind all the resentment that had grown up since the time of the Priestley Report. For its part, the Post Office insisted that narrow comparisons were possible.

The Armitage Committee tried to split the difference between these views. It insisted that pay research comparisons were possible and proposed that they could be made on the basis of analogies about skill and responsibility rather than by the general movement of wage rates. The Postmaster General at the time said he accepted this, but later described the Report with some justice as 'academic, confused and I regret to say ridiculous'.[104] However, it did force the parties back into negotiation. The Report was published on 11 June 1964 and on 26 June the first discussions with the Post Office began.[105]

In his later account of these matters, Bevins said that the Union's Executive might earlier have settled for a 5 per cent pay increase, but the Government had refused to accept this as beyond what was then its 'guiding light' of 4 per cent. Be that as it may, the atmosphere was changing rapidly over these weeks. These were the last days of a weak and discredited Government which hung on until the latest possible time in the autumn General Election. In any case, the expectations of the postmen themselves, who clearly had wide public support, had grown greatly since coming back from the brink in mid-April. The Union felt that it had won something from Armitage, and the *Financial Times* of 19 May described the position with reasonable accuracy when it said that the Union 'lost a point of principle but gained an equally valuable point in practice'. At all events a substantial offer was the only way to avoid further conflict. This was not at first forthcoming. On 8 July Bevins repeated the 4 per cent offer of earlier in the year together with a speeded up pay research exercise, carried out by the same team as in 1963. The Union negotiators made it clear that there was no possibility of this being agreed. 'If I were to accept', said Ron Smith, 'it would bring coals of fire upon my head.' He agreed to take it back to the Executive but said that 'it would be quite wrong for me to imply that there is any chance of them accepting it'. This indeed proved to be the attitude of the Executive at its meeting later in the day, the only doubt expressed being whether they should meet Bevins again before taking industrial action. The predominant view, however, was that it was worth a try.[106]

By the time that this meeting actually took place two days later on the afternoon of Friday 10 July, Union members were already making their feelings very clear. At a number of London offices, notably at Paddington and Hammersmith, there were unofficial walk-outs. By the Friday afternoon when the entire UPW Executive went to the Post Office Headquarters at St Martin's-le-Grand, at least 2,000 postmen had already walked off the job at the Mount Pleasant Sorting Office. They marched down the same road as their predecessors in 1890, and clearly demonstrated their feelings outside the talks with such chants as 'Why Are We Waiting?' and 'Bevins must go!'. Bevins himself seems to have been particularly upset by this 'raucous demonstration' which he said was so noisy 'that it was difficult to hear what was being said'. Against the din, Bevins made it clear that he was still not in a position to go beyond 4 per cent, and all he tried to do was to get Ron Smith to agree that the Union's claim was now in the region of 12 per cent. When Ron Smith left the building he met, according to a report in *The Times* of the following day, this reaction on speaking to the assembled postmen:

> An angry roar met his announcement that the Post Office were not prepared to improve on the offer that they made on Wednesday of a 4 per cent pay increase and an inquiry to see what further sum might be justified. This offer, Mr. Smith said, the Union Executive had rejected, and they had decided on the spot to call a one day strike next Thursday.
>
> Immediately there were shouts of 'Why not now?' and 'Why not to-morrow?'. With difficulty Mr. Smith obtained enough silence to explain that the Executive wanted the members to demonstrate not in anger as they were then doing but in a cool and disciplined manner. He was shouted down and hustled from the improvised platform.
>
> Surrounded by the crowd, who were now booing loudly, Mr. Smith was eventually rescued by half a dozen policemen, who forced a way for him back into the Post Office building. Once he was safely inside, the big iron gates were shut in the face of the demonstrators.

Other newspapers reported widespread walk-outs in many London offices as well as in Birmingham, Crawley, St Helen's and Wolverhampton. At the East Central District Office there was a unanimous vote on Friday evening to walk out. One report quoted a 'union official' as saying: 'It was against the wishes of the Union Officials but we had to go along with the decision. You cannot hold men in the raving temper they are in now.'[107]

Over the next few days the Union's leaders prepared for the national one-day strike called for 16 July and the ban on overtime planned for the succeeding fortnight.[108] They appealed to the members to avoid 'undisciplined action', but there was a good deal over the next few days. Members in many parts of the country initiated overtime bans. On Monday 13th, *The Times* published pictures of mounds of unsorted mail and an estimate that about 10,000 of inner London's 12,500 postmen had already been involved in some sort of unofficial action. Over the weekend many branches held meetings at which it was decided to ban overtime forthwith. From Derby and Wolverhampton, strike action was reported. On Monday night a noisy meeting of 800 members of the Sheffield Amalgamated Branch overthrew the proposal of the Branch Committee for an overtime ban. The meeting passed a unanimous vote for a twenty-four-hour strike on Tuesday before the overtime ban.[109] Postmaster General Bevins on the same Monday was subject to angry attack in Parliament and the only Conservative MP who spoke urged him to increase the 4 per cent offer. Later in the day he suspended the parcel service altogether, the printed paper service and the delivery of unaddressed circulars. On the following morning, Tuesday 14 July, the *Guardian* reported as follows:

> By last night, more than 30 cities and towns were experiencing overtime bans at all or some of their Post Offices. In addition to Crewe – a nerve centre of the

postal system – Leicester, Nottingham, Ipswich, Cardiff, Kettering, Leamington, Nuneaton and Southampton were among those to join the unofficial movement.

Overtime bans continued in all of London's 11 major sorting offices and at Manchester, Stafford, Coventry and Newcastle-upon-Tyne and other centres. At Derby 500 men remained on strike; they are due to report for work at 5 a.m. to-day, but will not work overtime. There were unofficial strikes also at Wolverhampton and Worcester.

Particular trouble was caused at the Mount Pleasant Sorting Office by a notice that went up on that same Monday night asserting 'that officers who deserted their posts or absented themselves without leave on 10/11 July or any strike on the 16 July will lose pay'. They were further warned of the possibility of prosecution or disciplinary penalties and of their liability to do overtime. The night shift on Monday 14 July walked out in protest against this, and all the following shifts did the same. The evening shift on the Tuesday voted almost unanimously to do so despite an appeal at a mass meeting from Executive members Tom Jackson and Ray Dobson who warned them that they were 'degenerating into a rabble'. They did not in the event return to work until the end of the general stoppage on Thursday 16th.[110]

The Union Executive at its meeting on 14 July voted to deplore all such unofficial action. At the same time they worked hard to organise the national strike they had planned for Thursday 16th. By now further walk-outs were reported from other London offices, as well as from Sheffield, Hereford, Pwllheli, Dover, Birkenhead and Norwich. Postal delays of two or three days were now reported in most parts of the country. In the final hours before the official strike at 4 p.m. on Wednesday 15 July, a Union delegation was summoned to see Chancellor of the Exchequer Maudling. The meeting had the purpose, according to Maudling, of 'clearing the air'. In the discussion he tried to fly the kite of a recall of the Armitage Committee to consider a settlement. The Union delegation was manifestly not in any position to accept anything other than more cash for the members. The Chancellor was perhaps hoping to plant the seed for further discussion.[111]

Thursday 16 July proved, as the *Daily Mirror* put it next day, 'A Lovely Day for a Strike'. As many as 20,000 postmen were reported to have marched in the blazing sunshine to Hyde Park in a massive show of strength organised by the postmen's section of the London District Committee. Similar demonstrations were held up and down the land. One particularly conspicuous feature was the level of public support. The delegation of almost 1,000 from the South Western District Office on its way to Hyde Park found 'obvious support . . . from well-wishers waving from many well-known business houses and many lines of pedestrians from the pavements smilingly offering their "good luck, lads," with many a friendly nod of approval'. Similarly one of a 'column of about 500 men' who marched for an hour round York said that 'at no time did I hear any adverse remarks'.[112] Ron Smith said that the response to the strike call was '99·9 percent recurring', and later analysis revealed that only 265 postmen and PHGs reported for work out of what was said to be a possible 64,239. One other conspicuous feature of that day was the fact that when it ended there was a disciplined return to work everywhere, even at Mount Pleasant where the offending poster had been tactfully removed. The ban on over-time now began, with no Sunday working. Little of the backlog was cleared. Fewer letters were being posted, but a lot fewer were being delivered also.[113]

Over the three or four days following the strike the most important participants in the drama ceased to be the foot soldiers and the stage was taken over by the generals. The attitude of the rest of the trade union movement was of considerable importance. TUC General Secretary George Woodcock had kept in close touch with the dispute and made a number of attempts at conciliation. He met Chancellor Maudling on Tuesday morning 21 July and in a discussion lasting eight minutes which he described as 'short and sour', he was offered nothing but an even speedier pay research exercise. This could not be taken seriously. At its meeting on the following morning the TUC General Council pledged a loan of £50,000 to the UPW for the purpose of pursuing its dispute further. By this time similar large loans had been pledged from other unions – £100,000 each from Frank Cousins's Transport and General Workers and the same amount from Bill Carron's Amalgamated Engineering Union. Even the Society of Telecommunication Engineers was offering a loan of £1,000 and a grant of £100 from its 6,000 odd members in managerial grades. The total available by the middle of the week was said to amount to over £300,000. As the money and promises poured in, attitudes at UPW House began to change. Ron Smith in particular made a number of public statements which belied the reasonable and moderate manner of earlier years. The *Guardian* of 17 July reported him as saying:

> I believe you have to have a substantial pay offer now to recover the goodwill which the Post Office began destroying in April 1963. We have seen the gradual destruction of a moderate sensible trade union leadership. That is what Mr. Bevins does not understand he has done over the last 18 months.

The *Financial Times* on the same day recorded some similar statements along with the report that 'I will not let myself be destroyed vis-à-vis my membership'. The next day the *Guardian* reported that he had said that 'if some people think I am Jack Easy and can be kicked around then I will have to change my approach'.

This was indeed what happened. At the fateful Executive meeting on Wednesday 22 July Ron Smith made a proposal which 'surprised even his closest advisers' and which Norman Stagg later characterised with some justice as 'the most momentous motion ever tabled before the Executive Council':

> that from midnight on Saturday July 25, there shall be a directive to Postmen and Postmen Higher Grade to withdraw their labour until further notice.

The Union was also to pay a hardship allowance of £2 per week which was then around 15 per cent of their normal wage. After lengthy discussion, this proposal was agreed without dissent.[114] Ron Smith was reported in all the press next day as having taken this unexpected decision because 'we particularly want the public to appreciate we are right slap-bang up against a brick wall'. He thought an all-out strike more likely to retain this support and settle the issue than the 'guerrilla' actions that had, until then, been considered sufficient.

This was indeed the turning point of the conflict.[115] The Government which only the day before had rejected any further compromise set up a Special Committee of four Ministers – PMG Bevins, Minister of Labour John Godber, Home Secretary Henry Brooke and William Deedes, Minister without Portfolio. By 10.30 p.m. they had decided on the outline of the solution, though Bevins, who found the whole day 'awful', was discussing until one in the morning. A further Cabinet meeting took place later that morning of Thursday 23 July. Here a new increase above the 4 per cent 'guiding light' was agreed. It had to be within 7 per cent so that it could be claimed that there was room left for the postmen to obtain only a further ½ per cent in the following January and thus be within the amount granted other civil servants. Bevins, who attended the meeting said that 'his colleagues had no stomach for the fight, but were prepared to settle on almost any terms. They gave Maudling a free hand.'

Ron Smith met Chancellor Maudling at noon to discuss the new proposals. No new figures were mentioned, but Maudling did refer for the first time to backdating some of the 3½ per cent due to civil servants in the following January. The pay research exercise would then be used to determine how much more of the 3½ per cent they would obtain. Maudling also made much of the demand that the strike should be called off before any 'concrete offer would be made'. This was somewhat spurious, however, since the postmen were clearly going to need a good deal more than talk before they would call off their action. What they got was 'clarification', which amounted to an actual cash offer.

A series of further meetings took place later on that day, 23 July. One was between Prime Minister Sir Alex Douglas Home and Opposition Leader Harold Wilson. This underlined the gravity of the conflict, but did not affect its outcome. In the afternoon Ron Smith and his negotiating team met George Woodcock and other TUC leaders who in turn went to see the Chancellor. Their main purpose was to clarify the precise figures being offered. At 5.15 Ron Smith and his colleagues went on their second visit to the Treasury that day. Smith had at this point agreed to go down to 7 per cent, and it was now clear that the Government would at least go up to 5 per cent. Further discussion took place on the Friday morning 24 July between Smith and Bevins, who found it all 'a nightmare'. By 2.30 in the afternoon, Smith was in a position to put to his Executive a series of proposals of which the most important was that in return for calling off the strike there would be negotiations within the range of 5–7 per cent, with the final settlement worked out by pay research backdated to 1 January 1964. The UPW Executive discussed this for three hours and at 5.25 agreed to accept it.

With the strike now called off, UPW negotiators went to see Bevins again. Discussions continued for four hours and were reported by Smith as follows:

. . . we met the Postmaster General at 6.30 p.m. The Postmaster General said 5½ per cent, but I said 7. Again we debated. I suggested the Postmaster General might care to consult which he did. He came back and said 6 per cent, and I said 7. The Postmaster General consulted again at length, and I am bound to tell you that I am satisfied that you must now make a decision as to whether a 6½ per cent increase as an interim settlement is now acceptable.

This was discussed at an Executive meeting at 10.20 p.m. and accepted by 23 votes to 5.[116] There was still one problem which was the insistence from the Government on a formula that the interim increase would be taken off anything gained the following January. At a press conference held at midnight, Maudling said that the 6½ per cent 'being subject to pay research, could be adjusted *either* way in future'. Smith agreed that this was theoretically so, but one reporter thought 'it sounded as if no one had better try to take any of the 6 per cent away again. Not after all this.'[117]

This outcome was seen as a victory for the postmen and their Union. The postmen had in the course of a punishing period of action retained the support of press and public. The atmosphere of the final weeks of a thirteen-year period of Tory administrations, and the shock value of the novelty of a civil servants' strike had the desired effect. The election of a new Labour Government on 8 October 1964 not initially committed to any specific means of holding down wages also contributed to the success of subsequent negotiations. As the Union had predicted, the pay research survey took a good deal more than the few weeks constantly promised in mid-1964. In fact it took eight months, during which time the Union itself spoke to outside industrial consultants about the sort of comparisons that could be made with postmen. A claim for the reduction of the working week of postmen from forty-five hours to forty-three was also submitted in September 1964.

The first meeting with the Director General of the Post Office was held on 18 March 1965 to take stock of the pay research material. The Union argued that the position was now greatly changed from the previous July and a substantial increase had been indicated by the pay research exercise. One interesting aspect of the proposal was to tie the postmen to 'contract pay' – the phrase used for long-term pay agreements common at the time elsewhere in the civil service. In particular, most other UPW grades, including P&TOs, telegraphists and telephonists, had recently settled for such arrangements with a 3½ per cent increase from January 1965 and January 1966. This was without prejudice to a new batch of pay research exercises, and was approved at a Special Conference in February 1965. For the postmen, a further meeting with PHG Benn on 15 March produced a series of proposals which amounted to initially all of what the Union had been demanding in the protracted struggle of the previous year. There was a 19 per cent increase back-dated to the previous January, incorporating the interim 6½ per cent. They also obtained the reduction in hours to forty-three, the abolition of household deliveries except for public services, and moves to deal with the problems of part-time workers. The one sting in the tail was an agreement to increases of 4 per cent from January 1965 and 3½ per cent from January 1966. This was approved at the May 1965 Annual Conference, though there was still some opposition, especially from London delegates.[118]

YEARS OF CHANGE AND CONFLICT: 1964–70

The period of Labour Government in the 1960s saw changes for the Post Office and its workers as well as in the economy as a whole which had a considerable impact on all the main fields which are described in this book. In Chapter 9 some detail has been given of developments during this period in methods of government economic intervention and the consequent changes in the way that the Post Office was run. In Chapter 11 and elsewhere something has been said of how the spirit and ethos of the UPW changed under the impact of these forces. Now something must be said of how the style and stance of the Union changed in the 1960s, how it was pushed from the carpeted corridors of civil service protocol into a more rumbustuous bargaining market place. Behind all this lay real changes in economic conditions and social attitudes. Although it is difficult to quantify this trend, there can be no doubt that the 1960s saw for the first time the reduction in the numbers of those who felt themselves to be 'Post Office people', perhaps of the second or third generation, and who came in from the armed forces or through the promotion path as boy messengers. From the late 1940s it was no longer possible to begin with an apprenticeship in this grade. Improved conditions in other industries, and a labour shortage generally, meant that people could come and go as they had never done before. For the very first time during this period, leaders of Post Office trade unionism included people who had not been in the Post Office since their youth.

Some reference has been made elsewhere to the rather authoritarian style of General Secretary Charles Geddes in contrast to his predecessors and successors. After Ron Smith inherited this mantle in 1957, the realities faced by the Union began to change, and with it the attitude of the members. The growth of unofficial industrial action in the Union and the great success of the 1964 strike, were part of a series of developments that affected the style of leadership by the time Ron Smith himself retired in 1966. Many individual events and trends in the life of the Union, which remain at the time of writing matters of passionate memory, were part of this new phase in the UPW's history.

These remarks apply in particular to the events of 1963–5, including the expulsion of members of the London District Committee postmen's group, called 'LDC 3'. This group, of whom the guiding light was clearly J. R. ('Dickie') Lawlor, had long been a thorn in the flesh of the Union leadership. As far back as 1951 they initiated unofficial industrial action and became the targets of the strongest anti-Communist statements of Charles Geddes. They had, naturally, been at the forefront of unofficial action in the 1962 work to rule and in the events leading to the 1964 strike. During this period a series of complex disputes developed between various active members in the London area and the national leadership.[119] They centred on a number of issues of which the most concrete was the refusal of London postmen to accept the household delivery agreement arrived at nationally. There were also allegations about the conduct of the Metropolitan District Branch. An Executive inquiry failed to blame anybody, though it did cause a good deal of local resentment.[120]

These disputes came to a head over a meeting called by London District Committee postmen in Trafalgar Square on Sunday 24 November 1963. It was a mass meeting called apparently without any consent or knowledge of the Union leadership and certainly without their participation. It reflected the discontent of London postmen with the arbitration award earlier in the year and generally argued for increased pressure on the Post Office and Treasury. Over 4,000 postmen attended the demonstration, whose impact was weakened by the enormous effect of a major event in world politics on 22 November, the assassination of President Kennedy in the United States. A brief account of the meeting did appear in London editions of the *Guardian* on Monday 25 November where an unnamed 'senior official' of the Union was quoted as saying that it was 'completely unofficial'. This caused a good deal of chagrin amongst those who had set up the meeting, particularly because it had been entirely orderly and had included no criticism of any kind of the Union leadership. An angry delegation visited the Union Headquarters on Tuesday 26 November consisting of all the members of the LDC '3' Executive. They insisted on seeing all the officers. After a few harsh words on either side and the exchange of more formal correspondence, it was eventually agreed that the LDC members had no intention of challenging the Executive, and the Union leadership for their part did not publicly condemn the Trafalgar Square meeting emphasising that they were now actively pursuing the question of postmen's pay.[121]

Over the following weeks tension remained high between Union Headquarters and London postmen's leaders. Though at times this was expressed in terms of personal differences between individuals and has undoubtedly been seen in these terms since that time, what clearly lay behind it was the growing discontent of London postmen. There had been a good deal of unofficial action in London offices in July, but there had been no need for the local leadership to provoke it. At times they discouraged it, as when Dickie Lawlor on 13 August got postmen to return to work at Wimbledon when they had walked out over a local grievance. Lawlor had written privately to Ron Smith on 23 July warning him that any retreat on their 10½ per cent claim would 'smash our Union'. LDC Secretary Dennis Coughlan also wrote to him on 17 August that following the industrial action 'the postman now sees his Union as an entirely new machine; one which is stronger and more forceful'.[122]

It was in this atmosphere of increased expectation that Ron Smith was informed on 12 August that the London Region postal management was proposing to re-introduce part-time labour. Part-time labour had been introduced in London for a year or two after the agreement of 1955 and had been stopped after discussion with the Union in 1962, though some part-timers were employed in other parts of the country. In London in particular temporary workers, usually women, were especially resented. This was partly because they were thought to obtain preferential treatment in their shift patterns, but more because they would limit overtime working for those who felt it necessary to make up their earnings in this way. A delegation of UPW officers met the regional management on 24 August urging them to negotiate the change office by office. It was already clear that the London District Committee '3' would not accept any compromise. As Secretary, Lawlor immediately circulated his affiliates urging them not to co-operate with any new entrants and to ban overtime where they were introduced. This line was confirmed on 15 September by 190 votes to 9 at a meeting of delegates to the postmen's District Council.

This was clearly a threat not simply to the plans of the Post Office, but also to the system of authority within the Union. The rules made it quite clear that only the Executive Committee had the right to call a strike. Even beyond this, however, the postmen's District Council insisted on operating quite independently of the other grade sections of the LDC. Thus is was only a partially representative delegation that met the London management on 16 September. Dennis Coughlan, who was Secretary of the LDC as a whole, presented the postmen's case forcibly enough, maintaining that there was much else the management could do besides introducing part-timers or temporaries. They could, for example, transfer people between different offices, or give overtime duties in sorting offices to P&TOs who served on counters. Meanwhile, on 21 September, Ron Smith met PMG Bevins who reminded him of the 1955 agreement. Smith in return referred to the difficulties arising from the delay in discussing improvements since the strike in July. On the 23rd he proposed for the Executive meeting on the following day that the only alternative in the immediate situation was 'accepting the use of part-time labour providing there are adequate safeguards'.[123]

On the following day, 24 September 1964, there took place a most extraordinary meeting of the UPW's Executive.[124] Without any notice being given, a resolution was proposed by Ron Smith and seconded by Lionel Andrews of which this is the most important part:

That the Executive Council takes note of the declared intention of the members of
the LDC Sectional Council 3 Committee to adhere to its own decisions and those
of its Sectional Council taken contrary to the National Rules of the Union and its
own authority as a Section of the Union's London District Council.

The Executive Council declares these decisions both to be ultra vires and not in
the best interests of the membership served by the Union.

It resolves in accordance with the authority vested in it by the National Rules to
expel forthwith from membership:- Mr. H. J. Jones, Mr. J. R. Lawlor,
Mr. M. H. Styles, Mr. J. R. Cooper, Mr. C. Kirk, Mr. J. P. Regan.

Harry Jones was at that time Chairman of the LDC Sectional Committee '3' and
Dickie Lawlor its Secretary. Maurice Styles was Assistant Secretary and also a
member of the Union's Executive. He took no part in the discussion on the
resolution or in the vote, which passed it by 20 to 3. Only Willie Failes asked for his
dissent to be recorded. Other efforts to get a more lenient or deferred punishment
were either declared out of order or defeated. One of the other dissentients
described the proceedings as 'quiet and dignified', with 'no bitterness'. There was
more difficulty involved in taking over the property of the Sectional Committee and
attempting to arrange a meeting to elect new officers. The Executive meanwhile
agreed to accept very limited part-time labour to cover the tasks expected in the
forthcoming General Election. However, this was only in return for a series of other
measures including the suspension of the household delivery service. Union leaders
met the management on this on 30 September and much of it was accepted.[125] They
also published news of the expulsion of eighty or so London postmen who had been
blacklegs during the one-day strike in July.

However it was the expulsions of the LDC officers that had the greatest significance for the Union. It soon became clear that those expelled had a good deal of
support among London postmen. Thus Tony Clarke and Harry Klein, the only two
members of the Sectional Committee who had not been expelled, indicated that
they were in complete support of their colleagues.[126] Resolutions were passed and
petitions circulated throughout London. On 5 October a demonstration of about
180 branch officials sent a delegation that met Ron Smith and presented him with
statements on behalf of the expelled men signed by 5,333 members. In the meantime the expelled men met the solicitors Gaster and Turner and on 6 October issued
a writ against the Executive and gave notice of their intention to go to the High
Court to obtain an injunction to reverse the expulsions. The case went ahead
despite the fact that one of those expelled, Harry Jones, decided to direct his appeal
to the Executive itself. On 20 October the case for the others was presented at the
High Court by Bernard Caulfield, QC. He maintained that they had been given no
notice of the charge against them and had been unable to defend themselves so that
the proceedings against them were contrary to 'natural justice'. On 29 October, Mr
Justice Ungoed Thomas issued a writ against the Executive on the grounds that 'the
rules of natural justice were necessarily to be implied from the Union's rules and
had not been observed here'.[127] This was given effect permanently on 24 November.

The reinstatement of Dickie Lawlor and his colleagues not only to their
membership but also to the positions they had held, had a number of important
consequences. A good deal of bitterness remained, with Executive members
insisting that the LDC '3' leaders had no alternative to offer to part-time labour
other than higher wages or less services. The men who had been expelled persisted

in their view that they had not broken any of the rules of the Union in calling the industrial action, especially as a similar call in 1963 had not been challenged. The legal proceedings were slightly extended in order to deal with this question, which was never in the end decided, and Ron Smith claimed that the pursuance of this issue was the only use to which the money raised from postmen on behalf of those expelled was put. The Executive was also compelled to rescind their expulsion of the 1964 strike blacklegs because they could now appeal on exactly the same grounds as the militants. Other arguments continued over a meeting of the LDC as a whole held during the expulsions where a determined group had prevented the transaction of any business in the absence of the LDC '3' officials or the considera- tion of their case.[128] Dick Lawlor – not a master of tact – went so far as to publish an article entitled 'Reform or Surgery?' questioning whether amalgamation had served the postman's grade. The very raising of this question, rarely if ever mentioned in the history of the Union in that form, met an abusive response from many quarters.[129]

In the meantime, Ron Smith and the Executive were insisting on a retraction from the reinstated members of their right to initiate strike action.[130] Essentially those who had been expelled insisted that they had not gone outside the rules as they understood them, and the Executive insisted that they alone had the right to call industrial action under the rules. The situation was complicated by the appearance in the *Daily Mail* on 30 January 1965 of a report that further proceed- ings were to be taken within the Union against the LDC '3' leaders. For their part, the LDC leaders called for an outside inquiry.[131]

It had long since become clear that these arguments were not likely to resolve much. Further court cases over such matters as the real meaning of the Union's strike rule could run for years, as could correspondence demanding undertakings on future conduct. In any case the LDC Annual General Meeting on 30 March elected one of those expelled, Maurice Styles, as its Secretary against his predecessor Dennis Coughlan who had not been directly involved. On 5 March the Executive had decided already that it was not worth continuing to pursue the matter. A long letter was sent to the LDC '3' officers reminding them of the undertakings they had given and of the powers of the Executive. A Special Branch Circular was sent out to the same effect. It began in this way:

> The Executive Council has been advised that if they were involved in any further legal action, such action might not be resolved in time to allow Annual Conference to have before it, for discussion and for decision, a full report on the differences which led to the High Court Action of October 1964. In these circum- stances it has resolved not to take any further action on the written explanation sought from 9 London Colleagues, and reported to Branches in the Annual Report contained in THE POST of January 23rd, 1965.
>
> At the same time it had directed that it wants it clearly understood that in future it will insist upon the strictest compliance with the Rules and Authorities of the Union and that it would regard itself, if necessary, entitled to reconsider its decision.

These same points were made in a long report to a Special Conference on 16 May 1965 which strongly endorsed the Executive Council's stand, by 3 and 4 to 1. Some- thing of the bitterness which had crept into this effort to reassert constitutional authority can be gathered from this extract from Ron Smith's speech:

> . . . he did not like having to be escorted from gatherings of Union members by Metropolitan Police after informing them that the EC had decided to withdraw their labour. He resented, too, being abused for the shortcomings of Tory Ministers . . . 'And I have seen enough of crowds on the lawns of UPW House shouting for "him" to be brought out – as if the fact that people pay 3d. or 4d. a year towards my salary entitled them to a lynching party. I dislike, particularly, sawdust Caesars ranting through UPW House followed by their minions trying to intimidate people who have been entrusted by this Conference with the carrying out of a task on their behalf . . .'[132]

When passions remained as strong as these, there were clearly conflicts abroad which could not easily be resolved. Feelings of bitterness have not quite disappeared at the present day. However time has healed many of the differences. Three of the seven expelled were subsequently elected officers of the Union along with one of their closest supporters. Later battles have to some degree moved elsewhere, and have become concerned with different issues. There can be no doubt however that the Union itself changed in a profound way in the mid-1960s. The retirement of Ron Smith in 1966 and the succession of Tom Jackson represented a new style of leadership to some degree associated with the rebellious elements within the Union. Tom Jackson was also the first General Secretary since Bill Bowen to have originated in the postman grade, though in fact he was a postman higher grade at the time he first became a full-time official in 1964. It is of some interest that a number of the other main negotiation officers changed during this period – Norman Stagg went from Editor to replace Lionel Andrews as Deputy General Secretary in 1967. Tom Jackson was himself replaced as Assistant Secretary Outdoor by Willie Failes, a Communist. Perhaps the most symbolic change was the creation of a new assistant secretary position to help the General Secretary and his Deputy, and the election to it of Dickie Lawlor in July 1969. The new militant style and spirit in the leadership reflected a membership that had become at the same time less deferential and less content.

Many of the great changes that affected Post Office workers during this same period of the mid-1960s have been mentioned in various contexts in other chapters of this book. In particular the changes in the organisation of the Post Office itself from a department of state to a public corporation were discussed in Chapter 9. The existence of a Labour Government between 1964 and 1970 meant that UPW leaders, as in the late 1940s, felt a loyalty to Government policies of planning incomes which had a profound effect on bargaining in the late 1960s. The UPW was a comparatively militant union in this period in a way it had not been before, and this was shown by the various forms of industrial action, official and unofficial, in 1968 and 1969. The careful marshalling of argument for arbitration court or outside inquiry, which was central to Post Office pay bargaining right back to the 1890s, was in the 1960s forgotten for the most part. Though the 'annual wage round' had now become the norm and direct negotiations the most usual way of discussing it, this new position in no way implied a simple untroubled progression, especially at a time of wage constraint of various sorts.

The change in status of the Post Office first announced in 1966 was brought into effect in 1969. Within the UPW there was a great deal of discussion with a Special

Joint Committee consisting of the Union's officers and Post Office management presenting four reports to the membership on a wide range of issues. Perhaps the most complex problem was superannuation, and perhaps the most extraordinary proposal was the one to increase the retirement age to 65.[133] As discussed elsewhere, the Union did not succeed in its efforts to obtain unity with others in the new Corporation, though it did eventually get recognition withdrawn from the secessionist National Guild of Telephonists. A Council of Post Office Unions was also set up with the new Corporation, and a compulsory membership agreement was also eventually secured. Despite the creation of quite separate regions for posts and telecommunications, and some strengthening of the machinery of the London District Committee, there were fewer structural changes in trade union organisation that were at first expected, at least in the short term. The opportunity was taken to standardise some procedures with regard to discipline and contracts of employment. The old 'non-established' section of the workforce had now largely disappeared and the new system of superannuation that emerged from negotiation was generally thought to be an improvement. The new arrangements were not an unqualified success, however, for reasons which were discussed in Chapter 9.

From the point of view of the Union, the most important change was the disappearance of the names and institutions of collective bargaining that had been familiar over two generations, particularly those associated with the Whitley Council system. Some of the differences were of little more than nomenclature. National and local negotiating machinery were not suddenly transformed with their names. Special arrangements for London continued as before, for example. Similarly, the Post Office's own arbitration machinery was expected to work in much the same way as the old civil service tribunal. For reasons quite apart from the setting up of the new Corporation, however, the Post Office Arbitration Board was used a good deal less than before. 'Pay research' came to an end for the Post Office workers in 1969. As various groups of Post Office workers gradually extracted themselves from their links with civil service grades, their wages and conditions came to be negotiated directly with the Post Office authorities. The entire pattern of negotiations in the 1966–9 period was extremely messy and complicated. The most important reason for this was the development of Government incomes policy and its continuous impact on the actions of the UPW and every other union.

During the years 1964–70 the Labour Government attempted to introduce various forms of income restraint, with diminishing support for the trade unions. This was at a time when the annual inflation rate varied between about 3 and 5 per cent. From July 1966 there was a period of wage standstill followed in December by 'severe restraint' and a year later by a 'twelve months rule' for settlements tied to productivity improvements. After March 1968 pay increases were supposed to be up to 3½ per cent with exceptions only for special cases. During the final period of the Labour Government that came to an end in June 1970, increases were supposed to be between 2½ and 4½ per cent. Trade union attitudes to these policies grew increasingly hostile and became almost universally so after the publication in January 1969 of the White Paper *In Place of Strife* which proposed various restrictions on trade union activities.

Each of these developments had a profound effect on the activities and attitudes of the UPW, to a greater extent than the various institutional changes which were taking place at the same time. Thus in the second of the reports on reorganisation, published towards the end of 1967, it was said that 'the largest single factor' in a 'sound wage policy would have to be the economic condition of the country'. The most important secondary factor was thought of as 'the state of the industry in which we work'. Such statements would not have been made in earlier periods. Another result of attitudes which perhaps reflected more traditional efforts to achieve orderly methods of collective bargaining was the support for the Prices and Incomes Board set up to obtain such ends in the early part of 1965. A PIB Report a year later met a good deal less approval on account of its effort to take account of overtime in its calculations about earnings. UPW leaders loyally accepted the July 1966 wages standstill, but not without 'doubts' and 'anxieties'. Even a visit by Prime Minister Harold Wilson to a meeting of the Executive on 31 March 1967 did not keep the Union faithful to 'severe restraint' for very long. By the early part of 1968, General Secretary Tom Jackson was a strong opponent of any possible legislation that limited collective bargaining, and in 1969 the UPW campaigned with other unions against *In Place of Strife*.[134]

Meanwhile, problems were building up for Union members. As already indicated, postmen and PHGs were generally considered to have done well out of the various negotiations that followed their industrial action of 1964. As labour shortages built up in the main cities it became increasingly possible to supplement earnings through overtime working. Postmen were also generally thought to have done well in the negotiations that culminated in a temporary 5 per cent increase approved at a Special UPW Conference in November 1967.[135] Such changes were to some degree matters of fortuitous timing between phases of incomes policy, and by no means all Union members were so lucky.

This applied in particular to postal and telegraph officers in this period. Although they were able to supplement their incomes through overtime working, there can be no doubt that they also grew a good deal more discontented. Once an educated and superior elite, those who served at counters felt themselves with some justice to have fallen back in the pay research race. As already noted, the 1965 UPW Conference decided to break from the historic claim of this group, now achieved, of alignment with the general clerical grades in the civil service. P&TOs now felt that they had to go beyond the largely routine duties of clerical officers with intensified duties caused by the abolition of specialised services at counters, and with increasing functions such as work on the newly established Giro. They retained long incremental scales now considered anachronistic, and had limited prospects of promotion.[136] The fact that similarly qualified people could secure other work was shown by the shortage of new recruits to the grade from within the service. The management initiated a scheme of 'supplementary recruitment' from outside the service to deal with this problem. The scheme was accepted by UPW leaders but rejected by the delegates at the 1966 UPW Conference, and then imposed by the management just the same.[137] The 1966 wages standstill then affected the third stage of 'contract pay' for the civil service as a whole including P&TOs. As a result their expected pay increase did not materialise at the beginning of 1967.

During 1967 there was a good deal of discussion within the Post Office on the conditions of postal and telegraph officers. There was a continuing shortage of recruits, and a special study group discussed separating counter and writing duties altogether. It was also obvious that the term 'telegraph' was now largely out of date and it was eventually dropped in 1972. In the meantime the last of the protracted pay research exercises resulted in what was described as the most complicated of all the Pay Research Unit reports being presented to the Union on 29 December 1967.

In the early months of 1968 it was said that for the P&TOs there developed an 'atmosphere' that was 'similar to that which existed amongst our Postmen and PHG membership in the hectic days of 1963 and 1964'. All the previous interim claims were now withdrawn, but the Post Office authorities were slow to respond to the urgency pressed upon them by the Union. A new incomes policy was in the process of gestation and the newly invented 'twelve month rule' was used as an excuse to deny any agreement on the grounds that some increases had been obtained for junior members of the grade the previous October. There were fears from the Treasury and those making economic policy in the Government that civil service clerical officers would want the same improvements as might be obtained in the Post Office, a reversal of what had been the traditional order. There were uncertainties in the administration as Edward Short was succeeded by Roy Mason as Postmaster General for a brief four-month tenure.

In all these circumstances, there was a very slow response to the PRU Report. On 26, 29, 30 April and 1 May there were limited one-hour official stoppages and on 3 May a national two-hour stoppage of all P&TO members. At meetings held during these stoppages, members voted by 17,513 to 241 in favour of protracted industrial action. The calling of a national strike for 8 May at last produced a response, and it was called off so that General Secretary Tom Jackson could on that day meet the Chancellor of the Exchequer, Roy Jenkins. The fact that P&TOs had already agreed to balance their accounts less frequently aided the negotiations. It was possible to bring this in as a productivity element and to agree an increase of 8–10 per cent. This was accepted by delegates representing the grade at a Special Conference on 19 May 1968.[138]

The impetus created by these events affected many other sections of Union members. Preliminary negotiations on telephonists' pay before the Union's Annual Conference in May 1968 resulted in a large explosion of anger from members that pushed the offer at the maximum from 5s (25p) up to 17s 6d (87½p) – an increase of 5½ per cent. A further 2½ per cent was secured in a productivity deal at the beginning of 1969, and 3½ per cent under the civil service general deal for 1 July.[139]

There were some difficult negotiations on behalf of other sections of the membership during this period, most notably the overseas telegraphists. There were never many in this grade – up to 3,500 – and nearly all of them were at Electra House in London. They had been created as a separate group by the standardisation of the system in the mid-1960s, and tended to have special problems somewhat apart from the Union, in certain ways comparable to male telephonists in the 1920s. There was sharp conflict with the Union leaders at times and occasional talk of secessionism. An unofficial walk-out during the lunch hour of 20 October 1967 from Electra House was condemned by the Union Executive. In the following June a demand for 5 per cent – comparable with an overall civil service increase – was submitted on their behalf. The Post Office, however, insisted on productivity strings being attached to any increase.

On 11 October and 14 November there were unofficial walk-outs of more than 1,000 OTOs on the claim. After further negotiations and various offers, OTOs voted to strike, and on 20 January 1969 they were called out by the Union Executive. At this stage Postmaster General John Stonehouse spoke of taking the dispute to the Civil Service Arbitration Tribunal. However, this did not impress the Union. The strike itself was solid and on 24 January the Union Executive called an overtime ban of all its members as from the 27th. On 30 January there was a national

UPW strike in the nineteen largest towns in Britain. In the afternoon PMG Stonehouse announced the suspension of second class mail, a step strongly attacked by UPW MPs Ray Dobson and Dennis Hobden. On the 31st Stonehouse announced that he was now able to negotiate and after six hours with the entire Executive agreed to backdate the 5 per cent increase to 1 August and to make a further 2 per cent from 1 April dependent on productivity strings. On 1 February *The Times* said this amounted to a 'complete capitulation by the Government' and the next day the *Sunday Mirror* described the whole episode as 'a tale of almost unbelievable chaos and incredible feeblemindedness by all concerned – with the exception of the Postmen's leaders'. Electra House Branch Secretary Ron Beak echoed what many felt in the Union when he described this a victory for 'amalgamation in action'. Clearly the Government had not expected so sharp and disruptive a response from the Union, which was greatly strengthened as a result.[140]

This was not the end of disagreements between the OTOs and the UPW Executive. Following the dispute, there was a row when Ron Beak revealed details of a confidential Department of Employment report on industrial relations at Electra House. However, as mentioned elsewhere, efforts to discipline Beak were reversed at the Union's 1970 Annual Conference.[141]

By this time a new situation was beginning to develop for wage bargaining in the Post Office. All the separate negotiations for various grades over recent years had been rendered messy and complicated by the capricious timing of incomes policy, particularly as applied to the civil service. Many half-baked and temporary agreements had been made of which the one eventually emerging for OTOs in 1970 was but a conspicuous example. During 1969 it grew increasingly clear that a great deal of discontent was growing up amongst Union members. The Union's Jubilee Conference celebrated its first fifty years in May. It heard a moving speech from J. Craig Walker – one of the old PTCA rebels from before the First World War who had opposed the abandonment of the strike policy in 1921 – about the need to keep the faith. The Conference stood respectfully for Prime Minister Harold Wilson but it was not persuaded by his efforts to get them to support *In Place of Strife*. It even went on to hear Postmaster General Stonehouse praise the solidarity they had shown in the previous January on behalf of the OTOs.[142]

In fact the main bargaining steps were decided in a way now becoming normal in the UPW – by the holding of special conferences. In June 1969 there was announced the last of the civil service wage increases, which gave 5 per cent to P&TOs and added 3½ per cent to what had recently been won by OTOs. A Special Conference of P&TOs held in July showed that the problems of this grade had by no means been resolved. They threw out yet another scheme for supplementary recruitment and applauded with particular enthusiasm attacks on incremental scales. A further Special Conference held in October agreed to a general claim for a 'substantial increase' in pay and reductions in incremental scales. The negotiations that followed were of some interest for the future. At a time when the general rate of consumer prices was going up by 5–7 per cent the Union leaders were expecting to settle at around a 12 per cent wage increase. On 5 February 1970 an offer of 10 per cent was unanimously rejected by the Union's Executive. Eventually something nearer 15 per cent was obtained and accepted by the Executive. General Secretary Tom Jackson said this was the most the Union had ever obtained, and it was a very large proportion of what had been asked for in the first place. What was in some ways most significant of all, however, was the vote from Union branches for acceptance, which was 10,987 to 9,651. Behind these figures clearly lay a good deal of simmering discontent.[143]

Years of frustration and restraint were clearly now having an effect on UPW members. In this period price inflation was becoming accepted but wage increases were constantly being held back. Overtime working had become the normal means of making up wages. Incremental scales had become a major grievance. In April 1970 the Union's Executive brought out yet another *Special Report on Wages Policy* and this was discussed in detail at the May 1970 Annual Conference. This pointed out that while the Union had been prepared to accept productivity bargaining while wages were going up more than incomes policies might dictate, there was still a wide range of different grievances which could only be dealt with by a significant 'increase in the take home pay of our members without increasing the length of the working week'. There was already a joint working party on incremental scales and there could be further consideration of working methods. The Annual Conference in May wanted the working party to report by October and also voted for a substantial general wage claim.[144]

Before this decision could be put into effect there occurred one event of considerable significance, and this was the election in June 1970 of a Conservative Government with a majority of 40. This administration was determined to restrict the powers of the trade unions and was soon hard at work on its ill-fated Industrial Relations Act. At the same time it was determined to reduce the rate of wage increases. This was done initially with an incomes policy sometimes called 'n–1,' in other words trying to ensure that each settlement should be 1 per cent less than its predecessor. This was at a time when inflation was around 8 per cent and wage settlements were moving from 12 per cent up to 20 per cent or more. At the beginning of the wage round local authority manual workers went on strike from 29 September to 9 November and eventually obtained 15 per cent after a Committee of Enquiry under Sir Jack Scamp which was bitterly attacked by the Government. In November after a series of unofficial strikes, miners obtained an increase of 12 per cent or more. In mid-December electricity workers began to work to rule which brought power cuts and a cacophony of anti-trade union abuse unprecedented since the 'Sheffield outrages' of the 1860s. The dispute went to a Court of Enquiry under Lord Wilberforce which reported in the following February bringing a complicated settlement probably amounting to 15 per cent.

This was the industrial context in which the UPW Executive met on 29 October 1970 to consider the policy agreed at its May Conference. On the following day it submitted a claim for a basic increase of 15 per cent on all pay scales. Where 15 per cent would not produce £3 more on the maximum, then it should be brought up to this amount with a similar percentage lower down the scales. (In practice this meant that low-paid grades like cleaners and cooks would get up to 24 per cent and other grades less – postmen for example 16 per cent and telephonists 17 per cent.) To this was added a call for substantial but unspecified reductions on incremental scales.[145] The claim that was submitted was thus well within the 'going rate' of the time, and below the level of a number of well publicised settlements. However, it came up against a senior management under considerable pressure from the Government, not just to keep down wages. The pressures they were under were clearly indicated in November 1970 by the dismissal of Lord Hall, the first Chairman of the new Corporation. Against this unmoving object was now gathering an irresistible force. Years of frustration and discontent for Post Office workers were coming to the surface. The low basic wages, the long hours of overtime, the years taken to reach the maximum, all now resulted in the greatest explosion of anger in the history of the Post Office. Truly, the new Corporation was about to receive its baptism of fire.

1971 –'SAY NOT THE STRUGGLE NAUGHT AVAILETH'

There can be no doubt that the national UPW strike of 20 January to 7 March 1971 was not only the most well known event in the history of industrial relations in the Post Office, it also affected the attitudes of all those who took part, or who have heard of it since.[146] It was the longest single official strike in terms of the length and number of working days lost since the 1926 General Strike, and was after this exceeded only by the miners in January–February 1972 and the – discontinuous – engineering strikes in 1979. The Union itself reckoned the figure of working days lost up to 8 million, the Post Office calculated it as 6,273,777, and the Department of Employment at 6,229,100. According to the Post Office, the highest number of strikers was 189,581 and at the end there were 175,576. The Department of Employment figure was 179,675. The Union, more vaguely, normally said 200,000 or more.[147]

Whatever its precise extent, no other national strike can have had so direct and continuous an effect on so many people. It was one of the epic battles in the history of the British working-class movement, disciplined and tumultuous. It was also a significant episode in the relations between the social classes in Britain. Those who participated will always remember it as a great experience in hundreds of thousands of lives. There can be no doubt that it will be seen for generations to come as a watershed in the history of the Union and in the efforts to settle wages and conditions in the Post Office. It was the culmination of a significant phase in the life of the UPW and is generally remembered a decade later as a defeat for the Union, although a temporary one. It is therefore seen by those with various points of view as an indication of the need to proceed differently in the future, either without strikes at all or else by organising them more effectively. The following account sets out the main events of the struggle, and discusses some of the issues that arise from a consideration of its course and outcome.

Before setting out these details, it is necessary to see the 1971 strike in its historical context. It was just a century after strikes of telegraphists and letter carriers which have been described in Chapter 5. It took place just over eighty years after the London postmen in 1890 walked out and were defeated. It was also almost exactly fifty years after those anguished weeks in 1921 when the decision was taken just after the foundation of the UPW to abandon the strike weapon altogether. Those who participated in 1971 knew little of this. They were, no doubt, more affected by the growth of militancy in the Union in the various unofficial actions from the 1950s onwards, and by the great success of the postmen's strike of 1964 and the actions in 1967 and 1968 on behalf of the postal and telegraph officers and overseas telegraphists. In particular they were no doubt emboldened by the great success of the trade union movement as a whole in keeping up with the ravages of inflation against increasingly strident efforts to put a stop to effective trade union activity. Also, the strikers of 1971 had seen a world where great demonstrations throughout the West were helping to undermine the military forces of the United States in their war in Indo China. Recently also millions of French workers in May and June of 1968 had for a moment brought the social order into question. While the issues behind these events were not at the centre of what the UPW strikers thought about, they helped to make acceptable a norm of behaviour which would have been quite foreign to previous generations. The students and others in Britain were demonstrating against the expulsion of the wounded former activist Rudi Dutschke to Germany and against the arrest of another activist, Angela Davis, in the United States. However dimly aware of all this, the London Post Office workers marched every week to Hyde Park on the same 'Ho Chi Minh Trail' as many other demonstrations, and their struggle took on a style which belonged to its time, as perhaps to no other.

The first discussion of the claim submitted on 29 October 1970 took place on 10 November. The Post Office Director of Personnel, Dorothy Fothergill, did not present any offer but instead suggested reference of the claim to the Post Office arbitration machinery. This became a constant theme in arguments presented by the Post Office over the following weeks, and was often taken up by hostile Conservative politicians and press. However, it was a more peculiar idea than many people realised. The Union's faith in arbitration machinery had been dented by the actions of Conservative administrations in the early 1960s. Such suspicions were confirmed by the abuse heaped on Sir Jack Scamp for his judgement on the recent local authority dispute, as well as the dismissal of Professor Hugh Clegg from his position on the Civil Service Arbitration Board in the following March. Despite any reservations induced by these events, the Union together with others in the Post Office had submitted names for a Post Office Arbitration Board in October 1970. The Post Office itself had not submitted any names, and did not in fact do so until the third week of the strike. Nor was there even a discussion about a chairman. Thus despite the sudden enthusiasm shown by the Post Office in November, frequently reasserted in succeeding weeks, arbitration was not a serious possibility for settling the differences between the two sides.[148]

Before the negotiations got beyond these preliminary parryings, a remarkable and almost unique incident occurred which showed something of the attitudes on both sides. On Wednesday 25 November, the first Chairman of the Post Office Corporation and a nominee of the previous Labour Government, Lord Hall, was compelled to resign his position at the behest of Christopher Chataway, Minister of Posts and Telecommunications. The precise reasons for this unusual event are not absolutely clear to this day. Behind it evidently lay sharp disagreement about the priority to be given to Post Office expansion, perhaps both for investment and wages. The Minister's public statements were that there were no policy differences, but nobody believed this.

Reports of Lord Hall's dismissal began to appear in the press on 26 November. He was quoted as feeling in his home in Belgravia 'like a virgin raped by force'. He attacked the 'dictatorial action' of the Minister and spoke of going to the law to defend his good character.[149] This clear manifestation of the insecurity of tenure of the head of the whole Corporation, and the obvious implications for the likely expansion of Post Office activities in any direction, had a profound effect on Lord Hall's subordinates. If this was going to happen at the top, then what would be the effect lower down? Such feelings were no doubt behind the spontaneous walk-outs reported not only from such well known centres of militancy as the East Central and Western District offices in London, but also from Manchester, York, Aberdeen and Portadown in Northern Ireland. These walk-outs included the members of other

unions besides the UPW, and they were officially supported by the POEU. On 26
November UPW leaders met Chataway who asserted that there was no question of
the reinstatement of Lord Hall. Both Tom Jackson and Lord Hall himself issued
statements urging an end to the industrial action, which then ceased.

The Acting Chairman of the Post Office then came to be A. W. C. Ryland, who
had had a long career in Post Office management, one of the very few of its heads to
have come from such a background. His determination to make his mark as a leader
of the enterprise at a time when his tenure at the top was uncertain was clearly a
factor in subsequent developments. At first, however, there was some hesitation
about what to do about the UPW wage claim. On 9 December, a fortnight after the
dismissal of Lord Hall, Tom Jackson wrote again to ask for a reply. It was not until
a further fortnight had passed, on 23 December, that further discussion took place.
While UPW representatives urged a rapid and reasonable settlement, Miss
Fothergill now expressed the ominous view that 'there had recently been a tendency
for the size of settlements, certainly in the public sector, to be somewhat smaller
than those quoted by the Union when the claim was discussed at a previous
meeting'.

Another fortnight passed after this until Friday 8 January 1971, when Miss
Fothergill finally replied with an offer of a 7 per cent all-round increase. 'The Post
Office', said Tom Jackson, 'must be joking if they expect our members to accept
seven per cent'. Already on 1 January Union branches had been circulated with
details about forms and methods of industrial action. Within the Post Office,
regional authorities were now discussing what to do in such an event, in addition to
the details which had been discussed some months before.[150]

Both sides were now tooling up for a conflict without even having discussed the
management offer. Such a position was quite unprecedented in the Post Office.
When the UPW Executive met on 11 January it unanimously rejected the offer and
declared 7 per cent to be 'totally and absolutely unacceptable'. Tom Jackson pointed
out that this was almost certainly below the retail price index and said that 'the Post
Office would have to raise its offer quickly and substantially to meet the Union's
requirements'. There was a further meeting on Thursday 14 January, this time
between the Post Office Board and all the officers of the Union. Acting Chairman
Ryland emphasised his view that 'a most important and relevant factor was the
serious financial position of the postal service', as well as the low level of investment
in telecommunications. To this the UPW delegation replied that their members
could not be expected to pay for the past and even future deficiencies of the system.
Ryland declared that he was prepared to make a final offer of 8 per cent, but Jackson
replied that this left the two sides too far apart.

It was quite clear now to everybody that industrial action of some sort was
inevitable. There were some outside the Union who called for a ballot, but few
within the Union doubted what the outcome would be. Tom Jackson was reported
as saying that 'if we go on negotiating for a few weeks we might lose control of our
members'. He was later said to have argued for a 'short sharp shock', in which a
national strike of all the Union's members would cause a complete closure of the
postal system and a major disruption of telecommunications.[151] Perhaps the most
important argument for this approach was the extraordinary unpopularity which
had been induced a month before by the protracted work to rule of the power
workers. A combination of sudden action and careful publicity might, it was
thought, do something to produce a more sympathetic public attitude and a more

favourable outcome. Thus it was that when the UPW Executive met on Friday 15 January 1971, there were some among their number who favoured the gradual build up of action, but there was eventually a unanimous vote for a national strike from the following Wednesday 20 January. The Executive decided to suspend all the other activities of the Union and set its next meeting for more than a week later, Sunday 25 January.[152]

In the days before the strike actually started the temper of the members was made clear from the resounding 'Yes' they gave at a number of large meetings to the question 'Are you prepared to take strike action knowing you will not get strike pay?' Advertisements began to appear in the press portraying the conditions of the low paid members of the Union belonging to the grades of postmen, telephonist and P&TO. On Saturday 16th *The Times* reported the opinion of Professor Wedderburn of the London School of Economics that the strike might be illegal and the response of William Ryland that their preliminary view was that 'he is incorrect. But whether he is incorrect or not, the union is going on strike.' On Sunday, students marched in London against the deportation of Rudi Dutschke. On Monday the *Daily Mail* called for attacks against the postmen like those that had recently been against the power workers. On Tuesday, after days of waiting, Secretary of State for Employment Robert Carr finally summoned both sides to his Ministry for talks which offered nothing new and broke down after eight hours. Jackson said the Minister and his subordinates 'had worked to produce circumstances in which a settlement could be reached', but Ryland insisted that what had been made clear was 'that the differences between us were unbridgeable'.

Wednesday 20 January, day one of the strike, was a cold clear winter day. Every sorting office in the land, many post offices, and nearly every major telephone exchange was surrounded by pickets. There was very little for them to do, with a tiny number of non-members on counters and a few non-union telephonists in the exchanges. Some of these were pictured in the press entering the Faraday Exchange, which happened to be near Fleet Street. There was some trouble there and five arrests on the second day of the strike. Such incidents were rare, however. On that same day, 21 January, a crowd of strikers variously estimated at 15,000 and 20,000, marched from Lincoln's Inn Fields to Hyde Park via the Post Office Headquarters. Jack London, Chairman of London District Council, said this showed the greatest solidarity in the history of the Union, and Mary Spurr of Eastern District Telephonists said the blacklegs were only a tiny minority. Norman Stagg and Tom Jackson repudiated Post Office statements that they could not afford to pay, or that the matter could be settled by arbitration. Ryland's latest statement to this effect was relayed to the crowd from a portable radio. On Friday 22nd, members for the first time voluntarily worked at counters where they distributed pensions.

On the first Sunday of the strike, 22 January, the Executive met for four-and-a-half hours. 'The strike response', they were told, 'was better than could ever have been expected though there were some weaknesses.' The Executive agreed to continue the strike and also to accept any mediation or negotiation that was offered. It was agreed to set up a hardship fund with a preliminary donation of £100,000 from the Union's own 'Defence Fund'. The longest discussion was on emergency work at counters where there were also blacklegs, an issue which caused controversy throughout the strike.[153] That night, on television, Tom Jackson said they would accept arbitration only from some such figure as Frank Cousins, former General Secretary of the Transport and General Workers Union. This pleasantry was intended to illustrate both the self-confidence of the Union and the absurdity of the suggestion.

Nevertheless, this was taken seriously by the Post Office Board at its meeting on Monday morning 25 January. William Ryland wrote during the day to ask for discussion about possible arbitration. Tom Jackson placed this 'before those members of the Executive Council who were present at the Headquarters when it arrived'. Inevitably they were 'not satisfied that it would be possible to obtain a tribunal that would be impartial', and they simply called for more negotiations. There was some feeling that this showed a weakening resolve on the part of the Post Office. There was certainly no such weakening in the Union. Large rallies that day disrupted traffic in Liverpool and York, despite threats to local Union officials in anonymous telephone calls. On Tuesday 26th a meeting of representatives of other Post Office unions expressed full support for the UPW and a refusal to perform any of their work. Meetings were also held with transport unions and the first large donations to the Hardship Fund were announced – £1,000 each from ASTMS, the Scottish Miners and the Foundry Section of the Engineering Workers. Donations were coming in from many other sources, and a scale of payments for hardship could be announced. [154]

As the strike entered its second week on Wednesday 27 January, it was clear that all the initiative and self-confidence remained with the Union. Tom Jackson was quoted as saying that they could continue 'indefinitely'. Although a number of papers echoed the management call for arbitration, the level of public support for the strikers seemed high. On Tuesday 26th a reporter from the London *Evening News* saw seven blackleg counter clerks inside the Chief Office in St Martin's-le-Grand, with a hundred pickets outside and nobody entering the building. Money was now pouring into the Hardship Fund, and the *Strike Bulletin* on 28 January contained a message from the Executive: 'WE ARE PRIVILEGED TO BE YOUR ELECTED LEADERS – YOU ARE MAGNIFICENT – KEEP IT UP!' At the third weekly demonstration at Hyde Park on the same day Tom Jackson was kissed and hugged by women telephonists. One banner said: 'We Won't Kneel for Crumbs, we'll Stand up for Bread'. [155] On Friday 29th, workers came out on strike at Ford's and Posts Minister Chataway was jostled by Post Office strikers at Reading.

Over the following week-end there occurred a set of negotiations which remain confused and unsatisfactory even in retrospect. After talking to Tom Jackson on Friday, TUC General Secretary Victor Feather publicly offered to intervene, in advance of a special meeting of the Post Office Board on the Saturday. Immediately after this, the conciliation services of Robert Carr's Department of Employment – from whom nothing had been heard since before the strike – offered to meet both sides for discussion. This action was described in the *Sunday Telegraph* as 'one of the most remarkable examples of political manoeuvring over an industrial dispute since the war'. It was certainly seen at the time as the attempt by a Conservative Minister to 'upstage' the TUC and its General Secretary. At all events the discussion which followed did nothing to resolve the dispute. After various preliminary exchanges, a UPW negotiating team met the Post Office Board for half an hour. 'We were not', said William Ryland afterwards, 'on the same wavelength.' Feelings on the other side were stronger still, since absolutely nothing was offered. Tom Jackson was particularly incensed by the 'cold calculating' air of the Post Office representatives and 'said that he will refuse to get round the table with the Post Office again – unless it comes up with another offer'. Later on a great deal was made of a message from Ryland to local managers saying that 'despite the gap between us it was deemed expedient for political and public relations reasons to meet the UPW'. When the Executive met it was decided not to participate in the voluntary payment of pensions where blacklegs were working. Ship-to-shore radio operators were also to be brought out even though they were not directly involved. However, this was later found to be unnecessary.[156]

February began on the thirteenth day of the strike. Tom Jackson reflected the mood of strikers in Birmingham. 'This is not a strike about pay any longer. It is a strike about self-respect and dignity. They cannot starve us out, for we will win.' Warming to this theme at Glasgow two days later, he said the strike had become 'a revolution, an explosion of layer upon layer of discontent piling upon the Post Office year after year'. The fourth Hyde Park rally on Thursday 4th was presented with £7,500 from Jack Jones of the Transport and General Workers. 'Each time we come back' said Tom Jackson, 'we are stronger and there are more of us.' In that same week, he also took up a new theme in his public speeches. At Leeds on Tuesday 2nd he suggested that Posts Minister Chataway might dismiss Ryland and set up a new Post Office Board with people prepared to negotiate with the Union. He also gave vent to a feeling familiar in Union statements of the time about the number of administrators in the Post Office 'multiplying like sex-mad rabbits'.[157]

At this point it could perhaps be said that the entire contest had ground to a halt. 'Have you noticed how quiet it's gone?' asked the Union's *Strike Bulletin* on Friday 5 February. Both sides were now waiting for the report of the Wilberforce Enquiry into the pay of the electricity workers, which was to appear on Wednesday 10 February. The following Monday, 15th, was Decimalisation Day, when historic shillings and pence were due to disappear for ever. It was hoped that this change could make the Post Office keener to compromise. But during the days of anticipation of these events there was some indication of hardening attitudes in the Post Office. On Tuesday 2nd, notices were put up in post offices blaming the strikers for delays in the issue of benefits when they refused to work alongside blacklegs. The Post Office also began to publish statistics of the numbers of Crown Post Offices being kept open. The first figure given was 300 and this later rose gradually day by day to 533. It was rarely mentioned that this was out of a total of 1,660, and was only possible by the judicious spreading of very small numbers of people with the most limited impact on the strike as a whole. However, as well as publishing these figures, the management began to leak to the press their alleged proposals for closing down sections of the service, like parcels. If such statements were intended to demoralise the strikers there was little indication that they were successful, and they soon stopped.

Two other indications of increasing intensity of feeling were noted early in the second week of February. On Tuesday 9 February a delegation of wives of strikers from Norwich led by Mrs Sheila Ramsbottom and Mrs Doreen Mingay marched to the Post Office Headquarters. They managed to meet Sir Richard Hayward, Board member for industrial relations, and former UPW Deputy General Secretary. They asked him how they were expected to live when their husbands brought home £16 a week. Sir Richard, who had not had such a wage since his distant days as a P&TO, agreed that it would not be easy. Meanwhile at Totton in Hampshire Mrs Judy Walker collected £15. 40 for her local striking postman Jim Butt, only to find it confiscated by the police. Eventually the hamfisted guardians of the law decided that there was nothing else they could do but pass on the well-meaning contribution to Mr Butt who, it was said, much appreciated it.[158]

When the Wilberforce Report finally appeared on 10 February, it had a good deal less effect than anticipated. For one thing there was some disagreement about how much money it offered the electricians. Tom Jackson put it at 14–15 per cent, but Employment Secretary Carr tried to argue that it was as low as 10·9 per cent. At any rate, Ryland soon issued a statement that he saw no reason to change his 8 per cent offer. A rather sombre Hyde Park rally on 11 February – said to be only 4,000 strong by TV and press – was told by Tom Jackson that the only aim of the Post Office now seemed to be to break the Union. Privately the Union leadership had little doubt that the strike remained effective but thought there was some loss of morale in places and the possibility, which never in fact materialised, of a much more substantial return to work.[159]

The Union leaders continued, despite the rebuff following the Wilberforce Report, to try to get negotiations going.[160] During the week a delegation from the Council of Post Office Unions met Carr. Tom Jackson secretly met William Ryland on Thursday evening, the 11th. Finally on Saturday 13th, the Post Office again expressed its willingness to negotiate. The first meeting took place between teams from both sides that evening from 8 to 9.30 p.m. Ryland argued that they might be able to increase by 2 per cent the 8 per cent offer to telephonists and by ½ per cent the offer to postmen and PHGs, in return for productivity improvements. However, this was to add nothing to what had previously been negotiated, and the Post Office side firmly stated that 'any extra money' had to be 'found without imposing any net increase in our wage bill . . .' Various possibilities were suggested, like expansion in the use of part-timers and the delivery of unaddressed mail. Tom Jackson's preliminary response to this was that it was quite unacceptable, but that they would like to return for further discussions. 'Nothing I have heard so far', he was reported as saying, 'gives me cause to be hopeful.'[161]

The UPW Executive met on Monday morning 14 February. There was no disagreement that 'the future productivity aspects' of the Post Office proposals 'be rejected'. There was somewhat more argument about whether to push for a formula which had emerged from discussions with other Post Office unions for negotiations under an independent chairman, in the event of an increase of 1 per cent in the offer. This had not finally been resolved when the Union's negotiating team, now including officers covering the various grades, returned to Post Office Headquarters at Howland Street at 4.30 p.m. The Union negotiators began by making some very large concessions. Tom Jackson said that the Union was 'not sticking rigidly to its 19½ per cent claim', but was prepared to 'agree to something less'. He suggested that the Post Office should accept the old Priestley principle of 'fair comparisons', together with something along the lines of the going rate to retain labour. The response of Ryland to this was totally inflexible. They 'could not', he said, 'accept the civil service fair comparison principle' nor indeed any other arguments from Wilberforce. Any increase would have to have productivity strings attached.

The next negotiating meeting was held on the following afternoon, Monday 15th. The Union representatives now said that they were prepared to go down to 13 per cent, though improvements in incremental scales would have to go beyond this. In response to this, the Post Office at last showed some movement. They were prepared to go up to 8 per cent, though only if the Union agreed to a programme of improvements in productivity, including 'a wide range of work study and measurement techniques such as activity sampling and traffic measurement forecasting'. In other words, postmen for an extra 18 pence a week were to help prepare major changes in their work patterns. Tom Jackson said that while they might be prepared to consider this, if the wage increase was 13 per cent, it would only be possible to get the members to accept it 'as a result of discussion and explanation'. He clarified this in a letter published in *The Times* on 17 February. 'It is of no value that full-time trade union officials should presume to deliver the cooperation of 200,000 men and women. We who negotiate must have the consent of our members.' The UPW Executive considered the Post Office offer at a meeting on Monday evening the 15th. It was agreed now to put forward its own proposals for an independent mediator together with a claim for 'at least 15 per cent'. At the same time further loans were sought.[162]

On the basis of a letter from the Union suggesting mediation, the Post Office approached the Department of Employment. Representatives of both sides spent the whole of the following day, Tuesday 16th, at the Department. The Union made it clear that they did not intend possible arbitration to have any binding power. At five minutes to midnight Tom Jackson reported to his Executive that he had just received a letter, dictated like so many others in those days, over the telephone. In this the Post Office rejected any mediation and once again argued for arbitration. After five hours of discussion on the following morning, the Union Executive voted to continue to strike.

The struggle was now beginning to reach epic proportions, both in terms of its size and scope and the intensity of feeling that was being displayed. A number of things had now become clear as the days passed. The Wilberforce Enquiry, from which something had been expected, was being ignored. Decimalisation Day had come and gone without any appreciable effect. The employers and those who stood behind them were growing more and more determined. 'Having held out for so long', advised the *Financial Times* on 17 February, 'the Post Office would be foolish to make large last-minute concessions.' 'It is more important to the Government', asserted *The Times* on the following day, 'not to "lose" this strike than to preserve the postal service from contraction.'

If determination was increasing on the one side it was by no means lacking on the other. Keith Harper wrote in the *Guardian* on 17 February that the Post Office had 'completely failed to break the backbone of the strike'. Strikers, it was reported from Northern Ireland and the West Country, were marching in the snow. The largest of the London rallies yet on the 18th was attended by strikers from many parts of the country. 'This is like the Blitz for our members', said Tom Jackson. 'They are reacting like the Londoners did during the war – getting closer together and more determined.' The *Evening Standard* perceived 'a new note of defiance' and the *Guardian* the next day said that despite 'no apparent hope of winning concessions from their employers, the postal workers were obviously determined to stick out'. A large delegation of Union members was cheered to the echo by the enormous demonstration of trade unionists held in Trafalgar Square on the following Sunday, 21st, against the Conservative Industrial Relations Bill.

Behind all these public events there was a great deal of effort to get some sort of meaningful negotiations, largely initiated by UPW leaders. On Wednesday 17th, following the Executive vote to continue the strike, there were talks with TUC General Secretary Victor Feather followed by a meeting with Robert Carr, at which he refused to take up the issue. Union leaders now looked to Labour MPs in Parliament, who on Thursday the 18th again urged Carr to intervene and called for an emergency debate. Over the week-end Shadow Employment Secretary Barbara

Castle and Opposition leader Harold Wilson issued calls for a committee of inquiry. It is interesting to notice the way press comment was now turning. In the popular tabloid the *Sun* on the 19th there appeared a piece on 'The Man Behind the Man Behind the Post Strike' centring on the fact that Union Chairman Maurice Styles was a member of the Communist Party. Norman Stagg had little difficulty replying to this the next day by talking of the '200,000-strong Army behind Tom Jackson'. More seriously, the quality papers were taking up a theme about the UPW becoming what the *Sunday Times* described on the 21st as the 'stalking horse and pace maker' for other big unions. It was even implied that the intervention of Labour politicians had delayed further intervention by Carr.[163] This theme was taken up by Carr himself on Monday 2nd when he said in the emergency debate that the big unions were 'using the Post Office dispute for political ends'. He also attacked the TUC and Labour opposition for good measure. However, he did agree to keep his conciliation efforts open, and soon further talks began.

These talks took place in a series of meetings held between the 22nd and 24th, as the strike entered its fifth week. Carr discussed with both sides. Various possible conciliators were suggested. Possible further productivity strings within a 10 per cent increase were mentioned. Tom Jackson was quoted in *The Times* on the 24th, in the quaint language of the day. 'I am not sure', he is alleged to have said, 'if we are in a breakthrough or a breakdown situation.' This soon became clear in further discussion lasting seven hours that day. During talks when Carr left UPW negotiators cooling their heels while he went off to vote for his infamous Industrial Relations Bill, he said that any increase above 8 per cent could only be 'on a basis which obviates any further net increase on their wages bill and any further financial burden to the customer'. After this there was little to discuss. The press picture of Norman Stagg walking out giving the thumbs down sign said it all. The proceedings were described as a 'charade' by the Union's *Strike Bulletin*. Tom Jackson was quoted in the *Guardian*: 'We are in exactly the same situation we were at the beginning, and that's a bloody shame. There has been no indication either formally or informally that any more money will be offered to us.'

As these discussions continued, the greatest worry for Union leaders was their growing debts. After Decimalisation Day on 15 February there was thought to be only enough left for two weeks of hardship money. Expenditure was now rapidly outpacing income. Most of the large amounts from other unions came as loans rather than outright grants, in the case of the NUR for example accompanied by fairly stringent repayment terms. After Tom Jackson met the TUC Finance and General Purposes Committee on 18 February, further money began to flow in, but the hardship claims also increased. Besides the £100,000 loan from the NUR, there were loans of half of that from the Transport and General Workers, the Engineers and the Furniture Trade Operatives, as well as £10,000 from the shop workers. There was soon talk of the Co-operative Bank demanding the deeds of the UPW's own Headquarters as security against any further loans. It was clearly pressure of this kind that lay behind Tom Jackson's distinctly sober speech to the enormous TUC demonstration in Trafalgar Square on Sunday 21st against the Industrial Relations Bill:

If we are defeated it will not be for lack of resolve. It will not be for lack of guts and determination. It will be for lack of funds. Sympathy we can get by the bucketful. We have the generous and wholehearted support of the public. What we want now is money – and fast.

Dickie Lawlor – now in the unaccustomed role of spokesman for the Union leadership – told strikers in Glasgow on the 23rd that they 'would rather sell the Union headquarters brick by brick than go crawling back'. On the next day, Wednesday 24 February, as the strike was entering its sixth week, Tom Jackson attended a meeting of the General Council of the TUC. It was this meeting which, according to one account, indicated once and for all that the scale of financial support from other sections of the trade union movement was simply not going to be such as to meet the requirements of the Union's Hardship Fund.[164]

It was not that general support from the trade union movement was by any means exhausted at this point. The General Council sent out an unprecedented general appeal for 'shop floor collections'. However, little ever came back from these. Other unions in the Post Office began to show more concrete support. There were perhaps 10,000 POEU members in the Hyde Park demonstration on 25 February on a limited strike. There was also support from POMSA, whose members walked out for the demonstration. Other walk-outs of POEU and POMSA members were reported from Birmingham and Glasgow in the next few days. Money continued to flow in from elsewhere.

All of this however was felt to be too little too late. Already on the 24th the Executive had surveyed the financial position with some disquiet. £746,000 had been paid out, including all but £50,000 of the Hardship Fund. Donations now amounted to £168,300, loans to £195,000 and £364,000 in hand – a total of £727,700. The expenses of local branches were also rising rapidly. Tom Jackson told the Executive that they could not go into debt above £600,000. After considering this melancholy prospect and attending the Hyde Park demonstration the Executive agreed to let the General Secretary consider 'a project that would have the objective of ensuring that the entire case is heard'. On 1 March Tom Jackson outlined the position. He said that although a few branches wanted to return, an increasing number were now calling for wider action from other Post Office unions. They could not continue hardship payments, however, and in his opinion the only course of action which did not entail enormous risk was to support the setting up of a court of inquiry whose outcome would be binding on both sides.[165]

This plan was presented to a meeting of the UPW Executive on Tuesday 2 March, together with a further statement of the Union's severe financial problems. The bank overdraft was now £340,000. The Executive agreed with only two dissentients to present the committee of inquiry proposal to Robert Carr, and they went in a body to the Department of Employment to do so. A great deal of discussion followed the next day, Wednesday 3 March, at the Department of Employment. The inquiry would be 'broadly based', and there would be separate discussion on the general matter of pay determination. The terms were finally accepted by the UPW Executive at 1.45 a.m. on Thursday 4 March. When the Executive met later in the morning, the main item to be settled was the arrangements for a ballot of members on this. It was also agreed to suspend payments of all hardship claims after 1 March. The Union was now £690,000 'in the red'.

That morning some papers spoke of 'a complete climb-down' by the Union. 'If we had more money', Tom Jackson was quoted as saying, 'the strike could have gone on. Facing the realities, this was the best way out of a bad situation.' The mood of the last of the Hyde Park demonstrations later that morning was different from its predecessors. It was held on a frosty, raw early spring day. Grey banks of snow clouds could be seen beyond the Serpentine over the City of London. One home-made banner dominated the rows of bewildered and angry strikers. It read 'My Vote Is No!' Tom Jackson was greeted by a vociferous group with a sardonic echo of recent anti-war demonstrations on the same spot. 'Eh, eh Tommy J, what about our £3 pay?' 'I am not claiming that this is the happiest day of my life', he responded, but 'I am convinced that our decision is absolutely right.' It was 'not the end of the road', but the only possible decision had been taken unanimously by the Executive. 'If you vote to stay out, I will lead you in that struggle but I think you would be totally wrong . . .' Tony Clarke, at the time the Secretary of the LDC, was the only other speaker. 'Whatever the sacrifice we shall continue', he said. Tom Jackson told journalists afterwards that he could understand the feelings of those who heckled him. 'They were naturally angry. If I had been there to-day I would have felt exactly as they did.'[166]

However, there was no rearguard action against the Executive's proposals because no alternatives were seriously offered. It was possible to say that even if there was no more money on the table, the argument would be carried forward to a forum that could not have been secured at the beginning of the strike. The South East London Office voted against the return, as also did the Edinburgh Outdoor Branch and the Liverpool Amalgamated. However, when the votes came to be counted there were only 1,427 to stay out against 19,614 to return. There were a few local disputes on the return, where efforts were made to enforce slightly different conditions from what had existed before the strike. There was a particularly sharp alteration at West Bromwich. There was also a rather bizarre proposal from the Post Office that the Union should not under its own rules 'victimise' its own members who had been blacklegs. Generally speaking, there were few serious problems, and the entire postal and telecommunications system was working smoothly and normally a mere matter of hours after the return to work on Monday 8 March.

AFTER THE BATTLE

The Committee of Enquiry which followed was under the chairmanship of Sir Henry Hardman, retired Permanent Secretary of the Ministry of Defence. The employers' representative was Thomas Carlile, Managing Director of Babcock and Willcox, and the Union nominated John Hughes, Vice-Principal of Ruskin College. The Enquiry was held a month after the end of the strike on 6–8 April at Church House, Westminster. The proceedings had something of the form of the old Arbitration Court, and indeed were not dissimilar to the discussions of the Tweedmouth Enquiry held a few hundred yards away three quarters of a century earlier. The case was well presented from the Union side, and with somewhat less success by the Post Office.[167]

The Union placed its claim firmly in the context of recent claims and increases, including 16 per cent for agricultural workers, 15 per cent for local authority manual workers and 12 per cent for miners. It described the very slow progress on the incremental scales and declared that the Post Office had 'unilaterally abandoned the "fair comparison" principle', which was 'a solemn promise made by the Government to all Post Office workers' at the time of incorporation. Details were given to show that the claim did 'no more than seek to restore the relative position of the Union's membership since the last claim was settled'. The Union also argued with some justice that 'never before had the "financial situation of the business" been the criterion on which a pay claim was to be judged'. If all decisions in the Post Office were to be on a commercial basis then the entire rural postal system would be abandoned. The Union had always agreed to participate in efforts to improve productivity, despite all assertions to the contrary. The Union's evidence pointed to increased discontent within the Post Office shown for example by unofficial strikes. It also repeated the usual points about increases in the numbers of managers and claimed there was a lack of real concern with industrial relations matters. There was a bleak summary of the changes with incorporation. 'Management has become more inflexible and stubborn in its purpose, and does not seem to have the same concern for people it once had.'

The Union's arguments were presented to the Committee with much skill and with some little concern for theatrical effect. Ordinary members made a number of good points. Thus PHG Eric Berry had to work fifty-nine hours to get the £33 claimed to be average for his grade. Young telephonists like 21-year-old Sue Metcalfe from Birmingham with two years' experience earned a great deal less than older colleagues with none at all. The 'star witness' for the Union was former Labour Postmaster General Edward Short who asserted that civil service conditions including 'fair comparisons' were promised to the unions when corporate status was being discussed. He even said that William Ryland had been present at meetings where explicit promises were made. Ryland said that he took this as 'a personal affront'. Tom Jackson, whose performance was compared both with Perry Mason and Clarence Darrow, centred on the contradiction between the alleged commercial yardstick being applied to Post Office employees but not to its operations. This was a 'dichotomy' which Jackson said William Ryland found it difficult to see because he was not earning £18 a week. John Buckley, postmaster of London's South Western District Office, was supposed to show that the Union was not co-operating with productivity improvements. In fact under Tom Jackson's cross-questioning he agreed that the former women's prison in which he was operating was unpleasant, with bays far too small for loading mail, and altogether in need of rapid replacement.

On the level of presentation, there was no doubt that the Post Office's case was less well produced than that of the Union. Their printed evidence argued their case almost solely in terms of their financial position. On this basis an 8 per cent increase would produce a 'fair wage' without comparability or any other such criterion. Far more briefly they argued that this would keep actual earnings up to the cost of living, and the more recent trend of settlements. They quoted Tom Jackson on how good the 1970 settlement had been, one of their few telling arguments. The case was led by William Ryland at very short notice because of the indisposition of Board member Richard Hayward. His most publicised point was the statement that prices would have to rise now in any case, and his most interesting assertion was that he had been under no direct pressure from the Government to stick rigidly to 8 per cent. It was generally agreed that the best part of the Post Office case was presented by Dorothy Fothergill, Director of Postal Personnel, who argued for the general inflationary character of the claim. Overall, however, one observer writing in the *Guardian* thought 'the employer's case for sticking to an 8 percent basic offer emerged muffled with overpowering detail, unsupported assertions and solid witnesses'.[168]

The same journalist thought that perhaps 'the public airing of grievances' had had a 'cathartic effect'. Certainly those Post Office workers in the gallery who applauded at the end were happy with the proceedings, and one Executive member thought there had been 'a marvellous three days'.[169] Such had often been the reaction to the presentation of the Post Office workers' case in the past. Experience should have shown however that higher wages are not necessarily secured by superior arguments or more skilful pleading. When the Hardman Report was published on 5 May it proved as bitterly disappointing to Post Office workers as had been the reports of Tweedmouth, Hobhouse and Holt before the First World War. The three members of the Committee asserted that neither Union nor Post Office had done enough to improve the productivity of the service. They thought that 'until recently, the two parties have opted for a cosy life and have been anxious to avoid pursuing measures which would disturb traditional work patterns and relationships'. After amongst other things defending the increase in the numbers of managers, all three committee members said that there was no basis for using fair comparison criteria, recommending instead 'a performance linked pay system'. It was at this point that Hardman and Carlile put forward their case for a mere 9 per cent wage increase. Although they thought it necessary to take into account such factors as the cost of living, the financial position of the Post Office and other conditions in service such as recent improvements in superannuation arrangements, there was one argument which they considered of over-riding importance and this was the 'national interest'. It is interesting to notice that the recent Wilberforce Enquiry had arrived at different conclusions when asked to take account of the same 'national interest'. Messrs Hardman and Carlile who had not been asked to take account of it, decided that 'the requirements of the general economic situation' necessitated 'realism' in wage settlements, by which they meant much lower increases. They threw in for good measure a proposal for higher wages in areas of labour shortage, an idea which afterwards sank without trace. The 'minority report' of the Union's nominee J. D. Hughes attacked these conclusions with some passion as 'inequitable' and 'unjustified'. Hughes did not accept the unprecedented use of the concept of 'national interest' in wage settlements, since it negated any serious basis for arbitration. The 'national interest' argument was damaging because it was based 'on an inadequate understanding of the causes and real nature of cost inflation and demand management problems in the national economy', it 'distracted the Committee from close concern with the merits of the pay claim' and 'introduced a new degree of inequitable distribution into British pay settlements'. Nine per cent was not only unjust, it was unlikely to recruit new staff and was alien to any rational planning of wages.

These views, to which the Union naturally gave a good deal of publicity, were nevertheless to no avail. The award of the Committee majority was final. All that the Union could do was accept this and then to present a new claim for 5 per cent, while re-establishing its own finances and its equilibrium.

The great strike had thus achieved very little, at least in the short term. There were some who argued that the very form of the Hardman Enquiry had been a step forward. It was also maintained that the improvements in incremental scales and superannuation arrangements as well as the 1972 settlement later made the theory of defeat a 'great myth'. However, as one District Organiser put it, 'we were beaten and we might as well admit it'.[170] There can be no doubt that this perception coloured the attitude of the UPW and its members after 1971. It made many members of the Union revert to earlier and more hesitant attitudes on industrial action, and also on general political matters. The Union has not called a national strike since then, nor is it likely that the generation that remembers 1971 will do so easily. Yet there was no mood of demoralisation and despair at the end of the strike. Many members insisted on marching back to the telephone exchanges and sorting offices behind bands and banners. A not untypical sentiment was expressed to an Executive member by one ordinary, inactive union member. 'We didn't half give them a run for their money . . . We'll beat the bastards next time.'[171]

Although many such individual reactions could be quoted it is not easy even a decade later to assess the significance of an event with tens of thousands of passionate participants and millions of interested onlookers. Some discussion however is possible on the central paradox expressed by one perceptive commentator on the last weekend of the strike when he said that 'Tom Jackson was successful in everything except actually winning'.[172] The fact was that the propaganda of the Union was effective, its solidarity second to none, public support was enormous and the leadership was generally clear and decisive. And yet the battle was seen as having been lost. This merits some discussion.

This was an industrial dispute conducted, as perhaps no other had been before, under the harsh glare of TV lights and the continual coverage of the other media. It followed the power workers' action which had produced a remarkably vitriolic reaction 'from 10,000 darkened drawing-rooms in Chelsea and the Surrey hills' with violence of language almost spilling over into deeds. There had been 'a notable state of national humbug' when TV 'personality' David Frost was seen 'bullying a few power workers, with a studio audience, hand-picked for their utter insensitive self-righteousness, baying at his back'.[173] When the Post Office dispute was about to begin it was this image perhaps more than any other which dominated the calculations of the Union leadership. The issues for them were perhaps more simple, but the effects of a strike in the Post Office were likely to be even more direct and universal. In the face of this a carefully thought out public relations effort was organised by the UPW. Advertisements were published in the press on the opening days portraying Union members and their conditions. There was a young telephonist called Jenny Meritt who got 'more rings than most' and only took home £10. 75 a week. There was Ian Moyes, a fully trained P&TO, who needed overtime for what was still a low wage. Postman Albert Edmondson with a lively 'sense of duty', but perhaps needing people to 'take a collection' in order to earn enough to maintain his family. The Union also placed a good deal of emphasis on its volunteers opening offices for pensions, and going out to deliver blood donor cards and urgent medical supplies, despite occasional brushes with blacklegs and resentful managers. Details of how the Plymouth Amalgamated Branch had done this and the thanks it received were presented in evidence to the Hardman Enquiry. 'Rarely', said one newspaper, 'can a strike have been so carefully planned, or shown such consideration to the public.'[174]

This is part of the reason at least why the efforts of some sections of the press to stimulate anti-Communism and general hysteria against the Post Office workers did not succeed. One popular newspaper reproduced precisely the sort of message the Union wished to convey when it looked at the conditions of a young postman called Don Failes and concluded that 'even under a system of rigid wage restraint, there are principles of equity . . . that should be upheld'. The Union had not been 'particularly militant or extreme' and the pay offer to those who were 'amongst the lowest paid in the country' was 'manifestly lower than that gained by other groups of workers'. Even at the end of the dispute the Catholic *Universe* had been convinced that 'real public interest should dictate that no public servant should be recompensed so poorly that his main problem in life is just making ends meet'. One public opinion poll published during the strike found that 47 per cent of those questioned thought the Post Office workers were justified in going on strike, even apart from their claim itself, though 45 per cent thought they should not have done so. This is a high level of support for an industrial dispute, and is confirmed by the virtual absence of hostility to the numerous demonstrations and the collections for the Hardship Fund that were going on in every corner of the land. Seven-year-old Kevin Butler was from a Post Office family, but he reflected the attitude of many others when he brought his collection of 1,782 old pennies (£7. 47) to present to 'Uncle Tom Jackson' in the sixth week of the strike. 'It is not much', said Kevin, 'but it is from a young heart.'[175]

Another perhaps unique aspect of this strike which must be mentioned is the extent to which its leader Tom Jackson succeeded in conveying the bluff friendly image of the local postman. He stamped a picture of himself in the media which made him for years afterwards perhaps the most readily recognised of all British trade union leaders. The press every day carried not only his picture but articles about his moustache, his diet, his weight, his hours of rising, and his family. It must be said that beyond the trivia, there was some basis for concentrating on the personality of the UPW General Secretary. It was certainly Tom Jackson who argued for the decision to call the strike, and in particular for the crucial point that it needed to be instantaneous and complete. It was he who proposed all the main tactical decisions during the strike itself, and it was he who initiated the discussion on the form of its ending. There can be little serious doubt that well beyond the hugs and kisses in Hyde Park, he was popular amongst UPW members, perhaps universally so until the end of the strike. 'Every union leader', said one newspaper before that, 'would be in church if he thought that he could pray for the loyalty Uncle Tom gets.'[176]

In the face of this presentation of the postmen's case, there was the extraordinary phenomenon of the media presenting the development of the struggle at times in terms more favourable to the Union than to management. It must have been particularly galling for the Post Office Board to see the negotiations over the week-end of 13–14 February presented on the BBC and ITV as their rejection of mediation rather than as Union rejection of 9 per cent. On top of this the Union made great play of the message from William Ryland to local officials about the discussions being necessary for public relations reasons. Whatever his private charm, Ryland never managed to project an image that was anything other than unfeeling and unbending. This to some extent arose from the difficulties Ryland had in trying to establish himself before his position was confirmed. He may well as a result have shown a determination that went beyond even that desired or required at the time by the Government. One newspaper saw Ryland's style in this way: 'His rock-like resistance and unflappability made less impact on the public than Mr. Jackson's astute publicity, but there were moments when even Mr. Carr quailed before his determination not to give an inch'.[177]

Yet whatever the public relations, whatever the uncertainties on the employers' side and their lack of popularity at the time, the management was seen, generally speaking, as having triumphed. The fact was that the propaganda successes of the Union were not enough. The tactic of calling a complete walk-out on 20 January may have avoided the unfortunate experiences of the electricity workers a month before, but it did not win the strike. One other thing which it is only possible to see in retrospect was the fundamental problem which faced the strikers after the first day, and this was that the effects of their action were not as they anticipated. They were defeated most of all by a force which had crept up unawares on the strikers and on almost everyone else, and this was the changes that had already taken place in communication technology. Perhaps it needed the strike to confirm this in a way no other event could have done.

There can be no doubt, despite the unconvincing claims of the Post Office, that the national postal system ceased to function for all significant purposes. The private operators who tried their hand when the monopoly was suspended simply served to underline the incapacity of such people to run the system. Their efforts varied from the pathetic to the farcical. A certain Colin Ward of Norwich found that virtually the only people to take an interest in his operation were philatelists. The Dowager Lady Birdwood, better known for her adherence to such distasteful causes as the Racial Preservation Society, attempted before the end of January to set up an Association of Private Postal Services. This seems to have been the last that was heard of these operations, until they handed back to the Post Office the mail they had accumulated at the end of the strike.[178] Those very few blacklegs who ran local services were of little significance either, and the claims of the Post Office to have increasing numbers of crown offices open as the days went by did not reflect itself in any significant amount of postal business.

There can be little doubt that many sections of business and industry were affected by the strike. Thus Littlewood's mail order company laid off 6,000 workers before the first week-end, and within a fortnight mail order companies generally were said to have lost 70 per cent of their business. Football pools were also affected and the manufacturers of greeting cards had to miss St Valentine's Day sales almost completely. All large enterprises faced problems. Thus in the third week it was reported that 30 per cent fewer cheques were being presented. However, soon Thorn Electric and other businesses began to advertise alternative arrangements in the press. Imperial Chemicals found a special courier service was adequate, at least for the short term. Banks and financial institutions were able to organise this also. Mail for abroad was sent through the Irish Republic. Chambers of Commerce arranged for messages to be carried. 'Although the postal strike' was certainly by 12 February 'hitting the pockets of industry, the majority of big companies regard it as a nuisance rather than a cause of serious disruption.' There may well have been, as the Union claimed, a conspiracy of silence about the real effects of the strike by companies who wanted to drive down wages, but one exporter was astonished to find, when he complained to the Ministry of Posts in the closing days about the effects on his business, that he was one of the first to do so.[179]

The plain fact was that although the closing of the postal system was not without effect, very few people, not just in the Union, had perceived the extent to which the sending of letters was already being superseded by new technology. New social habits and attitudes were being formed. The change even since the system had been closed down by the 1964 strike had perhaps been imperceptible, but it was crucial. It went well beyond the facetious comments heard in many conversations as the weeks went by. The strike, said one wit, was 'a merciful respite from creditors and a cast iron alibi for unwanted acquaintances'. 'How blissful', said a correspondent to *The Times* in the first days, 'is the postman's strike. Business back to simple principles again. No writing, acknowledging or confirming of orders. No filing, planning or indexing.' 'No service', concluded one newspaper four weeks later, 'is quite so essential as it looks.' At the end it was noted with some surprise that 'the nation's life has been upset far less than anyone – especially the union – expected'. The significance was perhaps more profound than had been realised:[180]

> We have now tasted the total absence of postal services without finding it half so unpalatable as we had expected. Letter writing is no longer our only or even principal means of shouting beyond shouting-distance. We have already outgrown the Railway Age: are we now outgrowing the Postal Age too? If we want to keep our friendly village postman we must pay him properly – or else do without him.

In 1971 the system of Subscriber Trunk Dialling was little more than a decade old. Although the number of letters being sent was not diminishing and there was still a future for posts, nevertheless, few people had yet quite realised the extent to which electronic communication was now replacing written messages, even before the days of the microchip. For most purposes the telephone system was now able, albeit for a higher price, to do more or less automatically what had until very recent times been done by letters and telegrams. Not only had the constant collections and deliveries of post in the Victorian cities long since gone for good. The need for and even the possibility of a continually functioning system had gone also. Sometimes human consciousness lags behind the reality of such change, especially when, as in the case of the Post Office workers, it is seen every day. Thus the new and unexpected reality of a postal system which had become more dispensable than at any time for 130 years was more than anything else what defeated the Post Office workers in 1971.

What then of the telephone system itself? The spread of automatic arrangements meant of course that there could never be the same immediate impact of the withdrawal of labour as with the posts. There were in any case more telephonists not in the Union in the first place, and some members who were even prepared to defy the decisions of their sisters and brothers. There was also the Telecommunications Staff Association, the transmogrified National Guild of Telephonists, now without its former officials and almost lost to public view. However it was now hoping to get some kind of recognition under the Industrial Relations Act, and as well as visiting Conservative Central Office to this end, it also advised 'all members not to join the strike action'. Some from the TSA are nevertheless said to have walked out, as also probably did the members of an even more shadowy body known as the Telecommunication Workers Union.[181]

There were operators therefore to keep the system going, though even on the figures published by the Post Office there were more on strike. However, it needed others to keep the telephones running also. There were stories of senior Post Office officials going round to empty coin boxes in public telephones, a task usually performed by postmen. It was also said that the telephones kept working because members of other unions maintained the exchanges and the lines. Be that as it may, members of other unions were instructed not to go beyond their normal tasks, and on the assumptions made at the beginning of the UPW's action, this was thought likely to be enough. As the days turned into weeks, telecommunications continued after a fashion, and the general significance of the struggle became clear. It was only towards the end that the militants and activists began to think in terms of the extension of action by other unions, and it was by then beginning to take place.

However, this was essentially after the issue had been decided. 'If the sister organisations had been consulted from the start', as may well be the case on some subsequent occasion, 'the necessary preparation will already have been made to get the willing cooperation of members.'[182]

There is of course much else that can be decided with the advantage of hindsight and perhaps in no other way. No doubt the biggest brickbats of all could have been directed at the members who in 1921 abandoned the strike fund. However, efforts had been made in more recent years to reverse the effects of this decision. It might also have been said that the Hardship Fund could have been set up earlier, but it is difficult to argue this except in retrospect. However there is another problem which is perhaps more subject to debate. 'We were beaten', said Tom Jackson at the May Conference, 'by lack of money.' Now it is certainly true that by the final week of the strike the Union was in a difficult financial position. However, an increase in subscriptions later in the year and steps to retrenchment dealt with this problem by 1972. Certainly, as a number of later studies were to show, members were able to survive. Despite many difficulties, and the small amounts obtained from the social security system, they showed few signs of flagging at the end.[183] However, it must remain a subjective judgement not susceptible to any form of easy proof either at the time or since to what extent this factor might have increased the drift back to work or diminishing enthusiasm for the strike. It certainly can be argued either way. It might be possible to go even further into the field of subjective judgement and passionate argument to decide whether the other unions could have given more. Certainly at least one newspaper thought this was the case at the time. 'The strike collapsed', it said, because other unions 'would not put their money where their fraternity is.' Tom Jackson thought it 'a shame how the trade union movement, in general, could not have rendered, as at that time, greater financial assistance than it did. But there were reasons.' Since then many have argued from varying viewpoints that it was lack of support from other TUC unions that lost the strike.[184]

Could things, in the end, have been different? It is possible to see a great deal only in retrospect. However, no analysis is valid either that goes to the opposite extreme and justifies everything that happened simply because it did happen. The fact remains that nearly everyone went into the 1971 struggle moulded by the experience of a peaceful union whose growing discontent had been expressed in a few brief but successful skirmishes in 1962, 1964, 1968 and 1969. The 1971 struggle was at a time when few had yet become quite aware of the change that had taken place in the balance of technology of the communications system. The tactical discussions on the timing and scope of the strike owed much to the particular circumstances of the wage rounds of that winter and to the recent experiences of the Union. The UPW had to be the first to face an intransigent employer backed by a hard-hearted Government. Against this, the successful propaganda of the Union and the public sympathy secured for its members were not enough. If new weapons could have been used, there were none to find and forge them.

The experience of 1971 dominated much of what the Union did and became during the following decade. At a national level the UPW took on some of the staid and conservative image it had once assumed, and this was reflected in the more cautious spirit in which it approached almost every issue. In Chapter 14 there are details of how the Union confronted the falling levels of wages and labour force in 1973–4, the threat to its right to strike since 1977, and the changes in form and constitution in the 1980s. Between 1974 and 1979 UPW leaders supported incomes policies, in the same way that their predecessors also sought for orderly and automatic forms of bargaining. Personalities at the top seemed to change also, even when they were embodied in the same individuals. No doubt in the longer term 1971 will be seen as an unusual event in the history of Post Office workers, succeeded by a return to the values and attitudes of Geddes and Bowen, or even of Stuart-Bunning and before. However, things changed in important ways after 1971. The carefully constructed system of collective bargaining in which the UPW participated from the days of Whitley and Tomlin and Priestley, with all the checks and balances, with national councils and arbitration boards, had gone never to return. It had been ended not just by institutional changes involved in moving out of the civil service, but even more by the decade of confrontation over wages and conditions between 1961 and 1971. The UPW had now matured as part of a trade union movement from which it had once been remote. The Union after 1971 dealt directly with those responsible for the welfare of its members in ways that had not existed before that time. For this reason, as for many others, the memory and effect of the 1971 struggle will mould the attitudes and actions of future generations just as surely as did the amalgamation of 1919, the strike of 1890, and the tender stifled buds of trade unionism in the 1870s and before.

NOTES

1 An account of the early history of these matters is to be found in the report of the (Norton) Committee appointed to consider the allocation of sorting duties at provincial offices, which came out in 1912, was reprinted at the time in association journals and on many subsequent occasions (eg. in *Post*, 3 September 1921, pp. 205ff.). There are also copies at F 223.

2 Report of the Joint Committee on the Allocation of Sorting Office Duties, 1928 (at F 223) and *Post*, 26 May 1928, pp. 463–9. See also ECM 13–15/7/26, 24–7, 20–23/4/27, 85–6.

3 ECM 16–17/4/29, 118–21; *Post*, 10 December 1932, p. 464.

4 ECM 2/4/37, 174–9, 12/11/37, 140–1; *Post*, 15 May 1937, p. 444, 30 October 1937, p. 348; *Postal Telegraph*, 1 June 1937, p. 264.

5 *Post* (7 April 1945); ECM 22–23/3/45, 293–324.

6 The first form is given in *Post*, 17 February 1945, and its final one in 27 April 1946.

7 *Post*, 25 June 1945, pp. 10–13, 8 December 1945, p. 407, 22 June 1946, p. 32.

8 ECM 18–24/10/45, 127.

9 ECM 18–24/10/45, 103–40, 22–24/11/45, 218–24; POC, 4038, 26 May 1948; *Post*, 5 June 1948, pp. 241–2.

10 ECM 22–24/11/45 and 9–11/5/46, 484–5.

11 *Post* (1 February 1947).

12 ECM 29/8/46, 641–2, 29–31/10–1/11/46, 709–15, 7–9/3/47, 930, 27–29/7/48, 466–71, 16–17/1/51, 217, 17–19/4/51, 222.

13 *Post*, 29 March, 26 April, 1947.

14 *Post*, 21 June 1947, pp. 8–14; ECM 4, 20/6/47, 19–26. Details of this and succeeding negotiations are at F 370. This includes the very comprehensive claim printed in a special issue of *The Post* which did not get into the bound volumes.

15 *Hansard* V, 441, 1486 (6 August 1947).

16 These discussions are at F 509.5.

17 All this and most of the subsequent details are at ECM 28–31/10–3–5/11/47, 115ff.

18 For this aspect see ECM 21–23/4/48, 406ff.

19 Reports in *Post*, 6 December 1947 and 3 January 1948.

20 White (1947).

21 Statement on Incomes, PP 1947–8 XXII reproduced in full in *Post*, 14 February 1948, pp. 63–4.

22 *Post*, 27 March 1948, p. 134, 19 June 1948, pp. 18, 35, 45; ECM 22/3/48, 319ff.

23 ECM 1/6/48, 444.

24 There is a full file covering all the negotiations including the Arbitration Court appearance at F 370 and all quotations are derived from this unless otherwise stated.

25 The main documents and discussions are given in *The Post* (including a good summary in the issue of 7 May) mostly after the settlement. There is more detail at F 370, including copies of the award, dated 31 May 1949.

26 ECM 26/11/48, 611–16; *Post*, 15 January 1949, pp. 28–30.

27 *Post*, 16 July 1949, pp. 23–4, 19 November 1949, pp. 577–8.

28 TUC 1950 Report, pp. 262ff.; *Post*, 11 February 1950, p. 55, 20 May 1950, p. 209.

29 TUC 1950 Report, pp. 267, 473. See also *Post*, 15 July 1950, p. 268, 21 October 1950, pp. 381–2.

30 *Post*, 8 April 1950, pp. 135, 17 June, p. 243, 15 July, p. 259; NWC (SS) Minutes, 2 March, 13 July 1950, p. 4.

31 *Post*, 1 July 1950, pp. 8–10, 15. There is a good deal on what follows at F 370 and some interesting discussions in ECM.

32 *Times* and *Daily Worker* (19 April 1951).

33 *Post*, 5 May 1951, p. 153.

34 These events were all reported in the press at the time and cuttings are collected at F 370. The Union's official publications say very little about them, except for a letter in *Post*, 19 May 1951, p. 189, protesting about the behaviour of the London members.

35 Details in *Post*, 5 May 1951, p. 151, 2 June, p. 199, 17 November, p. 474.

36 There are many thick files on these and subsequent Cable Room negotiations at F 370.

37 See *Post*, 18 August, 15 December 1951.

38 The fullest account of this is in the NWC (SS) Minutes.

39 *Post*, 3 January 1953, p. 13, 14 February, p. 136.

40 *Post*, 2 February 1952, p. 61, 31 January 1953, p. 68.

41 *Post*, 20 December 1952, p. 555; POC, 4292, 4 March 1953.

42 UPW (1953b) and *Post*, 4 July 1953, p. 20.
43 Details at F 370.
44 ECM 16/3/54, 271, 23/3/54, 279, 6/4/54, 285; *Post*, 3 July 1954, pp. 36, 48.
45 ECM, F 370 and *Post*, 23 October 1954, for this.
46 *Daily Worker* (11 September 1954).
47 *Post* (4 December 1954).
48 *Post*, 4 June 1955, p. 376, 13 August, p. 461, 24 September, pp. 527–9; F 370.
49 F 370; *Post*, 24 September 1955, p. 524, 28 January 1956, p. 110.
50 The main material on this is at F 000.3. The Royal Commission produced printed reports of the evidence given to it, some of which is given in *WBs*. The UPW's evidence is also given in *Post*, 14 August 1954. There is a full account of the attitude of another union in Mortimer and Ellis (1980), pp. 179–94.
51 ECM; *Post*, 19 December 1953, pp. 663–4.
52 Priestley Report, pp. 39, 45.
53 *Post*, 14 August 1954, p. 468; Priestley Report, p. 40, *Evidence*, pp. 499, 660.
54 See, for example, Job Evaluation Report, PP 1967–8 XXVIII.
55 Mortimer and Ellis (1980), p. 190; Wigham (1980), p. 133.
56 *Post*, 28 January 1956, pp. 134–5.
57 *WB*, April 1956; UPW (1956); *Post*, 6 July 1956, p. 393. NWC (SS) Minutes, 18 June 1956.
58 Details at F 370.
59 UPW (1957b), and *Post*, 6 July 1957, pp. 418–24.
60 *Post*, 17 May 1958, p. 313.
61 POC, 4531, 4 September 1957, 4609, 4 March 1959, 4707, 18 January 1961; *Post*, 7 January 1961, pp. 1–3.
62 See the Supplementary Report to the 1958 Conference and *Post*, 7 June 1958, pp. 340ff., 5 July, pp. 402ff., BC 19/58 and F 353.
63 *Post*, 2 February 1959, pp. 65–6, 13 April, pp. 256–8.
64 *Post*, 10 January 1959, pp. 10–11, 16 May, pp. 317–18, 23 January 1960, pp. 60ff., 27 February, pp. 208ff., 12 March, pp. 260–1, 16 April, p. 317.
65 *London Post*, December 1959, pp. 155ff.; ECM 25–27/11/59, 88–9.
66 *Post*, 9 January 1960, p. 30, 27 February, p. 241, 6 February, p. 180.
67 *Post*, 16 April 1960, p. 317, 29 October, pp. 705ff.; UPW (1960).
68 *Post*, 7 January 1961, p. 13, 21 January, p. 55, 22 April, pp. 323ff., 10 June, pp. 366–7.
69 F 330.6.
70 *Post*, 7 January 1960, pp. 21ff. See also Chapter 11.
71 *Post*, 21 April 1951, pp. 121ff.; F 322.
72 *Post*, 14 July 1959, pp. 286, 314, 2 January 1954, pp. 8–11, 3 July, p. 64.
73 *Post*, 25 June 1960, p. 483.
74 *Post*, 4 December 1954, pp. 674ff.; POC, 4554, 12 February 1958.
75 *Post*, 6 February 1960, p. 173; UPW (1965).
76 UPW (1965), pp. 5–6.
77 F 229.
78 *Post*, 4 July 1953, p. 32, 11 September 1949, p. 357.
79 *Post*, 25 September 1948, pp. 396–9, 1 July 1950, pp. 13–14, 4 July 1953, pp. 31–2, reprinted as a pamphlet.
80 *Post*, 10 February 1951, p. 23, 24 March, p. 96. For typical exchanges see *Red Tape*, December 1953, p. 78; *Post*, 2 January 1954, pp. 1–2.
81 BC 31/60, 2 August 1960; *Post*, 3 September 1960, pp. 645ff.
82 *Daily Mail* (5 June 1961).
83 *Post*, 11 July 1964, p. 444, 19 June 1965, pp. 438–40, 25 June 1966, pp. 176–7.
84 *Post*, 22 October 1949, 20 May 1950, p. 213, 1 July 1950, p. 8; POC, 4461, 2 March 1960.
85 *Post*, 15 April 1954, p. 274, 5 July 1954, p. 347.
86 Post Office Report and Accounts 1958–59, p. 4; *Hansard* V, 579, 644 (5 December 1957).
87 *Post*, 9 July 1960, pp. 516–8, 21 January 1961, pp. 60–2, 4 February, p. 189, 10 June, pp. 360–2, 368–9; *WB*, February 1961, pp. 21–2.
88 *Post*, 19 August 1961, pp. 477–9, 23 September, pp. 509, 519, 534–6.
89 An interesting document at F 353 summarises some of what is in ECM AD III for 1961–2.
90 ECM AD 1961–2 III, p. 1,618, 11/1/62, 183–4.
91 ECM 17–18/1/62, 189ff.; BC 10/62; *Hansard* V, 652, 13 (23 January 1962).
92 ECM 31/1/62, 222; AD 1961–2 IV, pp. 1,868ff.; *Post*, 9 June 1962, pp. 306–7. See also F 353.

93 ECM AD 15/2/62, pp. 233–6, 1961–2, pp. 1,984ff., 2,013ff.; *Post*, 31 March 1962, pp. 217–18, 28 April, pp. 273ff.

94 ECM 9/4/62, 281; *Post*, 28 April 1962, p. 278, 9 June, pp. 314–16.

95 *Post*, 9 June 1962, pp. 332–3, 30 June, pp. 361ff.

96 *Post*, 14 July 1962, p. 385.

97 *Post*, 9 February 1963, p. 145, 13 April, p. 267, 9 November, p. 539.

98 *Post*, 18 May 1963, p. 308, 15 June, pp. 318–21.

99 Pay Research Unit Survey No. 68 for January 1962, Postmen, pp. 1–5; *Post*, 3 August 1963, pp. 413–20, 17 August, p. 437, 7 September, pp. 644–6, *BOB*, 15 August 1963, p. 370.

100 *Post*, 21 September 1963, pp. 477ff., 18 August 1962.

101 *Post*, 11 January 1964, p. 7, 31 January, p. 140. The rest is in the separately produced Agenda and Report of the February 1964 Wages Conference. Full details of the background and following events are derived from Schneider (1966). See also Stagg (1964), pp. 468–73, Smith (1964) and Bevins (1965), pp. 127ff.

102 *Post*, 21 March 1964, pp. 237–9; ECM 13/3/64, 153; Bevins (1965), p. 129.

103 Armitage (1964). See also *Post*, 23 May 1964, pp. 329ff., 6 June, pp. 345ff.

104 Bevins (1965), p. 129.

105 There are full accounts at ECM AD 1964–5, pp. 140ff.

106 ECM 10/7/64, 15.

107 Quotations from *The Times* and *Financial Times* for 11 July 1964.

108 The best reports are in *The Times* and *Financial Times* for 13 July, *Guardian* and *Times* 14 July, *Daily Telegraph, Guardian, Financial Times, Evening Standard*, 15 July.

109 Details of these events are in a vivid letter from Sheffield Branch Secretary, Herbert Farniss, of 13 February 1965 to Norman Stagg, kept with a number of other such reports at F 370.

110 ECM 14/7/64, 19.

111 This is the burden of remarks in *The Times* and *Financial Times* of 16 July, which are clearly inspired by the Government.

112 Letters from F. C. Wells and L. K. White of SEDO and Les Simpson of York at F 370.

113 ECM AD 401 and 402/64; *Post*, 13 August 1964, p. 469.

114 *Post*, 13 August 1964, p. 470; ECM 22/7/64, 28.

115 See Bevins (1965), p. 131. The *Sunday Telegraph* of 26 July 1964 contains an extraordinarily well informed account of the denouement of the struggle, presumably by William Deedes, who reveals more of the Government's thinking than anybody else and says more about what happened in the UPW Executive than is recorded in its Minutes. Stagg (1964) also contains a good deal of interesting detail on this stage.

116 *Post*, 13 August 1964, p. 472; ECM 24/7/64, 32.

117 *Sunday Times* (26 April 1964).

118 For a useful explanation of the pay research exercise see Stagg (1965), pp. 222–4, 234–6. ECM AD 1964–5, pp. 1,085ff. for the first stage of the negotiations, and *Post*, 1 May 1965, pp. 358ff. and 19 June, pp. 404–7, for the rest.

119 Relevant documents on these matters are kept at F 107.3. However, there is little of significance that cannot be gathered from published press accounts or from *Post*, 23 January 1965, pp. 28ff.

120 ECM AD 1964–5, pp. 566–7.

121 *BOB* 47/63, 28 March 1963; *Post*, 22 February 1964, p. 170.

122 F 107.3; ECM AD 1964–5, p. 315.

123 *Financial Times* (22 September 1964); ECM AD 1964–5, p. 337.

124 ECM 24–25/9/64, 52–8, widely reported in the press on 25 September. See also ECM AD 1964–5, pp. 312–26 for various related documents.

125 Full details of these discussions are given in *Post*, 17 October 1964, pp. 537–9, 31 October, p. 554 and 23 January 1965, pp. 53–7. See also ECM AD 1964–5, pp. 499–501; *Financial Times* (26 September), *Guardian* (2 October).

126 ECM AD 1964–5, p. 476.

127 *Post*, 14 November 1964, p. 579.

128 *Post*, 12 December 1964, pp. 606–7.

129 *Post*, 20 March 1965, pp. 252–3, 10 April, p. 337; *London Post*, May–June 1965, pp. 49–50.

130 The documents are at ECM AD 1964–5, pp. 840–82, summarised in *Post*, 20 March 1965, pp. 249–51.

131 ECM 28–9/1/65, 147, 25/2/65, 175–6.

132 ECM AD 1964–5, pp. 1,077–80; *Post*, 20 March 1965, pp. 241, 249–57, 10 April, pp. 293ff., 19 June, pp. 398ff.

133 The reports were all published in special issues of *Post*, 22 April 1967, 25 November 1967, 13 April 1968 and 22 March 1969.
134 *Post*, 25 November 1967, p. 4, 22 May 1965, 5 February 1966, p. 42, 22 October 1966, p. 298, 15 April 1967, p. 4, 9 March 1968, 21 June 1969, p. 43.
135 *Post* (18 November 1967).
136 *Post*, 13 November 1965, pp. 660–1 and the dozens of letters printed in following issues.
137 *Post*, 14 January 1967, 24 June, pp. 16, 18.
138 *Post*, 29 April 1967, p. 1, 3 February 1968, p. 12, 17 February, 13, 20 July. See also F 353, and *BOB*, 5 July 1968.
139 *Post*, 24 June 1962, p. 32, 8 July, p. 1, 22 July, pp. 1–2.
140 1968 Conference Agenda, p. 6; F 535; *Post*, 25 January 1965, 15 February. Stonehouse (1975), p. 158, perhaps refers to Cabinet disagreements about his handling of this dispute.
141 *Post*, 8 April 1970, pp. 17–18. See above, p. 322.
142 *Post* (21 June 1969).
143 *Post*, 5 July 1969, p. 7, 19 July, 15 November, 14, 19 February 1970.
144 *Post*, 8 April 1970, 22 July, pp. 27–31.
145 These details are given in Hardman Report pp. 2, 60–5. See also *Post*, 7 November 1970.
146 The only published accounts of the strike are pamphlets brought out soon afterwards by left wingers – Foot (?1971), Weal (?1971), and the much slighter Jacobs (?1971). A fuller account of some of the issues is now to be found in Patel (1980) and L. Wills (?1980). There is a large collection of cuttings and associated documents in the UCW Research Department on which the following account is based. There is also some information in the daily *SB* published by the Union. The main negotiations are given in a special issue of *Post* for 10 May 1971, and the Union's case is set out in evidence to the Hardman Committee in an issue dated 7 April – also printed separately (UPW 1971). See also PO (1971) *Statement on Behalf of the Post Office*. Also of interest are the researches of Lasko and Gennard about how the strikers maintained themselves (1974a and b, 1975), as well as in Gennard (1977).
147 Patel (1980), p. 52; Department of Employment *Gazette*, January 1972, September 1980.
148 These points are set out in a letter to *The Times* by Tom Jackson published on 20 February 1971. See also *SB* 20.2.
149 *Daily Mirror, Financial Times* (26 November 1970).
150 All the negotiations are in *Post*, 10 May 1975, the quote in *Financial Times*, 9 January and Foot (?1971), p. 12 on management strike preparations.
151 *Guardian* (12 January, 18 January).
152 *Post* (10 May 1971); ECM 15/1/71.
153 ECM 24/1/71, but there is a fuller account in *Financial Times*, 25 January. The Executive was later defeated for continuing to keep counters open – see *Post*, 10 July 1971, p. 19.
154 *SB*, 26.1, 27.1.
155 *Daily Mail, Guardian* (29 January).
156 *Times* (3, 8 February); Union's evidence to Hardman, UPW (1971), p. 60; *SB* 31.1.
157 *Times* (2, 4 February).
158 *SB* 10.2; *Daily Mail* (9 February), *Daily Telegraph* (10 February).
159 ECM AD 75/71.
160 Nearly all of the points on these negotiations are in *Post*, 10 May, with some additions from ECM.
161 *Sunday Express* (14 February).
162 All significant points in *Post*, 10 May. See also ECM 14–19/2/71 and *SB* 15.2.
163 There is an interesting article on some of these points by Peter Jenkins in the *Guardian*, 24 February.
164 *SB* 21.2; *Morning Star* (24 February); Foot (?1971), p. 18.
165 ECM AD 83/71(F), 24–25/2/71, 28, AD 85/71.
166 *Telegraph, Guardian* (4 March), *Times, Guardian* (5 March).
167 See the documents referred to above in n. 146.
168 *Financial Times, Telegraph* (7 April), *Financial Times, Sun, Guardian* (8 April).
169 *Guardian* (10 April), *Tribune* (16 April).
170 Stagg (1971), Grace (1971), p. 3.
171 Tracey (1971).
172 Peter Paterson, *Sunday Telegraph* (7 March).
173 Thompson (1970 and 1980) vividly reproduces the mood of this campaign. See also Barker (1972), pp. 42–7.

174 *Daily Sketch, Guardian, Daily Mail* (15 January 1971), *Sunday Telegraph* (17 January).

175 *Daily Mirror* (15 January), *Universe* (12 March), *Evening Standard* (15 February), *South London Press* (26 February), *SB* 27.2.

176 *Daily Sketch* (18 February).

177 *Sunday Telegraph* (7 March).

178 *Times* (21 January), *Financial Times* (28 January).

179 *Sunday Times* (24 January), *Daily Telegraph* (11 February), *Financial Times* (12 February), *SB* 9.2, *Times* (2 March).

180 *Daily Mirror* (20 January), *Times* (25 January), *Daily Telegraph* (18 February), *Daily Mirror* (9 March), *Times* (10 March).

181 Weal (?1971), pp. 8, 31. See above, p. 379.

182 Patel (1980), p. 35.

183 These are outlined in the studies of Gennard and Lasko (1974a and b, 1975).

184 *Sunday Times* (7 March 1971); *Post*, 15 May 1971, p. 8. Dorfman (1979), p. 70 also expresses this view, and quotes others who agree with it.

14 From Post Office to Communication Workers

> Change is never comfortable but without change in a world that is itself changing the trade union movement can lose its cutting edge. The Executive Committee is therefore proposing change of a comparatively radical kind but in doing so they are sensitive to the history and the sentiment that exists in our organisation. (UCW, 'Special Report on Union Structure at National Level', *Special Conference Agenda*, November 1980, p. 1)

In 1980 the name of the Union of Post Office Workers was changed, along with many of its traditional forms of organisation. When the Executive and the members discussed these innovations they showed themselves very conscious of the fact that they did so in terms very much dictated by their history. As the last pages of this book are being written, it is still not possible to see what elements of these changes will be brought forward into the future. The time has not yet come either when it is possible to look back with real hindsight at the final decade of the unified Post Office from 1971 to 1981. Surveying this recent period from the perspective of 140 years of agitation about wages and conditions, we are presented with a picture that is too blurred, too close to our eyes, to discern trends and tendencies in the same way as for earlier times. This last chapter therefore sets out more briefly something of what now seems interesting and relevant in the recent activities of the UPW over and above the details given in earlier chapters about such matters as changes in the Union's structure and its participation in the administration of the old Post Office during its final years.

BARGAINING UNDER RESTRAINT: 1971–6

As might be expected, the discussion of wages and conditions in the Post Office after 1971 was dominated by the outcome of the great strike, or rather by how its outcome was perceived. In the first years after 1971, large-scale industrial action was no longer considered to be an option for the UPW. The national strike had been the culmination of a long period of developing militancy and discontent, but it did not inaugurate a period when wages and conditions were decided by industrial confrontation. The most obvious new characteristic of industrial bargaining on a national scale in the Post Office in the decade after 1971 was the fact that the main agreements were made as a direct result of annual negotiations held more or less directly with the Post Office and agreed with little or no reference to any outside agency such as arbitration. By the 1980s, this way of deciding things had become so commonplace that its novel features were no longer noticed.

In the 1970s also, wages and conditions in the Post Office were determined to a far greater extent than ever before with reference to what was happening with wages and prices elsewhere in the economy. Long since forgotten now was the historic opposition of Post Office workers and other civil servants to such comparisons being made at all. Generations had now grown used to the application of the formulae of Tomlin and Priestley, and to the more refined examination of tasks and rewards such as had been undertaken under the auspices of the Civil Service Pay Research Unit. By the time Post Office workers moved out of the civil service in the late 1960s, wages in the public sector were as a matter of course considered in terms of the movement of wages in the economy as a whole. Public sector wages were also at the centre of the efforts of governments to keep down the level of pay settlements. Thus during the 1970s it was government economic policy, with all the variations in the form and timing of incomes policy, that became the most important factor in the chief wage bargains in the Post Office. Claims no longer had any justification in themselves, but were seen usually as efforts to 'catch up' with what was obtained by other workers. Settlements came to be measured against movements elsewhere to an extent that would have been quite inconceivable in the past. This did much more than transform the rhetoric of bargaining. It opened the possibility of orderly and agreed forms of wage negotiation, which helps to explain the support given by the UPW to the incomes policies of Labour governments from 1974 to 1979.

Another significant feature of Post Office industrial relations during the last period of a single corporation was the increasing effect of technological change on the workers. Continual developments in telecommunications have transformed the character of the work performed there. On the postal side, there were also significant changes in the character of many tasks, and by the early 1980s new pressures developed which threatened all the work practices developed in the post-war economic boom, the results of which will only be seen in the distant future.

The three years immediately following the 1971 strike were difficult and unhappy both for UPW members and for the Post Office itself. This was the period of the bitterly fought and ultimately abortive Industrial Relations Act. During these years inflation rates rose to levels never before dreamed of. Efforts to deal with this led to the sharpest industrial conflict and the great social crisis of the winter of 1973–74, with the three-day working week and ultimate inglorious collapse of the Conservative administration in the General Election of February 1974. The fortunes of the Post Office itself during this period have been charted in Chapter 9. After pulling back from the problems of 1970 to make a slight profit in 1971, the enterprise came under increasing pressure as a result of government 'counter-inflation policies' which compelled it to adopt pricing policies that led to enormous losses by 1974, and to gigantic tariff increases in 1975 to 'catch up'. Post Office workers were caught between the caution which invariably characterised their attitudes after March 1971, and the timing of settlements which pushed them further and further behind the rate of inflation and the earnings received elsewhere. During this period the regular methods and accepted arguments of the Priestley Report and the Civil Service Pay Research Unit were abandoned. Instead there was a series of temporary agreements on wages and conditions which caused increasing resentment in the workforce.

The problems facing the Post Office had consequences which are still felt well into the 1980s. At the time they led to a number of rather ill-conceived efforts to save resources by such means as reducing rural services. Most of these schemes were opposed by the Union and eventually abandoned, though a reorganisation of the parcels service was more favourably received and carried through.[1] After the end of the strike in March 1971, wage settlements came under increasing pressure from the incomes policies of the Conservative Government. There were some improvements however. In December 1971, members were granted an extra 6·383 per cent on their pay, but this was only to compensate them for the switch to a contributory pension scheme. The first general post-Hardman settlement came in February 1972. This did much to further reduce incremental scales and also gave an overall wage increase of 7·5 per cent, not greatly different from the rate of inflation at the time. However, as it turned out, 24 February 1972 was not a good point for the UPW Executive to have accepted a 7·5 per cent settlement. On the next day the miners returned to work after a national strike which had lasted 6½ weeks – the same as the UPW a year earlier. For the 300,000 striking miners the outcome was different. Another Committee chaired by Lord Wilberforce granted increases said to amount to 27·7 per cent. In the following June railway workers received 16 per cent and the general level of settlements started to run to at least 13 per cent.

It was now the Union who began to look in a direction it had sometimes considered in the past. UPW leaders tried to initiate joint action with other unions in the public sector. A conference sponsored by the TUC and held in August 1972 did not do much to fulfil the hopes that brought it into being.[2] However, the UPW managed to get agreement with a number of unions with members in the Post Office – POMSA, the CPSA, the Society of Civil Servants, and the Telephone Sales Supervisors Association. Together they submitted a claim on 12 December 1972.[3] However, this was a few weeks after the Conservative Government announced a 'wages standstill', later known as 'Phase I' of its incomes policy. The result was that Post Office workers' leaders early in 1972 had to spend a great deal of time doing what they had been compelled to do exactly ten years earlier – to put pressure on a Conservative Government for the right to negotiate about wages at all. There were discussions with the Post Office and also, on 14 February 1973, with Employment Secretary Maurice MacMillan. Two days earlier UPW General Secretary Tom Jackson told delegates to a special conference at Bournemouth that the wage freeze was 'about as fair as a footpad with a big stick in the dark'. There was no settlement until 'Phase II' came into effect at the beginning of April and this was for £1+4 per cent, giving UPW members 7–8 per cent.[4]

The Union's Executive accepted these increases 'under protest' and immediately launched a campaign to take up the 'anomalies' that had hit the UPW as a result of the freeze and the timing of the settlements before it. The issue was taken to the Pay Board – a short-lived body which was supposed to settle disputes about the interpretation of the 'counter inflation policy'. Union leaders met the Board in June 1973, but its report in September offered such a narrow interpretation of 'anomalies' that Post Office workers could expect nothing at all.[5] On 3 October, Tom Jackson led a delegation to argue the case with Prime Minister Edward Heath. The Tory Government, however, had nothing to offer except what might be obtained under the ill-fated 'Phase III' announced a week later. With inflation picking up into double figures again, this was supposed to give 7 per cent or £2.25, whichever was the greater. It was also supposed to allow for anomalies again, for productivity agreements, for 'unsocial hours' and for threshold payments.

From October 1973 the UPW continued to take up the case on anomalies. The 'consortium' with other Post Office unions broke down, and some of the other unions associated with it embarked on limited industrial action. UPW leaders began to look around for other means to argue their claims. There were some strains on the incomes policies of the Conservative Government. On 13 December 1973 General Secretary Tom Jackson appeared on television and said that those who undermined Phase III would have a lot to answer for. (He was considered to be referring to miners, who were pursuing a large claim.) This view was not popular and there were many resolutions of protest within the UPW culminating in a vote of censure at the 1974 Annual Conference.[6]

In the meantime, Union leaders concentrated on trying to get something from the more flexible negotiations promised under Phase III. By the end of 1973 it could easily be shown that Post Office wages were lagging well behind those obtained elsewhere. General wage levels had gone up 53·9 per cent since 1970 and prices by 35·2 per cent. During the same period the wages of postmen had only gone up by 28·5 per cent, and those of postal officers by 30·8 per cent. At the same time the authorised establishment for postmen was 12 per cent down in London and 9 per cent nationally, while telephonists were 7·5 per cent down. These statistics were included in a detailed case presented to the Pay Board in November 1973.[7] The unusual feature of the representation was that it secured the general support of the Post Office Board, who were suffering from the labour shortage by the disruption of the mails and telephone service. The same people who had been holding the line in 1971 for government efforts to keep down wages were in 1974 complaining of 'the deep sense of unfairness and disquiet amongst Post Office staff'.[8] None of this convinced the Pay Board, however, and the Union had to continue to argue the case well into 1974 on the anomalies issue. Some of the less well paid grades were even deprived of extra leave entitlement under the incomes policy provisions.[9]

The agreement negotiated under Phase III gave some improvements to UPW members. They got what was aimed at under the policy – £2. 25 or 7 per cent, a good bit below the current rate of inflation. In addition, they got 'premium' payments for Saturday working and a 'threshold' agreement for 1 per cent extra every time there was a 1 per cent increase above 7 per cent on the Retail Price Index as at October. Other features of the settlement were a first step to equal pay for women cleaners and much reduced incremental scales for postal assistants, a new grade supplementing the work of postal officers.[10]

The quiet negotiations were soon overshadowed in 1974 by a social crisis at least as profound as that occasioned by the 1926 General Strike. The miners strike brought about the collapse of the Heath Government in February 1974 and the election of a minority Labour Government, which obtained a small majority after the subsequent General Election in October. These events went with climbing unemployment and inflation figures. The rise in prices in 1974 was 12 per cent, in 1975, 20 per cent, and in 1976, 23 per cent. The new Labour Government inevitably attempted to continue wage restraint, except in what were described as 'special cases'. However, Labour came into government on the basis of heightened expectations soon reflected in a general level of wage settlements at around 20 per cent. The great dam of restraint and insolvency built up by Conservative economic policies rendered large price increases in the Post Office inevitable, and UPW leaders felt obliged to accept the historically unprecedented rises announced early in 1975.[11]

A major part of the strategy of the Labour Government in dealing with the consequences of these economic events was to make an agreement with the unions known, without acknowledgement to the authorship or intention of Rousseau, as the 'Social Contract'. One step in getting this together was a visit from Prime Minister Harold Wilson to the May 1974 UPW Annual Conference. Delegates provided the requisite standing ovation, and certainly did not close the door on possible agreement with the Government. However there was a long and bitter debate on wages, and soon the anomalies issue was being taken up with some energy. Delegations met Employment Secretary Michael Foot on at least three occasions and Prime Minister Wilson once. These discussions eventually obtained a special pay supplement for all members of 11 per cent, not far short of what was then the rate of inflation. This was accepted by 17,720 votes to 565.[12] Meanwhile, climbing inflation rates were triggering threshold payments for UPW members and many others. During that summer of 1974 the first step in the Social Contract agreement between Government and TUC involved the abolition of the Pay Board in return for wage increases at the level of the cost of living.

After the second 1974 Election in October, therefore, the wages bargaining position was relatively flexible, but there was still much uncertainty and a high level of inflation. This was the background to the next major set of negotiations on behalf of UPW members. On 25 November 1974 the Union's Executive submitted a demand for the consolidation of threshold payments in such a way that wages kept up with the cost of living. This was directly in line with the TUC–Government agreement, though it also included a £30 per week minimum at 18. The settlement was for pay from the beginning of 1975 to be up to the level of the Retail Price Index. However the threshold payments were not consolidated and were to be triggered by 1 per cent increases for every increase in the RPI above 10 per cent during 1975. The members voted in March 1975 to accept this by 18,615 to 915.[13]

In the early part of 1975 inflation grew apace and negotiations for new forms of incomes policy continued. It is of interest to notice that during this period the Union went to the Post Office Arbitration Tribunal for the first time since 1969 on a claim to increase period covered for night allowance by two hours. The Tribunal split the difference and agreed to an extra hour. In the same period there was a 50 per cent increase in some allowances – the first since 1971.[14] On a national scale there were developments which altered the entire climate of industrial relations. The Trade Union and Labour Relations Act in 1974 replaced the hated Industrial Relations Act. At the same time the Health and Safety Act brought in reforms promised for some years which included a new role for the trade union movement. The 1975 Equal Pay Act gave statutory effect to an aim long held in the movement, and the Employment Protection Act gave new rights and responsibilities to trade unionists at every level. By mid-1975 discussions began on the implementation of 'industrial democracy' leading most notably to the Post Office 'experiment' described in Chapter 11.

The other side of the Social Contract consisted of various forms of wage restraint. The first of these was formalised as Phase 1 in July 1975. This provided for a £6 per week increase for everybody earning up to £8,500 per annum.[15] This policy, which tended to favour lower paid groups like many Post Office workers, was accepted with enthusiasm by UPW General Secretary Tom Jackson and his Executive. The case for a claim based on this was agreed at the 1975 Annual Conference, though not without a long debate and some modification. It was submitted in October, when the Union asked for a £6 increase including recently obtained threshold payments. This was accepted by the Post Office and when Union members began to be paid at the new rate on 1 January 1976, they were getting around 20 per cent more than a year before, because some of the earlier threshold payments were not included in the £6. Over this very inflationary year, therefore, the wages of UPW members had gone up not far short of the extraordinarily high rate of inflation.[16] The wage negotiations of 1976 again took place within Phase II of incomes policy for a 5 per cent increase within the range of increases of £2. 50–£4 per week. These were again reckoned as additions to basic wages. Although increases were now coming more or less in automatic succession, they were for the first time in living memory beginning to lag behind rises in prices generally. Furthermore, many difficulties were arising out of the fact that increases were not being consolidated into basic income. The most important of these was that real earnings from overtime were being reduced.[17]

There were many problems for Union negotiators which arose out of this form of bargaining. One result was the difficulties of the better off grades. For this reason a special joint study group on postal officers was set up in 1975. Although there could be little serious doubt that the tasks of postal officers were increasing and their relative pay was falling, the operation of incomes policy made it difficult to confront this and there were some delays in the study group producing any results. The 1978 Union Conference voted to demand the publication of a report on its work.[18]

THE UNION, GRUNWICK'S AND THE RIGHT TO STRIKE

Nor were these the only problems created by the great mass of legislation of the period 1974–6. Industrial peace there had certainly been, and inflation levels were beginning to fall. However the law had been introduced into the process of industrial relations in ways not previously known in Britain. In November 1976 the Labour Government lost its Parliamentary majority and began to rely for its existence on a tiny group of Liberal MPs. No longer was there significant new legislation which could be regarded as being of advantage to the trade union movement. Instead, there were various efforts to make and utilise the new laws to attack trade unionism. The quaintly named National Association For Freedom, a well financed front organisation for the social and ideological policies of the Conservative Party, took up the task of using the law in this way. In particular NAFF proved to be the stalking horse for a legal attack on trade union rights which were later implemented by the post-1979 Thatcher Government. One part of this offensive was directed against the right to strike of Post Office workers, and though this issue has not yet been resolved in the early 1980s, because of its considerable historical significance it is worth devoting some attention to it here.

During 1976–7 a comparatively minor trade union recognition dispute at the Grunwick factory in North West London took on a national significance greater than might normally have been expected. This was in part because it became a threat to the methods of industrial peace through legislation developed over the previous three years. The dispute was deliberately exploited and utilised by forces hostile to trade unionism in an effort to undermine the unions. From the point of view of the UPW, it is important to say that there were many precedents for the industrial action taken by UPW members in Cricklewood in November 1976. Nor was there anything new in the threat to boycott mails and telephones to South Africa in January 1977. Numerous examples have been quoted elsewhere in this book, from strike action taken in the 1870s and 1890s, unofficial industrial action in the 1950s and later, as well as national industrial disputes in the 1960s and 1970s. Nor was there anything particularly new about some of the conflicts of authority within the Union which occurred in the summer of 1977, either in the form of the determination of the UPW's leaders to pursue legal and constitutional methods, or the desire of sections of members to act differently. What was new was that serious questions were raised about the legality of Post Office workers going on strike at all.

Now it was certainly true that there was legislation to prevent mail being held up in the eighteenth century and before. However, it did not occur to anybody to claim that these laws – designed to deal with dishonesty and theft – were infringed by industrial action. This was the case even in the 1870s when the right to have a union was not accepted. The issue was not raised when postmen refused to handle the work of striking railway workers in 1911, nor when the UPW supported a boycott against right-wing terror in Hungary in 1921, or French nuclear tests in 1973. The issue of legality was not seriously raised either during the major industrial actions in 1964 and 1971. It is true that the question of the legality of Post Office strikes was occasionally considered, and reference is made elsewhere to such discussions during the bleak days of economic depression and the Trade Disputes Act in the 1930s. However, it was certainly assumed right up to the 1953 Post Office Act and beyond, that legislation directed against the dishonesty of those who wilfully delay or detain mails did not apply to industrial action. However, NAFF and the 'creative' legal decisions of Lord Denning and the Court of Appeal changed all that.

This is not the place to deal with all aspects of the story of the epic struggle to get a trade union into the Grunwick factory in North London.[19] The UPWs role was however of considerable importance. The dispute began in the 'dog days' of the 'long hot summer' of 1976 at the end of August, when 137 workers, mostly Asian women, who processed photographs largely supplied by mail order, walked out of their factory and joined the trade union APEX. A few days later, on 6 September 1976, APEX General Secretary Roy Grantham spoke at the TUC of 'conditions more appropriate to the nineteenth century' and said 'that Tom Jackson had pledged the full support of the UPW'. It soon became clear that the employer would not discuss with the Union, even at second hand, so on 14 September a formal letter was sent to the UPW asking for support. On 23 September the Executive considered this. Deciding against initiating any general boycott it nevertheless agreed to respect any picket lines at the factory. The onus was now placed on the workers at the local Cricklewood sorting office who, despite the ill-informed comments of Grunwick Managing Director George Ward, had no particular reputation as militants. Perhaps the only slight variation from the average in this Union Branch, was that they were more closely associated with the local community than most, and sent active participants to the local Trades Council. At any rate, they immediately stopped delivering letters to Grunwick's, but the company then sent people to collect their mail directly from the delivery office – as is normal in such circumstances. On 29 October the UPW Executive decided by 22 votes to 5 to take a further step and to black all Grunwick's mail.[20]

This action had a considerable impact. It was described by George Ward as a 'threat to our jugular'. Soon his supplies were stopped at a number of London offices and at this point, according to his own account, Ward approached NAFF and one of its supporters, John Gorst, who happened to be his MP. The day after the blacking started the company met the Advisory Conciliation and Arbitration

Service for the second time and agreed to continue discussion if the blacking stopped. After this Gorst, along with various Conservative front bench speakers, began to raise the unexpected issue of the legality of the blacking. At the same time Grunwick, in one of its numerous references to the law, began to sue the Post Office for the return of its mail. Union leaders were persuaded to sign affidavits to the effect that they would not call for any further obstruction of deliveries destined for Grunwicks. By the time there was a Parliamentary Debate on 4 November, Labour Employment Secretary Booth was able to announce that the Union had agreed to call off the blacking in the light of the employers' agreement to meet ACAS.[21]

Whatever may have been said in private discussions that took place at this time, it soon became obvious that Ward and his associates had no intention whatever of carrying out what was considered to have been agreed. Although from time to time he stalled and delayed, Ward never showed any inclination to enter serious negotiations with the strikers or their Union through ACAS, the Scarman Court of Enquiry or any other method whatsoever. On the other hand, he showed no hesitation in taking to court, under any law that could be discovered, anybody who seemed to be in his way. Many of these court cases were lost, but they always served to put pressure on his opponents. Thus the four days of official blacking by the UPW brought into question – though it did not resolve – the legal right to take such action at all. Afterwards the UPW did not decide again on a national level to take official direct action against the company.

Nevertheless, it soon became clear to local Union members and to anybody else who took an interest in the matter that Ward had no intention of carrying out the undertakings which had provided the basis for ending the UPW's action. Cricklewood postmen began to consider re-imposing their ban on Grunwick mail. On 12 December UPW Assistant Secretary, Maurice Styles, told a conference convened by the Brent Trades Council that the Union might consider re-imposing the blacking if the agreement to co-operate with ACAS was not honoured. However, the Executive in the following week, though convinced 'that this firm is seeking every means possible to frustrate the work of ACAS', simply agreed that they would 'keep the issue under review'.[22]

Before there were any further developments of significance to the Grunwick struggle, there were some events which further affected the position of the UPW. Following the shooting down of large numbers of black school children in Soweto in September 1976, the banning of all normal trade union activity and the death of a number of union leaders in detention, international trade union bodies called for a week of action against South Africa beginning on 17 January 1977. On 5 January, the UPW Executive voted unanimously to ban mail and telephone calls to South Africa during that week. As already mentioned, they had taken such sympathetic action on a number of previous occasions, most recently in June–July 1973 against French nuclear tests in the Pacific. However, that was before the National Association For Freedom came on the scene. On Friday 14 January 1977 its leader John Gouriet tried to get the Attorney General Sam Silkin to support him in taking legal action against the Union. This the Attorney General refused to do, and a High Court judge would not allow Gouriet to proceed on his own account. However, Gouriet soon found an ally in another quarter – Lord Denning and his Court of Appeal, who met specially on Saturday 15 January. Though Lord Denning could not persuade his two colleagues to condemn the Attorney General for not taking up the case, he did manage to get his words attacking Silkin on the front page of every national newspaper for most of the next week. Of more immediate and practical importance, the three judges did agree that Gouriet could bring his action and he could be granted an injunction to restrain the Union.

The first result of this was that the UPW decided to call off the boycott against South Africa. A great deal of high falutin discussion about the constitutional rights of various courts and the Attorney General kept journalists and lawyers busy for months. Eventually on 26 July the House of Lords, as court of final appeal, decided that the Attorney General had been entirely justified. Furthermore, it ruled that it was not the function of the Court of Appeal to define some law that stood above him, and Gouriet's injunction was withdrawn. As far as it went, this did not further infringe the right to strike. However, a new weapon had been placed in the armoury of those opposing strikes in the Post Office, so Union leaders began discussions with TUC and Government in an effort to get the law restored to the position that it had been assumed to be in before the action of NAFF. Employment Secretary Michael Foot addressed the UPW Conference in May 1977 on the issue. 'If the freedom of the people of this country', he said, 'especially the rights of trade unionists, if these precious things had in the past been left to the good sense and fairmindedness of judges, we would have few freedoms in this Country at all.'[23]

At the same UPW Annual Conference there was naturally a discussion on these issues, before even the limited clarification in the form of the House of Lords judgement in the Gouriet case. There were some complaints heard against the fact that the Executive had called off the South African boycott without consulting the members, but they were rebutted by speeches from those who supported the principle of taking some such action and the Conference voted overwhelmingly to endorse the decision. Another resolution called for the resumption of the blacking on Grunwick's. Delegates argued eloquently that their actions should not be decided by judges and the House of Lords. Tom Jackson however maintained that fines against the Union and the sequestration of its property would be 'too big a price to pay, for the UPW had been built over the years on the pennies of ordinary people and he did not believe that they had the right of running the risk of destroying the fabric of the Union'. The resolution calling for blacking was therefore lost, though another was carried against the advice of the Executive which called on the leadership with the TUC 'to undertake immediate collective action through the Labour movement'.[24]

These were the decisions on which the UPW Executive acted on the Grunwick issue over the following months. It is important to note that they were taken at a point when, although the strike was well known in the trade union movement, it had not yet assumed major political significance. ACAS had recently advised Ward to negotiate with APEX. Ward's response had been to sue ACAS on the bizarre grounds that they had not consulted those still working for Grunwick to whom Ward had not granted access. Had it not been for the self-righteous and reactionary attitudes that went with these actions, it might have seemed that the shade of Lewis Carroll had taken up residence at Grunwick's. The strikers were not amused, however, and in the absence of even a suggestion of compromise they began to call for mass pickets at the factory.

The first large-scale picket consisted mainly of women and was on Monday 13 June 1977. The picket line was attacked with considerable violence by the police and eighty-four people were arrested. That afternoon two postmen from the Cricklewood Office met the strikers and the next day they brought down two of the leaders of the LDC '3' Committee – Derek Walsh and John Taylor, the latter recently elected on to the UPW Executive for the first time. On their own responsibility, Walsh and Taylor sent out a letter calling for the blacking of Grunwick mail as from the following Thursday 16 June. On this basis the Cricklewood postmen, who had made a number of previous efforts to get backing for such a step, began to boycott the Grunwick mail. Soon dozens of untouched bags began to pile up in the office, and support came in from the West Central District Office and elsewhere. As soon as the UPW leadership heard of this they wrote informing the members that these actions were contrary to the rules of the Union and the decisions of the Annual Conference.[25]

The pressure was now again on Ward, and there were even hints of negotiations. These were soon dashed, however, when APEX General Secretary Roy Grantham was tricked into visiting the plant simply in order to be shouted down by blacklegs in front of TV cameras. On Friday 17 June, Attorney General Sam Silkin announced that he would not take legal action against the postal workers. Ward and his 'political advisers' from NAFF now decided to resort to law themselves, threatening the UPW members at Cricklewood. At the same time they refused all discussions, even with Government Ministers over the telephone. The size of the pickets outside the plant began to grow and the press and media generally began to give prominence to the dispute. However, they only gave passing reference to issues like union recognition and pay. Instead they concentrated on 'mob violence' and public order, which was portrayed as being defended by stouthearted policemen against subversives, terrorists and undesirables.

During the second week of large-scale picketing at Grunwick which began on Monday 20 June, the House of Lords began to consider the appeal against the Court of Appeal's line on the UPW South African boycott. At Grunwick's, Labour MPs and miners were amongst thousands on the picket line – Audrey Wise, MP, and Arthur Scargill of the Yorkshire miners were among many arrested. Tory MPs and journalists meanwhile savoured the vicarious joys of ramming their way in on the blacklegs bus. The press now hardly mentioned Ward's refusal to negotiate, concentrating on the NAFF/Tory theme of the need to enforce the law. A number of bottles were thrown on the picket line, in at least some cases by people later seen chatting amicably to policemen. On Thursday 23 June, after the picketing was over, a number of members of the Special Patrol Group jumped out of their van and weighed into the dispersing crowd. One of their number was hit by a bottle from another mysterious source and then left in a pool of blood for detailed attention by press photographers. The papers mourned this selected victim of violence on Friday 24th. By now all the main forces in state and society were involved in the dispute, including press, police, judiciary and Parliament. A Cabinet Committee was putting pressure on everybody possible not simply to tone down the picketing, but also to end the action of the postmen. In the absence of any agreement by Ward to negotiate, Employment Secretary Booth set up a Court of Enquiry in the next week under Lord Justice Scarman.

During the following week it was becoming increasingly clear that the action of the Cricklewood postmen was much the most potent weapon of the trade union movement against Grunwick. Ward himself later confessed to a fear that 'if a long time went by without our being able to get mail out of the Company, Grunwick would be slowly bled dry'. At the time one paper reported that Ward 'has made it clear that the blacking has begun to bite', and another expressed the view that 'the postmen have proved to be Apex's most effective allies because they threatened the company's film processing which is heavily reliant on mail order'. On Monday 27 June, the Tory Shadow Attorney General said that the dispute was now a great constitutional crisis, and it was essential to prosecute the postmen. On Tuesday 28th, the LDC '3' voted by 108 to 60 to support the action already taken by their officers and to black Grunwick mail throughout London. On Wednesday 29th, the Post Office announced that it would suspend all those who would not handle Grunwick mail. Notices to this effect were put up in the Cricklewood Office. Cricklewood Branch Secretary David Dodd was quoted in the press as making this simple statement:

> There is no way we are going to handle any Grunwick mail. As far as we are concerned, we are talking about the right of people to join a trade union and be represented by it. We must stand up and be counted.[26]

Until this time the attitude of the Union leadership had been to try to persuade the members to handle all mail, but in the absence of this to try to isolate the trouble to Cricklewood and to Grunwick's mail. Until 29 July they had succeeded in persuading the Post Office management that this was the most sensible course of action. When the Executive met on that day they were faced with the threats from the Post Office. While appealing to all members to work normally, the Executive nevertheless agreed by 16 votes to 4 'exceptionally and without creating a precedent' to pay hardship money to the Cricklewood men in the event of their suspension. On the same day Tom Jackson met Secretary of State Booth and agreed to attempt to prevent the dispute spreading elsewhere in London. On Thursday 30 June, he persuaded the Post Office management to postpone any action until he could address a meeting of the LDC '3' on the following Monday 4 July. At this meeting, he persuaded the District Council to withdraw its support for the blacking. However on the next day, Tuesday 5 July, the Cricklewood postmen voted by 63 to 41 that they would handle all but Grunwick mail. Twenty-six of their number were suspended that day as they individually carried out this decision, and eighty-seven more the day after. At first they tried to deal with all non-Grunwick mail using their own transport. On Thursday 7th, however, they were locked out and despite their clear willingness to work on all non-Grunwick mail, the postal system of NW2 was closed down. By this time the Cricklewood men had received over 200 telegrams and numerous other messages of support.[27]

Over the following weekend, two significant events occurred. Tom Jackson was upset by being heckled during a TUC demonstration in Manchester against racialism on 10 July for his role at Grunwick's. The Grunwick strikers disassociated themselves from this.[28] Meanwhile the press was reporting that the action of the postmen was 'increasingly squeezing the Company'. Under strong pressure, according to his own account from Tory MP John Gorst, Ward arranged for bags of mail to be taken from his factory at dead of night, processed by 250 NAFF supporters and then posted at various places around the country.[29] Meanwhile on Monday 11 July the largest of all the mass pickets, estimated at over 18,000, kept out the blackleg bus until noon. Those involved were then led away to an even larger demonstration organised by the TUC. On the following day the High Court ruled against Grunwick and in favour of ACAS in the latest court case brought by the company. While this was happening more and more sorting offices throughout the country were finding Grunwick mail. Members were instructed by General Secretary Tom Jackson to hold them until an Executive discussion on Tuesday 12 July. At this meeting Tom Jackson proposed to declare the Cricklewood action official, but after a lengthy and complicated debate, this was lost by 13 votes to 11, and by 14 votes to 11 it was agreed to tell members to handle all mail normally. On 13 July a Special Branch Circular instructed all members to this effect. The Cricklewood men continued to call for support. A delegation of them were summoned to UPW Headquarters and 'given a lecture on their conduct'.[30] However on the next day, Friday 15th, they picked up the first of the hardship money that had been agreed by the Executive, and on Saturday 16th the Branch voted 70 to 8 to continue their action.

During the following week the intensity of feeling began to diminish somewhat as the Court of Enquiry heard the case of Grunwick management and strikers. One thing established at this time was that it was no easy matter to take legal action against Post Office workers. On 14 July the High Court refused to allow local businessmen to collect their mail from the Cricklewood Office, and on the 18th even Lord Denning and the Court of Appeal could not find a legal basis to compel the Post Office to produce the mail. A few days later, on 26 July, Lord Denning's original judgement on the South Africa boycott was overturned in the House of Lords. At this point, according to one account, 'the winding down of the mass picket exposed the postal workers'.[31] In fact the only real effect of the action in support of the strikers at this stage was that no mail was being handled in NW2. UPW officers acted during the week to stop various boycotts and other unofficial actions against Grunwick mail at London offices, including WCDO, ECDO and the Foreign Section in the old King Edward Building next to St Martin's-le-Grand. Elsewhere it was reported that Grunwick mail was being misdirected and delayed, but this was more difficult to deal with. On Friday 22 July, the Cricklewood men received their second hardship payment. Efforts to get another meeting away from the scene of the strike itself so they could be told the views of the Executive were not successful.

On that same afternoon, UPW Headquarters was informed that the Post Office was considering a request from Grunwick to allow them to remove their mail from the Cricklewood office. No objection was raised, and on Saturday afternoon 23 July, sixty-three bags of Grunwick mail, stuck there since the boycott began, were removed. The Post Office then communicated individually with the Cricklewood men urging them to return to normal working. This was supported in a statement in the radio news by Norman Stagg, who was now Acting General Secretary in the absence of Tom Jackson on holiday. Perhaps not surprisingly, the Cricklewood men were not pleased with what had transpired. Branch Chairman Colin Maloney was quoted as being 'disgusted' about the Union leaders 'acting behind the membership's back without consultation'. 'They think all they need to do', he said, was 'whistle and we'll come, well they can think again.' A number of bad-tempered telephone conversations took place between Norman Stagg and various of the officers of the Branch who were meeting on Sunday 24th. The next day the Branch voted against listening to the case Norman Stagg wanted to present to it. Colin Maloney described as 'provocative' his statement that any individual returning to work on the Post Office's terms would be acting according to the Union's rules and Conference decisions. The meeting voted unanimously to return to work but not to handle Grunwick mail. They were once again locked out as a result.[32]

At this stage a battle of wills developed between the Union's Executive and the Cricklewood men. At a time when the temperature in the strike itself was diminishing, and the effect of events at the sorting office had been reduced almost to nothing, increasing pressure was brought upon the Cricklewood men to reverse their attitude. A lengthy Special Branch Circular on 25 July from Norman Stagg said that they could no longer be regarded as locked out, and that they could not discriminate against any Post Office customer 'without exposing the Union's funds to risk to the extent that the whole fabric of our organisation is at risk'. A meeting of LDC '3' attended by Norman Stagg on the following day accepted this argument and a resolution deploring the attitude of the Executive was withdrawn. Half a dozen or so London offices who voted to act in various ways against Grunwick mail were also dissuaded from doing so by UPW officers. The Executive met all day on Wednesday 27 July, and voted by 17 to 2 to suspend the hardship payments to the Cricklewood men. All members were contacted individually and asked to attend on Friday 29th for the last payment 'at a central point outside Grunwick strike head-quarters', which was to be the Conway Hall, Red Lion Square. Norman Stagg was reported to have told the locked-out men that not only had they now lost their hardship money, but they could be expelled from the Union, sacked, and deprived of their pension rights. They then voted by 49 votes to 46 to return to work on the terms dictated by Post Office management and the Union Executive. As always in the past, they all agreed to be bound by the majority, however small.

On that same Friday 29 July, two other significant events were occurring in other parts of London. At the Trades Hall in Brent the strikers, under threat of reductions in strike pay, were persuaded by APEX leaders to withdraw support for mass picketing. At the Court of Appeal, Lord Denning ruled in favour of Grunwick's claim that earlier recommendations from ACAS for recognition of APEX were invalid on the grounds that blacklegs to whom access had not been granted were not consulted. There might be some doubt as to the real effect of these discussions. However, because of their clear symbolic impact, there was a good deal of justice in the strikers' feeling that they had lived through a 'Black Friday'. Over the following weeks the level of support for the strike gradually diminished, though there was a large and peaceful 'Day of Action' on 9 August. The Scarman Report on 25 August proposed partial re-instatement of the strikers and was contemptuously brushed aside by Ward and his associates, including now the entire Conservative front bench and most of Fleet Street. There was a particularly vicious attack from Sir Keith Joseph, at the time head of policy formation for the Conservatives.

Although a rather weak resolution was passed at the TUC on 6 September calling for support for the Grunwick strikers, there was serious discussion between strike leaders and the TUC about efforts to cut off supplies. However, these largely foundered on the determination of all union leaders, not just from the UPW, to avoid any breach of the law. On 28 September only two members of the Union's Executive voted for further action if they could get more financial support from the TUC. The TUC General Secretary did issue a statement which called for support, but stopped short at condoning illegal action. This however was insufficient to produce any real results and mass picketing began again in October. On 7 November, the 'Day of Reckoning', there were 8,000 pickets. They were violently attacked by police who injured 243 of them in scenes which have been recorded for posterity on film. The reason for such actions is not easy to decide, except perhaps that the police now knew they would be certain of uncritical support for whatever they did from most of Fleet Street and all of the Conservative Opposition. On 22 November four of the leading strikers took up positions on the steps of the TUC in a hunger strike. They were punished by APEX by having their strike pay stopped for a time, and by the TUC General Council on 27 November by a statement that there was nothing further they could do. On 14 December the House of Lords ruled in support of Ward's refusal to canvass its workforce, and against ACAS. The strikers were not able to keep up the same level of activity over the winter, but in the end they were compelled to call off the struggle on 15 July 1978, after 690 days.

It was now almost a year since the Cricklewood men had returned. They did not do so with good grace. A number of subsidiary disputes arose, sometimes spreading to other offices and involving arguments about agreements that existed for dealing with re-directed mail or backlogs. Some further harsh words were exchanged within the Union in public, and no doubt harsher still in private.[33] Three days before Christmas, a disciplinary sub-committee of the Executive handed down a total of £1,300 in fines to seven responsible LDC officers who had breached the rules in the summer – John Taylor was to pay £500 and Derek Walsh £300. An appeal was launched in the following February to pay the fines supported by, amongst others, twenty-one Labour MPs. When the issue was discussed at the UPW Annual Conference in May 1978, Derek Walsh from the LDC '3' and Colin Maloney explained that they thought the action of the EC had been 'morally wrong' and complained that they had not had the opportunity to present their point of view before the membership. They said that the 1977 Conference decisions could not be regarded as binding in the changed situation in which they had acted. Colin Maloney said, 'we did what we believed to be right, and no one can take that away from us'. Furthermore:

It's no good going back to our Branches and saying that Cricklewood was wrong – they were against rules. There were no rules for George Ward. He made his own rules and the NAFF financed them . . . Had you been in the same situation as Cricklewood, passing the Grunwick people on the picket line every day, seeing them standing there looking for support, you would have done the same as we did.

Some representatives of smaller offices spoke in an opposite sense, but the strongest defence of the Executive decision came from Tom Jackson, arguing the case not simply on the basis of the legal and other threats against the Union, but also on the decisions it had taken:

One of the penalties of leadership . . . was to make difficult and hard decisions . . . Decisions you are not proud of, but decisions which have to be taken in the interests of your own Union.

The Executive view was supported by 9,694 to 9,033 votes. A further resolution condemning the hardship payments to the Cricklewood men was defeated. A resolution which condemned the TUC for its 'lack of action . . . in organising practical aid from affiliated Unions' was carried.[34]

This was not the end of the matter for the UPW. During the course of 1978 efforts were made by a number of back-bench Labour MPs to introduce measures to prevent employers and courts from threatening the work of ACAS. Norman

Buchan, MP, also introduced a Post Office Workers' (Industrial Action) Bill in February 1978. This would have allowed industrial action in disputes where the Post Office itself was involved, though not, significantly, in such cases as the South Africa and Grunwick boycotts. However, as in 1930 with the Trade Disputes Act, a Labour Government relying on Liberal support could not expect to carry measures favourable to the trade union movement. Thus in the following July Norman Buchan's Bill, as well as two others aiming to clarify the Employment Protection Act, were obstructed by the action of Conservative MPs.[35] When the Conservatives came to government in 1979, the possibility of changing the position with regard to industrial action in the Post Office was lost. The British Telecommunications Act of 1981, despite intense lobbying at the time of its passing, was not used to clarify the position in any way.

INTO THE SECOND CENTURY

The drama surrounding the Grunwick strike, and especially the events of the summer of 1977, brought the UPW into public prominence greater than at any time since the 1971 strike. These developments had causes and consequences of considerable long-term signficance for the UPW as well as for its successors. However, it should not be forgotten that there were also more humdrum negotiations taking place at the same time on wages and conditions which in their own way were not without long-term effects.

During the latter period of Labour Government from 1977–9, one of the few surviving parts of the Social Contract was the industrial democracy experiment in the Post Office. The most important aspects of this were brought to an end by the Conservatives. During these two years the UPW continued to support the Government's incomes policy. As already indicated, they accepted a settlement at the end of 1976 exactly in line with the 5 per cent limit of Phase II of Government incomes policy. Phase III came into operation in the summer of 1977, but without agreement with the TUC. This was for 10 per cent wage increases, plus productivity deals. When the UPW Conference discussed wages that May, efforts to repudiate the Social Contract were defeated. However, various demands were formulated beyond the Government guidelines, including calls for threshold payments and for further consolidation. Later in the year the Union Executive approached the Post Office with a set of productivity proposals as well as a call for wage increases designed to allow for the consolidation of threshold payments. These amounted to 7 per cent payable on 1 November 1977, and were apart from any other payments. This was rejected by the Post Office so the Union took the issue up directly with Employment Minister Eric Varley, but to no avail. On 13 February 1978 the Executive decided to cut its losses and to submit a general 10 per cent claim. This was obtained without much further difficulty.[36]

When delegates came to discuss the issue of pay at the UPW Annual Conference in May 1978, they again rejected efforts to break away from incomes policy. However, they wanted significant increases including equality between postal officers and telecommunications clerical officers, as well as a general public sector alliance on wages. The long debate did not make it easy to decide what the Union should do. Soon afterwards the Labour Government's Phase III of a 5 per cent maximum on wage increases was rejected by the TUC, and this was followed by a 'winter of discontent' as workers in hospitals and elsewhere struggled to defeat it. For the UPW it was necessary to hold a Special Conference on wages in Bournemouth in December 1978 to work out a claim for an 8 per cent overall increase, a three hours reduction in the working week, and a new threshold agreement. The Union once again argued for the consolidation of all supplements into basic pay, now with the support of the Post Office itself. However, when it came to the complex negotiations in the early part of 1979, the Post Office was prepared to concede 8 per cent but not the escalation clauses or the shorter working week. On 23 March 1979, the EC decided that this was the most that could be obtained and presented it to the membership. However, they had miscalculated the mood, and the proposals were rejected by a 6 to 1 margin. Later a further 1 per cent increase was obtained as an interim settlement from 1 January, and full consolidation was finally achieved in the latter part of 1979, worth over 5 per cent on pay. Also a further 7 per cent was negotiated from 1 July 1979 and 3½ per cent from 1 January 1980 in return for moving the review date to 1 April. There was a separate agreement for postal officers and postal assistants finally confirmed early in 1980.[37]

However, by this time the result of the May 1979 General Election had cast a baleful shadow over the Post Office and all who worked there. Ever since then the threat to erode the monopoly in telecommunications and to some extent also of posts has had a significant influence on every aspect of the development of both sectors, including the wages field. The apparent abandonment of the various forms of wage control created some new uncertainties in bargaining but did not abolish the 'going rate' or the pressure on wages, now intensified by frightening unemployment levels. The separation of posts and telecommunications bargaining was an inevitable result also of the new Government's policies, and may well have long-term consequences that cannot now be foreseen.

One other recent trend which will certainly be of significance in the future is the increasing effort to push up labour productivity in both of the new corporations. New machinery in posts has come since the days of Bevins and Ron Smith, but not at the speed many thought possible. It came into bargaining with the somewhat ineffectual Mails Operating Savings Scheme in the mid-1970s. However, after the great failure of the mails system in 1979 and the Monopolies Commission Report of 1980, the Union has entered productivity bargaining in the form of the Improved Working Methods Scheme which seems likely to have both a serious effect on working practices, and to lead to big increases in earnings. The working arrangements of the post-war boom are now beginning to change. One example of this was the effort made in the late 1970s to reduce working hours – the first such serious campaign for forty years. The abolition of Sunday collections in 1977 initially opposed and later supported by the Union indicated a new form of operation in the Post Office, and there was even talk in 1979 of abolishing Saturday services also. Productivity discussion in telecommunications has a longer history, but probably has achieved less for UPW/UCW members, at least since the time that the numbers of telephonists began to fall significantly in the 1970s. Nevertheless, new ideas have come since 1978, and no doubt the great scale of technological expansion in this field will open new possibilities for the future.

The period since the 1979 General Election saw changes in attitudes and institutions perhaps greater than ever before. The UPW became the UCW in June 1980. In October 1981 the separate Post Office and British Telecom began. For the new UCW, probably more important than the change of name were changes in the historic forms of the Union, with new regional structures and greater powers for separate Executives covering posts and telecommunications. New structures for co-operating with other unions in dealing with both employers have come into being and many and varied forms of possible amalgamation or joint working are in constant discussion for the future. Steps which might once have been feared as a threat to amalgamation are seen now as a means of dealing with new challenges. At the same time those who led the Union in the 1960s and 1970s have retired. Norman Stagg ended his period as Deputy General Secretary in 1980, Fred Moss retired as General Treasurer in 1981 and Tom Jackson as General Secretary in 1982. Soon an entirely new group of leaders will face many problems unknown to their predecessors.

It is impossible not to end without wondering what all the generations that went before would think of the story that has been told in this book. Would Robert Grapes from the 1840s or William Booth from the 1870s have thought that their blighted hopes were eventually fulfilled? If William Clery could have looked forward from 1891, or even Edith Howse from 1921 what would they have thought of the great changes in technology and organisation since that time? They would all undoubtedly have been shocked at first by the great machinery of the Union, with all the full-time officials, the great national strikes, and even representatives on the Board. The pioneers would undoubtedly be hard pressed to recognise in the modern UCW the great mansion that has been built on top of the foundations they laid and with the bricks they provided. Yet their bricks can be seen in the structure still, overlaid by dust and paint, yet essential for its maintenance and development. A century after the Postal Telegraph Clerks set up the first permanent organisation in 1881 their experiences are with their successors still.

As the last words of this book are being written, members of the Union and its leaders are having to cope anew with technological change, economic depression and mass unemployment. These phenomena confront our generation in ways which often look very different and more intense than before. Members of the UCW – like all those in the working-class movement – will need again all the sacrifice, resource-fulness and courage that was displayed by the dead generations who have made them what they are.

NOTES

1   *Post*, 13 November 1971, 11 November 1972, 28 February 1974, 4 January 1976, Special Issue.
2   *Post* (28 August 1971). For UPW pleas at the 1972 TUC see *Post*, 19 August 1972.
3   *Post* (12 December 1972).
4   *Post*, March 1973, p. 19, April 1973.
5   UPW (1973); Pay Board (1973).
6   *Post*, 1974 CS, p. 4.
7   *Post*, 27 October 1973, 16 November, 15 December.
8   Post Office Report and Accounts 1973–4 (HMSO 1974).
9   *Post*, 25 February 1974, p. 4.
10 *Post* (17 January 1974).
11 *Post* (18 January 1975).
12 *Post*, 31 July, 24 August 1974.
13 *Post*, 30 November 1974, 18 March, 31 March 1975.
14 *Post*, 31 January 1975, 28 December 1974.
15 See PP 1974–5 XXXI, Attack on Inflation.
16 *Post*, 9 August 1975, 1975 CS, pp. 14–16, 15 November 1975, p. 8, 1 January 1976, pp. 4–5.
17 *Post*, 31 August, 31 December 1976, 31 January 1977.
18 *Post*, 30 June 1978, p. 22.
19 The fullest account is in Dromey and Taylor (1978). See also Rogaly (1977) and Ward (1978) for the employers' viewpoint. Scarmen Report is also of interest as is Durkin (1978).
20 Scarman Report, pp. 6ff.; Dromey and Taylor (1978), pp. 51, 69–70; TUC 1976 Report, p. 466; Rogaly (1977), p. 93.
21 Ward (1978), pp. 54, 82; Scarman Report, p. 12; *Times* (5 November 1976).
22 Dromey and Taylor (1978), p. 98; *Daily Telegraph* (16 December 1976).
23 Rogaly (1977), pp. 152–9; Dromey and Taylor (1978), p. 82.
24 *Post*, 30 June 1977, pp. 25–8.
25 Dromey and Taylor (1978), pp. 114–15; UPW SBC 17/77.
26 Ward (1978), p. 86; *Financial Times* (29 June 1977), *Sunday Times* (3 July), *Daily Mail* (28 July), *Daily Telegraph* (30 June).
27 SBC 17 and 18/77, ECM AD 706/77.
28 *Post* (31 July 1977).
29 *Sunday Times* (10 July 1977); Ward (1978), pp. 86ff.
30 ECM AD 751/77 where Norman Stagg gives a full account of relations between Cricklewood men and Union leaders at this stage. See also his (1977) article.
31 Dromey and Taylor (1978), p. 165.
32 *Sunday Telegraph* (24 July 1977), *Guardian* (25 July).
33 *Times* (3, 6 August 1977), *Guardian* (9, 10 August); ECM AD 802/and 833/77.
34 *Post*, 30 June 1978, pp. 7–10.
35 *Post*, 30 September 1977, 31 January, 28 February 1978; *Financial Times* (15 July 1978).
36 *Post*, 30 June 1977, pp. 15–21, 17 November, 31 December 1977, 28 February, 3 April 1978.
37 *Post*, 30 June 1978, pp. 11–12, 31 December 1978, 31 March, 7 April, 10 May, 30 June, 15 September 1979, 19 January 1980.

Sources and Bibliography

I MAJOR ARCHIVES AND COLLECTIONS

The chief materials on which this book is based are to be found in the following locations:

1 UCW House, Crescent Lane, London SW4
The archives of the predecessors of the Union of Post Office Workers are arranged in a series of sequences generally by organisations and are referred to here as R or (UCW)R.

The files of the UPW/UCW are kept in the Research Department, arranged by a special numerical sequence. Many of them, especially of historical interest, are now on microfilm. They are referred to here as F or (UCW)F.

The UCW Library in the Research Department contains much relevant primary and secondary material including many of the periodicals of the predecessors of the UPW, some of the secessionists from it, and also the minutes from 1919 of the Executive Committee of the UPW/UCW (here referred to as ECM with AD, or Associated Documents from 1958), Branch Circulars (BC), *Branch Officers Bulletin (BOB)*, Whitley Council minutes, and much else besides.

2 Post Office Records, St Martin's-le-Grand, London EC1A 1LP
Referred to here as POR, this building contains the basic records of the old Post Office, which were all looked at before the two parts were torn asunder in 1981. This archive is arranged in a numerical series described in detail in Clinton (1981), p. 99.

3 Morten Postal History Collection (MC), Bruce Castle Museum, Tottenham, London N17
This collection, also described in more detail in Clinton (1981), was a private collection bought by the UPW in the 1920s and now on permanent loan to the London Borough of Harringay. It contains material on every aspect of the Post Office (including trade unionism) especially in the nineteenth century.

4 Nuffield College Library, Oxford
Useful in particular for the Cole Collection covering guild socialism and related matters.

5 Labour Party Archives, Walworth Road, London SE17
The Barber Collection (BAR) is valuable for aspects of the socialist and trade union movement in the 1880s.

6 The Library, Trades Union Congress, Great Russell Street, London WC1
Useful mainly on the TUC itself. Also has some primary material used here, largely duplicated elsewhere.

7 Modern Records Centre, The University of Warwick, Coventry CV4 7AC
Contains some unique documents from secessionist bodies, much more on organisations of supervisors and officials as well as the POEU. Also has a large number of duplicates of pre-UCW documents.

8 Manchester City Archives, St Peter's Square, Manchester 2
Fawcett Papers include a little about women in the nineteenth-century Post Office.

9 Lord's Day Observance Society, 47 Parish Lane, London SE20
Useful minutes and records.

10   Burns Papers in British Library in British Museum Additional Manuscripts

II OFFICIAL PUBLICATIONS

These provide a major source for the activities and developments of the Post Office when it was a department of state – and since.

Most of the official publications used in this book are to be found in the bound volumes of the Parliamentary Papers series, here generally referred to as PP followed by the parliamentary year and the volume number. Some of the publications in this series are simply given House of Commons session numbers, and some have command numbers which have been arranged in a number of sets (without prefix from 1833–69, C from 1870–99, Cd from 1900–18, Cmd from 1919–56 and Cmnd from 1956 to the present). Forms of reference used in the Notes in this book are generally those in which the relevant documents are most easily available. Thus the nineteenth-century references are always to Parliamentary Paper volumes. In more recent years command numbers may be used because they are often referred to elsewhere simply in this form, and from 1977–8 this appears to be the only kind of citation used. For ease of reference they are almost all listed under PP here.

Some heavily used documents in these series, notably the reports of the Postmaster General/Post Office are not given by their PP or command or session numbers since they vary so much and have normally been used from sets collected together at UCW House or the Post Office Archives. Major inquiries and commissions are referred to by the name of their chairman and are listed under Books, Pamphlets and Articles with a cross reference in the PP series. Individual Stationery Office publications not in any of these series appear in the list of Books and Pamphlets.

Parliamentary Papers (PP)

1806 VII	Report of the Commissioners Appointed by Act of Parliament to Enquire into the Fees, Gratuities, Perquisites and Emoluments, etc
1807 II	*see Palmer Report*
1817 XV	Accounts Relating to the Establishment of the Post Office
1828 V	Second Report of the Select Committee on Public Income and Expenditure
1828 XVI	List of Public Offices in the United Kingdom in 1797
1829	Reports of the Commissioners of Inquiry into the Collection and Management of the Revenues Arising in Ireland and Great Britain
1829 XI	18th Report on the Post Office Revenue in the United Kingdom
1829 XII	19th Report on Ireland
1830 XIV	20th Report on Scotland, 21st on England, Twopenny Post Office
1834 VI	Report from the Select Committee Appointed to Examine the Papers Respecting Sinecure Offices
1835 XLVIII	Commissioners to inquire into the mode of conducting the Post Office – Treasury minutes of appointment, and Report regarding the contract for mail-coaches. A Return of the Establishment of the General Post Office of the United Kingdom
1836 XXVIII	Fourth, Fifth and Sixth Reports of the Commissioners appointed to inquire into the management of the Post Office Department
1837 XXXIV, i	Seventh, Eighth and Ninth Reports of the Commissioners appointed to inquire into the management of the Post Office Department.
1837 L	Copies of correspondence between the Lords Commissioners of Her Majesty's Treasury and the Postmaster General on the subject of the detention of letters for the county on the Lord's Day
1837–8 XVI	Report from the Select Committee on Railroad Communications
1837–8 XX	Reports from the Select (Wallace) Committee on Postage
1837–8 XXXV	Tenth Report of the Commissioners appointed to inquire into the management of the Post Office Department

1898 XII	Report from the Select Committee on Telephones
1898 LII	Return Relating to the Pay of Sorters, Telegraphists, Sorting Clerks and Telegraphists, etc in the years 1872, 1881, 1890 and 1897
1898 LVII	Post Office Estimates
1899 LXXVII	Return of Appointments to Class I Clerkships in the Civil Service, 1886–1898
1903 XXXIII	Royal Commission on Civil Service Superannuation
1904 XXXIII	*see* Bradford
1905 VII	Report from the Select Committee on the Post Office (Telephone Agreement)
1905 XLIV	Memorandum to the Postmaster General, dated 24 March 1905, Setting Forth Changes about to be Made in the Wages of Certain Classes of Post Office Servants
1906 XII	Minutes of Evidence taken before the (Hobhouse) Select Committee on Post Office Servants
1907 VII	Report of the (Hobhouse) Select Committee on Post Office Servants
1908 XXXV	Second Report of the Departmental Committee on Industrial Diseases
1911 XXIX	Reports of the Standing Committee on Boy Labour in the Post Office (see also 1913 XXXVIII, 1914 XLIV and 1914–16 XXXII)
1911 XLI	Report of the Departmental Committee on Telegraphists Cramp
1911 L	Report of the Committee of Medical Officers Appointed to Inquire into the Conditions of Working of Telephonists
1912–13 IX	Report from the (Holt) Select Committee on Post Office Servants
1913 X-XIII	Evidence taken before the (Holt) Select Committee on Post Office Servants
1913 XVIII	*see* Macdonald Third Report
1914 XVI	*see* Macdonald Fourth Report
1914–16 XXXII	*see* Gibb First Report
1916 XIV	*see* Gibb Second Report
1918 VII	Report of the Proceedings of the Conciliation and Arbitration Board for Government Employees for 1917 (Cd 9017)
1918 X	Second Report of the Committee of the Ministry of Reconstruction on the Relations between Employers & Employed etc (Cd 9002)
1918 XVI	Civil Service Estimates
1919 XI	Report on the Application of the Whitley Report to the Administrative Departments of the Civil Service (Cmd 9)
1920 XXVII	Report of the Select Committee on Telephone Charges (HC Paper 247, 1920)
1921 VII,	Report from the Select Committee on the Telephone Service
1922 VI	(HC Paper 191, 1921 and 54, 1922)
1922 IX	*see* Geddes
1924–5 IX	*see* Blanesborough
1928 VII	Report of the Board of Enquiry Appointed by the Prime Minister to Investigate Certain Statements affecting Civil Servants
1928 XII	*Postal Cheque System*, March 1928 (Cmd 3151)
	Committee on the Inland Telegraph Service (Cmd 3058), reprinted in full in *Post*, 31 March 1928
1930–1 X	*see* Tomlin
1931–2 XII	*see* Bridgeman
1938–9 VII	Report of the Select Committee on Estimates (1938–9) (HC 145)
1940–1 VIII	Price Stabilisation and Industrial Policy (White Paper) (Cmd 6294)
1945–6 XI	Royal Commission on Equal Pay, Report (October 1946) (Cmd 6937)
1947–8 XXII	Statement on Personal Incomes, Costs and Prices (February 1948) (Cmd 7321)

1948–9 XII	Report of the Mastermann Committee on the Political Activities of Civil Servants
1950 IV	Fourth Report from the Select Committee on Estimates . . . The Post Office (July 1950) (HC 130)
1951–2 XVIII	Report of the Post Office (Departmental Classes) Reorganisation Committee (February 1952) (Cmd 8470)
1952–3 XXII	Report of the Committee on the Political Activities of Civil Servants
1955–6 XI	*see* Priestley
1955–6 XXVI	Report on Post Office Development and Finance (October 1955) (Cmd 9576)
1957–8 XXIV	Full Automation of the Telephone System (November 1957) (Cmnd 303)
1959–60 XXVII	The Status of the Post Office (March 1960) (Cmnd 989)
1960–1 XX	Control of Public Expenditure (July 1961) (Cmnd 1432)
1960–1 XXVII	The Financial and Economic Obligations of the Nationalised Industries (April 1961) (Cmnd 1337)
1960–1 XXVII	Memorandum on the Post Office Bill, Post Office Act, 1961 (December 1960) (Cmnd 1247)
1963–4 XXVI	The Inland Telephone Service in an Expanding Economy (November 1963) (Cmnd 2221)
1964–5 XXX	A Post Office Giro (August 1965) (Cmnd 2751)
1964–5 XXX	The National Plan (September 1965) (Cmnd 2764)
1966–7 XVII	First Report from the Select Committee on Nationalised Industries. The Post Office. Vol. I February 1967; Vol. II November 1967 (HC 340)
1966–7 LIX	Reorganisation of the Post Office (March 1967) (Cmnd 3233)
1967–8 XVIII	The Civil Service. Report of the Committee 1966–68 (June 1968) (Cmnd 3638)
1967–8 XXVII	National Board for Prices and Incomes. Report No. 58, *Post Office Charges* (March 1968) (Cmnd 3574)
1967–8 XXVIII	National Board for Prices and Incomes. Report No. 83 on Job Evaluation (September and December 1968) (Cmnd 3772, 3772-I)
1967–8 XXXIX	Nationalised Industries. A Review of Economic and Financial Objectives (November 1967) (Cmnd 3437)
1973–4 XIV	POUNC Annual Report 1973–4 (July 1974) (HC 343)
1974–5 XXX	POUNC Annual Report 1974–5 (December 1975) (HC 2)
1974–5 XXXI	The Attack on Inflation (July 1975) (Cmnd 6151)
1975–6 XXXIV	Second Report from the Select Committee on Nationalised Industries. 'The Post Office's Letter Post Services' (December 1975) (HC 73)
1975–6 XXXV	Fifth Report from the Select Committee on Nationalised Industries Service 1975–76: Cable and Wireless Ltd (May 1976) (HC 472)
1976–7 XVI	*see* Bullock
1976–7 XXXIX	*see* Carter
1977–8	The Post Office (July 1978) (Cmnd 7292)
1977–8	The Nationalised Industries (HM Treasury, April 1978) (Cmnd 7131)
1977–8	*see also* Scarman
1979–80	The Monopolies and Mergers Commission, *The Inner London Letter Post* (March 1980) (HC 515)

III POST OFFICE PUBLICATIONS

The first Annual Report of the Postmaster General came out in published form in 1854, and then each year until 1918. They were replaced by Commercial Accounts which appeared annually until 1939. These resumed from 1947–8, and from 1957–8 were restyled Report and Commercial Accounts in which form they continued until 1979–80 when they were split for the two sides of the operation. These are not separately listed.

Besides those contained in archival collections, some other Post Office publications have been cited. These include Green Papers – 47 pamphlets published by the Post Office between 1933 and 1939 – which are listed by author in the list of Books and Pamphlets.

Post Office, *Information Supplied by the Secretary to the Post Office* (1912). (Bound volume presented to the Holt Committee)
Post Office, Report on the Present System of Regionalisation in the Post Office by D. O. Lumley (1950) Vol. 1, p. 12
Post Office, *Report of the Advisory Committee on the Inland Telegraph Service* (HMSO July 1958)
Post Office, Telephone Service and the Customer (HMSO, 1959)

IV PERIODICAL SERIES

Some of the main periodical series used in this book are listed below with comments on the history of the most important of them.

B-H: Bee-Hive (newspaper) (1861?–1878)
BOB: Branch Officials Bulletin, published by the UPW since 1963
CC: Counter Clerk, journal of the secessionist ACC, October 1924–March 1947
Central London Review (1906–19): paper of the secessionist Central London Postmen's Association
Civilian: general paper for civil servants – later *New Civilian*
Controlling Officers Journal (COJ): journal of the Postal Telegraph and Telephone Controlling Officers Association
CSG: Civil Service Gazette (1853–1926)
EHR: English Historical Review
Engineering Officer
Gazette: produced by the Northern Ireland Postal Clerks. Issues covering 1926–45 are bound together at UCW House and occasional extracts appear in other journals
Manchester Postman: see *Postman, The*
Mets Journal: produced by the Metropolitan Districts branch of the UPW
MR View: see *Postman, The*
New Civilian: see *Civilian*
PA: Postmen's Alarm (1930–33), journal of the secessionist Postmen's Association/National Association of Postmen
P&TO: Journal of the secessionist National Association of Postal and Telegraph Officers, 1947–53
P&TR: Postal and Telegraph Record (1914–19), official organ of the P&TA incorporating the *Telegraph Chronicle* and the *Postal Clerks Herald*
PCH: Postal Clerks Herald (1898–1914), official organ of UKPCA, not a direct continuation of the *Postal Journal* but soon replacing it. Merged with the *Telegraph Chronicle* to form the *Postal and Telegraph Record*
PG: Postman's Gazette (1st series published by Postmen's Union 1889–90, 2nd series by the PF 1892–1919)
PJa: Postal Journal (1886?–99), until 1893 called the *Post Office Journal* and then in its new title and masthead became 'Organ of the Postal Clerks of the United Kingdom', associated with the UKPCA. In July 1896 the numbering changed and it was described as 'Representing the Major Establishment of the British Postal Service'. Collapsed soon after the setting up of the *Postal Clerks Herald*
PJb: Postmen's Journal (1933–44), published by the secessionist National Association of Postmen
Post Office Journal: original name of the journal associated with the UKPCA. Began some time after 1886 and became *Postal Journal* in 1893: *see PJa*

Post, The: periodical successively of the Fawcett Association (from 1890), the UPW and the UCW

Postal Advocate (1905–19): copies from July 1908 to December 1919 are in the BL

Postal Porter (1902–5): journal of the London Postal Porters Association

Postal Porters Journal (1895–1900): paper of the LPPA

Postal Telegraph (1914–19): journal of the P&TCA

Postman, The: later *Manchester Postman*, continuing as *MR View* to the present day

Postmaster, The

POEU Journal (1919–)

PSG: Postal Service Gazette (May 1888–June 1889)

PT: Postal Telegraphist (March 1921–April 1947), originally the journal of the secessionist National Federation of Postal and Telegraph Clerks, but by the mid-1930s only of the Sorters' Guild, part of the then defunct Federation

PTSG: Postal and Telegraph Service Gazette (1887–8?), merged with *The Telegraphist*

Red Tape: journal of the CPSA and its predecessors

Review, The (1905–26): journal of the Sorter Tracers Association

SB: Strike Bulletin (1971), UPW publication

SMLG: Saint Martin's-le-Grand (1890–1933): succeeded *Blackfriars Magazine* (published by the Post Office, 1885–9) and replaced by the *Post Office Magazine* in 1934

Summary: The Post Office: An Historical Summary (HMSO, 1911)

Supervising

TC: The Telegraph Chronicle and Civil Service Recorder (1893–1914), official organ of the PTCA merging with the *Postal Clerks Herald* in 1914

Telegraph Journal (November 1889–March 1893): PTCA journal replaced by *Telegraph Chronicle*

Telegraphist: The Telegraphist (1883–8), associated with the PTCA and apparently ceased publication as a result

Telephonist, The: produced by the National Guild of Telephonists from 1929 apparently to December 1970

TPWG: Temporary Postal Workers Gazette (1916–20), originally *TSA Gazette* from November 1915 to June 1916

Tracers Budget: a copy for 1894 is bound with an 1895 volume of *PG* in UCW House

Tracers Chronicle: two editions for 1900 and 1901 edited by Cheesman are in R IV/4

TSA Gazette (1915–16): became *TPWG*

TSG: Telegraph Services Gazette (PTCA May 1888–June? 1889). Incorporated the *Telegraphist* and the *Postal and Telegraph Services Gazette*. Replaced by the *Telegraph Journal*

WB: Whitley Bulletin, magazine published by the National Whitley Council staff side since 1920

V BOOKS, PAMPHLETS AND ARTICLES

The place of publication of all these is London unless otherwise stated.

Adams, Kathleen, 'The Union of Post Office Workers in relation to the General Strike' (unpub. paper, 1977)

Alderman, G., *The Railway Interest* (Leicester, 1973)

Alford, C. R., *The Sunday Post: A Sabbath Desecration* (1850)

'Aliquis', *Post Office Mysteries and Grievances Explained* (1868)

Allen, V. L., *Trade Unions and the Government* (1960)

Ammon, C., *The Cornering of the Civil Service, Being a Protest against the Abolition of Open Competition as a Means of Recruiting to the Post Office Service and a Comment on the Boy Labour Problem* (1911)

Andrews, Francis, *Jack and His Master: An Introduction to Democracy in Industry* (The Socialist Book Centre, 1946)

Anson, W. R., *The Laws and Customs of the Constitution*, Vol. 1 (Oxford, 1922 edn)
Armitage: Committee on the Pay of Postmen. Minutes of Evidence and Report (HMSO, 1964)
Armstrong, W., 'Whitleyism in the civil service', *Whitley Bulletin* (1969)
Ashley, M., *John Wildman, Plotter and Postmaster* (1947)
Attlee, C. R., *As It Happened* (n.d., 1954?)
Auden, W. H., 'Night Mail' (July 1935) in *The English Auden* (1977)
Austen, B., *English Provincial Posts 1633–1840: A Study Based on Kent Examples* (Chichester, 1978)
Bagwell, P. S., *The Railway Clearing House in the British Economy 1842–1922* (1968)
Bagwell, P. S., *Industrial Relations: Government and Society in Nineteenth Century Britain* (1974)
Baines, F. E., *Forty Years at the Post Office.* 2 Vols (1895a)
Baines, F. E., *On the Track of the Mail Coach* (1895b)
Baker, R. J. S., 'The postal service: a problem of identity', *Political Quarterly*, 47 (1976)
Baldwin, F. C. G., *The History of the Telephone in the United Kingdom* (1925)
Bank, J., and Jones, K. (eds), *Worker Directors Speak* (1977)
Barker, C., *The Power Game* (1972)
Batstone, E., Ferner, A., and Terry, M., *Interim Report on the Post Office Industrial Relations Experiment* (1980)
Baxter, A., 'Civil and municipal service', in Booth (1903)
Baxter, R. D., *National Income: The United Kingdom* (1868)
Bealey, Frank, *The Post Office Engineering Union: The History of the Post Office Engineers 1870–1970* (1976)
Belgrave, A. C., *Telephone Service* (POGP 37: November 1937)
Benn, A. W., *The Regeneration of Britain* (1965)
Benn, A. W., 'Why I welcome the users' council', *Labour Woman* (January 1966)
Beveridge, W., *The Public Service in War and Peace* (1920)
Bevins, R., *The Greasy Pole* (1965)
Binden, H., 'An old time punishment', *SMLG* (1907)
Binney, S. E. D., *British Public Finance and Administration* (Oxford, 1958)
Birch, T., *A Collection of State Papers of John Thurloe* (1742)
Blair, A., *The Case for Telegraph MP* (1905)
Blanesborough: Report of the Committee on the Parliamentary and other Candidatures of Crown Servants, March 1925 (Cmd 2408) (PP 1924–5 IX)
Booth, Charles (ed.), *Life and Labour of the People of London*, 2nd series, IV (1903)
Boston, S., *Women Workers in the Trade Union Movement* (1980)
Bowie, A. G., 'Women clerks in the Post Office', *SMLG* (1899)
Bowie, A. G., 'A short history of the post card', *SMLG*, X (1900)
Bowyer, P. C., 'Telegraph services: an account of discussions in the United Kingdom', *PTTI Studies* (Spring 1978)
Bradford: Committee on Post Office Wages, 1904, chaired by Sir Edward Bradford (PP 1904 XXXIII)
Brannen, P., Batstone, E., Fatchett, D. and White, P., *The Worker Directors* (1976)
Bridgeman: Report of the Committee of Enquiry into the Post Office (1932) (Cmd 4149) (PP 1931–2 XII)
Briggs, A., and Saville, J., *Essays in Labour History 1886–1923* (1971)
Brittan, S., *Steering the Economy* (1971)
Bronne, L., *La Reforme Postale en Angleterre* (Brussels, 1858)
Brown, F. J., *The Cable and Wireless Communication of the World* (1928)
Brown, K., 'Sub-postmasters: private traders or trade unionists', *British Journal of Industrial Relations* (1963)
Brown, R. G. S., and Steel, D. R., *The Administrative Process in Britain* (1979 edn)
Brown, W. J., *Whitleyism on its Trial* (n.d., 1921?)

Brown, W. J., *So Far* (1943)

Bruce, J., 'The history of our Post Office', *Notes and Queries*, I, 7, 1853

Buckley, E., and Ward, R., *Sheffield Postal History from Earliest Times to 1850* (Sheffield, 1969)

Budd, A., *The Politics of Economic Planning* (1978)

Bullock: Report of the Committee of Enquiry on Industrial Democracy (January 1977) (Cmnd 6706) (PP 1976-7 XVI)

Bullock, A., *The Life and Times of Ernest Bevin*, 2 Vols (1960)

Callaghan, J., *Whitleyism: A Study of Joint Consultation in the Civil Service* (1953)

Carey, H. S., 'Abolition of capital punishment in the Post Office', *SMLG* (1897)

Carpenter, N., *Guild Socialism* (1922)

Carter: Report of the Post Office Review Committee (July 1977) (Cmnd 6850) (PP 1976-7 XXXIX)

Carter: Appendix to the Report of the Post Office Review Committee (November 1977) (Cmnd 6954) (PP 1976-7 XXXIX)

Carter, W. G., *Post Office (London) Railway* (POGP 36: September 1937)

Central Office of Information, *A Customer Survey of the Telegram Service* (1957)

Chalmers, J. M., Mikardo, I., and Cole, G. D. H., *Consultation or Joint Management?* (1949)

Chambers, J. M., *Official Recognition, How it was Gained* (n.d.)

Chester, L., Leitch, D., and Simpson, C., *The Cleveland Street Affair* (1976)

Citrine, W., *Men and Work* (1976)

Clear, C. R., *Thomas Witherings and the Birth of the Postal Service* (POGP: 1935)

Clear, C. R., *John Palmer of Bath: Mail Coach Pioneer* (1955)

Clegg, H. A., and Adams, R., *Trade Union Education with Special Reference to the Pilot Areas* (1959)

Clegg, H. A., Fox, A., and Thompson, A. F., *A History of British Trade Unionism*, Vol. 1 (1964)

Clery, W. E., *An Exposition of the Fawcett Scheme* (1889)

Clery, W. E., *Civil Servitude, An Appeal to Public Opinion* (1892)

Clinton, A., 'A history of the salaries of the officers of the UPW' (unpub. paper, 1974)

Clinton, A., 'Education and the trade union movement: the Union of Post Office Workers, 1920-60' (unpub. paper, 1975)

Clinton, A., 'Post Office workers unions, strikes by other workers and general strike threats, 1911-25' (unpub. paper, 1976a)

Clinton, A., 'The UPW and the General Strike of 1926' (unpub. paper, 1976b)

Clinton, A., *The Trade Union Rank and File: Trades Councils in Britain 1900-40* (1977a)

Clinton, A., 'The failure of Victorian Sabbatarianism' (unpub. paper, 1977b)

Clinton, A., *Printed Ephemera* (1981)

Clinton, A., 'William Edward Clery', *Dictionary of Labour Biography*, V (1983)

Coase, R. H., 'Rowland Hill and the penny post', *Economica* (1939)

Coase, R. H., 'The postal monopoly in Great Britain: an historical survey', in Eastham (1955)

Cohen, E. W., *The Growth of the British Civil Service 1780-1939* (1941)

Cole, G. D. H., *Self-Government in Industry* (1920 edn)

Cole, G. D. H., 'Postal workers and Guild policy', *Post*, 5 November 1921

Cole, G. D. H., and Mellor, W. (eds), *Workers' Control and Self-Government in Industry* (1933)

Collins, W., 'Arbitration and Whitleyism applied in the public service', *CSG*, December 1919

Cook, C., and Ramsden, J. (eds), *By-Elections in British Politics* (1973)

Corby, M. E., *The Postal Business 1969-79: A Study in Public Sector Management* (1979)

Corfield, A. J., *Epoch in Workers' Education: A History of the Workers' Educational Trade Union Committee* (1969)

Craik, W. W., *The Central Labour College 1909-29* (1964)

Cripps, F., and Godley, W., *The Planning of Telecommunications in the United Kingdom* (Cambridge, 1978)

Crossley, W., *The Post Office: The Case for Improvement, Development and Extension as Advocated by the United Kingdom Postal Clerks' Association* (n.d., 1911?)

Crossman, R., *The Diaries of a Cabinet Minister* (1976)

Cruden, R., 'How a London postman lives', *SMLG* (1904)

Crutchley, E. T., *GPO* (Cambridge, 1938)

CSPD: *Calendar of State Papers. Domestic*, i.e. printed lists of government documents

Culley, R. S., 'The infancy of the electric telegraph', *Blackfriars Magazine*, VIII, 1889

Curran, J. W., 'The story of submarine telegraph 1880–1900', *SMLG*, X, 1900

David, E. (ed.), *Inside Asquith's Cabinet* (1977)

Davies, G., *National Giro: Modern Money Transfers* (1973)

Davin, A., 'Telegraphists and clerks', *Bulletin of the Society for the Study of Labour History*, 26, 1973

Defoe, D., *A Tour Through the Whole Island of Great Britain* (1962 edn)

Dicey, A. V., *Introduction to the Study of the Law of the Constitution* (10th edn, 1959)

DNB: *Dictionary of National Biography*

Doherty, W. C., *Mailman USA* (New York, 1960)

Donald, A. K., *Why There is Discontent in the Post Office: A Word to the British Public in Support of the Demands of the Postmen for Fair Treatment* (1890)

Donaldson, F., *The Marconi Scandal* (1962)

Dorfman, G. A., *Government Versus Trade Unions in British Politics since 1968* (1979)

Douglas, P. H., *Real Wages in the United States, 1890–1926* (New York, 1966)

Dow, J. C. R., *The Management of the British Economy 1945–60* (Cambridge, 1970)

Dromey, J., and Taylor, G., *Grunwick: The Workers' Story* (1978)

Dunlop, J. T. (ed.), *The Theory of Wage Determination* (1957)

Durkin, T., *Grunwick: Bravery and Betrayal* (1978)

Earl, R. A. J., *The Development of the Telephone in Oxford, 1877–1977* (1978)

Eastham, J. K. (ed.), *Dundee Economic Essays* (1955)

Eaton, J., and Gill, C., *The Trade Union Directory: A Guide to all TUC Unions* (1981)

Edwards, A. W., 'The telegraph service in wartime', *SMLG* (1917)

Elcho: Report upon the Post Office 1854 (PP 1854 XXVII)

Elliott, J., *Conflict or Co-operation: The Growth of Industrial Democracy* (1978)

Ellis, K., *The Post Office in the Eighteenth Century: A Study in Administrative History* (1958)

Emden, C. S., *The Civil Service and the Law of the Constitution* (1923)

Evans, D., *Women and the Civil Service* (1934)

Fels, A., *The British Prices and Incomes Board* (Cambridge, 1972)

Firth, C. H., 'Thurloe and the Post Office', *EHR*, 13, 1898

Foot, P., 'The postal workers and the Tory offensive' (*Socialist Worker*, 1971?)

Forester, T., 'Whatever happened to industrial democracy?', *New Society*, 17 July 1980

Foxell, J. T., and Spafford, A. O., *Monarchs of All They Surveyed: The Story of the Post Office Surveyors* (1952)

Garland, C. H., *Insurance Against Consumption . . . including an Historical Account of the Post Office Sanatorium Society* (1912)

Gash, N., *Politics in the Age of Peel* (1953)

Geddes: Third Report of the Committee on National Expenditure (PP 1922 IX)

Gennard, J., *Financing Strikers* (1977)

Gibb: First Report of the Committee Appointed to Examine the Issues Arising out of the Report of the Select Committee of the House of Commons on Post Office (PP 1914–16 XXXII)

Gibb: Second Report of the above Committee (PP 1916 XIV)

Gillett, E. W., *Transfer to Automatics* (POGP 29: August 1936)

Gladden, E. N., *Civil Service Staff Relationships* (1943)

Gladden, E. N., *Civil Services of the United Kingdom – 1855–1970* (1967)

Glass, S. T., *The Responsible Society: The Ideas of Guild Socialism* (1966)

Glenfield, L. J., *The Dial and the Countryside* (POGP 39: March 1938)

Gmür, F., 'The Postal Telegraph and Telephone International', *Labour World*, April 1959

Gnanapragasm, B. M., 'Industrial democracy – the Post Office experiment' (Polytechnic of Central London, BA dissertation, 1980)

Goodrich, C. L., *The Frontier of Control: A Study of British Workshop Politics* (1920)

Gosling, H., *Up and Down Stream* (1927)

Grace, P., Editorial, *Outpost* (1971)

Granville, R. K., *A Letter to the . . . Marquis of Clanricarde, Postmaster General* (1850)

Haldane, A. R. B., *Three Centuries of Scottish Posts: A Historical Summary to 1836* (Edinburgh, 1971)

Hall, C. E., *Thirty Years of Agitation: Being a Short Account of the Origin, Work and Progress of the Postal Telegraph Clerks' Association* (Liverpool, 1902)

Hanham, H. J., 'Political patronage at the Treasury', *Historical Journal*, 111 1960

Hardman: Report of the Committee (HMSO, 1971)

Harris, N., *Competition and the Corporate Society: British Conservatives, the State and Industry 1945–64* (1972)

Harris, S., *The Coaching Age* (1885)

Harrison, J. F. C., *The Early Victorian 1832–1851* (1973 edn)

Harrison, M., *Trade Unions and Labour Party since 1945* (1960)

Harrison, W., *Description of Britain* (1577)

Hatswell, R. W., 'The foundation and development of the Universal Postal Union', *SMLG*, XI, 1901

Hatswell, R. W., 'The history of street letter boxes', *SMLG*, XIII, 1903

Hay, I., *The Post Office Went to War* (1946)

Hazlett, W., 'The letter-bell', the *Mirror of Literature* (1831)

Hazlewood, A., 'Optimum pricing as applied to telephone service', *Review of Economic Studies*, 18, 1950–1

Heaton, J. H., 'Wanted! The end to political patronage', *Nineteenth Century and After*, 59, 1906

Hemmeon, J. C., *The History of the British Post Office* (Cambridge, Mass., 1912)

Herring, L. M., 'Feminism in the Post Office', *Post*, 6 August 1921

Herring, L. M., 'Women in the civil service', *Post*, 15 April 1922

Hill, C., *Sunday – Its Influence on Health and Prosperity* (1876)

Hill, L., 'Henry Fawcett as Postmaster General', *SMLG* (1909)

Hill, Rowland, *Post Office Reform: Its Importance and Practicability* (1st edn Jan., 2nd edn Feb., 3rd edn Nov. 1837)

Hill, Rowland, 'Results of the new postal arrangements', *Journal of the Statistical Society of London*, IV, 1841

Hill, R., and Hill, G. B., *The Life of Rowland Hill and the History of the Penny Postage*, 2 Vols (1880)

Hird, C., 'The struggle over £3 billion', *New Statesman*, 22 February 1980

Hobhouse: Select Committee on Post Office Servants, 1906–7, under Charles Hobhouse, MP (PP 1906 XII and 1907 VII). A volume of Appendices to the Minutes of Evidence was published by HMSO in 1907 but does not appear in the PP series

Hobhouse, H., *A Regency Survival in Clapham* (Crescent Grove (Private) Trust, 1967)

Hobsbawm, E. J., *Labouring Men, Studies in the History of Labour* (1964)

Hobson, S. G., *National Guilds: An Enquiry into the Wage System and the Way Out* (1914)

Hobson, S. G., *National Guilds and the State* (1920)

Hobson, S. G., *The House of Industry* (1931)

Hobson, S. G., *Pilgrim to the Left: Memoirs of a Modern Revolutionist* (1938)

Hodgson, E. P., 'The Federation of Post Office Supervising Officers', *Whitley Bulletin*, July 1947, pp. 104–5

Holcombe, L., *Victorian Ladies at Work* (Newton Abbot, 1973)

Holt: Select Committee on Post Office Servants, 1912–13, under R. D. Holt, MP (PP 1912–13 IX, 1913 X–XIII)

Holton, B., *British Syndicalism 1900–1914* (1976)

Horsfield, J. K., 'Post Office finance', *Lloyds Bank Review*, April 1956

Hosden, W., 'The Sunday Express delivery of letters in London', *SMLG* (1899)

Housden, J. A. J., 'Early posts in England', *EHR*, 19, 1903

Housden, J. A. J., 'The opening and detaining of letters in the post', *SMLG*, 14, 1904

Housden, J. A. J., 'The early posts and masters of the post', *SMLG*, 16, 1906

Hughes, E., 'The salaries of the excise officers and a cost of living index', *Economic History*, III, 1936

Humphreys, B. V., *Clerical Unions in the Civil Service* (Oxford, 1958)

Hunt, E. H., *Regional Wage Variations in Britain, 1850–1914* (Oxford, 1973)

Hyde, H. Montgomery, *The Cleveland Street Scandal* (1976)

Hyde, J. W., *A Hundred Years by Post* (1891)

Hyde, J. W. 'The Post Office bellman', *SMLG*, II, 1892

Hyde, J. W., *The Post in Grant and Farm* (1894)

Hyman, R., and Brough, I., *Social Values and Industrial Relations: A Study of Fairness and Equality* (Oxford, 1975)

Jackson, T., 'This was a man', *Post*, 16 August 1958

Jackson, T., 'Hope fades for one union', *Post*, June 1981

Jacobs, J., 'Sorting out the postal strike' (*Solidarity*, 1971)

Jenkins, R., *Tony Benn* (1980)

Jevons, W. S., 'On the analogy between Post Office telegraphs and other systems of conveyance of the United Kingdom, as regards government control', *Transaction of the Manchester Statistical Society* 1867 (April) 1866–7

Joyce: (Unpublished but printed) Report of the Committee chaired by H. Joyce (POR 60/91).

Joyce, H., *The History of the Post Office from its Establishment Down to 1836* (1893)

Kay, F. G., *The Royal Mail* (1951)

Kellner, P., and Crowther Hunt, Lord, *The Civil Servants: An Enquiry into Britain's Ruling Class* (1980)

Kent, W., *John Burns: Labour's Lost Leader* (1950)

Kerr, C., 'Wage relationships: the comparative impact of market and power forces', in Dunlop (1957)

Kiernan, E. J., *Arthur J. Penty: His Contribution to Social Thought* (Washington, 1941)

Kieve, J., *The Electric Telegraph: A Social and Economic History* (Newton Abbot, 1973)

Knowles, K. G. J. C., and Robertson, D. J., 'Differences between the wages of skilled and unskilled workers, 1880–1950', *Bulletin of the Oxford Institute of Statistics*, 13, 1951

Lascelles, G., 'Henry Cecil Raikes', *Post*, 15 November 1930

Lascelles, G., 'The Jubilee of the UKPCA', *Post*, 5 December 1936

Lasko, R., and Gennard, J., 'The impact of the 1971 postal dispute on industrial strikers in the Union of Post Office Workers: Liverpool (Amalgamated) Branch' (unpub. paper, December 1974a)

Lasko, R., and Gennard, J., 'Supplementary benefit and strikes', *British Journal of Industrial Relations*, March 1974b

Lasko, R., and Gennard, J., 'The individual and the strike', *British Journal of Industrial Relations*, November 1975

Layton, W. T., and Crowther, G., *An Introduction to the Study of Prices* (1938)

Lee, J., *The Economics of Telegraphs and Telephones* (1913)

Lerner, S., *Breakaway Unions and the Small Trade Unions* (1961)

Lewenhak, S., *Women and Trade Unions* (1977)

Lewins, W., *Her Majesty's Mail* (1864)

Lewis, W., 'On the health of the London postmen', *Transactions of the National Association for the Promotion of Social Science* (1862)

Lovell, J., and Roberts, B. C., *A Short History of the TUC* (1968)

MacDonnell: Third Report of the Royal Commission on the Civil Service (Minutes of Evidence) (PP 1913 XVIII)

MacDonnell: Fourth Report of the Royal Commission on the Civil Service (PP 1914 XVI)

Macrae-Gibson, J. M., *The Whitley System in the Civil Service* (1922)

MacKenzie, W. S., and Grove, J. W., *Central Administration in Britain* (1957)

Marsh, A., and Ryan, V., *Historical Directory of Trade Unions*: 2 Vols (1980)

Marshall, C. F. D., *The British Post Office from its Beginning to the End of 1925* (1926)

Martin, J. W., 'A strike of letter carriers in Warrington, 1872', *The Lancashire and Cheshire Mail*, VI, 1977

Martin, R. M., *TUC: The Growth of a Pressure Group 1868–1967* (1980)

Martindale, H., *Women Servants of the State 1870–1938* (1938)

Martinuzzi, L., 'The history of employment in the British Post Office' (Oxford University B.Litt thesis, 1952)

Mather, F. C., 'The railways, the electric telegraph and public order during the Chartist period, 1837–48', *History*, 38, 1953

Mather, F. C., *Public Order in the Age of the Chartists* (Manchester, 1959)

Matthison, A. L., *The Sun Shines on Wolverton* (Birmingham, 1957)

Meyer, H. R., *Public Ownership of the Telephone in Great Britain* (New York, 1901)

Meyer, H. R., *The British State Telegraphs* (New York, 1907)

Middleton, G., 'Self-government in industry', *Transactions of the Manchester Statistical Society* (1919)

Middleton, G., 'Guild Socialism and the Post Office', *The Guild Socialist*, September 1921

Middleton, G., 'An outrageous doubt', *Post*, 31 March 1928

Miller, J. P. M., *The Labour College Movement* (n.d., 1977?)

Milne-Bailey, W., *Towards a Postal Guild* (1921)

Monell, S. H., *The Cure for Writers' Cramp and Arm Troubles of Telegraphists and Ball Players* (New York, 1898)

Moran, M., *The Union of Post Office Workers: A Study in Political Sociology* (1974)

Morlay, E. J., *Women Workers in Seven Professions* (1914)

Morris, B., 'Workers' control in the Post Office', *Socialist Review*, March 1934

Morris, G., 'Equal pay for equal work. Is there an alternative?', *Post*, 28 May 1924

Mortimer, J. E., and Ellis, V., *A Professional Union: The Evolution of the Institution of Professional Civil Servants* (1980)

Moses, R., *The Civil Service of Great Britain* (New York, 1914)

Muller, W. D., *The 'Kept Men'? The First Century of Trade Union Representation in the British House of Commons 1874–1975* (1977)

Murikes, K., *Arthur Penty und der Nationalsozialismus* (Bonn, 1937)

Murray, G. E., *The Post Office* (1927)

Mustoe, E., *The Law and Organisation of the British Civil Service* (1932)

National Economic Development Office, *A Study of UK Nationalised Industries: their Role in the Economy and Control in the Future* (1976)

National Giro, Evidence to the Committee to Review the Functioning of Financial Institutions (1977)

Neale, W., *A History of the National Federation of Sub-Postmasters* (Bristol, 1913)

NFSPM, *1925–1935: A Summary of Ten Years Work* (1935)

Nortend, C., *Elihu Burritt: A Memorial Volume* (1880)

Northcote-Trevelyan: Report on the Organisation of the Permanent Civil Service (PP 1854 XXVII)

Norway, A. H., *History of the Post Office Packet Service Between the Years 1793–1815* (1895)

Ogilvie, A. M., 'The rise of the English Post Office', *Economic Journal*, III, 1893a

Ogilvie, A. M., 'Ralph Allen', *SMLG*, III, 1893b

Ogilvie, A. M., 'The revenue of the Post Office', *SMLG*, V, 1895

Ogilvie, A. M. (ed.), *By Way and Cross Road Posts* (1897)

Orage, A. R., *Political and Economic Writings* (ed. M. Butchart, 1936)

Paine, T., *The Rights of the Officers of Excise* (Lewes, 1772)

Palmer: Report from the Committee who were Appointed to Consider the Agreement Made with Mr. Palmer, for the Reform and Improvement of the Post Office and its Revenue (1797) (PP 1807 II)

Parris, H., *Staff Relations in the Civil Service: Fifty Years of Whitleyism* (1973)

Parrish, M. L. (ed.), *Four Lectures* (1938)

Patel, M., 'Strike in the Post Office' (BA dissertation, NE London Polytechnic, October 1980)

Paul, F., *Reminiscences of Early Efforts to Organise Post Office Workers at Brighton* (Brighton 1924?)

Pay Board, Advisory Report No. 1 (September 1973)

Paynter, W., *British Trade Unions and the Problem of Change* (1970)

PCE: *The Postmen's Case for Enquiry* (Postmen's Federation, 1896), largely consisting of their evidence to the Tweedmouth Enquiry but also including a brief 'Chapter of Postal Service History (from a Postman's Point of View)'

Pease, D., 'What we women think of Union policy', *Post*, 1 July 1939

Peers, R., *Adult Education: A Comparative Study* (1958)

Pelling, H., *Origins of the Labour Party 1880–1900* (1965 edn)

Penty, A. J., *The Restoration of the Guild System* (1906)

Penty, A. J., *Guilds and the Social Crisis* (1919)

Penty, A. J., *Tradition and Modernism in Politics* (1937)

Perry, C. R., 'The British Post Office 1836–1914: a study of nationalisation and administrative expansion' (PhD thesis, Harvard University, 1976)

Perry, C. R., 'The British experience 1876–1912', in Pool (ed.) (1977)

Perry, C. R., 'Frank Ives Scudamore and the Post Office telegraph', *Albion*, XII, 1980, pp. 350–67

PFSR, Postmen's Federation Secretary's Report, Vol. 1 (collected by the PF while the Committee was sitting: at UCW F 299.3)

Pitt, D. C., *The Telecommunications Function in the British Post Office: A Case Study of Bureaucratic Adaptation* (Farnborough, 1980)

Pool, I. S. (ed.), *The Social Impact of the Telephone* (Cambridge, Mass., 1977)

Porter, A., *The Life and Letters of John Henniker Heaton* (1916)

Poirier, P. P., *The Advent of the Labour Party* (1958)

POUNC, Report on Post Office Proposals for increased Postal, Telecommunications and Giro Remittance Service Charges (1975)

Preece, W. H., 'Telegraphy in the nineteenth century', *SMLG*, XI, 1901

Price, E. D. (ed.), *Hazell's Annual for 1891*

Priestley: Report of the Royal Commission on the Civil Service 1953–5 (November 1955) (Cmd 9613) (PP 1955–6 XI)

PTTI, *History of the Postal Telegraph and Telephone International* (1951)

PTTI, *British Unions and the PTTI* (1963)

Raikes, H. S., *The Life and Letters of Henry Cecil Raikes* (1898)

Ramsden, J., 'The Newport By-Election and the fall of the Coalition' in Cook and Ramsden (eds) (1973)

Raphael, M., *Pensions and Public Servants. A Study of the Origins of the British System* (Paris, 1964)

Rawlings, R. W., *The Civil Service and The People* (1945)

Raybould, S. G. (ed.), *Trends in English Adult Education* (1959)

Raynham, F. R., and Calvert, W. S. G., *Post Office Uniforms* (POGP 27: 1936)

Reckitt, M. B., and Bechhofer, C. E., *The Meaning of National Guilds* (1918, 1920)

Rees, J., *Foot-Prints of a Letter-Carrier* (Philadelphia, 1866)

Reeves, P., *Round About a Pound a Week* (1913)

Reith, J. C. W., *Into the Wind* (1949)

Reynolds, G. W., and Judge, A., *The Night the Police Went on Strike* (1968)

Reynolds, M., *Women's Labour in the Post Office* (1910) (copy in R II/12)

Rhodes, G., *Public Sector Pensions* (1965)

Richards, P. G., *Patronage in British Government* (Toronto, 1963)

Ridley: Royal Commission on the Civil Establishments, Second Report (PP 1888 XXVII)

Roberts, B. C., *Trade Union Government and Administration in Great Britain* (1956)

Roberts, B. C., *The Trades Union Congress 1868–1921* (1958)

Robinson, H., *The British Post Office: A History* (Princeton, NJ, 1948)

Robinson, H., *Britain's Post Office: A History of Development from the Beginning to the Present Day* (1953)

Robinson, H., *Carrying British Mail Overseas* (1964)

Rogaly, J., *Grunwick* (1977)

Rolland, L., *De la Correspondence Postale et Telegraphique dans les Relations Internationales* (Paris, 1901)

Routh, G., 'A study of the factors determining the level of pay in the British Civil Service since 1875' (London University PhD thesis, 1952)

Routh, G., 'Civil Service pay – 1875 to 1950', *Economica* (1954)

Ruggles, N., 'Recent developments in the theory of marginal cost pricing', *Review of Economic Studies*, 17: 1949–50

'RWH', 'Postmen's uniforms', *SMLG*, XXV, 1915

Rye, M. S., 'The rise and progress of telegraphs', *English Women's Journal* (1859)

Ryland, A. W. C., *The Post Office as a Business* (1971)

Samuel, H., *Memoirs* (1945)

Saxon Mills, J., *The Press and Communications of the Empire* (1924)

Scarman: Report of the Enquiry (August 1977) (Cmnd 6922) (PP 1977–8)

Schneider, B. V. H., 'The British Post Office Strike of 1964', *Personnel Report*, 662 (1966)

Scott, J. G. S., 'Sir Andrew Agnew and the Sunday posts', *Postal History* (1972)

Scott, W. R., *The Constitution and Finance of English, Scottish and Irish Joint Stock Companies to 1720* (Cambridge, 1911)

Seaton, S. A. R., 'The Association of Post Office Controlling Officers', *Whitley Bulletin*, April 1963, pp. 53–5

Secret Committee: Report from the Secret Committee on the Post Office (PP 1844, XIV)

Seebohm Rowntree, B., *The Human Needs of Labour* (1918)

Shepherd, E. C., *The Fixing of Wages in Government Employment* (1923)

Siedman, J., 'Collective bargaining in the postal service', *Industrial Relations*, IX, 1969

Simon, B., *Education and the Labour Movement 1870–1920* (1965)

Sinclair: Report of the Advisory Committee on the Inland Telegraph Service (HMSO, July 1958)

Sly, J. F., 'The genesis of the Universal Postal Union', *International Conciliation*, 233, October, 1927

Smee, W. R., *A Proposal to Increase Smaller Salaries in Government* (1860)

Smiles, S., *The Life of George Stephenson* (1858 edn)

Smith, A. D., *The Development of Rates of Postage: An Historical and Analytical Study* (1917)

Smith, H. W., 'The controversy regarding Sunday Labour in the Post Office', *Postal History*, 77–81, 1955

Smith, L. M., 'The history and working of trade unionism in the British Post Office' (Oxford University B.Litt thesis, 1931)

Smith, R., 'A hard day's strike', *Socialist Commentary*, September 1964

Smith, T., *The Politics of the Corporate Economy* (Oxford, 1979)

Snell, M., Taylor, D., and Wedderburn, D., *Interim Report on the Post Office Industrial Democracy Experiment: Regional and Area Levels* (1980)

Spero, S. D., *The Labour Movement in a Government Industry. Employee Organisation in the Postal Service* (New York, 1927)

Stack, F., 'Civil service associations and the Whitley Report of 1917', *Political Quarterly* (1969)

Staff, F., *The Penny Post 1680–1918* (1964)

Stagg, N., 'Nine days that shook the Post Office', *Post*, 15 August 1964

Stagg, N., 'Were we defeated? A note on the 1971 UK postal strike' (unpub., 1971)

Stagg, N., 'The Post Office Corporation in Great Britain', *PTTI Studies*, Winter 1973

Stagg, N., 'Don't blame the postmen', *Labour Weekly*, 2 September 1977

Stagg, N., *Industrial Democracy: The Post Office Experiment* (1978)

Stephen, L., *Life of Henry Fawcett* (1866 edn)

Stocks, M., *The Workers Educational Association: The First Fifty Years* (1953)

Stonehouse, J., *Death of an Idealist* (1975)

Summary: The Post Office: An Historical Summary (Published by Order of the Postmaster General, 1911)

Suthers, R. B., 'Union of Post Office Workers', *Labour Magazine*, June 1932

Swift, H. G., *A History of Postal Agitation – From Fifty Years Ago Till the Present Day – Including a Few Forgotten Pages in the Wider 'History of Our Own Times'* (1900). 'A new and Revised Edition' was published in Manchester in 1929. This is described as Book I but no Book II ever appeared. It is always cited here unless otherwise stated

Tallack, R. J., *The Post Office: What it Does for the Nation and what it Might Do* (1928?)

Tegg, W., *Posts and Telegraphs, Past and Present* (1878)

Telephone Development Association, *The Strangle-hold on the Telephones. A Practicable Remedy* (1931?)

Thomas, H., 'Towards a revision of the Official Secrets Act' in his *Crisis in the Civil Service* (1968)

Thompson, E. P., *William Morris: Romantic to Revolutionary* (1955)

Thompson, E. P., *Writing by Candlelight* (1980). Original article in *New Society*, 24 December 1970

Thompson, P., *Socialists, Liberal and Labour. The Struggle for London 1885–1914* (1967)

Todd, A., *On Parliamentary Government in England*, 2 Vols (1892), Vol 1

Tom Dredge Case, The, Anonymous pamphlet published by the *Postal Service Gazette* (1888)

Tombs, R. C., 'The London postal service at Christmas', *Blackfriars Magazine*, X, 1891

Tomlin: Report of the Royal Commission on the Civil Service 1929–31 (Cmd 3909) (PP 1930–1 X)

Tracey, B., 'Anatomy of a Strike', *MR View*, April 1971

Trollope, A., 'The civil service as a profession' (1861) in Parrish (ed.) (1938), p. 14

Trollope, A., *The Three Clerks* (1907)

Trollope, A., *Autobiography* (1923 edn)

Tupling, R. E., *A History of the Birmingham Telephone Area* (1978)

Turner, E. R., 'The secrecy of the post', *EHR*, 33, 1918

Tweedmouth: Interdepartmental Committee on Post Office Establishments chaired by Lord Tweedmouth, 1895–7 (PP 1897 XLIX)

UCW Executive, *Posts, Telecommunications and the New Technology* (1980): a response to Walsh *et al.* (1980)

UPW, *Wage Claim and Evidence 1926–7* (1927)

UPW, *Reorganisation of the Telegraphs* (April 1933)

UPW, *Wage Claim and Evidence 1938*

UPW, *Did we Fight for This? A Challenge to the TUC Conception of Industrial Control* (pamphlet, October 1945)

UPW, *Has the TUC Gone Wrong?* (March 1947)

UPW, *How We Began* (pamphlet, 1950)

UPW, *Post Office Joint Administrative Council* (1953a)

UPW, *Special Report on Wages Policy* (1953b)

UPW, *Supplementary Report to the Special Report on the Royal Commission* (1956)

UPW, *This Business of Workers' Control: The UPW Members' Introduction to Industrial Democracy* (1957a, repr. 1965)

UPW, *Special Report on Pay, Leave and Other Conditions of Service* (1957b)

UPW, *Special Report on Hours of Work* (1960)

UPW, *Special Report on Wages Policy* (1965)

UPW, *A Claim for Compulsory Trade Union Membership* (1969)

UPW, *Evidence of the Union of Post Office Workers* (1971)

UPW, *Post Office Workers Case for Special Treatment* (June 1973)

UPW, *Carter Review Committee. Evidence Submitted by the Union of Post Office Workers* (April 1976)

Vaughan, C. J., *A Letter on the Late Post Office Agitation* (1849)

Walker, G., *Haste, Post, Haste* (1938)

Walker, N., *Morale in the Civil Service: A Study of the Desk Worker* (Edinburgh, 1961)

Wallace, H., *Information on Boy Messengers* (1925)

Waller, R. D., *A Design for Democracy* (1956)

Walsh, V., Moulton-Abbot, J., and Senker, P., *New Technology, The Post Office and the Union of Post Office Workers* (September 1980)

Ward, C. A., 'The first idea of the penny post', *Notes and Queries*. VI, II, 1885

Ward, Dora, 'A question of equality', *Post*, 3 May 1924

Ward, G., *For Grunwick* (1978)

Weal, J., *The Post Office Workers and the State: The Great 1971 Post Office Strike* (International Marxist Group, 1971?)

Webb, S. (ed.), *How to Pay for the War* (Fabian Research Department, 1916)

Webb, S., and Webb, B., *Industrial Democracy* (1897)

Wells, E., *Postal Reform* (1930)

Whitaker, W. B., *Victorian and Edwardian Shopkeepers* (Newton Abbot, 1973)

White, L. C., *Whitley Councils in the British Civil Service* (Chicago, 1933)

White, L. C., 'A study in inconsistency: A disturbing analysis of the Government's attitude to wage claims', *Red Tape*, December 1947

White, L. C. (ed.), Bland, C. H., Sharp, W. R., and Marx, F. M., *Civil Service Abroad* (New York, 1935)

Wigham, E., *From Humble Petition to Militant Action: A History of the Civil and Public Services Association* (1980)

Wills, L., *1971 Strike* (1980? unpublished typescript)

Wolmer, Viscount, *Post Office Reform: Its Importance and Practicability* (1932)

Wood, G. H., 'Course of average wages between 1790 and 1860', *Economic Journal*, IX, 1899, pp. 588–92

Wood, G. H., 'Real wages and the standard of comfort since 1850', *Journal of the Royal Statistical Society*, vol. 72, 1909, pp. 91–103

Wootton, B., *The Social Foundations of Wage Policy* (1962)

Wright, M., *Treasury Control of the Civil Service 1854–1874* (Oxford, 1969)

Appendices

The following lists and tables add to the information given elsewhere. Most of the appendices are referred to in the text, but their main significance is as follows:

1–6   General information about the Post Office, relevant particularly to Chapters 2 and 9, and largely derived from the Post Office's own publications.

7–10   Various tables and indices on wages from 1793 to 1920 to accompany the arguments in Chapter 3.

11–12   Tables on First World War wage negotiations to accompany the closing sections of Chapter 7.

13–25   Statistics and lists of pre-amalgamation associations, 1881–1920, to accompany Chapter 8.

26–33   Tables on Post Office business and finances, 1911–80, to accompany Chapter 9.

34–36   Details on the UPW, mainly relevant to Chapter 10.

37   Details of Parliamentary candidatures referred to in Chapter 11.

38–41   Statistics to fill out details given in Chapter 12.

Appendix 1: POLITICAL HEADS OF THE POST OFFICE, 1835–1980

Postmaster General

30 May 1835	Earl of Lichfield
15 September 1841	Lord Lowther (Earl of Lonsdale)
2 January 1846	Earl of St German's
14 July 1846	Marquess of Clanricarde
6 May 1852	Earl of Hardwicke
8 January 1853	Viscount Canning (Earl Canning)
30 November 1855	Duke of Argyle
13 March 1858	Lord Colchester
24 June 1859	Earl of Elgin and Kincardine
11 May 1860	Duke of Argyle
28 August 1860	Lord Stanley of Alderley
19 July 1866	Duke of Montrose
30 December 1868	Marquess of Hartington
24 January 1871	William Monsell (Lord Emley)
13 November 1873	Lyon Playfair (Lord Playfair)
4 March 1874	Lord John Manners
14 May 1880	Henry Fawcett
7 November 1884	George J. Shaw-Lefevre (Lord Eversley)
29 June 1885	Lord John Manners
10 February 1886	Lord Wolverton
5 August 1886	Henry Cecil Raikes
21 September 1891	Sir James Ferguson
19 August 1892	Arnold Morley
5 July 1895	Duke of Norfolk
10 April 1900	Marquess of Londonderry
15 August 1902	J. Austen Chamberlain
9 October 1903	Lord Stanley
11 December 1905	Sydney Buxton
21 January 1910	Herbert Samuel (Viscount Samuel)
12 February 1914	C. E. H. Hobhouse
28 May 1915	Herbert Samuel
2 January 1916	J. A. Pease (Lord Gainford)
13 December 1916	A. H. Illingworth (Lord Illingworth)
15 April 1921	Frederick G. Kellaway
2 October 1922	Neville Chamberlain
12 March 1923	Sir W. Joynson-Hicks (Viscount Brentford)
29 May 1923	Sir Laming Worthington-Evans
23 January 1924	Vernon Hartshorn
13 November 1924	Sir William Mitchell-Thomson (Lord Selsdon)
10 June 1929	H. B. Lees-Smith
4 March 1931	C. R. Attlee
4 September 1931	W. G. A. Ormsby-Gore (Lord Harlech)
12 November 1931	Sir Kingsley Wood
7 June 1935	George C. Tryon (Lord Tryon)
5 April 1940	W. S. Morrison
6 February 1943	Captain Harry Crookshank

4 August 1945	Earl of Listowel
23 April 1947	Wilfred Paling
2 March 1950	Ness Edwards
5 November 1951	Earl De La Warr
7 April 1955	Charles Hill
16 January 1957	Ernest Marples
22 October 1959	Reginald Bevins
19 October 1964	A. W. Benn
4 July 1966	Edward Short
6 April 1968	Roy Mason
1 July 1968	John Stonehouse

(Post Office incorporated 1 October 1969)

Ministers responsible for Post Office Corporation

Minister of Posts and Telecommunications

1 October 1969	John Stonehouse
24 June 1970	Christopher Chataway
7 April 1972	Sir John Eden
9 April 1974	A. W. Benn

(office wound up on 29 March 1974)

Secretary of State for Industry

5 May 1974	A. W. Benn
10 June 1975	Eric Varley
5 May 1979	Sir Keith Joseph
14 September 1981	Patrick Jenkins

Appendix 2: PERMANENT HEADS OF THE POST OFFICE, 1798–1981

Post Office Secretary, 1798–1914

1798	Sir Francis Freeling
29 September 1836	Colonel W. L. Maberly
22 April 1854	Sir Rowland Hill (Secretary to the Postmaster-General, 1846–54)
15 March 1864	Sir John Tilley
1 May 1880	Sir S. A. Blackwood
10 November 1893	Sir Spencer Walpole
10 February 1899	Sir George H. Murray
1 October 1903	Sir H. Babington Smith
17 January 1910	Sir Matthew Nathan
7 August 1911	Sir Alexander F. King
24 August 1914	Sir G. Evelyn P. Murray

Director General, 1934–68

14 April 1934	Sir Donald Banks
9 August 1936	Sir Thomas Gardiner
1 January 1946	Sir Raymond Birchall
1 October 1949	Sir Alexander Little
1 October 1955	Sir George Radley
1 June 1960	Sir Ronald German
1 November 1966	(Sir) John Wall

Chairman of Post Office Board, 1969–81

1 October 1969	Viscount Hall
22 April 1971	(Sir) William Ryland
31 October 1977	(Sir) William Barlow
15 September 1980	Sir Henry Chilver

Chairman of the Post Office

1 October 1981	Ron Dearing

Chairman of British Telecom

1 October 1981	Sir George Jefferson

Appendix 3: POST OFFICE ACCOUNTS BEFORE 1911

(a) *Before the Penny Post*

	Income (£000s)	Profit (£000s)
1729–30	179	95
1739–40	194	91
1749–50	207	97
1759–60	230	83
1769–70	285	156
1779–80	373	139
1789–90	533	331
1799–00	1,084	721
1809–10	1,856	1,261
1819–20	2,192	1,522
1829–30	2,265	1,509

(b) *Post Office Reform and after, 1835–70*

	Income (£000s)	Profit (£000s)
1834–5	2,320	1,513
1839–40	2,390	1,633
1840–1	1,359	501
1844–5	1,705	719
1850–1	2,264	803
1855	2,716	1,065
1860	3,531	1,578
1865	4,424	1,482
1870	4,929	1,494

(c) *Accounts of the Post Office as a whole, 1874–1910*

	Income (£000s)	Profit (£000s)
1874–5	7,170	1,930
1879–80	8,452	2,898
1884–5	10,264	2,774
1889–90	12,086	3,531
1894–5	13,672	2,928
1899–00	16,855	3,422
1904–5	20,195	3,909
1909–10	23,627	3,780

620 *Post Office Workers*

(d) *Accounts of the Postal Service, 1874–1910*

	Income (£000s)	Profit (£000s)
1874–5	6,022	1,902
1879–80	6,982	2,601
1884–5	8,479	2,811
1889–90	9,721	3,446
1894–5	11,025	3,070
1899–00	13,394	3,710
1904–5	16,275	4,829
1909–10	18,710	4,911

(e) *Accounts of the Telegraph Service, 1870–1910*

	Income (£000s)	Profit (£000s)
1870–1	801	124
1874–5	1,148	28
1879–80	1,470	296
1884–5	1,785	− 36
1889–90	2,364	85
1894–5	2,646	− 142
1899–00	3,460	− 288
1904–5	3,920	− 919
1909–10	3,167	− 1,090

Main sources

Hemmeon (1912), Robinson (1953) and Annual Reports of the Postmaster General.

Notes

All prices are current. Accountancy years vary, coinciding with the calendar year only from 1855–70. Separate telephone accounts were only published at the very end of this period. In 1909–10 the total income of Post Office telephones was £1,750,000 and the deficit was £40,000. Expenditure on salaries was given as £423,000, 24 per cent of income.

Appendix 4: POST OFFICE WAGE COSTS BEFORE 1911

(a) Total

	Wages expenditure (£000s)	Wages/Income (%)
1855	1,022	35·6
1860	1,140	32·3
1865	1,295	29·3
1870	1,498	30·4
1874–5	2,075	28·9
1879–80	2,565	30·3
1884–5	3,769	36·7
1889–90	4,742	39·2
1894–5	6,431	47·0
1899–00	8,243	48·9
1904–5	9,824	48·6
1909–10	12,220	51·7

(b) Posts after 1870

1874–5	1,674	27·8
1879–80	1,967	28·2
1884–5	2,829	33·4
1889–90	3,360	34·5
1894–5	4,597	41·7
1899–00	6,018	44·9
1904–5	7,199	44·2
1909–10	9,185	49·1

(c) Telegraphs

1870–1	398	52·8
1874–5	598	52·1
1879–80	689	46·9
1884–5	939	52·6
1889–90	1,382	58·5
1894–5	1,834	69·3
1899–00	2,280	65·9
1904–5	2,625	66·9
1909–10	2,611	82·5

Main source

Annual Reports of the Postmaster General.

Appendix 5: SOME STATISTICS OF THE POST OFFICE WORKFORCE, 1835–1980

	Total	Women	Letter carriers/ Postmen
1835	9,505	–	–
1851	26,038	–	–
1875	58,644	–	16,389
1880	70,674	–	16,883
1885	95,583	23,844	16,034
1890	113,054	24,177	20,001
1895	138,738	28,280	27,218
1900	167,086	33,918	34,281
1905	192,454	40,189	40,818
1910	212,364	46,263	46,530
1914	226,744	46,040	
1925	220,066	51,299	
1930	230,675	53,952	
1935	241,560	55,015	
1939	268,083	65,546	
1950	321,782		
1955	337,465		
1960	339,013		89,727
1965	384,280		97,143
1970	409,721		102,563
1975	434,065		101,843
1980	422,902	96,350	107,400

Notes

These figures are given for the years in which they were published. They cannot be regarded as strictly comparable over time. The figures include part-timers counted as ½, though not necessarily at every point.

Appendix 6: POST OFFICE BUSINESS
1839–1980

	Letters and packets (millions)	Packets (millions)	Inland telegrams (millions)
1839	83	–	–
1840	169	–	–
1841–5 (av)	228	–	–
1846–50 (av)	327	–	–
1855–60 (av)	410	–	–
1860–65 (av)	648	–	–
1865–70 (av)	800	–	–
1870	993	–	10
1875	1,088	–	19
1880–1	1,662	–	29
1884–5	2,008	23	33
1890–1	2,578	46	66
1894–5	2,850	57	72
1900–1	2,327	89	90
1904–5	4,382	97	89
1909–10	4,987	118	87
1922–3	5,455	121	56
1929–30	6,400	160	42
1934–35	6,935	150	35
1939–40	7,360	192	55
1946–7	7,300	239	53
1949–50	8,350	243	42
1954–5	9,500	247	26
1959–60	10,200	244	14
1964–5	11,200	216	11
1969–70	11,400	208	8
1974–5	10,878	170	6
1979–80	10,207	180	3

Sources

All figures from Post Office or Postmaster General's Annual Reports. They cannot be regarded as strictly comparable over time.

Appendix 7: NUMBERS AND ANNUAL AVERAGE WAGES OF CERTAIN POST OFFICE GRADES, 1832–53

	London sub-sorters (inland only)	London metropolitan letter carriers[1]	Provincial letter carriers England and Wales	Edinburgh letter carriers	Scottish Provincial letter carriers, porters etc.	Scottish 'runners' (ie rural messengers)	Dublin letter carriers[2]	Irish Provincial letter carriers stampers and porters
1832		645 £54.98					103 £39.71	
1833								
1834							115 £43.19	
1835[3]	7 £80.36	787 £54.87	752 £20.20	44 £45.75	31 £35.17	197 £22.62	113 £44.85	63 £15.83
1836	7 £78.57	805 £54.82	844 £19.01	44 £46.06	34 £35.54	240 £19.83	109 £47.82	83 £19.64
1837	7 £77.95	807 £57.00	908 £18.15	44 £45.87	34 £36.19	247 £19.45	109 £47.53	94 £20.96
1838	7 £77.32	946 £50.00	1,070 £16.53	44 £45.28	166 £21.62	288 £17.29	109 £48.76	109 £20.30
1839	8 £75.00	979 £54.39	1,141 £16.65	47 £45.09	191 £20.00	303 £17.50	109 £47.79	126 £20.59
1840	11 £63.17	1,002 £56.06	1,229 £17.17	55 £45.48	191 £20.46	359 £15.11	126 £44.45	148 £19.55

Year	n	£	n	£	n	£	n	£	n	£	n	£	n	£	n	£
1841	14	£71.70	1,131	£54.92	1,348	£18.79	66	£45.19	204	£21.62	261	£21.35	134	£47.08	272	£14.07
1842	19	£66.42	1,225	£53.26	1,408	£19.13	66	£45.46	212	£21.65	254	£21.58	134	£50.71	348	£14.40
1843	19	£74.00	1,341	£50.42	1,457	£19.15	66	£46.24	237	£20.67	258	£21.41	135	£52.75	396	£13.61
1844	19	£74.21	1,347	£52.92	1,493	£18.91	66	£46.04	268	£19.18	256	£21.46	135	£53.65	411	£13.44
1845	23	£70.61	1,445	£53.30	1,589	£18.28	66	£46.00	322	£16.23	263	£21.57	135	£54.23	418	£13.50
1846	32	£67.43	1,520	£53.85	1,731	£20.66	66	£45.59	400	£14.05	329	£18.88	139	£54.32	433	£13.28
1847	31	£76.17	1,604	£57.76	1,810	£23.26	66	£46.97	417	£14.97	344	£19.62	141	£56.28	460	£12.94
1848	37	£71.62	1,711	£57.84	1,935	£23.26	66	£46.32	420	£16.34	377	£20.40	143	£56.53	492	£12.50
1849	37	£77.97	1,708	£58.89	2,131	£22.62	70	£46.09	421	£16.22	421	£21.29	143	£57.23	510	£12.43
1850	37	£78.84	1,670	£59.68	2,186	£22.70	70	£46.13	424	£15.06	420	£23.97	143	£54.51	521	£12.38
1851	41	£77.37	1,718	£58.27	2,193	£23.04	70	£46.23	425	£15.19	449	£23.16	143	£54.71	525	£12.27
1852–3							80	£45.50								

Notes

1 Includes both inland and metropolitan forces.
2 Includes a few messengers, stampers, and maidservants.
3 The main group of figures from 1835–51 is calculated from lists given in PP 1852 XLIX. They are based on overall totals earned by each grade and take no account of incremental scales and other complications. Other figures given are from PP 1835 XLVIII and POR 30E 4801/1861, and they take average figures within each sub-group.

Appendix 8: ANNUAL AVERAGE WAGES OF CHIEF POST OFFICE GRADES, 1793–1910

	London (£s p.a.)							Rest of UK (including Edinburgh and Dublin Chief Offices) (£s p.a.)			
	Letter carriers/ Postmen	Sub-sorters/ Sorters	Male tele-graphists	Female tele-graphists	Male CC&Ts	Female CC&Ts	Tele-phonists	Letter carriers/ Postmen	Male SC&Ts	Female SC&Ts	Tele-phonists
1793	25.52	58.36									
1816	54.67	63.71									
1836	54.82	78.57									
1845	53.30	70.61									
1850	59.68	78.84						22.80			
1855	58.37							20.03			
1860	(60.11)	84.33						22.20			
1861	63.29	83.59						(27.73)			
1862	62.11	78.45						33.99			
1865	60.38	76.22									
1872	59.33	59.36	71.07	45.58	84.46			36.66			
1875								42.70	(01.97)		
1881	64.08	73.02	85.19	61.97	91.43	60.02			74.32	51.78	
1885	65.22	73.90	74.97	59.37	89.48	56.98		51.57	70.63	51.57	
1890	64.10	88.40	92.08	66.73	93.60	64.35		(58.28)	81.25	55.68	
1896–7	65.63	(94.83)	97.50	58.28	102.48	65.52			86.02	54.60	
1897–8	69.12	103.35	100.75	67.60	100.75	67.60		60.88	87.35	59.80	
1905	78.00	118.73	116.57	67.17	117.65	71.93	39.22	66.95	92.08	60.45	43.55
1908	85.37	128.92	128.05	75.40	125.23	78.22	42.90		98.15	66.95	
1910	86.02	131.52	132.17	77.13	129.13	82.55	51.35	71.28	99.23	66.95	50.48

Notes

This table attempts to give some idea of the changes of the money wages of some of the main Post Office grades in the period. The different rows cannot be said to strictly compare throughout. This is not just because of the evolution of the grade structure described in Chapter 3 meaning that, for example, the London sorters and countermen are not really equivalent before and after 1854 or 1871. Some of the published provincial figures may well not include the Chief Offices outside London. Also, the range of sources used is so great that it cannot be ascertained whether the methods of calculating averages are the same in each case. The method used has been to find a total figure for each grade or sub-grade and calculate an average. The methods used by the Post Office to derive some of the latter figures were not explained. Nor is this method anything like as subtle as the one employed by Routh to compile the indices given in Appendix 10. Unfortunately, however, he does not give as much detail of the separate groups.

Chief sources

1793 and 1816: PP 1817 XV.
1836–50: PP 1852 XLIX.
1855: POR 30E 4801/1861.
1860: *ibid.* for sorters, estimates for provincial letter carriers and PP 1859 XIV for an (1859) figure for London letter carriers.
1861: *CSG*, 24 October 1861.
1862: PP 1863 XXXI.
1865: PP 1865 XXXI.
1872: Holt Committee Returns for London letter carriers; Estimates for countermen and an 1874 figure of provincial telegraphists; PP 1898 LII for the rest.
1881: *ibid.* for all except London letter carriers, again from Holt Returns.
1885: *Hansard*, V 32, 1765–6.
1890 and 1896–7: Holt Committee Returns for London postmen; PP 1898 LII for the rest.
1897–8 to 1910: *Hansard*, V 32, 1765–6, supplemented by Estimates.

Appendix 9: INDEX OF POST OFFICE WORKERS' WAGES, 1850–1910

| | London | | | | | | | | Rest of UK | | | | | | |
| | Letter carriers/ Postmen | | Sub-sorters/ Sorters | | Telegraphists (M) | | Telegraphists (F) | | CC&Ts (M) | | Letter carriers/ Postmen | | SC&Ts (M) | | Retail prices |
	N	R	N	R	N	R	N	R	N	R	N	R	N	R	
1850	101	115	133	151	–	–	–	–	–	–	–	–	–	–	88
1855	98	88	–	–	–	–	–	–	–	–	–	–	–	–	111
1860	101	103	142	145	–	–	–	–	–	–	–	–	–	–	98
1865	102	107	128	135	–	–	–	–	–	–	–	–	–	–	95
1872	100	100	100	100	100	100	100	100	100	100	100	100	100	100	100
1881	108	116	123	132	120	129	136	146	108	116	–	–	119	128	93
1885	110	129	124	146	105	123	130	153	106	125	121	142	114	134	85
1890	108	133	149	184	130	160	146	180	111	137	136	168	131	162	81
1897	111	146	160	210	137	180	128	168	121	159	–	–	139	183	76
1898	117	152	174	226	145	188	148	192	119	154	142	184	141	183	77
1905	131	162	200	247	164	202	147	181	139	172	157	194	149	184	81
1910	145	167	222	255	186	214	169	194	153	176	167	192	160	184	87

Notes

N = Nominal; R = Real; 1872 = 100

The money figures are based on Appendix 8 and translated into real terms with the retail price series derived from Layton and Crowther (1938), pp. 273–4.

Appendix 10: INDEX OF LONDON POST OFFICE WORKERS' WAGES, 1875–1920

	Telegraphists/ Counter clerks (M)[1]		Postmen/Sorters		Telegraphists Counter clerks (F)[2]		General wage rates	
	N	R	N	R	N	R	N	R
1875	100.0	96	100.0	96	100.0	96	104	100
1876	100.0	96	100.0	96	100.0	96	103	99
1877	100.0	96	100.0	96	100.0	96	102	98
1878	100.0	102	100.0	102	100.0	102	99	101
1879	100.0	105	100.0	105	100.0	105	97	102
1880	100.0	101	100.0	101	100.0	101	97	98
1881	107.0	110	112.5	116	112.1	115	97	100
1882	107.0	111	121.1	126	112.1	117	97	101
1883	107.0	111	121.1	126	112.1	117	98	102
1884	107.0	117	121.1	132	112.1	122	98	107
1885	107.0	124	121.1	140	112.1	130	97	113
1886	107.0	127	121.1	144	112.1	133	97	115
1887	107.0	130	121.1	148	112.1	137	97	118
1888	107.0	130	121.1	148	112.1	137	97	118
1889	107.0	127	121.1	144	112.1	131	100	119
1890	119.6	142	121.1	144	121.9	145	104	124
1891	119.6	142	123.5	147	121.9	145	104	124
1892	119.6	141	123.5	146	121.9	144	104	123
1893	119.6	142	123.5	147	121.9	145	103	123
1894	119.6	149	123.5	152	121.9	152	103	129
1895	119.6	153	123.5	158	121.9	156	102	131
1896	119.6	153	123.5	158	121.9	156	103	132
1897	117.0	149	132.4	165	132.5	166	104	130
1898	117.0	146	132.4	161	132.5	162	106	129
1899	117.0	147	132.4	163	132.5	163	108	133
1900	117.0	139	132.4	154	132.5	154	112	130
1901	117.0	138	132.4	156	132.5	156	111	131
1902	117.0	138	132.4	156	132.5	156	111	131
1903	117.0	138	132.4	154	132.5	154	110	128
1904	117.0	135	132.4	152	132.5	152	109	125
1905	120.8	139	136.4	157	135.7	156	109	125
1906	120.8	139	136.4	157	135.7	156	111	128
1907	120.8	134	136.4	151	135.7	151	111	123
1908	123.4	139	138.4	159	151.1	174	111	128
1909	123.4	138	138.4	158	151.1	172	111	127
1910	123.4	134	138.4	154	151.1	168	111	123
1911	123.4	132	138.4	151	151.1	165	112	122
1912	123.4	128	138.4	147	151.1	160	115	122
1913	123.4	126	138.4	144	151.1	157	119	124
1914	126.3	134	149.2	158	151.1	160	119	126
1915	134.0	115	158.5	136	159.5	137	128	110
1916	136.7	100	162.2	118	162.4	119	140	102

1917	150.1	92	178.0	109	182.6	111	166	101
1918	184.7	96	221.0	115	221.2	115	212	110
1919	226.3	111	264.4	130	266.2	130	255	125
1920	279.6	120	330.1	142	434.5	187	304	131

Source

Routh (1954).

Notes

N = Nominal   R = Real
1 Includes telegraphists from 1881 and telephonists (M) from 1912
2 Includes telephonists (F) from 1912.

Appendix 11: WAR-TIME BONUS CLAIMS AND THEIR RESULTS, 1915–1919

	Woodhouse Award 8 July 1915	Treasury Award 8 Sep 1916	Tribunal Award 1 May 1917	Tribunal Award 17 Dec 1917	Tribunal Award 9 July 1918	Tribunal Award 8 Nov 1918	Tribunal Award 31 March 1919[1]	Tribunal Award 11 Nov 1919[1]
Men on £1.50 p.w. (£78 p.a.) or less	20p–15p 7.80	40p–20p 10.40	50p–40p 20.80	75p–70p 36.40	£1–95p 49.40	£1.50–£1.15 59.80	£2–£1.20+20% (71.76–78.00)	£2.20+50%–£1.20+30% (76.44–85.80)
Men on £1.50 p.w. to £2 (£104 p.a.)	20p–15p 7.80	40p–20p 10.40	50p–40p 20.80	75p–70p 36.40	£1–95p 49.40	£1.50–£1.15 59.80	£2–£1.20+20% (83.02)	£2.20+50%–£1.20+30% (93.60)
Men on £2 to £2.50 p.w. (£130 p.a.)	15p–10p 5.20	30p–15p 7.80	40p–35p 18.20	75p–65p 33.80	£1–95p 49.40	£1.50–£1.15 59.80	£2–£1.20+20% (88.04)	£2.20+50%–£1.20+30% (101.40)
Men on £2.50 to £3 (£156 p.a.)	15p–10p 5.20	30p–15p 7.80	40p–35p 18.20	75p–65p 33.80	£1–95p 49.40	£1.50–£1.15 59.80	75%–£1.20+20% (135.02)	£2.20+50%–£1.20+30% (109.20)
Women on £1.50 or less (£78 p.a.)	10p–7½p 3.90	40p–10p 5.20	50p–30p 15.60	75p–35p 18.20	£1–62½p 32.50	£1.50–75p 35.00	£2–75p+20% (48.36–54.60)	£2.20+50%–75p+30% (53.04–62.40)
Women on £1.50 to £2 (£104 p.a.)	10p–7½p 3.90	40p–10p 5.20	50p–25p 13.00	75p–35p 18.20	£1–62½p 32.50	£1.50–75p 35.00	£2–75p+20% (59.80)	£2.20+50%–75p+30% (70.20)
Women on £2 to £2.50 (£130 p.a.)	10p–5p 2.60	30p–7½p 3.90	40p–22½p 11.70	75p–32½p 16.90	£1–62½p 32.50	£1.50–75p 35.00	£2–75p+20% (65.00)	£2.20+50%–75p+30% (78.00)
Women on £2.50 to £3 (£156 p.a.)	10p–5p 2.60	30p–7½p 3.90	40p–22½p 11.70	75p–32½p 16.90	£1–62½p 32.50	£1.50–75p 35.00	75%–75p+20% (70.20)	£2.20+50%–75p+30% (85.80)

Source

Smith (1931), p. 297.

Note

Top row for each date gives claim and award per week.
Bottom line gives annual increase obtained in £ per annum.
1 Maximum figures are translated into annual terms.

Appendix 12: PAY OF TEMPORARY POSTMEN AND POSTWOMEN, 1918–19

	To May 1918		After May 1918		After Nov 1918		After May 1919	
	£ per week	per annum	£ per week	per annum	£ per week	per annum	£ per week	per annum
London Division I	2.10	109.20	2.35	122.20	2.55	132.60	2.80	145.06
II & III	2.00	104.00	2.25	117.00	2.45	127.40	2.70	140.04
London Women	1.65	85.80	1.85	96.20	1.98½	103.22	2.18½	113.36
Provincial I (M)			2.25	117.00	2.45	127.40	2.70	140.40
(W)			1.75	91.00	1.87½	97.50	2.07½	107.90
Provincial II (M)			2.15	111.80	2.35	122.20	2.60	135.02
(W)			1.65	85.80	1.77½	92.30	1.97½	102.70
Provincial III (M)			2.00	104.00	2.20	114.40	2.45	127.40
(W)			1.55	80.60	1.67½	87.10	1.87½	97.50

Source

Civil Service Arbitration Board, *Awards and Agreements, 1917–1919* (1919).

Appendix 13: OFFICERS OF THE FAWCETT ASSOCIATION, 1889-1919

Chairman

1889–93	J. H. Williams
1893–1903	W. E. Clery
1903–04	G. W. Gains
1905–07	A. J. Mosedale
1908–11	E. J. Nevill
1911–19	C. G. Ammon

Secretary

1889–90	L. Leader
1890 February–June and August–September	W. E. Clery
1890 June–August	H. Hall
1891 September–1892 February	J. Guest
1892–1919	W. E. Cheesman

Treasurer

1889–99	H. Groves
1899–1902	W. E. Smith
1902–17	J. Fitzgerald
1917–19	C. P. Randall

Editor

1890 February–July	W. E. Clery
1890–91	H. Hall
1891 August–September	W. E. Clery
1891–92	J. Guest
1892–94	J. Cooke
1894–95	C. E. Raby
1895–99	H. G. Swift
1899 August–November	D. Griffiths
1900–01	W. E. Clery
1901–03	C. Durrant
1904 January–February	H. G. Swift
1904–11	C. G. Ammon
1911–18	H. Dubery
1918–19	C. G. Ammon
1919	T. E. Morris

Note

Both Williams and Groves resigned in August 1891 and Clery temporarily fulfilled the roles both of secretary and editor. The Fawcett Association also had two trustees and a registrar, as well as organising secretaries from 1895 to 1904. The latter position was filled in the first year by C. E. Raby, from 1896 to 1901 by E. J. Nevill and from 1901 to 1904 by E. Harvey.

Appendix 14: FAWCETT ASSOCIATION: MEMBERSHIP AND FINANCE

	Membership at beginning of year	% of possible[1]	Total income for year (£)	Balance at end of year (£)
1890	762		278	65
1891	2,600		1,509	39
1892	2,020		790	140
1893	2,620		1,015	134
1894	2,300		1,140	180
1895	2,464		1,353	246
1896	2,773		1,568	452
1897	2,810		2,004	614
1898	3,298	67	2,225	724
1899	3,392	67	2,478	592
1900	3,538	66	2,322	452
1901	3,465	61	1,851	166
1902	3,622	66	1,958	238
1903	3,682	69	2,023	141
1904	3,673	67	2,233	620
1905	4,211	76	3,032	1,056
1906	4,630	84	3,714	1,212
1907	4,983	86	4,123	1,515
1908	5,059	87	4,464	1,631
1909	5,144	86	4,511	1,655
1910	5,126	83	4,599	1,671
1911	5,090	83	4,611	1,542
1912	5,277	82	3,161	782
1913	5,670	85	4,315	814
1914	6,107	89	3,891	1,298
1915	6,305	90	4,879	1,292
1916	6,411	90	3,058	1,539
1917	6,391	89	4,752	1,662
1918	6,313	94	4,998	1,639
1919	6,229	95	6,181	505
1920	6,472	95		

Note

[1]Overseers and non-London members have been excluded in calculating percentages. The membership figures up to 1895 were reported to annual meetings in February. Thereafter they are more precisely dated as of 31 December of the previous year. War-time figures include many serving with the armed forces and not paying their subscriptions. All financial figures are rounded to the nearest £. Some of the early accounts only partly include income and expenditure on *The Post*.

Appendix 15: OFFICERS OF THE POSTMEN'S FEDERATION, 1891–1919

General Secretary

1891–1900	
1897 September–December	C. Churchfield
1900–09	H. M. Wilson
1910–11	A. MacLaren
1911–19	T. Robinson
	G. H. Stuart

Parliamentary Secretary

1902–11	
	G. H. Stuart

Organising Secretary

1911–19	
	T. Robinson

Assistant Secretary

1918–19	
	H. W. Wallace

MBS Secretary

1895–1900	
1900–10	H. Boaler
1910–19	T. G. Barnes
	J. W. Bowen

Treasurer

1891–92	
1892–1907	W. Rouse
1907–11	A. F. Harris
1911–19	W. Clubb
1919	A. F. Johnson
	J. W. Bowen

Editor

1892–96	
1896–1916	C. Churchfield
1916–19	J. C. Brown
	H. J. Lincoln

Note

Until 1909, chairmen were elected separately for the Executive and the Conference, nearly always for one year only. The combined position was held by H. J. Lincoln in 1914–15, and by W. Lockyer from 1916–19.

Appendix 16: POSTMEN'S FEDERATION: MEMBERSHIP AND FINANCE

	Membership	Total income (£)	Balance (£)	MBS income on class 'A' cases (£)	Gazette income (£)
1892	3,721	120	21	–	–
1893	6,109	326	158	–	–
1894	9,588	696	399	–	915
1895	11,100	967	235	183	–
1896	15,622	1,019	255	257	–
1897	22,928	1,346	284	4,925	2,667
1898	22,822	1,330	129	4,957	2,687
1899	22,026	934	331	6,596	1,994
1900	22,401	1,463	666	5,939	2,697
1901	23,112	1,897	316	5,155	2,970
1902	25,172	1,592	221	6,136	2,589
1903	25,074	2,813	925	6,324	3,145
1904	26,644	3,650	69	6,706	3,948
1905	29,206	3,149	7	7,462	3,665
1906	32,051	3,225	6	8,443	3,461
1907	33,132	4,037	147	8,626	5,157
1908	34,255	3,748	86	8,518	4,662
1909	35,441	3,804	30	9,383	4,126
1910	37,058	4,772	455	9,919	4,429
1911	37,892	5,566	1,581	9,635	5,111
1912	40,178	6,695	1,519	10,551	5,272
1913	42,607	7,712	1,926	12,580	6,670
1914	44,308	7,543	528	16,241	5,863
1915	44,107	6,432	2,163	19,881	5,530
1916	51,508	7,126	2,204	19,883	5,654
1917	54,441	6,626	1,880	25,850	5,836
1918	65,078	8,870	2,545	25,850	5,903
1919	61,910	13,009	1,820	23,285	6,462
1920	–	12,362	1,352	13,864	5,444

Notes:

1892–6 financial year ends in September, and 1897–8 on 1 August. From 1899 onwards it ends on 31 March, and in 1920 on 31 December 1919. *Gazette* income in the early period cannot be easily separated from that of the Federation as a whole. Membership figures are not always those published at the time.

Appendix 17: OFFICERS OF THE UKPCA, 1887–1914

General Secretary

1887–93	G. E. Lascelles
1893–95	P. Casey
1895–1901	G. A. Landsberry
1901–11	Ernest Lea
1911–14	Albert Varley

Assistant–later Organising Secretary

1896–99	James Lucas
1899–1901	Leo Brodie
1901–02	J. L. Cartwright
1903–04	W. S. Rickards
1904–06	Ben Sewards
1906–08	F. F. Riley
1908–11	J. F. Hunter
1911–14	G. B. Middleton

Treasurer

1895–98	E. W. Merry
1898–1900	J. A. Sweettenham
1900	A. Motgomorie
1900–01	E. Lea
1901–07	J. A. Sweettenham
1907–12	G. B. Middleton
1912–14	J. F. Hunter

Editor of Postal Clerks Herald

1898–1900	James Lucas
1901	Ernest Lea
1901–03	J. W. Wright
1903–12	R. R. Millard
1912–14	G. B. Middleton

Chairman of the Executive

1898–1901	A. E. D. Wilson
1901–08	G. A. Landsberry
1908–11	Albert Varley
1911–14	F. F. Riley

Note

The Association also had a publisher for the *Herald* from 1901, a Women's Organiser (Lucy Withringham, 1908–10 and May Reynolds 1910–14) and an Assistant General Secretary (Don Grant, 1911–14).

Appendix 18: UKPCA MEMBERSHIP AND FINANCE

	Income (£)	Balance (£)	PCH income (£)	Membership	Women
1894	35	3s 6d			
1895				700	
1896				1,587	
1897	128	86		2,888	
1898	150	4		2,590	
1899	–	3		2,324	19
1900	207	35	274	2,818	60
1901	258	49	326	3,270	99
1902	274	10	311	3,104	–
1903	269	19	328	2,500	–
1904	296	38	309	2,638	–
1905	545	84	437	3,753	–
1906	871	291	484	5,093	256
1907	1,143	222	1,018	5,858	–
1908	1,156	302	784	6,171	–
1909	1,307	291	860	6,521	–
1910	1,320	88	962	6,985	561
1911	1,373	−128	1,128	7,686	681
1912	1,418	13	1,180	7,715	719
1913	1,455	−35	1,616	8,109	–
1914	1,947	−451	1,395	8,499	–

Note

The financial figures from 1899 refer to 31 December of the previous year. Membership figures were always given at the same date but usually increased by the time of the conference the following year. The latest available figures are given, but they cannot be viewed with great confidence since they include half members paying only from June and it is never clear how they are counted. No records have survived from the early years.

Appendix 19: OFFICERS OF THE PTCA, 1881–1914

General Secretary

1881	T. Wilkinson
1881–86	T. Morris
1886–90	J. E. Scott
1890–97	T. D. Venables
1898–1903	C. E. Hall
1903–06	Thomas McKinney
1906–10	William Johnson
1910–14	E. R. Tuck

Deputy General Secretary

1894–97	C. E. Hall
1898–1904	Thomas McKinney
1904–07	William Johnson
1907–10	E. R. Tuck
1910–14	Fred Richardson

Parliamentary Secretary

1895–99	E. C. Fugler
1899–1908	Samuel Belderson
1908–13	E. H. Parker
1913–14	H. R. Young

Appendix 20: PTCA MEMBERSHIP AND FINANCE

	Membership	General income (£)	Account balance (£)
1881	1,413		
1882	1,542	346	281
1883	1,050	514	567
1884	704	(1,250)	(542)
1885	676	(1,246)	(780)
1886	1,593	n.a.	(952)
1887	2,125	61	26
1888	2,090	153	70
1889	2,015	154	83
1890	4,578	219	127
1891	4,648	331	207
1892	5,198	447	260
1893	5,557	487	357
1894	6,138	635	369
1895	6,255	662	408
1896	6,200	728	267
1897	7,065	590	224
1898	6,054	532	− 134
1899	4,811	632	63
1900	n.a.	707	124
1901	n.a.	836	20
1902	5,290	1,050	270
1903	5,567	1,069	276
1904	5,974	1,035	− 50
1905	6,822	1,042	106
1906	7,726	1,317	420
1907	8,583	1,554	41
1908	8,748	1,811	560
1909	8,927	2,121	652
1910	10,139	2,377	644
1911	10,701	2,313	426
1912	10,849	2,291	132
1913	11,014	2,419	− 219
1914	11,364	3,224	− 950

Note

The membership figure for 1881 is for 3 December, and thereafter the figures are those reported to the annual conferences for that year, generally as of the previous 31 December. It is not clear whether the insurance and general figures were added together in 1897–9, and in the two following years, when the totals were almost certainly lower, the figures of 5,500 and 5,000 were actually published. The financial figures for 1882 and 1883 are for 31 May, for 1884–93 for the last week in February and thereafter for 31 December of the previous year. In 1884–6 the insurance and general accounts were not given separately. The deficits for the last two years were paid for by selling off most of the stock in a small capital account kept from the general fund. A separate insurance capital account rose steadily from £1,080 in 1887 to £2,801 in 1911 when it was sold off and distributed to the members.

Appendix 21: P&TCA LEADERS, 1914–19

General Secretary

1914–19   J. G. Newlove
After Newlove's illness, A. Lynes was Acting General Secretary from August to December 1917 and F. F. Riley thereafter. Albert Lynes was elected his successor in 1919, but never served pending the amalgamation.

Editor

1914–19   George Middleton

Treasurer

1914–18   James Hunter
(Post then merged with Organising Secretary.)

Organising Secretary

1914–18   Fred Richardson
1918–19   Horace Nobbs

Parliamentary Secretary

1914–16   H. R. Young
1916–19   Walter Baker

Women's Organiser

1916–19   Edith Howse

Appendix 22: P&TCA MEMBERSHIP AND FINANCE

	Members	Women telephonists	All women	Income revenue A/C (£)	Balance (£)
1913	19,863	1,800	3,703	–	–
1914	17,773	2,500	4,800	3,510	572
1915	19,755	2,958	6,900	3,208	1,042
1916	25,641	5,086	9,529	4,036	408
1917	27,212	6,865	12,465	5,445	385
1918	30,346	8,586	16,217	7,652	1,216
1919	33,486	9,504	16,949	10,301	657

Note

All figures are as of 31 December. At the time of amalgamation there were 8,499 members in the United Kingdom Postal Clerks Association and 11,364 in the Postal Telegraph Clerks Association.

Appendix 23: PARLIAMENTARY ELECTION RESULTS OF POST OFFICE WORKERS' CANDIDATES, 1906–1918

York, January 1906
(2-member constituency)

Hamer Greenwood (Liberal)	6,413
G. D. Faber (Conservative)	6,108
J. G. Butcher (Conservative)	6,094
G. H. Stuart (Labour)	*4,573*

Dundee, May 1908

Winston Churchill (Liberal)	7,079
George Baxter (Unionist)	4,370
G. H. Stuart (Labour)	*4,013*
E. Scrymgeour (Prohibition)	655

Eccles, January 1910

G. H. Pollard (Liberal)	7,093
E. Assunder (Conservative)	6,682
G. H. Stuart (Labour)	*3,511*

North-West Durham, January 1914

A. Williams (Liberal)	7,241
J. O. Hardicker (Unionist)	5,564
G. H. Stuart (Labour)	*5,026*

General Election, December 1918
PF Candidates

Durham Consett

A. Williams (Liberal)	7,576
R. Gee (Coalition Labour)	7,283
G. H. Stuart-Bunning (Labour)	*7,268*

Willesden East

H. Mallaby-Deeley (Unionist)	12,044
H. J. Lincoln (Labour)	*4,941*
H. Doree (Liberal)	2,757

Newport

L. Haslam (Coalition Liberal)	14,080
J. W. Bowen (Labour)	*10,234*
B. O. Thomas (Independent)	647

Bury

C. Ainsworth (Unionist)	10,043
G. Toumlin (Coalition Liberal)	6,862
H. W. Wallace (Labour)	*4,973*

Fawcett Association (under ILP auspices)

Camberwell North

H. Newton Knights (Coalition U)	6,010
G. Hearn (Liberal)	2,177
G. C. Ammon (Labour)	*2,175*

P&TCA Candidates

Leicester South

J. A. Blane (Unionist)	18,498
F. Riley (Labour)	*5,463*

Heywood

A. H. Illingworth (Coalition Liberal)	14,350
H. Nobbs (Labour)	*6,827*

Altrincham

C. G. Hamilton (Unionist)	20,422
G. Middleton (Labour)	*7,686*

Harborough, Leicestershire

K. Frazer (Coalition Unionist)	8,466
P. A. Harris (Liberal)	4,608
W. J. Baker (Labour)	*4,496*

Appendix 24: VOTES ON AMALGAMATION, 1907–19

September 1907

UKPCA on amalgamation with the FA
For	1,902
Against	1,267
Majority	642
% poll	59

July 1913

UKPCA on amalgamation with the PTCA
For	6,003
Against	1,296
Majority	4,707
% poll	76

PTCA on amalgamation with the UKPCA
For	6,237
Against	563
Majority	5,674
% poll	63

May 1919

PF on amalgamation with P&TCA
For	24,398
Against	485
Majority	23,913
% poll	56

P&TCA on amalgamation with the PF
For	15,528
Against	975
Majority	14,553
% poll	46

FA on amalgamation with PF and P&TCA
For	4,467
Against	383
Majority	4,084
% poll	78

November 1919

London Postal Porters Association on joining the UPW

For	1,339
Against	78
Majority	1,261
% poll	94

Note

Percentages for May 1919 include those still in the armed forces, but not temporary members of the PF, who are excluded from voting.

Appendix 25: ASSOCIATIONS AND THEIR MEMBERSHIP IN 1912

(1) Manipulative Grades

	Grades	Membership	Possible	%
Postmen's Federation	Postmen	35,184	45,980	86·52
Postal Telegraph Clerks Association	SC&Ts, CC&Ts, Telegraphists, Telephonists	11,280	28,800	39·17
Amalgamated Society of Telephone Employees	Manipulative, Supervising Clerical & Engineering Officers	10,009	19,000	52·68
UK Postal Clerks Association	SC&Ts in postal work	7,724	11,000	70·22
Fawcett Association	London Sorters	5,277	6,413	82·29
Engineering & Stores Association	Workmen in engineering and stores	4,206	6,600	63·73
Irish Post Office Clerks	SC&Ts – Ireland	1,463	1,928	75·88
London Postal Porters' Association	London Porters	1,170	1,463	79·97
Central London Postmen's Association	ELDO Postmen	830	1,632	50·86
Women Sorters Association	London Women Sorters	646	845	76·45
Sorter-Tracers Association		166	177	93·78
Registry Assistants, 2nd Class Assistants		133	147	90·48
Tube Staff Association	Tube Assistants and Night Collectors	114	120	95·00
Postal Bagmen's Association		96	110	87·27
PO Telegraph Mechanicians Society	Mechanics in the Engineering Department	93	166	56·02
Tracers Association		84	105	80·00
Messengers Association		40	61	65·57

(2) Supervisory Grades

	Grades	Membership	Possible	%
Postal Telegraph and Telephone Controlling Association	Supervising Grades at provincial offices (M & F)	1,627	3,310	49·15

Association / Grade				
London Postal Superintending Officers Association	Assistant Superintendants and Overseers	673	966	69·67
Society of Post Office Engineers	Executive and Assistant Engineers	364	488	74·59
Association of National Telephone Engineers	Engineering Officers from the National Telephone Company	302	539	56·03
Central London Male Supervisors Association	Overseers and Assistant Superintendents, CTO	215	357	60·22
London Association of Head Postmen		194	217	89·40
Society of PO Engineering Inspectors		170	267	63·67
Assistant Head Postmen's Association	London	145	293	49·49
Head Porters Association	London	120	175	68·57
Association of PO Superintendents	Smaller provincial offices	81	220	36·82
Second Class Assistant Inspectors and Telegraph Messengers	London	56	87	64·37
Telephone Exchange Managers Association		51	63	80·95
Association of Inspectors of Messengers	London	42	48	87·50
Association of Inspectors of Tracing		26	28	92·86

(3) Clerical Grades

Association				
Women Clerks' Association	1st and 2nd class Women Clerks	1,865	2,498	74·66
General Association of Third Class Clerks		323	467	69·16
PO Engineering Clerks Association	3rd class Clerks in Provincial Engineers	274	286	95·81
London Postal Clerks Association		160	171	93·57
Association of Third Class Clerks (Surveyors)		139	140	99·29
Representative Committee of Metropolitan 3rd Class Clerks	of Superintending Engineers	121	123	98·37
London Telephone Service Association	Clerical and Supervising Males in London Telephone Services	96	112	85·71
Engineer-in-Chief's Office Supplementary Clerks' Association		67	67	100·00
1st and 2nd Class Clerks (Provinces) Association	of Provincial Superintending Engineers	39	53	58·21

(4) Others

National Federation of Sub-Postmasters	6,601	23,000	28·70
PO Medical Officers Association	600	3,291	18·23
Head Postmasters Association	494	750	65·87
Established Sub-Postmasters Association	49	369	13·28

Source

Post Office Information 1912. The precise date is not given and earlier appendices show that the figures are probably low for the larger associations, notably for the PF.

NOTES ON APPENDICES 26-32

None of these series can claim to be precisely comparable. Different figures are frequently published in different years, especially on matters of finance. These generally stick to those published at the time according to accountancy and other criteria of the time, though lines on the tables indicate major changes in the basis of the figures. Some of the most important are as follows:

a. After 1950–1 figures for Cable and Wireless are included in overseas telegrams.
b. In 1975–6 Inland Telex changed the measurement for units to calls.
c. In 1964–5 International Telex changed its unit of measurement for numbers of calls to numbers of minutes. Inward, outward and transit calls are all included.
d. International telephone calls: before 1937–8 Ireland is included; from 1949–50 ingoing as well as outgoing calls are given in the total.
e. Much financial information was not collected in war-time.
f. Wage statistics from 1955–6 include in all cases employers National Insurance contributions, but not Pension Contributions, as far as they are indicated as a separate category.
g. Wage statistics for 1960–1 include certain administrative and other staff who appear not to have been previously counted.
h. Post pay includes sub-postmasters.
i. From 1968–9 National Data Processing is included in the total, but not given separately. Giro and remittance services are also included from the time they are given separately.
j. In the mid-1970s figures are subject to government price restraint and consequent compensation. As far as possible, the actual operational figures are given here.

Appendix 26: POST OFFICE POSTAL BUSINESS, 1922–80

	Letters and packets (m)	Parcels (m)	Postal orders (m)	Broadcasting licences (radio & TV) (m)	Other licences issued (m)
1922–3	5,455	120·7	105·6	–	3·2
1928–9	6,230	154·5	149·0	2·7	–
1929–30	6,400	160·5	170·9	3·7	4·2
1930–1	6,475	161·9	191·2	3·6	4·2
1931–2	6,540	158·1	209·4	4·6	4·2
1932–3	6,640	151·7	212·3	5·5	4·1
1933–4	6,753	153·3	222·8	6·3	4·2
1934–5	6,935	149·7	260·2	7·0	4·1
1935–6	7,345	162·2	311·6	7·6	4·3
1936–7	7,690	174·3	343·9	8·1	4·4
1937–8	7,990	179·5	399·3	8·6	4·5
1938–9	8,150	184·8	422·5	9·0	4·6
1939–40	7,360	192·7	197·9	8·9	4·0
1946–7	7,300	238·7	344·4	10·8	4·3
1947–8	7,600	243·5	420·5	11·2	4·4
1948–9	8,050	239·6	423·8	11·7	4·8
1949–50	8,350	243·3	431·8	12·1	4·5
1950–1	8,500	232·6	480·2	12·4	5·0
1951–2	8,750	223·6	521·5	12·6	4·5
1952–3	8,800	243·4	575·8	12·8	5·0
1953–4	9,100	241·9	604·3	12·3	5·0
1954–5	9,500	247·1	616·1	15·1	5·0
1955–6	9,700	237·6	609·3	14·3	5·4

1956–7	9,700	249·0	631·3	14·5	5·8
1957–8	9,600	247·4	671·4	14·3	6·2
1958–9	9,700	243·3	693·9	15·7	6·4
1959–60	10,200	243·8	718·1	15·1	6·9
1960–1	10,600	248·1	735·9	15·2	7·0
1961–2	10,500	233·4	659·7	15·5	6·6
1962–3	10,600	224·2	591·3	15·8	7·6
1963–4	11,000	229·9	636·5	15·9	7·6
1964–5	11,200	216·0	643·9	16·2	8·1
1965–6	11,300	235·3	673·6	16·2	8·6
1966–7	11,400	222·3	667·2	16·9	8·8
1967–8	11,500	216·6	616·5	17·5	9·7
1968–9	11,300	212·3	544·9	17·8	9·7
1969–70	11,400	207·6	501·7	17·9	9·6
1970–1	10,500	180·8	434·6	17·6	9·8
1971–2	10,550	188·6	342·3	17·3	10·7
1972–3	10,790	194·3	358·1	17·7	11·2
1973–4	11,010	194·9	339·2	17·9	12·1
1974–5	10,878	200·5	304·0	17·2	13·1
1975–6	9,903	169·8	224·8	16·3	14·0
1976–7	9,458	152·3	192·2	16·4	15·9
1977–8	9,484	159·9	179·2	16·6	17·0
1978–9	9,965	171·5	172·8	16·6	18·5
1979–80	10,207	180·2	154·9	16·4	18·7
1980–1	9,969	172·4	118·4	16·4	19·5

Note

See *Notes* on p. 649 above.

Appendix 27: POST OFFICE TELECOMMUNICTIONS BUSINESS, 1922–80

	Inland telegrams (m.)	Inland Telex (m.)	Overseas telegrams (m.)	International Telex (m.)	Telephone calls Local (m.)	Trunk (m.)	International (m.)	Telephone stations (m.)
1922–3	55·8	—	14·7	—	730	59	·6	1·05
1929–30	42·4	—	14·0	—	1,322	117	2·2	1·88
1930–1	39·8	—	11·9	—	1,370	122	2·3	1·98
1931–2	37·2	—	10·8	—	1,305	124	2·5	2·07
1932–3	36·0	—	9·4	—	1,361	129	2·4	2·14
1933–4	36·2	—	9·3	—	1,440	139	1·3	2·22
1934–5	35·3	—	8·7	—	1,594	85	1·3	2·39
1935–6	44·5	—	8·7	—	1,725	98	1·5	2·58
1936–7	49·2	—	9·2	—	1,882	99	1·7	2·83
1937–8	49·2	—	9·2	—	2,059	106	1·9	3·05
1938–9	50·4	—	8·9	—	2,123	111	1·0	3·23
1939–40	54·7	—	9·1	—	2,076	117	0·9	3·34
1946–7	52·7	—	10·6	—	2,509	205	0·6	4·32
1947–8	47·4	—	10·6	—	2,681	217	0·8	4·65
1948–9	43·4	—	10·3	—	2,911	226	0·9	4·92
1949–50	42·0	—	10·5	—	2,940	235	1·1 / 2·2	5·17
1950–1	41·6	—	21·9	—	3,076	250	2·7	5·43
1951–2	38·6	—	21·3	0·3	3,230	261	3·0	5·71
1952–3	36·4	—	20·0	0·5	3,165	264	3·1	5·93
1953–4	34·2	—	20·4	0·8	3,370	278	3·4	6·14
1954–5	25·7	—	20·9	1·4	3,615	306	3·8	6·49
1955–6	20·5	—	21·1	2·1	3,865	333	4·1	6·89
1956–7	16·8	—	21·4	2·7	3,743	321	4·6	7·23

Year								
1957–8	15·2	2·8	20·9	3·2	3,671	327	5·2	7·36
1958–9	14·1	5·1	19·6	3·9	3,700	340	5·7	7·53
1959–60	13·8	11·7	20·3	4·8	3,900	383	6·3	7·86
1960–1	13·6	38·6	20·0	5·8	4,300	422	7·0	8·28
1961–2	13·3	77·1	19·8	8·0	4,500	477	7·7	8·62
1962–3	12·7	99·3	19·5	10·0	4,750	545	9·0	8·93
1963–4	10·0	125·3	19·8	12·8	5,100	624	10·1	9·36
				<u>16·3</u>				
1964–5	10·9	161·2	20·7	46·9	5,600	736	12·1	9·99
1965–6	10·3	174·2	20·9	55·2	6,050	841	14·8	10·72
1966–7	9·4	203·5	21·1	65·1	6,450	930	18·1	11·39
1967–8	8·8	229·6	21·6	75·8	6,450	1,064	18·1	12·11
1968–9	8·0	245·9	20·7	88·0	7,420	1,189	25·6	12·91
1969–70	7·9	258·5	21·0	104·6	8,270	1,325	32·7	13·96
1970–1	6·7	323·3	18·7	123·9	9,230	1,517	38·9	<u>14·98</u>
1971–2	6·8	353·5	19·7	145·6	10,330	1,699	46·9	16·16
1972–3	7·3	398·0	19·3	165·8	11,595	1,944	53·3	17·60
1973–4	7·2	363·5	19·9	201·2	12,707	2,138	61·5	19·14
1974–5	6·2	386·1	19·1	226·0	13,523	2,313	73·0	20·39
		<u>403·3</u>						
1975–6	4·2	64·3	16·6	237·6	13,736	2,356	93·1	21·09
1976–7	3·4	67·7	15·3	266·9	14,200	2,456	113·6	22·08
1977–8	3·2	74·9	13·9	292·9	14,600	3,703	150·7	23·26
1978–9	3·3	83·2	13·0	329·4	15,700	3,022	184·0	25·02
1979–80	3·3	86·0	12·0	367·9	16,600	3,257	222·6	26·74
1980–1	2·9	90·0	10·6	404·0	16,840	3,335	252·6	27·87

Note

See *Notes* on p. 649 above.

Appendix 28: POST OFFICE ACCOUNTS, 1911–1980 – I: TOTAL

	Total income (£m.)	Profit/Loss (£m.)	Wages paid (£m.)	Wages (% of income)
1911–12	26·2	4·5	<u>13·2</u>	<u>50·6</u>
1912–13	29·8	4·7	15·5	51·8
1913–14	31·7	5·2	16·1	50·6
1914–15	31·7	3·5	17·8	56·2
1915–16	–	3·4	–	–
1916–17	–	6·2	–	–
1917–18	–	6·6	–	–
1918–19	–	7·4	–	–
1919–20	–	−1·2	–	–
1920–1	–	−6·7	–	–
1921–2	64·6	−1·3	41·5	64·2
1922–3	58·3	4·4	31·1	53·2
1923–4	56·1	5·3	28·7	51·1
1924–5	58·6	5·4	29·6	50·5
1925–6	61·8	6·7	31·4	50·9
1926–7	62·3	5·6	31·7	50·7
1927–8	66·6	7·6	32·5	48·7
1928–9	68·5	9·0	32·3	46·8
1929–30	71·2	9·4	33·1	46·2
1930–1	71·9	9·2	32·9	45·5
1931–2	71·8	10·6	30·8	42·6
1932–3	72·7	11·1	30·3	41·4
1933–4	74·4	12·3	30·4	40·6
1934–5	75·8	11·9	31·3	41·1
1935–6	80·0	12·5	33·4	41·4
1936–7	84·1	12·3	35·0	41·3
1937–8	87·7	11·2	36·5	41·3
1938–9	90·6	10·2	38·2	42·0
1939–40	93·1	7·4	39·8	42·6
1940–1	–	22·4	–	–
1941–2	–	26·0	–	–
1943–4	–	37·3	–	–
1944–5	–	39·8	–	–
1945–6	–	36·1	–	–
1946–7	–	24·1	–	–
1947–8	182·3	19·5	80·0	43·9
1948–9	190·3	15·8	86·1	42·2
1949–50	199·6	13·8	89·8	45·0
1950–1	211·1	12·6	95·3	45·2
1951–2	231·1	5·4	107·7	46·6
1952–3	253·3	4·9	118·1	46·6
1953–4	269·1	7·4	123·8	46·3
1954–5	284·9	5·2	132·0	46·3
			<u>144·50</u>	<u>46·8</u>
1955–6	<u>308·7</u>	2·3	175·1	56·7

1956–7	356·3	−3·1	195·9	54·7
1957–8	389·2	2·6	210·2	54·0
1958–9	408·3	8·7	222·8	54·4
1959–60	442·5	20·9	230·2	52·0
			242·5	51·7
1960–1	468·6	24·3	278·6	59·4
1961–2	459·3	13·1	306·3	66·7
1962–3	530·3	12·1	325·2	61·3
1963–4	604·7	30·7	348·8	57·7
1964–5	646·6	20·1	398·3	61·6
1965–6	722·8	40·2	437·5	60·5
1966–7	782·4	44·3	462·0	59·0
1967–8	845·0	39·3	498·3	59·0
1968–9	950·0	44·4	539·5	56·8
1969–70	1,046·4	36·2	586·5	56·0
1970–1	1,135·3	20·5	635·4	56·0
1971–2	1,373·5	36·1	775·5	56·9
1972–3	1,530·3	−64·1	881·6	57·6
1973–4	1,762·5	−128·1	1,013·9	57·5
1974–5	2,122·7	−307·7	1,340·9	63·2
1975–6	3,205·7	147·9	1,662·4	51·9
1976–7	3,806·0	392·3	1,782·9	46·8
1977–8	4,813·2	367·7	1,942·4	46·4
1978–9	4,619·0	375·1	2,251·2	47·7
1979–80	5,193·3	297·0	2,660·2	51·2
1980–1	6,579·7	216·0		

Note

See *Notes* on p. 649 above.

Appendix 29: POST OFFICE ACCOUNTS, 1911–1980 – II: POSTS

	Total income (£m.)	Profit/Loss (£m.)	Wages paid (£m.)	Wages (% of income)
1912–13	20·9	5·5	10·0	47·9
1913–14	21·9	6·2	10·3	46·9
1914–15	21·8	4·9	11·4	52·1
1915–16	26·5	6·0	12·0	45·4
1916–17	28·0	6·5	12·0	42·9
1917–18	29·5	6·8	13·3	45·0
1918–19	34·9	8·2	16·8	48·3
1919–20	36·2	3·5	23·3	64·4
1920–1	43·9	1·7	29·9	68·1
1921–2	45·0	2·3	29·8	66·2
1922–3	38·8	5·2	22·5	57·8
1923–4	36·4	5·0	20·7	56·9
1924–5	38·4	6·6	21·3	55·4
1925–6	40·6	7·4	23·0	56·8
1926–7	40·0	6·8	23·1	57·7
1927–8	43·0	8·8	23·7	55·1
1928–9	43·5	9·2	23·7	54·3
1929–30	44·8	9·7	24·3	54·2
1930–1	45·1	9·8	24·3	53·8
1931–2	44·5	10·9	22·8	51·2
1932–3	44·9	11·5	22·6	50·3
1933–4	45·1	10·9	22·7	50·3
1934–5	45·5	11·2	23·4	51·5
1935–6	47·9	11·5	24·9	51·9
1936–7	50·0	11·5	26·1	52·2
1937–8	52·0	11·5	27·2	52·3
1938–9	52·8	10·8	28·4	53·7
1939–40	50·4	7·0	29·1	57·7
1940–1	–	19·3	–	–
1941–2	–	18·5	–	–
1942–3	–	19·7	–	–
1943–4	–	18·7	–	–
1944–5	–	16·9	–	–
1945–6	–	15·5	–	–
1946–7	–	11·9	–	–
1947–8	96·4	11·5	57·5	59·6
1948–9	102·0	11·0	60·7	59·5
1949–50	104·6	9·1	63·4	60·6
1950–1	106·5	6·8	65·8	61·7
1951–2	120·7	4·4	74·2	61·5
1952–3	132·7	4·8	81·7	61·6
1953–4	139·0	4·9	85·9	61·8
1954–5	145·4	3·3	91·6	63·0
			100·5	66·0
1955–6	152·9	−1·5	103·5	67·7

1956–7	175·2	−1·7	116·4	66·5
1957–8	190·0	−0·5	126·7	66·7
1958–9	202·4	3·0	132·1	65·4
1959–60	213·2	6·4	136·9	64·2
			143·8	64·5
1960–1	223·05	5·9	144·4	64·7
1961–2	233·0	1·0	156·6	67·2
1962–3	241·4	−8·1	167·8	69·5
1963–4	262·0	−7·8	177·5	67·7
1964–5	273·7	−19·6	201·6	73·7
1965–6	318·8	0·9	218·8	68·6
1966–7	340·6	6·6	228·9	67·2
1967–8	359·9	−4·0	245·0	68·1
1968–9	377·8	−5·8	261·8	69·3
1969–70	405·3	−24·8	283·1	69·8
1970–1	379·4	−72·6	296·2	78·1
1971–2	516·1	−12·6	359·3	69·6
1972–3	561·3	−42·5	396·4	70·6
1973–4	631·4	−57·5	461·4	73·1
1974–5	773·2	−109·2	615·3	79·6
1975–6	1,088·6	−9·2	762·6	70·0
1976–7	1,200·0	24·3	810·4	67·5
1977–8	1,325·1	40·4	881·9	66·5
1978–9	1,427·4	33·1	1,025·5	70·8
1979–80	1,708·8	49·3	1,198·3	70·1
1980–1	2,125·2	29·2		

Note

See *Notes* on p. 649 above.

Appendix 30: POST OFFICE ACCOUNTS
III: TELECOMMUNICATIONS, 1911–47

	Profit/Loss (£m.)	Inland telegram Profit/Loss (£m.)	Telephone Profit/Loss (£m.)
1911–12	+ 0·9	+1·2	+ 0·3
1912–13	+ 0·2	−1·2	+ 0·2
1913–14	− 1·3	−1·2	− 0·1
1914–15	− 0·6	−0·5	− 0·1
1915–16	− 0·3	−0·5	+ 0·2
1916–17	− 0·2	−0·6	+ 0·4
1917–18	− 0·7	−0·7	− 0·04
1918–19	− 4·6	−2·6	− 2·0
1919–20	− 8·4	−3·7	− 4·7
1920–1	− 3·6	−3·0	− 0·6
1921–2	− 0·8	−1·7	+ 0·9
1922–3	+ 0·3	−1·3	+ 1·6
1923–4	− 1·1	−1·6	+ 0·5
1924–5	− 0·8	−1·3	+ 0·5
1925–6	− 0·6	−1·3	+ 0·3
1926–7	− 1·3	−1·4	0·1
1927–8	− 1·3	−0·8	+ 0·5
1928–9	− 1·3	−0·8	+ 0·5
1929–30	− 0·7	−1·0	+ 0·3
1930–1	− 1·4	−0·8	+ 0·6
1931–2	− 1·2	−0·8	+ 0·4
1932–3	− 0·8	−0·6	+ 1·4
1933–4	− 1·1	−0·6	+ 1·7
1934–5	+ 1·3	−0·8	+ 2·1
1935–6	+ 0·9	−0·6	+ 1·5
1936–7	+ 0·8	−0·7	+ 1·5
1937–8	− 0·4	−0·8	+ 0·4
1938–9	− 0·5	−0·8	+ 0·3
1939–40	+ 0·4	−0·6	+ 1·0
1940–1	+ 3·2	−0·4	+ 3·6
1941–2	+ 7·4	−0·3	+ 7·7
1942–3	+12·3	−0·1	+12·4
1943–4	+18·5	−0·2	+18·7
1944–5	+23·0	−0·1	+23·1
1945–6	+20·6	−0·04	+20·6
1946–7	+12·2	−1·9	+14·1

Note

This table indicates the comparatively small role of telephone income in the overall Post Office service before the 1940s. The published figures do not make it possible to provide more information on income, proportion paid on wages and so forth. Between 1932 and 1940, the *average* annual income on inland telegrams was £3·98 m., the average expenditure on wages of £2·88 m., an average percentage on income of 72·3. The losses for these eight years were from £·55 m. to £·84 m. In 1950–1 the income on telegrams was £9·7 m., the loss £4·19 m. £8·48 m. went on wages, a proportion of 87·2% of income. In 1960–1 the income was £22·1 m., the loss £1·93 m., the wages £15·03 m., being 67·9% of income.
See also *Notes* on p. 649 above.

Appendix 31: POST OFFICE ACCOUNTS IV: TELECOMMUNICATIONS, 1947–80

	Income (£m.)	Profit (£m.)	Operators' & engineers' wages (£m.)	Wages (% of income)	Telephone inland (£m.)	Telephone profit (£m.)	Telephone wages (£m.)	Telephone wages (% of income)
1947–8	86·5	8·0	35·6	41·1	79·6	10·5	16·7	20·9
1948–9	88·4	4·2	39·3	44·2	82·3	8·1	18·8	22·9
1949–50	95·6	4·7	43·5	41·6	89·1	9·1	19·8	22·2
1950–1	105·3	0·2	45·6	43·3	95·5	9·9	21·1	22·1
1951–2	110·5	1·0	52·1	47·2	97·4	4·3	24·3	24·9
1952–3	120·6	0·1	56·8	47·1	106·3	3·7	26·7	25·1
1953–4	130·1	2·4	58·6	45·0	115·2	5·5	28·1	24·4
1954–5	139·5	1·8	63·9	45·8	123·3	4·3	30·6	24·8
1955–6	155·8	3·8	70·4	45·2	138·1	4·9	<u>34·0</u>	<u>24·6</u>
							59·5	43·1
1956–7	181·0	1·4	78·6	43·4	162·7	0·1	65·9	40·5
1957–8	199·2	3·1	83·5	41·9	180·6	5·2	70·3	38·9
1958–9	214·6	5·7	90·7	42·3	194·8	8·2	76·6	39·3
1959–60	229·3	14·6	93·3	40·7	208·5	16·9	79·0	37·9
			<u>98·7</u>	<u>40·2</u>				
1960–1	<u>245·5</u>	<u>18·4</u>	134·2	54·7	223·5	20·4	83·7	37·5
1961–2	262·3	12·6	149·8	57·1	–	–	–	–

1962-3	241·4	20·2	159·4	66·0
1963-4	342·7	38·5	171·3	50·0
1964-5	372·9	39·7	196·6	52·8
1965-6	404·0	39·3	218·7	54·1
1966-7	441·8	37·7	231·1	52·3
1967-8	485·1	35·3	253·3	52·2
1968-9	568·2	50·1	276·1	48·6
1969-70	652·3	61·3	301·1	46·1
1970-1	772·3	93·5	334·2	43·3
1971-2	884·1	58·0	404·5	45·7
1972-3	1,002·3	9·7	472·6	47·1
1973-4	1,160·5	61·4	536·5	46·2
1974-5	1,382·6	194·6	704·3	50·7
1975-6	2,166·8	154·7	872·9	40·3
1976-7	2,658·0	365·4	944·0	35·5
1977-8	2,920·0	326·6	1,047·8	35·9
1978-9	3,243·9	374·1	1,208·6	37·2
1979-80	3,558·9	236·1	1,434·7	40·3
1980-1	4,554·2			

Note

From the financial changes of 1960–1 it is no longer possible to give separate figures for telephone and telegraph, the latter now constituting a very much smaller proportion of the total than twenty years before.
See also *Notes* on p. 649 above.

Appendix 32: POST OFFICE STAFF
1950–80

	Total	
31 March 1950	321,782	
31 March 1955	337,465	
31 March 1960	339,013	(of which 89,727 were postmen, 22,490 PHGs, 22,490 P&TOs, 59,366 non-Engineering Telecoms.)
31 March 1965	384,280	(of which 97,143 were postmen, 20,994 PHGs, 22,337 P&TOs,) 85,000 non-Engineering Telecoms, 170,831 postal.)
31 March 1970	407,721	(162,885 postal, 200,263 Telecoms.)
31 March 1975	434,065	(177,625 postal, 247,205 Telecoms.)
31 March 1980	422,902	(176,486 postal, 249,056 Telecoms.)

Note

These figures are very difficult to compare over time because of the varied basis on which they are calculated. Generally speaking, part-timers count as ½ and sub-postmasters are not included (there were 22,907 of these in 1950, 22,918 in 1960, 22,628 in 1970 and 21,056 in 1980.)
See also *Notes* on p. 649 above.

Appendix 33: CAPITAL EXPENDITURE IN THE POST OFFICE, 1947–80

	Total (£m.)	% Return on capital	Telecomms (£m.)	% Return on capital	Posts (£m.)	% Return on capital
1947–8	32·0					
1948–9	38·3					
1949–50	45·3					
1950–1	48·3					
1951–2	55·3					
1952–3	67·0					
1953–4	74·2					
	69·6					
1954–5	72·0		69·3		2·7	
1955–6	85·4	4·4	82·3		3·1	
1956–7	95·7	6·9	91·4	6·9	4·3	7·7
1957–8	97·2	7·5	91·3	7·3	5·9	10·8
1958–9	94·0	8·0	88·8	7·4	5·2	18·0
1959–60	100·1	8·6	93·9	7·8	6·2	20·0
1960–1	105·2	8·5	98·2	7·9	7·0	16·2
1961–2	124·6	6·5	115·5	6·6	9·1	4·8
1962–3	131·1	6·2	121·6	7·2	9·5	−13·2
1963–4	163·8	7·8	150·9	8·8	12·9	−10·3
1964–5	187·3	6·9	173·7	8·6	13·6	−24·6
1965–6	209·7	8·1	193·5	8·2	16·2	7·7
1966–7	266·0	8·0	242·0	7·7	24·0	13·2
1967–8	318·3	7·4	290·7	7·3	27·6	9·1
1968–9	354·3		325·8	8·0	27·3	
1969–70	393·1		451·4	8·4	27·3	
1970–1	459·8		426·2	9·8	34·3	
1971–2	541·1		537·3	8·6	29·9	
1972–3	654·1		625·5	6·9	27·5	
1973–4	725·0		696·4	6·4	26·3	
1974–5	825·9		787·2	5·2	33·9	
1975–6	962·5		915·9	14·1	40·5	
1976–7	867·5		834·6	7·6	29·9	
1977–8	870·1		844·6	6·1	24·8	
1978–9	1,032·2		996·5	6·9	34·5	
1979–80	1,290·3		1,240·8	4·6	47·0	
1980–1				4·0		

Note

These figures were not published for every year.

Appendix 34: UPW OFFICERS, 1920–82

General Secretary

1919–36	J. W. Bowen
1936–44	T. J. Hodgson
1944–56	C. J. Geddes
1957–67	Ron Smith
1967–82	Tom Jackson
1982	A. D. Tuffin

Assistant (Deputy) General Secretary

1919–30	W. J. Baker
1931–41	J. Paterson
1941–4	C. J. Geddes
1944–51	G. A. Stevens
1951–6	R. A. Hayward
1956–67	L. V. Andrews
1967–80	N. Stagg
1980–82	A. D. Tuffin
1982	Tony Clarke

General Treasurer

1919–35	A. W. Lockyer
1935–47	W. T. Leicester
1947–53	A. H. Wood
1953–6	Ron Smith
1956–62	E. R. Mercer
1962–81	F. W. Moss
1981	F. J. Binks

Organising Secretary

1919–21	H. J. Lincoln
1921–28	C. Ammon
1928–40	H. Nobbs
1940–56	H. E. Randall
1956–64	A. Sampson
1964–76	A. R. T. Mash
1976	R. I. Rowley

Editor

1919–30	George Middleton
1931–45	Francis Andrews
1945–54	J. M. Chalmers
1954–6	E. R. Mercer
1956–67	Norman Stagg
1967–80	Harry Burnett
1980–2	Tony Clarke
1982	Allen Slater

Assistant Secretary (Outdoor)

1919–45	Harry Wallace
1945–9	J. Moohan
1949–55	C. Stennett
1955–64	L. Morgan
1964–7	Tom Jackson
1967–72	W. J. Failes
1972	M. Styles

Assistant Secretary (Indoor)

1919–20	W. B. Cheesman
1920–5	Fred Riley
1925–36	T. J. Hodgson
1936–40	John Coyne
1940–52	H. R. Williams
1952–6	J. Currie
1969–80	A. D. Tuffin
1980–1	R. Nelson
1981	E. Dudley

Assistant Secretary (Telephones/Telecommunications)
(originally Women's Organiser)

1919–37	Edith Howse
1937–44	M. Peake
1945–54	W. E. Rowe
1954–69	Nan Whitelaw
1969–80	J. M. McKinlay
1980	M. Spurr

Assistant Secretary (Legal and Medical)

1947–51	R. A. Hayward
1951–7	G. H. Edwards
1957–73	E. V. W. Marshall
1973–81	A. Reid
1981	P. Grace

Assistant Secretary (PHG and Revisions)

1953–65	D. L. Brown
1965–80	W. H. Wolfenden
1980	H. J. Jones

Assistant Secretary (GS/DGS Department)

1969–73	J. R. Lawlor
1973–82	W. M. Tracey
1982	L. Hewitt

Assistant Secretary (Male Telephonists)

1970–4	G. Forsyth
1974–7	J. Murchie
1978	K. McAllister

Research Officer (not elected)

1919–22	W. Milne Bailey
1922–6	G. Mackenzie
1926–64	E. R. Hardcastle
1964–6	J. Mathew
1967	E. A. Geaney

Appendix 35: UPW MEMBERSHIP FIGURES
1920–80

	Total[1]	Women members[2]	Postmen (& Postmen higher grade)[3]	Main indoor grades[4]	Telephonists[5]
1920	107,770	19,016	51,640	31,351	12,169
1921	83,807	14,125	44,804	22,876	9,624
1922	85,664	15,430	44,667	23,837	10,127
1923	86,194	15,355	44,444	23,600	9,848
1924	87,329	15,091	46,167	21,672	9,969
1925	91,359	16,280	47,973	22,525	11,080
1926	90,039	15,935	47,074	22,179	11,073
1927	92,743	16,607	48,491	22,709	11,193
1928	95,110	17,151	50,138	22,803	11,596
1929	99,843	17,973	52,433	23,198	12,257
1930	101,388	18,485	58,318	23,589	12,726
1931	98,389	17,618	51,169	23,548	11,975
1932	96,092	16,876	50,288	23,084	11,194
1933	98,449	17,421	51,194	23,723	11,468
1934	103,005	18,443	52,931	24,608	12,029
1935	108,701	19,509	55,600	24,599	12,969
1936	113,851	20,640	57,905	26,739	14,094
1937	120,089	22,098	60,610	27,921	15,647
1938	124,909	23,309	62,806	28,657	16,789
1939	132,152	25,545	65,035	30,998	18,295
1940	137,614	27,447	66,217	33,860	19,382
1941	149,827	42,648	55,635	29,197	20,673
1942	156,076		55,707	31,263	20,524
1943	153,903		52,978	31,874	20,515
1944	147,831		52,564	31,793	19,210
1945	145,280		56,357	31,949	18,941
1946	151,615		69,618	35,148	23,560
1947	146,947		72,713	29,648	24,223
1948	147,508		82,680	26,753	26,644
1949	144,118		86,772	23,328	21,162
1950	149,022		87,704	24,175	26,448
1951	155,602		90,510	24,848	29,047
1952	160,908		90,307	25,346	30,365
1953	161,290		94,607	25,392	30,163
1954	161,481		93,566	25,843	31,545
1955	159,816		93,512	24,855	31,167
1956	163,317		97,163	24,004	31,303
1957	165,438		100,528	24,497	29,948
1958	165,487		100,973	25,135	29,802
1959	166,573		100,518	25,413	31,441
1960	166,054		99,447	24,963	32,463
1961	174,354		103,405	25,124	37,212
1962	172,699		104,093	24,446	35,822

1963	171,200	101,722	25,129	36,075
1964	181,783	112,884	25,330	36,205
1965	175,492	113,831	(24,306)	31,009
1966	180,371	116,286	23,890	33,898
1967	185,388	117,696	25,071	35,599
1968	192,310	119,515	26,056	38,644
1969	198,037	122,068	26,647	39,447
1970	209,479			
1971	192,257	122,271	21,781	33,024
1972	191,076			
1973	194,208	117,324	23,566	38,197
1974	190,000			
1975	185,000			
1976	201,099	123,871	25,034	32,838
1977	197,247	121,056	25,351	31,624
1978	197,157	121,112	24,720	31,935
1979	203,452	125,599	25,766	34,042
1980	202,993	123,040	26,024	33,796

Notes

The source of these figures is the reports of the organising secretaries to the annual conferences, and refer to the last day of the year in each case. In the 1953 Report a table was given but the figures vary very slightly for 1928–35 and for 1943–4, probably because a different part of the year is taken. In each case I have used the originally published figure.

In March 1922, 2,717 members joined the Irish Postal Workers Union.

The figures for 1965 never appeared in the Organising Secretary's reports and have to be inferred from his comments on the 1966 figures. Those from 1970 onwards have not been published and, as can be seen, in some cases not calculated either.

1 In later years the figure for 1920 was given as 97,151 (see for example the list presented to the 1930 Conference), but the figure given here will be seen to correspond to the totals given by the three Organising Secretaries to the 1921 Conference. The lower figure was clearly calculated by some other method in order not to emphasise how far membership had since fallen.

2 The figures for Women's membership are taken from the Womens Organiser's Report issued to the annual conferences until 1941. They are not calculated separately thereafter.

3 Includes established and non-established staff, temporary and auxiliaries and also head postmen. From 1947 onwards I have also included in the group the postmen higher grade who performed many of the functions previously done by the main indoor grates. For some purposes therefore the figures before and after this date are not comparable.

4 Includes all those in these groups, whether established or not. For reasons explained above part of the figure for 1965 is simply the average of the adjacent years. Grades included: sorting clerks and telegraphists, counter clerks and telegraphists, telegraphists, postal and telegraph officers, postal assistants.

5 Includes night and temporary telephonists.

Groups not included with the above include messangers, cleaners, overseas telegraph operators, junior and preparatory grades, various other small grades and honorary members.

Appendix 36: UPW FINANCE, 1919–80

Year	Total income/ revenue account (£)	Total Political Fund income[1] (£)	Investments[2] (£)	Defence Fund investments (£)	Insurance Society funds[3] (£)
1919	10,301	4,891	168	—	4,906
1920	69,379	7,220	4,538	—	—
1921	68,734	13,888	8,569	—	6,938
1922	67,403	15,931	3,069	—	6,938
1923	71,368	13,648	16,980	—	6,938
1924	70,166	13,022	25,185	—	8,932
1925	71,179	12,890	33,117	—	11,931
1926	72,302	17,275	34,303	—	13,924
1927	74,729	16,215	34,976	—	18,885
1928	84,302	—	34,922	—	17,914
1929	93,132	—	36,239	—	21,907
1930	100,053	—	36,812	—	21,907
1931	73,592	—	34,421	—	21,907
1932	69,191	—	34,957	—	39,769
1933	69,709	—	40,512	—	48,683
1934	71,359	—	42,034	—	55,455
1935	76,293	—	43,331	—	57,351
1936	78,848	—	42,487	—	62,701
1937	80,394	—	490	—	63,702
1938	85,948	—	5,490	—	63,474
1939	88,396	—	30,213	—	65,097
1940	84,902	—	41,339	—	66,538
1941	90,416	—	52,707	—	67,947
1942	90,833	—	52,267	—	72,688
1943	97,102	—	52,757	—	75,614

	Total income/ revenue account (£)	Total Political Fund income[1] (£)	Investments[2] (£)	Defence Fund investments (£)	Insurance Society funds[3] (£)
1944	91,190	—	61,096	—	78,122
1945	91,496	—	50,184	—	80,636
1946	114,978	—	49,097	—	82,422
1947	122,527	8,867	50,130	—	86,438
1948	124,467	11,054	43,680	—	88,121
1949	133,155	13,040	57,681	—	91,020
1950	135,291	13,384	60,025	—	91,136
1051	145,375	12,734	65,076	—	93,917
1952	160,027	11,171	64,922	—	102,354
1953	175,917	14,886	72,208	—	110,983
1954	187,352	18,906	66,230	—	120,182
1955	208,034	22,203	55,056	—	129,582
1956	251,327	20,335	60,080	—	123,628
1957	251,398	27,449	59,814	—	134,836
1958	237,438	32,102	57,848	—	153,461
1959	257,122	26,419	56,286	—	179,312
1960	248,961	29,169	58,534	—	213,054
1961	262,978	33,397	57,902	—	244,360
1962	284,726	34,129	58,028	—	297,442
1963	346,804	38,254	58,247	—	337,657
1964	350,575	22,300	70,251	—	397,625
1965	478,672	22,672	70,251	—	442,632
1966	629,372	25,261	70,251	190,643	480,282
1967	619,430	25,261	155,975	302,127	560,270
1968	687,551	21,694	140,489	337,129	617,697
1969	687,583	20,756	166,171	312,129	608,424
1970	841,971	22,513	145,966	357,129	718,845
1971	1,114,875	39,460	25,000	130,908	807,538
1972	1,506,598	31,390	154,428	520,888	955,095
1973	1,468,841	38,314	328,337	580,971	1,040,697
1974	1,300,265	30,415	240,973	545,906	1,150,697
1975	1,959,547	30,475	180,396	650,888	1,352,287

1976	3,288,647	62,573	347,428	809,476	1,708,067
1977	3,813,837	72,538	752,517	1,129,482	2,157,177
1978	4,100,367	76,588	1,272,186	1,233,999	2,929,901
1979	4,075,851	81,605	1,335,786	1,433,837	3,721,711
1980	5,433,839	90,862		1,586,893	

Notes

1 The Political fund income is *less* branch grants.

2 The figures for investments are given at cost and not market value. They do not include mortgages for officers' houses, nor loans. They do include new savings certificates.

3 The Insurance Society was called the Mutual Benefit Society until 1937 and the Insurance and Endowment Society until 1967. It had 31,724 policies in 1919, 39,120 in 1929, 10,876 in 1939, 7,805 in 1949, 40,051 in 1959, 16,503 in 1969 and 22,723 in 1979, the later two figures calculated on a different basis.

Appendix 37: UPW PARLIAMENTARY CANDIDATES, 1922–79

April 1921 By-Election
Bedford
F. F. Riley (lost to Lib. by 4,666)

February 1922 By-Election
North Camberwell
C. Ammon (1,135 maj.)

October 1922 By-Election
Newport
J. W. Bowen (lost to Con. by 2,090)

November 1922 General Election
Bury
H. W. Wallace (lost to Con. by 1,187)

Carlisle
G. Middleton (1,301 maj.)

Market Harborough
W. J. Baker (lost to Con. and Lib.)

Newport
J. W. Bowen (lost to Con. by 3,019)

North Camberwell
C. Ammon (254 maj.)

Stockton-on-Tees
F. F. Riley (lost to Lib. by 1,213)

December 1923 General Election
Bristol East
W. J. Baker (2,036 maj.)

Bury
H. W. Wallace (lost to Con. by 1,112)

Carlisle
G. Middleton (276 maj.)

Newport
W. J. Bowen (lost to Con. by 324)

North Camberwell
C. Ammon (4,686 maj.)

Stockton-on-Tees
F. F. Riley (lost to Lib. and Con.)

October 1924 General Election
Bristol East
W. J. Baker (4,777 maj.)

Bury
H. W. Wallace (lost to Con. by 3,096)

Carlisle
G. Middleton (lost to Con. by 2,111)

Newport
J. W. Bowen (lost to Con. by 2,163)

North Camberwell
C. Ammon (3,736 maj.)

Stockton-on-Tees
F. F. Riley (lost to Con. by 3,215)

May 1929 General Election
Bristol East
W. J. Baker (11,621 maj.)

Carlisle
G. Middleton (2,417 maj.)

Crewe
J. W. Bowen (9,216 maj.)

East Walthamstow
H. W. Wallace (1,374 maj.)

North Camberwell
C. Ammon (7,823 maj.)

Stockton-on-Tees
F. F. Riley (2,389 maj.)

October 1931 General Election
Carlisle
G. Middleton (lost to Con. by 4,634)

Crewe
J. W. Bowen (lost to Con. by 6,790)

East Walthamstow
H. W. Wallace (lost to Con. by 8,832)

North Camberwell
C. Ammon (lost to Con. by 765)

Stockton-on-Tees
F. F. Riley (lost to Con. by 11,031)

November 1935 General Election
Crewe
J. W. Bowen (lost to Con. by 1,109)

East Walthamstow
H. W. Wallace (lost to Con. by 2,488)

North Camberwell
C. Ammon (5,777 maj.)

July 1945 General Election
Clitheroe
H. E. Randall (2,647 maj.)

East Walthamstow
H. W. Wallace (6,532 maj.)

Heston and Isleworth
W. R. Williams (6,569 maj.)

February 1950 General Election
Clitheroe
H. E. Randall (lost to Con. by 2,455)

East Walthamstow
H. W. Wallace (3,272 maj.)

Heston and Isleworth
W. R. Williams (lost to Con. by 4,279)

October 1951 General Election
Droylsden
W. R. Williams (1,870 maj.)

Dumfries
G. Douglas (lost to Nat. Lib. by 9,717)

East Walthamstow
H. W. Wallace (1,020 maj.)

Mitcham
H. E. Randall (lost to Con. by 5,869)

May 1955 General Election
East Walthamstow
H. W. Wallace (lost to Con. by 1,129)

Openshaw
W. R. Williams (8,042 maj.)

December 1955 By-Election
Gateshead West
H. E. Randall (6,535 maj.)

October 1959 General Election
Chedale
C. R. Morris (lost to Con. & Lib.)

Edinburgh South
A. Reid (lost to Con. by 11,514)

Enfield West
G. Hickman (lost to Con. by 13,808)

Gateshead West
H. E. Randall (9,768 maj.)

Lewes
Bill Reay (lost to Con. by 16,577)

Openshaw
W. R. Williams (8,438 maj.)

Torrington
R. Dobson (lost to Con. & Lib.)

December 1963 By-Election
Openshaw
C. R. Morris (8,962 maj.)

October 1964 General Election
Brighton Kemptown
D. H. Hobden (7 maj.)

Bristol North East
Ray Dobson (lost to Con. by 1,211)

Edinburgh North
A. D. Reid (lost to Con. by 4,830)

Gateshead West
H. E. Randall (11,767 maj.)

Openshaw
C. R. Morris (9,202 maj.)

March 1966 General Election
Basnet
G. Hickman (lost to Con. by 5,486)

Brighton Kemptown
D. H. Hobden (831 maj.)

Bristol North East
R. Dobson (3,972 maj.)

Gateshead West
H. E. Randall (13,503 maj.)

Openshaw
C. R. Morris (11,638 maj.)

June 1970 General Election
Brighton Kemptown
D. H. Hobden (lost to Con. by 3,103)

Bristol North East
R. Dobson (lost to Con. by 462)

Openshaw
C. R. Morris (7,101 maj.)

September 1971 By-Election
Stirling, Falkirk and Grangemouth
Harry Ewing (4,488 maj.)

February 1974 General Election
Brighton Kemptown
D. H. Hobden (lost to Con. by 4,020)

Hampstead, Camden
A. J. Clarke (lost to Con. by 2,257)

Openshaw
C. R. Morris (7,457 maj.)

Stirling, Falkirk and Grangemouth
H. Ewing (3,849 maj.)

Western Isles
A. W. Wilson (lost to Nat. by 7,200)

October 1974 General Election
Brighton Kempton
D. H. Hobden (lost to Con. by 2,665)

Openshaw
C. R. Morris (8,513 maj.)

Stirling, Falkirk and Grangemouth
H. Ewing (1,766 maj.)

May 1979 General Election
Openshaw
C. R. Morris (7,144 maj.)

Stirling, Falkirk and Grangemouth
H. Ewing (15,618 maj.)

Note

H. B. Morgan was not sponsored by the Union but as its Medical Adviser worked closely
with it. He stood unsuccessfully for Camberwell North West in 1922 and 1923 and was MP
for the Constituency in 1929-31. He was also MP for Rochdale (1940-50) and for
Warrington (1950-5).

Appendix 38: 1927 ARBITRATION SUBMISSION AND AWARD

Grade	Current rate	UPW claim	PO counter-claim	Arbitration award
CC&T (M) (15+)	15s ×21 to 67s 6d	21s ×17 to 82s	14s ×22 to 65s	16s ×22 to 72s 6d
CC&T (F) (15+)	15s ×17 to 45s	21s ×13 to 66s	14s ×18 to 43s	16s ×19 to 47s
London telegs (M) (15+)	15s ×20 to 67s 6d	21s ×16 to 88s	14s ×20 to 62s 6d	16s ×21 to 70s
London telegs (F) (15+)	15s ×17 to 45s	21s ×13 to 66s	14s ×17 to 42s	16s ×18 to 46s
Sorters (18+)	24s ×17 to 67s 6d	27s ×13 to 82s	20s ×17 to 60s	22s ×17 to 67s 6d
Outer London SC&Ts (M) (15+)	14s ×19 to 62s	21s ×16 to 82s	12s ×19 to 58s	14s ×20 to 64s 6d
Outer London SC&Ts (F) (15+)	14s ×17 to 43s	21s ×13 to 66s	12s ×16 to 38s	14s ×19 to 45s
Prov SC&Ts (M) (15+)	13s ×20 to 61s 12s ×19 to 55s 12s ×18 to 49s	19s ×16 to 74s	12s ×19 to 58s 11s ×18 to 52s 11s ×17 to 46s	14s ×20 to 62s 13s ×20 to 57s 12s ×20 to 54s

Grade	Current rate	UPW claim	PO counter-claim	Arbitration award
Prov SC&Ts (F) (15+)	13s ×15 to 40s 12s ×14 to 37s 12s ×13 to 34s	19s ×13 to 60s	12s ×16 to 38s 11s ×14 to 35s 11s ×12 to 32s	14s ×18 to 42s 13s ×17 to 39s 12s ×16 to 36s
London postmen (18+)	22s ×14 to 46s 20s ×13 to 41s	25s ×11 to 61s	19s ×14 to 43s 17s ×13 to 37s	22s ×14 to 46s 20s ×14 to 42s 6d
Prov postmen (18+)	20s ×13 to 40s 19s ×12 to 37s 18s ×12 to 34s	23s ×11 to 54s	17s ×13 to 37s 16s ×12 to 34s 15s ×12 to 31s	20s ×14 to 41s 19s ×14 to 39s 18s ×14 to 37s
London telephs. (F) (16+)	18s ×12 to 36s 17s ×12 to 34s	21s ×11 to 50s	16s ×11 to 35s 14s ×10 to 32s	18s ×16 to 40s 16s ×16 to 38s
Prov telephs. (F) (16+)	16s ×11 to 33s 15s ×10 to 31s 14s × 9 to 29s	19s ×11 to 45s	14s ×10 to 32s 13s × 9 to 30s 12s × 8 to 28s	16s ×15 to 37s 15s ×14 to 35s 14s ×13 to 33s
Night (IL) telephs. (OL) (Prov) (M) (18+)	22s ×12 to 43s 20s ×12 to 40s 20s ×12 to 39s	25s ×10 to 58s 23s ×10 to 51s	19s ×15 to 43s 17s ×15 to 39s	22s ×12 to 45s 20s ×12 to 43s 20s ×12 to 41s
London porters (22+)	47s × 8 to 67s 6d	56s 2d × 7 to 93s 11d	47s 8d × 5 to 59s 6d	47s 8d × 7 to 67s 6d

Note

These figures are in shillings per week, and with the number of steps in each actual or proposed incremental scale. Training grades omitted.

Appendix 39: 1938 ARBITRATION SUBMISSION AND AWARD

Grade	Current rate	UPW claim	Secessionist claim	Award
CC&T (M) (16+)	28s ×18 to 101s 6d 28s ×21 to 78s 6d	31s ×17 to 117s –	32s 8d×21 to 135s 1d (at 17)	30s ×18 to 108s 30s ×18 to 83s 6d
Telegs (M) (16+)	28s ×19 to 98s 6d	31s ×18 to 117s	–	30s ×19 to 105s
Telegs (F) (16+)	28s ×20 to 74s	–		30s ×18 to 79s
Sorters (18+)	34s ×16 to 95s 6d	40s ×15 to 117s	34s ×15 to 120s	36s ×16 to 102s
Outer London SC&Ts (M) (16+)	25s ×18 to 91s 6d	26s 6d×17 to 105s	–	27s ×18 to 97s
Outer London SC&Ts (F) (16+)	25s ×17 to 68s 6d	–	–	27s ×17 to 72s 6d
Prov SC&Ts (M)	25s ×18 to 88s 6d 23s 6d×18 to 82s 22s ×18 to 78s 6d	26s 6d×17 to 105s 24s 6d×17 to 94s 23s ×16 to 91s	– – –	27s ×18 to 94s 25s 6d×18 to 87s 6d 24s ×18 to 84s
Prov SC&Ts (F)	25s ×17 to 66s 6d 23s 6d×17 to 61s 6d 22s ×17 to 59s			27s ×17 to 70s 6d 25s 6d×17 to 65s 6d 24s ×17 to 63s

Grade	Current rate	UPW claim	Secessionist claim	Award
London postmen (18+)	34s ×13 to 69s 31s ×13 to 64s 6d	40s ×11 to 90s 35s 6d×11 to 75s	—	36s ×13 to 75s 33s ×13 to 70s
Prov postmen (19+)	31s ×13 to 63s 29s 6d×13 to 60s 6d 28s ×13 to 58s	35s ×11 to 73s 33s ×11 to 70s 31s ×11 to 68s		33s ×13 to 68s 31s 6d×13 to 65s 6d 30s ×13 to 62s 6d
London telephs. (F) (16+)	28s ×15 to 61s 6d 25s ×15 to 59s	31s ×14 to 77s 6d 26s ×14 to 68s	— —	30s ×14 to 66s 27s ×14 to 63s
Prov telephs. (F) (16+)	25s ×15 to 58s 6d 23s 6d×14 to 55s 6d 22s ×13 to 52s 6d	26s 6d×14 to 67s 6d 24s 6d×13 to 64s 23s ×12 to 60s	—	27s ×14 to 62s 6d 25s 6d×14 to 59s 6d 24s 6d×13 to 56s 6d
Night (IL) telephs. (OL) (Prov) (M) (18+)	34s ×13 to 69s 31s ×13 to 65s 31s ×13 to 63s	40s ×12 to 90s 35s 6d×11 to 75s 31s ×11 to 73s	34s ×17 to 98s 6d 31s ×17 to 91s 6d 31s ×17 to 88s 6d	36s ×12 to 75s 33s ×12 to 70s 33s ×12 to 67s 6d
London porters (22+)	45s × 6 to 64s	57s × 7 to 90s	—	47s × 6 to 68s 6d

Note

These figures are in shillings per week, and with the number of steps in each actual or proposed incremental scale. Training grades omitted.

Appendix 40: CIVIL SERVICE COST-OF-LIVING BONUS FIGURES, 1920–34

From		% above basic 1914 rates
March	1920	130
July	1920	135
November	1920	155
March	1921	165
September	1921	130
March	1922	105
September	1922	85
March	1923	80
September	1923	75
March	1924	80
Sepember	1924	75
March	1925	80
September	1925	75
March	1926	80
September	1926	70
March	1927	80
Sepember	1927	70
March	1928	70
September	1928	65
March	1929	70
September	1929	70[1]
March	1930	70
Sepember	1930	65[1]
March	1931	55
September	1931	50[2]
November	1934	52½
July	1935	55

Notes

[1] In September 1929 the figure based on the normal method of calculation would have been 65, and in September 1930 60.

[2] After September 1931, the figure was frozen during a further period when it was falling and the final consolidation proposals were the result of negotiation, rather than direct relationships with the Index.

Appendix 41: BONUS PAYMENTS IN THE SECOND WORLD WAR, 1940–45

	1 Feb 1940 (per week)	1 March 1941 (per week)	1 June 1942 (per week)	1 Dec 1942 (per week)	1 June 1943 (per week)	1 Nov 1943 (per week)	1 Nov 1944 (per week)	Consolidation 1 Nov 1945 (per week)
Under 16	1s 6d/7½p	3s /15p	4s /20p	4s /20p	5s /25p	5s /25p	6s 6d/32½p	12s /60p
16	1s 6d/7½p	3s /15p	4s /20p	4s /20p	5s 6d/27½p	6s 6d/32½p	8s /40p	12s /60p
17	1s 6d/7½p	3s /15p	4s /20p	4s /20p	6s /30p	7s 6d/37½p	9s /45p	15s /75p
18	2s /10p	5s /25p	6s 6d/32½p	6s 6d/32½p	8s 6d/42½p	10s /50p	12s /60p	18s /90p
19	2s /10p	5s /25p	6s 6d/32½p	7s 6d/37½p	9s 6d/47½p	11s /55p	13s 6d/67½p	21s /£1.05
20(F)	2s /10p	5s /25p	6s 6d/32½p	8s /40p	10s 6d/52½p	12s /60p	14s 6d/72½p	22s 6d/£1.12½
20(M)	2s /10p	5s /25p	6s 6d/32½p	8s /40p	10s 6d/52½p	13s /65p	16s /80p	24s /£1.20

Adult

	1 Feb 1940 (per week)	1 March 1941 (per week)	1 June 1942 (per week)	1 June 1943 (per week)	1 Nov 1943 (per week)	1 Nov 1944 (per week)	Consolidation 1 Nov 1945 (per week)
Up to £2 p.w. / £104 p.a.	3s /15p	Up to £4.75/£250 p.a.			Up to £850 p.a. (£1,000 on 1 July 1944)	Up to £1,500 p.a.	
£2–2.50 / £130	4s /20p	(M)10s /50p	13s 6d/67½p	(M)17s /85p	(M)19s /95p	(M)23s /£1.15	30s /£1.50
£2.50–4.75 / £250	5s /25p	(F) 7s 6d/37½p	10s /50p	(F) 13s 6d/67½p	(F) 15s 6d/77p	(F) 18s 6d/92½p	24s /£1.20
(M)£4.75–6.70 / £350	5s /25p	£250–350 p.a. / 5s /25p	£250–500 p.a. / (M) 5s /25p	£250–500 p.a. / (M)14s /70p; (F) 11s 6d/57½p			
(F)£4.75–5.75 / £300	4s /20p	£250–300 p.a. / 4s /20p	(F) 4s /20p	£500–850 p.a. / (M) £25 p.a.; (F) £20 p.a.			

Index